Newsmakers®

ISSN 0899-0417

Newsmakers®

The People Behind Today's Headlines

Laura Avery

Project Editor

2004

Cumulation

Includes Indexes from
1985 through 2004

THOMSON
GALE

Detroit • New York • San Francisco • San Diego • New Haven, Conn. • Waterville, Maine • London • Munich

Newsmakers 2004, Cumulation

Project Editor
Laura Avery

Research
Barbara McNeil

Editorial Support Services
Emmanuel T. Barrido, Venus Little

Permissions
Denise Buckley, Sheila Spencer, Ann Taylor

Imaging and Multimedia
Leitha Etheridge-Sims, Lezlie Light, Mike Logusz

Composition and Electronic Capture
Carolyn A. Roney

Manufacturing
Lori Kessler

ISBN 0-7876-6806-0
ISSN 0899-0417

Printed in the United States of America
10 9 8 7 6 5 4 3 2 1

Contents

Obituaries

Introduction

Newsmakers provides informative profiles of the world's most interesting people in a crisp, concise, contemporary format. Make *Newsmakers* the first place you look for biographical information on the people making today's headlines.

Important Features

- **Attractive, modern page design** pleases the eye while making it easy to locate the information you need.

- **Coverage of all the newsmakers** you want to know about: people in business, education, technology, law, politics, religion, entertainment, labor, sports, medicine, and other fields.

- **Clearly labeled data sections** allow quick access to vital personal statistics, career information, major awards, and mailing addresses.

- **Informative sidelights essays** include the kind of in-depth analysis you're looking for.

- **Sources for additional information** provide lists of books, magazines, newspapers, and internet sites where you can find out even more about *Newsmakers* listees.

- **Enlightening photographs** are specially selected to further enhance your knowledge of the subject.

- **Separate obituaries section** provides you with concise profiles of recently deceased newsmakers.

- **Publication schedule and price** fit your budget. *Newsmakers* is published in three paperback issues per year, each containing approximately 50 entries, and a hardcover cumulation, containing approximately 200 entries (those from the preceding three paperback issues plus an additional 50 entries), *all at a price you can afford!*

- And much, much more!

Indexes Provide Easy Access

Familiar and indispensable: The *Newsmakers* indexes! You can easily locate entries in a variety of ways through our four versatile, comprehensive indexes. The Nationality, Occupation, and Subject Indexes list names from the current year's *Newsmakers* issues. These are cumulated in the annual hardbound volume to include all names from the entire *Contemporary Newsmakers* and *Newsmakers* series. The Newsmakers Index is cumulated in all issues as well as the hardbound annuals to provide concise coverage of the entire series.

- **Nationality Index**—Names of newsmakers are arranged alphabetically under their respective nationalities.

- **Occupation Index**—Names are listed alphabetically under broad occupational categories.

- **Subject Index**—Includes key subjects, topical issues, company names, products, organizations, etc., that are discussed in *Newsmakers*. Under each subject heading are listed names of newsmakers associated with that topic. So the unique Subject Index provides access to the information in *Newsmakers* even when readers are unable to connect a name with a particular topic. This index also invites browsing, allowing *Newsmakers* users to discover topics they may wish to explore further.

- **Cumulative Newsmakers Index**—Listee names, along with birth and death dates, when available, are arranged alphabetically followed by the year and issue number in which their entries appear.

Available in Electronic Formats

Licensing. *Newsmakers* is available for licensing. The complete database is provided in a fielded format and is deliverable on such media as disk or CD-ROM. For more information, contact Thomson Gale's Business Development Group at 1-800-877-GALE, or visit our website at www.gale.com/bizdev.

Online. *Newsmakers* is available online as part of the Gale Biographies (GALBIO) database accessible through LexisNexis, P.O. Box 933, Dayton, OH 45401-0933; phone: (937) 865-6800, toll-free: 800-227-4908.

Suggestions Are Appreciated

The editors welcome your comments and suggestions. In fact, many popular *Newsmakers* features were implemented as a result of readers' suggestions. We will continue to shape the series to best meet the needs of the greatest number of users. Send comments or suggestions to:

The Editor
Newsmakers
Thomson Gale
27500 Drake Rd.
Farmington Hills, MI 48331-3535

Or, call toll-free at 1-800-877-GALE

Bashar al-Assad

President of Syria and physician

Born on September 11, 1965, in Damascus, Syria; married Asma (Emma) al–Akhras, December 31, 2000; children: Hafez. *Education:* Studied medicine at the University of Damascus.

Addresses: *Office*—Office of the President, Damascus, Syria. *Website*—Bashar al–Assad Official Website: http://www.basharassad.org.

Career

Studied medicine at the University of Damascus, late 1980s; medical residency in London, 1992; started preparations to assume leadership of Syria, 1994; became a colonel in Syrian army, 1999; elected President of Syria, 2000.

Sidelights

Bashar al–Assad, who spent years training to be a doctor, suddenly found himself, at the age of 34, occupying the most powerful position in Syria as its new head of state. He had inherited the presidency after the death of his father, Hafez al–Assad, in 2000. Since then, Syrians and the rest of the world have been watching him very closely to see if Assad will follow in the footsteps of his father, a shrewd and uncompromising man who ruled Syria for nearly 30 years with an iron fist.

Bashar al–Assad was born in Damascus, on September 11, 1965, the second son of Syria's late president Hafez al–Assad. Assad studied medicine at the Uni-

AP/Wide World Photos

versity of Damascus. In 1988, he continued his studies at a military hospital in the city, where he specialized in ophthalmology. He moved to London in 1992 to fulfill his medical residency at St. Mary's Hospital.

In January of 1994, Assad's medical career came to an abrupt halt when his older brother, Basil, died in a car crash. Assad flew back to Damascus to attend the funeral, not realizing at the time that this tragedy would change his life drastically, and that he would have to set aside his dream of practicing medicine. As the eldest son, Basil had been groomed from birth to be his father's successor. Upon his death, a plan was quickly put into action to prepare Bashar al–Assad to take his place. Assad was enrolled in a military academy for an accelerated course in leadership and Middle East diplomacy, recounted Nicholas Blanford in the *Christian Science Monitor.* Assad quickly rose through the ranks, making colonel by 1999. This was an important step, according to a British Broadcasting Corporation profile, because the army plays a key role in Syrian politics and the late president had been commander of both the army and the air force.

On June 10, 2000, Hafez al–Assad died. Ten days later, Assad was elected president through a public referendum, and his training and strength of character were put to the test. He had inherited one of the toughest jobs in the Middle East. Assad faced the challenge of holding on to the power he had inherited from his father. According to the *Christian Science Monitor*'s Blanford, a western observer noted, "There are sharks around and he has to tread carefully." Syrian expert Eyal Zisser, a professor at Tel Aviv University, said in a Federation of American Scientists interview, "You need to show that you are strong, that you are a leader, and you need to crush in the first moment any signs of opposition, resentment, or independence."

Syria's economy was in a dreadful state, according to Charles Foster in the *Contemporary Review*. In a serious recession since the mid–1990s, Syria had squandered its oil revenues. Foster noted, "A huge proportion of its income goes to finance an increasingly lame army, crippled by the cessation of Soviet support. There is a grotesquely over–staffed, corrupt bureaucracy, which makes it difficult for the private sector to make a start." On the foreign affairs front, Assad faced many critical problems, from trying to maintain Syria's military presence in Lebanon, to settling water quarrels with Turkey, to the volatile issue of Middle East peace.

Influenced by his Western education and a cosmopolitan upbringing, the young president was eager to begin implementing "his own cultural revolution," wrote Sami Moubayed in the *Washington Report on Middle East Affairs*. Assad was determined to push Syria into the 21st century and the world of computer technology, the Internet, and cellular telephones. At his inaugural speech on July 17, 2000, Assad promised many sweeping reforms. He attacked inefficient administration as an impediment to Syria's growth, and declared, "We have to fight waste and corruption." Assad wasted no time spearheading a campaign to weed out corrupt, high–level officials, a move which also served to eliminate potential rivals and opponents within the old guard.

On the second anniversary of his presidency, Assad was still struggling to introduce reforms. Wrote Donna Abu–Nasr for Yahoo! News, "On the surface, Syria today appears younger, livelier, and more efficient than it was a few years ago under Assad's father, the late Hafez Assad. There are cell phones, satellite television, trendy restaurants, and Internet cafes with operators who know how to find detours to websites blocked by the government. The country's first mall opened last year. However, below the surface, the system remains corrupt and decrepit, unable to make the changes that could propel Syria and its 17 million people into the 21st century."

Freedom of speech was only marginally restored. When Assad first took office, he encouraged "constructive criticism." The president received four open letters of appeal, published in the Lebanese press, from Syrian citizens asking for political, economic, and social reform, wrote the *Washington Report on Middle East Affairs*' Moubayed. To everyone's surprise, the letters were tolerated by the regime, signaling an end to the era of regulation of thought and speech. Feeling emboldened, others began to speak out. "In September [of 2000], 99 Syrian intellectuals issued a public manifesto in Beirut calling for freedom of speech, the lifting of martial law imposed on the country since 1963, political pluralism, a general amnesty and freeing of political prisoners," according to Moubayed. No measures were taken against them. Two years later, however, mounting calls for political liberalization led to a backlash, wrote the *Christian Science Monitor*'s Blanford. This resulted in the arrest of several dissidents, and an end to the public debate on reform.

On the issue of Middle East peace, Yahoo! News' Abu–Nasr noted that Assad has not deviated from his father's refusal to negotiate until Israel agrees to return the Golan Heights. Last year, in a speech welcoming Pope John Paul II, Assad shocked the West when he used unmistakably anti–Semitic language to attack "those who ... betrayed Jesus Christ and ... tried to betray and kill the Prophet Muhammad." Most blame the aging and still powerful old guard for this stance. According to Blanford in the *Christian Science Monitor*, Damascus University law professor Mohammed Shukri said, "I am very optimistic about [Assad]. He's open–minded, educated.... He will win because the people are backing him. Sooner or later he will rearrange his house." Assad, speaking to the *New York Times* in late 2003, acknowledged that some people will always compare him to his father. "The son is not a copy of his father," Assad philosophized. "He takes some things from his parents, but he will get many things from society.... As a president, the first thing is to make your decisions and your vision based on the society, the country, and the people."

The world's attention was drawn to Syria in March of 2003 when Assad took an outspoken stance against the impending United States–led invasion of Iraq. Though Syria and Iraq did not have a friendly relationship, Assad publicly stated that he hoped the mission would fail. In April of 2003, as Iraqi President Saddam Hussein's regime crumbled and Hussein himself went into hiding, it seemed like Assad's prediction of failure was incorrect. Attention was again drawn to Syria, as John Kampfner, writing in the *New Statesman,* observed, "George W. Bush is opening a third front. The war on terror, which took American might to Afghanistan and then Iraq, is now begin redirected against a new enemy, one conjured almost overnight—Syria."

Assad denied the allegation that Syria was cooperating with Iraq's ousted regime, stepped up patrols of the Syria/Iraq border, and remained committed to maintaining an amicable relationship with the United States in light of increasing chaos and instability in Iraq as 2003 drew to a close. "There can be no peace in the region without Syria. And Syria is important for the future stability [of] Iraq due to its credibility and its being a neighbor to Iraq," Assad stated to *New York Times* reporter Neil MacFarquhar. "The problem is whether the U.S. is going to become a power for achieving turbulence in the region instead of being an element of stability."

Sources

Periodicals

APS Review Gas Market Trends, April 15, 2002.
Asia Africa Intelligence Wire, December 16, 2001.
Christian Science Monitor, June 18, 2002.
Commonweal, June 15, 2001, p. 10.
Contemporary Review, October 2000.
Middle East, December 2001, p. 36.
New Statesman, April 21, 2003, p. 14.

New York Times, December 1, 2003.
Washington Report on Middle East Affairs, December 2000, p. 31, p. 80.

Online

"Acceptance Speech of Dr. Bashar Al–Assad," *Jewish Post of New York,* http://www.jewishpost.com/jp0610/jpn0610q.htm (December 22, 2003).
"Bashar al–Assad," *Encyclopaedia of the Orient,* http://i–cias.com/e.o/assad_bashar.htm (December 22, 2003).
"Bashar al–Assad: Eyeing the future," BBC News, http://news.bbc.co.uk/2/hi/middle_east/785921.stm (December 22, 2003).
"Israel's View of the Changes in Syria," Federation of American Scientists, http://www.fas.org/news/syria/000612–syria3.htm (December 22, 2003).
"Presidential Nominee Dr. Bashar al–Assad," *Café Syria,* http://www.cafe–syria.com/Dr_Bashar.htm (December 22, 2003).
"Two Years After Taking Office, Bashar Assad Still Struggling To Introduce Reforms," Yahoo! News, http://story.news.yahoo.com (December 22, 2003).

—Enid Yurman

Ashanti

Singer and songwriter

Born Ashanti Shequoiya Douglas, October 13, 1980, in Glen Cove, NY; daughter of Ken–Kaid (aka Thomas; Ashanti's road manager) and Tina (Ashanti's manager) Douglas.

Addresses: *Office*—Murder Inc. Records, 825 8th Ave., New York, NY 10019. *Website*—http://www. murderincrecords.com.

Career

Worked as a model and appeared in television commercials, 1980s; appeared in music videos, 1990s; signed and was dropped from both Jive Records and Epic, 1990s; made recording debut on Big Punisher's single "How We Roll," 2001; sang on Ja Rule's "Always on Time," 2001; sang on Fat Joe's "What's Luv" single; wrote a remix version of Jennifer Lopez's song "Ain't It Funny;" sang on the soundtrack of the film *The Fast and the Furious,* 2001; signed with the Murder Inc. label, 2001; released single, "Foolish," 2002; released debut album, *Ashanti,* 2002; published book of poems, *Foolish/ Unfoolish: Reflections on Love,* 2002; released *Chapter II,* 2003. Television appearances include: *Sabrina, The Teenage Witch,* 2002; *American Dreams,* 2002; *Buffy the Vampire Slayer,* 2003.

Awards: Entertainer of the Year, Aretha Franklin Award, Soul Train's Lady of Soul Awards, 2002; Best R&B/Soul or Rap New Artist, Soul Train's Lady of Soul Awards, 2002; Breakout Artist of the Year, Teen Choice Awards, 2002; R&B/hip–hop artist of the year, R&B/hip–hop female artist of the year, R&B/ hip–hop single of the year for "Foolish," R&B/hip–hop singles artist of the year, new R&B/hip–hop artist of the year, Hot 100 singles artist of the year, top new pop artist of the year, and female artist of the year, all Billboard Awards, 2002; favorite new artist (pop/rock), American Music Awards, 2003; favorite new artist (hip–hop/R&B), American Music Awards, 2003; Grammy Award for best contemporary R&B album, Recording Academy, for *Ashanti,* 2002.

Sidelights

Ashanti became the hottest R&B act of 2002 when her debut album, *Ashanti,* broke sales records for female recording artists, and three of its singles landed on the Top 10 charts simultaneously. The Long Island native had only recently graduated from high school when she first landed on the charts in 2001 with her vocals on the Big Punisher rap song "How We Roll." Contributions on the tracks of other stars from her record label, Murder Inc., pushed her star higher, culminating with the release of *Ashanti.* That album earned the singer/songwriter two Soul Train Lady of Soul Awards, eight Billboard Awards, and a Grammy. Her second album, *Chapter II,* released in the summer of 2003, also sold briskly, proving that Ashanti is here to stay.

Ashanti Douglas, named after a tribe in the country of Ghana, was born and raised in the Long Island, New York, community of Glen Cove. At Glen Cove High, she was a track star and an honor student. She began performing before the age of ten, modeling and appearing in TV commercials. Soon afterward, she appeared in music videos as a dancer. Music runs in her family; her father, Ken–Kaid, was a singer before leaving show business for more steady work as a computer systems administrator. Ashanti's little sister, Kenashia, also a singer, took home the grand prize for children on the *Showtime at the Apollo* television show at the age of six. Ashanti's grandfather, James Davis, was an advocate for civil rights, and served for many years as the head of the Long Island chapter of the National Association for the Advancement of Colored People (NAACP).

When Ashanti was 12 years old, her mother discovered her daughter's singing talent. She had asked Ashanti to turn off the radio while she did her chores, and left the room. Ashanti did as she was told, but she began to sing the songs from the radio herself. Her mother came back into the room to reprimand her for disobeying, and was astonished to find that it was Ashanti making beautiful music, not the radio. Soon afterward, Ashanti's parents entered their daughter in a local talent show, which she handily won. From then on, Ashanti's mother has acted as her co–manager.

At the age of 14, Ashanti landed her first recording contract, with Jive Records. This label also featured such top artists as the Backstreet Boys, 'N Sync, and Britney Spears. During that time, she divided her efforts between high school and recording sessions with the label. The company would send a limo to pick her up after school to take her to the recording studio, where she would do her best to catch up on her homework before recording and then while being driven home.

Ashanti and Jive ended their relationship after a year, before a single album was released. When she was 17, however, Ashanti was picked up by the Sony label Epic Records. It was a heady time for Ashanti, and the label took out a full page ad in her high school year book congratulating her on her graduation. That deal required her to move to Atlanta, Georgia, which, Ashanti told Nekesa Mumbi Moody in the *Gazette* of Montreal, "kind of broke up the family." Ashanti admitted that there were a lot of tears from family members the day she left home.

But after only a year in Atlanta, the person who had signed Ashanti to the label was let go, and the artists he had signed were also dismissed. Ashanti returned home, again without an album to show for her time with the new label. After graduating from high school in 1998, Ashanti was faced with a difficult decision: to go on to college as many of her friends were doing, or pursue her music career full time. She had been admitted to Hampton University in Virginia on a track scholarship, and her music career had yet to take off. Even so, she chose music over continuing her academic education. At first it was difficult for her not to feel discouraged as she struggled to gain broader recognition as a singer while her friends enjoyed their freshmen year of college.

Nevertheless, Ashanti stuck it out, recording demos in New York while looking for yet another record deal. After two years of hard work, she got her break in the form of Chris Gotti, the brother of the president of the Murder Inc. label. He introduced her to his brother, Irv, who hired Ashanti to sing backup on a Big Punisher album released after the hip–hop star's death. The song was "How We Roll," and Ashanti's backing vocals helped to propel the song to the top of the charts in early 2001.

Ashanti first hit the airwaves in a big way with her contribution to the Ja Rule song "Always on Time," which came out in the second half of 2001. The song, helped along by her refrain on the song, hit the Billboard 100 as the seventh most–played song in the United States. Hard on the heels of that release, she appeared on the television show *Saturday Night Live* with Ja Rule. Soon people were stopping her in the street to ask for her autograph.

Another collaboration soon followed, this time with Fat Joe, on a song called "What's Luv." This song was also a hit, and Murder Inc. signed Ashanti to her own contract. She began to play concerts with Ja Rule at the same time that she worked on her own album. Also during this time, Ashanti wrote a remix version of a song for Jennifer Lopez called "Ain't It Funny," and sang on the soundtrack for the film *The Fast and the Furious.*

The first single from Ashanti's debut album, released before the album itself, was "Foolish," which takes its melody from a DeBarge song, and which was made famous by Notorious B.I.G. in his hit rap "One More Chance." The song is based on Ashanti's experience breaking up with a boyfriend. That relationship, she told *Rolling Stone's* Matt Diehl, was "real, real serious," but could not stand up to the stress put on it by Ashanti's success and her heavy traveling schedule. According to Ashanti, the recording of the song benefited from the synergy created by the fact that everyone involved in the production, including the engineers, was going through similar relationship troubles.

The melody for Ashanti's debut was chosen by Irv Gotti, and Ashanti was nervous about having her debut single ride on the shoulders of such a big star as B.I.G., but she trusted Gotti to put the best possible sound on her debut. Gotti felt that the song needed "a familiar beat that people would recognize," as he told Richard Cromelin in the *Los Angeles Times*. His strategy, coupled with Ashanti's heartfelt lyrics and her sultry vocals proved a winning combination; her single became a hit, remaining at the top of the charts for ten weeks.

Ashanti continued to live at home, even after becoming a successful recording artist, albeit in a separate apartment with her own entrance. That situation had to change, she and her parents acknowledged in a 2001 *New York Times* interview with Seth Kugel, since she was just a bit too accessible to her ever–increasing numbers of fans. "They come right up to the house," Ashanti's mother told Kugel. "Then they bring kids from out of town." The family decided to move, but not far—their new home was also on Long Island, though much larger than their old one.

Ashanti's self–titled debut album hit the racks in April of 2002, immediately dislodging Celine Dion from her perch at the top of the charts by selling more than a million copies in a single month. The album eventually outsold not only Dion, but also every other female recording artist in history, with four million copies and counting. Ashanti also became the first recording artist since the Beatles to have three singles on the Top 10 charts at the same time. The album earned Ashanti no less than five Grammy nominations, one of which—Best Contemporary R&B Album—it won. The album also earned Ashanti eight Billboard Awards. Over at MTV she grabbed four nominations at the Video Music Awards and performed live at the popular event. She also scored "Breakout Artist of the Year" from the 2002 Teen Choice Awards. In January of 2003, she won two awards at the 30th annual American Music Awards.

However, one award she won in 2002 was also controversial. When it was announced that Ashanti would receive the Soul Train Aretha Franklin Award for "Entertainer of the Year" a high school boy in California took offense and started an on–line petition against her. He explained to the *Seattle Times* that she was too new to deserve the award and "she

lacks stage presence in the majority of her performances." Nearly 30,000 people agreed with him, signing the petition. Many pointed out that established artists such as Mary J. Blige and Missy Elliott or critically acclaimed singers like Alicia Keys and India.Arie were more deserving of an award that carries the name of a musical legend. However, veteran singer Patti LaBelle, who presented the award, said the singer was "extremely deserving of this wonderful recognition," according to a report in the *Cincinnati Post*. Ashanti also picked up the Soul Train Lady of Soul award for best new solo artist.

Despite chart–topping success, most reviewers panned Ashanti's debut effort. Other critics pointed to the fact that *Ashanti*'s phenomenal first week sales were propelled along by Island Def Jam Music Group, the parent company of Murder Inc. The company offered retailers a two–dollar rebate for each album sold in the first two weeks. While it is true that Ashanti was hot, Lyor Cohen, CEO of Island Def Jam, confessed to the *New York Times*, "We put gasoline in the carburetor." For Ashanti, who was happy just to have a record deal that actually resulted in a album, her debut's astounding success was just icing on the cake. "I never dreamed of all this," she told Glenn Gamboa in *Newsday*. "I just wanted the album to be released.... To have it finished and have it released and in stores was a major accomplishment."

Always conscious of her roots, Ashanti chose her hometown as the location for the music video for "Happy," one of the cuts on *Ashanti*. She remembered as a child waiting in vain for stars to visit Glen Cove, and as an R&B superstar, she decided to finally bring some star power to the little city. Her handlers suggested Los Angeles or Monte Carlo as possible locations, but Ashanti was firm; Glen Cove was her favorite place, and she wanted her hometown to share in her success. With that, dozens of crew members and 20 trailers full of production equipment descended on the city for three days of shooting. The mayor presented Ashanti with the key to the city, and the executive of Nassau County declared May 3, 2002, Ashanti Douglas Day.

Around this time, Ashanti also took a stab at bringing her verses to print with a book of poems titled *Foolish/Unfoolish: Reflections on Love*. Although her book is about love, she has admitted that she has been less than lucky in that department. She blamed it on being overworked with concerts and other public appearances, and also the fact that she is followed everywhere she goes by employees of her record label. As she told Peter Robinson in the *Ob-*

server, "It's a little difficult to meet people when I have a bunch of big brothers standing there everywhere I go. But I suppose it's a good thing. They do it out of love."

Ashanti's second album, *Chapter II,* was released in the summer of 2003. In the same vein as her debut, it features, in the words of the *Observer*'s Robinson, "fresh–sounding ... breezy beats and irresistible hooks underpinning Ashanti's silky R&B style." Ashanti has said that one of her favorite parts of the album is a short duet she sings with her then–14–year–old sister. The first single from *Chapter II,* called "Rock Wit U (Awww Baby)," immediately hit the charts and rose to the top 10.

In 2003, Ashanti was nominated for two American Music Awards: Favorite Female Artist—Hip–Hop/Rhythm & Blues Music and Favorite Album—Hip–Hop/Rhythm & Blues Music, for *Chapter II.*

Ashanti remained determined not to let success go to her head, knowing full well that disappointment in the music business is often not far away. "I take it one day at a time," she told *Newsday*'s Gamboa. "I've had to get used to so many letdowns."

Selected discography

(Contributor) *Endangered Species* by Big Punisher ("How We Roll"), Relativity, 2001.
(Contributor) *Pain Is Love* by Ja Rule ("Always on Time"), Def Jam, 2001.
(Contributor) *The Fast and the Furious* ("When a Man Does Wrong," "Justify My Love"), Universal, 2001.
(Contributor) *Jealous Ones Still Envy (J.O.S.E.)* by Fat Joe ("What's Luv?"), Atlantic, 2001.
Ashanti, Murder Inc./Universal, 2002.
(Contributor) *Irv Gotti Presents the Inc.,* Murder Inc./Universal, 2002.
(Contributor) *Disneymania,* Disney, 2002.
(Contributor) *Irv Gotti Presents the Remixes,* Murder Inc./Universal, 2002.
(Contributor) *The Last Temptation* by Ja Rule ("Mesmerize" and "The Pledge Remix"), 2002.
Chapter 2, Murder Inc/Universal, 2003.

Selected writings

Foolish/Unfoolish: Reflections on Love, Hyperion Press, 2002.

Sources

Periodicals

Cincinnati Post, August 26, 2002, p. 12C.
Daily News (New York), June 22, 2003, p. 2.
Gazette (Montreal), May 6, 2002, p. F6.
Houston Chronicle, March 2, 2003, p. 14.
Los Angeles Times, April 27, 2002, p. F1.
Newsday (New York), February 16, 2003, p. D20.
New York Times, December 30, 2001; May 12, 2002, p. 1, p. 15; June 9, 2002.
Observer, July 6, 2003, magazine section, p. 38.
Rolling Stone, May 23, 2002, p. 39.
Seattle Times, August 30, 2002, p. H6.

Online

"Ashanti Bio," MTV.com, http://www.mtv.com/bands/az/ashanti/bio.jhtml, (August 20, 2003).
"Ashanti, Nelly Top *Billboard* Awards," E! Online, http://www.eonline.com/News/Items/0,1,10954,00.html (August 20, 2003).
"Eighth Annual Soul Train Lady of Soul Awards," SoulTrain.com, http://www.soultrain.com/losa/8los.html (August 20, 2003).

—*Michael Belfiore*

Rachel Ashwell

Interior designer and entrepreneur

Born c. 1960 in Cambridge, England; married; children: two.

Career

Interior designer and entrepreneur. Left school at 16; set designer and wardrobe stylist, 1977–87; founded Shabby Chic, c. 1987; hosted décor shows on television.

Sidelights

In the late 1980s, Rachel Ashwell created Shabby Chic, an interior design concept that featured a light color palette, distressed furniture with character, slipcovers, and old–style designs. Comfort and function were favored in Ashwell's vision. Ashwell copyrighted the name and owned the concept. She was successful in owning a series of stores and product lines under the Shabby Chic name.

Ashwell is a native of Great Britain, where her parents got her involved in antiques from an early age. Her mother was a restorer of antique dolls and teddy bears, while her father was a secondhand, rare book dealer. Ashwell learned to love shopping in flea markets and antique stores as a young girl as she and her sister went to such places with their parents looking for dolls, books, and bears. By the time she was 13 years old, Ashwell was selling items in London antique markets.

By about 1983, Ashwell had moved to the United States, settling in California. She had a career as a set designer and stylist in the entertainment indus-

try, primarily working in as a commercial and print stylist. When she had her two children, she left this career behind to focus on her family.

Ashwell began doing what became Shabby Chic in her own home as she decorated the house to withstand the rigors of her children and pets. She made washable, design–friendly slipcovers for her furniture. Friends soon wanted them, which led to her first store.

In about 1989, Ashwell opened a store in Santa Monica, California, called Shabby Chic. By this time, she wanted to start a small business, though Shabby Chic soon became a large, successful company. She began by selling slipcovers, in such varied materials as velvet, denim, and linen. She later expanded to vintage furniture and accessories for the home, again emphasizing comfort as well as the beauty of imperfections.

To find pieces to sell in her store, Ashwell would hit garage sales and flea markets. While she might restore, sand and/or paint the dressers, tables, and cabinets that she would find, for the most part Ashwell was determined to keep the piece's character. She would buy furniture that was well–built but well–used, capitalizing on the flaws as a chance to be creative. These finds would form the core of Ashwell's Shabby Chic business for many years.

Though Ashwell emphasized practical furniture with character, she also had a touch of sophistication. She especially enjoyed finding and including crystal chandeliers in her decorating schemes. As Mary Berth Breckenridge of the *Pittsburgh Post–Gazette* wrote, "Ashwell's style is at once easy and elegant, making unlikely partners of elements like rumpled fabrics and crystal chandeliers. Most of all, it's practical."

By 1991, Ashwell had three Shabby Chic stores, opening additional locations in New York City and San Francisco, California. She later added a store in Chicago, Illinois. While each store sold Shabby Chic products, she geared what was found in each store toward the style and clientele it would attract in each city.

Shabby Chic also expanded the kind of products it carried. Ashwell first branched out into home textiles, like sheets and fabrics. Many of her fabrics were poplins and linens in her signature colors. In the late 1990s, she also added Shabby Chic Man to appeal to male consumers, Shabby Chic Home, which included bedding, and Rachel Ashwell Designs Collection, which featured new furniture in the mode of the restored pieces that she sold at her stores.

Some of these products created trends in the home decorating industry. Ashwell was among the first to popularize the concept of knitted bed sheets in the late 1990s. Because she favored a jeans and T–shirt lifestyle, she believed the latter fabric would make great bedding, a trend which other companies began to follow. Similarly, many companies started selling new, distressed furniture.

Ashwell continued to expand her own ideas to stay ahead of the market. She added pajamas and aromatherapy products to the Shabby Chic Home line. She also introduced three new product lines: Shabby Chic Studio, a less expensive line of furniture; Shabby Chic Baby, which featured bedding and accessories for infants; and Shabby Chic Accessories, a line of lampshades, chair pads, and backpacks.

Between 1996 and 2004, Ashwell penned four books showcasing different aspects of her Shabby Chic design concept. *Shabby Chic*, published in 1996, was primarily a book of photos of homes done in Ashwell's decorating style. In 1998, she published *Rachel Ashwell's Shabby Chic Treasure Hunting & Decorating Guide,* a handbook on how to shop at flea markets and garage sales to purchase and create one's own Shabby Chic furniture. She followed this with 2000's *The Shabby Chic Home* and 2001's *The Shabby Chic Gift of Giving*. The latter was a guide for finding unusual gifts in antique stores and flea markets and wrapping them with flair. *Shabby Chic: Sumptuous Settings and Other Lovely Things* was scheduled for publication in March of 2004.

Because of Ashwell's success with Shabby Chic, she was a guest on shows on HGTV (Home and Garden Television). By 2000, Ashwell was a home and how–to expert with her own program on E! Entertainment Television and its related Style Network. She displayed her style on her show *Rachel Ashwell's Shabby Chic*. Of her philosophy as an interior designer, Ashwell told Glenna Morton from about.com, "One of my pet peeves is too much matching, clutter, frills, and people being too quick to complete the decorating process. The solution is to simplify. Be without, rather than making a wrong quick choice. Less is more."

Selected writings

Shabby Chic, HarperCollins, 1996.
Rachel Ashwell's Shabby Chic Treasure Hunting & Decorating Guide, Regan Books, 1998.
The Shabby Chic Home, Regan Books, 2000.
The Shabby Chic Gift of Giving, Regan Books, 2001.
Shabby Chic: Sumptuous Settings and Other Lovely Things, Regan Books, 2004.

Sources

Periodicals

Book List, July 1998, p. 1844.
Chicago Sun–Times, June 3, 2001, p. 8.
Christian Science Monitor, September 16, 1998, p. B4.
Country Living, February 2002, p. 77.
HFN, March 24, 1997, p. 17.
Independent, March 5, 2003, p. 19.
Library Journal, September 15, 1998, p. 72.
Ottawa Citizen, September 5, 1998, p. I9.
Pittsburgh Post–Gazette, August 3, 1996, p. C1.
San Francisco Chronicle, August 28, 1991, p. 1; January 1, 2003, p. 2WB.
Times, April 5, 2002.

Online

"About Shabby Chic," Rachel Ashwell Shabby Chic, http://www.shabbychic.com/aboutus.html# (December 18, 2003).

"At Home with a Designer: An Interview with Rachel Ashwell," about.com, http://interiordec.about.com/library/designers/bl_ashwell.htm (December 18, 2003).

"Furniture gets protection in new cover-up scheme," SouthCoast Today, http://www.s-t.com/daily/05-00/05-28-00/h01ho201.htm (December 18, 2003).

"Not Too Shabby a Life," Groovy Art Gal, http://www.groovyartgal.com/beyondthecover/departments/lifestyles.asp (December 18, 2003).

"Rachel Ashwell's Shabby Chic," Style Network, http://www.stylenetwork.com/Popup/Shows/shabby.html (December 18, 2003).

—Annette Petruso

Rowan Atkinson

Actor and comedian

Born Rowan Sebastian Atkinson, January 6, 1955, in Newcastle–Upon–Tyne, England; son of Eric and Ella May Atkinson; married Sunetra Sastry (a makeup artist), 1990; children: Benjamin, Lily. *Education:* University of Newcastle, BS; the Queen's College at Oxford University, MS.

Addresses: *Management*—PGJ Management Ltd., 7 Soho St., London, England W1D 3DQ.

Career

Actor on stage, including: *Beyond a Joke,* Hampstead, England, 1978; *The 1979 Amnesty International Comedy Gala,* Her Majesty's Theatre, London, 1979; *Rowan Atkinson in Revue,* Globe Theatre, London, 1981; *The Secret Policeman's Other Ball* (comedy gala), Drury Lane Theatre, London, 1981; *One Man Show,* 1981 and 1986; *Not in Front of the Audience,* Drury Lane Theatre, 1982; *The Nerd,* Aldwych Theatre, London, 1984; *Rowan Atkinson: The New Revue,* Shaftesbury Theatre, London, 1986; *Rowan Atkinson at the Atkinson,* Brooks Atkinson Theatre, New York City, 1986; *Mime Gala,* London International Mime Festival, Bloomsbury Theatre, London, 1987; *The Sneeze,* Aldwych Theatre, 1988; one–man–show tours to Australia, Canada, United States, and Far East. Also appeared in *Oxford University Revues,* Edinburgh Festival Fringe. Writer of theatrical works, including: (with Richard Curtis) *Rowan Atkinson in Revue,* Globe Theatre, 1981; (with Richard Curtis and Ben Elton) *Rowan Atkinson: The New Revue,* Shaftesbury Theatre, 1986; (with Richard Curtis and Ben Elton) *Rowan Atkinson at the Atkinson,* Brooks Atkinson Theatre, 1986.

Television appearances include: *Doctor Who,* 1963; *The Innes Book of Records,* 1979; *Canned Laughter* (movie), 1979; *Not The Nine O'Clock News,* 1979–82; *The Blackadder,* BBC, 1983; *Blackadder II,* BBC, 1985; *Comic Relief,* BBC1, 1986; *Blackadder the Third,* BBC, 1987; "Just for Laughs II," *Showtime Comedy Spotlight,* Showtime, 1987; "Live from London," *HBO Comedy Hour,* HBO, 1988; *Blackadder: The Cavalier Years* (movie), 1988; *Blackadder Goes Forth,* 1989; "Montreal International Comedy Festival," *HBO Comedy Hour,* HBO, 1989; *Blackadder's Christmas Carol,* BBC, then A&E, 1989; *The Appointments of Dennis Jennings,* HBO, 1989; *Mr. Bean,* 1990–95; *The Return of Mr. Bean,* 1990; *A Bit of Fry and Laurie,* 1990; *The Curse of Mr. Bean,* 1991; *Mr. Bean Goes to Town,* 1991; *Bernard and the Genie* (movie), 1991; *The Trouble with Mr. Bean,* 1992; "Rowan Atkinson: Not Just Another Pretty Face," *HBO Comedy Hour,* HBO, 1992; *Mr. Bean Rides Again,* ITV, 1992; *Merry Christmas Mr. Bean,* 1992; *Mr. Bean in Room 426,* 1993; *Laughing Matters* (also known as *Funny Business*), Showtime, 1993; *Rowan Atkinson On Location in Boston,* 1993; *Mind the Baby Mr. Bean,* 1994; *Do–It–Yourself Mr. Bean,* 1994; *Back to School Mr. Bean,* 1994; *Full Throttle,* 1994; *The Thin Blue Line,* 1995–96; *The Story of Bean* (movie), 1997; *Ohh Nooo! Mr. Bill Presents,* Fox Family Channel, 1998; *A Royal Birthday Celebration* (movie), 1998; *Mr Bean* (animated series), 2003—. Creator of television programs, including: *Not the*

Nine O'Clock News, 1980; *The Blackadder,* 1983; *Blackadder the Third,* 1987; *Laughing Matters,* 1993. Writer of television programs, including: (with others) *Not the Nine O'Clock News,* 1979–82; *Canned Laughter,* 1979; (with Richard Curtis) *Blackadder,* 1983; *Blackadder II,* 1985; *Blackadder the Third,* 1987; *Blackadder Goes Forth,* 1989; (with Robin Driscoll, Richard Curtis, and Ben Elton) *Mr. Bean,* 1989–91; "Rowan Atkinson: Not Just Another Pretty Face," *HBO Comedy Hour,* 1992; *Merry Christmas, Mr. Bean,* 1992; *The Driven Man,* 1993; (contributor) *Laughing Matters* (also known as *Funny Business*), 1993; *Ohh Nooo! Mr. Bill Presents,* 1998; *Blackadder Back & Forth,* 1999.

Film appearances include: *Monty Python Meets Beyond the Fringe* (also known as *Pleasure at Her Majesty's*), 1977; *The Secret Policeman's Ball,* 1979; *The Secret Policeman's Other Ball,* 1981; *Fundamental Frolics,* 1981; *Dead on Time,* 1982; *Never Say Never Again* (also known as *Warhead*), 1983; *The Tall Guy,* 1989; *The Witches,* 1990; *Hot Shots—Part Deux,* 1993; *The Driven Man,* 1993; *Four Weddings and a Funeral,* 1994; *The Lion King* (voice), 1994; *Bean,* 1997; *Blackadder Back and Forth,* 1999; *Maybe Baby,* 2000; *Rat Race,* 2001; *Scooby Doo,* 2002; *Johnny English,* 2003; *Love Actually,* 2003. Producer of films, including: *Bean,* 1997. Writer of screenplays, including: *The Secret Policeman's Ball,* 1979; *Bean,* 1997.

Awards: BBC TV Personality of the Year, 1980 and 1989; British Academy Award for best light entertainment television performance, British Academy of Film and Television Arts, for *Not the Nine O'Clock News,* 1980; Laurence Olivier Award, best comedy performance of the year, Society of West End Theatre, for *Rowan Atkinson in Revue,* 1981; British Academy Award for best light entertainment television performance, British Academy of Film and Television Arts, for *Blackadder Goes Forth,* 1989; Golden Rose Award for *Mr. Bean,* 1990; Montreaux Television Festival Award for *Mr. Bean,* 1990; SWET Award for Comedy Performance of the Year, for *One Man Show;* award for best cable television comedy, for *Blackadder.*

Sidelights

Rowan Atkinson is a British comic actor with international popularity, best known as the star of the films *Bean,* in which he played the kooky Mr. Bean made popular by the television series with the same name, and 2003's *Johnny English,* in which he played another wacky character, this time a spy named Johnny English. The black–haired, bug–eyed comedian has become one of England's most popular funnymen and his keen, often black comedy has earned him an international following.

Atkinson began performing in 1979 while still at Oxford University where he studied electrical engineering. It was at the university that he met Richard Curtis, who continues to work with him. They began writing comedy material together and collaborated on several projects. Together, they created *Not the Nine O'Clock News,* a series that began airing on the BBC in 1979. In 1981, Atkinson became the youngest performer to have a one–man show in London's West End when he performed in *Rowan Atkinson in Revue* at the Globe Theatre.

One of his most popular roles was on *The Blackadder,* a hysterical historical farce. This BBC series ran from 1983 to 1989, with some specials airing after the series concluded. Atkinson played the title character, Edmund Blackadder, described variously as "a priggish, upper–crust weasel" and "dastardly aristocrat." The show also ran in the United States on PBS.

In 1992, his stand–up act was filmed for HBO as *Rowan Atkinson Live.* In the program, said Ty Burr in *Entertainment Weekly,* "all the comedian's sides merrily collide. You can see his debt to Monty Python in the 'dead student' sketch, and even an echo of Benny Hill…. Quite simply, he's one of the finest silent comedians alive. I mean that in the classic, Mack Sennett sense." Atkinson was, in 1996, the top–earning British actor. According to *Entertainment Weekly,* he made more than eleven million pounds sterling. He also has a production company called Tiger Aspect.

Largely responsible for his success was the character of Mr. Bean and the eponymous television show. The Bean character was born in 1979 when Atkinson and Curtis created the strange and silent man for a performance at a comedy festival. According to the Mr. Bean website, the character was loveable and always needed to be helped out of sticky situations. The character was given his own 13–episode series essentially to preserve the Bean performances. *Mr. Bean* was the highest–rated comedy series in British history and it has, according to *Maclean's,* "entered a kind of permanent orbit like the original *Star Trek.* The series has been broadcast in more than 80 countries, and some nine million videos have been sold around the world."

Atkinson has a fond view of the Mr. Bean character. According to the Mr. Bean website, he said, "I have a huge faith and a huge liking of the character…. The essence of Mr. Bean is that he's entirely selfish and self–centered and doesn't actually acknowledge the outside world." The 1997 film based on

Atkinson's character from the BBC series made about $130 million in the United Kingdom before being released in North America later that year. At the time, this was a box office record. Perhaps it could be attributed to the fact that—for the first time—Bean spoke.

American audiences, however, did not take a liking to the character and the film only earned about $45 million in the United States. Perhaps, Atkinson told *Entertainment Weekly,* audiences did not get the satire. "Americans don't quite see the joke of why you shouldn't make a beer mug or plastic whistle from a [famous James Whistler] painting."

Some British critics do not get Bean either. As Atkinson told *Maclean's,* "The more educated critics have decided he's the least–amusing comedy character ever created. There was really quite a lot of extremely dismissive criticism of the movie in some of the trendier, more intelligent newspapers. But that wasn't so much about the movie as about seven years of pent–up frustration over the popularity of a character they've never enjoyed."

Apart from his television roles, Atkinson had scene–stealing parts in several films. Most notable were a small part in 1983's *Never Say Never Again,* the last Bond film starring Sean Connery; 1989's *The Tall Guy,* in which he played Ron Anderson, a snarky standup comic, opposite Jeff Goldblum; and the tongue–tied priest in 1994's *Four Weddings and a Funeral.*

According to John Howard–Davies, who worked with Atkinson on *Not the Nine O'Clock News* and produced and directed him in the television series *Mr. Bean,* Atkinson "brings a touch of genius to everything he does," he said in an interview with *Variety.* "He is a painstaking performer who can drive people mad with his obsession with perfection.... Rowan has very good judgement. He only does what he wants to do and what he believes in. It's quite probable that his best work is still to come."

In 2003, Atkinson was riding high on the international success of *Johnny English.* In this Bond spoof, Atkinson played a bumbling incompetent yet again, this time trying to block a plot to steal the Crown Jewels. "It's no accident that English is played ... by the extraordinary British comedian Rowan Atkinson," *Entertainment Weekly's* Lisa Schwarzbaum wrote in a 2003 review. "Those, therefore, who don't respond to the mesmerizing self–centeredness of the nitwit Bean may feel equally underentertained

by the antics of English, who is chosen for assignment only because he has accidentally caused the demise of every one of his superiors. English has little of [Austin] Powers' sophisticated cheekiness." Atkinson did many guest spots on American television shows to plug the film, such as his appearance on *The Tonight Show with Jay Leno.* His goal, he told *Entertainment Weekly,* was to move beyond his cult figure status with American viewers: "Achieving success in the U.S. isn't something I hanker for on a personal level, and it's not really necessary for commercial reasons. But it would be nice. It's nice when two people like you, but it's even nicer when three like you."

Also in 2003, Atkinson's animated television series debuted. In addition to being the executive producer and supplying all of the vocal sounds for the series, Atkinson was "filmed for every script so that the animators could capture the movements of this unique character," the Mr. Bean website stated. Each episode was set in the real world, but found Mr. Bean in situations that escalated into mayhem. Series producer Claudia Lloyd stated on the Mr. Bean website, "Moving into animation just seemed a natural evolution for such a self–contained and defined character." That same year, Atkinson appeared in *Love Actually,* an ensemble romantic comedy that followed the love lives of some very different couples in various interrelated stories, all set in the week before Christmas in London, England.

Atkinson, who lives in suburban London, is married to Sunetra Sastry, a makeup artist, with whom he has two children. He rarely gives interviews and when he does, reveals little information about his personal life and reportedly does not relish making personal appearances. When not working, Atkinson enjoys racing and collecting cars; he is especially fond of Aston Martins and Ferraris.

Selected writings

(With Robin Driscoll) *Mr. Bean's Diary,* Boxtree, 1992.

Sources

Books

Contemporary Theatre, Film and Television, volume 27, Gale Group, 2000.
Debrett's People of Today, Debrett's Peerage Ltd., 2004.
Marquis Who's Who, Marquis Who's Who, 2004.

Periodicals

Entertainment Weekly, November 21, 1997; March 27, 1998; July 25, 2003, p. 51; August 1, 2003, p. 32.

Maclean's, October 20, 1997.

People, November 24, 1997; December 1, 1997.

Variety, June 23, 1997.

Online

"Credits," E! Online, http://www.eonline.com/Facts/People/0,12,909,00.html?celfact2 (March 4, 2004).

"Mr. Bean," Mr. Bean—The Animated Series, http://www.mrbean.co.uk/site.htm (March 4, 2004).

"Rowan Atkinson," All Movie Guide, http://www.allmovie.com/cg/avg.dll?p=avg&sql=2:2727 (March 10, 2004).

"Rowan Atkinson," E! Online, http://www.eonline.com/Facts/People/Bio/0,128,909,00.html (March 4, 2004).

—Linda Dailey Paulson

Mark Badgley and James Mischka

Fashion designers

Born Mark Badgley, January 12, 1961, in East St. Louis, MO; son of Paul (a department–store executive) and Marjorie (a homemaker) Badgley. *Education:* Attended the University of Oregon; attended University of Southern California; graduated from Parsons School of Design, New York, NY, 1985. Born James Mischka, December 23, 1960, in Burlington, WI; son of Carl (a sales executive) and Judith (a homemaker) Mischka. *Education:* Earned a degree from Rice University, c. 1982; graduated from Parsons School of Design, New York, NY, 1985.

Addresses: *Office*—Badgley Mischka, 525 Seventh Ave., 11th Fl., New York, NY 10018.

Career

Launched line of women's eveningwear under label Badgley Mischka, 1988, after jobs as design assistants at Jackie Rogers and Donna Karan (Badgley), and Yves St. Laurent and Willi Smith (Mischka); line backed financially by Escada AG, 1992–2004; introduced bridal line, 1996, and footwear, 1999; opened store in Beverly Hills, CA, 2000.

Awards: Mouton Cadet Young Designer Award, 1989.

Sidelights

American designers Mark Badgley and James Mischka create elegant, ultra–luxurious evening gowns that are red–carpet favorites for some of the entertainment industry's best–dressed actresses. The beaded, form–fitting Badgley Mischka–label designs seem to hearken back to a bygone era of Hollywood dazzle. "Our philosophy is, 'One zip and you're glamorous,'" Badgley told Janice Min when she profiled the duo for *People*. "When you get dressed for evening, you shouldn't have to work hard at it."

Though the two designers—partners in business and in life—have lived in the New York City area since the early 1980s, each have ties to California. Badgley was born in East St. Louis, Missouri, in 1961, and grew up in suburb called Belleville. His father was a department–store executive whose job took the family to Lake Oswego, Oregon, when Badgley and his twin sister, O'Hara, were seven. The future designer claimed to have sketched evening clothes since he was a child. "I remember drawing women and clothes when I could barely hold a crayon," he told Min in *People*. He studied art at the University of Oregon, and then moved on to the University of Southern California, where he took business courses. Around 1982, he enrolled at the Parsons School of Design in New York City.

Mischka was a native of California, the eldest of three boys and born just before Christmas of 1960. The family moved from the beach town of Malibu to New Jersey when he was 12, however, and Mischka recalled it as a rather difficult transition. "In Malibu we would make love beads and dye our clothes," he said in the *People* interview with Min. "In New Jersey, it was totally chinos and button-down shirts." During his senior year of high school, Mischka won a National Merit Scholarship, and used it at Rice University. A biomedical engineering major there, he planned on designing artificial limbs as a career, but eventually switched to an arts-management program at the Houston, Texas, school. Around 1982, he, too moved to New York to study at Parsons.

Badgley and Mischka met at Parsons, and after graduating in 1985 began careers on Seventh Avenue. Badgley worked as a design assistant for Jackie Rogers and Donna Karan, while Mischka did a stint in Paris at Yves St. Laurent before working for the menswear line of designer Willi Smith. In 1988, the duo put together $250,000 in loans from their families, and formed their own company. They used their own names, though having an eponymous label initially seemed a bit of a drawback. "People thought Badgley Mischka was some old Russian lady," Badgley joked in the *People* article.

From the start, Badgley and Mischka were determined to only design eveningwear, keeping clear of the far more fickle, highly competitive sportswear and career sectors of women's fashion. Though their first showing of evening gowns was not much of a success, their second one resulted in orders from Saks Fifth Avenue, Barneys New York, and Neiman Marcus. Buyers and customers alike loved their ultra-feminine, sleek dresses, and a minor cult following developed, despite price tags that sometimes reached $5,000. Their designs were sewn from a variety of delicate fabrics, often in a subdued metal palette that became part of their signature style, and were usually elaborately beaded or embellished. The designers even aged some of their materials on purpose, so "they're not plastic and new-looking," Badgley told *St. Louis Post–Dispatch* writer Becky Homan. For example, they use Drano and a dry-cleaning fluid to take the orange sheen from gold thread, and soaked pearls in a Drano bath to achieve a more antiqued patina.

In their early years in business, despite doing $2 million in sales a year, Badgley and Mischka struggled to keep their business solvent, and were sometimes forced to resort to credit-card advances to make ends meet. In 1992, German ready-to-wear powerhouse Escada AG bought a controlling stake in their company. "We're really excited," Badgley told Constance C.R. White for a *WWD* article at the time. "Escada has unbelievable resources so we'll be able to use more luxurious fabrics." Within a few years, their dresses were favorites of actresses like Winona Ryder, Angela Bassett, and Sharon Stone, but well-heeled young executive women also liked them as well. "Our customer almost dresses like a man for day, in a real modern way," Mischka explained to Homan in the *St. Louis Post–Dispatch* about their line's appeal. "But she's bored dressing like that for evening. She wants over-the-top glamour by night."

In 1996, after devoted clients began clamoring for specially made dresses from the Badgley Mischka collection in white or off-white for their weddings, the designers decided to launch a bridal line sold out of the high-end salon at Saks. "A lot of the women who come to us wear designer clothes, and they want that look for their bridal dresses," Mischka said in a 1997 interview with White for the *New York Times.* The fashion journalist described the new Badgley Mischka venture as representative of a trend toward a more daring, couture-inspired elegance in bridal wear, but Mischka did admit that reality sometimes intruded on fantasy. "When we envision our evening gowns we see them being worn in palaces and on marble staircases," Mischka told the newspaper. "In reality, they're going to the Marriott."

With the Escada backing, Badgley Mischka were able to expand into daywear, evening bags, and shoes by 2000. They also opened their first store, a Beverly Hills boutique, which placed them near the epicenter of the old-style Hollywood glamor that continued to inspire their line. Overhead costs for their company remained high, however: the luxurious fabrics came from Europe, and were then cut, sewn, and fitted in Badgley Mischka's Seventh Avenue workshop. From there, a dress was boxed and flown to a beading factory in Bombay, India. By the time it returned ready for sale, it had logged some 70,000 air miles. Though their company did $40 million in sales in 2003, Badgley Mischka's label failed to turn a profit in tough economic times after 2001. Escada, struggling to stay afloat as well, began seeking a buyer for its 80 percent stake in late 2003, and several high-profile luxury-goods makers were reportedly interested. The designers were pragmatic about the pending sale. "We are ready to branch out, like open up another store," Mischka told *San Francisco Chronicle* writer Sylvia Rubin. "We want to do fragrance, eyewear, loungewear, and you need deep pockets for that. We're very, very close to signing a new deal; we're all geared up and ready to rock and roll."

Sources

Books

Contemporary Fashion, 2nd edition, St. James Press, 2002.

Periodicals

Footwear News, July 19, 1999, p. 4S.
New York Times, May 6, 1997, p. B11.
People, April 1, 1996, p. 101.

San Francisco Chronicle, June 6, 2000, p. E6; November 9, 2003, p. E6.
San Francisco Examiner, June 6, 2000, p. B3.
St. Louis Post–Dispatch, May 8, 1997, p. 1.
WWD, June 11, 1991, p. 7; January 28, 1992, p. 2; January 26, 1999, p. 2; June 8, 2000, p. 15; September 8, 2000, p. 11; February 4, 2003, p. 8; May 8, 2003, p. 7; October 13, 2003, p. 2; December 15, 2003, p. 2.

—Carol Brennan

Brian Becker

Chair and Chief Executive Officer of Clear Channel Entertainment

Born c. 1957, in Texas; son of Allen Becker (an insurance salesman and event promoter); married Stacy; children: four. *Education:* Earned undergraduate degree from Stanford University, 1979; University of California—Los Angeles, M.B.A., 1982.

Addresses: *Office*—Clear Channel Entertainment, 200 Basse Rd., San Antonio, TX 78209.

Career

Concert promoter at Stanford University, late 1970s; worked in the marketing department for Britrail, c. 1979–80; associate with a pay–television channel in southern California, and assistant in the office of a film producer, both early 1980s; PACE Entertainment, Houston, TX, employee in its theatrical division, after 1982; president and chief executive officer, 1994–98; after merger with SFX Entertainment served as executive vice president, 1998–2000; chair and chief executive officer of Clear Channel Entertainment, San Antonio, TX, 2000—.

Sidelights

Brian Becker serves as board chair and chief executive officer of Clear Channel Entertainment, a subsidiary of the media giant Clear Channel Communications. His father launched the promotions company that eventually became part of the Clear Channel empire, and Becker had worked for the predecessor since his teen years. In the 1990s, he was instrumental in helping make Clear Channel Entertainment into the world's largest tour and concert producer, and the industry–wide influence he wields landed him in the No. 11 spot on *Entertainment Weekly'* "Power 2003" list of movers and shakers in the business.

Becker was born in the late 1950s, and grew up in Houston, Texas. In 1966, his insurance salesperson father, Allen, formed PACE Entertainment with a partner to operate the annual boat show in Houston. The company soon branched out to demolition derbies and motorcycle races, and during his formative years Becker and his siblings enjoyed backstage access to celebrities like daredevil motorcyclist Evel Knievel. Becker's interests were of a more college–track variety, however: he led his Bellaire High School debate team to a 1975 Texas championship, was active in the Jewish service organization B'nai Brith, was an avid baseball and tennis player, and worked during the summer as an intern in the offices of the publicity firm that handled PACE events.

PACE entered the music business after winning the contract for a 1975 Houston concert by the British rock band the Who, then at the height of their fame. Not long afterward, Becker enrolled at Stanford University in California, where he honed his concert–promotion skills by bringing such acts as Parliament/Funkadelic to campus. After graduating in 1979, he spent a year in England working for the marketing department of Britrail, the British national passenger rail service, and then returned Stateside to begin business school at the University of California at Los Angeles.

Armed with his M.B.A., Becker headed back to Texas in 1982 and began working for PACE's recently launched theatrical division. His office helped make regional tours of hit Broadway shows standard fare in many American cities. It was an innovative move by PACE management at the time, for few Broadway producers wanted to work with regional promoters. Their first shows in Memphis and Nashville—*Hello, Dolly!* with Carol Channing and a *King and I* production that starred Yul Brynner—fared poorly, and PACE lost some $400,000. "Even today that's a big loss, but back then it was a huge loss," Becker recalled in an interview with *Houston Chronicle* writer Clifford Pugh. "But we paid the bills. In New York, the general managers and producers said, 'Wait a second, these guys in Texas paid their bills. We ought to sell them some more dates.'"

Becker helped PACE become the leading producer of regional theater events in several American cities, and urged his father and the other executives to make investments into building their own venues for musical events. He had noticed that open-air amphitheaters often did well, despite their limited summer-weather seasons, and recognized that they were relatively cheap to build and operate. In 1994, he became president and CEO of PACE Entertainment, and helped negotiate a deal with SFX Entertainment that gave the company dominance in the newly emerging national network for live-event promotions. From 1998 to 2000 he served as an executive vice president at SFX, and was given another top job when Clear Channel Communications bought SFX for $4 million in 2000.

Since then, Becker has served as chair and CEO of Clear Channel Entertainment, the company's live-event division. It produces the immensely successful tours of acts from Ozzfest to Madonna's "Drowned World" tour, and is still involved financing such theatrical productions like the smash New York musical *The Producers*. Becker even appeared onstage at the 2001 Antoinette Perry awards ceremony to accept the Tony for Broadway's best musical of the year. Some assert that the larger, highly profitable Clear Channel Communications, with its ownership of radio stations across the country, is too dominant a player in the entertainment business. A Clear Channel show that Becker is promoting, for example, enjoys tie-ins in various markets that are home to the 1,200 radio stations that Clear Channel owns.

Becker dismisses charges that Clear Channel wields too much power and is only interested in working with established, money-making acts. "We'll do some 8,000 concert events this year," he told *Hollywood Reporter* journalist Tamara Conniff, and noted that nearly three-quarters "of those events are being done in theaters and being done in clubs where we make little to no money or lose money. We do it because we are providing a forum for new and emerging artists to be exposed and develop their careers." Becker was also enthusiastic about his company's new "InstantLive CD" program, in which concert-goers can immediately purchase a CD of the performance after the last encore.

Under Becker's guidance, Clear Channel Entertainment is moving into Europe as well, promoting the popular music festivals there that are a staple of the summer season. Again, his company faced charges of using its brand-name power to gain a foothold. "We are the largest, and by definition that creates a rallying cry for those that want to be the largest," Becker reflected in an article by *Billboard*'s Ray Waddell. "I will tell you this: It's not based upon the merit of how we operate. There are people that are going to say, 'Big is bad.' And it's not going to matter why or how, it's just going to be a matter of fact."

Becker is married to a former bond broker whom he met when she interviewed for a job with PACE in 1996. They have four children. His father, Allen, still serves as a consultant to the company, though officially retired, and his brother, Gary, is also an executive with Clear Channel. "I get a tremendous amount of enjoyment out of doing my job well," Becker told Pugh in the *Houston Chronicle*. "There is truly nothing like being part of the universe based upon the creativity of the human spirit. There's nothing like the live experience."

Sources

Billboard, December 6, 2003, p. 66.
Entertainment Weekly, October 24, 2003, p. 26.
Hollywood Reporter, October 17, 2003, p. 1.
Houston Chronicle, September 2, 2001, p. 8; October 15, 2003, p. 3.

—*Carol Brennan*

Oscar Berger

AP/Wide World Photos

President of Guatemala

Born Oscar Berger Perdomo, November 8, 1946, in Guatemala City, Guatemala. *Education:* Earned law degree from Universidad Rafael Landivar.

Addresses: *Office*—Office of the President, Palacio Nacional, Guatemala City, Guatemala.

Career

Worked in family businesses; formed political group, Comite Civico Plan de Avanzada Nacional, with other business leaders, 1985; became Guatemala City city council member, 1985; mayor of Guatemala City, 1991–99; ran for presidency and lost, 1999; ran again as candidate of new party, Gran Alianza Nacional, 2003; took office as president of Guatemala, 2004.

Sidelights

Oscar Berger twice ran for president of Guatemala, and won on his second attempt, in 2003. Berger had been a popular mayor of Guatemala's capital, Guatemala City, but swore to leave politics after he lost his presidential bid in 1999. Conflict within the political party he had helped found led to Berger's apparent retirement from politics. But he nevertheless returned to the stage in 2003 at the head of a new political party. Berger won in a second round runoff election with a narrow majority. Praised as a good administrator and a skillful broker of compromises, Berger inherited a country plagued by poverty, famine, and an uncomfortable legacy of military dictatorship. Berger's nickname is *el conejo,* or "the rabbit," and some analysts judged him too manageable in the hands of Guatemala's entrenched business interests. Nevertheless, immediately on taking office, Berger took several bold steps, cutting the size of the army in accordance with a 1996 peace treaty, and endeavoring to cut corruption in government. Early into his presidency, Berger had a high approval rating among Guatemalans.

Berger was born in Guatemala City in 1946 to a wealthy family with business interests in coffee and sugar plantations. Berger went to the country's best private schools, and later earned a degree in law and the title of notary public. After law school, Berger managed various business interests, and he did not begin his political career until he was almost 40 years old. In 1985, Guatemala ended years of military dictatorship, though the country was still entrenched in a civil war that lasted from 1960 to 1996. Berger joined with other businessmen and his friend, Alvaro Arzu, and created the liberal policy group Comite Civico Plan de Avanzada Nacional (Civic Committee for National Advancement Strategy) in 1985. This group evolved into the national political party Partido de Avanzada Nacional

(Party of National Advancement, known as PAN). Arzu won the mayoral election in Guatemala City in 1985, and Berger held his first political post that year, becoming a city council member. In 1990 Berger got the PAN party blessing to run for mayor, replacing Arzu. Berger won the election, and took office as mayor of Guatemala City in January of 1991.

In his first term as mayor, Berger confronted the complex problem of traffic in the city. Berger wished to stimulate public transportation, but was stymied by the owners of the bus companies. The owners banded together and raised bus ticket prices unilaterally. Berger won the good opinion of the citizens of Guatemala City for taking the side of the people against the bus owners. This led to his re-election in 1995. The transportation situation only got more difficult in his second term. In 1996, the bus owners went on strike. Berger eventually called on the military to preserve order in the streets, and he also hired private trucks to carry people to work. Berger successfully resolved the bus strike, with concessions on both sides, and in 1998 the city acquired its own fleet of buses.

The PAN party suffered internal dissension, but nonetheless promoted Berger as its presidential candidate in 1999. Berger ran a race building on his image as a populist, promising to fight poverty and urban crime. But Berger was not a great orator, and this hindered his presidential bid. Berger lost the election that year to Alfonso Portillo of the conservative party Guatemalan Republican Front (FRG). Though Portillo had also campaigned as a populist, his FRG party was led by Guatemala's former dictator General Efrain Rios Montt. Berger's loss embittered him, and he declared that he was leaving politics forever. Portillo's administration, meanwhile, was beset by scandals involving drugs and corruption, and the FRG party was roiled by dissension over Rios Montt. Rios Montt had been banned from seeking election because of his past actions, but he managed to have this ruling overturned by a sympathetic court. Faced with what looked like a weakened FRG, in 2003 Oscar Berger decided to return to politics. He won the PAN party nomination as presidential candidate. Months after winning the PAN nomination and gaining the support of his old friend, Arzu, Berger defected from the party and became the candidate of a much smaller party, the Gran Alianza Nacional (GANA). GANA was a coalition of three still-smaller parties, and was considered a center-right wing group.

The 2003 election made international waves because former dictator Rios Montt ran as the FRG party candidate. The general was accused of crimes against humanity, and courts both in Guatemala and in Spain were considering trying him for his part in the deaths of thousands of peasants in the months after he took power in a coup in 1982. His election would have strained Guatemala's relations with many other countries. But Rios Montt did poorly, and Oscar Berger won the first round of polling. Berger faced off against Alvaro Colom, a textile executive with much support in the indigenous Mayan community, for a second round of voting. Berger won the second round with about 54 percent of the vote. Yet his GANA party won only 47 seats in the 158-seat congress. Immediately after the election, Berger began putting together a legislative coalition with PAN and other political parties.

In a sense, Berger's win seemed unenviable. Guatemala was racked by poverty, famine, government corruption, and organized crime. Berger had carried the nickname "rabbit" since childhood, and he had been ridiculed for gaffes and verbal flubs while on the campaign trail. Some political analysts doubted that he was a strong enough figure to make a dent in Guatemala's problems. But after taking office in January of 2004, Berger began making good on some difficult campaign promises. Under terms of a peace treaty negotiated in 1996, the Guatemalan government had pledged to reduce its armed forces. While previous administrations had delayed implementing the treaty, Berger cut the size of the army by more than 40 percent and closed most of Guatemala's barracks. This finally put the size of Guatemala's army in line with armies in neighboring Latin American countries. Berger also publicly confronted his government's unsavory past. In April of 2004, Berger held a ceremony with the heads of Congress and the Supreme Court, and acknowledged government complicity in the 1990 murder of human rights worker Myrna Mack. Berger also moved against government corruption, making all his ministers and officials sign a code of ethics. Though he had won only 54 percent of the vote, in an election that many voters sat out, early in his term Berger was very popular. A Mexican consulting group took a poll showing that 83 percent of Guatemala's citizens approved of Berger. This was the highest approval rating of any Latin American head of state at that time. Berger vowed to use his time in office to fight poverty and hunger, problems which all sides agreed were extremely pressing.

Sources

Periodicals

Economist, November 13, 1999, p. 36.
Latin American Weekly Report, January 6, 2004; April 6, 2004.

Latin America Regional Reports, June 17, 2003, p. 2.
Latinnews Daily, April 1, 2004.
New York Times, November 11, 2003, p. A9.

Online

"Conservative Ex–Mayor Wins Guatemalan Presidential Election," CNN.com, http://www.cnn. com/2003/WORLD/americas/12/29/guatemala. election.ap/index.html (January 5, 2004).

—A. Woodward

Orlando Bloom

Actor

Born January 13, 1977, in Canterbury, Kent, England; son of Harry Bloom (an activist) and Sonia Copeland–Bloom (a language instructor). *Education:* National Youth Theatre of London; British American Drama Academy; Guildhall School of Music and Drama, 1996–99.

Addresses: *Agent*—c/o ICM, Oxford House, 76 Oxford St., London W1D 1BS, England.

Career

Actor in films, including: *Wilde,* 1997; *Black Hawk Down,* 2001; *The Lord of the Rings: The Fellowship of the Ring,* 2001; *The Lord of the Rings: The Two Towers,* 2002; *Pirates of the Caribbean: The Curse of the Black Pearl,* 2003; *The Lord of the Rings: The Return of the King,* 2003; *Ned Kelly,* 2003. Television appearances include: *Midsomer Murders,* 2000; *Smack the Pony,* 2000. Stage appearances include: *Casualty, London's Burning, Twelfth Night, Uncle Vanya, Little Me, Peer Gynt.*

Awards: Empire Award for best debut for *Lord of the Rings: The Fellowship of the Ring,* 2001; best breakthrough star award, MTV Movie Awards, for *Lord of the Rings: The Fellowship of the Ring,* 2002.

Sidelights

Actor Orlando Bloom got his first big break when he was cast as the elven archer Legolas Greenleaf in the film trilogy *Lord of the Rings.* His good looks and acting ability quickly transformed him from an unknown to a young heartthrob, but he also garnered favorable critical reviews. Since filming the trilogy, Bloom has worked steadily on a variety of films, and his career continues to grow.

Bloom grew up in Canterbury, England, where his mother ran a language academy for foreign students; his father, Harry Bloom, was a Jewish South African anti–apartheid activist and author of a novel, *Transvaal Episode.* Harry Bloom died when his son was four years old. Bloom became interested in acting at a very early age; he was captivated with television and movie characters, as well as by street performers. He was particularly fascinated by the fact that one actor could portray many different people so convincingly. "I loved James Dean," he told Cindy Pearlman in the *Houston Chronicle,* "because he put so much passion in his work."

Bloom's mother encouraged him and his sister to participate in local poetry and Bible readings, feeding his interest in drama and performance. When Bloom was 16, after winning several contests for reciting poetry and Bible verses, he left school and moved to London to join the National Youth Theatre. After spending two seasons with the theater, he earned a scholarship to train with the British American Drama Academy. While training, he auditioned for a variety of television and film roles, and won small parts in the plays *Casualty* and *London's Burning.* His appearance in a play at London's Tricycle Theater led him to acquire an agent, a big step for a young actor. Bloom then spent three years at the Guildhall School of Music and Drama. At Guildhall, he appeared in a number of plays, including *Twelfth Night, Uncle Vanya, Little Me,* and *Peer Gynt.* He also made his film debut in the film *Wilde,* a biography of Oscar Wilde, which was critically acclaimed; in the film, Bloom played a young prostitute.

While at Guildhall, Bloom suffered an accident that could have ended his career, if not his life. In 1998, at the age of 21, he was the home of friends, who told him that the door to their roof terrace was warped and couldn't be opened from the inside. Someone would have to get to it from the outside, and kick it in. Bloom climbed out a window and onto a drainpipe, planning to climb along to the roof, where he could open the door. However, his weight was too much for the pipe, which gave way. Bloom fell three stories to the ground below, breaking his back, and was unable to move. He spent the next four days in a hospital, trying to understand what the doctors were telling him: that he would never walk again. He underwent surgery in which metal plates were bolted to his spine, but the doctors warned him that this was risky, that it would probably not be successful, and that at best, he would still have severe damage to his bones and nerves. Despite this depressing prognosis, he left the hospital 12 days later—walking, though with crutches. Shortly after, he was able to walk without the crutches. He did have to learn to walk again, reminding himself how to do it by repeating "heel–ball–toe" with each step.

Bloom told Jeff Dawson in the *Weekend Australian,* "It was kind of the making of me, really. I feel like it really tested my belief in myself and everything else because they told me I'd be in a wheelchair. It took a while for me to really comprehend what had happened." He continued to pursue his interest in sports and horseback riding, although he admitted to Pearlman that he became more cautious: "If I'm going to get on a snowboard, I'm aware that I could do serious damage to myself. So I don't just fly off a cliff and hope there will be a big pile of snow beneath me instead of a rock. I check to make sure that the snow is there." He also considered buying a motorcycle, but rejected the idea because it was too risky.

Although Bloom had planned on a career in the theater, soon after graduating from Guildhall he landed a part in a television series, *Midsomer Murders.* He had also attracted the interest of casting agents for director Peter Jackson, who was planning the three–film trilogy *The Lord of the Rings,* based on the fantasy trilogy of that name by J.R.R. Tolkien. The trilogy would be filmed in New Zealand. Within a year of his fall from the drainpipe, Bloom was riding horses through the trilogy's fictional land of Middle Earth, playing an elf, Legolas Greenleaf. The role would be a breakout for Bloom, since it not only guaranteed him work in three films, but the films would garner international attention. For the role, Bloom had to hide his brown hair under a long blond wig, transform his brown eyes to blue with contact lenses, and wear pointed elf ears over his own, but he was nevertheless recognizable as a new talent on the big screen. Female fans in particular went wild over Bloom, making him the newest teen heartthrob. For his role in the trilogy, he won an Empire Award for Best Debut as well as an MTV Movie Award for Best Breakthrough Star.

While filming the trilogy, Bloom fell off a horse and broke several ribs, but this did not prevent him from continuing to work. All three parts of the trilogy were filmed simultaneously, which required Bloom and the other cast members to spend a year and a half in New Zealand. Bloom told Henry Cabot Beck in *Interview,* "It was like winning the lottery. I mean, imagine being flown to this amazing country and being taught how to shoot a bow and arrow, learn to ride horses and study swordplay.... Not until I'd filmed a few scenes did I finally believe it was actually happening." Bloom enjoyed learning these skills, and became quite proficient at archery. He was able to shoot paper plates out of the sky and while riding a horse, dropping the reins to loose arrows at enemies. During the filming, much of the movie had to be kept secret, so Bloom and the other actors were not allowed to take photographs of themselves in costume, and while riding back and forth to work with makeup on, had to wear hooded jackets to hide their appearance. By the time the long period of filming ended, the cast and crew had become very close, and when Jackson called the end of the final scene, they were all crying. The stuntmen, in tribute to the film and those who worked on it, did a Maori dance called a "hucker." "It was really sad and hugely emotional," Bloom told Amy Longsdorf in the *Record.* The trilogy, which was released in 2001, 2002, and 2003, was a hit with audiences as well as with critics.

Bloom's other 2001 film, *Black Hawk Down,* provided an odd reflection of Bloom's real life: his character in the film was a United States marine who fell out of a helicopter and was similarly injured. Unlike Bloom, the character was carried out of the action on a stretcher early in the film, and did not return. In 2003's *Pirates of the Caribbean: The Curse of the Black Pearl*, Bloom played the romantic lead, Will Turner, a former blacksmith–turned–pirate who joins Jack Sparrow, played by Johnny Depp, in mayhem on the high seas. Together, the two must rescue a beautiful maiden from an evil pirate. Bloom thought he would enjoy the movie because as a child he had watched many pirate movies on long Sunday afternoons, and like many other children, had imagined being involved in boat–to–boat battles, swinging on ropes and brandishing swords. In addition, Bloom, who as a young man had idolized Depp, told the *Houston Chronicle*'s Pearlman, "Knowing that Johnny Depp was involved in this movie made it a no–brainer for me. Johnny is such a hero of mine." Depp advised Bloom that he should take roles that were meaningful to him, not simply go for the money, and to give his career time if it needed to develop. However, Bloom's career was not slow to develop, and he did not have to wait to make money. *Pirates of the Caribbean* director Gore Verbinski told Jeff Chu in *Time International* that Bloom's appeal was that he was both "beautiful and accessible. As cool as Orlando can be, there is also something there you can relate to." Bloom admitted that all the attention he was getting made him nervous, telling Chu, "Celebrity and stardom are never things I wanted. To acknowledge that's what's happening is odd. To admit it to yourself, that seems wrong."

Bloom next appeared in *Ned Kelly,* directed by Gregor Jordan. The film, about the life of Australian outback robber Ned Kelly, featured Bloom as a member of Kelly's gang. Jordan told the *Record*'s Longsdorf, "Orlando is a movie star waiting to happen.... He's in the long tradition of guys like James Dean and Russell Crowe. There's just something about him that makes people want to sit in the dark and watch him on the movie screen."

Bloom was cast as the romantic lead, Paris, in *Troy,* based on the ancient epic, the Iliad. He told the *Weekend Australian*'s Dawson, "I suppose I'm getting into that position, which I suppose all actors want to be in, where I have some control over what I'm doing, yet what goes with that is a whole new series of pressures." He told Dawson that while

filming the movie, he and costar Brad Pitt went out to dinner and were mobbed with photographers and crowds of fans. Of Pitt's response, Bloom said, "I was so impressed with the way he kind of kept his composure. But it's bizarre to see how one person can have that kind of effect on that many people just immediately. It was really scary." Bloom also began filming or contracted for roles in *The Calcium Kid, Kingdom of Heaven, Pirates of the Caribbean 2,* and *Haven* (which he is co–producing). In addition, Bloom told Dawson that his own growing fame, as well as his busy film schedule, was beginning to catch up with him. "It's been such a whirlwind since the release of the first *Rings* film.... I guess the novelty's wearing off—all the travel, all the excitement of doing the press stuff." When told he had been named one of 2003's "It" people by *Entertainment Weekly*, he laughed and said, according to the *Houston Chronicle*'s Pearlman, "That's huge. Massive. What is 'it'?" Bloom told the *Record*'s Longsdorf, "You know, the heartthrob thing—I hope that it won't stop me from making more interesting choices, because that's what I intend to try and do."

Sources

Periodicals

Houston Chronicle, July 13, 2003, p. 8.
Interview, November 2001, p. 50.
Newsweek, July 14, 2003, p. 56.
Record (Bergen County, New Jersey), July 6, 2003, p. E1.
Teen People, December 1, 2002, p. 80.
Time International, August 11, 2003, p. 52.
Weekend Australian (Sydney, Australia), August 30, 2003, p. B1.

Online

"Biography for Orlando Bloom," Internet Movie Database, http://www.imdb.com/name/nm0089217/bio (December 1, 2003).
Biography Resource Center, Gale Group, 2003.

—*Kelly Winters*

Michele Bohbot

Fashion designer

Born c. 1959, in Morocco; married Marc Bohbot, c. 1979; children: Yoann, Sandra, Steven, Stephanie, Noah, Chloe, Celine.

Addresses: *Home*—Beverly Hills, CA. *Office*—Bisou–Bisou, Inc., 2025 S. Figueroa St., Los Angeles, CA 90007.

Career

Manager of Paris boutique chain until 1987; jeans importer in Los Angeles, late 1980s; founder, Bisou–Bisou, Inc., 1989.

Sidelights

Los Angeles, California–based designer Michele Bohbot inked a 2002 deal that would put her Bisou Bisou line of contemporary sportswear across hundreds of square feet on the floors of one of the biggest retailers in the United States. Bohbot and her company had enjoyed tremendous success in the 1990s, but a recessionary climate and resulting retail losses made it harder for mid–size companies like hers to survive on their own. A French–Moroccan mother of seven, Bohbot had never actually been inside a J.C. Penney store before the deal to carry her line exclusively was discussed, but was looking forward to the new partnership. "It was a tough decision, but I have the opportunity to dress more people," she told Anne D'Innocenzio for an article that appeared in the Bergen County, New Jersey, *Record.*

Bohbot hails from the fabled city of Casablanca, Morocco, where her father owned a boat–building company. Morocco was a protectorate of France until 1956, and her family was one of many European–heritage expatriates who had settled and prospered in the North African country. She met her future husband, also French–Moroccan, when she was 19, and Marc Bohbot proposed to her four days later. The newlyweds settled in Paris, France, where her husband ran a clothing–boutique business that he ultimately suggested she join. Bohbot was aghast at the prospect, as she recalled in an interview with *People*'s Allison Adato. "I didn't think this was normal for a man to send me to work," she remembered. "I married to raise children! But I wanted him to love me, and I wanted to impress him, so I did it."

In 1987, the Bohbots moved to Los Angeles to establish a clothing–import business. The line of French jeans they sold failed to do well, however, so Bohbot decided to start designing her own line of casual tops for women with a fitted, colorful style she found quintessentially Californian. Bisou Bisou, a name that means "small kiss" in French, was formally launched in 1989, and within a few years it was a thriving sportswear company. The trendy clothes that Bohbot designed were sold in upscale retailers like Nordstrom, and by 1999 her company was posting sales of $60 million. Bisou Bisou also operated some two dozen freestanding stores by 2000, but the economic slump that began in earnest the next year hampered the company's growth. Some of its department–store clients experienced problems meeting their contractual obligations, for example, and suddenly retail real–estate space was prohibitively expensive. Early in 2002, Bohbot and her husband, who serves as the company's chief executive officer, were forced to file for Chapter 11 bankruptcy protection.

In December of 2002, Bisou Bisou entered into a deal with Plano, Texas–based J.C. Penney that would give the American department–store chain exclusive rights to sell her Bisou Bisou line. The 500 accounts at competing retailers were closed, as were most of the Bisou Bisou stores. From that point, Bohbot's line would be available only in about 450 stores across the United States—about half of the total number of the J.C. Penney empire. If they sold well, however, more would be added at a later date. Bohbot had never been inside any one of those 900–plus Penney's stores before the deal was signed, but she was pragmatic about the new venture. "Sometimes in life you have opportunities," she *WWD* writer David Moin. "And if you are a little bit smart, you need to adapt yourself to what is happening. I never went to a J.C. Penney. It was really strange to see it, but I was really open and I said, 'why not?' It was comfortable to stay where we were, but we were comfortable to go to the next level."

Bohbot still retained creative control of her company, but the Penney deal necessitated a few changes to meet the mass–retail market. Bisou Bisou would now offer a wider range of sizes, and the seasonal–collection presentations to buyers and journalists twice yearly in New York City were jettisoned. Bohbot's new arrangement, however, also meant that the average price for a Bisou Bisou item would be significantly reduced, because working under the manufacturing, shipping, and distribution umbrella of such a large retailer helped to defray costs significantly. A few months into the deal, Bohbot told *WWD*'s Moin that things were going well. "Nobody has ever removed some trim or changed the fabric. The production is beautiful." Apart from the larger sizes, there was a slight shift in what Bisou Bisou now offered its devoted customers. "The collection is more balanced than what it used to be," Bohbot admitted, when Moin

asked her if any of its trademark body–conscious look had been compromised. "There are some sexy pieces and some less sexy pieces."

Bisou Bisou sales were predicted to easily reach the $100 million mark in 2004. The daring move on the part of J.C. Penney executives to make the exclusive offer followed an important new trend in the American retail industry, one in which mass–market purveyors sought to land a bit of cool for their shelves. Following the Martha Stewart/Kmart success came Minnesota–based Target and its cache of designer lines, from architect Michael Graves to Seventh Avenue stalwart Isaac Mizrahi.

Despite her career successes, Bohbot also found the time to fulfill her original goal of starting a family. Her first child, a son named Yoann, was born in the early 1980s, followed at two– and three–year intervals by his brothers and sisters, including twins Chloe and Celine, who were the last of Bohbot's seven. Her husband told *People* that he never thought he would have such a large brood, and had once considered two a sufficient goal, "but she would come up to me and say, 'Hi. I'm pregnant.'" The family of nine resides in a palatial Beverly Hills home with 18 bathrooms and eleven bedrooms. To get through her busy day, Bohbot employs a driver, nanny, cook, and housekeeping help, and is able to finish her Bisou Bisou workday by 5 p.m. She also teaches yoga in her spare time, and insists that all children be home for dinner nightly. Those close to her credit her remarkable organizational skills for giving her serenity despite her hectic lifestyle. "It's like our family lives in a hotel that my mother manages," her eldest son told *People*.

Sources

Cincinnati Post, March 11, 2003, p. C7.
Los Angeles Business Journal, February 18, 2002, p. 9.
People, March 24, 2003, pp. 99–100.
Record (Bergen County, NJ), March 13, 2003, p. B1.
WWD, July 19, 2000, p. 9; December 4, 2002, p. 1.

—Carol Brennan

Lee Bontecou

Artist

Born in 1931, in Providence, RI; daughter of Russell Bontecou (a salesman); married William Giles (an artist), 1965; children: Valerie. *Education:* Graduated from Bedford Junior College, 1952; studied art at Arts Students League of New York; studied metal welding at Skowhegan Art School.

Addresses: *Gallery*—c/o Knoedler Gallery, 19 E. 70th St., New York, NY 10021.

Career

Became interested in art, c. 1950; artist in New York City, NY, and PA, c. 1952— first group exhibition, Castelli Gallery, 1959; first solo exhibition, Castelli Gallery, 1960; art teacher at Brooklyn College, 1971–91.

Sidelights

Artist Lee Bontecou was a popular figure in the New York art world from the late 1950s through the early 1970s, in part because of her unique constructions and sculptures as well as her intense drawings. She dropped out of the art scene in the early 1970s to work on her art out of the limelight and at her own pace. Though she primarily lived on a farm in Pennsylvania and focused much of her energy on raising her daughter, she also found time to teach art for 20 years at the Brooklyn College. In the 1990s and early 2000s, Bontecou's work was rediscovered and she was the subject of a career retrospective in 2003. Considered one of the most important, original sculptors of her generation, Dodie

Kazanjian described Bontecou's art in *Vogue*: "Her work is sui generis, entirely her own in its constant oscillation between abstract and figurative, toughness and lyricism, the intimate and the infinite, the natural world and the world of her imagination."

Born in 1931 in Providence, Rhode Island, Bontecou was the daughter of Russell Bontecou, a salesman who loved fishing. Bontecou's father and her uncle helped invent and later sell the aluminum canoe. She and her older brother, Frank, were raised in Westchester County, New York, where she attended public schools. Summers were spent with her grandmother in Nova Scotia, Canada. As a child, she was very attracted to natural history, which would later inform her work as did machines, especially those created for the war effort. She was also influenced by World War II, which was fought during her childhood. Her mother worked in a factory wiring submarine parts.

Bontecou was not particularly interested in art until she went to college. She took her first art class at Bedford Junior College. After Bontecou graduated from that Massachusetts–based school in 1952, she moved to New York City. There, she spent three years studying at the Arts Student League in New York City, while working to support herself. She also spent one summer at Maine's Skowhegan Art School learning to do metal welding on scholarship. While there, she created a partially abstract sculpture in cast iron of a man who was 13 feet tall. As a young artist, Surrealists, especially Alberto Giacometti, were among her influences.

From 1957–58, Bontecou lived in Rome, Italy, studying art on a Fulbright Scholarship. There, she began experimenting with black in drawings. She began creating soot drawings by employing an acetylene torch but turning down the oxygen to create a uniquely deep black. The black had depth and a velvet look that slowly graduated. The drawings that Bontecou created using this technique were called "worldscapes." This discovery changed the way she looked at her world. In Italy, she also created some animals, birds, and people in semi-abstract form primarily in terra cotta, but also a few cast in bronze.

When Bontecou returned to New York City in 1958, she continued to experiment with black in drawings. In the late 1950s and early 1960s, she also moved from worldscapes to bigger constructions, with black still a key feature. Her first important works in the art world were wall constructions fabricated primarily from found objects. Living above a laundry, she used worn–out laundry conveyor belts made of heavy canvas, as well as canvas and/or muslin, airplane parts, industrial sawtooths, and black velvet. Bontecou sewed or constructed these materials together with copper wire on steel frames. The finished works projected out several feet from the wall and into the viewers' space.

These works and others were shown at her first show, a group show, at Leo Castelli's gallery in New York in 1959. Castelli, one of the most high profile and highly respected dealers of new art of the time, gave her a solo show in 1960. Bontecou's work received much critical praise and soon made her a popular figure on the New York art scene. Years later, her work was still praised. Reviewing Bontecou's 2003 retrospective, Doug Harvey of *LA Weekly* wrote, "Her large, labor–intensive wall reliefs—constructed from fragments of worn and discolored canvas stretched and attached with twisted wire onto elaborately welded geometric steel structures, almost invariably framing a central circular void darkened with black soot—struck a disturbing balance between a delicate but assured abstract formal genius and a brooding fascination with the visual vocabulary of the military–industrial complex."

By the early 1960s, Bontecou was regarded as a connection between 1950s Abstract Expressionism and pop art and minimalism that was becoming popu-

lar in the 1960s. She continued to create constructions, welding frames into shapes and attaching found materials to it. Many of her works in this time period featured handles, grommets, canvas straps, and other materials available at hardware stores and Army surplus stores. Bontecou's works in this time period included "The Prisons," which consisted of small rectangular metal pieces, and 1961's "Untitled," which had iron bars forming a vertical grid with a figure trapped behind them. Museums began buying her work, and she was included in a 1961 exhibit at the Museum of Modern Art, *The Age of Assemblage.*

Bontecou was commissioned to create art by the mid–1960s. One of her better–known works was a large relief created for the New York State Theater Lobby in New York City's Lincoln Center. This was one of the largest pieces she ever did, and it was created using a banner and other airplane parts from a World War II–era bomber. The finished product looked like an airplane wing. At the time, Bontecou was fascinated with jets taking off and would watch them on a regular basis. She also made model airplanes in her spare time.

Bontecou's other works in this time period were also influenced by airplanes and their materials. In addition being more streamlined, aerodynamic, and full of metallic elements, many of her canvas works featured panels that were tinted in shades of grays and blacks. She also began using hardwood and was sometimes influenced by architecture. Bontecou's sculptures continued to evolve from the abstract to include plants, insects, and undersea creatures in her forms. Though most of Bontecou's work consisted of constructions, she always continued to draw.

Though Bontecou had some artist friends, she gradually began withdrawing from the art world by the late 1960s. She slowly went to fewer shows and soon became out of touch with what other artists were doing. She already had a farm in rural Pennsylvania, and growing less enchanted with New York City. Her personal life began changing. After being friends with artist William Giles for several years, the pair became a couple in 1964 and married the following year. In 1966, Bontecou gave birth to their daughter, Valerie. By this time, the family had moved out of New York and lived variously in Gettysburg, Pennsylvania; Long Island; Rockland County, New York; and Bryn Athyn, Pennsylvania, before settling permanently on their farm.

Bontecou still showed her work through the early 1970s in New York City. By this time, she was experimenting with carving objects out of Styrofoam and placing them in a vacuum press. In this process, she created plastic fish, flowers, and plants, some of which were very large. One work from 1970 featured a plastic fish hanging from the ceiling with the tail of another fish in its mouth. Her comment on the way the world was changing and becoming very plastic was not well–received at the time, though this social commentary was later regarded as meaningful, innovative, and political. Her last exhibit for many years came in 1971 and featured the plastic flowers and fish.

Negative criticism was not the reason why Bontecou dropped out of the art scene for many years. She wanted to work at her own pace instead of meeting the demands of a gallery–shown artist. She also wanted to raise her daughter and play a large role in her life, and took care of her ill father during the last years of his life. Though some critics believed otherwise, Bontecou did not disappear entirely. In 1971, she took a job as an art teacher at the Brooklyn College. There, she taught design, sculpture, and drawing for the next 20 years. She commuted from her farm to the city a few days a week to meet the requirements of teaching.

While Bontecou was out of the art scene, the museums that had bought her work in the 1960s did not display it very often in the 1970s and 1980s, and she fell off the art radar. Though the art world had basically forgotten her, she continued to create works on her own, primarily small sculptures and drawings, that were influenced by both industry and nature. Her sculptures in the 1980s and 1990s were constructions of steel wires with other elements worked into them that included smaller metal or ceramic pieces and wire mesh. Bontecou's larger sculptures often had a natural form to them while the smaller works were more abstract. Some pieces were mobile reliefs; many were complex and very original. As the 2000s approached, Bontecou's work featured skulls, skeletal structures, and animal bones in her delicate sculptures of wire, porcelain beads, and cloth with some color. She created these works in her private studio located in a barn on her farm. In 1993, Bontecou's profile was raised when the Los Angeles–based Museum of Contemporary Art featured a retrospective of some of her work from the 1960s and 1970s, both reliefs and drawings, that later moved to the Parrish Art Museum. It was her first show in 16 years. Bontecou did not organize it and none of her post–early 1970s work was included. At the time, she was adamant about not displaying her "new" work. Her attitude changed after she suffered a life–threatening illness in the late 1990s and early 2000s. She suffered from

aplastic anemia, a disease of the bone marrow, but was nursed back to health by her husband. The incident prompted her to access the whole of her career.

By the early 2000s, Bontecou allowed her new works to be shown as part of exhibits about her career. A display of 27 of her drawings, some recent, was shown at the Daniel Weinberg Gallery in Los Angeles, California, in 2001. The pieces showed Bontecou's skill in this area, but also reflected her style in her sculptures and reliefs. Reviewing the show, Christopher Miles of *Artforum International* wrote, "The drawings involve strange jumblings of serene and sinister, sensual and clinical, comical and foreboding. And all reflect Bontecou's odd penchant for mixing feminine with masculine and hybridizing attributes of the natural with those of the machine–made, and the machine itself."

Bontecou also played a hand in organizing her first major retrospective, which was organized at the Hammer Museum at the University of California at Los Angeles in 2002. About half of the show included post–1971 works, many of which had never been displayed before. There was some controversy for the artist. She was offended by an essay included in the show's catalog that was written by New York art critic Robert Storr that featured commentary on her, her career, and influences. She wrote an "Artist's Statement" to indirectly address related issues, including her influences and decision to drop out of the art scene for so long. Despite this problem, the show and her work were praised by critics. Christopher Knight of the *Los Angeles Times* wrote, "Bontecou's art is a masterful tour de force, mesmerizing and poignant."

With the success of this retrospective, Bontecou began showing at a gallery in New York City again. She agreed to work with the Knoedler Gallery, and among her first shows there was a display of her drawings in 2004. Of her decades–long withdrawal from the art scene, she was quoted by Calvin Tomkins of the *New Yorker* as saying "I've never left the art world. I'm in the real art world."

Selected exhibitions

Castelli Gallery (group shows), 1959, 1994; (solo shows), 1960–71, 2000.
(With others) *The Art of Assemblage,* Museum of Modern Art, New York City, 1961.
(With others) *Americans 1963,* Museum of Modern Art, New York City, 1963.
Museum of Contemporary Art (mid–career retrospective), Chicago, IL, 1972.

The Museum of Contemporary Art, Los Angeles, CA, 1993, then Parrish Museum of Art.

The Daniel Weinberg Gallery (drawings), Los Angeles, CA, 2001.

Lee Bontecou: A Retrospective, Hammer Museum, University of California at Los Angeles, Los Angeles, CA, 2002, then Museum of Contemporary Art, Chicago, IL, 2002–03, then Museum of Modern Arts, New York City, 2003.

Knoedler Gallery (drawings), New York City, 2004.

Sources

Artforum International, December 2001, p. 125.

Art in America, December 1994, p. 99; February 2000, p. 122.

Art Journal, Winter 1994, p. 56.

LA Weekly, October 3, 2003.

Los Angeles Times, October 4, 2003, p. E1; October 7, 2003, p. E1.

Newsweek, December 15, 2003, p. 66.

New Yorker, August 4, 2003, p. 36.

New York Times, October 3, 1993, sec. 2, p. 42; October 5, 2003, p. AR34.

San Diego Union–Tribune, October 19, 2003, p. F4.

Time, October 13, 2003, pp. 77–78.

Vogue, March 2004, pp. 532–37.

—*A. Petruso*

Sandra Boynton

Illustrator and author

Born Sandra K. Boynton, April 3, 1953, in Orange, NJ; married Jamie McEwan (an author); children: Caitlin, Keith, Devin, Darcy. *Education:* Yale University, B.A., 1974; attended University of California—Berkeley Drama School and Yale Drama School.

Addresses: *Publishing company*—Children's Division Editorial Department, Simon & Schuster, 1230 Avenue of the Americas, New York, NY 10020.

Career

Designed greeting cards as college student, 1973; signed with Recycled Paper Products, 1974; published first children's book, *Hippos Go Berserk!* 1979; published first adult humor title, *The Compleat Turkey,* 1980; peaked in popularity in the greeting card industry, 1980s; made *New York Times* bestseller list with adult humor title *Chocolate: A Consuming Passion,* 1982; signed with Portal Productions, 1995; published first children's book–and–CD set, *Rhinoceros Tap: And 14 Other Seriously Silly Songs,* 1996; made *New York Times* bestseller list with children's book–and–CD set *Philadelphia Chickens,* 2003.

Awards: Irma Simonton Black Award, for *Chloe & Maude,* 1985; National Cartoonists Society Award, 1993; National Parenting Publications Awards Gold Medal, for *Barnyard Dance!,* 1994.

Sidelights

The illustrator and author Sandra Boynton became a sensation in the 1980s when her humorous animal characters and clever text filled picture books and graced greeting cards, mugs, stickers, posters, stationary, and more. At the peak of her career in the mid–'80s, she created some 150 designs and sold more than 80 million cards a year. Key to Boynton's success was her mastery of the "alternative" greeting card—a style that avoided sentimentality and cliché and instead delivered humor, whimsy, and wit. When her one–of–a–kind cards spawned hordes of imitators, she staked out her own territory with some three dozen illustrated books and an array of merchandise, including a line of children's clothing.

Boynton's publications have ranged from toddlers' board books like 1979's *Hippos Go Berserk!* to adult humor titles like 1982's *Chocolate: A Consuming Passion,* which spent 24 weeks on the *New York Times* bestseller list. In the 1990s she started pairing her children's books with music, releasing popular book–and–CD sets—including 2002's *Philadelphia Chicken,* with a celebrity–cast CD. The musical book spent more than 40 weeks on the *New York Times* bestseller list in 2003, pulling Boynton back into the spotlight.

One of four daughters raised by a teacher and a school secretary, Boynton grew up in Philadelphia, Pennsylvania, attending the Germantown Friends School (where her father taught English) from kindergarten through high school. Her school's rich art program would have a lasting influence, though the self–effacing Boynton would often deny her natural abilities. "Growing up, I never had any particular talent for art," Boynton said in a 2001 interview with Simon & Schuster Children's Publishing, as quoted at Barnes&Noble.com. "I just always loved to draw and make things." A prolific doodler, she created her own cartoon characters, including an animal–like sports car named Furrari.

Entering Yale University in 1970, Boynton had planned to major in art but found herself drawn to courses in English. At Yale, she took a course on writing and illustrating for children by the celebrated author/illustrator Maurice Sendak. Boynton was not yet convinced that she would become an illustrator, however. Upon graduation she intended to pursue a career as a theater director, entering a graduate program in drama—first at the University of California at Berkeley, and later back at Yale.

In need of spending money for college, Boynton made her first foray into greeting cards during the summer of 1973. An uncle printed the cards, some 60,000 of them—all drawn, hand–colored, and packaged by Boynton. She distributed them herself, hitting craft shops along the East Coast. More than 100 stores accepted her cards, and only three turned her away. "I can't believe they sold," she told Paula Span of the *Washington Post*. By the following summer, she had made between $3,000 and $4,000 from the venture.

The next step for Boynton was to attend a trade show in New York City in the hopes of finding a marketer. At the show she was impressed with the work of an environmentally responsible business called Recycled Paper Products, run by two recent college graduates. A deal was struck that gave Boynton royalty rights and nearly complete control over her material and its marketing. Boynton would produce two card lines distributed by Recycled Paper Products: Animal Farm and Kulture Kards.

With their witty word play and disarming animal illustrations, Boynton's cards appealed to a wide audience. Among her best–selling items, one birthday card depicted a menagerie of animals with the words "Hippo Birdie Two Ewe." A thank–you card featured two pigs in a bathtub with the message "Not the usual hogwash. Just thanks." Making her cards feel personal was important to Boynton. "When you get a card that says 'Just for you....' it seems very impersonal," she told Victoria Irwin of the *Christian Science Monitor*. "My cards are actually from me to someone."

Early in her career, Boynton still considered the greeting cards a side project to support herself through graduate school. It was not until she had a family that Boynton fully embraced illustrating as her vocation. "When my first daughter was born," she told Simon & Schuster, "I realized that the drawing and writing were much more compatible with a reasonable family life than theater would be, so I followed that path."

After achieving commercial success, Boynton bought a 1700s farmhouse on 40 acres in Connecticut's Housatonic Valley with her husband, Jamie McEwan. A writer as well as a bronze medal canoeist in the 1976 Olympics, McEwan shared parenting responsibilities with his wife. Boynton set up her studio and workplace in a restored barn on the property, where a day's work might yield between five and 20 new card designs. Her family kept a dog and a cat, but farm animals would only populate Boynton's drawings.

Boynton also started writing and illustrating books, the first of which was 1979's children's counting book *Hippos Go Berserk!* The same year, she published *Hester in the Wild* and *Gopher Baroque and Other Beastly Conceits*. The following year brought her first adult humor title, *The Compleat Turkey*, with cartoons poking fun at life's difficult people, the so-called "turkeys." Successive adult books have served as an outlet for Boynton's ironic observations about life.

By 1980, Boynton was making news as a best–selling greeting card designer, cartoonist, and author. Her animal illustrations were appearing on stuffed animals with mock–literary names like Gustave Flaubear, Harry Elephonte, and Emily Chickinson. Her designs graced sheets, quilts, wallpaper, and even a line of Carter's children's clothing. In 1982, her illustrated book *Chocolate: The Consuming Passion* graced the *New York Times* bestseller list for 24 weeks.

Boynton's cast of characters has included hippos, cats, turkeys, and gophers—all surrogates for people. Frequently asked why she has not directly represented people, Boynton has joked that she does not know how to draw them. Yet she has also noted the benefits of depicting only animals. "[U]sing [animals], an artist becomes largely freed from the constraints of age, gender, race, and so on," Boynton explained to Simon & Schuster. She creates her cartoons with a technical pen and watercolors, using a computer only for typography.

"Inspiration almost never happens to me," Boynton told Sandy Coleman of the *Boston Globe*. "I work when I work. If I need to do ten card ideas, I sit down and go: idea No. 1.... It's almost like a math problem: What direction do I want to go? What direction have I gone?"

In the 1980s Boynton's popular cards spawned a slew of imitators. Although the attention flattered the illustrator, it also worked against her. When a new line from Hallmark Card Inc. directly copied a Boynton birthday card in 1986, she decided to sue for copyright infringement. The Hallmark card in question featured the same text and a similar illustration to a Boynton card featuring several pigs holding quiches, with the message "Hogs and Quiches on Your Birthday." After Hallmark's new line appeared, sales of Boynton's cards dipped for the first time in five years. "That's upsetting," she told Marilyn A. Harris of *BusinessWeek.* "I get so offended. I'm worried about people mistaking the cards for mine."

Boynton had always enjoyed almost absolute control over her material. Early in her career, some companies had offered to buy her designs, but she refused. Recycled Paper Products gave her the freedom that she needed, and the business had grown at a rate of about 30 percent a year since it had started marketing Boynton's cards. But both Boynton and Recycled Paper Products began to suffer after Hallmark launched its Shoebox Greetings line, which attempted to break into the alternative greeting card market with knockoffs of Boynton's cards. Recycled Paper Products was forced to compete with stationary giant Hallmark, which commanded prominent shelf space in stationary stores across the country. Boynton, however, continued to prosper from her books, clothing, and merchandise.

The illustrator remained with Recycled Paper Products until the mid–1990s, when she decided to end her 20–year relationship with the Chicago–based company. According to Boynton, her quibble with the company was largely philosophical. "They went in a direction that I found distasteful," she told Karen Heller of the *Houston Chronicle.* Speaking with Denise Lavoie of the Associated Press, as quoted at SouthCoastToday.com, she elaborated: "An increasingly large percentage of their line were cards they called risqué. They weren't risqué—they were obscene. They were rude and offensive, flip, trendy, but nasty in various ways."

To express her dissatisfaction with Recycled Paper Products, Boynton refused to create new card designs for a year. When her contract ran out at the end of 1994, she did not renew it. But a spokesperson for the company explained the split differently,

telling the Associated Press that declining sales in Boynton's cards led to the falling out. Between 1987 and 1995, Boynton had dropped in status from Recycled Paper Products' top–selling artist to No. 8.

Boynton then signed with a small company called Portal Productions, a California–based card and fine art poster company, which inherited the rights to thousands of vintage Boynton cards, including her 60 bestsellers. In addition, Boynton would keep the new cards coming. She continued to handle almost every aspect of her cards' production, including proofreading, contracts, design, and licensing for Boynton merchandise. "I find doing cards very easy," she told the *Houston Chronicle*'s Heller. "I still find I have room to grow."

In 1996 Boynton entered new territory, complementing her children's books with companion CDs. Her book–and–CD set *Rhinoceros Tap: And 14 Other Seriously Silly Songs* featured tunes with names like "Perfect Piggies" and "I Love You More Than Cheese," written with composer/arranger Michael Ford and performed with Adam Bryant. The pairing of her words and pictures with music came naturally to Boynton, who once sang with her high school and college choirs. Inspiration for the project came from a desire to give children's music a touch more sophistication. Often, Boynton told Stephanie Dunnewind of the *Seattle Times,* children's music can be "very condescending and repetitive. It doesn't move you." That same year, Boynton also published an illustrated book and CD for adults, *Grunt: Pigorian Chant from Snouto Domoinko de Silo,* a funny twist on Gregorian Chant recordings, substituting pigs for monks.

In the late 1990s Boynton stopped creating new greeting cards, though her classic designs remained available. Instead she concentrated her efforts on writing children's songbooks and other music, occasionally teaming up with celebrity actors and singers. Actress Meryl Streep, whose children attended the same school as Boynton's, was the first to collaborate with the illustrator. Streep then helped to enlist actor Kevin Kline and others to record songs for Boynton's 2002 book–and–CD set *Philadelphia Chickens,* which spent more than 40 weeks on the *New York Times* bestseller list in 2003.

An illustrator and author with dozens of titles to her credit, Boynton shows no signs of slowing her pace. Said the artist to the Associated Press's Lavoie, "I still have the same pleasure a child has in creating something, finishing it, looking at it, and saying, 'I made that.'"

Selected writings

Hippos Go Berserk! (children's book), Little, Brown, 1979.
Hester the Wild (children's book), HarperCollins, 1979.
Gopher Baroque and Other Beastly Conceits (children's book), Dutton/Plume, 1979.
If at First.... (children's book), Little, Brown, 1980.
The Compleat Turkey (adult humor), Little, Brown, 1980.
The Going to Bed Book (children's book), Simon & Schuster, 1982.
But Not the Hippopotamus (children's book), Simon & Schuster, 1982.
Chocolate: The Consuming Passion (adult humor), Workman Publishing Co., 1982.
Moo, Baa, La La La (children's book), Simon & Schuster, 1982.
Opposites (children's book), Simon & Schuster, 1982.
A to Z (children's book), Simon & Schuster, 1984.
Blue Hat, Green Hat (children's book), Simon & Schuster, 1984.
Horns to Toes and in Between (children's book), Simon & Schuster, 1984.
Chloe and Maude (children's book), Little, Brown, 1985.
Good Night, Good Night: Based on the Going to Bed Book (children's book), Random House, 1985.
Don't Let the Turkeys Get You Down (adult humor), Workman Publishing Co., 1986.
A is for Angry: An Animal and Adjective Alphabet (children's book), Workman Publishing Co., 1987.
Hey! What's That? (children's book), Random House, 1987.
Christmastime (children's book), Workman Publishing Co., 1987.
The Classic Prints: A Portfolio of Twelve Great Drawings and Three Pretty Good Ones (adult humor), Workman Publishing Co., 1991.
Barnyard Dance! (children's book), Workman Publishing Co., 1993.
Birthday Monsters! (children's book), Workman Publishing Co., 1993.
One, Two, Three! (children's book), Workman Publishing Co., 1993.
Oh My Oh My Oh Dinosaurs! (children's book), Workman Publishing Co., 1993.
Doggies: A Counting and Barking Book (children's book), Simon & Schuster, 1995.
Rhinoceros Tap (children's book and CD), Workman Publishing Co., 1996.
Grunt: Pigorian Chant from Snouto Domoinko de Silo (adult illustrated book and CD), Workman Publishing Co., 1996.
Snoozers: 7 Short Short Bedtime Stories for Lively Little Kids (children's book), Simon & Schuster, 1997.
Dinosaur's Binkit (children's book), Simon & Schuster, 1998.
Bob and 6 More Christmas Stories (children's book), Simon & Schuster, 1999.
Hey! Wake Up! (children's book), Workman Publishing Co., 2000.
Pajama Time! (children's book), Workman Publishing Co., 2000.
Dinos to Go: 7 Nifty Dinosaurs in 1 Swell Book (children's book), Simon & Schuster, 2000.
Hippos Go Berserk! (children's book, revised and rewritten), Simon & Schuster, 2000.
Yay, You! Moving Out, Moving Up, Moving On (children's book), Simon & Schuster, 2001.
Consider Love (children's book), Simon & Schuster, 2002.
Philadelphia Chickens (children's book and CD), Workman Publishing Co., 2002.
Snuggle Puppy (children's book), Workman Publishing Co., 2003.

Sources

Periodicals

Boston Globe, May 19, 1997, p. C6.
BusinessWeek, July 21, 1986, p. 96.
Christian Science Monitor, December 30, 1980, p. 19; April 22, 1999, p. 1.
Houston Chronicle, December 21, 1996, p. 5.
People, November 11, 2002, p. 96.
Seattle Times, May 3, 2003, p. E1.
Washington Post, March 23, 1986, p. K1.

Online

"Here's Looking at Ewe, Sandra," SouthCoastToday.com, http://www.s-t.com/daily/03-96/03-03-96/1boynton.htm (August 26, 2003).
"Meet the Writers: Sandra Boynton," Barnes&Noble.com, http://www.barnesandnoble.com/writers/writer.asp?userid=2W7DNF9IIO&cds2Pid=1302&cid=1004078 (July 11, 2003).

—Wendy Kagan

L. Paul Bremer

United States diplomat

Born Lewis Paul Bremer III, September 30, 1941, in Hartford, CT; married Frances Winfield, 1966; children: two. *Education:* Graduated from Yale University, 1963; studied political science in Paris, France; earned graduate business degree from Harvard University, 1966.

Addresses: *Field address*—Ambassador Paul Bremer CPA–EXSEC, APO AE 09335. *Office*—The Pentagon, 1000 Defense Pentagon, Washington, DC 20301.

Career

Executive Assistant to Secretary of State Henry Kissinger; 1974–76; deputy chief of mission, American Embassy, Oslo, Norway; Ambassador to the Netherlands, 1983–86; served as Executive Secretary of the State Department, 1980s; appointed Ambassador at Large for Counter Terrorism, 1989; managing director of Kissinger Associates, 1989–2000; appointed Chairman of the National Commission on Terrorism, 1999; ran Marsh Crisis Consulting, 2001; appointed to the President's Homeland Security Council, 2002; named Presidential Envoy to Iraq, Administrator of the Coalition Provisional Authority, 2003.

Awards: Superior Honor award, U.S. State Department, 1974; two Presidential Meritorious Service Awards; Distinguished Honor Award from the Secretary of State.

Sidelights

Retired diplomat L. Paul Bremer was named Presidential Envoy to Iraq by President George W. Bush on May 6, 2003. In that position, Bremer serves as the Administrator of the Coalition Provisional Authority, the interim governing body in Iraq following the ousted regime of Saddam Hussein. A counter–terrorism expert and member of Washington's neoconservative political establishment, Bremer was judged to possess the consensus–building skills and tough managerial style necessary for the job. In the weeks following a successful United States military ouster of Saddam Hussein and his Baath Party, Iraq's cities remained plagued by violence, and large sections were still without water and electricity. However, the American troops scored a significant victory with the capture of Hussein on December 13, 2003, and Bremer looked forward to making substantial progress in the rebuilding of Iraq.

A native of Hartford, Connecticut, Bremer was born in 1941 and graduated from Yale University 22 years later. He spent a year studying political science in Paris, France, and earned a graduate business degree from Harvard University in 1966. Joining the

U.S. Foreign Service, he spent the next several years in various postings around the world. In 1974, he became executive assistant to U.S. Secretary of State Henry A. Kissinger, and two years later served as deputy chief of mission at the American Embassy in Oslo, Norway. He returned to Washington and held various State Department posts during the Reagan era, and also served as ambassador to The Netherlands for three years. In 1989, he was made ambassador–at–large for United States counter–terrorism efforts.

Bremer retired from government in 1989 and took a job with a firm run by Kissinger. Toward the end of 2001, he signed on to run Marsh Crisis Consulting, a firm that provides risk–management advice to corporations with investments or personnel in foreign lands. His extensive counter–terrorism background made him a well–known figure in Washington and State Department circles. Some six years before the September 11, 2001, attacks on the Pentagon and World Trade Center, Bremer had warned of the growing threat from radical Islamic groups overseas; he also claimed that America itself was liable to be attacked in a future holy war. President Bush named him to the Homeland Security Advisory Council in June of 2002.

Before the United States launched military operations against Iraq in March of 2003 in coalition with British troops, it had already established an Office of Reconstruction and Humanitarian Assistance to provide the administrative framework for a post–Hussein Iraq. A retired U.S Army general, Jay Garner, was appointed to head it, and Garner and his team arrived just days after Baghdad was seized. Yet there were conflicts over what type of leadership the new Iraq would have—Pentagon brass were thought to take a more drastic approach than State Department experts with knowledge of Middle Eastern history and politics. One debate concerned the number of Iraqi exiles allowed to form a transitional government. Another issue was the continuing United States military presence itself—international aid organizations often were prevented by their own bylaws from working with occupying military authorities in a war–torn country.

News organizations reported that many Iraqis were still without water and electricity weeks later, and on May 6, 2003, the Bush White House seemed to strike a compromise by appointing Bremer—a State Department veteran—to become the new civilian administrator in Iraq. The announcement was made in an Oval Office ceremony, and Bremer appeared with Bush and U.S. Secretary of Defense Donald Rumsfeld. Senior administration officials said that Bush appointed Bremer "because he is widely viewed as having both the diplomatic polish and the neoconservative credentials to win support from both the State Department and the Pentagon," wrote *New York Times* journalist James Dao.

Bremer reported for duty on May 12, 2003, and upon arriving in Baghdad briefly spoke to the press. He emphasized that the goal was to restore stability to the long–suffering country. "We are not here as a colonial power. We are here to turn over to the Iraqi people ... as quickly as possible," a report published in the *New York Times* quoted him as saying.

In his first week on the job, Bremer sent out patrols to curb the violence in Baghdad. He also announced that his team was working to defuse the tensions caused by the ouster of Hussein's defunct Baath Party from power. "We have hunted down and will continue to deal with those members of the old regime who are sabotaging the country and the coalition's efforts," *New York Times* reporter Terence Neilan quoted him as saying.

The violence in Iraq continued well after President Bush declared major combat over in May of 2003. Bremer had to answer many questions about ongoing security concerns in Iraq, while attempting to build a new governing council of Iraqis. During a televised interview with Fox News reporter Brit Hume, Bremer fielded questions about continued attacks on American troops: "We're not losing," he insisted. "Ninety–five percent of these attacks on the coalition forces are taking place in a very small part of the country.... They pose no strategic threat to our operations here."

The capture of Saddam Hussein on December 13, 2003, boosted Bremer's claims that the situation in Iraq was under control. Bremer announced the capture to American troops in Iraq during a news conference the following day. "Ladies and gentlemen," he began, "we got him."

Sources

Periodicals

America's Intelligence Wire, October 26, 2003; November 16, 2003.
Financial Times, May 7, 2003.
Knight Ridder/Tribune Business News, November 13, 2003.
Los Angeles Times, May 2, 2003; May 7, 2003.
Newsweek, October 6, 2003.

New York Times, May 2, 2003; May 8, 2003; May 12, 2003; May 15, 2003.
Washington Post, December 14, 2003.

Online

"Ambassador L. Paul Bremer," Coalition Provisional Authority, http://www.cpa–iraq.org/bremerbio.html (December 1, 2003).

—Carol Brennan

Dan Brown

Author

Born June 22, 1964, in Exeter, NH; married Blythe (an art historian and painter). *Education:* Amherst College, B.A., 1986; studied art history at University of Seville, Spain.

Addresses: *Office*—c/o Author Mail, Random House, 1745 Broadway, New York, NY 10019.

Career

Taught English at Phillips Exeter Academy, New Hampshire; first novel published by St. Martin's Press, 1998; film rights to fourth novel, *The Da Vinci Code,* acquired by Columbia Pictures, 2003.

Sidelights

Dan Brown's 2003 novel, *The Da Vinci Code,* spent more than a year at or near the top of the *New York Times* best–seller list. Brown was the author of three previous techno–cryptic thrillers that received little critical attention before the runaway success of *The Da Vinci Code.* Its plot revolved around arcane symbology, Renaissance art, ancient religious texts, and a devious scheme involving the Roman Catholic church, and it became one of the most discussed books of the year. Even a writer for *U.S. Catholic,* Patrick McCormick, called it "a vastly entertaining read that mixes the thrill of a high–speed chase with the magical pleasures of a quest through an enchanted forest of art, literature, and history."

Brown was born in 1964 in Exeter, New Hampshire. His father was a respected professor of mathematics, and his mother was a musician who specialized in religious works. While earning a degree from Amherst College, Brown spent time studying art history at the University of Seville in Spain, which piqued his interest in the mysteries of the medieval Christian church. After earning his Amherst degree in 1986, Brown taught English at Phillips Exeter Academy in his hometown, and it was an event there that inspired him to write his first novel, *Digital Fortress.* One of his students had engaged in a political debate via e–mail with some friends, and the next day U.S. Secret Service agents came to the school to question the student. Whether or not the government might actually be able to read the ordinary e–mail of citizens, which is encrypted, became the basis of his 1998 debut novel.

Digital Fortress features Susan Fletcher, a government cryptographer, who discovers a code that the powerful e–mail monitoring government computer known as "TRNSLTR" cannot crack. The code seems to be the work of a National Security Agency programmer Ensei Tankado, who dies early on in the book, but the ingenious strategy Tankado put in place to force the government to admit the existence of TRNSLTR survives him. Interconnected intrigues at the Agency and in Seville, where Fletcher's romantic partner, linguist Dave Becker, works to solve the mystery, thicken the plot. *Publishers Weekly* called it an "inventive debut thriller" and a "fast–paced, plausible tale."

Brown's second novel, *Angels and Demons,* was the first to feature *The Da Vinci Code* hero, Robert Langdon. An expert in religious symbols and professor at Harvard University, Langdon is perpetually erudite, well–dressed, and a step ahead of his enemies in this 2000 novel. He is called in to help when the brilliant scientist who discovered antimatter is found murdered in his Swiss lab, and Langdon identifies the markings that were left on the man's body as the possible work of the Illuminati. The term refers to a group of 15th and 16th–century figures who claimed to enjoy direct communion with the Holy Spirit, rejecting the trappings and sacraments of the established churches as superfluous. In Brown's book, the Illuminati survived in secret until the modern era, and the action takes Langdon from Switzerland to Rome, where a potentially explosive vial of antimatter leads him to a nefarious plot at the Vatican, the holy city inside the Italian capital where the business of the church is conducted. A critic for *Library Journal,* Jeff Ayers, called *Angels and Demons* "one of the best international thrillers of recent years."

Both of Brown's novels attracted little media attention save for the standard publishing and library trade publication reviews. The same lukewarm reception occurred with *Deception Point,* his 2001 thriller and second for Pocket Books. Its plot centers around a mysterious meteor discovered by National Aeronautics and Space Administration (NASA) scientists in the Arctic. The meteor apparently crashed to Earth in 1716, and allegedly contains insect fossils, which seems to provide exciting, irrefutable evidence of extraterrestrial life. Others believe the meteor to be a NASA hoax engineered to revive the space agency's declining reputation. Assessing it for *Booklist,* David Pitt found that *Deception Point* "has characters that range from inventive to wooden [and] dialogue that bounces between evocative and clichéd."

Brown's editor at Pocket Books had more faith in his talents, however, and took the writer and an as–yet–unpublished manuscript with him when he was hired at Doubleday. In the fall of 2002, the publishing house handed out advance review copies of *The Da Vinci Code* to booksellers and publishing insiders at book–industry trade events, and word came back that many could not put the book down. The early buzz caused Brown's novel to debut at the No. 1 spot on the *New York Times* best–seller list in mid–March, and it would remain there for more than a year.

The Da Vinci Code opens with a presentation of two crucial "facts," one of which roused the ire of religious scholars and historians. The first fact declares the existence of a secret society dating back to 1099 called the Priory of Sion, and notes that "in 1975, Paris's *Bibliothèque Nationale* discovered parchments known as *Les Dossiers Secrets,*" which listed the society's roster of famous members throughout the ages. Those same documents were exposed as a hoax in a 1996 British Broadcasting Corporation (BBC) documentary. The second "fact" presented was subject to less dispute, and involved the existence a conservative Catholic organization known as Opus Dei. Each group figures prominently in the plot, which begins with the imminent death of Louvre Museum chief curator Jacques Saunière, the current leader of the Sion order. A malevolent albino monk is the culprit, and leaves Saunière to die a painful death in the darkened museum—but in his last moments Saunière manages to arrange enough tantalizing clues on or around his body to point to a much wider conspiracy involving Opus Dei.

Langdon is summoned to the scene to help read the clues, but had been scheduled to meet with Saunière and instead finds himself the prime suspect. He teams with the slain curator's granddaughter, Sophie—a cryptologist with the Paris police—and they go underground to find the true killer, partly with the help of clues found in Da Vinci's works. "Together the intrepid investigators use their talents to move through a maze of artistic, linguistic, and mathematical codes and puzzles," noted McCormick in the *U.S. Catholic* article, "unraveling the mystery of [Saunière]'s murder and uncovering the greater mystery of his identity as the head of an ancient secret society entrusted with a secret about Christianity's founder and origins." Supposedly the Italian Renaissance artist Leonardo Da Vinci also belonged to the Sion group, whose ostensible mission was to guard the Holy Grail. In medieval times, lore surrounding this alleged chalice claimed it was used by Christ at the Last Supper (when He dined with His apostles before the crucifixion) and possesses healing and restorative powers. It figures into both Arthurian legend and the lengthy series of battles to secure Christian domination in the Middle East known as the Crusades.

In Brown's book, Opus Dei wants to eliminate the Sion group and the secret surrounding the chalice forever. "Though for many readers the notions about Christian history in *The Da Vinci Code* seem new and startling, the novel introduces to a popular audience some of the debates that have gripped scholars of early Christian history for decades," noted *New York Times* writer Laurie Goodstein. These involve the true identity of Mary Magdalene, the follower of Christ once touted by Church teachings as a reformed prostitute, and the suppression of gospels written by the Gnostics, members of a spiritual movement that may have predated Christianity. The rest of *The Da Vinci Code* takes on several other provocative theories, including the idea that Christ did not die on the cross, that Mary Magdalene was pregnant with his child, that she—perhaps even both of them—settled in the south of France, and that their descendants created France's early–medieval Merovingian dynasty. This "secret" is the Holy Grail guarded by members of the Priory of Sion in Brown's book.

Even the most resolute of literary critics commended *The Da Vinci Code* for the sheer inventiveness of its author as he wove together so many disparate yet intriguing elements. The *New York Times'* Janet Maslin called it a "gleefully erudite suspense novel.... Not since the advent of Harry Potter has an author so flagrantly delighted in leading readers on a breathless chase and coaxing them through hoops." Maslin liked the book's well–plotted pace and cliffhanger at the close of nearly every chapter. "As Langdon and Sophie follow clues planted by Leonardo, they arrive at some jaw–dropping suppositions, some of which bring *The Da Vinci Code* to the brink of overkill," she conceded. "But in the end Mr. Brown gracefully lays to rest all the questions he has raised."

Salon reviewer Charles Taylor made a similar claim, noting that Brown "falls into the danger that always awaits a thriller writer so adept at twists, by supplying so many last–minute surprises he nearly twists the plot into total implausibility." Taylor had high praise for the end result, however, noting that its minor flaws fail "to ruin the pleasure of this hugely entertaining book. As a thriller writer, Brown is like a showboat academic, using facts to spin one grand theory after another. It may be an inch deep, but it has the thrill of a terrific performance." Writing in *U.S. Catholic*, McCormick predicted the book had tremendous film potential. "Brown has crafted a great thriller with the sort of smart, resourceful hero who could easily go Hollywood.... With the breakneck pacing, serpentine plotting, and conspiratorial tone of the best of Tom Clancy or Michael Crichton, *The Da Vinci Code* has all the stuff for a major blockbuster," McCormick asserted.

As these and other laudatory reviews, plus word–of–mouth, helped keep the book at the top of the *New York Times* best–seller list and selling at a rate of 100,000 copies per week, some scholars took umbrage with its recounting of the 325 C.E. Council of Nicaea, which declared Christ's divine nature as Church doctrine and spelled the end for the Gnostic movement. Other analysts contended that part of the appeal of Brown's best–seller could be attributed to recent revelations that Church hierarchy had covered up sexual–abuse cases by its priests for decades. A *U.S. News & World Report* article noted that Brown's book "owes part of its popularity to impeccable timing. Published at a moment when doubts about institutional integrity were running high, the book confirms many readers' worst suspicions."

Given such theories, some sensed an anti–Catholic bias in *The Da Vinci Code*. A *National Catholic Reporter* essay by best–selling novelist and Roman Catholic priest Andrew M. Greeley found several factual errors, and termed it merely the latest in a long list of slightly veiled novelistic jabs at the Church and Vatican hierarchy over the decades. "As usual in such stories, the Roman curia is pictured as smooth, sophisticated schemers who will stop at nothing to preserve the power of the church," Greeley wrote.

The Da Vinci Code aroused so much debate that it spawned an entire subgenre: ABC television aired a special in November of 2003 that featured a panel of experts who clarified some of the book's assertions. Several books were published in the spring of 2004, including *Secrets of the Code: The Unauthorized Guide to the Mysteries Behind the Da Vinci Code,* a collection of critical essays, and *Breaking the Da Vinci Code: Answers to the Questions Everybody's Asking.* In addition to the mainstream books, both Roman Catholic and Protestant denominations sponsored workshops and lectures refuting some of the book's claims, or issued pamphlets and study guides.

In early 2004, Brown's book became the all–time best–selling work of fiction in hardcover, with sales of 6.2 million and nudging out the previous record–holder for hardcover fiction, *The Bridges of Madison County* by Robert James Waller. Film rights to *The Da Vinci Code* were acquired by Columbia Pictures, and Ron Howard was reportedly interested in directing. Brown had declared an informal media quarantine so that he could concentrate on writing his fifth novel. He is married to Blythe, an art historian and painter.

Selected writings

Digital Fortress, St. Martin's Press (New York City), 1998.
Angels and Demons, Pocket Books (New York City), 2000.

Deception Point, Pocket Books, 2001.
The Da Vinci Code, Doubleday (New York City), 2003.

Sources

Books

Brown, Dan, *The Da Vinci Code,* Doubleday, 2003.

Periodicals

Booklist, September 15, 2001, p. 198.
Christian Century, March 9, 2004, p. 13.
Entertainment Weekly, December 12, 2003, p. 39.
Independent (London, England), March 18, 2004, p. 6.
Library Journal, November 15, 2000, p. 124.
M2 Best Books, March 1, 2004.

National Catholic Reporter, October 3, 2003, p. 18.
Newsweek, June 9, 2003, p. 57.
New York Times, March 17, 2003, p. E8; February 22, 2004, sec. 7, p. 23; April 27, 2004.
Publishers Weekly, December 22, 1997, p. 39; May 1, 2000, p. 51; September 10, 2001, p. 56; January 27, 2003, p. 117; February 9, 2004, p. 18.
U.S. Catholic, November 2003, p. 36.
U.S. News and World Report, December 22, 2003, pp. 45–49.

Online

Contemporary Authors Online, Gale, 2004.
"*The Da Vinci Code* by Dan Brown," *Salon.com,* http://archive.salon.com/books/review/2003/03/27/da_vinci/ (April 30, 2004).

—*Carol Brennan*

John Seely Brown

AP/Wide World Photos

Scientist

Born in 1940 in Utica, NY; married. *Education:* Brown University, B.S., 1962; University of Michigan, M.S., 1964, Ph.D., 1970.

Addresses: *Office*—Xerox Corporation, 800 Long Ridge Rd., Stamford, CT 06904.

Career

Assistant professor, University of California at Irvine, 1969–73; senior scientist, Bolt Baranek and Newman, Cambridge, MA, 1973–78; principal scientist in cognitive and instructional sciences, Xerox Corporation, Palo Alto Research Center (PARC), 1978–84, Intelligent Systems Laboratory director, 1984–86, vice president for advanced research, 1986–90, corporate vice president and PARC director, 1989–2000; associate director, Institute for Research on Learning, 1986–90; chief scientist, Xerox Corp., 1992—; Batten fellow, University of Virginia Darden Graduate School of Business Administration, 2003; fellow of the American Association for Artificial Intelligence, fellow of the American Association for the Advancement of Science, trustee of Brown University, trustee of the MacArthur Foundation.

Awards: Industrial Research Institute Medal for outstanding accomplishments in technological innovation, 1998.

Sidelights

John Seely Brown bears the impressive title of "chief scientist" at the Xerox Corporation, the American imaging–technology giant. Brown directed the company's celebrated Palo Alto Research Center, known as PARC, until 2000. Usually described by interviewers as both engaging in his conversational style and exhausting in his intellectual range, Brown is considered one of the leading contemporary thinkers on how technology impacts modern life.

A native of Utica, New York, Brown was fascinated by computers even as a teenager in the 1950s. While still in high school he became proficient on an IBM 650, one of first units ever built for commercial use. He participated in a summer business–training program at Colgate University in New York State before entering Brown University in Providence, Rhode Island, where he finished in 1962 with an undergraduate degree in mathematics and physics. He then spent the rest of the decade at the University of Michigan, where he earned a math degree and a Ph.D. in computer and communication sciences. One of his first jobs was teaching both computer science and psychology courses at the University of California at Irvine. In 1973, he joined Bolt Baranek and Newman, a prestigious technology–consulting firm in Cambridge, Massachusetts. It devised the "@" symbol signifying a domain name in the digital era, among many other innovations, and Brown served as senior scientist there for five years when it was perfecting the ARPANET, the forerunner of the Internet.

Brown moved to northern California in 1978 to take a post with the Xerox Corporation's Palo Alto Research Center (PARC). The legendary spin–off of the copier maker had a lavish budget and a mission to define what it called "the office of the future." At PARC, Brown served as a principal scientist in its cognitive and instructional sciences division, when PARC was developing the first prototypes of the spell–checking and thesaurus applications that would later become standard features in word–processing programs. In 1984, he was named director of PARC's Intelligent Systems Laboratory, which worked on developing the artificial–intelligence programming systems. He became a vice president for advanced research two years later, and by 1989 was serving as PARC's director. In this post, he commanded a staff of some 400 scientists and programmers who were renowned as some of the brightest minds in the field. PARC teams had already developed the laser printer and the graphical user interface (GUI), and by the time Brown took over were working on the first generation of handheld devices like the Palm Pilot.

Brown's leadership and visionary ideas earned him another job title in 1992: chief scientist at Xerox. His time in the job coincided with a crucial developmental period for the company, and his ideas helped re–focus attention back to its core business as "The Document Company." Back in the early days of his career, at the onset of computer–technology boom, experts predicted a "paperless office" of the future. This was an illusory goal, Brown argued. "Paper itself is one of the most wonderful media that we have ever created," he told *Management Review* interviewer Barbara Ettorre. "It is lightweight. It has high contrast ratio. It has no power requirements. There's no chance in the near future that we will find a digital replacement for paper."

At the time of that 1995 interview, Brown also predicted that increased networking capabilities would soon bring what he called a virtual social reality. He explained to Ettorre, "It is the question of how you start to have fairly in–depth social relationships in this digital cyberspace world and how you actually complement the physical world with the virtual world…. There's a sense of coming together in this digital space with the kind of full–blooded interactions that you have associated in the past solely with shared physical space." Brown further explored such ideas in his 2000 book, *The Social Life of Information*, written with University of California—Berkeley researcher Paul Duguid. The chapters discuss what the authors term "communities of practice," the setting in which knowledge is shared. Innovation, they contend, is often not the result of individual genius, but rather an improvisational process that originates inside a group and meets a need. Brown and Duguid provide examples of technological advances that failed in practice, but also recount one intriguing success story: when investors in the fledgling telephone company founded by Alexander Graham Bell's device became leery about its potential for catching on with the public, Bell had telephones placed where people could see others using them—in offices with heavy foot traffic, for example, and near busy lunch counters.

At PARC, Brown devised workable ideas that illustrated his theories about "communities of practice." For example, he once wired the office coffeemaker so that engineers at their desks received alerts when a fresh pot was ready. Electronic white boards near the coffee station served as a notepad so that employees could discuss current projects. "I am looking for ways that we don't have to attend so many meetings by creating technologies that appeal directly to people," Brown explained to *Financial Times* journalist Philip Manchester. As an observer of the modern corporation, he was adamant about how companies fail their employees when they implement the latest management strategies du jour, such as project teams. This, combined with a new era of information–overload from e–mail, creates a form of tyranny within a corporation, he believed. "I am getting angry about the profound flakiness of many modern systems and I think we will have a backlash against technology unless we make it better," he asserted to Manchester. "We must make technology that fits people—rather than expect people to fit the technology."

Brown served as director of PARC until 2000. He is a trustee of Brown University and the MacArthur Foundation, and is a fellow of the American Association for the Advancement of Science. Married to an architect, Brown enjoys sailing and motorcycle trips in his spare time. The holder of several patents in document imaging, he was once asked *Forbes ASAP*'s Karen Southwick about his "favorite technology;" Brown confessed that it was "a very, very lightweight printer. It weighs about an ounce. It never runs out of batteries, even though it's portable. It prints at astounding resolution…. I spend a lot of time finding good pens."

Selected writings

(Editor) *Seeing Differently: Insights on Innovation*, Harvard Business School Press (Boston, MA) 1997.
(With Paul Duguid) *The Social Life of Information*, Harvard Business School Press (Boston, MA), 2000.

Sources

Periodicals

Economist, April 15, 2000, p. 4.
Electronic Business, May 2000, p. 146.
Financial Times, January 19, 2000, p. 10; September 7, 2002, p. 11.
Forbes ASAP, March 25, 2002, pp. 46–47.
Inc., March 2000, p. 119.
Information Outlook, June 2000, p. 39.
Management Review, February 1995, p. 9.
Training, September 2002, p. 28.

Online

"Batten Fellows," Darden—University of Virginia, http://www.darden.edu/batten/btr_fellows_fellows_s–brown.htm (July 21, 2003).

—*Carol Brennan*

Linda Buck

Neurobiologist

Born Linda B. Buck, c. 1956, in Seattle, WA. *Education:* University of Washington, Seattle, WA, B.S. (psychology and microbiology); University of Texas Southwestern Medical Center, Dallas, TX, Ph.D. (immunology)

Addresses: *Office*—Fred Hutchinson Cancer Research Center, 1100 Fairview Ave. N., A3–020, Seattle, WA 98109.

Career

Took a postdoctoral position at Columbia University working with Richard Axel on olfactory system in mammals; identified genes for olfactory receptors with Axel, 1991; set up own lab at Harvard, 1991; explained organization of odor receptor neurons in the nose, 1994; deciphered combinatorial code that allows odor receptors to work together, 1999; transferred lab to Fred Hutchinson Cancer Research Center, 2002.

Member: American Association for the Advancement of Science; National Academy of Sciences.

Awards: Lewis S. Rosenstiel Award; Louis Vuitton–Moët Hennessy Science for Art Prize; R.H. Wright Award in olfactory research; Unilever Science Award; Perl/University of North Carolina Neuroscience Prize; Gairdner Foundations International Award.

Sidelights

Linda Buck is a preeminent researcher in the science of sense perception. She is responsible for groundbreaking work on the olfactory system in mammals. Buck made clear for the first time how odors are perceived and identified. Before Buck's work, scientists had only surmised that the nose contained special receptors to identify smells. Buck showed that mammals have as many as a thousand different receptors that allow us to receive and categorize odors. The olfactory system is more primitive and complex than other sensory systems. The eye, for example, uses only three receptors for color, but is able to identify thousands of different shades. In the nose, thousands of receptors track tens of thousands of odors, and mapping this system was thought to be impossibly difficult. Buck showed it could be done. Her work has many implications for medicine and industry. She looks at how scents affect behavior, emotion and memory. Buck is also investigating ways to help cancer patients who often have to take unpalatable drugs. Chemicals that block bitter tastes, for instance, might help patients tolerate their drugs better. Chemicals that enhance taste or odor could also induce ill people to eat.

Buck was born and raised in Seattle, Washington. She enrolled in the University of Washington for her undergraduate education, eventually earning a double degree in psychology and microbiology. From there she moved to the University of Texas Southwestern Medical Center in Dallas, where she earned her doctorate in immunology. Her first postdoctoral position took her to Columbia University in New York. At Columbia she worked with Richard Axel on a baffling, unsolved problem: how the sense of smell works.

The sense of smell is evolutionarily more primitive than our other sensory systems. Neuroscientists had thought that mammals used specific smell receptors to identify particular scents, but no one had identified the actual receptors yet. Researchers surmised that there must be several groups or classes of receptors, but nothing was known for sure. It was known that humans, for example, have five specific taste receptors—bitter, sour, sweet, salty, and umani (the taste associated with monosodium glutamate or MSG)—and from these the brain puts together all the complex tastes of meals we enjoy.

Neuroscientists believed odor might also be divided into a few main classes of receptors. A team of researchers led by Solomon Snyder at Johns Hopkins University worked on finding olfactory receptors in the 1980s. After years of work, Snyder's team was unable to solve the problem. Buck read Snyder's work when she arrived at Columbia and got excited about it. Her work in immunology gave her a good background for olfactory research, because she was used to dealing with molecular systems that had to recognize and code complex data. She and Axel began working on the olfactory system of rats. Buck was looking for a family of genes that would be found only in one place in the back of the nose, called the olfactory epithelium. If she could find these genes, she believed she would have located the olfactory receptors. Buck refined her methods several times when her early attempts ran into dead ends. She was completely dedicated to her work. She told Daniel Lyons of *Forbes* that she worked round–the–clock for three years. "I was putting in 12 to 15 hours a day," she said. "Basically I just got up and went to the lab, and stayed there until the wee hours of the morning."

Buck's final results were astonishing. In 1991 she and Axel published their olfactory study, which identified at least 1,000 different genes that were active exclusively in the noses of rats. No one, including Buck herself, had predicted such a large number of genes. This seemed to mean that processing of odors was done more at the level of the nose than in the brain itself. Though this was unexpected, it also made sense. Early animals that were highly reliant on sense of smell for survival would not have needed large brains to process odor information if the nose itself was doing most of the work. Vision, where most of the processing is done in the brain, developed later.

After Buck's work with Axel was lauded, she secured a position in the neurobiology department of Harvard Medical School. Here she refined her work on the olfactory system. In 1993 and 1994 Buck published explanations of how the nerve cells in the nose function. Buck claimed that neurons on the olfactory epithelium are grouped by type, with about 5,000 neurons for each of the 1,000 different odor receptors. She described the shape of the neurons, which stretch from the olfactory epithelium in the nose into a part of the brain called the olfactory bulb.

She fitted more pieces into the puzzle in 1999, when she laid out the method by which receptors work together to identify particular odors. Even though she had identified as many as 1,000 receptors, mammals can distinguish ten times that many individual scents. Buck's research revealed a kind of code by which several receptors together spell out a particular odor. In 2001, members of her laboratory team traced the neural connections between the olfactory bulb and the larger olfactory cortex that controls it. This led Buck into more complex explorations of behaviors or instincts that are triggered by smell. Certain scents called pheromones that animals release can trigger aggressive behavior, for example. Buck hoped to figure out which odor receptors were linked to unique behaviors, and how the connection worked in the brain. Buck also became interested in aging and life span. She began to investigate whether pheromone perception could be linked to the onset of puberty in animals. She also began a study with roundworms looking for chemicals that influenced these primitive animals' life span. In 2001 Buck also published a report that possibly identified a specific gene for the perception of sweetness. In popular parlance this was called "the sweet tooth gene."

In 2002 Buck moved back to Seattle to take a post at the Fred Hutchinson Cancer Research Center. It was important to Buck that her work find applications that help people. In locating her lab in a cancer research center, Buck hoped to collaborate with researchers who could apply her work with smell and taste to new pharmaceuticals. While she worked to broaden our basic understanding of the olfactory system, she hoped others would build on her achievements, perhaps by developing chemicals that blocked the bitter taste of some cancer medicines. Other possible applications of her work included chemicals that would block our perception of foul odors; this was imagined as a solution to smelly public restrooms. Another possibility was the artificial reproduction of the scent receptors dogs use to sniff explosives. This might mean a machine could do that job more accurately and reliably than trained animals. While others dreamed of possible applications of her research, Buck herself continued to work on the basic science of scent perception.

Sources

Chemistry and Industry, May 7, 2001, p. 270.
FHRCRC Faculty & Staff Newsletter, April 18, 2002.
Forbes, December 23, 2002, p. 278.

New York Times, April 5, 1991, p. A1, p. D18.
Science, April 12, 1991, pp. 209–10.

—*A. Woodward*

Martha Burk

Activist

Born Martha Gertrude Burk, October 18, 1941, in Tyler, TX; daughter of Ivan Lee Burk (an oil company engineer) and Dorothy May Dean (a dress–business owner); married Eddie C. Talley (a pharmacist), September 2, 1960 (divorced, 1985); married Ralph Estes (a professor), 1986; children: (first marriage) Edward, Mark. *Education:* University of Houston, B.S., 1962; University of Texas at Arlington, M.S., 1968, Ph.D., 1974.

Addresses: *Office*—National Council of Women's Organizations, 733 15th St. NW, Ste. 1011, Washington, DC 20005.

Career

Licensed psychologist. University of Texas at Arlington, research director of its Graduate School of Social Work, 1974–76, assistant professor of management, 1976–79; co–founder and partner, A.U. Software, Inc., Wichita, KS, 1981–90; elected president of the Wichita National Organization for Women (NOW) chapter; national board of directors, National Organization for Women, 1988–90; co–founder, Center for the Advancement of Public Policy, early 1990s, president, 1990—; chair, National Council of Women's Organizations, Washington, DC; served on National Task Force on Pay Equity, 1993.

Sidelights

Martha Burk, chairperson of the National Council of Women's Organizations, stepped into a media fracas in 2002 when she challenged the Au-

gusta National golf club's men–only membership policy. The posh, private Georgia club plays annual host to the famed Masters Tournament, one of golf's most prestigious events, and Burk spent several months involved in the matter. In the end, her mission failed, but she predicted that calling public attention to the matter would eventually effect change at clubs like Augusta. "This is symbolic of all the ways women are left out," *New York Times* reporter Kate Zernike quoted her as saying. "It legitimizes sex discrimination when American [chief executive officers] are engaging in it with impunity."

Born in 1941, Burk grew up in Pasadena, Texas, a suburb of Houston. She earned top grades in high school and finished at age 16; her studies at the University of Houston were interrupted by marriage and the birth of her first child. Living in Dallas with her pharmacist husband, who ran a chain of drug stores, she became a parent again in 1965 and found herself increasingly dissatisfied with her role as a wife and mother. As she told Peter J. Boyer in a profile that appeared in the *New Yorker*, "the most radicalizing experience in my life was being a stay–at–home mother.... It forced isolation for women in that situation."

Returning to school, Burk received a master's degree in psychology and computer science from the

University of Texas at Arlington, and then a Ph.D. in experimental psychology in 1974. Armed with top credentials, she was shocked to find that her gender nevertheless hampered her in the workforce; when she tried to land one university teaching job, she was asked to take a typing test. Around 1979, while at the University of Texas, she developed an educational software program that became the basis for her own company. The business became so successful that she was able to quit her teaching job, and she then turned to political activism. After a divorce, she married an accounting professor, Ralph Estes, with a strong political streak himself, and when he took a teaching job in Kansas, the couple settled in Wichita. There Burk became involved in a contentious battle over a local women's–health clinic in the mid–1980s, and eventually headed the Wichita chapter of the National Organization for Women.

In 1990, Burk and her husband moved to Washington, D.C., where they established the Center for the Advancement of Public Policy, an advocacy group. Burk eventually became chair of the National Council of Women's Organizations (NCOW), an umbrella association of various groups that range from the Association of Junior Leagues International to the League of Women Voters. Burk's job entailed calling public attention to women's issues such as pay equity in the workplace and violations of the Title IX federal law that guarantees equal athletic opportunity for men and women at schools and colleges.

Burk, an occasional golfer from years back, cared little about the game until she read an article about the Augusta National golf club's men–only membership that appeared in *USA Today* around the time of the 2002 Masters Tournament. Irked, she decided to write a letter on NCOW letterhead to the club's president, William W. "Hootie" Johnson, that questioned the decades–old ban and urged him to revise it. Founded in 1932, the Augusta golf club is one of the most elite private clubs in the United States. Women are ineligible to join, but they may play the course at the invitation of a member. The roster includes some of the most celebrated business leaders in America, such as Sanford (Sandy) Weill, outgoing head of Citigroup, and longtime General Electric chair Jack Welch.

To her surprise, Johnson responded with a blistering 18–paragraph statement released to the media. "The message delivered to us was clearly coercive," it stated, according to the *New Yorker* article by Boyer. Johnson asserted that "there may well come a day when women will be invited to join our membership but that timetable will be ours and not at the point of a bayonet." Burk was suddenly bombarded with requests for media interviews, and gained the support of the NCOW board to pressure CBS, which televises the Masters Tournament, and launch a letter–writing campaign to Tournament sponsors and Augusta members.

Over the next few months, Burk and Johnson fought a war of words in the press. The Augusta golf club released CBS and the sponsors from their signed contracts for the 2003 Masters Tournament—a $20 million shortfall that the club agreed to cover—and Burk announced her intention to hold formal protests outside the Tournament the following April. Supporters of Burk's cause, which included the *New York Times* editorial pages, denounced the Augusta club as a stiff, elitist organization, while Johnson argued that it was a private organization and was not bound by any law to admit women.

Burk and the NCOW applied for a permit to protest outside of the club's main gates during the 2003 Masters Tournament, but the local sheriff claimed it might prove a safety hazard, and they were forced to stage their demonstration a half–mile down the road. The demonstrations proved neither a public danger nor enough to sway Johnson, but a few weeks later Swedish–born golfer Annika Sorenstam was allowed to play in a Professional Golfers' Association event in Texas. The Augusta National golf club remained a staunchly men–only enclave. In June of 2003, two House of Representative Democrats introduced a bill that would prohibit tax deductions for business–entertaining expenses at private clubs that discriminate on the basis of gender. Burk supported the legislation, which targets 24 private clubs in the United States that, like Augusta, either bar women from membership or restrict access to facilities. "If corporate CEOs believe that entertaining at clubs is necessary for business," a Knight Ridder/Tribune Business News report quoted her as saying, "and that such business expenses should be tax–deductible, there are many, many fine clubs that do not discriminate."

Sources

Golf World, July 19, 2002, p. 13.
Knight Ridder/Tribune Business News, June 12, 2003.
Los Angeles Times, September 5, 2002, p. D3.
New Yorker, February 17, 2003, p. 78.
New York Times, February 25, 2003, p. D1; April 11, 2003, p. S1; April 13, 2003, p. 4; April 14, 2003, p. D1; April 16, 2003, p. S3; May 25, 2003, p. 9; June 12, 2003, p. D4.
People, November 25, 2002, pp. 87–88.
Sports Illustrated, April 21, 2003, p. G20, p. G46.

—*Carol Brennan*

Candace Bushnell

Author

Born c. 1959, in Connecticut; daughter of Calvin (a scientist) and Camille (a travel–agency owner) Bushnell; married Charles Askegard (a ballet dancer), July 4, 2002. *Education:* Attended Rice University and New York University.

Addresses: *Office*—c/o Atlantic Monthly Press, 841 Broadway, New York, NY 10003.

Career

Writer and journalist. Staff and freelance writer for *Ladies' Home Journal, Good Housekeeping, Self, Mademoiselle, Cosmo Beauty and Fitness, Family Circle, GQ,* and *Vogue,* 1980s–94; columnist, *New York Observer,* New York, NY, 1994–c. 1998; columns collected into 1996 book, *Sex and the City,* which was made into HBO series of the same name, 1998–2004; first novel published, 2003.

Sidelights

Author Candace Bushnell served as the whip–smart, amusing, and well–shod prototype for Carrie Bradshaw, the character played by Sarah Jessica Parker on the hit HBO series *Sex and the City.* Bushnell penned a much–read column about the travails of Manhattan single life that inspired the show and its premise, and then went on to author far lengthier exposés with *Four Blondes,* a collection of novellas published in 2000, and *Trading Up,* her first novel.

Dimitrios Kambouris/WireImage.com

Trading Up, which appeared in 2003, earned Bushnell more than a few comparisons to both Jane Austen and Edith Wharton for her mordantly relentless dissection of the mysterious code phrases, barely concealed snubs, and restaurant–seating patterns that add up to the ever–shifting hierarchy of status among New York's media, fashion, and Wall Street elite. "Bushnell succeeds because she provides what readers and audiences have always craved," noted Stephanie Merritt in London's *Observer,* "from Molière down through Wilde and Mitford to *Dynasty* and the rash of current celebrity magazines—a window on to the stupidities and weaknesses of the rich and powerful, inspiring an addictive mix of envy and moral superiority."

Bushnell was born in the late 1950s and grew up in Glastonbury, a bedroom community in central Connecticut. Her family boasted impressive New England Yankee roots: the Bushnell brothers arrived in the 1630s and one of them married into a Mayflower family; a later ancestor invented the first submarine ever deployed in combat, the *American Turtle,* which scared off a British frigate near the Connecticut coastline during the Revolutionary War. Her own father was a scientist who invented the fuel cell used on the Apollo space missions of the 1960s. But Bushnell, the eldest of three daughters, was eager to leave quaint New England. "We used to call it Glastonboring," she explained to *Times* of London writer Joe Warwick. "It doesn't have a movie theatre and everybody likes horses. It's that sort of place."

Bushnell was an imaginative and savvy youngster who made up stories, recorded them on cassette, and then charged neighborhood kids a fee to hear them. After high school, she entered Rice University in Houston, Texas, but left before earning her degree in order to move to New York City. She had impressively ambitious plans at the time. "I thought I could make money as an actress and I'd be able to support myself as a novelist, which of course is incredibly stupid," she recalled in an *Entertainment Weekly* interview with Troy Patterson. Bushnell's closest claim to an entertainment–industry credit was a Burger King commercial that she almost landed. Instead, she went out a lot. It was the late 1970s and the heady discotheque era, and she landed her first success as a writer with an arch magazine piece that she titled, "How to Act in a Disco."

Over the next decade, Bushnell served time on the mastheads of magazines like *Ladies' Home Journal, Good Housekeeping, Cosmo Beauty and Fitness,* and *Self.* "I'd write about spastic colons, foot fungus, you name it," she told Minneapolis *Star Tribune* journalist Rick Nelson. "It was really good training, and great discipline. You have to write to a prescribed word length, and make whatever you're writing interesting, to keep the reader turning the page." Eventually she went solo, and got off to a good start in the early 1990s with pieces published in *GQ, Mademoiselle, Health,* and even *Family Circle.* But the freelance life proved tenuous, and Bushnell struggled financially. Behind in her rent, she was evicted from her apartment, which she told the *Evening Standard*'s Lydia Slater, "was my lowest point." In the Cinderella–type moment that she later skillfully deployed in her fiction, Bushnell was offered her own column in the *New York Observer,* the highbrow media and arts weekly, while still sleeping on her friend's couch.

Bushnell's *New York Observer* column, "Sex and the City," debuted in 1994. It cynically examined the dating scene among Manhattan's upper echelon of strivers, and was based simply on Bushnell's own experiences and those of her friends. Her acerbic, witty tone struck a chord with readers, who easily recognized many of her newly named archetypes. There was the "modelizer," or man who dated only models, who was a subspecies of the "toxic bachelor," but Bushnell was an equal–opportunity satirist: there were also women who selected boyfriends based on real estate holdings. "The idea of the desperate single woman is somewhat true," she told Warwick in the *Times* of London about her subject matter. "New York is a city where men don't want relationships." It was a theme she often discussed in interviews when a collection of her columns became her first book, *Sex and the City,* in 1996. "Because of how men are raised, they're ill–equipped to provide love and support," she said of the anti–heroes who populated her column in a Knight Ridder/Tribune News Service interview with Jennifer Weiner. "They're raised to be self–centered, to be entitled."

Bushnell herself was romantically linked with Alfonse D'Amato—a former Republican senator from New York—and *Vogue* magazine publisher Ron Galotti, widely believed to have been the inspiration for the elusive "Mr. Big," the chauffeur–driven exec who occasionally romanced her column's alter ego, Carrie. *Independent* journalist Deborah Ross asked Bushnell about what was New York's most obvious secret for a time in the mid–1990s. "I don't think he took it very seriously," she said of Galotti's reaction. "It was obviously fictionalised, but he was the big inspiration for the character. I was in love with him. When I saw him I would get so excited. My heart would flip–flop, which was great, except I don't think he had the same feelings about me."

Galotti allegedly broke up with Bushnell on the day the galley proofs arrived for her book. It earned mixed reviews, and those who came to it after the subsequent HBO series may have been surprised to find a tone that was far bleaker than the small–screen version. The 25 essays, wrote Ginia Bellafante in *Time,* "should serve to dissuade any single person in America from ever moving to Manhattan." A *Times* of London review from Amanda Craig deemed it "riveting, trivial and completely vile," but commended Bushnell's talent for observation and the minutiae of class–demarcation detail. "Sharp, gritty, and so hard you could use it to bore holes in granite, Bushnell's wit is like an industrial diamond," Craig declared.

Bushnell's book was optioned by Darren Star, the *Melrose Place* creator, and the series debuted on HBO in 1998. Her alter ego, Carrie Bradshaw, was joined by a trio of best friends that had either been characters or composite characters in the original column: cynical corporate attorney Miranda (Cynthia Nixon), art dealer and aspiring Connecticut housewife Charlotte (Kristin Davis), and publicist Samantha (Kim Cattrall), a commitment–phobe. The series quickly generated a buzz, lured new HBO subscribers by the thousands, and was nominated for numerous Emmy awards. *Nation* critic Alyssa Katz asserted that "one of its pleasures is that it lampoons its glossy Manhattan universe as much as it tries to sell it to the tourists."

In the meantime, Bushnell carried on with her anthropological field work. Journalists almost always asked her about her personal life. She admitted to having been engaged once, but claimed that she was simply not marriage material—a famous line from the TV series that Big delivers when Carrie gloats about her impending nuptials. Later, Carrie suffers a panic attack when she tries on a wedding dress in a bridal salon. Bushnell recalled in the *Independent* interview with Ross that she "had an engagement ring and everything, but it didn't feel right. I called it off. I literally felt as if I was suffocating. I felt like I was drowning. It felt like an ending, not a beginning...."

Bushnell also began working on the novellas that would become *Four Blondes*, her 2000 best-seller. The last story of the quartet chronicled an American woman's romance with a well-heeled English aristocrat, mirroring Bushnell's own romance with a British-born venture capitalist. The other stories skewer a paranoid, drug-addled model who is married to an Italian prince, and the marriage of a pair of well-connected Manhattan journalists whose female half loathes her mate and pines for a more ambitious one. The first of the four blondes, however, was Janey Wilcox—an aging, shrewd, but not very bright model who endures a near-comical level of emotional abuse from the viper-like men she insists upon dating. Desperate to parlay her looks into an advantageous marriage, Janey summers at various Hamptons houses and trips herself up at every turn. Just when she is forced to contemplate selling real estate as a career, she wins a lucrative modeling contract for Victoria's Secret. A *Publishers Weekly* contributor asserted that Bushnell's characters seemed to be driven by "their fear of mortality.... Mercilessly satirical, Bushnell's scathing insights and razor wit are laced with an understanding of this universal human fear, and they inspire fear and pity in the reader."

Bushnell took the Janey Wilcox story and turned it into her 2003 novel, *Trading Up*. The plot centers around Janey's marriage to entertainment executive Selden Rose. Janey finally possesses all the wealth and status she craved, but now wants more. She is envious of her even more well-married best friend's affair with a handsome polo player, worries about the abusive former beau who seems to be trying to blackmail her, and once again besmirches her repu-

tation by her own shallow-minded decisions. Some of it, many critics noted, seemed to be lifted from the classic Edith Wharton novel *The House of Mirth*, but Janey fails to meet the doomed end that befell Wharton's more delicate Lily Bart.

Indeed, Bushnell's protagonist was far more amoral than the delicate Lily, many reviewers noted. "Selfish, fickle, and occasionally outright deluded," noted *Entertainment Weekly*'s Laura Miller, "Janey makes an unlikely heroine: Her chief claim on our sympathy is her indomitable will, though she can never quite settle on what she really wants." Miller dismissed previous critical comparisons to Lily Bart. "Unlike Wharton's tragic characters," Miller pointed out, "Janey isn't trapped by anything bigger than her own laziness, pretensions, and greed." The London *Observer* review from Merritt assessed comparisons to the other literary figure with whom Bushnell was often mentioned—Jane Austen—finding "flashes of the same viper wit, the same piercing observation of detail, the same joyfully bitchy spotlight turned on the posturing and insincerity of society."

Penelope Mesic, writing in *Book*, called Janey "doubly gratifying as a heroine, since readers can fantasize about being her and then congratulate themselves that they're not." That dichotomy was what helped propel the book to the *New York Times* best-seller list and land its author another television deal. In August of 2003, ABC and Touchstone Television acquired the rights to *Trading Up* for what would likely become a weekly prime-time series. Bushnell was also slated to write another Janey Wilcox book, according to her contract with Hyperion. Meanwhile, HBO's *Sex and the City* series was coming to a close, slated for a 2004 grand finale. In it, Carrie finally finds love with the most unlikely of suitors: a Russian-born, world-renowned painter.

The fictional paramour was played by actor Mikhail Baryshnikov, whose previous career was as ballet's most appealing male dancer of the twentieth century. The show had a neatly symmetrical parallel with Bushnell's own life, for in 2002 she wed a principal dancer with the New York City Ballet, Charles Askegard. The two were married on a Nantucket beach after just a seven-week courtship. "I wasn't ready to get married until I was 43," she told D. Parvaz of the *Seattle Post-Intelligencer*.

Times had changed, Bushnell believed, and the ruthless scene chronicled in her original column was now a bygone era. Her new husband was ten years her junior, and she told Slater in the *Evening Stan-*

dard interview, "in the past five years, relationships between the sexes have really changed. There's a whole group of men born in the Seventies who tend not to be as sexist, because they grew up with the idea of women working.... There seem to be more and more people who will take a partner as a person, as opposed to someone who will fit into a box."

Selected writings

Sex and the City (essays), Atlantic Monthly Press (New York City), 1996.
Four Blondes (short stories), Atlantic Monthly Press (New York City), 2000.
Trading Up (novel), Hyperion (New York City), 2003.

Sources

Periodicals

Atlantic Monthly, October 2000, p. 138.
Book, July–August 2003, p. 72.
Daily Variety, August 12, 2003, p. 1.
Entertainment Weekly, August 23, 1996, p. 116; June 6, 2003, p. 36; June 27, 2003, p. 140.

Evening Standard (London, England), September 12, 2003, p. 20.
Independent (London, England), February 5, 2001, p. 1.
Independent Sunday (London, England), August 31, 2003, p. 3.
Knight Ridder/Tribune News Service, October 6, 2000.
Nation, August 24, 1998, p. 36.
New York Post, June 22, 2003, p. 50.
New York Times, July 13, 2003, p. 4.
Observer (London, England), July 28, 2002, p. 4; August 3, 2003, p. 16.
Publishers Weekly, July 3, 2000, p. 46.
San Francisco Chronicle, August 7, 2003, p. E1.
Seattle Post–Intelligencer, August 2, 2003, p. E1.
Star Tribune (Minneapolis, MN), July 26, 2003, p. 1E.
Time, August 12, 1996, p. 66.
Times (London, England), February 22, 1997, p. 11; July 10, 1999, p. 6.

Online

"Candace Bushnell," *Contemporary Authors Online,* Gale, 2003.

—Carol Brennan

James Caan

Actor

Born March 26, 1939, in Bronx, NY; son of Arthur (a meat dealer) and Sophie Caan; married Dee-Jay Mathis (a dancer), 1961 (divorced, 1966); married Sheila Ryan (a model and actress), 1976 (divorced, 1977); married Ingrid Hajek (a pastry chef), September 9, 1990 (divorced, 1995); married Linda Stokes, October 7, 1995; children: Tara (from first marriage), Scott Andrew (an actor; from second marriage), Alexander James (from third marriage), James Arthur, Jacob Nicholas (from fourth marriage). *Education:* Studied economics at Michigan State University; studied theater at Hofstra University, Long Island, NY; studied acting at the Neighborhood Playhouse School of the Theatre, New York, NY, and with Wynn Handman.

Addresses: *Contact*—P.O. Box 6646, Denver, CO 80206–0646; 644 Amalfi Dr., Pacific Palisades, CA 90272.

Career

Actor in films, including: *Irma La Douce* (uncredited), 1963; *Lady in a Cage,* 1964; *The Glory Guys,* 1965; *Red Line 7000,* 1965; *El Dorado,* 1966; *Games,* 1967; *Countdown,* 1968; *Journey to Shiloh,* 1968; *Submarine X–1,* 1968; *The Rain People,* 1969; *Rabbit, Run,* 1970; *T.R. Baskin,* 1971; *The Godfather,* 1972; *Slither,* 1972; *Cinderella Liberty,* 1973; *The Gambler,* 1974; *The Godfather: Part II* (uncredited), 1974; *Freebie and the Bean,* 1974; *Funny Lady,* 1975; *Rollerball,* 1975; *The Killer Elite,* 1975; *Gone with the West,* 1976; *Silent Movie,* 1976; *Harry and Walter Go to New York,* 1976; *A Bridge Too Far,* 1977; *Another Man, Another Chance,* 1977; *Comes a Horseman,* 1978; *Chapter Two,* 1979; *1941* (uncredited), 1979; *Hide in Plain Sight* (also director), 1980; *Thief,* 1981; *Kiss Me Goodbye,* 1982; *Gardens of Stone,* 1987; *Alien Nation,* 1988; *Dick Tracy,* 1990; *Misery,* 1990; *For the Boys,* 1991; *The Dark Backward,* 1991; *Honeymoon in Vegas,* 1992; *The Program,* 1993; *Flesh and Bone,* 1993; *Tashunga,* 1996; *A Boy Called Hate,* 1996; *Bottle Rocket,* 1996; *Eraser,* 1996; *Bulletproof,* 1996; *This Is My Father,* 1998; *Mickey Blue Eyes,* 1999; *Luckytown,* 2000; *The Way of the Gun,* 2000; *The Yards,* 2000; *Viva Las Nowhere,* 2001; *In the Shadows,* 2001; *Night at the Golden Eagle* (uncredited), 2002; *City of Ghosts,* 2002; *Dogville,* 2003; *Jericho Mansions,* 2003; *Elf,* 2003; *Dallas 362,* 2003; *This Thing of Ours,* 2003. Television appearances include: *Naked City,* ABC, 1961; *Route 66,* 1961; *Alcoa Premiere,* 1962; *The Untouchables,* 1962; *The Wide Country,* 1962; *Dr. Kildare,* 1963; *Death Valley Days,* 1963; *Ben Casey,* 1963; *Combat!,* 1963; *Kraft Suspense Theatre,* 1963; *The Alfred Hitchcock Hour,* 1964; *Wagon Train,* 1965; *The F.B.I.,* 1969; *Get Smart,* 1969; *Brian's Song* (movie), ABC, 1971; *Rowan & Martin's Laugh–In,* 1972; *Superstunt* (movie), 1978; *Bolero* (miniseries), 1981; *NewsRadio,* 1996; *Poodle Springs* (movie), HBO, 1998; *A Glimpse of Hell* (movie), FX, 2001; *Warden of Red Rock* (movie), Showtime, 2001; *Hearts of Men* (movie), USA, 2002; *Lathe of Heaven* (movie), 2002; *Blood Crime* (movie), 2002; *Las Vegas,* NBC, 2003—; *The Incredible*

Mrs. Ritchie (movie), 2003. Stage appearances include: (as Jimmy Caan) *La Ronde,* 1960; *Blood, Sweat, and Stanley Poole,* 1961.

Sidelights

Though American actor James Caan was a leading man in the 1970s—his best–known role was as Sonny Corleone in Francis Ford Coppola's *The Godfather*—he stopped acting for five years in the 1980s. Even before he left the industry behind, he was already playing more character roles, a trend that would continue into the early 2000s. His up–and–down career was slowly rebuilt after his hiatus, primarily after the success of 1990's *Misery.* Caan was often cast in tough guy roles, especially mafia types, but he also succeeded in doing comedy, singing, and dancing. His tough reputation spilled over into Caan's personal life which was marred by several arrests for violence.

Caan was born on March 26, 1939, in the Bronx, New York, the son of Arthur and Sophie Caan. His father was employed as a kosher meat wholesaler. Caan grew up in Sunnyside, Queens, New York, and Long Island City, with his brother, Ronald, who became a producer, and his sister, Barbara. As a child, Caan attended PS 150 in Brownsville, Brooklyn, New York. When he was a high school student at Rhodes High School, Caan was an athlete and class president.

After graduating from Rhodes, Caan entered Michigan State University where he studied economics and wanted to play football so that he could have a career as a professional football player. However, when he came to Michigan State, he was too small to make the team and had to give up his football dreams. Caan then transferred to Hofstra University where he studied theater. Caan later studied acting at the Neighborhood Playhouse School of the Theatre with Sanford Meisner in New York City and with Wynn Handman.

Caan began his professional acting career on stage in New York City. His stage debut came in 1960 in *La Ronde.* The following year, Caan made his Broadway debut in *Blood, Sweat, and Stanley Poole* in 1961. He then moved to Los Angeles, California, where he began working in television. Caan appeared in some episodic television roles on shows like *Naked City.* Within a short time, Caan was also appearing in feature films. His first role was an uncredited part in 1963's *Irma La Douce.* His first real film role came in 1964's *Lady in a Cage.*

In 1969, Caan appeared in *The Rain People,* a film directed by Francis Ford Coppola. It was Coppola who soon helped Caan's career take off. In the early

1970s, Caan had two breakout roles that were among the best of his career. The first was the part of Brian Piccolo in the 1971 television movie, *Brian's Song.* Piccolo was a professional football player for the Chicago Bears who was stricken with cancer at the height of his career. Caan was nominated for an Emmy Award for his work in the television movie. Coppola then cast Caan in a role the actor was forever identified with in *The Godfather.*

In 1972's *The Godfather,* Caan played Sonny Corleone, the eldest son of the mafia capo. Caan's character was a violent man who was tapped to run the family business until he was killed at a tollbooth in one of the film's most famous scenes. Caan was nominated for an Academy Award as a best supporting actor for his work. Caan's success in *The Godfather* led to many starring roles in film in the 1970s and early 1980s, though he also had a problem from being typecast as a Sonny Corleone type. The actor also turned down roles in what became some of the big leading roles of the decade. He was offered, but refused, roles in many critically acclaimed films, including: *M*A*S*H, Love Story, One Flew Over the Cuckoo's Nest, Kramer vs. Kramer, Apocalypse Now,* and *Superman.*

One of the roles that Caan did take in the 1970s was the lead in 1974's *The Gambler.* He was praised for his work, and later had a co–starring role in *Freebie and the Bean* in the same year. In 1975, Caan was able to show off his other talents when he played Billy Rose in *Funny Lady,* the Barbra Streisand vehicle in which she played Fanny Brice. Caan sang in the film. While working on his directorial debut, Caan took a role in 1979's *Chapter Two* to raise funds to finish his film. *Chapter Two* was based on a play of the same name, and Caan played the character based on the playwright.

In 1980, Caan's directorial debut, *Hide in Plain Sight* was released. He also had the starring role in the film. *Hide in Plain Sight* had taken Caan two and a half years to make, and he said he never wanted to direct again. The film was based on the true story of a divorced father who lost touch with his children when their stepfather was put in the witness protection program because he was an informant on the mob. The father, played by Caan, had to sue to find his children. Caan wanted to make to a simple, powerful film, but was upset that the film studio executives added music to the soundtrack that he did not want. In addition to that and other other clashes with the production company, *Hidden in Plain Sight* was a failure at the box office.

Caan went on to star in a few films in the early 1980s. In 1981, he played the title role in *Thief.* Caan was proud of his work in the film, though it did not do well at the box office. The following year, he played the ghost of the husband of a character played by Sally Field in *Kiss Me Goodbye*. Caan later said he disliked this film, as he did several films he appeared in just to work or for the money.

Kiss Me Goodbye was one of the last film that Caan would make for several years. He did not make any films between 1982 and 1987. During that time, he suffered some personal tragedies. His sister, Barbara, died of leukemia. Caan had run–ins with the law, including a 1980 arrest when he was charged with beating Sheila Ryan, his ex–wife, after she told him she was re–marrying. Caan also had problems with his temper, drug use, abuse, and depression. But he also found joy in raising his son, Scott, of whom he had custody. Caan spent as much time as possible with him; he even coached his son's sports teams.

Though Caan said he had no intention of returning to acting, in 1987, he was forced to restart his career because he was having financial problems because an associate mismanaged his funds. Coppola gave Caan his first film role in five years when the director cast the actor as a burnt–out career military officer working burial duty at Arlington National Cemetery in the Vietnam–era *Gardens of Stone*. In 1988, Caan took on an entirely different film role when he appeared in *Alien Nation*, an adventure set in the future when space aliens were moving to the United States. Caan played a veteran police detective who was partnered with an alien.

Within a few years of the reawakening of his acting career, Caan was in one of his biggest box office hits. In 1990, he was given a lead role in *Misery*, based on a story by Stephen King, when Warren Beatty was dropped from the project. Caan played a romance novelist who has a car accident near the home of an overenthusiastic fan, played by Kathy Bates. The fan is angry with the changes the author has made in some of his recent works, and holds him captive and inflicts injury on him. Caan receive good reviews for the role he called the most physically demanding of his career as he had to stay in bed most of the time. *Misery* helped put Caan's career back on track.

In the early 1990s, Caan appeared in a number of hit movies, including 1991's big budget spectacle, *For the Boys*. In the film, Caan played Eddie Sparks, a member of a song–and–dance team with Bette Midler. The film explores their relationship as they entertain troops from World War II to Vietnam. The role allowed Caan to show more of his singing and dancing skills. Midler complimented her co–star, telling Bernard Weinraub of *New York Times*, "Somehow Jimmy's acting never shows.... He has a more languid way of working. And everything he does is very small—he's a master of the small gesture, the flickering eyelash; everything was exquisitely right. He has all these deep layers of macho stuff; he's very boisterous, very outgoing, but then you work with him and get him in a corner, and you realize he's very smart and very sensitive."

Caan went on to appear in a number of other films of significance in the 1990s. He played a gangster the 1992 romantic comedy *Honeymoon in Vegas*, a box office hit. In 1993, Caan played a football coach in the controversial film, *The Program*. Caan's son, Scott, also began an acting career, and the pair appeared together in 1996's *A Boy Called Hate*. The breadth of his film choices could be seen by two films released in 1996, *Eraser*, an action picture starring Arnold Schwarzenegger, and the comedy *Bulletproof*.

While Caan's career was rebounding during this time period, he was still having numerous run–ins with the law and with tragic incidents. In 1993, while Caan was staying at a friend's apartment, a young aspiring actor, Mark Alan Schwartz, fell from the fire escape to his death. A year later, he was arrested for showing his gun in public to Derek Lee, a rap artist, and for beating up a woman. Both cases never went to trial. Caan checked himself into drug rehabilitation in 1995 at the Exodus Recovery Center and remained clean after that date.

Many of Caan's film roles in the late 1990s and early 2000s were again tough guys, often mafia types. In 1999's *Mickey Blue Eyes*, he played a gangster opposite Hugh Grant who played his future son–in–law. In the 2000 thriller *The Way of the Gun*, Caan's character was the muscle for a mafia lawyer, but was a bad guy with good intentions and the moral character in the film. Caan went on to play Uncle Frank, a subway contractor in New York City who operates a company which has been corrupted by mafia connections, in 2000's *The Yards*. Not all his films were dark, however. In 2003, he played a publishing company executive who learns his long–lost son was raised by elves, in the holiday hit, *Elf*. Both the film and Caan received good reviews.

Caan also began working in television more in this time period. After playing detective Philip Marlowe in the 1998 television movie *Poodle Springs*, based on an unfinished novel by Raymond Chandler, he appeared in two more television movies in 2001,

FX's *A Glimpse of Hell* and Showtime's *Warden of Red Rock*. In the former, Caan played a navy captain in the 1989 real–life tragedy that occurred on the USS Iowa, while in the latter, a western, he played a warden of a local prison. In 2003, Caan began starring in his first major television series, the NBC drama *Las Vegas*. He played "Big Ed" Deline, the head of security at a casino. *Las Vegas* was one of the most popular new dramas on television that season, and Caan was the senior member of an ensemble cast. In 2004, Caan began filming the motion picture *Santa's Slay*.

Having been at both the bottom and the top of the acting business, Caan was able to offer sage advice to aspiring actors. He told Denis Hamill of *Daily News*, "[W]hat is inevitable, no matter what heights you achieve, is that there is a slide down. The degree varies of course, but if your whole life is [acting], you're nuts. Because then when your career slides, your life goes with it. So acting is not my life, it's my job. It's very, very important to me. But my life, my family, my wife, my children, my friends, my health, their health. After that, of course, I'd also like to be the best actor in the world."

Sources

Books

Celebrity Biographies, Baseline II, Inc., 2004.

Periodicals

Atlanta Journal–Constitution, November 7, 2003, p. 1D.
Boston Globe, November 27, 1991, p. 23; September 22, 2003, p. B7; January 3, 2004, p. C8.
Chicago Sun–Times, August 15, 1999, p. 3.
Christian Science Monitor, April 11, 1980, p. 19.
Daily News (New York), March 19, 1998, p. 2.
Esquire, May 1998, p. 82.
Houston Chronicle, March 16, 2001, p. 10.
Independent (London, England), October 19, 2000, p. 7.
New York Times, April 3, 1981, p. C6; November 17, 1991, sec. 2, p. 13; September 8, 2000, p. E10.
Observer, August 22, 1999, p. 12.
People, October 4, 1993, p. 53; December 15, 2003, p. 24.
San Francisco Chronicle, November 7, 2003, p. D1.
St. Louis Post–Dispatch, December 7, 1990, p. 1F.
Sunday Herald Sun (Melbourne, Australia), April 19, 2001, p. 54.
Time, November 24, 2003, p. 89.
Toronto Star, May 26, 1987, p. G1; October 5, 1988, p. F1; November 30, 1990, p. D16; September 21, 2003, p. TV2.
USA Today, July 21, 1994, p. 2D.
Washington Post, March 21, 1980, p. D1.

—A. Petruso

Keisha Castle-Hughes

Actress

Born March 24, 1990, in Donnybrook, Western Australia, Australia; daughter of Tim Castle and Desrae Hughes.

Addresses: *Agent*—Auckland Actors, P.O. Box 56460, Dominion Rd., Auckland 1003, New Zealand.

Career

Made debut film appearance in *Whale Rider,* 2002; also appeared in *Star Wars: Episode III,* 2005.

Sidelights

Keisha Castle–Hughes wowed film audiences around the world with her performance in the 2002 indie hit, *Whale Rider,* the tale of one young New Zealander teen's struggle against misogynistic traditions in her Maori fishing village. Though she was just eleven years old when cast and had no prior acting experience, it earned her an Academy Award nomination at the age of 13. Castle–Hughes, noted *Newsweek*'s David Ansen, "possesses an innate grace that makes her transformation from outcast adolescent to spiritual warrior seem utterly natural."

Castle–Hughes was born in 1990 in Donnybrook, Western Australia. Her mother, Desrae Hughes, is of Maori heritage, while her father, Tim Castle, is Australian. Castle–Hughes and her two younger brothers moved to New Zealand with their mother when she was four years old, and settled in Mount Wellington, a suburb just outside of New Zealand's largest city, Auckland. She always dreamed of acting, Castle–Hughes recalled, but had never even appeared in a school play when a casting agent for a movie to be filmed on New Zealand's North Island arrived at her school. Diana Rowan, who had found a young Anna Paquin to play Holly Hunter's daughter in the acclaimed 1993 film, *The Piano,* felt that Castle–Hughes possessed the necessary blend of guilelessness and perseverance to take on what would prove to be a challenging role for any actress.

Just a few days after her formal audition for *Whale Rider,* Castle–Hughes took part in a career–day event at her school, and hinted that she would like a career in the performing arts. "People were like, 'It's not going to happen. It's a great dream, but let's get real here,'" she recalled in an interview with *Entertainment Weekly* writer Sumeet Bal. In the end, *Whale Rider*'s director, Niki Caro, who also wrote the screenplay, agreed with Rowan and cast Castle–Hughes in the lead.

Whale Rider featured an entirely Maori cast. Castle–Hughes, her brothers, and mother moved to the fishing village of Whangara for the shoot, which was a homecoming of sorts, for her mother's family was originally from the area. Caro's screenplay was based on a book from the 1980s by Witi Ihimaera, a well–known Maori writer, and recounted the story of a young girl who is the sole heir in her family to the tribal–chief seat held by her grandfather. He refuses to acknowledge the possibility of a girl serving as the local leader, however, despite her increasingly obvious suitability for the challenges of the job.

Castle–Hughes played Paikea, nicknamed "Pai," a young woman given the controversial name by her artist father, who soon vanished to Europe. In Maori lore, the original Paikea was the male ancestor who came to Whangara from Polynesia a thousand years earlier on the back of a whale. Tradition among the Ngati Kanohi of Whangara, who are considered descendants of the first Paikea, holds that the firstborn son among Paikea's direct descendants should become chief. Pai is her grandfather's sole remaining progeny, however. Both a twin brother and her mother died in childbirth, and the orphaned girl lives with her prickly grandfather Koro (Rawiri Paratene) and his more supportive wife, Nanny Flowers (Vicky Haughton). Koro treats Pai with contempt, and announces his intention to begin searching for a new chief from among the boys in the village.

Secretly, Pai learns the customs and songs she needs to lead, and also trains in *taiaha*, the Maori stick–fighting martial art permitted only for boys. When Koro tosses his whale–tooth pendant into the sea—the symbol of his authority—it is Pai who finds it. In one moving movement, she delivers a speech at a school event, and dedicates it to Koro, but she realizes as she talks about her culture that her grandfather has not even bothered to show up. When a group of whales beaches in Whangara following a storm, villagers wonder who might lead them back out to sea, as their custom dictates. Pai takes the job and proves her mettle.

Castle–Hughes admitted that in the whale–riding scene, it was a mechanical mammal she rode, but the sequence was filmed a mile out at sea. She also had a stunt double for part of the scenes, since she was not a strong–enough swimmer yet for ocean currents. For all her other scenes, however, Castle–Hughes won enthusiastic praise from critics when *Whale Rider* was released in the United States in the summer of 2003. The *New York Times* film reviewer, Elvis Mitchell, described it as "wickedly absorbing. Much of the film's power comes from the delicate charisma of" its young star, and the critic added that though she appeared untrained as an actress, Castle–Hughes "instead communicates her feelings

through a wary hesitation. It doesn't matter that her voice makes her sound a little lost, still trying to find her way into a world that disdains her. Her intelligent, dark eyes are so expressive that she has the piquant confidence of a silent–film heroine." *Time International*'s Marlene Sorensen also wrote favorably of the performance. Castle–Hughes's "Pai navigates all obstacles with a quiet self–belief," asserted Sorensen. "The character could have come across as irritatingly self–righteous, but Castle–Hughes' performance is so subtle and sincere that Pai remains likable throughout the film."

In January of 2004, Castle–Hughes's name appeared on the list of Academy Award nominations in the Best Actress in a Leading Role category. Her competitors were Diane Keaton, Samantha Morton, Charlize Theron, and Naomi Watts, and Castle–Hughes was the youngest woman ever to be nominated in the category, breaking a previous record held since 1975 by a 20–year–old Isabelle Adjani. The New Zealand high–school student's next film role would be in 2005's *Star Wars: Episode III* as the Queen of Naboo. As for her future in film, she was pleased that *Whale Rider*, one of few internationally released films to depict Maori life, had done so well. "Fifteen percent of the population in New Zealand is Maori," she explained to *Times* of London writer Dave Calhoun, "and we went through a little time when it was forbidden to speak the Maori language and things like that. But it's all good now."

Sources

Periodicals

Entertainment Weekly, June 13, 2003, p. 73; February 6, 2004, p. 50.
Film Journal International, June 2003, p. 43.
Newsweek, June 9, 2003, p. 59.
New York Times, June 6, 2003, p. E14; December 7, 2003, p. ST4.
O: The Oprah Magazine, June 2003, p. 62.
Record (Bergen County, NJ), March 22, 2004, p. F2.
Time International, August 11, 2003, p. 58.
Times (London, England), July 10, 2003, p. 16.

Online

"NZ girl youngest Oscar nominee," CNN.com, http://www.cnn.com/2004/SHOWBIZ/Movies/01/27/kiwi.nominee.ap/index.html (June 1, 2004).

—*Carol Brennan*

Edwin E. Catmull

President of Pixar Animation Studios

Born March 31, 1945, in Parkersburg, WV; married Susan; children: five. *Education:* University of Utah, B.S. (computer science), B.S. (physics), Ph.D.

Addresses: *Office*—Pixar Animation Studios, 1200 Park Ave., Emeryville, CA 94608.

Career

Computer–animation pioneer. Began career as director of the Computer Graphics Lab, 1975; vice president of Computer Division, Lucasfilm Ltd., 1979–86; co–founder and chief technical officer, Pixar Animation Studios, 1986&mdash, president, 1986–95, 2001—.

Member: Academy of Motion Picture Arts and Sciences.

Awards: Co–recipient, Academy Award for Scientific & Technical Engineering Achievement, Academy of Motion Picture Arts and Sciences, 1993 and 1996; co–recipient, Academy Award of Merit, Significant Advances in the Field of Motion Picture Rendering, 2001.

Sidelights

Edwin E. Catmull heads Pixar Animation Studios, the California–based enterprise that pioneered digital animation for film. The company, which made the hit movies *Toy Story* and *Finding Nemo,* has become one of the entertainment industry's surprise financial success stories, but bringing computer–drawn figures to life on the big screen proved a greater challenge than Catmull, who has spent much of his career working in the field, ever expected. "I thought it would probably take ten years to get to the point where we could really use computer graphics in movies," he told *Guardian* writer David Teather. "The reality is it took more like 20 years."

Catmull was born in West Virginia in 1945, but grew up with his four siblings in Utah, where his father was a school principal. From an early age, he dreamed of a career with the Walt Disney Company, the world's leading feature–film animation studio for much of the twentieth century, but realized as he came of age that perhaps he lacked the artistic ability to land a job with the prestigious Disney corps of animators. Instead, Catmull studied physics and computer science at the University of Utah, earning degrees in each, before entering the school's Ph.D. program in computer science, which he finished in 1974.

While completing his doctorate, Catmull worked on some of first computer–generated experiments that made it into Hollywood film. He created an animated version of his own hand, for example, that was seen in the 1976 sci–fi thriller *Futureworld*. The University of Utah was a hotbed of innovation in the field at the time, and its reputation landed Catmull and some other newly minted Ph.D.s jobs with the New York Institute of Technology in 1975. This was the brainchild of an unconventional New York millionaire, Alexander Schure, who hoped to make the first–ever computer–animated feature film. Catmull ran the Computer Graphics Lab for Schure, but he eventually realized that the Long Island enterprise lacked the technical expertise to make a credible animated film.

In 1979, Catmull moved west to take a job with Lucasfilm Ltd. in northern California. Named after its founder, noted *Star Wars* director George Lucas, the studio was also interested in creating an entirely computer–animated feature film, and Catmull was hired to set up this division. Some of the technological breakthroughs that Catmull made during this time found their way into Lucas' other projects, such as a minute–long transformation of a barren planet to life in *Star Trek II: The Wrath of Khan* in 1982. He also developed the first computer program to mimic "motion blur," a crucial element in making animation realistic to the human eye. Lucasfilm made one computer–animated short film, *Andre and Wally B.,* in 1984, before Lucas decided to unload the division for financial reasons. Catmull was determined to find a committed buyer, and approached Steven P. Jobs, co–founder of Apple Computer. Jobs had recently departed Apple with an immense amount of capital, but was initially wary of getting into the entertainment business. Finally, nearly a year later, Jobs agreed to take over, and Catmull and the other pioneers were able to keep their jobs.

Jobs bought the company Catmull was running in 1986 for $10 million, and rechristened it Pixar Animation Studios, a name taken from the computer hardware it had developed that processed images. Later that year, Pixar premiered the short *Luxo, Jr.* at the Special Interest Group on Computer Graphics (SIGGRAPH) convention in Dallas, Texas, an event that earned a mention in *Time* magazine. The cartoon featured two iconic Luxo desk lamps playing catch with one another, and incited an industry buzz. "The crowd had greeted some earlier offerings with hoots and good–natured catcalls," noted *Time* journalist Philip Elmer–DeWitt. "But when the Luxo lamps appeared, bathed in each other's light and seemingly imbued with human emotions, the hall burst into prolonged and enthusiastic applause."

Luxo, Jr. was even nominated for an Academy Award, and Catmull termed this a crucial turning point for the company. "Even though it didn't win, I think it was really the milestone," he recalled in an interview with *Variety*'s Laura A. Ackley. "When people saw this, they said, 'Oh, this is what computer animation is all about.'" It would be nearly another decade before Pixar was able to finish and release its first full–length feature, however. Only when another short, *Tin Toy* from 1988, won the Academy Award in its category did Pixar find a studio willing to take on the onerous production costs in return for a share of the box–office take. That studio was Disney, and the result was *Toy Story* in 1995. "The reason we picked toys was that we could do them," Catmull told Teather in the *Guardian*. "They are made of plastic. We were at the hairy edge of what we could do."

An initial public offering (IPO) of Pixar stock, buoyed by *Toy Story*'s box–office success, helped put the company on more solid financial ground in the late 1990s. The IPO even forced Catmull to relinquish his chief executive officer title to Jobs for a time, in order to provide Wall Street with a recognizable name. He still led the team, however, and it went on produce a string of hits, from the *Toy Story II* sequel to *Monsters, Inc.* Catmull remained, as *BusinessWeek* writer Peter Burrows asserted, "keeper of the company's unique corporate culture, which blends Silicon Valley techies, Hollywood production pros, and artsy animators." He regained his title of Pixar's president in 2001. *Finding Nemo*, the studio's 2003 release about a hapless clown fish in search of his son, became the top–grossing film in Pixar history: four months after its release, it had taken in more than $336 million, and also became the highest–grossing animated film in history.

Catmull, married and the father of five, oversees a studio that employs 750 at its offices in Emeryville, California, near the city of Oakland. At Pixar, employees are forbidden to work more than 50 hours per week without authorization, and many enjoy perks Catmull has instituted, such as an in–house masseuse and regular Pilates classes. He and his team were now working on the next big step in computer animation: the human form. Pixar's next project was titled *The Incredibles,* about a gang of suburban crime–fighters. "It is a totally different challenge," Catmull told the *Guardian*'s Teather. "The humans in our previous films were not the strongest element."

Sources

BusinessWeek, June 30, 2003, p. 68.
Guardian (London, England), October 11, 2003, p. 34.
PC, November 15, 1998, p. 98.
Time, September 1, 1986, p. 66.
Variety, July 20, 1998, p. 32.

—*Carol Brennan*

Roberto Cavalli

AP/Wide World Photos

Fashion designer

Born November 15, 1940, in Florence, Italy; son of Giorgio (a mine surveyor) and Marcella (a tailor; maiden name, Rossi) Cavalli; married Silvanella Giannoni, 1964 (divorced, 1974); married Eva Duringer; children: Christiana, Tommaso (from first marriage), Rachele, Daniele (son), Robin (son) (from second marriage). *Education:* Attended the Academy of Art of Florence, Italy, after 1957.

Addresses: *Office*—Roberto Cavalli, 711 Madison Ave., New York, NY 10021–8003.

Career

Began career as a textile printer for an Italian knitwear line, 1960; started a T–shirt, denim, and leather design company; worked for the design house of Mario Valentino; opened namesake boutique in Saint–Tropez, France; showed first women's collection in Florence, Italy, 1972; launched short–lived men's line, 1974; design house revived in early 1990s with the success of Cavalli Jeans line (renamed Just Cavalli); began showing women's lines during Milan Fashion Week, 1994; opened Madison Avenue boutique, September, 1999; also designs Roberto Cavalli Casa, a housewares division, and has ten product licenses, from fragrance to footwear.

Sidelights

Italian designer Roberto Cavalli's flamboyant, creatively embellished clothes have earned him a loyal following among fashion–forward men, women, and pop stars. Cavalli had enjoyed a fleet-ing burst of fame when he began his business in the early 1970s for his innovative printed leathers, but faded into relative obscurity as styles grew more minimalist. Fashionistas and celebrities rediscovered his still–extravagant designs in the '90s, and helped make them among the most–coveted of items from the runways each season. Writing in London's *Observer,* Polly Vernon termed Cavalli the "king of bling" and his line "the absurd, trashy, slag–luxe fashion choice of the footballer, the footballer's wife, and the super–ornate superstar."

Born in 1940, Cavalli is a native of the Tuscan capital of Florence. His father, Giorgio, was a mine surveyor by profession, and his mother, Marcella, a tailor. Marcella was the daughter of artist Giuseppe Rossi, a member of the Macchiaoli group of painters in Italy. The Macchiaoli movement was an offshoot of French Impressionists, and works by Cavalli's grandfather are among those that hang in Florence's esteemed Uffizi Museum. When Italy was drawn into World War II, military units from Nazi Germany arrived in Florence, and Cavalli's father was slain. "Something happened between the partisans and the Germans and my father was involved," Cavalli told a writer for London's *Evening Standard,* Nick Foulkes, "so my mother took care of me and my sister. It made my character more deep, more strong."

In 1957, Cavalli enrolled at Florence's Academy of Art with plans to either follow in his grandfather's footsteps or become an architect. He began dating a fellow art student, however, and those plans took a detour. "She was a classic, very pretty Italian girl," Cavalli said of his first wife in the *Evening Standard* interview with Foulkes. "Her parents were dreaming for her to marry a doctor or a lawyer and I was just a poor art–school student." His fortunes improved considerably in 1960, when a friend was launching a knitwear line and asked him to hand–paint some of the sweaters. They proved a hit, and Cavalli began researching the art of textile printing in earnest. He started making T–shirts and jeans with a luxe–hippie look that caught on with young Italians. For a time, he worked for Mario Valentino, the Naples designer known for his well–crafted leathers and suedes. While there, he recalled in the interview with the *Evening Standard*'s Foulkes, "I had this idea to print on leather. I used glove skin from a French tannery, and when I started to print, I saw it was possible to make evening gowns in leather … in pink—unbelievable." Cavalli opened his own boutique in Saint–Tropez, on the French Riviera.

Cavalli formally launched his own women's line in 1972 with an extravagant event at Florence's Pitti Palace. His form–fitting, vividly colored clothes quickly became a hit with trend–setting Europeans of the more idle class. One of the first celebrities to wear his designs was the French film star Brigitte Bardot, and soon his eponymous boutiques were providing discotheque–wear for the jet–set crowd of the 1970s. Later, Cavalli's over–the–top designs would sometimes be compared to those of a fellow Italian, the late Gianni Versace, whose name became synonymous with embellished extravagance in the 1980s. "It would be easy to say that Cavalli is the new Versace," asserted Foulkes in the *Evening Standard* article, "except that when he was alive it would have been more accurate to call Versace the new Cavalli." Similarly, *New York Times* writer Ruth La Ferla claimed that Cavalli's "feathered evening clothes, rhinestone–encrusted jeans, and python pants were precursors to the rock 'n' roll fashions of Versace and Dolce & Gabbana."

During the 1980s, however, Cavalli seemed to lose his footing in fashion as other Italians, among them the Milan–based Versace and Giorgio Armani, began to gain a strong international following. Cavalli remained in Florence, by contrast, and did not take part in the seasonal presentations of new collections for spring/summer and fall/winter that were known as Milan Fashion Week. Moreover, his glitzy clothes were lost in the parade of more minimalist–chic wear that began to dominate fashion in the

1990s. "Cavalli refused to adapt his style," wrote Vernon in the *Observer*, "and his label seemed destined to languish forever in a fashiony no–man's–land, drip–fed life support by a dwindling trickle of ageing, tasteless, mindlessly loaded Euro trash." Cavalli's second wife, Eva, is credited as the behind–the–scenes force in the renaissance of his design house in the 1990s. He met the former Miss Austria when she was 18 years old and a contestant in the 1977 Miss Universe pageant in Santo Domingo, Dominican Republic. At the time, Cavalli was 37, the divorced father of two, and a pageant judge, and the blonde Eva Duringer had been named in an unofficial pre–pageant poll as the front–runner for the crown. Instead she was the first–runner up to Miss Trinidad and Tobago, the first black Miss Universe, and won Cavalli's heart. They wed and began a family, and as their children grew more independent in the early 1990s, Eva set her sights on improving her husband's business fortunes. "I was thinking maybe to stop," her husband confessed to *Time International* writer Lauren Goldstein. "But then Eva became interested so I started—for her—to involve myself again."

Devising a method of printing patterns onto stretch denim, Cavalli launched a jeans line that boosted his revenues considerably. He began showing his dressier line at Milan's Fashion Week in 1994, and soon his racy, abbreviated chiffon dresses and signature zebra–print items were appealing to an entirely new generation of celebrities—some of whom were around the same age as his company. They included singers Jennifer Lopez and Christina Aguilera, British soccer star David Beckham, and rap mogul Sean "P. Diddy" Combs. "The celebrity connection is very important," Cavalli explained to *WWD*'s Eric Wilson. "It's more important to me personally than to anyone else because it makes me feel important. Sometimes in Italy you don't know how important you are. It's important because it's adrenaline, and that's what starts creativity."

Cavalli's clothes also caught on with a more difficult segment to win over. What *Independent Sunday* writer Rebecca Lowthorpe termed "the Cavalli cult" included "not only … every big rock, pop, and rap star, from Madonna to Mary J. Blige, and the entire cast of *Sex and the City*, but, strangely, on fashion folk—traditionally the most resistant of all to colourful, busy clothes." A Cavalli dress even became a plot point on *Sex and the City*, when Sarah Jessica Parker's Carrie character was forced to clean out her overstuffed closet to make room for her boyfriend's clothes. Their battle over space later escalates, and she tells him, "It's Roberto Cavalli! I threw it out and I love it. What more do you want?"

Cavalli began courting the American market in earnest in the late 1990s. He began advertising in magazines like *Cosmopolitan,* and hired a management team to work with top United States retailers that carried his line, like Bergdorf Goodman. A Roberto Cavalli store with a posh Madison Avenue address opened in September of 1999. The effort paid off, and by 2002 Cavalli's United States sales had tripled in just two years. Some of it, he believed, could be credited to a weariness with the somber minimalist shades that had continued to dominate women's styles. As he insisted to *People* writer Galina Espinoza, "My fashion has become a success because other designers have become so monotonous."

Cavalli has been the target of occasional criticism for what some consider an excess of fur in his collections. His men's collection, re–launched in 1999, features clothes as equally spirited as his women's line. The first attempt, back in 1974, was not a success, he recalled in an interview with Luisa Zargani of the *Daily News Record.* "The collection was too feminine, too colorful and artistic. I was not happy about it at all. I had tall and androgynous women walk down the runway wearing men's clothes, but the final effect simply made no sense." He retains a sharp eye for what a certain segment of the female populus wants to wear. "For a long time, designers tried to dress women like men," he told *Wall Street Journal* writer Cecilie Rohwedder. "I changed that. I try to bring out the feminine, sexy side that every woman has inside her."

Cavalli's sportswear and jeans line, Just Cavalli, is also the name of a Milan restaurant that he owns. He designs housewares— not surprisingly, empress–red tones and zebra prints predominate—under the name Roberto Cavalli Casa, and also has accessories, fragrance, footwear, swimsuit, and eyewear licenses. He allocates money for marketing efforts only reluctantly, he told Lowthorpe in the *Independent Sunday* interview. "I never liked to spend too much on advertising," he asserted. "All my life, I thought fashion should never be advertised like the washing machines."

Cavalli's company enjoyed United States sales in what were estimated would be $150 million for 2004. The designer plans a further expansion into the North American market that will include a New York City café—modeled on one he launched in Milan, which features his tableware designs—and a boutique on Beverly Hills's poshest shopping street, Rodeo Drive. It would be the 39th among Roberto Cavalli boutiques, including the first one still operating in Saint–Tropez.

Cavalli and his family, however, remain primarily in Florence, where his hilltop home outside the city plays host to celebrity–studded galas rumored to be as opulent as his clothes. He and his wife, with whom he has three children, breed thoroughbred horses, own vineyards in the Chianti region, and oversee a chocolate factory in Italy. Cavalli pilots his own helicopter and 62–foot speedboat that features cushions with his signature zebra print, and also owns three Ferrari luxury sports cars, each of which possesses its own set of custom luggage. In person, note many journalists who interview him, he retains the look of the 1970s–era rake with his fitted jeans, shirts unbuttoned to the waist, and a flowing mane of hair that has turned silver. In mid–2003, he appeared in court in Florence after Italian authorities charged him with tax fraud. It was a not–uncommon practice for moguls in Italy, a country where the estimated tax tables actually take into account the percentage that taxpayers are likely to cheat. The evasion charges stem from renovations done to his Tuscan villa, parts of which date back to the year 1200, that were charged to his business.

In 2003, Cavalli was chosen to serve as grand marshal of New York City's Columbus Day parade. Notable personalities of Italian heritage are usually selected for the honor, and past grand marshals have included Frank Sinatra and Luciano Pavarotti. Cavalli, however, was the first fashion designer to lead the parade. On that same October day, an article he wrote titled "America La Bella" appeared in the *Wall Street Journal.* In it, he identified with the Italian–American community whose achievements the parade celebrates. "This country gave us all an opportunity and that's exactly why I have always loved America," he wrote. "Because it embraces whoever has the desire to build. It's a blend of family and entrepreneurship."

Sources

Cardline, September 19, 2003, p. 1.

Daily News Record (Los Angeles, CA), June 12, 2000, p. 12.

Evening Standard (London, England), July 9, 2001, p. 23.

Footwear News, July 17, 2000, p. 6S.

Global Cosmetic Industry, March 2003, p. 11.

HFN: The Weekly Newspaper for the Home Furnishing Network, November 3, 2003, p. 18.

Independent (London, England), January 12, 2002, p. 9.

Independent Sunday (London, England), February 25, 2001, p. 24.

International Herald Tribune, February 28, 2004, p. 14.

New York Times, September 9, 2001, p. 1.

Observer (London, England), August 17, 2003, p. 16.

People, December 17, 2001, p. 125.

Time International, March 10, 2003, p. 56.

Times (London, England), July 27, 2002, p. 58.

Wall Street Journal, October 22, 2002, p. B1; October 13, 2003, p. A18.

WWD, February 4, 1998, p. 18; April 13, 2001, p. 9; May 2, 2003, p. 3; July 2, 2003, p. 3; July 11, 2003, p. 2; August 4, 2003, p. 4; October 14, 2003, p. 10; January 14, 2004, p. 2; February 11, 2004, p. 7.

—*Carol Brennan*

Paul Charron

President and Chief Executive Officer of Liz Claiborne

Born Paul Richard Charron, August 24, 1942, in Schenectady, NY; son of Richard Armand and Helen Marie (Barringer) Charron; married Kathy Lyn Herdt (an interior designer), June 29, 1974; children: Bradley, Ashley. *Education:* Notre Dame University, B.A, 1964; Harvard University, M.B.A., 1971.

Addresses: *Home*—Darien, CT. *Office*—Liz Claiborne Inc., 1441 Broadway, Fl. 22, New York, NY 10018–2088.

Career

Served as a lieutenant in the U.S. Navy during the Vietnam War, 1964–69; brand manager, Procter & Gamble Corporation, Cincinnati, OH, 1971–78; category manager, General Foods Corporation, White Plains, NY, 1978–81; senior vice president for sales and marketing, Cannon Mills Company, New York and North Carolina, 1981–83; president, chief operating officer, Brown & Bigelow, St. Paul, MN, 1983–87; group vice president, VF Corporation, Wyomissing, PA, 1988–March 1993, executive vice president, March 1993–May 1994; vice chair, chief operating officer, Liz Claiborne Inc., New York, NY, May 1994–February 1995, president and chief executive officer, February 1995—.

Awards: Decorated with the Meritorious Service medal, U.S. Department of Defense, for service in Vietnam.

Sidelights

Paul Charron has run Liz Claiborne Inc., the apparel group, since 1995. Charron revitalized the company's fortunes after a sharp downturn when its namesake founder left the business, and it entered a period of unprecedented growth and profit that helped make it the fourth–largest American apparel–maker in its class. A former Navy officer, Charron is known for his pragmatic approach to women's fashions. "The Navy taught me how to operate in a combat zone," he told *Forbes*'s Nancy Rotenier.

Charron was born in Schenectady, New York, in 1942, but grew up in Louisville, Kentucky, where he attended Roman Catholic parochial schools. As his eighth–grade year ended, he chose the city's highly regarded St. Xavier High School, which necessitated an early rise and a two–bus crosstown commute. But its "reputation for athletics and academics really held a lot of allure for me at the time," he told Mark Coomes, a writer for Louisville's *Courier–Journal.* "As an eighth–grader, I was one of those individuals who needed a little extra discipline to stay focused in the classroom."

Charron went on to another renowned Catholic school, Notre Dame University, from which he graduated in 1964. He planned to earn a law degree and enter Louisville politics someday, but served a stint in the Navy as a communications specialist on board destroyer ships in the South China Sea during the Vietnam War first. After reaching the rank of lieutenant and earning a Meritorious Service medal, Charron was discharged in 1969 and decided to apply to just one graduate business program instead of law school—Harvard's. He won admission and earned his M.B.A. two years later.

Hired by Cincinnati's consumer–brands giant, Procter & Gamble, Charron spent seven years as a brand manager for such products as Dawn dishwashing liquid and Cheer laundry detergent. In 1978 he took a similar job with the General Foods Corporation, and three years later was offered an executive post with towel–maker Cannon Mills as a senior vice president for sales and marketing. Charron spent two years there before heading to the Minneapolis/St. Paul area to run a specialty advertising firm. His first foray into the apparel industry came when he was made a group vice president at the VF Corporation in 1988. The Wyomissing, Pennsylvania, company was the maker of Vanity Fair lingerie, but also had several successful other lines it had acquired through licensing deals.

Just a year after being made VF's executive vice president, Charron left the company when Liz Claiborne, Inc. offered him its recently vacated chief operating officer slot. The move surprised many in the garment industry in and around New York City's Seventh Avenue, for such top posts are usually the preserve of industry veterans. But the Liz Claiborne board had been under pressure from financial analysts to bring in an outsider to help it revive its flagging balance sheet, and Charron had a strong record at VF with its sportswear division. Founded in 1976 by the real Liz Claiborne, the company thrived in the 1980s by cornering the women's career and sportswear markets at a time when competition in the field was scarce. After Claiborne retired to become an environmentalist in 1989, however, the company's fortunes sank, and its moribund designs went unsold in stores. Sales and profits had flatlined for four years straight in the early 1990s.

Within a year, Charron had become chief executive officer (CEO) and president, and worked on reviving the namesake brand's designs. He also okayed an unprecedentedly lavish ad campaign that featured model Niki Taylor, and renovated its free-standing stores. Management turnover was high in the first two years, but Charron brought in seasoned veterans and offered bonuses tied to sales performance. At the time, Liz Claiborne, Inc. had

just a few other brands in its stable—the moderately priced department–store staples Russ, Villager, and Crazy Horse. Charron went to work acquiring more prestigious lines via licensing deals, following the success of its nearest rival—the Jones Apparel Group, which had once been on the verge of bankruptcy.

Under Charron, Liz Claiborne, Inc. acquired several more brands, beginning with prestigious handbag maker Dooney & Bourke, and the Dana Buchman, Sigrid Olsen, and Kenneth Cole New York lines of women's clothing. It also snapped up Lucky Brand Dungarees and Laundry, each strong sellers among trendier shoppers. By 2001 the empire was so vast that seven products were manufactured in its plants every second that year. In 2002, the company posted $3.7 billion in sales, a seven–percent growth spike from the previous year—though overall figures for the women's apparel market had declined.

To capture those buyers, Charron firmly believed in giving the customer what she wanted—or, in this case, what she thought she wanted. The company spends some $1.5 million annually on market research, and retains a quiet New York trend–watching company that is staffed by consumer–spending analysts and psychologists. The firm comes up with directional trends for upcoming seasons, and the 250 designers of the 30 Liz Claiborne brands follow the ideas suggested. As Charron explained to Kristin Larson in a *WWD* interview, "This company has the disadvantage of not having a 'name designer' on premise who tells what the color red is going to be and whether skirts are going to go up or down. That's a tremendous disadvantage, but one of our greatest advantages is that we don't have a 'name designer' on premise to tell us this is the color red and whether skirts are going up or down."

For his track record in turning around the Liz Claiborne brand, Charron is well compensated. The board rewarded him with $4.3 million in salary, bonuses, and stock in 2002. He and his wife, Kathy, have two grow children and live in Darien, Connecticut. "This is what I've always wanted to be—a CEO of a major corporation," he told *WWD*'s Larson. He is proud of the company's turnaround since he took over, with 28 consecutive quarters of sales growth since 1996. "Early on, I said to my management team that they had the opportunity to be a participant in an event that would only happen once or twice in a career—maybe for a lot of people never—and that is the rejuvenation of one of America's great brands," he said in the same interview. "And we did it."

Sources

Courier–Journal (Louisville, KY), October 25, 2000, p. 1F.

Crain's New York Business, September 30, 1996, p. 1.

Daily News Record, November 22, 2000, p. 1B.

Forbes, January 13, 1997, p. 96; April 15, 2002, pp. 66–72.

WWD, April 25, 1994, p. 2; February 1, 1995, p. 1; April 22, 2002, p. 10B; March 31, 2003, p. 2; May 23, 2003, p. 11.

—Carol Brennan

Bruce Chizen

Courtesy of Adobe Systems Inc.

Chief Executive Officer of Adobe Systems Inc.

Born c. 1955, in New York, NY. *Education:* Received degree from Brooklyn College.

Addresses: *Office*—Adobe Systems Inc., 345 Park Ave., San Jose, CA 95110–2704.

Career

Began as sales representative for housewares in the catalog–showroom industry, late 1970s; with Mattel Electronics after 1980, and became merchandising manager for the company's Eastern U.S. region; joined Microsoft Corporation, 1983, and served as East Coast sales director; senior founding executive with Apple Computer's Claris Corporation after 1987; vice president and general manager of Claris Clear Choice; joined Adobe Systems Inc., 1994, and rose to vice president of products and marketing, became president, April, 2000; became chief executive officer, December, 2000.

Sidelights

Since becoming president and chief executive officer of Adobe Systems Inc., Bruce Chizen has taken the image–creation software powerhouse toward major market domination. One of the company's innovations, the Adobe Reader, is installed on some 500 million computers around the world, but it remains freeware. Chizen's mission since taking over at its Silicon Valley headquarters in late 2000 has been to deploy a strategy that will make the $250 Adobe software the leading product in document management companies on the planet.

Chizen was born in the mid–1950s and grew up in the Brooklyn neighborhood of Canarsie, just outside New York City. He was the middle child in a family of three, and was a shy, slightly overweight adolescent when his parents divorced. The situation placed him even more outside the realm of standard teenage life at the time, he told *Forbes* writer Erika Brown. "I had a tough upbringing, but I was determined to overcome it," he recalled. There was a family owned appliance store in the Flatbush part of Brooklyn, where Chizen's father worked as a salesperson, and after graduation from Brooklyn College he followed in his father's footsteps, taking a job hawking merchandise to the catalog–showroom retail industry. He remained leery about his future prospects for a career in sales, however. "I hated it," he said in the *Forbes* interview. "I always wanted to be more than a sales guy."

Despite his aversion, Chizen nevertheless did stay in sales. In 1980, he was hired by Mattel Electronics, and within a few years had reached the executive level as a marketing person for its thriving videogame sector. From there he went on to a job with a promising newcomer, the Microsoft Corporation, in 1983. He eventually became the company's East Coast sales director, and jumped ship in 1987 to take a post with Microsoft's arch–rival, Apple Computer. Chizen was a founding executive at Apple's software spin–off, the Claris Corporation, and held positions in sales and worldwide marketing before becoming vice president and general manager of Claris Clear Choice, a utility suite for data protection.

Chizen joined Adobe in 1994, just a year after the company launched its innovative Adobe Acrobat software. It was the next in a long series of successes for the Silicon Valley firm, founded in 1982 by Chuck Geschke and John Warnock, two former Xerox employees. The company first made inroads into the nascent computer industry with its Postscript printing software, and made the some of the first widely used products—Adobe Illustrator and Photoshop—that launched the desktop-publishing revolution. Acrobat, which went on the market in 1993, enabled relatively novice computer users to create a Portable Document Format (PDF) file, which yielded a legible screen document that printed exactly as it appeared. Acrobat was a great innovation in document-imaging software, and the company gave away a half-billion copies of the Reader, which was needed to view such files; they were either bundled into new computer software packages or available as a free download on the company website. Adobe executives hoped that users would eventually buy the $250 Acrobat software needed to create such PDFs, but the idea never caught on outside of the publishing and advertising world.

At Adobe, Chizen served as vice president of products and marketing, and had great success with the launch of PhotoDeluxe, a consumer-friendly version of its best-selling Photoshop. But Chizen began to see that the company had no long-term strategy in place to keep up with the ever-changing market, and began to strategize how Acrobat might become more of a revenue-generator. The chance to implement his ideas came when Geschke decided to leave the president post in early 2000, and Chizen was named to replace him. Later that year, Warnock also stepped aside as chief executive officer to became the company's first chief technology officer instead; Chizen took the CEO position. After nearly 20 years of running the company, the 60-year-old Warnock told Knight Ridder/Tribune Business News writer Jon Fortt, "I don't want to go to these operations meetings anymore."

Chizen began pushing the idea of selling Acrobat to a wider spectrum of clients. It was already the standard format for annual corporate reports, school-board meeting minutes, and other unwieldy documents available online, and Chizen's newly created marketing team began successfully touting it to companies like Pfizer, the pharmaceutical giant, which used it to create and manage the stringent, complex application process necessary for Food and Drug Administration product approval. Adobe also

began selling Acrobat to governmental agencies that utilized it to speed up the permit process. Under Chizen's watch, Adobe acquired the Canadian data-management company, Accelio.

With the downturn in the economy in 2001, Chizen's vision was all the more crucial to the company's fortunes: the advertising market suddenly bottomed out, and it was necessary to find new revenue sources. He still reported to Geschke and Warnock, but obtained approval for a restructuring plan that laid off or reassigned nearly 700 employees out of 3,000 worldwide in 2002. A new marketing strategy divided Acrobat's potential customers into three distinct groups—corporations, design professionals, and consumers—and in mid-2002 the company launched an expensive print campaign in the mainstream media, touting Acrobat's multitude of uses. That was followed several months later by a series of lavishly produced television commercials for the newly renamed Adobe Reader. By September of 2003, Adobe stock had continued its strong earnings performance, thanks to Chizen's well-executed plans. The price of a share rose eight percent in just one day, to $39.46, after it announced that revenues for the third quarter for Acrobat had jumped 12 percent.

In an article he wrote for London's *Daily Telegraph* in 2002, Chizen chronicled one meeting-packed business trip to Europe that entailed "six cities, four countries, 18,000 air miles, and innumerable airport check-ins—and all within five days," he wrote. He met with new clients like the UK Online Initiative, a British plan to put all available government services online, but admitted that though his company's innovative Acrobat software was designed to make information-sharing among far-flung work teams much easier, a personal appearance was still a necessity. "Although we do more and more digitally and remotely," he concluded, "you simply cannot replace face-to-face meetings."

Sources

Brandweek, May 19, 2003, p. 16.
Computer Reseller News, December 9, 2002, p. 26.
Daily Telegraph (London, England), May 16, 2002, p. 67.
Knight Ridder/Tribune Business News, December 14, 2000.
Forbes, July 7, 2003, p. 105.
New York Times, July 7, 2003, p. C1; September 12, 2003, p. C4.
Publishers Weekly, March 11, 2002, p. 14.

—*Carol Brennan*

Carlo Azeglio Ciampi

President of Italy

AP/Wide World Photos

Born December 9, 1920, in Livorno, Italy; married; children: one son, one daughter. *Education:* Earned diploma from the Scuola Normale Superiore of Pisa; received B.A. and LLB. degrees from the University of Pisa.

Addresses: *Office*—c/o Embassy of Italy, 3000 Whitehaven St. NW, Washington, DC 20008.

Career

Began at Banca d'Italia (Bank of Italy), 1946; rose through administrative ranks and served as branch inspector, 1950s; became economist in its research department, 1960; named head of research department, 1970, secretary general after 1973, deputy director general after 1976, director general after 1977, and governor, 1979–1993; appointed prime minister of Italy, 1993; Bank of International Settlements, vice president, 1994–96; appointed Italy's Treasury Minister, 1996—; elected president of Italy, 1999.

Sidelights

Italy's octogenarian president Carlo Azeglio Ciampi is one of the most respected figures in his country. A sober banker who headed Italy's central bank for a number of years, he was elected president by the Italian parliament in 1999 for a seven–year term. He has proved a surprisingly formidable foil for the country's controversial prime minister, media tycoon Silvio Berlusconi. Ciampi is also a staunch supporter of the European Union (EU), whose origins date to the post–World War II period and the hopes of many of his generation who wished to never again see European blood shed on the continent.

Ciampi was born in 1920 and attended Pisa's Scuola Normale Superiore and its university as well. Though he eventually earned a law degree, early in his academic career he studied German language and literature, and even spent time in that country in 1938 just before the Nazi German government began invading neighboring countries, which sparked a world war. His fellow students came from across Europe and North America, and as Ciampi recalled in an interview that appeared in the *Economist*, "we used to hang out on the banks of the Rhine—and would talk about ending up as enemies as if it were a joke. And then it happened."

During the war, Ciampi served in the Italian Army for three years. In 1946, he joined the Banca d'Italia, or national bank of Italy, and rose through its ranks as an economist and branch inspector. He was named head of its research department in 1970, and went on to hold three senior posts before he become its governor in 1979. Over the next 14 years, he earned a reputation as a sound financial manager as well as a figure impervious to the taint of corruption that had become endemic among Italy's business and political elite. Ciampi was also instrumental in guiding Italy's entry into the European Monetary Union, the plan to link the currencies of the EU member nations in order to lessen inflation and prevent fluctuations in foreign–exchange rates. After urging Prime Minister Giulio Andreotti to accept the terms of the Maastricht Treaty of European Union in the early 1990s, *il governatore,* as he was known, began to enact measures at the Banca d'Italia that would help Italy meet the necessary requirements to join a single European currency by the target date of 1999. Ciampi's sterling reputation made him a dark–horse favorite to become the country's next prime minister in an unexpected turn of events in the early 1990s. A series of corruption scandals rocked Italy, and decimated an entire generation of postwar business tycoons and elected officials. One after another, governments dissolved in discord as a result, and finally the president, Oscar Luigi Scalfaro, appointed Ciampi as prime minister in April of 1993. The power to appoint a prime minister is one of few powers the Italian president enjoys, and Ciampi's accession helped to soothe frayed nerves. "Ciampi appears to be light–years away from career Italian politicians," wrote *Europe* journalist Niccolo d'Aquino. "He is polite yet solitary, steely as far as work is concerned, and his dark blue suits cut an elegant figure in a gentlemanly, if old–fashioned, way."

Ciampi had a reform plan to help stabilize the government, but the lingering wake of the scandals caused dissension within his cabinet, and he was replaced by Berlusconi in the 1994 national elections. For a time, he left government service altogether, taking a vice presidency at the Bank of International Settlements, but in 1996 a new prime minister and ardent pro–European Union figure, Romano Prodi, appointed Ciampi to serve as Italy's Treasury Minister. European Monetary Union deadlines were coming, and there were several requirements Italy had to meet before the introduction of the Euro, or single EU currency, in 1999. Even Prodi's replacement, Massimo D'Alema, kept Ciampi on as Treasury minister when yet another new government came to power in 1998.

Ciampi stood for the presidency in the spring of 1999, and won election by two–thirds of the parliament vote. At the time, Italy had endured 56 different governments since the end of World War II, and though the presidency had little actual power, it was viewed as an office of inestimable respect and influence. *Financial Times* writer James Blitz described Ciampi's new role as "the ultimate arbiter of the Italian political 'game', with the right to pronounce in public when he thinks politicians are over–stepping the mark."

Ciampi did not disappoint. He took on Berlusconi, who returned as prime minister in 2001, and his center–right party often, most notably in a 2003 fracas over media–ownership laws. Berlusconi's array of companies control a majority of Italy's radio and television networks, and in December of that year Ciampi refused to sign a new media bill that would have given Berlusconi's empire increased power and possibly even greater advertising revenues. The bill had made it through parliament despite intense debate over a potential conflict of interest, and was derided by the EU's press–freedom watchdog group. Ciampi's veto forced it back to parliament for more debate, an act that was roundly applauded by many Italians, EU member nations, and the *Economist,* which described one of the Berlusconi–held television stations as "a channel whose evening news bulletins exude pro–government sycophancy." The article commended Ciampi's stance. "This brave and principled refusal is the best news Italy's constitution has had during the two–and–a–half years of Mr. Berlusconi's prime ministership," it asserted.

Ciampi also stepped into a debate over whether Italian schools should display the crucifix, as a 1924 law compels. The nation still retains a strongly Roman Catholic character, but its population of 58 million has tentatively welcomed many new immigrants from North Africa and southern European countries like Albania since the 1990s. A Muslim activist filed suit objecting to the crucifixes displayed in his son's school, and a judge ruled in October of 2003 that they should be removed. Ciampi sided with Roman Catholic church officials in support of the archaic law. "The crucifix has always been considered not only as a distinctive sign of a particular religious credo," CNN.com quoted him as saying, "but above all as a symbol of the values that are at the base of our Italian identity."

Ciampi's term expires in 2006, the same year he will turn 86. He is married and has two children, and still reads German literature in his leisure time.

Sources

Periodicals

Economist, May 22, 1999, p. 60; December 20, 2003, p. 13.
Europe, July/August 1997.
Financial Times, May 14, 1999, p. 23; May 10, 2001, p. 10; April 20, 2002, p. 7; July 24, 2002, p. 8; December 18, 2003, p. 4.
Guardian (London, England), December 16, 2003, p. 11.
Independent (London, England), December 17, 2003, p. 12.

Online

"Carlo Azeglio Ciampi," *Biography Resource Center Online,* Gale Group, 2002.

"Carlo Azeglio Ciampi," Embassy of Italy, http://www.italyemb.org/Ciampi.htm (February 24, 2004).

"Italy president in crucifix row," CNN.com, http://www.cnn.com/2003/WORLD/europe/10/27/italy.president.crucafix.ap/ (October 27, 2003).

—Carol Brennan

J. M. Coetzee

Author

Born John Maxwell Coetzee, February 9, 1940, in Cape Town, South Africa; married, 1963 (divorced, 1980); children: Nicholas, Gisela. *Education:* University of Cape Town, B.A., 1960, M.A., 1963; University of Texas, Austin, Ph.D., 1969.

Addresses: *Agent*—Peter Lampack, 551 Fifth Ave., New York, NY 10017. *Home*—Australia.

Career

Applications programmer, International Business Machines (IBM), London, England, 1962–63; systems programmer, International Computers, Bracknell, Berkshire, England, 1964–65; State University of New York at Buffalo, NY, assistant professor, 1968–71, Butler Professor of English, 1984, 1986; University of Cape Town, Cape Town, South Africa, lecturer in English, 1972–82, professor of general literature, 1983–2001; Hinkley Professor of English, Johns Hopkins University, 1986, 1989; visiting professor of English, Harvard University, 1991.

Member: International Comparative Literature Association, Modern Language Association of America.

Awards: CNA literary award for *In the Heart of the Country,* 1977; CNA literary award for *Waiting for the Barbarians,* 1980; James Tait Black memorial prize for *Waiting for the Barbarians,* 1980; Geoffrey Faber Award for *Waiting for the Barbarians,* 1980; CNA literary award for *The Life and Times of Michael K,* 1984; Booker–McConnell Prize for *The Life and Times of Michael K,* 1984; Prix Femina Etranger for *The Life and Times of Michael K,* 1984; D. Litt., University of Strathclyde, Glasgow, 1985; Jerusalem Prize for the Freedom of the Individual in Society, 1987; Sunday Express book of the year prize for *Age of Iron,* 1990; Premio Modello for *The Master of Petersburg,* 1994; *Irish Times* international fiction prize for *The Master of Petersburg,* 1995; Booker prize for *Disgrace,* 1999; National Book League and Commonwealth Writer's prize for best novel for *Disgrace,* 1999; Life Fellow, University of Cape Town; Nobel Prize for literature, 2003.

Sidelights

J. M. Coetzee explores the implications of oppressive societies on the lives of their inhabitants, often using his native South Africa as a backdrop. As a South African, however, Coetzee is "too intelligent a novelist to cater for moralistic voyeurs," Peter Lewis declared in the *Times Literary Supplement.* "This does not mean that he avoids the social and political crises edging his country towards catastrophe. But he chooses not to handle such themes in the direct, realistic way that writers of older generations, such as Alan Paton, preferred to employ. Instead, Coetzee has developed a symbolic and even allegorical mode of fiction—not to escape the living nightmare of South Africa but to define the psychopathological underlying the sociological, and in doing so to locate the archetypal in the particular."

Though many of his stories are set in South Africa, Coetzee's lessons are relevant to all countries, as *Books Abroad*'s Ursula A. Barnett wrote of 1974's *Dusklands,* which contains the novellas *The Vietnam Project* and *The Narrative of Jacobus Coetzee.* "By publishing the two stories side by side," Barnett remarked, "Coetzee has deliberately given a wider horizon to his South African subject. Left on its own, *The Narrative of Jacobus Coetzee* would immediately have suggested yet another tale of African black–white confrontation to the reader." Although each is a complete story, "their nature and design are such that the book can and should be read as a single work," Roger Owen commented in the *Times Literary Supplement. Dusklands* "is a kind of diptych, carefully hinged and aligned, and of a texture so glassy and mirror–like that each story throws light on the other." Together the tales present two very different outcomes in confrontations between the individual and society.

Coetzee's second novel, 1977's *From the Heart of the Country,* also explores racial conflict and mental deterioration. A spinster daughter, Magda, tells the story in diary form, recalling the consequences of her father's seduction of his African workman's wife. Both jealous of and repulsed by the relationship, Magda murders her father, then begins her own affair with the workman. The integrity of Magda's story eventually proves questionable. "The reader soon realizes that these are the untrustworthy ravings of a hysterical, demented individual consumed by loneliness and her love/hate relationship with her patriarchal father," Barend J. Toerien reported in *World Literature Today.*

Coetzee followed *From the Heart of the Country* with 1980's *Waiting for the Barbarians,* in which he, "with laconic brilliance, articulates one of the basic problems of our time—how to *understand* ... [the] mentality behind the brutality and injustice," Anthony Burgess wrote in *New York.* In the novel, a magistrate attempting to protect the peaceful nomadic people of his district is imprisoned and tortured by the army that arrives at the frontier town to destroy the "barbarians" on behalf of the Empire. The horror of what he has seen and experienced affects the magistrate in inalterable ways, bringing changes in his personality that he cannot understand.

Coetzee's fourth novel, *The Life and Times of Michael K,* was published in 1983. According to CNN.com, it was "the story of a young gardener abandoned after his mother's death in a South Africa whose administration is collapsing after years of civil strife." The book won the Booker Prize in 1984.

In 1987's *Foe,* a retelling of Daniel Defoe's *Robinson Crusoe,* Coetzee tells the story of the mute Friday, whose tongue was cut out by slavers, and Susan Barton, the castaway who struggles to communicate with him. Daniel Foe, the author who endeavors to tell Barton's story, is also affected by Friday's speechlessness. Both Barton and Foe recognize their duty to provide a means by which Friday can relate the story of his escape from the fate of his fellow slaves who drowned, still shackled, when their ship sank; but both also question their right to speak for him. "The author, whether Foe or Coetzee, ... wonders if he has any right to speak for the one person whose story most needs to be told," *West Coast Review*'s Maureen Nicholson noted. "Friday is ... the tongueless voice of millions."

In 1990's *Age of Iron* Coetzee addresses the crisis of South Africa in direct, rather than allegorical, form. The story of Mrs. Curren, a retired professor dying of cancer and attempting to deal with the realities of apartheid in Cape Town, *Age of Iron* is "an unrelenting yet gorgeously written parable of modern South Africa, ... a story filled with foreboding and violence about a land where even the ability of children to love is too great a luxury," Michael Dorris wrote in *Tribune Books.*

In Coetzee's next novel, 1994's *The Master of Petersburg,* the central character is the Russian novelist Fyodor Dostoevsky, but the plot is only loosely based on his real life. In Coetzee's story, the novelist goes to St. Petersburg upon the death of his stepson, Pavel. He is devastated by grief for the young man, and begins an inquiry into his death. He discovers that Pavel was involved with a group of nihilists and was probably murdered either by their leader or by the police. During the course of his anguished investigation, Dostoevsky's creative processes are exposed; Coetzee shows him beginning work on his novel *The Possessed.*

Coetzee's nonfiction works include 1988's *White Writing: On the Culture of Letters in South Africa,* 1992's *Doubling the Point: Essays and Interviews,* and 1996's *Giving Offense: Essays on Censorship.* In *White Writing,* the author "collects his critical reflections on the mixed fortunes of 'white writing' in South Africa, 'a body of writing [not] different in nature from black writing,' but 'generated by the concerns of people no longer European, yet not African,'" Shaun Irlam observed in *MLN.* The seven essays included in the book discuss writings from the late seventeenth century to the present, through which Coetzee examines the foundations of modern South African writers' attitudes. In *Doubling the Point: Essays and Interviews,* a collection of critical essays on Samuel Beckett, Franz Kafka, D. H. Lawrence, Nadine Gordimer, and others, Coetzee presents a "literary autobiography," according to Ann Irvine in a *Library Journal* review. Discussions of issues including censorship and popular culture; interviews with the author preceding each section round out the collection.

Giving Offense: Essays on Censorship was Coetzee's first collection of essays in nearly ten years, since *White Writing* appeared. The essays collected in *Giving Offense* were written over a period of about six years. Coetzee discusses three tyrannical regimes: Nazism, Communism, and apartheid; and, drawing upon his training as an academic scholar as well as his experiences as a fiction writer, argues that the censor and the writer have often been "brother-enemies, mirror images one of the other" in their struggle to claim the truth of their position.

In 1997's *Boyhood: Scenes from Provincial Life,* Coetzee experiments with autobiography, a surprising turn for a writer, as Caryl Phillips noted in the *New Republic,* "whose literary output has successfully resisted an autobiographical reading." *Boyhood,* written in the third person, "reads more like a novella than a true autobiography. Coetzee develops his character, a young boy on the verge of adolescence, through a richly detailed interior monolog," wrote Denise S. Sticha in *Library Journal.* He recounts his life growing up in Worcester, South Africa, where he moved with his family from Cape Town after his father's latest business failure. There, he observes the contradictions of apartheid and the subtle distinctions of class and ethnicity with a precociously writerly eye. Coetzee, an Afrikaaner whose parents chose to speak English, finds himself between worlds, neither properly Afrikaaner nor English. Throughout his boyhood, he encounters the stupid brutalities inflicted by arbitrary divisions between white and black, Afrikaaner and English.

The Lives of Animals, published in 1999, is a unique effort by Coetzee, incorporating his own lectures on animal rights with the fictional story of Elizabeth Costello, a novelist obsessed by the horrors of human cruelty to animals. In this "wonderfully inventive and inconclusive book," as Stephen H. Webb described it in *Christian Century,* Coetzee poses questions about the morality of vegetarianism and the guilt of those who use animal products. But his arguments are not simplistic: he wonders, for example, if vegetarians are really trying to save animals, or only trying to put themselves in a morally superior position to other humans. Following the novella, there are responses to Costello's arguments from four scholars who have written about animals: Barbara Smuts, Peter Singer, Marjorie Garber, and Wendy Doniger. The sum of the book, wrote Marlene Chamberlain in *Booklist,* is valuable "for Coetzee fans and others interested in the links between philosophy, reason, and the rights of nonhumans."

Coetzee's next novel, 1999's *Disgrace,* is a strong statement on the political climate in post–apartheid South Africa. The main character, David Lurie, is an English professor at the University of Cape Town. He sees himself as an aging, but still handsome, Lothario. He has seduced many young women in his day, but an affair with one of his students finally proves his undoing. Charged with sexual harassment, he leaves his post in disgrace, seeking refuge at the small farm owned by his daughter, Lucy. While David's world is refined and highly intellectualized, Lucy works at hard physical labor in simple surroundings. David's notions of orderliness are overturned when three men come to the farm, set him afire, and rape Lucy. Father and daughter survive the ordeal, only to learn that Lucy has become pregnant. Eventually, in order to protect herself and her simple way of life, she consents to become the third wife in her neighbor's polygamous family, even though he may have arranged the attack on her in order to gain control of her property. The novel won the Booker Prize in 1999; Coetzee made history by becoming the the first author to win the award twice.

Antioch Review contributor John Kennedy noted, "In its honest and relentless probing of character and motive ... this novel secures Coetzee's place among today's major novelists.... The impulses and crimes of passion, the inadequacies of justice, and the rare possibilities for redemption are played out on many levels in this brilliantly crafted book." The author's deft handling of the ambiguities of his story was also praised by Rebecca Saunders, who in *Review of Contemporary Fiction* warned that *Disgrace* is "not for the ethically faint of heart." Saunders felt Coetzee has "strewn nettles in the bed of the comfortable social conscience," and his book is written in the style "we have come to expect" from him, "at once taciturn and blurting out the unspeakable."

On December 10, 2003, Coetzee was awarded the Nobel Prize in Literature. He dedicated the award to his mother. In 2004, Coetzee edited and translated *Landscape with Rowers: Poetry from the Netherlands.* The novelist introduced and translated one poem each by five 20th centrury Dutch poets and three by a sixth. In April of that year, Coetzee was nominated for the Christine Stead Prize for fiction, one of the New South Wales Literary Awards, which are one of Australia's top literary events. The event marked the first time that a Nobel laureate had been nominated for one of the awards. He also was on the shortlist for Australia's Miles Franklin Literary Award for his 2003 novel *Elizabeth Costello*. That same month, five of Coetzee's novels were released in China for the first time. The books included *Waiting for the Barbarians, Youth,* and *Disgrace*.

In addition to his writing, Coetzee has produced translations of works in Dutch, German, French, and Afrikaans, served as editor for others' work, and taught at the University of Cape Town. "He's a rare phenomenon, a writer–scholar," Ian Glenn, a colleague of Coetzee's, told the *Washington Post's* Allister Sparks. "Even if he hadn't had a career as a novelist he would have had a very considerable one as an academic." Coetzee told Sparks that he finds writing burdensome. "I don't like writing so I have to push myself," he said. "It's bad if I write but it's worse if I don't." Coetzee hesitates to discuss his works in progress, and views his opinion of his published works as no more important than that of anyone else. "The writer is simply another reader when it is a matter of discussing the books he has already written," he told Sparks. "They don't belong to him anymore and he has nothing privileged to say about them—while the book he is engaged in writing is far too private and important a matter to be talked about."

Selected writings

Novels

Dusklands (contains two novellas, *The Vietnam Project* and *The Narrative of Jacobus Coetzee*), Ravan Press (Johannesburg, South Africa), 1974; Penguin Books (New York, NY), 1985.
From the Heart of the Country, Harper (New York, NY), 1977; published in England as *In the Heart of the Country,* Secker & Warburg (London, England), 1977.
Waiting for the Barbarians, Secker & Warburg (London, England), 1980; Penguin Books (New York, NY), 1982.
The Life and Times of Michael K., Secker & Warburg (London, England), 1983; Viking (New York, NY), 1984.
Foe, Viking (New York, NY), 1987.
Age of Iron, Random House (New York, NY), 1990.
The Master of Petersburg, Viking (New York, NY), 1994.

(With others) *The Lives of Animals,* edited with an introduction by Amy Gutmann, Princeton University Press (Princeton, NJ), 1999.
Disgrace, Viking (New York, NY), 1999.
Youth, Viking (New York, NY), 2002.
Elizabeth Costello, Secker & Warburg (London, England), 2003.

Other works

(Translator) Marcellus Emants, *A Posthumous Confession,* Twayne (Boston, MA), 1976.
(Translator) Wilma Stockenstroem, *The Expedition to the Baobab Tree,* Faber (London, England), 1983.
(Editor, with Andre Brink) *A Land Apart: A Contemporary South African Reader,* Viking (New York, NY), 1987.
White Writing: On the Culture of Letters in South Africa (essays), Yale University Press (New Haven, CT), 1988.
Doubling the Point: Essays and Interviews, edited by David Attwell, Harvard University Press (Cambridge, MA), 1992.
(With Graham Swift, John Lanchester, and Ian Jack) *Food: The Vital Stuff,* Penguin (New York, NY), 1995.
Giving Offense: Essays on Censorship, University of Chicago Press (Chicago, IL), 1996.
Boyhood: Scenes from Provincial Life, Viking (New York, NY), 1997.
(With Bill Reichblum) *What Is Realism?,* Bennington College (Bennington, VT), 1997.
(With Dan Cameron and Carolyn Christov–Bakargiev) *William Kentridge,* Phaidon (London, England), 1999.
Stranger Shores: Literary Essays, 1986–1999, Viking (New York, NY), 2001.
The Humanities in Africa/Die Geisteswissenschaften in Afrika, Carl Friedrich von Siemens Stiftung (Munich, Germany), 2001.
Contributor of introduction, *The Confusions of Young Törless,* by Robert Musil, Penguin (New York, NY), 2001.
(Translator and author of introduction) *Landscape With Rowers: Poetry from the Netherlands,* Princeton University Press, 2004.
Contributor of reviews to periodicals, including *New York Review of Books*.

Media adaptations

An adaptation of *In the Heart of the Country* was filmed as *Dust,* by ICA (England), 1986.

Sources

Books

Attwell, David, *J. M. Coetzee: South Africa and the Politics of Writing*, University of California Press (Berkeley, CA), 1993.

Coetzee, J. M., *Giving Offense: Essays on Censorship*, University of Chicago Press (Chicago, IL), 1996.

Gallagher, Susan V., *A Story of South Africa: J. M. Coetzee's Fiction in Context*, Harvard University Press (Cambridge, MA), 1991.

Goddard, Kevin, *J. M. Coetzee: A Bibliography*, National English Literary Museum, 1990.

Head, Dominic, *J. M. Coetzee*, Cambridge University Press (New York, NY), 1998.

Huggan, Graham, and Stephen Watson, editors, *Critical Perspectives on J. M. Coetzee*, introduction by Nadine Gordimer, St. Martin's Press (New York, NY), 1996.

Jolly, Rosemary Jane, *Colonization, Violence, and Narration in White South African Writing: Andre Brink, Breyten Breytenbach, and J. M. Coetzee*, Ohio University Press (Athens, OH), 1996.

Kossew, Sue, editor, *Critical Essays on J. M. Coetzee*, G. K. Hall (Boston, MA), 1998.

Kossew, Sue, *Pen and Power: A Post–Colonial Reading of J. M. Coetzee and Andre Brink*, Rodopi (Atlanta, GA), 1996.

Moses, Michael Valdez, editor, *The Writings of J. M. Coetzee*, Duke University Press (Durham, NC), 1994.

Penner, Dick, *Countries of the Mind: The Fiction of J. M. Coetzee*, Greenwood Press (New York, NY), 1989.

Periodicals

African Business, November 1999, p. 42.

Africa Today, number 3, 1980.

America, September 25, 1982.

Animals' Agenda, July–August 1999, p. 38.

Antioch Review, summer 2000, p. 375.

Ariel: A Review of International English Literature, April 1985, pp. 47–56; July 1986, pp. 3–21; October 1988, pp. 55–72.

Atlantic Monthly, March 2000, p. 116.

Booklist, November 1, 1994, p. 477; April 1, 1996, p. 1328; August 1997, p. 1869; March 15, 1999, p. 1262; November 15, 1999, p. 579; March 15, 2001, p. 1362; August 2001, p. 2075; February 1, 2004, p. 943.

Books Abroad, spring 1976.

Books and Culture, March 1997, p. 30.

Books in Canada, August/September 1982.

Boston Globe, November 20, 1994, p. B16.

British Book News, April 1981.

Charlotte Observer, December 29, 1999.

Chicago Tribune Book World, April 25, 1982; January 22, 1984, sec. 14, p. 27; November 27, 1994, p. 3.

Choice, November 1999, p. 552.

Christian Century, May 19, 1999, p. 569; August 16, 2000, p. 840.

Christian Science Monitor, December 12, 1983; May 18, 1988, pp. 503–05; November 10, 1999, p. 20; November 18, 1999, p. 12.

Commentary, March 2000, p. 62.

Contemporary Literature, summer 1988, pp. 277–85; fall 1992, pp. 419–31.

Critique: Studies in Modern Fiction, winter 1986, pp. 67–77; spring 1989, pp. 143–54; spring 2001, p. 309.

Economist (U.S.), December 4, 1999, p. S4; September 15, 2001, p. 93; March 16, 2002.

Encounter, October 1977; January 1984.

English Journal, March 1994, p. 97.

Globe and Mail (Toronto, Ontario, Canada), August 30, 1986; October 2, 1999, p. D18; November 27, 1999, p. D49.

Harper's, June 1999, p. 76.

Hudson Review, summer 2000, p. 333, p. 336.

Kirkus Reviews, February 15, 1999, p. 264.

Library Journal, June 1, 1992, p. 124; September 1, 1994, p. 213; March 15, 1996, p. 70; September 1, 1997, p. 181; December 1999, p. 182; July 2001, p. 89.

Listener, August 18, 1977.

London Review of Books, September 13, 1990, pp. 17–18; October 14, 1999, p. 12.

Los Angeles Times Book Review, May 23, 1982, p. 4; January 15, 1984; February 22, 1987; November 20, 1994, p. 3; December 12, 1999, p. 2.

Maclean's, January 30, 1984, p. 49.

MLN, December, 1988, pp. 1147–50; December 17, 1990, pp. 777–80.

M2 Best Books, April 19, 2004; April 21, 2004; April 29, 2004.

Nation, March 28, 1987, pp. 402–05; March 6, 2000, p. 30.

Natural History, June 1999, p. 18.

New Leader, December 13, 1999, p. 27.

New Republic, December 19, 1983; February 6, 1995, pp. 170–72; October 16, 1995, p. 53; November 18, 1996, p. 30; February 9, 1998, p. 37; December 20, 1999, p. 42.

New Statesman, October 18, 1999, p. 57; November 29, 1999, pp. 79–80.

New Statesman and Society, September 21, 1990, p. 40; February 25, 1994, p. 41; November 21, 1997, p. 50.

Newsweek, May 31, 1982; January 2, 1984; February 23, 1987; November 15, 1999, p. 90.

Newsweek International, November 8, 1999, p. 72.

New York, April 26, 1982, p. 88, p. 90.

New Yorker, July 12, 1982; July 5, 1999, p. 80; November 15, 1999, p. 110.

New York Review of Books, December 2, 1982; February 2, 1984; November 8, 1990, pp. 8–10; November 17, 1994, p. 35; June 29, 2000, p. 20; January 20, 2000, p. 23.

New York Times, December 6, 1983, p. C22; February 11, 1987; April 11, 1987; November 18, 1994, p. C35; October 7, 1997, p. B7; November 11, 1999, p. B10; November 14, 1999, p. WK1.

New York Times Book Review, April 18, 1982; December 11, 1983, p. 1, p. 26; February 22, 1987; September 23, 1990, p. 7; November 20, 1994, p. 9; September 22, 1996, p. 33; November 2, 1997, p. 7; November 28, 1999, p. 7; December 5, 1999, p. 8; September 16, 2001, p. 29.

Novel, fall 2000, p. 98.

Observer (London, England), July 18, 1999, p. 13.

Publishers Weekly, September 5, 1994, p. 88; January 22, 1996, p. 52; July 28, 1997, p. 59; February 8, 1999, p. 193; November 22, 1999, p. 42.

Quadrant, December 1999, p. 80.

Quarterly Review of Biology, June 2001, p. 215.

Reference and User Services Quarterly, spring 2001, p. 251.

Research in African Literatures, fall 1986, pp. 370–92.

Review of Contemporary Fiction, summer 2000, p. 167.

SciTech Book News, June 1999, p. 13.

Sewanee Review, winter 1990, pp. 152–59; April 1995, p. R48; fall 2000, p. 648; summer 2001, p. 462.

South Atlantic Quarterly, winter 1994, pp. 1–9, 33–58, 83–110.

Southern Humanities Review, fall 1987, pp. 384–86.

Spectator, December 13, 1980; September 20, 1986; April 3, 1999, p. 41; July 10, 1999, p. 34; November 20, 1999, p. 47; September 22, 2001, p. 46.

Sun–Sentinel, December 22, 1999.

Time, March 23, 1987; November 28, 1994, pp. 89–90; November 29, 1999, p. 82.

Time International, November 15, 1999, p. 96.

Times (London, England), September 29, 1983; September 11, 1986; May 28, 1988.

Times Literary Supplement, July 22, 1977; November 7, 1980, p. 1270; January 14, 1983; September 30, 1983; September 23, 1988, p. 1043; September 28, 1990, p. 1037; March 4, 1994, p. 19; April 16, 1999, p. 25; June 25, 1999, p. 23; May 19, 2000, p. 14; October 5, 2001, p. 23.

Tribune Books (Chicago, IL), February 15, 1987, p. 3, p. 11; September 16, 1990, p. 3.

Tri–Quarterly, spring–summer 1987, pp. 454–64.

Village Voice, March 20, 1984.

Voice Literary Supplement, April 1982.

Wall Street Journal, November 3, 1994, p. A16; November 26, 1999, p. W8.

Washington Post, October 29, 1983.

Washington Post Book World, May 2, 1982, pp. 1–2, 12; December 11, 1983; March 8, 1987; September 23, 1990, pp. 1, 10; November 27, 1994, p. 6.

West Coast Review, spring 1987, pp. 52–58.

Whole Earth Review, summer 1999, p. 13.

World Literature Today, spring 1978, pp. 245–47; summer 1978, p. 510; autumn 1981; autumn 1988, pp. 718–19; winter 1990, pp. 54–57; winter 1995, p. 207; autumn 1996, p. 1038; winter 2000, p. 228.

World Literature Written in English, spring 1980, pp. 19–36; spring 1986, pp. 34–45; autumn 1987, pp. 153–161, 174–184, 207–215.

Online

"J. M. Coetzee Honored with Booker Prize, Top British Fiction Award," *University of Chicago Chronicle,* http://chronicle.uchicago.edu/991104/coetzee.shtml (July 6, 2004).

"Shy Nobel winner dedicates prize to mother," CNN.com, http://www.cnn.com/2003/WORLD/africa/12/10/nobel.coetzee.reut/index.html (July 6, 2004).

Coldplay

Rock group

Members include Guy Berryman (born April 12, 1978, in Fife, Scotland), bass; Jonny Buckland (born September 11, 1977, in London, England), gui-

tar; Will Champion (born July 31, 1978, in Hampshire, England), drums; Chris Martin (born March 2, 1977, in Devon, England; married Gwyneth Pal-

trow, 2003; children: Apple), vocals, piano. *Education:* All attended University College, London, England.

Addresses: *Record company*—Capitol Records, 1750 N. Vine St., Los Angeles, CA 90028–5209. *Website*—http://www.coldplay.com.

Career

Group formed in London, England, mid–1990s; made debut with *Safety* EP, 1998; released first album, *Parachutes,* 2000; released follow–up album, *A Rush of Blood to the Head,* 2002.

Awards: Brit Award for best British group, 2001; Brit Award for best British album, for *Parachutes,* 2001; New Music Express Carling Award for best new artist, 2001; New Music Express Carling Award for best single, for "Yellow," 2001; New Music Express Carling Award for Session of the Year, for a live BBC show, 2001; Brit Award for best British group, 2003; Brit Award for best British album, for *A Rush of Blood to the Head,* 2003; Grammy Award for best rock performance by a duo or group with vocal, Recording Academy, for "In My Place," from *Coldplay Live 2003,* 2003; Grammy Award for best alternative music album, Recording Academy, for *A Rush of Blood to the Head,* 2003; MTV Video Music Award for best group video for "The Scientist," 2003; MTV Video Music Award for breakthrough video for "The Scientist," 2003; MTV Video Music Award for best direction for "The Scientist," 2003; Grammy Award for record of the year, Recording Academy, for "Clocks," 2004.

Sidelights

British rock quartet Coldplay burst onto the music scene with its debut album *Parachutes,* released in 2000. Fresh, heartrending, and passionate, the album proved popular on both sides of the Atlantic Ocean, capturing honors at both the Brit Awards and the Grammy Awards. Since then, Coldplay has become one of Britain's leading musical exports, filling venues across the United States with fans yearning to hear their searing love songs and haunting ballads. In 2002, the band released its second album, *A Rush of Blood to the Head,* which also captured top musical honors. Ironically, lead singer Chris Martin credits the band's insecurity for its success. "I think our strength is not being sure if we're ever good enough, and so we're always trying to write a better song—or get a better suit," Martin told *Sound & Vision* writer Mike Mettler.

Martin is backed up by guitarist Jonny Buckland, bassist Guy Berryman, and drummer Will Champion. The four met in the mid–1990s at University College in London and became steadfast friends. Music had always been a part of Martin's life. As a youngster, he banged out songs on the family piano and joined his first band at 15. He grew up the oldest of five kids. Likewise, the other band members had been involved with music most of their lives. Soon after meeting, Martin and Buckland started writing songs together. Buckland had taken up the guitar after he discovered the psychedelic pop band the Stone Roses. Berryman liked Buckland and Martin's work and added his bass, which he had taken up at age 13. Champion thought the trio had a lot of potential and wanted to join. He ended up on drums, though he had never played them before. Growing up, Champion had concentrated on guitar, bass, and piano, but those positions were already filled.

Eager and anxious to see what they could come up with, the group rehearsed nearly every night during those first years. "We used to play in bathrooms, the basement, even in the park," Martin said in the group's biography posted on its website. "Anywhere we could find to play." The bandmates all lived in the same residence hall and stole the name Coldplay from another resident. It was the name his own band used, but he decided it was too depressing.

Eventually, all of those rehearsals paid off and the young men felt confident enough to make a recording, which they called *Safety.* The 500–copy, independently produced EP, released in 1998, earned the band a performance slot in the 1998 In the City music festival in Manchester, England, which featured unsigned bands. At the festival, they were discovered by Simon Williams, who offered to produce *Brothers and Sisters* on his Fierce Panda label. That EP was released in 1999 and Coldplay subsequently signed with Parlophone Records, who in the past had signed the Beatles and Queen. That year, Coldplay also released a 5,000–copy EP, *The Blue Room,* which included five new tracks.

In 2000, Coldplay released its first album, *Parachutes,* which quickly shot to the top of the British charts. It remained in the top ten for more than 30 weeks. For a rock album, it had a quieter sound than most bands, yet was full of raging emotion. "We were trying to say that there is an alternative," Martin said on the band's website. "That you can try to be catchy without being slick, poppy without being pop, and you can be uplifting without being pompous. Because we're sometimes playing quieter stuff, it's hard to sound like we're trying to change things, but we wanted to be a reaction against soulless rubbish."

Their approach worked. In sum, the album sold about five million copies worldwide and earned them a stack of honors. At the 2001 Brit Awards (the British Grammys), the band went home with both the Best British Group and Best British Album awards. That same year, Coldplay also won three NME (New Music Express) Carling Awards, for Best New Artist, Best Single ("Yellow"), and Session of the Year, for a live BBC show. Before releasing their album, the band had been playing in small pubs across Britain, but after the success of *Parachutes*, band members headed to the United States for their first headlining tour.

In October of 2001, the band started work on its second album, *A Rush of Blood to the Head*. By Christmas, the producers were satisfied that the album was complete. Coldplay members, however, felt the album needed something more. "There was a feeling it was almost going too smoothly," Buckland related on the band's website. "We were pleased with it, but then we took a step back and realized that it wasn't right. It would have been easy to say we'd done enough, to release an album to keep up the momentum, but we didn't." In the end, Buckland is glad they went back to the studio so they would have an album they were satisfied with and would be proud to tour with for two years.

The resulting album, released in August of 2002, was a bit more upbeat from the first and chock full of emotional beauty and maturity. By September, it sat atop both the UK and Canadian LP charts. Once again, the band's efforts proved award-winning. At the 2003 Brit Awards, *A Rush of Blood to the Head* captured awards for Best British Group and Best British Album. Coldplay also won two Grammy Awards, one for Best Rock Performance by a Duo or Group with Vocal for "In My Place" and Best Alternative Music Album. The band spent 2003 on tour. Coldplay also collected several video awards at that year's MTV Video Music Awards, including Best Group Video, Breakthrough Video, and Best Direction, all for "The Scientist."

Coldplay has used its position in the rock world to promote its own political ideologies. Lead singer Martin has become a champion spokesman for Ox-Fam, a British humanitarian organization that campaigns for fair-trade practices in an effort to reduce worldwide poverty. After traveling to Haiti and the Dominican Republic to find out what some global-

trade policies do to real people, the band was hooked on the cause. At concerts, Martin's piano often has the words "Make Trade Fair" scrawled across it. He scribbled the OxFam web address on his hand during the MTV Video Music Awards so he would be sure to include it in his winning speech. Martin also plugs the cause relentlessly during Coldplay's shows. Before a 2003 concert in Mexico City, the band visited with local farmers in the town of Santa Isabel Tepetzala. In 2003, Martin attended a World Trade Organization (WTO) meeting and presented the WTO with a four–million–signature petition seeking trade–rule reform; signatures had been collected at shows.

"Anyone in our position has a certain responsibility," Berryman noted on the band's website biography. He said the band has a great platform through its television appearances, records, and notoriety. "You can make people aware of issues. It isn't very much effort for us at all, but if it can help people, then we want to do it."

Martin used the 2004 Grammy Awards to stump for another cause. During the ceremony, Coldplay won the Record of the Year award for "Clocks." When Martin accepted the award, he took the opportunity to do a little political campaigning. According to *Scotsman* writer Tracey Lawson, Martin accepted the award by saying, "We would like to dedicate this to Johnny Cash [the late country singer] and to John Kerry, who hopefully will be your president some day." He also used the Brit Awards to call for an end to military action in Iraq.

Viewed as a cutting–edge alternative rock band in the United States, Coldplay remains wildly popular there, but often takes a beating back home. British tabloids love to poke fun at the clean–cut, public–educated rock stars, whom they label as terminally boring. There are no bad boys of rock 'n' roll here. Berryman, after all, earned a degree in engineering and Martin, whose degree is in ancient world studies, is thought to be the dullest of all. Martin reportedly loves cricket and rarely drinks. When he started dating actress Gwyneth Paltrow, the press had a heyday. The couple met in October of 2002 backstage at a Coldplay concert. According to *Independent* writers Ian Burrell and Andrew Gumbel, one British tabloid described the couple as "anti–starlet Paltrow (no wheat, no dairy, no fun) hooked up with anti–rock star Martin (no sex, no drugs, even less fun)." The couple had a daughter, Apple Blythe Alison Martin, born May 14, 2004. They plan to raise her in London. Martin did, however, generate some headlines in July of 2003 when he allegedly chased down a photographer in Australia. Though Martin was arrested, the charges were eventually dropped.

Q magazine's Gareth Grundy told the *Independent* that the band is getting a bad rap for its good–boy image. "People probably say they are boring because they are not cool and everybody likes to like things that are cool. But whether they are cool or not they are a really great band, both on record and live."

According to *Time* magazine writer Josh Tyrangiel, rock manager Alan McGee, the man who discovered Oasis, dubbed Coldplay "music for bed wetters." Martin, however, defended the group to *Entertainment Weekly* writer Mary Kaye Schilling: "We take s*** for being boring. It just means that instead of doing coke or partying with the Dallas Cowboy Cheerleaders, we lock ourselves away and think of a new chord."

Sitting around thinking about their music, however, is precisely what has made Coldplay so successful. They take the time to be involved in every aspect of album production, down to shooting their own album cover art. Even though their albums are produced with a major label, Coldplay members remain ardently independent in their approach. They keep tabs on everything from the videos to the artwork. They want to have a hand in everything that has their name on it.

Of course, when it comes right down to it, it is Coldplay's songs that makes them so popular. Speaking to *Sound & Vision*, Martin talked about what makes a good song good. "Songwriting is the crux, but the best records ... are those where the sounds fit the song. There's no use putting amazing techno sounds on a song that just needs to be played on a blues harp; similarly, there's no point in having a nice oboe sound on a Nirvana record. But I'm not pretending to be an expert, because I sometimes hear our stuff and think, 'Ecch.'"

Selected discography

Safety EP, independently produced, 1998.
Brothers and Sisters EP, Fierce Panda, 1999.
The Blue Room EP, Parlophone, 1999.
Parachutes, Parlophone, 2000.
"Yellow" (single), Parlophone, 2000.
A Rush of Blood to the Head, Capitol, 2002.
Coldplay Live 2003, Capitol, 2003.
"Clocks" (single), Capitol, 2003.

Sources

Periodicals

Entertainment Weekly, December 26, 2003–January 2, 2004, pp. 36–37.
Independent (London, England), February 10, 2004, pp. 20–21.
Rolling Stone, October 16, 2003, p. 30; December 25, 2003/January 8, 2004, p. 83.
Scotsman, February 10, 2004, p. 7.
Sound & Vision, July/August 2001, p. 17.
Time, September 2, 2002, p. 71.
Time International, March 12, 2001, p. 58.

Online

"Biography," Coldplay, http://coldplay.com/biogpage.php (May 15, 2004).
"Coldplay," Rock on the Net, http://www.rockonthenet.com/artists–c/coldplay.htm (May 27, 2004).

—*Lisa Frick*

Jackie Collins

Author

Born Jacqueline Jill Collins in 1941, in London, England; daughter of Joseph (a theatrical agent) and Elsa (a dancer) Collins; married Wallace Austin (a businessman), 1959 (divorced, 1963); married Oscar Lerman (a nightclub owner and art dealer), 1966 (died, 1992); children: Tracy (from first marriage), Tiffany, Rory.

Addresses: *Home*—Los Angeles, CA. *Office*—c/o Simon & Schuster, 1230 Avenue of the Americas, New York, NY 10020.

Career

Novelist and actress. First novel, *The World Is Full of Married Men,* issued by World Publishing, 1968; penned screenplay for the feature film *The Stud,* 1978; also wrote screenplays for the television films *Lady Boss* and *Hollywood Wives: The New Generation;* producer of television miniseries and specials for CBS–TV, including *Hollywood Wives: The New Generation* and *Sexual Secrets of Men.* Film appearances include: *Barnacle Bill,* 1957; *Undercover Girl,* 1957; *Rock You Sinners,* 1957; *The Safecracker,* 1958; *Intent to Kill,* 1958; *Passport to Shame,* 1958; *During One Night,* 1961. Television appearances include: *Kraft Television Theatre,* 1949; *Danger Man,* 1961; *The Saint,* 1963. Many of Collins's novels have been adapted by herself or others for film or television, beginning with *The World is Full of Married Men,* 1979; *The Bitch, Chances, Lucky, Hollywood Wives,* and *Hollywood Kids* were produced as television miniseries; *Hollywood Wives: The New Generation* aired as a CBS feature film, 2003.

AP/Wide World Photos

Sidelights

British–born author Jackie Collins regularly lands on best–seller lists with her racy page–turners that chronicle the scandalous doings of various fictional movie stars, rock stars, up–and–coming stars, and has–been stars. Best known for her immensely successful "Hollywood" series that kicked off with the 1983 bestseller *Hollywood Wives,* Collins has mined her own experiences in celebrity–ville for the plots of nearly two dozen books. Critics have not always been kind to Collins, but the 400 million books sold under her name attest to her enduring appeal.

Collins is the sister of veteran actress Joan Collins, who has been married five times and regularly lands in the tabloids on both sides of the Atlantic. The younger Collins daughter prefers a quieter life, and described herself as a stay–at–home mom through much of her career as a best–selling author. Yet nearly all of her novels feature "tawdry tales of fabulous people," remarked *Entertainment Weekly* writer Rebecca Ascher–Walsh, "who get into the kind of trouble only the very rich can afford." A high–school drop–out who had a brief career as a film actress in the 1950s herself and then married twice, Collins views her remarkable success in publishing as an inspirational tale. "People can look at me and say, 'If she can do it, there's hope for anybody,'" she told *People.*

Collins's official birthdate is 1941, but other sources peg it as early as 1937. She was born in London, England, to a mother who had once been a dancer and a father who earned a good living as a theatrical agent. Jacqueline Jill Collins arrived some eight years—or four, depending on the birthdate—after her sister, Joan Henrietta. At a young age, she was determined to break free of her middle–class home's constraints. "I read the whole time and lived in a fantasy world," Collins once recalled in an interview for *Los Angeles Magazine* with Eve Babitz. "I was English but pretended I was American and couldn't reveal my own identity, and I wouldn't hang out with other kids."

During her school years, Collins was an admittedly bad student who regularly earned only one good grade—in her composition class. She also penned limericks with scandalous lines, and charged her friends six cents a page to read them. "I guess I was really a juvenile delinquent," she told *People*'s Scot Haller. "I would pad my bed at night with pillows and be out the window. My parents were constantly threatening juvenile hall." At the age of 15, her various transgressions—which included smoking and mocking the local flasher—caused school officials to expel her. Eventually, her parents agreed to let her go live with her sister, who had some success in British films in the early 1950s and then moved on to conquer Hollywood. There, Joan had some early success with roles in films like *The Girl in the Red Velvet Swing,* and even greater luck dating the most sought–after of young actors in town, among them Warren Beatty.

Collins joined her sister in Hollywood in 1956, settling into an attic room at the swanky Chateau Marmont. She dallied with a few young heartthrobs herself, including Marlon Brando, but eventually returned to London, where she married a man 12 years her senior. She has described Wallace Austin in various interviews as a compulsive gambler, mentally unstable, and a substance abuser, but did say once that the first months of her life as a newlywed were exciting. "We would do wild things like go for dinner in London and end up on a plane to the south of France, where we would gamble for 24 hours," she told *Los Angeles Magazine*'s Babitz. Motherhood sobered her, as did the life–threatening illness of her own mother, and she left Austin. "It was a very unfortunate first marriage," she told *People.* "Wallace was a drug addict, and he ultimately killed himself of an overdose. I divorced him because I knew he was going to do it."

Collins decided to try her luck in film, and between 1957 and 1958 appeared in a half–dozen films, among them *Undercover Girl* and *Passport to Shame.* She went through an admittedly carefree period as a single woman, but in 1966 wed Oscar Lerman, a nightclub owner and art dealer. They had two daughters, and Lerman encouraged his wife to begin writing fiction based on her experiences. Her first book, *The World Is Full of Married Men,* was published in 1968 to some notoriety. Its plot follows the downfall of a philandering London advertising executive. Collins wrote it, she told Babitz in the *Los Angeles Magazine* interview, to make a statement. "I was fed up with the way married men came on to me. I'd say, 'Well, what about your wife?' and they'd all say, 'Oh, my wife's different—she's happy staying at home.'"

Critics were shocked by Collins's literary debut. "One review called it 'the most disgusting book ever written,'" noted Haller in *People,* but it quickly became a bestseller in Britain. She followed it with *The Stud* a year later, which centered on a wealthy nightclub owner and the young, handsome man who enters her life. Collins said she wrote the part of "Fontaine," the main character, with her sister Joan in mind. She signed over the rights to her sister, and it would take Joan several years to find a backer willing to make the film version. A visit to the Cannes Film Festival in France in 1977 finally yielded a deal to make *The Stud.* As Joan recalled in the interview with Haller in *People,* "I suggested Jackie write the screenplay. She said, 'Oh, I've never written a screenplay,' and I said, 'Listen, we can't afford to hire a good screenwriter. Write the screenplay!'" Collins finished it six weeks later, and the 1979 film became a cult hit in Europe. It also revived her actress–sister's flagging career. Joan's portrayal of Fontaine, the assertive, scheming nightclub owner, was widely thought to have been the basis for Alexis Carrington, the vixen she played on the hit ABC series *Dynasty* in the 1980s that launched her star in the United States.

Collins wrote several other novels during the 1970s, among them *The World Is Full of Divorced Women,* and in 1979 brought two more of her own novels to the big screen—*The Bitch,* which also starred her sister, and *The World Is Full of Married Men.* Yet Collins only hit her stride after she and her husband moved to the Los Angeles, California, area in 1980. Lerman had run a successful London discotheque called Tramp, and opened an L.A. branch. The new cast of characters that Collins encountered in Hollywood and Beverly Hills enlivened the already–sensational plots of her books, and she had a hit with her 1981 novel *Chances,* which marked the first appearance of Lucky Santangelo, the determined daughter of a former mobster. Her next book, *Hollywood Wives,* was her first for Simon & Schuster, the powerful New York publishing house, and remained on the best–seller lists for much of 1983. It made Collins a household name, and boosted sales of her backlist as well.

Hollywood Wives was a scathing indictment of Hollywood and the sordid lives behind the glamour. The "wives" were a certain breed of Beverly Hills housewife, the wealthy spouses of powerful entertainment–industry executives and leading–men actors. They shopped, schemed, and relished the occasional fall from grace of a particularly unfaithful husband. Collins' book sold ten million copies and became the talk of Hollywood. Though the characters were entirely fictitious, guessing who Collins had based her wives and executives on occupied restaurant–table and poolside gossip sessions for months. She was often asked about her inspiration and her sources, since so much of it seemed to ring true. "I have a great many acquaintances who are Hollywood wives," she admitted in a *People* interview in 1983. "They call me and say, 'Who is this one and who is that one?' I tell them my characters are composites. They never recognize themselves."

The guessing game continued with Collins's other novels. *Rock Star* was another best–seller for her in 1988, and she brought Lucky Santangelo back in *Lady Boss* in 1990 and *Vendetta* six years after that. The "Hollywood" franchise proved her most enduring, however: she wrote *Hollywood Husbands, Hollywood Kids,* and *Hollywood Wives: The New Generation* in a 15–year span. *Hollywood Kids* proved a bit prophetic: one young character runs an expensive prostitution ring, and the book was published in 1994 just as the story of real–life Hollywood madam Heidi Fleiss broke. "Overlapping plot lines are propelled by rude energy and blazing tabloid–style tales of suicide, substance abuse, towering egos, dubious parentage, and truly star–crossed lovers," assessed a reviewer for *Publishers Weekly* of the book.

At the start of the twenty–first century, Collins wrote an update of sorts with the book *Hollywood Wives: The New Generation,* which reflected a new generation of power couples in the entertainment biz: the women held impressive studio jobs themselves now. Another "wife" is actually a gay man. "Collins recounts her two main narrative strands—a kidnapping and a celebrity's dalliance with her bodyguard—in her inimitably breathless staccato," noted *Harper's Bazaar*'s Henry Alford, who went on to mimic her. "Jackie Collins. Jackie Collins's prose style. Jackie Collins's prose style is a snowball from hell."

The mobster–daughter device that Collins deployed in the "Lucky" books proved so successful that she reinvented it for *Lethal Seduction,* a 2000 novel that starred the daring and beautiful Madison Castelli. In 2002's *Deadly Embrace,* Madison finds herself embroiled in a hostage situation in, most improbably, a hip restaurant. Collins' 23rd book, *Hollywood Divorces,* appeared on bookshelves in 2003. It featured the by–now familiar mix of infidelity, designer gowns, and romantic scheming. *Publishers Weekly* found it "jampacked with glamorous characters as believable as paper dolls and situations as familiar and credible as in any Collins classic."

Other book critics have been less than kind in judging Collins's immensely successful "sex–and–shopping" fiction category. "The only original thing that Collins brings to this exhausted genre is remarkably foul dialogue," wrote Campbell Geeslin about *Lucky* in a 1985 *People* review. Lucky's reappearance in *Lady Boss* five years later prompted *Time*'s John Skow to point out that the book "offers the reader a rare opportunity to watch adverbs mate." But Collins remains unfazed by bad reviews, as someone who has sold some 400 million books and seen several of the titles turned into miniseries might indeed be. "The people who really put me down do so because I'm Jackie Collins and I write a supposed kind of book, but they never read them," she told *People.*

Coinciding with the publication of her 23rd book in 2003 was the made–for–television movie version of *Hollywood Wives: The New Generation,* which starred Farrah Fawcett. In a twist that only the combination of Hollywood and Collins' fiction could provide, the veteran Hollywood blond actress was once thought to have been the inspiration for a character in *Hollywood Husbands,* Whitney Valentine. Though her own life has been nearly as fascinating as any of her characters, Collins is proud of her quietest accomplishment: her three daughters. The eldest, Tracy, is a makeup artist. Rory, one of her two daughters with Lerman, is a children's book editor in London; the other, Tiffany, designs her own line of handbags. Lerman died in 1992, and for a time in the late 1990s Collins was engaged to a shopping–mall developer, but he also died of cancer. She still writes for ten hours daily, in longhand. "I plan to write a hundred books," she told *Good Housekeeping* writer Maria Speidel. A memoir, she admitted, could only be published if she was ready to retire from mining Hollywood gossip. "I'll only write my story," she told the magazine, "when I'm ready to leave town."

Selected writings

The World Is Full of Married Men, World Publishing (New York, NY), 1968.

The Stud, W. H. Allen (London), 1969; World Publishing, 1970.

Sunday Simmons and Charlie Brick, W. H. Allen, 1971; published as *The Hollywood Zoo,* Pinnacle Books (New York, NY), 1975.

Lovehead, W. H. Allen, 1974; published as *The Love Killers,* Warner Books (New York City), 1975.

The World Is Full of Divorced Women, W. H. Allen, 1975.

Lovers and Gamblers, W. H. Allen, 1977; Grosset (New York, NY), 1978.

The Bitch, Pan Books (London), 1979.

Chances, Warner Books, 1981.

Hollywood Wives, Simon & Schuster (New York, NY), 1983.

Sinners, Pan Books, 1984.

Lucky, Simon & Schuster, 1985.

Hollywood Husbands, Simon & Schuster, 1986.

Rock Star, Simon & Schuster, 1988.

Lady Boss, Simon & Schuster, 1990.

American Star: A Love Story, Simon & Schuster, 1993.

Hollywood Kids, Simon & Schuster, 1994.

Vendetta: Lucky's Revenge, HarperCollins (New York, NY), 1996.

Thrill!, Simon & Schuster, 1997.

Dangerous Kiss, Simon & Schuster, 1999.

Lethal Seduction, Simon & Schuster, 2000.

Hollywood Wives: The New Generation, Simon & Schuster, 2001.

Deadly Embrace, Simon & Schuster, 2002.

Hollywood Divorces, Simon & Schuster, 2003.

Sources

Periodicals

Advocate, June 19, 2001, p. 94.
Booklist, June 1, 2002, p. 1644.
Bookseller, July 4, 2003, p. 25.
Broadcasting & Cable, June 15, 1998, p. 40.
Entertainment Weekly, August 3, 2001, p. 34; December 19, 2003, p. 84.
Fortune, March 22, 1993, p. 180.
Good Housekeeping, August 2001, p. 73.
Harper's Bazaar, July 2001, p. 74.
Library Journal, April 1, 1999, p. 146.
Los Angeles Magazine, September 1994, p. 96.
New York Times, October 18, 2003, p. B17.
People, September 26, 1983, p. 64; November 12, 1984, p. 55; August 26, 1985, p. 20; January 12, 1987, p. 80; May 16, 1988, p. 57; May 23, 1988, p. 31; Spring 1991 Special Issue, p. 4; April 19, 1993, p. 28; February 3, 1997, p. 33; December 15, 1997, p. 105.
Publishers Weekly, August 29, 1994, p. 61; May 28, 2001, p. 48; July 2, 2001, p. 18; November 10, 2003, p. 43.
Time, October 15, 1990, p. 86.

Online

Contemporary Authors Online, Gale Group, 2003.

—Carol Brennan

Chris Cooper

Actor

Born Christopher W. Cooper, July 9, 1951, in Kansas City, MO; son of Charles (a military doctor and cattle rancher) and Mary Ann (a homemaker) Cooper; married Marianne Leone (a screenwriter and actress), July, 1983; children: Jesse (son). *Education:* University of Missouri, B.G.S. (theater and agriculture), 1976.

Addresses: *Publicist*—PMK, 8500 Wilshire Blvd., Ste. 700, Beverly Hills, CA 90211–3105.

Career

Actor in films, including: *Bad Timing*, 1980; *Matewan*, 1987; *Thousand Pieces of Gold*, 1991; *Guilty by Suspicion*, 1991; *City of Hope*, 1991; *This Boy's Life*, 1993; *Ned Blessing: The True Story of My Life*, 1994; *Pharaoh's Army*, 1995; *Money Train*, 1995; *A Time to Kill*, 1996; *Boys*, 1996; *Lone Star*, 1996; *The Horse Whisperer*, 1998; *Great Expectations*, 1998; *American Beauty*, 1999; *October Sky*, 1999; *The 24–Hour Woman*, 1999; *The Patriot*, 2000; *Me, Myself, and Irene*, 2000; *Interstate 60*, 2001; *The Bourne Identity*, 2002; *Adaptation*, 2002; *Seabiscuit*, 2003.

Television appearances include: *The Edge of Night*, c. 1985; *The Equalizer*, 1987; *Miami Vice*, 1988; *American Playhouse* (special), 1988; 1991; *Lonesome Dove* (miniseries), 1989; *Lifestories*, 1990; *To the Moon, Alice* (movie), 1990; *In Broad Daylight* (movie), 1991; *Bed of Lies* (movie), 1992; *Return to Lonesome Dove* (miniseries), 1993; *One More Mountain* (movie), 1994; *Law and Order*, 1996; *Breast Men* (movie), 1997; *Alone* (movie), 1997; *My House in Umbria* (movie), 2003.

AP/Wide World Photos/Fashion Wire Daily

Stage appearances include: *Of the Fields, Lately,* New York, NY, 1980; *A Different Moon,* New York, 1983; *The Ballad of Soapy Smith,* Seattle, WA, 1983; New York, 1984; *Sweet Bird of Youth,* London, England, 1985; *Cobb,* New Haven, CT, 1989.

Awards: Best actor award, Cowboy Hall of Fame, for *Thousand Pieces of Gold,* 1991; Screen Actors Guild Award for outstanding performance of a cast in a motion picture, Screen Actors Guild, for *American Beauty,* 2000; best supporting actor, Los Angeles Film Critics Association, for *Adaptation,* 2002; best supporting actor, San Francisco Film Critics Circle, for *Adaptation,* 2002; best supporting actor, National Board of Review Awards, for *Adaptation,* 2002; best supporting actor, Broadcast Film Critics Association, for *Adaptation,* 2003; Golden Globe Award for best supporting actor, Hollywood Foreign Press Association, for *Adaptation,* 2003; Academy Award for best supporting actor, Academy of Motion Picture Arts and Sciences, for *Adaptation,* 2003.

Sidelights

After more than two decades of quietly providing solid support in quirky character roles on stage, film, and television, actor Chris Cooper in

2003 was finally thrust into the spotlight. For his portrayal of John Laroche, the orchid–fancying, dentally challenged swamp rat at the center of 2002's *Adaptation,* the Missouri–born Cooper walked away with both an Oscar and a Golden Globe as best supporting actor. For Cooper the recognition was proof positive that he had accomplished his central goal in life, a goal he had defined for Pam Lambert in *People* in 1996 when he said he wanted to be "an actor, not a star."

In accepting the Academy Award for his work in *Adaptation,* Cooper was characteristically modest. "To all the nominees," he was quoted as saying on the University of Missouri's website, "it's a pleasure to be thought in your same company. To all the people in *Adaptation* who helped to make this the most enjoyable job I ever had, thank you. Charlie Kaufman, Spike Jonze, Nicolas Cage, the fabulous, beautiful, wonderful Meryl Streep. Working with this woman was like making great jazz. You had a lot to do with this, so I thank you. To my wife, Marianne, you took on all the burden, thank you. And in light of all the troubles in this world, I wish us all peace. Thank you."

Over the course of his acting career, Cooper has created dozens of memorable characters, ranging from a murderous, retired military man tortured by the pain of concealing his homosexuality in *American Beauty,* to a small–town Texas sheriff in *Lone Star.* He has managed to leave a lasting impression on millions of moviegoers, most of whom find his face familiar but would be hard–pressed to come up with his name. Whether the publicity accompanying his Oscar and Golden Globe wins in 2003 will change all that remains to be seen. But many critics have little doubt that Cooper will continue to display the range of his acting skills for years to come.

He was born Christopher W. Cooper in Kansas City, Missouri, on July 9, 1951. His father, Charles, a transplanted Texan, served for several years as a doctor in the U.S. Air Force and later operated a cattle ranch in Kansas, while his mother, Mary Ann, kept the household running smoothly while looking after Cooper and his older brother, Chuck. Cooper grew up in a home in the Kansas City suburbs but spent his summers on the Cooper family cattle ranch in nearby Kansas. Agonizingly shy as a boy, he was overshadowed in his early years by his outgoing older brother. His first exposure to the stage and public appearances came as a participant in the church choir and school choral group. One of Cooper's teachers, worried about his painful shyness, was instrumental in getting him into the school chorus. In his teens, Cooper and some of his high school buddies began to get into trouble, including a few incidents of petty theft. To get himself off the streets and out of trouble, he volunteered to help build sets for productions at local community theaters, further increasing his interest in the stage.

Cooper's budding interest in the stage and performing won him little encouragement at home. As he told Jeff Jensen in *Entertainment Weekly,* "I remember my mother saying, 'But, honey, you don't have *any* imagination.' I understood what she meant—I just wasn't outgoing. But I *knew* what was in my head, and it was *full* of imagination."

To avoid being drafted into the military and sent off to fight in Vietnam, Cooper served a tour in the U.S. Coast Guard Reserve after graduating from high school. He also worked briefly as a carpenter's assistant, but in 1972 he enrolled at the University of Missouri to study technical theater, the behind–the–scenes tasks including set design and construction and lighting. He was, however, intrigued by the notion of acting and before long was playing leading roles in theater department productions. In the college production of Harold Pinter's *The Birthday Party,* he played Stanley. Other roles included Teddy in Mark Medoff's *When You Comin' Back, Red Ryder?* and the King in Eugene Ionesco's *Exit the King.*

Cooper also found himself drawn to musical theater, taking both big and small roles in college productions. He even enrolled in a ballet class at nearby Stephens College, a predominantly women's college. His foray into the study of ballet offered an unexpected bonus. As he told *People*'s Lambert, "Probably the best thing that ever happened to me was taking dance, because I made a total fool of myself every day in front of a classroom full of women. It helped to break through the shyness that I'd always had." Hedging his bets, just in case his dreams of an acting career should prove unattainable, Cooper also took some agricultural classes in college.

After graduating from the University of Missouri in 1976 with a bachelor's degree in theater and agriculture, Cooper headed for the bright lights of Broadway, hoping to break into the acting business with roles on the stage. To further hone his acting skills, he enrolled in classes with well–known drama coach Stella Adler. Cooper made both his professional stage and film debuts in 1980. On Broadway, he appeared as Ben Mercer in *Of the Fields, Lately* at the Century Theatre, while on film, he landed a role in the British movie, *Bad Timing*. Although he continued to work on stage in and around New York over the next several years, *Bad Timing* proved exactly that for Cooper as far as film work was concerned. It was to be seven years before he landed his next movie role.

From 1980 into 1981 Cooper appeared in several productions staged by the Actors Theatre of Louisville, Kentucky. In 1983 he played Tyler Biars in a New York production of *A Different Moon* by the Workshop of the Performing Arts. In July of that year, he married screenwriter/actress Marianne Leone, with whom he has since appeared in a couple of movies. At the Seattle Repertory Theatre in 1983, Cooper played the role of Paul Anthony MacAleer in *The Ballad of Soapy Smith*, a role he recreated at the New York Shakespeare Festival the following year. In 1985 Cooper played opposite Lauren Bacall in a London production of Tennessee Williams' *Sweet Bird of Youth*.

Cooper's career expanded into film and television in a big way during the late 1980s. On TV, he made guest appearances on several series popular at the time, including *Miami Vice, American Playhouse,* and *The Equalizer.* He also appeared for a time as Sam Cranshaw in ABC's daily soap opera, *The Edge of Night.* In 1987 he made his American film debut, playing Joe Kenehan in John Sayles's production of *Matewan.*

Although Cooper's acting career had truly begun to take off during this period, he and his wife experienced a personal tragedy in the fall of 1987. Six months pregnant with their first child, Marianne in October of 1987 came down with a bad case of the flu. Their son, Jesse, was delivered three months prematurely. Relatively healthy for a "preemie" during the first three days of his life, Jesse then suffered a massive cerebral hemorrhage. For several days, the infant's ability to survive was in doubt. Jesse did pull through but was left with cerebral palsy, which has severely limited his mobility and ability to communicate.

Director/screenwriter Sayles, who gave Cooper his first major role in an American film, 1987's *Matewan,* was obviously pleased with the actor's performance, for he has since featured the Missourian in two of his subsequent films—1991's *City of Hope* and 1996's *Lone Star.* In the latter film, Cooper won wide acclaim for his portrayal of Sam Deeds, a small-town Texas sheriff who is investigating the role played in a murder by his late father, his predecessor in the job. Seven years earlier, Cooper earned critical praise in the role of cowboy July Johnson in *Lonesome Dove,* the TV miniseries of Larry McMurtry's epic novel of the West.

With the exception of *Lone Star,* in which he received top billing, most of Cooper's film work has been as a supporting player. Along the way he has created some truly memorable characters. Among the most impressive of his supporting performances was his portrayal of the conflicted, overbearing ex–Marine neighbor in Sam Mendes's 1999 film *American Beauty.* Of that performance, Bob Ivry of the Bergen County, New Jersey, *Record* wrote: "Chris Cooper is so affecting as the Marine colonel that you might be willing to forgive the facile obviousness of his revealed sexuality...." For that performance Cooper was nominated for Best Supporting Actor by the Screen Actors Guild (SAG) and shared in the SAG Award for Outstanding Performance of a Cast in a Motion Picture.

For the second time in his acting career, Cooper portrayed a coal miner in 1999's *October Sky,* playing John Hickam, father of aspiring teenage rocket scientist Homer Hickam. Cooper's first role as a coal miner came in *Matewan,* in which he played union organizer Joe Kenehan who leads oppressed miners in a revolt against the mine's owners. In an interview with Ivry shortly before the release of *October Sky,* the actor offered some insight into how his film career had evolved. "I'm beginning to get a little bit of recognition. As far as studio films go, I've done well with small, supporting roles. *October Sky* was a much larger role, and *American Beauty* is a good supporting piece.... *Lone Star* brought me some attention, but is that going to make me a Hollywood leading man? I don't think the studios know what to do with me."

Clearly, the crowning achievement of Cooper's film career thus far has been his award–winning portrayal of orchid thief John Laroche in 2002's *Adaptation.* In February of 2003, the film's producer, Edward Saxon, discussed with *Entertainment Weekly*'s Jensen both the part and how well suited Cooper was to play it. Of the Laroche character, Saxon observed, "A great antihero. A guy who isn't rich or beautiful, but extremely special. And a little bit cracked. What I love about this part for Chris is that he's usually playing a guy who's fundamentally unhappy. Here, he's this passionate force of nature. He's the guy everyone wants to be." As for the emergence of his Laroche as something of a sex symbol in the film, no one seems more amazed than Cooper. As he told Elaine Dutka of the *Los Angeles Times,* "It scares me. If the female public says that, they befuddle me, as they have all my life."

Cooper and his family live in a seaside home not far from Plymouth, Massachusetts. He told Dutka that their son is "the best thing that has happened to us. Like many husbands, I was reluctant to have a child, but Jesse has instilled in us what's really important. He seems so normal to us now. And what a great teacher: His patience is extraordinary and, because he's so limited, he's very, very focused. At the expense of sounding ghoulish, Jesse has fueled the characters I've played. He's filled my emotional life."

Sources

Books

Contemporary Theatre, Film, and Television, volume 14, Gale Research, 1995; volume 38, Gale Group, 2002.

Periodicals

Agence France Presse, March 24, 2003.
Entertainment Weekly, February 21, 2003, p. 42; March 21, 2003, pp. 47–50.
Kansas City Star, March 23, 2003.
Newsday, March 13, 2003, p. D7.
People, August 5, 1996, p. 103.
Record (Bergen County, NJ), February 16, 1999, p. 1; March 26, 2000, p. 1.

Online

"Chris Cooper," Filmbug, http://www.filmbug.com/db/260566 (June 19, 2003).
"Chris Cooper," Hollywood.com, http://www.Hollywood.com/celebs/bio/celeb/1672554 (June 19, 2003).
"Chris Cooper," Yahoo! Movies, http://movies.yahoo.com/shop?d=hc&id=1800018625&cf=biog&intl=us (June 19, 2003).
"The Facts: Chris Cooper," E! Online, http://www.eonline.com/Facts/People/Bio/0,128,3544,00.html (June 19, 2003).
"MU Alumnus Wins Academy Award," University of Missouri–Columbia, http://atmizzou.missouri.edu/apr03/cooper.htm (June 19, 2003).

—Don Amerman

Sofia Coppola

Filmmaker

Born May 14, 1971, in New York, NY; daughter of Francis Ford (a filmmaker) and Eleanor (a photographer and documentary filmmaker) Coppola; married Spike Jonze (a director), 1999 (divorced, 2004). *Education:* Attended California Institute of the Arts, early 1990s.

Addresses: *Agent*—William Morris Agency, 1325 Avenue of the Americas, New York, NY 10019.

Career

Actress in films, including: *The Godfather* (uncredited), 1972; *The Godfather: Part II* (uncredited), 1974; *The Outsiders,* 1983; *Rumble Fish,* 1983; *The Cotton Club,* 1984; *Peggy Sue Got Married,* 1986; *Anna,* 1987; *The Godfather: Part III,* 1990; *Star Wars: Episode I—The Phantom Menace,* 1999; *CQ,* 2001. Writer of screenplays, including: "Life without Zoe" for *New York Stories,* 1989; *Lick the Star,* 1998; *The Virgin Suicides,* 1999; *Lost in Translation,* 2003. Director of films, including: *Lick the Star,* 1998; *The Virgin Suicides,* 1999; *Lost in Translation,* 2003. Has also worked at the Paris offices of the House of Chanel, and as a photographer for *Vogue* and *Allure;* co–hosted a Comedy Central show called *Hi–Octane,* 1993; launched clothing line, Milk Fed, 1995.

Awards: New York Film Critics Circle Award for best director, for *Lost in Translation,* 2003; Golden Globe Award for best screenplay, Hollywood Foreign Press Association, for *Lost in Translation,* 2004; Academy Award for best screenplay, Academy of Motion Picture Arts and Sciences, for *Lost in Translation,* 2004.

Sidelights

Sofia Coppola emerged from her family's shadow to become one of Hollywood's most surprising success stories. The daughter of auteur Francis Ford Coppola, she was roundly excoriated in her teens for her performance in *The Godfather: Part III.* Moving behind the lens, however, Coppola has since become an acclaimed filmmaker in her own right. At the age of just 32, she won an Academy Award for best screenplay for her first original work, 2003's *Lost in Translation,* as well as critical praise for creating a stunningly subtle yet luminous film as its director. "I can't believe I am standing here," a clearly unnerved Coppola said during her acceptance speech, according the *New York Times.* "Thank you to my dad for all he taught me."

Coppola's film debut came just after her birth in May of 1971, when her father cast her as the infant in the baptism scene that concludes his epic, *The Godfather.* The senior Coppola is perhaps best known for his adaptation of the Mario Puzo saga about an Italian–American family and the criminal underworld, which regularly appears on lists of the greatest films of all time. As a toddler, Coppola also appeared in an uncredited role in the sequel, as a child onboard a boat approaching New York's Statue of Liberty scene in 1974's *The Godfather: Part II*. She and her brothers, Roman and Gian Carlo, were often taken along to locations where their father was shooting his films, including the grueling, trouble–plagued Philippines production of his other classic, *Apocalypse Now*. She also took bit roles (under the screen name "Domino") in *The Outsiders, Rumble Fish,* and *The Cotton Club,* her father's films from the early 1980s.

Most of Coppola's childhood, however, was spent in California's Napa Valley, where her parents owned a vineyard. Both recalled her as an imaginative, persuasive child. Eleanor Coppola, a photographer and documentary filmmaker, told *Time* writer Kate Betts that when her only daughter "played with her friends, she always wanted them to play her way—her story, her costumes. And I would have to say, 'Sofia, not everyone wants to play your way.' She had that pattern of somehow gathering everyone's enthusiasms, which is very much like a director." Her teen years were at first charmed ones, and included a stint as an intern at the Chanel atelier in Paris, working for Karl Lagerfeld, when she was just 15. "At one point I tripped over the phone wire and disconnected his call," she told *W* writer Christopher Bagley, "but he was always really nice." Tragedy struck Coppola and her family, however, in 1986, when Gian Carlo was killed in a boating accident. Coppola was at home in Napa Valley with her mother, and recalled it as "a heartbreaking time," she told *New York Times* writer Lynn Hirschberg. "You never really get over something like that."

Coppola's first foray into screenwriting came when she and her father wrote a segment for Woody Allen's 1989 trilogy, *New York Stories,* which he then directed. Their short film, "Life without Zoe," featured a precocious 12–year–old who lived at the Sherry–Netherland Hotel. Critical reviews were mixed, but journalistic venom came out full–force for the senior Coppola's next project, the long–anticipated final installment of *The Godfather: Part III*. Actress Winona Ryder had dropped out after being cast as Mary Corleone, daughter of Al Pacino's Michael Corleone, and Coppola's father put her in the part instead. The film was judged a half–baked conclusion after the cinematic accomplishment of the first two, but Coppola's performance was singled out as particularly regretful. "Though Mary is not on screen that much, she is crucial to the action," noted *National Review* film critic John Simon. "To have a gross–looking, totally non–acting, personality less person impersonating the movie's love interest is a costly impertinence. And to think that, because of daughter Sofia's Valley–girl accent, some-

one else had to dub her voice! But at least the dubbing is perfect: the voice is as inept as the body."

Mortified, Coppola steered clear of Hollywood for a time. She took classes at the California Institute of the Arts, appeared in a few music videos—including an early Black Crowes production—and co–hosted a 1993 cable television show with her friend Zoe Cassavetes, daughter of another cinematic legend, John Cassavetes. The show, *Hi–Octane,* featured the pair driving around the Los Angeles area in a vintage muscle car and interviewing their celebrity friends. She also learned photography, got a photo agent, and did work for French *Vogue* and *Allure,* but felt like she was floundering, career–wise. "I became a dilettante," she confessed to the *New York Times'* Hirschberg about this time in her life. "I wanted to do something creative, but I didn't know what it would be." In 1995, she started her own clothing company, Milk Fed, with a friend from grade school, Stephanie Hayman. The company became such a success in Japan that it gave Coppola a certain degree of financial freedom.

Coppola's varied interests in music and fashion eventually led her back into film. She was friends with designer Marc Jacobs, who introduced her to Sonic Youth's Kim Gordon and Thurston Moore. They, in turn, introduced her to her future husband, video director Spike Jonze, but Moore also gave her a copy of Jeffrey Eugenides acclaimed debut novel, *The Virgin Suicides*. Coppola was enchanted by the story of five sisters in a posh Midwestern suburb who commit suicide one by one. The story is narrated in flashback by one of the boys that knew the ethereally lovely Lisbon sisters, and when Coppola heard about a screenplay adaptation in the works that would add a bit more sex and violence to the story, she decided to write her own. She did so, quietly, without telling anyone and landed the project and the director's job as well.

Coppola had actually made her directing debut with a little–seen 1998 indie film called *Lick the Star,* but *The Virgin Suicides* was her first her major studio release. The work earned laudatory reviews, with critics noting she seemed particularly skilled in creating a pitch–perfect period piece of 1970s teen life. "Coppola has carefully preserved the spirit of her source and, for the most part, succeeded in her efforts to find a visual idiom appropriate to the lush melancholy of the novel's language," remarked A. O. Scott, the *New York Times* critic. *Esquire* called it "hypnotic," with its critic asserting "the film has a deeply photographic quality, like a romantic, super-saturated snapshot capturing the surrealism of 1970s suburbia. Entirely absent of the mocking condescension of films such as *Welcome to the Dollhouse* or the glibness of *American Pie,* it is one of the most authentic portraits of adolescence in years."

The Virgin Suicides was not only a tour–de–force of a movie, but also served to redeem Coppola's reputation in Hollywood after the *Godfather* debacle. Scott, writing in the *New York Times,* conceded that any filmmaker who tackled the *Suicides* story was working with a project with some holes, for Eugenides' novel had little in the way of character development or plot. As director, Scott noted, Coppola was required to make a film that would "hold the viewer's interest through moods, associations, and resonant images. That she has done so is impressive, and *The Virgin Suicides* should quiet the buzz of skepticism that has preceded this film. Yes, Ms. Coppola is the daughter of one famous director and the wife of another, but she is also an assured and imaginative filmmaker in her own right." In the profile for *W,* Bagley asserted that though Coppola had enjoyed a few "quasi–careers" that included "muse to Marc Jacobs [and] all–around poster girl for low–key West Coast cool," her filmmaking debut "was so assuredly deft and original that it lent an instant credibility to her new calling and, retroactively, to her old ones."

Coppola's forays to Tokyo, Japan, inspired her next screen project, the luminous *Lost in Translation.* She and Hayman, her business partner, traveled there often for Milk Fed, which was manufactured in Japan and had its own Tokyo store called Heaven 27. They preferred to stay at the ultra–modern Park Hyatt, and Coppola wrote a screenplay about two drifting Americans who meet in its hotel bar. She was determined to film only at the Park Hyatt, and equally determined to have actor Bill Murray play the lead—that of an aging Hollywood star who comes to Japan to appear in a whiskey commercial for a $2 million paycheck. While there, he meets a young, moribund American woman, played by Scarlett Johansson, whose flighty fashion–photographer husband (Giovanni Ribisi, who provided the wistful narrative voice–overs in *The Virgin Suicides*) leaves her to fend for herself in the strange city.

Lost in Translation won unanimously positive reviews. The *New York Times's* Elvis Mitchell called it "the first grown–up starring part that Mr. Murray has had," and "one of the purest and simplest examples ever of a director falling in love with her star's gifts." David Denby, writing in the *New Yorker,* also assessed it in glowing terms. "Not much happens, but Coppola is so gentle and witty an observer that the movie casts a spell," Denby wrote. "She captures the sleek pomp of a luxury Japanese hotel, with its intimidating high–tech look, its abundant staff mysteriously stepping out of the shadows and offering unwanted assistance in beautifully mangled English." *BusinessWeek* critic Thane Peterson hailed her as one of American film's new visionaries. "At the moment, Coppola is the only woman in a band of young auteurs who represent the best and brightest of Hollywood's next generation," Peterson declared, and listed her only rivals as Paul Thomas Anderson (*Punch Drink Love*), Wes Anderson (*The Royal Tenenbaums*), and her husband, who had a hit with *Adaptation* the year before. Yet the *BusinessWeek* writer further noted that the men of the bunch "tend to fall back on quirkiness to make their movies distinctive.... Coppola doesn't bother with that sort of thing. She just comes straight at you with an unabashed art film that unfolds at a languid, European pace—but is also sufficiently unpretentious to appeal to a wide audience."

Coppola, taking a cue from her father, enthusiastically mixes her professional and personal lives. Her film soundtracks are supervised by Brian Reitzell, drummer for the French band Air whom she knew when he played with the cult–favorite L.A. punk outfit Redd Kross. Another old friend, Lance Acord, became *Lost in Translation's* cinematographer. Her brother, Roman, served as its second unit director, and in turn she appeared in a brief but glamorous cameo in his 2001 paean to Sixties Euro–cool, *CQ.* Ribisi's photographer character, meanwhile, was said to bear an uncanny resemblance in mannerisms to Coppola's husband. She and Jonze, born Adam Spiegel, wed in a 1999 Napa ceremony at which Tom Waits sang and an all–star guest list from the worlds of film, music, and fashion intersected. The couple had a home in Los Angeles, but Coppola spent much of the summer of 2003 in New York City editing *Lost in Translation,* prompting rumors that their union was on the rocks. Their split was announced later that year.

Coppola avoids publicity and the outspokenness for which her father is known. His battles with Hollywood studios over the years were legendary, and in some cases even involved litigation. Coppola's style is a more reticent one. She recalled in the *New York Times* interview with Hirschberg that her famous parent "came on the set of *The Virgin Suicides* and told me, 'You should say "Action" louder, more from your diaphragm.' I thought, 'O.K., you can go now.'"

Sources

Books

Contemporary Theatre, Film and Television, volume 30, Gale Group, 2000.

Periodicals

Back Stage West, September 11, 2003, p. 8.
BusinessWeek, October 21, 2003.
Cineaste, Winter 2003, p. 26.
Daily Variety, November 12, 2003, p. A14.
Entertainment Weekly, October 3, 2003, p. 51.
Esquire, May 2000, p. 146.
Independent (London, England), January 2, 2004, p. 8.
Independent Sunday (London, England), December 21, 2003, p. 9.
Interview, April 2000, p. 46; October 2003, p. 54.
Nation, January 7, 1991, p. 22.
National Review, January 28, 1991, p. 65.
New Republic, March 27, 1989, p. 24.
New Yorker, September 15, 2003, p. 100.
New York Observer, September 29, 2003, p. 29.
New York Times, April 21, 2000; August 31, 2003, p. 35; September 12, 2003; February 3, 2004, p. E8; March 1, 2004.
Observer (London, England), February 13, 2000, p. 6; May 21, 2000, p. 8.
Time, September 15, 2003, pp. 70–72.
USA Today Magazine, January 2004, p. 59.
W, September 2003, pp. 350–54.
WWD, June 16, 2003, p. 7.

Online

"The Coppola Clan's Best Director?" *Salon.com,* http://www.salon.com/ent/movies/int/2003/09/23/sofia_coppola (September 23, 2003).
"Lost in Translation," *Salon.com,* http://www.salon.com/ent/movies/review/2003/09/12/translation (September 12, 2003).
"Sofia Coppola," Internet Movie Database, http://www.imdb.com/name/nm00010681 (February 11, 2004).

—Carol Brennan

John Corbett

Actor

Born May 9, 1962 (some sources say 1961), in Wheeling, WV. *Education:* Attended cosmetology school and Cerritos Community College.

Addresses: *Agent*—Creative Artists Agency, 9830 Wilshire Blvd., Beverly Hills, CA 90212. *Home*—Seattle, WA, and Los Angeles, CA.

Career

Worked as a welder and pipe–fitter in a steel factory for six years in the 1980s; briefly worked as a hairdresser before landing first professional acting job in a television commercial. Television appearances include: *The Wonder Years,* ABC, 1988; *Northern Exposure,* CBS, 1990–95; *Web of Life* (documentary; voice), PBS, 1995; *Duckman* (voice), 1996; *Innocent Victims* (movie), 1996; *Don't Look Back* (movie), 1996; *The Morrison Murders* (movie), 1996; *The Visitor,* FOX, 1997–98; *Warlord: The Battle for the Galaxy* (movie), 1998; *The Sky's On Fire* (movie), 1998; *To Serve and Protect* (miniseries), 1999; *The Love Chronicles,* 1999; *Sex and the City,* HBO, 2000–02; *On Hostile Ground* (movie), 2000; *Rocky Times* (movie), 2000; *Private Lies* (movie), 2000; *The Chris Isaak Show,* 2002; *The Griffin and the Minor Canon* (voice), 2002; *Lucky,* FX, mid–2003. Film appearances include: *Flight of the Intruder,* 1991; *Tombstone,* 1993; *Wedding Bell Blues,* 1996; *Volcano,* 1997; *Desperate but Not Serious,* 1999; *Dinner Rush,* 2000; *Serendipity,* 2001; *Prancer Returns,* 2001; *My Big Fat Greek Wedding,* 2002; *My Dinner with Jimi,* 2003; *Raising Helen,* 2004.

Steve Granitz/WireImage.com

Sidelights

Actor John Corbett ventured into new on–screen territory in 2003 when he appeared in the FX Channel series *Lucky.* Eternally cast as the romantic male lead in properties ranging from the slightly risqué HBO series *Sex and the City* to the feel–good romantic comedy hit of 2002, *My Big Fat Greek Wedding,* Corbett possesses a mellifluous voice and mellow demeanor that translates well on screens both large and small. His title role in the comic–noir FX series was a departure from what *Arizona Republic* writer Kathy Cano–Murillo termed his "knack for portraying rugged, handsome boyfriends who aren't afraid to show their sensitive sides," because Michael "Lucky" Linkletter was a disastrously unlucky compulsive gambler. Though critics found the series and Corbett's role intriguing, *Lucky* failed to find an audience and was cancelled after a three–month run.

Born in the early 1960s, Corbett grew up in Wheeling, West Virginia. He moved to California after he finished high school, and worked in a steel factory for six years as a welder and pipe–fitter. When a back injury compelled him to find another career, he decided to try acting, but enrolled in cosmetology school as a back–up plan while taking drama classes at Cerritos Community College. A week after graduating from the hairdressing program, Corbett landed his first television commercial. Other roles arrived soon afterward: he appeared in an episode of *The Wonder Years,* ABC's sentimental retro comedy that was a strong ratings–winner in the late 1980s, and made his feature–film debut in *Flight of the Intruder,* a 1991 Paramount wartime drama that cast him alongside Danny Glover and Willem Dafoe.

By then, however, Corbett had already won a somewhat nonconformist role on a quirky new series on CBS called *Northern Exposure.* The show debuted in July of 1990 and quickly caught on with viewers and critics alike for its erudite humor and eccentric but likable characters. Corbett played Christopher Danforth Stevens, a.k.a. "Chris in the Morning," the local DJ on the sole radio station in a fictional Alaskan town called Cicely. Will Lee, writing in *Entertainment Weekly,* described the show as "something of a misfit. Neither comedy nor drama, both highbrow and homespun, and teeming with eccentric characters ... [the show] nonetheless proved to be a bracingly cool frontier–scented breeze in the dead of summer."

Northern Exposure's lead, an unknown actor named Rob Morrow, led the cast as Dr. Joel Fleischman, an ardent New Yorker and recently minted physician who must live and practice in the town to satisfy a medical–school scholarship agreement. "Corbett played a kind of wise space cadet," noted *Buffalo News* writer Jeff Simon, "always on hand to shepherd the perennially uptight hero through the more notable Alaskan eccentricities." As Chris, Corbett spun a compelling mix of music mixed in with his arch philosophical musings, and another dimension was added to his character when it was revealed he was on the lam from West Virginia parole authorities and had served time in prison for grand theft auto. During its first few seasons, the show won both high ratings and Emmy awards, but Morrow departed and the show came to an end a few months later in 1995.

Corbett's co–star Morrow, and an attractive pilot played by Janine Turner, were hailed as *Northern Exposure*'s breakout stars, but both went on to feature–film careers that sputtered. During the show's successful run, the press hype was intense for a time, but Corbett eventually stopped giving interviews. As he recalled later, "it became less and less about what I was doing with my life everyday, which was acting, and more about what kind of press I could get or what magazine cover or what talk show I could get on," he told *Los Angeles Times* journalist Jon Matsumoto.

After *Northern Exposure* ended, the roles dwindled for Corbett for a time. He made *Wedding Bell Blues,* an ill–fated matrimony comedy, and the blockbuster *Volcano* in 1997 before landing back on the small screen with a Fox Network science–fiction series/ *X–Files* copycat called *The Visitor.* Corbett starred as a 1940s American military pilot who disappeared over the Bermuda Triangle, and returns to the present day with paranormal powers. The show lasted just a season, however, and Corbett supplemented his film work with a three–year stint as a spokesperson for the Ford Motor Company.

Corbett was back in West Virginia on a visit when producers for the smash HBO series *Sex and the City* tracked him down. "I hadn't worked in years," Corbett told *Houston Chronicle* writer Mike McDaniel, "and they go, 'You want to be Sarah Parker's boyfriend for a couple of seasons?' And I said, 'I don't know, send me some tapes and let me see it.'" He agreed to take the role, and debuted in the third season as nice–guy furniture designer Aidan Shaw, the new love interest for Sarah Jessica Parker's Carrie Bradshaw character. They fall in love, she even quits smoking for him, and the show's fans "swooned at his lazy, good–natured sensuality," wrote *New York Times* critic A.J. Frutkin. Then Carrie dallies with her elusive ex, Mr. Big (Chris Noth), and just before the lavish wedding of Carrie's friend, Charlotte, she confesses her transgression to Aidan; he breaks up with her outside the church.

Corbett had only been signed for one season, but ardent *Sex and the City* fans inundated HBO's offices with letters pleading with the show's producers and writers to reunite Carrie with Aidan. He agreed to come back, and in the fourth season Carrie woos a newly buff and short–haired Aidan back. Corbett admitted he didn't lose that much weight for the on–screen transformation, he told Frutkin in the *New York Times.* He claimed the haircut tricked the eye, as did "sucking my stomach in when they said 'Action,'" he said. "That goes a long way." His character departed the show for good in a January of 2002 episode in which he nearly succeeds in evicting Carrie from her apartment after a disastrous broken engagement.

Returning to the big screen, Corbett had a small but comic role in the John Cusack/Kate Beckinsale romantic comedy *Serendipity* in 2001. He played Beckinsale's overly earnest, moderately famous musician boyfriend, Lars. Corbett told the *Arizona Republic*'s Cano–Murillo that the film's writing team "let me improvise; like, I got to pick out my own clothes and my instrument. I picked the Shanai. It's an Indian instrument. They tame the cobras with it." He and the cast headed to Toronto—a common stand–in for New York City in the entertainment industry—to shoot some of the movie's final scenes, and it was in a hotel bar that a genuinely serendipitous moment for Corbett's career occurred: he had been sent a quirky script for a small independent film about a Greek–American woman and her romance outside "the clan." Corbett was interested in playing the male lead, but the producers did not return his agent's call. At the Toronto hotel bar Corbett was telling someone, "'I've just read this great script called *My Big Fat Greek Wedding*,'" as he recalled in an interview with the *Birmingham Post*'s Alison Jones. Little did he know that Nia Vardalos, who wrote the script based on her one–woman stage play *My Big Fat Greek Wedding*, and the producer were standing nearby and overheard. "Nia said, 'You're talking about my script. I wrote that,'" Corbett told Jones. "She had seen me come in and knew that I was the guy. I swear to God ten minutes later I was offered the role, just like that."

My Big Fat Greek Wedding, released in the spring of 2002, turned out to be the surprise indie hit of the year and ended its successful run as the highest–grossing romantic comedy in box–office history. Vardalos played 30–ish Toula Portokalos, single and perennially unlucky in love. She works at her parents' Greek–cuisine restaurant, Dancing Zorba's, where she meets Ian Miller, a handsome teacher played by Corbett. Her fiercely nationalist family objects to the romance, and the conflict makes up the balance of the plot and ends on a predictably happy note. The movie, shot on a budget, wound up earning $30 million at the box office, and even spawned a spin–off television series.

Corbett, however, was unavailable for the television version of *My Big Fat Greek Wedding*, having already committed to FX's *Lucky*. Though he had been wary about taking on another television series after *Sex and the City*, fate intervened once again to guide his career. He was sent the *Lucky* script by an FX executive, and threw it away. "And it literally bounced back," *Houston Chronicle* writer Clifford Pugh quoted Corbett as saying. "I tried to throw it in again and it landed on top of the trash can, flat. And so I set it back up on the desk and I read it the next day."

The show's premise—that of a compulsive gambler trying to stay out of trouble while living in Las Vegas—appealed to Corbett as a way to break out of the "sensitive boyfriend" typecasting. "I never was asked to play a moody or darker role," the actor told Frutkin in the *New York Times*. "So I started to believe I wasn't right for them." The pilot episode kicked off with his character, Michael "Lucky" Linkletter, winning $1 million in a Las Vegas poker championship; in a flash–forward to several months later, he has lost it all, including his new bride. Now a used–car salesperson and Gamblers' Anonymous member, Linkletter needs to come up with a few thousand dollars to pay for his wife's funeral expenses. "Corbett is so likable," series co–creator Mark Cullen told the *Houston Chronicle*'s Pugh, "that even when he's not a great guy, you'll still follow him."

Lucky earned good reviews for its April of 2003 debut, and an Emmy nomination made it the first ever for a comedy series that aired on a basic cable channel. "Corbett is excellent as the eternally conflicted Lucky, torn between his compulsion to gamble and desire to make something of his life," declared *Hollywood Reporter* reviewer Barry Garron, who called *Lucky* "a daring and darkly humorous show spiced with wonderfully eccentric characters." Alan Sepinwall, writing in the *Star–Ledger* of Newark, New Jersey, claimed the actor delivered "the funniest, loosest, and most confident performance of his life," and commended him for passing on the *Greek Wedding* television series whose cast must "mug their way through terrible punchlines." In *Lucky*, Sepinwall wrote, "Corbett has a vehicle that taps deep into the well of his laid–back charisma while showing more depth and comic talent than he ever has before."

But ratings for the series slipped as the weeks passed, and FX executives cancelled its run in early August. Never unemployed for too long, Corbett had already lined up parts in *My Dinner with Jimi*, a tale of 1960s–era rock–star life, *Raising Helen*, a Kate Hudson comedy, and *Elvis Has Left the Building*. He maintains homes in Seattle and Los Angeles, and has never been married—though he has been romantically linked with the original *Sex and the City* columnist and author Candace Bushnell, and actresses Brittany Daniel and Bo Derek. His ability to shine on screen as the ideal male mate is a credit to his acting abilities, for he claims to be ardently single. "I'm not monogamous at all," he told *Independent Sunday*'s Tiffany Rose, and said that is why he is not married: "I don't want to be a guy who cheats on his wife." Rose asked him if he might still be a welder or hairdresser had stardom not happened for him. "Acting is not my life," he told the *Independent Sunday* journalist. "It's just something I do because I like it. I'm sure I would have found something else that I would have enjoyed doing. I'm a blue–collar worker at heart. If I wasn't in front of the camera, I would probably be an electrician."

Sources

Books

Contemporary Theatre, Film and Television, volume 32, Gale Group, 2000.

Periodicals

Arizona Republic, October 11, 2001, p. 8.
Atlanta Journal–Constitution, May 9, 2002, p. E1.
Birmingham Post (Birmingham, England), September 21, 2002, p. 4.
Boston Herald, July 24, 2002, p. 51.
Buffalo News, August 8, 1999; April 20, 2003.
Cosmopolitan, July 2002, p. 39.

Entertainment Weekly, October 23, 1992, p. 64; July 9, 1999, p. 88; April 11, 2003, p. 65.
Guardian (London, England), September 20, 2002, p. 13.
Hollywood Reporter, April 7, 2003, p. 9.
Houston Chronicle, May 18, 2002, p. 9; April 6, 2003, p. 10.
Independent Sunday (London, England), February 3, 2002, p. 3.
Los Angeles Times, September 14, 1997, p. 5.
New York Times, April 6, 2003, p. 31; April 8, 2003, p. E1.
People, December 2, 2002, pp. 84–85.
Seattle Times, January 21, 1996, p. 2.
Star–Ledger (Newark, NJ), April 8, 2003, p. 71.
Variety, September 29, 1997, p. 38.
WWD, October 2, 2001, p. 16.

—Carol Brennan

Nilo Cruz

Playwright

Born c. 1961, in Matanzas, Cuba; son of Nilo and Tina Cruz; married (divorced); children: Chloe Garcia–Cruz. *Education:* Attended Miami Dade College; Brown University, M.F.A., 1994.

Addresses: *Agent*—Peregrine Whittlesey, Peregrine Whittlesey Agency, 345 E. 80th St., New York, NY 10021. *Home*—New York, NY.

Career

Playwright. McCarter Theatre, Princeton, NJ, playwright–in–residence, 2000; New Theatre, Coral Gables, FL, playwright–in–residence, 2001–02. Has taught drama at Brown University, University of Iowa, and Yale University.

Member: New Dramatists.

Awards: Grants from National Endowment of the Arts, Rockefeller Foundation, and Theatre Communications Group; W. Alton Jones Award for *Night Train to Bolina;* Kennedy Center Fund for New American Plays award for *Two Sisters and a Piano;* American Theatre Critics/Steinberg New Play Award, Humana Festival for New American Plays, for *Anna in the Tropics,* 2003; Pulitzer Prize for drama, for *Anna in the Tropics,* 2003.

Sidelights

Nilo Cruz shot to national prominence in 2003 when he won the Pulitzer Prize for drama for his play *Anna in the Tropics,* a Depression–era tale about migrant Cubans working in a Tampa, Florida, cigar factory. The play "is about the power of art and how art can actually change your life," Cruz told Michael Kuchwara in a *Boston Globe* article. Cruz's tale of the Cuban–American experience centers on the "lector" of the factory, a man hired to provide cultural enrichment to the workers as they toil. The lector chooses to read Leo Tolstoy's *Anna Karenina* to the workers, and as the play progresses their lives come to mirror those of the characters in the Russian classic. The immigrant experience is a common theme in many of Cruz's plays. "He gives voice to the stories, the struggles and the sensibilities of the Cuban American," Rafael de Acha, the director of *Anna in the Topics,* was quoted as saying in the *Miami Herald,* "with grace, sensitivity, imagination and immense theatricality." In addition, Cruz is often praised for his poetic language and his ability to weave strains of other literary traditions, such as magic realism, into his works.

Cruz was born in Matanzas, Cuba, and for the first few years of his life, his father was in jail for attempting to emigrate. When Cruz was nine, his family successfully fled to the United States in 1970 and settled in the Little Havana area of Miami. He became interested in theater in the early 1980s as an actor, and in 1988 he directed *Mud,* by playwright Maria Irene Fornés, who in 1990 became the only other Latin American ever nominated for a Pulitzer Prize for drama. Fornés invited Cruz to join her In-tar Hispanic Playwrights Laboratory, and it was there that he began writing plays in earnest. Cruz's plays were soon produced in theaters across the country, from San Francisco to Princeton. Though several of his works have been staged by the Joseph Papp Public Theater in New York, Cruz is one of the few playwrights to win a Pulitzer without hav-ing a major presence on the New York theater scene. In fact, none of the Pulitzer judges had seen a per-formance of *Anna in the Tropics*; it won on the strength of its script alone.

In 2001, Cruz served as the playwright–in–residence for the New Theatre in Coral Gables, Florida, which commissioned *Anna in the Tropics*. The main action of the play pits the women against the men, with the dashing lector as the central figure of both ad-miration and contempt. The impoverished women, led by Ofelia and her two daughters, Conchita and Marela, are mesmerized by Juan Julian and are swept away from their dreary Ybor City lives by his recitation of *Anna Karenina*. But the men feel differently. Some, like Ofelia's brother–in–law Cheche, view Juan with ambivalence, but others, like Conchita's unfaithful husband, see him as un-welcome competition. Tensions mount when at-tempts to keep their tight–knit community together are imperiled by encroaching industrialization; cigar–making machines are on the horizon, and soon the lector—not to mention the workers' own positions—may be obsolete. The play opened to good reviews for both the playwright and the cast. Despite the characters' flaws, wrote Christine Dolen of the *Miami Herald*, "each of Cruz's characters com-mands attention and elicits empathy." Bruce Weber of the *New York Times* called it "a lyrical paean to a lost pocket of culture and a lost way of life," which exudes "the romance and tragedy of Tolstoy."

One of Cruz's first plays to be produced, the semi–autobiographical *A Park in Our House,* harkens back to the playwright's youth in Cuba, when Fidel Cas-tro rolled out his "Ten Million Tons of Sugar Har-vest" program in 1970. When a Russian botanist comes to stay with a Cuban family as part of an ex-change program, the family is distracted from their economic deprivations by his presence. The mother of the family, Ofelina, is the emotional fulcrum of the play; she dreams of a romantic reconciliation with her husband, Hilario. But Hilario, a low–ranking government official, is obsessed with his desire to build a park in order to boost his reputa-tion within the administration. The allegorical na-ture of the play is borne out through those who share their house. Ofelina and Hilario's gay nephew, Camilo, regains his voice after years of being mute; their niece, Pilar, longs to seek happiness in the So-

viet Union. Their cousin, Fifo, a photographer, cap-tures the symbolism of their predicament through his photographs. According to Cruz, the play at-tempts to understand the human reaction to op-pression: "They take flight and move into the imagi-nation in order to transcend their immediate reality," he said in *American Theater.* In terms of its autobiographical elements, Cruz said that writing *A Park in Our House* "helped me understand my own loss of innocence."

Another of Cruz's early plays, *A Bicycle Country,* takes place on a raft manned by three refugees, known as *baseleros,* who are making the treacherous journey from Cuba to Florida. They pass the time by telling the stories of their lives, and as their situ-ation becomes more desperate, their stories take on mythical and hallucinatory qualities. Julio is a wheelchair–bound widower recovering from a stroke who is sure that all the misfortunes of his life will evaporate once he sets foot on American soil. Julio's gloom is tempered only moderately by his traveling companions: Ines, the nurse who cares for him, and his friend, Pepe. Like Cruz's other plays, *A Bicycle Country* concerns both the prisons of the physical world and the psychological shackles the human spirit seeks to overcome in order to be free. According to Diane Thiel of *Brown Alumni Maga-zine,* "the waters of the Straits of Florida seem to have their own role" in the play as the metaphori-cal walls of the jail that must be breached for the characters to gain their freedom. Other reviewers also noticed the play's use of water as a symbol. Madeleine Shaner of *Back Stage West* wrote that "Cruz's language is uncluttered, simplistic, some-times banal, but informed by an unpretentious po-etry that rocks with the inevitable bonding of the first act and the rhythm of the unforgiving ocean in the second."

Two Sisters and a Piano, though not autobiographi-cal, features characters based on Cruz's sisters as well as on the Cuban poet Maria Elena Cruz Varela, who was imprisoned by Castro for her writings. The play is set in Havana in 1991, where the sisters Maria, a romance novelist, and Sofia, a pianist, are under house arrest following Maria's release from prison. Her crime was writing a letter to Castro urg-ing him to support the Soviet reforms known as *perestroika.* In order to get her hands on the letters her exiled husband has mailed to her from Europe, Maria offers to tell some of her romantic stories to her police protector. The sympathetic policeman, Lieutenant Portuondo, is secretly a fan of Maria's novels, and eventually he seduces her. Sofia's ro-mantic interest is the piano tuner, Victor, who flirts with her as he tunes her piano, but their relation-ship goes stale when Sofia's house arrest prevents her from seeing him on a regular basis. Above all, the sisters are tied to each other in their isolation and in their memories, as the regime's grip around their lives tightens.

Critics recognized *Two Sisters and a Piano* as a mature continuation of Cruz's earlier works. Robert L. Daniels of *Variety* called it "a provocative observation of the snail–paced changes of Cuba's political landscape" that is "layered with lyrical flights of romanticism." Ben Brantley of the *New York Times* noted parallels to Anton Chekhov's *Three Sisters,* saying that Cruz's play "somehow seems more old–fashioned than its Russian antecedent," even though it "fitfully evokes a poetic appreciation of the visions of phantom lives bred in circumscribed existences." David A. Rosenberg of *Back Stage* praised the play, calling it an "affecting piece, even if stronger on releasing passion than explaining politics." Similarly, noted *Variety*'s Daniels, "there is a restless ambiguity in the narrative, and an undercurrent of tragedy that is never fully realized." Survival instincts are more the point than politics, according to Cruz, who told Randy Gener in the *New York Times* that "*Two Sisters and a Piano* is about two women who, even though they live in very harsh conditions, make the best of their lives. They create a little paradise in their house. Even though they are under house arrest, they bring out the beautiful china and use a tablecloth. It's the integrity of that, the dignity of it, that moves me."

In 2002, Cruz adapted Colombian author Gabriel García Marquéz's short story "A Very Old Man with Enormous Wings" as a musical that premiered at the Children's Theatre in Minneapolis, Minnesota. The story concerns an injured angel who falls to earth and is nursed back to health by two children. Though the children try to protect him, the adults in their village see the old man as a curiosity to be exploited. Soon he is caged and put on display where he is at the mercy of people's misguided desire to be cured of all their physical and spiritual pain. Rohan Preston of the Minneapolis *Star Tribune* wrote that the play "is full of the layering common in Caribbean and Latin American cultures," in which ancient Earth–based religions coexist with Christianity. While Marquéz's story is steeped in his trademark blend of magic realism, Cruz told Preston that for him, the question is not so much magic as it is religion: "It's this mesh of Catholicism and Yoruba religions, for example—that's reality." Or, as Robert Simonson of *Playbill* quoted Cruz as saying, his plays are "realism that is magical."

In 2003, Cruz's Pulitzer Prize–winning play, *Anna in the Tropics,* eventually opened on Broadway at the Royale Theater, starring Jimmy Smits in the role of the lector. In January of 2004, his play *Beauty of the Father* debuted in Coral Gables, Florida. That same year, Cruz began working on his next play, which was about a Caribbean hurricane.

Consistently, critics have commented favorably on Cruz's poetic language. "The words of Nilo Cruz waft from a stage like a scented breeze," wrote the *Miami Herald*'s Dolen. "They sparkle and prickle and swirl, enveloping those who listen in both a specific place and time." In addition, Cruz's works are steeped in his cultural heritage. His plays are "imagistic dramatic poems," wrote John Williams of *American Theatre,* that are "rich in myth, symbol and metaphor." Commenting on *A Bicycle Country, Brown Alumni*'s Thiel similarly wrote that Cruz's "language becomes increasingly rich with [the characters'] 'hallucinations' and evocative surreal visions."

Though Cruz is acknowledged as a rising star of the Cuban–American literary scene, he says he doesn't aim to speak for the community as a whole, nor is he trying to advocate for political change in his homeland. As he told Gener in the *New York Times,* "Ultimately my plays are about being an individual. Belonging to a particular group, left or right, entails a political loss. When you embrace your whole being and all that you can be in this world, that's the strongest position."

Selected writings

A Park in Our House, Magic Theatre, San Francisco, CA, 1996.

Dancing on Her Knees, Joseph Papp Public Theater, New York, NY, 1996.

A Bicycle Country, Florida Stage, Manalapan, FL, 1999.

Two Sisters and a Piano, McCarter Theater, Princeton, NJ, 1999.

(Adapter) Gabriel García Marquéz, *A Very Old Man with Enormous Wings,* Children's Theater, Minneapolis, MN, 2002.

Anna in the Tropics, New Theatre, Coral Gables, FL, 2002; New York, NY, November, 2003.

Lorca in a Green Dress, produced at the Oregon Shakespeare Festival, 2003.

Beauty of the Father, New Theatre, Coral Gables, FL, 2004.

Also author of the plays *Night Train to Bolina,* produced in San Francisco, CA, *Hortensia and the Museum of Dreams,* and *Graffiti.* Translator of Federico García Lorca's *The House of Bernarda Alba* and *Dona Rosita, the Spinster.*

Sources

Periodicals

American Theatre, July–August, 1996, p. 8.
Back Stage, March 15, 1996, p. 60; March 3, 2000, p. 56.
Back Stage West, April 12, 2001, p. 16.
Boston Globe, April 7, 2003.
Brown Alumni, March–April 2001.
Entertainment Weekly, December 12, 2003, p. 41.

Miami Herald, October 14, 2002.
New York Times, February 16, 2000, p. E1; February 27, 2000, p. 8, p. 22; April 9, 2003.
Playbill, April 7, 2003.
Star Tribune (Minneapolis, MN), September 6, 2002.
United Press International, December 8, 2003.
Variety, March 1, 1999, p. 93.

Online

"The Pulitzer Prize Winners: 2003," Pulitzer Prize, http://www.pulitzer.org (July 3, 2004).

Ben Curtis

AP/Wide World Photos

Professional golfer

Born May 26, 1977, in Ostrander, OH; son of Bob and Janice Curtis; married Candace Beatty, August, 2003. *Education:* Graduated from Kent State University (recreation management degree), 2000.

Addresses: *Agent*—Jay Danzi, IMG, 420 West 45th St., New York, NY 10036.

Career

Professional golfer, 2002—. Won Ohio Amateur Tournament, 1999; won Players' Amateur Open, 1999; won Ohio Amateur Tournament, 2000; qualified for United States PGA Tour on his third attempt, 2002; played 13 PGA events, 2003; won British Open, 2003.

Sidelights

Ben Curtis was a Professional Golf Association (PGA) Tour rookie, ranked 396th in the world rankings, and was a 500–to–1 shot to win the 2003 British Open, his first major championship. To the surprise of the golf world, win he did, beating the world's best golfers. He was the first player to win a major championship on the first try since Francis Ouimet won the 1913 U.S. Open.

Curtis, who was born in Ostrander, Ohio, grew up playing golf; his family's home was only 50 yards from the practice putting green of the Millcreek Golf Course, which his maternal grandfather had built in 1973. He first swung a club when he was three years old, and became so obsessed by the game that when he was 12, his parents moved to another house two miles from the course, hoping the distance would distract him into thinking about something else so he could develop more diverse interests. However, this ploy did not work, and Curtis remained obsessed with golf.

At Buckeye Valley High School, Curtis was already an elite player, and was recruited by almost every major college golf program in the United States. He chose to go to Kent State University because it was small and close to his family's home. While there, he became a three–time All–American and in 2000, was ranked No. 1 among world amateurs. As an amateur, Curtis was a two–time winner of the Ohio State Amateur Tournament, and also won the Players' Amateur Open. Interestingly, other than a few lessons he took from a local pro as a teenager, and coaching from Kent State's Herb Page, he has received no formal instruction in golf. "He likes his mind uncluttered," Page told Seth Davis in *Sports Illustrated.* Page noted that the one time he tried to give Curtis detailed instructions on his swing, Curtis became so distracted that it took him six months to clear his mind and go back to his much more effective, natural swing. Curtis himself told Davis, "I grew up on a driving range where you had to pick up your own balls after you hit them, so I learned the game by playing."

After his senior year at Kent State, Curtis received offers from several sports management agencies, which typically do not recruit such young players. Curtis told *Sports Illustrated*'s Davis, "That gave me a lot of confidence because if they believed in me, why shouldn't I?" He signed with the well–known agency IMG, which got him a two–year sponsorship with golf equipment manufacturer Titleist.

In December of 2000, Curtis qualified to play on the PGA Tour on his third try. In 2003, he traveled to England to play in the British Open, paying his own way because unlike the other players, he did not have a sponsor. He took only two cousins with him, hired a caddy from the European PGA Tour, and settled in to play. As an unknown, he was not expected to win, and he only wanted to hold his ground. However, he did win, decisively.

Curtis won by closing with a 2–under 69, the only player to break par at 283. He told a *SI.com* reporter, "I came in here this week just trying to play the best I could, hopefully make the cut and compete on the weekend. Obviously, I did that and went out there and probably played the best weekend of my life." Of all the other golfers at the Open, none could match him, including famed golfers Tiger Woods and Vijay Singh.

After winning the British Open, Curtis told *SI.com* that he was aware that some observers thought his win was a fluke and that he did not belong among the ranks of the world's best golfers. "But I know I do, so that's all that matters," he said. As a result of his win, he earned more than $1.1 million. "I'm very fortunate to be a winner with all the great names on that trophy—Jack Nicklaus, Arnold Palmer, Ben Hogan, Bobby Jones," he said.

After winning the British Open, Curtis garnered more publicity than he had bargained for. As a result, his every move was scrutinized by reporters and others in the golf world. When he decided to withdraw from the Greater Hartford Open the week after the British Open, he was attacked by some reporters, as well as by fellow golfers. Peter Jacobsen, who won the tournament, told *Sports Illustrated*'s Davis, "I was disappointed that Ben withdrew. You don't do that. I know you have to think about yourself and your health, but in the short term you have

to keep your obligation." Curtis said he regretted withdrawing, but did it so that he could spend time with family members who had been unable to go to England for the British Open.

Curtis was also distracted in August of 2003 by his wedding to Candace Beatty; he had proposed to her during a Caribbean cruise in December of 2001. Beatty had played golf for the Kent State women's team, and she and Curtis were close friends for two years before he confessed to her that he was in love with her. "I'm shy in everything," Curtis told *Sports Illustrated*'s Davis. "You can kind of control what happens on the course, but you can't control a situation like that." Fortunately, Beatty said yes to his proposal. The wedding took place on the same day as the NEC Invitational, where Curtis calmly made par to conclude his third round; three hours later, he and Beatty were wed. His cousin, Mike Birkenheier, told Dennis Manoloff in the Cleveland *Plain Dealer*, "About 400 people are going to be at the wedding, and I'm proud of the fact that only a few were invited after the British [Open]. He's the kind of guy who will try to be more normal after something like that. He doesn't need to be ridiculous." In *Crain's Cleveland Business*, Brian Tucker commented on Curtis's unassuming personality: "It couldn't happen to a nicer guy…. He's the kind of pro golfer you wish they all were: genuine, friendly, sincerely interested in his playing partners."

Sources

Periodicals

Crain's Cleveland Business, July 28, 2003, p. 10.
Daily Telegraph, October 15, 2003, p. 7.
Plain Dealer (Cleveland, OH), July 23, 2003, p. B8; August 24, 2003, p. A1.
Sports Illustrated, August 11, 2003, p. G20.
Weekend Australian (Sydney, Australia), July 26, 2003, p. T15.

Online

"Ben Curtis," PGATour.com, http://www.golfweb.com/players/02/26/21/bio.html (November 17, 2003).
"Big Ben," *SI.com*, http://www.sportsillustrated.cnn.com/golfonline/2003/british_open/news/2003/07/20/open_Sunday_ap/ (December 26, 2003).

—Kelly Winters

Crispin Davis

Courtesy of Reed Elsevier

Chief Executive Officer of Reed Elsevier

Born March 19, 1949, in England; married; children: three daughters. *Education:* Oriel College, Oxford University, M.A. (history).

Addresses: *E–mail*—crispin.davis@reedelsevier.co. uk. *Home*—Hills End, Titlarks Hill, Sunningdale, Berkshire SL5 0JO, United Kingdom. *Office*—c/o Reed Elsevier PLC, 25 Victoria St., London SW1H 0EX, United Kingdom.

Career

Assistant brand manager, Procter & Gamble (P&G), 1970; served as marketing director of United Kingdom operations, P&G, 1978–82; marketing director of German operations, P&G, 1982–85; division manager of North American Foods Division, P&G, 1985–86; president of North American Foods Division, P&G, 1986–1990; managing director of European operations, United Distillers, 1990–92; group managing director, 1992–93; chief executive, Aegis Group, 1994–99; chief executive officer, Reed Elsevier, 1999—.

Sidelights

One of the hottest properties in the publishing world today, British executive Crispin Davis engineered a near–miraculous turnaround at Reed Elsevier Group, the Anglo–Dutch media giant that is a dominant force in the business, educational, legal, and medical/scientific information business. Named chief executive officer of Reed Elsevier in mid–1999, Davis quickly realigned the company's management structure and has steadily increased profit margins. Davis has also managed to position Reed Elsevier as one of the Internet's top revenue–makers, a significant factor in the company's consistent outperformance of other companies in the media sector, most of which has been mired in recession over the last few years.

Davis's strategy for the future of Reed Elsevier is built on innovation. In an interview with Raymond Snoddy of London, England's *Times,* Davis said, "We are not just waiting for the economy to recover. Let's assume there is no recovery. How do we get faster top–line growth? We are emphasizing innovation much more." He told Snoddy that each division at Reed Elsevier has been charged with bringing to market each year a set number of new initiatives in order to keep growing company revenue: "What I am looking for is a constant stream of new initiatives." Division managers have been instructed to closely examine the activity of their customers in order to identify new services that might prove useful.

Born on March 19, 1949, Davis, the son of an attorney, grew up in the English county of Kent, southeast of London. A healthy sibling rivalry pitted Davis against his three brothers, all of whom have gone on to make successful lives for themselves. Opting for careers in the business world were Davis and his brother, Ian, who on July 1, 2003, took over as the new managing director of McKinsey & Company, the international management consulting organization. Their two brothers followed their father into the practice of law. One maintains law offices in the City of London, the mile–square business heart of the city, while the other serves as a judge. Davis studied at Charterhouse, an exclusive boarding school in nearby Sussex.

After completing his studies at Oxford University's Oriel College, Davis in 1970 began his business career as an assistant brand manager for Procter & Gamble. During his two decades with P&G, he served as United Kingdom marketing director, managing director of German operations, and president of the company's North American Foods Division. In 1990 Davis left P&G to take over as managing director of European operations for United Distillers (UD), the subsidiary of Guinness PLC responsible for the brewer's hard spirits sales. In mid–1992 Davis was named managing director of UD, but he resigned 15 months later after clashing with Guinness chairman Tony Greener over the direction the company should take. During this period Davis also served as a director on the Guinness board.

Somewhat chastened by his experience at UD, Davis did a good deal of soul searching. As he told Neil Bennett of the *Sunday Telegraph*, "It was the first time I had failed at something, but you learn more from your failures than from your successes. It made me think what I would have done differently. I would have put much greater emphasis on building trust in me within the organization. Here I was, going into a company that had been extremely successful and saying, 'This is how we should do things.' A lot of people were somewhere between skeptical and hostile. I should have spent more time building their trust."

Davis entertained a number of offers—including executive posts with both PepsiCo and Fisons—but in the end decided to accept the challenge of pulling once–powerful advertising agency Aegis Group PLC back from the brink of bankruptcy. He signed on as Aegis chief executive officer in 1994, and under his direction the company's market capitalization grew from £180 million to more than £2 billion. But, mindful of his missteps at UD, he took a radically different approach at Aegis. Rather than going off on his own to develop a management plan, as he had done at UD, Davis called upon the entire Aegis team to help him come up with a strategy for turning the company around. It made all the difference in the world, he told Bennett. "They owned the plan."

The wonders worked by Davis at Aegis did not go unnoticed. Shortly after Morris Tabaksblat, former chairman of Unilever, hired on as Reed Elsevier's new chairman in 1999, he brought in Davis as the company's sole chief executive. For his part, Davis wasted no time in getting things turned around. As one of his first moves, he cleaned house at the senior management level, replacing eleven of the company's top 12 executives and cutting head–office personnel by 40 percent. In its first full three fiscal years under Davis's direction, Reed Elsevier steadily improved its net profit margin: from just under one percent in fiscal 2000 to 3.6 percent in fiscal 2002.

In a June of 2002 interview with *BusinessWeek*'s Diane Brady, Davis discussed his strategy for the company: "The most fundamental decision was to focus on the four core businesses—science, legal, business–to–business, and education. At the time, it was thought we should break the company up, but I thought they were all great assets we could grow. There were two gaps: medical publishing and U.S.–schools education. Harcourt was the ideal acquisition that filled the gap perfectly." (In 2001, Davis engineered the acquisition of Harcourt General, the American textbook publisher, giving Reed Elsevier a solid foothold in the United States educational market.)

Another key to Reed Elsevier's success under Davis has been the company's decision to sharply increase its investments in the Internet, moving an ever–larger share of its businesses online. In announcing the company's Internet strategy, Davis told Paula J. Hane of *Information Today*: "Reed Elsevier has powerful and valuable assets: leading brands and market positions, high–quality and in–depth content, scale, professional people, and financial strength. Coupled with the exciting opportunities opened up to us by the Internet, this represents a strong platform for growth. We are determined to build aggressively on this with a new management team and new strategy in place."

Sources

Books

Complete Marquis Who's Who, Marquis Who's Who, 2003.

Periodicals

BusinessWeek, June 26, 2002.
Forbes, November 11, 2002, p. 130.
Information Today, September 1999; April 2000.

Online, May 2000.
Publishers Weekly, July 26, 1999, p. 17.
Reuters Business Report, February 24, 2000.
Sunday Telegraph, February 27, 2000, p. 8.
Times (London, England), June 16, 2003.

Online

"Announcement of Mr. Crispin Davis as Chief Executive of Reed Elsevier," Investis, http://produc
tioninvestis.com/ReedElsevierPlc/pressreleases/press1999/1999–7–20/ (June 16, 2003).
Biography Resource Center Online, Gale Group, 2003.
"Crispin Davis–Chief Executive Officer," Reed Elsevier, http://www.reedelsevier.co.uk/reed
mediacentre/crispindavis/ (June 18, 2003).

—*Don Amerman*

Paige Davis

Amy Graves/WireImage.com

Host of *Trading Spaces*

Born Mindy Paige Davis, October 15, 1969, in Philadelphia, PA; married Patrick Page (a stage actor), 2001. *Education:* Attended Meadow School of Arts at Southern Methodist University, Dallas, TX.

Addresses: *Home*—New York, NY. *Office*—c/o Discovery Communications, Inc., One Discovery Pl., Silver Spring, MD 20910.

Career

Commercial actress in Los Angeles, early 1990s; performed as a dancer on a Beach Boys tour; appeared in the national touring company of *Beauty and the Beast,* c. 1995–98; understudy to Chita Rivera and Marilu Henner in the national tour of *Chicago;* joined the cast of *Trading Spaces,* the Learning Channel show, 2001; first book published, 2003.

Sidelights

Former Broadway actress Paige Davis hosts the cult–favorite home–decorating reality–TV show *Trading Spaces* on cable staple The Learning Channel (TLC). The show invites pairs of neighbors to re-decorate one room in each other's house, and Davis is on hand to walk them through the "reveal," or moment of truth at the end of the show when they return home to a sometimes spectacular, sometimes stomach–turning new room. The show has attracted a devoted fan base, with season DVDs available and even a behind–the–scenes tell–all from its perky host published in 2003. Prior to joining the show, the onetime *Beauty and the Beast* dancer and singer

had little experience with tools or paint. "Home improvement was not my specialty at all," the Manhattanite confessed in an interview with Thomas Nord of the *Courier–Journal*. "Now I hear myself saying things like, 'No! That needs to dry first.'"

Born in 1969, Davis grew up in several different locales. She was born in Philadelphia, Pennsylvania, spent some elementary–school years in Sun Prairie, Wisconsin, and finished high school at the Youth Performing Arts School of Louisville, Kentucky. A dedicated gymnast, Davis found a new calling at the age of 13 when she discovered her mother's *West Side Story* cast recording. "I would play Anita ..., Maria, Tony—the whole bit. I would do the whole show," Davis said of the ill–fated romantic characters in the *Courier–Journal* interview with Nord. "That's how it started."

Davis was a performing–arts major at the Southern Methodist University in Dallas, Texas. When she graduated, she moved to Los Angeles, California, and began winning television commercial and video work. Once, she landed a job as a back–up dancer for a Beach Boys tour, but her first real break came when she was cast in the role of Babette the Featherduster in the national touring company of *Beauty and the Beast,* the Disney musical that premiered on

Broadway in the early 1990s. Davis also served as an understudy to Chita Rivera and Marilu Henner in a tour of the hit musical *Chicago.*

The *Trading Spaces* job came to Davis almost by accident—a friend of hers who enjoyed the show during its first season learned that the host had quit, and suggested that Davis try to get an audition. Her effusive personality won over the show's producers, though she had little on–camera experience to date. Based on a hit British television show called *Changing Rooms, Trading Spaces* debuted on TLC in September of 2000. Its premise involves a pair of neighbors who exchange house keys for two days and buckle down to a major room re–do with the help of a design professional. Each are given a $1,000 budget to work with, and a carpenter is on hand to help out as well, but the guest homeowners do much of the grunt work.

With her cheery enthusiasm, Davis seemed a natural for the job, and the show climbed steadily in the ratings after she joined in 2001. She was stunned by this turn of events, as she told the *Sarasota Herald Tribune*'s Charlie Huisking. "When I auditioned, I had no idea what it would become," Davis said. "I figured it would be a chance to spread my wings and cut my chops on TV, hidden away on cable on a show no one would see. Boy, was I wrong." Soon, *Trading Spaces*'s Saturday–night new–episode slot began landing No. 1 regular–cable ratings numbers, luring an average of 6.4 million viewers, and TLC executives increased the episodes per season from 45 to 60.

Essentially, Davis's job is to introduce the couples and their room challenges to viewers, and then show the renovation project in its speeded–up stages, but she is also the soother when the situation warrants it. Despite the potential for tears, there seemed to be no shortage of Americans who were willing to spend a weekend with Davis and the *Trading Spaces* team for a free room re–do. When the show's crew arrives in a neighborhood, people often sit outside on lawn chairs. The crux of the show comes at the end, when Davis takes the homeowners through to see what their neighbors did to their house. "A traditional how–to show says your home is an expression of your personality," *Time* critic James Poniewozik asserted in trying to define the show's appeal. "*Trading Spaces* says your home is an expression of your personality—and not everybody likes you."

Sometimes those rooms are changed back the same day, Davis divulged in her book, *Paige by Paige: A Year of Trading Spaces.* Published as the fourth

season's taping schedule was underway in mid–2003, the tome contains an insider's view of the show, based on a diary she kept for several months. In it, she also recounts some episodes that became legendary among the show's cast, crew, and viewers. One participant could be heard sobbing off–camera when she saw that her beloved fireplace mantle had been hidden, and Davis admitted that was part of the show's allure for viewers. "It does make good television," she told the *Courier–Journal*'s Nord. "I have friends who tell me they love it when that happens. I hate it. It's terribly awkward and sad."

Trading Spaces has spun off into special celebrity–week shows and even a "sequel," *Trading Spaces: Family,* which features the brutally frank opinions of teenagers on aesthetic matters. Davis also has a minor celebrity following herself, and has appeared on *The Tonight Show* and *Hollywood Squares.* Davis's most memorable small–screen performance, however, was on another TLC staple, *A Wedding Story,* which aired in December of 2001. She wed fellow stage actor Patrick Page, whom she met while on the *Beauty and the Beast* tour. Forced to keep her maiden name, lest she become "Paige Page," Davis and her husband share a Manhattan apartment whose decorating scheme is mundane, she claims. "It's very Pottery Barn," she told *Boston Herald*'s Stephanie Schorow. "I want Ligne Roset [a contemporary–furnishings company]."

Selected writings

Paige by Paige: A Year of Trading Spaces, Meredith Books (Des Moines, IA), 2003.

Sources

Arizona Republic, April 20, 2003, p. E2.
Boston Herald, August 17, 2003, p. 49.
Broadcasting and Cable, December 9, 2002, p. 16.
Courier–Journal (Louisville, Kentucky), August 6, 2002, p. 1C.
Entertainment Weekly, March 22, 2002, p. 26; April 11, 2003, p. 50.
Good Housekeeping, June 2003, p. 240.
People, May 27, 2002, p. 151; July 20, 2002, p. 66.
Sarasota Herald Tribune, May 13, 2003, p. E1.
Time, April 22, 2002, p. 62.
Wisconsin State Journal, August 20, 2003, p. D1.

—*Carol Brennan*

Dido

Singer and songwriter

Born Dido Armstrong, December 25, 1971, in London, England; daughter of William (a book publisher) and Claire Armstrong. *Education:* Attended Guildhall School of Music, London, England; attended law school.

Addresses: *Record company*—Arista Records, 6 W. 57th St., New York, NY 10019; http://www.arista. com. *Website*—http://www.didomusic.com/.

Career

Performed as a backup singer for Faithless, 1996–99; signed with Arista label, 1997; released *No Angel,* 1999; rapper Eminem sampled "Thank You" in his hit single "Stan," 2000; released *Life for Rent,* 2003.

Awards:

Brit Award for best British female, 2002; Brit Award for best British album for *No Angel,* 2002; World Music Award for best–selling British artist, 2002; World Music Award for top pop female, 2002; World Music Award for top adult contemporary artist, 2002; Bambi Award (Germany) for best international pop act, 2003; Brit Award for best British single for "White Flag," 2004; Brit Award for best British female, 2004.

Sidelights

Famed for writing songs that seemed to have an Everywoman spirit, British pop singer Dido started as a backup singer for her brother's band,

Faithless. With her very first solo effort, *No Angel,* she soared to the top of the charts and into the hearts of millions around the world. To those looking from the outside in, her success seemed to happen overnight, but in reality Dido's road to stardom was a lifelong process.

Dido Armstrong was born and raised in London, England; she was the daughter of book publisher William Armstrong and his wife, Claire, a homemaker whose hobby was writing poetry. Her parents named her after a Carthaginian queen. "Dido, she was an African queen, and in Latin literature, she was sort of a warrior queen, who actually ended up killing herself over a guy, which was a bit depressing," Dido explained to iAfrica.com.

The Armstrong household did not have a television during Dido's childhood, so she found other ways to entertain herself. At the age of five, she stole a recorder from her school's lost and found and discovered a passion for music as a result. Without any prompting from her parents, she practiced for six hours a day and sometimes more. The following year, she began attending the Guildhall School of Music in London, where she added the violin and piano to her talents. Dido discussed her early dedication in an interview with Jeff Chu at *Time Europe.*

"I'd do like two hours on each instrument and maybe an hour on harmony and composition.... I have respect for how I was when I was younger, because I'm so not that cool now," she said.

As a teenager, Dido toured the United Kingdom with a classical music ensemble, primarily focused on her chosen instruments. But when she was 16, her focus started to shift. She discovered the music of Ella Fitzgerald and became very interested in singing. Dido's brother, Rollo, who had begun pursuing his own musical career, discouraged her from her new direction. "I used to tell Rollo that Dido had a lovely voice," Faithless lead singer Sister Bliss told *People,* "and he looked at me and said, 'My sister can't sing!'"

Undaunted like her warrior namesake, Dido followed her dream anyway and began performing with a variety of bands in London. At the same time, she worked for a book publishing company and attended law school. She started in publishing as an assistant and eventually moved up to become a literary agent.

In the mid–1990s, Dido finally convinced her brother of her abilities and landed a spot as a backup singer with Rollo's trip–hop group Faithless. The group's 1996 debut album, *Reverence,* sold more than five million copies, and Dido decided to explore the idea of writing and performing her own music. "The Faithless thing was such a good experience, but I knew that had really nothing to do with me," Dido told Charlie Craine of Hip Online. "I was just singing backup vocals. It's such a different thing when I went on alone. I was like, 'Why is everyone looking at me?'"

Although she had been making good money as a literary agent, she decided to take a year off, with her supervisor's blessing, to work on her music career full time. Her boss assured her that she could have her old job back if things did not work out. She spent part of her new free time touring with Faithless and part of the time writing and recording her own songs. A year to the day after she left her job, she signed a recording contract with the Arista label. Although she had not sent her demo tape to anyone at Arista, the record company invited her to meet with the head of the company, Clive Davis, at the Dorchester Hotel in London. "I think my demo tape just drifted around the music industry through friends and by word–of–mouth, basically," Dido told *Time Europe*'s Chu. It became clear that the meeting was a success when Davis became enthused enough to jump in with backing vocals for her performance.

Dido released her debut, *No Angel,* in the United States in June of 1999. Accompanying it was the single "Here With Me," which was later chosen as the theme song for the WB television show *Roswell.* Dido produced the album with the help of her brother, Rollo (who had become one of her biggest supporters), Rick Nowels, and former Verve and Crowded House producer Youth. "Dreamy pop, electronica shadings, folk guitars, and soulful vocals bend and blend together on *No Angel,*" Christopher John Farley wrote in his *Time* review. That same year, Dido appeared on Faithless's second release, *Sunday 8pm,* which included her song "My Lover's Gone."

Dido had to wait until October of 2000 to release *No Angel* in Europe due to contractual disputes with her European label, Cheeky Records. The CD was released after BMG Records purchased the small label. *No Angel*'s success in the United States did not come quickly. Dido toured small venues around the country until one day she received a letter from rapper Eminem in which he explained that he wanted to sample her tune "Thank You" in a song he was working on, "Stan." He included a CD containing the song so she could hear how he would use it. By this time, "Thank You" had already appeared on the soundtrack for the film *Sliding Doors,* starring Gwyneth Paltrow. Dido gave Eminem permission to use the sample—a decision that launched her career into superstardom.

"I'm blown away that so many people decided to investigate or buy my record on the strength of hearing six lines of it on 'Stan,'" Dido said in her website biography. "I think that's brilliant." The outcome of this brilliance was that *No Angel* spent 100 weeks on the British album charts and sold more than 12 million copies.

In 2001, Dido wrote the song "I'm Not a Girl, Not Yet a Woman" for Britney Spears and witnessed Elton John singing her lines from "Stan" when he performed with Eminem at the Grammy Awards ceremony. "It was too surreal for me, just too surreal to see Elton John singing my song," Dido told Tom Lanham of *Teen People.* "He's one of the biggest singer–songwriters in the world. And there he was, singing my funny little song."

In June of 2001, Dido launched her first tour as a headliner after nearly two years on the road. Her tour in support of *No Angel* finally came to an end in May of 2002, and she found herself in a completely different place in her life from where she had been when she started. "When I made *No An-*

gel, I was in my early 20s, and now I'm 30," Dido told Corey Moss of VH1.com. "I'm a completely different person. My world has changed."

Before she returned to the studio to record her second album, Dido decided to take some time off for herself and traveled to various places, including New York, Thailand, Canada, and Ireland. Refreshed and ready to start the process again, she released *Life for Rent* on September 29, 2003. The album included the single "White Flag," and for the video of that song Dido invited David Boreanaz, star of the television show *Angel,* to appear with her.

On *Life for Rent,* Dido took a more philosophical approach to her songwriting, particularly on the title track. "It's about not being afraid to take chances or to live life to the full," Dido said in her website biography. "It's so easy to slip into complacency or to disengage from the world. This album works as a reminder to myself not to do that." In 2004, Dido headed out on a North American tour in support of the album, before heading to Europe.

Dido's success continued with *Life for Rent,* which debuted at number one on the European top 100 albums chart. But despite all of her success, Dido still considered herself an underdog. "No matter how successful I am, I'm always going to be trying to be a better singer or songwriter or producer or player or whatever," she explained on her website. "In my own mind, I'm always going to be coming from behind, and that seems to suit me."

Selected discography

Solo

(Contributor) *Sliding Doors* (soundtrack), MCA, 1998.
No Angel, Arista, 1999.
Roswell (soundtrack), Nettwerk, 2002.
Life for Rent, Arista, 2003.

With Faithless

Reverence, Arista, 1996.
Sunday 8pm, Arista, 1998.
Outrospective, Arista, 2001.

Sources

Periodicals

Billboard Bulletin, October 10, 2003; October 17, 2003.
Entertainment Weekly, October 20, 2000; December 1, 2000; August 1, 2003.
People, April 30, 2001; October 20, 2003; December 1, 2003.
Teen People, May 15, 2001.
Time, June 7, 1999.

Online

"Dido Biography," *RollingStone.com,* http://www.rollingstone.com/?searchtype=RSArtist&query=dido (July 3, 2004).
"Dido Gets Extreme on 'Life,'" *RollingStone.com,* http://www.rollingstone.com/news/story?id=5935759&pageid=rs.ArtistArticles&pageregion=mainRegion (July 3, 2004).
Dido Official Website, http://www.didomusic.com (July 3, 2004).
"Dido: The Dreamlife of Angels," VH1.com, http://www.vh1.com/artists/interview/1478218/09152003/dido.jhtml (July 3, 2004).
"Dido, Travis Take Vancouver," *RollingStone.com,* http://www.rollingstone.com/news/story?id=5931792&pageid=rs.ArtistArticles&pageregion=mainRegion (July 3, 2004).
"Dido Won't Let Success Go to Her Head," VH1.com, http://www.vh1.com/artists/news/1459637/01222003/dido.jhtml (July 3, 2004).
"Hip Online: Dido," Hip Online, http://www.hiponline.com/artist/music/d/dido/interview/100201ii.html (July 3, 2004).
"No Angel, Just a Star," *Time Europe,* http://www.time.com/time/europe/webonly/europe/2001/01/dido.html (July 3, 2004).
"No Angel With an Angelic Voice," iAfrica, http://entertainment.iafrica.com/music/interviews/237875.htm (July 3, 2004).

—Sonya Shelton

Vin Diesel

Actor

Born Mark Vincent, July 18, 1967, in New York, NY; son of Delora (an astrologer) and stepson of Irving (a theater director and teacher) Vincent. *Education:* Attended Hunter College, New York, NY.

Addresses: *Production company*—One Race Productions, 2029 Century Park East #1060, Los Angeles, CA 90067. *Representative*—Endeavor Talent Agency, 9701 Wilshire Blvd., 10th Floor, Beverly Hills, CA 90210.

Career

Actor in films, including: *Multi–Facial* (also writer, producer, director), 1994; *Strays* (also writer, producer, director), 1997; *Saving Private Ryan,* 1998; *The Iron Giant* (voice), 1999; *Boiler Room,* 2000; *Pitch Black,* 2000; *The Fast and the Furious,* 2001; *Knockaround Guys,* 2001; *XXX,* 2002; *A Man Apart,* 2003.

Awards: Best on–screen team (with Paul Walker), MTV Movie Awards, for *The Fast and the Furious,* 2002.

Sidelights

A small role in the award–winning movie *Saving Private Ryan* provided Vin Diesel with the recognition he needed to make his move on Hollywood. The film *The Fast and the Furious* catapulted him into action–hero stardom. With roles in that film and *XXX,* he is set to take over where previous action stars like Bruce Willis, Sylvester Stallone, and Arnold Schwarzenegger have left off.

AP/Wide World Photos

His fast and furious ride to the top of the A–list of action movie stars may seem like a smooth ride to those on the outside, but it is the result of years of preparation plus a life–changing phone call from Steven Spielberg. Diesel's smooth, deep voice and shaved head are the trademarks of a driven man who made his own way when no one else would give him a chance. John Horn of *Newsweek* wrote of Diesel, "His real draw is a mysterious multicultural look that links him to young men and a surprising number of women of all ethnicities."

Born Mark Vincent on July 18, 1969, in New York, New York, Diesel never knew his biological father. He was raised by his mother, Delora, and stepfather, Irving Vincent. Delora was an astrologer and Irving was a theater director and teacher. Diesel grew up with his fraternal twin, Paul, who is now a film editor, and his two sisters in Greenwich Village. Because he never knew his biological father, Diesel is reluctant to discuss his racial background. Instead he chooses to remain mysterious about it, insisting that his ethnicity is of no consequence to the kinds of roles he can play.

Diesel and his family lived in Westbeth Artists Housing in Greenwich Village. The government–funded housing was built in the 1960s as a way to assist artists struggling at the beginning of their careers by providing them with affordable housing. By virtue of Irving Vincent's work as a theater director and drama teacher the family was able to live in the project during Diesel's childhood.

When Diesel was seven years old, he and some friends broke into a local theater. As they were messing around inside they were discovered by the artistic director of the Theater of the New City, Crystal Field. Instead of calling the police or kicking them out, Field gave the children scripts as well as $20. She told them to come back every day after school, learn lines from the script, and she would give them each $20 a week for their participation. Diesel claims that from then on he was hooked on acting. He appeared in Off–Off–Broadway productions throughout his teen years and into his twenties.

At age 17, Diesel decided to take advantage of his big physique (he is more than six feet tall and muscle–bound) by working as a bouncer. This line of work left his days open for auditions and gave him his new name. He explained to Jess Cagle of *Time*, "The name Vin Diesel came out of the bouncing thing. We all had nicknames. It was a wonderful thing to detach a little bit." Diesel worked as a bouncer for nine years while trying to make his way as an actor.

While Diesel was working as a bouncer at such hotspots as the Tunnel, he attended Hunter College. He majored in English and studied creative writing, learning how to write screenplays. After three years at Hunter College, Diesel dropped out and moved to Hollywood. A year in Hollywood left Diesel with no offers and a sense of failure. He returned to New York where the gift of a book helped him refocus.

That book, *Feature Filmmaking at Used–Car Prices* by Rick Schmidt, inspired him; he went on to write, produce, direct, and star in a short film called *Multi–Facial*. Echoing Diesel's own experiences, the short was about an actor who couldn't find work because he was never the right color for the part he was auditioning for, even though he always excelled at playing the parts. Made for around $3,000, the film was shot on 16mm film and made in three days.

Multi–Facial premiered at the Anthology Film Archives in Manhattan. Diesel described the effect of that night to Jamie Allen of CNN.com, "That night changed my life completely. I still went through a few more years of sleeping on couches and struggling and taking odd jobs outside film. But I knew my life had changed." From its premier in Manhattan the film went on to play at the Cannes Film Festival in 1995.

Multi–Facial changed Diesel's life, but it was almost shelved. During the making of the film, Diesel was receiving feedback that was not positive; he did not want to continue making the movie. However, advice from Diesel's stepfather put him back on track to finishing the film. He told CNN.com's Allen, "It was an important lesson for me to learn, to be thorough, to finish what you start."

Feeling confident from the success of his short film at Cannes, Diesel returned to Hollywood intent on making a feature–length film. Diesel worked as a telemarketer selling tools and raised $50,000 to make *Strays*. Once again, he wrote, produced, directed, and starred in the film about a streetwise New Yorker who falls in love with a midwestern "girl next door" and the effect that relationship has on his friends. In 1997 the film was accepted to the Sundance Film Festival. Although the film was reviewed positively, Diesel was unable to find a distributor for it. He returned to New York to figure out what to do next.

While dealing with the disappointment of not finding a distributor for his film *Strays*, Diesel received a call out of the blue. Steven Spielberg, the noted director of such films as *Schindler's List* and *Jurassic Park*, was calling to ask Diesel to be in his next film. Spielberg had seen Diesel's short *Multi–Facial* at the Cannes Film Festival and was impressed with the actor's abilities. The role of Private Adrian Caparzo had been written into the already finished script of *Saving Private Ryan* to accommodate Spielberg's desire to cast the actor. Spielberg's interest did not stop with casting. While filming, Spielberg discussed shots with Diesel and even allowed him to film a few scenes.

Saving Private Ryan was successful and won several awards. The film gave Diesel the exposure he needed to launch his career in Hollywood. From there, Diesel went on to the lead voice role in the animated film *The Iron Giant*. He also played a crooked stock broker in the film *Boiler Room*. That film has special relevance for Diesel who feels the film helped him pay his dues for his telemarketing days. He told CNN.com's Allen, "I did *Boiler Room* to redeem myself... By doing this film, I put out the message that anytime anybody calls you to sell anything, hang up the phone."

From playing an Italian–American stock broker dressed in expensive suits, Diesel went on to play a serial killer in a muscle shirt in the Australian film *Pitch Black*. In the film, Diesel plays Richard Riddick, a convicted killer who has crash landed on a deserted planet with his captors. He becomes the only means of survival for the crew once the inhabitants of the planet, large man–eating creatures, start killing off everything that walks.

Pitch Black brought Diesel a small—yet adoring—set of science fiction fans. That fan base grew when he starred in *The Fast and the Furious,* which was released in 2001. As Dominic Toretto, Diesel plays the leader of a gang that hijacks trucks for their cargo. The gangs are also into high–speed street racing. The slick action film highlighted Diesel's sex appeal and became one of the top ten grossing films of 2001.

Riding high on the wave of excitement created by *The Fast and the Furious,* Diesel teamed up with its director, Rob Cohen, to star in *XXX,* which was released in 2002. Branded as the secret agent for the extreme sports generation, Diesel's Xander Cage is meant to replace the martini–sipping image created by the James Bond films with a tattooed, hard–edged thrill seeker. He explained his attraction to the character and the film to *Jet:* "The idea of giving birth to a new breed of secret agent was interesting and challenging.... I like the idea that someone like Xander could be called upon to step into the shoes of professional secret agents. Taking a guy who's the least likely to want to save the world, and having him do just that, fascinates me."

Diesel's sudden rise to stardom also helped bring another film back from the dead. He had been part of an ensemble cast in a gangster film called *Knockaround Guys.* Its distributor, New Line Cinema, had shelved the film, which contained appearances by veteran actors John Malkovich and Dennis Hopper. The fame that Diesel gained from *The Fast and the Furious* convinced New Line Cinema to finally release the film.

Stardom has also allowed Diesel to command increasingly higher salaries. For *Saving Private Ryan,* Diesel earned $100,000. His role in *The Fast and the Furious* earned him $2.5 million. After the success of *The Fast and the Furious* his salary rocketed up to $10 and $11 million dollars for *XXX* and the sequel to *Pitch Black* respectively. For the sequel to *XXX,* to be released in 2005, he will be earning $20 million.

With the power that comes from being an A–list action hero, Diesel still takes the time to indulge his other interests. A fan of video games as well as Dungeons and Dragons–style multiple–player games, Diesel announced in 2002 his decision to form a videogame company. He was being asked to contribute to so many other video game projects that he decided to form Tigon Games to see if he could

do it on his own. He reported that his first game will be based on a 1970s New York policeman named Perrone.

Diesel also formed his own production company called One Race Productions. One Race is responsible for producing the sequel to *XXX* as well as an upcoming film about Hannibal Barca, the Carthaginian general who led an unsuccessful attack on Rome in the third century B.C. Diesel also continues to write screenplays. He is working on one based on his years as a bouncer called *Doormen.*

Diesel lives in Los Angeles with his Staffordshire bull terrier named Winston. He claims not to be romantically involved with anyone. In fact, he is amused by who the media often state he is dating. He told Anderson Jones of E! Online, "If I'm not playing Sony PlayStation or rereading a classic ... my friends and I get on the Internet and find out who I'm dating, and it's always hysterical."

Diesel's biggest hope for the future is to play roles outside the action–hero genre. His talent and interests span a wide range of genres. Tigon Games and One Race Productions are likely to keep Diesel busy in between film shoots. While it is obvious that Diesel worked hard to gain the recognition that got him started in Hollywood, he told Nick Charles of *People,* "At the end of the day, I'm just a lucky kid from New York."

Sources

Periodicals

BusinessWeek, October 14, 2002.
Electronic Gaming Monthly, April 1, 2003.
Entertainment Weekly, February 25, 2000, p. 58.
Jet, July 9, 2001, pp. 53–54; July 29, 2002, pp. 58–62.
Newsweek, July 9, 2001, p. 57; August 5, 2002, pp. 56–57.
People, October 12, 1998, pp. 162–64; August 19, 2002, pp. 87–88.
Time, August 5, 2002, pp. 61–62.

Online

"The Drive of Vin Diesel," CNN.com, http://www.cnn.com/2000/SHOWBIZ/Movies/02/21/vin.diesel/ (August 26, 2003).
"Hollywood's new antihero on cars, classics and his *Fast and Furious* road to stardom," E! Online, http://www.eonline.com/Celebs/Qa/Vin Diesel/ (August 26, 2003).

—*Eve M. B. Hermann*

Elizabeth Diller and Ricardo Scofidio

Architects and artists

Born Elizabeth Diller, in 1954, in Poland; married Ricardo Scofidio. *Education:* Cooper Union School of Architecture, B.A., 1979. Born Ricardo Scofidio, in 1935, in New York, NY; married first wife (divorced); married Elizabeth Diller. *Education:* Attended Cooper Union School of Architecture, 1952–55; Columbia University, B.A., 1960.

Addresses: *Office*—Diller + Scofidio, 38 Cooper Sq., New York, NY 10003. *Website*—www.dillerscofidio. com.

Career

Diller worked as assistant professor, Cooper Union School of Architecture, 1981–90; associate professor of architecture at Princeton University, 1990—; director of graduate studies, 1993—. Scofidio worked as architect, 1960–79; professor at Cooper Union School of Architecture, 1965—. Together, formed Diller + Scofido, 1979.

Awards: Together: Graham Foundation for Advance Study in the Fine Arts fellowship, 1986; New York Foundation for the Arts fellowships, 1986, 1987, and 1989; Bessie Schoenberg Dance and Performance Award for design, 1987; Chicago Institute for Architecture and Urbanism fellowship, 1989; Tiffany Foundation Award for Emerging Artists, 1990; Award from *Progressive Architecture* magazine, for Slow House, 1991; Chrysler Award for Achievement and Design, 1997; John D. and Catherine T. MacArthur Foundation Fellowship, 1999; Eugene Mac-Dermott Award for creative achievement from Mas- sachusetts Institute of Technology, 1999; Brunner Prize, Architecture from the American Academy of Arts and Letters, 2003; James Beard Foundation Award for best new restaurant design for the Brasserie; Progressive Architecture Design Award for Blur Building; Obie Award for creative achievement, *Village Voice,* for *Jet Lag.*

Sidelights

In 1999, Elizabeth Diller and Ricardo Scofidio, working under the name Diller + Scofidio, became the first architects to be awarded the MacArthur Foundation "genius" grant. The married couple, who began working together in 1979, did not initially do many traditional architecture projects, but cultivated their own version of modernism in their art projects, primarily installations, sculptures, and constructions as well as sets, design, and other art works. By the late 1990s and early 2000s, Diller + Scofidio began being commissioned for more buildings and other works normally associated with architects while retaining their very individual vision for these pieces. As the curator of their retrospective show in 2003 Aaron Betsky told Arthur Lubow of the *New York Times,* "In experimental architecture and design, they are the only ones who made as the core of their work the question 'What do we mean by architecture?'"

Though Diller and Scofidio were both trained as architects, they come from somewhat dissimilar backgrounds. Diller was born in 1954 in Poland, the daughter of a Jewish couple. After spending her early years in Lodz, Poland, Diller emigrated with her parents to the United States when she was five years old. They settled in New York City. Scofidio was born in 1935 in New York City. His father was a band leader.

Both Diller and Scofidio studied at New York City's Cooper Union. Scofidio was a student in the Cooper Union School of Architecture from 1952–55, but earned his undergraduate degree from Columbia University's architecture school in 1960. He began his career in traditional architecture firms after graduation, and became a professor of architecture at Cooper Union in 1965. It was there that they met when Diller began studying at Cooper Union's School of Architecture in the 1970s. She originally began her studies at Cooper Union in art, but took an architecture class because she was interested in ideas about space and culture, two concepts that would be central to her work with Scofidio.

While Diller was Scofidio's student, he was already married, though he later divorced his wife. The pair did not date nor marry until after she graduated from Cooper Union in 1979. After she graduated, she began teaching at Cooper Union as an assistant professor beginning in the early 1980s. She later lectured at Harvard University, and beginning in 1990, was an associate professor at Princeton University. By this time, Diller and Scofidio were firmly established architects in their own right as Diller + Scofidio.

The couple began working together in 1979. Many of their early works were rather small, and included stage sets, site–specific art installations, and performance pieces. They were already using space and form to explore social behavior. Summarizing their approach, Aaron Betsky of *Architecture* wrote, "they are less concerned with traditional architectural form and construction than with analyzing the way social conventions or rules dictate the way people use places, objects, and events. Diller + Scofidio's job as they see it is to reveal those roles, and where it makes sense, to free us from them."

Some of their early works were very simple. In 1981, for example, Diller + Scofidio put 2,500 orange cones in New York City's Columbus Circle for 24 hours to show traffic patterns. Three years later, the pair designed a new entrance gate, sign, and pole–based windsocks for the site of the annual Art on the Beach, a sculpture show in New York City. Diller herself had previously designed part of the set for a participatory work of art at the 1983 Art on the Beach called *Civic Plots* with sculptor James Aholl and performance artist Kaylynn Sullivan.

Other early works of Diller + Scofidio's were also related to performance and art space. In 1986, the pair provided the stage design for a performance piece called *The Rotary Notary and His Hot Plate, or a Delay in Glass*. The theater troupe Creation Production Company staged *The Rotary Notary and His Hot Plate* and the rest of the title referred to the staging which was inspired by Marcel Duchamp's work "The Large Glass" which was originally done on a window. Diller + Scofidio put a large mirror angled on the divided stage. The actors behind a divider could be seen by the audience in the mirror. Ten years later, the pair did a set for the Charleroi/Dances Troupe's performance called *Moving Targets* that used a mirror in similar fashion. It featured a mirror angled over the stage giving the audience an unusual view of the dancers and the stage.

On a completely different front, Diller + Scofidio did *The WithDrawing Room* with sculptor David Ireland. They took a house in San Francisco, California, and transformed it into a gallery/studio as well as a work of art that commented on domestic ideas. For example, in the dining room, the table hung from the ceiling and its chairs were attached by hinges.

One of Diller + Scofidio's first important commissions was a piece at New York's Museum of Modern Art in 1989 called *Para–Site*. The multi–media work was unusual in that nothing touched the floor—everything was hanging from the walls or ceiling. *Para–Site* featured a number of high–tech gadgets including live video cameras, monitors, mirrors, and chairs, as well as a hole in the wall that showed plumbing and wiring. The cameras were set to capture images from other parts of the building, including the museum's escalators, as a comment on the nature of modern society. Critics gave the project cautious praise.

Another pivotal early work was the design for a private home called *Slow House* in 1989. The home was to be located on the ocean in Long Island, New York, and built for a Japanese art investor. Because of his financial issues, only the foundation was built, but it still became part of the Museum of Modern Art's collection. Diller + Scofidio designed a house that was shaped like a crescent with a glass wall at one end. A video camera was set up to record the view which could be re–played on the window. This would allow the home to always be sunny.

In the 1990s, Diller + Scofidio continued to explore the tension between architecture and art. While they were both considered highbrow artists, they were also highly reputable architects. This success led to such honors as a media residency at the Centre for New Media Research at the Banff Centre for the Arts from 1993–95. Throughout the decade, their works were commissioned for or shown at leading art institutions, and toured around the world.

In 1991, Diller + Scofidio created *Tourism: SuitCase Studies,* which was originally displayed at the Walker Art Center in Minneapolis, Minnesota. It consisted of 50 suitcases—all the same gray–colored Samsonite pieces—hung up, one for each of the United States. Each suitcase represented one state and was opened to reveal small items inside including tourist attractions and historical figures.

Two years later, the pair created a controversial installation located outside of New York City's Rialto Theatre, a former pornographic theater. As part of the 42nd Street Project, Diller + Scofidio did *Soft Sell* on commission. *Soft Sell* featured a pair of big red lipsticked lips projected via video image on the exterior of the theater. The lips uttered phrases such as "Wanna buy a new lifestyle?" to passersby.

Another significant work for Diller + Scofidio was *Bad Press,* a 1993 gallery installation that toured through 1996. This work featured 18 men's white shirts ironed into individualistic shapes and displayed on ironing boards, with text. This was another work that commented on domesticity.

Diller + Scofidio continued to push the barriers of their art into other mediums. In the mid–1990s, they published two books. The 1994 tome, *Back to the Front,* to which they contributed two multi–media projects and also edited and designed, focused on the link between summer travel and war as conquest, and explored related architecture. They followed this with *Flesh: Architectural Probes* in 1995. In 1997, Diller + Scofidio created a series of drinking glasses called Vice–Virtue Glasses, each about a different drug and a means of taking it.

In 1998, Diller + Scofidio moved into theater performance pieces with *Jet Lag.* Originally presented at the Lantaren Theater in Rotterdam, the Netherlands, and later staged Off–Broadway, *Jet Lag* consisted of two stories. One focused on the true story of a grandmother who wanted to obtain custody of her grandson from his father, and took him on 167 trans–Atlantic flights to keep him. *Jet Lag* focuses on their stops in airports. The other story was about a sailor who went alone on an around–the–world yacht race and filmed himself. His footage was projected as part of *Jet Lag.*

While Diller + Scofidio explored other mediums, they continued to create installations for museums and galleries. In 1998, they did *The American Lawn: Surface of Everyday Lawn,* about the meaning of lawns in American life and how unnatural lawns can really be. More unusual was 1999's piece, *Master/Slave,* originally displayed in France. The pair used a toy robot collection lined up on a 300–foot–long conveyor belt that moved along and passed through an airport security device. The robots were videotaped by security cameras, and the images appeared on monitors located in other parts of the gallery. Such works led to the MacArthur Foundation giving Diller + Scofidio a $375,000 grant in 1999 to continue their work.

After the grant, Diller + Scofidio began designing more traditional architecture works, including buildings and interiors, albeit with their unconventional touch. In 2000, they renovated a restaurant in New York City called the Brassiere. Already a modernist place, they balanced their art with clients' needs. Among their touches was having video screens above the bar airing the entrance of each patron. Diller + Scofidio also created a low–income housing project in Gifu, Japan, which personalized the often limited space of public housing, and with others, a controversial viewing platform on Fulton Street in Lower Manhattan to give viewers a closer look at Ground Zero after the September 11, 2001, World Trade Center disaster.

A more challenging and high profile project was the Blur Building created on Yverdon–les–Bains over Lake Neuchatel for the Swiss Expo in 2002. Diller + Scofidio worked for two years to create the unusual space. The Blur Building consisted of a steel structure that people could walk into and be inside a misty cloud as the structure was surrounded by fog–creating water nozzles. It was later the subject of a 2002 book by Diller + Scofidio entitled *Blur: the making of nothing.*

At the time, the Blur Building was considered to be Diller + Scofidio's defining work, but they soon received commissions to design larger projects such as the Institute for Contemporary Art in Boston, Massachusetts, and the Eyebeam Museum of Art and Technology in New York City, as well as smaller works such as a permanent installation in the John F. Kennedy International Airport and helping with the master plan for a cultural district around the Brooklyn Academy of Music. Of their work and influence, Parsons School of Design architecture department chairman Peter Wheelwright told Peter Marks of the *New York Times,* "The thing about Liz and Ric that makes them as important as they are becoming is they have been in the forefront of thinking about architecture as a social product."

Selected works

Diller (solo)

(With James Holl and Kaylynn Sullivan) "Civic Plots," Art on the Beach, Battery Park City Landfill, New York, NY, 1983.

Diller + Scofidio

The Rotary Notary and His Hot Plate, or a Delay in Glass, 1986.
The WithDrawing Room, San Francisco, CA, 1986.
Para–Site, Museum of Modern Art, New York, NY, 1989.
Slow House, Long Island, NY, 1989.
SuitCase Studies, Walker Art Center, Minneapolis, MN, 1991.
Soft Sell, outside of Rialto Theatre, New York, NY, 1993.
Bad Press, Richard Anderson, New York City, 1994, and other locations, 1993–96.
Pageant, Johannesburg Biennial and Rotterdam Film Festival, 1996.
Moving Targets (set), 1996.
Vice–Virtue Glasses, 1997.
Jet Lag, 1998.
The American Lawn: Surface of Everyday Life, Canadian Centre for Architecture, 1998.
Master/Slave, Cartier Foundation, Paris, France, 1999.
The Brassiere (restaurant interior), 2000.
The Blur Building, Swiss Expo '02, 2002.
Scanning: The Aberrant Architecture of Diller + Scofidio (retrospective), Whitney Museum of American Art, New York, NY, 2003.

Selected writings

Back to the Front, Princeton Architectural Press with F.R.A.C. Basse–Normandie, 1994.
Flesh: Architectural Probes, Princeton Architectural Press, 1995.
Blur: the making of nothing, Abrams, 2002.

Sources

Periodicals

Architecture, June 2000, p. 129.
Artforum International, June 2003, p. 180.
Art in America, May 1994, p. 114; October 2003, p. 90.
Boston Globe, April 6, 2003, p. N8.
Interior Design, January 1, 2003, p. 166.
Newsweek, March 17, 2003, p. 64.
New York Times, December 10, 1981, p. C10; February 3, 1983, p. C18; July 31, 1983, section 2, p. 25; July 21, 1989, p. C30; August 1, 1993, section 2, p. 34; July 10, 1994, section 2, p. 30; July 13, 1984, p. C22; May 23, 2001, p. E1; November 10, 2002, section 2, p. 34; February 16, 2003, section 6, p. 36; February 28, 2003, p. E2.
Time, February 14, 2000, p. 85.
Washington Post, March 30, 2003, p. G1.

Online

"Diller + Scofidio," Gallery MA, http://www.toto.co.jp/GALLERMA/hist/en/biogra/diller.htm (February 9, 2004).
"Diller & Scofidio, Top Architectural Team, Speaks at Free Lecture April 14 at NJIT," New Jersey Institute of Technology, http://www.njit.edu/old/News/Releases/345.html (February 9, 2004).
"Elizabeth Diller," Princeton University, http://www.princeton.edu/cgi–bin/Phone/phonecg.pl?Qname=elizabeth+diller (February 9, 2004.)
"Howard Johnson, Diller + Scofidio awarded Arts Council Prizes," TechTalk, http://web.mit.edu/newsoffice/tt/1999/oct27/artscami.html (February 9, 2004).
"Princeton Architect, Four Ph.D. Alumni are Among This Year's MacArthur Fellows," Princeton University, http://www.princeton.edu/pr/news/99/q2/0623–macarthur.htm (February 9, 2004).
"Thinking about architecture," Princeton Weekly Bulletin, http://www.princeton.edu/pr/pwb/00/0327/p/archit.shtml (February 9, 2004).

—*A. Petruso*

Tim Donahue

President and Chief Executive Officer of Nextel Communications

Born Timothy M. Donahue, c. 1950; married Jayne. *Education:* John Carroll University, Cleveland, OH, B.A., 1971.

Addresses: *Office*—Nextel Communications Inc., 2001 Edmund Halley Dr., Reston VA 20191–3421.

Career

Began career as owner and operator of Ben Franklin craft stores; joined MCI Communications Corp., 1984; president, paging division, McCaw Cellular Communications, 1986–89; president, U.S. central region, McCaw Cellular Communications, 1989–91; president/general manager, AT&T Wireless of N.Y. and N.J. and also president/general manager, AT&T Wireless, northeast operations, 1991–96; president and chief operating officer, Nextel Communications, 1996–99; president and chief executive officer, Nextel Communications, 1999—.

Member: Board member, Eastman Kodak Co., 2001—.

Awards: Ernst & Young Entrepreneur of the Year, Networking and Communications division, 2003; Ernst & Young's Greater Washington Master Entrepreneur of the Year, 2003.

Sidelights

In the competitive and sometimes cutthroat world of telecommunications, one business leader has put his company in front of the pack. That person is Tim Donahue, president and chief executive officer (CEO) of Nextel Communications. In 2003, the Reston, Virginia–based wireless carrier enjoyed its best year ever, adding 2.3 million subscribers. That year, Nextel also had earnings of $1.47 billion, leaving other cell–phone service providers scrambling to copy the company's business practices. Under the direction of Donahue, Nextel has shed its underdog status. In an article posted on *The Street.com,* Scott Moritz summed it up best when he wrote that Nextel had "rebounded from being the wireless industry's David to the Goliath of business services."

One of the people behind Nextel's success is Donahue, who earned a bachelor of arts degree in English literature in 1971 from John Carroll University, located in Cleveland, Ohio. Donahue began his career in the business world as an owner and operator of retail outlets in the Ben Franklin craft–store chain. While working at Ben Franklin, Donahue realized that customer satisfaction was the key to any successful business venture. In time, Donahue transferred that knowledge to the communications field, joining MCI Communications Corp. in 1984. In 1986, MCI sold its paging division, where Donahue worked, to McCaw Cellular Communications and Donahue became president of the paging division at McCaw. In 1989, Donahue was named McCaw Cellular's president for the U.S. central region. However, in 1991, AT&T bought McCaw and renamed its new acquisition AT&T Wireless. Donahue stayed on, becoming president and general manager of AT&T's New York and New Jersey wireless services. In time, Donahue was named president and general manager of northeast operations for AT&T Wireless.

In 1995, Craig McCaw, the man who pioneered McCaw Cellular, hooked up with Nextel and by 1996 hired Donahue, his former employee, to be president and chief operating officer. By 1999, Donahue was Nextel's president and CEO. At the time, Donahue took over what some considered a sinking ship. The company had yet to turn a profit. With a clear vision of what Nextel could become, Donahue initiated a new concept for the company—"Be first, Be better, Be different"—which drove every business decision. Instead of trying to copy what his competitors were doing, Donahue charted a new path. "In an industry overrun with competition, Chief Executive Timothy Donahue figured he had little to lose by being different," business writer Scott Woolley remarked in *Forbes*.

Under Donahue's direction, Nextel positioned itself as a different kind of wireless carrier, eager to launch services others did not provide. Nextel turned its phones into walkie–talkies, allowing customers to connect to business associates, friends, or family who were also Nextel users without placing a phone call. Nextel was also the first to offer packages with no roaming fees outside a customer's home area and also began rounding bills to the nearest second instead of rounding up to the next minute, a practice most carriers at the time used but which made customers feel cheated. Nextel was also the first wireless carrier to release Internet–ready phones, which allowed customers access anytime, anywhere, to e–mail, wireless–enabled Internet sites, and company databases. Another unique Nextel feature was eDispatch.com, which allowed business customers to use their phones to connect to their corporate website so they could find out things such as if a delivery had been made on time.

Nextel was also ahead of the pack when it released a new wireless phone in 2000 that could be used in 65 countries. The phone gave jet–setting executives the ability to have just one phone and one phone number no matter where they were. As soon as the new phone was unveiled, France Telecom ordered 10,000 of them for its customers. Under Donahue, Nextel's customer retention rate rose due to his drive for customer satisfaction, culled during his years at Ben Franklin. According to *Forbes*, four out of five Nextel users will not switch to a different carrier.

As a manager, Donahue is known as a likeable people–person. During his time at Nextel, he used these skills to turn the place around. Looking at the numbers, Donahue's turnaround is apparent. When he joined Nextel in 1996, it serviced 100,000 customers; by the start of 2004, the communications company boasted 13 million customers. Nextel also turned a profit for the first time in 2003—and the industry took notice. Frost and Sullivan named Nextel the 2003 Mobile Communications Company of the Year and *BusinessWeek* placed Nextel atop its 2003 list of the top 100 IT companies. That publication also named Donahue one of the "best managers" around. He also earned accolades from Ernst & Young, who named Donahue its Entrepreneur of the Year for 2003 in the Networking and Communications division.

Nextel itself took note of Donahue's accomplishments and in the summer of 2003, offered him a lucrative contract extension, which raised his salary by 43 percent. While his base salary stood at $1 million, the contract included bonuses and stock options that could potentially make Donahue tens of millions of dollars through 2006, when the contract ends. But Donahue does not take all of the credit. In a press release, quoted on *The Street.com*'s website, Donahue thanked his staff for the success. "At Nextel, I'm surrounded by the most dedicated, innovative and results–driven team I've ever seen."

Despite Nextel's recent gains, long–standing success is not guaranteed. In recent years, telecom companies have been gobbling each other up and consolidating in an effort to streamline services and make money. MCI WorldCom bought Sprint, Bell Atlantic joined forces with GTE, and Cingular Wireless acquired AT&T, but Donahue believes Nextel can stand alone. "At the end of the day, there will be four or five [wireless] players," Donahue told *BusinessWeek*'s Amy Borrus. "We will be one of them."

Sources

Periodicals

BusinessWeek, April 10, 2000, p. 92; January 13, 2003, p. 70.
Forbes, January 12, 2004, p. 172.
Washington Post, June 11, 1999, p. E1.

Online

"Nextel Communications' Tim Donahue Named 2003 Ernst & Young Entrepreneur of the Year

Award Winner," Ernst & Young, http://www.ey.com/global/content.nsf/US/Media_-_Release_-_11–22–03FDC (February 16, 2004).

"Nextel Touts Great 2003, but 4Q Profit Dips," Telephony Online, http://telephonyonline.com/ar/telecom_nextel_touts_great/index.htm (February 26, 2004).

"Rich Reward for Nextel Chief," TheStreet.com, http://www.thestreet.com/tech/scottmoritz/10107363.html (February 16, 2004).

Additional information was obtained through correspondence with Nextel media relations in March of 2004.

—Lisa Frick

Hilary Duff

Actress and singer

Born Hilary Ann Lisa Duff, September 28, 1987, in Houston, TX; daughter of Bob (a retail executive) and Susan (a business manager) Duff.

Addresses: *Office*—c/o Boo Management and Consulting, 10061 Riverside Dr., Ste. 1061, Toluca Lake, CA 91602.

Career

Appeared in a BalletMet Columbus tour of *The Nutcracker,* c. 1993; cast in television commercials. Film appearances include: *True Women* (uncredited), 1997; *Casper Meets Wendy,* 1998; *Human Nature,* 2001; *Agent Cody Banks,* 2003; *The Lizzie McGuire Movie,* 2003; *Cheaper by the Dozen,* 2003; *A Cinderella Story,* 2004; *Raise Your Voice,* 2004; *The Perfect Man,* 2004; *Outward Blonde,* 2005. Television appearances include: *The Soul Collector* (movie), 1999; *Chicago Hope,* 2000; *Lizzie McGuire,* 2001–03; *Cadet Kelly* (movie), 2002; *George Lopez,* 2003; *American Dreams,* 2003; *Frasier* (voice), 2004. Launched singing career with "Santa Clause Lane," included on the soundtrack to *The Santa Clause 2,* 2002, and on her own Christmas album *Santa Claus Lane,* 2002; released *Metamorphosis,* 2003; released single "So Yesterday," 2003; released single "Come Clean," 2004; contributed to *A Cinderella Story* soundtrack, 2004.

Sidelights

Hilary Duff became a household name and a worldwide phenomenon thanks to her starring role in the hit Disney series *Lizzie McGuire.* With her wholesome blonde looks and exuberant personality, Duff stepped into the part of the likable middle–schooler with ease, though she had very little professional experience before the show debuted in early 2001.

Duff was suddenly dubbed the new "tween queen" in the media, a superstar for a generation of pre–teens whose age group had now grown to include ten–year–olds. This new "tween" category was a marketing phenomenon that took off with Duff and her cohorts around 2002. But as *Newsweek*'s Kate Stroup noted, the Texas teen was a cut above. "Duff, who's got a giddy charm and unexpected vulnerability in person, has established herself as the best actress of her generation," Stroup asserted, "easily outclassing the Olsen twins and Nickelodeon's Amanda Bynes."

Duff was born on September 28, 1987, and grew up in Boerne, Texas, a part of the state known as Hill Country. She was close to her older sister, Haylie, who was two years her senior, and took gymnastics and ballet lessons from an early age. She eventually won a part in *The Nutcracker* with BalletMet Columbus in the Ohio company's tour of the Christmas-time classic. Their mother, Susan, who had once worked as a makeup artist, decided to take the girls to Los Angeles, California, to try their luck in television commercials. Right away, they landed jobs. "We were like, 'This is so easy!'" Duff recalled when Taylor Hanson spoke with her for an *Interview* article. "Then we went back to Texas ... and came back to L.A. for the next pilot season. We thought that would be easy, too, but you audition and audition, and you don't get anything."

On that second trip to Los Angeles in 1996, Duff's mother had decided to resettle there in order to be closer to the entertainment business. Their father, Bob, was a partner in a chain of convenience stores back in Texas, and agreed to the plan, with visits from him every three weeks. The Duff women headed to Hollywood in a car with all their belongings, which included a pair of goldfish, a hermit crab, gerbil, and rabbit. Both Duff and her sister won parts in a television miniseries, *True Women*, in 1997, and Duff also appeared in a movie that went straight to video, *Casper Meets Wendy*.

A rough patch followed, and Duff did not work for almost two years. "Some kids have success too quickly, and they take it for granted, but it definitely didn't come too fast for us," she reflected in an article that *Texas Monthly* invited her to write. She appeared in the pilot episode of an NBC sitcom, *Daddio*, but the show's producers replaced her when casting the regular series, which did not last anyway. After that, she won a guest role on a *Chicago Hope* episode that aired in March of 2000, but was beginning to feel disillusioned by the search for work. "I was, like, wanting to quit," she recalled in an interview with *Entertainment Weekly* journalist Tim Carvell, "and I had one audition left, and it was *Lizzie McGuire*."

Duff actually auditioned for the Disney show four separate times, as the network's entertainment-division president Rich Ross told Stroup in the *Newsweek* article. "She wasn't doing anything wrong," Ross said of the multiple auditions. "She just wore such great outfits, and we wanted to see what she'd come in with next." Clearly, Duff had a natural star quality, and Ross and his colleagues decided she was a perfect fit in the role of a normal middle–school student with an amusing animated alter ego. *Lizzie McGuire* debuted in January of 2001, and quickly garnered a huge following among younger viewers for its lighthearted look at the ups and downs in the life of a klutzy middle–schooler.

With plots revolving around Lizzie's adventures at home and at school, and helped out by her two best friends, Gordo and Miranda, the show was a hit with critics and even older viewers, too. Many of the storylines "typically prey upon Lizzie's insecurities, which are more about what she wants to do when she grows up than about the size of her tummy, or crushes on boys," the *New York Times'* Hillary Frey reflected. "In one episode Lizzie, who has quit many an extracurricular activity, worries that she isn't as talented as" Gordo, a wannabe filmmaker, and Miranda, a violin prodigy. "In stark contrast to the contrivances of prime–time teenage dramas," Frey continued, "Lizzie's problems are plausible, her character believable. This is key: Lizzie is the luminous and loyal friend any kid would want to have at a stage of adolescence when the world just begins to seem very dark."

More than one television critic and celebrity confessed to being a fan of *Lizzie McGuire*. "Lizzie's fizzy middle–school misadventures, like buying a bra and scoring a first kiss, are always sweet, never syrupy—making the show palatable for parents and even twentysomethings," declared Stroup in *Newsweek*. Carvell, writing in *Entertainment Weekly*, noted that Duff's hit show "amounts to *Ally McBeal* with longer skirts and homework: Lizzie negotiates all the crises of middle school, while her cartoon alter ego supplies fantasy sequences and wry commentary." Duff herself explained Lizzie's particular appeal. "She doesn't exactly fit in at school," the actress reflected in an interview with *Time's* Richard Corliss. "Even though she's cool, and she dresses cool, she doesn't know who she is yet."

Lizzie McGuire became the Disney Channel's highest–rated program, and also the highest–rated program on basic cable in its 7:30 p.m. time slot. The Disney marketing machine went into overdrive, merchandising tie–in material that included a series of Lizzie McGuire novels, a clothing line, and then a big–screen version. That was slated for a spring release in 2003, and Duff's status as the new "Tween Queen" was cemented by a *Vanity Fair* cover for its annual Hollywood issue. Though *The Lizzie McGuire Movie* was savaged by many critics, it took in $17.3 million on its opening weekend, a testament to the legions of Duff/McGuire fans. Its plot began with the end of her middle–school career for McGuire, and an exciting summer class trip to Rome, where Lizzie becomes involved with a handsome Italian teen pop star named Paolo (Yani Gellman).

Disney also owned the ABC network, and had planned to move Duff into prime–time on the broadcast network with a new series that would feature Lizzie as a high–schooler. There were, however, reportedly two other broadcast networks vying for a chance to give Duff her own prime–time sitcom, and Duff's mother, who served as her business manager, was reportedly unhappy with Disney's offer for a big–screen sequel. There was further rancor involving an alleged $500,000 bonus Disney had promised when *The Lizzie McGuire Movie* had earned $50 million at the box office. "Disney thought they'd be able to bully us into accepting whatever offer they wanted to make, and they couldn't," Susan Duff told *Entertainment Weekly* writer Allison Hope Weiner. "We walked away from a sequel. They walked away from a franchise."

Duff was already a feature–film veteran by then, with a role in another tween hit, *Agent Cody Banks* with Frankie Muniz, and signed to a $2 million paycheck for the lead in *A Cinderella Story*. She had also segued into a recording career, with a CD, *Metamorphosis,* on Buena Vista/Hollywood Records—also owned by Disney but part of a separate contract from her film and television work. Her debut record of pop tunes went platinum weeks after its release in August of 2003, yet further evidence of Duff's ongoing appeal to her vast *Lizzie McGuire* audience. Her move to pop stardom was somewhat unexpected, she told *Billboard* writer Craig Rosen, but certainly not unwelcome. In 2001, she had taken part in a Radio Disney concert, and saw "all these pop acts backstage at the concert," Duff told Rosen. "They were all getting ready backstage and warming up, and I was like, 'I want to do this so bad.'"

Despite her thriving career in television and film, Duff's first actual singing appearance before a live audience was unnerving, she confessed. It came at the American Music Awards telecast in November of 2003, with several industry heavy–hitters, among them country superstar Faith Hill, sitting in the front row. "I was so nervous I thought I was going to throw up," she wrote in the article for *Texas Monthly.* But Duff then embarked on a concert tour to promote *Metamorphosis,* and the tour dates also served to boost her profile for her next project: her appearance in the Steve Martin family comedy *Cheaper by the Dozen,* which hit theaters in time for the holiday 2003 season.

Duff's career in television seemed to end with the 65–episode run of *Lizzie McGuire.* She was the object of a bidding war between networks in the fall of 2003, and walked away with a sitcom development deal with CBS. A few months later, however, the network announced that there would not be a new Duff series, after writers and producers failed to come up with a suitable project for the teen star.

Her career in Hollywood and on stage, meanwhile, continued at an exciting pace: in June of 2004, she and her sister, Haylie, released a single, the remake of the early 1980s Go–Go's classic, "Our Lips Are Sealed," which was slated to appear on *A Cinderella Story*'s soundtrack. The movie was set in California's San Fernando Valley, and starred Duff as Sam, a high–schooler whose father dies and leaves his restaurant to Sam's brutish stepmother, played by Jennifer Coolidge (*Legally Blonde, American Pie*). Sam is overworked at home and at the restaurant, and ignored at school, until she begins receiving mysterious text messages from the cute boy at school, played by Chad Michael Murray (*Freaky Friday, The Gilmore Girls*). Duff was also slated to appear in *The Perfect Man,* opposite Heather Locklear and Chris Noth, about a daughter determined to find a mate for her single mom.

As for herself, Duff has had a difficult time dating with such a high public profile. The press avidly chronicled the perceived ups and downs of her relationship with pop singer Aaron Carter for most of 2003. Despite the multimillion–dollar contracts and endless business meetings, she remains very much a teenager. She travels with a tutor, who assigns typical high–school homework for her to complete, and for months she told reporters that she could only think about turning 16 and being able to get her driver's license. Nor is she immune to standard bouts of freak–out. "I think I have about two really good cries a year about being so overwhelmed and having so much stress," she confessed to *CosmoGirl!* writer Lori Berger. "Sometimes you don't even know what you're crying about because you've held it inside for so long."

Selected discography

"Santa Clause Lane," *The Santa Clause 2* (soundtrack), Disney, 2002.
Santa Claus Lane, Disney, 2002.
Metamorphosis, Buena Vista, 2003.
"So Yesterday" (single), Festival, 2003.
"Come Clean" (single), Festival, 2004.
(Contributor) *A Cinderella Story* (soundtrack), Hollywood, 2004.

Sources

Periodicals

Billboard, January 31, 2004, p. 10; June 5, 2004, p. 32.
Billboard Bulletin, September 11, 2003, p. 1.
CosmoGirl!, March 2004, p. 126.
Daily Variety, May 2, 2003, p. 8; March 22, 2004, p. 7.
DSN Retailing Today, January 5, 2004, p. 2.
Entertainment Weekly, May 9, 2003, pp. 34–36; June 13, 2003, pp. 14–15.

Film Journal International, April 2003, p. 57.

Girls' Life, August–September 2003, p. 46.

Interview, February 2004, p. 122.

New Statesman, September 8, 2003, p. 46.

Newsweek, March 17, 2003, pp. 56–57.

New York Times, April 27, 2003, p. 13.

People, May 12, 2003, p. 37; May 19, 2003, pp. 83–84; April 5, 2004, p. 20.

Texas Monthly, April 2004, p. 80.

Time, April 14, 2003, pp. 76–79.

WWD, December 18, 2003, p. 2.

Online

"Sizzlin' 16, 2003: Hilary Duff," E! Online, http://www.eonline.com/Features/Features/Sizzlin2003/Girls/index2.html (January 31, 2003).

—*Carol Brennan*

Dale Earnhardt, Jr.

Professional race car driver

Born Ralph Dale Earnhardt, Jr., October 10, 1974, in Concord, NC; son of Dale, Sr. (a race car driver and team owner) and Brenda Earnhardt.

Addresses: *Fan club*—Club E JR, PO Box 5190, Concord, NC 28027. *Home*—Mooresville, NC. *Office*—Dale Earnhardt, Inc., 1675 Coddle Creek Highway, Mooresville, NC 28115.

Career

Began racing c. 1990; competed in the street stock division, Concord (NC), Speedway, c. early 1990s; racer, NASCAR's Late Model Stock Division, c. mid–1990s; race car driver, NASCAR Winston Racing Series, c. 1995–98, winning three races; Busch Grand National Series, race car driver #1 car, 1998–99; Busch Grand National Champion, 1998, 1999. Busch Grand National Series victories: Coca–Cola 300, Texas Motor Speedway, 1998; MBNA Platinum 200, Dover Speedway, 1999; Textilease Medique 300, South Boston Speedway, 1999; Lysol 200, Watkins Glen International, 1999; Carqueset Auto Parts 250, Gateway International Raceway; NAPA 200, Michigan International Speedway, 1999; Autolite Platinum 205, Richmond International Raceway, 1999; EAS/GNC Live Well 3000, Daytona International Speedway, 2002; Funai 250, Richmond International Raceway, 2002; Koolerz 300, Daytona International Speedway, 2003; Aaron's 312, Talladega Superspeedway, 2003; Winn–Dixie 250, Daytona International Speedway, 2003; Hershey's Kisses 300, Daytona International Speedway, 2004. Winston Cup Circuit (known as Nextel Cup beginning in 2004), race car driver #8 car, 1999—; Winston Cup/Nextel Cup

wins: The Winston (all–star race), 2000; Samsung/RadioShock 500, 2000; Pontiac Excitement 400, 2000; Pepsi 400, Daytona, FL, 2001; Dover 400, 2001; EA Sports 500, 2001; Aaron's 499, 2002; EA Sports 500, 2002; Budweiser Shootout, 2003; Gatorade 125 Race 2, 2003; Checker Auto Parts 500, Phoenix, AZ, 2003; Aaron's 499, 2003; Checker Auto Parts 500, 2003; Gatorade 125 Race 1, 2004; Daytona 500, 2004; Golden Corral 500, 2004; Atlanta 500, 2004; Chevy American Revolution 400, Richmond, VA, 2004. Chance2 team, co–owner, 2002—. Published *Driver #8* (memoir), 2002.

Sidelights

When Dale Earnhardt, Jr., decided to become a race car driver, he was following in the footsteps of a legend in NASCAR, his father, Dale Earnhardt, Sr., known as "The Intimidator." His son, known as "Little E" and "Junior," began racing as a teenager and within a short time he was racing professionally. Though he twice won the Busch Grand National Series and did well on the Winston Cup (later known as the Nextel Cup) circuit, it was not until the death of his father on the race track at the Daytona 500 in 2001 that he emerged from his father's shadow and came into his own both as a driver and public figure. One of the highlights of

Earnhardt's career was winning the Daytona 500 in 2004, three years after his father's death.

Earnhardt was born on October 10, 1974, in Concord, North Carolina, the son of Dale Earnhardt and his second wife, Brenda. His grandfather was Ralph Earnhardt, a NASCAR race car driver who also built cars for other drivers in North Carolina. Dale Earnhardt, Sr., had been a race car driver from an early age and won a number of Winston Cup championships in the 1980s and 1990s. He went on to own his racing team, for which his son later raced. Earnhardt, his older sister, Kelly, and half-siblings, Kerry and Taylor, were raised around racing and race car operations from an early age. Earnhardt and his brother, Kerry, were especially interested in the sport.

Earnhardt and his sister lived with their mother for the first six years of Earnhardt's life, then they lived with their father and his third wife in Mooresville, North Carolina. His father was often not there, but off racing. He did not have a close relationship with his father because of the demands of his father's career, and often suffered from low self-esteem. Earnhardt only attended a few races of his father's as a child. After racing go-karts on occasion as a kid, Earnhardt became more interested in the sport by the time he was 16 years old, though his father claimed he was not interested at all. His father wanted him to start by sweeping floors at the garage before working on cars, but Earnhardt was not particularly a fan of this plan.

After Earnhardt graduated from high school—mostly because his father insisted that he do so (his father dropped out after ninth grade), though Earnhardt, Sr., did not show up at his graduation—Earnhardt became serious about racing. He and his brother, Kerry, fixed up a car and traded off racing the car for one season at local short tracks. Impressed by their efforts, their father bought them each a car to race in as well as their sister, Kelly. The siblings raced at local tracks, though not against each other.

In the early to mid-1990s, Earnhardt moved up in the racing world. After racing in the street stock division at the Concord, North Carolina, Speedway, he moved to NASCAR's Late Model Stock Division in the mid-1990s. Within a few years, Earnhardt was racing primarily on the NASCAR Winston Racing Series. He won three races on that circuit in three years. Earnhardt did well and showed he had talent. As Leigh Montville of *Sports Illustrated* wrote of Earnhardt in this time period, "He found he had a capacity for hard work, an interest in improvement that no one had suspected in him—certainly his father hadn't. He spent time in the garage and on the track. He developed the driving style of a veteran, picking his spots to challenge, to lay back."

In 1998, Earnhardt became a full-time driver in the Busch Grand National series, after competing in several races on the circuit on 1996 and 1997. He was racing in the Busch series in preparation of becoming a full-time driver on the Winston Cup Circuit. In 1998, he won at least one race on the Busch Grand National series as well as the series title. Earnhardt then signed a six-year sponsorship deal with Budweiser from $42–50 million. Those in the know were impressed by Earnhardt's growth as a driver. H.A. Wheeler, president of the Charlotte Motor Speedway, told Liz Clarke of the *Washington Post,* "Dale Jr. is very deliberate, but moves when he needs to. He uses his head a lot and doesn't try to overrun his machine."

Earnhardt raced primarily on the Busch series again in 1999, winning six races and repeated as Busch series champion. That year was also the first in which Earnhardt raced professionally against his father. Competing directly against him or not, racing brought Earnhardt closer to his father. When asked if he raced to be close to his father, who was rather distant, he told Daniel McGinn and Bret Begun of *Newsweek,* "I wanted to impress him. I could have ... done other things, but no matter how successful I'd been ... it wouldn't have been as impressive to him as winning a race."

In 2000, Earnhardt made the jump up to the Winston Cup circuit, though he still occasionally competed on the Busch National Grand series each year. With the jump to the highest level of NASCAR competition, he faced more pressure and bigger sponsors. At the circuit's biggest race, the Daytona 500, Earnhardt finished 13th while his father finished 21st, the first time in six races that Earnhardt had beat his father. Earnhardt posted his first victory on the circuit in his 12th race, then won again the following week. In the rest of his races, he finished on average in the top 25.

Despite this impressive rookie campaign, Earnhardt was accused of being not very focused on racing all the time. One week, he went to Cancun on vacation while his crew remained at the garage working on his car. He also missed some press appearances. Earnhardt claimed that he took such actions so that he could have a normal life while dealing with pressures of being a high-profile race car driver. Earnhardt finished the 2000 Winston Cup season 16th in points and was the runner–up for rookie of the year honors. Two years later, in 2002, he a wrote book about his rookie year on the circuit, *Driver #8,* which was a best seller.

Earnhardt faced even more pressure in the 2001 season. His father was trying to win the Winston Cup championship that season so that he could set a record for most Winston Cup wins. Earnhardt, Sr., died in the biggest race on the circuit, the Daytona 500, which opened the season. He was in a fatal accident in the last lap of the race. Despite this tragedy, Earnhardt finished second in the race. He credited his father for his success. Earnhardt told Lars Anderson of *Sports Illustrated,* "The key to all the success I've had is my dad. It's that simple. He's taught me how to drive, how to live with integrity and how to be a man."

Upon his father's death, Earnhardt did not just inherit the mantle of the Earnhardt family racing legacy, but the whole company, including Dale Earnhardt, Inc., which his father had founded in 1996. His father had done a lot of merchandising and had managed the careers of three drivers racing for him. Earnhardt had to grow up fast and take charge, while his father's death followed him everywhere. He also was still improving as a driver himself, getting better with his car, learning more about how it ran, and diagnosing problems by feel.

The week following Earnhardt's father's death, the young race car driver got into an accident similar to the one that killed his father. The accident occurred at the Dura–Lube 400 at the North Carolina Speedway, but he was not hurt. Fellow team driver Steve Park won the race. Less than five months after the fatal accident, Earnhardt was racing again at the Daytona International Speedway in a different race, the Pepsi 400. He won the race. Earnhardt won three Winston Cup races, and finished eighth in the point standings. His prize money for the year was $5.8 million.

As Earnhardt's success gave him a higher profile, he was signed to additional valuable endorsement deals that brought him millions of dollars in income. One such deal was with Drakkar Noir cologne which signed him to a three–year contract during which he would serve as the face of the fragrance. He also was invited to throw the first pitch at a baseball game and had a hand in developing video games. One reason for Earnhardt's higher exposure was that his fan base greatly increased after his father's death. Many of his father's fans became his

at that time. Unlike his father, Earnhardt was able to cross over into a mainstream sensibility; he was an MTV–friendly NASCAR driver. In 2004, he was named one of *People* magazine's "50 Most Beautiful People." Despite this increased adulation, Earnhardt was not altogether comfortable with his celebrity.

While the 2002 season was profitable for Earnhardt off the track, he suffered on the track. In addition to clashing with his crew, he suffered injuries in a number of races. In one race at Fontana, he sprained an ankle, hurt his shoulder, and was bruised in an on–track accident. Earnhardt later suffered a severe concussion from a crash at a race at the California Speedway. He did not do well in many races at the beginning of the season, but in the season's last eight races, he finished in the top ten six times. By the end of the season, he had become more consistent as a driver and more mature as a person because of his tribulations. He also took on more responsibilities by becoming the co–owner of Chance2, a racing team that competed on the Busch series.

Earnhardt did much better as a driver in 2003, after changing some of his crew members. At the beginning of the season, he finished third in a race at Martinsville, and second at a race in Las Vegas. He began spending more time at the track, and learned more about his car and how the race preparation process worked. Earnhardt won a number of races during the season, but did not win the Winston Cup Championship. To help run the company he had inherited as well as his team, Earnhardt moved to Mooresville to be closer to Dale Earnhardt, Inc.

In 2004, Earnhardt grew even stronger as a driver and had a goal of winning the Nextel Cup (as the Winston Cup began being called in 2004, after a sponsorship change) that season. Though other drivers accused Earnhardt of being the beneficiary of favoritism by NASCAR which led to many victories at certain tracks (Daytona and Talladega), Earnhardt had improved and knew how to legally garner information about other drivers and their cars. Earnhardt's new–found strength showed as he won the Daytona 500 on February 15, 2004, the anniversary of his father's death. He told Bill Coats of *St. Louis Post–Dispatch,* "He was over in the passenger side. I'm sure he was having a blast."

After this popular win, Earnhardt won another race the next day, the Hershey's Kisses 300. This win made him the points leader in the standings, the first time he ever held the lead while racing on the premiere circuit. However, it was only a temporary hold on the number–one spot. In addition to winning several other races that year, Earnhardt became more involved with his own company, Junior Motor Sports.

On July 18, 2004, Earnhardt wrecked his vehicle during a warmup for an American Le Mans Series race in Sonoma, California. The accident occurred when he lost control of his car which then went into a spin and slid backward into a concrete barrier. The crash caused his car to burst into flames, leaving him with second–degree burns on parts of his body. A spokesperson for Earnhardt said he was not badly injured and planned to compete in the Nextel Cup race at New Hampshire International Speedway.

Though he was proud of his father and what he meant in his life, Earnhardt wanted to be known for his own successes. He told Pam Lambert and Michaele Ballard in *People,* "The biggest compliment you can give me is that I remind you of my dad. But when is the day going to come when I don't have to reflect back? When will I stand on my own merit?"

Sources

Periodicals

Brandweek, August 19, 2002, p. 16.
Global Cosmetic Industry, August 2003, p. 50.
Los Angeles Times, February 16, 2004, p. D1.
Milwaukee Journal Sentinel (WI), February 16, 2004, p. 1C.
Newsweek, April 15, 2002, pp. 46–47.
People, March 12, 2001, p. 56; July 23, 2001, p. 75; March 8, 2004, pp. 71–72; May 10, 2004, p. 140.
Sports Illustrated, November 17, 1997, p. 60; December 22, 1999, p. 78; December 6, 2000, p. 88; February 28, 2001, p. 60; December 3, 2001, p. 34; July 1, 2002, p. 60; June 23, 2003, p. 48.
St. Louis Post–Dispatch (MO), February 16, 2004, p. D1.
St. Petersburg Times (FL), February 13, 2004, p. 8Y.
USA Today, February 6, 2004, p. 1C.
Washington Post, February 12, 1999, p. G1.

Online

"A Dale Earnhardt, Jr. Biography," Dale Earnhardt Jr., http://www.dalejrpitstop.com/bio8/bio.html (April 13, 2004).

"Biography and Favorites," Dale Jr., http://www.dalejr.com/bio.html (April 13, 2004).
"Dale Earnhardt Jr.," CBS Sports Line, http://cbs.sportsline.com/autoracing/drivers/driverpage/275370 (April 13, 2004).
"Dale Earnhardt Jr.," ESPN.com, http://sports.espn.go.com/rpm/driver?series=wc&id=dearnhardtjr (April 17, 2004).
"8 Budweiser Driver: Dale Earnhardt Jr.," Dale Earnhardt Inc., http://www.daleearnhardtinc.com/content/motorsports/t_driver.aspx?t=8 (April 13, 2004).
"Frequently Asked Questions," Dale Jr., http://www.dalejr.com/faq.html (April 13, 2004).
"Junior burned in crash during Le Mans practice," *SI.com,* http://sportsillustrated.cnn.com/2004/racing/07/18/earnhardt.injured/index.html (July 19, 2004).
"1999 Results for Dale Earnhardt Jr.," ESPN.com, http://sports.espn.go.com/rpm/drivers/results?year=1999&driverId=150 (April 17, 2004).
"Race by Race: Dale Earnhardt Jr. 1999 Busch," NASCAR Racing, http://www.racingone.com/driver_ytd.asp?driverid=67&subseries=2&raceyear=1999 (April 17, 2004).
"Race by Race: Dale Earnhardt Jr. 2004 Busch," NASCAR Racing, http://www.racingone.com/driver_ytd.asp?driverid=67&subseries=2&raceyear=2004 (April 17, 2004).
"Race by Race: Dale Earnhardt Jr. 2003 Busch," NASCAR Racing, http://www.racingone.com/driver_ytd.asp?driverid=67&subseries=2&raceyear=2003 (April 17, 2004).
"Race by Race: Dale Earnhardt Jr. 2002 Busch," NASCAR Racing, http://www.racingone.com/driver_ytd.asp?driverid=67&subseries=2&raceyear=2002 (April 17, 2004).
"2000 Results for Dale Earnhardt Jr.," ESPN.com, http://sports.espn.go.com/rpm/drivers/results?year=2000&driverId=150 (April 17, 2004).
"2004 Results for Dale Earnhardt Jr.," ESPN.com, http://sports.espn.go.com/rpm/drivers/results?driverId=150 (April 17, 2004).
"2001 Results for Dale Earnhardt Jr.," ESPN.com, http://sports.espn.go.com/rpm/drivers/results?year=2001&driverId=150 (April 17, 2004).
"2003 Results for Dale Earnhardt Jr.," ESPN.com, http://sports.espn.go.com/rpm/drivers/results?year=2003&driverId=150 (April 17, 2004).
"2002 Results for Dale Earnhardt Jr.," ESPN.com, http://sports.espn.go.com/rpm/drivers/results?year=2002&driverId=150 (April 17, 2004).

—*A. Petruso*

Shirin Ebadi

Human-rights activist

Born in 1947, in Hamadan, Iran; daughter of Mino Ebadi; married to Javad Tavassolian (an electrical engineer); children: two daughters. *Education:* Studied law at Tehran University.

Addresses: *Office*—c/o The Nobel Foundation, Box 5232, SE–102 45 Stockholm, Sweden.

Career

Judge in Tehran, Iran, until 1979; human–rights lawyer; children's advocate and founder of non-governmental organization for children's rights; author of several books on women's rights and law in Islamic societies; professor of law, Tehran University.

Awards: Nobel Prize for Peace, Norwegian Nobel Committee, 2003.

Sidelights

Iranian human–rights activist Shirin Ebadi became the first Muslim woman to win the Nobel Peace Prize in the prestigious award's 103–year history. Since her country's 1979 Islamic Revolution, Ebadi has worked to secure civil rights for Iranian women, children, and political prisoners, which has often put her at odds with the country's conservative Muslim clergy who wield immense influence in the Islamic republic. Her win, noted *Time International* writer Scott Macleod, "is proof that while Muslim women continue to endure severe inequality, many

are nonetheless making remarkable efforts to re-shape their own lives as well as the societies that shackle them."

Ebadi was born in Hamadan, Iran, in 1947. Her father was a lawyer who authored a work on Iranian commercial law that served as a standard law–school text for a number of years, and he also served in the government of Iran's Shah, Mohammad Reza Pahlavi. During Ebadi's youth and early adulthood, Iran was both a progressive and repressive place on the Middle Eastern map: the Shah courted Western investment, encouraged literacy and education, and granted Iranian women equality on many fronts, but the nation's oil wealth was unevenly distrib-uted, and a secret police force carried out harsh re-prisals against those who opposed the Shah's regime.

Ebadi followed in her father's footsteps and studied law at Tehran University. In 1975, she became presi-dent of the city court of Tehran and the first female judge in the country. Her promising career, how-ever, was cut short by the 1979 revolution, when groups of Islamic extremists began rioting and forced the Shah into exile. A fundamentalist cleric, Ayatollah Ruhollah Khomeini, became Iran's new leader, and an Islamic republic was declared. Ebadi was herself a devout Muslim, and supported the revolution and the new government, but she lost her job when new decrees based on strict interpretations of the Koran, or Muslim holy text, declared women unfit to hold decision–making positions in the judiciary.

Ebadi instead turned to writing books on civil rights and children's advocacy issues, an area of interest roused by the abuse cases she had heard as a Tehran jurist. Their plight was closely linked to the legal status of women in conservative Islam, and Ebadi began taking cases that other lawyers were unwilling to defend in the repressive political climate. In one notorious incident, a father was accused of killing his nine–year–old daughter. The girl's mother had lost custody after the divorce—a common practice in Iran, though the woman claimed her ex–husband was a drug user and kept the girl out of school. Initially the court declared the man guilty of murder, but he was not given any jail time, on the grounds that a father has ultimate control over his offspring. The highly publicized case and verdict angered many in Iran, and Ebadi campaigned to force the court to jail the man for a year. Her crusade also forced lawmakers to amend the family law statutes to make drug abuse and neglect of a child's education grounds for losing custody.

In 1997, many in Iran and the outside world were hopeful when a moderate, Mohammed Khatami, became president. Khatami began a cautious liberalization effort, but fundamentalist elements fought back decisively. Intellectuals and others who argued in support of speeding the reform process were harassed, and several dissidents were slain in a string of heinous, unsolved murders. Some believed that vigilantes in the hire of conservative factions in Iran were responsible, and Ebadi began collecting evidence to prove it. One thug's videotaped confession admitted that hardliners in the government were indeed linked to the slayings, and Ebadi secretly distributed the tape. Authorities caught on, and in June of 2000 she turned herself in to the local magistrate when she learned that her arrest was imminent.

Ebadi spent 23 days in solitary confinement in Tehran's notoriously brutal Evin Prison. International human–rights groups pressured the Khatami government to release her, and she was convicted on a charge of defaming the Islamic republic and given a suspended sentence. She was also banned from practicing law for five years. In Paris, France, in October of 2003 to deliver a speech, she learned that she had won the Nobel Peace Prize from a news report on the car radio. She became the first Iranian

in history to win it, and only the third Muslim. Government–run news sources in Iran initially downplayed the honor, but popular support was effusive; when Ebadi flew home, thousands of women turned out at Tehran's airport to greet her. Her 79–year–old mother confessed to Macleod in the *Time International* interview that she herself cried all day when she heard the news. "I always wanted to become just like Shirin became," Mino Ebadi told the magazine.

Ebadi received death threats both before and after her acceptance speech in Oslo, Norway, in December of 2003, and was grudgingly provided with a bodyguard, car, and driver by Iranian authorities. The prize was not without controversy abroad as well: some in international human–rights community claimed the choice of Ebadi was a tacit victory for Islamic fundamentalism. The activist has long asserted that democracy and an Islamic–based society are not mutually exclusive goals. "There is no contradiction between an Islamic republic, Islam, and human rights," she said in an interview with *Newsweek International* writer Marie Valla. "We need an interpretation of Islam that leaves much more space for women to take action. We need an Islam that is compatible with democracy and one that's respectful of individual rights."

In February of 2004, Ebadi joined in a widespread boycott of parliamentary elections after the cleric–controlled Guardian Council of the government summarily disqualified some 2,000 liberal candidates. She lives and works in a modest Tehran apartment she shares with her husband, an electrical engineer, and is the mother of two daughters. One of them is a law student, and Ebadi has said that one unexpected benefit of a strict Muslim society has been a rise in the number of Iranian women earning university degrees, for the schools are segregated by gender and thus the more tradition–minded Muslim fathers do not disapprove of their daughters' educational goals. She was also heartened by the rise of new channels of information–sharing. "My generation had very little means to keep itself informed," she told Valla. "When I was young we had neither computers nor the Internet.... I hope that today's young people can do much more and do better for our country than I did."

Sources

Books

Contemporary Theatre, Film and Television, volume 27, Gale Group, 2000.

Periodicals

Independent (London, England), October 11, 2003, p. 5.

Middle East, November 2003, p. 32.

Nation, January 12, 2004, p. 11.

Newsweek International, October 20, 2003, p. 92.

New York Times, December 11, 2003, p. A20; February 18, 2004, p. A6.

Time, October 20, 2003, p. 39.

Time International (Europe Edition), December 15, 2003, p. 44.

Online

"Iranian rights activist wins Nobel," CNN.com, http://www.cnn.com/2003/WORLD/europe/10/10/nobel.peace/index.html (October 10, 2003).

—*Carol Brennan*

Larry Ellison

AP/Wide World Photos

Founder and Chief Executive Officer of Oracle Corporation

Born Lawrence Joseph Ellison, August 17, 1944, in New York, NY; son of Florence Spellman; adopted at nine months by Florence's aunt, Lillian Ellison, and her husband, Louis; married Adda Quinn, 1967 (divorced, 1974); married Nancy Wheeler, 1976 (divorced, 1978); married Barbara Boothe, 1983 (divorced, 1987); married Melanie Craft (a romance novelist), 2003; children: David, Margaret (with Boothe). *Education:* Attended University of Illinois, Champaign, IL, 1962–64, and University of Chicago, 1966.

Addresses: *Office*—Oracle Corp., 500 Oracle Pkwy., Redwood City, CA 94065.

Career

Worked as a programmer in California for various companies, late 1960s; became vice president, Precision Instruments Co., 1976; founded Software Development Laboratories, with Robert Miner and Edward Oates, 1977; took company public (as Oracle Corp.), 1986; ceded some executive responsibility to new president and chief financial officer, 1991, following accounting scandal; deposed president Ray Lane and assumed sole control of Oracle, 2000; resigned as chairman but remained CEO of Oracle, 2004.

Sidelights

Larry Ellison founded a software company that makes little-noticed but ubiquitous database programs that are indispensable to modern commerce. His Oracle Corporation began with three employees in 1977 and now employs more than 40,000, with annual sales of $9.5 billion. Ellison, who owns 26 percent of Oracle's stock, is the richest man in California, and ranks in the top ten of the Forbes 400 list of the world's wealthiest individuals. His personal fortune is estimated at $21.9 billion. Ellison started the firm with two partners, and was always the chief salesman and architect of Oracle's growth. Oracle has a reputation for ruthless competitiveness, which stems at least in part from the electric personality of its chief executive. Ellison was born in 1944 in Manhattan to a 19–year–old woman. His mother found it impossible to raise the child alone, and after the baby suffered a severe bout of pneumonia at nine months, she gave him up to her aunt, Lillian Ellison, and Lillian's husband, Louis. Louis Ellison had emigrated from Russia in 1905 and arrived in New York virtually empty–handed. He moved to Chicago, Illinois, where he married and became an accountant and possibly the owner of apartment buildings. Louis Ellison married Lillian, his second wife, during the Great Depression, and their adopted son was their only child. They did not tell Larry he was adopted until he was 12 years old, and then kept from him the fact that his biological mother was the niece of his adoptive mother. Ellison never learned anything about his biological father. The family lived on the

North Side of Chicago for most of Ellison's youth, then moved to the South Shore, on the other side of town, when he was in high school. Ellison was prone to describe his background as rough, though a biographer, Mike Wilson, claimed the South Shore of that era was a comfortable, middle–class neighborhood. Ellison graduated from South Shore High School in 1962 and enrolled at the University of Illinois at Urbana–Champaign. His aim was to become a doctor. Ellison's academic career was undistinguished, and he dropped out of college after two years, after his adoptive mother died of cancer. He enrolled for one semester at the University of Chicago, but never graduated.

Ellison moved to Berkeley, California, in 1966. He worked at various jobs, mostly related to computers. He worked mainly night and weekend shifts backing up data and doing routine maintenance work. It was neither highly skilled nor challenging work, but the future entrepreneur was at that point not very ambitious. He married Adda Quinn in 1967, shortly after meeting her at a Berkeley employment agency. They lived in a one–room apartment for three years, until buying a house in Oakland in 1970. Neither made much money, and Ellison often took a pay cut when he changed jobs. His passions were bike riding and boating, and he borrowed money to buy a 34–foot sailboat before he had finished paying off a smaller vessel. His wife divorced him in 1974, apparently worn out by his aimlessness and his debts. According to Wilson's *The Difference Between God and Larry Ellison,* it was at a session with a marriage counselor while he and Adda were breaking up that Ellison decided to become a millionaire. He had never talked about money or any concrete success before this. Quinn advised him to go make his million for his own sake; she was leaving anyway.

Ellison continued to work with computers, eventually learning a lot about programming IBM machines. While working at a small company called Ampex, Ellison met Robert Miner and Edward Oates, who became his partners in Oracle. At Ampex the three worked on writing a database program for the Central Intelligence Agency (CIA). In those days, computers could store lots of information, but managing it and recalling it were complicated and inefficient processes. Ampex was working on a way to maintain a database of information on videotape as opposed to traditional magnetic tape. The Ampex machine could search and rewind videotape at high speed. Miner, Oates, and Ellison wrote the program for the Ampex video database, which was called Oracle. Ellison left Ampex for a sales and marketing position at another company, but he remained friends with Oates and Miner, and

the three met often for lunch, chess, or tennis. Ellison ended up vice president of a small firm called Precision Instruments Co. Precision Instruments was working on a project similar to Ampex's, trying to find a way to store and retrieve masses of data, this time on microfilm. Precision Instruments needed to hire a contract company to program its software. Ellison convinced Miner and Oates to go into business with him, and the three formed Software Development Laboratories in 1977. The new company existed at that point solely to write programs for Precision Instruments, and its offices were inside the Precision Instruments building. Ellison, who had instigated the venture, took 60 percent of the shares, with Oates and Miner each taking 20 percent.

While the three young men were busy writing Precision Instruments software, they discovered something else. Programmers at IBM had been working on what was called a relational database. This was a database that could be queried, or asked to retrieve certain pieces of information. The databases that existed up until then were good at holding information, such as lists of employees and how much money they made. But to find out how many employees, for instance, made more than a certain figure, the user had to go in and look at the data. The relational database, however, could tell the user who made how much money, and even go in and give selected employees a raise. This was what everybody wanted, and IBM programmers figured out how to do this using a simple computer language that could be typed on a keyboard. When a paper on the relational database program appeared in a trade journal, Ellison and his partners got very interested. They realized their new company could finish its contract work for Precision Instruments and then drum up similar work for other companies. But the better alternative was to find a really good software product and sell that to whoever wanted it. Using the IBM paper, the three figured out how to write their own relational database software. They named their program Oracle, after the CIA project they had worked on earlier.

Ellison met his second wife, Nancy Wheeler, in 1976, and they married about six months before the founding of Software Development Laboratories. In 1978, the couple divorced. Wheeler gave up any claim on her husband's company for $500. The company moved into new quarters and changed its name to Relational Software Inc. (RSI). Its first customer outside of Precision Instruments was the CIA. RSI also sold a copy of its new database program to the Navy. Even with only two customers, the company had to write its software to work on three different types of computer. This prompted Ellison to develop a marketing strategy that eventually led Oracle to dominate the database market. His idea was to make the Oracle program truly portable, that is, it would work on any kind of computer. The CIA used IBM computers as well as other brands, and so did many large corporations. Ellison promised that Oracle would work with whatever equipment a company used.

Ellison became a relentless marketer, demonstrating Oracle at trade shows and training corporate technical staff in its use. By 1982, the company employed only several dozen people, and had sales of $2.4 million, but it was on a steep upward trajectory. It managed to double or nearly double sales year by year, and Oracle surpassed its competitors. Ellison married for the third time in 1983. Barbara Boothe, a former receptionist at RSI, had borne him a son, David, and pressed Ellison to marry her before the baby turned one. The couple had a second child, Margaret, in 1986. That year, RSI became a public company, taking the name of its software, Oracle. It debuted on Wall Street one day before Microsoft. While Microsoft's programs soon became part of a majority of American households, Oracle's growth was more behind the scenes. Its database program made possible such things as computerized hotel and airline reservation systems, inventory tracking for chain stores, and management of supplier and client databases for large manufacturers. Oracle aggressively outsold its competitors, and by the late 1980s it was still doubling sales yearly, making it by far the largest company in the database market. By the time Ellison and Barbara Boothe filed for divorce in 1986, he was a millionaire several times over, as were many of the top people at Oracle. Oracle's revenue that year was more than $55 million, and Ellison's stake in the company was valued at $90 million.

Ellison had urged his sales team to push Oracle hard, and there were few traditional corporate controls at the rapidly growing company. Ellison was an entrepreneur with a genius for marketing and the savvy to make the most of an opportunity. But he had no experience running a multimillion dollar corporation. So perhaps not surprisingly, Oracle began to rocket out of control. The sales team routinely cut corners, turning in contracts on April 2 but recording them as March sales, for example. The company also booked sales to companies that had only a dubious ability to pay. Even though the company was showing tremendous sales figures, it was not actually collecting all the money that was due it. Ellison cultivated a bad–boy image, racing cars and yachts, building a home for himself that was a reproduction of a Japanese medieval villa, investing in a Hollywood magazine and flying fighter

jets. He was also well–known for coming late to meetings, whether of his own board or with Washington dignitaries. Meanwhile the company instituted a sales incentive program called "Go for the Gold," where employees who met or exceeded sales goals were paid in actual gold coins. Ellison's flamboyant style had extended through the whole company, leading it to flout Securities and Exchange Commission rules. Finally, Oracle's financial auditors demanded that the company restate its earnings to reflect accurate sales. In 1990 Oracle was forced to restate $15 million in earnings for the previous quarter, meaning it had to announce that that $15 million had never existed in the first place. As a result, its stock price sank, and angry investors sued the company. Oracle's board considered replacing Ellison, but he stayed on, determined to keep his mind on the business. He also hired an experienced president and chief financial officer. The company righted itself after the disaster, and progressed at a more moderate pace through the 1990s. Oracle added $1 billion in sales annually between 1992 and 1998.

In 1997, Ellison took a new tack, pushing Oracle to get more involved in so–called applications software. Applications run on top of existing programs, doing things like billing. While the market for database programs was shrinking, the applications market was expected to continue to grow well into the 2000s. In 1998, Ellison sailed his yacht, the "Sayonara," in a disastrous 725–mile ocean race. A storm sank six of his competitors, four men died, and Ellison was unable to control his boat in the immense waves. This near–death experience apparently shook Ellison into devoting more time to his company. He began to take back power he had assigned to his president and chief financial officer. Oracle's president, Raymond Lane, resigned in 2000, and many other top executives also moved on to other companies. Oracle's new applications software, 11i, debuted in 2000 but was full of problems. The company's stock price fell, and 2001 also turned out to be a poor year for Oracle.

However, by 2003 Oracle's revenue had risen to $9 billion, and the company was still profitable despite an overall downturn in the technology industry. Ellison's love live was looking better, too. At the end of 2003, he married romance novelist Melanie Craft. The couple had met while leaving a San Francisco, California, restaurant in 1996. Business–wise, Ellison's new mantra was the NC, a small, cheap computer that ran off software stored on the Internet. He repeatedly predicted that the personal computer was dead, and that the NC would surpass it. He seemed determined to keep Oracle growing, and in 2003 he launched a hostile bid to take over a rival company called PeopleSoft. PeopleSoft was run by a former Oracle executive, Craig Conway. Ellison and Conway displayed a lot of personal animosity over the deal. Oracle's offer was being reviewed by government regulators at the close of 2003. Ellison was sure the deal would go through, while Conway was convinced of the opposite. Whatever the result, Ellison's maverick style clearly still dominated Oracle.

Ellison resigned as chairman of Oracle effective January 19, 2004, but remained CEO of the company. On February 26, 2004, the Justice department ruled that Oracle's attempt to take over rival PeopleSoft would be bad for competition, effectively blocking Ellison's hopes of acquiring the competing firm. On March 18, 2004, Ellison bought and sold one million shares of Oracle Corp. for a profit and gave another 911,744 shares to his wife. He still owned more than 1.3 billion shares in the company.

Sources

Books

Stone, Florence M., *The Oracle of Oracle*, AMACOM, 2002.
Wilson, Mike, *The Difference Between God and Larry Ellison*, William Morrow, 1997.

Periodicals

BusinessWeek, August 25, 2003, pp. 120–121.
Computer Weekly, May 30, 1996, p. 136.
Daily Telegraph (London, England), February 27, 2004.
eWeek, September 11, 2003.
Forbes, August 20, 2001, p. 82.
Fortune, November 13, 2000, p. 98.
Knight Ridder/Tribune Business News, January 14, 2004.
Newsweek, January 11, 1999, p. 68.
Time, June 23, 2003, pp. 47–49.
U.S. News & World Report, January 18, 1999, p. 38; May 8, 2000, p. 10.
Vanity Fair, June 1997, pp. 146–152, 188–193.

Online

Oracle's Ellison buys, sells $1M shares, *Silicon Valley/San Jose Business Journal,* http://sanjose.bizjournals.com/sanjose/stories/2004/03/15/daily28.html (July 9, 2004).

—A. Woodward

Robert Evans

AP/Wide World Photos

Film producer

Born Robert J. Shapera, June 29, 1930, in New York, NY; son of Archie (a dentist) and Florence (a homemaker) Shapera; married Sharon Hugueny (an actor), May 28, 1961 (divorced, 1962); married Camilla Sparv (a model and actor), c. 1963 (marriage ended); married Ali MacGraw (an actor), October 24, 1969 (divorced, 1972); married Phyllis George (an actor), 1977 (marriage ended, 1978); married Catherine Oxenberg (an actress), July 12, 1998 (annulled, July 21, 1998); married Leslie Ann Woodward (a model), November 2, 2002 (divorced, 2003); children: Joshua (with MacGraw).

Addresses: *Publisher*—Dove Books, 301 North Canon Dr., Beverly Hills, CA 90210.

Career

Began career in entertainment as a radio and television actor while still in junior high school, 1940s; became an executive and stakeholder in his brother's clothing company, Evan–Picone, 1950s; cast in his first film, *The Man of a Thousand Faces*, 1957; appeared in *The Sun Also Rises*, 1957; appeared in several more films before leaving Hollywood to return to the clothing business, 1960s; sold his stake in Evan–Picone and left the company to return to Hollywood as a producer, 1966; landed three–picture producing deal with 20th Century Fox, 1966; headed world–wide production at Paramount, where he produced numerous hit films, 1966–1974; produced films as an independent producer, 1974—; published autobiography, *The Kid Stays in the Picture*, 1994; narrated movie version of *The Kid Stays in the Picture*, 2002; narrated cartoon *Kid Notorious*, Comedy Central, 2003—.

Sidelights

Film mogul Robert Evans rescued the Paramount movie studio from financial ruin when he became head of worldwide production in 1966. Under his leadership, which lasted until 1974, Paramount's earnings grew from five percent of Gulf and Western's (its parent company) income to 55 percent. Propelled by such hits as *Rosemary's Baby* and *The Godfather*, Evans' Paramount became the top–grossing film studio in Hollywood. But after leaving Paramount to become an independent producer, Evans fell on hard times, flirting with financial ruin himself, and running afoul of the law with a drug conviction. Evans' star rose again, however, with the 2002 film *The Kid Stays in the Picture*, based on his autobiography of the same name. The film was a hit, turning Evans into a celebrity, and once again, offers began to roll in for him.

Robert Evans was born Robert J. Shapera in New York City in 1930—the beginning of the Great Depression. Evans' father, Archie, was a dentist, and he ran his own clinic in Harlem. Archie worked seven days a week at the clinic to support the family, which included Evans' mother, older brother, and younger sister. "Both my parents were second–

generation Jews," Evans said in his 1994 autobiography, *The Kid Stays in the Picture.* "That was all they had in common." Evans admired his father, who was also well liked by his patients in Harlem. Unusual for the time, Archie had a staff of both white and African–American dentists and assistants.

Very early on, while still in elementary school, Evans decided he wanted to become an actor. His inspiration was the stars of the silver screen—James Cagney, Humphrey Bogart, and others. While Evans was growing up, radio was king, employing more actors than any other medium, including film. So Evans set his sights on becoming a radio actor. When he was 12 years old, Evans began to audition regularly for roles in radio, and within a few months, he landed his first part—that of a Nazi colonel on a show called *Radio Mystery Theater.* By the time Evans turned 14, he was acting regularly on a program called *Let's Pretend.* More radio roles followed in rapid succession.

Evans changed his last name while in junior high school at the insistence of his father, who had always felt that his boys should be named after his mother (Ms. Evan before she was married; Evans added the "s") rather than his father, who was not a good parent. Evans continued his acting career in radio through high school, also picking up occasional roles on television, which was just starting to take hold as a viable medium for entertainment.

After an unsuccessful bid to become an film actor in Hollywood, Evans headed back East, where he worked for his brother's by–then–thriving women's clothing manufacturing business. Evans and his brother struck it rich, and before he turned 25, Evans was a millionaire. The company's label, Evan–Picone, continued to be a trend–setter in women's fashion into the 21st century.

Wealthy and 26 years old, Evans thought his acting career was well behind him. But while in Beverly Hills on business in 1956, he was spotted poolside at the hotel he was staying in by the female star of a new film in production by Universal, *The Man of a Thousand Faces.* The film also starred one of Evans' early idols, James Cagney. The female star, Norma Shearer, wanted Evans to play a role in the film. He screen–tested with Cagney that day, and was cast the following day. And so, Evans, without even trying, finally broke into films.

Shortly after finishing his work on his first film, Evans was spotted by Twentieth Century Fox producer Darryl Zanuck in a night club. Zanuck did

not even know that Evans was an actor, but he saw in him star potential, and he cast Evans in a film version of the Hemingway novel *The Sun Also Rises.* In it, he played opposite Ava Gardner as her Mexican bullfighter lover.

It was during the making of this film that Evans found his true calling. Arriving on set in Mexico, he was instantly disliked by the cast, the writer, and the director, all of whom told Zanuck in no uncertain terms that Evans would make the film a failure. Zanuck came to the Mexican set to see for himself why Evans was so disliked. Evans turned on the charm for Zanuck during the filming of his scenes in the bullring. Afterward, Zanuck pronounced, as Evans reported in his autobiography, "The kid stays in the picture. And anybody who doesn't like it can quit!" Zanuck left the set without further discussion. Evans, who did indeed stay in the picture, decided then and there that what he really wanted to do was become a producer. As he put it in his autobiography, "It was then I learned what a producer was—a Boss. It was then I learned I wanted to be D.Z., not some ... actor ... desperate for a nod of approval."

Both *The Man of a Thousand Faces* and *The Sun Also Rises* came out within a few weeks of each other in 1957, to critical acclaim. For a brief while, Evans, by his account, was one of the most sought–after actors in Hollywood. But the offers quickly boiled down to roles in second–rate films. Evans, by his own admission, did not have the talents of a major film star. Then, too, his heart was in producing, not acting. After acting in several unmemorable minor films, Evans was given an ultimatum by his brother's company: either return to New York as an executive, or sell out his stake in the company.

By this time, Evans had married the first of what was to be six wives: Hollywood starlet Sharon Hugueny. Evans had a tough decision to make. As he said in his autobiography, "Looking at yourself in the mirror, calling a spade a spade ain't easy—Evans, you're not good enough to make it all the way. The parts you're offered you don't want, and the parts you want you're not offered. Paul Newman? No shot. Tab Hunter? More like it. Not for me. I wanted to be the next Darryl Zanuck, and I paid the price, making the most difficult decision of my life. I gave up the glamour of Hollywood, two firm pictures with Zanuck, a storybook existence, and returned to New York City with my child bride, back to Evan–Picone's showroom on Broadway."

Within six months of bringing his new wife to New York, Evans and Hugueny divorced. He hated his work at the clothing company, dreaming only of

California's beaches and his friends in the film business back in Los Angeles. Not long after Evans's return to New York, in 1966, he and his partners sold their company to Revlon, Inc., making a reported $10 million in the process. Evans and his new bosses did not get along, and he left the company soon after, leaving him free once again to pursue his dream of becoming a producer.

By this time, he had married model Camilla Sparv. He took his new wife back to Los Angeles. There, with the money and the contacts to acquire literary properties to make into films, he started his new career as a film producer. Almost at once, he landed a three–picture contract with 20th Century Fox. Meanwhile, he grew restless in his marriage, and after Sparv caught him being unfaithful, and he refused to stop seeing other women, they got divorced.

Even as his marriage fell apart, Evans' star as a producer rose. A feature article about him the *New York Times* brought him to the attention of the heads of the Paramount movie studio, who hired him in 1966 to head the studio's European production office in London, England. It was an offer he could not refuse, and he had to back out of his contract with 20th Century Fox—all this before he produced a single film. Evans later credited the *New York Times* article, which was written by Peter Bart, with landing him the Paramount deal. Evans returned the favor a few months later by hiring Bart to be on his staff at Paramount after Evans was promoted and moved to Hollywood.

Evans' promotion put him in charge of production at the entire studio. At the time Paramount was dead last in earnings among the major Hollywood movie studios, and its owners were counting on Evans to improve its fortunes—they were not disappointed. The studio's first big hit under Evans was the 1968 film *The Odd Couple.* Based on the play by the same name by Neil Simon, the film became a smash hit, eventually spawning numerous sequels and a TV series.

Under the leadership of Evans, Paramount, tottering dangerously close to financial ruin when he took the helm, pulled back into the black. He followed up the success of *The Odd Couple* with *Rosemary's Baby,* also in 1968. It became the best–grossing film of the summer, and made its lead actress, Mia Farrow, a star.

Goodbye Columbus in 1969 was the next hit for Paramount, and it too catapulted its lead actress, Ali MacGraw, to stardom. Evans was just as taken with MacGraw as the movie–going public; he married her the year the film came out. They had one child, a son named Joshua, before divorcing in 1972.

Paramount produced many more hits under Evans, including 1968's *Romeo and Juliet,* 1970's *Love Story,* which starred MacGraw, and 1972's *The Godfather.* Under Evans, Paramount went from earning just five percent of the revenues of its parent company, to 55 percent, and became the top movie studio in Hollywood.

But while Paramount's fortunes soared, Evans' did not. Never earning percentages of his film company's profits, nor bonuses in addition to his salary, Evans found himself sliding into debt, and he left Paramount in 1974 to produce films on his own. His first effort as an independent producer, 1974's *Chinatown,* starring Jack Nicholson, was a hit. In 1977, Evans married his fourth wife, former Miss America Phyllis George. That marriage lasted eleven months.

In 1980, Evans was prosecuted along with his brother for purchasing thousands of dollars worth of cocaine. He stayed out of jail, spending a year on probation. But it was the beginning of a decline for the producer. Two films ruined him financially in 1990. These were *The Cotton Club* and *The Two Jakes.* After his old friend Nicholson helped him financially, he attempted a comeback later in the 1990s by producing what turned out to be unmemorable thrillers. It was during this time, in 1994, that he published his autobiography, *The Kid Stays in the Picture.*

Evans suffered a series of debilitating strokes in 1998, and he required extensive rehabilitation. During his recovery period, he married Catherine Oxenberg after a five–day courtship. This fifth marriage was his briefest, lasting only a few days. "My fault," he later told *People*'s Jim Jerome. "My brain wasn't working right."

The Kid Stays in the Picture was made into a movie narrated by Evans himself, and released in 2002, to critical and popular acclaim. It made Evans into a celebrity once again. In May of 2002, he was given a star on the Hollywood Walk of Fame. Offers came rolling in, and he was soon back producing. Among his first efforts in this, his second comeback, was *How to Lose a Guy in 10 Days.* The film, starring Kate Hudson and Matthew McConaughey, was released in 2003.

Evans married for the sixth time in 2002. His bride was model and actress Leslie Ann Woodward; however, in 2003 the couple divorced. That same year,

Evans was at work on a sequel to his autobiography called *The Fat Lady Sang.* Also in 2003, he lent his voice to cable channel Comedy Central's cartoon *Kid Notorious,* which was based on his life. According to CNN.com, the cartoon followed "the adventures of "Kid" Evans; his butler, English; his cat, Puss Puss; and his housekeeper, Tollie Mae, as Evans cuts show business deals, romances women, and schmoozes Hollywood." Evans wrote his own dialogue for the cartoon because "he figured no one else could capture his original style," CNN.com explained. Asked by the *San Francisco Chronicle*'s Edward Guthmann to name his biggest accomplishment, Evans replied, "Being alive today.... The doctors thought I would never walk and I'm playing tennis today. I'm still in the picture."

Selected writings

The Kid Stays in the Picture, Hyperion Press, 1994.

Sources

Periodicals

Boston Globe, August 4, 2002, p. L9.
InStyle, February 2003, p. 254.
New York Times, August 9, 1966, p. 29; November 4, 1966, p. 32; December 21, 1966, p. 46; August 5, 1972, p. 13; September 22, 1980, p. C15; May 20, 1993, p. C15.
People, August 12, 2002, pp. 135–38.
San Francisco Chronicle, August 4, 2002, p. 32.

Online

"Outta the way—it's Kid Notorious," CNN.com, http://www.cnn.com/2003/SHOWBIZ/TV/10/22/apontv.kidnotorious.ap/index.html (October 22, 2003).

—*Michael Belfiore*

Eve

AP/Wide World Photos

Rapper, actress, and fashion designer

Born Eve Jihan Jeffers, November 10, 1978, in Philadelphia, PA; daughter of Jerry Jeffers (a chemical–plant supervisor) and Julie Wilcher (a medical publishing–company supervisor).

Addresses: *Record label*—Ruff Ryder/Interscope Records, 2220 Colorado Ave., Santa Monica, CA 90404. *Official website*—http://www.evefansonly.com.

Career

Joined Ruff Ryder hip–hop collective, 1998; appeared on *Bulworth* soundtrack, 1998; appeared on compilation *Ryde or Die Vol. 1*, 1999; released *Let There Be Eve...Ruff Ryder's First Lady*, 1999; released *Scorpion*, 2001; released *Eve–Olution*, 2002. Television appearances include: *Third Watch*, 2003; *Eve*, UPN, 2003—; *One on One*, 2004. Producer of television shows, including: *Eve*, 2003—. Film appearances include: *XXX*, 2002; *Barbershop*, 2002; *Barbershop 2*, 2004; *The Woodsman*, 2004; *The Cookout*, 2004. Debuted fashion line, 2003.

Awards: Video music award for best female video (with Gwen Stefani), MTV, for "Let Me Blow Ya Mind," 2001; Grammy award for best rap/sung collaboration (with Gwen Stefani), Recording Academy, for "Let Me Blow Ya Mind," 2002.

Sidelights

One of the most successful women in hip–hop, Eve rode her connection with the Ruff Ryders rap collective to quick stardom. Her music and per-sona claim a successful middle ground between hip–hop women who have embraced feminism and neo–soul and those who trade on a tough image and sex appeal. Her success has reached beyond music: she has shot several films and stars in a television comedy named after her.

Eve was born to a single mother and grew up in housing projects in Philadelphia, Pennsylvania. She went through her teenage years without seeing her father and has said she has no relationship with him now. As a kid, she toured Philadelphia talent shows in the all–girl singing group Dope Girl Posse, but switched to rapping at the age of 13. "I did any talent show, ever," she told *Rolling Stone*'s Touré. "Anytime they [were having] one, I was there. If I won last week, [I'd be] back." She and her friend, Jennifer Pardue, performed as the rap duo Edjp (which stood for Eve of Destruction Jenny–Poo and was pronounced Egypt) as teenagers. They recorded an album, which helped cement Eve's interest in a music career.

After graduating from high school, Eve dedicated herself to breaking into the music business and began auditioning for a record deal, while working at a record store in Philadelphia and, briefly, at a strip club in New York City (an experience she will not talk about in interviews anymore). "I didn't want to have a regular life—have a baby, get a boyfriend, get married. I just wanted to do things," she told Christian Wright in *Allure*. Her backup plan was to become a makeup artist, but hitting it big in the music world made that unnecessary.

When she was only 18 years old, hip–hop icon Dr. Dre signed her to his label, Aftermath. Eve moved to Los Angeles, California, and adopted the stage name Eve of Destruction. However, eight months later, Aftermath dropped her, and she returned to Philadelphia, although a song she recorded for the label did end up on the *Bulworth* soundtrack in 1998. Fortunately, Eve met rap star DMX, who introduced her to the Ruff Ryders, a collective of producers and rappers based in New York. They made her audition on the spot. "They just put a beat on and said, 'All right, yo, let her spit,'" she told *Rolling Stone*'s Touré. "I said rhymes I had written for Dre. If I [had] failed that, I don't know where I'd be now." Instead, she impressed the Ruff Ryders, and they took her in as their only female member. "They made me write and recite, write and recite," Eve told *Newsweek*'s Lorraine Ali. "It was like boot camp. You had to prove yourself to them, and that's what made me a better MC."

Eve's song "What Y'all Want" appeared on the Ruff Ryders' top–selling compilation *Ryde or Die Vol. 1*, and she guested on The Roots' "You Got Me" and on "Girlfriend/Boyfriend" with Janet Jackson and Blackstreet to build buzz. Her first album, *Let There Be Eve...Ruff Ryder's First Lady,* released in late 1999, debuted at number one—making her one of the few female rappers to accomplish that feat—and sold more than two million copies. Touré, reviewing the album in *Rolling Stone,* described her as having "an oven–roasted voice, smooth flows and a thuggish attitude for days." The album ranged from drinking and partying anthems to a fantasy about taking revenge on a friend's abusive boyfriend ("Love Is Blind") to her father's absence and her youthful attraction to older men: "Didn't have a daddy/So I put a daddy in his space," she rapped on "Heaven Only Knows."

Mostly produced by Ruff Ryder member Swizz Beatz, the debut album featured the Ryders' tough, fast signature sound. The press responded by endlessly repeating her self–description as a "pit bull in a skirt." Actually, she was striking a balance compared to other female rappers. "It established her persona—sexy but not pornographic, in your face but somewhat introspective," wrote Christopher John Farley in *Time,* while *Newsweek*'s Ali described her as "playing as tough as the boys, but with a

stealthy female elegance. She walks the fine line between the empowering, old–school style of Queen Latifah and the trashy titillation of Lil' Kim." She took pride in being an independent woman. "I don't need a man to support me or keep me happy," she told *Interview*'s Vivien Goldman. Her blond hair, which she had bleached since high school, added to her striking image, though she would later dye it red and bright pink, among other colors.

Her second album, *Scorpion,* with tracks produced by Stephen and Damian Marley and her then–boyfriend Stevie J, was released in 2001. Dre produced two songs on the album, to help mend fences. *Rolling Stone*'s Arion Berger gave it three stars, but complained that her rhymes were "endless old–school sass with no point deeper than striking a pose." *Time*'s Farley also had a mixed reaction: "Her rapping is more controlled and confident, though she sometimes sacrifices coherence for rhythm, spouting half–thoughts and sentence fragments just to keep her flow going." But the album also included a more creative mix of music, including reggae and Latin horns, and she let down her guard for the hurt of "Life Is So Hard," which she called her favorite song on the album, a soulful duet with R&B singer Teena Marie. "I think it's a good balance of the hard core from the first album and the artist I wanna become as I get older," she told *Newsweek*'s Ali. "Before, the lyrics were mine, but the vision was pretty much [the Ruff Ryders']. Like, there was a song about a heist that was totally the guys' idea. After that, I promised myself I would never make a song about shooting, robbing, anything like that, 'cause it's not me."

Scorpion (named after Eve's astrological sign, Scorpio) went gold within two months, and in the summer of 2001 she toured with R&B group Destiny's Child, pop singer Jessica Simpson, and rapper Nelly on MTV's *TRL* (Total Request Live) tour. Touré's *Rolling Stone* profile caught her enjoying her fame and the fortune that followed it: it described Eve and Stevie J driving around Manhattan in Eve's gold BMW, Eve buying diamond rings, earrings, and a necklace worth a total of $100,000, and Eve's accountant, Horace Madison, making her sign a "stupid letter" acknowledging that too many purchases like that could wreck her finances. By this time, the 22–year–old already had a house in New Jersey, a retirement plan, and an portfolio of investments. "From a financial–stability standpoint, Eve's ahead of 85 percent of people in the urban–music business right now," Madison told Touré.

Eve had no reason to worry about her future. *Scorpion*'s second single, "Let Me Blow Ya Mind," her duet with Gwen Stefani of No Doubt, became her biggest success; it won an MTV Video Music Award in 2001 and a Grammy award in 2002. Near the end of 2001, Eve raved to *Rolling Stone*'s Mark Binelli about meeting Courtney Love, and her description of Love could easily work as a description of herself: "She's just raw. She just is who she is, period. She doesn't care, doesn't bite her tongue." Another sign of Eve's success was her entourage; by the summer of 2002, reported *Newsweek*'s Ali, Eve was traveling with five handlers: a publicist, hairstylist, makeup artist, clothing stylist, and bodyguard.

Eve described her next album, 2002's *Eve–olution,* as more melodic. It featured more neo–soul singing mixed in with the raps. She told *Newsweek*'s Ali that she was listening to reggae and rock more than rap. "I don't listen to a lot of hip–hop anymore because I can't respect it," she added, saying she was tired of hearing her peers rap about guns and selling drugs. But she still considered herself a rapper. "I do enjoy singing, but I'm not a singer," she told Rory Evans in *Teen People.* "I would never try to hit notes. I'm not Brandy, Monica or Alicia [Keys]. I can hold a note and that's good enough." Still, she did include Keys as a new duet partner, on the album's first single, "Gangsta Lovin.'" She explained to *Entertainment Weekly*'s Tom Sinclair, "Gangsta is just slang that we use for something that's good, or something we love or something that's hot."

The same year, Eve broke into acting with a supporting role in the Vin Diesel action flick *XXX* and a star turn with fellow rapper Ice Cube and controversial comic Cedric the Entertainer in the successful comedy *Barbershop,* filmed in an actual Chicago barbershop. She spent a week in barber school to prepare for the movie. Her UPN television series, *Eve,* debuted in late 2003. "Never, ever in my wildest dreams could I have imagined doing this," she told Margena A. Christian in *Jet.* "My basic overall goal is to be successful and happy. This is just something that's a bonus." Eve plays a fashion designer living in Miami named Shelly Williams, and the show focuses on Shelly's search for love and the advice she receives from her friends. The show, which had a working title of *The Opposite Sex,* was written for a white actress, then revamped and renamed for her.

Reviews were mostly terrible. "The good news is, it's only 30 minutes long," wrote the *Hollywood Reporter*'s Ray Richmond. "The star, while sexy, isn't much of an actress, and the writing is lazy and obvious," wrote Terry Kelleher in *People,* who was irritated by the show's predictable take on relationship

issues. But the program's ratings took off after a brief lull, and UPN ordered a full season of the show. Meanwhile, Eve starred in the sequel *Barbershop 2: Back in Business,* released in early 2004.

Though she started out looking tomboyish, Eve has embraced fashion and shown off a more feminine look in more recent videos. *People* named her one of the magazine's 50 most beautiful people in 2003. "There is almost no one else who can pull off just about every hair color imaginable and pair those signature paw print tattoos on her chest with an Alexander McQueen gown," wrote Julee Greenberg in the fashion publication *WWD.* Eve debuted her own sportswear line for young women, Fetish, in the fall of 2003. She appeared in a Victoria's Secret fashion show that November, where *People*'s Steven Cojocaru reported that she "insisted on being covered from head to toe in Francesca Guerrera's Sunset Bronze Loose Powder." Interviewers often find her chatting about her two Yorkshire terriers, Spunky and Bear.

Eve has also filmed a dark movie with Kevin Bacon called *The Woodsman,* about a pedophile trying to resurrect his career. But she insists acting will not take her away from recording. "I miss my music," she told Christian in *Jet.* "I miss the world. I do love the stability of acting, but it becomes monotonous after awhile." She planned to enter the studio in the spring of 2004 to record an album for the following fall. However, she did not plan on being a recording star forever. "I don't want to be with a record label for the rest of my life," she told *Allure.* "Music is the loneliest business. It makes you feel much older than you are. I could live without being in the spotlight. I want to know that when I'm 30, I can settle down if I want to."

Selected discography

Bulworth (soundtrack), Interscope Records, 1998.
(Contributor) *Ryde or Die Vol. 1,* Ruff Ryder Records, 1999.
Let There Be Eve...Ruff Ryder's First Lady, Ruff Ryder/Interscope Records, 1999.
Scorpion, Ruff Ryder/Interscope Records, 2001.
Eve–Olution, Ruff Ryder/Interscope Records, 2002.

Sources

Periodicals

Allure, July 2003, pp. 158–61, p. 164.
Daily Variety, November 12, 2003, p. A1.
Entertainment Weekly, March 9, 2001, p. 78; September 20, 2002.

Hollywood Reporter, January 16, 2003, p. 50; September 15, 2003, p. 18.

Interview, November 2000, p. 155.

Jet, April 9, 2001, p. 58; November 10, 2003, p. 60.

Newsweek, March 12, 2001, p. 70; September 2, 2002, p. 61.

People, March 19, 2001, p. 41; September 23, 2002, p. 204; May 12, 2003, p. 149; November 17, 2003, p. 38; December 15, 2003, p. 144; February 16, 2004, p. 27.

Rolling Stone, October 14, 1999, p. 119–120; March 29, 2001, p. 64; July 5, 2001, pp. 58–60; December 6, 2001, p. 124.

Teen People, December 1, 2002, p. 88.

Time, March 19, 2001, p. 74; September 2, 2002, p. 70.

Variety, September 1, 2003, p. S18.

WWD, June 19, 2003, p. 1; August 27, 2003, p. 5; September 4, 2003, p. 20B.

Online

"Eve," All Music Guide, http://www.allmusic. com/cg/amg.dll?p=amg&uid=UIDSUB04 0312131553210342&sql=B5m5tk6ax9kr0 (March 6, 2004).

"Eve," Internet Movie Database, http://www.imdb. com/name/nm1073992/ (March 7, 2004).

"Rock on the Net: MTV Video Music Awards 2001," http://www.rockonthenet.com/archive/2001/ mtvvmas.htm (March 6, 2004).

—Erick Trickey

Colin Farrell

Actor

Born March 31, 1976, in Dublin, Ireland; son of Eamon (a professional soccer player) and Rita Farrell; married Amelia Warner (an actress), July 17, 2001 (divorced, November, 2001); children: one son (with model Kim Bordenave). *Education:* Studied acting at Gaiety School of Drama, Dublin, Ireland.

Addresses: *Agent*—Creative Artists Agency, 9830 Wilshire Blvd., Beverly Hills, CA 90212. *Home*—Dublin, Ireland.

Career

Worked as a warehouse painter and busboy in Dublin, Ireland, and performed with a country line–dance group; appeared in the television series *Pie in the Sky,* 1994; cast in the British Broadcasting Corporation television comedy *Ballykissangel;* appeared onstage in the play *A Little World of Our Own,* Donmar Warehouse, 1998. Film appearances include: *Drinking Crude,* 1997; *Ordinary Decent Criminal,* 2000; *Tigerland,* 2000; *American Outlaws,* 2001; *Hart's War,* 2002; *Minority Report,* 2002, *Phone Booth,* 2003; *Veronica Guerin,* 2003; *S.W.A.T.,* 2003; *Intermission,* 2003; *Alexander,* 2004.

Sidelights

Irish actor Colin Farrell emerged in 2002 as Hollywood's most–sought–after new leading man with roles in Steven Spielberg's *Minority Report* and a string of other major feature films released over the next year. Farrell had little trouble submerging a thick Irish brogue to play American characters, such as a maverick L.A.P.D. cop in *S.W.A.T.* and a sleazy, philandering publicist in *Phone Booth,* both released in 2003. *Entertainment Weekly* critic Lisa Schwarzbaum asserted that Hollywood typecasting standards requiring a certain "taciturn iconoclasm suits Farrell's scruffy handsomeness, and the Irish actor seems more at ease than ever portraying rule–breaking American men." Part of Farrell's appeal seemed linked with reports of his penchant for drinking, brawling, and randy public behavior. He admitted to *Esquire* writer Chris Jones that his infamous, hard–drinking, bad–boy image and fast–moving career were inextricably linked. "I'm chasing something I'll never catch with this job," he said. "I'm chasing a feeling of peace that I don't think I'll ever experience."

Born on March 31, 1976, in Dublin, Ireland, Farrell was the last of four children in his family. His father, Eamon, had been a professional soccer player in Ireland in the 1960s, and his parents' marital union eventually dissolved. Farrell and his siblings lived with their mother in Castleknock, an area of newer homes just outside Dublin, near one of the world's largest parks. But Farrell remembered Castleknock more for its suburban pall, as he said in a *Vanity Fair* interview with Ned Zeman, and likened it to Los Angeles. "People here are ... suspect," Farrell told Zeman. "Everyone has a hidden agenda. They live in a bubble, and it's a very nice bubble to live in."

Farrell attended Castleknock College, but eschewed higher educational pursuits for a series of menial jobs. He worked as a warehouse painter, and as a busboy at a Dublin pub called the Elephant & Castle. When a country line–dancing fad swept through Ireland briefly, he joined a touring company and traveled in a van with other teens demonstrating the dances. "I did it until I couldn't look at myself," Farrell recalled in the *Vanity Fair* interview. "I looked at myself in the mirror and I had a ... Stetson, and I looked like what the Village People's idea of what a cowboy is, and I was like, 'I can't ... do this anymore.'"

By his own account, Farrell was a discontented young adult, drinking himself into further despondency. His brother, Eamon, who would become a director of a Dublin performing–arts academy for youth, talked him into taking an acting class, and he went on to classes at the Gaiety School of Drama in the city. He landed a television commercial for his first job, and then a part in a comedy series called *Pie in the Sky* in 1994. He was soon cast in recurring role in a British Broadcasting Corporation television series, *Ballykissangel,* about an English priest transferred to a small Irish village. His feature film debut came in a 1997 Irish movie, *Drinking Crude.*

Farrell moved to London, England, to further his career, and in 1998 was appearing onstage in the play *A Little World of Our Own* at the über–hip Donmar Warehouse theater. American actor Kevin Spacey saw the play one night, and was impressed with Farrell's performance. Spacey cast Farrell in his Dublin–set gangster flick, *Ordinary Decent Criminal,* and made the necessary calls back in Hollywood. Farrell soon arrived in Los Angeles, California, taking a room at the Holiday Inn in Santa Monica, and with Spacey's introduction went for a meeting at the talent–firm powerhouse, Creative Artists Agency (CAA). Farrell's first meeting there involved some 25 CAA associates assembled to greet him in a conference room. "I rabbited on for 15 minutes," Farrell *Vanity Fair*'s Zeman. "It was scary.... I mean, I was 22. I didn't even know what this was about."

Not one to turn down an invitation, Farrell was soon a fixture at Hollywood A–list parties, and his brazen attitude was not the type of networking that was common to the industry. Determined nevertheless, Farrell learned of auditions to be held in London by *Lost Boys/Batman Forever* director Joel Schumacher for a small–budget Vietnam–era story, *Tigerland.* Without having read the script, Farrell talked his way into an audition, and Schumacher sent him away with orders to make an audition tape. Farrell did so with his sister's help—the tape is included on *Tigerland*'s DVD release—and won one of the leads. The 2000 release was not a box–office hit, but earned critical accolades for its gritty look at a United States Army boot camp in 1971 Louisiana. Farrell's character, the Texan rebel of the group, helps some of his fellow grunts avoid being shipped off to the war overseas. To deliver a convincing Texas accent, Farrell submerged his thick Irish brogue by spending a few weeks in Texas and carousing at honky–tonk bars there.

By the spring of 2001, there was a serious press buzz about Farrell. In May, *Time International*'s Jumana Farouky called him "The Man Who Stole The Movies," noting that the relatively unheard–of actor was earning $2 million per picture. "Farrell won't be unknown for long," Farouky predicted, and asserted that in *Tigerland,* "Farrell displays a kind of cool that's rare in today's leading men. A sensitive brooder with rugged good looks, he's Russell Crowe without the ego." Farouky explained that Farrell's arrival in Hollywood as worries about a potential Screen Actors' Guild strike intensified gave his career an unexpected boon: fears about a walkout made some of the top names choosier about their next parts, and thus other roles were up for grabs for newcomers.

Farrell's next choice of a role did not bode well for his future, but it would be one of the few missteps of his career. He starred as nineteenth–century rebel Jesse James in *American Outlaws,* and the film bombed at the box office in August of 2001. Critical assessments were scathing, but Farrell had better luck with his next part, which came thanks to the fears about a strike: Edward Norton bowed out of a role in *Hart's War,* and Farrell was offered it instead. The World War II–era drama was set in a German–run prisoner–of–war camp, and featured him alongside veteran leading man Bruce Willis. Again, the film failed to lure audiences in any great number, but critics liked it and wrote favorably of Farrell's performance.

Farrell was stunned to land a role in *Minority Report,* director Steven Spielberg's summer of 2002 blockbuster. Again, he won the role after Matt Damon dropped out, and did not have to submit an audition tape, either; in this case, he dropped by

Spielberg's office on the set of another movie, shared a sardine sandwich with him, and was offered the role opposite Tom Cruise that same day. Spielberg's picture was based on a story by cult–favorite sci–fi writer Philip K. Dick, and described as "a thriller confident and complex enough to mix mayhem with meditations on predestination and free will" by *Newsweek*'s film reviewer, David Ansen. *Minority Report* is set in Washington, D.C. in 2054, where Cruise's character is a "pre–crime" detective. Law–enforcement authorities now have the power to stop crime before it happens, thanks to a trio of psychic "Pre–Cogs" submerged in a top–secret tank, but Farrell's Justice Department agent arrives to keep an eye on Cruise's zealous detective. The plot takes a sinister and high–speed turn when Cruise's up–right character shows up on one of the pre–cog screens. Though Farrell's role was a somewhat thankless one as merely a foil to the star, the movie was a huge box–office draw, and helped make the Irish actor a household name.

By early 2003 Farrell's asking price had climbed to $5 million per picture, and the caliber of roles offered him continued to escalate as well. He starred next in *The Recruit*, opposite Al Pacino, as a whiz–kid from the Massachusetts Institute of Technology recruited by Pacino's Central Intelligence Agency veteran. The film opened as the No. 1 box–office draw its first weekend, but his next film, the comic–book adaptation *Daredevil* with Ben Affleck, fared less well. Farrell sported a shaved head and a bulls–eye target on his forehead, the latter an eerie harbinger for his next role.

In *Phone Booth*, Farrell played a man trapped a phone booth by a sniper's cross–hatch. It was also the first film in which he received top billing, and was expected to carry with a minimum of special effects. Farrell was cast by *Tigerland* director Schumacher as New York media publicist Stu Shepard, a man of dubious moral character with a penchant for expensive suits and waifish, up–and–coming actresses. Hoping to romance one of these clients, Stu calls her daily from a pay phone so that his wife will not see the calls on his cell phone. She spurns him, but then the phone rings, and Stu answers it. In short order, the man on the other end reveals far too many unsavory details about Stu's life for the call to be a prank, and tells him to reform. The caller also trains a gun on him, and Farrell's character is then pinned inside the booth as prostitutes, the police, the media, and finally his wife clamor for him to come out. The part, with just one location to keep the viewer's interest, was a challenging one for any actor, and critics asserted that Farrell handled it masterfully. "Slippery and defensive, with panicky eyes and a touch of beard accenting his chin, Farrell jabbers and implodes...." declared *Entertainment Weekly*'s Owen Gleiberman. "He has the intensity to play two conflicting states at once—cockiness and anxiety—and the flow of the movie is in watching the former give way to the latter."

In all, Farrell appeared in six movies released in 2003, including *S.W.A.T.,* a genre action–thriller featuring yet another example of Hollywood's penchant for formulaic action movies with a Los Angeles Police Department plotline, and *Veronica Guerin,* Schumacher's tale of a slain Irish journalist. He had a supporting part in *Intermission,* filmed in Dublin, carrying one of eleven linked subplots related to the break–up of a couple, and was also to appear in *The Home at the End of the World,* an adaptation of a novel by Michael Cunningham. Oliver Stone cast Farrell in the title role in *Alexander,* a sweeping, big–budget epic about the Macedonian king who conquered large parts of the known world in the fourth century B.C.

With a price now reportedly in the $8 million range, Farrell seems relatively unaffected by his stardom. Profanity–laced interviews are still the norm, and his reputation for carousing remains: in the summer of 2003 he reportedly spent $20,000 at a New York City strip club in a single evening. His entourage, however, often includes family members such as his brother, Eamon, and sister, Catherine, an actress. Another sister, Claudine, serves as his assistant. Farrell has been romantically linked with a number of actresses and celebrities, and was even wed briefly to Amelia Warner for four months in 2001. Model Kim Bordenave, 33, gave birth to Farrell's first child in September of 2003, but the pair were never a couple. He bought a Los Angeles home for her and the child, and keeps one of his own back in Ireland, in the Dublin section of Irishtown near the city's Grand Canal. "I'm fairly low–maintenance," the actor, who obtained the first credit card of his life in 2002, told *Vanity Fair*'s Zeman. "Packets of smokes and a few pints and I'm a happy man. I have all this [money] that I never thought I'd have. And I wouldn't know what to do with it, apart from just let it sit there. People will think it's from me being smart, but it's from me not knowing what to do with it. They pay me this money for a job that I would gladly do for … minimum wage, and it's insane."

Sources

Economist, April 19, 2003.
Entertainment Weekly, November 3, 2000, p. 23; August 24, 2001, p. 103; February 15, 2002, p. 42; February 14, 2003, pp. 8–9; April 11, 2003, p. 52; April 18, 2003, p. 16; August 15, 2003, p. 50.

Esquire, September 2003, pp. 162–167.
Film Journal International, September 2001, p. 65.
Newsweek, February 18, 2002, p. 69; July 1, 2002, p. 57.
New York Times, February 2, 2003, p. 1; February 16, 2003, p. 11.
People, March 3, 2003, pp. 61–62; May 12, 2003, p. 114; August 11, 2003, p. 92.

Time International, May 28, 2001, p. 69.
Vanity Fair, July 2002, pp. 106–110, 156–158.
Variety, August 5, 2002, p. 11; February 17, 2003, p. 39.

—*Carol Brennan*

Anthony S. Fauci

Director of the National Institute of Allergy and Infectious Diseases

Born Anthony Stephen Fauci, December 24, 1940, in Brooklyn, NY; son of Stephen (a pharmacist) and Eugenia A. Fauci; married Christine Grady (a nurse), 1985; children: Jennifer, Megan, Alison. *Education:* Holy Cross College, Worcester, MA, B.A., 1962; Cornell University, M.D., 1966. *Religion:* Roman Catholic.

Addresses: National Institute of Allergy and Infectious Diseases, Office of the Director, Bldg. 31, Rm. 7AO3, 31 Center Dr. MSC 2520, Bethesda, MD 20892.

Career

Began as clinical associate at the National Institutes of Health (NIH), 1968; head of NIH Clinical Section, 1974; appointed Chief of Laboratory of Immunoregulation, 1980; head of National Institute of Allergy and Infectious Diseases, 1984—.

Member: National Academy of Sciences, Philosophical Society, Institute of Medicine of the National Academy of Sciences, American Academy of Arts and Sciences, Royal Danish Academy of Science and Letters, American College of Physicians, American Society for Clinical Investigation, Association of American Physicians, Infectious Diseases Society of America, American Association of Immunologists, American Academy of Allergy Asthma and Immunology.

Awards: Arthur S. Flemming Award, 1979; U.S. Public Health Service Distinguished Service Medal, 1984; National Medical Research Award, National Health Council, 1989; Dr. Nathan Davis Award for Outstanding Public Service, American Medical Association, 1992; Frank Annunzio Award, 2001; Albany Medical Center Prize in Medicine and Biomedical Research, 2002; Ellis Island Family Heritage Award for Medicine and Science, 2003.

Sidelights

Dr. Anthony S. Fauci is one of the best–known members of the American public health establishment and has been at the forefront of the fight against Acquired Immunodeficiency Syndrome (AIDS) since the 1980s. Honored worldwide for his research, Fauci is a hands–on doctor, and he still sees patients twice a week. Fauci helped change the tenor of AIDS research at a time when AIDS patients and activists felt shut out by the medical establishment. Fauci was singled out by furious activists in the mid–1980s, who blamed him for the government's slowness in reacting to the epidemic. Fauci turned the situation around by meeting with his critics and listening to their complaints. As a result, Fauci is credited with making huge changes in the way public health agencies handle AIDS. He got the Food and Drug Administration (FDA) to speed up its approval process for AIDS drugs and to make certain drugs more widely available. He set in place public policies that included the voices of patients and their advocates, setting an unprecedented tone of inclusiveness. He went from villain to hero of the gay community by the end of the 1980s.

As director of the National Institute of Allergy and Infectious Diseases (NAIAD), Fauci oversees a budget that grew from $320 million in 1984 to more than $2.4 billion by 2001, while at the same time, deaths in the United States from AIDS dropped precipitously. Since 2001, Fauci has also been one of the top government advisors on bioterrorism. He began working with Health and Human Services Secretary Tommy Thompson after the 2001 anthrax attacks. He has led the government's preparations for a possible biological weapons attack by speeding up the production of smallpox vaccine.

Fauci was born in Brooklyn, New York, in 1940, and grew up working in his father's pharmacy. He graduated from Cornell University Medical College in 1966, and then completed a two–year residency at New York Hospital–Cornell Medical Center. This was at the height of the Vietnam War, and after his residency Fauci chose to work for the Public Health Service rather than serve as a military doctor. He began working at the National Institutes of Health (NIH) in 1968, and spent the rest of his career there. In 1974, he was promoted to head of the Clinical Section, and in 1980, he became Chief of the Laboratory of Immunoregulation. Around this time, Fauci began seeing the first reports of an unusual and baffling disease that primarily afflicted gay men: AIDS. Fauci was in on the ground floor of the AIDS epidemic. He met his wife, a nurse, while caring for an AIDS patient. The couple continued to work with infected people even while expecting their first child, though at the time, no one was sure exactly how the disease was transmitted and if health workers were at risk.

In 1984 Fauci was appointed to his present position, head of the NAIAD. He became a prominent name in AIDS research, but his public eminence brought him notoriety. AIDS advocacy groups like ACT UP were convinced that the government was dragging its feet on fighting the epidemic. New medications were slow in coming, and proven treatments were sometimes denied patients who could not qualify for them. The playwright and AIDS advocate Larry Kramer called Fauci a monster. Activists chanted "murderer" throughout one of Fauci's speeches to the New York Academy of Sciences, and at one point Fauci was even hanged in effigy. In 1988 Fauci sat down with one of his virulent critics, a San Francisco AIDS activist who was going blind from an AIDS–related infection. The man explained that a drug existed to treat his eye problem, but that government regulations prevented him from using it.

Fauci was immeasurably moved by the man's dilemma, and from that point he changed his philosophy about dealing with the outspoken AIDS advocates. He met with Kramer and others, he toured gay bathhouses, and he began lobbying the FDA to speed up drug approval. Fauci's actions turned the tide, bringing more money for research, and quieted the raucous criticism of government AIDS policy. When President Bush offered Fauci the top job at the NIH in 1989, Fauci turned it down. He was too involved in AIDS research to give it up for an administrative position. Fauci's research helped pin down our understanding of the way the AIDS virus destroys the body's immune defenses. His research has also shown ways of rebuilding the immune system, and he has contributed to the search for an AIDS vaccine.

Fauci is known as a straight talker, and he has been a useful bridge between the scientific community and the politicians who control the purse strings of public health. He has been very successful at expanding the budget of the NAIAD. About half the agency's budget goes to AIDS research, Fauci's specialty, but he has also persuaded Congress to allocate more money for other problems, such as emerging and unknown infectious diseases. Diseases like ebola, Hanta virus, and SARS are frightening prospects for public health researchers, because there are as yet no vaccines and antibiotics are of limited use. Fauci has also been a sane and somber voice in the dialogue about bioterror. After the anthrax attacks on the United States in 2001, Fauci insisted that more bioterror attacks were inevitable, and the best thing was to be prepared. Fauci prefers that people understand their risk, so that they are frightened enough to act, but not too scared to act wisely. Fauci told *U.S. News and World Report* in January of 2002: "What I learned from HIV/AIDS was that from the beginning you gotta level with people, you gotta tell them what you don't know, and you've got to explain risks in a way that is realistic without making someone feel better than they should." He has helped prepare the United States for future biological attacks by overseeing the production of smallpox vaccine, channeling money to new vaccine research, and speeding up existing antibioterror projects.

Sources

Journal of the American Medical Association, January 17, 1996, p. 173.
Parade, June 8, 2003, p. 5.
Scientist, May 5, 2003, p. 11.
Time, August 20, 2001, pp. 45–46.
U.S. News & World Report, January 28, 2002, p. 32.

—A. Woodward

Roger Federer

Professional tennis player

Born August 8, 1981, in Basel, Switzerland; son of Robert (a pharmaceutical company employee) and Lynette Federer (a pharmaceutical company employee). *Education:* Attended tennis training centers in Switzerland.

Addresses: *Office*—c/o Lynette Federer, Postfach, CH–4103 Bottmingen, Switzerland.

Career

Tennis player; won junior Wimbledon singles and doubles and the Orange Bowl (Miami, Florida) title, 1998; ranked No. 1 in juniors in the world by International Tennis Federation, 1998; won first Association of Tennis Professionals title at Milan, 2001; won men's Wimbledon final, 2003; ranked No. 3 after Wimbledon win; won Australian Open, 2004; won Dubai Open championship, 2004; won Hamburg Masters championship, 2004; won Gerry Weber Open in Halle, Germany, 2004; won men's Wimbledon final, 2004; won Swiss open, 2004.

Sidelights

Swiss tennis champ Roger Federer fulfilled what many believed was his destiny with a Wimbledon win in straight sets in July of 2003. After dominating junior tennis, expectations ran high for the powerful player, but he had a knack for sliding into valleys after reaching peaks at the start of his professional career. The Wimbledon victory—his first major title—marked both a physical and psychological victory. In addition, he went down in the

record books as the first Swiss man to win a Wimbledon's men's title. "He may not be the 17–year–old symbol of a nation, as Boris Becker was when he won the title," wrote Christopher Clarey in the *New York Times,* "and he may not exude the Nordic mystery of Björn Borg or have the Big Apple mouth of John McEnroe. But there is something magnetic about Federer's tennis: an attractive blend of smooth moving and creative thinking, of tact and force that has the potential to cut across borders."

Born in Basel, Switzerland, on August 8, 1981, Federer is the son of Robert and Lynette Federer, who both work for the pharmaceutical corporation Ciba–Geigy. His father met his mother while on a business trip to South Africa. They also have a daughter, Diana, who studies nursing. Federer grew up in the suburban Basel town of Munchenstein, and started playing tennis at age eight. His parents, who were weekend amateurs, got him interested in the game, but he took it to another level. *Tennis*'s Cindy Shmerler wrote, "His earliest tennis–related memory is of watching his idol, Boris Becker, battle Stefan Edberg on television in the 1988 Wimbledon final. When Becker lost, Federer wept."

Federer's home town is in the German–speaking region of Switzerland, and he moved to the French–speaking area while in his early teens to train. Fellow players made fun of him, but he learned French and speaks English as well. From age 10 to 14 and on and off until 1999, he trained with Peter Carter, who was killed in a car crash in 2002. Later in his career he trained under Swedish coach Peter Lundgren. As a youth, Federer had a temper on the court. "I was hotheaded," he admitted to *Tennis's* Shmerler, "always acting bad on the court, throwing my racquets like ten meters from me, or into the curtain." He matured, however, into a soft-spoken athlete highly regarded by other players and members of the media.

In 1998, Federer won the Wimbledon junior title and finished that year as the number–one junior in the world. That year, he also reached the finals at the U.S. Open and semifinals at the Australian Open, and took the title and the Orange Bowl in Miami, Florida. In 1999, he was the youngest player—at 18 years, four months—to finish in the top 100. He then advanced to his first Association of Tennis Professionals (ATP) semifinals in Vienna, Austria, and went on to quarterfinals in Marseille, France; Rotterdam, Netherlands; and his hometown of Basel. In 2000, he was the number–two–ranked tennis player in Switzerland and lost the bronze medal at the Olympic Games that year to Arnaud Di Pasquale.

The next year, 2001, Federer became the one to watch as he broke seven–time champ Pete Sampras's 31–match Wimbledon winning streak in the fourth round. Up to this point, Federer still had never made it past quarterfinals at a Grand Slam tournament. Also, his stunning performances were often followed by massive upsets. For instance, after showing up Sampras, he lost three first–round matches at majors, including at Wimbledon in 2002, the Australian Open in January of 2003, and the French Open in May of 2003. The Wimbledon loss was a huge setback, because it was in straight sets against Mario Ancic, ranked number 154 in the world. However, he snagged a Tennis Masters Series shield in Hamburg, Germany, in 2002 and qualified for the Tennis Masters Cup later that year in Shanghai, China. He reached the semifinals with a perfect 3–0 record before losing to eventual victor Lleyton Hewitt in three close sets.

Building on the momentum, Federer captured four titles in the first half of 2003 at Marseille, France; Dubai, United Arab Emirates; Munich, Germany; and Halle, Germany. The 2003 Wimbledon win would finally put an end to questions of whether he could overcome his anxiety to capture a major title. After beating fifth–seeded Andy Roddick, he advanced to his first Grand Slam final. On July 6,

2003, with a calm demeanor throughout, he triumphed over Mark Philippoussis, 7–6 (5), 6–2, 7–6 (3). Immediately upon winning, Federer unleashed his emotions, dropping to his knees on the court and holding his arms in the air. Then he sobbed for joy in his courtside chair. "There was pressure from all sides—also from myself," he said, as reported on *Sports Illustrated*'s website. "It's an absolute dream for me. I was always joking around when I was a boy: 'I'm going to win this.'" The victory netted the 21–year–old Federer $959,100.

Following Wimbledon 2003, Federer lost to David Nalbandian at the U.S. Open in September in their fourth–round match. Later that month, he fell to Hewitt at the Davis Cup final as well. However, in October he bounced back by successfully defending his CA Trophy against Spain's Carlos Moya. This gave him his sixth ATP title of the year, and he also set a new record for ATP best season with 67 wins, 14 losses. In addition, it put Federer in a three–way tie with Roddick and Spaniard Juan Carlos Ferrero for the year–end ATP number–one spot. "Becoming the ATP number one is my aim," he said afterward, according to Harry Miltner of AP Worldstream. "I am not far away and I will hang on and see what happens."

Federer is six feet, one inch tall and 177 pounds, with dark–brown hair and dark–brown eyes. On his official website, he cites his favorite colors as blue, white, and red, and his favorite animals as the lion and tiger. He also reveals that his bands of choice are AC/DC and Lenny Kravitz, and that he prefers roses and orchids to any other flowers. When he is not on the court, Federer enjoys golf, soccer, skiing, video games, card games, and the company of friends. In July of 2003, he launched his own fragrance called "RF—Roger Federer," with the slogan, "Feel the touch."

As of 2003, Federer was dating Miroslava Vavrinec, a fellow Swiss tennis pro whom he met at the 2000 Olympic Games in Sydney, Australia. While some professional athletes live the high life after reaching a certain point in their careers, Federer appears to be attached to his family and friends near his hometown. Instead of buying his own home once he had enough earnings, he and his parents split the cost of a larger home in hilly Bottmingen, Switzerland. He also shares an apartment in Biel, near the Swiss national training center. "My family is the thing I miss most on tour," Federer told Shmerler in *Tennis.* "Why should I have my own place? Who is going to clean it for me?"

On December 9, 2003, Federer fired Lundgren, his coach of three years. Being without a coach did not seem to affect his game, however, because on February 1, 2004, he won the Australian Open. Federer went on to win the Dubai Open championship on March 7, the Hamburg Masters championship on May 16, and the Gerry Weber Open on June 13. On July 6, 2004, he successfully defended his Wimbledon title when he defeated Andy Roddick. Roddick told BBC.com, "Roger just played too good today. I threw the kitchen sink at him he went to the bathroom and got his tub." This win was Federer's third career Grand Slam. Federer went on to win the Swiss Open in Gstaad, Switzerland, defeating Igor Andreev, 6-2, 6-3, 5-7, 6-3. It was his first career title in his native country. Federer won his third straight title on August 1, 2004, with his defeat of Roddick at the final of the Tennis Masters Canada.

Sources

Periodicals

AP Worldstream, September 21, 2003; October 12, 2003.
New York Times, July 5, 2003, p. D1; July 7, 2003, p. D1; September 5, 2003, p. D1.
Palm Beach Post (Florida), July 5, 2003, p. 1C.
Sports Illustrated, July 14, 2003, p. 46.
Tennis, March 2003, pp. 28–34.

Online

"Federer captures Gerry Weber Open," Sports Network, http://www.sportsnetwork.com/default/asp.?c=sportsnetwork&page=tennis-m/news/BCN3292934.htm (July 9, 2004).
"Federer continues streak with Swiss Open win," *SI.com,* http://sportsillustrated.cnn.com/2004/tennis/07/11/bc.ten.lgns.gstaadtennis.r/ (July 26, 2004).

"Federer dumps coach," *Clarion-Ledger* (Mississippi), http://www.clarionledger.com/news/0312/10/sbriefs.html (July 8, 2004).
"Federer fights back to retain title," BBC.com, http://news.bbc.co.uk/sport1/hi/tennis/3865037.stm (July 9, 2004).
"Federer retains Dubai title," BBC.com, http://news.bbc.co.uk/sport1/hi/tennis/3541605.stm (July 9, 2004).
"Federer wins Wimbledon crown," News24.com, http://www.news24.com/News24/Sport/Tennis/0,,2-9-30_1552703,00.html (July 9, 2004).
"Master of Canada," *SI.com,* http://sportsillustrated.cnn.com/2004/tennis/08/01/bc.ten.toronto.ap/index.html (August 2, 2004).
"Pursuit of Perfection," Tennis Masters Cup, http://masters–cup.com/news/federer_bio.asp (November 9, 2003).
"Roger Federer," ATPtennis.com, http://www.atptennis.com/en/players/playerprofiles/Highlights/default.asp?playernumber=F324 (November 9, 2002).
"Roger Federer beats Marat Safin to win the German Masters tennis tourney," Slam Sports, http://www.slam.ca/SlamResults020519/ten_germany-ap.html (July 9, 2004).
Roger Federer official website, http://www.rogerfederer.com (November 9, 2003).
"Swiss success: Federer wins men's Wimbledon final in straight sets," *SI.com,* http://sportsillustrated.cnn.com/tennis/2003/wimbledon/news/2003/07/06/wimbledon_Sunday_ap/ (November 9, 2003).
"Swiss Sweep," *SI.com,* http://sportsillustrated.cnn.com/2004/tennis/specials/australian_open/2004/02/01/men.final.ap/index.html (July 9, 2004).

—*Geri Koeppel*

Will Ferrell

Actor and screenwriter

Born John William Ferrell, July 16, 1968, in Irvine, CA; son of Lee (a musician) and Kay (a schoolteacher) Ferrell; married Viveca Paulin (an art–house auctioneer), August, 2000; children: Magnus Paulin. *Education:* University of Southern California (sports journalism), 1990.

Addresses: *Agent*—United Talent Agency, 9560 Wilshire Blvd., Ste. 500, Beverly Hills, CA 90212.

Career

Actor in television, including: *Saturday Night Live,* NBC, 1995–2002; *Bucket of Blood,* Showtime, 1995; *Living Single,* FOX, 1995; *Grace Under Fire,* ABC, 1995; *The George Wendt Show,* CBS, 1995; *Cow and Chicken* (voice), 1997; *Disney's Hercules,* ABC and syndicated, 1998; *King of the Hill* (voice), FOX, 1999; *Family Guy,* 2000; *Strangers with Candy,* 2000; *The Oblongs* (voice), 2001; *Family Guy,* 2001; *Undeclared,* 2001; *The Guardian,* 2003. Film appearances include: *Criminal Hearts* (uncredited), 1995; *Austin Powers: International Man of Mystery,* 1997; *Men Seeking Women* 1997; *A Night at the Roxbury,* 1998; *The Whistleblower,* 1999; *The Thin Pink Line,* 1998; *The Suburbans,* 1999; *Austin Powers: The Spy Who Shagged Me,* 1999; *Dick,* 1999; *Superstar,* 1999; *Drowning Mona,* 2000; *The Ladies Man,* 2000; *Jay and Silent Bob Strike Back,* 2001; *Zoolander,* 2001; *Boat Trip* (uncredited), 2002; *Old School,* 2003; *Elf,* 2003; *Starsky and Hutch,* 2004; *Anchorman,* 2004. Author of screenplays, including: *A Night at the Roxbury,* 1998; *Anchorman,* 2004.

Awards: Emmy award for outstanding individual performance in a variety or music program, Academy of Television Arts and Sciences, for *Saturday Night Live,* 2001.

Sidelights

Actor Will Ferrell is best known for his seven seasons of appearances on the NBC comedy show *Saturday Night Live,* on which he impersonated United States President George W. Bush, Attorney General Janet Reno, Iraqi President Saddam Hussein, and many others. The Emmy Award–winning actor portrayed a variety of other characters on the show, and has also appeared in several hit films, including *Elf* and *Old School.*

Born and raised in the Los Angeles, California, suburb of Irvine, in 1968, Ferrell was an easygoing child. "He was born like that," his mother, Kay, told Scott Raab in *Esquire.* "You know those little Matchbox cars? Will would line up his Matchbox cars, by himself, and be totally happy. You'd say, 'You wanna go to Disneyland today or line up your cars?' and he'd have to think about it." Ferrell was known as a funny kid even in elementary school, where he would punch himself in the head just to make girls laugh.

Ferrell's father, Lee, was a musician who toured with the Righteous Brothers, and as Ferrell grew up, he decided he would never go into show business like his father had. He saw that performing was uncertain and financially unstable, and vowed to become a businessperson. However, he didn't count on the fact that he was inherently talented at performing. He got his first taste of performing when he read daily announcements to students over his high school's public address system. He also re-enacted comedy skits he had seen on television to entertain his friends.

During his college years at the University of Southern California (USC), where he majored in sports journalism, Ferrell took whatever job he could get. For one job, he worked as a parking garage valet at the Meridien Hotel in Newport Beach. On the second night of that job, he drove a van into a parking garage that did not have enough clearance for it. The entire luggage rack came off when the van hit the low ceiling. Surprisingly, Ferrell was not fired for this mishap. Another disastrous job involved working as a bank teller; on the first day, his cash drawer was short $330, and on the second day he was short $280. He had not taken the money; the job was just not suited to him.

After graduating from USC, he worked as a sports-caster for a local cable series. He did stand–up comedy routines at comedy clubs and coffeehouses. He also took classes with the Groundlings, a Los Angeles–based comedy and improvisation troupe that had helped *Saturday Night Live* stars Laraine Newman, Jon Lovitz, Phil Hartman, Cheri Oteri, and *Friends* star Lisa Kudrow start their careers; six months after he began his studies with them, the group asked him to become a member. In addition to his work with the Groundlings, Ferrell spent a summer studying scene construction, dialects, movement, and writing at South Coast Repertory in Costa Mesa, California.

In 1995, Lorne Michaels, the producer of *Saturday Night Live,* came to town looking for fresh talent for his show. Ferrell told *Esquire*'s Raab how he made it through the first audition and what occurred when he was called back for the second, which involved a meeting with Michaels in New York City. Ferrell hoped to make an impression by being funny at this meeting, and brought a briefcase full of fake money, planning to do a mock bribe of Michaels. However, when he got there, the meeting was dead serious, so he kept quiet and never brought out the fake money at all. The show's producer, Steve Higgins, was present, and after Michaels said everything he wanted to say, he asked Higgins what he thought. Higgins looked at Ferrell and said, "Nice briefcase." Ferrell eventually won a slot on *Saturday Night Live,* leading to seven seasons of performances

made notable by Ferrell's imitations of President George W. Bush, Attorney General Janet Reno, pompous television host James Lipton, and singer Neil Diamond, as well as a cheerleader and a "ladies man," among many others. His impressions of Bush became wildly popular during the 2000 presidential election. Ironically, the president did not recognize Ferrell when they met on the *Saturday Night Live* set one day; in Bush's defense, "I was wearing a beard for another piece," Ferrell explained to *Newsweek*'s Marc Peyser. In addition to meeting Bush, Ferrell also met another target of his lampoons when Reno appeared on the show. Ferrell told Peyser that he told Reno that "we've always portrayed her as a take–charge, almost superhero kind of character, and she kind of went, 'Oh, be quiet!'"

Although Ferrell worried that he might be bothered by fans when he was out in public, his characters—not the actor himself—were what viewers remembered. Out of makeup, in his own clothes, he could often go out in public and never be noticed. Joel Stein commented in *Time* that Ferrell "doesn't stick out. He looks backgroundy, and his shockingly mellow demeanor makes him extra–unnoticeable." Ferrell told *Newsweek*'s Peyser, "[Before I began working on the show] I remember thinking I'd better take the subways a lot, because once we do our first show, I'm going to be mobbed. I'm still taking the subways." Nevertheless, Michaels told Peyser, "He's the center pillar [of the show]. He's as good as anyone who's ever done the show."

Ferrell made his feature film debut in 1997 with the role of Mustafa in the Mike Myers comedy, *Austin Powers: International Man of Mystery.* He also appeared in spinoffs from *Saturday Night Live,* including *A Night at the Roxbury, Superstar,* and *The Ladies Man.*

He continued to star on *Saturday Night Live,* but he was always aware that he might become stuck in a rut with the show, and he wanted to avoid that. "It's an interesting show to be a part of," he told Ed Bark in a Knight Ridder/Tribune News Service article. "Some people leave too early, some people stay too long." Ferrell wanted to leave while he was on top of the wave, and he did. In 2002, Ferrell left *Saturday Night Live* to pursue a film career. He knew this was risky; as he told Jeff Jensen in *Entertainment Weekly,* "There's an argument that maintaining a presence on the show means you have a nice platform in front of the public. At the same time, at some point you just have to take a flying leap."

In the 2003 film *Old School,* Ferrell played Frank the Tank, a middle–aged man who, longing for those good old partying college days, joins with his friends to form a fraternity to relive them. Costar Luke Wilson told *Entertainment Weekly*'s Jensen that Ferrell has "this total thousand–yard stare that's scary–hilarious. There were times in a scene where I couldn't look at him—I'd look just off to the side of him—because otherwise I'd crack up."

In one scene for that film, Ferrell streaked, running nude down a long street full of shops. Ferrell joked with *Newsweek*'s Bret Begun about that scene: "When you have certain physical gifts, I think you should share them. I've gotten a lot of mileage out of this body." Ferrell does get a lot of mileage out of his body; when he is not acting, he is an avid long–distance runner, a fact that became apparent to many of his fans in April of 2003, when he ran the Boston Marathon—his third marathon race. According to *Esquire*'s Raab, Ferrell spent the entire 26.2 miles of the race hearing spectators yell "Frank the Tank!" when he sped past them. "Kids were running next to me, snapping pictures," he told Raab. "Runners were running up ahead and then having their buddies stand next to me, snapping. It was insane."

Old School opened doors for Farrell. He told *Time*'s Stein, "I like to think it was because everyone saw how funny it was, but it's because it made a lot of money." Farrell went on to star in *Elf,* a Christmas comedy in which he played Buddy, an orphaned human who is raised at the North Pole and is told he is an elf. When he discovers the truth, he sets off to New York City to find his birth father at the suggestion of his kindly adoptive elf father. His human father turns out to be a hardnosed workaholic who has no time or patience for his long–lost son.

The six–foot–three actor might have seemed like a stretch in the part of a human elf, but as the film's producer Jon Berg told Glenn Lovell in a Knight Ridder/Tribune News Service article, Ferrell is funny because he is so down–to–earth. "Whether he's screaming like a madman or acting like a goofball, he's always going to be a sympathetic character because his humor comes from a really sweet place." Ferrell told *Newsweek*'s Peyser that he feels the pressure to be funny, but that it is not like him to be humorous all the time: "Sometimes I feel like I'm continuously letting people down by being normal." Michaels told Peyser that Ferrell "exudes a kind of goodness. There's something sunny about what he does." The film's director, Jon Favreau, told *Time*'s Stein, "His humor has a real vulnerability to it." In *Daily Variety,* David Rooney commented that the film "achieves much of its buoyancy from Ferrell's exuberant physical comedy and the character's immensely likeable guilelessness."

Ferrell married his wife, Viveca, an art–house auctioneer, in 2000, after knowing her for six years. "I knew when I met her," he told *Esquire*'s Raab. "She's the one…. I'm just gonna wait for her to come around the bend." The couple has a son, Magnus, who was born on March 7, 2004.

In 2003, Ferrell began working on a film by Woody Allen, titled *Melinda and Melinda.* According to *Time*'s Stein, he was chosen to replace actor Robert Downey, Jr. in the lead role because Allen did not want to pay the cost of insuring Downey. At CNN.com, Stephanie Snipes asked him what that film was about. "That's a good question," he said. "I'm in the midst of it and I don't even know." He was allowed to read the script once, but it was then taken away from him, apparently so that the storyline would not become public knowledge. He also told *Time*'s Stein that he had some trouble relating to Allen: "Woody Allen has been nothing but nice and complimentary to me, but every time I've tried to joke with him, I get nothing. He thanked me for doing the script and asked me if I liked it, and I said I really liked the car crashes. He went, 'Uh–huh. Anyway.'"

Also in 2003, Ferrell was cast as Darrin Stephens in a movie remake of the 1960s sitcom show *Bewitched* and as the lead in a film version of the John Kennedy Toole novel *A Confederacy of Dunces.* Ferrell played a pompous 1970s newscaster in *Anchorman,* released in the summer of 2004, and in the same year, he appeared in a dramatic role in *Winter Passing.* The year 2004 continued to be busy for Ferrell, as he filmed the soccer comedy *Kicking & Screaming* and the dramedy *The Wendell Baker Story* and provided the voice of the Man in the Yellow Hat for the film version of the classic children's book, *Curious George.* Ferrell was also scheduled to appear in the film adaptation of Broadway's *The Producers* and cowrite and star in *Talladega Nights,* a stock–car racing comedy planned for 2006.

Ferrell told CNN.com's Snipes that his career role model was Bill Murray, another *Saturday Night Live* performer who went on to do many landmark comedies, and who then moved to more serious films. Whatever he chooses to do, he vows to put all of his talent into it. He told *Esquire*'s Raab, "What I recognized when I started doing comedy was that I'm probably not the wittiest, not the fastest on my feet, but the one thing I can guarantee is that I won't hold anything back."

Sources

Books

Contemporary Theatre, Film, and Television, vol. 25, Gale Group, 2000.

Periodicals

America's Intelligence Wire, February 24, 2004; March 11, 2004.
Daily Variety, October 27, 2003, p. 4.
Entertainment Weekly, February 28, 2003, pp. 33–34; November 28, 2003, pp. 15–17.
Esquire, December 2003, p. 162.
Knight Ridder/Tribune News Service, May 8, 2002, p. K5221; November 6, 2003, p. K5196.
Newsweek, February 19, 2001, p. 56; February 24, 2003, p. 13.

People, November 24, 2003, pp. 71–72.
Time, November 10, 2003, p. 90.

Online

"A Chat With Will Ferrell," CNN.com, http://www.cnn.com/2003/SHOWBIZ/Movies/11/07/sprj.caf03.qa.Ferrell/index.html (November 10, 2003).
Biography Resource Center Online, Gale Group, 2003.

—Kelly Winters

Alberta Ferretti

AP/Wide World Photos

Fashion designer

Born in Cattolica, Italy, c. 1950; married, c. 1967 (divorced); married Giuseppe Campanella (an anesthesiologist); children: sons Simone, Giacomo (first marriage).

Addresses: *Home*—Cattolica, Italy. *Office*—Aeffe, Via delle Querce, 51, 47842 S. Giovanni, Marignano, Italy.

Career

Opened boutique in Cattolica, Italy, called "Jolly," c. 1968; designed first collection, c. 1973; co–founder of Aeffe (a clothing manufacturer and distributor), 1976; began showing seasonal collections on runways of Milan, Italy, 1981; launched Ferretti Jeans Philosophy, 1989, renamed Philosophy di Alberta Ferretti, 1994; renovated a 13th–century castle into the Palazzo Viviani hotel, Montegridolfo, Italy, 1994; signed licensing deal with Proctor & Gamble for a fragrance line, 2000.

Member: Foundation of the Cassa di Risparmio di Rimini (a bank), 1989—.

Awards: Named best female entrepreneur in the state of Emilia Romagna, Italy, 1991.

Sidelights

Designer Alberta Ferretti built a thriving fashion empire from a small boutique she opened in a seaside Italian village in the late 1960s. A savvy en-

trepreneur best known for her translucent, gossamer dresses, Ferretti also heads a manufacturing company that makes and distributes the lines of designers Narciso Rodriguez and Jean Paul Gaultier, among others. Her business acumen is combined with a characteristically Italian respect for *la dolce vita*, or "the good life": she renovated a medieval village near her hometown, complete with castle/ luxury hotel, and she prefers to spend time in both places rather than Milan. In a 2001 *Times* of London feature titled "Italy's Quiet Achiever," Lisa Armstrong described Ferretti as "a formidable industrialist," and representative of a country with "a sufficiently developed aesthetic sensibility to be able to accept captains of industry who waft around in floaty wisps of chiffon." Ferretti did not view herself as paradoxical in the least, she told Armstrong. "I don't see any reason why you can't look delicate and act tough." Ferretti grew up in Cattolica, Italy, in the 1950s and '60s. This seaside town lies on the Adriatic Sea near Rimini, in the state of Emilia Romagna. Her mother owned a dressmaking atelier in town, and Ferretti was cutting fabric for it by the time she was 12. At age 17, she left school and married not long afterward. With a small loan from her parents, she opened her own clothing store in Cattolica, calling it "Jolly." It had a workshop upstairs as well as living quarters, and within a few years she had two little boys and a thriving business to look after. "I could hold it all together only by giving up everything that was to do with having time to myself," she recalled in the interview with Armstrong for the *Times*.

By the early 1970s, Jolly was selling the work of then–unknown Italian designers like Mariuccia Mandelli, Giorgio Armani, and Gianni Versace, and Ferretti had started to run up some of her own design ideas as well for sale there. A sales representative visited her store one day, liked the frocks, and suggested she sell them elsewhere. Thus Ferretti's own line took shape around 1973, and within a short time proved such a hit with Italian women that she had to hire more seamstresses and move them into a 400–square–foot shed. From her perspective, Ferretti realized how problematic it could prove to have a seasonal collection sewn perfectly and then delivered on time, and so she began contracting her workshop to take in the work of other designers. Her business sense coincided with a boom in Italian fashion in the mid–1970s, when Milan's biannual "fashion weeks" began attracting an international crowd of buyers and journalists and Italian fashion became synonymous with well made and modern. Ferretti formally launched her second company in 1976, calling it "Aeffe" after the Italian pronunciation of her initials, and asked her younger brother Massimo to run it. By 1980 they had landed their first major contract, signing with an up–and–coming Italian designer, Enrico Coveri.

Ferretti began showing her own line in Milan in 1981, a debut she described to *Interview*'s Ingrid Sischy as "an experience which was very, very frightening for me." Her designs were both feminine and modern, made from the most delicate of fabrics like chiffon, gazar, or georgette. They caught on with style–conscious women on both sides of the Atlantic. By the mid–1990s, Ferretti's dresses were sold at upscale American retailers like Bergdorf Goodman and Neiman Marcus. Writing in the *Times*, Armstrong described Ferretti's signature style as "a kind of Valentino look for a younger, slightly more bohemian woman." Reviewing her Spring 2002 line, a writer for *WWD* listed the variations on the diaphanous—"bias–cut and pleated, ruched and side–draped, Empire–waisted and wrapped obi–style"—that had become the signature Ferretti frock. Her profile was boosted by a celebrity clientele that included Julia Roberts, Nicole Kidman, Sarah Jessica Parker, and Andie MacDowell; for the 2000 Academy Awards ceremony, Uma Thurman appeared in a red Alberta Ferretti number that won rave reviews. Ferretti summed up her design ethos in a talk with Tamsin Blanchard of London's *Independent* newspaper. "My clothes are not trendy at all costs," she declared. "They are an extension of a woman's personality, not for the woman who identifies with a Seventies or a Forties look."

A jeans line, Ferretti Jeans Philosophy, was launched in 1989, but by 1994 had morphed into a pret–a–porter division called Philosophy di Alberta Ferretti. For this the designer produced a more whimsical look. "The line allows me to let my creativity run wild," she told *WWD* journalist Samantha Conti. "Because the prices are contained and well below my top line, I feel much more free in designing." She also began opening boutiques—both Alberta Ferretti and Philosophy brands—in some of the world's best–dressed cities, from Milan and London to Tokyo and New York. Aeffe operations continued to expand, and by the late 1990s its state–of–the–art computerized factory near Cattolica was producing the lines of Narciso Rodriguez, Jean–Paul Gaultier, Rifat Ozbek, and Moschino. Ferretti also takes an occasional assignment for film, such as the outfit worn by Madonna in one crucial scene of the 2002 film *Swept Away*. "It was a caftan, and she had to keep falling off a yacht into the water," Ferretti told *WWD*. "So of course that meant a lot of caftans."

Ferretti keeps a seaside villa in Cattolica, and a winter place a few miles inland in San Giovanni in Marignano, where her Aeffe headquarters are located. One of her adult sons, Simone, works as a computer programmer for her company; his younger brother Giacomo raises mussels. After her first marriage ended, Ferretti wed anesthesiologist and acupuncturist Giuseppe Campanella. In the mid–1990s, she bought and renovated an entire hillside town, not far from Cattolica, called Montegridolfo. With structures dating back to the 1200s, the medieval town was in ruins, but the castle was turned into a four–star hotel, the Palazzo Viviani.

Ferretti's success, she notes, has but one drawback: she misses the daily interaction with clients that came from running a single store. "For me it's very important not to lose perspective when you become famous," she told *Guardian* writer Susannah Frankel. "I work all day. I'm a real woman. I cater for different needs. I'm not tall and I'm a bit, shall we say, rounded. I understand such problems and always design clothes that I myself would like to wear."

Sources

Books

Contemporary Fashion, second edition, St. James Press, 2002.

Periodicals

Guardian (London, England), April 5, 1997, p. 42.
Independent (London, England), April 13, 1997, p. 46.
InStyle, April 1998, p. 86.
Interview, October 1998.
People, January 26, 1998, p. 81.

Times (London, England), July 23, 2001, p. 13.
WWD, February 22, 1993, p. ID12; March 9, 1995, p. 12; January 30, 1996, p. 16; September 17, 1997, p. 13; October 27, 2000, p. 27; October 2, 2001, p. 6; March 25, 2002, p. 14; May 31, 2002, p. 13.

—*Carol Brennan*

Harvey Fierstein

© 2003 Harvey Fierstein

Playwright, actor, and gay-rights activist

Born Harvey Forbes Fierstein, June 6, 1954, in Brooklyn, NY; son of Irving (a handkerchief manufacturer) and Jacqueline (a housewife; maiden name, Gilbert) Fierstein. *Education:* Pratt Institute, Brooklyn, NY, B.F.A., 1973.

Addresses: *Office*—RF Entertainment Inc., 29 Haines Rd., Bedford Hills, NY 10507.

Career

Actor on stage, including: *Pork,* La Mama Experimental Theater Club (E.T.C.), New York, NY, 1971; *International Stud,* La Mama E.T.C., New York, NY, 1972; *Fugue in a Nursery* and *Widows and Children First!,* both onstage in New York, NY, 1979; *Torch Song Trilogy,* 1981–83; *Hairspray,* Neil Simon Theatre, New York, NY, August 2002—. Television appearances include: *The Demon Murder Case* (movie), 1983; *Miami Vice,* 1986; *Apology* (movie), 1986; *Tidy Endings,* 1988; *The Simpsons* (voice), 1990–91; *Cheers,* 1992; *In the Shadow of Love: A Teen AIDS Story* (movie), 1992; *Murder She Wrote,* 1992; *Daddy's Girls,* 1994; *Loving,* 1994; *Happily Ever After: Fairy Tales For Every Child* (voice), 1995; *The Larry Sanders Show,* 1997; *Ellen,* 1998; *Stories From My Childhood* (voice), 1998; *Double Platinum* (movie), 1999; *The Sissy Duckling* (movie; voice), 1999; *X–Chromosome* (voice), 1999; *Common Ground* (movie), 2000. Film appearances include: *The Times of Harvey Milk* (narrator), 1984; *Garbo Talks,* 1984; *Torch Song Trilogy,* 1988; *The Harvest,* 1993; *Mrs. Doubtfire,* 1993; *Bullets Over Broadway,* 1994; *Dr. Jekyll and Ms. Hyde,* 1995; *The Celluloid Closet,* 1996; *Everything Relative,* 1996; *Elmo Saves Christmas,* 1996; *White Lies,* 1996; *Independence Day,* 1996; *Kull the Conqueror,* 1997; *Safe Men,* 1998; *Mulan* (voice), 1998; *Jump,* 1999; *Playing Mona Lisa,* 2000; *Death to Smoochy,* 2002; *Duplex,* 2003. Works as a writer include: *Spookhouse* (play), 1984; *Tidy Endings,* 1988; *Torch Song Trilogy,* 1988; *Forget Him* (play), 1988; *Legs Diamond* (book for a Broadway musical), 1988; *The Sissy Duckling,* 1999; *Common Ground,* 2000. Works as a producer include: *Safe Sex* (play), 1987. Recording appearances include: *This Is Not Going To Be Pretty: Live at The Bottom Line,* Plump Records, 1995.

Awards: OBIE Award, *Village Voice,* for *Torch Song Trilogy,* 1982; George Oppenheimer–Newsday Playwriting Award for *Torch Song Trilogy,* 1982; Fund for Human Dignity Award, 1983; Theatre World Award for outstanding new performer, *Torch Song Trilogy,* 1983; Drama Desk Award for outstanding new play for *Torch Song Trilogy,* 1983; Drama Desk Award for outstanding actor in a play for *Torch Song Trilogy,* 1983; Tony Award for best play for *Torch Song Trilogy,* 1983; Tony Award for best performance by a leading actor in a play for *Torch Song Trilogy,* 1983; Tony Award for best book of a musical for *La Cage Aux Folles,* 1984; L.A. Drama Critics Circle Award for *La Cage Aux Folles,* 1984; Dramatists Guild Award for *La Cage Aux Folles,* 1984; Cable ACE Award for best writing in a special drama for *Tidy Endings,* 1989; GLAAD Award for Visibility, 1994;

Humanitas Prize for children's animation for *Happily Ever After: Fairy Tales for Every Child* for "The Sissy Duckling" episode, 2000; Tony Award for best performance by a leading actor in a musical for *Hairspray*, 2003; Drama Desk Award for outstanding actor in a musical, *Hairspray*, 2003; Drama League Award for distinguished performance for *Hairspray*, 2003.

Sidelights

As an actor and playwright, Harvey Fierstein has made a career of turning unconventional shows into Broadway sensations. Fierstein (pronounced Fire–steen) first rose to fame in the early 1980s with his smash play *Torch Song Trilogy*, for which he earned two Tony Awards in 1983, one for Best Actor and one for Best Play. The stage show, which Fierstein wrote and which featured him as a drag queen, was a breakthrough piece because it proved that a gay–themed show could turn a profit on Broadway. In 2002, Fierstein returned to Broadway and became the show–stopping centerpiece of *Hairspray*, winning another Tony Award. What made his comeback so remarkable was that he won the lead actor Tony Award for playing a woman. Furthermore, Fierstein holds the distinction of being only the second person in history to earn four Tony Awards in different categories.

The youngest of two sons born into a Jewish family in Brooklyn, New York, Fierstein attended the city's public schools. His father, Irving, was a handkerchief manufacturer and his mother, Jackie, stayed home to tend to the kids and the household. The future playwright took creative writing in high school but said he did not do well. What Fierstein did do well in high school was perform in drag. As a 270–pound teenager, Fierstein specialized in impersonations of the brassy–voiced Broadway musical comedy star Ethel Merman. He became a hit in some of New York's lesser–known clubs as he transformed himself into characters with names like Virginia Hamm, Kitty Litter, and Bertha Venation. "But I was living very much of a triple life," Fierstein told Michiko Kakutani of the *New York Times*. "I had my night life there, I was living at home with my parents in Bensonhurst, and like my mother says, 'Remember to say you were going to school full–time, too.'"

Despite the demands of his busy life, Fierstein made a name for himself and got his first break in 1971 when he was offered a role in *Pork*, one of pop icon Andy Warhol's few theater productions. The play, which featured Fierstein as an asthmatic lesbian, made its debut at New York's La Mama Experimental Theater Club in 1971. Soon, Fierstein was writing his own plays, inspired by other La Mama actors who wrote plays for Fierstein to perform. Fierstein returned the favor, writing his colleagues into his plays. Fierstein's first production was a play titled *International Stud*, which debuted at La Mama in 1972. The play featured a drag queen on a visit to a backroom bar. While the play was well–liked within the gay community, most people did not think Fierstein or his thought–provoking material would ever hit Broadway.

"I don't think I would ever have written again, except that the *Village Voice* sent a critic who called me the devil come to earth for writing this horrible thing," Fierstein told Peter Stone in an interview for *Broadway Song & Story*. "So I figured this is a talent I should work on."

Fierstein's parents, however, encouraged him to study art education, figuring it would provide a steady income. He enrolled at the Pratt Institute in Brooklyn, New York, earning a bachelor of fine arts degree in 1973. Fierstein taught briefly, then returned to the theater and playwriting. Over the next several years, Fierstein continued writing, reworking, and performing his plays. In 1979, he penned and starred in two one–act plays, *Fugue in a Nursery* and *Widows and Children First!*. These would one day be combined with *International Stud* to form *Torch Song Trilogy*, a trio of amusing yet moving plays that dealt with contemporary gay life.

The main character in *Torch Song Trilogy* is Arnold Beckoff, a drag queen who yearns for an ordinary life. Arnold wants nothing more than to settle down, adopt a child, and live happily ever after and sees no reason his sexual orientation should hinder that goal. Fierstein, who is gay, acknowledges that some of the plot was inspired by his own life experiences. For instance, both Arnold and Fierstein had lovers who dumped them to get married. Both had friends who were battered and killed, had thought about adopting a child, and were close to their widowed mothers.

Torch Song debuted Off Off Broadway in 1981, featuring Fierstein in the role of Arnold, with John Glines as one of the producers. Glines thought the play would appeal to gay audiences but never figured it would have commercial potential. The play's initial run was scheduled to last eight weeks, but after two weeks, the producers wanted to close it down for lack of interest—and profit. Then came an upbeat review in the *New York Times*, which resulted in capacity crowds and a move to an Off Broadway theater, where it ran for five months before hitting Broadway in 1982. At every step, Fierstein continued in the part of Arnold, never seeming to wear out, even though the role required him to be onstage for nearly all of the duration of the four–hour play, up to six performances a week. The hard work, however, paid off in the form of two Tony Awards in 1983, one for Best Play and one for Best Actor in a Play.

The success of *Torch Song* showed the world that gay–themed shows could be successful. Before *Torch Song,* playwrights shied away from dealing openly with homosexual characters. Instead, metaphors were used, or perhaps gays and lesbians were referenced indirectly. They were never, however, a significant and sympathetic character. Fierstein was successful because he was able to use laughter and dramatic truth to humanize drag queens, who most often had been portrayed as exotic divas or victims of circumstance. Through his carefully written words and acting, Fierstein made Arnold worthy of empathy from the audience.

Glines said he believed the play was a hit because everyone, gay or straight, could identify with Arnold, who wanted out of life what most people want: a job he liked pretty well, a comfortable life, and someone to share it with. Speaking to Leslie Bennetts of the *New York Times,* Glines put it this way: "What Harvey proved was that you could use a gay context and a gay experience and speak in universal truths."

Fierstein's success as a playwright prompted him to write a musical adaptation of *La Cage Aux Folles,* based on the French–Italian film and French play of the same name. Because *Torch Song* kept his schedule full, Fierstein did most of his writing on the subway, going to or from performances. *La Cage Aux Folles* opened at New York's Palace Theater in August of 1983 and ran for 1,761 performances, winning Fierstein another Tony Award, this one for Best Book of a Musical. Other plays followed, including *Spookhouse,* 1984, and *Forget Him,* 1988. In 1987, Fierstein produced *Safe Sex,* a set of three one–act plays on gay themes, though it opened and quickly folded. In 1988, he wrote the book for the Broadway musical *Legs Diamond.*

In 1988, Fierstein returned to the role of Arnold, turning the play into a film. After that, Fierstein quit drag. "I said, 'I've done that for a large part of my career and I do not need to do that anymore,'" he told the *Baltimore Sun*'s J. Wynn Rousuck. "Drag is a mask that you wear when you don't want people to see who you are."

Over the next several years, Fierstein appeared in some 30 films in supporting roles, including *Mrs. Doubtfire, Independence Day, Playing Mona Lisa,* and *Duplex.* He also starred on several television shows, including *Miami Vice, Murder She Wrote,* and *The Larry Sanders Show.* In 1992, he earned an Emmy nomination for his supporting role on the smash hit *Cheers,* playing Rebecca's lover. Fierstein also added his voice to many shows, including *The Simpsons,* where his distinctively gravelly voice became Homer's executive secretary in 1990–91. He also did the voice of Yao for Disney's animated film *Mulan* in 1998.

Fierstein returned to Broadway in 2002, accepting a part in the quirky musical *Hairspray,* based on John Waters' 1988 cult movie of the same name. Fierstein quickly became the star of the show in his role as Edna Turnblad, mother of the heroine, Tracy. The musical, which takes place in 1962 Baltimore, is about Tracy, a sizeable teen with large hair and big dreams. Though Fierstein was once again donning dresses on Broadway, this time he was not playing a drag queen; rather, he was playing a real woman. Director Jack O'Brien told the *Baltimore Sun* that Fierstein was so good that the audience readily accepted him as a woman. "I contend that there are certain factions of our audiences who totally believe that he is Edna.... They accept that relationship of being mother–daughter."

For Fierstein, playing Turnblad was a grueling experience. His performance–night dressing ritual included more than 90 minutes of shaving, make–up application, and body wrapping for womanly curves. In addition, he attached bouffant wigs and 35–pound breasts, then stepped onto the stage to sing and dance, though he had never been in a musical before. So brilliant was his performance that he captured his fourth Tony Award in 2003, for Best Actor in a Musical. The musical itself won eight Tonys, including Best Musical. *Hairspray* itself was an unlikely candidate for a Broadway hit, but the cast pulled it off, garnering rave reviews from the *New York Times* and *New Yorker.* The show, which cost $10.5 million to produce, turned a profit after only nine months due to the sellout crowds.

As a gay activist, Fierstein realizes that he must be sensitive to the roles he takes because they will influence people's opinions about gay people. As he told Scottie Campbell in an interview for *Watermark* posted on Walt Disney World's Gayday 2004 website, "There are times when I don't take roles because I don't want to be perceived a certain way. For example, I was offered the role as the monster in Stephen King's *It*—a clown who ate children. I wouldn't do it. Even though it was a great role, I felt that I didn't want to be perceived in that way because of the horrible lie that gay people want children. I wasn't even going to put that in the back of people's minds."

Over the years, Fierstein has been a vocal gay–rights activist, speaking out for gay people, queer theater, and AIDS causes. He has been a spokesman for the Services Legal Defense Fund, a group that advocates for the rights of gays and lesbians in the military. As far as his legacy is concerned, Fierstein told Campbell: "Time will tell us what we did and didn't do. The way that I look at it, the only thing that I will definitely take credit for is that *Torch Song* and *La Cage Aux Folles*—two of my shows—were the first ever gay–themed shows to make money on Broadway. And I think that counts more than anything."

Selected writings

International Stud (play), 1972.
In Search of the Cobra Jewels (play), 1973.
Feaky Pussy (play), 1975.
Flatbush Tosca (play), 1976.
Cannibals Just Don't Know Better (play), 1978.
Fugue in a Nursery (play), 1979.
Widows and Children First! (play), 1979.
Torch Song Trilogy (play), 1981.
La Cage Aux Folles (musical), 1983.
Spookhouse (play), 1984.
Safe Sex (play), 1987.
Forget Him (play), 1988.
Legs Diamond (play), 1988.

Sources

Books

Botto, Louis, *At This Theatre: 100 Years of Broadway Shows, Stories and Stars,* Applause Theatre and Cinema Books, 2002.
Guernsey, Otis L., Jr., ed., *Broadway Song & Story,* Dodd, Mead & Company, 1985.

Periodicals

New York Times, July 14, 1982, p. C17; June 26, 1983.
Sun (Baltimore, Maryland), August 11, 2002, p. 3E; June 9, 2003, p. 1A.
USA Today, September 5, 2002, p. 2D.

Online

"Color Me Harvey," Gayday 2004, http://www.gayday.com/news/2000/watermark_000525b.asp (November 14, 2003).
"Harvey Fierstein," E! Online, http://www.eonline.com/facts/people/0,12,5340,00.html?celfact2 (November 10, 2003).

—*Lisa Frick*

Claudia Fleming

Food director for Pret a Manger USA

Born April 11, 1959, in Brentwood, NY; married Gerry Hayden (a chef). *Education:* Studied at Peter Kump's New York Cooking School (now known as the Institute of Culinary Education).

Addresses: *Office*—c/o Pret a Manger USA, 145 W. 30th St., New York, NY 10001.

Career

Began career in food service industry as a server at Jams in New York City in the early 1980s; took server's job at New York's Union Square Café while she studied at New York Cooking School, moving up to entry–level kitchen position after graduation; polished pastry cooking skills in Paris; returned to New York to work in dessert preparation at several New York restaurants, including Montrachet, the Tribeca Grill, and Luxe; executive pastry chef, Gramercy Tavern, New York, 1994–2002; food director, Pret a Manger USA, New York, 2002—.

Awards: James Beard Foundation, Outstanding Pastry Chef Award, 2000; named to Ten Best Pastry Chefs in America, *Pastry Art & Design,* 2000.

Sidelights

At first glance, award–winning pastry chef Claudia Fleming seemed a curious choice as food director for Pret a Manger USA, the American sub-

sidiary of the rapidly growing British chain of "quick casual" food boutiques. The transition from whipping up elaborate pastries at New York's Gramercy Tavern to supervising Pret a Manger's menu of prewrapped sandwiches struck many in the restaurant business as a very dramatic change of pace indeed. Fleming does not see it as much of a leap at all. As she told Bret Begun of *Newsweek,* "At Gramercy, we changed the way people thought about dining. I feel strongly about the ability of Pret to change the way people think about eating quick meals."

Fleming also believes passionately that so–called fast food need not be unhealthy food. It was Pret a Manger's dedication to quality that first attracted her, Fleming told Paul Frumkin of *Nation's Restaurant News.* "It's a great company. The philosophy is very much the same as it was at Gramercy. It's fresh, natural, trying to be as seasonal as possible. It's all hormone–free, antibiotic–free. It really speaks to me." Also appealing to Fleming is the sandwich, centerpiece of the Pret a Manger menu. As she told Frumkin, "People say to me, 'What a weird transition—pastry to sandwiches.' But the sandwich thing has always been something I've wanted to do. It's the perfect meal if it's made well."

Born in Brentwood on New York's Long Island on April 11, 1959, Fleming grew up wanting to be a professional dancer and began taking dance lessons while little more than a toddler. Her ascendancy to the highest ranks of the American culinary industry did not even begin until, at age 25, she gave up on her dreams of a career in dance. Because of the central role dance played in her life as a girl, food and eating took a relatively low profile. "I never cooked with my grandmother or with my mom," Fleming told Frumkin. "I was dancing as far back as I can remember, and you're almost trained not to eat when you're practicing ballet. I think I was on a diet from the time I was five years old."

With high school and years of ballet lessons behind her, Fleming headed off to Hartford, Connecticut, to study at the dance school associated with the Hartford Ballet Company (now known as Dance Connecticut). Moving to New York City at the age of 21, Fleming joined a small modern dance troupe but found it necessary to take jobs in the food service industry to support herself. In the first half of the 1980s, she worked as a server in two popular New York eateries—Jams and Union Square Café. When she turned 25 in April of 1984 and still had not made it into a major dance company, Fleming decided it was time to hang up her ballet slippers.

Captivated by the mysteries of the food preparation side of the restaurant business, Fleming decided to make the transition from dining room to kitchen. To do so, she enrolled in classes at Peter Kump's New York Cooking School (which has since been renamed the Institute of Culinary Education) while still working as a server at the Union Square Café. After completing her studies, Michael Romano, the restaurant's executive chef, rewarded Fleming with an entry–level job in the kitchen. After further broadening her cooking skills with a summer in the kitchen at Gordon's Restaurant in Aspen, Colorado, she returned to New York to accept a job as assistant pastry chef at Union Square.

In an interview with Amy Zuber of *Nation's Restaurant News,* Fleming elaborated further on her decision to specialize in pastry. "I loved that it was a world within the restaurant industry. It is pretty independent, and there is a lot of autonomy in pastry. I also love dessert. I remember eating Pepperidge Farm cookies and Haagen–Dazs ice cream for dinner when I first moved to New York and couldn't afford much else. Being a pastry chef offers great immediate gratification, and I was good at it. It came naturally to me, and it suited my personality."

Fleming moved from the Union Square Café to an assistant pastry chef position at the trendy Tribeca Grill in New York. It was while working there that she met her future husband, Gerry Hayden, who is today the executive chef at New York's Aureole Restaurant. To learn even more about the art of pastry making, Fleming next flew off to Paris, France, where she worked for a time at Paris's upscale Fauchon restaurant and in a Biarritz pastry shop. While in France, she was also introduced to a new concept in sandwich making at the original Cosi in Paris. Recalling her stint at Cosi, Fleming told Frumkin, "I worked there for several months. It was bread baked on premises in a wood–fired oven and really fresh ingredients, like grilled sardines and onions and greens. I loved it. At one point I even thought about staying and managing a second store."

Instead, homesick for New York, Fleming returned to the Big Apple where she landed a job as an assistant pastry chef at Luxe. When the restaurant closed, she was persuaded by a friend to interview with partners Danny Meyer and chef Tom Colicchio who were looking for a pastry chef to work at their soon–to–open Gramercy Tavern. Impressed by Fleming's ideas, as she was by their plans for the new restaurant, Meyer and Colicchio gave her the job. Both the restaurant and the pastries and other desserts conceived by Fleming were a solid hit with New York diners. For some eight years food critics lavished praise on the elaborate confections whipped up by Fleming, but then in 2002 along came Pret a Manger with an offer she simply could not refuse. Although she remained enthusiastic about her work with pastries, Fleming acknowledged to *Newsweek's* Begun that some of her passion for the work had faded. She recalled that when she began at the Gramercy in 1994, "every waking moment was spent thinking about desserts. That stopped. I miss being obsessed."

For the moment, at least, Fleming seems to be very much obsessed with her new responsibilities, which include managing the sandwich menu at Pret a Manger and looking for new and exciting additions to the chain's line. Asked by Rob Patronite of *New York* magazine what makes a good sandwich, Fleming replied: "Balance of flavor and texture, stripping it down to its essentials. I love stripping things down; it's what I do best. They're the same principles that apply to creating a dessert: I'm looking for contrast—you want something soft in there, but you also want something crispy—and a lot of it has to do with the bread."

Selected writings

(With Melissa Clark) *The Last Course: The Desserts of Gramercy Tavern,* Random House, 2001.

Sources

Periodicals

Nation's Restaurant News, December 2, 2002; January 27, 2003.
Newsweek, November 4, 2002, p. 52.
Publishers Weekly, July 2, 2001.
Time, November 13, 2000, p. 98.

Online

Biography Resource Center Online, Gale Group, 2003.
"Claudia Fleming, Pastry Chef," StarChefs, http://www.starchefs.com/women/bio_fleming.html (July 1, 2003).
"The Fast (Food) Lane," *New York,* http://www.newyorkmetro.com/urban/articles/02/fallpreview/restaurants/fleming.htm (July 1, 2003).

—*Don Amerman*

George Foreman

Spokesperson and former professional boxer

B orn George Edward Foreman, January 10, 1949, in Marshall, TX; son of J.D. (a railroad worker) and Nancy Ree Foreman; married and divorced four times; married Mary Foreman; children: Michi, Freeda George, Georgetta, Natalie, Leola, George Edward II, George Edward III, George Edward IV, George Edward V, George Edward VI.

Addresses: *Office*—George Foreman Youth Center, PO Box 14267, Humble, TX 77347.

Career

B oxer, 1969–1977, 1987–1997; pastor, 1977—; product representative, 1994—.

Awards: Olympic gold medal in boxing, 1968; World Heavyweight Championship, 1973, 1994.

Sidelights

O lympic gold medalist and boxing champion George Foreman has held the world heavyweight title twice, and became the oldest man ever to win it after making a comeback to regain the honor in 1994. Although he retired from boxing in 1997, he is still a popular and highly visible figure, and has made millions by selling a home grill, the Lean, Mean, Fat–Reducing Grilling Machine. He is also a preacher and the founder of a youth center in Houston, Texas.

AP/Wide World Photos

Born in Marshall, Texas, Foreman grew up there and later in Houston's rough Fifth Ward, where his mother moved to look for work. When Foreman was five, J.D. Foreman, the man Foreman believed was his father, left the family, leaving Foreman and his six siblings with their mother. It was a daunting load for a single mother, and Foreman often roamed the streets of Houston, getting into trouble. He was bigger and stronger than most boys his age, and he wandered the streets, living in abandoned houses, picking pockets, mugging drunks, and making trouble for everyone he met. His mother, overwhelmed by his bad behavior, was hospitalized for emotional collapse when he was 14. While in the hospital, she sent $45 home to pay for Foreman's sister's graduation ring, but Foreman stole the money and spent it to buy wine and presents for himself. By the time he was 16, he was tough and street–smart, but he could barely read or write.

One night, however, he had an experience that woke him up to the truth about his life. He told Hans J. Massaquoi in *Ebony* that after mugging some people, he crawled under a house to hide from the pursuing police and their dogs: "I started remembering from television shows that whenever the criminals were getting pursued, they would go into the water so the dogs couldn't sniff them. So I started digging myself under the mud. And for the first time I realized that I had become a criminal. I had dropped out of school and didn't know what to do with my life."

At this point, he remembered seeing a television commercial for the Job Corps, a program that educated young people and gave them job skills. He signed up the next day, and after an initial period of adjustment, learned bricklaying, forestry, and carpentry; he also learned to read and write. To siphon off the energy he used to spend street fighting, he learned the sport of boxing. Each month, he sent $50 home to his mother.

Only 20 months after his first boxing match, Foreman's talent for the sport led him to win a gold medal at the 1968 Olympic Games in Mexico City. After winning, he waved an American flag around the ring, causing a controversy among many African–American civil rights activists, who saw this patriotic move as a way of appeasing the oppressive white–run American society of the time. His move was in sharp contrast to that of other African–American athletes at the Games; instead of raising the American flag, they proclaimed their pride and protest by giving the Black Power salute—a raised, clenched fist—after their Olympic wins. Foreman told *Ebony*'s Massaquoi, "I was so proud that I had won. I wanted the whole world to know that I was from America."

Hurt by the criticism, Foreman adopted a tough-guy image, habitually wearing a menacing grimace; after he turned professional in 1969, he was known for his mean facial expression and tough demeanor. This persona made him unpopular among the public, as did the fact that he did not serve in the military during the Vietnam War. In fact, Foreman did register for the draft, but drew a high number in the lottery, so he did not have to serve, and chose a civilian career. In contrast, boxer Muhammad Ali, who refused to be drafted, was stripped of his boxing title as a result, but still became a popular hero to the public because he was not considered to be surly, as Foreman was. Foreman's lawyer and friend, Henry Holmes, told *People,* "He was a guy who never smiled. He was feared and rejected by the public."

On January 22, 1973, after fighting his way through the ranks of boxers, winning his first 37 fights—including 34 knockouts—he won the heavyweight championship from Joe Frazier after only two rounds. He continued to box for the next four years. During those years, his most ignominious fight was with Muhammad Ali, who soundly beat him in

1974. Foreman bolstered his flagging self–confidence with money, toys, and women, buying several houses, a pet lion and tiger, and fancy cars. He retained deep bitterness toward Ali and dreamed of a rematch, but it never happened.

In 1977, Foreman experienced a profound religious conversion that led him to leave the boxing world, as well as to forego millions in potential boxing winnings. After losing a difficult 12–round match against Jimmy Young in San Juan, Puerto Rico, Foreman was bleeding from his forehead, hands, and feet, and exhausted. In the dressing room, he felt as if he had spiritually died and needed to be reborn. "Jesus is coming alive in me!" he shouted, according to *Ebony*'s Massaquoi, and from that moment, became a born–again Christian. Eventually, he cofounded a small church, the Church of the Lord Jesus Christ, in a poor area of Houston, and hit the road as a traveling evangelical preacher.

Foreman cut his hair, as well as his ties with boxing, and told Massaquoi that even the general public failed to recognize him anymore. "So you see, I had disappeared. I had become just a regular guy in the crowd." Along with his hair, Foreman rid himself of all his luxury cars, several houses, his pet tiger and lion, and stopped flying first class. He also gave up exercising, ate whatever he wanted, and gained a great deal of weight.

With his brother, Reid, Foreman founded the George Foreman Youth and Community Development Center in Houston. Intended to keep young people active and away from crime and drugs, the center offered basketball, weight lifting, boxing, and a library. However, the center eventually ran out of funding. Foreman, not wanting to close it down, decided that the only way to save it was for him to make some money. The only way he knew how to make money was through boxing, so he decided to return to the ring. It was a difficult decision, because he was unsure how the members of his church would view a pastor who beat people up for a living.

When he decided to return to boxing in 1987, Foreman was the subject of many scornful press commentaries, as reporters were skeptical of his ability to make a comeback. Some viewed it as a publicity stunt, partly because Foreman, to supplement his income, found work as a pitchman for hamburgers and other fast food, and boasted of his huge appetite. He was no longer the fit young man he had been in his prime, and he looked it. Still, despite his increased girth and weight, he began beating younger and fitter boxers, slowly earning respect from boxers and the sports press. In addition, his persona had changed; instead of a surly young man, he was now a pleasant and funny middle-aged man. In addition, he had a sense of humor about himself, yelling during interviews, "I might be the fattest guy in the world, but I got the hardest punch!" according to Julie Sloane in *Fortune.*

After 24 wins, including 23 knockouts, he was viewed as a true contender to regain the heavyweight title. In 1991 he fought Evander Holyfield for the title, but lost by a decision. On November 5, 1994, Foreman fought Michael Moorer for the World Boxing Association and International Boxing Federation heavyweight titles, and won after knocking out Moorer in the tenth round.

As a result of his win, Foreman received endorsement offers from many companies, but the one that has had the greatest publicity is his association with the Lean, Mean, Fat-Reducing Grilling Machine, manufactured by Salton. Foreman began pitching the grill in 1995. In 1997, Foreman retired from boxing for good, with a record of 76–5, with 68 knockouts. Meanwhile, after a slow start, sales of the grill skyrocketed; in 2002 alone, the company made $922 million from the product, and by 2003, it had sold 50 million grills over the years. *Advertising Age* writer Bob Garfield told *Fortune*'s Sloane that Foreman was largely responsible for the sales: "He was a highly charged personality, very likable, a noted carnivore who was selling a good and inexpensive product." Sloane observed that Foreman had the unique ability to appeal to both men and women, for different reasons: "Women see him as warm and cuddly, while men see him as a champ."

Foreman has ten children—five girls and five boys. The boys are all named George Edward, after Foreman, with the addition of numerals: George Edward II, George Edward III, George Edward IV, George Edward V, George Edward VI. Foreman told *Ebony*'s Massaquoi why he named all his sons after himself: "I wanted my boys to have something that nobody could ever take from them, and I figured, give them a name that they could run into whenever they had problems or if they ever got lost...." He also explained that he was deeply affected by the fact that he did not know who his real father was until 1976, and he wanted to make sure his own sons never had any doubt about their own origins.

In 2003, Foreman was inducted into the International Boxing Hall of Fame. He told a reporter for *Jet,* "It's wonderful.... I'm a boxing Hall of Famer, and I love it." In the same year, he published a book, *George Foreman's Guide to Life,* with coauthor Linda Kulman. In an interview with Jeff Zaleski in *Publishers Weekly,* Foreman said that the most important piece of advice he wanted to pass on to people was, "Learn to trust in yourself. There's not a better person you're going to meet in this life, and there's not anyone you're going to know any better than you. The best advice will come from within you." He told *People,* "I wasted a lot of time not being nice. The thing I covet more than anything is to be seen as the nicest guy in the world."

Selected writings

(With Linda Kulman) *George Foreman's Guide to Life,* Simon & Schuster, 2003.

Sources

Ebony, July 1995, p. 86.
Fortune, June 9, 2003, p. 168B.
Jet, June 23, 2003, p. 51.
Men's Health, April 1995, p. 120.
People, April 28, 2003, pp. 115–18.
Publishers Weekly, January 6, 2003, p. 53.
Texas Monthly, February 1995, p. 98.
Time, April 28, 2003, p. G10.

—*Kelly Winters*

Tommy Franks

AP/Wide World Photos

United States Army general

Born Tommy Ray Franks, June 17, 1945, in Wynnewood, OK; married Cathryn (maiden name, Carley; March 22, 1969); children: Jacqueline. *Education:* Attended University of Texas at Austin, 1963–65; graduated from U.S. Army Artillery Officer Candidate School, Fort Sill, OK, 1967; University of Texas, Arlington, B.A. (business administration), 1971; graduated from Armed Forces Staff College, Norfolk, VA, 1976; graduated from U.S. Army War College, Carlisle, PA; Shippensburg University, Shippensburg, PA, M.S. (public administration), 1985.

Addresses: *Office*—U.S. Army Central Command, 7115 S Boundary Blvd., MacDill Air Force Base, FL 33621–5101.

Career

Commissioned as Second Lieutenant in U.S. Army, 1967; served as battery assistant executive officer at Fort Sill, OK; assigned to Ninth Infantry Division in Vietnam, serving as forward observer, aerial observer, and assistant S–3 with Second Battalion, Fourth Field Artillery; served as fire support officer with Fifth Battalion, 60th infantry; returned to Fort Sill to command cannon battery in Artillery Training Center, 1968; assigned to Second Armored Calvary Regiment in West Germany, 1973; commanded the 84th Armored Engineer Company and served as regimental assistant S–3; posted to Pentagon as Army Inspector General in the Investigations Division, 1976–78; served on Congressional Activities Team and as executive assistant, Office of the Army Chief of Staff, 1977; as-

sumed command of Second Battalion, 78th Field Artillery in West Germany, 1981–84; returned to United States in 1984 to attend Army War College, after which he was posted to Fort Hood, TX, as III Corps Deputy Assistant G3; given command of Division Artillery, First Cavalry Division, 1987; chief of staff, First Cavalry Division; named Assistant Division Commander (Maneuver), First Cavalry Division during Operations Desert Shield and Desert Storm, 1991; assistant commandant of Field Artillery School at Fort Sill, 1991–92; director of Louisiana Maneuvers Task Force, Office of Chief of Staff of the Army, 1992–94; dispatched to South Korea to assume command of U.S. Forces Korea and the Combined Forces Command, 1994; commander of Second Infantry (Warrior) Division in Korea, 1995–97; assumed command of Third Army/Army Forces Central Command in Atlanta, GA, 1997–2000; promoted to general and named commander–in–chief of U.S. Central Command at MacDill Air Force Base, Tampa, FL, 2000; commanded United States–led invasion of Afghanistan, 2001–03; commanded Operation Iraqi Freedom, 2003.

Awards: Defense Distinguished Service Medal, Distinguished Service Medal (two awards), Legion of Merit (four awards), Bronze Star Medal with "V" (three awards), Purple Heart (three awards), Air Medal with "V", Army Commendation Medal with "V", numerous United States and foreign service awards.

Sidelights

After a distinguished military career spanning five decades, General Tommy Franks retired from active duty in July of 2003. The head of the U.S. Central Command (CENTCOM) during the American invasion of Iraq during the spring of 2003, Franks in May was offered the post of Army chief of staff—the top job in the U.S. Army—but turned it down, mostly because he had little heart for the political infighting of the Pentagon bureaucracy. As one Defense Department official told CNN, "This is a man, a combat commander, who has won two wars. He's not really excited about a desk job."

In the first two major American military engagements of the new millennium—Operation Enduring Freedom in Afghanistan and Operation Iraqi Freedom—Franks deftly commanded United States troops to quick victories. In the early days of the Iraqi campaign, he, along with the rest of the Bush defense team, endured searing criticism from opponents of the war, most of whom decried the slow pace of coalition advances and suggested that the United States ran the risk of a much broader war in the Middle East. In the end, Franks and his lieutenants were able to demonstrate the essential soundness of their military strategy, concluding the all-out battle phase of the operation in a relatively short period of time. Although there were lingering questions about the accuracy of the intelligence used as a pretext for launching the war, this had little to do with Franks' role in the conflict and did nothing to tarnish his image as a military leader.

The general's military experience extends from the Vietnam War of the late 1960s through the second United States war against Iraq. In between Franks was involved in United States military operations around the world. In the mid–1970s, he commanded a howitzer battery in West Germany, and he later served as commander of the Second Battalion, 78th Field Artillery in Germany during the first half of the 1980s. During the Gulf conflict of 1990–91, Franks was assistant division commander for operations Desert Shield and Desert Storm. Between 1995 and 1997, he commanded the Second Infantry Division in South Korea. From CENTCOM's headquarters in Tampa, Florida, Franks directed Operation Enduring Freedom in Afghanistan beginning in late 2001. To lead United States military operations in 2003's Operation Iraqi Freedom, Franks alternated between CENTCOM's Tampa headquarters and a command base in Doha, Qatar.

Born in Wynnewood, Oklahoma, on June 17, 1945, Franks grew up in Midland, Texas, where his family had moved shortly after his birth. He attended Robert E. Lee High School in Midland, where he played linebacker on the Rebels football team. Other distinguished alumni of the high school include President George W. Bush and the First Lady, the former Laura Welch. After high school graduation in 1963, Franks headed to the University of Texas at Austin, where he studied business administration. He dropped out two years later to join the Army as the United States became increasingly entangled in the conflict between North and South Vietnam.

After completing basic training and Artillery Officer Candidate School at Fort Sill, Oklahoma, Franks was commissioned as a second lieutenant. He served briefly as a battery assistant executive officer at Fort Sill before being dispatched in 1967 to Vietnam, where he was assigned to the Ninth Infantry Division. During his tour in Vietnam, Franks served as a forward observer, aerial observer, and assistant S–3 with the Second Battalion, Fourth Field Artillery. He also served as a fire support officer with the Fifth Battalion (mechanized), 60th Infantry, while in Vietnam. He was wounded three times in combat in Vietnam.

Returning to Fort Sill in 1968, Franks assumed command of a cannon battery in the Artillery Training Center. Selected to participate in the Army's Boot Strap Degree Completion Program the following year, he took classes at the University of Texas in Arlington, earning his bachelor's degree in business administration in 1971. Franks next attended the Artillery Advance Course, after the completion of which he was assigned to the Second Armored Calvary Regiment in West Germany in 1973. During the time he was attached to the Second Regiment, he commanded the First Squadron Howitzer Battery and served as Squadron S–3. He subsequently assumed command of the 84th Armored Engineer Company and served as Regimental Assistant S–3.

Back in the United States, Franks attended the Armed Forces Staff College in Norfolk, Virginia. Upon graduation in 1976, he was assigned to the Pentagon where he served as an army inspector general in the Investigations Division. The following year he was posted to the Office of the Army Chief of Staff, serving first on its Congressional Activities Team and later as an executive assistant. After spending five years at the Pentagon, Franks in 1981 was once again assigned to West Germany where for the next three years he commanded Second Battalion, 78th Field Artillery.

In 1984 Franks returned to the United States from West Germany to attend the U.S. Army War College at Carlisle, Pennsylvania. At the same time, he also managed to complete work on a master's degree in public administration at nearby Shippensburg University. After completing his studies in Pennsylvania, Franks in 1985 was assigned to Fort Hood, Texas, where he served until 1987 as III Corps Deputy Assistant G3. He assumed command of Division Artillery, First Calvary Division, in 1987, also serving as chief of staff, First Cavalry Division during this tour.

Franks' first assignment as a general officer came during Operations Desert Shield and Desert Storm in the Persian Gulf region at the beginning of the 1990s. During that first American conflict with Iraq, he served as assistant division commander (maneuver) of the First Calvary Division. At the close of hostilities with Iraq, Franks was assigned to the Field Artillery School at Fort Sill as assistant commandant. In 1992 he was named first director of the Louisiana Maneuvers Task Force, Office of the Chief of Staff of the Army, at Fort Monroe, Virginia, in which post he continued until 1994. In March of that year Franks was reassigned to South Korea as commanding general of the Second Infantry (Warrior) Division, First Army. Promoted to lieutenant general in 1997, Franks spent the rest of the 1990s as deputy commanding general of the Third Army at Fort McPherson in Georgia.

Franks was made commander–in–chief of CENTCOM in July of 2000. Headquartered at MacDill Air Force Base in Tampa, CENTCOM was responsible for military operations in the Middle East as well as much of the former Soviet Union. Franks moved into this critical post only months before Middle East terrorists launched a new series of devastating attacks against western—mostly American—targets. Suicide bombers struck the U.S.S. Cole, an American destroyer anchored off the Yemeni port of Aden, in October of 2000. The attack not only crippled the Cole but left 17 American sailors dead and 39 injured. But far worse was yet to come. On the morning of September 11, 2001, al–Qaeda terrorists launched a deadly attack on the United States. Al–Qaeda operatives hijacked four aircraft, two of which were crashed into the twin towers of the World Trade Center in New York City while another was flown into the Pentagon, just outside Washington, D.C. The fourth hijacked craft was believed to be headed for the White House or another target in the nation's capital when passengers aboard the jet, seeking to regain control of the plane, struggled with the hijackers. The plane crash–landed in the southwestern Pennsylvania countryside, well short of its intended target. The terrorists's September 11 attacks left more than 3,000 dead and called into question the adequacy of United States security measures.

In the wake of the terrorists' attack, President George W. Bush declared war on al–Qaeda and other terrorist organizations, as well as the countries harboring them. In the case of al–Qaeda, clearly implicated in the September 11 attacks, Afghanistan, under the oppressive rule of the Taliban regime, was known to strongly support the terrorist group and its leader, Osama bin Laden. On October 7, 2001, less than a month after the attacks on the World Trade Center and Pentagon, American forces launched operations designed to rout both al–Qaeda and the Taliban from Afghanistan. Franks was named commander of American forces in Afghanistan.

Under the direction of Franks, most of the initial goals of Operation Enduring Freedom—including the dismantlement of Taliban rule and destruction of al–Qaeda training camps—were quickly accomplished, but despite exhaustive searches in the rugged, mountainous country, most Taliban and al–Qaeda leaders remained at large. More than a year after the American offensive in Afghanistan was launched, Franks told Mike Eckel of the Associated Press, "While an awful lot has been done in Afghanistan, this is Afghanistan. We're just going to have to stay with it for as long as it takes ... to be sure that we don't permit terrorism to retake Afghanistan." As of mid–2003 American military operations in Afghanistan were continuing.

Even as American military operations continued in Afghanistan, the Bush administration began expressing growing concern about the threat posed by the regime of President Saddam Hussein in Iraq. American concerns focused on widespread reports that the Iraqi regime possessed weapons of mass destruction (WMD) and was continuing to develop still other such weapons. Although teams of United Nations weapons inspectors failed to uncover definitive evidence of Iraqi WMD, the United States, along with the United Kingdom and a handful of other allies, decided to invade Iraq with the twin goals of finding and destroying WMD and ending Hussein's repressive regime. Once again, as commander–in–chief of CENTCOM, Franks was assigned to direct the American offensive in Iraq.

Perhaps because of the speed and low casualties with which the goals of Operations Desert Shield and Desert Storm were accomplished in 1990–1991, many Americans seemed confident that Operation Iraqi Freedom similarly would go off with barely a hitch. When a couple of weeks had passed without coalition troops yet occupying Baghdad, the seat of government in Iraq, Franks and other American military strategists came under fire for their supposed failure to put together a viable plan for the invasion. However, the critics were soon quieted as American troops entered the Iraqi capital and effectively dismantled what remnants of the Hussein regime remained. The location of Hussein himself remained uncertain, but his oppressive regime was toppled once and for all.

In an interview with *Newsweek* after the end of the war, Franks reported that the United States war strategy had originally been expected to take up to four months to fully implement. As it happened, however, Hussein was toppled in less than three weeks. Anxious to accomplish American goals in Iraq with a far leaner force than many thought would be needed, President Bush ordered Defense Secretary Donald Rumsfeld to come up with such a war plan. Rumsfeld turned to Franks for assistance, and together the two hammered out the plan that was eventually put into action. Their planning sessions, on which General Peter Pace, vice chairman of the Joint Chiefs of Staff, often sat in, were sometimes tension-filled, but Franks told *Newsweek* that he never found the defense secretary abrasive. "His style is direct. He doesn't waste a lot of time. But in-your-face, absolutely not." Together the two mapped out a war strategy that took full advantage of new technology to accomplish what previously might have taken far more American troops to do.

On May 22, 2003, Rumsfeld announced that Franks would retire from active duty the following summer. Rumsfeld had offered Franks the post of Army chief of staff—the highest job in the Army—but Franks turned it down. In October of 2003, it was announced that Franks had agreed to write his memoirs. The book will be published by ReganBooks, an imprint of HarperCollins; Franks had reportedly sought a seven-figure deal. Married since 1969 to the former Cathryn Carley, Franks lives with his wife in Tampa, home of MacDill Air Force Base and CENTCOM. Whether he will stay in the Tampa Bay area after stepping down from the military remains to be seen, but if he does he will join scores of other retired military leaders living in the area. So big a fan is Franks of the Super Bowl-winning Tampa Bay Buccaneers that he made special arrangements to watch 2003's big game from his hotel room in Pakistan. Fellow Tampa resident George Steinbrenner, owner of the New York Yankees, told the *Tampa Tribune*, "It means something great for our community that Gen. Franks and his wife are fans of Tampa Bay."

On May 25, 2004, Franks received the honorary Knight Commander of the Order of the British Empire for his "inspirational leadership." A defense ministry spokesman told CNN.com, "Gen. Tommy Franks has been a sterling friend of the United Kingdom during a period of turbulence in world affairs." The honor came with controversy, however, because the United States-led invasion of Iraq had become increasingly unpopular with the British public. Some felt that it was not the right time to be honoring an American military figure.

Sources

Books

Complete Marquis Who's Who, Marquis Who's Who, 2003.
Carroll's Federal Directory, Carroll Publishing, 2002.

Periodicals

AP Online, November 29, 2002.
Esquire, August 2002.
Newsweek, December 30, 2002; January 6, 2003, pp. 60–61; April 7, 2003, p. 24; May 19, 2003.
Seattle Post–Intelligencer, April 4, 2003.
Tampa Tribune, May 23, 2003.
Time, March 8, 2002.

Online

"Biography: General Tommy Franks," United States Central Command, http://www.usembassy.uz/centcom/frankbio.htm (June 22, 2003).
Biography Resource Center Online, Gale Group, 2002.
"Gen. Tommy Franks Signs Book Deal," CNN.com, http://www.cnn.com/2003/SHOWBIZ/books/10/07/franks.ap/index.html (October 7, 2003).
"Gen. Tommy Franks to Retire," CNN.com, http://edition.cnn.com/2003/US/05/22/franks.retires (June 22, 2003).
"Interview with Army General Tommy Franks," *Arizona Reporter*, http://www.azreporter.com/news/features/articles/tommyfranks.html (June 22, 2003).
"U.S. general knighthood sparks row," CNN.com, http://www.cnn.com/2004/WORLD/meast/05/25/iraq.franks.knighthood/index.html (July 9, 2004).

Transcripts

All Things Considered, National Public Radio, November 8, 2001.
Morning Edition, National Public Radio, November 21, 2001.

—*Don Amerman*

John Frieda

Hairstylist and entrepreneur

Born July 5, 1951, in England; married Lulu (a pop singer; born Marie McDonald McLaughlin Lawrie), 1976 (divorced, 1994); children: Jordan (son).

Addresses: *Home*—New York, NY, Connecticut, and London, England. *Office*—John Frieda Professional Hair Care Inc., 333 Ludlow St., Stamford, CT 06902–6987.

Career

Apprenticed in the London, England, salon of Leonard, late 1960s; opened first London salon with Nicky Clarke, 1976; opened namesake salon, London, 1979; began selling small hair–care product line in the British drugstore chain Boots, 1988; formed John Frieda Professional Hair Care Inc., 1989; opened first New York City salon, 1990; sold hair–care product company to Kao Corporation, 2002.

Sidelights

British hairdresser John Frieda leveraged his celebrity status to create a tremendously successful line of hair–care products bearing his name. The road from well–heeled salon owner to brand name was a short one for Frieda; he launched his first products in drug stores—an unusually daring start for a line with roots in the professional salon world—and quickly captured a mass–market share with products like Frizz–Ease Serum and the Sheer Blonde line. In 2002, Frieda and his longtime business partner sold the company to Japanese giant Kao Corporation, which also owns the Andrew Jergens brand. With this new marketing muscle, industry analysts predicted that the Frieda line would continue its unparalleled growth as the one of the most successful hair–care lines in history. The handsome, 50–ish mogul, with his close–cropped salt–and–pepper hair and understated dark suits, asserted that all the expertise in the world would not help a shampoo, gel, or hair spray if it did not do the job. "People will pay if they know a product will make a difference," he told *Sunday Times* writer Claire Oldfield, "and the reason why we are successful is because the products really do work."

Frieda is a third–generation coiffeur. His grandfather was a barber on Fleet Street, the epicenter of London's newspaper world. By the time Frieda was born in 1951, his father owned a hair salon in Ealing, a district in West London, and had a small real–estate business on the side. Frieda proved to be an academically gifted child, and his family hoped he might choose medicine as a profession and become the first doctor in the family. Sent to King's School in Harrow, England, Frieda found his interest in schoolwork abruptly waning as a teen. "Girls appeared on the horizon," he recalled in an interview with Rachelle Thackray of London's *Independent* newspaper. "I must have stopped working—I failed all my exams. My motivation was to get out of studying."

Frieda decided that he wanted to join his father's business. "Dad tried to talk me out of it, but I was quite determined," he told a *Financial Times* journalist. Realizing that his Ealing establishment would not launch a necessarily impressive career for his son, Frieda senior arranged an apprenticeship at the salon of Leonard, a famed London stylist of the late 1960s. Frieda rose quickly in the job and soon became Leonard's assistant, which placed him at editorial shoots for top British fashion magazines like *Harper's & Queen*. Frieda also styled his first celebrity clients during this era, including Jacqueline Kennedy Onassis and Diana Ross.

Frieda followed in his father's footsteps in investment habits as well, and owned three houses by the time he was 20 years old. In 1976, he used some of his accumulated capital to open his first salon on Marylebone Road in London with another defector from Leonard, future celebrity hairstylist Nicky Clarke. At the salon, Frieda created what is known in Britain as the Purdey cut, named after the character played by actress Joanna Lumley, later of *Absolutely Fabulous* fame. Frieda cropped Lumley's hair into a bowl–shaped bob for her 1976–78 run on a revival of the hit British television series *The Avengers* that was widely imitated. The brief fad of the Purdey cut helped make Frieda famous, and he even married a celebrity himself—1960s pop star Lulu, best known for her appearance in the 1967 Sidney Poitier film *To Sir With Love* and her hit single of the same name.

The first actual "John Frieda" salon opened in 1979 in London's New Cavendish Street, and there Frieda gained a devoted clientele in the 1980s that even included the late Diana, Princess of Wales, and former Beatle Paul McCartney. As always, though, the ambitious Frieda was looking for new opportunities. "I wanted to expand, but didn't want to open lots of salons," he told Thackray in the *Independent* article. "Products were the way to go. The only professional line was Vidal Sassoon's; I knew the products people needed, the ones I used on models, which weren't available to anybody else."

Frieda was a veteran of day–long fashion shoots in which the models' hairstyles needed to be changed and perfected quickly. Stylists used an array of tricks to achieve the effects needed, and Frieda joined with a chemist to come up with a viable product of a similar nature for the consumer market. His small line was at first only sold in his salon, but then "people who were not clients were coming to the salon just for bottles of the lotion," he recalled in the *Sunday Times* interview with Oldfield. In 1988 Boots, a ubiquitous British drugstore chain, invited him to do a line of products for its shelves. His first success came with a thickening lotion, and to promote it Frieda went on television and performed a "before" and "after" demonstration with a model;

the British station was immediately flooded with calls from viewers wanting to know where they could buy the product.

By this point Frieda had met Gail Federici at a trade show. Federici was a vice president at Zotos, a U.S.–based hair–care company. "I was running the company out of a basement in my salon; a logistical nightmare," Frieda remembered of this time in the interview with Thackray. "Then I got an order for 1.2 [million] bottles of thickening lotion—it was like having a hit record. And it was the one moment when Gail was available to join me." With each owning half of the new business, John Frieda Professional Hair Care Inc., they set out to conquer the American market with a miniscule marketing budget of just $30,000. Frieda spent these early years in shopping malls and elsewhere, demonstrating his products first–hand.

Frieda's first big seller was Frizz–Ease Serum, launched in Britain in 1989 and in the United States two years later. The struggling company received a lucky break when a buyer for Eckerd, a large drug store chain that dominated the southeastern United States, agreed to give the Frieda Frizz–Ease Serum some shelf space. In the face of tremendous—and well–funded—brand–name competition, Frieda was convinced that his products were superior. "We couldn't out–spend the opposition, so we had to out–think them," he told the *Financial Times*. "We had to target areas that nobody else had targeted, so when people used our products they thought, 'God, I can't live without this'. If we really worked, people would stick with us."

The success of Frizz–Ease Serum and its successors proved Frieda correct. When it was launched, it sold for a much higher retail price than its rivals—a strategy that Frieda was warned was a gamble. "No one was charging over $5 for a hairstyling product when we entered the market," Frieda told *Chain Drug Review* in 1994, "but we were confident that when women saw what Frizz–Ease could do for their hair they would be willing to pay what we were asking for it." His gamble worked. "What Frieda recognised," noted Tina Gaudoin in an *Independent* article, "that the rest of the American haircare market did not—was that American women probably spend half of their adult lives trying valiantly to calm their frizzy hair."

Throughout the 1990s, Frieda worked tirelessly to promote his products and even appeared in television commercials. He also worked on developing new formulas for different niches of the hair–care market. His second line, aimed at fine hair, was called Ready to Wear. It failed to catch on as quickly as the growing line of Frizz–Ease products, however, but Frieda's 1998 launch of the Sheer Blonde line made him a household name in North America and gave him an impressive amount of shelf space in drug stores and mass–market retailers across the continent. It also became a top–seller in Scandinavia. Relax, an ethnic hair–care line, came out in 2001 after Frieda learned that African–American women were using Frizz–Ease to tame their locks.

All of Frieda hair–care lines have products ranging from shampoo and conditioner to texturing sprays and glossers. His company has posted steady growth, and Frieda attributes the success to a maxim he once learned from his father: "[O]nly two businesses are recession and war proof. Groceries and hair," he told the *Financial Times*. "When people are a bit down, they still get their hair cut." By 2002, Frieda's company enjoyed worldwide sales of $160 million. In August of that year, Frieda and Federici sold it to the Kao Corporation, a Japanese company whose American consumer–products unit is the Cincinnati–based Andrew Jergens Company. The infusion of capital meant that Frieda's products could now be promoted in stylish television commercials that resembled music videos—some of them starring Federici's twin teenaged daughters, the signature faces of the Sheer Blonde line. The company also planned to gain a better foothold in the continental European market. Frieda still remained heavily involved. "In many respects, my job is very much the same as it was before we sold John Frieda, except without the responsibility—it's quite nice," he told *WWD*'s Andrea M.G. Nagel and Jennifer Weil. "I don't own the company anymore, but I still feel the same. I am just as passionate about the products."

Frieda rarely cuts hair any more, but still owns a handful of salons, including his New Cavendish Street space. Other addresses included one at 797 Madison Avenue, and a lavish Los Angeles one called Sally Hershberger @ John Frieda. Hershberger, best known for shaping Meg Ryan's sought–after late 1990s coif, worked with Frieda on developing the Sheer Blonde line and holds the title of style director at the Frieda company. The posh L.A. salon includes a courtyard pool and in–house video–monitor system that lets clients accurately assess their $400 haircuts from television screens situated at the stylists' stations. Frizz–Ease, meanwhile, continues to be the biggest seller in the Frieda line, with some $60 million in sales annually and a bottle sold every 30 seconds.

Frieda and Lulu divorced in the early 1990s, and their son Jordan, a Cambridge University graduate, is an actor and lives in New York City. Frieda spends much of his time in his Manhattan penthouse and at a Connecticut home near to his company headquarters in Stamford. He also keeps homes in London and the Spanish hot–spot of Ibiza. Famously unflashy, the hairdresser favors sober suits and is known for generously supporting Conservative Party politicians in Britain like Iain Duncan Smith. He likes to ski in Austria and is a devoted cricket player who plays on a team with Broadway lyricist Sir Tim Rice. For a famously successful beauty mogul, he is surprisingly low–key, assessed journalist Shane Watson of London's *Evening Standard*. "The fabulous life of Frieda is unusual—as superrich businessmen's go—in that it combines the fastidiousness peculiar to the world of fashion, the obsession with control typical of the successful entrepreneur, and a robust sporty outlook and abhorrence of all things flash that's more English public schoolboy," Watson wrote.

While Frieda admits that the beauty business has brought him great success, he maintains that looks are indeed a superficial attribute. "People are so impressed by impressions, but your happiness should not depend on how you look," he told the *Financial Times*. "I've known many people who were beautiful but once you got to know them they were horrible—and the other way 'round."

Sources

Advertising Age, May 12, 2003, p. 18.
Chain Drug Review, December 5, 1994, p. 58.
Evening Standard (London, England), November 8, 2002, p. 29.
Fairfield County Business Journal (Fairfield County, CT), April 7, 2003.
Financial Times, January 26, 2002, p. 3.
Independent (London, England), November 24, 1999, p. 8; June 18, 2002, p. 8.
New York Times, September 29, 2002, p. 14.
SalonNews, May 2000, p. 52.
Sunday Times (London, England), June 27, 1999, p. 15.
WWD, March 17, 1995, p. 8; November 5, 1999, p. 14; November 10, 2000, p. 10; September 28, 2001, p. 10; August 2, 2002, p. 1; December 10, 2002, p. 16; April 25, 2003, p. 14.

—Carol Brennan

Jim Furyk

Professional golfer

Born May 12, 1970, in West Chester, PA; son of Michael and Linda Furyk; married Tabitha Skartved, 2000; children: Caleigh Lynn. *Education:* Graduated from University of Arizona, 1992.

Addresses: *Agent*—c/o Goal Marketing, 230 Park Ave., Ste. 840, New York, NY 10169.

Career

Professional golfer, 1992—. PGA Tour victories: Las Vegas Invitational, 1995, 1998, 1999; United Airlines Hawaiian Open, 1996; Doral–Ryder Open, 2000; Mercedes Championships, 2001; Memorial Tournament, 2002; U.S. Open Championship, 2003; Buick Open, 2003. Nationwide Tour victories: Nike Mississippi Gulf Coast Classic, 1993. International victories: Argentine Open, 1997.

Sidelights

Known for his idiosyncratic swing, golfer Jim Furyk turned professional in 1992. Over the years, he has become noted for his methodical approach to golf, which emphasizes straight driving and conservative shots. He worked his way up the ranks of golf quietly, but took the golf world by storm in 2003, when he beat the world's best golfers with ease at the U.S. Open and the Buick Open.

As a high school student, Furyk was a standout on the football, basketball, and baseball teams at Manheim Township High School in Lancaster, Pennsylvania. Although he was well regarded for his all–around talent in these sports, he secretly yearned to play golf, but felt embarrassed about his love for the game. On days when he had a golf match, he asked his mother to drive him to school early so he could hide his clubs in his locker before his friends arrived at school and saw him carrying them.

Furyk learned to play golf from his father, who encouraged him to stick with his quirky swing, which defied all conventional wisdom about body form in golf, but which worked for him. Furyk is also noted for his pre–swing ritual, which was described by Michael Silver in *Sports Illustrated*: "The 33–year–old grinder's grinder prepares for each herky–jerky swing like a geologist conducting a seismic survey." Before each swing, Furyk hitches up his pants with his right hand. Before every putt, Furyk reads the line, addresses the ball, steps away, and then repeats the routine. Furyk told Silver, "I got a lot of recognition early in my career because of my goofy swing, and it was a positive for me. I'm a guy who finds a comfort zone and sticks to his guns." Furyk's father added, "If you have a manufactured golf swing, I'm a firm believer that you won't hold up under pressure. If you've got a swing that's natural, whatever it looks like, you've got a chance." In addition to his father's emphasis on what came naturally, Furyk also inherited his focus on hard work and his perfectionism. In *Golf World,* John Hawkins commented on their relationship, "The two have formed an effective, low–key team since Furyk began winning on the PGA Tour ..., not so much in terms of mechanical alterations, but in strengthening the kid's two biggest assets: his head and heart."

Furyk turned professional in 1992, and in 1993, won the Nike Mississippi Gulf Coast Classic. He followed this with a series of PGA victories: the Las Vegas Invitational in 1995, 1998, and 1999, the United Airlines Hawaiian Open in 1996, and the Doral–Ryder Open in 2000. In late 2000, Furyk was sidelined by a wrist injury, which happened while he was attending a Baltimore Ravens football game. Furyk was crossing the parking lot at the Ravens game when he saw some people playing catch. When a pass came toward him, he tried to catch it but slipped, falling on his left wrist and tearing the cartilage. As a result, he was knocked out of contention for the Tour Championship, the Sun City Million Dollar Challenge, and the World Match Play in Australia.

In that same year, Furyk married his long–time girlfriend, Tabitha Skartved, and the two began building a home in Maui, Hawaii, which Furyk told *Sports Illustrated*'s Alan Shipnuck was "my favorite spot in the entire world." By the end of 2000, Furyk healed from his injury and made a dramatic comeback at the Mercedes Championship in January of 2001. Although Furyk seemed destined to lose the championship as South African Rory Sabbatini took the lead, on the final day Sabbatini missed a three–footer on the 72nd hole. Furyk took the victory, and told *Sports Illustrated*'s Shipnuck, "There was one key: attitude. Whenever I started to get mad at myself, I would remember that my goal was to be able to complete all 72 holes [of the tournament]."

Furyk's wife, Tabitha, told *Sports Illustrated*'s Silver that Furyk often got ready for tournaments in a highly organized manner, but that "sometimes it gets away from him. Before we left home, he made a big point of having all of his pants for the [103rd U.S. Open in 2003] dry–cleaned and hanging them neatly in the closet. Then we got on the plane, and, of course, he realized he had forgotten to pack them." The two headed out to shop in Chicago three days before the Open, and despite the mix–up, Furyk performed, Silver noted, "almost flawlessly, dominating the planet's best golfers and winning his first major with an ease that suggested this won't be his last."

In 2002, Furyk won the Memorial Tournament and ended the year with nine Top Ten finishes. In August of 2003, Furyk had another decisive victory at the Buick Open, where he outplayed famed golfer Tiger Woods, remaining calm and collected throughout the tournament. Later, he told *Sports Illustrated*'s Shipnuck, "I wanted to go out and get a low number, and whether I'm playing with Tiger Woods or someone else, it doesn't make that much of a difference." The win put him second on the earnings list for 2003, just $400,000 behind Woods.

In an interview with Joan Alexander of *ASAP Sports,* Furyk said that after he won the U.S. Open, many people told him his life would undergo a drastic change. He admitted that he had gotten more demands on his time and energy, as well as more demands for autographs and more questions from the press: "For some reason, my opinion matters more now," he observed. He also noted, "It's a good problem to have and it goes with the territory. You realize that we all want to win major championships and win golf tournaments, and the more you do that, the more your time becomes in demand. That's part of it.... It's really not a bad problem to have."

Sources

Periodicals

Golf World, November 17, 2000, p. 36; January 19, 2001, p. 29; June 20, 2003, p. 22.
Sports Illustrated, January 22, 2001, p. 33; June 23, 2003, p. 34; August 11, 2003, p. G25.

Online

"Jim Furyk," PGATour.com, http://www.golfweb.com/players/01/08/09/bio.html (November 17, 2003).
"Jim Furyk: Ready to finish the year strong," ASAP Sports, http://www.golfserv.com/gdc/news/article.asp?id=16126 (December 1, 2003).

—Kelly Winters

Peter Gallagher

Actor

Born August 19, 1955, in New York, NY; son of Tom (an advertising executive) and Mary (a bacteriologist) Gallagher; married Paula Harwood (a music video producer), 1983; children: James, Kathryn. *Education:* Earned degree in economics from Tufts University, mid–1970s; attended the New England Conservatory of Music and the University of California—Berkeley.

Addresses: *Agent*—Steve Alexander, Creative Artists Agency, 9830 Wilshire Blvd., Beverly Hills, CA 90212. *Website*—http://www.petergallagher.com.

Career

Actor in television, including: *Skag*, 1980; *Private Contentment* (movie), 1982; *Terrible Joe Moran* (movie), 1984; *A Different Twist* (movie), 1984; *Long Day's Journey Into Night* (movie), 1987; *Private Eye*, 1987; *The Murder of Mary Phagan* (miniseries), 1988; *The Caine Mutiny Court Martial* (movie), 1988; *The Big Knife* (movie), 1988; *I'll Be Home for Christmas* (movie), 1988; *Love and Lies* (movie), 1990; *An Inconvenient Woman* (miniseries), 1991; *Fallen Angels*, 1993; *White Mile* (movie), 1994; *Titanic* (movie), 1996; *Path to Paradise: The Untold Story of the World Trade Center Bombing* (movie), 1997; *Homicide: Life on the Street*, 1998; *Superman* (voice), 1998; *Host* (movie), 1998; *Brave New World* (movie), 1998; *The Secret Lives of Men*, 1998–99; *Brotherhood of Murder* (movie), 1999; *Cupid & Cate* (movie), 2000; *The Last Debate* (movie), 2000; *Anne Rice's The Feast of All Saints* (miniseries), 2001; *Family Guy* (voice), 2001; *Double Bill* (movie), 2003; *The O.C.*, 2003—. Film appearances include: *The Idolmaker*, 1980; *Summer Lovers*, 1982; *Dreamchild*,

1985; *My Little Girl*, 1986; *High Spirits*, 1988; *sex, lies, and videotape*, 1989; *Tune in Tomorrow*, 1990; *The Cabinet of Dr. Ramirez*, 1991; *Late for Dinner*, 1991; *Milena* (also known as *The Lover*), 1991; *Bob Roberts*, 1992; *The Player*, 1992; *Malice*, 1993; *Short Cuts*, 1993; *Watch It*, 1993; *The Hudsucker Proxy*, 1994; *Mother's Boys*, 1994; *Mrs. Parker and the Vicious Circle*, 1994; *While You Were Sleeping*, 1995; *The Underneath*, 1995; *Cafe Society*, 1995; *To Gillian on Her 37th Birthday*, 1996; *Last Dance*, 1996; *The Man Who Knew Too Little*, 1997; *Johnny Skidmarks*, 1998; *American Beauty*, 1999; *The House on Haunted Hill*, 1999; *Other Voices*, 2000; *Center Stage*, 2000; *Perfume*, 2001; *Lunar Girl*, 2001; *Protection*, 2001; *Mr. Deeds*, 2002; *How to Deal*, 2003. Writer of screenplays, including: *The Cabinet of Dr. Ramirez*, 1991. Stage appearances include: *Grease*, 1977; *A Doll's Life*, 1982; *The Corn Is Green*, 1983; *The Real Thing*, 1984; *Long Day's Journey into Night*, 1986; *Guys and Dolls*, 1992; *Noises Off*, 2001. Also performed with the Boston Shakespere Company, and at the Priscilla Beach Theatre, Whitehorse Beach, MA, and Long Wharf Theatre, Connecticut.

Awards: Theatre World Award, for *A Doll's Life*, 1982; Clarence Derwent Award, for *The Real Thing*, 1985.

Sidelights

Peter Gallagher became a familiar presence to an entirely new generation of viewers as beleaguered dad Sandy Cohen on the hit Fox Television series that debuted in 2003, *The O.C.* A veteran actor who started out as Danny Zuko in the Broadway musical *Grease*, Gallagher had endured sporadic career highs, and a few lows, in the 25 years since. Handsome to the point of distraction, he seemed the victim of his own looks, with Hollywood usually typecasting him in the role of cad or shark. In *The O.C.*, Gallagher took the role of a do–gooder for a change. "I generally play really ambitious people, cutthroat and conniving and all that stuff," he told *Daily News* writer Bob Strauss. "But I'm completely inept. I've scratched my way to the middle after all these years."

Like Cohen, his *O.C.* character, Gallagher's roots are in the New York City borough of the Bronx. He was born during a storm at Lenox Hill Hospital in Manhattan, and it was a difficult delivery. As he wrote in a biography that appeared on his official website, the doctor came in to see his mother during it, "offered her a drink and a cigarette, informed her that the umbilical cord was wrapped around my neck, and that they had done all they could. Things looked bad. The doctor suggested that my mother have a drink and a smoke and pray. She managed all three and I arrived intact." Gallagher was the last of three born to Mary, a bacteriologist, and Tom Gallagher, an outdoor–advertising executive. The family lived in Yonkers, just outside of New York City, before relocating to suburban Armonk.

Gallagher appeared in high school plays in Armonk, but claimed that he was anything but a heartthrob during his teens. "I had fat lips, glasses and big eyebrows," he told *InStyle* writer Mark Morrison. "If I'd had a designer bag I would've put it over my head." Both parents tried to instill middle–class values in their children, Gallagher recalled in an interview with the *New York Times*'s Patrick Pacheco. "My mother had always told us that her father had been a kindly grocer during the Depression," he said. "But I later found out that he'd run a speakeasy and was a bartender in the Bronx. There was a great desire to measure up and not bring your backward ways with you." Thus the performing arts were not on his career agenda, Gallagher noted, when he entered Tufts University in Boston as an economics major. "My father was paying for my education, so I wanted him to get his money's worth," he explained in an interview with *People* writer Michael A. Lipton, adding, "I was scared to study acting because I was afraid I'd lose my passion for it."

For three years, Gallagher performed with the Boston Shakespeare Company, and spent summers working at the Priscilla Beach Theatre in Whitehorse Beach, Massachusetts. Before starting his senior year, he took some courses in non–Western economic thought at the University of California's Berkeley campus, and returned to Boston dismayed. He realized he had little interest in business or economics as a career path. "I resolved to finish school and give myself six or seven years to make a living onstage," he recalled on his Web site.

Moving to New York, Gallagher began attending open–call auditions for Broadway musicals. "You get there around dawn, sign up and then stand in line for about eight hours before you go in and sing a few bars of a song," he explained in the web biography. "In both cases, there were well over a thousand people ahead of me." But success came almost immediately: he was offered a plum role in a 1977 Broadway revival of *Hair*, the hit hippie musical, but before it opened a casting director offered him a part in the touring version of another top Broadway show, *Grease*, as the lead, Danny Zuko. Leaving *Hair* before it opened, Gallagher made his Broadway debut in *Grease* in 1978.

Within a year he was signed to appear in an NBC television series and as the lead in a movie. The series was *Skag*, and Gallagher was cast as one of the sons of a Pittsburgh steelworker played by Karl Malden. The series debuted in early 1980, but was not renewed for a new season. By then, however, Gallagher was already pegged as a big–screen up–and–comer for his part in *The Idolmaker*. The movie musical was loosely based on the life of Bob Marucci, who helped make Frankie Avalon and Fabian stars in the 1950s. Gallagher played a Bronx busboy discovered by Vinnie Vacarri (Ray Sharkey), who christens him Caesare and grooms him for stardom. *The Idolmaker* tanked at the box office. Years later, the *New York Times*'s Pacheco noted that the massive hype surrounding Gallagher's film debut "seemingly came out of an old M–G–M publicity manual," he wrote, "replete with chest–hair waxings and posters of his smoldering features plastered across buses. 'Caesare is coming,' they announced."

Gallagher's famously bushy eyebrows earned their first press mention in Janet Maslin's *New York Times* review of *The Idolmaker*, and he admitted years later that he was indeed sent for a body wax. He recalled in the *InStyle* interview with Morrison that the aesthetician "ripped the strip off, and I almost went into cardiac arrest. Afterward, I sat in my car and wept." He was subject to the same treatment for his many shirtless scenes in *Summer Lovers,* his next film, which co–starred him opposite a pre–*Splash* Daryl Hannah. The two played young Americans vacationing on a freewheeling Greek island for the summer, but their romance is threatened by his affair with a French woman. Soon, all three are caught up in the island's intoxicating atmosphere. Again, it earned dismal reviews.

Gallagher returned to the New York stage for the next few years, taking only the occasional film role that came his way. On Broadway, he appeared in *A Doll's Life,* the 1982 season's ill–conceived musical sequel to the Henrik Ibsen classic, *A Doll's House.* Two years later he originated a lead in *The Real Thing,* a new Tom Stoppard play, but considered quitting acting altogether for a time. In 1985 he was seen in *Dreamchild,* a forgotten film about the life of *Alice in Wonderland* author Lewis Carroll that was the work of the legendary British television writer Dennis Potter. The film later became a cult classic, a term that would generally not be applied to most of the films Gallagher made during the rest of the decade. He did earn a Tony nomination and outstanding reviews—including one from the *New York Times'* notoriously candid theater critic at the time, Frank Rich—for his part in the Eugene O'Neill revival, *Long Day's Journey into Night,* at the Broadhurst Theatre in 1986.

Gallagher seemingly reappeared out of nowhere in 1989 in the surprise indie film hit, *sex, lies, and videotape.* The work of an unknown 26–year–old filmmaker named Steven Soderbergh, it won the prestigious Palme d'Or at the Cannes Film Festival, and went on to become one of the first independent films to make a killing at the box office. Gallagher played an odious Louisiana lawyer named John, married to Andie MacDowell's repressed Southern belle, Anne. John's friend from college, Graham (James Spader) comes to visit, and Graham's odd hobby of interviewing women on camera about their private lives serves to unleash a series of events that exposes John's affair with Anne's reckless sister Cynthia, played by Laura San Giacomo. The ensemble cast won rave reviews for their performances, which were culled out of them by Soderbergh's insistence on run–through rehearsals more commonly used in the theater world. Unfortunately, when the film was released nationwide in the United States, Gallagher's role as the slick, vacuous John went unmentioned in the publicity blurbs. Irate, the actor called those responsible, he told Pacheco in the *New York Times* interview, "and said, 'What are you guys trying to do to me?' And they said, 'We couldn't find anything nice.' And I screamed, 'That's because I was playing the jerk. If I hadn't played this guy so well, this picture wouldn't have been so successful!'"

Gallagher's career seemed to falter again during the 1990s, save for two well–reviewed appearances in films by Robert Altman, *The Player* in 1992 and *Short Cuts* a year later. He had small parts in *The Hudsucker Proxy, Mrs. Parker and the Vicious Circle,* and the 1995 Sandra Bullock comedy *While You Were Sleeping.* He was cast somewhat against type as a grieving widower in *To Gillian on Her 37th Birthday,* and played Bill Murray's brother in *The Man Who Knew Too Little* in 1997. After another short–lived television series, *The Secret Lives of Men* on ABC, Gallagher returned to the big screen once again and stunned audiences in another role as a loathsome cad: Buddy Kane, the real–estate king in the Academy–Award–winning *American Beauty.*

Not surprisingly, Gallagher was again cast in such a part by a director with far more experience in theater than Hollywood. *American Beauty* was the work of British stage director Sam Mendes, and the 1999 film, with its bleak yet funny portrayal of placid suburban life gone awry, swept the Academy Awards the following year, including taking the best–picture statuette. Kevin Spacey played Lester Burnham, a mid–career schlump whose wife and teenage daughter openly disdain him. Rose– and status–obsessed spouse Carolyn (Annette Bening) judges him against her local house–selling rival, Gallagher's Kane, and is swept into a torrid extramarital affair.

Gallagher returned to Broadway in a revival of the farce *Noises Off* in 2001, and played the man out to steal *Mr. Deeds's* fortune in the 2002 Adam Sandler film. His role as Mandy Moore's disc–jockey father in the 2003 teen romance, *How to Deal,* was a foreshadowing of his next part: that of Sandy Cohen, the ultra–liberal public–defender dad in the television program, *The O.C.* Set in Orange County, California, the large swath of suburban communities that stretch south of Los Angeles, down the Pacific coast, the series proved to be an immediate hit with viewers. Gallagher's intensely idealistic Cohen married into wealth, but chafes against the rules at times. His character is originally from the Bronx, and feels sympathy for some of the young troublemakers who wind up on his caseload. In the first season, he brings one of them home to live, installing him in the pool house of the lavish Newport Beach estate he shares with wife, Kirsten (Kelly Rowan), and son, Seth (Adam Brody). The series earned strong critical plaudits as well as high ratings during its first season. *Entertainment Weekly* critic Carina Chocano wrote, "Somewhere in all the high–stakes soapiness ... and often deft and subtle drama, there is a pretty wicked satire of baby–boomer values. Gallagher, in particular, is sublime as the Bronx–raised, [BMW]–driving fairy godfather whose moral compass is stuck on do–gooder even when he is headed in the opposite direction."

Unlike the caddish screen roles of his past, Gallagher asserts that the role of Sandy Cohen is far closer to his real persona. He married Paula Harwood, a classmate from Tufts, in 1983, and they have two children. Gallagher has resolutely resisted relocating to California for much of his career, and commutes to the set of *The O.C.* from New York and Connecticut, where he and his family have homes. His young son was wary when he heard about the new TV role, Gallagher confessed to Eric Messinger in *InStyle,* and asked if he would be playing "another bad guy." Gallagher was indifferent to the opinion of non–family members, however, when it came to his career. "Whatever the role, I've tried to be in films that I like and respect," he told Messinger. "This philosophy has served me well. I have a career I'm not only proud of but still excited about. In a way, I feel like I'm just coming into my prime."

Sources

Books

Contemporary Theatre, Film and Television, volume 28, Gale Group, 2000.

Periodicals

Daily News (Los Angeles, CA), October 27, 1996, p. L3.
Entertainment Weekly, October 1, 1993, p. 36; October 25, 1996, p. 94; September 17, 1999, p. 49; November 9, 2001, p. 101; August 15, 2003, p. 61.
InStyle, December 1997, p. 107; August 1, 2003, p. 252.
National Review, May 29, 1995, p. 64.
New Leader, October 2, 1989, p. 20.
New Republic, September 4, 1989, p. 26.
Newsweek, May 1, 1995, p. 70.
New York Times, November 14, 1980, p. C8; October 24, 1993, pp. H16–17; September 15, 1999; June 28, 2002; July 18, 2003.
People, August 18, 2003, p. 73.
Time, April 27, 1992, p. 65.

Online

"Background," Peter Gallagher Official Website, http://www.petergallagher.com/background.htm (March 3, 2004).

—Carol Brennan

Julie Gerberding

AP/Wide World Photos

Director of the Centers for Disease Control and Prevention

Born Julie Louise Gerberding, August 22, 1955, in Estelline, SD; married David Rose (a computer software engineer); children: Renada (stepdaughter). *Education:* Case Western Reserve University, Cleveland, OH, B.S. (chemistry/biology), 1977, M.D., 1981; University of California, Berkeley, M.S. (public health), 1990.

Addresses: *Office*—c/o Centers for Disease Control and Prevention, 1600 Clifton Rd., Atlanta, GA 30333.

Career

Director, University of California, San Francisco, Epidemiology Prevention and Interventions (EPI) Center, 1990–98; director of healthcare quality promotion, Centers for Disease Control and Prevention (CDC), 1998–2001; acting deputy director, National Center for Infectious Diseases, CDC, 2001–02; director, CDC, and administrator, Toxic Substances and Disease Registry, 2002—; associate clinical professor of medicine, Emory University, Atlanta, GA, and associate professor of medicine, University of California, San Francisco, CA.

Sidelights

Barely six months after she took over as the 13th director of the Centers for Disease Control and Prevention (CDC), Julie Gerberding found herself faced with an ominous threat to public health—a potentially fatal viral infection labeled severe acute respiratory syndrome, or SARS. No stranger to the

front lines of the war against emerging diseases, Gerberding is a specialist in infectious diseases who first earned her stripes two decades earlier in the battle against AIDS, a scourge she still considers the major worldwide public health issue for the next decade. Under Gerberding's direction, the CDC moved promptly to prevent the spread of the disease (which appeared to have originated in eastern Asia) within the United States. By mid–2003, the SARS epidemic appeared to have been largely contained—at least temporarily—but Gerberding and her colleagues at CDC were taking no chances. In the event that SARS may reappear on a seasonal basis—much like influenza—the CDC drafted a plan to cope with a possible return of SARS. Gerberding, quoted by the *International Herald Tribune,* said her agency would focus on "detecting cases, responding to WHO's [World Health Organization] call for technical assistance or field team assistance in various parts of the world, and having reliable diagnostic tests available where they are needed. It would be foolish to not have that kind of plan available for us."

Even before the frightening SARS headlines had disappeared completely from the front pages of United States newspapers, Gerberding was confronted by yet more frightening medical news, including an American outbreak of the rare monkeypox disease and the return of the seasonal threat from West Nile virus. Fortunately, the monkeypox scare, tentatively linked to the infection of pet prairie dogs exposed to infected giant rats from Africa, seemed to be quickly brought under control. In late June of 2003, Gerberding told the Center for Infectious Disease Research & Policy (CIDRAP), "I think we have optimism that this particular outbreak of monkeypox can be contained. We have so far been able to link human cases to affected animals, and they directly link back to the source that has been described already today," in a reference to the African rodents.

Potentially far more problematic for Gerberding and the CDC was the return of the summertime threat of the West Nile virus, which was first detected in New York in 1999. In mid–June of 2003, according to Agence France Presse, Gerberding told reporters, "We have documented West Nile virus activity in 24 states. We have not documented human cases yet. It is too soon to predict if it will be better or more severe than last summer." The disease, spread mostly by mosquitoes although it has also been transmitted through blood transfusion and organ transplants, in 2002 infected 4,156 Americans, 284 of whom died, for a mortality rate of nearly 7 percent. A number of health experts have predicted more cases in 2003, largely because of the heavy rains that hit much of the eastern United States in the spring. Most susceptible to the West Nile virus are people with weak immune systems, most notably the elderly. Ironically, one of the Americans infected with West Nile virus in 2002 was Gerberding's husband, computer software engineer David Rose. When the couple found a dead bird in the backyard of their Atlanta, Georgia–area home, Gerberding promptly reported the finding to local health authorities. She later told CWRU (Case Western Reserve University) magazine, "I have a fair amount of experience with a lot of different viral agents. I was not surprised with the test results and was very thankful that it was just a mild case."

A native of Estelline, South Dakota, where she was born on August 22, 1955, Gerberding is the daughter of the town's police chief and his schoolteacher wife. By the age of four, she had decided that more than anything she wanted to be a doctor when she grew up. In pursuit of that goal, Gerberding enrolled at Cleveland, Ohio's Case Western Reserve University, earning her bachelor's degree in chemistry and biology in 1977. Four years later she received her medical degree from Case Western. In an interview published in the Spring 2003 issue of CWRU, she discussed the selection of the school for her studies. "I did a lot of research about where I wanted to go to medical school. I was extremely

impressed with the concept at Case that you were there to learn and the emphasis on the organ system curriculum, the problem–oriented curriculum, and the early exposure to patients. I was interested in going to Case as an undergraduate, because I wanted to go to medical school there." She served her internship and residency in internal medicine at the University of California, San Francisco (UCSF) and in 1990 was named director of the school's Epidemiology Prevention and Interventions (EPI) Center. Her years in San Francisco coincided with the emergence of the AIDS epidemic, which struck particularly hard in that city. Against this backdrop, Gerberding developed a passionate interest in combating infectious disease.

Of her involvement in the battle against AIDS, Gerberding told CWRU, "I started my training at UCSF at the very beginning of the AIDS epidemic and took care of the earliest patients there, who, in retrospect, we recognize had AIDS. My clinical training really evolved with the AIDS epidemic, and it was natural to get started in the infectious disease area during that time." While at UCSF, Gerberding helped write guidelines to protect hospital workers from contracting the disease, winning recognition for her pioneering efforts in this area of the war against HIV infection.

Julius Krevans, chancellor emeritus of UCSF, told Anita Manning in USA Today that Gerberding was "considered one of the bright stars" almost from the outset of her years at the institution. The early emergence of the AIDS crisis coincided with research Gerberding was already conducting into the nature of hospital infections and how best to prevent their spread. Under the circumstances, it was logical that she would broaden her research to include this new mystery disease and how it might be communicated from patients to hospital personnel. According to Krevans, research conducted by Gerberding and her colleagues helped to establish ground rules for ways in which large institutions—including hospitals and large corporations—could deal with HIV–infected people in the workplace.

The guidelines developed by Gerberding and her colleagues were adopted by major Bay Area companies, including Levi Strauss, and eventually by the San Francisco Chamber of Commerce as well. Of Gerberding's contribution to the early battle against HIV/AIDS, Krevans told USA Today's Manning, "From the beginning of her career, she had thrust upon her a responsibility to think through something that affected not just an individual patient, but something that affects a community, the larger society." Dr. David Bangsberg, who succeeded Gerberding as director of UCSF's EPI Center, was interviewed by the *Atlanta Journal–Constitution* about his predecessor's research: "She quickly became a leading authority in establishing that the risk of HIV infection was low among health care workers and that the risk could be further reduced" through the use of post–exposure drugs.

In 1998 Gerberding joined the CDC as director of its healthcare quality promotion division. In that position, she continued to pursue her research into the area of hospital safety, focusing in particular on medical errors and drug–resistant infections. Three years later, Gerberding was named acting deputy director of the CDC's National Center for Infectious Diseases (NCID). Her new position put Gerberding at the center of the CDC's response to the anthrax terrorist incidents of late 2001. It was Gerberding who helped to quiet the widespread panic that gripped the United States in the wake of a handful of anthrax cases traced to disease spores sent through the mail. By mid–November of 2001, when a couple of weeks had passed with no further anthrax–tainted letters, Gerberding shifted the focus of the CDC's response to specific target groups. The CDC's recommended 60–day regimen of preventive antibiotics was aimed specifically at postal workers, media representatives, and congressional staff members, all of whom had been among the handful previously exposed. In explaining the agency's rationale, Gerberding told United Press International, "The circle of people who need to be treated has narrowed substantially," adding that the federal agency was cooperating with state and local health organizations "to do everything possible to promote adherence to the antimicrobial regimen."

When CDC Director Jeffrey Koplan stepped down in the spring of 2002, it soon became apparent that Gerberding was prominently featured on the short list of candidates to replace him. In late June of 2002, the race had been narrowed down to Gerberding and Dr. Robert Redfield, an AIDS vaccine researcher based at the University of Maryland, both of whose names were submitted to President George W. Bush. Speaking out in support of Gerberding's candidacy was Dr. James Curran, dean of the Rollins School of Public Health at Atlanta's Emory University and the former chief of HIV/AIDS programs at the CDC. Curran told the *Atlanta Journal–Constitution,* "She has been given increasing responsibility quickly, which is a sign of the confidence that people within the CDC have in her. She is a solid scientist, personable and reasonable, and she's knowledgeable about infectious disease at a time when that has the attention and concern of the American public and the administration."

In the end, Gerberding got Bush's nod, influenced in no small part by strong support from Secretary of Health and Human Services Tommy Thompson. In announcing that the Bush administration had decided to go with Gerberding, Thompson told reporters, as quoted by Mike Fleming in the *Washington Blade,* "I can think of no one better equipped to take the helm. Dr. Gerberding knows public health, she knows infectious diseases, and she knows bioterrorism preparedness." For her part, Gerberding pledged to do all that she could to see that CDC pursued the priorities of both Thompson and Bush. According to Fleming, she said, "Most importantly, I intend to listen to voices that may not have been heard, especially those from external constituencies in communities, academic environments, and the private sector, whose input—sometimes painful input—is absolutely essential to our success."

The first woman ever to serve as director of the CDC, Gerberding faced a number of daunting challenges in her first 18 months on the job. In addition to the emergence of SARS, an outbreak of monkeypox, and the continuing battle against HIV/AIDS, she also faced an internal CDC debate about the magnitude of the agency's vaccination campaign to protect key groups against a possible smallpox bioterror attack. Originally targeted at health care workers, the vaccination program was later expanded to cover other first responders, including police officers and firefighters. Citing the incidence of heart inflammation and heart attack among vaccine recipients, the CDC's Advisory Committee on Immunization Practices (ACIP) in June of 2003 recommended limiting vaccinations to health care workers. However, Gerberding came down in favor of the broadened approach to smallpox vaccination, telling the *Atlanta Journal–Constitution,* "We respect the ACIP perspective, but we also recognize that we still have work to do, including ongoing immunization."

As director of the CDC, Gerberding has been forced to follow a grueling schedule, flying frequently between the CDC's headquarters in Atlanta and the nation's capital to confer with Thompson and other federal health officials. The demands of her job have forced her to be creative in carving out time to spend with her husband, stepdaughter Renada, and the family's three cats. As she told *USA Today*'s Manning in June of 2003, "We've only been married less than three years. This is not exactly how I'd recommend spending your honeymoon."

Sources

Periodicals

Agence France Presse, June 19, 2003.

Atlanta Journal–Constitution, October 19, 2001, p. A1; June 29, 2002, p. A1; July 3, 2002, p. A1; June 20, 2003, p. A11; June 27, 2003, p. A5.

CWRU, Spring 2003, pp. 28–31.
International Herald Tribune, June 23, 2003.
National Journal, October 10, 2002.
United Press International, November 15, 2001.
USA Today, June 12, 2003, p. 4D.
Washington Post, July 3, 2002, p. A21.

Online

"AIDS Expert Named to Head Federal Health Agency," *Washington Blade,* http://www.aegis.com/news/wb/2002/WB020705.html (June 29, 2003).

Biography Resource Center Online, Gale Group, 2002.

"CDC Director Confident of Monkeypox Containment," CIDRAP, http://www.cidrap.umn.edu/cidrap/content/hot/monkeypox/news/june2003monkeypox.html (June 29, 2003).

"CDC 'Very Concerned' SARS Could Spread in Workplace," CNN.com http://www.cnn.com/2003/HEALTH/04/10/sars.virus.us.ap/index.html (April 11, 2003).

—*Don Amerman*

Jean-Sebastien Giguere

Professional hockey player

Born on May 16, 1977, in Montreal, Quebec, Canada; son of Claude (a bus driver) and Gisele Giguere; married Kristen Fawthrop, 2003.

Addresses: *Office*—Mighty Ducks of Anaheim, Attn: Jean–Sebastien Giguere, 2965 E. Katella Ave., Anaheim, CA 92806.

Career

Began playing hockey at the age of five, 1982; first–round draft pick in the National Hockey League by the Hartford Whalers, 1995; traded to Calgary Flames, 1998; traded to Anaheim Mighty Ducks, 2000; lead the Mighty Ducks to the Stanley Cup Finals, 2003.

Awards: Conn Smythe Trophy, National Hockey League, 2003.

Sidelights

Though he seemed to emerge out of nowhere, Jean–Sebastien Giguere dominated the Stanley Cup playoffs in 2003. The goalie for the Anaheim Mighty Ducks, he led his team to the finals, defeating some of the best teams in the National Hockey League (NHL), before losing in game seven to the New Jersey Devils. For his run, Giguere won the Conn Smythe Trophy as Most Valuable Player of the playoffs.

Born on May 16, 1977, in Montreal, Canada, Giguere is the son of Claude and Gisele Giguere. His father was a prison guard turned school bus driver, while his mother also used to drive a bus. The Gigueres encouraged their children to play hockey. Giguere is their youngest son; he has two brothers and two sisters, all of whom played hockey.

Giguere began playing hockey when he was five. He played goalie because his oldest brother, Stephane, did. Of all his siblings, however, Giguere made it the farthest as a player, though Stephane did play minor league hockey. Giguere's promise began to show when he played junior hockey in Canada; when he was 17 years old, he was considered a world–class goalie on the junior level.

In 1995, based on his potential, Giguere was drafted in the first round of the NHL draft by the Hartford Whalers. His National Hockey League career was relatively undistinguished. Giguere played for the Hartford Whalers in the 1996–97 season, then was traded to the Calgary Flames. From 1998 to 2000, he played for the Flames, but spent much of his time in the minors.

What had made Giguere great as a goalie was his simplicity and patience. By the time he landed in Calgary, he slumped more often and lost his technique. He became a more complicated player, one who reacted to the situations he faced instead of controlling them. Calgary gave up on Giguere and traded him to Anaheim in 2000 for a second–round draft pick.

Over several seasons with Anaheim, Giguere returned to his original form. One reason his career was revitalized was the Ducks' goaltending consultant, Francois Allaire. He helped Giguere make his game simple again. Allaire had taught Giguere when he was a 12–year–old boy living in Quebec; even at an early age, Giguere had had a strong work ethic, but lost his confidence as a professional by playing for bad teams and because he was often sent to the minors. Allaire re–taught Giguere how to be a goalie again, by becoming more conservative in play, not handling the puck much, and controlling rebounds.

Giguere's changes, however, did not click until the middle of the 2002–03 season. He ended that season strongly after playing well in the second half of the regular season. Until this time, the Mighty Ducks were not a great team, and had never made it past the second round of the playoffs. Seeded seventh in the Western Conference, Anaheim proceeded to destroy the West.

After sweeping the defending Stanley Cup champion Detroit Red Wings in the first round in four games, Anaheim eliminated the number–one seed in the West, the Dallas Stars, in six games. Anaheim then faced another upstart team, the Minnesota Wild, defeating them to win the Western Conference title. It was Giguere who often carried his team, playing many minutes of confident shut–out hockey. Of Giguere's zone in the playoffs, ESPN analyst Bill Clement told Eric Adelson of *ESPN the Magazine*, "He's found a way not to let his mind control him. It's just incredible. He never beats himself."

In the Stanley Cup Finals, Giguere and the Ducks faced the New Jersey Devils in the finals, a team with more experience winning (having won two Stanley Cups in the previous eight years). Anaheim and Giguere pushed the Devils to seven games, before finally losing, and for his outstanding play, Giguere was named the Most Valuable Player of the playoffs. He finished the playoffs with an astounding 1.62 goals–against average, as well as the longest playoff scoreless streak (168 minutes and 27 seconds).

Despite this defeat, Giguere re–signed with the Ducks for a contract worth $20 million over five years. The lineup of the Ducks changed between the 2002–03 and 2003–04 seasons, with popular left wing Paul Kariya leaving for the Colorado Avalanche and superstar center Sergei Fedorov joining the team. Speaking of the changes, Giguere remarked to Knight Ridder/Tribune News Service reporter Steve Bisheff, "It was huge. It just shows you that the team and the organization, they're in this to win. It's great to see that. It shows other players around the league that you have to respect the Ducks."

Sources

Associated Press, June 11, 2003.
ESPN the Magazine, June 11, 2003.
Knight Ridder/Tribune News Service, May 30, 2003; June 3, 2003; June 9, 2003; September 10, 2003.
Sports Illustrated, May 12, 2003.
Time International, June 2, 2003, p. 42.

—*A. Petruso*

Brian Graden

President of Entertainment for MTV and VH1

Born March 23, 1963, in Hillsboro, IL. *Education:* Oral Roberts University, Tulsa, OK, B.A, 1985; Harvard Business School, Boston, MA, M.B.A., 1989.

Addresses: *Office*—2600 Colorado Ave., Santa Monica, CA 90404–3556; 1515 Broadway, New York, NY 10036–8901.

Career

Executive for Fox Television Stations Productions, 1989–95; named vice president of program development, 1993; head of Foxlab, 1995–96; executive vice president of *South Park*, 1996–97; principal, Brian Graden Productions; executive vice president of programming for MTV, 1997–2000; president of programming for MTV and MTV2, 2000–02; named president of entertainment for MTV and VH1, 2002.

Awards: CableAce Award for animated programming special or series, National Academy of Cable Programming, for *South Park,* 1997; Tom Stoddard National Role Model Award, PrideFest America, for distinguished contribution to social change for the gay, lesbian, bisexual and transgender community, 2002.

Sidelights

Brian Graden serves as president of entertainment for the cable–music channels MTV and VH1, two properties in the immense Viacom multi-media empire. Both are tremendous advertising–revenue generators for Viacom, but it is Graden's task to ensure that they remain fresh and up–to–date with viewers across a difficult–to–nail demographic. In that he has succeeded: Graden is the executive who greenlighted the shows *Jackass* and *The Osbournes,* among several other ratings–winners. "Graden's touch in the late 1990s brought new hits to basic cable that broke the old rules with raw, anything–goes humor," noted *New York Times* writer Jim Rutenberg, "and ultimately pushed the barriers of taste for all television."

Born in 1963, Graden is a native of Hillsboro, Illinois, a small, semi–rural community outside of St. Louis, Missouri. He played the piano as a youngster, and became an ardent rock–music fan as a teenager. He recalled his first experience with the music–video medium that revolutionized the entertainment industry in an *Advocate* interview with Jeffrey Epstein. "I was 16 or 17 when MTV first came on the scene," he said. "Nobody had cable, but there was one person in the whole city who had satellite. So we would go over to his basement and just watch for hours and hours."

Graden was elected president of his senior class, and played in a rock band called Ace Oxygen and the Ozones. When one bandmate's father, a conservative preacher, ordered his son to attend Oral Roberts University in Oklahoma, the rest of the band followed. The Ozones broke up midway through their college years, but Graden stayed on at the Tulsa school and earned his degree in 1985. He entered Harvard Business School, and in the summer of 1988 took an unpaid internship at the fledgling Fox Television network. "I worked on a show called *King of the Mountain* in the middle of the desert in 100–degree heat and loved it," he recalled in an interview with *Mediaweek* writer Sue Karlin.

Graden's career direction did not crystallize for him, however, until his final year at Harvard, when he made the rounds of Wall Street firms on the job–prospecting interviews that are standard for soon–to–be–minted business–school graduates. He decided that high finance was not for him after one meeting with a leading investment bank in which the executive across from him asked him why he wanted to be in the interviewer's chair someday. "I had a rare moment of clarity," Graden recalled to *Broadcasting & Cable*'s Allison Romano, "and thought, 'I can't imagine anything more horrifying than being you.'"

Deciding that the entertainment industry was a better fit, Graden went back to Fox. He won a slot on the network's production staff, working on the creative team that brought such shows as *Studs* and *Cops* to the air, and by 1993 had become a vice president for program development. For a year in the mid–1990s, he headed Foxlab, its alternative programming division. After meeting two renegade animators, Trey Parker and Matt Stone, Graden thought it wise to sign them to some sort of contract before a rival company poached them from Fox. So, he commissioned them to make a Christmas video card for $2,000. The cartoon—a crudely animated debate over the merits of Santa Claus versus Jesus Christ—generated a buzz when it arrived on the desks of executives across town, and convinced Graden that he indeed had a potential hit with Parker and Stone. From that video came the *South Park* cartoon series.

Fox, however, was uninterested in *South Park,* and so Graden decided that his time there was up. He spent 18 months as executive vice president for *South Park,* and helped make the series, which debuted on the cable network Comedy Central in 1997, a huge hit. *Entertainment Weekly* critic Ken Tucker described the series as "the ongoing chronicle of four genially vile, mitten–wearing eight–year–olds," and asserted that it "has replaced Beavis and Butt–head as America's premiere gross national product." Despite the success, Graden left to form his own production company.

Brian Graden Productions was a short–lived venture, however: in 1997 its principal was contacted by a head–hunting firm putting out feelers on behalf of a major cable enterprise. The channel was MTV, and Graden was hired in August of 1997; four months later he was named executive vice president in charge of programming. At the time, MTV was flagging in the ratings, and relying on a raucous dating game show called *Singled Out,* hosted by actor Chris Hardwick and former *Playboy* centerfold Jenny McCarthy, to lure viewers nightly. Graden went to work, easing *Singled Out* to the door and bringing in Canadian prankster Tom Green and his on–camera stunts that usually involved an innocent bystander or animal body parts. Graden also greenlighted *Total Request Live,* a type of live on–air jukebox that became a top ratings grabber with the after–school pre–teen and tween crowd, and *Jackass,* a stunt show that incited controversy even in the halls of Congress when younger viewers began imitating its sometimes–dangerous pranks.

In 2000, Graden was promoted to president of programming for MTV and MTV2, its video–only sister channel, and ratings for MTV continued to improve considerably under his watch. Nearly all of the shows lured new viewers, and kept previous ones tuned in as well. For 19 quarters straight, the station was No. 1 in cable ratings with 12– to 24–year–old viewers. His biggest success during this two–year executive slot was landing *The Osbournes,* a reality–TV show centered around the Beverly Hills household of rock star Ozzy Osbourne and his family. Graden came up with the idea for the show after Osbourne and his wife, Sharon, appeared in a segment of *Cribs,* the MTV show that gave viewers a look inside the homes—down to the refrigerators and closets—of their favorite performers.

The Osbournes became a huge hit for MTV after its debut in the spring of 2002, with ratings spiking 57 percent for the nights it aired; some of the weekly episodes lured an audience of five million—phenomenal numbers in the cable industry. Even President George W. Bush admitted to being a fan of the show. Cultural pundits from across the spectrum weighed in on why the show was so entrancing. "What MTV has done right," remarked *Time* writer James Poniewozik, "is a case study in what TV often does wrong. The Osbournes is the oldest thing on TV since the test pattern: a nuclear family that eats meals together, shares its problems (even if every third word is bleeped) and survives wacky scenarios."

In early 2002, Graden was named president of entertainment for both MTV and its spin–off, VH1, which essentially gave him double duties at both.

VH1 was originally launched as a less–boisterous alternative to MTV's youth–oriented fare, aimed at the baby–boomer generation, and had come into its own in the 1990s with interesting original programming, such as *Behind the Music* and *Pop–Up Video*. When Graden took over, however, *Behind the Music* was daily fare for the channel, and it had lost record numbers of viewers. In one year, ratings plummeted 20 percent alone. That sent advertising revenues into a tailspin, and Graden was brought in to do for VH1 what he had at MTV.

Taking over at VH1, Graden reshuffled the creative management and okayed a raft of new shows and specials. One reality–show concept, based on the life of newlyweds Liza Minnelli and David Gest, was slated to premiere in October of 2002, but fell quietly by the wayside; the couple separated months later amidst allegations of spousal abuse and financial misdeeds. Graden had better luck, however, with specials like *25 Greatest Fads* and an ongoing series, *I Love the '80s,* each episode of which singled out the music, movie, and sartorial trends for a specific year in that decade. "VH1 should act like a pop–culture magazine, like *US Weekly* or *People,*" he told Romano in a *Broadcasting & Cable* interview. "Whenever we put on quasi–current specials, they do disproportionately well."

Graden is regularly hailed in entertainment–industry sources as a genius for reviving MTV. *Daily Variety* journalist Melissa Grego once termed him the "MTV content king," while *Broadcasting & Cable's* Romano called him "a development machine, willing to take ideas from almost anyone at MTV and relentless on keeping up with pop culture." Even his boss, MTV president Van Toffler, claimed that "Brian's got the best creative instincts in TV today," Toffler told *Mediaweek* writer Becky Ebenkamp. "His other head is like that of a 20–year–old boy or girl. He pushes his people to be open to ideas from the creative community or anywhere it bubbles up. He's not that arrogant executive who feels his ideas are better than everyone else's." Graden claimed it was a simple formula that made his career thrive via groundbreaking new television fare. "I believe in constantly being open and never thinking you know too much," he told Rutenberg in the *New York Times* not long after taking over at VH1. "Sometimes the good ideas are the ones that borrow nothing from the world before them. If somebody came in a year ago and pitched Ozzy Osbourne as the next big thing, on paper nobody would have bought that."

Graden, who is openly gay, has earned high marks for using his position at MTV to help raise public awareness of social issues via its public–service messages, specials, and shows. One of them was *Flipped,* a short–lived series that presented "poignant social messages with sometimes graphic and unsettling effects," asserted *Boston Herald* writer Mike Saucier. "The show arranges role reversals for parents and teens, cops and gangsters, bullies and the bullied, and plays them out. In one episode, a girl who rails against fat people is transformed into a 200–pound woman." Graden told Saucier in the same article that "*Flipped* is by far my favorite show in the network right now. It made these topics come alive." Another outstanding moment in Graden's career came in early 2001 when MTV aired *Anatomy of a Hate Crime,* a film about the 1998 slaying of Wyoming college student Matthew Shepard, and then scrolled the names of hate–crime victims at the bottom of the screen for the next 17 hours. That programming decision earned him kudos that year from the *Advocate,* the politically minded journal of gay and lesbian life in America that issues an annual honor list, as well as the Tom Stoddard National Role Model Award at PrideFest America in 2002.

Despite his keen sense for what brings in viewers, Graden is more pragmatic about mapping out his own life and career. He claims to set few career goals for himself. "At some point I'll grow out of it," he told the *New York Times's* Rutenberg about his MTV post, "and I'll just program VH1." When Rutenberg inquired what might follow that, Graden asserted, "I'll go program the AARP [American Association of Retired Persons] channel." Such attitudes extended to his personal life as well. "After planning all these things that I should do, like get married and get a job, all failed, and I decided never to have plans after that," he said in the interview with Epstein in the *Advocate.* "I have absolutely no idea. I just want to keep being true to the moment."

Sources

Periodicals

Advocate, May 23, 2000, p. 76; August 14, 2001, p. 82.

Boston Herald, February 14, 2002, p. 46.

Broadcasting & Cable, February 3, 2003, p. 13; September 8, 2003, p. 40.

Daily Variety, January 24, 2002, p. 1; April 18, 2002, p. 3; May 21, 2002, p. 11; July 25, 2002, p. 1.

Electronic Media, September 29, 1997, p. 44.

Entertainment Weekly, January 16, 1998, p. 53.

Houston Chronicle, July 14, 2000, p. 1.

Mediaweek, October 14, 1991, p. 18; April 19, 1999, p. 10; July 29, 2002, p. 4; October 20, 2003, p. 28.

Multichannel News, July 17, 2000, p. 62.

New York Times, May 20, 2002.

St. Petersburg Times, July 10, 2000, p. 1D.
Time, April 15, 2002, p. 64.
Variety, December 22, 1997, p. 28; October 8, 2001, p. A2.

Online

"Brian Graden," *Biography Resource Center Online,* Gale Group, 2003.

—*Carol Brennan*

Christopher Guest

Actor, writer, and director

Born Christopher Haden–Guest, February 5, 1948, in New York, NY; son of Peter (an editor) and Jean (maiden name, Hindes; a network executive) Haden–Guest; married Jamie Lee Curtis (an actress), December 18, 1984; children: one son, one daughter. *Education:* Attended Bard College, 1967; attended New York University, 1968–70.

Addresses: *Agent*—Creative Artists Agency, 9830 Wilshire Blvd., Beverly Hills, CA 90212.

Career

Actor, writer, and director. Appeared in New York City stage plays beginning in 1969 with *Little Murders;* co–writer of music and lyrics for, and actor in *National Lampoon's Lemmings* at the Village Gate Theater, New York City, 1973. Film appearances include: *The Hospital* (uncredited), 1971; *The Hot Rock* (also known as *How to Steal a Diamond in Four Uneasy Lessons*), 1972; *Death Wish,* 1974; *The Fortune,* 1975; *Girlfriends,* 1978; *The Last Word,* 1979; *The Long Riders,* 1980; *Heartbeeps,* 1981; *This is Spinal Tap,* 1984; *Little Shop of Horrors,* 1986; *Beyond Therapy,* 1987; *The Princess Bride,* 1987; *Sticky Fingers,* 1988; *A Few Good Men,* 1992; *Waiting for Guffman,* 1996; *Small Soldiers* (voice), 1998; *Best in Show,* 2000; *A Mighty Wind,* 2003. Television appearances include: *Saturday Night Live With Howard Cosell,* 1975; *The Lily Tomlin Special* (also co–writer), ABC, 1975; *All in the Family,* CBS, 1977; *It Happened One Christmas* (movie), 1977; *Laverne & Shirley,* 1978; *The T.V. Show* (movie), 1979; *Blind Ambition* (miniseries), 1979; *Hay-*wire, 1980; *Likely Stories, Volume 1* (also producer), 1981; *St. Elsewhere,* 1982; *Million Dollar Infield* (movie), 1982; *A Piano for Mrs. Cimino* (movie), 1982; *Close Ties* (movie), 1983; *Likely Stories, Volume 3,* 1983; *Saturday Night Live,* NBC, 1984–85; *Morton & Hayes* (also producer), 1991; *The Simpsons* (voice), 1992; *Animaniacs* (voice), 1993; *Attack of the 50–Ft. Woman* (also songwriter), HBO, 1993; *D.O.A.* (movie), 1999; *Mad TV,* 2003. Works as a director include: *The Big Picture,* HBO, 1989; *Morton & Hayes,* 1991; *Attack of the 50–Ft. Woman,* 1993; *Waiting for Guffman,* 1996; *Almost Heroes,* 1998; *D.O.A.,* 1999; *Best in Show,* 2000; *A Mighty Wind,* 2003. Works as a writer include: *The T.V. Show,* 1979; *Likely Stories, Volume 1,* 1981; *Likely Stories, Volume 3,* 1983; *Saturday Night Live,* 1984–85; *This is Spinal Tap,* 1984; *The Big Picture,* 1989; *Morton & Hayes,* 1991; *Waiting for Guffman,* 1996; *D.O.A.,* 1999; *Best in Show,* 2000; *A Mighty Wind,* 2003. Works as a composer include: *The T.V. Show,* 1979; *This is Spinal Tap,* 1984; *Morton & Hayes,* 1991; *Waiting for Guffman,* 1996; *Best in Show,* 2000; *A Mighty Wind,* 2003. Also toured as a musician with *This Is Spinal Tap* co–stars.

Awards: Emmy Award for best writing for a comedy special, Academy of Television Arts and Sciences, for *The Lily Tomlin Special,* 1976; Critics' Choice Award for best song, Broadcast Film Critics

Assocation, for "A Mighty Wind," 2004; Grammy Award for best song written for a motion picture, television or other visual media, Recording Academy, for "A Mighty Wind," 2004.

Sidelights

Filmmaker Christopher Guest is the comic talent behind such spoof films as *Best in Show* and *A Mighty Wind,* both gems in the "mockumentary" genre. Guest's roots in these biting, satirical glimpses into the purported world of purebred dog shows or the folk–music scene stretch back to his appearance in the cult classic, *This Is Spinal Tap,* in which he played a pompous but slow–witted rock guitarist. Guest's brilliant rips depict, as *Independent Sunday* journalist James Wolcott asserted, "middle-aged, middle–class also–rans who've deluded themselves into thinking that the only thing separating them from stardom is a lucky break." Yet *New York Times* film reviewer Elvis Mitchell noted that there seemed a more thoughtful side to Guest's movies that made them so funny. "The crucial element in all of his behind–the–scenes comedies," Mitchell maintained, "is that he allows the characters their dignity, and understands how important it is to all of them."

Of British heritage, Guest was born in 1948 in New York City, where his father, Peter, worked at the United Nations as a publications editor. His grandfather was made a baron in the 1950s for his child-health advocacy in Great Britain, and Guest would eventually inherit the title himself. His show–biz acumen may have been inherited from his mother, Jean, an executive at CBS. As a teen in the early 1960s, he attended New York's High School for the Performing Arts, where he became friends with Arlo Guthrie, the son of folk singer Woody Guthrie. The two even played in a folk act together, with Guest on the mandolin, that landed gigs in Greenwich Village coffeehouses during the folk–music heyday of the era.

Guest spent a year at Bard College in 1967, before switching to New York University (NYU) and its newly formed Tisch School of the Arts, where he studied acting. With its stellar faculty and lofty goals, Tisch was a "Mecca of pretension," Guest recalled in an interview with the *New York Times*'s Mitchell. But it was there that he met Michael McKean, whose first big success came on the hit ABC sitcom *Laverne and Shirley* in the mid–1970s. Despite cautions from his professors that he was not ready for the stage, Guest began winning roles in Off Broadway theater productions, including *Little Murders,* a 1969 play from the pen of political cartoonist

Jules Feiffer. He made his film debut—albeit uncredited—in the 1971 Paddy Chayefsky farce *The Hospital,* and went on to win roles in such films as *The Hot Rock* and *Death Wish,* the Charles Bronson classic.

Guest hit his stride when he became involved with writing both the script and music for *National Lampoon's Lemmings* at the Village Gate Theater. The 1973 musical revue, a spoof of the legendary Woodstock music festival, was the Off Broadway hit of the year and led to steady television work for Guest. He was hired as a co–writer and performer for a 1975 ABC event, *The Lily Tomlin Special,* for which he won an Emmy award, and spent the rest of the decade appearing in feature and made–for-television movies, including *Blind Ambition* in 1979, in which he was cast as Jeb Stuart Magruder, a crony of President Richard M. Nixon jailed for his part in the 1973 Watergate scandal.

Guest also began working with former *All in the Family* star Rob Reiner on television writing projects in the late 1970s, and then co–wrote the script for Reiner's directorial debut, *This is Spinal Tap,* along with former NYU alum McKean and a writer for *Saturday Night Live,* Harry Shearer. Its premise was a faux documentary about an enduring British rock band called Spinal Tap, played by Guest, McKean, and Shearer. Hapless to a fault, the bombastic metal act had weathered several career low points, including what appeared to be a curse on their drummers, one of whom had choked to death on vomit, "but not his own," as the band members sadly explain to Reiner's filmmaker–fan character, Marty DiBergi.

The script and soundtrack that Guest co–wrote for *Spinal Tap* parodied nearly every rock cliché from the past two decades, but a certain deadpan skill was needed for the three actors to pull it off. As the band's guitarist, Nigel Tufnel, "Guest catches the perfect combination of gormlessness and tongue-pulling enthusiasm," wrote Anthony Quinn in London's *Independent* newspaper some years later, "and gets many of the most famous scenes, confusing 'sexy' and 'sexist,' playing his tender piano piece in D minor ('the saddest of all keys') and, of course, explaining to DiBergi how the amplifiers go to eleven." Somewhat misunderstood when it was released—many thought the band actually existed—*Spinal Tap* took time to find its audience, but eventually earned its creators a small fortune.

Guest spent one season as a regular cast member on *Saturday Night Live* between 1984 and 1985, where his most memorable skit came as the coach of an all–male synchronized–swimming duo. Returning to film, he appeared in the remake of *Little Shop of Horrors* as well as *The Princess Bride,* and made his own directorial debut in *The Big Picture,* an original HBO movie. The comedy starred Kevin Bacon as the idealistic young winner of a student filmmaking award who is lured into the dismal business of big-budget Hollywood blockbusters. Outside of his writing and directing projects, Guest continued to take the occasional film role—including one in the 1992 Reiner–directed drama *A Few Good Men*—and made another HBO film, this one spoofing the schlock sci–fi movies in the 1950s, *Attack of the 50-Ft. Woman.*

Guest's career as a "mockumentary" filmmaker in the vein of *Spinal Tap* came into being in 1996 when he put out the small–budget *Waiting for Guffman.* After a basic script outlined with former *Second City Television* comedian Eugene Levy, Guest directed and starred in this drily comic take on a Missouri town staging a musical review in honor of its sesquicentennial celebration. Guest played Corky St. Claire, a former New Yorker who now teaches drama at the high school. Corky pulls together an improbable cast of Broadway hopefuls from amongst the town's citizenry, including its dentist (Levy), and a Dairy Queen cashier played by Parker Posey.

Though *Waiting for Guffman* barely made a blip in theatrical release, it went on to garner a cult following on video and DVD. Guest won praise for both his performance and as the filmmaker behind the satirical look at small–town boosterism and show-business dreamers. "Corky caresses his words like silk pajamas, and his rage keeps bursting out with jack–in–the–box abandon," noted *Entertainment Weekly* critic Owen Gleiberman. Writing in *Newsweek,* David Ansen also liked Guest's portrayal of a sensitive "artist," as he is often referred to by other cast members. "Guest's Corky is a triumph, a queenly stereotype invested with such enthusiastic conviction it transcends offensiveness," opined Ansen.

Guest's long–awaited follow–up to *Waiting for Guffman* was *Best in Show,* a spoof of the world of purebred dog competitions. The film reunited him with the ensemble from *Guffman,* which included Levy, Posey, Fred Willard, and Catherine O'Hara. Guest took a smaller role this time as bloodhound lover Harlan Pepper, a performance that often seemed overshadowed by the fictional couples who also arrived in Philadelphia, Pennsylvania, for the national purebred dog show. Levy and O'Hara played Gerry and Cookie Fleck, a Florida pair with a beloved ter-rier named Winky; Gerry has, literally, two left feet, while Cookie runs into evidence of her former single–gal escapades on an almost–daily basis. At the other end of the spectrum are weimaraner parents/attorneys Meg and Hamilton Swan, played by Posey and Michael Hitchcock, "a highly caffeinated couple whose tense shallowness is like a sheet of glass about to shatter," noted Wolcott in the *Independent Sunday* article. McKean and John Michael Higgins played an outlandishly swish couple with a prize shih–tzu. Again, Guest and Levy penned the script, and the actors improvised their dialogue and even went so far as to select their own wardrobes. "They're the best people at this I think that there are," Guest told Wolcott about his stellar cast. "And that is my joy in doing this. These are not money-making propositions. These are small movies, but I think the value for people working in them is that they get to do what they do, and they're not given the chance to do that in a conventional movie."

In 2003, Guest took on an even riper target for satire in *A Mighty Wind,* a fictional behind–the–scenes glimpse of a reunion of 1960s folk acts. Once again, he took a role—this time as part of a trio that included McKean and Shearer together for the first time since they performed in *Spinal Tap.* The project was based on a *Saturday Night Live* skit they did together back in 1984 as a trio of aging, hapless folksingers, the Folksmen. Guest, with balding pate and flowing curls, was the Folksmen's Alan Barrows, a singer who "baas" his lyrics and bickers with Shearer, who sports an outlandish Amish beard. The rest of the cast included Levy and O'Hara as a once popular duet act, Mitch & Mickey—since divorced and one embittered, the other nearly brain–dead—but "the bigger guffaws are inspired by the New Main Street Singers, led by John Michael Higgins and Jane Lynch as husband and wife straight arrows who are also bent about as far as they can be," noted Gleiberman in *Entertainment Weekly.*

Again, Guest won critical raves for his film. Gleiberman termed it a "sublime, dizzying satire of American folk music," while *New York Times* reviewer David Hajdu found that the "seasoned troupe of ensemble players captures [folk–music] types in all their blithe vapidity." Guest asserted that the folk scene—to which he once belonged himself—was ripe for parody. "I was a bluegrass player early on," he told Mitchell in the *New York Times* interview, "and we looked down on all other kinds of folk music. And that was because you had to be able to technically play, and play fast, for bluegrass." He explained to *Time* writers Richard Corliss and Josh Tyrangiel that he targeted the quasi–pop early 1960s pre–Bob Dylan folk scene in part because of "the earnestness that this kind of folk music has. Those people took themselves too seriously—way too seriously. And any group of people that takes itself seriously is fodder." On January 10, 2004, Guest, McKean, and Levy shared a Grammy Award for best song written for a motion picture, television, or other visual media from the Recording Academy for "A Mighty Wind." The song also won a Critics' Choice Award from the Broadcast Film Critics Association.

Guest is a centrifugal entertainment–industry presence. In an addition to a roster of famous comedian friends, he is married to actress Jamie Lee Curtis, daughter of actors Tony Curtis and Janet Leigh, and his half–brother is New York–based journalist and veteran partygoer Anthony Haden–Guest, reportedly the role model for the British writer in Tom Wolfe's 1987 bestseller, *The Bonfire of the Vanities*. Guest inherited his family's royal designation in 1996 when his father passed away. Technically he is the fifth Baron Haden–Guest of Saling, a district outside of London, and has taken Curtis along when he dons an heirloom ermine robe to attend the opening of the British Parliament, a starchy annual affair for which Queen Elizabeth II delivers the opening address. "It feels as if you're in a movie," Guest told *Maclean's* film critic Brian D. Johnson. "It's as surreal as the Spinal Tap thing, which is awfully surreal." He and Curtis have two children.

Though he avoids the most commonly used term that critics deploy when discussing his work—"I hate the word mockumentary, that's not my word," he told the *New York Times*'s Mitchell—Guest remains fascinated by the banal. He summed up his artistic vision in an *Esquire* interview with Genevieve A. Roth. "In my experience, we don't come close to describing how weird people in this world are," he reflected. "I mean, there are whole conventions for people who like thimbles."

Sources

Periodicals

Entertainment Weekly, February 14, 1997, p. 43; October 6, 2000, p. 58; April 25, 2003, p. 123.
Esquire, May 2003, p. 68.
Independent (London, England), October 13, 2000, p. 10; March 9, 2001, p. 10.
Independent Sunday (London, England), March 4, 2001, p. 6; March 11, 2001, p. 3.
Maclean's, September 25, 2000, p. 73; April 21, 2003, p. 55.
Nation, October 9, 1989, p. 398; May 5, 2003, p. 34.
Newsweek, February 10, 1997, p. 66.
New York Times, March 19, 2003, p. E1; April 13, 2003.
People, April 29, 1996, p. 56.
San Francisco Chronicle, March 7, 1997, p. D3.
Shoot, October 16, 1998, p. S45.
Time, March 5, 1984, p. 86; October 9, 2000, p. 106; April 21, 2003, p. 68.

Online

Contemporary Authors Online, Gale, 2002.
"Critics Choice Awards," BFCA.org, http://www. bfca.org/cca_vote_data.asp?year=2003 (July 9, 2004).
"List of Grammy winners," CNN.com, http://www. cnn.com/2004/SHOWBIZ/Music/02/08/ grammy.winners/ (July 9, 2004).

—*Carol Brennan*

E. Lynn Harris

Author

Reproduced by permission of E. Lynn Harris

Born Everette Lynn Harris, in 1955, in Flint, MI; son of James Jeter and Etta W. Harris (a factory worker). *Education:* Graduated from the University of Arkansas at Fayetteville, 1977. *Religion:* Baptist.

Addresses: *Publisher*—Doubleday, 1540 Broadway, New York, NY 10036. *Website*—Official Website of E. Lynn Harris: http://www.elynnharris.com. *E–mail*—heyelynn@aol.com.

Career

Worked as a salesman for IBM, 1977–82; worked for Wang Labs and AT&T, 1982–1990; self–published first novel, *Invisible Life,* through his own Consortium Press, 1991; signed deal with Doubleday, 1992; *Invisible Life* reprinted as a trade paperback by Anchor Books, 1994; sequel *Just As I Am* published by Doubleday, 1994; narrated *Dreamgirls* on Broadway, 2001; taught English, University of Arkansas at Fayetteville, 2003.

Awards: Blackboard's Novel of the Year (for best African–American novel), 1996, 2002, and 2003; James Baldwin Award for Literary Excellence for *If This World Were Mine,* 1997; Arkansas Black Hall of Fame, 2000; *Poets & Writers* "Writers For Writing" Award, 2002; University of Arkansas Citation of Distinguished Alumni, 1999.

Sidelights

E. Lynn Harris, "the bestselling African–American male novelist of the '90s," according to *Publishers Weekly*'s Alissa Quart, has sold more than three million copies of his novels about successful black professionals in dramatic romances. His vivid tales of black men who date women yet carry on hidden relationships with other men shocked and fascinated his readers, who made his self–published first novel a grassroots phenomenon and attracted a major publisher's attention. The novel's title, *Invisible Life,* became a metaphor for the experiences of closeted gay and bisexual blacks. His novels were often semi–autobiographical, yet his 2003 memoir, *What Becomes of the Brokenhearted,* still shocked readers with Harris' painful stories of surviving child abuse, alcoholism, depression, and the struggles of being a closeted gay man.

Born in Flint, Michigan, in the summer of 1955, Harris moved to Little Rock, Arkansas, with his mother at age three and grew up believing his stepfather, Ben Harris, was his father. He was the oldest of four children in the house and the only son. Harris' memoir is full of heart–wrenching stories of his stepfather beating and verbally abusing him. A babysitter showed him his birth certificate—which included his real father's name—at age 12 as a way of consoling him about the abuse. His mother, Etta, divorced his stepfather when Harris was 13. Two years later, Harris met his father, James Jeter, while visiting relatives in Michigan. Their reunion was tragically brief; Jeter was killed in a car accident the next year.

Harris attended high school in Little Rock. He secretly began to consider himself gay in high school, especially after visits to gay pride dances at George Washington University while in Washington, D.C. for a program that gave low–income black students brief internships in government agencies. He went to the University of Arkansas at Fayetteville, where he became a cheerleader and the first black yearbook editor at a major southern university. Harris casually dated women in college, but the college romance that meant the most to him was a secret relationship with a male athlete who would later inspire a central character in *Invisible Life*.

Though he graduated with a degree in journalism in 1977, Harris got a job as a salesman for IBM in Dallas. He stepped into social circles that defined his life for years and his fiction for years after that. "With a good–paying job, I had become a member of the black brunch–eating bourgeoisie," he recalled in his memoir, *What Becomes of the Brokenhearted*. As he had done in high school and college, he pretended to be from a middle–class family, embarrassed by his actual working–class roots. "My employment with IBM was like an entry card with the A crowd, and I quickly became friends with television personalities, doctors, sports figures, and lot of beautiful black women," he wrote. He also frequented a gay club in Dallas, a fact he kept secret from his straight friends. He was making more than $100,000 a year before he turned 26. He moved to New York City in 1982, worked for Wang Labs and AT&T and cultivated circles of friends that included Lencola Harris, a former Miss Arkansas. Later, he lived in Chicago and Washington, D.C. and continued to work in computer sales. He still mostly kept his straight friends and gay friends separate, and struggled with depression and difficult romantic relationships.

Some of Harris' friends fell sick with AIDS in the late '80s, and when visiting them made him too sad, he wrote them letters. "One of my sick friends was so moved by these letters that he said, 'Promise me, you will write; you have to tell our story,'" Harris told *Publishers Weekly*'s Quart. Profiles of Harris often stated that he left a lucrative sales job to write *Invisible Life*, and as of late 2003 his website still asserts this, but the version of the story recounted in *What Becomes of the Brokenhearted* is more complicated. Harris attempted suicide in 1990 after a long slide into severe depression and alcoholism left him isolated from work and most friends, broke,

and facing eviction. He entered therapy, quit drinking, and began living with friends, first in Washington, then in Atlanta. He interviewed for computer sales jobs there, but turned down a job offer after deciding he needed to do something new. He was still unemployed, living off disability insurance and money from friends and family, and staying with a friend when he began writing *Invisible Life*.

Its main character, Raymond Winston Tyler Jr., was a bisexual black lawyer and Harris' luckier alter ego. "I gave Raymond the life I would have wanted for myself," he told the *Detroit Free Press*. "Two parents who adored me, middle–class lifestyle, popularity." He wrote in the first person, expressing his feelings through Raymond's. Several publishers rejected his manuscript, so Harris formed his own company, Consortium Press, and began selling his book himself in late 1991 to black beauty salons, AIDS organizations, and independent book stores. *Invisible Life* quickly became popular in Atlanta, and an article about the book in an Atlanta newspaper helped Harris get the attention of an agent and a publisher. Harris signed with Doubleday in 1992, and in 1994, Anchor Press republished *Invisible Life* as a trade paperback, while Doubleday released the sequel, *Just As I Am*.

Harris' philosophy was simple, he told *Publishers Weekly*'s Quart: "It's 'let me tell you a story about the people I know.'" Tales of his friends and ex-lovers, transformed into fiction, earned Harris a huge following. "Though the characters were fictional—sort of—the soap opera–like drama in their lives was so real it kept readers talking long after they'd finished the last pages," the *Detroit Free Press* journalist stated. "Talking and wondering, especially about how many supposedly straight men were keeping sexual trysts with men on the down low, secretly, as several of Harris's characters did." Harris debuted a new set of characters for 1996's *And This Too Shall Pass*, about a star athlete accused of rape, which made the *New York Times* best–seller list. He won the James Baldwin Award for Literary Excellence with the novel, *If This World Were Mine*, about four friends and the secrets they record while in a journal–writing group. Doubleday paid him more than a million dollars for 1999's *Abide With Me*, the final book in the trilogy that began with *Invisible Life*. Soon, readers began to look forward to a new Harris book coming out every summer. *Not A Day Goes By*, published in 2000, and 2001's *Any Way the Wind Blows* both debuted at number two on the *New York Times* best–seller list.

Though Harris' protagonists and anti–heroes are usually gay or bisexual black men, most of his readers are black women, he acknowledges. "The fit is not entirely surprising," observed *Publishers Weekly*'s Quart, "as Harris has a passion for both black men and the minutiae of everyday romantic relationships." Still, Harris told *Ebony*, "I want anyone who enjoys reading to pick up my book." Critical appraisal of his novels is torn between those who accept them for what they are—dramatic, steamy romance novels that glamorize and sometimes satirize upwardly mobile black life—and those who do not, such as Cleveland *Plain Dealer* critic Rochelle O'Gorman, who compared Harris to pulp romance novelist Jackie Collins and called his work "simplistic" and "hackneyed." Harris has reacted angrily to being identified as a black commercial writer, but has also admitted he is not a great writer like less–known, critically acclaimed novelists, and he has claimed to keep critics' points in mind while writing subsequent novels.

In interviews, Harris revealed some of the pain of his life before writing, but saved the full story of his struggles for *What Becomes of the Brokenhearted*, a memoir that took several years to write. The book opens with the story of his suicide attempt, then cuts to his childhood and the abuse his stepfather inflicted on him. It ends at the close of 1991, as he emerges from depression and *Invisible Life* begins to find an audience. "This story has a happy ending," he told the *Advocate*'s Austin Foxxe. "I'm here to say that brokenhearted people, whether they've had their hearts broken by love or family members or what have you, can survive it. They can find happiness, and they can find love."

Harris appeared on Broadway in 2001, as the narrator of the play *Dreamgirls*. His E. Lynn Harris Better Days Foundation, which supports aspiring writers, won the *Poets & Writers* "Writers for Writing" Award in 2002. He became the first three–time winner of Blackboard's Novel of the Year award for best novel by a black writer in 2003. As 2003 ended, Harris was teaching an English class at his alma mater, the University of Arkansas at Fayetteville and was working on his next novel. He had recently moved into a condo in Atlanta, and also had an apartment in Chicago. Harris had completed a screenplay for a so–far–unproduced remake of the film *Sparkle* and signed three options that may lead to seeing his novels adapted as films.

Selected writings

Invisible Life, Consortium Press, 1991.
Just As I Am, Doubleday, 1994.
And This Too Shall Pass, Doubleday, 1996.
If This World Were Mine, Doubleday, 1997.
Abide With Me, Doubleday, 1999.
Not A Day Goes By, Doubleday, 2000.
"Money Can't Buy Me Love" (novella), published in *Got To Be Real: Four Original Love Stories*, New American Library, 2000.
Any Way the Wind Blows, Doubleday, 2001.
A Love of My Own, Doubleday, 2002.
"The Dinner Party" (short story), published in *Gumbo: A Celebration of African–American Writers*, co–edited by E. Lynn Harris and Marita Golden, Harlem Moon, 2002.
What Becomes of the Brokenhearted (memoir), Doubleday, 2003.

Sources

Books

Harris, E. Lynn. *What Becomes of the Brokenhearted*, Doubleday, 2003.

Periodicals

Advocate, July 8, 2003, pp. 62–64.
Cincinnati Enquirer, August 13, 2002, p. 3C.
Detroit Free Press, July 20, 2003, p. 1H.
Ebony, October 2000, pp. 23–24.
Essence, April 1996, p. 88.
People, May 15, 1995, p. 115.
Philadelphia Inquirer, July 15, 2003, p. C1.
Plain Dealer (Cleveland, Ohio), September 3, 2000, p. 10J.
Publishers Weekly, December 6, 1993, p. 29; April 19, 1999, pp. 44–45; July 30, 2001, pp. 53–54.

Online

Official Website of E. Lynn Harris, http://www.elynnharris.com (November 23, 2003).

—*Erick Trickey*

Bruce Hayse

Conservationist

Born c. 1949, in Burns, OR; son of Joe (stepfather, a civil engineer) and Laura; married to Jan; children: two daughters. *Education:* University of Wisconsin, M.S.; University of Oregon, M.D.

Addresses: *Office*—African Rainforest and Rivers Conservation, P.O. Box 2594, Jackson, WY 83001.

Career

Worked as a guide for the Idaho Forest Service; co–founded radical environmental group Earth First!, 1979; moved to Jackson Hole, Wyoming, and set up a family medical practice, 1983; began traveling recreationally in Africa; founded Africa Rainforest and River Conservation, 1998.

Awards: Citizen of the Year, Jackson Hole Chamber of Commerce, 1992.

Sidelights

Dr. Bruce Hayse is an unusual environmentalist. He co–founded Earth First! in the 1970s, a group that advocated extreme measures in fighting for conservation, such as tree–sitting and jamming logging machinery. Hayse ran a medical practice in Jackson Hole, Wyoming, that often served immigrants and the uninsured. An avid hiker all his life, Hayse began taking adventurous trips down African rivers. He was particularly struck by the devastation of the forest in the Central African Republic (CAR). The land and rivers had been ravaged by mining, logging, and poaching. In some places, 95 percent of the wildlife had been killed off. Hayse was inspired to found a group, African Rainforest and Rivers Conservation (ARRC), in 1998. The group worked with the government of the CAR, and took the unprecedented step of hiring and training a 400–man militia to protect the Chinko river basin, a gigantic wilderness area, against poachers. This combative strategy discomfited some more traditional conservation groups, such as the World Wildlife Fund. But Hayse believed there was no other way to win against the well–armed poachers.

Hayse grew up in the town of Burns, in eastern Oregon. He came from a family of four, and from an early age he was attracted to the mountains and wilderness around his home. He worked for the Forest Service in Idaho, both on the fire crew and as a guide on mule packing expeditions. He considered himself first and foremost an outdoorsman. He moved to Wisconsin to complete a master's degree in plant ecology, and then turned to medicine. He earned his medical degree from the University of Oregon, and then specialized in family practice. However, his duties as a physician did not curtail his interest in wilderness and land preservation. In 1979 he co–founded the group Earth First!, which remains one of the most extreme factions of the American environmental movement. In 1983 Hayse and his wife and daughters moved to Jackson Hole, Wyoming. The area is known for its spectacular scenery and abundance of wildlife. Hayse became a prominent citizen, known both for his medical work with the poor and for his involvement in local land issues. He took frequent hiking and skiing trips around Wyoming, and since the 1980s took a yearly adventurous vacation to Africa.

Hayse was not a sedate tourist, and he seemed to enjoy risk. Hayse eventually contracted malaria three times and faced down poisonous snakes and surly hippos. He told James Gorman of the *New York Times* that he thought getting malaria was a good idea for a lot of people. "It can teach you compassion for those Africans who are, millions of them, shivering in these oppressive huts every day," he said. "You really don't have any comprehension of what that's like unless you can get one of these horrible life–threatening illnesses yourselves. I think that's really important to do." Hayse had lived for weeks at a time with a remote pygmy tribe in the Congo river basin, and had survived tse tse flies, vicious wasps, and many kinds of everyday African dangers.

His interest in working on conservation issues in Africa began seriously in 1998, on a 300–mile rafting trip down the Chinko river. The Chinko was a wild river snaking through dense forest. Its name means "River of Elephants," and at one time it housed tens of thousands of the huge mammals. But Hayse's 1998 trip down the Chinko was strangely quiet. The elephants were gone, and little other wildlife was evident. In fact, conservationists estimated that 95 percent of the wildlife in the Chinko area had been killed off. Hayse's party came across abandoned campsites littered with elephant bones and spent ammunition, evidence of poachers. When at the mouth of the river Hayse's party finally encountered a populated village, the people there begged him to help them. The poachers were heavily armed, and the native people were unable to stop their brutal trade in so–called bushmeat, which included the flesh of rhinos, buffalo, giraffe, and giant eland, as well as elephants. The poachers pillaged the indigenous communities, raping women and taking men captive. Hayse felt that he had little choice but to find a way to help. He and his friend, orthopedist Christian Guier, founded ARRC with their own money. They brokered an agreement with the president of the CAR to let them arm and train a defense group to fight back against the poachers.

This was quite an unusual tactic for an American conservation group. But Hayse believed the situation in the CAR was dire, and that he had a responsibility to do what he could. The World Wildlife Fund and Conservation International, two large multinational conservation groups, distanced themselves from Hayse's group, explicitly condemning the use of force. But the government of the CAR, plagued by instability and short of funds, could not afford to send its own army against the poachers, who were a formidable threat. Hayse told *National Geographic Adventure* magazine, "The poachers are obviously well armed and they're in a lucrative business and aren't going to be interested in listening to advice from us.... These people are lawless; they're basically criminals who are not easily intimidated."

Hayse was not easily intimidated, either, and he kept on with his group despite difficulty raising money. In 2001 he attempted to raft down the Lindi river in the Democratic Republic of the Congo (DRC) to raise the visibility of ARRC. The Lindi ran through Maiko National Park, a wildlife preserve that had been essentially abandoned and closed off to Westerners because of the political turmoil in the DRC. The DRC was criss–crossed with competing military groups who terrorized and pillaged the countryside, and one of these groups put a stop to the ARRC trip. Hayse, Guier, and their party, were arrested, threatened, and told they needed a letter of permission to continue their journey. After two of their guides were taken hostage, Hayse and Guier ransomed them with $500 and left the country.

Nevertheless, Hayse was determined to investigate Maiko National Park, and a year later he returned. This time he arranged with a militia leader for an expensive letter of permission, and brought along various other things to barter with. Hayse packed a liquor bottle spiked with sleeping pills, just in case he needed to drug anyone who captured him. The militia chieftain Hayse had bribed for the letter of permission insisted on sending an armed escort, which was entirely unwelcome. Hayse had to bribe the men to take themselves and their machine guns away. The river itself was extremely dangerous, filled with rapids, waterfalls, and whirlpools. At one point, Hayse and another party member got lost in the jungle near their campsite. The brush was so dense that they couldn't walk and had to crawl. It got dark, and they had no flashlight. Eventually their friends found them and brought them back to camp. Later they came across another militia leader, one who was a particular enemy of one of their party, a former conservator of Maiko Park. Only another bribe and Guier's lie that the party was in constant satellite contact with the United States government saved the conservator's life.

Harrowing as the trip was, Hayse was buoyed by the elephant dung he found. He believed that the armed groups that made Maiko Park so dangerous actually kept out poachers and loggers, and so the wilderness there was probably relatively unspoiled. Hayse began making plans to return to Maiko Park to do a more complete wildlife study. Meanwhile, ARRC continued to solicit funds for its wildlife protection work. Hayse and Guier had spent some $350,000 of their own money to fund the CAR militia. They hoped to raise $3.5 million more to keep the group going.

Selected writings

Unobscured Horizons, Untravelled Trails, Olive Press, 1979.

Sources

Periodicals

National Geographic Adventure, January/February 2002.
New York Times, November 26, 2002, p. F5.
People, June 2, 2003, pp. 115–16.
Sports Illustrated, July 1, 2002, p. A4.

Online

"Wyoming doctor, 'extreme environmentalist,' recruits army in Africa to save animals from poachers," PlanetSave, http://www.planetsave.com/ViewStory.asp?ID=3176 (March 30, 2003).

—*A. Woodward*

David Hempleman-Adams

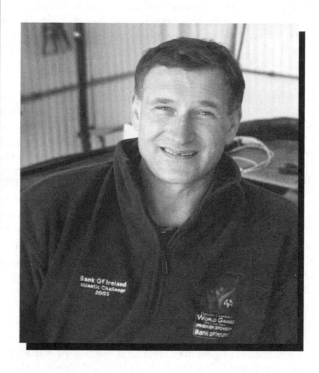

Explorer

Born 1956, in Swindon, England; married Claire (an attorney); children: Alicia, Camilla, Amelia. *Education:* Studied business at a Manchester, England college.

Addresses: *Office*—Global Resins, Ltd., Unit 7, Park Lane Industrial Estate, Corsham, Wiltshire, SN13 9LG, United Kingdom.

Career

Executive with family resins–manufacturing business; climbed first of the highest peaks on each continent with his ascent of Mt. McKinley, Alaska, 1980; completed several solo and unsupported treks to the magnetic and geographical North and South Poles during the 1980s and '90s; became the first person in history to make a solo open–basket, hot–air balloon flight across the Atlantic Ocean, 2003.

Awards: Two bronze medals for bravery, Royal Humane Society; Member of the Order of the British Empire, 1995; Officer of the Order of the British Empire, 1998.

Sidelights

In 2003, David Hempleman–Adams became the first person to cross the Atlantic Ocean in an open–basket, hot–air balloon. Forty–six years old at the time, the British chemical–company executive had made a second career out of such adventure stunts, including treks to the North and South Poles.

Despite several close calls with danger, Hempleman–Adams asserted he was unafraid of so–called death by misadventure. "I have a feeling that when I do die, it will be doing something relatively safe," he told *Sunday Telegraph* writer Emily Bearn. "In 25 years, I've never called out the rescue services and I've never made an insurance claim. I'd like that to go on my tombstone."

Born in 1956, Hempleman–Adams was entranced by altitudes since a school skiing trip to Austria when he was 13. "It was the first time I had climbed in the Alps and vividly remember getting to the top and wondering why the teachers were struggling with the altitude," he recalled in an interview with *Geographical.* As a young man, he went on to study business in Manchester, England, and became a skilled mountaineer as well. The first major peak he scaled was Alaska's Mt. McKinley in 1980. He eventually married and settled into a job running a family owned resins business in Wiltshire, England.

In his spare time, however, Hempleman–Adams set about completing the "Adventurers' Grand Slam," which no other person had done successfully to date. Climbing each of the highest peaks on each continent was the effortless part of the challenge; conquering both magnetic and geographical poles at the top and bottom of the Earth would prove the far trickier. His first polar trek was in 1983, but two cracked ribs from a bad fall forced him to turn back before he reached the geographic North Pole. An attempt the following year to conquer the magnetic North Pole was temporarily interrupted by a polar-bear attack.

By 1995, Hempleman–Adams had scaled both Mt. Everest in Nepal (the world's tallest peak) and Mt. Vinson in Antarctica, which was the last of his climbs to the highest summits on each continent. Returning to the Poles challenge, he became the first Briton to make a solo, unsupported 680–mile trek to the geographic South Pole in January of 1996. Most of the way involved trudging against strong headwinds, and he averaged just eight miles a day. He dragged a 285–pound sled, but ate three pounds' worth of it daily. A month later, he sailed by boat to the magnetic South Pole, becoming the first person in history to reach both South Poles in the same year.

In May of 1996, Hempleman–Adams and a team finally reached the magnetic North Pole on Ellesmere Island, the largest in Canada's Arctic archipelago. The geographic North Pole remained the elusive final goal. He and a Norwegian friend, Rune Gjeldnes, tried in 1997, but were waylaid when a fellow explorer fell through the ice; on the attempt, Gjeldnes's sled fell apart, and because they were trying to set the unsupported record, they refused an offer of an airlifted new sled and turned back. Hempleman–Adams described this and his successful 1998 trip in *Walking on Thin Ice: In Pursuit of the North Pole.* The proceeds from the sale of this and his previous work, *Toughing It Out: The Adventures of a Polar Explorer and Mountaineer,* went to a charity that funds an adventure camp for disadvantaged children in England.

Hempleman–Adams claims he is better suited to colder climates, recalling one Venezuelan expedition through the rainforest that proved particularly arduous for him. "There are people who have natural jungle skills but I don't have any," he told *Geographical.* "The daily struggle of not getting dehydrated in the intense heat and humidity, putting up the hammock and mosquito net every night, avoiding snakes, spiders, and the like was a complete nightmare." He returned to frostier climes in 2003 with an entirely solo trip to the magnetic North Pole, taking neither sled dogs nor Gjeldnes, and declared it to be his last.

Hot–air ballooning was Hempleman–Adams' next adventure sport. He was determined to become the first person to make a transatlantic trip in an open-

basket, hot–air balloon alone. The solo crossing had been done once before, in 1984, but in an enclosed heated basket. Hempleman–Adams' plan, by contrast, was to dress warmly, knock off the two–foot icicles that formed at 14,000 feet by hand, and hope for good winds. He made his first attempt in 2002, but a mechanical failure with his autopilot device forced him to turn back. He started out once again in June of 2003, but this time a lack of wind stymied the trip from North America to England. One route that his meteorologist on the ground discovered would have taken him over Camp David, the United States presidential retreat in Maryland, but security concerns made it impossible to even try. "We asked permission, and were told very simply by e–mail, 'Pass over Camp David and you will be shot down,'" Hempleman–Adams told a journalist for London's *Times* newspaper, Rupert Mellor.

Later that year, on September 26, Hempleman–Adams set off in his balloon once again from New Brunswick, Canada. He survived the 83–hour sleepless trip by eating canned soup that he heated on a Bunsen burner in his seven–by–four–foot basket. His most frightening moment came when the Concorde supersonic airliner passed overhead, and its sonic booms caused his basket to plunge precipitously. Sailing through heavy rains and bitterly cold temperatures proved far more challenging than his Arctic trips, he was surprised to discover. "There was no heater and some nights my teeth were chattering so hard that I couldn't get on the radio to talk," he told Bearn in the *Sunday Telegraph.* "It was colder than going to the North Pole because at the North Pole you're skiing and keeping warm. But here it was just endurance."

On the fourth day, Hempleman–Adams touched down in a field in Hambleton, Lancashire, England. He vowed that his extreme–adventuring days are over, having taken a toll on his physique. He returned to his home in Box, outside of Bath, England, where he lives with his wife, Claire, a former attorney, and three daughters. He claims that out of all of his escapades to date, the most arduous have been with his "three young children," he told *Geographical,* "on a long–haul flight to Los Angeles when your knees are up to your chin."

Selected writings

Toughing It Out: The Adventures of a Polar Explorer and Mountaineer, Trafalgar Square, 1998.
(With Robert Uhlig) *Walking on Thin Ice: In Pursuit of the North Pole,* Orion/Trafalgar Square, 1999.

Sources

Capper's, April 29, 2003, p. 18.

Geographical, June 2000, p. 114; October 2001, p. 74; December 2001, p. 66; December 2003, p. 14.

Independent (London, England), May 1, 1998, p. 3.

Library Journal, January 1999, p. 137.

Money Marketing, June 8, 2000, p. 5.

Sunday Telegraph (London, England), August 25, 2002, p. 2; October 5, 2003.

Times (London, England), November 15, 2003, p. 21.

—*Carol Brennan*

Justine Henin-Hardenne

Professional tennis player

Born Justine Henin, June 1, 1982, in Liège, Belgium; daughter of Jose (a postal worker) and Françoise Henin; married Pierre–Yves Hardenne, November 16, 2002.

Addresses: *Office*—c/o Association Francophone de Tennis, Galerie de la Porte Louise, 203 bte 12 (8ème étage), 1050 Brussels, Belgium. *Website*—http://www.justine–henin.be/.

Career

Won juniors titles at the Orange Bowl (Miami, FL) and the European Junior Championships (San Remo, Italy), both 1996; won the Belgian Open, 1999; advanced to semi–finals at French Open, and finals at Wimbledon, both 2001; won German Open, 2002; won eight tournaments in 2003, including the U.S. Open, the French Open, and German Open women's singles titles; won the Australian Open, January, 2004.

Sidelights

Justine Henin–Hardenne emerged as the newest star in women's tennis after trouncing rivals to win the 2003 French Open, the 2003 U.S. Open, and the 2004 Australian Open. The 21–year–old Belgian was just one of a handful of players to hold three of the four Grand Slam tennis titles in a single year, and became the No. 1–ranked female player in the world after her string of victories.

Those who have met Henin–Hardenne refer to her dedication to the game and determination to succeed, but her entry into the game came via a much harder path than that of many of her fellow competitors. Born in 1982 in the French–speaking city of Liège, she grew up as one of four children of Jose, a postal worker, and Françoise, who encouraged her interest in tennis at a young age. Henin–Hardenne won a ten–and–under contest and a prize trip to Roland Garros Stadium, the legendary site of the French Open. Her prowess in the sport continued to impress those who saw her, but Henin–Hardenne's budding career nearly ended with the death of her mother from cancer when she was 12. Suddenly, she was forced into a caretaker role in her family. "It is wrong to say I became the mother of the family, because I didn't cook or do anything like that," she explained in an interview with Richard Evans of the *Sunday Times*. "But I was mature very early and they all used to come to me with their problems."

Adding to the stress in Henin–Hardenne's life was the fact that her father was her coach, but at age 14 she began working with an Argentine, Carlos Rodriguez, who was affiliated with Belgium's tennis federation. As Rodriguez told Evans in the *Sunday Times*, "He, the father, and the whole family, wanted to appropriate her. They did not respect her needs. I saw what they were doing to her and I spoke up very quickly." Henin–Hardenne's problems with her father escalated when she began dating her future husband, Pierre–Yves Hardenne, the son of a butcher in a nearby village whom she at a trophy presentation. Her father opposed the romance, and she left home at age 17 to move in with Hardenne above his family's butcher shop. Virtually penniless, she depended on the largesse of the Belgian tennis federation as well as financial help from two sympathetic aunts and a family friend.

The year 2001 proved a trying one for Henin–Hardenne, who attempted an unsuccessful reconciliation with her family when her infant nephew died. She won three trophies that year, and even advanced to the French Open semi–finals and the finals at Wimbledon as the season progressed, but learned of her grandfather's death just after losing that last match to Venus Williams, the reigning champion of women's tennis. Both Williams and her sister, Serena, would prove two of the most formidable competitors for Henin–Hardenne. Several weeks after her 2001 Wimbledon loss, Henin–Hardenne went up against Serena during the early rounds of the 2001 U.S. Open and lost again, but bested the younger Williams at the 2002 German Open in Berlin for the title.

Back in Belgium, however, the media–incited rivalry was between Henin–Hardenne and another young tennis star, Kim Clijsters, who was also quickly advancing to the top ranks of women's tennis. Both were young, talented, and photogenic, and Clijsters was the first Belgian woman to be ranked No. 1 in singles. A year younger than Henin–Hardenne, Clijsters hailed from the Dutch–speaking part of the country, and the competition between the two became front–page news in the Belgian media.

Henin–Hardenne emerged as a strong player as the 2003 tennis season got underway. Watchers of the sport found her one–handed backhand particularly graceful and a welcome departure from the customary two–handed power–shot common in women's tennis. In early June, Henin–Hardenne she returned to Roland Garros for the 2003 French Open and trounced the previous year's winner, Serena Williams. Writing in London's *Guardian* newspaper, Stephen Bierley called it "a semi–final of high drama, controversy, and thrills." At one point, Henin–Hardenne raised her hand, signaling that perhaps she was not yet ready to receive Williams's serve, which prompted Williams to fault. The umpire claimed not to have seen Henin–Hardenne

make the gesture, and Williams tearfully excoriated her at the post–game press conference. Next, Henin–Hardenne went up against Clijsters in a match whose television broadcast was the central focus of Belgian life that day, and defeated her rival to become the new French Open women's champion.

Just two weeks later at Wimbledon, the famed English tournament that is the second of the Grand Slam tennis events, Serena Williams seemed to take her revenge by eliminating Henin–Hardenne in the semi–finals. In early August of 2003, at the Acura Classic tournament in San Diego, the rivalry between Henin–Hardenne and Clijsters took a nasty turn. Henin–Hardenne won after a grueling round of give–and–take with Clijsters, but Clijsters then claimed that Henin–Hardenne faked injuries to give herself time to collect herself in the midst of the heavy psychological duress of such matches. Later that August, when Henin–Hardenne won the 2003 U.S. Open after beating Clijsters, some in Clijsters' camp voiced suspicion about Henin–Hardenne's suddenly stronger physique, but later retracted their statements. The competition continued as the 2004 season began on the other side of the world, when summer comes in December, at the Australian Open in late January. Again, it was another tense final for Henin–Hardenne, and the crowd even appeared to be siding with Clijsters for a time. After Henin–Hardenne hit the shot that her rival missed and the game was over 6–3, 4–6, 6–3, she tossed her racket aside, dropped to her knees, and covered her face in elation.

Henin–Hardenne was anticipating defending her French Open title in June of 2004, and following that with her first Wimbledon Cup win. She has said that she will play until she turns 30. "By then I will have decided what I want to do with the rest of my life," she told Evans in the *Sunday Times* interview. "But I enjoy playing so much that I don't see any reason to stop before then."

Sources

Financial Times, November 5, 2003, p. 4.
Guardian (London, England), June 6, 2003, p. 33; July 3, 2003, p. 35; August 6, 2003, p. 30; January 16, 2004, p. 32.
Houston Chronicle, September 9, 2003, p. 1.
New York Times, January 31, 2004, p. D1; February 1, 2004, p. SP4.
Sunday Times (London, England), June 22, 2003, p. 12.

—*Carol Brennan*

Sam Houser

President of Rockstar Games

Born c. 1972, in England; son of a jazz–club owner.

Addresses: *Office*—Take Two Interactive Software, Inc., 622 Broadway, New York, NY 10012. *Website*—http://www.rockstargames.com.

Career

Began in the promotions department of Bertelsmann Music Group (BMG) in London, England; directed music videos and worked in artists–and–repertoire (A&R) at BMG; headed international product development for BMG Interactive; co-founder and president, Rockstar Games, New York, NY, 1998—.

Sidelights

Sam Houser is president of Rockstar Games, the company behind the *Grand Theft Auto* game for Sony PlayStation 2 consoles. He co–founded the company with fellow Brit Terry Donovan, a friend from his school years, to develop and bring to the market the kind of games they wanted to play. *Grand Theft Auto* earned a slew of bad press for its ostensibly violent content, but Houser compares the criticism to the kind often leveled at the music business. "We get into trouble every now and again, it's raw," the former record–label executive told *Guardian* writer Steven Poole. "That's what the record business was like when it started. It's supposed to be energetic and fun."

Houser was born in England the early 1970s and grew up in London, where his father ran a well–known jazz club called Ronnie Scott's. As a youngster, he was a first–generation devotee of the new arcade–game culture, and met Donovan at the prep school they both attended. During their early adult years, each worked in the music business. Houser's experience included working in promotions at Bertelsmann Music Group (BMG), and he went on to direct videos for performers under the BMG labels before taking an artists–and–repertoire position with the company. When BMG launched a new Interactive division, he was named head of international product development for the new multimedia venture. When BMG decided to spin it off into an independent, New York–based company, Houser went with it.

Houser was in charge of finding and bringing to market new products for gaming systems like the popular PlayStation 2 and X–Box. One day, the first prototype for *Grand Theft Auto* arrived on his desk. It was the work of a Scottish game developer, DMA Design, and its carjacking premise intrigued Houser and his office–mates. At the time, the industry was eager to land the next *Lara Croft: Tomb Raider*–type success. "Graphically it wasn't nearly as sharp as *Tomb Raider*," Houser recalled in a *Rolling Stone* interview with David Kushner, "but it was deeply immersive. You were put into a world and given choices."

An early version of *Grand Theft Auto* was released in Europe, where it became a cult favorite and gained a measure of bad press for its violent content. Yet BMG's Interactive division was about to tank, and so in 1998 Houser asked Donovan to join him in New York in order to launch their own company around *Grand Theft Auto,* which would be financed by a more established company called Take Two Interactive. They named their new venture Rockstar Games, and began releasing PlayStation games that lured a devoted following, including *Smuggler's Run* and *Midnight Club Street Racing.* Among denizens of New York City's Lower East Side and a subset of Silicon Alley tech–industry workers, Houser and Donovan became known for their "Rockstar" nights at bars and dance clubs that promoted their new releases.

Grand Theft Auto III was released for the new, highly anticipated Sony PlayStation 2 system in 2001, and went on to become the best–selling title in the gaming industry that year. It had an aggressive theme and some choices could be construed as borderline sociopath: a player can choose to solicit and then rob a prostitute, or win extra points for carrying out a hit–and–run accident. Its "runaway success," noted *Newsweek*'s N'Gai Croal—"is proof that the 12–year–olds who grew up on [Nintendo's Super Mario Brothers] are looking for something very different now that they're in their 20s: games whose look, feel, and sound are drawn from the edgy movies, comic books, and music that reflect a twentysomething's interests."

The prospect of pre–teens being exposed to such a world prompted a flurry of media coverage and even a political moment: the U.S. Senator from Connecticut, Joseph I. Lieberman, cited it as an example of the trend toward overly violent content in the entertainment industry in general. "Games like *Grand Theft Auto* are particularly troubling because they go beyond just celebrating violence generally, and actually reward players for engaging in organized crime, murdering innocent people, and other forms of perverse, antisocial behavior," the *New York Times* journalist John Leland quoted the senator as saying.

Houser and Donovan often pointed out that *Grand Theft Auto III* and its successful 2002 sequel, *Grand Theft Auto: Vice City,* were rated "M" for mature content, and thus advisable for sale only to those 17 and older. *Vice City* proved as successful as the first *Grand Theft Auto,* and sold a million copies in United States alone during its first week of release. The story is set in Miami during the mid–1980s, and positions the player as a low–level mobster trying to

determine who may have stolen his contraband. "Other games may offer more killing and gore, but few are as ethically ambiguous," noted the *New York Times*'s Leland. In defense of the bad press, Houser said that he had met members of the New York City police department, and told the *Guardian*'s Poole that they had said they liked his game. "And I said, 'What about the fact that [the player can] kill cops?,'" he recounted, "and they said, 'Well, you know what? There's a lot of people out there trying to kill cops and we'd rather they did it in your game than on the street.'"

Despite the controversial content, *Vice City* landed on the short list for Britain's Designer of the Year competition, sponsored by the prestigious Design Museum. Its immersive world is rife with pitch–perfect period detail, including a choice of nine radio stations featuring various Eighties pop–music genres. Museum director Alice Rawsthorn told a writer for *Design Week,* Paul Murphy, that *Vice City* had made it onto the list of finalists "totally on its design merits. Visually and technically, in terms of the narrative it's much more complex than any other game—it is a genuine leap forward."

Houser serves as president of Rockstar, and concentrates on product development, while Donovan handles the marketing work; Houser's brother, Dan, writes dialogue for the games. Their company's name, Houser noted, continues to reflect their goal—to deliver products with attitude. "At the end of the day you can't [mess] with Keith Richards," Houser explained in the *Rolling Stone* interview with Kushner. "You can't argue with Keith Moon riding down the street in a Rolls Royce.... That guy is the original punk rock. And if we can bring a fraction of a percent of that to games, then we're doing something."

Sources

Design Week, February 27, 2003, p. 15.
Financial Times, October 29, 2002, p. 94; November 26, 2002, p. 32.
Guardian (London, England), November 3, 1999, p. 14.
Newsweek, March 18, 2002, p. 50.
New York Times, October 27, 2002.
Rolling Stone, November 28, 2002, p. 61.

—*Carol Brennan*

Hu Jintao

President of China

Born in December of 1942 in Shanghai, China; married Liu Yongqing; children: one son, one daughter. *Education:* Tsinghua University, degree in hydraulic engineering, 1964; Central Party School, 1980.

Addresses: *Office*—Office of the President, State Council Secretariat, Zhong Nan Hai, Beijing, China.

Career

Political instructor in Water Conservancy Department of Tsinghua University, 1964–65; worked in hydropower research, 1965–68; laborer on Gansu Liujiaxia Power Station project, 1968–69; joined staff of Ministry of Water Conservancy and Power, working his way up through the ranks, 1969–74; deputy chief, Project Design Management Division, Gansu Provincial Construction Commission, 1974–1980; deputy secretary, Gansu Provincial Communist Youth League, 1980–82; alternate member, Central Committee of Chinese Communist Party, 1982; head of Communist Youth League, 1984; secretary, Guizhou Provincial Party Committee, 1985–88; party secretary, Tibet Autonomous Region, 1988–92; member, Politburo Standing Committee, 1992–98; director, Central Party School, 1993–2002; vice president, People's Republic of China, 1998–2002; general secretary, Chinese Communist Party, 2002—; president, People's Republic of China, 2003—.

Sidelights

For the leader of a country of 1.3 billion people, Hu Jintao remains something of a mystery to much of the outside world. Although Hu became China's president in March of 2003, he had already ascended to the highest office in the land in the fall of 2002 when he was named to succeed Jiang Zemin as general secretary of the Chinese Communist Party. Active in Chinese politics for nearly four decades, Hu has nevertheless spent much of his public life toiling in the background, out of the spotlight. But it is a sign of the high regard in which he has long been held by party leaders that for nearly a decade Hu served as director of the country's Central Party School. Based in Beijing, the school provides training for almost all of China's top–tier national leaders and also arbitrates most national debates over party ideology.

One of China's youngest leaders of the communist era, Hu is the only member of the communist party's previous politburo standing committee to be carried over onto the new committee, which formally took office in November of 2002. Although he is clearly the group's leader, his ability to significantly alter party policy—and thus the future course of the country—is likely to be inhibited by the presence on the committee of so many close allies of outgoing party leader Jiang Zemin. A technocrat by training, Hu is seen by many China observers as a champion of the country's poor, in contrast to his predecessor who focused much of his time and energy on working for the interests of China's growing middle class.

Another major question mark hanging over Hu's administration is the future direction of China's policy toward the United States. In a February of 2002 assessment of China's prospective new leader, John Tkacik of the Heritage Foundation's Asian Studies Center wrote, "For a man destined to be China's supreme leader, he has rarely dealt with U.S. issues. In the past, he has complained of Cold War 'hegemony' and has voiced suspicion of American power. In 1994 a Hong Kong journal reported that Hu told a secret party meeting that 'strangling China's development' was 'a strategic principle pursued by the United States.' And one pseudonymous Chinese scholar reports that after the NATO bombing of the Chinese Embassy in Belgrade in spring 1999, Hu told a closed–door conference of party and government workers that 'the hostile forces in the United States will never give up its attempt to subjugate China.'"

One of the first big challenges faced by Hu was the epidemic of the potentially deadly viral infection known as severe acute respiratory syndrome (SARS), believed to have originated in China. In June of 2003, according to Agence France Presse, Hu told reporters, "The Chinese people are full of confidence and determination ... to bring this epidemic under proper control and we are sure mankind will be victorious over the epidemic." By the end of that month, the World Health Organization dropped Beijing—the last of the Chinese cities hard hit by SARS—from its health–related travel advisories. Although the Chinese government came under fire for its early failure to fully disclose the full extent of its SARS outbreak, it appeared that the measures taken to halt the spread of SARS had been successful.

The eldest of three children, Hu was born in Shanghai in December of 1942. His family, which previously had enjoyed prosperity in the tea trade, had fallen on hard times, undoubtedly exacerbated by the ever–tightening Japanese occupation of China's largest city. The family's chain of tea shops, which once were found in cities throughout several of the country's coastal provinces, had been reduced to a single outlet in Shanghai by the time of Hu's birth. While he was still an infant, the family moved from Shanghai to Taizhou county in Jiangsu Province, where Hu grew up and attended high school.

In 1959 Hu was granted admission to China's prestigious Tsinghua University in Beijing. A promising scholar and the youngest student in his class, Hu specialized in hydropower generation in the school's hydraulic engineering department and eventually earned his degree in hydraulic engineering. Early in his college career, he was identified as a potential leader by senior members of the school's party organization and groomed for eventual membership in the party. He also developed a close relationship with Tsinghua President Jiang Nanxiang, who maintained close ties with local leaders in Beijing and the Central Committee of the Chinese Communist Party. With Jiang's approval Hu was accepted into the party on a probationary basis in April of 1964. He had already completed his studies at Tsinghua and had stayed on as a political assistant. With his elevation to probationary status, Hu was appointed a researcher at the university and also became a political instructor. He attained full party membership in 1965. During his years at Tsinghua Hu met and married a young woman named Liu Yongqing. The couple has two grown children.

Hu was still a political instructor at Tsinghua University when China's Cultural Revolution began in the fall of 1966. For the next two years the Chinese capital—particularly its institutions of higher learning—was torn by civil strife between thousands of college students of the so–called Heaven Faction and others in the Earth Faction. Caught up in the struggle, Hu was eventually denounced for his role in the civil turmoil and banished, along with thousands of others—students and instructors as well—to the hinterlands.

Hu, sent to the poverty–stricken, desert province of Gansu, was selected to work on the Gansu Liujiaxia Power Station project because of his background in hydropower engineering. After serving for a year as a laborer on the power station project, he was assigned to another local project managed by the national government's Ministry of Water Resources and Electric Power. He quickly rose through the ranks to a party position with some clout. Transferred in 1974 to work as a secretary and deputy chief of the Gansu Provincial Construction Commission's Project Design Management Division, Hu soon came to the attention of provincial party chief Song Ping, an ultra–conservative revolutionary. It was at Song's recommendation that Hu in 1980 was accepted into the Central Party School in Beijing in 1980. While attending Beijing classes for cadre leaders, Hu was named by Song to serve as deputy secretary of the Gansu Provincial Communist Youth League (CYL).

In 1982, Song managed to win for Hu an appointment to the secretariat of the national CYL. Hu also became president of the All–China Youth Federation. By the end of 1984, Hu had advanced to the top post in the CYL secretariat. His involvement in the CYL soon brought Hu into close contact with Hu Yaobang, a pioneering revolutionary who at the time was seeking to promote both economic reforms and great political openness. For his support of the elder Hu's goals, which brought him into conflict with some factions within the CYL, Hu was rescued from possible repercussions and further entanglements in Beijing by being named provincial party committee secretary in Guizhou province.

As he had during his years of service in Gansu, Hu made it his business to familiarize himself with the land and people of the new province to which he had been assigned. He eventually visited virtually every corner of the Guizhou. During his very first month in the province, Hu embarked on an eleven–day tour that brought him to some of Guizhou's more remote counties. As he traveled, Hu frequently dropped into the homes of local residents to inquire into the problems of day–to–day life they found most pressing. Fred Hu, who is unrelated but knew Hu Jintao while the latter was a student at Tsinghua, told *Time* of a visit made to the Guizhou home of a former classmate. Although his friend was out at the time, Hu spent a couple of hours drinking tea and speaking with the classmate's parents. "Only after he left did the parents slowly realize that he was the new party secretary," Fred Hu said.

It was in Guizhou that Hu first provided a clue as to his policies for dealing with dissent. When student demonstrators at Guizhou University, in a burst of pro–democracy fervor, seized the school's main lecture hall in late 1986, Hu rejected a hard–line approach and instead visited the campus personally to persuade students to end their protest. Writer Ge Shiru, who witnessed the events, told *Time* that Hu "did a beautiful job winning over the students by treating them as equals." Hu's masterful handling of the Guizhou crisis helped win for him in December of 1988 an appointment as party secretary for the Tibet Autonomous Region.

For some years Tibetans had enjoyed a degree of cultural freedom, but it was not enough to satisfy the mountainous region's people who continued to press for independence. Only three months after taking the party's reins in Tibet, Hu found himself faced with another political crisis when a group of monks demonstrated in the streets of Lhasa with homemade Tibetan flags. This time, the crisis was not handled nearly as well as had been the case in Guizhou. Government police fired upon the demonstrators, setting off even more widespread civil unrest, which forced Beijing to declare martial law. Approximately 70 Tibetans were killed in the riots that followed. Although Hu remained the nominal party chief in Tibet for the next three years, he spent most of his time in Beijing and not Lhasa.

Despite the unfortunate outcome of the political standoff in Tibet, Hu managed to stay in the good graces of the country's top leaders. In 1992 Deng Xiaoping, who had resigned most of his official posts but remained one of the most powerful figures in China, brought Hu into the politburo's seven–member Standing Committee. Most observers believed that Hu, the youngest member on the committee, had been selected to be groomed as a successor to Jiang Zemin. Only a year later Hu was given control of the Central Party School, where he moved the focus away from old–line Marxist orthodoxy to the consideration of fresh new ideas, including political reform.

Chinese liberal intellectuals developed nicknames for each of the seven members of the politburo's Standing Committee. According to Yao Jin in a *China Brief* article, Hu was nicknamed "sunzi," which literally means "grandson" but is often used to denote "yes–man." Hu, the youngest man on the committee, was frequently assigned thankless tasks by Jiang as a test of the younger man's loyalty. One such assignment was briefing party workers on the implications of the NATO bombing of the Chinese embassy in Belgrade in the spring of 1999. In another thorny task, Hu was assigned by Jiang in 2001 to counter hardliners' attacks on Jiang's proposal to open the party to capitalists. Walking a fine line in order to avoid infuriating either conservatives or reformists, Hu temporarily suspended two left–wing publications for "rectification" (according to Yao) but declined to close them down altogether. He also warned the rest of the nation's media not to publish future articles critical of Jiang's policy change.

Hu's ability to deal quickly and efficiently with the tasks assigned him by Jiang as well as his stewardship of the Central Party School accelerated his rise to the very top ranks of China's leadership. In March of 1998 Hu was named state vice president by Jiang, who also took pains to point out that while Hu had proven his ability to quiet political turmoil, particularly from the party's left wing, former premier Li Peng had shown an equal ability to put down turmoil from the right. Jiang thus set up a power struggle between Hu as leader of the party's reform movement and Li as its leading hardliner. In the end, the reformers prevailed, lifting Hu to the highest office in the land in 2003.

Considering his dramatic rise to the top of China's Communist Party and government, Hu has ruffled relatively few feathers in the process. His ability to keep almost everyone happy may well be attributed to the deliberately low profile he's assigned to his own political philosophy, only fragments of which have been subtly hinted. As Yao observed in the *China Brief* article, "A Chinese saying best describes the risk of showing one's clear political or ideological leanings: 'The bird that sticks its head out gets shot.'" Hu Jintao ... has been careful enough to act as 'a bird that keeps its head down.'"

Sources

Books

Complete Marquis Who's Who, Marquis Who's Who, 2003.

Periodicals

Agence France Presse, June 3, 2003.
Business Asia, February 2003, p. 28.
China Brief, November 21, 2001; January 14, 2003, p. 3.
Economist, March 1, 2003.
Fortune, November 11, 2002, p. 155.
Newsweek, November 25, 2002, p. 36; December 30, 2002/January 6, 2003, p. 76.
Time International, April 22, 2002, p. 14.
U.S. News & World Report, November 25, 2002, p. 14.

Online

"Background Information on Hu Jintao," International Campaign for Tibet, http://www.savetibet.org/news/NewsPrint.cfm?ID=981&c=27 (June 24, 2003).

"Hu Jintao," People's Daily, http://english.people daily.com.cn/data/people/hujintao.shtml (June 24, 2003).
"Profile: Hu Jintao," BBC News, http://news.bbc.co.uk/2/hi/asia–pacific/2404129.stm (June 24, 2003).
"Heritage Lectures: Who's Hu? Assessing China's Heir Apparent, Hu Jintao," Heritage Foundation, http://www.heritage.org/Research/AsiaandthePacific/HL739.cfm (June 24, 2003).

Transcripts

Morning Edition, National Public Radio, November 15, 2002; March 19, 2003.

—Don Amerman

Hugh Jackman

Actor

Born October 10, 1968, in Sydney, New South Wales, Australia; son of Chris Jackman (an accountant); married Deborra–Lee Furness (an actress), February, 1996; children: Oscar Maximilan. *Education*: Studied journalism at the University of Technology, Sydney; attended Actor's Centre, Sydney; theater diploma from the West Australian Academy of Performing Arts, 1994.

Addresses: *Agent*—Creative Artists Agency, 9830 Wilshire Blvd., Beverly Hills, CA 90212–1825.

Career

Actor in films, including: *Paperback Hero*, 1999; *Erskineville Kings*, 1999; *X–Men*, 2000; *Someone Like You*, 2001; *Swordfish*, 2001; *Kate and Leopold*, 2001; *X2: X–Men United*, 2003; *Standing Room Only*, 2004; *Van Helsing*, 2004. Television appearances include: *Law of the Land*, 1995; *Blue Heelers*, 1995; *Corelli*, 1995; *Snowy River: The McGregor Saga*, 1996; *Halifax f.p.: Afraid of the Dark* (movie), 1998; *Making the Grade* (movie), 2004. Stage appearances include: *Beauty and the Beast*, 1995–96; *Sunset Boulevard*, Melbourne, Australia, 1996; *Oklahoma!*, National Theatre, London, England, 1998; *The Boy From Oz*, Imperial Theater, New York City, 2003. Host of the Antoinette Perry (Tony) Awards ceremony, 2003, 2004.

Awards: Named Star of the Year in Australia, 1999; Astaire award for best male dancer, Theatre Development Fund, 2004; Antoinette Perry (Tony) award for best actor in a musical, League of American Theaters and Producers and the American Theatre Wing, for *The Boy From Oz*, 2004.

Sidelights

Actor Hugh Jackman followed fellow Australians Mel Gibson and Russell Crowe into Hollywood stardom and a top ranking as the big screen's newest romantic hero. A versatile performer, his roles have ranged from the cowboy Curly in the popular stage musical *Oklahoma!* to Wolverine, the mutant hero of the *X–Men* films. In 2003, he made a surprising move by signing on to play the lead in a Broadway musical for a year's run. In *The Boy from Oz*, Jackman starred as the late singer/songwriter Peter Allen, the Australian once married to Liza Minnelli and known for penning a raft of treacly pop tunes. *Entertainment Weekly*'s Benjamin Svetkey noted that Jackman, though a talented singer and dancer, headed toward potential "careericide" by taking the *Oz* part, but "it turned out to be a shockingly smart choice," Svetkey asserted. "Jackman's performance in *Oz* has wowed critics even if the show hasn't and made him a rare bright light in a rocky Broadway season."

Jackman was born in 1968 in Sydney, Australia, the last of five children in a family that had emigrated from England just a year before he was born. When he was eight years old, his mother left and returned to England, informing Jackman's father, an accountant, by telegram of her whereabouts. Jackman credits his father for holding the family together after the devastating event. "He, more than anyone, has instilled in me a sense of pride and dedication," the actor told *Weekend Australian*'s Bryce Hallett. "When Mum left, Dad did the week's shopping every Saturday morning and learned to become a fine cook. All the family are big achievers."

Jackman attended a private school in Sydney where the uniform for boys included a kilt. Gangly during much of his adolescent years, he bore the nickname "Worm" for it, but he was also an extrovert and skilled rugby player. He entered the journalism program at the University of Technology in Sydney, but as he told Bruce Wilson in a *Sunday Herald Sun* interview, "my heart wasn't in it. I thought, it's damned hard to get a job, and when you do get a job there's going to be bits of it you don't like.... And so I went for acting, where it is probably ten times harder to get a job." One early low point in his career was a job with the National Parks and Wildlife Foundation in Australia, which required dressing up in a giant koala suit and handing out leaflets. "I lost track of how many times I passed out," he recalled in an *Entertainment Weekly* interview.

Already involved in community theater, Jackman left journalism school early to enroll in a one–year course at the Actor's Centre in Sydney. The instructors at the school initially disliked him, he confessed to Belinda Luscombe in a *Time* article. "They admitted it later, after they were my friends," said Jackman. "I was very clean–cut, hammy and let's–put–on–a–show. They were very Beckett and Chekhov." He then landed a place at the West Australian Academy of Performing Arts in Perth, but was offered a part in a in hugely successful Australian soap opera, *Neighbours,* that same week. *Neighbours* had provided breakout roles for Russell Crowe, Kylie Minogue, Guy Pearce, and Natalie Imbruglia, among many others, but Jackman turned down the part.

By the time he finished the Academy in 1994, Jackman already had an agent by then, thanks to a job at a Melbourne fitness club he had taken to help pay the bills. The wife of cinematographer Dean Semler (*Bruce Almighty, Dances With Wolves*) was a client of the gym, and one day she told Jackman, "'I'm a white witch,'" Jackman recalled her saying, as he told *Los Angeles Magazine* writer Margot Dougherty, "'and you're going to be a big star.'" The Semlers helped him find an agent, which led to a role in an Australian television series, *Corelli,* in

1995. From there he landed the lead in Disney's *Beauty and the Beast* stage musical in Australia, though producers were initially wary of his inexperience and would not even let him audition at first.

Jackman's impressive talents, however, caught the attention of renowned stage director Trevor Nunn, who cast him as the lead in the musical *Sunset Boulevard,* the 1950 film classic adapted for the stage by Andrew Lloyd Webber. Jackman played the part in Melbourne in 1996, and went on to roles in two Aussie films, *Paperback Hero* and *Erskineville Kings.* Landing the part of Curly in the London revival of *Oklahoma!* in 1998 would make him a star on a more international stage. The classic American musical enjoyed an impressive run at London's National Theatre, with Queen Elizabeth II in attendance once. More importantly, a largely female contingent of journalists from Britain's print media wrote enthusiastically about Jackman, his acting abilities, and his heartthrob looks. *New Statesman* reviewer Kate Kellaway called him "intoxicating to watch," while others tagged him as Down Under's next important export and musical theater's newest star.

Jackman and his wife, actress Deborra–Lee Furness—whom he had met on the set of *Corelli*—had only recently relocated to Los Angeles when he won the lead in the much–anticipated *X–Men* movie, the big–screen adaptation of the cult Marvel Comics series. Jackman was cast as the furry, sharp–clawed mutant Wolverine, and the part effectively launched him Stateside. He co–starred with Patrick Stewart, Ian McKellen, Famke Janssen, and Halle Berry, but Jackman's character had little dialogue, and so he prepared for the role by watching the Clint Eastwood *Dirty Harry* movies and Mel Gibson's post–apocalyptic hero in *Road Warrior,* as he told Melbourne *Herald Sun* journalist Nui Te Koha. "Here were guys who had relatively little dialogue, like Wolverine had, but you knew and felt everything," Jackman said. "I'm not normally one to copy, but I wanted to see how those guys achieved it because I'm relatively inexperienced on the big screen."

X–Men was a box–office hit in the summer of 2000, and Jackman earned high marks from *New York Times* critic Elvis Mitchell in an otherwise negative review. "Wolverine, well played by Mr. Jackman, is perhaps the only other semi–rounded character who animates the picture besides Xavier and Magneto," Mitchell noted, mentioning the Stewart and McKellen roles. "He lives to fight, a boisterous tragic hero without complication." The star turn in *X–Men,* twinned with Jackman's lanky good looks, suddenly made him hot box–office property in Hollywood. Casting directors were eager to put him in romantic comedies or action films as the dashing hero, and he covered up his Australian accent convincingly to play opposite Ashley Judd in *Someone Like You* in 2001, based on the Laura Zigman book *Animal Husbandry.*

Jackman went on to play a computer hacker in a little–seen heist film, *Swordfish,* alongside John Travolta, and then delivered the accent of a nineteenth–century British aristocrat in *Kate and Leopold,* the third film of his released in 2001. A cute Meg Ryan vehicle largely dismissed by critics, *Kate and Leopold* nevertheless helped boost Jackman's profile immensely. Reviewing it for the *New York Times,* Stephen Holden noted that the actor "lends Leopold's haughty pronouncements enough good humor to keep his character from turning into an insufferable twit."

Jackman admitted to one misstep along the lightning–fast trajectory of his career: turning down the lead that later went to Richard Gere in the movie version of the musical *Chicago.* "I just felt I was too young for the part," he told Svetkey in *Entertainment Weekly.* Instead he reprised Wolverine for *X2: X–Men United,* in 2003, which earned more laudatory reviews than the first. *Time*'s Richard Corliss found it a longer, more complex film, and "Jackman, on the verge of stardom for three years, grows ever more appealing."

The buzz surrounding Jackman continued to grow: *Entertainment Weekly* termed him the new "It" leading man of 2003, while *Elle*'s Jesse Green asserted "his is an unusually virile kind of charm—part beefcake, part heartbreak." Having conquered Hollywood, Jackman was surprised to win over New York as well: after a successful one–nighter as host of the 2003 Antoinette Perry Awards—the ceremony better known as the Tonys, which honors Broadway's best shows and stars of the past season—Jackman was approached to take the lead in a big–budgeted stage production that would be the first Australian musical to make it to Broadway, *The Boy From Oz.*

Oz was a daring role for any actor. It was based on the life of flamboyant singer–songwriter Peter Allen, who died of AIDS–related complications in 1992, and its title was a play on the slang term for Australia as well as Allen's link to *Wizard of Oz* star Judy Garland. Born into an impoverished rural family, Allen became a popular entertainer in Australia before Garland discovered him singing in a Hong Kong hotel in 1964. Though he was bisexual, Allen was briefly married to Garland's daughter Liza Min-

nelli for a time in the early 1970s. He wrote a number of popular tunes that were featured in *The Boy From Oz,* including "Don't Cry Out Loud" and "I Go to Rio," his signature song, which he often performed with maracas and a balloon–sleeved shirt on 1970s–era television variety programs.

Jackman was signed to sing and dance through *The Boy from Oz* for a one–year run, a rather unusual move for a film actor, whose agents consider such long–term commitments inadvisable. While the Broadway show earned mixed critical assessments, it broke box–office records at the Imperial Theater. Reviewers termed it fatuous at best, but most gave high marks to Jackman. Hilton Als of the *New Yorker* termed him "a charming, wildly hardworking performer," but one who "has been put in the awkward position of having to prove that Allen is worthy of our attention." Writing in *Entertainment Weekly,* Lawrence Frascella called it a "sexy, ingratiating performance.... Forget Wolverine. This slim, loose–limbed Jackman bumps and grinds his way across the stage, winks flirtatiously at the balcony, and endlessly flashes his irresistible smile. Even more surprisingly, he possesses a big, throaty Broadway voice, which serves him best during Allen's bombastic ballads."

Though Jackman was often seen around New York with his wife and toddler son, Oscar, in tow, rumors arose that he was gay because of the *Oz* role, which amused him greatly. He was also tagged in the press as the epitome of the "metrosexual"—the urbane, well–groomed urban male. *People* named him one of its 50 Most Beautiful People in 2004.

His next film roles included *Standing Room Only* and *Van Helsing.* The latter was predicted to become the summer of 2004's must–see movie and perhaps even revive the entire monster–movie genre from Hollywood's golden era of the 1930s and '40s. Jackman was cast as the titular Roman Catholic priest who moonlights as a vampire slayer. *Van Helsing* was loosely based on a character from the 1897 Bram Stoker novel *Dracula,* and also featured a wolfman and Frankenstein. Director Stephen Sommers (*The Mummy*) cast Jackman because, "I needed a man for the part, not a boy," he told *Entertainment Weekly.* "And the only guys out there are either in their 20s or cost $15 million. Ewan McGregor and Viggo Mortensen were the only other possibilities, but they already have their big swashbuckling franchises."

In 2004, Jackman hosted the Tony Awards for the second year in a row. He won a Tony that year for best actor in a musical for his role in *The Boy From*

Oz. Rumors also arose that Jackman might take the lead in Darren Aronofsky's *The Fountain,* or become the next James Bond. In an interview with the *Herald Sun,* Jackman was cavalier about his future. "I'm the same as anyone else in the audience," he told journalist Simon Ferguson. "I get sick of seeing the same faces after a while and I know that this amazing run of roles I've been getting will one day just grind to a halt and nobody will want to know me for ages."

Sources

Books

Contemporary Theatre, Film, and Television, vol. 28, Gale Group, 2000.

Periodicals

Daily Variety, May 20, 2003, p. 1.
Elle, September 2003, p. 252.
Entertainment Weekly, November 16, 2001, p. 98; May 9, 2003, p. 49; June 27/July 4, 2003, pp. 26–29; October 24, 2003, p. 114; March 26, 2004, p. 22.

Herald Sun (Melbourne, Australia), June 13, 1998, p. 4; June 30, 2001, p. W4.
Independent Sunday (London, England), July 19, 1998, p. 7.
InStyle, December 1, 2001, p. 193.
Interview, September 2003, p. 170.
Los Angeles Magazine, August 2000, p. 38.
New Statesman, July 24, 1998, p. 41.
Newsweek, June 18, 2001, p. 53.
Newsweek International, March 25, 2002, p. 68.
New Yorker, October 27, 2003, p. 108.
New York Times, July 14, 2000; March 30, 2001; December 25, 2001; May 2, 2003; October 17, 2003; October 27, 2003, p. E1.
People, May 14, 2001, p. 95; May 13, 2002, p. 89; June 9, 2003, p. 22; December 1, 2003, p. 88.
Sunday Herald Sun (Melbourne, Australia), March 21, 1999, p. 14.
Time, May 5, 2003, p. 79; October 20, 2003, p. 72.
Time International, June 9, 2003, p. 66.
United Press International, December 3, 2003.
Weekend Australian (Sydney, Australia), October 26, 1996, p. R10.

—Carol Brennan

Peter Jackson

Film director and screenwriter

Born October 31, 1961, in Pukerua Bay, North Island, New Zealand; son of Bill (a civil servant) and Joan Jackson; companion of Frances Walsh; children: Billy, Katie.

Addresses: *Agent*—United Talent Agency, 9560 Wilshire Blvd., #500, Beverly Hills, CA 90212. *Home*—Karaka Bay, New Zealand.

Career

Made amateur fiction shorts, including *The Dwarf Patrol, Curse of the Gravewalker,* and *The Valley.* Worked as a newspaper photo engraver, *Evening Post,* Wellington; named top New Zealand photo–engraving apprentice three years running; started making feature film *Roast of the Day* on weekends with friends and colleagues; renamed *Bad Taste,* film was completed after funding received from New Zealand Film Commission, 1986; set up own studio, Wingnut Films, in Wellington, with computer–driven special effects division, WETA; purchased National Film Unit, New Zealand, 1998. Film work: director, producer, cinematographer, special effects and makeup effects, and editor (with Jamie Selkirk), *Bad Taste,* 1988; director, producer, camera operator, and puppet maker, *Meet the Feebles,* 1989; second assistant director, *Ted and Venus,* 1991; director and stop motion animator, *Braindead,* 1991; assistant director, *Deadly Bet,* 1992; stunt double, *Grampire,* 1992; associate producer, production manager, and first assistant director, *Married People Single Sex,* 1993; producer (with Jim Booth and Hanno Huth) and director, *Heavenly Creatures,* 1994; associate producer (with Willie Boudevin and Helen

Haxton) *Night Fire,* 1994; executive producer and second unit director, *Jack Brown, Genius,* 1995; co–writer and director, *Forgotten Silver,* 1995; director and producer, *The Frighteners,* 1996; special effects, *Contact,* 1997; co–producer and director, *The Lord of the Rings: The Fellowship of the Ring,* 2001; director, *The Lord of the Rings: The Two Towers,* 2002; director, *The Lord of the Rings: The Return of the King,* 2003. Film appearances include: *Bad Taste,* 1988; *Braindead,* 1991; *The Last Dance,* 1993; *Heavenly Creatures* (uncredited), 1994; *Forgotten Silver,* 1996; *The Frighteners* (uncredited), 1996. Television cinematographer, including: *Romance on the Orient Express,* 1985; "Cloud Waltzing," *Harlequin Romance Movie,* Showtime, 1987; "Out of the Shadows," *Harlequin Romance Movie,* Showtime, 1988; *The Attic: The Hiding of Anne Frank,* 1988.

Awards: Film Award for best screenplay, for *Braindead,* 1993; New Zealand Film and TV Awards, for *Braindead,* 1993; International Fantasy Film Award for best film, for *Braindead,* 1993; Silver Scream Award, for *Braindead,* 1993; Amsterdam Fantastic Film Festival, for *Braindead,* 1993; Grand Prize, Avoriaz Fantastic Film Festival, for *Braindead,* 1993; Silver Lion Award, Toronto International Film Festival, for *Heavenly Creatures,* 1994; Metro Media Award, Toronto International Film Festival, for *Heavenly Creatures,* 1994; Film Award for best director,

New Zealand Film and TV Awards, for *Heavenly Creatures,* 1995; Grand Prize, Gerardmer Film Festival, for *Heavenly Creatures,* 1995; ALFS Award for director of the year, London Critics Circle Film Awards, for *Heavenly Creatures,* 1996; TV Award for best director, New Zealand Film and TV Awards, for *Forgotten Silver,* 1996; Audience Jury Award, Fantasporto, for *Forgotten Silver,* 1997; KCFCC Award for best director, for *The Lord of the Rings: The Fellowship of the Ring,* 2001; AFI Film Award (with others), for *The Lord of the Rings: The Fellowship of the Ring,* 2002; Saturn Award for best direction, for *The Lord of the Rings: The Fellowship of the Ring,* 2002; British Academy of Film and Television Artists Award for best film, for *The Lord of the Rings: The Fellowship of the Ring,* 2002; David Lean Award for Direction, for *The Lord of the Rings: The Fellowship of the Ring,* 2002; Bodil Award for best American film, for *The Lord of the Rings: The Fellowship of the Ring,* 2002; Sierra Award for best director, for *The Lord of the Rings: The Fellowship of the Ring,* 2002; Companion of the New Zealand Order of Merit, 2002; honorary degree, Wellington Massey University, 2002; New York Film Critics' Circle Award for best film, for *The Lord of the Rings: The Return of the King,* 2003; Critics' Choice Award for best picture, Broadcast Film Critics Association, for *The Lord of the Rings: The Return of the King,* 2004; Critics' Choice Award for best director, Broadcast Film Critics Association, for *The Lord of the Rings: The Return of the King,* 2004; Critics Award for best director, Los Angeles Film Critics Association, 2004; Golden Globe for best director in a motion picture, Hollywood Foreign Press Association, for *The Lord of the Rings: The Return of the King,* 2004; Golden Globe for best picture (drama), Hollywood Foreign Press Association, for *The Lord of the Rings: The Return of the King,* 2004; Modern Master Award, Santa Barbara Film Festival, 2004; best director, Directors Guild of America, for *The Lord of the Rings: The Return of the King,* 2004; best international film, Directors Guild of Great Britain, for *The Lord of the Rings: The Return of the King,* 2004; Academy Awards for best writing (adapted screenplay), best director, and best picture for *The Lord of the Rings: The Return of the King,* 2004.

Sidelights

"If you were entrusting $270 million to someone making three movies, you wouldn't choose me," quipped New Zealand director and writer Peter Jackson, to Melissa J. Perenson on *Scifi.com.* But that is exactly what New Line Cinema did when it chose Jackson to direct its lavish production of author J. R. R. Tolkien's *Lord of the Rings,* a seven–hour marathon that is divided into three separate movies released a year apart. Jackson, known as a specialist in what he calls "splatstick"—the comic horror film—was hardly known for flights of Tolkien–like fantasy up to that time. His debut feature, *Bad Taste,* was a sci–fi comedy about aliens who harvest Earth folk for fast–food dining, and was "awash with vomit and blood," according to BBC.com. That cult classic attracted viewers to his next films, a gory zombie comedy, *Braindead,* and an off–the–wall horror parody, *Meet the Feebles,* that has been likened to "the Muppet show on drugs," according to BBC.com.

Though Jackson earned a certain celebrity from such features, he was still an outsider to mainstream filmmaking in two ways: because of his interest in a genre that had seemingly peaked in popularity and because he continued to produce films in his home country. His breakthrough, however, came with the 1994 critically acclaimed *Heavenly Creatures,* starring a then–unknown Kate Winslet in a story about a New Zealand murder case. Oscar nominations for Jackson and his screenwriting and life partner, Frances Walsh, brought him to the attention of studio heads in Hollywood.

However, even Jackson was surprised when he got the nod for *The Lord of the Rings.* The move from small–scale productions to a mega–production like *Titanic* and *Gone with the Wind* was a big step. Yet after 15 months of filming on location in New Zealand, Jackson produced a popular box–office hit as well as a critical success with the release of the first part of the trilogy, *Lord of the Rings: The Fellowship of the Ring,* in 2001. As Dade Hayes noted in *Variety,* Jackson proved that "he is the best director in the contemporary lead–the–troops sense of the word." Jackson told Paul Fischer of the *iofilm* website that he is not a Tolkien addict, but rather a fantasy fan. "I've not had a lifelong ambition to make *The Lord of the Rings,* which is what a lot of people are sort of assuming that I've had.... I've had a lifelong passion to make a fantasy adventure film, because when I was younger I loved Ray Harryhausen's movies, as well as stuff like *Jason and the Argonauts,* and the original *King Kong.* I've always had a desire to make one of those fantasy adventure type of films, and they don't do those movies much any more."

Born in Pukerua Bay, just west of Wellington, New Zealand, in 1961, Jackson was raised on a television diet that included *Monty Python's Flying Circus, Batman,* and a British science–fiction program featuring marionettes called *Thunderbirds.* At the age of eight, he got his hands on his parents' 8mm camera, and began experimenting with it, shooting his own home movies. His fascination was focused at about age 12 when he saw the original 1933 version of

King Kong and discovered the magazine *Famous Monsters of Filmland.* That year he and a couple of friends dug a hole in the Jacksons' back garden and made a World War II movie, simulating gunshots by making holes in the celluloid next to where the guns were to simulate muzzle flash; it was his first venture into special effects. Jackson left school at 17 hoping to get work in the New Zealand film industry. All he could find initially was a minor acting job in a Swedish movie. To pay the bills, he took a position with the *Evening Post,* a local newspaper, as a photo–engraving apprentice. Employed, he could now afford his own camera and bought a 16mm Bolex in 1983.

Jackson collected a group of friends to help make a movie, initially intended as a ten–minute short film about aliens snacking on humans. Shooting on weekends and holidays, Jackson soon discovered that this short, with the working title *Roast of the Day,* was turning in a feature–length film. He re-titled the film *Bad Taste,* and served as director, editor, actor, and makeup man. This low–budget fare was financed at the outset by Jackson's newspaper salary. Applying to the New Zealand Film Commission for a grant so that he could do post–production work on the movie, Jackson luckily found favor with one of the chairmen, who used discretionary money to help fund the film project. It ultimately took four years to film *Bad Taste,* the story of a government attempt to fight aliens who are eating humans. When it was finally finished, the New Zealand Film Commission was sufficiently pleased with the gory comedy to take it to the Cannes Film Festival, where this movie of excesses met with polar extremes of criticism. Subsequently, the film was sold to 30 countries, quickly paying off its costs. Jackson met his future love and writing partner, Fran Walsh, at a screening for the film. Asked by *Time*'s Jess Cagle what she saw in Jackson, Walsh replied, "I think it was the brain–eating sequence." Walsh shares Jackson's macabre sense of humor.

Bad Taste was the first in a series of comedic horror films from Jackson. In this film, the extra–terrestrials have emptied the tiny New Zealand town of Kaihoro of all its inhabitants, and the government sends its top unit, Astro Investigations and Defense Service, to investigate. Things go from bad to worse as the team discovers the ghoulish reason for ET interest: prepackaging the humans for a galactic fast food chain. Chainsaw and bazooka massacres punctuate this edgy comedy, which pokes fun at the horror genre and at middle class life in New Zealand. The government agents are not the typical good–looking heroes seen in most Hollywood takes on the horror genre. Instead, Jackson's agents are "inept, nerdish, and post–adolescent," according to a

contributor in *International Dictionary of Films and Filmmakers.* The film was nominated for an International Fantasy Film Award for Best Film in 1987 and an Audience Award at the FantaFestival in 1989.

Jackson continued in a similar vein when he made 1989's *Meet the Feebles,* an adult film with a cast of puppets that do drugs, have sex, and even commit mass murder. This film is even more outlandish in its choice of target, taking on the squeaky–clean world of Jim Henson's Muppets. "Hijacking the standard Muppet narrative framework of backstage shenanigans, Jackson gleefully subverts the perky ethos of the puppet troupe with lavish helpings of booze, filth, sex, and drugs, culminating in one of his trademark bloodbaths," wrote a critic for *International Dictionary of Films and Filmmakers.* The film was nominated for an International Fantasy Film Award for Best Film in 1989 and Best Direction at the FantaFestival in 1991.

Jackson's next film was the gore–fest *Braindead* (distributed as *Dead Alive* in the United States), in which a monkey bite turns a New Zealand woman into a zombie. The condition is contagious, and soon the film's hero must try to stop the devastation caused by a growing herd of the undead. *Entertainment Weekly* reviewer Owen Gleiberman noted that Jackson's film "manages to stay breezy and good–natured even as you're watching heads get snapped off of spurting torsos." Regarding the gruesome special effects, Gleiberman perceived that there were "no rules in Jackson's slapstick carnival of gore." A reviewer for *Time* cautioned the prospective viewer to "forget profound," but commended the "good, broad humor amid the very gross gore effects." Film critic Leonard Maltin called the film "astonishing, vigorous, [and] inventively gruesome," in his *Movie and Video Guide.*

"After his first three features, most critics thought they had Peter Jackson neatly pegged," wrote a critic for *International Dictionary of Films and Filmmakers:* "an antipodean maverick whose films made up for their zero–budget limitations with comic gusto, and creative ingenuity; films ... [with] gross-out excesses of spurting bodily fluids and splattered guts." This fascination with outrage, with the consequences of pushing beyond the bounds of convention, carries through into 1994's *Heavenly Creatures.* Based on an infamous New Zealand murder in the 1950s, the Parker–Hulme case, the film traces the progress of two 15–year–old schoolgirls into an increasingly unhinged world of ritual and fantasy. Pauline and Juliet are loners who bond together to turn their outsider status into an exclusive, closed society that has overtones of lesbianism. They are attracted to certain famous people—actors Mario Lanza and James Mason—turning them into icons of their friendship, and develop a medieval fantasy kingdom of Borovnia. Drawing on real case documents (Pauline's diaries and the girls' own Borovnian "novels"), Jackson creates a mood of intense pubescent obsession sliding steadily out of control until—as the borders between the two worlds collide—it culminates in brutal murder.

Jackson was determined not to present his heroines as the "evil lesbian killers" they were called in the press of the day, portraying them instead with sympathy and insight. In doing so, he captures the creative energy of their shared fantasies, a reaction to the sterile society around them. Jackson's depiction of 1950s Christchurch in garish pastels peopled by shallow gentility, appears as perhaps a more bizarre and unbalanced world than the one the girls create for themselves. However, the killing—of Pauline's well-meaning but bumbling mother when the girls believe they are going to be separated from one another—is done with none of the sick humor of Jackson's previous films, but rather is shown as clumsy, painful, and horrific in the true sense of the word. The film was a stylistic departure for Jackson that earned him international recognition. His screenplay—written with Walsh, with whom he has two children—was nominated for an Academy Award for Best Original Screenplay; the film also won awards at film festivals in Venice and Toronto. Writing in *Film Comment,* Michael Atkinson declared *Heavenly Creatures* "a masterpiece that ... marks a quantum leap from the crude emotional syntax of zombie comedies."

As co-writer (with Costa Botes) and director of 1995's *Forgotten Silver,* Jackson turned in another piece of quirky filmmaking. This time, he crafted a careful mock documentary that purports to tell the story of a New Zealand filmmaker named Colin McKenzie. Supposedly, McKenzie was not only the creator of the silent film classic *Salome,* but was responsible for numerous film "firsts," including the first tracking shot, the first feature-length film, and the first color film. Reportedly, the technological and stylistic deftness of the production left many New Zealanders, who were the first to see the production on television, convinced that it was a real documentary.

Stanley Kauffmann, reviewing *Forgotten Silver* for *New Republic,* was not surprised by the deceptive effect of the film and noted, "New Zealand, with only three and a half million people, has inched slowly into the world's film consciousness, and it's against the smallness of its film history that the sly

joke of *Forgotten Silver* really registers." Jacqui Sadashige, writing in the *American Historical Review,* put the film into a larger context, however, when she commented that "the dazzling bricolage that is *Forgotten Silver* implicitly laments the loss of an era in which one could actually make history and not merely rewrite it or artfully deploy its remains."

When Jackson made the 1996 film *The Frighteners* for the United States film studio Universal, he returned to the familiar territory of the comic horror film, this time as an independent filmmaker who had clearly entered the big leagues. He had a big-name star in Michael J. Fox and a big-name producer in Robert Zemeckis. The combination resulted in a wacky blend of humor and horror, which he called "*Casper* meets *The Silence of the Lambs*" in an interview with Andy Webster in *Premiere.* In the film, Fox plays a ghost-hunter who is befriended by a trio of helpful ghosts after he survives a car crash that kills his wife; later, however, he is beset by some very evil and violent spirits. Jackson was aided by his own special effects in this movie; he created almost 600 computer graphics shots at his own New Zealand studio, making *The Frighteners* "the first CG movie produced entirely outside Hollywood," according to Anne Thompson in *Entertainment Weekly.* "My natural tendency is to want to deliver the goods," Jackson told Thompson. "To suspend people's disbelief, you want a lot of effects." *Entertainment Weekly* reviewer Ken Tucker perceived the completed film to be a "smart, subtle movie disguised as a dumb, noisy one" and "that rare horror film that actually gets better as it proceeds; this scare machine has a heart and a brain." To the contrary, *People's* Ralph Novak described the film as "lame comedy" and commented, "[it] fails to mine the rich satiric possibilities of America's obsession with the paranormal." The film was nominated for the Best Film Award at the Catalonian International Film Festival in 1996.

Before *The Frighteners* was completed, Jackson had already been enlisted to direct a remake of *King Kong* for Universal; in *Premiere* he remarked, "It's like repaying a debt—I'm doing what I'm doing now because of that film." However, funding for *King Kong* never materialized, and soon Jackson found himself engaged in the most ambitious project of his career.

Jackson was approached as early as 1995—after the success of *Heavenly Creatures*—by Miramax to do another movie. The head of the studio had the rights to Tolkien's *Lord of the Rings* trilogy, and Jackson, along with Walsh and first-time screenwriter Philippa Boyens, worked on the script for a time. At first, Jackson saw the film as a two–part movie, but Miramax wanted only one. New Line Cinema was interested in the project, as well, and felt that there was a possibility for three movies in all, reflecting the trilogy of books themselves. When *King Kong* fell through, Jackson busied himself in earnest with *Lord of the Rings*. "In adapting the screenplay, we were very much aware that we had to make changes to the book," Jackson told Scifi.com's Perenson. "We tried to keep the spirit of the story and the plot, but the details are different." A fantasy classic since its first publication in England in the 1950s, the *Lord of the Rings* novels have captivated more than 100 million readers of all ages in many languages around the world. The trilogy chronicles the quest for the One Ring, which gives the wearer mastery over all. Hobbits, wee folk who love "peace and quiet and good tilled earth," as Tolkien wrote in *The Fellowship of the Ring,* have held this powerful Ring for many years, but now Sauron, the dark lord of Mordor—who created the Ring—wants it back. Frodo, together with a Fellowship that includes his loyal Hobbit friends, Humans, a Wizard, a Dwarf and an Elf, must take the One Ring across Middle–earth to Mount Doom, where it first was forged, and destroy it forever. The members of the Fellowship set out on a long and dangerous journey, attacked on all sides by many strange enemies, and also by the enemy within themselves: the temptation to use the power of the Ring, a power that corrupts all those who employ it.

As with his other movies, Jackson chose to produce this one in New Zealand, and also chose a New Zealand setting to resemble Middle–earth. While Jackson and his collaborators adapted much of the book freely, they took Tolkien "as the bible … in terms of descriptions," as he told Scifi.com's Perenson. Employing models, miniatures, matte paintings, and computer graphics, he enhanced the landscape into the fantasy world of Middle–earth. Painstaking care was taken, for example, in the creation of the hobbit hall at Bilbo Baggins' house. Jackson's crew created two separate scales of that set, exact duplicates of each other except for size, in order to give the illusion of a four–foot–tall hobbit.

Additionally, Jackson determined early on in the project to shoot all three parts of the movie at the same time. "I felt that in order to do the tale's epic nature justice, we had to shoot it as one big story because that's what it is," Jackson explained on *The Lord of the Rings* website. "It's three movies that will take you through three very unique experiences but it all adds up to one unforgettable story." Jackson further commented, "As a director, it has given me an enormous canvas on which to try all sorts of things. The story has so much variety to it. In each

installment there is intimate, heart–wrenching drama, huge battle scenes, intense special effects, sudden changes for the characters, every emotion in the realm." Filmed during a 15–month shoot, the films were given a $270 million budget (which eventually rose to $310 million). Starring Elijah Wood as Frodo, along with Cate Blanchett, Viggo Mortensen, Christopher Lee, Liv Tyler, and Sir Ian McKellen, the first of the three films appeared in December of 2001 to critical acclaim.

David Ansen, reviewing the film in *Newsweek,* confessed he was no Tolkien groupie. "Before I saw *The Lord of the Rings: The Fellowship of the Ring,* I didn't know the difference between an orc and an elf, or what Middle–earth was in the middle of…. I went in to Peter Jackson's movie … with no preconceptions. I came out, three hours later, sorry I'd have to wait a year to see what happens next…. The movie works. It has real passion, real emotion, real terror." *Time* reviewer Richard Corliss noted that Jackson's movie "is not simply a sumptuous illustration of a favorite fable; though faithful in every way to Tolkien it has a vigorous life of its own…. His movie achieves what the best fairy tales do: the creation of an alternate world, plausible and persuasive, where the young—and not only the young—can lose themselves." David Hunter, writing in *Hollywood Reporter,* had similar praise for the film, calling it "masterfully paced and one of those rewarding movies that seems to get better and better as it progresses."

Nominated for 13 Academy Awards, *The Fellowship of the Ring* was an auspicious debut for the trilogy. Jackson, somewhat hobbit–like himself in demeanor, credits the success of the film in part to the sincerity with which it was produced. "Everybody working on the film took the attitude that *The Lord of the Rings* is true," the director told Daniel Steinhart in *Film Journal International.* "Tolkien didn't make it up. It's 7,000 years ago, the records have all been lost, but this is a true story about real people, whether you're a hobbit, a wizard, or an elf. The monsters really lived and existed, and we're just going to present it the way it was. That was our philosophy for everything on the film." The film won Academy Awards for cinematography, makeup, music, and visual effects. Jackson himself was nominated for a Golden Globe for best director and was a BSFC Award runner–up for best director in 2001, and was nominated for a Saturn Award for Best Writing, a DGA Award for outstanding directorial achievement, and an Empire Award in 2002. The film was nominated for a Golden Globe for best picture, drama.

The Fellowship of the Ring was the second–highest–grossing release of 2001, earning $860 million worldwide. Its sequel, *The Lord of the Rings: The Two*

Towers, was released in late 2002 and took a darker turn, with more violence, doom, and an epic battle scene in Helm's Deep. According to *Entertainment Weekly's* Gleiberman, this battle is a "spectacular deathly cataclysm" that is "downright biblical (or, at the very least, virtually so), with a dimension of David–and–Goliath suspense." In this film, Frodo and his best friend, Sam, are forced to split off from the rest of the Fellowship and are guided to Mordor by Gollum, a "creepy creature who has been corrupted by having once possessed the Ring," explained *Time's* Corliss. The film won Academy Awards for sound editing and visual effects. For his work on *The Two Towers,* Jackman (along with Barrie M. Osborne and Walsh) was nominated for an Academy Award and Golden Globe for Best Picture. He was also nominated for a Best Director Golden Globe.

The third film in the trilogy, *The Lord of the Rings: The Return of the King,* opened in 2003. Focusing on the final battle, the forces of good battle the evil army gathered by Saruman, an evil wizard and ally of Sauron. Although the forces of good are outnumbered, they persist with their fight to give Frodo time to complete his quest. "The film is a majestic finish to what may be the greatest sustained piece of entertainment in the history of movies, and the most emotionally rich," declared Steve Vineberg in *Christian Century.* For this film, Jackson won many honors, including a Los Angeles Film Critics Association Award for Best Director, Modern Master Award from the Santa Barbara Film Festival, and a Directors Guild of America Award. The film won a record–tying eleven Oscars. Jackman himself won an Academy Award for Best Directing, Best Picture (with Osborne and Walsh), and Writing (adapted screenplay) (with Walsh and Boyens). He also won a Golden Globe for Best Picture (drama) and Best Director.

The shoot for the trilogy had been exhausting for Jackson. "My brain was shrinking. My imagination was drying up, and that was freaking me out," Jackson told Gilliam Flynn in *Entertainment Weekly.* To recharge, Jackson would watch films such as *Good-Fellas, Saving Private Ryan,* and *JFK.* "These movies are just wonderful examples of verve and imagination. They gave me a slap around the face: 'You know what your job is now—go back and do it,'" he explained to Flynn.

Next on Jackson's horizon was an autobiography he was working on with Brian Sibley. Plus, his dream of directing a remake of *King Kong* was finally coming true. He had signed a "20/20" deal to direct the film, in which he would be paid $20 million for di-

recting, plus 20% of the box office profits. The deal made him one of the highest–paid directors of all time. Jackson was scheduled to start shooting a new version in August of 2004 in New Zealand. The film is set in 1933, like the original, with actors Naomi Watts, Adrien Brody, and Jack Black playing the lead human roles. Jackson was also in negotiations to direct a film adaptation of Alice Sebold's best–selling *The Lovely Bones,* which he would shoot after releasing *King Kong.*

Moving from filming aliens with the munchies to a fantasy in the world of Tolkien to a giant ape were immense leaps, but Jackson's fertile imagination seems to be game for anything. As Jeff Giles concluded in a *Newsweek* profile, "Jackson is a director with a hundred boxes in his brain. There will be time to open every one."

Selected works as screenwriter

(With Tony Hiles and Ken Hammon) *Bad Taste,* Blue Dolphin, 1987.
Meet the Feebles, Wingnut Films, 1989.
(With Stephen Sinclair and Frances Walsh) *Braindead,* Wingnut Productions, 1991; released as *Dead Alive,* Trimark Pictures, 1992.
(With Walsh) *Heavenly Creatures,* Miramax, 1994.
Jack Brown, Genius, Senator Film International, 1995.
(With Costa Botes) *Forgotten Silver,* 1995.
(With Walsh) *The Frighteners,* Universal, 1996.
(With others) *The Lord of the Rings: The Fellowship of the Ring,* New Line, 2001.
(With others) *The Lord of the Rings: The Two Towers,* New Line, 2002.
(With others) *The Lord of the Rings: The Return of the King,* New Line, 2003.

Sources

Books

International Dictionary of Films and Filmmakers, vol. 2, St. James Press, 1996.
Maltin, Leonard, *Leonard Maltin's 1996 Movie and Video Guide,* Signet (New York, NY), 1995, pp. 76, 307.
Tolkien, J. R. R., *The Fellowship of the Ring,* Ballantine Books (New York, NY), 1965, p. 19.

Periodicals

American Historical Review, June 1997, pp. 938–39.
Christian Century, January 2, 2002, p. 35; January 13, 2004, p. 41.

Cineaste, fall 1995, p. 51; summer 2001, p. 55.

Entertainment Weekly, March 5, 1993, pp. 40–41; November 25, 1994, p. 48; March 10, 1995, p. 46; December 8, 1995, pp. 81–82; July 26, 1996, pp. 34–35; August 2, 1996, p. 41; June 12, 1998, p. 84; December 14, 2001, p. 50; February 22, 2002, p. 92; December 13, 2002, p. 55; February 6, 2004, p. 92; April 30, 2004, p. 20; May 17, 2004, p. 38.

Film Comment, May–June 1995, pp. 31–36.

Film Journal International, January 2002, pp. 14–15.

Film Quarterly, fall 1995, pp. 33–38.

Hollywood Reporter, December 4, 2001, pp. 8–9; May 28, 2002, p. 14.

Library Journal, June 1, 2004, p. 138.

Maclean's, January 30, 1995, p. 86; December 17, 2001, p. 44.

New Republic, November 3, 1997, p. 29.

New Statesman, February 10, 1995, p. 39.

Newsweek, December 10, 2001, p. 72, p. 75.

New Yorker, December 24, 2001, pp. 124–27.

New York Review of Books, January 17, 2002, pp. 8–9.

New York Times, September 9, 2001, p. AR40.

People, July 29, 1996, p. 18; December 23, 2002, p. 31.

Premiere, August 1996, pp. 33–37.

Rolling Stone, January 17, 2002, pp. 55–56.

Time, February 8, 1993, p. 83; November 21, 1994, p. 110; December 24, 2001, p. 64; December 31, 2001, p. 139; December 23, 2002, p. 71; December 2, 2004, pp. 84–91.

Variety, October 16, 2000, p. 105; December 10, 2001, p. 31; March 18, 2002, p. 44; January 29, 2004, p. 19; February 2, 2004, p. 40; February 6, 2004, p. A1.

Online

Academy of Motion Picture Arts & Sciences, http://awardsdatabase.oscars.org/ampas_awards/BasicSearchInput.jsp (July 7, 2004).

"Director Peter Jackson Proves to Be the Lord of *The Fellowship of the Ring,*" Scifi.com, http://www.scifi.com/sfw/issue244/interview.html (July 7, 2004).

Golden Globes, http://www.thegoldenglobes.com (July 7, 2004).

"'Hobbit Man' Talks Tolkien," iofilm, http://www.iofilm.co.uk/feats/interviews/p/peter_jackson.shtml (July 7, 2004).

Official Lord of the Rings Site, http://www.lordoftherings.net (July 7, 2004).

"Peter Jackson: King of the Rings," BBC.com, http://news.bbc.co.uk/1/hi/in_depth/uk/2000/newsmakers/1697355.stm (July 7, 2004).

Jesse James

Television host and motorcycle-customizing shop owner

Born Jesse Gregory James in 1969, in Long Beach, CA; son of an antiques dealer; married Karla (divorced); married Janine Lindemulder (an actress), 2002 (divorced, 2004); children: Jesse (son), Chandler (daughter, from first marriage), Sunny (daughter), one stepson (from second marriage).

Education: Attended the University of California—Riverside, c. 1987.

Addresses: *Office*—Discovery Communications, One Discovery Place, Silver Spring, MD 20910–3354.

AP/Wide World Photos

Career

Worked as professional bodyguard for rock bands; founded West Coast Choppers in Long Beach, CA, 1992; first television appearance in *Motorcycle Mania I,* Discovery Channel, 2001; became host of *Monster Garage,* June, 2002; signed endorsement deal with Yoo–Hoo Beverages, 2003.

Sidelights

Jesse James hosts the cult–favorite Discovery Channel series *Monster Garage,* a reality show in which he and his team transform ordinary cars for shockingly inappropriate new uses. *Monster Garage* has had several memorable success stories, including a Chevy Impala that became a fully functioning Zamboni–style ice–resurfacing machine, and the show has garnered a devoted following as well as impressive ratings. James owns his own motorcycle–customizing shop in Long Beach, California, and initially took the television job merely as a fluke. Its success owes much to his frequently displayed sense of the absurd. "Everyone I talked to said I shouldn't do this show, that I'm an idiot," he recalled in an interview with the *Boston Herald*'s Mark A. Perigard, "and that let me know I was on the right track."

Born in 1969, James was a self–professed gearhead as a kid. He was given his first motorbike at age seven, which developed into a passion for motorcycles as a teen, and he became an avid garage tinkerer. Yet the Long Beach native was also a formidable football player, and admitted to being "kicked out of practice once a week for hitting the quarterback too hard" in high school, he told *Men's Fitness* writer Andrew Vontz.

James was indeed named after the infamous American outlaw slain in 1882, with a great–great–grandfather who was a cousin to the first, and he confessed to possessing his own lawless streak for a time in his teens. Caught stealing cars, he spent enough time in a juvenile lockup to straighten out and steer clear of further trouble with the law. He never lost his penchant for being argumentative, however. "I inherited the inability to take crap from anybody," he told *USA Today* writer Elizabeth Kaye McCall about his famous ancestor's legacy. Finding his niche in athletics, he earned a football scholarship for the University of California's Riverside team, but was sidelined by an injury. After some training, he worked as a professional bodyguard for rock bands like Soundgarden, Danzig, and Slayer.

James still loved to tinker, and found his calling in customizing motorcycles. "I never had money, and I always wanted expensive bikes," he explained to McCall in the *USA Today* article. "So I learned how to do it myself. I would build everything. I'd paint everything, build my own motor, and show up with a cool bike, and people couldn't believe it. They were like, 'Yeah—you bought that.'" He eventually opened his own shop in 1992 in Long Beach called West Coast Choppers. Over the next few years the business became immensely successful, with a client list that grew to include basketball player Shaquille O'Neal, actor Keanu Reeves, and rock–rapper Kid Rock. He and his few dozen employees customized bikes for fees that ranged from $50,000 to $250,000.

A producer for the Discovery Channel, Thom Beers, came in one day to have his bike overhauled at James's increasingly well–known shop, and Beers liked his attitude. He suggested a special about custom bikes that would feature James, and *Motorcycle Mania I* aired on the cable channel in 2001 to high ratings. A sequel was equally successful, and Discovery Channel producers then offered James his own show. *Monster Garage* would have a challenge–type concept each week, with James leading a team of fellow gearheads in transforming a mundane car or sport–utility vehicle into an outrageously new vehicle. The show made its debut in June of 2002 with a challenge to modify a Ford Explorer into a working garbage truck via various parts, blowtorches, and sheer ingenuity, and was an immediate hit with viewers.

James and his ever–revolving cast of customizers are given one week to re–tool and re–fit a vehicle, and a budget of just $3,000 with which to do it. *Monster Garage*'s impressive transformations include a Mazda Miata that became a personal watercraft, a BMW Mini–Cooper that emerged as a working snowmobile, and a Chrysler PT Cruiser that found a new life as a tree mulcher. The show's producers rein in some of his more extravagant ideas, James told FOX News network's John Gibson in a broadcast whose transcript was reprinted on America's Intelligence Wire. "Every car would do a wheelie and shoot flames if I had total control," he joked. He also told Gibson that there was no mystery to his team's success in transforming vehicles, crediting it to "just getting over the fear of ... taking a brand new car that's got pretty decent value and, you know, don't be afraid to cut it in half."

Monster Garage regularly scores some of the highest ratings on cable for its Monday–night shows, garnering up to 1.6 million viewers. It spawned a *Mon-*

ster House series that also airs on the Discovery Channel, and provided some of the inspiration for MTV's *Pimp My Ride*. James credits part of the appeal of his series to serving as a welcome antidote to other reality–TV fare. "All the other shows show people at their absolute worst," he told Gibson on the FOX News broadcast. "They're conniving and trying to marry a rich guy and stuff like that. This is the only show that focuses on teamwork, hard work, skills, and, you know, it pays off at the end."

Covered in tattoos, James stands more than six feet in height and packs 200–plus pounds of attitude. He has an endorsement contract with the Yoo–Hoo brand chocolate beverage, and has appeared in a beer commercial with Kid Rock. He hopes to reprise the original *Motorcycle Mania* for a big–screen project featuring himself, Rock, and Metallica singer and guitarist James Hetfield. A participant in celebrity Grand Prix races and long–distance rallies, James remains a gearhead at heart. He collects classic cars, and one of his prizes is a rare 1949 Mercury, the kind driven by James Dean in the cult classic *Rebel Without a Cause*. In December of 2003, James began dating actress Sandra Bullock. His estranged second wife, Janine Lindemulder, gave birth to their daughter, Sunny, on January 1, 2004.

James still lives in Long Beach and runs his custom–bike shop. The success of his show made him unlikely celebrity, and the twice–married father of two finds what he calls the "rock star" treatment somewhat unsettling still. "Part of me really appreciates the attention," he told the *Boston Herald*'s Perigard, "but part of me thinks of all the metal guys, all the craftsmen who came before me and all they did is work and punch a clock and no one gave them a TV show."

Sources

Periodicals

America's Intelligence Wire, March 1, 2003.
Boston Herald, June 21, 2002, p. S39.
Brandweek, October 13, 2003, p. 16.
Daily News (Los Angeles, CA), June 2, 2003, p. U12.
Knight–Ridder/Tribune News Service, May 2, 2003; May 9, 2003.
Men's Fitness, January 2004, p. 62.
People, December 2, 2002, p. 112; April 26, 2004.
USA Today, March 2, 2003.
Welding Design & Fabrication, March 2003, p. 6.

Online

"How 'Monster Garage' Works," Howstuffworks.com, http://entertainment.howstuffworks.com/monster–garage2.htm (April 21, 2004)

—*Carol Brennan*

Diane Johnson

Author

Born Diane Lain, April 28, 1934, in Moline, IL; daughter of Dolph and Frances (Elder) Lain; married B. Lamar Johnson Jr., July, 1953 (divorced); married John Frederic Murray (a professor of medicine), May 31, 1968; children: Kevin, Darcy, Amanda, Simon (from first marriage). *Education:* Attended Stephens College, Columbia, Missouri, 1951–53, A.A. 1953; University of Utah, Salt Lake City, B.A., 1957; University of California, Los Angeles (Woodrow Wilson fellow), M.A., 1966, Ph.D., 1968.

Addresses: *Home*—24 Edith St., San Francisco, CA 94133. *Office*—Department of English, University of California, Davis, CA 95616. *Agent*—Lynn Nesbit, Janklow, & Nesbit, 598 Madison Ave., New York, NY 10022.

Career

Author. University of California at Davis, assistant professor, then professor of English, 1968–87; held Harold and Mildred Strauss Living Stipend from the American Academy of Arts and Letters, 1988–92. Contributor of essays and book reviews to periodicals, including the *New York Times, New York Review of Books, San Francisco Chronicle,* and *Washington Post.*

Member: International PEN.

Awards: American Association of University Women fellowship, 1968; Guggenheim fellowship, 1977–78; Rosenthal Award, American Academy and Institute of Arts and Letters, 1979; Strauss Living award, 1987; *Los Angeles Times* medal, 1994.

Jeffrey Mayer/WireImage.com

Sidelights

In an age when writers tend to be pigeonholed, Diane Johnson remains a difficult author to categorize. Perhaps best known as an essayist and biographer, she got her start as a novelist and continues to write successfully in this vein. She is a teacher and scholar with expertise in nineteenth-century literature, yet she also lent a hand in writing the screenplay for *The Shining,* a popular horror film. And while her initial focus was on women and their problems in society, she has since written sympathetically of a man who faced similar difficulties in *Dashiell Hammett: A Life.* Even her early works, which have been claimed as the province of feminists, were intended to cast a wider net, as Johnson explained to Susan Groag Bell in *Women Writers of the West Coast:* "The kinds of crises, the particular troubles that I assign to my women characters, these are not necessarily meant to be feminist complaints.... In my mind, they may be more metaphysical or general. That sounds awfully pretentious, but I guess what I mean is that I'm not trying to write manifestos about female independence, but human lives."

Like many artists, Johnson sees herself as a craftsperson whose work should be judged on its merits as literature, not—as is often the case with female writers—on moral or extraliterary grounds. In her Pulitzer Prize–nominated collection of book reviews and essays, *Terrorists and Novelists,* Johnson addresses the particular problems faced by female novelists, chiding those male critics who "have not learned to read books by women and imagine them all to be feminist polemics."

Johnson was born and raised in Moline, Illinois. The first child of middle–aged parents, she lived in the same house surrounded by neighboring aunts and uncles until she went away to college at 17. She described herself as a "puny, bookish little child, with thick glasses," and told *Los Angeles Times* reporter Beverly Beyette that she was "the kind of whom you say, 'Let's take her to the library on Saturday.' I was typecast, but I was a type." When she was 19, Johnson married her first husband, then a UCLA medical student, and relocated to the West Coast where she has remained.

Despite her long residence in California, Johnson told *Women Writers'* Bell that "a certain view of life, which I very much obtained from my Illinois childhood, does inform my work. In a couple of my books I have put a middle–western protagonist, always somebody who's displaced like I am, looking at the mess of today. This person remembers an orderly society from which subsequent events have seemed to depart." She maintains that it is the turmoil of modern society, rather than a personal preoccupation with disorder, that leads to the prevalence of violence in her books. "She is not sensational, sentimental, nor simple–minded," suggested *Critique: Studies in Modern Fiction* contributor Marjorie Ryan, who pointed out that Johnson writes in "the satiric–comic–realistic tradition, in a mode that may not appeal to readers nurtured on the personal, subjective, and doctrinaire."

In her early fiction, *Fair Game, Loving Hands at Home,* and *Burning,* Johnson employs "a comic tone" as well as "a central female character who is uncertain about how to conduct her life," according to Judith S. Baughman in the *Dictionary of Literary Biography Yearbook.* In each of these novels, a woman who has ventured outside the boundaries of convention "has a shocking experience which sends her back inside, but only temporarily until another experience … either sends her outside again or changes her whole perspective," *Critique's* Ryan explained.

Much criticism was leveled at Johnson's choice of subject. A Southern California story of disaster, *Burning* was viewed as a genre novel that had been approached in the same fashion many times before.

Though *Newsweek's* Peter Prescott found Johnson "witty and serious," he contended that she "tries to be both at once and doesn't make it. Her book should have been either much funnier, or much grimmer or, failing that, she should have been much better."

Her competence established, Johnson began to attract more serious attention, and her fourth novel, *The Shadow Knows,* was widely reviewed. Originally set in Los Angeles, the story was relocated to Sacramento because, as the author explained to *Women Writers'* Bell, "I decided after the reception of *Burning* that Los Angeles was too loaded a place in the minds of readers." The novel takes its title from an old radio melodrama (which featured the line, "Who knows what evil lurks in the hearts of men? The Shadow knows.") and focuses on one terror–filled week in the life of a young divorcée and mother of four, known simply as N. When someone slashes her tires, leaves a strangled cat on her doorstep, threatens her over the telephone, and beats up her babysitter in the basement laundry room, N. becomes convinced that she is marked for murder. But who is the assailant? Her spiteful former husband? The wife of her married lover? The psychotic woman who used to care for her children? Her jealous friend, Bess, who comes to visit with a hunting knife in her purse? Or, worst of all, is it some nameless stranger, an embodiment of evil she does not even know? N.'s attempt to identify her enemy, and her imaginary dialogue with the Famous Inspector she conjures up to help her, make up the heart of the book.

Writing in the *New Statesman,* A. S. Byatt described the novel as a "cunning cross between the intensely articulate plaint of the under–extended intelligent woman and a conventional mystery, shading into a psychological horror–story." *Nation* contributor Sandra M. Gilbert called it "a sort of bitter parody of a genre invented by nineteenth–century men: the detective novel." Some reviewers went so far as to suggest that N.'s problems are more imagined than real. "Understandably, N. would like to know who's doing all these bad things to her, if only to be sure that she's not making it all up," wrote Thomas R. Edwards in the *New York Review of Books.* "And since we also wonder if she may not be doing that, we share her desire for knowledge."

In her interview with *Women Writers'* Bell, Johnson asserted that such disbelief stems more from readers' biases than from the way the protagonist is portrayed. "There's [a] problem that comes from having as your central character a female person," said Johnson. "The male narrative voice is still accorded more authority. The female narrative voice is always questioned—is she crazy? Are the things she's saying a delusion, or reality?.... Nonetheless, I write about women of childbearing age, because I like to fly in the face of these prejudices and hope that I can make them authoritative and trustworthy reporters."

While women still figure prominently in Johnson's next novel, *Lying Low*, the focus shifted from psychological to political concerns and from one protagonist to several. The book, which covers four days in the lives of four characters who inhabit a boarding house in Orris, California, is a "mosaic-like juxtaposition of small paragraphs, each containing a short description, a bit of action, reflections of one of the principal characters, or a mixture of all three," according to Robert Towers in the *New York Times Book Review*. Praising its artful construction, elegant style, and delicate perceptions, Towers called *Lying Low* "a nearly flawless performance...." The book was nominated for a National Book Award.

Johnson was nominated for a Pulitzer Prize for her 1987 novel, *Persian Nights*. This book chronicles the story of Chloe Fowler, a woman who accidentally finds herself traveling in Iran just prior to the revolution. Fowler is a physician's wife, and the couple looks forward to a trip to Iran where the husband will teach in a local hospital. Just before they arrive, he is called away on an emergency and Fowler decides to continue to Iran without him. Alone in a country where single women are suspect, she finds herself the target of government attention. Fowler tries to help a dissatisfied Iranian woman leave the country, and gets involved in several affairs, before she is forced to leave the country.

Critics noted Johnson's success in portraying an imperfect protagonist. Paul Gray of *Time* believed that "in creating such a selfish, flawed heroine, Johnson took a calculated risk: readers might not be able to see themselves and their prejudices through Chloe and make the appropriate adjustments toward the truth." However, he concluded that the book is "neither a bodice ripper nor a treatise on the Iranian revolution, but an intriguing compromise: an attempt to show major upheavals as a progress of small shocks."

In addition to novels, Johnson has written two biographies. Her portrait of the first Mrs. George Meredith, *Lesser Lives: The True History of the First Mrs. Meredith,* grew out of her doctoral dissertation. "In biographies of Meredith, there would always be

this little paragraph about how he was first married to Mary Ellen Peacock who ran off and left him and then, of course, died, deserted and forlorn—like the woman in a Victorian story," Johnson told Bell. "I always thought, I bet there is her side of it too. This was when my own marriage was breaking up, and I was particularly interested in the woman's side of things."

Working from evidence she exhumed from letters and diaries, Johnson hypothesizes that the real Mary Ellen was a strong–willed, intelligent, free spirit, whose main sin was being out of step with her times. Raised by her father in the tradition of eighteenth–century individualism, she incited the wrath of her decidedly Victorian second husband, the famous novelist George Meredith, when she abandoned their loveless marriage to lead a life of her own. *Lesser Lives* received a National Book Award nomination.

Even when her subject is a contemporary figure, about whom concrete facts and anecdotes are readily available, Johnson prefers an artistic to an exhaustive approach. "A biography has a responsibility which is to present the facts and get all of them straight, so that people can get the basic outlines of a person's life," Johnson explained to Miriam Berkley in *Publishers Weekly*. "And then, I think, it has to have a point of view and a shape which has to come out of the biographer as artist. I guess I am arguing for the interpretive biography, you might call it an art biography, as opposed to a compendious ... presentation of a lot of facts."

Johnson's commitment to biography as art presented special challenges in her study of mystery writer Dashiell Hammett and the writing of *Dashiell Hammett: A Life*. The first "authorized" Hammett biographer, Johnson had access to all his personal papers and the cooperation of his family and friends. But in exchange for these privileges, Hammett's executrix and long–time companion Lillian Hellman insisted that she be shown the final manuscript and be granted the right to decide whether or not the quoted material could stand.

"She set out to be pleasant and wonderful, then, when she stopped being wonderful, I stopped going to see her," Johnson told Beverly Beyette in the *Los Angeles Times*. The problem was one of vision: "She saw him very much as her guru, this wonderfully strong, terrifically honest, fabulously intelligent dream man. I saw him as an intelligent, troubled man, an alcoholic with terrible writer's block. She didn't like to think of his life having been painful, unsuccessful." Johnson eventually obtained Hellman's permission to use Hammett's letters in her own way. "She had to agree, I guess, that it *was* the best way of presenting Hammett," Johnson told Berkley. "He was a difficult man and not entirely sympathetic, but he was certainly at his most sympathetic in his own voice."

Johnson, a woman who has reluctantly traveled all over the globe with her second husband, a physician, published the autobiographical work, *Natural Opium,* in 1993. The book is narrated by D., a character conspicuously similar to Johnson, who travels the globe while her husband J., an expert in infectious diseases, conducts his research. Critics have praised the book for its realistic feel, writer's attention to detail, and humor and intelligence. "What Ms. Johnson describes is not merely what the place was like, but—far more interesting—what it was like to be there," claimed Roxana Robinson in the *New York Times Book Review.* A tragic sled ride following a dinner in Switzerland, ethical physicians being drawn into the heart of corruption, and trying to visit her children who live at opposite ends of the globe are some of the topics she explores; disaster and destruction are almost always the themes.

A pair of *fin–de–siecle* novels, 1997's *Le Divorce* and 2000's *Le Mariage,* lend a French flavor to Johnson's work. In the former, the action begins as Roxanne (Roxy) de Persand, a Californian living in Paris, is pregnant with her second child when she learns that her French husband is leaving the marriage. Roxy's tale is narrated by her younger sister, Isabel Walker, "a film–school dropout who is good at describing scenes but doesn't always catch on to what they're really about," as Christopher Lehmann–Haupt described her in a *New York Times* review.

Isabel's arrival in Paris to help see Roxy through her pregnancy and "le divorce" sets in motion the younger sister's quest to become more worldly. The author, said a *Kirkus Reviews* article, is noteworthy for "catching the class–bound, cool, utter self– assurance" of the upper–class French characters as well as the "determinedly frank, aggressive innocence of their American counterparts."

Following *Le Divorce* was *Le Mariage,* Johnson's second take on cross–cultural relations. The players this time include American journalist Tim Nolinger, engaged to Parisian Anne–Sophie d'Arget, who runs a whimsical boutique. The passionate young couple comes to grips with doubts as the wedding day draws nearer. Johnson counters their story with the tale of another Franco–American couple. This time

glamorous Clara Holly, a former actress, realizes her longtime marriage to reclusive film director Serge Cray is on its last legs.

Clara takes in another American, the tourist Delia, who's had her passport stolen on her first day in Paris. The addition of the militant Delia to Clara and Serge's home life results in domestic confusion, political extremism, and even Y2K paranoia. Through it all, Johnson "sprinkles the novel with McGuffins as if they were spices," according to Cathleen Schine. Writing in the *New York Review of Books,* Schine added that "besides a murder, *Le Mariage* offers a medieval apocalyptic manuscript stolen from the Morgan Library just at the time Delia leaves the country, an apocalyptic right–wing extremist plot based in Oregon, and a dispute over bloods sports and French national monuments that threatens to turn into an international incident."

Schine admired the author's ability to integrate so many spins into one narrative: "More or less amusing on their own," she said, the plot points "blend together to create the satisfying aroma, if not the full flavor, of suspense. They also serve to bring Clara, Serge and Delia together with [Tim and Anne–Sophie]."

On August 8, 2003, Johnson's novel *Le Divorce* was adapted as a film by Ruth Prawer Jhabvala and James Ivory, directed by Ivory, and starred Kate Hudson and Naomi Watts. The film was released by Fox Searchlight Pictures. Later that year, the third novel in the trio with *Le Divorce* and *Le Mariage*— *L'Affaire*—was published. The novel was "about cultural misunderstandings and amorous entanglements," according to *People*'s Francine Prose. Thomas Mallon of *Atlantic Monthly* declared that Johnson "has a lightness of touch that has nearly disappeared from literary fiction, comic or otherwise." The novel also echoed Johnson's uneasiness about the state of her home country's political views. Since she and her husband split their time between Paris, France, and San Francisco, California, she is very aware of the hard feelings other countries have toward the United States. "America knows its heart is pure and its intentions are good, and that ought to be enough, right? It seems to assume that the values of Western democracy are self– evident and that therefore people will eagerly embrace them—without any willingness to think about other traditions that are completely incompatible. People can't just peel off tradition like that. We all feel that they ought to, but of course they can't," Johnson told Sarah Lyall in *Elle.*

Selected writings

Novels

Fair Game, Harcourt, 1965.
Loving Hands at Home, Harcourt, 1968.
Burning, Harcourt, 1971.
The Shadow Knows, Knopf, 1974.
Lying Low, Knopf, 1978.
Persian Nights, Knopf, 1987.
Health and Happiness, Knopf, 1990.
Le Divorce, Dutton, 1997.
Le Mariage, Dutton, 2000.
L'Affaire, Dutton, 2003.

Biographies

Lesser Lives: The True History of the First Mrs. Meredith, Knopf, 1973, published as *The True History of the First Mrs. Meredith and Other Lesser Lives,* Heinemann (London), 1973.
Dashiell Hammett: A Life, Random House, 1983.

Screenplays

(With Stanley Kubrick) *The Shining* (based on the Stephen King novel of the same title), Warner Brothers, 1980.
Also author of unproduced screenplays *Grand Hotel, The Shadow Knows* (based on her novel of the same title), and *Hammett* (based on her biography *Dashiell Hammett: A Life*).

Other writings

(Author of preface) John Ruskin, *King of the Golden River,* Garland Publishing (New York, NY), 1976.
(Author of preface) Charles Dickens, *A Holiday Romance,* Garland Publishing (New York, NY), 1976.
(Author of preface) Tom Hood, *Petsetilla's Posy,* Garland Publishing (New York, NY), 1976.
(Author of preface) Margaret Gatty, *Parables of Nature,* Garland Publishing, 1976.
(Author of preface) George Sand, *Mauprat,* Da Capo Press (New York City), 1977.
(Author of preface) *Frankenstein* by Mary Shelley, c. 1979.
Terrorists and Novelists (collected essays), Knopf, 1982.
(Author of preface) *Josephine Herhst: Collected Works,* 1990.
(Author of preface) *Tales and Stories of E. A. Poe,* Vintage, 1991.
Natural Opium: Some Travelers' Tales, Knopf, 1993.
Contributor of essays and book reviews to periodicals, including the *New York Times, New York Review of Books, San Francisco Chronicle,* and the *Washington Post.*

Media adaptations

Le Divorce was released by Merchant–Ivory Productions in 2003.

Sources

Books

Dictionary of Literary Biography Yearbook: 1980, Gale, 1981.
Yalom, Marilyn, editor, *Women Writers of the West Coast: Speaking of Their Lives and Careers,* Capra, 1983.

Periodicals

Atlantic Monthly, October 2003, p. 124.
Critique: Studies in Modern Fiction, Volume 16, number 1, 1974.
Elle, October 2003, pp. 208–10.
Kirkus Reviews, November 1, 1996.
Los Angeles Times, October 6, 1982; April 27, 1983.
Nation, June 14, 1975.
New Statesman, June 6, 1975.
Newsweek, December 23, 1974; May 5, 1975; October 16, 1978; October 17, 1983; March 30, 1987, p. 69.
New York Review of Books, February 20, 1975; May 25, 2000, p. 29.
New York Times, January 23, 1997; April 16, 1997; August 8, 2003.
New York Times Book Review, November 19, 1978; January 24, 1993, p. 8; February 2, 1997, p. 10; April 16, 2000, p. 8; April 16, 2000, p. 10.
People, October 27, 2003, p. 48.
Publishers Weekly, September 9, 1983.
Time, March 23, 1987, p. 83.

Norah Jones

Singer

Born March 30, 1979, in New York, NY; daughter of Ravi Shankar (a world renowned sitar player) and Sue Jones (a nurse). *Education:* Attended University of North Texas.

Addresses: *Booking agent*—Monterey Peninsula Artists, Attn: Joe Brauner, 24 E. 21st St., Ste. #802, New York, NY 10010. *Manager*—Macklam Feldman Management, Ste. 200, 1505 West 2nd Ave., Vancouver, BC V6H 3Y4. *Record company*—Blue Note Records, 304 Park Ave. South, 3rd Floor, New York, NY 10010.

Career

Sang in church choirs starting at age five; began taking piano lessons at age seven; performed first gig at an open mic night on her 16th birthday; performed with band, Laszlo, throughout high school; solo gigs at a restaurant, 1997–99; moved to New York and started playing nights in Greenwich Village, 1999; performed with Wax Poetic, 1999–2000; recorded with Peter Malick Group, 2000; released Blue Note EP, *First Sessions,* 2001; *Come Away with Me* released, 2002; appeared on the *Tonight Show,* 2002; toured with John Mayer and Charlie Hunter, 2002; performed at a Willie Nelson tribute show, 2002; toured Japan and Europe, 2002; performed at the Montreal Jazz Festival, 2003; performed at the Tribeca Film Festival, 2003.

Awards: Student Music Award for best jazz vocalist and best original composition, *Down Beat,* 1996; Student Music Award for best jazz vocalist, *Down Beat,* 1997; Grammy Awards for album of the year, record of the year, best new artist, best female pop vocal performance, and best pop vocal album, Recording Academy, 2003.

Sidelights

She has been compared to some of the greatest singers in music history, from Nina Simone to Billie Holiday as well as Sarah Vaughan and Joni Mitchell. Norah Jones came to widespread fame quickly and almost effortlessly. She was signed to a record contract the day she auditioned. Her quiet, reflective album took the Grammys by storm in 2003 despite competing with such established artists as rocker Bruce Springsteen and rapper Eminem.

Jones is a combination of hard–working jazz musician and guileless young woman. Her voice is what captures her listeners. Jeff Gordinier of *Entertainment Weekly* described it as follows, "Precociously rich and seductive, her voice seems to well up from the age of Dinah Washington and Nina Simone." She had dreams of a future cultivating her piano playing and her singing repertoire. Jones never expected her first album to go triple platinum and beat out the professionals in the pop music category.

Jones was born March 30, 1979, in New York, New York, the daughter of Sue Jones and the famous sitar player, Ravi Shankar. Jones's mother and Shankar were never married, and eventually separated after Norah's birth. Soon afterward, the younger Jones and her mother moved to Texas, where Sue worked as a nurse to support them. Jones grew up in Grapevine, a suburb of Dallas, but moved into the city of Dallas so that she could attend the Booker T. Washington High School for the Performing and Visual Arts.

While growing up, Jones had very little interaction with her father, who had become famous in the United States for his work with the British rock group the Beatles. Despite years of separation, she ended up establishing a closer relationship with him while she was in college. She explained to *Entertainment Weekly's* Gordinier, "It's not a secret. But I didn't grow up with my dad. [I]t's not something that contributed to my musical upbringing."

Jones' musical influences came from her mother's record collection, which included artists such as Aretha Franklin and Etta James. She also found a set of Billie Holiday records that she listened to constantly throughout high school. She discovered singer/songwriter Joni Mitchell while in college. Other early influences included musicals. She recalled to Jim Macnie of VH1.com that she memorized the songs from both *Cats* and *Phantom of the Opera.* She also enjoyed the film *West Side Story* for the energy of the gang scenes, not the romance of the love story.

Jones exhibited musical interest at age three when her parents noticed her listening intently while Shankar practiced his sitar. By age five she was singing in her church choir. She eventually learned to play several instruments but felt most comfortable with piano. She briefly attended Grapevine High School where she played saxophone in the marching band. Her interest in jazz blossomed when she was in high school. Her talents were recognized early on by the premiere jazz magazine, *Down Beat.* She was awarded the Student Music Award (SMA) for Best Jazz Vocalist two years in a row. She also showed talent as a composer. In 1996, she was awarded an SMA for Best Original Composition.

Jones's first public performance as a solo pianist and singer came on the day of her 16th birthday. She performed "I'll Be Seeing You," a song made famous by Holiday, during an open mic night at a coffeehouse. She continued to hone her performing skills by playing in the band Laszlo, named for a character from the film *Casablanca.* After high school she attended the University of North Texas where

she majored in jazz piano. On weekends she would perform solo at a restaurant, an experience which she claims as an important part of her development as an artist. She told VH1.com's Macnie, "[T]hat was the best practice I could have ever had. That's where I learned to coordinate my singing and my piano playing."

The summer after her sophomore year in college, Jones moved to New York City to get a taste of the jazz scene there. She subleased a friend's apartment and worked as a waitress during the day; nights she would perform at venues throughout Greenwich Village. In addition to her solo gigs, she contributed her talents to bands such as the Peter Malick Group and Wax Poetic. She told Josh Tyrangiel of *Time,* "It was pretty much everything I wanted." Even though she was satisfied with the work she was doing, she became frustrated when she was not signed to a record label after almost a year of passing her demo around. She wanted to return to Texas, but her mother encouraged her to stay in New York and keep trying. Jones told *People,* "My mom said, 'As much as I want you to come back, you should stay. Otherwise you'll feel like a failure.'"

Failure was not in Jones's future. Instead, she won the dedication of Blue Note employee Shell White. White was in the audience the night of Jones's 21st birthday, and was so impressed by Jones's performance that she vowed to help Jones get a recording contract. Through White's intercession, Jones presented her demo to Blue Note chief executive officer Bruce Lundvall. Lundvall, who has always accepted unsolicited material, met with Jones and was impressed. He explained to *Time's* Tyrangiel, "Norah doesn't have one of those over–the–top instruments. It's just a signature voice, right from the heart to you. When you're lucky enough to hear that, you don't hesitate. You sign it." It was only the second time during his tenure as head of the record label that Lundvall had signed an artist on the spot.

Right off the bat, Jones recorded an EP with Blue Note titled *First Sessions,* which was released in 2001. She continued to record throughout 2001, working with legendary producer Arif Mardin, who had produced for singing stars such as Aretha Franklin and Dusty Springfield. Her voice and the piano were emphasized, and even though Blue Note is decidedly focused on jazz, Jones was allowed to interpret songs her own way. The end result was an album that defied categorization. When Lundvall first heard it, he wanted Jones to rerecord some of the songs. However, Jones was eventually allowed to maintain her musical integrity, remaining true to the style she had cultivated for years. Produced at a legendary jazz label, containing jazz standards as well as old country hits and new songs with hints of the blues and pop, *Come Away With Me* added up to a best–selling debut album.

Released in February of 2002, *Come Away With Me* slowly accumulated interest as listeners discovered Jones's quiet and sultry sound. The media campaign for the album was based on giving those who heard it a sense of discovery. Mardin, the producer on *Come Away With Me,* explained the appeal of Jones's style of music to *Entertainment Weekly*'s Gordinier, "People are bored with formula records. There's a certain age group that would like to get their hands on records that feel natural...."

Despite the low–key marketing of the album, it was gaining increased attention as 2002 wound down. *Rolling Stone* and *Entertainment Weekly* both included Jones on their lists of top new artists. By late 2002, the album had created a low–level buzz. On January 7, 2003, that buzz was turned up several notches when the Recording Academy published their list of Grammy nominees. Jones's subtle and nuanced debut album had received a not–so–subtle eight nominations. As testament to Jones's unassuming nature, she was sleeping when the Grammy announcements were made.

On Grammy night, Jones walked away with an armload of awards. She won in each category for which she was nominated: Album of the Year, Record of the Year, Best New Artist, Best Pop Vocal Album, and Best Female Pop Vocal Performance. The album also won three other awards: songwriter Jesse Harris won for Song of the Year for "Don't Know Why," Arif Mardin won Producer of the Year, and Jay Newland and S. Husky Höskulds won the Best–Engineered Album of the Year. In total, *Come Away With Me* won eight awards, putting Jones in a tie with Lauryn Hill and Alicia Keys—other women whose albums had won as many awards at the Grammys.

Throughout the hype that led to Grammy night and afterward, Jones maintained a nervous humility. She explained to Larry Flick of *Billboard,* "It's such a blessing. It's so far beyond what I could ever imagine might happen for me and my music." When questioned about what she would do next, she told Flick, "I just keep doing what I'm doing, nothing more. This is a once–in–a–lifetime moment.... My objective is to enjoy this moment and then put it on the side and get on with what I've been doing all along, which is to make music."

At 24 years of age, Jones has made plenty of good music. What she hasn't done a lot of is prepare for the pop starlight. She is nervous at interviews, afraid of saying too much. When asked who made the dress she wore Grammy night, she had to ask someone to check the tag. Jones excused herself from a press conference by stating she had to go to the bathroom. She is not a contrived pop star. She explained her intentions to *RollingStone.com,* "I didn't want to be on a pop label, because I know what comes with that. I didn't want to make videos. I didn't want to be expected to sell millions of records. I didn't ever want to be a celebrity."

One reason for wanting to eschew celebrity is her inherent shyness. Her sound and her performing style have been portrayed in many articles as seductive, moody, and romantic. Jones takes issue with these portrayals, explaining to Chris Willman of *Entertainment Weekly,* "It's funny, this image thing, because I'm not soft–spoken and romantic.... I'm pretty much loudmouthed, obnoxious, and silly." She further explained, though, that she is nervous around strangers and that her nervousness probably comes off as mysteriousness.

Despite her intentions, Jones has become a pop star. Her recording label asked her to do a video for her album. Then they asked her to do it again. Her album has sold millions. She told *RollingStone.com* that she had agreed to do a lot of the things she originally had said she did not want to do. Still, she takes it all in stride, recognizing that she has a larger audience than she ever dreamed of attaining. Already gifted with an incredible talent, she has the time to mature into an even more impressive expression of that talent. Eric Felten of the *Washington Times* reviewed a concert she performed in June of 2003, "Miss Jones' voice had more strength to it than on her debut record, with a potent emotional core more yearning than vulnerable, more womanly than girlish. The young singer, already impressive in her subtle ability to emote, is clearly growing as an artist."

Selected discography

First Sessions, Blue Note, 2001.
(Vocals) *Songs From the Analog Playground,* Blue Note, 2001.
Come Away With Me, Blue Note, 2002.
(Guest appearance) *Get Your Glow On,* 301, 2003.
(Piano and vocals) *Peter Malick Group/Norah Jones,* Koch, 2003.
(Guest appearance) *Willie Nelson and Friends: Live and Kickin',* Lost Highway, 2003.
Feels Like Home, Blue Note, 2004.

Sources

Periodicals

Billboard, March 8, 2003, p. 1.

Entertainment Weekly, March 22, 2002, pp. 72–73; December 20, 2002, p. 36.
Knight Ridder/Tribune News Service, February 24, 2003; March 6, 2003.
People, February 24, 2003, pp. 61–62.
Time, March 18, 2002, p. 84.
Washington Times, June 23, 2003, p. B5.

Online

"Jones Sweeps Major Grammys," CNN.com, http://www.cnn.com/2003/SHOWBIZ/Music/02/03/grammys/ (August 16, 2003).

"Norah Jones," AskMen.com, http://www.askmen.com/women/singer_100/149c_norah_jones.html (August 16, 2003).
"Norah Jones," *RollingStone.com,* http://www.rollingstone.com/features/coverstory/featuregen.asp?pid=1255 (August 16, 2003).
"Norah Jones: Quiet Is the New Gold," VH1.com, http://www.vh1.com/artists/news/1459679/05082002/jones_norah.jhtml (August 16, 2003).

—Eve M. B. Hermann

Juanes

Singer

Born Juan Esteban Aristizábal, August 9, 1972, in Medellín, Colombia; married Karen Martínez (a model and actress); children: Luna (daughter).

Addresses: *Record label*—Universal Music and Video, 5713 N. Figueroa St., Los Angeles, CA 90042.

Career

Founded the band Ekhymosis in Medellín, Colombia, 1990s; disbanded Ekhymosis and relocated to Los Angeles, CA, to pursue a recording career, 1998; signed to producer Gustavo Santaolalla's Surco label, 1999; released first solo album, *Fíjate Bien*, 2000; released *Un Día Normal*, 2002.

Awards: Latin Grammy award for best new artist, Latin Academy of Recording Arts and Sciences, 2001; Latin Grammy award for best rock solo vocal album for *Fíjate Bien*, 2001; Latin Grammy award for best rock song for "Fíjate Bien," 2001; Latin Grammy award for best rock song for "A Dios le Pido," 2002; Latin Grammy award for album of the year *Un Día Normal*, 2003; Latin Grammy award for best rock solo vocal album for *Un Día Normal*, 2003; Latin Grammy award for song of the year for "Es Por Ti," 2003; Latin Grammy award for record of the year for "Es Por Ti," 2003; Latin Grammy award for best rock song for "Mala Gente," 2003.

Sidelights

Colombian–born singer Juanes collected a total of nine Latin Grammy awards just three years after his major–label debut, and his impressive number of wins has been hailed as a harbinger of a new era in Latin music. With music that is less pop, more reflective, and definitely wider in musical range, Juanes's hit albums were chosen overwhelmingly by his peers in the Latin music world as representative of the best it had to offer when the Grammy votes were counted. His second release, *Un Día Normal* ("A Normal Day") won five Latin Grammys alone in 2003.

The singer–songwriter's striking looks have lured fans to his music, but it is his straightforward rock that has propelled him to the top of the charts throughout Latin America. Juanes considers himself a musical ambassador for Colombia, where a few of his tracks have become rallying cries for political change. "Everyone knows about the war in our country," a *Chicago Tribune* article by Achy Obejas reproduced in the Knight Ridder/Tribune News Service quoted him as saying. "Everyone knows about the violence, about all our political and social problems. But there is another country too: The one where people are sick of all that, where there are so many hard–working people struggling for a better life, and where the arts are—and have been—flourishing." Juanes's name is the shortened version of Juan Esteban Aristizábal, which his parents, a farmer and a homemaker, named him when he arrived in the world in August of 1972. He was born in Medellín, one of Colombia's main cities. His only formal musical training came from his father and his brothers, who began teaching him to play guitar when he was seven years old. In his teen years, he discovered the music of bands like Led Zeppelin, Pink Floyd, Black Sabbath, Iron Maiden, and Metallica. "I felt a lot of strength when I heard that music," he explained to *Houston Chronicle* writer Ramiro Burr. "I didn't understand the lyrics, but I liked the sound of the guitars and the strength they transmitted."

By the time he was 16, Juanes had formed a rock band in Medellín called Ekhymosis, a name they chose from a Greek word meaning the first stage of a bruise. He fronted the band as its singer and guitarist, and his piercings and eye makeup were a bit daring for Colombia even in the mid–1990s. The band lasted a decade, releasing five records. The first was a full–on metal extravaganza, while the others blended traditional Colombian sounds into standard rock chords. The group's greatest success was their 1997 LP, *La Tierra.*

When the members of Ekhymosis decided to part ways in 1998, Juanes sold his computer, stereo, and scooter, and used the proceeds to buy a plane ticket to Los Angeles, California. Knowing almost no one in the city, he arrived on a tourist visa and lived in a dicey motel. At night, he earned money by finding work as a freelance musician at Sunset Boulevard bars, and by day tried to break into the music business by getting his demo tapes into the hands of producers and executives. Finally, one of those tapes made it to Gustavo Santaolalla, a respected Argentinean musician and producer who ran an L.A.–based label affiliated with Universal Music. Santaolalla was widely respected in the *rock–en–español* world, having produced records for acts like Café Tacuba, Julieta Venegas, and Puya, and was already familiar with Juanes because of the success of Ekhymosis.

The two set up a meeting at a coffee house, and it went even better than Juanes expected. "When he told me he liked my music, I almost cried," the artist recalled in a Los Angeles *Daily News* interview. Juanes was living on the edge of dire poverty at the time, writing songs and eating up his savings. Santaolalla signed him to his label, Surco, and the two spent the next six months working on his debut solo record.

Fíjate Bien, or "Pay Close Attention," was released on Universal/Surco in October of 2000. It featured 12 Spanish–language tracks of rock, hip–hop, and pop, some of which utilized salsa flavors, and oth-

ers that deployed the Colombian musical strains of *vallenato,* the romantic–themed, accordion– and bongo–heavy music of Colombia's coastal–region cowboys. But the record was also a somber affair, with lyrics about the violence and civil strife that had plagued Colombia for years. Medellín, Juanes's native city, lent its name to a notoriously vicious drug cartel, while a Marxist rebel group had been seizing territory in the Colombian countryside during the 1990s. While land mines dotted the countryside, the cities were also dangerous because of frequent kidnappings. Juanes knew several people who had died: his best friend was killed when a nightclub was sprayed by gunfire, and his cousin was kidnapped and slain, even though the ransom had been paid. The title track of Juanes's debut came out of a telephone conversation he had had with his mother about the land mines that still dotted the Colombian countryside, which maimed or killed innocent people every year.

Critics who discovered *Fíjate Bien* wrote glowing reviews, but sales were slow until July of 2001, when it suddenly earned seven Latin Grammy Award nominations. Juanes had not wanted to attend the press conference at which the nominations were announced, but his manager, Fernán Martínez—who had previously managed the career of Enrique Iglesias—encouraged him to show up. Juanes brought just one change of clothes, and was wearing a T–shirt and freshly washed sneakers that were still wet. "I kept telling Fernán, 'I don't want to be there,'" the singer recalled in an interview with Jordan Levin that appeared in the Knight Ridder/Tribune News Service. "What if my name is not on the list? No one knows who I am and I'm going to be standing up there like a freak." With his sneakers making a squishing noise when he walked, Juanes answered the occasional query. "Someone asked me, 'Who are you?'" he told Levin. "And I said, 'I'm Juanes. I have an album. I'm from Colombia.'"

Sales for *Fíjate Bien* quadrupled after the Latin Grammy nominations were announced. The title track, the song he had penned about land mines, became a hit, as did "Podemos Hacernos Daño." They began to air on Spanish–music radio, and Universal put Juanes on tour. He played his first American dates on the Watcha Tour. A critic for the Los Angeles *Daily News* reviewed one performance at the Universal Amphitheatre, and found the Colombian singer a compelling performer. "On stage, Juanes merged with the music and the beat: jerking, bobbing, and banging away on his Fender Telecaster in a muscle shirt like a young Bruce Springsteen," the newspaper reported. "In contrast to this disheveled ecstasy, his playing was clean and precise, his despairing voice given passion by the urgency of his lyrics."

The Latin Grammy ceremony was scheduled for September 11, 2001, but was canceled that day after hijacked planes hit the World Trade Center in New York City. When the winners were finally announced, Juanes won Best New Artist of the Year, *Fíjate Bien* won Best Rock Solo Vocal Album, and its title track took the award for Best Rock Song. Juanes missed his chance to perform at the Miami ceremony that fateful day, but later said in the *Chicago Tribune* article by Obejas that the day changed his life in a more profound way. The songwriter who had written about Colombia's violence had felt relatively safe in the United States until 9/11. "I saw it on TV, like so many other people," he told Obejas. "All I could think about was that my family was traveling that day, and that nowhere was safe."

Following the Latin Grammy wins, Juanes worked on his next solo record for several months with Santaolalla in a Los Angeles studio. *Un Día Normal* was released in May of 2002, and was a marked change, at least in themes, from his first. "I wanted to show a different side of my soul," he told *Dallas Morning News* journalist Mario Tarradell, according to a Knight Ridder/Tribune News Service report. "*Fíjate Bien* was a very dark, depressing album. But when I was writing *Un Día Normal* I wanted to share with the audience different things. I didn't want to talk about the storms exploding in my country. I wanted to talk about the hope, the family, and the good things. *Un Día Normal* is a positive album."

The first single from *Un Día Normal*, "A Dios le Pido (Of God I Ask)," quickly became a huge hit in Colombia and elsewhere in the Latin–American diaspora. The song's lyrics celebrated love—of family, of country, of being alive—despite the pervasive violence and fear that shook the lives of ordinary Colombians on a daily basis. The song hit the charts in Colombia just as its presidential election race was coming to a close, and later that month Colombians elected Alvaro Uribe Vélez, who campaigned on a promise to rid the country of the sectarian violence. In the build–up to Vélez's August inauguration, Juanes's song became an anthem for Colombians both there and abroad who hoped for a new era. It stayed at No. 1 in Colombia for seven weeks, and topped the charts in other Latin American countries as well. It sat in the Top Ten Billboard Latin Albums chart for a stunning 65 weeks.

At the 2002 Latin Grammy Awards, Juanes performed "A Dios le Pido," and it won him his fourth Latin Grammy, this one for Best Rock Song of the Year. The following year, the record took another five Latin Grammys: Album of the Year, Best Rock Solo Vocal Album, Best Rock Song for "Mala Gente," and Song of the Year and Record of the Year for "Es Por Ti (It's For You)." One song from *Un Día Normal* that did not win an award was "Fotografía," Juanes's duet with a pop star of Canadian–Portuguese heritage, Nelly Furtado. Writing in the *Houston Chronicle*, Burr termed it "a reflective and instantly catchy midtempo rocker with gorgeous harmonies … [T]he pair resemble a rejuvenated Fleetwood Mac when they harmonize."

At the 2003 Latin Grammy ceremony, Juanes performed with the Black Eyed Peas, an alternative hip–hop act. The show's producers, hoping to win potential crossover sales, asked him to deliver his acceptance speech in English, to which he agreed—but he wore a T–shirt that read "Se Habla Español," or "Spanish spoken." He remains committed to reversing the international reputation Colombia has endured since the 1980s as the province of vast drug wealth, corruption, and random violence. "I know a lot of times, people have a bad image of my country," New Jersey *Star–Ledger* reporter Adrian Sainz quoted him as saying on the night of the 2003 Latin Grammys. "That's why it's so important for me to be here, to represent the other side of Colombia."

Juanes and his wife, Colombian model and actress Karen Martínez, welcomed the birth of their daughter, Luna, on September 6, 2003. The family moved from Los Angeles to Miami, which made it easier to visit home. "I go to Colombia to visit my family, even if it's just for a day or two," he told Burr in the *Houston Chronicle*. "I always miss Colombian food."

Selected discography

With Ekhymosis

Niño Gigante, Codiscos, 1993.
Ciudad Pacifico, Codiscos.
Amor Bilingue, Codiscos.
La Tierra, 1997.
Ekhymosis, Fonovisa, 1997.

Solo

Fíjate Bien, Universal, 2000.
Un Día Normal, Universal, 2002.

Sources

Books

Contemporary Musicians, vol. 43, Gale Group, 2004.

Periodicals

Billboard, September 13, 2003, p. 3.

Boston Herald, September 27, 2002, p. S24.

Business Wire, August 27, 2003, p. 5166; September 9, 2003, p. 5940.

Daily News (Los Angeles, CA), September 11, 2001, p. L3.

Hollywood Reporter, October 18, 2002, p. 18.

Houston Chronicle, March 24, 2002, p. 7; June 16, 2002, p. 7; December 14, 2002, p. 9.

Knight Ridder/Tribune News Service, August 8, 2001; September 30, 2002; December 13, 2002.

New York Times, November 3, 2002, p. 6.

Star–Ledger (Newark, NJ), September 4, 2003, p. 27.

—Carol Brennan

Karen Jurgensen

Former editor of *USA Today*

Born c. 1949, in NC; daughter of Kai (a drama teacher) and Peggy Jurgensen; married first husband (divorced); married Bill Leary (an attorney); children: Kirsten (from first marriage). *Education:* University of North Carolina, Chapel Hill, B.A., 1971.

Addresses: *Home*—Virginia.

Career

Began journalism career as editorial and features writer, columnist, and layout editor of the editorial page, *Charlotte (North Carolina) News,* 1972–75; became writer and editor at the University of North Carolina, Raleigh, Sea Grant College Program, 1976–79; assistant lifestyle editor and then lifestyle editor, *Miami News,* 1979–82, assistant city editor, 1982; joined *USA Today,* 1982, held several posts, including topics editor, 1982, special projects editor, 1983–85, managing editor, life department, 1985–86, managing editor, cover stories department, 1986–87, senior editor, special projects, 1987–91, editorial page editor, 1991–99, editor of newspaper, 1999-2004.

Member: American Society of Newspaper Editors, future of newspapers committee, 1988–90, 1991; writing awards board, 1989–91; vice chair, literacy committee, 1989–91; convention committee, 1991–94; chair/vice chair press bar committee, 1993–95; vice chair convention committee, 1995–96.

Awards: Association for Women in Communications' Matrix Professional Achievement Award for outstanding contributions to the field of communications, 2000.

Sidelights

As the first female editor of the largest–circulation newspaper in the United States, Karen Jurgensen is among the most influential women in the industry. Yet, the former *USA Today* editor refuses to see herself as a trailblazer and believes her achievement is merely a part of the natural progression of women through the workforce.

Following her 1999 appointment to become *USA Today*'s editor, Jurgensen downplayed the role of gender as media outlets across the world lauded her promotion as a great advancement for women. For Jurgensen, it was no big deal. As she told *Washington Post* writer Howard Kurtz, "It's only appropriate that a newspaper that calls itself the nation's newspaper reflect that diversity in its staffing."

Raised in North Carolina, Jurgensen was born around 1949 to Kai and Peggy Jurgensen. Her Danish roots run deep and are reflected in her name, Karen, which she pronounces in the Danish style of CAR–in. Jurgensen's father taught drama at the University of North Carolina; her mother died when she was in her teens.

As early as eighth grade, Jurgensen got involved with her first newspaper and followed that passion through college. In 1971, she earned an English degree from the University of North Carolina at Chapel Hill. By 1972, Jurgensen was employed by the *Charlotte News* in North Carolina. She stayed there until 1975, working as both an editorial and features writer, as well as a columnist and layout editor.

In 1976, Jurgensen joined the Sea Grant College Program at the University of North Carolina at Raleigh. She was a writer and editor for the program, which worked to promote the sustainable use of the state's marine resources. In 1979, Jurgensen headed back to the newsroom, becoming the assistant lifestyle editor at the *Miami News.* While there, Jurgensen worked her way up to lifestyle editor but yearned for a change of pace. In the 1970s, women were entering journalism in greater numbers, but, as Jurgensen found out, they were mostly kept in the lifestyle section. In time, Jurgensen took a demotion to become a metro editor assistant so she could gain hard news experience.

By the early 1980s, plans for the launch of *USA Today* were well under way, and Jurgensen was offered a job. With the job came great opportunity, but also risk. Jurgensen was a single mother with a five–year–old daughter. She wrestled with the idea of leaving her stable job in Miami, Florida, to relocate 1,000 miles away to work at a paper that did not even exist. In the end, she decided to head to Arlington, Virginia, where *USA Today* would be produced. "It was a leap of faith," Jurgensen told Bob Dart of the *Atlanta Journal and Constitution.* "I thought then and still think that *USA Today* is the most exciting thing going on in journalism in the country, and I wanted to be a part of it."

Jurgensen began at *USA Today* as a topics editor in the life section. Later, she became special projects editor and was also deputy managing editor in the life section. By 1991, Jurgensen was in charge of the editorial page and on May 1, 1999, she became the paper's fifth editor. She had just turned 50. At the time, publisher Tom Curley said Jurgensen was selected for her leadership skills. As Curley told the *Washington Post's* Kurtz, "I was most impressed with the transformation she led on the editorial page. She has really boosted the quality of writing, subject matter, approach.... She has an expansive vision for what the newspaper should be." Colleagues refer to her as a calm, cool–headed, and highly organized leader.

During her tenure at *USA Today,* Jurgensen initiated many changes. One change included a new accuracy program, prompted by the coverage Jurgensen read about herself upon her appointment to editor. Papers across the world carried her story, but she said she noted minor mistakes in many of them. In her accuracy program, the paper chose random stories, then called the sources to see if any mistakes had been made. Naturally, the program discouraged errors in the first place. Other changes included the addition of page–one ads, which first appeared in October of 1999.

Jurgensen's success, however, was not without consequences and sacrifices. From the beginning, Jurgensen told the *Atlanta Journal and Constitution,* "I had my daughter in a day–care center that closed at 6 o'clock and was, at minimum, a 45–minute drive away at rush hour. Well, it very soon became obvious that there was no way this was going to be a workable plan, so I hired someone to come and be at the house with my daughter." In the end, Jurgensen said her daughter is proud of her achievements.

Jurgensen also made headlines in 1990 when she wrote a chilling, first–person account of her experience as a rape victim when she was 26 and lived in Charlotte. Jurgensen wanted to be counted among the victims, to put a face to the crime since most papers reported rapes, but left out victims' names. Recalling the event in *USA Today,* she wrote, "I want you to know the police treated me as though I were the criminal. The case went nowhere. I was the bad one because I hadn't gone to the hospital for yet another invasion to prove the first one had occurred."

While *USA Today* makes its way into more hands than any other paper, it still struggles to be taken seriously by long–established papers, such as the *New York Times.* Over the years, *USA Today* has taken a beating for its colorful graphics and quick–fix articles meant to appeal to a broad national audience. It was nicknamed a "McPaper."

But the paper's writers know their influence is far–reaching. Mark Halperin, political director for ABC News, explained it this way to James Poniewozik of *Time,* "The media elites in Washington and New York who don't read *USA Today* unless they're traveling underestimate its influence in the lives of Americans." *USA Today* political columnist Walter Shapiro told Poniewozik, "There's no greater feeling than being out somewhere in Iowa, New Hampshire, South Carolina, and realizing that one has a choice of two newspapers for the entire press corps and the entire campaign: the local paper and *USA Today.*" Jurgensen's goal as editor is simple: to turn a successful product into a lasting institution. She hopes that someday, the paper will carry more authority and can be viewed as a heavyweight by peers.

On April 20, 2004, Jurgensen abruptly resigned, "citing her failure to intercept what were apparently fabrications in articles by Jack Kelley, who was the newspaper's star foreign correspondent," according to Jacques Steinberg in the *New York Times*. Jurgensen resigned a week after Craig Moon, the paper's publisher, received a confidential report from three outside journalists who had been asked to find out how Kelley's fabrications had gone into the paper unnoticed. The managing editor of news, Hal Ritter, who oversaw Kelley's work most directly, also resigned.

Sources

Periodicals

American Journalism Review, April 1999, p. 9.
Atlanta Journal and Constitution, May 4, 1999, p. 2C.
Independent (London, England), March 23, 1999, p. 13.

New York Times, April 21, 2004, p. A1.
Time, July 21, 2003, pp. 48–50.
USA Today, April 4, 1990, p. 8A.
Washington Post, March 10, 1999, p. C1; May 6, 1999, p. C3.

Online

"Eight Women To Watch," *Washingtonian,* http://www.washingtonian.com/people/powerful women/womentowatch.html (February 26, 2004).

"Women in the News," Association for Women in Communications, http://www.awic–dc.org/womennews_jurgensen.shtml (February 18, 2004).

—Lisa Frick

David Kirk

Author and illustrator

Born c. 1956; married (divorced); married Kathy Anne Dropp (a museum curator), 2000; children: Violet, Primrose, Wisteria. *Education:* Cleveland Institute of Art, B.A. (painting).

Addresses: *Publisher*—Callaway, 54 7th Ave. S., New York, NY 10014.

Career

Founded toy production company, Hoobert Toys, 1970s; published first children's book, *Miss Spider's Tea Party*, 1994; published many popular children's books afterward, including: *Miss Spider's Wedding*, 1995; *Nova's Arc*, 1999; *Little Miss Spider: A Christmas Wish*, 2001; *Little Bird, Biddle Bird*, 2001; *Little Bunny, Biddle Bunny*, 2002; *Little Miss Spider*, 2003.

Sidelights

David Kirk is the best–selling author and illustrator of the "Miss Spider" series of books for children, as well as the "Biddle" series, and *Nova's Arc*. With stories in verse, and bright, colorful illustrations of animals and robots, Kirk has captured the hearts and minds of millions of children around the world, as well as many adults. His books have been spun off into a television special and a series for the Nickelodeon network as well as a line of designer clothing, accessories, and furniture produced and sold by Target Stores beginning in 2003.

Kirk grew up in Columbus, Ohio. His father was an insurance salesperson who also worked with his wife as a professional puppeteer, giving shows at conventions and birthday parties. Kirk found himself at an early age drawn toward creating toys himself, although he later denied that his parents's unusual sideline had anything to do with it. "My interest in making toys came from my liking toys," he told the *Plain Dealer*'s Carolyn Jack. At first, Kirk took toys apart to see how they worked and put them back together again. Then he graduated to making his own toys, an activity he continued into adulthood.

After graduating from high school, Kirk attended the Cleveland Art Institute. The experience was not a positive one for him. He railed against what he considered limiting assignments—paintings inspired by the Victorian era. He was also frustrated at not being allowed to use the tools of the design department; since he was a painting student and not a design student, he was not given the freedom he needed to continue to develop his interested in designing and building objects rather than just painting them. However, Kirk did not fit in among the design students either, since the program was mostly focused on industrial design, teaching students how to design automobile bodies, and other products that did not interest Kirk.

His time at the Art Institute, Kirk later affirmed, did not help him much in his future career. Nor did he think studying in general art makes one a better artist. "Much of the stuff that I use came from my childhood or from my own effort," Kirk told the *Plain Dealer*'s Jack. In fact, Kirk went on, being a student at the Institute taught him, more than anything else, "how not to be bullied."

Kirk graduated from the Cleveland Art Institute with a degree in painting, and went on to continue his studies in England. From there, he moved to New York City to try to find work. In New York, he lived with his brother, who was a writer. This experience also failed to inspire the budding artist. Although he and his brother worked hard, they had little money, so Kirk relocated to the Finger Lakes region in upstate New York, where it was less expensive to live, and whose surroundings he found more inspiring.

In the Finger Lakes area, Kirk began to make toys and market them to area craft shops. Although the toys sold well, especially to collectors and other adults, he soon found himself frustrated by his inability to produce them fast enough, or cheaply enough to sell to children. He then decided to try to mass produce them. He founded a company called Hoobert Toys, but, unfortunately, his manufacturing ventures were not successful. However, his illustrations for the packages in which he planned to sell the toys later became the basis of the illustrations for his first books.

Although his first efforts at toy manufacturing proved ultimately unsuccessful, his prototypes did catch the eye of a publisher named Nicholas Callaway. Callaway had his own publishing company, and he thought Kirk's toys would make excellent characters for children's literature. Callaway found Kirk in the phone book and asked him if he would be interested in writing books for children; as luck would have it, Kirk had been thinking about doing such a thing. In fact, Kirk had already been approached by other publishers about creating children's books inspired by his toys. But Callaway was the only publisher willing to offer Kirk an advance—$20,000—before he sold a single copy. Callaway and Kirk hit it off, and after they made the deal, Callaway opened Kirk's first book, *Miss Spider's Tea Party*, to auction among 15 different major children's book publishers. Just one publisher, Scholastic, offered a deal for the book.

Callaway's company, in conjunction with Scholastic, published *Miss Spider's Tea Party* in 1994. Callaway, although successful as a publisher, had never published any children's literature. In fact, his company

was perhaps best known up until the time of *Little Miss Spider* as the publisher of pop singer Madonna's book, *Sex*. Asked why he had never published books for kids until Miss Spider came along, Callaway said it was because he had never seen anything "special enough," as he told the *Plain Dealer*'s Jack. *Miss Spider's Tea Party* landed on the best-seller lists in its first month of publication.

Kirk found the calmer, more rural aspect of the Finger Lakes area much more conducive to writing and illustrating than he did New York City. He married, and he and his wife had a daughter named Violet. He and his wife eventually divorced, but Kirk remarried, and had two more daughters named after flowers: Primrose and Wisteria. He constructed a two-story, Victorian-style treehouse on his property, which he uses as his studio. It was there that he first gained prominence as the writer and illustrator of his series of children's books featuring Miss Spider and a cast of other bugs.

Miss Spider's Tea Party features Miss Spider as a vegetarian spider who has trouble making friends among the other bugs in her neighborhood because they are afraid they will be eaten. But Miss Spider shows the others that she only eats flowers, and at last they become her friends and come to her tea party. Kirk went on to write more books with Miss Spider as the main character. In the sequels to *Miss Spider's Tea Party*, Kirk wrote about Miss Spider marrying (*Miss Spider's Wedding*), buying a new car (*Miss Spider's New Car*), and going to school (*Little Miss Spider at Sunny Patch School*).

Miss Spider's Tea Party and the other books in the series sold more than four and a half million copies by early 2003, including editions in seven languages. This was all the more remarkable considering that Kirk had never written anything before these books. The book are written in verse, and, according the Kirk, appeal to children because of their bright colors, feel-good stories, and characters that readers identify with. Calloway further related the books' appeal to their life-affirming themes.

But Miss Spider's appeal is not limited to children. In 1995, pop star Madonna read *Miss Spider's Tea Party* on a show that was broadcast on MTV. From then on, it was cool to be friends with Miss Spider, and her books have found fans among college students and many others besides her original audience. The book got an additional boost in 1997 when first lady Hillary Rodham Clinton selected the book to promote a national children's literacy program.

Following his success with the Miss Spider books, Kirk went on to write and illustrate other successful children's books, such as his "Biddle" series, which features baby animals. Kirk also followed the Miss Spider books with a series of Little Miss Spider books, which feature Miss Spider as a youngster. In 1999, Kirk published *Nova's Arc,* about a robot who looks like a little boy and crash–lands on a lifeless planet and builds other, animal–inspired robots to keep loneliness at bay. Instead of drawing the illustrations himself for this book, he worked closely with a computer graphics company to produce them.

Late in 1996, Kirk met the woman who was to become his second wife. Kathy Anne Dropp approached Kirk at a book signing for an autograph, and the two got to know each other the following year when Dropp, who was a museum curator, presented an exhibition of drawings and paintings, including Kirk's, at the Roberson Museum and Science Center in Binghamton, NY, where she worked. The two discovered in each other a mutual love of animals, and after Dropp accompanied Kirk on one of his regular trips to rescue toads from country roads, they fell in love. The two were married in 2000 in a ceremony that included only 22 guests. The wedding featured a mole theme, with bride and bridegroom mole characters on top of the wedding cake. Kirk explained that the moles were inspired by a story he was writing about a mole who finds fulfillment in the company of another mole.

In 2003, Kirk branched out from illustrating and writing books to creating merchandise for Target stores. Beginning in 2003, Target featured a line of Miss Spider children's clothing, furniture, and gardening tools—all of which Kirk designed. The line of Miss Spider merchandise is called "Sunny Patch," and it is unusual in that, unlike other children's merchandise based on fictional characters, it was offered in stores before a link was established between it and a television program. But it was not the first time that the retailer had worked with Kirk's creations: in 1996, Target featured Miss Spider in an advertising campaign. The Sunny Patch line is Target's first designer brand for children.

Speaking to the *Plain Dealer*'s Jack, Callaway called the idea of selling Miss Spider products through Target his own brainstorm. The products feature the bright colors of Kirk's illustrations, and include caterpillar brooms, ladybug rockers, and spider watering cans—more than 100 items in all. More products were planned for later in the year, including Halloween costumes and furniture for children's bedrooms.

Also in 2003, the Nickelodeon television network produced a cartoon special based on Kirk's work called *Miss Spider's Sunny Patch Kids.* Rendered in computer–generated 3–D graphics, the show aired in March of 2003. Future plans for Kirk's work on TV included a series based on the Nickelodeon special to be aired on a daily basis on Nick Jr. starting in 2004. A book titled *Miss Spider's Babies* was scheduled to be published in April of 2004.

Kirk has said that part of his secret to success with creating products and books for children is that his own outlook on life has changed little from the time he was seven years old. He sees the world, he has said, through the eyes of a child, and that keeps him young at heart. Kirk has also said that he would not let success go to his head. Preferring a quiet lifestyle, Kirk works with a single assistant, engaging in negotiations and delivering his designs and writings by mail, phone, and email.

Kirk enjoys spending time with his family more than spending time in the limelight, and he intends to change little about his life and work, no matter how popular his work becomes. "David likes to live in a hole and not be disturbed," his brother, Dan, told Lois Smith Brady in the *New York Times,* "He doesn't like the phone to ring. He doesn't like to travel. He likes to be quiet." Kirk has cited as his biggest reward writing books that people enjoy reading.

Selected writings

Miss Spider's Tea Party, Scholastic (New York), 1994.
Miss Spider's Wedding, Scholastic, 1995.
Miss Spider's Tea Party: The Counting Book, Scholastic, 1997.
Miss Spider's New Car, Scholastic, 1997.
Nova's Arc, Scholastic, 1999.
Little Miss Spider at Sunny Patch School, Scholastic, 2000.
Miss Spider's ABC, Scholastic, 2000.
Little Miss Spider: A Christmas Wish, Scholastic, 2001.
Little Bird, Biddle Bird, Scholastic, 2001.
Little Pig, Biddle Pig, Scholastic, 2001.
Little Mouse, Biddle Mouse, Scholastic, 2002.
Little Bunny, Biddle Bunny, Scholastic, 2002.
Little Miss Spider, Scholastic, 2003.
Biddle, Scholastic, 2003.
Little Miss Spider at Sunny Patch, Scholastic, 2003.

Sources

Periodicals

Los Angeles Times, November 18, 1999, p. 46.
New York Times, February 20, 2000, p. 9.
Plain Dealer, February 22, 2003, p. E1.
Time, January 20, 2003, pp. 131–32.

Online

"About Callaway: Who We Are," Callaway, http://www.callaway.com/About_Callaway/AC-whoweare.html (August 25, 2003).

"Author David Kirk," Scholastic, http://www.scholastic.com/titles/missspider/author.htm (July 11, 2003).

—Michael Belfiore

Jim Koch

President of Boston Beer

Born C. James Koch, May 27, 1949, in Cincinnati, OH; married first wife (divorced); married Cynthia A. Fisher (a biotechnology entrepreneur); children: four (two from each marriage). *Education:* Harvard University, B.A. 1971, J.D./M.B.A., 1978.

Addresses: *Office*—Boston Beer Co., 75 Arlington St., Boston, MA 02116.

Career

Instructor for Outward Bound, 1973–77; business consultant, Boston Consulting Group, 1979–84; founded Boston Beer Co., 1984.

Sidelights

Jim Koch gave up a lucrative career as a business consultant to become a brewer. His family had been brewers back to his great–great–grandfather, but Koch's parents had steered him to a different profession. Koch (pronounced "Cook") founded Boston Beer Company in 1984, and brought American drinkers a domestic beer, Samuel Adams, that competed with imports on taste and quality. Koch's marketing skill made Samuel Adams the best–selling craft beer in the United States. Koch began by aggressively promoting his beer at bar after bar, trying to persuade Boston innkeepers to stock Samuel Adams. Now he presides over a company with sales of more than $200 million, at what might be called the largest small brewer in the country. A fanatic for taste, Koch still personally samples every batch of Samuel Adams.

Koch was born in Cincinnati, Ohio, to a family of German descent. His ancestors had made beer in the old country, and his father was a brewer for a Cincinnati beer–maker. Koch did well in school, and was accepted to prestigious Harvard University. After completing an undergraduate degree in government, Koch went on to a combined program at Harvard that offered both a law degree and a master's in business. It was a particularly difficult course of study that attracted some stellar candidates. One of Koch's classmates was Mitt Romney, who went on to become governor of Massachusetts. But Koch was dissatisfied with life at Harvard. At the age of 23, he felt he had done nothing in his life yet but go to school. He wanted different kinds of experience. So he left his graduate program and became an instructor at the outdoor adventure school Outward Bound.

Outward Bound was a rigorous wilderness program that taught often troubled teens how to survive the outdoors, work in a group, make good decisions, and assess risks. Koch was keenly aware that he held the lives of his students in his hands. During his four years with Outward Bound, he traveled across the West, gaining insights that helped him later in his business career. In a story he wrote for the *New York Times* in 2003, Koch recalled how his Outward Bound groups always used a lot of nylon string. So he started out giving everyone more string than they would need, just in case. That group failed to take care of its string, and ended up with too little. For his next group, he doled out less string than necessary. This group learned to conserve the essential asset, and finished the adventure with string left over. Though it was years later that Koch started his company, it stuck with him that it was possible to do more with less.

Koch eventually returned to Harvard and finished his double degree. He then got a job with a business consulting company called the Boston Consulting Group. He worked there for five years, but he found he was still not doing what he really wanted. He decided to quit the consulting group and invest his savings in brewing beer. His father, a lifelong brewery worker, was appalled. When Koch told his story for *Reader's Digest,* he said, "When I told Dad, I was hoping he'd put his arm around me and get misty about reviving tradition. Instead he said, 'Jim, that is the dumbest thing I've ever heard!'"

Yet Koch's plan was far from naïve. He had carefully researched the market, and he believed beer drinkers were ready for a good domestic beer. In the early 1980s, sales of imported beer were growing. European beers had a reputation for better quality than mass–market American brands such as Coors and Miller. Yet European brewers frequently resorted to preservatives and fillers in order to make their products last for overseas shipment. At the same time, the United States market was seeing a flood of domestic beers made by very small brewers, called microbreweries. While these microbrews often won big on taste, their makers rarely had the marketing know–how to get their beers to a wide audience. Plus, most microbrewers had made large financial commitments to their physical plants, and had little money left over to push for wider distribution or to run advertising. Koch planned to make a fine–quality domestic beer that would compete with both imports and microbrews. But he aimed to grow beyond a regional market and become a national player.

Koch started out with $100,000 of his own savings, plus $140,000 in loans from family and friends. Instead of buying a brewery with his capital, Koch took his great–great–grandfather's authentic German beer recipe to a contract brewer in Pittsburgh. He named his creation Samuel Adams, after the Revolutionary War hero and brewer. Though he saved an estimated $10 million by not building his own brewery, Samuel Adams still turned out to be an expensive beer. Using the quality ingredients Koch insisted on, Samuel Adams retailed for about 15 percent more than leading imported beers. This made it very difficult to sell. Koch roamed Boston, serving samples to bartenders and bar owners while telling them about his new company and his family tradition. Koch claimed he sometimes had to make 15 visits to a bar before he could persuade the owner to carry his brand.

Boston Beer began advertising heavily in 1986. Unlike other beer advertising, which relied primarily on images of attractive, happy drinkers, Koch depicted Samuel Adams as simply a quality brew. Early advertising also emphasized that Samuel Adams was a domestic brand, with slogans like "Declare your independence from foreign beer." Perhaps because it was so different from established beer advertising, the Samuel Adams campaign attracted a lot of media attention. The brand caught on, and in 1992 it went into markets across the country. Sales grew by over 60 percent that year. By 1994, Koch's company was bringing in $50 million in sales, and Samuel Adams was the best–selling specialty beer in the United States.

Sales continued to grow, and Koch's company was bringing in about $200 million by the mid–1990s. Koch took Boston Beer Company public in 1995. Koch told Gerry Khermouch of *BusinessWeek* that he could have sold the company any time he wanted, and never worked again. But that did not appeal to him. "What would I do if I did sell?" he asked Khermouch. "I'd go looking for a brewery to buy so I could launch my own brand." Even as his company grew to have hundreds of employees, Koch remained intimately connected with the brewing process. The company began experimenting with unusual beers in the late 1990s, including pricey, extra–strong brews, and special seasonal flavors. Koch confided to Sarah Theodore, of *Beverage Industry,* that he still tasted every batch Boston Beer produced. "I'm still the protector of the beer," he told her. Not only did he make sure his company's beer tasted good straight out of the cask, but he traveled to bars, restaurants, and convenience stores to check how the beer was selling and make sure draft kegs were the right temperature and not beyond the sell date.

After two years of research and development, Koch's company brought out a light (low–calorie) beer in 2002. Light beers were often disdained by the kind of beer connoisseurs who relished Samuel Adams and other craft beers. But Sam Adams Light aimed for a different kind of flavor than the typical light beer, and it was evidently very successful. Sales at Boston Beer climbed more than ten percent the year the light brew came out.

By 2004, Koch was in his fifties and celebrated 20 years as head of Boston Beer. He was clearly not ready to retire, and brushed off talk of selling the company. His share of the company was then worth about $70 million. He was keen on introducing Samuel Adams to younger beer drinkers, who often bypassed the brand for more exotic–sounding microbrews. He continued to tinker with beer recipes, brewing what he believed to be the world's strongest beer, a 50–proof special edition, to keep himself interested.

Sources

Beverage Industry, May 2003, p. 32.
BusinessWeek, September 1, 2003, pp. 54–56.
Management Review, April 1994, p. 16.

New York Times, July 20, 2003, sec. 3, p. 12.
Reader's Digest, February 1, 2000, pp. 28–30.

—A. Woodward

Mike Korchinsky

Founder and Chief Executive Officer of Wildlife Works

Born Michael Korchinsky, September 21, 1961, in Brookville, Ontario, Canada; son of Walter (a chemical engineering professor) and Gloria Korchinsky; married Linda Hanson (an insurance–firm owner), 1993. *Education:* Birmingham University, Birmingham, England, B.S.E. (chemical engineering), 1982.

Addresses: *Office*—475 Gate 5 Rd., No. 120, Sausalito, CA 94965–1443.

Career

Worked for Shell Oil; consultant, Anderson Consulting, London, England, 1982–85, Chicago office, 1985; consulting manager, Myers Holum, San Francisco, CA, 1986–88; co–founder and president, Axiom Consulting, San Francisco, 1988–95; senior vice president, Cambridge Technology Partners, 1995–97; founder and chief executive officer, Wildlife Works, San Francisco (moved to Sausalito, CA), 1997—.

Sidelights

Mike Korchinsky, founder of Wildlife Works, is thrilled to see celebrities appearing in national magazines wearing his company's apparel. But he is not a fashion designer, and he is not planning to make a name on the runways of Paris or Milan. Instead, he is an entrepreneur and conservationist who hopes that by selling more clothes, he will help save animals and raise awareness of the need for more conservation. Talk show host Oprah Winfrey and actresses Helen Hunt, Catherine Zeta–Jones, and Charlize Theron, among others, have been spotted wearing the Wildlife Works brand. The clothes also showed up in the on–set closet of actress Debra Messing, star of the hit television sitcom *Will & Grace.* Non–famous customers across the country are scooping up sporty Wildlife Works apparel at department stores like Nordstrom and local boutiques. Korchinsky started the company after a trip to Africa in 1996 left him assessing his goals. "I wondered whether I really wanted to spend the rest of my life helping big companies become more successful or trying to help wildlife find a way in this world," he remarked in an article in *People.*

Korchinsky was born September 21, 1961, in Brookville, Ontario, Canada, to Walter and Gloria Korchinsky. His mother died when he was six and his father, a chemical engineering professor, raised him and his brother on his own. This left the two boys with plenty of time on their hands, so Korchinsky used to read a lot and he liked learning about animals. As a child, he had a collection of elephant figurines. Growing up in Stockport, England, he had dogs and cats as pets, but "never saw anything remotely resembling a wild animal," he said in a telephone interview with *Newsmakers.*

Following in his father's footsteps, Korchinsky earned a bachelor's degree in chemical engineering from Birmingham University in Birmingham, England. Afterward, he spent a summer working for Shell Oil. "It was so incredibly dull that I decided I didn't want to be a chemical engineer," he told *Newsmakers.* Anderson Consulting recruited him in 1982 and trained him to be a business consultant. Korchinsky traveled to the United States, Belgium, France, and Spain during this time, and in 1985, he was transferred to the Chicago, Illinois, office.

In 1986, Korchinsky took a job as a consulting manager with Myers Holum in San Francisco, California. In these consulting jobs, he advised businesses to be innovative, but as he told Michael Barrier in *Nation's Business,* "There was an inherent contradiction, because, internally, they were just as bureaucratic and old–fashioned" as the firms they were trying to help. After two years there, he co–founded Axiom Consulting.

With Axiom Consulting, Korchinsky established a business that incorporated the practices it was recommending for others. For one, he instituted a "productive dress code," which meant employees could dress however they felt most productive. If that meant jeans and short–sleeved shirts, that was fine. He also set up offices in San Francisco's South of Market area that had more natural light and only two or three floors, as opposed to 50 in a high–rise. He felt this would make the workplace more enjoyable for employees. By 1994, Axiom Consulting posted sales of $12 million and boasted a client list that included Wells Fargo, Transamerica, and Shell Oil. In 1995, Korchinsky sold Axiom to Cambridge Technology Partners, but stayed on with the new company as senior vice president.

On a vacation to Africa in 1996, according to Keri Brenner of the *Marin Independent Journal* article, Korchinsky's entire life began to change. After observing majestic animals lounging in their natural splendor for a few days, "I began seeing skittish animals [and] electric fences," he told Brenner. "I began to ask questions." He found out animals were being hunted by poor locals who poached them to eat their meat and sell their hides; trees were being destroyed for fuel. Angry, Korchinsky resolved to do something about it. Instead of trying to force change on Africans, he founded a model of

"consumer–powered conservation," wrote Nichole L. Torres in *Entrepreneur.* He envisioned a business that would provide an economic engine for the area to help the people and at the same time preserve the local environment. "Many people, after they've made their money," Korchinsky stated to Brenner, "give their money and hearts to conservation, but very few give their business acumen."

In 1997 Korchinsky put his model into practice with Wildlife Works. He decided on a clothing company, according to a reporter for Planetsave.com, for these reasons: "Fashion is trendy enough to get celebrity and media attention. It can be made with environmentally friendly materials. It has a high–labor content but a low–skill level." Creative director Tammy Hulva comes up with themes for each seasonal collection. Some of the clothes, which are made of organically grown cotton, feature endangered species like silverback gorillas and Bengal tigers, while others have slogans like "Tree Hugger." T–shirts sell for about $28 and up.

The company got started with help from private investors and in 1999, Wildlife Works bought a failing cattle ranch in Tsavo National Park in Kenya to convert into a garment factory and wildlife sanctuary. The 80,000–acre Rukinga Wildlife Sanctuary is home to 47 mammal species and several endangered species. As of late 2003, the factory in Kenya employed 56 locals who earn $50 a week with health benefits (the average annual salary in Kenya is $300 a year). Korchinsky gives back 20 percent of the company's proceeds to fund community projects like schools and libraries in addition to the sanctuary, and hopes to increase that amount to 25 percent, according to Brenner. Estimated sales for 2003 were $2 million.

Korchinsky is married to Linda Hanson, who owns an insurance firm, and they have two dogs, Joey and Tess, and one cat, Ben. A self–confessed "nature channel addict," as he said in the telephone interview with *Newsmakers,* he is also a vegetarian. Korchinsky plans to continue to grow his business in order to expand conservation efforts to more places in the world such as India and South America, he noted in the telephone interview. "I would like to measure success in ten years based on how many species we save," he said in *People.*

Sources

Periodicals

Entrepreneur, June 2002, p. 132.
Environment, September 2001, p. 6.

Forbes, March 14, 1994, p. 152.

Forbes FYI, Spring 2001, p. 22.

Knight Ridder/Tribune Business News, February 6, 2002, p. 1.

Los Angeles Times, August 17, 2001, p. E2.

Marin Independent Journal (California), April 9, 2002.

Nation's Business, July 1994, p. 18.

People, January 20, 2003, pp. 89–90.

PR Newswire, November 7, 2001.

San Francisco Chronicle, August 26, 2001.

Online

"Clothing company goes to work for its community," Planetsave, http://www.planetsave.com/ViewStory.asp?ID=3844 (November 17, 2003).

Additional information was obtained through a telephone interview with Mike Korchinsky on November 18, 2003.

—*Geri Koeppel*

Dick Kovacevich

Chairman, President, and Chief Executive Officer of Wells Fargo & Co.

Born Richard M. Kovacevich in 1943, in Enumclaw, WA; married Mary Jo; children: three. *Education:* Stanford University, B.S. (industrial engineering); Stanford University, M.B.A., 1967.

Addresses: *Office*—Wells Fargo & Co., 420 Montgomery St., San Francisco, CA 94163.

Career

Worked in strategic planning, General Mills, c. 1968–69; general manager, Kenner Products, 1970–71; head of American Photographics Corp., 1972–75; consumer banking positions at Citibank, 1975–85; chief operating officer, Norwest Bank, 1986; named president, Norwest, 1989; became Norwest's CEO, 1993; became CEO of Wells Fargo after merger with Norwest, 1998.

Member: Board member, Cargill, Inc.; Target Corp.; San Francisco Symphony; trustee, San Francisco Museum of Modern Art; chairman, California Business Roundtable.

Awards: *American Banker*'s Banker of the Year, 2003.

Sidelights

Richard Kovacevich heads Wells Fargo, one of the biggest banks in the United States. After putting together a risky merger of the Minneapolis–based Norwest Corp. with Wells Fargo in 1998, Kovacevich proved industry analysts wrong by dovetailing the two companies and then outperforming all major rivals. While many banks had trouble righting themselves after mergers, Kovacevich handled the integration of Norwest and the San Francisco–based Wells Fargo with particular care so that customers were not alienated. Wells Fargo went on to perform well above expectation in the 2000s, though economic conditions were poor and other banks stumbled. Kovacevich is described as a contrarian by many in the banking industry. His philosophy is to look beyond current business conditions and figure out what his customers will need in the future. Kovacevich also stands out among bankers for his concern with consumers. He refers to Wells Fargo branches as "stores," and his growth plan while he headed Norwest was compared to the strategy of proliferating chains like Starbucks and McDonald's. This is an unorthodox vision of banking, yet Kovacevich has the numbers to prove his way works. Since the late 1990s, Norwest and then Wells Fargo have showed earnings growth of close to 15 percent annually, nearly twice that of the banking industry average.

Kovacevich was born in the small town of Enumclaw, Washington, 20 miles east of Tacoma. He excelled at both academics and athletics, and played baseball for Stanford University. He earned a degree in industrial engineering at Stanford, where he was a star pitcher. He considered a career as a professional baseball player, but a shoulder injury made that impossible. Kovacevich continued at Stanford, earning a graduate degree in business administration. He told a classmate at the time that he would never go into banking. He preferred a less hierarchical business, where he would have more responsibility for key decisions. His first job out of graduate school was with General Mills in Minneapolis, Minnesota. He spent two years doing strategic planning for that company, and then took a position as general manager of General Mills' toy division, Kenner Products, in Cincinnati, Ohio.

After several years at Kenner, Kovacevich decided to go into something entrepreneurial. He took over American Photographic Corp., a small photography business on Long Island in New York, started by former General Mills executives. The company reproduced family photos from damaged originals. After three years there, a management recruiter convinced him to meet with an executive at the New York bank Citicorp. Citicorp was a large urban bank with many layers of management, exactly the kind of business Kovacevich was sure he did not like. But after talking several times with the head of Citibank's consumer division, Kovacevich was convinced working for the bank would present new and interesting challenges. He was also promised responsibility and the leeway to do things how he saw fit. Kovacevich started in the consumer division in October of 1975, and by 1977 he was in charge of the bank's branch system in New York City.

Kovacevich showed his empathy with consumers and his ability to inspire his employees while at Citibank. The bank had just reorganized, taking large corporate accounts out of the branches and putting them under an umbrella corporate banking group. The bank had also just begun to install automated teller machines (ATMs) throughout the city. Branch employees resented the new equipment, fearing that it would replace human beings. Customers also were not comfortable with ATMs at that point. These combined changes had taken their toll on the New York City branch system, which had 273 outposts, and the division was losing money. Within three years, Kovacevich had made the branch system profitable. He was apparently able to promote the use of ATMs to customers, while reassuring employees that their jobs were not threatened. He worked closely with the bank's technology section as well, and ended up satisfying all the parties involved in the ATM deployment.

Kovacevich clearly did a great job handling Citibank's branch banking system. But after working there ten years, another man was promoted ahead of him to head Citibank's consumer division. Kovacevich was looking for more responsibility, and it seemed like he might not get it at Citibank. So he

left his post and moved back to Minneapolis, where he became chief operating officer of the regional bank Norwest. Norwest had been a leading farm lender in the 1980s, but then suffered as the agriculture and real estate sectors in the Midwest did poorly. The bank had a heavy portfolio of bad loans by the mid–1980s, and its return on equity (a key measure of a bank's profitability) was very low, at eight percent. The bank had also had plain bad luck. The bank's president was electrocuted during a thunderstorm in 1979, and in 1982 the bank's headquarters burned down. A new chief executive took over just before Kovacevich came in, and management began to turn Norwest around. Kovacevich traveled extensively, so that within two years at Norwest he had visited all its more than 200 offices.

Kovacevich was known for inspiring employees, sometimes resorting to theatrical antics to fire up team spirit. His aim was to make Norwest a superior local bank, even as it began to spread beyond the Midwest. Kovacevich inspired Norwest's branches to seek out small customers instead of big businesses. The bank also moved into areas such as consumer finance, insurance, and mortgages, where it had done little business before. Kovacevich also promoted cross–selling, meaning he hooked customers who used one bank service to sign up for others. Selling more products to existing customers seemed to make more sense to Kovacevich than angling to bring in customers of other banks. Cross–selling became one of the hallmarks of Norwest's success.

By the end of 1988, Norwest was showing remarkable improvement, with a return on equity of close to 20 percent. Kovacevich became president of Norwest in 1989, and then chairman in 1995. In the early 1990s, Norwest added close to 1,400 branches (or stores, as Kovacevich liked to call them). Kovacevich's cross–selling strategy had paid off, and Norwest's customers used close to four of the bank's products, on average, by the mid–1990s. Norwest grew into a so–called superregional bank, with assets of about $78 billion by 1996.

In 1998 Kovacevich put together a merger of Norwest and Wells Fargo, a deal worth $31 billion that Wall Street claimed would not work. Bank mergers were notoriously ticklish, and several big mergers in the 1990s had left the new company with a sagging stock price and complaints that the acquiring bank had paid too much. Often the merged company cut costs by eliminating jobs, and this sometimes drove customers away. Wells Fargo itself had made a bad merger in 1996, buying First Interstate and then finding its customers fleeing. Because it had this unhappy merger behind it, Wells Fargo was something of a bargain. Kovacevich viewed the merger as a combination of equals. The combined company took the Wells Fargo name and moved its headquarters to San Francisco, California. Then Kovacevich did everything the "wrong" way round. Instead of trimming costs in the range of 30 to 45 percent, like other merged banks had tried, he only aimed to cut costs by a modest 17 percent. Instead of rushing through new technology that would bring both companies together within a year, Kovacevich laid out a leisurely schedule of three years for full integration. Thousands of Wells Fargo employees could have lost their jobs because of the merger, but Kovacevich offered retraining and kept on almost 60 percent of the Wells Fargo workers whose positions became redundant. This all sounded like nice–guy decisions, but the bank made money, too. Wells Fargo's earnings rose more than 90 percent in 1999. Its revenue rose almost ten percent, outperforming rivals, and its share price also went up.

Kovacevich made Wells Fargo a high–performing bank even as the long bull market of the 1990s ended and many other banks found themselves burdened with bad loans. Wells Fargo made some smaller acquisitions in the 2000s, building up its insurance business. Its stock price rose at a compound rate of four percent annually in the early 2000s, when comparable regional banks were seeing their stock sink. The bank also prospered on refinancing mortgages. Kovacevich continued to stress cross–selling, aiming to get Wells Fargo customers using as many as eight of the bank's services. The banking industry journal *American Banker* chose Kovacevich as its banker of the year for 2003. Kovacevich explained an element of his philosophy to the magazine's Laura Mandaro, telling her how he looked for the next business environment, not what was happening now. "If you look at most financial institutions, they're always chasing today's environment, where in fact that should probably be a signal to do the opposite," he said. "We start shifting resources two or three years before probably anything's going to occur." Although Wells Fargo had handled some $221 billion in new mortgages in 2002, Kovacevich hinted that he would probably scale back the bank's mortgage business. At one point, Kovacevich's contrarian streak may have seemed foolish, but his success with Wells Fargo showed that he knew what he was doing. Kovacevich, who had sworn he would never go into banking, had become the banker to watch.

Sources

American Banker, March 22, 2002, p. 2; December 2003 Supplement, p. 2A; December 4, 2003, p. 1.
BusinessWeek, January 13, 2003, pp. 68–69.
Chief Executive, May 2001, p. 23.
Fortune, July 6, 1998, p. 126; May 15, 2000, p. 299.
Institutional Investor, December 1996, p. 43.
U.S. Banker, November 2002, p. 46.

—*A. Woodward*

Heinz Krogner

Deputy Chairman and Group Chief Executive Officer of Esprit Holdings Ltd.

Born Heinz Jü Krogner–Kornalik, c. 1941, in Czechoslovakia. *Education:* Earned degree in business administration and industrial engineering.

Addresses: *Office*—Esprit Europe GmbH, Esprit–Allee, D–40882 Ratingen, Germany.

Career

Worked as a retail consultant with Kurt Salmon Associates; worked as a textile–company executive; joined Esprit, January, 1995; became chief executive officer of Esprit Europe; named chief executive officer of Esprit International; named deputy chairman and group chief executive officer of Esprit Holdings Ltd., November, 2002.

Sidelights

Heinz Krogner has grand plans to revive the Esprit clothing line in the United States and make it a serious contender in the range of fashionable, affordable styles, featuring good quality for democratic prices. As the focused, somewhat fierce new chief executive officer of Esprit International, Krogner has guided the company's once–moribund performance to an impressive turnaround in Europe, and by 2003 had set his sights on re–conquering the U.S. market, Esprit's original home turf.

Krogner was born in the early 1940s in Czechoslovakia into a German èmigrè family there. He grew up in the post–World War II Communist bloc, first in Czechoslovakia and later, after the age of 17, in what was then known as the German Democratic Republic, or Communist East Germany. Later he became one of the many young adults who fled the restrictions of Soviet–style socialism in Eastern Europe, and he eventually earned a degree in business administration and industrial engineering in what was then West Germany.

Krogner was a highly successful retail consultant in Germany for a number of years, working with Kurt Salmon Associates, and also held executive posts with various textile companies. He joined Esprit in January of 1995, at a time when the company was still doing well in Europe and Asia, but was being run by creditor banks in the United States. The irony behind Esprit's plummeting U.S. fortunes was one that was almost a quintessentially American tragedy: founded in California in 1968 by two design–conscious hippies, Esprit enjoyed tremendous success in the 1980s, with sales peaking at $400 million in 1987. Its fresh styles were instantly recognizable by their bright hues and modern textile patterns, and its mail–order catalogue and print campaigns were the innovative work of Oliveiro Toscani, who later went on to take a similar approach for Benetton. Esprit also pioneered the socially conscious advertising campaign. It moved into Europe in the 1980s, and the Hong Kong office, established to reach a potentially huge Asian market, was established in the late 1980s.

By the time Krogner joined the company, Esprit's founders, Douglas and Susie Tompkins, had gone through a bitter divorce, and the legal proceedings on how the company's assets should be split between them dragged on for years. Meanwhile, the company faltered, and began losing market share to brands like The Gap. In 1996, creditor banks gained control of Esprit de Corp, as the company was formally known in the United States. Its brands in Europe and Asia, meanwhile, were managed separately, and the latter did particularly well under the guidance of a Hong Kong businessman, Michael Ying, whose links to the company dated back to the early 1970s.

Krogner served as head of Esprit's Europe division, which in 1996 was acquired by the Asian arm. Under the newly named Esprit Holdings Ltd., the company moved to recapture its lost European market share. He ran a tight ship out of Esprit Europe's Düsseldorf, Germany, offices, and made the division a more cohesive unit. For example, he eradicated the practice of pricing items differently in the various countries, which was common practice for many retailers in Europe. The introduction of the Euro, the common currency adopted by most Europe union member nations, ended that business practice. "You can not ask for more money in Britain than you would on the Continent," Krogner told *Sunday Times* journalist Dominic Rushe. "All the price tags will be in euros and people will know they are being cheated. People who try it will not survive."

By the new millennium, Krogner was a key executive in a thriving empire that did business in some 44 countries and rang in retail sales in the $2 billion range. In the fall of 2002, Ying named him chief executive officer of Esprit Holdings, and stepped aside to take a post as chairman of the supervisory board. It was a move that signaled the company's determination to become a truly global player, along the lines of hip, affordable clothing chains like H&M and Zara, which had captured the European market and then headed into North American cities. That same year, Esprit Holdings, the parent company, bought the rights to the "Esprit de Corp" name from the company's ailing U.S. operations.

Krogner's mission was to re–integrate the company's operations and position it as a global presence. During his first year, noted *Forbes* writer Leigh Gallagher, "he fired the company's six division heads, eliminated 100 additional positions, and reorganized the company's structure by business unit instead of by function. He also nearly quadrupled revenues." Esprit was even planning 20 company–owned, entirely new megastores for the United States. The American retail sector was ripe for such a move, Krogner told *Brandweek*'s Sandra Dolbow. "There's too much sameness and too much discounting," he asserted, noting that the climate was similar to that of department stores in Europe in the early 1990s. After losing sales to H&M, the department stores revamped their clothing lines, and "they went with companies like Esprit. We bring differentiation to the market and a new flavor to the table." The cost–conscious CEO had no plans to create an "Old Navy"–style marketing blitz to re–launch, however. He claimed that sixty percent "of American women still know Esprit," according to Dolbow in the *Brandweek* interview.

The company's stock, listed in the Hong Kong and London exchanges, was one of the few retail–industry successes during the recession–plagued first years of the 21st century. Krogner oversaw this newly global company from his Düsseldorf office; Esprit's financial staff was still in Hong Kong, and there was an "image" headquarters slated to open in New York City around 2004. The CEO spends two hours a day on videoconference calls. "We are becoming more or less a virtual company," he told *Forbes*'s Gallagher. "I am sitting in the middle, like the spider in the net." Taking a page from the immensely successful H&M, Esprit would no longer offer regional lines geared toward an American, Asian, or European consumer. "People have become more international," he said in the *Forbes* interview. "They travel, and their taste level has become more similar." Market research had also declared Esprit's new target customer as the 28–year–old—in mind and spirit, that is. "A 20–year–old wouldn't mind becoming 28—it represents career and marriage and family," Krogner told *Wall Street Journal* writer Sarah McBride. "And a 40–year–old woman wouldn't mind becoming 28." Krogner summed up this feeling when he said, as noted on the Esprit.com website, "Esprit is not an age, but an attitude."

Sources

Periodicals

Brandweek, April 15, 2002, p. 11.
Financial Times, September 19, 2003, p. 31.
Forbes, June 9, 2003, p. 80.
Hong Kong iMail, February 1, 2001.

New York Post, July 10, 2003, p. 35.

San Francisco Chronicle, July 8, 2003, p. B1.

Scotsman (Edinburgh, Scotland), December 15, 1998, p. 22.

Sunday Times (London, England), November 28, 1999, p. 2.

Times (London, England), December 15, 1998, p. 25.

Wall Street Journal, June 17, 2002.

Online

"Company Executive Board Members," Esprit.com, http://www.esprit.com/company/board.cfm (December 26, 2003).

"Company Profile," Esprit.com, http://www.esprit.com/company/profile.cfm (December 26, 2003).

—*Carol Brennan*

Nick Lachey and Jessica Simpson

Singers and actors

Born Nicholas Scott Lachey, November 9, 1973, in Harlan, KY; son of John Lachey and Cate Fopma–Leimbach; married Jessica Simpson (a singer and actress), October 26, 2002. *Education:* Attended the University of Southern California; attended Miami (Ohio) University. Born Jessica Ann Simpson, July 10, 1980, in Dallas, TX; daughter of Joe (a minister, psychologist, and talent manager) and Tina (a stylist) Simpson; married Nick Lachey (a singer and actor), October 26, 2002.

Addresses: (Lachey) *Record label*—Universal Records, 1755 Broadway, New York, NY 10019. *Website*—www.nicklachey.com. (Simpson) *Fan club*—P.O. Box 452588, Garland, TX 75045–2588. *Office*—c/o Top 40 Entertainment, 156 W. 56th St., 5th Fl., New York, NY 10019. *Website*—www.jessicasimpson. com.

Career

Lachey joined pop group 98 Degrees, 1995; signed to Motown Records, 1996; released *98 Degrees,* 1997; released *98 Degrees and Rising,* 1998; released *Revelation,* 2000; left 98 Degrees, 2001; solo artist, 2003—; released *SoulO,* 2003. Television appearances include: *American Dreams,* NBC, 2004; *I'm With Her,* 2004; *Hot Momma* (pilot), ABC, 2004. Simpson began working as a singer, c. 1997; released *Sweet Kisses,* 1999; released *Irresistible,* 2001; released *In This Skin,* 2003. Film appearances include: *Master of Disguise,* 2002. Television appearances include: *That '70s Show,* Fox, 2002–03; *The Twilight Zone,* UPN, 2003; VH1 Divas, 2004; ABC television pilot, 2004. Television appearances together: *Newlyweds: Nick and Jessica,*

MTV, 2003—; *Dick Clark's New Year's Rockin' Eve* (co–hosts), 2003; *Saturday Night Live* (co–hosts), NBC, 2004; *The Nick and Jessica Variety Hour,* ABC, 2004.

Awards: (Lachey) Love song of the year, Teen Choice Awards, for "Where You Are," 2000; most requested song of the year, Radio Music Awards, for "Give Me Just One Night (Una Noche)," 2000. (Simpson) Breakout artist and love song of the year, Teen Choice Awards, for "Where You Are," 2000.

Sidelights

Though Nick Lachey and Jessica Simpson had at least moderately successful singing careers before their marriage—he with boy band 98 Degrees then as a solo artist, and she as a pop solo artist—it was their reality show, *Newlyweds: Nick and Jessica,* that made them celebrities. The show was a big hit, due in part to Simpson's jaw–dropping gaffes and Lachey's patience with his wife's lack of common sense. *Newlyweds* proved so popular that MTV aired a second season in 2004, and ABC gave them a variety special, *The Nick and Jessica Variety Hour* to try to make them into the next Sonny and Cher.

Simpson was born on July 10, 1980, in Dallas, Texas, the daughter of a Baptist minister, Joe Simpson, and his wife, Tina. She was raised in Texas with her younger sister, Ashlee, who is also a singer, in a very Christian household. Simpson began her singing career early in life, singing gospel at her father's church from at least the age of five, if not earlier. Simpson also wanted to try acting.

When Simpson was 12 years old, she auditioned for *The New Mickey Mouse Club* but she did not make it. However, her future pop singing rivals, Britney Spears and Christina Aguilera, did secure roles on the show. Despite this setback, Simpson continued singing, including appearances at church camps.

It was at such a camp that an executive from a Christian gospel label, CCM, discovered Simpson and signed her to a recording contract. From the ages of 13 to 16, Simpson worked on her debut record for the label. However, the label folded before her record could be released. Simpson's grandmother paid for some copies to be pressed, but there was little attention paid to the recording.

While still attending high school at J.J. Pearce High School in Richardson, Texas, Simpson built her career on the Christian youth conference circuit where she was a very popular singer. Before she graduated, Simpson was able to finally secure some mainstream notice. In 1997, she was signed to a record deal by Sony after singing "Amazing Grace" a cappella for the company's chief executive officer. Her voice proved to be one of her strongest points as a singer, often acclaimed as being natural and full of soul. She was also attracted to the label because it allowed her to be honest about herself in public, including talking about her faith and her decision to remain a virgin until she married.

Simpson graduated from Pearce with her GED in 1998, and continued working on her first release for Sony. Her father became her manager while her mother was her stylist. In 1999, she released her debut album, *Sweet Kisses* which sold more than two million copies. One single, "I Wanna Love You Forever," was a top ten hit. Simpson was praised by *Billboard* critic Larry Flick who called her a "diva-in-training, capable of transcending age demographics" and her album "a measured blend of kid-friendly up-tempo pop ditties and mature, gospel-laced ballads."

Before the release of *Sweet Kisses,* Simpson had met her future husband at the 1998 Hollywood Christmas Parade. After her album's release, she toured in support of it as an opening act for Lachey's band, 98 Degrees, as well as Latin-pop sensation Ricky Martin. Simpson and Lachey began dating in 1999,

and recorded a single together, "Where You Are," which appeared in the film *Here on Earth.* Simpson went on in 2001 to release the album *Irresistible,* which went gold.

Lachey was born on November 9, 1973, in Harlan, Kentucky, the son of John Lachey, a pharmacist, and Cate Fopma–Leimbach, a substance abuse program coordinator. From his childhood growing up in Cincinnati, Lachey had a love of performing. To that end, he attended the School for Creative and Performing Arts in that city.

After graduating from high school, Lachey entered the University of Southern California, then transferred to Miami University in Ohio. There, he studied exercise science and athletic training, and was the trainer for the women's volleyball team. Lachey also sang with a local band, the Avenues, in Cincinnati, sometimes letting the band interfere with his studies.

The summer before his senior year of college, Lachey was invited by an old friend, Jeff Timmons, to move to Los Angeles and joining a vocal group. Lachey dropped out of Miami University, took his younger brother, Drew, and another friend from Ohio, Justin Jeffre, with him. The four formed 98 Degrees, a vocal group, in 1995.

Success did not come easily for Lachey and 98 Degrees. The four men worked other jobs as they tried to get noticed and become successful. They finally got a break after trying to crash the backstage area at a Boys II Men around 1996. This incident led to an appearance on a local radio station. 98 Degrees soon found a manager, Paris d'Jon, and a record deal with Motown.

In 1997, 98 Degrees released their first self–titled first record. With the hit single "Invisible Man," *98 Degrees* went gold. Their follow–up release was even more popular. *98 Degrees and Rising* went multi–platinum and was popular world wide. In 2000, 98 Degrees released *Revelation* which went platinum. This was the same year the group was sued by their former managers for $25 million. The group had fired this management team after they had been on the road constantly for several years and saw little in return for the effort.

One point of dissension between 98 Degrees and their first managers was the pressure to lie about their ages. They refused to be a "teeny bopper" band. 98 Degrees wanted to be different than most boy vocal bands who were popular at the time. They focused on an urban soul/R&B sound more than other boy bands, which were often pop–oriented. They wanted to be more like Boys II Men than N'Sync. 98 Degrees also performed well live and wrote most of their own material. The foursome also owned their name and merchandise rights. They were not a studio creation, but four solid singers.

Of the way 98 Degrees performed in concert, Lachey told Sarah Rodman of *Boston Herald,* "We're not going to get up there and overwhelm you with dance moves; that's not what we're about. When we put the group together, we were singers, and we want to remain singers and all this other stuff comes second."

By the early 2000s, 98 Degrees was less popular, especially while touring. They did not attract as large of a crowd when they toured in 2001, and went on indefinite hiatus in 2002. Lachey found more success with his wife. He and Simpson continued to date until April of 2001, when their relationship temporarily ended. They got back together after the September 11, 2001, terrorist attacks on the east coast of the United States, and were engaged in February of 2002.

Simpson and Lachey married on October 26, 2002, in Austin, Texas. Their early days of wedded bliss were the subject of a reality series on MTV, *Newlyweds: Nick and Jessica.* The show was taped during the first year of their marriage, following them in their personal and professional lives, and aired in 2003. When it was originally aired, *Newlyweds* was not expected to be a hit, but it found a large audience, attracting about 2.4–2.7 million viewers per week. Its biggest audience was found among viewers between 12 and 34 years old.

One aspect that attracted viewers was Simpson's personality, alternately described as dumb, ditzy, spoiled, and whiny. Some of her mistakes and misunderstandings were highly amusing. In one episode, she wondered aloud whether or not Chicken of the Sea tuna contained chicken, and in another, why buffalo wings were not made of buffalo. In contrast, Lachey was both patient with her and exasperated by her, especially her sloppiness, as he had "neat freak" tendencies.

Many critics believed that *Newlyweds* made Simpson, especially, more of a star than her singing ever did. Richard Roeper of *Chicago Sun–Times* declared, "Out of nowhere, Simpson has become the surprise breakout TV star of the season. She's more fascinating than Ozzy Osbourne, more embarrassing than Paris Hilton, and funnier than all five Queer Eye guys put together." *Newlyweds* was renewed for a second season which aired in 2004.

Even before *Newlyweds* had hit the airwaves, Simpson was already working on an acting career. The WB television network was considering developing a weekly series for her. She also had several television shows of note. In 2003, she had a recurring role as Annette, Kelso's girlfriend, on Fox's *That '70s Show,* and a guest role as Miranda Evans on an episode of *The Twilight Zone* on UPN. In the episode entitled "The Collection," Simpson's Evans was a babysitter of a girl who possesses a doll collection of which Evans soon may be a member.

Simpson also tried to jumpstart her singing career, which played a minor role in *Newlyweds.* In 2003, she released her third album, *In This Skin,* which was initially a flop. The record featured slick, glossy production values, and more adult themes than her previous releases. Though *In This Skin* debuted in the top ten on *Billboard*'s album charts, it soon dropped significantly. Sales rebounded for a time when there was a bonus DVD added with extra tracks in 2004. She was also selected to be a part of VH1's annual "Divas" show in 2004. Simpson had a pilot in the works with ABC for the fall of 2004, but it was not picked up. In May of 2004, it was announced that Simpson would play the role of Daisy Duke in the film based on the television show *The Dukes of Hazzard.* Plus, she was scheduled to appear in the 2005 film, *Walk On.* Along with her sister, Ashlee, Simpson became a spokesperson for Hershey's Ice Breakers Liquid Ice mints. She also promoted an edible cosmetics and fragrance line, Dessert, which launched in Sephora stores in April of 2004. "It's like vanilla cupcakes—yummy, really yummy," Simpson told *Allure*'s Alexandra Jacobs. Simpson kicked off a North American tour on June 4, 2004.

Like Simpson, Lachey also worked on his acting and singing careers. In 2004, he appeared in the NBC drama *American Dreams* as Tom Jones. Lachey was cast opposite Gina Gershon on the fall 2004 ABC situation comedy *Hot Mamma,* but the show was not picked up. In 2003, Lachey released his first solo album, *SoulO,* of which he wrote or co–wrote eight tracks. Though the track "This I Swear" was used as the theme song of *Newlyweds,* Lachey's album sold even worse than Simpson's.

The success of *Newlyweds* also led to joint work for the couple, primary on television. They co–hosted *Dick Clark's New Years Rockin' Eve* in 2003. In 2004,

ABC selected them to host a variety special, *The Nick and Jessica Variety Hour*, which drew on their ability to sing, do comedy, and act together. After the success of the first, they were signed to do a second special in December of that year, with more possible in the future. The couple was also considering recording an album of duets together. In 2004, they both were named to *People* magazine's "50 Most Beautiful People" list. In July of that year, Simpson announced that the second season of *Newlyweds* would be their last. "We're not newlyweds anymore," she explained on E! Online.

Lachey said he was glad that many of his and Simpson's career triumphs had come together. He told Donna Freydkin of *USA Today*, "We were the poor man's stars. It's cool that our biggest success in this industry has come as a married couple. It's gratifying to know that people were wrong and being married is not a bad thing." Simpson explained to *Allure*'s Jacobs, "We did *Newlyweds* to show we're not a perfect couple. We let our guards down, fight, cuss each other out, whatever it may be, and people ended up embracing it more than the celebrity life. Our success came from being ourselves. That's the best kind of success to have."

Selected discography

Nick Lachey (with 98 Degrees)

98 Degrees, Motown, 1997.
98 Degrees and Rising, Motown, 1998.
Heat It Up, Motown, 1999.
This Christmas, Universal, 1999.
Revelation, Universal, 2000.
The Collection, Universal, 2002.

Nick Lachey (solo)

SoulO, Universal, 2003.

Jessica Simpson

Sweet Kisses, Columbia Records, 1999.
Irresistible, Columbia Records, 2001.
This Is The Remix, Columbia Records, 2002.
In This Skin, Sony, 2003.

Lachey & Simpson

"Where You Are," *Here on Earth* (soundtrack), 2000.

Sources

Books

Celebrity Biographies, Baseline II, 2004.

Periodicals

Allure, April 2004, pp. 190–95.
Billboard, November 6, 1999, p. 13; February 26, 2000, p. 89; March 20, 2004, p. 77.
Boston Globe, November 11, 2003, p. F4.
Boston Herald, June 25, 1999, p. S21; August 19, 2003, p. 43.
Brandweek, March 1, 2004, p. 22.
Chicago Sun–Times, October 14, 2003, p. 11.
Columbus Dispatch, December 17, 2003, p. 1B.
Daily News (New York), August 3, 2003, p. 14; September 30, 2003, p. 44; October 7, 2003, p. 86; January 16, 2004, p. 120; April 13, 2004, p. 79.
Entertainment Weekly, December 26, 2003/January 2, 2004, pp. 70–71; January 16, 2004, pp. 22–28.
Houston Chronicle, March 1, 2001, p. 4.
Los Angeles Times, March 11, 2004, p. E8.
Ottawa Citizen, December 13, 2003, p. J12.
People, November 15, 1999, p. 182; March 20, 2000, p. 113; November 11, 2002, p. 60; September 1, 2003, p. 127; December 1, 2003, p. 133.
San Francisco Chronicle, March 28, 1999, p. 39; October 19, 2003, p. D6.
Seattle Times, May 11, 2001, p. G12; May 14, 2001, p. E3.
Straits Times, August 25, 2000, p. 13.
Toronto Sun, January 28, 2000, p. 39; September 12, 2000, p. 54; August 24, 2003, p. S20.
USA Today, September 25, 2000, p. 6D; January 21, 2004, p. 2D.
Washington Post, September 10, 2003, p. C5; April 16, 2004, p. C7.

Online

"First Look," E! Online, http://www.eonline.com/News/firstlook.html?eol.tkr (July 15, 2004).
"Jessica Puts Up Her Dukes," E! Online, http://www.eonline.com/News/Items/0,1,14155,00.html?tnews (May 21, 2004).
"Where's Jessica Simpson?," CNN.com, http://www.cnn.com/2004/SHOWBIZ/05/25/showbuzz/index.html#2 (May 25, 2004).

—*A. Petruso*

Bill Laimbeer

Basketball coach and entrepreneur

Born William Laimbeer, Jr., May 19, 1957, in Boston, MA; son of William, Sr. (a business executive) and Mary Laimbeer; married Chris Skiver; children: Eric, Keriann. *Education:* Attended Notre Dame; attended Owens Technical College, Toledo, OH; graduated from Notre Dame, B.S. (economics), 1979.

Addresses: *Office*—c/o Detroit Shock, Palace of Auburn Hills, 2 Championship Dr., Auburn Hills, MI 48326.

Career

Played college basketball, Notre Dame University, c. 1975–76, 1977–79; drafted by Cleveland Cavaliers, 1979; played with the Italian League's Pinti Inox of Brescia, 1979–80; played in Southern California summer league, 1980; played for Cleveland Cavaliers, 1980–82; traded to Detroit Pistons, 1982; played for Detroit Pistons, 1982–1993; won two NBA championships with Pistons, 1989 and 1990; principal, Laimbeer Packaging Corp., 1993–2001; worked in community relations department for Pistons, 2001; television commentator for Pistons, 2001—; named special consultant to, then coach/director of player personnel for the WNBA's Detroit Shock, 2002; coach/director of player personnel for Detroit Shock—; won WNBA championship with Detroit Shock, 2003.

Awards: NBA All–Star, 1983, 1984, 1985, and 1987; named WNBA Coach of the Year, 2003.

AP/Wide World Photos

Sidelights

While playing center for the Detroit Pistons in the National Basketball Association (NBA) for a number of years, Bill Laimbeer was known as a dirty player who was hated, sometimes by even his own teammates. The head of the so–called "Bad Boys," he did whatever he had to do to win. With the Pistons, Laimbeer won two NBA championships in 1989 and 1990. After retiring in 1993, Laimbeer ran a box manufacturing factory for several years, before returning to a front office position with the Pistons. In 2002, he was hired as a special consultant for the Detroit Shock, the Pistons' Women's National Basketball Association (WNBA) team. When the team got off to a bad start in the 2002 season, Laimbeer was hired as head coach and player personnel director, though he had no professional experience in either area. Within a season and a half, Laimbeer led the Shock to the WNBA championship.

Born in 1957, in Boston, Massachusetts, Laimbeer is the son of an executive at Owens–Illinois, which was a company that made glass containers and paper products. Laimbeer was raised with his two sisters, Susan and Lee Ann, in the Chicago suburb of Clarendon Hills, where he had a privileged upbringing. While he played basketball as a child, he did not take the pursuit particularly seriously. Laimbeer continued to play basketball in high school, even after he transferred to Paso Verdes High School when the family moved to that California city during his junior year of high school.

For college, Laimbeer entered Notre Dame where he played basketball, but he flunked out after his freshman year. To regain his eligibility, he spent two semesters at Owens Technical College in Toledo, Ohio. Laimbeer then re–entered Notre Dame. He spent two years playing for Notre Dame's basketball team, though he was not a star in any sense. For his last two years of college, he averaged 7.3 points and 6.0 rebounds per game while playing 20 minutes a game, primarily as a substitute. With the Fighting Irish, Laimbeer appeared in the Final Four in the NCAA basketball tournament in 1978, and the regional finals of the same tournament in 1979.

After graduating with a degree in economics in 1979, Laimbeer did not intend to become a professional basketball player. It was just a fun job, though in many ways, Laimbeer liked the game of golf much better. After he was drafted by the Cleveland Cavaliers in the third round of the June 1979 NBA draft with the 65th pick, the team did not make him an offer. Laimbeer then signed with a professional team in Italy. Before he left the country, the Cavaliers tried to sign him, but it was already too late. He played for one season with the Italian League's Pinti Inox of Brescia. He played well, averaging 21.1 points and 12.5 rebounds per game.

When Laimbeer returned to the United States, the 6'11" center played in the Southern California summer league. He also tried out for the United States Olympic team that was going to play at the Olympic Games in 1980. The team never went because of the United States' boycott of the Moscow, U.S.S.R.–based games. Laimbeer then signed with the Cavaliers for the 1980–81 season. He had a solid rookie NBA season before the Cavaliers traded him to the Detroit Pistons in February of 1982 with Kenny Carr for Phil Hubbard, Paul Mokeski, and two draft picks.

It was while playing in Detroit that Laimbeer really learned his game, enhanced his concentration, and came into his own. With the Pistons, he successfully drew on his desire to be the best and win, but in his way. Laimbeer told Clifton Brown of the *New York Times,* "A lot of basketball is mental. Some people find the way I play very frustrating. They can't handle it. I throw them off their game. I'm playing

to win, and I'll use all my tools both physically and mentally to win the game. Other players don't like that and I can't help that. I have to do what I do best. I call it gamesmanship."

Laimbeer had to draw on his competitive nature because he knew he was not the best player, but willing to sacrifice and use what he had to get his team to win. He had no speed and could not jump. But he had great defensive skills and ability to nail free throws, as well as good parameter and jump shots. Laimbeer would use his elbows, complain a lot, and agitate others to get his way. He also had a reputation for being a great actor on the court to get the referee's calls to go his way, a quality that did not endear him to other players. Fellow player Kevin McHale told Jack McCallum of *Sports Illustrated,* "I got to know Bill a little at the All–Star Game. He's a really nice guy. He might even be a good guy to have on your team. But he flops. That's why players don't like him."

In 1984, Laimbeer's tough play on what was still a relatively mediocre team prompted the Pistons to sign him to a five–year deal worth $3.5 million. He had already been an All–Star in 1983 and 1984, and would go on to be a member of the 1985 and 1987 squads. His reputation as a dirty player and bad guy were cemented when he started several fights on the court in the mid–1980s, though he did not punch anyone until the late 1980s. Laimbeer was more than a physical player. In 1985–86, he led the NBA in rebounds, averaging 12.9 rebounds per game. His scoring also improved from 16.3 points per game in 1985 to 17.4 in 1986.

By the late 1980s, the Pistons were a much improved team. In 1988, Laimbeer and the Pistons reached the NBA finals, losing in seven games to the Los Angeles Lakers. It was at this time that the Pistons became known as the "Bad Boys," and Laimbeer did much of his team's dirty work. As the *New York Times'* Brown wrote, "Laimbeer infuriates opposing players so much largely because he may be the league's most physical player. An elbow here, a shove there, a hard foul against anyone who dares to drive into the lane—there are many tricks that Laimbeer uses to keep opponents off stride." When the Lakers and Pistons met again in the 1989 finals, the Pistons prevailed. Detroit won a second championship in 1990, defeating the Portland Trail Blazers four games to one.

Laimbeer remained physically tough throughout his career. He played in 685 consecutive games through January of 1989, when he was suspended for one game for fighting Brad Daugherty. He did not miss one game due to injury through 1990. After the Pistons went into a decline in the early 1990s with key players in the championship teams leaving, injuries also began catching up with Laimbeer. He retired on December 1, 1993, when he had problems with his back and knees and he believed he was unable to play to the professional level he set for himself.

When Laimbeer retired, he was the Pistons' all–time leader in rebounds with 9,430. Over the course of his career, he averaged 12.9 points per game and 9.7 rebounds per game. After he retired, Laimbeer retained season tickets to the Pistons and would often go to games. On February 4, 1995, Laimbeer's number was retired by the Pistons.

In 1993, Laimbeer founded his own company, Laimbeer Packaging Corp., which he owned with his father and other investors. The company made boxes in a factory in Detroit, and later added a second factory in Melvindale, Michigan, that made corrugated boxes. Laimbeer ran the company, which had 240 employees and $60 million in projected sales in 1995. He sold the Detroit plant in 2000 as he focused his company on the large box and heavy weight container manufacturing business. Laimbeer left the business entirely in October of 2001.

Laimbeer then returned to the Detroit Pistons. He was initially hired to work for the Pistons in the community relations department. He also began doing television commentary for certain Pistons games. His career took another turn a year later when he was hired to be a special consultant for the Detroit Shock, the WNBA team owned by the Pistons. The Shock played poorly under coach Greg Williams, starting the 2002 season with an 0–10 record. Williams was then fired, and Laimbeer was hired in his place, even though he had no experience except for coaching his daughter Keriann's AAU (Amateur Athletic Union) team for several years. (Laimbeer is married to Chris Skiver, with whom he also has a son, Eric.)

While some observers believed the hiring of Laimbeer was just a publicity stunt, the Shock greatly improved under him. Detroit finished the 2002 season with a 9–23 record. He also developed the team's fundamentals like rebounding, scoring, and free throws. His work saved the team from folding or moving after the 2002 season, and changed the attitude of the players toward the game. Laimbeer had an effective touch as coach. He told Andrea Woo of *Sports Illustrated,* "Being out of basketball helped me become more patient and understand

that not everyone thinks the same. I'm still demanding, but I get my point across by using playing time and not by getting into someone's face. I never wanted a screamer as a coach."

The Shock blossomed in 2003, going from worst to first in the league. As director of player personnel, Laimbeer traded all but two of the players he started with and drafted well, including center Ruth Riley and college rebounding expert Cheryl Ford. The players were not his only concern. Laimbeer even helped sell tickets by calling season ticket holders and personally asking for their help. Detroit's regular season record was 25–9, with home court advantage in the playoffs.

The Shock reached the WNBA finals against the Los Angeles Sparks, who were coached by Laimbeer's old NBA nemesis, Michael Cooper. After losing the series' first game to the Sparks, the Shock won the series' next two games. One game set a WNBA attendance record with 22,076 people present. For his extraordinary effort, Laimbeer was named the WNBA coach of the year in 2003.

Many were amazed at Laimbeer's ability to succeed as a coach of women, but his team liked to play for him. Ford, who was named WNBA rookie of the year, told Larry Lage of the Associated Press, "Everyone loves him to death and loves playing for him. He gives us all the confidence in the world and he doesn't beat around the bush when he has something to say. He'll tell it to you straight if you're messing up. I haven't seen the Bad Boy side of him, and I'm not ready to see it. I love him as he is."

Sources

Periodicals

Associated Press, June 19, 2003; June 21, 2003; September 12, 2003.
Baltimore Sun, August 23, 2003, p. 1C.
Boston Globe, February 9, 1994, p. 57; May 12, 2002, p. D1.
Boston Herald, December 31, 1995, p. B12.
Los Angeles Times, September 17, 2003, p. D1.
New York Times, February 7, 1989, p. D25; June 12, 1990, p. B12; June 20, 2002, p. D7; September 7, 2003, sec. 8, p. 14.
Sports Illustrated, April 7, 1986, p. 71; November 5, 1990, p. 136; November 10, 1997, p. 23; August 11, 2003, p. R6.
USA Today, December 2, 1994, p. 7C; July 25, 2002, p. 8C.

Online

"Bill Laimbeer Bio," NBA.com, http://www.nba.com/history/players/laimbeer_bio.html (February 9, 2004).

"Bill Laimbeer Coach Info," WNBA.com, http://www.wnba.com/coachfile/bill_laimbeer (February 9, 2004).

"Shock dethrone Sparks as WNBA champs," SI.com, http://sportsillustrated.cnn.com/2003/basketball/wnba/09/16/shock_champions.ap/index.html (February 9, 2004).

—A. Petruso

Robert Lanza

Biologist and medical researcher

Born Robert Paul Lanza, February 11, 1956, in Stoughton, MA. *Education:* University of Pennsylvania, B.A., 1978, M.D., 1983.

Addresses: *Office*—Advanced Cell Technology, One Innovation Dr., Biotech Three, Worcester, MA 01605.

Career

Researcher in the lab of Gerald Edelman, Rockefeller University, 1976; moved to the Salk Institute, 1978; became senior scientist at Biohybrid Technologies, 1990–93; clinical associate professor in surgery, Tufts University, Boston, MA, 1994–95; vice president of medical and scientific development, Advanced Cell Technology, 1999—.

Sidelights

Dr. Robert Lanza is a medical researcher at the forefront of headline–making developments in cloning and organ transplantation. Lanza, who works for a private biotechnology firm called Advanced Cell Technology, has cloned extinct and near–extinct mammals. He cloned a guar, an endangered oxlike Asian animal, in 2001, and in 2003 cloned a rare South Asian cowlike creature called a banteng. The guar died within days of its birth, but the banteng, born out of an Iowa farm cow, survived and lives at the San Diego zoo. Lanza is also involved in so–called xenotransplantation, the science of transplanting cells, tissues or organs from one species into another. Lanza wrote a book for a general audience on the subject. He also edited a

book about world health problems, eliciting contributions from leading scientists and from luminaries such as former United States president Jimmy Carter and former United Nations Secretary General Boutros Boutros–Ghali.

Lanza was born in Stoughton, Massachusetts, south of Boston, in 1956. As a child he was always interested in animals. Once he healed the leg of an injured rooster and kept it as a pet. He credits a high school science teacher with encouraging him to go to college and study biology. Only two of his four siblings made it through high school, so going to the University of Pennsylvania was a big step for Lanza. He earned a degree in biology in 1978. Lanza stayed at Pennsylvania for a medical degree, which he completed in 1983. Along the way he studied with many prestigious scientists. While still an undergraduate, he worked in the laboratory of Gerald Edelman, who won the Nobel Prize in Medicine in 1972 for his work on the chemical structure of antibodies. Lanza won a Fulbright fellowship, which sent him to Oxford University in England. There he worked with Rodney Porter, who had shared Edelman's Nobel. Lanza later also worked with Richard Hynes, at the Massachusetts Institute of Technology, and with the eminent Harvard psychologist B.F. Skinner. He also worked with Dr. Christiaan Barnard, the pioneer of heart transplantation. Lanza co–authored research papers with Skinner and Barnard, and a year after receiving his medical degree he published a book on heart transplantation.

Lanza's interests were broad. He combined a love for animals with a flair for medicine, coupled with an overarching concern for the environment and the ultimate fate of the world's creatures. In the early 1990s Lanza worked as senior scientist at a Boston biotechnology firm called Biohybrid Technologies. The company specialized in diabetes research, particularly in the development of an artificial pancreas. Between 1994 and 1995 he worked as a professor of surgery at Boston's Tufts University. All the time he continued to write. He published a book called *Medical Science and the Advancement of World Health* in 1985, and then published a three–volume series on pancreatic islet transplantation in 1994. His next book, though, was something of a departure. Lanza solicited essays from dozens of scientists as well as politicians for a compilation called *One World: The Health and Survival of the Human Species in the 21st Century*. The book was intended to provide a multifaceted glimpse of pressing global problems, with hope for finding solutions. Lanza's contributors included some of the world's best–known scientists, such as Jonas Salk, discoverer of the polio vaccine; Lanza's former mentor, Christiaan Barnard; the essayist Carl Sagan, and leading AIDS researchers Robert Gallo and Luc Mantagnier. *One World* ranged well beyond sheerly medical problems, discussing subjects such as population growth, global warming, the education of women, and the role of poverty in disease.

Lanza followed this tome with another academic medical text, this one on tissue transplantation, and then put out another book for a more general audience in 2000, *Xeno: The Promise of Transplanting Animal Organs into Humans* (with co–author David Cooper). *Xeno* discussed the range of issues raised by animal transplants, as well as the fascinating history of the science. The book covered the medical challenges of xenotransplantation, explained animal and human immune systems, and attempted to sort out the ethics of using animals in this way. In July of 2004, Lanza's two–volume set, *Handbook of Stem Cells*, was published.

In 1999, Lanza began working for another Boston–area private biotechnology company, Advanced Cell Technology, Inc. (ACT). He was vice president of medical and scientific development at the firm, which specialized in cloning and stem cell research. The company was formed in 1994, and it was responsible for several advances in cloning. In 1998

ACT announced it had successfully cloned two calves, named Charlie and George, and later that year the company claimed it had treated Parkinson's disease in rats using fetal brain cells from cloned cows. When Lanza joined the company, ACT began to work on cloning endangered animals. This was both exciting and controversial research.

Lanza argued that cloning endangered animals was one way of conserving them. Lanza began work in 2000 on cloning a guar, a kind of wild ox from Southeast Asia that was on the verge of extinction. Lanza inserted DNA from a dead guar into an altered egg from a domestic cow. He fertilized the egg with a chemical process, and the fertile egg was then implanted into the cow. In 2000, Lanza's lab brought the guar to a late stage of fetal development, but it wasn't until the next year that a cloned guar survived through birth. The cloned guar, named Noah, was born in January of 2001, but it died within two days. Lanza claimed its death was due to dysentery, and probably had little to do with the fact that the animal was a clone.

Lanza's lab also began work on cloning a Spanish mountain goat called the bucardo. Whereas the guar was endangered, the very last bucardo had died in 2000. The Spanish government contracted with ACT to try to clone a bucardo using preserved tissue. Some conservationists thought Lanza's approach to saving endangered animals was of little use. All the money it cost to bring a clone to life did little to preserve the endangered animal's habitat. So cloning seemed to some a narrow–minded approach to conservation. But Lanza argued that if there were only a few individuals left in an endangered species, cloning was an important way to ensure that the species continued to exist. The bucardo was a good example, as there were none left in the wild. The South China tiger was another example. There were only 30 South China tigers known to exist as of 2003.

Lanza had more success in 2003, when he successfully cloned a cow–like animal from Southeast Asia, the banteng. Like Noah, the ill–fated guar, Stockings the banteng was born out of an ordinary dairy cow. Stockings survived and was moved to the San Diego zoo, where he grew to more than 300 pounds. Lanza encouraged zoos to freeze genetic material from rare animals, so that more could be cloned in the future. Lanza hoped to possibly clone a giant panda, of which there were only a thousand left by 2003. The cloned panda's host would presumably be a black bear. Another possibility would be to clone the Texas Ocelot, an extremely rare wildcat found in Mexico and the southwestern United States. Its host would be the common domestic cat.

Cloning endangered animals was only the most sensational part of Lanza's work. He continued to research cloning for human medical advancement at ACT. Lanza thought the health risks were too immense to consider cloning humans, but he believed that cloning and stem cell research might lead to effective new therapies for a variety of diseases such as Parkinson's, Alzheimer's, cancer, and diabetes.

Selected writings

Heart Transplantation (ed., with D.K.C. Cooper), MTP Press, 1984.

Medical Science and the Advancement of World Health, Praeger, 1985.

Procurement of Pancreatic Islets, R.G. Landes Co., 1994.

Immunomodulation of Pancreatic Islets, Springer Verlag, 1994.

Pancreatic Islet Transplantation: Immunoisolation of Pancreatic Islets, Dimensions, 1994.

One World: The Health and Survival of the Human Species in the 21st Century, Health Press, 1996.

Principles of Tissue Engineering (ed., with R. Langer and W. L. Chick), R.G. Landes, 1997.

Cell Encapsulation Technology and Therapeutics, (ed., with W. Kuhtreiber and W.L. Chick), Birkhauser, 1999.

Xeno: The Promise of Transplanting Animal Organs into Humans (with David Cooper), Oxford University Press, 2000.

Methods of Tissue Engineering (ed., with A. Atala), Academic Press, 2002.

Handbook of Stem Cells, Academic Press, 2004.

Sources

American Scientist, May 2000, p. 270.

Bioscience, March 1997, p. 193.

New Scientist, May 20, 2000, p. 48; January 19, 2002, p. 9.

Newsweek, October 23, 2000, p. 76.

People, September 8, 2003, pp. 89–90.

—A. Woodward

Anthony LaPaglia

Actor

Born Anthony M. LaPaglia, January 31, 1959, in Adelaide, Australia; married Gia Carides (an actress).

Addresses: *Agent*—International Creative Management, 8942 Wilshire Blvd., Beverly Hills, CA 90211.

Career

Actor in television, including: *Amazing Stories*, 1985; *Magnum, P.I.*, 1986; *The Twilight Zone*, CBS, 1986; *Trapper John, M.D.*, 1986; *Hunter*, 1987; *Frank Nitti: The Enforcer* (movie), 1988; *Police Story: Gladiator School* (movie), 1988; *Hardball*, NBC, 1989; *Criminal Justice* (movie), 1990; *Father Dowling Mysteries*, 1990; *Tales from the Crypt*, HBO, 1991; *The Brotherhood* (movie), ABC, 1991; *Keeper of the City* (movie), 1991; *Black Magic* (movie), 1992; *Past Tense* (movie), 1994; *Murder One*, ABC, 1996–97; *Murder One*, 1996–97; *Murder One: Diary of a Serial Killer* (miniseries), 1997; *The Garden of Redemption* (movie), 1997; *Lansky* (movie), 1999; *Black and Blue* (movie), 1999; *Frasier*, NBC, 2000; *Normal, Ohio*, 2000; *On the Edge* (movie), 2001; *Frasier*, 2002; *Without a Trace*, 2002—; *Frasier*, 2004. Film appearances include: *Cold Steel*, 1987; *Slaves of New York*, 1989; *Betsy's Wedding*, 1990; *Mortal Sins*, 1990; *He Said, She Said*, 1991; *One Good Cop*, 1991; *29th Street*, 1991; *Innocent Blood*, 1992; *Whispers in the Dark*, 1992; *So I Married an Axe Murderer*, 1993; *The Custodian*, 1993; *Bulletproof Heart*, 1994; *Mixed Nuts*, 1994; *Paperback Romance*, 1994; *The Client*, 1994; *Lucky Break*, 1994; *Killer* (aka *Bulletproof Heart*), 1994; *Empire Records*, 1995; *Chameleon*, 1995; *Trees Lounge*, 1996; *Brilliant Lies*, 1996; *Commandments*, 1997; *Phoenix*, 1998; *The Repair Shop*, 1998; *Mob Law: A Film Portrait of Oscar Goodman* (narrator), 1998; *Summer of Sam*, 1999; *Sweet and Lowdown*, 1999; *Autumn in New York*, 2000; *House of Mirth*, 2000; *Company Man*, 2000; *Looking for Alibrandi*, 2000; *The Bank*, 2001; *Lantana*, 2001; *Jack the Dog*, 2001; *The Salton Sea*, 2002; *The Road to Perdition*, 2002; *The Guys*, 2002; *I'm With Lucy*, 2002; *Salton Sea*, 2002; *Dead Heat*, 2002; *Analyze That*, 2002; *Spinning Boris*, 2003; *Happy Hour*, 2003; *Manhood*, 2003; *Winter Solstice*, 2004. Producer of films, including: *Winter Solstice*, 2004. Stage appearances include: *Bouncers*, Minetta Lane Theatre, New York, NY, 1987; *The Rose Tattoo*, Circle in the Square, New York, NY, 1997; *A View from the Bridge*, Roundabout Theatre, New York, NY, c. 1997–98; *On the Open Road*, Public Theatre/Martinson Hall, New York, NY, 1998; *After the Fall*, 2002.

Awards: Drama Desk award, for *The Rose Tattoo*, 1997; Antoinette Perry (Tony) award for best actor in a play, League of American Theaters and Producers and the American Theatre Wing, for *A View from the Bridge*, 1998; best film and best actor, for *Lantana*, Australian Film Institute, 2002; Emmy award for best guest star, Academy of Television Arts and Sciences, for *Frasier*, 2002; PRISM Award, 2004; Golden Globe for best actor in a drama series, Hollywood Foreign Press Association, for *Without a Trace*, 2004.

Sidelights

Best known for playing cops and crooks, actor Anthony LaPaglia has had a prolific and versatile career on stage as well as in television and film. In tribute to his versatility, LaPaglia has won both an Emmy and a Tony award.

Born in Adelaide, Australia, in 1959, LaPaglia (pronounced La–PAY–lee–ah) grew up in a family of first–generation Italian immigrants. However, his grandparents on his mother's side were Dutch, and he lived in a neighborhood of immigrants from Germany, Croatia, Greece, and other places; this exposure to different people and their accents would later prove to be an asset in his acting career.

Before LaPaglia immigrated to the United States in 1984, he worked as an elementary school teacher in Adelaide. When he was 20 years old, he saw his first play, William Congreve's *The Way of the World,* and decided that he wanted to be an actor. However, in addition to this dream, vague at the time, he mainly wanted to live in New York City, so he moved there. LaPaglia told Rob Kendt in *Back Stage West,* "I felt like I was missing out on something, and I really wanted to live in New York City." Even if he had not dreamed of becoming an actor, he would have moved to the city anyway, "with or without acting. Acting wasn't the lure."

In New York, LaPaglia studied with Kim Stanley and, like many actors, worked at a variety of jobs to make ends meet while pursuing his acting career. He worked as a shoe salesman, furniture restorer, and sprinkler system installer. He also worked as a production assistant for a commercial company; for one commercial, he had to cut up bananas. "Man, I was the best banana cutter," he told Dan Snierson in *Entertainment Weekly,* "Coulda made a career out of it." He told Rebecca Ascher–Walsh in *Entertainment Weekly* that his agent told him, "Lose the [Australian] accent and change your name." LaPaglia learned to use an American accent by watching and imitating Al Pacino in *Dog Day Afternoon,* but he refused to change his name, despite his agent's predictions that the Italian name would limit him to playing tough guys.

LaPaglia admitted to Ascher–Walsh that his agent was right, but he still managed to break into acting anyway. His first stage appearance was in *Bouncers,* an Off Broadway comedy in which he played eight of the 30 roles in the play. He first achieved critical attention in 1990, when he played a mobster in *Betsy's Wedding.* After several years of playing similar small parts in films, in 1994 LaPaglia played a hit man in *Killer,* a stylish black comedy. *Killer* was a low–budget ($1.5 million) film that appeared only at film festivals and art houses, but it showcased a stellar performance by LaPaglia. "This is the best part I've been given, and I can't get people to see it," he told Glenn Lovell in a Knight Ridder/Tribune News Service article.

In that same year, LaPaglia played mafia thug Barry "the Blade" Muldano in the film *The Client,* which was based on the John Grisham thriller by the same name. He appeared in the film at the request of his agents, who insisted that it would help his career if he had a role in a major motion picture. LaPaglia explained to Knight Ridder's Lovell, "The people who have the power to give you a job don't care how good your work it. They look at something and go, 'How much money did it make?'" He noted that an actor could be excellent, but if he has only appeared in films that did not make money, studios will instead hire a terrible actor whose films were profitable.

Ironically, and to his dismay, *The Client* proved to be LaPaglia's big break. At an interview at the 1994 Toronto International Film Festival, LaPaglia told Lovell, "It's depressing. I do this goofy little movie called *The Client.* Which is pulp. I turn in a one–dimensional performance. Which is what they wanted. I get paid a lot of money. It makes $85 million. And all these doors swing open."

LaPaglia became a favorite of audiences in 1996, for his role on the television show *Murder One.* In 1998, he won a Tony award for his performance in Arthur Miller's play *A View from the Bridge.* LaPaglia had always been interested in Arthur Miller's plays, and told Simi Horwitz in *Back Stage,* "His writing is very specific and lean. There's nothing to add. At the same time, there's a big difference between what's on the page and the staged version. I believe that's more true of Miller than many other writers."

LaPaglia still retains a trace of his original Australian accent, but his speaking style is usually a blend of Brooklyn and Australia. Often cast as a mobster, in 2001 LaPaglia began turning down roles that typecast him as an Italian–American thug, characters "whose names end in a vowel or who carry a gun," he remarked to Snierson in *Entertainment Weekly.* He told *Back Stage West's* Kendt that he believes it is an actor's responsibility to avoid being slotted into a narrow range of roles, even if that means turning down work at times. Although he will turn down work if it seems to be typecasting, he does not consider the size of the part to be important. If a part is small, but interesting, LaPaglia will take it.

His willingness to take a variety of small parts has led some observers to consider his career trajectory a bit disappointing. LaPaglia told *Back Stage West's* Kendt, "People have flat–out said to me, 'I thought you were going to be such a big movie star.'" But, he remarked, he feels quite successful and happy with the course of his career and with the variety of opportunities he has had. "I wanted to be a working actor, and that's exactly what I got," he told Kendt. He also told Daniel Fienberg, in a Knight Ridder/Tribune News Service article, that he finds his fans' (and his detractors') honesty refreshing. "I've had people say to me, 'I really love your show, I love your work' and I've had other people say, 'I hate your stuff. I hate what you do.' But they're not saying it to be hostile, just in a really honest way." He added, "[In New York City], they stab you in the front, they don't stab you in the back."

Although most of LaPaglia's career has involved American television, film, and stage, he occasionally travels back to Australia to work. He told *Back Stage West's* Kendt, "There's a freshness to the filmmaking scene [in Australia] that seems to have disappeared" in the United States. "It's a raw energy that I really love—a maverick, everyone's–in–it–together kind of feeling, which I prefer."

In the 2001 film *Lantana,* LaPaglia played police officer Leon Zat, an introspective, self–questioning man who is troubled by guilt about his extramarital affair. *Back Stage West's* Kendt wrote that as portrayed by LaPaglia, "Leon has a nuanced impassivity that borders on inscrutable, until despair at last cracks the surface. It's a beautifully modulated performance, in other words—one that takes us off guard, even from an actor of LaPaglia's gifts." LaPaglia told Kendt that as he has matured as a person and as an actor, he has learned to do "less acting and more being," portraying characters with increasing subtlety. "The camera just picks up everything if it's in the right spot," he said. LaPaglia described what it was like to work on the film in a Knight Ridder/Tribune News Service article by Moira Macdonald: "[Director Ray Lawrence] kept saying, 'Just tell the truth in every scene.' It's a very simple statement, very hard to do. Always stripping away … because the writing was so good…. You spend more time stripping stuff away, as opposed to building it."

For his role as Leon in *Lantana,* LaPaglia won a Best Actor Award from the Australian Film Institute; the film won Best Film from the same organization.

LaPaglia told *Entertainment Weekly's* Ascher–Walsh, "The irony has totally not been lost on me that I ran away from Australia to build a career, but the movie that's doing the most for my career is from Australia."

Although LaPaglia considered retiring after his performance in *Lantana,* he went back to work after his accountant informed him that he needed the money. In 2002, LaPaglia went back to television in the series, *Without a Trace.* In the show, which became a quiet hit, he played Jack Malone, the head of an FBI team of Missing Persons investigators. For each episode, the team reconstructed the final hours before an individual's disappearance. The cases were often similar to those in news headlines, and each show featured a real missing person fact sheet at the end of the episode. "The day somebody gets found because of one of those, I'll be a really happy guy," LaPaglia told Fienberg in the Knight Ridder/Tribune News Service article.

Also in 2002, LaPaglia won a Best Guest Star Emmy Award for a role on the comedy television series *Frasier. Entertainment Weekly's* Bruce Fretts asked LaPaglia if he was surprised to win the award for a comedy. "I was just surprised to win one in general," LaPaglia replied. However, he explained that throughout his career, he has never made the distinction between comedy and drama. "I've always prided myself on the idea that I could do both," he said.

The year 2002 was a busy one for LaPaglia, who completed work on five feature films, several episodes of the television show *Frasier*, a film version of *A View from the Bridge,* and a stage production of Arthur Miller's play *After the Fall.* He told Knight Ridder's Macdonald that he did not distinguish between all the genres. "I'm more interested in the material," he remarked. "If it's a great play, that's what I want to do; if it's a great character on TV, that's what I want to do. The whole point of me becoming an actor was variety."

In 2004, LaPaglia won a Golden Globe Award for Best Actor in a drama series, for his work in *Without a Trace.* In *Television Week,* executive producer Hank Steinberg noted that in police procedural dramas, "It is difficult to get into a character's personal life," but LaPaglia successfully "shows us what makes his character tick— all while he solves the mystery."

LaPaglia's career is still on the rise. When he began acting, he was in an age category that does not have many leading parts; he was not young enough to fit the "leading man" category, and was not old enough for character parts. He told *Back Stage West*'s Kendt that he always knew his career would take off after he hit the age of 40: "The last couple of years have been by far the best." He also noted that although he never set out to be a leading man in films and actually considered the idea rather "uninteresting," according to *Entertainment Weekly*'s Ascher–Walsh, he would take such a role if it were offered to him. "If the material warrants it, I'll do it. And if the check is big enough, I'm there," he said with a laugh.

Sources

Back Stage, December 19, 1997, p. 6.
Back Stage West, December 13, 2001, p. 8.
Entertainment Weekly, October 11, 1996, p. 81; January 11, 2002, p. 49; December 6, 2002, p. 82.
Europe Intelligence Wire, April 30, 2004.
Knight Ridder/Tribune News Service, November 10, 1994; January 24, 2002; April 30, 2003.
Television Week January 19, 2004, p. S11.

—Kelly Winters

Arthur Levitt

Financial expert

Born Arthur Levitt Jr. in 1931, in New York, NY; son of Arthur Sr. (a government official) and Dorothy (a teacher) Levitt; married Marylin Blauner (a psychiatry professor), 1955; children: two. *Education:* Williams College, B.A., 1952.

Addresses: *Office*—Pantheon Books Publicity Dept., 1745 Broadway, New York, NY 10019.

Career

Worked in the marketing department of *Time* magazine, New York City, 1950s; tax–shelter salesperson with Oppenheimer Industries in Kansas City, 1959–63; broker, Carter, Berlind & Weill, New York City, 1963, became partner, then president by 1970; chair and chief executive officer of the American Stock Exchange, 1978–89; founder of Levitt Media, 1986; co–founder of a small–business lobbying organization, the American Business Conference; chair, New York City Economic Development Corporation, 1989–93; appointed to chair of the U.S. Securities and Exchange Commission by President Bill Clinton, July, 1993; re–appointed, 1998; retired, 2001; worked for the Carlyle Group; signed book deal with Pantheon that produced book about investing, 2002.

Awards: Hunter College/Franklin and Eleanor Roosevelt Institute, Distinguished Public Service award, 2003.

AP/Wide World Photos

Sidelights

Arthur Levitt's eight–year tenure as chair of the U.S. Securities and Exchange Commission (SEC) was the longest in the 70–year history of the regulatory office. Yet it was notable for a far greater achievement—or near–achievement, as it were: from 1993 to 2001 Levitt battled with some of the most powerful executives in corporate America in an attempt to reform the way in which they presented their financial data to Wall Street and, ultimately, the stock–market investing public.

Levitt's efforts were met with resistance from Wall Street executives, corporate boards, the accounting industry, and finally even members of Congress. Some of those same politicians later expressed outrage when Texas–based Enron collapsed just eleven months after Levitt left office, due to exactly the kind of financial malfeasance, sanctioned by its accounting firm, that the SEC chair had predicted. Levitt detailed this battle in his 2002 book, *Take on the Street: What Wall Street and Corporate America Don't Want You to Know: What You Can Do to Fight Back*. In it, declared *New York Times* reviewer Thomas A. Bass, "Levitt is unsparing in his criticism of corporate greed and puffery."

Born in 1931, Levitt was an only child who grew up in the Crown Heights section of Brooklyn, New York. His grandparents were Orthodox Jewish immigrants who lived with the family, and an aunt was Broadway star Ethel Merman. Levitt's father was elected New York State comptroller six times, serving for 24 years that included a period of the 1970s when New York City faced bankruptcy. Levitt Sr., in charge of keeping an eye on the New York State employee pension funds, adamantly refused the appeals of politicians that some of those reserves be used to purchase municipal bond issues, which would have temporarily staved off the city's looming financial crisis—though at the expense of the workers' pension funds. Both his and the retirement fund of Levitt's mother—a second-grade teacher in a Brooklyn public school for 38 years—were there, as well as those of thousands of others, and "my father ... placed the well-being of New York retirees above all other considerations," Levitt wrote in *Take On the Street*.

Levitt did not immediately pursue finance as a career path. He studied English at Williams College, penning a senior thesis on the playwright Lillian Hellman before he graduated in 1952, and worked in the marketing department of *Time* magazine as his first full-time job. In 1959, the now-married Levitt moved to Kansas City to take a post with Oppenheimer Industries, and sold cattle herds and ranches to the wealthy as tax shelters for the next few years. One of his clients suggested he would do well on Wall Street, and so in 1963 Levitt returned to the New York area with his family and began at Carter, Berlind & Weill, a brokerage firm, to sell securities and bonds in a cutthroat, highly competitive environment.

Levitt rose through the ranks at the firm, garnering an increasingly high-profile roster of clients that included conductor Leonard Bernstein and composer Aaron Copland, and eventually became its president by the end of the decade. The firm eventually became Shearson Hayden Stone, which was sold to the American Express Corporation in 1981 and later became Citigroup. But Levitt also began to see a change in business ethics during the decade, as brokerage firms scrambled to stay profitable in the merger-mania of the era and became increasingly focused on the bottom line. Brokers, for example, earned their commissions not on how well their clients' money performed, but on the number of transactions they executed. "I grew uncomfortable with practices and attitudes that were misleading and sometimes deceptive," Levitt wrote in his book.

Invited to head the search committee for a new chair and chief executive officer for the American Stock Exchange, Levitt was offered the job himself and took over in 1978. The Amex, as it was called, was the smaller fish on Wall Street, nowhere near as powerful as the New York Stock Exchange (NYSE), in poor financial shape at the time and, some predicted, on the verge of folding altogether. Levitt was credited with rescuing it, in part by modernizing its operations and trading floor during his eleven-year tenure. Some began to suggest that he might do well in politics, and even New York State Governor Mario Cuomo urged him to run for a U.S. Senate seat. However, Levitt's wife was said to be adamantly disinterested in public life.

After he left the Amex in 1989, Levitt chaired the New York City Economic Development Corporation and, with onetime Commerce Secretary Robert Mosbacher, established a small-business lobbying organization in Washington called the American Business Conference. A skilled political fund-raiser with a wealth of Wall Street and Washington contacts of both party stripes, he set up a 1992 dinner for Democratic presidential hopeful Bill Clinton that raised $750,000. When Clinton took office, Levitt was stunned to learn that he was being considered for the SEC job.

The SEC is a federally funded agency that monitors Wall Street. It was created in 1934 by President Franklin D. Roosevelt, who battled tremendous opposition from America's financial elite over its creation and regulatory authority. Its mandate was to protect the average investor from fraudulent practices on the part of brokerage firms—practices that had led, in part, to the October of 1929 stock market crash and subsequent worldwide economic depression. Levitt accepted the post, and quickly went to work putting through reforms that helped the average investor better understand the market. He forced mutual-fund companies to issue prospectuses in plain English, for example, and instituted new rules for the municipal bond market.

Levitt next went after the National Association of Securities Dealers, and forced it to institute new rules in response to charges of price-fixing on its NASDAQ trading floor. He was also wary about the practice of allowing stock options granted to employees as part of their compensation packages to be treated as an expense on corporate income statements—a little accounting trick that would have major repercussions in the booming bull market of the late 1990s. This was one of the battles he lost, however, along with the one he launched against the accounting industry that sanctioned such practices. Technically, the major American accounting firms—Price Waterhouse, Coopers & Lybrand, Deloitte & Touche, Ernst & Young, K.P.M.G., and

Arthur Andersen—were not part of the SEC's domain, but they nevertheless played a key role in corporate finance: such firms had risen to prominence in the twentieth century by their auditing expertise. Any publicly traded company had to hire such a firm to review its books and ensure that its quarterly and annual financial statements—on whose publication the company's share price either rose or fell—were accurate and not misleading.

In the 1980s, however, those Big Six accounting firms—which became the Big Five during Levitt's tenure after Price Waterhouse's merger with Coopers & Lybrand—began selling an array of other services to their corporate clients. Consulting—for management compensation, information–technology systems, merger analysis, and other services—proved a far more lucrative revenue source than auditing, but presented a potential conflict of interest. As Levitt explained in *Take On the Street,* as quoted in *BusinessWeek,* at some companies more than three–quarters of management compensation was in stock options, which "gave executives an incentive to use accounting tricks to boost the share price on which their compensation depended.... We [at the SEC] began to see a pattern. Corporations were playing with their earnings calculations until they arrived at the best possible number. Earnings press releases revealed only the good news. Auditors, increasingly captive of their clients, would give them the clean audits they wanted, despite lots of chicanery."

In a few cases, companies were caught red–handed, and were compelled by law to issue a restatement of their earnings; as a result, irate shareholders who had lost money on the company's stock then filed lawsuits. Two years into his tenure, Levitt fought a Republican–sponsored initiative that made it harder for shareholders to sue in such cases, but his power was no match against the business interests allied to lobby for the passage of the Private Securities Litigation Reform Act, and he stepped out of the fight. It set the tone for the rest of his tenure, however: lobbyist Jeffrey Peck told *New Yorker* writer Jane Mayer that that particular battle was the starting point for a "really bad feeling" between the accounting profession and Levitt. "It was as if two people had gone out on a first date and had a bad time," Peck explained. "But the rules required them to keep dating."

In 1998, President Clinton re–nominated Levitt for a second five–year term, a rarity for an SEC chief, and Levitt began a more determined campaign to force the accounting industry to reform. He went to the Financial Accounting Standards Board, an inde-

pendent body located in Norwalk, Connecticut, which sets rules for the accounting profession, but they proved less than willing to agree to his proposals, arguing that the industry did an effective job of policing itself. Levitt, his critics claimed, didn't understand the rules of the "New Economy" and, furthermore, there was simply no "smoking gun"—no genuine proof of any instance of wide-scale fraud between corporations and the accounting firms that provided both auditing and consulting services.

As the war of words intensified, Levitt was contacted by no less than 47 members of Congress urging him to reconsider his stance, and became even more irate when he learned of the massive campaign donations made by the accounting industry to many legislators. "It was the ultimate nexus of business and politics," Levitt told Mayer in the *New Yorker.* "If there was ever an example where money and lobbying damaged the public interest, this was clearly it." Finally, when some politicians threatened to reduce the SEC budget, Levitt agreed to a compromise in November of 2000 that forced the Big Five firms to simply disclose the amount of non–audit services they provided to their corporate clients. He stepped down as SEC chair three months later, along with the rest of the Clinton team.

Eight months later, in October of 2001, the failure of Enron became front–page headlines. It was revealed that executives at the Houston–based oil pipeline and energy–trading company had inflated its net income by $600 million. Its auditor, Arthur Andersen, was eventually indicted on obstruction of justice charges for feverishly shredding those "smoking gun"–type documents in the weeks following the initial reports. Millions of dollars invested in Enron's stock were lost overnight, and it became the biggest bankruptcy in United States history.

Levitt was by then absorbed in writing *Take on the Street* with finance journalist Paula Dwyer. The book earned laudatory reviews and even became a best–seller. The *Economist* noted that Levitt's "expose of the bad behavior and conflicts of interest that beset investment banks, stock exchanges, and company bosses is devastating," and that his tales of the political maneuvering to block his attempts at reform "are sobering to believers in American democracy."

In his other post–SEC career, Levitt has an office at the Carlyle Group, a private equity firm. An avid power–boater, Levitt regularly takes friends, Wall Street executives, and politicians on wilderness retreats out West. His own fortune was once estimated at $30 million, and he has homes in Connecticut, Santa Fe, New Mexico; Washington, D.C., and New York City. The same year his book was published, his successor at the SEC was forced to resign, and President Bush signed the Sarbanes–Oxley Act into law, which prohibits accounting firms from doing consulting work for companies that they audit. In the rounds of interviews he did to promote his book, Levitt was often asked if the United States economy could ever recover after the crisis of confidence that came in the wake of Enron and other revelations of corporate fraud. "I believe that embarrassment and humiliation have already caused societal change," he told *Fortune*'s Janice Revell. "You've seen CEOs of companies that have been in the limelight suddenly sounding like latter–day Elmer Gantrys, calling for the expensing of stock options and so on. This would have been laughed at a few years ago."

Selected writings

(With Paula Dwyer) *Take on the Street: What Wall Street and Corporate America Don't Want You to Know: What You Can Do to Fight Back,* Pantheon Books (New York City), 2002.

Sources

Books

Levitt, Arthur, with Paula Dwyer, *Take On the Street: What Wall Street and Corporate America Don't Want You to Know: What You Can Do to Fight Back,* Pantheon Books (New York City), 2002.

Periodicals

Bond Buyer, October 22, 1993, p. 3.
BusinessWeek, September 30, 2002, pp. 74–80.
CFO: The Magazine for Senior Financial Executives, May 2003, p. 63.
Corporate Board, January–February 2003, p. 32.
Economist, October 26, 2002.
Fortune, October 14, 2002, p. 64.
Institutional Investor, January 1998, p. 48.
Investment News, June 10, 2002, p. 22.
Money, November 1, 2002, p. 65.
Newsweek International, July 15, 2002, p. 64.
New Yorker, April 22, 2002, p. 64.
New York Times, November 24, 2002, p. 28; June 8, 2003.

—Carol Brennan

Eugene Levy

Actor, writer, and director

Born December 17, 1946, in Hamilton, Ontario, Canada; married Deborah Devine, 1977; children: Dan, Sarah. *Education:* Graduated from McMaster University, 1970.

Addresses: *Home*—Toronto, Ontario, Canada.

Career

Actor in television, including: *Stay Tuned,* 1976; *Sunshine Hour,* 1976; *Second City TV* (also known as *SCTV* and *SCTV Network 90*), CBC, NBC, and Cinemax, 1976–84; *The Last Polka* (movie), HBO, 1984; *The Canadian Conspiracy* (movie), 1985; *Bride of Boogedy* (movie), 1987; *Biographies: The Enigma of Bobby Bittman* (movie), Cinemax, 1988; *Second City's 15th Anniversary Special* (also producer and director), 1988; *Camp Candy* (voice), 1989; *Partners 'n Love* (movie; also directed), Family Channel, 1992; *Harrison Bergeron* (movie), 1995; *Hiller and Diller,* 1997; *Hercules* (voice), 1998; *D.O.A.* (movie), 1999; *The Sports Pages* (movie), 2001; *Club Land* (movie; uncredited), 2001; *Committed* (voice), 2001; *The Kid* (movie; voice), 2001; *Greg the Bunny,* Fox, 2002.

Film appearances include: *Cannibal Girls,* 1973; *Running,* 1979; *Nothing Personal,* 1980; *Double Negative,* 1980; *Heavy Metal* (voice), 1981; *National Lampoon's Vacation,* 1983; *Going Berserk,* 1983; *Splash,* 1984; *Club Paradise,* 1986; *Armed and Dangerous,* 1986; *Speed Zone!,* 1989; *Father of the Bride,* 1991; *Stay Tuned,* 1992; *I Love Trouble,* 1994; *Father of the Bride II,* 1995; *Multiplicity,* 1996; *Waiting for Guffman,* 1996; *Dogmatic,* 1996; *Almost Heroes,* 1998; *Holy Man* (uncredited), 1998; *Akbar's Adventure Tours,* 1998; *The Secret Life of Girls,* 1999; *American Pie,* 1999; *Best in Show,* 2000; *The Ladies Man,* 2000; *Silver Man,* 2000; *American Pie 2,* 2001; *Down to Earth,* 2001; *Serendipity,* 2001; *Repli-Kate,* 2002; *Like Mike,* 2002; *A Mighty Wind,* 2003; *Bringing Down the House,* 2003; *Dumb and Dumberer: When Harry Met Lloyd,* 2003; *American Wedding,* 2003.

Television and film writing includes: *Second City TV,* 1976–81; *SCTV Channel,* 1983; *The Last Polka* (also executive producer), 1984; *Biographies: The Enigma of Bobby Bittman* (also director and executive producer), 1988; *Maniac Mansion* (also executive producer and director of certain episodes), Family Channel, 1990; *Sodbusters* (also songwriter, director, and executive producer), 1994; *The Martin Short Show,* 1994; *Waiting for Guffman,* 1996; *D.O.A.,* 1999; *Best in Show* (also songwriter), 2000; *A Mighty Wind* (also songwriter), 2003.

Director of films, including: *I, Martin Short, Goes Hollywood* (TV), 1989; *Once Upon a Crime,* 1992; *Partners 'n Love,* 1992; *Sodbusters* (TV), 1994. Stage appearances include: *Godspell,* Toronto, Ontario, Canada, 1972–73; Second City productions, Toronto.

Awards: Emmy Award (with others) for outstanding writing in a variety or music program, for *SCTV Network,* 1992; New York Film Critics Circle Award for best supporting actor, for *A Mighty Wind*, 2003; Critics' Choice Award (with Christopher Guest and Michael McKean) for best song, Broadcast Film Critics Association, for "A Mighty Wind," 2003; Grammy Award (with Christopher Guest and Michael McKean) for best song written for a motion picture, television, or other visual media, Recording Academy, for "A Mighty Wind," 2004.

Sidelights

Though film audiences have become familiar with comedic actor Eugene Levy through such movies as the 1999 teen flick *American Pie* and its sequels as well as such independent fare as the 2000 dog show fictional documentary *Best in Show,* he already had a long career working in film and television. Years before these films, Levy began in Canadian television as a star of the hit sketch comedy show *Second City TV.* He then embarked on a career that included small roles in film and television, writing or co–writing films and television specials, and some directing assignments in film and television movies, both in the United States and Canada. Despite his late success as an actor, Levy shunned the Hollywood life, keeping his native Canada as his primary home.

Born in 1946 in the steel town of Hamilton, Ontario, Canada, Levy was the son of a foreman at an automotive plant, while his mother worked as a homemaker. Performing was part of Levy's life by the time he was a student at Hamilton's Westdale High School. Music was also one of his interests. He was a member of a folk trio called the Tri–tones as a teenager. For college, Levy attended McMaster University in Hamilton. There, he met many future collaborators including Dave Thomas, Martin Short, and Ivan Reitman. Levy graduated from McMaster in 1970.

Levy's acting career began in 1970. That year, he made his film debut in the second feature directed by Reitman, the horror comedy *Cannibal Girls*. The film was not released until 1973, and also featured future *Second City TV* castmate Andrea Martin. Film was not Levy's only genre in this time period; he appeared in theater productions as well. In 1972–73, Levy appeared in the Toronto, Ontario, Canada, production of *Godspell,* with McMaster alumni Short and Thomas, as well as Martin. Levy and several of his castmates then appeared with the Second City comedy troupe in live productions in Toronto. Second City's live comedy theater including sketches and improv.

After moving to California to start a new theatre company with fellow Second City troupe members John Candy and Joe Flaherty, the trio returned to Toronto when their venture failed. Soon after they returned, the comedy of Toronto's Second City moved to television. The program was a sketch comedy show that originally aired on television in Toronto only, then moved to the Canadian Broadcast Company (CBC) and later aired on American networks, including NBC and Cinemax, and other international networks. Originally titled *Second City TV,* the show was commonly known as *SCTV,* and later re–titled *SCTV Network 90* and *SCTV Network.*

With *SCTV,* Levy was part of what many considered one of the best comedy shows produced in Canada for much of its run, which lasted from 1976–84. The cast included Candy, Thomas, Martin, and Short. In addition to writing for *SCTV* Levy also created a number of memorable characters, including fake comic Bobby Bittman and Stan Shmenge, one of the polka king brothers. Levy also did a number of celebrity impersonations such as Floyd the barber from *The Andy Griffith Show,* Gene Shalit the movie critic, and actor Ricardo Montalban.

Long after the run of *SCTV* ended, the show was still watched in reruns, and on video and DVD. Of the show's continuing popularity, Levy told Rob Salem of the *Toronto Star,* "With *SCTV,* we created an entire world, which was insulated from the real world and insulated from timely events. And in doing that, I think, the show survives well without being dated."

While a part of *SCTV,* Levy also appeared in several films, including the 1979 drama *Running* and as a voice actor in the 1981 animated feature *Heavy Metal.* After the end of *SCTV,* many of Levy's castmates went on to bigger and better things, including Candy who had a long career in Hollywood comedies. While Levy also had a film career after *SCTV,* he chose to remain in Canada instead of moving to Los Angeles, California. He and his wife, Deborah Divine, whom he married in 1977, wanted to raise their two children, Dan and Sarah, there. Levy told Lewis Beale of *Daily News* in 1997, "If I was career–oriented, I wouldn't be living in Toronto. I [just] wanna make a decent living, and I wanna do the jobs I wanna do.… When I got my first stage job, I couldn't believe I was going to get paid every week for doing this… I still can't believe I'm getting paid for what it is I do." Levy remained Toronto–based throughout his career.

Levy still compiled credits in Hollywood comedies in the 1980s, but was primarily relegated to small or supporting roles. Levy played a car salesman in 1983's *National Lampoon's Vacation,* and a scientist who wants to capture the mermaid played by Daryl Hannah in the 1984 romantic comedy, *Splash*. The 1986 comedy *Club Paradise* featured many *SCTV* alumni. Levy played a swinger named Barry who was a patron at the failing resort. Levy's first larger role came in 1986's comedy about a security guard, *Armed and Dangerous*, which co–starred Candy.

Acting was not Levy's only post–*SCTV* pursuit; he also did some producing, writing, and directing. Many of his early projects were based on characters from *SCTV*. In 1984, Levy served as co–writer and executive producer of *The Last Polka* for HBO. This was a fake documentary based on his *SCTV* sketch about the Shmenge brothers and their polka band. Levy and co–writer Candy appeared as the brothers. Four years later, Levy wrote, directed, and served as executive producer on *Autobiographies: The Enigma of Bobby Bittman*, which aired on Cinemax. He also produced, directed, and acted in *Second City's 15th Anniversary Special* in 1988.

In the early 1990s, Levy continued to work in behind–the–scenes capacities. In 1990, he created the television series *Maniac Mansion* which was based on a computer game produced by Lucas Film and aired on the Family Channel. He also served as the show's executive producer, and wrote and directed certain episodes. In 1992, Levy directed the television movie, *Partners 'n Love*, for the Family Channel. That same year, Levy directed his first feature film, *Once Upon a Crime*. The film was a failure at the box office and among critics. In 1994, he served as a writer, director, executive producer, and song writer for the television movie *Sodbusters*, a comic take on westerns.

Levy continued to appear in films in the early 1990s as well, though primarily in small comic roles. His films included 1992's *Stay Tuned*, the 1994 Julia Roberts vehicle, *I Love Trouble*, and 1995's *Father of the Bride Part II*. While Levy's roles were still supporting or part of a large ensemble, in the late 1990s, his career and profile blossomed. The change came in the mid–1990s when he began working with Christopher Guest, a writer, director, and actor best known for his role in the cult classic from 1984, *This Is Spinal Tap*.

Guest tapped Levy to help him write the script for a new "mockumentary," 1996's *Waiting for Guffman*. The script was basically an outline with plot points, basic story line, and defined characters which left room for the actors to improvise. *Guffman* was set in the small town of Blaine, Missouri, where the locals were putting on a musical revue for the 150th anniversary of the city's founding. Levy played Dr. Allan Pearl, a cross–eyed dentist who has no real talent but much ambition to be a talk show host like Johnny Carson. Levy's Pearl hosts the show. Levy was praised for his work in the film and was considered by many critics to be one of the best in the cast.

After the success of *Guffman*, Levy worked on a number of Guest's subsequent films. Levy again co–wrote the script for 2000's *Best in Show*, a mockumentary about dog shows. Levy also had a prominent role in the ensemble film, playing an obsessive dog owner named Gerry Fleck who literally has two left feet and a formerly promiscuous wife named Cookie. As with *Guffman*, much of the film was improvised, and Levy shone in the critically acclaimed film.

While Levy was building a reputation in ensemble mockumentaries, he also found an audience in an unexpected place. In 1999, Levy was cast in *American Pie* in a supporting role known only as Jim's Dad. *American Pie* was a teen comedy film, and Levy's character was the father of the main character, played by Jason Biggs. Jim's Dad was loving and full of fatherly advice, but bumbling and known for his bad timing.

Levy's role remained prominent in the two sequels: 2001's *American Pie 2* and 2003's *American Wedding*. Of his role in the films, Levy told Bruce Kirkland of the *Toronto Sun*, "I haven't heard a negative thing about the character since the first movie came out. So I'm very proud to carry the moniker of 'Jim's Dad' now. I find myself picking up some things from the character, just in terms of trying to stay on an even keel. I've actually tried to adopt a few personality traits of the character."

These successes led to more roles in Hollywood films for Levy. In 2001, he appeared in *Down to Earth*, a *Heaven Can Wait* remake directed by the Weitz brothers (Paul and Chris) who were part of the original *American Pie* movie. Levy played Keyes, an angel who is not great at his job. Levy also played a small but important role as a salesman in the 2001 romantic film, *Serendipity*. In 2003, Levy played rich lawyer Howie Rottman, the friend to Steve Martin's lead character, in *Bringing Down the House*. The film was panned by critics but Levy's work received their praise; the film did well at the box office despite less–than–favorable reviews. Levy was similarly acclaimed for his role as the cheating high school principal in 2003's *Dumb and Dumberer: When Harry Met Lloyd*, though the movie did not do well.

While Levy was building up a career in film, he still worked in television on occasion. In 2001, he provided a voice for *Committed,* a CTV (Canadian television) animated comedy, also with *SCTV* alums Martin and Catherine O'Hara. Levy was the voice of Joe Larsen, a freelance writer who works at home with his kids. Levy appeared in the short–lived 2002 television series, *Greg the Bunny,* on Fox. The show was a behind–the–scenes look at a puppet show, *Sweetknuckle Junction,* in which the puppets were as real as the humans who worked on the program. While the show barely lasted its first season, it did develop a cult following.

In 2003, Levy again collaborated with Guest as co–writer and performer in *A Mighty Wind,* a mockumentary about folk artists reuniting for a tribute show. Levy played Mitch Cohen, a 1960s folk singer who is trying to make a career comeback. Cohen had been part of a folk duo, Mitch & Mickey. O'Hara played Mickey, Cohen's ex–wife and ex–partner. Though Levy had to play music live for the first time in many years, he still managed to garner several awards for a song he co–wrote for the film, including a Grammy.

Levy enjoyed his success, gladly accepting the fact that he would not be a lead actor. He told Tim Carvell of *Entertainment Weekly,* "I'm a character actor. That gives you the ability to go in knowing that you've only got a handful of scenes. And you don't necessarily have to carry the movie, you just have to score. It's a great way to work."

Sources

Books

Celebrity Biographies, Baseline II, 2004.

Periodicals

Daily News (New York), January 27, 1997, p. 32.
Entertainment Weekly, April 25, 2003, pp. 50–52.
Houston Chronicle, April 20, 2003, p. 8.
Maclean's, March 19, 2001, p. 47; April 21, 2003, p. 59.
Newsweek, February 10, 1997, p. 66.
Ottawa Citizen, August 16, 2003, p. J3.
People, July 1, 1985, p. 8; August 11, 2003, p. 64.
Time, April 1, 2002, p. 67A.
Toronto Star, July 5, 1986, p. F1; February 28, 1997, p. D1; October 31, 1998, p. SW4; March 9, 2002, p. SS04.
Toronto Sun, March 3, 1997, p. 36; March 10, 2001, p. 38; August 7, 2001, p. 27.
Vanity Fair, April 2003, p. 162.
Variety, February 19, 2001, p. 37.

Online

"Eugene Levy," Internet Movie Database, http://www.imdb.com/name/nm0506405/ (February 9, 2004).
"OutKast Snag Top Grammy, Eugene Levy Represents Canada," Chartattack, http://www.chartattack.com/damn/2004/02/0907.cfm (February 18, 2004).

—*A. Petruso*

Daniel Libeskind

Architect

Born May 12, 1946, in Lódz, Poland; married Nina Lewis (an architectural–office manager), c. 1969; children: two sons, one daughter. *Education:* Cooper Union for the Advancement of Science and Art, New York, NY, B.A., 1970; Essex University, Colchester, England, M.A., 1972.

Addresses: *Home*—New York, NY. *Office*—Studio Daniel Libeskind, 2 Rector St., New York, NY 10006.

Career

Worked for architect Richard Meier, early 1970s; taught architecture at universities in Kentucky, London, England, and Toronto, Canada; head of architecture school, Cranbrook Academy of Art, Bloomfield Hills, MI, 1978–85; founded private graduate academy, Architecture Intermundium, Milan, Italy, 1985; won first architectural commission for the Jewish Museum, Berlin, and opened Studio Daniel Libeskind in Berlin, 1989; selected as primary architect for the rebuilding of the World Trade Center site, New York City, 2003.

Sidelights

An imaginative proposal submitted by architect Daniel Libeskind trounced some stiff competition and was chosen in early 2003 to serve as the master plan for the rebuilding of the 16–acre World Trade Center (WTC) site in New York City. While Libeskind is a respected name in his field, he was primarily known as an architectural theorist and teacher, having won just a handful of museum–

design commissions before landing the WTC project, but he was considered an adroit diplomat in dealing with the sometimes–conflicting private–interest and municipal goals that often play out in the realm of urban architecture. As such, critics considered him the ideal architect to transform the ill–fated landscape of Lower Manhattan where, noted *New Yorker* writer Paul Goldberger, "the goal is to meld sacred space with a functioning city, and Libeskind has a natural instinct for that."

Libeskind is of Polish–Jewish heritage. Both parents had separately fled Poland after Nazi Germany's invasion of the country in 1939, fearing anti–Semitic reprisals, and made it to the Soviet Union border, where they were arrested and interned in Siberia. They returned after the war to Lódz, the hometown of Libeskind's father, and learned that nearly all of their family on each side had died in the Holocaust—some 85 victims in all. Libeskind was born in the city in 1946, and proved a talented young accordionist as a child. His parents had chosen the instrument for him over the piano, for to have brought one in via the common courtyard in their apartment building would have made the distinctly wrong impression on their neighbors, as Libeskind recalled in an interview with Stanley Meisler in the *Smithsonian.*

"Anti–Semitism," he said, "is the only memory I still have of Poland.... It wasn't what most people think happened after the war was over."

Libeskind's talents were so impressive that he even delivered the first live musical performance on Polish television at the age of six. When he was eleven, the family, which included a sister, left Poland for Israel and settled in Tel Aviv. A year later, Libeskind won a coveted America–Israel Cultural Foundation scholarship, whose past recipients included violinist Itzhak Perlman, and with it a visa for his family to emigrate. They settled in the New York City borough of the Bronx, and not long afterward Libeskind enrolled in the prestigious Bronx High School of Science. He continued to pursue his musical interests, and even gave the occasional piano concert. He became a naturalized American citizen in 1965.

In the early 1960s, Libeskind entered the architecture program at Cooper Union for the Advancement of Science and Art. He chose the field, in part, because it "combines so many of my interests," Newsweek's Cathleen McGuigan quoted him as saying. "Mathematics, painting, arts. It's about people, space, music." He completed a graduate degree in the history and theory of architecture at Essex University in Colchester, England, in 1972, and though he was hired by top firms such as Richard Meier's office, Libeskind rarely lasted longer than a week on any job at a practice. "I didn't like the smell, the atmosphere, the hierarchy" of such offices, he wryly admitted in a talk before the Royal Geographical Society of London, according to Building Design writer Catherine Croft.

Instead Libeskind took teaching posts at universities in Kentucky, London, and Toronto, and in 1978 was named head of the school of architecture at the Cranbrook Academy of Art in Bloomfield Hills, Michigan. It was a prestigious job for someone just 32 years old, for Cranbrook was a world–renowned, highly selective training ground for the creative professions. After seven years there, Libeskind left to establish his own educational community, Architecture Intermundium, in Milan, Italy. He was its only professor, and taught just a dozen students at a time.

Libeskind opened his own practice in Berlin, Germany, after winning the commission to build a Jewish Museum in the city in 1989. The project was an emotionally resonant one: the city had once served as home to Germany's thriving Jewish culture in the decades before World War II, but a Nazi regime with headquarters in this German capital set out to

rid the nation, and then the rest of conquered Europe, of its Jewish population with a ruthless bureaucratic efficiency. Taking into account this historical tragedy, Libeskind read the case files of German–Jewish families who lived in the neighborhood of the proposed museum site, most of whom were deported and died in Nazi concentration camps. He created a matrix based on the geographical addresses of famed Berliner Jews, and from those points mapped out the zigzag design of the building, which gave it a Star of David shape.

Libeskind was compelled to settle in Berlin—at his wife's urging—when several roadblocks occurred before the Jewish Museum finally came to fruition. At first, the entire project was cancelled due to fiscal shortfalls in the city, and even when it was completed in 1999, but not yet officially open, a debate raged over its purpose, and the various factions finally agreed that it would serve as museum dedicated to German–Jewish history. Since September of 2001, it has become the second–most–visited museum in the city after the Pergamon in what was formerly East Berlin, and is one of those rare structures that elicit paeans from the architectural community but has a strong emotional appeal to the public as well. Its modernist zinc exterior houses a narrative hall containing the stories of 19 German–Jewish families, and visitors then enters a Holocaust Tower, closed off by an immense iron door that seems to entrap. That leads on to the Garden of Exile, which features 48 columns topped by foliage and earth from Berlin. The number 48 corresponds to the year that Israel was founded, and a 49th column contains soil from Jerusalem, Israel's capital.

After the success of the Jewish Museum, Libeskind began entering more competitions. His next major project was the Felix Nussbaum Museum in Osnabrück, Germany, which was finished in 1998. The site houses the works of a German–Jewish artist who died in World War II. For a time before his deportation, Nussbaum hid in a basement and painted there; part of Libeskind's design shows these paintings in a dark, small space not unlike the one where the artist originally painted them. The façade of the building is a large concrete slab, representing the blank canvas of Nussbaum's truncated career, but the exterior is beautified by a bed of sunflowers, the artist's favorite flower. Another unusual commission that Libeskind won was for the Imperial War Museum of the North, in Manchester, England. The building houses a panoply of ships, artillery, tanks, and fighter planes, but Libeskind designed a "shattered–globe" space in which visitors contemplate how wars alter the landscape permanently.

When the terms of an international competition were announced to create a master plan for the site of the former World Trade Center towers in August of 2002, nearly a year after the modernist towers, 110 stories each, were reduced to rubble in an attack that involved hijacked airliners, Libeskind went to work on his submission. To prepare, he re–read the Declaration of Independence, as well as nineteenth–century American fiction about New York from Herman Melville and Walt Whitman. The commission, however, presented an unusually tough challenge for any architect: it was the site of the first–attack ever on American soil, where scores died, but it was also a valuable parcel of real estate and nexus for transportation in and out of the city. Several competing parties had a voice in what ultimately would become of the WTC site: the Lower Manhattan Development Corporation, which was created after 9/11 and made up of 15 prominent board members; the office of New York City Mayor Michael Bloomberg; New York's governor, George Pataki; the Port Authority of New York and New Jersey, the transit management group that actually owned the land; and Larry A. Silverstein, a developer who had signed a 99–year lease on the WTC towers that gave him ownership of all of its office space just days before they fell. Lastly—but by no means least—was the public input. New Yorkers who had lost family members argued that the site should be preserved as a memorial; residents of the area maintained that a mixed–use plan might be a more viable compromise.

Libeskind's plan, unveiled in December of 2002, fulfilled each of these objectives. The 70–foot–deep excavation pit would remain; this part of the site had become known as Ground Zero, where rescue workers and construction personnel toiled for months to clear rubble and remains. In Libeskind's plan, visitors could peer down from a semi–circular curving walkway into a large empty space below. There, the original slurry walls erected in the early 1970s when the WTC went up were visible. These were devised to keep the waters of the Hudson River from flooding the subterranean section of the original site. Libeskind's plan also included office and residential space, but his tallest tower boasted a rooftop garden that would serve as an eye–catching skyline fixture for Manhattan, "because gardens are a constant affirmation of life," Libeskind explained to Meisler in the *Smithsonian*. This tower would be 1,776 feet in height, a reference to the year that America gained its independence and, if built, would be the world's tallest building. Other elements of his plan included a "Park of Heroes," with the names of fire and police units who lost personnel in the rescue effort engraved into the pavement. Finally, Libeskind's proposed buildings would be configured so that each September 11, from 8:46 a.m., when the first plane struck the North Tower,

to 10:28 a.m., when that tower followed the South one's collapse by 23 minutes, a wedge of light would fall below in commemoration of the tragedy and the 2,800–plus lives lost. No shadows would be visible on the site during that time.

In February of 2003, the finalists were winnowed down to the plans of two contenders: Libeskind's and that of the "Think" team, comprised of several other prominent architects and landscape designers. The latter centered on two towers that mimicked the original, but were instead two empty lattice-work frames that could later house cultural facilities. A press war waged over the next few weeks. Some deemed Libeskind's gaping memorial pit ghoulish, while others considered the Think's group's empty towers skeletal. Both sides retained public–relations firms to put their opposing viewpoints before the public, but in the end, Bloomberg was said to have liked Libeskind's public squares and park, and the governor's office favored it as well.

Architecture critics, media pundits, and average New Yorkers hailed Libeskind's plan for the WTC site. As McGuigan pointed out in *Newsweek*, New York City is "a place with fewer great examples of contemporary design than any major Western metropolis, a place where development decisions are made by big–shouldered moneymen." Choosing "someone of Libeskind's caliber for this historic project," McGuigan continued, "is a turning point for architecture and for the city, and it sends a clear signal that the public has an appetite for innovative design." It was a sentiment echoed by Goldberger in the *New Yorker*. "The architectural bar has been raised in New York," he noted. "Ten months ago, it was hard to imagine that the official plan for Ground Zero would be produced by one of the most innovative architects in the world."

Libeskind was planning to move to New York City, to a home and office in Lower Manhattan, to begin work on the project. He has two adult sons and a young daughter. His wife, Nina, works closely with him in his practice, managing the 130–employee office and dealing with the plethora of non–creative details involving new projects, including an extension to the Denver Art Museum in Colorado, a new addition to the Royal Ontario Museum (adding 40,000 square feet) in Toronto, Canada, and a new Jewish Museum in San Francisco, California. He still dabbles in music, and even designed and directed an opera based on the life of St. Francis of Assisi at Berlin's Deutsche Oper in 2002. Architecture remained his primary passion, however, and he was eager to begin work on the Lower Manhattan project, slated for completion by September 11, 2006. As he told *Time* journalist Richard Lacayo just after his plan was chosen, "I shaped the entire site to speak to the traces of the event and to its significance," he reflected. "But we also want to reassert its vitality."

Selected writings

Between Zero and Infinity: Selected Projects in Architecture, Rizzoli International (New York City), 1981.

Chamber Works: Architectural Meditations on Themes from Heraclitus, Architectural Association (London, England), 1983.

Fishing from the Pavement, Nai Publishers (Rotterdam, The Netherlands), 1997.

Daniel Libeskind, Radix–Matrix: Architecture and Writings, translated from the German by Peter Green, Prestel (New York City), 1997.

Daniel Libeskind: The Space of Encounter, Universe/St. Martin's Press (New York City), 2000.

Sources

Periodicals

Building Design, September 15, 2000, p. 8.
BusinessWeek, February 24, 2003, pp. 110–12.
New Statesman, June 24, 2002, p. 36.
Newsweek, February 10, 2003, pp. 62–64; March 10, 2003, pp. 58–60.
New Yorker, March 10, 2003, p. 78.
New York Times, February 23, 2003, p. 54; July 15, 2003; August 1, 2003, p. A1; August 25, 2003.
Smithsonian, March 2003, p. 76.
Time, March 10, 2003, p. 58.

Online

"Renaissance ROM announces $30 million lead gift from Michael Lee–Chin," Royal Ontario Museum, http://www.rom.on.ca/news/releases/public. php?mediakey=gfosuo3dvn (October 28, 2003).

—*Carol Brennan*

Ray Lines

Chief Executive Officer of CleanFlicks

Born c. 1960, in Utah; married Sharon; children: Rashelle, Tiffani, Elisse, Camille, Celeste, Savanna, Makenna. *Education:* Brigham Young University, B.A. (broadcast news).

Addresses: *Office*—CleanFlicks, 533 West Center, Pleasant Grove, UT 84062.

Career

Served as a Mormon missionary in Tonga, 1978–80; worked as a sports broadcaster for an ABC–TV station in Rapid City, SD; promoted to position of sports director; moved into production work, traveling around the country in a TV production truck to cover sporting events, concerts, and conventions, 1990s; edited material he considered offensive from *Titanic* for rental by a video store, 1999; founded CleanFlicks chain of video rental stores, 2000.

Sidelights

CleanFlicks chief executive officer Ray Lines has raise the ire of Hollywood by renting and selling edited versions of popular movies. Lines removes from the movies he distributes material that he deems offensive, including nudity, violence, and profanity. With more than 70 successful CleanFlicks video stores around the United States, Lines has proven that he is not alone in his desire to watch sanitized films, and says he is fulfilling a definite need, particularly among those whose religious beliefs make unedited movies offensive to them. The Directors Guild of America—along with a group of movie studios—believes otherwise, however, and in 2002 named CleanFlicks and several other companies engaged in the same business in a lawsuit alleging copyright infringement.

Lines grew up in Provo, Utah. His father supported his family by working as a safety engineer while his mother was a homemaker. Early on, he developed a love of movies, fostered by weekly trips to a nearby drive–in movie theater. He later recalled the movies of those days as much cleaner and more wholesome than the movies of his adulthood. His favorite movie is *It's a Wonderful Life.*

After graduating from high school in 1978, Lines traveled to Tonga—a group of islands in the Pacific Ocean—as a missionary for the Church of Jesus Christ of Latter–day Saints (the Mormon church). He returned home after two years of service, and shortly thereafter, an event occurred which was to plant the seeds of his future career: he took a girl-friend to see a movie. The film was rated PG, so he thought it would be free of any material he or his date would find offensive. He was therefore caught off guard when a woman in the firm exposed her breasts. "I was totally embarrassed," Lines later told *People.*

Lines attended college at Brigham Young University in Utah and graduated with a B.A. in broadcast news. Soon after graduating, he went to work at an ABC affiliate in Rapid City, South Dakota, as a weekend sports anchor. He moved up rapidly in the company, and not long after he started at the television station, he was promoted to the position of sports director. In this capacity, he anchored sports on weekdays, not only on television, but also on radio. He also broadcast play–by–play for both the professional and college sports teams in the area.

After three years as an on–air personality, Lines shifted his focus to production work, moving behind the scenes to a television production truck he put together himself. In the truck, Lines covered sporting events all over the western United States. He also branched out to cover not only sporting events, but conferences and concerts. A highlight of his career at this time was covering the 1996 Olympic Games in Atlanta, Georgia.

Wanting to help other people avoid the embarrassment he had suffered on his date in 1980, particularly fellow Mormons, Lines put his video production skills to use by creating edited versions of popular films. For instance, in 1989, Lines used video editing equipment to remove profanity from the film *Top Gun* for a family member. He went on to edit films for viewing by his seven daughters.

A personal crusade turned into a career in 1999. This was when he helped a local video store cut nudity from the film *Titanic*. The store did need help: employees of the store, lacking Lines's skills, had resorted to using scissors to cut the offending material from the film. Lines was only too happy to show them a better way to edit video, and he soon realized that there was a wider market for cleaned–up films, especially in Utah, where 70 percent of the population is Mormon.

In 2000, Lines opened his own stores that rented edited videos. These first CleanFlicks stores were in Utah, and soon he was turning out cut versions of major Hollywood films for anyone who wanted them. His primary motivation, he told *People*, is to sanitize films "so that families can watch the movies in their homes."

By 2003, more than 70 video stores around the country were offering videos of films edited by Lines's company. CleanFlicks also launched a website to sell and rent movies online. Thus, Lines became the first company to widely distribute cleaned–up versions of major films. Features edited out of Clean-Flicks versions of films include sex, nudity, violence, profanity, and even bathroom humor. Lines, working with a single assistant, still does the bulk of the editing work himself.

This activity met with strong disapproval from the motion picture industry. In 2002, the Directors Guild of America, along with a group of major movie studios, named CleanFlicks, along with a dozen other companies who edit films, with copyright infringement. Lines and his colleagues, the suit argued, have no right to edit for broad distribution materials whose copyright they do not own. Lines remained resolute, saying he had every right to edit copies of films he owns. To suggest otherwise, he asserted in *People*, would be like trying to forbid the purchaser of a pair of jeans from making shorts out of them.

A University of Southern California law professor, Daniel Klerman, predicted that Lines and his co–defendants would lose the lawsuit because, he told *People,* copyright law gives movie studios the exclusive right to edit their own material. But he did acknowledge that the demand for edited movies was there, and wondered why the movie studios did not get into this business themselves. However, studios have in fact long been in the business of editing films for television and airline viewing.

Lines, for his part, feels that his company, rather than harming Hollywood, is bringing its films to audiences who would not otherwise watch many of them. Since the studios do not offer edited versions of their films to the video renting public, it is up to companies like CleanFlicks to provide them. "I'm not cramming anything down anyone's throat or campaigning for anything or trying to get Steven Spielberg to edit or direct in a certain way," Lines told Michael Janofsky in the *New York Times*. "I'd never do that. I'm just providing the community an option."

Sources

Periodicals

People, February 17, 2003, pp. 111–12.
New York Times, January 31, 2001, p. A11.

Online

"Executive Biographies: CEO Ray Lines," Clean-Flicks, http://www.cleanflicks.com/company/index.php?file=bios (July 11, 2003).
"Startups in Utah Clean Hollywood's Act," *Wall Street Journal,* http://www.startupjournal.com/ideas/services/20020720–buckman.html (July 11, 2003).

—*Michael Belfiore*

Lisa Ling

AP/Wide World Photos/Fashion Wire Daily

Television host

Born August 30, 1973, in Sacramento, CA; daughter of Doug (an aviation manager) and Mary Ling. *Education:* Attended the University of Southern California.

Addresses: *Office*—c/o National Geographic Society, P.O. Box 98199, Washington, DC 20090–8199.

Career

Served as host of *Scratch,* a television magazine show for teens from northern California, c. 1989–91; reporter and then primary war correspondent for *Channel One,* a satellite television service for schools, 1991–99; freelance reporter and producer for ABC News, 1997–99; co–host of ABC's *The View,* May, 1999–November, 2002; host, *National Geographic Ultimate Explorer,* December, 2002—; has also served as a senior political correspondent for the College Television Network, contributing editor to *USA Today* magazine, and writer for the *New York Times* wire service.

Sidelights

Television journalist Lisa Ling is the host of *National Geographic Ultimate Explorer,* a Sunday–night staple that airs on the MSNBC cable network. Ling journeys to some of the world's most exotic, remote, and even dangerous locales to report stories that range from prisons in India to the women who jump out of planes to fight wildfires in the western United States. Offered the National Geographic job just before she turned 30, Ling did so with little

hesitation, she told *People.* "I'm not married and I don't have kids," she told the magazine. "If I don't do this now, I don't know if I could do it in a couple of years."

Ling was born in 1973 in Sacramento, California, to Doug, an aviation manager, and Mary Ling. Her parents divorced when she was seven, and Ling and her sister lived with their father, though they saw their mother regularly. She attended a school in which she was one of just a handful of Asian–American students enrolled. "As a kid I was embarrassed to be Asian because I didn't look like everyone else," she recalled in an interview with *Transpacific* writer Steve Hirano. "People would tease me. I wasn't an outcast, but I didn't like being different."

Ling excelled academically and proved to be a formidable debater, and her debate–team coach suggested she try out for a spot on a local television show for teens called *Scratch.* She showed up for an audition that required her to stand in front of a camera for half a minute and talk about herself. "How I got the job I don't know," she joked with *Transpacific*'s Hirano. "When I look back at those tapes...." *Scratch*—and Ling—proved to be a hit with younger viewers, and even turned into a nationally syndicated show. It required a heavy travel schedule in addition to her schoolwork, however. "I sacrificed my whole junior and senior years," she recalled in the *Transpacific* interview. "I mean, I still had a good time, always, but at the same time, I missed a lot of school. We would leave Thursday in the late afternoon and come back Sunday evening."

While on *Scratch,* Ling regularly received viewer mail and was stunned to learn that she had an actual fan club. Hers was a tough audience, she admitted to Hirano. "Students are extremely critical. They are really, really critical people. There are times when I think to myself that if I was sitting in the classroom I would have thought that I was acting geeky." Back home, she was slightly miffed by her high–school yearbook page, which termed her "The Next Connie Chung." As she explained in the *Transpacific* interview with Hirano, "I was kind of insulted. They're associating me with this Asian woman. Would you associate the blond girl on our show with Jane Pauley or with Diane Sawyer?"

Ling postponed college for a year to stay on *Scratch,* but her plans to enter Boston University in 1991 were further delayed when a producer in New York called and asked her to audition for a slot on a much–ballyhooed new educational television experiment called Channel One. A satellite news service broadcast directly into thousands of American schools, Channel One was created by the Whittle Educational Network as a way to supplement school curricula via a medium that appealed to students. Ling easily won the job, though she was Channel One's youngest reporter at the time. For the next seven years, her reports on news stories of the day reached some eight million student viewers daily, in 12,000 middle and high schools. She eventually began taking the toughest foreign assignments that required her to travel to places like Colombia, where she and her crew once filmed a cocaine bust, and Afghanistan during its messy civil war, where she disguised herself as Muslim woman. She later said that the Afghanistan experience was her most unforgettable: "I saw boys who looked about ten years old carrying weapons larger than they were," she told *Psychology Today*'s Carin Gorrell. "They had no light in their eyes; they looked like they could shoot me right then and there with no remorse whatsoever. And I never saw one woman's face."

The job for Channel One was based out of Los Angeles, California, and Ling spent several years as a history major at the University of Southern California while working and traveling full–time for the show. Despite the opportunity, her family had been less than enthusiastic about her taking the job. "My parents, being of a traditional Chinese family, were pretty opposed to me pursuing any aspect of television," she confessed to Hirano in the *Transpacific* interview. "They wanted me to be a doctor or a lawyer, of course." To further her career prospects, Ling and her Channel One producer also teamed up to make documentary films for KCET, the Los Angeles PBS affiliate. In one of them, Ling heart–wrenchingly chronicled her 13–year–old cousin's battle with fatal liver cancer.

The extra assignments paid off: In July of 1997 Ling landed a freelance contract with ABC News to deliver ten news feature stories. Her resulting work attracted the attention of ABC veteran journalist Barbara Walters, who offered her a job on her top–rated daytime talk show, *The View,* in May of 1999. The show was nearly two years old by then, and had been a surprise hit for the network with its round–table format that had Walters and four other women discussing the day's stories, dishing with celebrity guests, and delivering the latest news in health, fashion, and family matters. Each of the women represented different generations, and the original 20–something host, Debbie Matenopoulos, had become the subject of much criticism and even ridicule. Walters and the other executives involved in the show decided to go with a less lightweight representative of that age group, and the serious and elegant Ling easily beat out more than 12,000 applicants for the job.

Ling was 25 years old when she joined Walters, journalist–turned–suburban mother Meredith Vieira, former prosecuting attorney Star Jones, and comic Joy Behar on the show, which aired weekdays at 11 a.m. "My perspective is just fundamentally younger," she told Knight Ridder/Tribune News Service writer Al Brumley. "But it wasn't like, 'You have to spew the young agenda.' I'm representing a younger point of view just by being myself." *Time*'s James Poniewozik wrote about the show's appeal to a viewing audience that is 72 percent female—many of whom, he theorized, are not just stay–at–home mothers, but working part–time, or working out of the home—as a daily dose of water–cooler–type workplace chat. "Trying to get through the day without murdering the kids, they want to escape not to a surrogate home but to a surrogate office."

Ling quickly proved a popular addition to the mix, with ratings shooting up some 15 percent after she came on board, though she occasionally struggled to get a word in during the sometimes boisterous give–and–take. "To have to be so forceful with my voice runs contrary to everything I was taught growing up," she told *Psychology Today's* Gorrell. "Coming from an Asian culture, I was always taught to respect my elders, to be a better listener than a talker." *The View* garnered the usual industry markers of success: Emmy nominations and *Saturday Night Live* parodies.

Ling's duties on *The View* required her to wear many hats, not all of them common to journalism. She demonstrated glute–tightening exercises, had her navel pierced on camera, and even trained for the Boston Marathon, which she finished in four hours and 34 minutes. The foundation established in memory of her cousin, the Ali Pierce Endowment Fund, had won some charity slots for the prestigious race, and Ling decided to volunteer, partly in honor of her uncle who had started the pediatric–cancer research charity, and then died of a heart attack while running a mini–marathon. "I wanted to do something, and I thought I would love to run in my uncle's honor and finish what he was never able to do," she told *Psychology Today's* Gorrell.

While appearing on *The View,* Ling wrote for *USA Today* magazine and for the *New York Times* wire service, but missed the hard news and war–torn locales of her former job. As she told *People* writer Michael A. Lipton, the hit ABC show "raised my profile a lot, [but] it's not where you want to spend the rest of your career." One morning in November of 2002, Walters made the congratulatory announcement on *The View* that Ling was leaving the show to take over as host of *National Geographic Ultimate Explorer,* an eight–year–old cable newsmagazine show. Walters, Ling later said, had been a supportive mentor all along. "From day one," Ling told *Newsweek* writer Marc Peyser, "she said, 'I want to keep you forever. But if you come across your dream job, tell me.'"

The *National Geographic Ultimate Explorer* was indeed Ling's professional goal, and those first–person segments she had done on *The View* were now expanded into long mountain treks with a camera crew in search of a story, or jumping out of an airplane for the MSNBC adventure–series program. Her reports began airing in May of 2003, and in one of her first, she journeyed to Shanghai with Houston Rockets basketball player Yao Ming to revisit the neighborhood of his youth. In another, she examined the differences between women incarcerated in the American and Indian prison systems who become mothers while serving time. Returning to an arduous global travel schedule, she trekked to the Himalayas to report on the black–market trade for the fur of the chiru, a rare Tibetan antelope, and traveled to Baghdad just after the museums there

were looted during the 2003 United States–Iraq war. Such stories, Ling told *Psychology Today's* Gorrell, were the kind she always hoped to do as a journalist. "I've been so disenchanted with the apathy amongst young people for what's going on around the world," she said in the interview. "Our generation will inevitably assume the problems our country is faced with, and we are so ill–equipped to do so. My hope is that I can somehow raise the level of consciousness about world events."

The *National Geographic Ultimate Explorer* job forced Ling to move to Washington, D.C., where she shares a house with two male roommates. She has been romantically linked to actor Rick Yune, but declares she has no plans to settle down just yet. "I feel like a kid, like I haven't even stopped growing yet," she told *People.* Never having finished her USC degree, she nevertheless put her education and reporting skills to excellent use when she and her mother traveled to Taiwan: Intrigued by the reasons behind her parents' divorce, Ling began delving further into her family's past, and learned that her grandfather ran brothels in Taiwan and had three wives. Her sleuthing inspired her to begin writing a book on her family's history.

The *Ultimate Explorer* host seemed well–suited for the job, for Ling has claimed in several interviews that it is the hard–news, mettle–testing stories that truly thrill her. Recalling her Iraq visit in the *People* interview with Lipton, she said she climbed into a cab and found herself "with this driver who didn't speak a word of English, and it was a 13–hour drive to Amman, and I was thinking, 'I love my life right now being out here in the middle of nowhere, just experiencing history.'"

Sources

Daily Variety, November 19, 2002, p. 2.
Dayton Daily News, April 10, 2000, p. 2A.
Fresno Bee, February 9, 2000, p. A2.
Good Housekeeping, November 1999, p. 118; April 2000, p. 30.
InStyle, August 15, 1999, p. 67.
Knight Ridder/Tribune News Service, August 4, 1999.
Newsweek, December 2, 2002, p. 91.
People, May 24, 1999, p. 125; April 30, 2001, p. 15; March 11, 2002, p. 118; December 2, 2002, p. 24; August 25, 2003, p. 79.
Psychology Today, January–February 2003, p. 37.
Time, May 22, 2000, p. 126.
Transpacific, June 1994, p. 18.
Virginian Pilot, May 30, 2003, p. E1.

—*Carol Brennan*

Lewis Lucke

United States government official

Born c. 1951, in North Carolina; married Joy; children: three. *Education:* Earned degree from University of North Carolina at Chapel Hill; American Graduate School of International Management, M.B.A., 1977.

Addresses: *Office*—c/o United States Agency for International Development (USAID), Department of State, 2201 C St. NW, Washington, DC 20520.

Career

U.S. State Department, United States Agency for International Development (USAID), junior program officer in Mali, late 1970s, posted to Senegal and Costa Rica; assistant mission director for Tunisia, 1990–92; also served as special assistant to the USAID assistant administrator for Europe and chief of project development and finance for South America; USAID deputy mission director in La Paz, Bolivia, after 1994, and mission director in Amman, Jordan, 1996–2000, and Port–au–Prince, Haiti, 2000–01; retired from State Department post and worked for Carana, an economic development company; returned to government service in the fall of 2002 at the State Department; named to staff of newly created Office of Reconstruction and Humanitarian Assistance, a branch of the Pentagon, as coordinator for reconstruction, January, 2003; U.S. Agency for International Development, Iraq mission director, July, 2003—.

Awards: Presidential Merit Service Award, 2000; Administrator's Distinguished Career Award, U.S. Agency for International Development, 2001; five U.S. Agency for International Development Superior Honor and Meritorious Honor Awards.

Sidelights

Lewis Lucke serves in one of postwar Iraq's most essential executive posts as local mission director for the U.S. Agency for International Development (USAID). Lucke's task is to coordinate the necessary resources to fix the war–torn country, and which includes rebuilding power stations, roads, and schools. Giving Iraqis a sense of permanency and confidence in the postwar transitional regime was his office's primary objective, and Lucke was optimistic about the end result. "They're special people, smart, talented, and artistic," he said in an interview with Dick Stanley of the *Austin American–Statesman.* "The more you deal with them the more you know we'll go home and they'll be fine."

Born in the early 1950s in North Carolina, Lucke earned an undergraduate degree in international studies from the University of North Carolina at Chapel Hill. He spent his junior year in Lyon, France, and took part in an archeological dig in Israel after college, which piqued his interest in the Middle East. In 1977, he graduated from the American Graduate School of International Management in Arizona with a master's degree in business administration, and landed a spot in a training program for foreign–service officers with USAID, the branch of the State Department responsible for administering the economic and humanitarian aid for countries around the world.

Lucke's first USAID posting was in Mali, and he went on to serve in Senegal and Costa Rica before becoming assistant mission director in Tunisia in the early 1990s. In 1994, he was USAID's deputy mission director in La Paz, Bolivia, and named head of the agency's Jordan office in Amman in 1996. He served there for four years, during which time his wife—whom he had met in graduate school—and three children also lived with him. They moved to Texas when he accepted his last posting, to Port–au–Prince, Haiti. As USAID mission director in the troubled Caribbean nation, he headed the largest United States aid program in the western hemisphere.

Lucke retired from USAID in 2001 and spent some months working for Carana, an economic development company, before returning to government service after 9/11. As a State Department veteran with a working knowledge of Arabic, he was a highly sought–after bureaucrat at the time. His job in Iraq actually began in October of 2002, as U.S. President George W. Bush and his administration considered taking military action to oust Iraqi leader Saddam Hussein, and were seeking United Nations approval for it. Lucke began drawing up a post–war plan and signing contracts with companies that could help with reconstruction efforts. In January of 2003, when Bush signed the executive order that established the U.S. Office of Reconstruction and Humanitarian Assistance, Lucke joined it. The office was set up within the Department of Defense, which vetted all personnel, and minor internecine battles plagued its first months in operation: the State Department had submitted eight names for the job of reconstruction coordinator, and Pentagon officials rejected all of them before Lucke's was submitted.

Lucke arrived in Baghdad from Kuwait not long after the Iraqi capital was captured by American forces. His new office was located in the Baghdad Convention Center, and during his first few months on the job he often worked 16–hour days for seven days a week, as did many of his 90–member staff. Lucke was responsible for coordinating the work of some 500 independent contractors working to rebuild the country, and the task was enormous. In the waning years of Hussein's three–plus decades in power, the country's infrastructure had been poorly maintained, and international sanctions against Hussein's regime meant that legitimately obtaining crucial electronics components or construction equipment from the rest of the world was almost impossible. Even the vital port city of Umm Qasr had to be dredged before ships carrying direly needed cargo could enter. "We're putting back together a system abused by years of neglect," Lucke told Stanley in the *Austin American–Statesman*. "It was incredibly degraded."

The first major goal of Lucke's office was to restore full electricity, water, and phone service in Baghdad and the rest of the country. It also worked with international agencies to staff and supply hospitals, and with UNICEF set a target of re–opening 1,000 schools by September of 2003; Lucke was immensely pleased that his team and many others surpassed that number by almost 600. He credited some of the success for his office's undertakings to the resourcefulness of the Iraqis with whom they worked, describing them as a "very capable people," in an interview with *Newsweek*'s Christian Caryl and John Barry. "They kept all these systems going for decades with very little outside assistance."

Lucke's office also oversaw the immunization of children and encouraged Iraqis to form neighborhood advisory councils that could take care of trash collection and other badly needed services. Fixing rail lines and the highway system was next on his office's agenda. "It has been humbling," he admitted to *Forbes* writer Nathan Vardi. "However much time you spend planning something like this, being able to put it together on the ground is complex and depends on things that are not in your control."

In the fall of 2003, Lucke returned to Austin for a brief respite—noting it would be his only chance to see his son play with his high school football team that season—and was dismayed by the grim tone of the news coverage about the rebuilding of Iraq. "There's just an incredible amount of productive stuff going on over there, with a lot of Iraqi participation," he told the *Austin American–Statesman*'s Stanley. "To come here and see it portrayed as a failure in the making—it's very superficial and inaccurate."

The dangers of Lucke's job intensified when he returned, with hostilities reaching a crisis point in April of 2004, the first anniversary of the White House–declared victory in Iraq. Lucke's office is located inside the heavily guarded Green Zone, and when outside of it he usually wears a bulletproof vest and travels in an armored vehicle. He had no plans to leave, and cautioned that the United States should not, either. "The thing we have to struggle against is the American tendency to think this is like a baseball game, you play a few hours and you win or you lose," he told the *Newsweek* journalists. "This is a long–term process."

Selected writings

Waiting for Rain: Life and Development in Mali, West Africa, Christopher Publishing House, 1998.

Sources

Periodicals

Austin American–Statesman, October 4, 2003, p. A1.
Forbes, May 26, 2003, p. 62.
Newsweek, November 3, 2003, p. 34.

Online

"Lewis W. Lucke," http://www.whitehouse.gov/government/lucke–bio.html (April 26, 2004).

—Carol Brennan

Laurie MacDonald and Walter Parkes

Movie producers

Born Laurie MacDonald, c. 1954, in Watsonville, CA; married Walter Parkes, 1983. Born Walter Parkes, c. 1952, in Bakersfield, CA; married Laurie MacDonald, 1983; children: two. *Education:* Parkes graduated from Yale University, studied documentary film at Stanford.

Addresses: *Office*—DreamWorks SKG, Motion Picture Division, 1000 Flower St., Glendale, CA 91201.

Career

MacDonald modeled for a year in her twenties; produced a television talk show in San Francisco, CA; became junior executive at Columbia Pictures; co–produced *True Believers* with Parkes, 1988; co–head of Steven Spielberg's Amblin Entertainment, 1994; co–head of DreamWorks motion picture division, 1994—. Parkes began working in film industry after graduate school; first noted for his documentary *The California Reich,* 1975; wrote screenplays in the 1980s; produced *Awakenings,* 1990; co–head of Steven Spielberg's Amblin Entertainment, 1994; co–head of DreamWorks motion picture division, 1994—. Couple co–produced DreamWorks' first film, *The Peacemaker,* 1997; co–produced many popular mainstream movies, including *Men in Black, Gladiator, The Tuxedo, Road to Perdition, The Ring,* and *Catch Me If You Can.*

Sidelights

Laurie MacDonald and Walter Parkes belong to a rare breed in Hollywood. They have been married for more than 20 years, and they work together every day as co–heads of the motion picture division of DreamWorks SKG. The couple produced DreamWorks' first film in 1997, and went on to produce a string of hits. MacDonald and Parkes produced seven films in 2002 alone. These included some of the highest–grossing movies of the year, such as *Men in Black II* and *Minority Report.* The two claim to have a remarkably unified vision, agreeing about most things movie–related, and their films seem to have a knack of attracting a very wide audience. MacDonald is said to be the more business–minded of the two, while Parkes, a former screenwriter, brings more writerly skills to movie producing. Few couples in any industry share a job of this magnitude.

MacDonald was born in Watsonville, California, where her father was a mining engineer. The family moved around, and she grew up in Las Vegas, Nevada, and in Pasadena, California. After modeling for a year in Paris, MacDonald went to work for a local television news program in San Francisco, California. She eventually began producing a live news talk show five nights a week. MacDonald began working as an executive at Columbia Pictures in the early 1980s. In 1982 she met Parkes, who was then a screenwriter. By 1985, MacDonald was vice president of production at Columbia. Her first collaboration with Parkes was in 1988, when they co–produced the film *True Believers*.

Parkes, the son of a plastic surgeon, grew up in Bakersfield, California. He attended Yale University, where he majored in anthropology, and then took graduate courses at Stanford in documentary film. He directed a film called *The California Reich* in 1975, about the American Nazi party. *The California Reich* was nominated for an Academy Award for Best Documentary Film that year. When Parkes met MacDonald, he was writing a film which won him his second Academy Award nomination, *War Games*. Parkes moved from writing to producing films. He produced *Volunteers* for TriStar in 1985 and *Project X* for Fox in 1987. After collaborating with MacDonald in 1988, the duo's careers became more and more intertwined.

The job of movie producer is a complex one, encompassing all aspects of developing a film, from the initial idea to the final product. As producers, MacDonald and Parkes read scripts or listen to pitches, set budgets, arrange financing, find locations, and develop marketing plans. After they married, the couple had two children, and they found that they could incorporate their family life into their careers by working together. Though the job was exhausting, it offered flexibility, and MacDonald and Parkes brought their children with them as they traveled to filming locations. Parkes produced a several movies in the early 1990s, including *Awakenings* in 1990 (for which he received an Academy Award nomination), *Sneakers* in 1992, and *Little Giants* in 1994. That year, the couple got an unusual offer from Steven Spielberg. Spielberg, one of Hollywood's best–known directors, traveled in the same social circle as MacDonald and Parkes. One day Spielberg and his wife got together with MacDonald and Parkes to watch an old movie, and a friendship blossomed. Spielberg soon asked MacDonald and Parkes to work for him. He made them co–heads of his film production company, Amblin Entertainment. A few months later, Spielberg formed a film, television, and music production company, DreamWorks SKG, with David Geffen and Jeffrey Katzenberg. MacDonald and Parkes then took the position of co–heads of the DreamWorks film division. DreamWorks' first film was *The Peacemaker* in 1997, starring George Clooney and Nicole Kidman, which MacDonald and Parkes produced. They also contributed to DreamWorks' next film, and first big hit, *Saving Private Ryan*. The couple continued to produce movies for other studios as well, including the very successful *Men in Black* for Sony in 1997.

MacDonald and Parkes seemed to have a clear vision of what made good general entertainment. In an interview with *Daily Variety* in January of 2003, Parkes described *Men in Black* as "the ultimate family movie in that it appealed equally to kids and adults." While others in the industry may have been looking more narrowly at marketing categories aimed at specific age groups, MacDonald and Parkes had a feel for mass–market films that brought in a mixed crowd. Working with Spielberg, they had the pick of good scripts, and Parkes had long–standing connections with successful scriptwriters. In the late 1990s, the couple rode a wave of hit films. They produced *The Mask of Zorro* for Sony in 1998, which eventually grossed $94 million at the box office in the United States. Their next picture for DreamWorks, 2000's *Gladiator,* grossed more than twice that. There was no doubt that the couple had an outstanding sense of what made a popular film. In 2001, the couple viewed a Japanese horror film called *Ringu*. Within hours of watching *Ringu*, they had bought the rights to it, and this became the heralded DreamWorks picture *The Ring* in 2002. That year, they produced an extraordinary seven films, five for DreamWorks, one for Fox, and the sequel to *Men in Black* for Sony. These were all strong movies, including the critically acclaimed science fiction film *Minority Report* and the Leonardo DiCaprio vehicle *Catch Me If You Can.* By 2002, the couple had more than two dozen films to their combined credit, and these had grossed some $4.3 billion worldwide.

MacDonald and Parkes had no intention of stopping after that banner year. They planned to follow up over the next few years with a sequel to *The Ring,* another remake of a Japanese film called *Ikiru, Gladiator 2,* and a film written by playwright Tom Stoppard, among other projects. The couple had an opulent deal with DreamWorks, giving them up to five percent of revenues from films they produced. In a world of three–week marriages and high–level executive fallings out, MacDonald and Parkes seemed uniquely talented in maintaining their flourishing dual careers.

Sources

Daily Variety, January 13, 2003.
Forbes, March 3, 2003, pp. 86–87.
More, June 2002, pp. 54–55.

—A. Woodward

Jo Malone

Fragrance executive

Born c. 1964, in England; daughter of Peter (a painter) and Elaine (a facialist) Malone; married Gary Willcox, 1984; children: Josh.

Addresses: *Office*—Jo Malone, The Old Imperial Laundry, Warriner Gardens, London SW11 4XW, England.

Career

Worked as a facialist out of her apartment in London, England; began mixing bath oils for clients in her kitchen; opened first eponymous store in London, England, October, 1994; opened store inside Bergdorf Goodman, New York City, 1998; sold share of company to Estée Lauder, 1999; opened New York City store, 2001; introduced skin–care line, 2002.

Sidelights

Jo Malone's eponymous line of fragrances lured a cult–like following of celebrity customers to her London, England, store in the mid–1990s. Malone had began concocting her addictive, nature–based signature scents in her kitchen some years before, but when beauty–industry giant Estée Lauder acquired a stake in the company in 1999 for an amount rumored to be astronomical, she gained access to state–of–the–art laboratories.

A *Town & Country* profile by Pamela Fiori described Malone as "a walking advertisement for the brand— understated, modern and seemingly uncompli-

cated." In interviews, Malone has been forthright about her less–than–posh childhood while growing up in a council flat, as England's post–World War II government–subsidized housing units are called, in Bexley Heath, a town in Kent. Born in the early 1960s, she learned her trade at an early age: her mother was a facialist, and worked for a woman who owned a small skin–care line marketed under a specious aristocratic title, Countess Labatti. Malone often went along to the Countess's apartment, which served as the company headquarters, and as she recalled in the interview with Fiori, "When I was nine years old, the countess said to me, 'I want you to make your first face mask.' And I did, under her tutelage. She also told me, 'Life has something very special in store for you, so if you are going to do something, do it brilliantly.'"

When Labatti died, Malone's mother took over the business and Malone continued to help out. She also learned entrepreneurial skills from her father, an artist: she accompanied him when he sold his paintings at the local weekend market fair. In her teens, she began making and selling her own T–shirts. "I am intrigued by the whole concept of buying and selling," she told *Financial Times* journalist Kate Burgess. "I love creating something and making someone want to buy it. I am a merchant at heart."

In her early twenties, Malone followed in her mother's footsteps and became a facialist. Her style emphasized massage and various aromatic topical ointments. Unable to afford her own business space, she worked out of her apartment. As her business grew, she came upon the idea of giving her clients a small token of appreciation, and began mixing batches of bath oil on her stove. Her first was a nutmeg and ginger concoction, and her clients loved it. "Then a customer bought 100 bottles to put by each place setting at a party," she recalled in the *Financial Times* interview. "Eighty–six people came back to me for more." Soon, Malone's husband had quit his job as a surveyor to help bottle and sell her wares.

Malone began making perfumes as well, though she had no formal training. Her scents had only one or two notes, in contrast to most fragrances, which have a complex blend of light, medium, and heavy notes. Malone's line featured lime, vetiver, mandarin, and other scents, and they could be layered with one another. The fledgling business took off, and her husband—weary of working long into the night in their apartment—found and renovated a London retail space that became the site of her eponymously named store. When it opened in an upscale shopping area in October of 1994, lines of customers formed down Walton Street.

Malone's line became a favorite of fashion–industry insiders and celebrities. Serena Linley, the daughter–in–law of the late Princess Margaret, was an early fan, and as was Isabel Ettedgui (the wife of clothing designer Joseph Ettedgui), who helped create Malone's signature cream–and–black logo for her squarish, vintage apothecary–style bottles. Another devotee was Dawn Mello, president of luxe Manhattan retailer Bergdorf Goodman, who signed Malone to a deal that brought her line to the Fifth Avenue store in 1998. Soon, the Estée Lauder company began making overtures, but Malone was initially reluctant to give up a company she had founded in her kitchen in 1983, no matter what the price.

Estée Lauder chair Leonard Lauder, however, allayed Malone's fears by reminding her that his mother had also started her company in her kitchen. The deal was announced in late 1999, and it allowed Malone to retain creative control while freeing her and her husband from the financial stresses of running a transatlantic business. It was, she told Burgess in the *Financial Times*, "like a weight had been taken off my shoulders. And I am still very much involved. I have total autonomy. After all, Lauder bought my expertise in creating fragrances. They bought what is in my head, not what is on the shelf at the moment."

The Lauder deal helped Malone obtain counter space inside upscale American department stores Saks Fifth Avenue and Neiman Marcus, and she was also able to open her first freestanding American store in early 2001, located in New York's landmark Flatiron Building. There, one of her first successes remains one of the top sellers: Lime, Basil & Mandarin. Other top sellers include Amber & Lavender, the coffee–like Black Vetyver Café, and French Lime Blossom, which was inspired by a walk along Paris's Champs–Elysées. Malone admits to finding ideas for new scents from rather unusual sources. "The inside of a horse's harness might give me an idea for a new fragrance," she told Simon Brooke of the *Daily Telegraph*. "The other day I was in a Chinese restaurant and the smell of ginger tea suddenly inspired me."

In 2002, Malone's company launched a skin–care line of cleansers, moisturizers, and specialty products. The elixirs used many of her trademark ingredients, from lavender to eucalyptus, and she tested batches at both the modern laboratory facilities she now had access to via the Lauder partnership, and also at home in her kitchen, as Fiori found her doing with some vitamin E serum when she interviewed her. Reminded of the countess's prophetic words to her as a child, she conceded, "I know I have a gift," she told the *Town & Country* writer. "But in the end, I'll always be the girl in the store making face creams. That's really who I am, and that's just fine with me."

Sources

Chain Store Age, June 2001, p. 114.
Daily Telegraph (London, England), November 10, 2001.
Financial Times, July 26, 2000, p. 17.
Harper's Bazaar, November 2000, p. 160.
People, August 10, 1998, p. 75.
Town & Country, April 2002, p. 132.
W, December 1999, p. 156.
WWD, May 10, 2001, p. 3; May 23, 2001, p. 26S; February 1, 2002, p. 4.

—*Carol Brennan*

Brian Marsden

Astronomer

Born Brian Geoffrey Marsden, August, 1937, in Cambridge, England; married Nancy Zissell, 1964; children: two. *Education:* Attended Oxford University; Yale University, Ph.D., 1965.

Addresses: *Office*—Minor Planet Center, Smithsonian Astrophysical Observatory, 60 Garden St., Cambridge, MA 02138.

Career

Began working for Smithsonian Astrophysical Observatory, 1965; made head of Smithsonian's Central Bureau for Astronomical Telegrams, 1968; head of Smithsonian's Minor Planet Center, 1978—.

Member: Chairman, American Astronomical Society Division on Dynamical Astronomy, 1976–78; president, International Astronomical Union Commission on the Positions and Motions of Minor Planets, Comets, and Satellites, 1976–79; board of directors, Spaceguard Foundation, 1996.

Awards: Van Biesbroeck Award, University of Arizona, for services to astronomy, 1989; Brouwer Award, American Astronomical Society, for research in dynamical astronomy, 1995.

Sidelights

Brian Marsden is on the front line for new discoveries in space. As head of the Minor Planet Center at the Smithsonian Astrophysical Observa-

tory in Cambridge, Massachusetts, Marsden sifts through reports sent in from observatories around the world about unknown celestial objects. Marsden and his co–workers pore through thousands of astronomical observations every day, to confirm reports of new comets, asteroids, and supernovas. Marsden's office then publishes the International Astronomical Union (IAU) Circular, which serves as an official list of celestial discoveries. "If it moves or it's fuzzy, it goes through us," he told *Astronomy* magazine's David H. Freedman and Robert Naeye. Amateur astronomers as well as the biggest observatories in the world send in their suspicious sightings to Marsden. Marsden caught the world's attention in 1998, when he warned that a newly discovered asteroid might come dangerously close to the earth in the year 2028. As the clearinghouse for new celestial sightings, it was Marsden's job to disseminate this bad news. He was also able to gather enough new information within 24 hours that he could offer a revised calculation. This one showed the asteroid zooming safely past the earth. Anyone worried about cataclysmic collisions or eager to name a new comet must pay attention to Marsden.

Marsden was born in Cambridge, England, in August of 1937. While still in high school, Marsden became an expert on calculating the initial orbits of newly discovered comets. Young as he was, there were only a few other people in the world who could manage these laborious calculations. A member of the British Astronomical Association befriended Marsden, and lent him a large mechanical calculator. With this bulky machine and a logarithm table, the young man worked away at the difficult orbital formulations. He did his undergraduate work at Oxford University, and then in 1959 enrolled at Yale University's graduate program in celestial mechanics. Yale was one of the few places offering advanced work in this field. Marsden wrote his dissertation on the orbits of the Galilean satellites of Jupiter, and received his Ph.D. in 1965.

Though Marsden had found few compatriots who shared his interest in comets and asteroids, the United States was beginning to pour money into astronomy programs. After the Soviet Union successfully launched its Sputnik satellite in 1957, the United States government began its race to get into space. In 1965, Marsden accepted a position at one of the most flourishing centers of celestial research, the Smithsonian Astrophysical Observatory, an institution affiliated with Harvard University. That year, the Smithsonian Astrophysical Observatory also became home to the Central Bureau for Astronomical Telegrams, a research clearinghouse that had been based in Copenhagen, Denmark, since the 1920s. In 1968, Marsden became head of this organization. In 1978, Marsden also became head of the Minor Planet Center. The Minor Planet Center had been based in Cincinnati, Ohio, since 1947, but it moved to Cambridge under the aegis of the Smithsonian. The Minor Planet Center's mission was to catalog discoveries and observations about small orbiting bodies such as asteroids.

The Minor Planet Center and the Central Bureau for Astronomical Telegrams function as the news service for celestial events. All new discoveries come through these offices. Marsden's offices publish circulars that list new asteroids, comets, and newly determined orbits, and prints predictions of events such as a comet colliding with Jupiter. Marsden's personal interest was in conducting an inventory of the solar system, and he also rediscovered some so-called lost comets. Marsden predicted the return in 1992 of comet Swift–Tuttle, which was last seen in 1862. Marsden also became known in the 1980s for his contention that Pluto was not a planet and should be reclassified as an asteroid. Marsden was not alone in holding this opinion, but he was outspoken in this rather unpopular cause. But Marsden really grabbed headlines with his ominous predictions of possible collisions of comets or asteroids with the earth. Most scientists now believe that some kind of celestial object colliding with the earth led to the demise of the dinosaurs. Early in the twentieth century, an asteroid or comet 100 meters wide struck the earth, causing massive damage in remote Siberia. As the breaking news service for celestial bodies, Marsden several times warned of impending close calls. In 1983, Marsden verified that a comet known as IRAS–Araki–Alcock would pass closer to the earth than any known comet (except one that had passed in 1770). Knowing that such news causes alarm, Marsden told John Noble Wilford of the New York Times that there was "Nothing to fear." However, in 1998, Marsden came up with a prediction that was not so comforting. Marsden's office issued a circular on March 11, 1998, noting that an asteroid known as 1997 XF11 was in a possible collision course with the earth, and could hit in 2028. Even though the possible collision was 30 years away, and Marsden judged the actual chance of a collision as very small, his announcement sparked fearful news stories around the globe. Marsden's office called for more data, and within 24 hours, it received a photograph that gave some more information on the comet's orbit. Using the data from the photograph, Marsden recalculated the course of 1997 XF11, and found that it would pass well clear of the earth. Marsden dealt with the crisis quickly, but the incident did call attention to his organizations, and ultimately attracted more funding. Several organizations, including the Spaceguard Foundation, which Marsden once headed, now focus on finding so–called near–earth objects (NEOs) that might pose a threat to the planet.

Marsden works long hours with only a very small staff for support. Now in his sixties, Marsden is considering retiring. On the other hand, some of his colleagues believe that he is not nearly ready to retire. He is too good at what he does, and his position is too crucial. Marsden would like to see more money spent on new telescopes that can spot smaller NEOs. He also recommends that scientists plan now for what to do if a comet or asteroid is found that really is on a collision course with the earth. He told Steve Nadis of Scientific American that "we have to do more than the dinosaurs."

Sources

Astronomy, September 1998, p. 58.
New York Times, May 6, 1983, p. A21; March 30, 1987, p. B6; March 13, 1998, p. A1.
Scientific American, August 2003, pp. 84–85.
Smithsonian, May 2000, p. 28.

—A. Woodward

Paul Martin

AP/Wide World Photos

Canadian Prime Minister

Born Paul Edgar Philippe Martin, August 28, 1938, in Windsor, Ontario, Canada; son of Paul Joseph James (a legislator and cabinet official) and Eleanor "Nell" Martin; married Sheila Ann Cowan, 1965; children: Paul, Jamie, David. *Education:* University of Toronto, B.A., 1962; earned law degree from the University of Toronto, 1965.

Addresses: *Office*—Office of the Prime Minister, 80 Wellington St., Ottawa K1A 0A2, Canada.

Career

Merchant seaman and oil–field worker in Alberta, Canada, c. 1962–64; European Coal and Steel Community offices, assistant in the legal department; Power Corporation, special assistant to the president, 1965; vice president after 1969; Canada Steamship Lines Ltd., president, 1973, co-owner, 1981–88, owner, 1988—; elected to Canada's House of Commons from the riding of LaSalle–Émard, Montreal, Quebec, 1988—; Minister of Finance in the cabinet of Prime Minister Jean Chrétien, November, 1993–June, 2002; elected Liberal Party chair, November, 2003; sworn in as prime minister, December 12, 2003.

Sidelights

Paul Martin fought a long, bitter battle to become head of Canada's Liberal Party that even cost him his post as the country's Finance Minister. One of his party's more conservative policy–makers, Martin won the leadership post after a long, strate-gic insider campaign against veteran Liberal Party chair Jean Chrétien, prime minister since 1993. Martin became Liberal Party leader in November of 2003, and weeks later was sworn in as the twenty–first prime minister of Canada.

Martin belongs to a relatively rare breed in Canadian politics: a political dynasty. He was born in 1938 in Windsor, Ontario, the border city that elected his father, also named Paul Martin, to represent it in Ottawa's House of Commons in 1935. Martin senior went on to a distinguished career in Liberal Party politics as one of its more left–leaning members, and would serve in the cabinets of four prime ministers. He was instrumental in the creation of postwar Canada's national health–care system, which provided universal coverage to all Canadian citizens, and he was a leader in the effort to eradicate polio in the country, after his own son survived a bout with the disease. Twice the senior Martin made a bid for the Liberal leadership at party conventions, which could have made him prime minister—in Canadian politics, the party that wins a majority of seats in the legislature forms the mandate, or government—but lost to Lester Pearson in 1958 and Pierre Trudeau a decade later.

As a youngster, Martin lived in Windsor but moved to Ottawa with his family, which included a sister, in 1945 when his father became Canada's federal Health and Welfare Minister. His parents believed it best that he become bilingual, and he was sent to a French school in the federal capital. Politically astute even at a young age from campaigning alongside his father, he once caused a minor schoolboy incident when he threw stones at the Soviet Embassy in Ottawa during the tense Cold War years. In 1957, he entered St. Michael's College at the University of Toronto, finishing five years later with a degree in philosophy and history. Before entering law school, he spent time in Canada's merchant navy and worked in an oil field in the Alberta province. He took a less taxing position at one point with the European Coal and Steel Community in Luxembourg—a forerunner organization of the European Union—in its legal department. By 1965, he had finished his course at the University of Toronto Law School and married Sheila Cowan, whose father was a partner in his own father's law firm.

Martin began his career as a special assistant to Paul Desmarais, a friend of his father's and a man often referred to as Canada's wealthiest citizen. Desmarais was the force behind the creation of the Power Corporation, an immense conglomerate with stakes in the pulp and paper industry, the media, public transport, and insurance services. By 1969 Martin had risen to a vice presidency at the Montreal–based giant, and four years later Desmarais put him in charge of one of its subsidiaries, Canada Steamship Lines Ltd. (CSL). Martin worked to improve the flagging finances of the shipping company, and in 1981 he and a business partner bought CSL for $116 million. They had to borrow the funds for the purchase, and interest rates were above 20 percent at the time. On the day that Martin signed the loan papers, a well–known Wall Street analyst predicted that rates might rise as high as 30 percent. "I gambled everything that interest rates had reached their peak," Martin recalled in an interview with Anthony Wilson–Smith in *Maclean's*. "If they had continued to rise, I was cooked."

Fortunately for Martin, interest rates fell, and in 1988 he was able to buy out his original partner and become sole owner of CSL. That same year, however, he ran for and was elected a Member of Parliament (MP) as the Liberal Party candidate from Montreal's LaSalle–Émard riding, as electoral districts are called in Canada. The party was the official opposition at the time, with its rival, the Progressive Conservative Party (PC) in power since 1984 under Brian Mulroney. In June of 1990, Martin made his first bid to chair the Liberal Party at its leadership caucus in Calgary. He came in second to Chrétien, a veteran politician with several cabinet posts on his resume by then. In 1993, Chrétien took

the Liberals to a major victory in national elections, and named Martin his new Minister of Finance.

As a federal minister, Martin avoided charges of a possible conflict of interest over his ownership of CSL by handing over the reins of his company to his sons. He concentrated on improving Canada's ailing economy, which was on the verge of a serious crisis by 1994: its generous social programs were draining resources, and economic growth was stalled because the country's higher corporate tax rates discouraged new investment. By 1995, the federal government was saddled with a $26 billion deficit, and Martin announce a program of drastic cutbacks. His work to balance Canada's budget and avoid financial catastrophe helped the Liberals maintain the majority in 1997 national elections, and the country's budget went into surplus–status the following year. By 2001, the surplus had reached an impressive $11 billion.

Political pundits had long pegged Martin as one of the likeliest of successors to Chrétien, beginning with his energetic bid for the Liberal Party leadership back as a political novice with a famous name in the 1989–90 season. Within the party itself, some believed that Chrétien was perhaps remaining too long at the top, and there came increasing calls for him to step down. A lengthy list of scandals was also blackening the Liberals' reputation as well, with members of Chrétien's government linked to apparent backroom deals that proved profitable for them or business associates who had been campaign donors. Internal strife among Liberal Party members intensified in 2000, after Chrétien led the party to a third term in power and continued on as prime minister.

In June of 2002, the battle between Martin's supporters and the Chrétien camp caused Martin to lose his post as Finance Minister. Chrétien asserted that Martin had quit, while Martin told the press that he had been fired. The break between the two seemed to accelerate the divisions within the party, and at a parliamentary caucus meeting in Saguenay, Quebec, in August of 2002, Chrétien announced he would retire from the leadership at a later, as–yet–undetermined date. Martin seemed to be positioning himself for a larger leadership role. "There is a great debate in the world about the sovereignty of nations, about how in the shadow of the United States, other nations can find their niche," he told a crowd of Liberal Party supporters in September, according to *Maclean's*. "Well, I can tell you that we can find ours by being the most successful nation in the world, by being a place where the best and the brightest will want to come."

Finally, it was the threat of a newly reconstituted PC that spurred Liberals to act to end Chrétien's reign. In October of 2003, the PC allied with Canadian Alliance to form a coalition. The Canadian Alliance had originally been constituted as the Reform Party, which split from the PC in the 1980s after dissatisfaction over Ottawa's policies toward the country's western provinces like Alberta and Saskatchewan. On November 14, 2003, at the Liberal Party leadership convention, Martin made a bid for the party chair post, and took 94 percent of the vote. The gathering was notable for presence of Irish rock star and international political activist Bono, lead singer of the group U2, whom Martin had invited to the convention to speak to delegates about global poverty. On November 18, Chrétien announced he would leave office on December 12, 2003. On that day, Martin was sworn in as the country's twenty–first prime minister.

Martin replaced much of the Chrétien cabinet when he took office, and was obligated to set a date for new national elections before 2005. In February of 2004, a political scandal threatened to bring down his new Liberal government. Martin and his party were castigated in a report from the Auditor General of Canada, Sheila Fraser, which showed that a complex system of financial transfers had enriched the business bank accounts of a number of party supporters. The so–called sponsorship scandal involved the misuse of some $75 million in funds that had been allocated for a public–relations campaign in the mid–1990s to bolster support for federalism, or a united Canada, in the province of Quebec. Over the years, the Public Works Ministry plan apparently degenerated into a number of financial transactions that moved millions from one government agency to another and provided payments to the public–relations firms—owned by leading Liberal Party donors—as commissions for the transactions. There also seemed to have been little actual public-relations work done.

Martin's first response was to peg the sponsorship scandal on a wayward cadre of bureaucrats in Ottawa, and noted that he had cancelled the program almost immediately after taking office in December. But a letter to him from a policy official in his own party dating back to 2002 surfaced in the press; in it, the colleague sounded a warning that the sponsorship program's abuses might be ruinous to the party. Martin also claimed that though he was Finance Minister during much of the time of the program, strained relations with Chrétien and his camp kept him out of the party's Quebec–strategy issues. He was also excoriated in the Canadian media for this assertion, and finally called for an official judicial inquiry. "I am sick and deeply, deeply troubled about what happened," New York Times writer Clifford Krauss quoted him as saying. "Heads will roll."

One of the first on the chopping block was Alfonso Gagliano, the former Public Works Minister under Chrétien who had recently become ambassador to Denmark. Martin immediately recalled him from the post. In late April, the Public Works Department official who had run the sponsorship program, Charles Guité, told a parliamentary–inquiry committee that in a 1994 conversation, Martin's former chief of staff in his finance ministry mentioned specific PR firms that "would efficiently distribute the sponsorship funds," according to Krauss in the New York Times. "The firms included Earnscliffe Research and Communications, a consultancy firm that included senior managers who advised Mr. Martin during his effort to wrest the Liberal Party leadership from Mr. Chrétien."

After a period of intense media scrutiny, in late May Martin finally called elections for June 28, 2004. Public–opinion polls showed that support for and confidence in the prime minister and the Liberals had dropped significantly as a result of the scandal, but the party had been working to shore up support from among younger voters with legislation designed to curry favor, such as a marijuana decriminalization bill. The parliamentary elections would pit Martin against PC leader Stephen Harper, a staunch social conservative from Alberta. Harper has supported the idea of a closer alliance, in military and economic matters, with the United States. Martin and his Liberal Party won the election but a strong showing by separatists in Quebec helped rob him of an outright majority.

Martin succeeded where his father had not: in leading the most influential political party in Canadian history. His political career had actually started at a very young age. "What I would do a lot with my dad is travel the riding with him," he once recalled, according to Maclean's journalist John Geddes. "I went to church picnics, that kind of thing. That's one of the ways that we stayed close, my dad and I. He was a tremendous constituency politician. He—probably as much as anyone—built the modern constituency organization."

Sources

Periodicals

BusinessWeek, December 29, 2003, p. 54.
Economist, November 22, 2003, p. 36; February 7, 2004, p. 37; March 20, 2004, p. 38.

Maclean's, December 13, 1993, p. 22; June 17, 2002, p. 32; September 2, 2002, p. 18; October 7, 2002, p. 20.

New Leader, November–December 2003, p. 9.

New York Times, February 15, 2004, p. A4; April 24, 2004; May 24, 2004.

Time Canada, December 22, 2003, p. 36; February 23, 2004, p. 12.

Time International, December 30, 2002, p. 50, p. 58.

Online

"Canadian PM wins election but with minority government," CNN.com, http://www.cnn.com/2004/WORLD/americas/06/29/canada.election/index.html (June 29, 2004).

"In Depth: Paul Martin," CBC News, http://www.cbc.ca/news/background/martin_paul/ (May 1, 2004).

"Liberal cabinet discusses election timing," CBC News, http://www.cbc.ca/stories/2004/04/27/liberals040427 (April 29, 2004).

"Options running out for spring election call," CBC News, http://www.cbc.ca/stories/2004/04/27/canada/liberalselexn040427 (April 29, 2004).

"Pundit Poll," CBC News, http://www.cbc.ca/news/background/cdnelection2004 (May 6, 2004).

—Carol Brennan

309

Frances Mayes

AP/Wide World Photos

Author

Born c. 1940, in Fitzgerald, GA; daughter of Gar-bert (a cotton mill manager) and Frankye (Davis) Mayes; married William Frank King (a computer research scientist; divorced, 1988); married Ed Kleinschmidt (a creative writing professor), 1998; children: Ashley (from first marriage). *Education:* Attended Randolph–Macon College; earned B.A. from University of Florida; San Francisco State University, M.A., 1975.

Addresses: *Home*—2022 Broderick St., San Francisco, CA 94115; and Cortona, Italy.

Career

Taught English and creative writing at San Francisco State University since the late 1970s, eventually become chair of the creative writing department; freelance copywriter for cookbook publishers and newspapers; first collection of poetry, *Sunday in Another Country,* published by Heyeck Press, 1977; contributor of poetry to *Atlantic, Carolina Quarterly, Gettysburg Review,* and *Southern Review,* and of travel articles to the *New York Times* after 1988. Her memoir, *Under the Tuscan Sun,* was made into a film by Touchstone Pictures, 2003.

Awards: Award from Academy of American Poets, 1975.

Sidelights

Frances Mayes was virtually unknown as a writer until her 1996 memoir, *Under the Tuscan Sun: At Home in Italy,* went on to spend much of the remain-der of the decade on the best–seller lists. The account of her renovation of an abandoned villa in the Italian countryside was even made into a 2003 feature film that starred Diane Lane. "I think people responded to a woman in her midlife taking a big risk and making a change," Mayes told *WWD* writer Luisa Zargani about the book's appeal. "I believe a lot of people have this dream."

Mayes was born in the early 1940s and grew up in a small Georgia town called Fitzgerald, where her father managed a family owned cotton mill. One of three daughters in her family, she was a bookworm from an early age, preferring to while away the hours perched on a tree branch in her backyard with Nancy Drew mysteries. She left Fitzgerald in 1958 to attend Randolph–Macon College in Virginia, but eventually transferred to the University of Florida to earn her undergraduate English degree. While there she met her first husband, who would go on to a career as a computer–research scientist. The couple moved to northern California in the early 1960s, and had a daughter, Ashley, in 1964.

Mayes continued her studies, eventually earning a graduate degree from San Francisco State University (SFSU) in 1975. She began teaching there, and published her first book of poetry in 1977, the prophetically titled *Sunday in Another Country*. Several more volumes followed, but Mayes toiled on the verge of obscurity as a poet while rising to a post as head of SFSU's creative–writing department. Collections of her verse—which included *After Such Pleasures* in 1979 and *Hours,* a 1984 tome that drew heavily upon her Southern roots—earned good reviews in the literary world, but she remained a relative unknown outside of it.

Mayes' life changed after her 1988 divorce. She had already been spending time in Italy during her summer teaching breaks, but decided to use her divorce settlement money to acquire a more permanent address there. In 1989, she found an abandoned 250–year–old villa for sale just outside of Cortona. The place was about 60 miles southeast of Florence, the Tuscan capital, and was one of many in the area that had sat crumbling for a generation and was badly in need of repair. Since the 1950s, Italians had been leaving the countryside in droves for the cities, and high taxes on such estates also made keeping the venerable ancestral homes impossible.

Mayes paid dearly for the property, Bramasole, but also knew it was far more reasonable a price than buying a vacation home somewhere on the California coast. She and her boyfriend, Ed Kleinschmidt—also an academic—began restoring it with the help of local artisans known as *muratori*. She also began a journal of the renovation process, which also chronicled her increasing passion for the Tuscan hills, a fertile agricultural region, and her idyllic days there.

Mayes began writing articles for the *New York Times* about the charms of Florence and region, and a 1992 piece on a weekly market fair became the basis for her memoir. "I just had such a good time writing the article that I started writing other chapters, other essays," she recalled in an interview with Lee Svitak Dean of the *Star Tribune*. The result was *Under the Tuscan Sun,* published by San Francisco's Chronicle Books in 1996. *New York Times* reviewer Alida Becker delivered one of the first mainstream press reviews. "Casual and conversational, her chapters are filled with craftsmen and cooks, with exploratory jaunts into the countryside—but what they all boil down to is an intense celebration of what she calls 'the voluptuousness of Italian life,'" Becker noted. The critic did grant that Mayes' passion for her adopted land at times "leads to the sort of gushy observations you might expect from a besotted lover. But more often it produces an appealing and very vivid snapshot imagery."

In her book, Mayes writes that her rustic house yielded many surprises that first year. Told that its water supply was excellent and dated back to a sys-

tem built by the great Medici patrons in medieval times, Mayes found out otherwise during a shower just six weeks later. She was forced to pay dearly for a truckload of water to keep her supplied for the rest of their summer. Another time, prepping the dining–room walls for a paint job, they uncovered a fresco. "Every swipe reveals more: two people by a shore, water, distant hills," she writes. "The biscuit–colored houses are the same colors we see all around us." Ed concentrates on refurbishing the long–neglected garden, and Mayes devotes herself to shopping for local produce in the meantime. The Cortona market brings inspiration. At certain intervals in her book, she includes many casual recipes for such Italian delights as basil and mint sorbet and wild mushroom lasagna.

Mayes' San Francisco publisher had little marketing money to promote the book when it was first published, but it soon caught on with readers, and word of mouth helped propel it to the best–seller lists after Broadway Books released it as a trade paperback in late 1997. It remained on the *New York Times* bestseller lists until July of 2000, an astonishing 142–week run. Mayes' account of her new life in Italy, juxtaposed with her more hectic one back in the United States, seemed to strike a chord with readers. Italy and its pleasures have intoxicated centuries of travelers back to the pilgrim of the early Christian era. In more modern times, food, family, and enjoying life's simple pleasures—*la dolce vita,* or "the sweet life"—seem to be the preoccupying goal of Italians, who appear to outsiders to be a nation of impossibly fashionable and attractive people whose days revolve around spirited political arguments at outdoor cafes and long, genial evening meals. "I had a feeling it would sell," Mayes confessed to *San Francisco Chronicle* writer Jerry Carroll, "because … I absorbed the sense of the mania people have for Italy, not only as a travel destination and a place to have a vacation, but as a lifestyle. There is a sense that the Italians are having more fun." The restorative, escapist fantasy was not lost on United States President Bill Clinton, whom reporters followed to a bookstore one day in the middle of his impeachment trial in early 1999, where he became one of the one million readers who bought a copy of *Under the Tuscan Sun.*

The success of *Under the Tuscan Sun* freed Mayes financially. "I've always been trying to squeeze writing in around the edges of teaching," she told *Entertainment Weekly* journalist Lisa Schwarzbaum. "Now I just have the responsibility of being a writer, which is what everyone in my department dreams of, to write their way out of that horrible job." There had been some professional derision, Mayes granted, that after so many years contributing poetry to small literary journals that she then earned a mint out of a combination travelogue/home–restoration diary complete with recipes for polenta and gelato. "Sometimes my colleagues have been a little weird about this, and I've been shocked, because I expected all my friends and associates to be thrilled for me," she told Schwarzbaum. "One of my colleagues referred to my book as 'your little food book.'"

Mayes wrote a sequel, *Bella Tuscany: The Sweet Life in Italy,* that takes up where her first memoir ended: she and Ed finish the house, plant a garden, and begin to use Bramasole as a base to explore Tuscany and Italian treasures elsewhere. The pair, who had married by then, collaborated on the lavishly illustrated *In Tuscany* in 2000, a coffee–table–style work that prompted some book reviewers to declare that perhaps Mayes had finally exhausted her subject matter.

In 1987, she wrote *The Discovery of Poetry: A Field Guide to Reading and Writing Poems,* and started a novel she had begun some years earlier but then misplaced. Mayes rewrote the first 50 pages of the novel, called *Swan,* which was published by Broadway in 2002. She had always wanted to tackle the form, but was stymied by the necessity of devising a credible plot. Then, she explained to *Atlanta Journal–Constitution* writer Bob Longino, she realized she could build a story around the "things that always obsessed me about the South and growing up there. Unlike other parts of the country, the actions of your ancestors play out on you in a pretty direct way. I think in the South there has always been that sense that your dead grandmother might walk into the room at any minute."

Swan is set in a small Georgia town of same name—not coincidentally also the earlier name of her Fitzgerald birthplace—and centers on a grown brother and sister, J.J. and Ginger, whose mother committed suicide nearly two decades before. Ginger, an archaeologist, has been living in Italy for many years, but returns home when their mother's body is found illegally exhumed. The plot reaches back into possible skeletons in the family closet, and is helped along by a number of memorable side characters drawn from townsfolk and extended family members. "Mayes pulls off the drama while eschewing melodrama, imbuing the book with a strong core," asserted *Houston Chronicle* writer Melanie Danburg.

Mayes' Tuscan reveries were revived for the big screen when the film version of *Under the Tuscan Sun* was released in 2003. Diane Lane played the

Mayes character, but director Audrey Wells, who had adapted the book for the screen, changed some elements of the story. The steady Ed vanished, and instead she finds romance with an Italian man. "I didn't mind the changes at all, I actually expected them," Mayes told *WWD*'s Zargani just before the film was released in United States theaters. "The spirit of the book is there, it's the same as the film's."

Mayes still lives in Bramasole, and because of her books Cortona became a thriving tourist destination. The city began hosting a Tuscan Sun Festival, and even made Mayes an honorary citizen. The occasion required her to deliver a ten–minute speech in Italian, which she claimed was the "the scariest thing I have ever done apart from having a baby," she told Schwarzbaum in *Entertainment Weekly.* Her love of Italy remains strong, despite her still–shaky language abilities, and often in her books she has compared the welcome she received in her new homeland to the famous Southern hospitality with which she was raised. "They have this warmth and gift for friendship that just constantly amazes us, " she told Dean in the *Star Tribune* interview. "They are the most giving people. Surely that's a gross generalization. I'm sure there are some horrid Italians, but we've never met them."

Mayes was tapped as a consulting designer for the "Tuscan Home" line of furniture by Drexel–Heritage, and was working on another nonfiction book, *Tuscan Home,* slated for 2004 publication. She and Ed—who took her last name when they wed in 1998—also acquired another property in Tuscany. This one might prove even more challenging: 900 years old, it was built by hermits and sits perched on a mountainside. Back at Bramasole, travelers still stop on the road to get a view at her beloved, immortalized home. "I've heard them say it's even more beautiful than they thought," she told *People* writer Peter Ames Carlin. "But I also heard someone on the road say, 'Is that it? Why don't they fix it up?'"

Selected writings

Sunday in Another Country (poetry), Heyeck Press (Woodside, CA), 1977.
Climbing Aconcagua (poetry), Seven Woods Press (New York, NY), 1977.
After Such Pleasures (poetry), Seven Woods Press, 1979.
The Arts of Fire (poetry), Heyeck Press, 1982.
Hours (poetry), Lost Roads Publishers (Providence, RI), 1984.

The Discovery of Poetry, Harcourt (San Diego, CA), 1987.
Ex Voto (poetry), Lost Roads Publishers, 1995.
Under the Tuscan Sun: At Home in Italy (memoir), Chronicle Books, 1996.
Bella Tuscany: The Sweet Life in Italy, Broadway Books, 1999.
(Coauthor) *In Tuscany,* Broadway Books, 2000.
Swan (novel), Broadway, 2002.
(Editor) *The Best American Travel Writing 2002,* Houghton Mifflin, 2002.

Sources

Books

Mayes, Frances, *Under the Tuscan Sun: At Home in Italy,* Chronicle Books, 1996.

Periodicals

Atlanta Journal–Constitution, October 10, 2002, p. F1.
Booklist, November 15, 2000, p. 594.
Entertainment Weekly, April 16, 1999, p. 32; December 8, 2000, p. 85.
Houston Chronicle, October 20, 2002, p. 23.
Library Journal, September 1, 2003, p. 236.
New York Times, November 17, 1996; September 26, 2003, p. E15.
People, August 23, 1999, p. 154.
Publishers Weekly, August 26, 2002, p. 57.
San Francisco Chronicle, September 16, 1997, p. E1.
Star Tribune (Minneapolis, MN), November 7, 2001, p. 1E; November 8, 2001, p. 6T.
WWD, August 29, 2003, p. 4.

Online

"Frances Mayes," *Contemporary Authors Online,* Gale, 2003.

—Carol Brennan

Camille McDonald

AP/Wide World Photos/Fashion Wire Daily

President and Chief Executive Officer of Parfums Givenchy North America

Born c. 1953. *Education:* Smith College, Northampton, MA, B.A.

Addresses: *Office*—Parfums Givenchy Inc., 717 5th Ave., Ste. 4, New York, NY 10022.

Career

Began career at Charles of the Ritz as product manager for mass–distribution fragrances, 1979–82; spent a year as a marketing director at Revlon International, and worked in Cosmair, Inc.'s marketing division, 1984–86; briefly served as vice president of marketing at Parfums Phenix, 1987, before returning to Cosmair and reaching the post of vice president for global development and United States marketing of its Ralph Lauren Fragrances division; became senior vice president of sales at Chanel Parfums, April, 1997; named president and chief executive officer of Parfums Givenchy North America, January, 1998; given responsibility for its Guerlain brand, November, 2001.

Member: Fragrance Foundation and Cosmetic Executive Women.

Sidelights

In 1998, Camille McDonald became president and chief executive officer of Parfums Givenchy North America, part of the LVMH Moet Hennessy Louis Vuitton empire. Her realm includes overseeing the development, launch, and marketing for an array of Givenchy fragrances, from Eau de Givenchy to Organza. In 2001, she was given responsibility for the Guerlain division as well, which includes Shalimar, one of the world's best–selling women's perfumes. "The exciting news isn't about me—it's about LVMH and a very exciting time in its development as a force in the U.S. beauty business," she told *WWD* journalist Julie Naughton when her Guerlain duties were announced, and said she was looking forward to the challenge of reviving what some felt was a moribund brand. "The smartest companies see difficult times as an opportunity," McDonald asserted. "They look for synergies—and they also look for how they can break the rules. Guerlain and Givenchy have numerous synergies in magic, prestige, and products."

Born in the early 1950s, McDonald earned a degree in American studies from Smith College, the prestigious women's school in Northampton, Massachusetts. She began her career in the cosmetics industry in 1979 with a job at Charles of the Ritz, where she served as product manager for its mass–distribution fragrances, including the highly successful Enjoli and Jean Naté lines at the time. Moving over to Cosmair, the United States licensee of the Paris–based L'Oreal Group, McDonald became brand manager for the 1984 launch of Paloma

Picasso's signature fragrance. At Parfums Phenix in 1987, she helped launch another signature scent, this one from legendary French actress Catherine Deneuve. Back at Cosmair by 1989, McDonald marketed the lines in its Ralph Lauren Fragrances division. Over the next few years, she oversaw the development of five new popular Lauren fragrances, from Safari to Polo Sport Woman.

McDonald's marketing savvy led to an executive job with Cosmair's Lauren division in global development. She joined the venerable House of Chanel's fragrance division for a time as senior vice president of sales, but after less than a year on the job there through much of 1997, McDonald was hired by luxury–goods group LVMH Moet Hennessy Louis Vuitton as president and chief executive officer of its Parfums Givenchy North America unit. The Givenchy fragrance line dated back to designer Hubert de Givenchy's creation of a signature scent called L'Interdit for his muse, the actress Audrey Hepburn, in 1957. British maverick Alexander McQueen had been head designer at Givenchy since 1996, and was credited with revitalizing the classic French couture house. "Among our immediate strategies," the newly appointed McDonald told WWD writer Pete Born, "will be an accelerated pace for new product launches, as well as tightening the connection between Givenchy fragrances and Givenchy fashion, which has enormous potential under the brilliant design direction of Alexander McQueen."

Several new scents were launched during McDonald's first years on the job at Parfums Givenchy, including an entirely new "American Designers" line, which included fragrances from American designers Michael Kors, Marc Jacobs, and Kenneth Cole. In the fall of 2001, LVMH restructured its American fragrances and cosmetics divisions, and McDonald was given responsibility for Guerlain Inc., the American subsidiary of the French fragrance house, as well. The perfume–maker, thought to be world's oldest fragrance and cosmetics line, dates back to 1828 and includes the famed Guerlain house brands like Shalimar and Samsara, plus the newer Kenzo and Celine scents. "Guerlain is the oldest fragrance company in the world, and it has flourished in pure creativity without the equity of a designer name," McDonald told WWD's Naughton at the time. She adroitly sidestepped the issue of moribund sales for the brand in what had become an extremely competitive market. "The best product in the world won't succeed if the communications aren't right, and there have been challenges with that in the U.S. at retail," she noted. "But there is an American voice that can be employed without changing the Frenchness of the brand."

In 2002, McDonald oversaw the launch of Kenneth Cole New York Men and Kenneth Cole New York Women scents. But within a year, LVMH had started to sell off its non–core beauty businesses, beginning with the sale of the Kors fragrance license to Estée Lauder, Inc., in May of 2003 for what industry sources believed to be in the neighborhood of $20 million. A Lauder executive, Patrick Bousquet–Chavanne, told Born of WWD that his company had "inherited a good business. The people at LVMH, under Camille's leadership have done a good job of bringing this product to market." McDonald told the same writer that the announcement of the Kors deacquisition "[i]s a bittersweet time for us. We never like to see our children grow up and move out of the house. But it's something that could be harvested for the benefit of the more core business and the delivered value could be reinvested elsewhere." A few weeks later, LVMH okayed the sale of the Jacobs and Cole scents to Coty, another cosmetics–licensing powerhouse, for an amount rumored to be in the $50 million neighborhood for both brands. Rumors circulated at the time that perhaps McDonald would be leaving the company as well, but she told WWD's Born and Naughton, "I have no plans to leave LVMH," and asserted elsewhere that by letting go of the LVMH's American Designers experiment, she and her team "will be able to focus our resources and creativity on capitalizing on the success of Parfums Givenchy and Guerlain in the U.S market."

McDonald is a board member of two industry groups, the Fragrance Foundation and Cosmetic Executive Women. She admitted once that her dressing for her job sometimes presented a challenge, she told More magazine in 2001. "The reality is I have to portray leadership and credibility.... Believe me, there are days when all I want to wear are my Bugs Bunny slippers and Nick & Nora pjs."

Sources

Periodicals

Drug & Cosmetic Industry, March 1994, p. 16.
More, October 2001, p. 117.
WWD, January 9, 1987, p. 8; January 7, 1998, p. 2; July 27, 2001, p. 13; November 2, 2001, p. 1; May 9, 2003, p. 1; May 30, 2003, p. 1.

Online

"The First Annual Newsmakers Panel," Essec Business School, http://www.essecusa.com/news makers/mcdonald.htm (August 11, 2003).

—Carol Brennan

Ian McEwan

Author

Born Ian Russell McEwan, June 21, 1948, in Aldershot, England; son of David (an army officer) and Rose Lilian Violet (Moore) McEwan; married Penny Allen (a healer and astrologer), 1982 (divorced, 1995); married Annalena McAfee (a journalist); children: Gregory, William (from first marriage), two stepdaughters. *Education:* University of Sussex, B.A. (honors), 1970; University of East Anglia, M.A., 1971.

Addresses: *Office*—Publicity Dept., Doubleday Books, 1745 Broadway, New York, NY 10019.

Career

Master's thesis of short stories published in 1975 as *First Love, Last Rites*; first novel, *The Cement Garden,* published, 1978; author of a banned British Broadcasting Corporation play, *Solid Geometry,* 1979; wrote screenplays for the 1983 film *The Ploughman's Lunch* and *The Good Son,* 1992, among others; his 1981 novel *The Comfort of Strangers* was adapted for film by Harold Pinter and director Paul Schrader, 1991; *The Cement Garden* was adapted for film by writer–director Andrew Birkin, 1993; *Atonement* was adapted for a film directed by Sir Richard Eyre and written by Christopher Hampton.

Awards: Somerset Maugham Award for *First Love, Last Rites,* 1976; Evening Standard award for best screenplay for *The Ploughman's Lunch,* 1983; Whitbread Award for *The Child in Time,* 1987; Man Booker Prize for *Amsterdam,* 1998; W.H. Smith Literary Award for *Atonement,* 2002; National Book Critics Circle Award for fiction for *Atonement,* 2003; Los Angeles Times Book Award for *Atonement,* 2003.

Sidelights

Ian McEwan, winner of Britain's prestigious Booker Prize for *Amsterdam* in 1998, is a writer with a well–established and, at times, even somewhat infamous literary reputation before his novels began to gain a North American readership. For many years he was known primarily for a literary style that delivered horrifically visceral passages but remained compellingly eloquent throughout. In his middle age McEwan began toning down the explicit with horrors that were far more accessible: the loss of a child, the betrayal of a friend, the disintegration of a family. His 2001 novel, *Atonement,* spent seven months on the best–seller lists in Britain. "McEwan forces his readers to turn the pages with greater dread and anticipation than does perhaps any other 'literary' writer working in English today," declared *Atlantic Monthly* critic Claire Messud.

McEwan was born in 1948 and spent part of his youth in Singapore and North Africa, where his father was stationed as a British Army officer. He finished his education at a boarding school in England, and went on to earn an undergraduate degree from the University of Sussex in 1970. Enrolling at the University of East Anglia in its graduate literature program, McEwan was part of the university's first–ever creative writing class, led by young British writer Malcolm Bradbury. The course reading list was heavily skewed to the postwar American canon, with selections from Philip Roth, Norman Mailer, John Barth, and others, and McEwan began submitting short fiction pieces along with his coursework to Bradbury. The latter influenced the former, he reflected later in a *Guardian* article he penned in 2000. "The ambition, the social range, the expressive freedom of American writing made English fiction seem poky and grey," McEwan explained. "To find bold and violent colors became my imperative."

The first story McEwan wrote and handed in to Bradbury was "Conversation With a Cupboardman," a morbid tale about a man who lived in a closet. It was followed by several others of a macabre nature—rife with themes of incest, assault, and even necrophilia—that appeared in *First Love, Last Rites,* published in 1975. McEwan attributed a crisis of confidence in himself for stoking such unusual creative fires. "I had been invisible to myself in my teens," he told journalist Phil Daoust in an interview that appeared in London's *Guardian* newspaper some years later. "A lot of my terror of things was in those stories—my terror of not making full or rich emotional relationships."

Other short stories followed, which were collected into a second volume, *In Between the Sheets,* in 1978. Soon afterward, McEwan was commissioned to write a play for the British Broadcasting Corporation (BBC), and based it on a short story that appeared in his debut collection. But *Solid Geometry* was halted by the BBC mid–production, after executives deemed it "untransmittable" due to its subject matter: the plot concerned a man who keeps a sexual organ, purchased by an ancestor in 1875, pickled in a jar on his desk. The incident caused a minor stir in Britain, with many siding with McEwan, but others asserting that with Britain on the eve of electing its first–ever female prime minister, the story was beyond the realm of being politically insensitive and in just plain bad taste.

McEwan's first novel, *The Cement Garden,* was published in 1978, and served to further bolster his reputation as a literary maverick. The story concerned four orphaned siblings and was filled with some shocking scenes, including incest and the burial of their deceased mother inside a cement box in the house. In 1981, his second novel, *The Comfort of Strangers* appeared. Its plot concerned a couple vacationing in Venice who become involved with a mysterious expatriate, who leads them into a dangerous sadomasochistic game. Ten years later, the novel was adapted for film by the playwright Harold Pinter, with Paul Schrader directing a cast that included Rupert Everett, Christopher Walken, and Helen Mirren.

McEwan's fiction changed course in the mid–1980s when he became a parent. The violence in his work began to subside, and the protagonists became less openly deviant. In the *The Child in Time,* his 1987 novel, children's book author Stephen Lewis mourns the loss of his three–year–old daughter Kate, who simply disappeared one day in a grocery store and was never seen again. *Time* critic R. Z. Sheppard hailed it as "a death–defying story, inventive, eventful, and affirmative without being sentimental."

In his fourth novel, *The Innocent,* McEwan presents the unusual dilemma of English telephone technician Leonard Marnham, who is co–opted into a Cold War spy plot in 1955 Berlin involving a secret tunnel beneath the divided but not yet walled city. Leonard begins an affair with a German woman, but the plot turns truly sinister when they murder her husband. Leonard carves the victim up in what literary critics called a perfect example of McEwan's talent for writing famously gruesome passages. "He should not have been going through bone," the novel reads, as quoted in the *Guardian.* "His idea was to get between the joint. His idea of it was vague, derived from roast chicken Sunday lunches." The scene endures for some six pages, and Leonard then carries the cumbersome suitcases containing the parts around the city, looking for an appropriate place to leave them—a section "told with all McEwan's frigid skill," noted a *Time* review from Martha Duffy, who also compared him to author Evelyn Waugh for "sheer, mirthful heartlessness."

McEwan's 1992 novel, *Black Dogs,* took a more prosaic setting, with its protagonist simply attempting to write the memoir of his wife's aging, but still spirited parents. The title is drawn from the couple's 1946 walk in Provence, when the wife sees a terrifying apparition that comes to symbolize to her the darkest part of the human soul. "McEwan's meticulous prose, his shaping of his material to create suspense, and his adept use of specific settings produce a haunting fable," noted a *Publishers Weekly* contributor.

Around this same time, McEwan had his first experience with the Hollywood film industry. A short story he wrote, "The Good Child," was optioned for a film that eventually starred Macaulay Culkin and Elijah Wood. Wood plays a boy sent to live with relatives after his mother dies, and finds that his cousin Henry (Culkin) is a far more sinister force than he can handle by himself. The film was directed by Joseph Ruben, and *Entertainment Weekly* reviewer Ty Burr felt that both director and writer "tap into something we rarely admit about childhood: Where most kids learn to temper any innate sadism with ethics, some just don't." But McEwan was released from his contract by order of Culkin's famously influence–wielding father, and the experience soured him. He once described Hollywood screenwriting as "an opportunity to fly first–class, be treated like a celebrity, sit around the pool, and be betrayed," the *Guardian* profile by Daoust quoted him as saying.

McEwan's 1998 novel, *Enduring Love,* followed the travails of science writer Joe Rose who, on an idyllic picnic day with his beloved wife, spies a hot–air balloon in the sky that is failing; he and several others nearby grab its ropes, but then the wind kicks up again, with the rescuers left hanging—and so the "crew enacted morality's ancient, irresolvable dilemma: us, or me," the novel reads, and Rose and the others let go. A religious zealot is among the group, and then begins to stalk him. The coolly rational Rose diagnoses the man with a form of erotomania, named after a long–dead French psychiatrist, but the man's actions prove the undoing of Rose's ostensibly happy marriage. "McEwan does a superb job of making us believe what seems so unlikely, and that is the book's great power," noted *Independent Sunday*'s Jan Dallcy.

Only with McEwan's next novel, *Amsterdam,* did his work begin to gain a wider appreciation outside of Britain. Published in the United States in 1998, the story involves two longtime friends who make a pact after the London funeral of their former lover, Molly. She died a painful death, and Vernon Halliday and Clive Linley vow to one another that should the same fate befall them, they would help one another get to the Netherlands, where physician–assisted suicide is legal. McEwan's premise behind the plot is the possibility that euthanasia might be misused, a story that gets underway when Halliday, the newspaper editor, plans to publish incriminating photos of a British politician they both know that were found among Molly's possessions; Linley, the composer, objects strenuously on moral grounds. The novel finally won McEwan the Booker Prize for contemporary fiction, given to the best work of the year by a writer from Britain or its Commonwealth nations. Two of his previous works had also made it onto the estimable Booker list of finalists: *The Comfort of Strangers* in 1981 and *Black Dogs* in 1992.

Atonement, McEwan's eighth novel, was also short–listed for the Booker in 2001, and hailed as a tour–de–force on both sides of the Atlantic. It took "the British novel into the twenty–first century," declared Geoff Dyer in the *Guardian* in 2001. The story begins on a summer day in 1935 at a Surrey country estate at which the members of the Tallis family have gathered. There is Leon, the eldest son and a young London banker, who arrives with his wealthy

friend; Cecilia, the older Tallis daughter, comes from Cambridge University, as does Robbie, whose mother is the longtime housekeeper at the Tallis estate. There are also cousins Lola, 15 years old, and her homesick twin brothers. Robbie wrestles with his growing attraction to Cecilia. He writes a letter that concludes with a salacious line, but decides to rewrite it; he accidentally sends the first one via her 13–year–old sister Briony, who reads it, and then when Lola is assaulted later on that evening, claims that Robbie is the culprit. Lola colludes in the accusation, and Robbie is convicted and imprisoned.

The next section of the book shifts ahead five years later to World War II, with Robbie freed from jail but now serving in the military as the Battle of Dunkirk rages—passages which McEwan based on his own father's stories—and Briony a nurse in London. *Atonement* progresses with a series of fateful pairings and consequences, but in the final section some of this is revealed to be merely the fiction of Briony, who became an acclaimed writer but is haunted by her guilt over that 1935 incident. When she was a young nurse taking the bandages from her patients' battle–ravaged faces, she realized "that a person is, among all else, a material thing, easily torn, not easily mended," the novel reads, according to *Atlantic Monthly*'s Messud.

Atonement earned overwhelmingly enthusiastic reviews. Boyd Tonkin, writing in London's *Independent,* termed it "a magnificent novel, shaped and paced with awesome confidence and eloquence; as searching an account of error, shame, and reparation as any in modern fiction." *New Yorker* fiction critic John Updike reflected that McEwan's previous "novels have tended to be short, smart, and saturnine," and called *Atonement* "a beautiful and majestic fictional panorama."

McEwan has never failed to tout his first and only writing teacher as the source of his confidence as a writer. He recalled a magical incident in which he became separated from his publicity handlers in the heady Booker Prize announcement ceremony and round of press interviews, and found himself in a deserted hall that led to another corridor. "Coming towards me, from some distance away, were Malcolm and his wife, Elizabeth," McEwan wrote in the *Guardian.* "We approached each other as in dream, and I remember thinking, half seriously, that this was what it might be like to be dead. In the warmth of his embrace was concentrated all the generosity of this gifted teacher and writer."

Selected writings

First Love, Last Rites (short stories), Random House (New York City), 1975.

In Between the Sheets, and Other Stories, Simon & Schuster (New York City), 1978.

The Cement Garden (novel), Simon & Schuster (New York City), 1978.

The Comfort of Strangers (novel), Simon & Schuster (New York City), 1981.

The Ploughman's Lunch (screenplay), Methuen (London), 1985.

Rose Blanche (children's book), J. Cape (London), 1985.

The Child in Time (novel), Houghton (Boston), 1987.

The Innocent (novel), Doubleday (Garden City, NY), 1990.

Black Dogs (novel), Doubleday (Garden City, NY), 1992.

The Innocent (screenplay), Lakeheart/Miramax/Sievernich, 1993.

The Good Son (screenplay), Twentieth Century–Fox, 1993.

The Daydreamer (children's book), illustrated by Anthony Browne, HarperCollins (New York City), 1994.

The Short Stories, J. Cape (London), 1995.

Enduring Love (novel), Doubleday (Garden City, NY), 1998.

Amsterdam (novel), J. Cape, 1997, Doubleday (Garden City, NY), 1998.

Atonement (novel), Doubleday (Garden City, NY), 2002.

Sources

Periodicals

Atlantic Monthly, March 2002, p. 106.

Booklist, September 1, 1994, p. 43.

Contemporary Review, June 1995, p. 320.

Entertainment Weekly, October 1, 1993, p. 38; March 22, 2002, p. 101.

Guardian (London, England), August 4, 1997, p. 6; August 16, 1999, p. 8; November 29, 2000, p. 2; September 22, 2001, p. 8.

Independent (London, England), September 3, 1999, p. 5; September 10, 1999, p. 11; September 15, 2001, p. 3.

Independent Sunday (London, England), August 31, 1997, p. 22.

Maclean's, November 17, 1997, p. 106.

New Republic, October 15, 1984, p. 24; November 16, 1992, p. 41; March 25, 2002, p. 28.

New Statesman, September 11, 1998, p. 47.

Newsweek International, April 8, 2002, p. 94.

New Yorker, March 4, 2002, p. 80.

Publishers Weekly, September 14, 1992, p. 103.

Time, September 21, 1987, p. 76; June 25, 1990, p. 69.

Online

Contemporary Authors Online, Gale, 2003.

—*Carol Brennan*

Ted McGinley

Actor

Born Ted M. McGinley, May 30, 1958, in Newport Beach, CA; married Gigi Rice (an actress); children: Beau Martin, another son. *Education:* Attended University of Southern California, c. 1976–79.

Addresses: *Contact*—1999 Ave. of the Stars, #2850, Los Angeles, CA 90067; 14951 Alva Dr., Pacific Palisades, CA 90272.

Career

Actor in television, including: *Happy Days,* 1980–84; *Love Boat,* ABC, 1984–86; *Dynasty,* ABC, 1986–87; *Baby Talk,* ABC, 1991; *Married ... With Children,* FOX, 1991–97; *Sports Night,* 1998–99; *The West Wing,* NBC, 2000–01; *Charlie Lawrence,* CBS, 2003; *Hope & Faith,* 2003—. Television movies include: *Valentine,* ABC, 1979; *The Making of a Male Model,* 1983; *The Love Boat: The Christmas Cruise,* ABC, 1986; *The Love Boat: The Shipshape Cruise,* ABC, 1986; *The Love Boat: Who Killed Maxwell Thorn?,* 1987; *Revenge of the Nerds III: The Next Generation,* FOX, 1992; *Linda,* USA, 1993; *Wild Justice* (miniseries), 1993; *Revenge of the Nerds IV: Nerds in Love,* FOX, 1994; *Tails You Live, Heads You're Dead,* 1995; *Deadly Web,* NBC, 1996; *Every Mother's Worst Fear,* USA, 1998; *Hard Time: Hostage Hotel,* TNT, 1999; *N.T.S.B.: The Crash of Flight 323,* ABC, 2001; *Frozen Impact,* 2003. Television guest star roles include: *Fantasy Island,* 1982; *The Love Boat,* 1983; *Hotel,* 1985–87; *Perfect Strangers,* 1988; *B.L. Stryker,* ABC, 1989; *Married ... With Children,* FOX, 1989; *Evening Shade,* CBS, 1990; *Dream On,* 1995; *The John Larroquette Show,* NBC, 1995–96; *The Practice,* ABC, 2001; *Justice League* (voice), Cartoon Network, 2002–03; *Wednesday 9:30 (8:30 Central),* ABC, 2002.

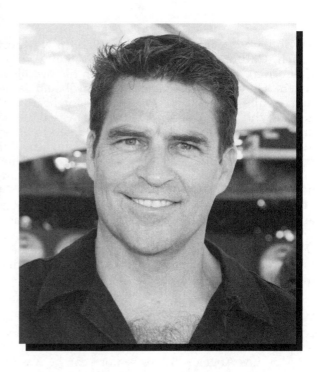

AP/Wide World Photos

Television pilots include: *Herndon,* ABC, 1983; *Work with Me,* CBS, 1999; *Life of the Party,* CBS, 2002. Film appearances include: *Young Doctors in Love,* 1982; *Revenge of the Nerds,* 1984; *Troop Beverly Hills,* Columbia, 1989; *Physical Evidence,* 1989; *Blue Tornado,* 1991; *Wayne's World 2,* 1993; *Covert Assassin,* 1994; *Major League: Back to the Minors,* 1998; *Follow Your Heart,* 1998; *Dick,* 1999; *The Big Tease,* 1999; *Face the Music,* 2000; *Daybreak,* 2000; *Cahoots,* 2000; *Pearl Harbor,* 2001. Worked as a model c. 1976–80.

Sidelights

Classically handsome actor Ted McGinley appeared in supporting roles on a number of successful television series including *Happy Days, Love Boat, Dynasty,* and *Married ... With Children.* He often joined these shows mid–run. Sometimes the shows had reached their peak and/or were canceled within a few years of his joining the cast. Because of this trend, McGinley was named the patron saint of a website which chronicled this so–called "Jump the Shark" phenomenon. McGinley did not just appear in television shows, but also had roles in television movies and on film. One of his most popular film roles was a supporting role as an antagonist in the hit comedy *Revenge of the Nerds* and two of its sequels. As McGinley told Christian Toto of the

Washington Times, "I've made a living out of not being the main person. I consider myself a utility player."

McGinley was born on May 30, 1958, in Newport Beach, California (some sources say San Marino, California), where he was raised with his two older sisters. His father was a successful cardboard salesman, while his mother was a nurse for heart surgeons who had a second career as a real estate broker. From childhood, McGinley wanted to be an actor and appeared in musicals and theater productions. Sports were also a big part of his life. He played little league baseball and began swimming to lose weight. By the time McGinley was 14 years old, he was a member of an elite swim team and won some championships. He also surfed and worked as a lifeguard on the beach at Newport Beach. McGinley was already attracting attention for his looks on the beach, but did not like getting into the water to save people unless he had to.

Water sports proved to be McGinley's ticket to college. He was given a full scholarship to play water polo at the University of Southern California, located in Los Angeles. By his senior year, he was the captain of the team. While a college student, McGinley also began a modeling career. He saw this as the first step to an acting career. However, modeling led to McGinley losing his athletic scholarship. He appeared in a sporting goods ad that was seen as violating NCAA rules of amateurism. After losing his scholarship, McGinley left school and went to New York City for a time to model.

While working as a model, McGinley appeared on boxes of Sun–In hair lightener and in a dozen television commercials. Within a short time, he was making his acting debut. McGinley's first role was as a jogger in an ABC television movie, 1979's *Valentine.* Producer–director Garry Marshall soon discovered McGinley and added him to the cast of his hit television show, *Happy Days.* McGinley joined the show in 1980, playing Roger Phillips, the cousin of main character Richie Cunningham. McGinley's Phillips was also a high school English teacher and basketball coach.

When McGinley took the role, he had minimal professional acting experience and had to learn on the job. It was a very hard adjustment for him, and McGinley thought his acting on the show was very bad at times. He considered leaving acting behind during the run of *Happy Days* to become a heart surgeon. Just as McGinley considered quitting, Marshall called him with a film offer that the actor decided he wanted.

Marshall cast McGinley in the 1982 film he was directing, *Young Doctors in Love,* which was a parody of the soap opera genre. McGinley played Dr. Bucky De Vol, an orthopedic surgeon who was also a jock. The character was in love with a hooker who favored roller skates. This film led to more roles for McGinley. He appeared in the 1983 television movie *The Making of a Male Model* with future *Dynasty* co–star Joan Collins. McGinley also continued to appear on *Happy Days* until the end of its run in 1984.

As soon as *Happy Days* ended, McGinley was cast in a role on another hit television series already well into its run, *The Love Boat.* He played Ashley "Ace" Covington–Evans, the ship's photographer and social director. McGinley stuck with the show until it was canceled by ABC in 1986. After its end as a television series, *The Love Boat* continued on in television movies; McGinley appeared in three: *The Love Boat: The Christmas Cruise, The Love Boat: The Shipshape Cruise,* and *The Love Boat: Who Killed Maxwell Thorn?.*

In 1984, McGinley also had his first big–screen role of significance. In the hit comedy *Revenge of the Nerds,* he played Stan Gable, the quarterback of the fictional college's football team and president of the Alpha Beta fraternity. McGinley's Gable was the primary enemy of the nerds at the center of the film. McGinley reprised the role in two sequels which were aired as television movies, 1992's *Revenge of the Nerds III: The Next Generation* and 1994's *Revenge of the Nerds IV: Nerds in Love.*

Until this point, most of McGinley's significant roles had been in comedies. After the run of *The Love Boat* ended, he was cast in a role on another production produced by Aaron Spelling, the already–popular prime–time soap opera, *Dynasty.* McGinley spent a little more than a season, 1986–87, playing Clay Falmont, a senator's son who was both a rebel and a rogue. McGinley believed that this dramatic role helped make him a better actor. During the run, he also volunteered his time to work at a paradise camp for kids suffering from terminal cancer.

In the late 1980s and early 1990s, McGinley worked on a number of different film and television projects. In 1989, he had a role in the dramatic mystery *Physical Evidence,* directed by Michael Crichton and starring Burt Reynolds. McGinley played the boyfriend of a female lawyer played by Theresa Russell. McGinley continued to alternate between film and television roles. In 1991, he played Craig Palmer on the short–lived situation comedy, *Baby Talk.* The ABC show was derived from the hit film *Look Who's Talking.*

After the end of *Baby Talk*, McGinley was added to the cast of yet another already–successful show, the over–the–top situation comedy *Married ... With Children* on FOX. He played Jefferson D'Arcy, the second husband of Marcy D'Arcy, a controlling career woman, from 1991 until the show ended its run in 1997. McGinley's character was a hunky freeloader who was "kept" by his wife. He told Eirik Knutzen of Copley News Service, "I guess I'm part of television history, because I have appeared in four successful shows but I really can't take the credit, because I came in late on all of them. I've always been the low man on the totem pole. I'd be thrilled to be part of a TV series from day one and ride that cow until it died."

During and shortly after the run of *Married ... With Children*, McGinley was a part of many film and television movies, playing different types of characters. In 1993, he played Mr. Scream in *Wayne's World 2*. That same year, McGinley used a Southern accent in his role in the miniseries *Wild Justice* which did not go over well with critics. Some of his television movie roles were very dark. In 1996, he was the star of *Deadly Web*, a movie that aired on NBC in 1996 and co–starred his wife, Gigi Rice. The movie was about a woman who was stalked on the Internet. One of McGinley's darkest roles came in 1998 in the television movie *Every Mother's Worst Fear*. He played Mitch Carson (also known as Scanman), a sexual predator who lures a teenage girl upset by her parents' divorce into his lair. He holds her captive and tortures her.

Bigger film roles came McGinley's way in the late 1990s and early 2000s. In 1998, he appeared in *Major League: Back to the Minors*, the third film in the *Major League* series. He played Leonard Huff, the manager of the Minnesota Twins, who was incompetent, vain, and arrogant. The film received some praise, and was seen as better than part two in the series, *Major League II*, but did not do well at the box office. Of the actor's performance, Michael Saunders of the *Boston Globe* declared: "McGinley has made a career of playing well–groomed twits and does a great job here."

Soon after *Major League: Back to the Minors*, McGinley filmed *Dick*, a comedy about President Richard Nixon's Watergate break in. The story focused on two teenage girls who accidentally stumble on the crime in progress. McGinley's character was an aide of Nixon who has to interrogate the girls. The film was released in 1999. McGinley was also a part of big Hollywood productions such as 2001's *Pearl Harbor*, in a small role as an Army Corps major.

In the late 1990s and early 2000s, McGinley's television career had its ups and downs. He joined the critically successful show *Sports Night* mid–season.

McGinley played Gordon until the show was canceled in 1999. In 1999, he played Murray Epstein on the CBS pilot *Work With Me* that was not picked up. In 2001, McGinley joined the hit drama *The West Wing*, first in a guest–starring role that turned into a recurring role. Two years later, he was selected for a role in *Charlie Lawrence*, a situation comedy about a freshman congressman from New Mexico, played by Nathan Lane. McGinley played Graydon Cord, the neighbor of Lane's title character, who was a member of the opposing political party. McGinley was also in the pilot for the 2002 CBS show *Life of the Party*, playing a senator.

Because of McGinley's checkered television history, he was picked as the epitome of the phenomenon known as "Jump the Shark." This concept was begun by Jon Hein on a website (www.jumptheshark. com) in 1997. Hein claimed that whenever McGinley—or certain other actors—appeared on a show, its run soon ended or at least its best days were behind it. The name comes from what Hein considered the zenith of *Happy Days*, when one of the characters jumped over a shark on water skis. Hein named McGinley the patron saint of Jump the Shark, but meant no malice against the actor. For his part, McGinley disagreed with Hein's assessment, pointing out that several of the shows he was on ended long after he was on them. McGinley told Melanie McFarland of the *Seattle Post–Intelligencer*, "I've had a lot of fun with it. To be honest with you, it's meant people are still talking about me. It's kind of doing me a favor. And people keep hiring me, so I know that I'm OK."

Indeed, McGinley kept working. In 2003, he was cast in yet another situation comedy, *Hope & Faith*. The show focused on the relationship between stay–at–home mom, Hope (played by Faith Ford), and her sister, Faith, a washed–up soap actress (played by Kelly Ripa). McGinley played Charlie, an orthodontist married to Hope whose life is turned upside down when Faith moves in. While the show had some initial success, it struggled to keep an audience during its first season on the air. Despite its potential Jump the Shark status, McGinley was not worried about its longevity. He told Scott D. Pierce of Deseret News, "Look, it took me 3 1/2 years to kill *The Love Boat*, 4 1/2 years to kill *Happy Days*, 7 1/2 years to kill *Married ... With Children*. So I'm hoping it takes me ten years to kill this one."

Sources

Books

Celebrity Biographies, Baseline II, 2004.
Contemporary Theatre, Film and Television, vol. 51, Gale Group, 2003.

Periodicals

Boston Globe, April 18, 1998, p. C5; September 26, 2003, p. D4.
BPI Entertainment News Wire, April 20, 1998.
Chicago Sun–Times, April 26, 1998, p. 403.
Copley News Service, August 13, 1998.
Daily Variety, June 24, 2003, p. 18.
Deseret News (Salt Lake City, UT), December 5, 2003, p. C8.
Entertainment Weekly, October 17, 2003, pp. 50–52.
Houston Chronicle, November 1, 2000, p. 1.
People, August 29, 1983, p. 9; February 13, 1989, p. 20; May 31, 1993, p. 11.
Pittsburgh Post–Gazette, June 14, 1984, p. D8.
Seattle Post–Intelligencer (Seattle, Washington), July 25, 2003, p. E1.
Seattle Times, April 20, 1998, p. E5.
Sunday Mail (Queensland, Australia), October 25, 1987.

Toronto Star, June 21, 1986, p. F3.
Toronto Sun, July 16, 2003, p. 56.
Washington Post, September 2, 1984, p. H1.
Washington Times, September 24, 2003, p. B6.

Online

"Charlie Lawrence," CBS.com, http://www.cbs.com/primetime/charlie_lawrence/about.shtml (April 13, 2004).
"Ted McGinley," Hollywood.com, http://www.hollywood.com/celebs/bio/celeb/1672413 (April 13, 2004).
"Ted McGinley," Internet Movie Database, http://www.imdb.com/name/nm0569337/ (April 13, 2004).

—A. Petruso

Betsy McLaughlin

President and Chief Executive Officer of Hot Topic, Inc.

Born Elizabeth M. McLaughlin, c. 1962, in California; daughter of Bob (a salesperson) and Karin (a homemaker) McLaughlin. *Education:* Attended the University of California, Irvine.

Addresses: *Home*—Manhattan Beach, CA. *Office*—Hot Topic, Inc., 18305 E. San Jose Ave., City of Industry, CA 91748.

Career

Began retail career in selling men's suits in a California department store, late 1970s; held merchandising and buyer's positions with Millers Outpost and Broadway department stores; vice-president of store operations, Hot Topic, Inc., 1993–95, head of merchandising, 1996–99, president after 1999, chief executive officer, 2000—.

Sidelights

Betsy McLaughlin runs Hot Topic, the chain of alternative clothing stores that became one of the surprise retail success stories of the 1990s. McLaughlin was also instrumental in launching a new division, Torrid, which features plus-size teen fashions. The chief executive officer helped promote the daring new Torrid retail concept personally, noting her own struggles to find fashionable gear as a full-figured woman. "It's about style, not about size," McLaughlin told *Time*'s Dody Tsiantar.

Born in the early 1960s, McLaughlin grew up in Orange County, California, and earned straight A's at Costa Mesa's Estancia High. She began her career in retail while studying economics at the University of California's Irvine campus. As her father, Bob, a sales veteran, recalled in an interview with *People,* his daughter was a natural at selling men's suits in a local department store. "She'd get one guy in and sell to him," he told the magazine, "and then he'd come back with his whole football team!" After graduating, McLaughlin worked in merchandising for a West Coast mall clothier, Millers Outpost, and went on to the department–store chain Broadway. She began at Hot Topic in 1993, when the California-based company was just a few years old.

McLaughlin was hired as vice–president of store operations at Hot Topic, and oversaw its rapid expansion over the rest of the decade. Hot Topic lured young shoppers into its funkily designed emporiums by selling a range of daring gear, from band T–shirts to skull rings to unisex vinyl wear. It carried its own products as well as those from more outré vendors such as Lip Service, which usually refused to deal with chain stores but made an exception for Hot Topic. The mall–based retailer, noted *Fortune*'s Kimberly L. Allers, quickly attained phenomenal sales numbers by "following the pulse of the alternative teen demographic more closely than most any other big company. For years, angst–ridden teens sought their edgy wares in ... urban hotbeds of pseudo–subversive underground culture" like Greenwich Village in New York City or Belmont Avenue in Chicago, Allers noted. "Hot Topic has taken that antiestablishment vibe and put it in, of all places, the suburban mall."

McLaughlin was promoted to head of merchandising at Hot Topic in 1996, and was named company president in 1999; a year later she took over the chief executive officer position. As the company grew to some 400–plus stores, she made certain that it still retained its reputation for seeking out and bringing cutting–edge merchandise to its mall addresses with a turnaround time that was unprecedented in the retail sector. The company encouraged its buyers and other employees to delve into field research personally, and even reimbursed the cost of a concert ticket if an employee attended a show and submitted a report on the band or new clothing trends spotted in the crowd. McLaughlin also utilized the company's Internet site, which was launched in 1997 and proved a profit–maker almost from the start. "We can put a message out on our Web site and ask if our customers have heard of a particular band," she told *WWD* writer Kristin Young. "The next day, we get hundreds, if not thousands, of responses from every area of the country saying what they think about the band. It's that kind of information flow that's so valuable."

That kind of customer feedback was crucial in launching Hot Topic's new division, Torrid, in 2001. At every Hot Topic store, suggestion cards sat near the cash register, and when the company tested size–15 vinyl jeans in the stores, the messages began arriving on McLaughlin's desk with the same plea. "Customers started writing in, saying, 'I see you have this one item; why can't you have more?'" she said in the interview with *People.* "We realized this customer didn't have anywhere to go." McLaughlin recalled her own difficult experiences finding fun clothes as a size–14 teen, and realized that there was an untapped market of more than 50 percent of American women who wore a size 14 and up. Plus–size clothing had become a hot, new apparel category in recent years, but no other retailer was offering heavier teens the same stylish, curve–accentuating fashions that dominated standard–size junior styles.

The first Torrid store opened at the Brea Mall in Orange County in April of 2001. It carried its own Torrid line of clothes, plus sizes 12 to 26 from other vendors. That and the Torrid stores that followed were overnight sensations, McLaughlin recalled. "Some people thought we had staged customers," she told *People,* "because when they went into a store, they saw a mom or daughter screaming with joy or crying." The chain quickly expanded to more than three dozen across the United States, and helped make Hot Topic one of the most impressive retail stocks on Wall Street. The company's stock price rose 33 percent between 2001 and 2002, and in 2003 the company posted sales of $546 million across 494 stores, making it one of the highest sales–per–square–foot performers in the industry. It was No. 47 on *Fortune* magazine's list of the 100 fastest-growing companies in America that year.

McLaughlin's company jumped from twelfth place to fourth on *Forbes*'s "200 Best Small Companies in America" rankings in 2003 as well, in part because of the dynamic, decidedly non–corporate structure at its City of Industry headquarters just outside Los Angeles, California. McLaughlin does her job from a desk situated in the middle of a large room amidst dozens of other employees, for example, while music videos play on screens overhead. The conference room resembles a dance club, and bands sometimes stop by for special in–house performances. McLaughlin encourages all employees to e–mail her with ideas and suggestions, and works hard to eliminate roadblocks that keep staff from voicing their opinions. Part of her job involves attending rock concerts herself, but she still carefully monitors the customer–comment cards for both Hot Topic and Torrid. "This is serious stuff because not many people ask teenagers what they think," she explained in the interview with Young for *WWD.* "You learn with teenagers that you don't presume anything. They are a segment that tells you what they think and they're not shy about it. The best thing to do is put it out there and listen [to] what they have to say. They'll vote with their words and they'll vote with their money."

Sources

Periodicals

Advertising Age, November 17, 2003, p. S2.
BusinessWeek, June 9, 2003, pp. 84–86.
Chain Store Age, September 2003, p. 96.
DSN Retailing Today, May 1, 2001, p. 2.
Fortune, September 1, 2003, p. 81; November 10, 2003.
Investor's Business Daily, June 25, 2001, p. A4; December 5, 2003, p. A3.
Los Angeles Business Journal, November 25, 2002, p. 10.
New York Times, February 9, 2003.
People, May 26, 2003, pp. 153–54.
Time, May 6, 2002, p. Y17.
U.S. News & World Report, April 30, 2001, p. 44.
WWD, February 1, 2001, p. 16B; March 15, 2001, p. 18; May 7, 2001, p. 20.

Online

"200 Best Small Companies 2003," *Forbes.com,* http://www.forbes.com/finance/lists/23/2003/LIR.jhtml?passListId=23&passYear=2003&passListType=Company&uniqueId=TO7Z&datatype=Company (February 12, 2004).

—*Carol Brennan*

Debra Messing

AP/Wide World Photos

Actress

Born August 15, 1968, in Brooklyn, NY; daughter of Brian (a sales executive) and Sandy Messing; married Daniel Zelman (a screenwriter and actor), September 3, 2000; children: Roman Walker Zelman. *Education:* Earned undergraduate degree from Brandeis University; received M.F.A. from New York University.

Addresses: *Office*—NBC, 30 Rockefeller Plaza, New York, NY 10112.

Career

Actress in television, including: *NYPD Blue*, 1994 and 1995; *Seinfeld*, 1996 and 1997; *Ned and Stacey*, 1995–97; *Prey*, 1997–98; *Will and Grace*, 1998—; *Jesus* (movie), 1999; *King of the Hill* (voice), 2002. Film appearances include: *A Walk in the Clouds*, 1995; *McHale's Navy*, 1997; *Celebrity*, 1998; *The Mothman Prophecies*, 2002; *Hollywood Ending*, 2002; *Along Came Polly*, 2004; *Garfield* (voice), 2004; *Something Borrowed*, 2004. Stage appearances include: Off Broadway theater productions, early 1990s; *Collected Stories*, Manhattan Theater Club, 1997.

Awards: TV Guide award for actress of the year in a comedy series, for *Will & Grace*, 2001; Golden Satellite award for best performance by an actress in a series, comedy or musical, International Press Academy, for *Will & Grace*, 2002; Golden Satellite award for best performance by an actress in a series, comedy or musical, International Press Academy, for *Will & Grace*, 2003; Emmy award for outstanding lead actress in a comedy series, Academy of Television Arts and Sciences, for *Will & Grace*, 2003.

Sidelights

In 2003, Debra Messing finally won the Emmy for television's best comic actress after five seasons on *Will & Grace*. It was the fourth nomination for Messing's role as the slightly daft but immensely likable interior designer Grace Adler Markus on the top–rated NBC sitcom. Tom Carson, writing in *Esquire*, compared Messing to actresses Julie Christie and Lucille Ball, calling her "unique and something splendidly unprecedented on TV."

Born in 1968, Messing spent the first three years of her life in Brooklyn, New York, before settling with her parents and brother in a small Rhode Island town. She gravitated toward the performing arts at an early age, taking dance classes and appearing in local youth–theater productions. By her teens, she was competing in beauty pageants, and in 1986, the year she turned 18, she won the crown of Rhode Island's Junior Miss. Still, Messing loved comedy, and had spent countless hours in front of the television watching actresses like Mary Tyler Moore and Carol Burnett, each of whom had eponymous shows that ruled prime–time TV during the 1970s. She was also fascinated by reruns of *I Love Lucy*, the Lucille Ball–Desi Arnaz classic that was one of the most–

watched series of the 1950s. "I knew every line from their shows," Messing recalled in an interview with *Cosmopolitan* writer Robert Abele. "I would watch the repeats over and over and over again, because these women just inspired my comedic sensibilities. I felt somehow like I knew them, and they were teaching me something."

Messing also loved the television show *Fame,* an hour–long drama that aired in the early 1980s after a hit movie of the same name, and had pleaded—unsuccessfully—with her parents to let her attend New York City's High School for the Performing Arts, the school that inspired the show. Her parents also nixed her plans to major in theater at Brandeis University in Waltham, Massachusetts, but did strike a bargain with her: if she completed a liberal arts education there, they would foot the bill for graduate school if she still wanted to pursue a drama degree. Messing was able to spend part of her junior year in London, England, in a program for aspiring theater hopefuls, which intensified her ambitions, and she moved to New York City immediately following graduation.

Messing had landed a coveted spot in the graduate theater program at New York University, which accepted just 15 or so new students each year. In her class was future film star Billy Crudup, and she also met her future husband, Daniel Zelman, in the program. For a time, she worked as a nanny to support herself, but began landing theater parts in off–Broadway and Broadway productions. Her big break came with a 1995 film, *A Walk in the Clouds.* The film's director was Alfonso Arau, coming off the success of his *Like Water for Chocolate,* and it featured Keanu Reeves as a returning World War II veteran who falls in love with a young woman from a conservative Mexican family with roots in Napa Valley's wine country. Messing had a small role as Betty, the promiscuous wife of Reeves' character.

From there, Messing won a recurring role as Dana Abandando, the sister of an *NYPD Blue* character, and then the Fox Network offered her a lead role in a new sitcom opposite Thomas Haden Church, who had been a regular on the hit NBC series *Wings.* The show was *Ned and Stacey,* and debuted as one of the more promising new series of the 1995 fall season. *Entertainment Weekly* critic Ken Tucker described it as "conceived in cynicism and redeemed by talent" for its premise: Ned is a scheming advertising executive who suddenly believes he needs to have a wife to further his career prospects; Stacey is the left–leaning flake—a writer of airline–magazine articles—who still lives with her parents and agrees to the marital arrangement. Critics loved the dia-

logue, with *Time's* Ginia Bellafante terming it "the rare modern TV comedy that has been bold enough to create a not very feminist–minded imbalance between romantic sparring partners. Stacey is an empty–headed liberal prone to statements like, 'I'm not interested in things that are frivolous and superficial!'"

Ned and Stacey was canceled after its second season, and Messing had to decide whether or not to return to New York permanently. Then two competing offers came: a lead in a new off–Broadway play by acclaimed playwright Donald Margulies back in New York, or another lead on a network sitcom. "One was going to afford me money and fame," she recalled in an interview with *Cosmopolitan* writer Jennifer Kasle Furmaniak. "The other would take me back to the reason I'm an actor—the theater—and I'd be paid next to nothing." She agreed to do the play, *Collected Stories,* and earned impressive reviews for her performance in the two–person show when it opened in May of 1997 at the Manhattan Theater Club. She played Lisa, a Columbia University student who finds an unlikely mentor in Ruth (Maria Tucci), a celebrated writer of short stories. Over the next six years, Lisa moves from naïve hopeful to savvy publishing success, but her fame comes after she uses a confidential and painful episode of Ruth's life for literary inspiration. "Messing is good at rendering goofy callowness with a reflexive edge of self–interest," asserted the theater critic for the *New York Times,* Ben Brantley.

Messing later said that accepting the *Collected Stories* role "was the most important decision I've ever made in my professional life," she told Furmaniak in *Cosmopolitan.* "It was about risk taking and not looking back." During the play's run, she was offered a starring role in a sci–fi television series for ABC, *Prey,* which aired in 1997 as a mid–season replacement. She played scientist Sloan Parker, whose colleague and friend has been murdered. Parker continues the other bioanthropologist's research in secret, which seems to point to a new super–species created by global warning. The New York theater gig also led to a part for Messing in a Woody Allen film, *Celebrity.*

When *Prey* finished a shooting schedule that had stretched to 18–hour days, Messing informed her agent that she was exhausted and planned to take a few weeks off before auditioning for any new roles. The next day, she was informed that a production team for a new network comedy wanted her to read for a starring role. The show was *Will & Grace,* and its director, James Burrows, was a sitcom veteran with a string of successes behind him, among them

Taxi, Cheers, and *Frasier.* Her role was a New York City single with a history of failed relationships, who moves in with her old college flame in the pilot episode. Will is an attentive, attractive Manhattan lawyer who has since come to terms with his sexual orientation. The heterosexual actor playing him, Eric McCormack, was cast as the first openly gay leading male character in a network sitcom. Burrows and the show's creators, David Kohan and Max Mutchnick, came to Messing's home personally to plead their case. They brought vodka and asked her what would seal the deal for her. "So I told them, 'I need to meet Eric and work with him. Actually sit in a room and read with him and make sure it's there. Because you may think he is the perfect Will and I am the perfect Grace, but this show will not work unless there is real chemistry between the two of us—you can't fake it.'"

The principals agreed with her, and McCormack and Messing found their footing with one another immediately after a read-through. When it debuted in September of 1998, *Will & Grace* was a hit with viewers and critics alike. Messing's character was appealing from several standpoints: she ran her own successful interior design firm in SoHo, but had to endure an abrasive socialite assistant to help her land new clients. Exotically attractive and warm-hearted, Grace has nothing but war stories from the dating zone. The friendship with Will provides much-needed support and stability in her life. Both Messing and McCormick earned high marks for their on-screen repartee, while their two outrageous sidekicks—Grace's assistant, Karen (Megan Mullally), and Will's Broadway-bound friend, Jack (Sean Hayes)—provided additional comic fodder.

Critics wrote enthusiastically of *Will & Grace*'s charms. Reviewing it for the *Nation,* television critic Alyssa Katz commended the show's "winningly smart writing that makes a friendship between a gay man and a straight woman feel more fully realized than most TV relationships." Messing was also singled out by *Esquire*'s Carson for her talents. "No matter how smug *Will & Grace* can be about its own sophistication in making homosexuality safe for prime-time laughs," he noted, "Messing's presence keeps reminding you that sitcoms have barely tackled female heterosexuality yet. In her erotic scheming and frustration, she's a miniature Scarlett O'Hara. Without her, *Will & Grace* would be as disposable as it is clever."

Grace's dating travails over the next six seasons included a doomed romance with a boorish neighbor (Woody Harrelson), and marriage to the man of her dreams—a nice Jewish doctor played by heartthrob singer/pianist Harry Connick Jr. The show's success inspired an all-star roster of supporting characters and guest stars, from John Cleese to Madonna. It regularly scored in the Top 20 of television ratings each week, and McCormick, Mullally, and Hayes had all won Emmy awards. Messing herself had been nominated three times and lost to competitors like Patricia Heaton of *Everybody Loves Raymond,* but won in September of 2003 on her fourth go-round. "I was dumbstruck," she told *Houston Chronicle* writer David Kronke. "I was as relaxed as I've ever been at one of those events—they're pretty nerve-racking—because I was absolutely convinced that they would not be calling my name."

Not long afterward, Messing was forced to take an unscheduled hiatus from the last few episodes of Season Six when her pregnancy became too obvious to conceal, and her doctor ordered bed rest. She and Zelman, an actor and screenwriter, had married in September of 2000, and the show's writers had actually toyed with the idea of writing a possible pregnancy into the plot, with Grace carrying Will's child via artificial insemination. That plotline was thrown off by her wedding to Connick's do-gooder doctor, and Messing could not even appear in a special hour-long finale in April of 2004 that featured Karen's Las Vegas wedding and guest star Jennifer Lopez.

Messing has taken the occasional film role after her *A Walk in the Clouds* debut. They include a bit part as Richard Gere's wife in *The Mothman Prophecies,* a 2002 thriller, and a larger comic role in another Woody Allen film, *Hollywood Ending,* that same year. In the latter, she was cast as the dimwit actress/girlfriend of Allen's haughty auteur film-director character. Early in 2004 she appeared in *Along Came Polly* as Ben Stiller's wife, and later that year was slated to take on her first lead role in a film with *Something Borrowed.* The feature paired her with Dermot Mulroney in the story of a single woman whose desperation to take a date to her sister's London wedding inspires her to hire a male escort.

Will & Grace is filmed in Studio City, California, and Messing and Zelman make their home in the Hollywood Hills. She recalled in the interview with *Cosmopolitan*'s Abele that their early days as struggling Greenwich Village graduate students did not seem that far distant. "We lived in small studios with Murphy beds," she said. "We used to go out in the East Village and have soy-burger dinners for $2.95, and that would be our big splurge."

Sources

Cosmopolitan, May 2000, p. 218; February 2001, p. 194.
Daily Variety, September 22, 2003, p. 49.

Entertainment Weekly, September 8, 1995, p. 61; October 23, 1998, p. 24; May 14, 1999, p. 58; December 10, 1999, p. 87; October 13, 2000, p. 38; May 18, 2001, p. 64.

Esquire, October 2000, p. 170.

Houston Chronicle, February 26, 2004, p. 4.

Marie Claire, December 2002, p. 94.

Nation, November 2, 1998, p. 32.

Newsweek, January 28, 2002, p. 61; April 19, 2004, p. 71.

New York Times, November 21, 1996, p. C20; April 24, 1997; May 21, 1997; August 14, 1998.

People, May 13, 2002, p. 170; January 19, 2004, p. 24; April 19, 2004, p. 62.

Time, December 2, 1996, p. 92; April 19, 2004, p. 103.

Variety, April 29, 2002, p. 23.

—*Carol Brennan*

Metallica

Heavy metal group

Members include Kirk Hammett (replaced Dave Mustaine, 1983, who had replaced Lloyd Grant), lead guitar; James Hetfield, vocals, rhythm-guitar; Jason Newsted (replaced Cliff Burton, who died in a tour bus accident, 1986; left group, 2001), bass; Robert Trujillo (replaced Newsted), bass; Lars Ulrich, drums.

Addresses: *Record company*—Elektra Entertainment, 75 Rockefeller Plaza, New York, NY 10019, http://www.elektra.com. *Website*—http://www.metallica.com.

Career

Group formed, 1981; recorded *Kill 'Em All* on Elektra/Asylum Records, 1983; released multiplatinum–selling *Metallica*, 1991; released *Load*, 1996; released *Reload*, 1997; released *S&M*, a collection of concerts with the San Francisco Symphony, 1999; filed lawsuit against Napster for copyright violations, 2000; released *St. Anger*, 2003.

Awards: Grammy Award for best metal performance, Recording Academy, 1989; Grammy Award for best metal performance, Recording Academy, 1990; Grammy Award for best metal performance with vocal, Recording Academy, 1991; Grammy Award for best metal performance, Recording Academy, 1998; Grammy Award for best hard rock performance, Recording Academy, 1999; Grammy Award for best rock instrumental performance, 2000. Grammy Award for best metal performance, Recording Academy, for "St. Anger," 2004.

Sidelights

After more than 20 years, eleven albums, and six Grammy Awards, Metallica has more than proven its staying power as rock's preeminent metal group. The group paid its dues during the hair–band era of the 1980s, but Metallica's 1991 release addressed the decidedly adult topics of nuclear holocaust, mental illness, suicide, and the dangers of drug addiction. Yet despite these grim themes, Metallica's music runs contrary to heavy metal's one–dimensional image; their sound involves more than just bone–breaking chords and fire–and–brimstone lyrics. The band has distinguished itself with a grungy sophistication well beyond the work of its predecessors to become the seventh–largest–selling act in the history of American music as of 2001. Members of Metallica are rude and cheeky, but they are proficient. *Bass Player* magazine attested, "Their famous 'Metal Up Your A**' T–shirt ensured Metallica a notorious place in rock–and–roll history." Taste in merchandising notwithstanding, *Spin*'s Alec Foege called Metallica "a burnished black gem."

Metallica coalesced in 1981 with singer–guitarist James Hetfield, drummer Lars Ulrich, bass player Cliff Burton, and lead guitarist Dave Mustaine. Mustaine, who had taken over for early collaborator Lloyd Grant, was replaced in 1983 by Kirk Hammett. Their first album, *Kill 'Em All*, attracted droves of "head–banging" fans. The follow–up releases, *Ride the Lightning* and *Master of Puppets*, were greeted with even more enthusiasm by the world's heavy metal constituency, which enabled the band to strut their stuff with fellow "metalheads" on the enormous Monsters of Rock Tour. That outing featured a free concert in Moscow that was attended by 500,000 Soviet metal fans. Metallica was increasingly credited with single–handedly revitalizing heavy metal music, paving the way for other thrash bands like Slayer and Megadeath.

Tragedy struck Metallica on September 27, 1986, when the band's tour bus went into a ditch in Sweden, killing bassist Cliff Burton. After a brief hiatus, the band reassembled and began looking for a replacement for Burton. Attempting to fill the bass player's shoes and duplicate his eccentric, unbridled style seemed impossible. Burton had never been a particularly smooth player, but other band members had not attempted to reign him in. They did try once, however, to persuade him to forego his bell–bottom jeans in favor of more traditional heavy metal garb, but quickly realized the attempt was futile; Burton was set in his ways and rarely influenced by others. In truly bizarre heavy metal fashion, one of his dreams had been to invent a gun that shot knives instead of bullets.

To refurbish their lineup, the members of Metallica decided to settle on someone completely different from Burton: Jason Newsted, then with the Phoenix band Flotsam & Jetsam. Newsted was raised in Niles, Michigan, and had decided to turn professional after playing in bands throughout high school. He told *Bass Player*, "I heard Cliff had died the day after the accident.... I was a huge Metallica fan at the time. When I was looking at the blurb in the paper, I was sad, but things started flashing through my mind.... I just thought if I could play 'Four Horsemen' once with those guys, I'd be really happy."

Burton had been a remarkable soloist, but Newsted provided Metallica with a more cohesive sound. Burton's sound had not been well–defined, particularly when he played low on the guitar's neck. Newsted chose to mirror the band's guitar riffs precisely instead, producing a newly unified guitar effect. This sound dominated the new band's 1988 double album. Titled *... And Justice for All*, the record went multiplatinum by 1989 and earned a Grammy Award nomination, despite a dearth of radio airplay. The release of *Justice* coincided with Metallica's return to its musical roots: the groundbreaking metal stylings of 1970s rock giants Led Zeppelin and Black Sabbath. This resolve became the cornerstone for the 1991 release, *Metallica,* also known as the "Black" album.

Still steely, but a little slicker, *Metallica* was produced by Bob Rock, who had also worked with metal acts Mötley Crüe, Loverboy, and Bon Jovi. Buoyed by the dark, driving single "Enter Sandman," *Metallica* sold 2.2 million copies in its first week and has sold more than 15 million copies worldwide since its release. Metallica's hard–won versatility is showcased on the record with guitarist Hammett's winsome wah–wah, and open–throated, more melodic vocals from Hetfield. The band earned Grammys in both 1990 and 1991 and effectively ascended to a new strata of heavy metal superstardom. Featured on the covers of both *Rolling Stone* and *Spin,* Metallica's popularity seemed to know no bounds. With increased media coverage, it became clear that the band's appeal was not narrowly bohemian, political, or reflective of any trend—except perhaps anger. *Village Voice* contributor Erik Davis wrote that "Metallica's 'image'—dark shades, frowns, and poorly conceived facial hair—allies them with a musical culture of refusal. They haven't stopped dragging mud onto the carpet and slamming their bedroom doors without saying hello. 'Enter Sandman' has touched the brains of fry cooks and beer guzzlers across the land."

Analysis of Metallica's lyrics reveals the band's unique penchant for conjuring up the timeless grandiosity of myth by placing the object of a line before its subject: "This fight he cannot win," and "Off the beaten path I reign" are two examples. The band's head–banging thrash metal songs are short, but not sweet; they're delivered with grim, tight expressions, and a minimum of emotion, which gives the impression that the entire band is grimacing. Metallica's albums have few tender spots; songs range from the brutal "Sad But True" to the sweet and gritty "Ride the Lightning," from the praised pagan slant found on "Of Wolf And Man" to the metaphysical musings of "Through the Never." Commenting on their larger musical style— "Metallica's riffs crack like glaciers"—the *Village Voice's* Davis said of the band, "They hew thrash to a rigorous minimalism."

Worn out from touring during the early 1990s and a contract suit against Elektra, Metallica's next release was not to come until 1996. *Load,* the longest of the group's work with 14 songs, was a marked change in style and sound from the *Metallica* album. As described in the group's biography at its official website, the material was "loose, powerful and eclectic,

the sound thick and punchy and the image one which screamed out change and freedom from the enslavement to the Black album era." The group built on the critical success of the album and released an additional set of *Load* session tracks as *Reload* in 1997. Instead of simply revisiting *Load's* eclecticism, *Reload* offers "enough left curves to make it a better record," according to *All Music Guide's* Stephen Thomas Erlewine. *Spin's* Foege waxed mathematic in his assessment of Metallica, writing, "At turns algebraically elegant and geometrically raucous, present–day Metallica can stop and start on a dime."

The late 1990s and early 2000s brought new challenges for the group, both inside the studio and out. The group toured in support of *Load* and *Reload* in 1997 and 1998, and ventured into new musical territory in 1999 with *S&M,* a two–disc collection of concert performances with the San Francisco Symphony. The innovative collaboration between the groups featured orchestral arrangements behind Metallica classics such as "Master of Puppets," "One," "For Whom the Bell Tolls," "Sad But True," and "Of Wolf and Man." On April 14, 2000, the group, along with rapper Dr. Dre, filed suit against Napster, the website that facilitated the sharing of music files between personal computers for free, alleging violation of copyright laws. During a prolonged battle against the site by Metallica, Dre, and the Recording Industry Association of America (RIAA), the group managed to block 300,000 users who had downloaded copies of Metallica songs. The group and Dre settled their suit against Napster for an undisclosed amount in July of 2001.

In January of 2001, Newsted announced that he planned to leave Metallica after 14 years "due to private and personal reasons, and the physical damage that I have done to myself over the years while playing the music that I love.... This is the most difficult decision of my life, made in the best interest of my family, myself, and the continued growth of Metallica," according to comments at the Elektra Records website.

The group searched for a replacement for Newsted, ultimately deciding on Robert Trujillo to fill the spot. Trujillo had previously played bass in the rock group Suicidal Tendencies and backed up Ozzy Osbourne on a tour. Speaking to Charles Brookford for *Bass Player,* Trujillo confessed that he had a tough job ahead of him. "The biggest challenge for me is to come into a band like this and follow the footsteps of Cliff Burton and Jason Newsted. These guys are key parts of the band's history. This is a new Metallica, but they carry so much weight and I have full respect for them." Still, he concluded, "It's a great time to be a part of Metallica."

Hetfield entered an alcohol rehabilitation program in 2002, and committed himself to a sober lifestyle. When he emerged from rehab, the band began recording their next album, *St. Anger,* which was released in mid–2003. *St. Anger* was an immediate success, selling more than two million copies in less than two months. It was also a hit with critics, who praised the stripped–down urgency of the music. Brian McCollum of the Knight Ridder/Tribune News Service called the bare bones approach a "dirty, jagged rattle that recalls the band's early material. The careful textures and high–end gloss that had marked Metallica's past decade were abandoned in favor of a clanging, garage–metal crunch." In an interview with Ben Wener of the Knight Ridder/Tribune News Service, Hetfield credited his renewed sense of purpose and joy of playing with Metallica for allowing the band to continue through the rough patches of their two decades together. "Almost losing everything and then coming back and being extremely grateful for what *is* there—you know, brothers in the band—that's what it's all about."

Selected discography

Kill 'Em All, Elektra, 1983.

Ride the Lightning, Elektra, 1984.

Master of Puppets, Elektra, 1986.

... And Justice for All, Elektra, 1988.

Metallica, Elektra, 1991.

Live Sh**: Binge and Purge, Elektra, 1993.

Load, Elektra, 1996.

Reload, Elektra, 1997.

Garage, Inc., Polygram, 1998.

S&M, Elektra, 1999.

St. Anger, Elektra, 2003.

Sources

Periodicals

Bass Player, September/October 1991; August 2003.
EContent, August/September 2003.
Entertainment Weekly, June 13, 2003; June 20, 2003.
Knight Ridder/Tribune News Service, June 4, 2003; July 16, 2003; August 11, 2003.
Newsweek, September 23, 1991; June 9, 2003.
PC Magazine (United Kingdom), July 2000.
People, July 14, 2003.
Rolling Stone, November 14, 1991; March 19, 1992.
Spin, October 1991; December 1991.
Time, June 16, 2003.
Village Voice, September 18, 1991.
Washington Post, July 12, 2000, p. A23.
Wilson Library Bulletin, January 1992.

Online

"Metallica," *All Music Guide,* http://www.allmusic. com (December 1, 2003).
"Metallica, Dre Settle with Napster," Netscape, http://dailynews.netscape.com/mynsnews/ story.tmpl?table=n&cat=50880&id= 20010713071400120526 (December 1, 2003).
"Metallica News," Elektra Records, http://www. elektra.com/elektra/metallica/news.jhtml?qt= %22Metallica%22 (December 1, 2003).
Metallica Official Website, http://www.metallica. com (December 1, 2003).
"Napster, MusicNet Forge Deal With Strings Attached," *Billboard.com,* http://www.billboard.com (December 1, 2003).
The Recording Academy, http://www.grammy.com (December 1, 2003).

—*B. Kimberly Taylor*

Phil Mickelson

AP/Wide World Photos

Professional golfer

Born Philip Alfred Mickelson, June 16, 1970, in San Diego, CA; son of Phil (a pilot) and Mary Mickelson; married Amy; children: Amanda Brynn, Sophia, Evan. *Education:* Graduated from Arizona State University, bachelor's degree (psychology).

Addresses: *Home*—California. *Website*— http://www.phil–mickelson.com.

Career

Professional golfer. Wins include: Northern Telecom Open, 1991; Buick Invitational, 1993; Sprint International, 1993; Mercedes Championship, 1994; Northern Telecom, 1995; Nortel Open, 1996; Phoenix Open, 1996; GTE Byron Nelson, 1996; NEC World Series, 1996; Bay Hill Invitational, 1997; Sprint International, 1997; Mercedes Championship, 1998; AT&T Pebble Beach, 1998; Buick Invitational, 2000; Bellsouth Classic, 2000; Mastercard Colonial, 2000; Bob Hope Chrysler Classic, 2002; Bob Hope Chrysler Classic, 2004; Masters, 2004; Exelon Invitational, 2004.

Awards: Golf Digest Byron Nelson Award recipient (most wins on PGA TOUR), 1996; ESPY award for best championship performance, 2004; ESPY award for best male golfer, 2004.

Sidelights

Phil Mickelson, once crowned the golden boy of golf by many sportswriters, hall of fame golfers, and fans, was known for many years as "the best

player never to have won a major," noted *Sports Illustrated*. However, Mickelson taught not only his fellow competitors, but also golf fans, that loving your family and your sport is more important than winning. His determination paid off in 2004, when he won the Masters for his first major championship in more than 40 tries.

Phil Mickelson was born on June 16, 1970, in San Diego, California. And, as his website noted, he was "born to be a golfer." With a homemade golf club in his hand at only one–and–a–half, Mickelson, a natural right–hander, became a left–handed golfer when he stood in front of his father and mirrored his swing. In love with the game so much, Mickelson, at three, wanted to golf with his father one weekend that when he was told that he could not, he tried to run away. Finally, when he was almost four, he played his first 18 holes. He cried at the eighteenth green because he did not want to stop playing. "Phil would hit the ball and run to hit it again, never tiring," his website further noted.

In 1975, Mickelson entered and won the Harry McCarthy Putting Contest at the age of five, beating competitors who were as old as 13. His practice time turned into a game when he would "redesign the course to make things more interesting," his website stated. For example, he would stand on the seventh tee and hit to the fourth hole green. By the 1980s, he had not only won four junior events, he had also brought golf into his schoolwork. For his sixth grade science project, Mickelson tested golf balls to see which had the best compression for junior golfers. By age 14, he was studying with Dean Reinmuth, a popular teacher at the Golf Digest School. Reinmuth was so impressed with Mickelson that he became his coach.

Throughout his high school years, Mickelson continued his winning ways. Not only did he qualify for the San Diego and Los Angeles Opens as a junior, he also won 16 San Diego junior events and 12 American Junior Golf Association events. Yet, golf was not Mickelson's only interest. Encouraged by his mother, he took a music appreciation class. However, he incorporated golf into his studies by "comparing [composers'] music tempo to the tempo of the golf swing for different clubs," noted his website. "He associated every classic artist with a golf club."

In 1988, Mickelson entered Arizona State University to study psychology. However, as his college golf wins increased, including three NCAA Championships, many sportswriters, fans, and golf pros began to wonder why Mickelson had not left college to become a professional golfer. "School is a commitment I made," Mickelson told *Sports Illustrated,* "and I don't feel that the degree is as important as fulfilling my commitment." Mickelson also felt that the tournaments he played in college helped him progress and mature as a player. "I kind of set a four–year plan. I felt that in four years [while in college] I could advance my game and be strong enough to compete on the PGA [Professional Golf Association] Tour," he told *Sports Illustrated*. Mickelson, as an amateur, did play in PGA events, and won five of them. After graduating with a bachelor's degree in psychology, Mickelson turned pro.

In 1995, Mickelson entered the world of professional golf with great fanfare. One reporter for the *London Financial Times Weekend* enthusiastically announced, "Not since Jack Nicklaus ... has a young amateur excited the world of golf like Mickelson." At the 1992 U.S. Open, Mickelson's first PGA event as a professional was unsuccessful. He did not qualify for the tournament. However, he did anchor the team for the Ryder Cup competition and won all three of his matches.

Throughout the 1990s, Mickelson won many PGA tour events and became the second youngest player after Jack Nicklaus to win eleven of those events.

However, it was his demeanor and his inability to win a Major—the Masters, the U.S. Open, the British Open, and the PGA—which became the focus of critics and fans alike. Mickelson had always loved the game of golf, had studied its history and heritage, and had always impressed the U.S. Golf Association with both. Yet, many others felt that he had manufactured this image. Mickelson acknowledged to *Sports Illustrated* that "A golfer is an entertainer, much like an actor. People pay money to go out and watch you play, and I don't think they pay just to watch you hit a drive down the middle, hit a shot on the green, and two–putt."

By 1999, still unsuccessful at the Majors, Mickelson entered the U.S. Open and played to a tie for first place with Payne Stewart. However, a more important event was about to take place—the birth of his child, and Mickelson was ready to step off the course to see it—even if he had to step off during a possible playoff hole with Payne Stewart. "There's going to be a U.S. Open every year. The birth of my child was an experience that I will cherish for the rest of my life," he told *People*. Mickelson completed the tournament and watched Stewart break the tie with a 15–foot putt on the final hole. Nine hours later, he watched his baby daughter's birth.

By early 2002, Mickelson had still not won a major while still weathering his critics, who focused more on his style of play. "His pedal–to–the–metal mentality and slipshod course management skills," noted *Golf World,* had cost Mickelson many tournament wins. However, there was also another player preventing Mickelson from winning—Tiger Woods. And, unlike Woods, a methodical, quiet player, Mickelson would "rather crash and burn than play it safe," noted Knight Ridder/Tribune News Service. Mickelson further commented that "I need to go out and play an attacking style and try to make some noise."

Yet, no matter how much Mickelson attacks the course, he will always be considered a nice guy. The nice guy, who *Sports Illustrated* noted, "signs autographs 10 minutes past forever ... [who has] the manners of Jeeves and the charm of Bond." Despite being criticized for his risky play, Mickelson has not changed his demeanor or his game, "If I try to just hit fairways with irons, hit the middle of greens, it's not fun."

The year 2003 was not a good one for Mickelson. In March of that year, his wife, Amy, had nearly died in childbirth and their son, Evan, had gone seven minutes without a breath. "Phil was so shaken by the trauma that he sleepwalked through the 2003 season, his worst in 12 years on the PGA Tour," wrote *Sports Illustrated*'s Alan Shipnuck. He failed to win a tournament all year. At the year's end, Mickelson took a hard look at his body and his swing. He began watching what he ate and working out six times a week, which resulted in 15 pounds dropping off of him. He also reshaped his swing.

Mickelson's hard work paid off on January 25, 2004, when he won the Bob Hope Chrysler Classic. This was his fourth time as a professional that he began the season with a win. He had announced at the beginning of the tournament that he would donate $100 per birdie and $500 per eagle in 2004 to the Special Operations Warrior Foundation. The charity funds college educations for children of military special operations personnel killed in operational or training missions. In this tournament, Mickelson had 37 birdies and no eagles, which totaled $3,700 for the foundation.

Mickelson finally won a major golf championship on April 11, 2004, with his victory at the U.S. Masters tournament. He "completed the back nine in five–under 31, the lowest by a winner at Augusta National since Jack Nicklaus scorched round in 30 in 1986," according to the Asia Africa Intelligence Wire. It was his first major championship in more than 40 tries. According to *Sports Illustrated*'s Shipnuck, after his win Mickelson said, "It was an amazing, amazing day, the fulfillment of all my dreams."

Mickelson continued his winning ways. On June 7, 2004, Mickelson won the Exelon Invitational in Avondale, Pennsylvania. The event was hosted by fellow golfer Jim Furyk, who was sidelined after arthroscopic wrist surgery.

In 2004, Mickelson had finally proven to himself, his fans, and sports writers that he had the talent and determination to win a major tournament. Shipnuck declared that the "Masters should be not the culmination of a career but the beginning of a wondrous second act."

Sources

Periodicals

Asia Africa Intelligence Wire, April 13, 2004.
Golf World, March 23, 2001.
Knight Ridder/Tribune News Service, April 13, 2002.
London Financial Times Weekend, June 20, 1992.
Orange County Register (Santa Ana, CA), January 25, 2004.
People, July 12, 1999.
Philadelphia Enquirer, June 8, 2004.
Sports Illustrated, May 6, 1991; August 27, 2001; April 15, 2002; August 19, 2002, pp. 62–73; April 19, 2004, p. 52, p. 92.

Online

"Mickelson prevails in sudden–death chip–off," *SI.com*, http://sportsillustrated.cnn.com/2004/golf/06/07/bc.glf.exelon.ap/index.html (July 3, 2004).
"Phil Good Story," *SI.com*, http://sportsillustrated.cnn.com/2004/golf/specials/masters/2004/04/11/vansickle.mickelson/index.html (July 3, 2004).
"Phil's Facts," Phil Mickelson Online, http://www.phil–mickelson.com/x12.xml (July 3 , 2004).
"The Thrill of Victory," *SI.com*, http://si.cnn.com/2004/golf/01/25/bc.glf.hopeclassic.ap/index.html (July 3, 2004).

Anthony Minghella

AP/Wide World Photos

Playwright, screenwriter, director, and producer

Born January 6, 1954, in Ryde, Isle of Wight, England; married Carolyn Choa (a producer and choreographer); children: two. *Education:* University of Hull, Yorkshire, B.A. (drama, with honors), 1975.

Addresses: *Agent*—Michael Peretzian, CAA, 9830 Wiltshire Blvd., Beverly Hills, CA 90212; Judy Daish Associates, 2 St. Charles Place, London W10 6EG, England.

Career

Lecturer in drama, University of Hull, Yorkshire, 1976–81; chair, British Film Institute, 2003. Writer and director of plays, including: *Mobius the Stripper, Child's Play, Whale Music, Two Planks and a Passion, A Little Like Drowning,* 1984; *Made in Bangkok,* 1986. Director and screenwriter of films, including: *Truly, Madly, Deeply,* 1991; *Mr. Wonderful* (director only), 1993; *The English Patient,* 1996; *The Talented Mr. Ripley,* 1999; *Play,* 2000; *Cold Mountain,* 2003. Producer of films, including: *Iris,* 2001; *Heaven,* 2002; *The Quiet American,* 2002. Writer for television, including: *What If It's Raining* (movie), 1985; *Boon,* 1986; *Inspector Morse,* 1987; *Jim Henson's The Storyteller,* 1987; *Living with Dinosaurs* (movie), 1989.

Member: Directors Guild of America, Writers Guild of America, Writers Guild of Great Britain, European Film Academy.

Awards: Most promising playwright, London Theatre Critics Awards, for *A Little Like Drowning,* 1984; best play, London Theatre Critics Awards, for *Made in Bangkok,* 1986; best drama, Sony and Giles Cooper Award, for *Cigarettes and Chocolate,* 1988; Prix Italia for Radio Fiction, for *Hang Up,* 1988; best original screenplay, British Academy of Film and Television Arts, for *Truly, Madly, Deeply,* 1991; Academy Award for best director, Academy of Motion Picture Arts and Sciences, for *The English Patient,* 1997; Academy Award for best picture, Academy of Motion Picture Arts and Sciences, for *The English Patient,* 1997; Directors Guild of America Award for outstanding directorial achievement in motion pictures, for *The English Patient,* 1997; Golden Globe Award for best best director, Hollywood Foreign Press Association, for *The English Patient,* 1997; Golden Globe Award for best screenplay, Hollywood Foreign Press Association, for *The English Patient,* 1997; best film, British Academy of Film and Television Arts, for *The English Patient,* 1997; best adapted screenplay, British Academy of Film and Television Arts, for *The English Patient,* 1997; University of Hull, Yorkshire, D.Litt. (honorary), 1997; appointed a CBE (Commander of the British Empire) by the Queen of England, 2001.

Sidelights

Anthony Minghella received critical acclaim in 1996 as the screenwriter and director of *The English Patient,* a movie that garnered nine Academy

Awards (it was nominated for 12), including Best Picture and Best Director. Based on the 1992 Michael Ondaatje novel of the same name, it tells of two love affairs played out in the waning days of World War II.

The story of one of the affairs unfolds like a puzzle from the raspy voice of an aristocrat slowly dying from massive burns suffered when the two–seater airplane he piloted was shot down by the Germans over a vast expanse of North African desert. His lover, the woman in the passenger seat, did not survive. As he spins his romantic yarn to the French Canadian nurse who comforts him at his deathbed, flashbacks color in the details of a tragic love triangle that led to the fateful flight. The nurse is accustomed to loss as well. The war has claimed both her lover and her best friend. Tentatively, she begins another affair with an Indian mine sweeper in the employ of the British army. The movie intercuts between the two stories. "Backward into memory, forward into loss and desire," wrote critic Roger Ebert of the *Chicago Sun–Times,* "*The English Patient* searches for answers that will answer nothing. This poetic, evocative film ... circles down through the layers of mystery until all of the puzzles in the story have been solved, and only the great wound of a doomed love remains." That the nearly three–hour movie succeeds as an epic and as intimate psychological drama, as historical pageant and as lyric poem (it received wide critical acclaim and was a commercial success), is a testimony to Minghella's artistry.

Many believed that Ondaatje's Booker Prize-winning novel was unfilmmable because of its difficult narrative structure. In an online *Mr. Showbiz* interview Minghella said, "The book, can, in a single page, change voice and location and period a dozen times.... The novel is a bit like a notebook, a book of ideas and thoughts and images. Parading through every page are these incredible images which arrest you, but storytelling in film is very significant, and Michael's book is anti–narrative and anti-psychology. The burden for the film was to lasso all these images, or as many as I could collect, and make it into a film that felt coherent and had some psychological density." The *Chicago Sun–Times'* Ebert wrote, "The novel is so labyrinthine that it's a miracle it was filmed at all, and the writer–director, Anthony Minghella, has done a creative job of finding visual ways to show how the rich language slowly unveils layers of the past." The achievement is all the more remarkable when one considers that Minghella had directed only two feature films— both enjoying only moderate success—before *The English Patient.*

Minghella, the son of Italian immigrants (his father is an ice–cream maker), was born in 1954 on the Isle of Wight. "I don't consider myself to be remotely English," Minghella told Kathleen O'Steen of the *Washington Post,* "and yet when I come to the States, I become the token Englishman. It's very strange." A movie theater stood next door to the Minghella house. The theater's projectionist befriended the young Minghella and he viewed many movies for free. He remembers in particular a Fellini film about boys living in a seaside Italian resort town. Minghella recalled for O'Steen, "The tone and everything about the film was so familiar to me that it was then I truly realized I wasn't English."

Minghella graduated from the University of Hull in England, and subsequently accepted a position as a lecturer there, writing and directing plays on the side. Early on the variety of his dramatic efforts won him praise. *Whale Music* has an unwanted pregnancy as its subject. *A Little Like Drowning* shows the destructive effects of adultery on an Italian Catholic family. *Two Planks and a Passion* is set in fourteenth–century York as its citizens prepare for staging the Mystery Plays for the Feast of Corpus Christi for King Richard II. *Made in Bangkok* is a comedy about the sexual opportunism of a group of tourists in Thailand. The London Theatre Critics named Minghella the most promising playwright in 1984 and named *Made in Bangkok* best play of the year in 1986.

Minghella branched out into radio and television productions of his plays in the 1980s. Beginning in 1987 he wrote several episodes for the Emmy-winning NBC anthology series, *Jim Henson's The Storyteller.* The show recounted folk tales and myths in an entertaining manner and Minghella directed the short film *Living with Dinosaurs* for *The Storyteller.* Minghella also wrote episodes for *Inspector Morse,* a popular British detective series.

Truly, Madly, Deeply, Minghella's first attempt at writing and directing a feature film, met with great success in England, but only moderate success elsewhere. An unconventional comic love story, *Truly, Madly, Deeply* opens with the main character grieving over the death of her boyfriend. His ghost comes back with a bunch of his friends and they wreak emotional havoc like the dearly departed who haunt Noel Coward's classic play *Blithe Spirits.* Critic Stanley Kauffmann of the *New Republic* called the movie "neat, well–acted, and literate," but added that "its story is sentimental slush, and old slush at that." *Nation* contributor Stuart Klawans stated that "the dialogue is ... smarter than what you're used to hearing; and Minghella's direction ... accomplishes what it sets out to do, by letting the events sneak up on you."

Mr. Wonderful, Minghella's first Hollywood directorial effort (he did not write the screenplay), was less successful. In the film, a New York City electrical worker tries to get his ex–wife married off so that he can recoup on the alimony he's been paying and invest it in a bowling alley. Of the "matchmaker" plot, *Entertainment Weekly* critic Owen Gleiberman wrote, "This low–watt gimmick … is like something you'd see in a hack comedy…. What's more, it's obvious that Minghella couldn't care less about it. He's looking for feelings, not farce." On the experience of making a "Hollywood" film like *Mr. Wonderful,* Minghella told Jonathan Coe of the *New Statesman,* "Language in an American film is always used as a character device…. Characters always tell you what they're feeling and thinking and what they need, whereas I'd never come across that in my life. I think it's often the failure to speak, the inability to say what we feel, which is intriguing." It is this sentiment that informs so much of his writing in the screenplay of *The English Patient.*

Minghella spoke of the joys of the writing and directing films to Tomm Carroll of *DGA Magazine:* "One thing is clear to me—that the writing process in film is a continuous one, and I mean that in a literal and a metaphorical sense, insofar as that not only does the writer need to work throughout the film process and into the cutting room, but also the director is a writer in the film. Essentially, the director is the author. I know that's a contentious remark. I'm a writer first and foremost, but it's quite evident to me that the camera is the second pen at work in the film. So, if you're interested in being a filmmaker, it seems imperative that you continue that writing process with a camera."

The public had to wait three years until Minghella's next film, *The Talented Mr. Ripley,* was released. Adapted from Patricia Highsmith's 1953 suspense novel, the film is the story of a love triangle between a playboy, his girlfriend, and a fellow tourist that they meet during a trip through Italy; it starred Matt Damon, Jude Law, and Gwyneth Paltrow. Minghella told *WWD*'s Hilary de Vries, "The film is very concerned with the beguiling surface and the chaos that lurks beneath that…. It's about beauty with thorns." Filled with "enough betrayal and passion to fill a season's worth of soaps," according to *Entertainment Weekly*'s Rebecca Ascher–Walsh, the film performed well at the box office. Minghella received Academy Award and Golden Globe nominations for his screenplay and a Golden Globe nomination for directing the film.

Minghella's next film, *Cold Mountain,* almost did not happen. Minghella had first heard of the National Book Award–winning Charles Frazier novel

when he received a copy while staying at a friend's cabin. However, since he had no interest in doing another adaptation, he did not read it. However, when he arrived home, he found three more copies, sent by an editor and two film companies. So, he read the book and fell in love with the "collisions of cruelty and generiosity" in the novel, according to Jeff Giles of *Newsweek.* Minghella's film adaptation of the novel tells the story of a Confederate deserter and the girlfriend he is trying to get home to late in the Civil War. Although the film had a $90 million budget, the director met nothing but hardship. Filmed in Romania (to stand in for North Carolina and Virginia), the cast and crew dealt with "punishing heat and 20–odd consecutive days of rain," Giles explained. While the film was yet another one based on a previously published source, Minghella explained to Bruce Newman of Knight Ridder/Tribune News Service, "I want to think I have a film in me that is not an adaptation, that is not historical. But I know it's likely that I will do another book. The trouble is that I love the canvas of film, love the scale of it." The film was released on December 25, 2003. It earned eight Golden Globe nominations from the Hollywood Foreign Press Association, including best director and best screenplay nods for Minghella.

In 2004, Minghella executive produced *The Interpreter,* and was working on producing, directing, and writing the script for *The Assumption.* In February of that year, he announced that he would write and direct an adaptation of the Liz Jensen novel, *The Ninth Life of Louis Drax.* He also planned to direct a film version of Alexander McCall Smith's *The No. 1 Ladies' Detective Agency.* Plus, Minghella planned to produce a film called *Appearances* in 2005. With many projects in the works, it seems certain that he will be in the public eye for a long time.

Selected writings

Plays

Mobius the Stripper (adapted from a story by Gabriel Josipovici; also director), produced in Hull, England, 1975.
Child's Play (also director) produced in Hull, England, 1978.
Whale Music (produced in London and Methuen, 1987; also director), S. French (New York, NY), 1983, reprinted, with *A Little Like Drowning* and *Two Planks and a Passion,* as *Whale Music: Three Plays,* 1987.
A Little Like Drowning (produced at Hampstead Theatre, London, England, 1984), published in *Whale Music: Three Plays,* 1987.

Two Planks and a Passion (produced in Exeter, 1983; London, 1984), published in *Whale Music: Three Plays,* 1987.

Love Bites, produced in Derby, England, 1984.

Made in Bangkok, produced in Lond, 1986.

Interior: Room, Exterior: City (includes *Cigarettes and Chocolate, Hang Up,* and *What If It's Raining?*), produced in Methuen, 1989.

Plays 1 (includes *Made in Bangkok, Whale Music, A Little Like Drowning,* and *Two Planks and a Passion*), produced in London, 1992.

Living with Dinosaurs and One–Act Plays and Sketches, produced in London, 1995.

Plays 2, produced in London and Methuen, 1997.

Screenplays

Truly, Madly, Deeply (also director), Heinemann (London), 1991.

The English Patient (also director), Hyperion Miramax (New York, NY), 1996.

The Talented Mr. Ripley (also director; based on the book by Patricia Highsmith), Paramount/Miramax, 1999.

Cold Mountain (also director), Miramax Films, 2003.

Also adapted *Made in Bangkok* for film.

Television plays

Studio series, 1983.

What If It's Raining, 1986.

Inspector Morse (based on the characters created by Colin Dexter), 1987 and 1990.

"Hans My Hedgehog?" (also known as "The Grovelhog"), "Fearnot," "A Short Story," "The Lucky Child," all for *Jim Henson's The Storyteller,* NBC, 1987–88.

Signals (opera), 1989.

Radio plays

Hang Up, 1987.

Cigarettes and Chocolate, 1988.

Sources

Periodicals

Chicago Sun–Times, November 22, 1996.

Daily Variety, December 19, 2003, p. A3.

DGA Magazine, vol. 22–2, May/June 1997.

Entertainment Weekly, October 29, 1993, pp. 42–43; January 22, 1999, p. 46.

Knight Ridder/Tribune News Service, December 18, 2003; December 29, 2003.

Nation, June 24, 1991, pp. 862–64.

New Republic, May 27, 1991, pp. 26–27.

New Statesman, March 7, 1997, pp. 38–40.

Newsweek, September 1, 2003, pp. 50–52.

People, December 22, 2003, p. 27.

Washington Post, November 22, 1996.

WWD, November 30, 1999, p. 4.

Online

"Against all odds, *English Patient* hits the big screen," CNN.com, http://cnn.com/SHOWBIZ/9611/14/english.patient (April 6, 2004).

"Anthony Minghella," Internet Movie Database, http://us.imdb.com/name/nm0005237 (April 6, 2004).

"Minghella wins Directors Guild Award," E! Online, http://www.eonline.com/News/Items/0,1,769,00.html (April 6, 2004).

Mr. Showbiz, http://www.mrshowbiz.com/interviews/308_1.html (December 31, 1998).

Monica

AP/Wide World Photos

R&B singer

Born Monica Denise Arnold, October 24, 1980, in College Park, GA; daughter of M.C. Arnold, Jr. (a mechanic) and Marilyn Best (a consumer affairs officer for an airline).

Addresses: *Record company*—J Records, 745 Fifth Ave., New York, NY 10051, http://www.j–records. com. *Website*—http://www.monica.com.

Career

Joined Charles Thompson and the Majestics (traveling gospel choir) at the age of ten; signed to Rowdy Records, 1993; signed to Arista Records, c. 1994; released debut album, *Miss Thang,* 1995; song "For You I Will," on *Space Jam* soundtrack, 1996; released album *The Boy Is Mine,* 1998; released *After the Storm,* 2003.

Awards: Grammy Award for best R&B duo with vocal (with Brandy), Recording Academy, for "The Boy is Mine," 1998.

Sidelights

In 1995 Atlanta, Georgia, native Monica became the youngest artist ever to achieve two No. 1 hits on the *Billboard* R&B singles chart in the same year. In an era when her teen cohorts in the industry, such as Brandy and Aaliyah, also enjoy massive chart success, the gospel–trained singer easily won praise for both her talent, self–possession, and her down–to–earth demeanor. "Monica stood apart from the crowd of one–name teenage divas with her rich, soulful voice and her unbridled confidence," wrote Melissa Ewey in *Ebony.* Some of that soul and maturity may be the result of her child-hood—she was raised with three brothers in a single–parent household, and has battled various critical snipes and salacious rumors since the start of her career. "You can hear the struggle in her voice; it's husky, gospel–tinged, knowing," declared Veronica Chambers in *Newsweek.* "Forget about her age—unlike her teen counterparts, Monica makes music for grown–ups," she added.

Born Monica Arnold on October 24, 1980, she was joined by a quick succession of three brothers be-fore her parents split when she was just four. She would have little contact with her mechanic father, M.C. Arnold, Jr., until she became a celebrity. Monica and her brothers were raised by her mother, Marilyn, who worked full–time to support them, with help from her own mother. Monica's mother eventually became a consumer affairs official at Delta Air Lines and was remarried to a minister, Dr. E.J. Best, in 1993. While the singer was on promo-tional tours for her first album, she told *Ebony*'s Ewey, she met other teens who had also been through less–than–idyllic childhoods. "They were surprised that I went through a lot of the same things they had, like there were nights when my mother didn't eat so I could," Monica said.

Despite her rough work schedule, Marilyn was also devoted to her church and choir, and passed on that love of gospel music to her daughter. Growing up in College Park, Georgia—a suburb of Atlanta—Monica began singing in the church choir alongside her mother when she was just a toddler. As a child in the mid–1980s, Monica was a huge fan of Whitney Houston, who enjoyed a string of hits throughout the decade. One song in Houston's repertoire—which also reflected her own heavy–duty gospel background—was "The Greatest Love of All," and Monica made this song her own when she first sang it publicly at the age of nine. An obvious vocal prodigy, she joined a traveling gospel choir, Charles Thompson and the Majestics, at the age of ten.

Soon Monica was winning honors in Atlanta–area talent shows with "The Greatest Love of All," and at one of them a record–industry scout introduced himself and set up an introduction for her with one of his friends, famed producer Dallas Austin. An executive of Atlanta's Rowdy Records, Austin's resume included work with Madonna and Boyz II Men. Though the Rowdy label later went under, Austin had an affiliation with Arista Records, one of the music industry's pop and rock giants. Monica began working with Austin on improving her voice and developing her songwriting skills, and at the age of 13 sang for Arista's legendary president, Clive Davis. Davis had been instrumental in charting the careers of Toni Braxton and Houston, and signed Monica to the label.

When her debut album, *Miss Thang,* was released in 1995, Monica was just 14 years old. The LP reached No. 7 on the *Billboard* R&B album charts, and she scored a No. 1 hit with the first single, "Don't Take It Personal (Just One of Dem Days)," which featured a young woman telling her boyfriend she needed her space. The next single, "Before You Walk Out of My Life," also reached No. 1 that same year, which earned Monica a spot in chart history as the youngest artist ever to have two hit singles. "Why I Love You So Much," a third single from *Miss Thang,* was released in 1996.

Monica had co–written the songs with Austin over a two–year period when she was between the ages of 12 and 14. Given the all–knowing, heartache–laden themes of her vocals, Austin and Arista were criticized for burdening such a young talent with decidedly adult topics. But as Monica told Elysa

Gardner in the *Los Angeles Times*, the songs reflected her own peer–group experiences and were collaborative efforts based on incidents in her life. "People may wonder how I know about relationships, but I think the fact is that society is producing more adult teenagers. I would definitely say that a lot of my friends grew up faster. I mean, you're just a product of your environment," the singer said.

Few teens, no matter how mature, could enjoy a single on the soundtrack of a Michael Jordan movie ("For You I Will," featured in the animated film *Space Jam*) at the same time she graduated from an exclusive private school a year ahead of schedule with a 4.0 grade–point average. Monica had accomplished this despite a heavy touring schedule since the 1995 release of *Miss Thang*; Atlanta Country Day School had provided a tutor who went with her on tour and allowed Monica to fit her classtime in according to her energy level—meaning she was often hitting the books late at night after a performance. "There really wasn't a tough subject, there were just tough times," the singer told *Jet* magazine about her accomplishment.

Still, Monica did face tough times in the press after her stellar debut. During the long hiatus between *Miss Thang* and *The Boy Is Mine,* released by Arista in 1998, her career was continually plagued by rumors that she and another teen R&B one–name star, Brandy, were intense rivals; the two had become singing stars around the same time and were nearly the same age. There were also rumors that Monica had had a child, which she adamantly denied—a pregnancy that with her size–two frame and touring schedule would have been difficult to conceal at some point.

In interviews Monica always stressed the close and positive relationship she enjoyed with her own mother. Furthermore, her singing career is managed by her cousin, Melinda Dancil. Her aunt is the proprietor of an Atlanta salon, but Monica has encountered far less hospitable receptions at other establishments. "I'm a young black woman, and I may walk into a certain area where the women are older and they're housewives and they don't really relate to me and how I dress," Monica told Jancee Dunn in *Rolling Stone*. "It's so odd—you see the difference on the days that I dress up and put on the jewelry that I own and the days that I put my hair in a ponytail and wear sweats. I walk into some jewelry stores, I can't get help. It always goes that way," she continued.

Like *Miss Thang, The Boy Is Mine* would earn its own place in R&B chart history. It gave Monica another platinum record for the creative collaboration with Austin; Rodney Jerkins and Jermaine Dupri were among some other notable names involved as songwriters or producers. The first hit single, however, came before the LP was even released: the extremely successful duet with Brandy, "The Boy Is Mine." The song, which spent two months at No. 1 on the *Billboard* R&B chart in the summer of 1998, was an antagonistic vocal duel between two young women fighting over the same two–timing heel. It was designed as a remake of sorts on the Paul McCartney–Michael Jackson hit "The Girl Is Mine."

But rumors about the Monica–Brandy acrimony, that the song had ostensibly aimed to put to rest, only increased. The single was released in May, did very well, and then Brandy performed it by herself on the *Tonight Show with Jay Leno*; then, as Craig Seymour of the *Village Voice* chronicled, "Monica fires off a statement to MTV that Brandy's solo performance 'hurt our song.' Meanwhile, Brandy's off on the sneak recording a solo remix that is leaked to radio, only to be pulled because, according to a label source, contracts forbade altering the song in any way. At this point, Monica has 'had about enough' and decides to name her whole ... album *The Boy Is Mine*."

Monica's second album enjoyed success equal to her debut and received positive reviews. Other singles from it also did well, such as "The First Night"—celebrating a young woman's refusal to acquiesce to sex—as well as "Angel of Mine" and "Street Symphony," a sad teen lament about a girl's attempt to halt her boyfriend's forays into drug dealing; the Atlanta Symphony Orchestra was brought in to back Monica on the song in the studio.

Despite the success, the Monica–Brandy issue again arose after the 1998 MTV Music Awards, held in September of that year in Los Angeles, California. The pair performed the song for the first time live together, but rumors erupted that they had come to blows during rehearsals, and this was the reason for the great distance between them on stage during the number. A black eye and swollen lip were supposedly camouflaged by makeup and lighting. A joint press release denied the altercation, blaming unnamed persons for creating a media rift when none existed between the two. The statement maintained that the stars were on friendly terms. "Such ongoing negativity is totally unfair to these two talented teenagers, both of whom are simply working hard to build successful careers in a very tough business," it concluded.

Monica and Brandy shared a Grammy Award for Best R&B Duo with Vocal for "The Boy is Mine." The alleged rift between the two stars soon fell off the media radar as Monica had more serious problems to face. Less than a year after her Grammy win, Monica's best friend and cousin Selena Glenn died of a sudden brain aneurysm at the age of 25. The next year, Monica received a phone call from a distraught Jarvis Weems, her first boyfriend. She rushed to meet him, but could not stop him from taking his own life. Unable to do anything, Monica watched as Weems shot himself in a locked car. As Monica struggled to get over the shock of Weems' death, her current beau, rapper C–Murder (born Corey Miller, and the brother of No Limit founder Master P), was convicted of second–degree murder and sentenced to life in prison.

Just one of these events would have been devastating; having to go through all three in two years, and at such a young age, tested Monica's strength and faith. "Most people I love are either dead or in jail," she told Steve Dougherty in *People*. "For a while it was one day at a time. I didn't eat, didn't sleep or drink. I wondered how I would ever heal." Monica chose not to seek professional counseling, relying on her family and close friends to help her through the difficult years. She entered the studio again after a four–year absence and began recording her third album, *After the Storm*. Debuting at the number–one spot on the *Billboard* Top 200 charts, *After the Storm* was produced by Monica's close friend Missy "Misdemeanor" Elliott and features collaborations with R&B singer Tyrese and rapper DMX.

After her hiatus from the music business, Monica has a fresh take on fame and success. Her time away helped her to realize the importance of her family and friends, and allowed her to emotionally prepare to return to the spotlight after a trying couple of years. "It's easy for me [to return] just because I've been gone for so long. I've had the time to really get to know myself ... and do things that most women get a chance to do if they are not involved in the music industry," she confessed to *Jet* writer Margena Christian. "I appreciate coming back in a different way."

Selected discography

(Contributor) *Panther* (soundtrack), Mercury, 1995.
Miss Thang, Rowdy/Arista, 1995.
(Contributor) *Nutty Professor* (soundtrack), Def Jam, 1996.
(Contributor) *Fled* (soundtrack), Rowdy, 1996.
(Contributor) *Space Jam* (soundtrack), Atlantic, 1996.
(Contributor) *Soul Food* (soundtrack), La Face, 1997.
The Boy Is Mine, Arista, 1998.

(Contributor) *Big Momma's House* (soundtrack), Sony, 2000.
After the Storm, J Records, 2003.

Sources

Periodicals

Billboard, June 20, 1998; October 3, 1998; July 5, 2003.
Ebony, September 1998; August 2000; October 2003.
Entertainment Weekly, July 18, 2003.
Hollywood Reporter, June 26, 2003.
Jet, July 7, 1997; October 5, 1998; July 19, 1999; July 28, 2003.
Los Angeles Times, July 7, 1998.

Newsweek, July 27, 1998.
People, August 3, 1998; May 10, 1999; June 30, 2003.
Rolling Stone, December 24, 1998.
Vibe, October 1998.
Village Voice, July 29, 1998.
WWD, June 13, 2003.

Online

"Monica," *All Music Guide,* http://www.allmusic.com (November 20, 2003).
Monica Official Website, http://www.monica.com (November 20, 2003).

—Carol Brennan

Les Moonves

AP/Wide World Photos

Co-President and Co-Chief Operating Officer of Viacom, Inc.

Born October 6, 1949, in New York; married Nancy Wiesenfeld (an actress); children: three. *Education:* Earned degree from Bucknell University, 1971; took acting classes at the Neighborhood Playhouse, New York City.

Addresses: *Office*—Viacom, 1515 Broadway, New York, NY 10036.

Career

Actor and bartender in New York City, c. 1972–77, and in Los Angeles, CA, 1977–79; made guest appearances in the television shows *The Six Million Dollar Man* and *Cannon*; producer of plays in Los Angeles, including *The Hasty Heart*; worked in development for Saul Ilson Productions, a part of Columbia Pictures Television, c. 1979–81; worked for Twentieth Century Fox in its movies and miniseries development department after 1981; became head miniseries production, 1983; development executive, Lorimar Television, 1984–86, head of creative affairs, 1988, president, 1989; president, Warner Bros. Television, after 1991; became president of entertainment, CBS Television, July, 1995; became president of CBS Television, August, 1997; became chair and chief executive officer, April, 1998; named head of UPN by Viacom, CBS's parent company, 2002; named co-president and co-chief operating officer, Viacom Inc., 2004.

Sidelights

Les Moonves has been deemed the network television executive responsible for bringing *Survivor* and the reality–TV craze that followed to the airwaves. As chair and chief executive officer of the CBS Television network, this tanned, affable, former actor known as "Mr. Hollywood" in entertainment circles is regularly ranked as one of the most powerful people in show business. Moonves came aboard at CBS at a time when the once–dominant broadcaster was suffering from low ratings, a paucity of new hit shows, and general industry ridicule. In the space of a few short years, he became the force credited with "resuscitating it from cobwebbed irrelevance and reasserting its dominance through a combination of classically mainstream hits," noted *New York Observer* reporter Jason Gay. "Along the way, Mr. Moonves has also revived the faded concept of the single–headed entertainment empire.... For better and for worse, he's become indistinguishable from his network, and his network has become indistinguishable from him."

Born in 1949, Moonves grew up in Valley Stream, a community in Long Island's Nassau County. His father owned gas stations in the New York City area, and Moonves recalled "Saturday mornings: getting up with him in the middle of winter in Long Island, driving into Brooklyn," he told *Variety* writers Josef Adalian and Michael Schneider. "I hated it. I said, 'This sucks.' My father didn't mind, and he made a good living, but that wasn't what I wanted." Instead, Moonves planned on becoming a doctor, and spent four years at Bucknell University in Pennsylvania in its pre–med curriculum. By the time he graduated in 1971, however, he had changed his mind and decided to move to New York City to become an actor. "Needless to say, my parents were a little upset," he admitted a 1990 interview that appeared in *Broadcasting.*

For the next six years, Moonves lived in Greenwich Village, took acting classes at the Neighborhood Playhouse, and supported himself as a bartender at the famed Tavern on the Green restaurant. He wed a fellow thespian, Nancy Wiesenfeld, and the two moved to Los Angeles in 1977. Forced to bartend there as well to earn a living, Moonves had a difficult time finding work outside of an occasional thug role on television series like *The Six Million Dollar Man* and *Cannon,* but he found his way into producing plays in small venues around town. "I finally realized that as an actor you're sort of dependent on other people to take care of your career," he told *Broadcasting,* "and I didn't like that."

Moonves produced a winner with *The Hasty Heart,* a drama that went on to enjoy a successful run at the Ahmanson Theater and even won the Los Angeles Drama Critics Award. The coup helped him land a job with a production company on the Columbia Pictures Television lot, where he worked in comedy development. Less than a year later, he moved over to Twentieth Century Fox, working in TV–movie development. In 1984 he went to work at Lorimar Television, one of the most successful small–screen content providers of the era. There, Moonves brought miniseries like *The Two Mrs. Grenvilles,* based on the Dominick Dunne book, and the Emmy–nominated *I Know My First Name Is Steven* to the screen in the late 1980s, and also became head of series production in 1986, which entailed supervising such hit shows as *Dallas, Knots Landing,* and *Falcon Crest.* In 1988, he was named head of creative affairs, and given the president's chair the next year.

Moonves' career took off in earnest when Lorimar merged with a Warner–empire business in 1991 to become Warner Bros. Television. WBTV was a well–funded entity with access to some of the best creative minds in Hollywood, and under Moonves' guidance produced a slew of hit shows for all of the networks. He placed some 20 hit shows on the

1995–96 fall schedule alone, including *Friends* and *ER,* but before that season started, Moonves was lured to CBS to take over as the network's entertainment–division president.

At the time, CBS was in last place among the three major broadcast networks. It had been "the network that both created and defined television," noted Nancy Hass in *Los Angeles Magazine,* and "the most influential network in history.... NBC and ABC were pale reflections that only set off CBS's originality, its sense of purpose, its credibility." That reputation was severely tarnished by the mid–1990s, however. A decade earlier, its chief, Laurence Tisch, had taken over and made a slew of profit–focused decisions that essentially gutted the network. It missed out on the cable boom, lost the National Football League (NFL) broadcast contract to the upstart Fox network—and with it eight big–city affiliate stations—and failed to launch any promising new series. In the ratings game, it was the most–watched network in rural households in the United States, with a programming slate heavy with shows that appealed to older viewers, such as *Touched by an Angel* and *Dr. Quinn, Medicine Woman*; the Candace Bergen sitcom *Murphy Brown* was its sole across–the–board hit. CBS was roundly derided as the "geezer" network when Moonves took over, despite a recent attempt to lure a younger, hip audience with shows like *Central Park West.* Its ratings for the fall 1995 season were abysmal.

"For the first eight months of this job I woke up every morning thinking, 'God, what have I done?,'" Moonves told Hass in the *Los Angeles Magazine* interview. Yet the well–liked executive with a solid track record was given free rein, and immediately began contacting teams of writers and producers to come up with new ideas. One result was *Everybody Loves Raymond,* a retro–style sitcom about a married couple and their in–laws that debuted in the fall of 1996. Critics largely ignored it, but the show caught on with viewers despite a tough Friday–night time slot, and within a few years it was racking up Emmy nominations. Named president of CBS Television in August of 1997, Moonves went on to engineer a deal that brought the NFL back to the network, which returned the all–important opportunity to promote new CBS shows to a younger audience. In early 1998, CBS came in first in the February sweeps for the first time since 1995, boosted by its broadcast of the Winter Olympics in Nagano, Japan. A few months later, Moonves was made president and chief executive officer of CBS, which gave him more input into the news division, once the crown jewel of the network. He was responsible for a weeknight version of the CBS staple, *60 Minutes II,* and greenlighted the fall 1999 debut of *Judging Amy,* another popular Emmy–winning series.

Moonves nearly missed out on what would prove to be the network's turnaround show: *Survivor*. The show belonged to a new wave of reality–TV shows, borrowed in part from European hits. *Survivor* grouped several strangers on a deserted island and forced them to participate in various tests of strength, endurance, and meals of stomach–turning cuisine. Each week, the participants voted someone off the island. Once it debuted in May of 2000, the characters quickly became household names and the show added new viewers every week, until 58 million viewers tuned in for the first–season finale. Moonves had initially been skeptical about the show, as he told *Broadcasting & Cable* reporter Paige Albiniak. "The first two times I heard it pitched to me, I almost threw [CBS's head of alternative programming] Ghen Maynard out of my office. I told him, 'This is CBS; this isn't some cable network.' But Ghen had the fortitude to keep pushing me."

Moonves and the network scored another hit later that year with the debut of *CSI: Crime Scene Investigation,* and it was his decision to move the popular drama and the subsequent *Survivor* sequels to Thursday night, in order to battle it out in the ratings with NBC. It was a risky maneuver, forcing the shows to compete against both *Friends* and *Will & Grace* and, moreover, to challenge NBC's longstanding lead in the Thursday–night ratings race—but the CBS shows began beating the competition. "That changed the face of the network," Moonves told Gay in the *New York Observer* article, though he admitted it was a daring move. "We could have been destroyed."

The turnaround that Moonves achieved at CBS was so impressive that the entertainment–industry bible *Variety* named him "Showman of the Year" in 2000, and he began topping *Entertainment Weekly*'s annual "Suits" Power List that year as well. He became so well–known that David Letterman even began knocking him on his late–night CBS show. Irate at one point, Moonves reportedly walked over from his CBS offices to Letterman's in the Ed Sullivan Theater and the two had an unfruitful meeting that resulted in Letterman ribbing his boss further with a Top Ten list, "Things Overheard at a Meeting with Les Moonves."

In early 2002, Viacom, CBS's parent company, named Moonves head of the ailing UPN, a money–losing property that had bled $1 billion since 1995. The added duty made Moonves the first executive in history to run two networks. "I did sort of sit back the day after it happened and say, 'This is pretty amazing,'" he told *Broadcasting & Cable*'s Joe Schlosser. "But you don't look at history while on the job. There are days when I sit back and say, 'Who was great in this business?'" He named several legendary broadcast visionaries, including the late Brandon Tartikoff, who brought NBC to dominance in the 1980s, and Grant Tinker, creator of the *Mary Tyler Moore* show. "I guess the answer is that none of them had this opportunity to play on two playing fields with very different demographics," Moonves reflected. "I think I would like to be remembered for running successful networks, not running two networks."

In 2002, CBS attained the number–one spot for total viewership, and was much closer to NBC than ever before in the crucial 18–to–49 age group. It was a solidly profit–earning network as well, and by this point Moonves' kingdom included all CBS programming, including news and sports, the daily operations of UPN, some 39 television stations, and King World, the company that produces both *Oprah* and the *Dr. Phil* show. In 2003, CBS racked up a record seven Emmy awards, coming in second just after HBO. In a nod to his former career, Moonves occasionally steps in for guest appearances on television shows written or produced by his longtime friends. He has appeared on the sitcom *The Nanny*, the soap opera *The Young and the Restless,* and even the ABC drama *The Practice.* With his trademark raspy voice, quick wit, and charismatic personality, Moonves has become a entertainment industry legend, "a throwback to a time when TV executives were showmen, not suits," asserted *Newsweek* writer Johnnie L. Roberts.

The power Moonves wields was no match, however, for the "Boycott CBS" movement that gained momentum in the weeks before CBS's planned November sweeps miniseries, *The Reagans,* in 2003. Objecting to what it claimed was a liberal bias in the script, and dialogue described as fictitious and inflammatory, Republican and conservative political forces objected vehemently, and Moonves ordered it to be re–edited just weeks before its scheduled air date. When James Brolin and Judy Davis, the actors playing Ronald and Nancy Reagan, announced they would not assist in publicizing the edited version, Moonves cancelled the series. It ran on Showtime, a Viacom property, instead.

Moonves is a distant relative of David Ben–Gurion, founder of the modern Israeli state, via a 1917 marriage on his father's side of the family. His wife, Nancy, made several appearances on the hit show *Beverly Hills 90210,* and they are the parents of three, including Sara Moonves, who played Terri on *Full House* in the early 1990s. Reflecting on what a show business–involved family he has, Moonves recalled in a Knight Ridder/Tribune News Service interview with Gail Shister that his daughter brought him an early morning fax with the overnight Nielsen ratings and told him, "Dad, you did terrible last night."

On June 1, 2004, Moonves, along with MTV chairman and chief executive officer Tom Freston, was named co-president and co-chief operating officer of Viacom, Inc., the parent company of MTV and CBS. Outgoing Viacom chairman and chief executive officer Sumner Redstone said that he expects one of them to replace him when he leaves, which, he says, will be sometime in the next three years.

Sources

Broadcasting, July 16, 1990, p. 111; October 22, 1990, p. 50.
Broadcasting & Cable, January 21, 2002, p. 26; September 29, 2003, p. 1.
Electronic Media, July 28, 1997, p. 1; March 26, 2001, p. 10.

Entertainment Weekly, February 13, 1998, p. 32; October 24, 2003, p. 26.
Fortune, February 4, 2002, p. 28.
Knight Ridder/Tribune News Service, January 15, 1996.
Los Angeles Magazine, September 1996, p. 68.
Mediaweek, June 12, 1995, p. 5; October 30, 2000, p. 46.
Newsweek, November 19, 2001, p. 60.
New York Observer, May 19, 2003, p. 1.
New York Times, November 5, 2003.
TelevisionWeek, March 17, 2003, p. 3; April 21, 2003, p. 4.
Variety, April 13, 1998, p. 17; August 28, 2000, p. 63, p. 71.

Online

"Viacom: Farewell, Mel," CNN Money, http://money.cnn.com/2004/06/01/news/fortune500/Karmazin/index.htm (June 3, 2004).

—*Carol Brennan*

Mandy Moore

Singer and actress

Born Amanda Leigh Moore, April 10, 1984, in Nashua, NH; daughter of Don (an airline pilot) and Stacy (a homemaker and former reporter) Moore.

Addresses: *Fan club*—Mandy Moore International Fan Club, P.O. Box 6079, Bellingham, WA 98227. *Record company*—Epic, 550 Madison Ave., New York, NY 10022–3211. *Website*—http://www.mandy moore.com.

Career

Signed with Sony label, c. 1999; released *So Real* and single "Candy," 1999; released *I Wanna Be With You*, 2000; released *Mandy Moore*, 2001; released *Coverage*, 2003. Hosted MTV show *Mandy*, 2000. Film appearances include: *The Princess Diaries*, 2001; *A Walk to Remember*, 2002; *How to Deal*, 2003; *Chasing Liberty*, 2004; *Saved*, 2004.

Awards: MTV Movie Award, breakthrough performance—female, for *A Walk to Remember*, 2002; Teen Choice Awards for choice breakout performance—actress and choice chemistry (with Shane West), for *A Walk to Remember*, 2002.

Sidelights

One of the teen singers who emerged from Orlando, Florida's late–1990s star factory, Mandy Moore has developed a reputation as a sweet, squeaky–clean pop diva. Her youth–oriented dance–pop and blonde hair brought early comparisons to Britney Spears, but her many movie roles, her romance with tennis champion Andy Roddick, and her fourth album, made up of songs by acclaimed songwriters, have distinguished her from her peers and are starting to give her a more mature reputation.

Born in New Hampshire in 1984, Moore grew up in Florida and decided she wanted to be a singer at age six, when she saw a school production of the musical *Oklahoma*. Voice lessons, a musical theater camp, and appearances in local musicals, such as a staging of *Guys & Dolls* in sixth grade, led her to sing "The Star–Spangled Banner" at an Orlando Magic basketball game at age nine, and soon she was nicknamed the "National Anthem Girl" and singing at several local sporting events. Work taping voice–overs, filming pilot episodes for Disney and Nickelodeon at their Orlando studios, and appearing in commercials led to her big break. A FedEx deliveryman who heard her sing for a commercial asked her for a demo tape, and he passed it on to his friend, Dave McPherson, a talent scout for Sony Records, who signed her to a recording contract with Sony's Epic/550 Records when she was 14.

Moore's first album, *So Real,* recorded in early 1999, was produced by Jive Records, hit–makers who had worked with Spears, the Backstreet Boys, and 'N Sync. Epic/550 and Transcontinental Media, instrumental in the success of the two boy bands, both debuted websites about Moore in March of 1999 to build interest in her. She toured with the two bands as an opening act in the summer of 1999, and kids flooded her autograph sessions after the shows (though a few Backstreet fans were hostile to her because of a false rumor she was dating Backstreet Boy Nick Carter). *So Real,* which *Rolling Stone*'s Matt Hendrickson described as "combining the requisite formula of up–tempo R&B ditties and sappy ballads," was released in fall 1999, and its early sales— 40,000 to 60,000 copies a week—were modest for teen–pop acts with such aggressive promotion. But her first single, "Candy," caught on, and Moore returned in 2000 with the album *I Wanna Be With You,* which included new songs and remixed versions of "Candy" and other *So Real* tracks, while *So Real* itself reached the platinum million–selling mark. Moore was surprised by the sudden success. "It's really surreal," she told Hendrickson. "I thought a record company would sign an artist my age and wait until I was 17 or 18 before they started having me do stuff. But I just jumped right in."

By summer 2000, Moore was hosting *Mandy,* a daily half–hour call–in and video show on MTV, co-hosted by Carson Daly. That year, she signed a deal to appear in Neutrogena commercials. The press noticed that she was projecting a more innocent image than other pop stars; *TV Guide* noted that "she shuns the midriff–baring tops preferred by Britney Spears and Christina Aguilera and wears almost no makeup," while *People* declared she "packs a punch—without raunch." The next year, she released the album *Mandy Moore,* which stuck to conventional love–song sentiments ("I learned what love is/From loving you/I held you, I held everything I ever dreamed of," she sang on "From Loving You"). *Entertainment Weekly*'s Beth Johnson gave the album a B–, complaining that its lyrics were predictable, but saying its "Eastern rhythms [and] jangly percussives ... help separate her from the pack," while All Music Guide's Stephen Thomas Erlewine gave it 4½ stars, writing, "*Mandy Moore* manages to pack more hooks, melody, beats, clever production flourishes, and fun into its 13 tracks than nearly all of its peers—remarkably, it's a stronger album, through and through, than either of Britney's first two albums or Christina's record."

Moore appeared in her first film in 2001, *The Princess Diaries,* but said acting would not replace music in her life. "I probably will always be more passionate about singing. There's a rush I get performing live that's missing when I'm in front of the camera," she told Heather Matarazzo, another actress in the film, when they interviewed each other for *Seventeen.* (When filming started, Matarazzo disdainfully called Moore "Britney," so Moore got revenge by calling Matarazzo "Wiener Dog," the cruel nickname of her character in *Welcome to the Dollhouse;* the two eventually became friends.) Moore dated actor Wilmer Valderrama of *That '70s Show* throughout 2001; they broke up later that year.

Movie stardom came in 2002, when Moore got the lead role in the melodramatic teen love story *A Walk to Remember,* playing an awkwardly dressed minister's daughter who falls in love with a popular boy. Though *Entertainment Weekly*'s Lisa Schwarzbaum called the movie a "teen–angel sobathon" and Moore's charms "unexceptional," *Time* declared that Moore showed "screen appeal and poise" and predicted that "when pop–star status deserts her, she might become a movie star, or something more precious: a fine actress." The movie earned more than $30 million within a month of its release, and Moore's portrayal of a pious character enhanced her clean image. In a *People* profile headlined "Gee Rated," Daly, her MTV co-host, called her "one of the most genuine, sweetest young female talents I've ever met" and wondered what it would be like to see her angry: "She's got to blow a gasket sometime, right? Maybe throw a teddy bear?" Moore discovered another way to stand out from other blonde pop stars: After *A Walk to Remember*'s director told her she would have to dye her hair brown to get the part, she decided to remain a brunette. It made her feel "more confident," she told *People* when the magazine named her one of its 50 most beautiful people of 2002 in May of that year. "I look at pictures of myself with blonde hair and cringe."

In her next major film role, 2003's *How To Deal,* Moore played a teen turned cynical about love by watching her parents and close friend struggle with relationship troubles. She spent part of 2003 in Prague filming *Chasing Liberty,* in which she stars as a First Daughter who falls for a Secret Service agent. The script called for her character to be nude in one scene, but she refused to take her clothes off on camera and selected a body double instead. She toyed with her image a little in *Seventeen,* listing 60 things she wanted to do before turning 30, including "Shave my head," "Drive a motorcycle," and "Get a tattoo." Meanwhile, a new romance developed with tennis star Andy Roddick. They met while she was filming *How to Deal* in Toronto and he was playing in a tournament there; when her mother went to watch the tournament, Moore had her invite Roddick to the set. Moore watched him win the U.S.

Open in September of 2003. But when Roddick signed up to star in a reality show, *The Tour,* she did not want any part of it. "My personal life is my personal life, and it's behind closed doors," the *Chicago Tribune* quoted her as saying.

In fall 2003, she turned back to music. Just before her new album's release, she hosted cable network Lifetime's "Women Rock! Songs From the Movies," a special highlighting breast cancer awareness. "It's fun to take a break and be creative in another way, but it's nice to step back into these shoes," she told the *Los Angeles Times.* "I haven't really done anything music–related for the past two years, so this event comes at a time when I want to get my mind going on something else."

Her new CD, *Coverage,* was made up of songs by critically acclaimed '70s and '80s singer–songwriters such as Joni Mitchell, Carly Simon, and John Hiatt. "We kind of did it unbeknownst to the record company. I found a producer I wanted to work with and we worked out of his garage studio and just did it," she told *Entertainment Weekly*'s Liane Bonin. "At 19, my musical tastes have changed.... I know it's a left turn for me, but I want people my age to hear this music." Reviews varied wildly. Ron Harris of the Associated Press, as quoted in the *Chicago Tribune,* wrote that the album sounded "like karaoke at a bachelorette party gone bad" and declared that Moore had "no personal touch" to add to the songs. But *Spin* declared it "the best collection of other people's songs since David Bowie's 1973 classic, *Pinups.*"

Moore lives with her parents and younger brother, Kyle, in a Los Angeles, California, home she bought for $1.7 million. (She also has an older brother, Scott.) With *Chasing Liberty* and the teen film *Saved* set for release in early 2004, and other film roles set to follow, some in the press speculated that Moore might have an even brighter future as an actress than a singer. "There's nothing like being onstage," she told the *Los Angeles Times* in late 2003—but talking to a writer for the *Cincinnati Post* a few months earlier, she seemed happy to see her career go either way. "If a record is successful, then there will be a tour and that takes time," she said. "If a film is successful and other opportunities are presented to me, then I want to take advantage of that, too."

Selected discography

So Real, Sony, 1999.
I Wanna Be With You, Epic/500 Music, 2000.
Mandy Moore, Epic, 2001.
Coverage, Epic, 2003.

Sources

Books

Bankston, John, *Mandy Moore: A Real–Life Reader Biography,* Mitchell Lane Publishers, 2002.

Periodicals

Chicago Tribune, October 23, 2003, p. 32; November 5, 2003, p. 62.
Cincinnati Post, July 17, 2003, p. T5.
Entertainment Weekly, June 18, 2001; February 8, 2002; May 29, 2003; June 27/July 4, 2003, p. 30; July 16, 2003; October 24, 2003.
Interview, August 2003, p. 125.
Los Angeles Times, October 19, 2003.
People, July 3, 2000, p. 110; March 4, 2002, pp. 59–60; May 13, 2002, p. 175; August 25, 2003, pp. 106–09; September 1, 2003, pp. 81–82.
Rolling Stone, March 16, 2000, pp. 23–24.
Seventeen, July 2001, p. 122; August 2003, pp. 185–87.
Spin, November 2003, p. 28.
Teen, August 2001, pp. 155–58.
Time, February 25, 2002, pp. 62–63.
TV Guide, July 15, 2000, pp. 38–40.
Washington Post, September 8, 2003, p. D1.

Online

"Mandy Moore," All Music Guide, http://www.allmusic.com/ (November 30, 2003).
"Mandy Moore," Internet Movie Database, http://www.imdb.com/name/nm0601553 (November 23, 2003).
"Mandy Moore," Rock On The Net, http://www.rockonthenet.com/artists–m/mandymoore.htm (November 30, 2003).
Official Mandy Moore Website, http://www.mandymoore.com (November 23, 2003).

—*Erick Trickey*

Carrie-Anne Moss

Actress

Born August 21, 1967, in Vancouver, BC, Canada; married Steven Roy (an actor and director), 1999; children: one. *Education:* Attended the American Academy of Dramatic Arts, Pasadena, CA, early 1990s.

Addresses: *Agent*—Metropolitan Talent Agency, 4526 Wilshire Blvd., Los Angeles, CA 90010–3801.

Career

Actress in television, including: *Dark Justice,* 1991–93; *Nightmare Cafe,* 1992; *Forever Knight,* 1992; *Down the Shore,* 1992; *Matrix,* 1993; *Flashfire* (movie), 1993; *Street Justice,* 1993; *Doorways* (movie), 1993; *L.A. Law,* 1993; *Silk Stalkings,* 1993; *Spider–Man* (voice), 1994; *Baywatch,* 1994; *Models, Inc.,* 1994–95; *Nowhere Man,* 1995; *Due South,* 1996; *F/X: The Series,* 1996–97; *Viper,* 1997. Film appearances include: *The Soft Kill,* 1994; *Terrified,* 1996; *Sabotage* (uncredited), 1996; *Lethal Tender,* 1997; *The Secret Life of Algernon,* 1997; *The Matrix,* 1999; *New Blood,* 1999; *The Crew,* 2000; *Memento,* 2000; *Red Planet,* 2000; *Chocolat,* 2000; *The Matrix Reloaded,* 2003; *The Matrix Revolutions,* 2003; *Suspect Zero,* 2004. Stage appearances include: *Outward Bound,* Hudson Theatre, Los Angeles, CA. Also worked as a model in Spain and Japan during the 1980s.

Sidelights

Carrie–Anne Moss, star of the immensely successful *Matrix* trilogy of sci–fi thrillers, found herself an unlikely action heroine after a career in television and several straight–to–video movies. "Not since George Lucas's *Star Wars* has a sci–fi film captivated a mass audience as *The Matrix* has, nor inspired such slavish devotion from a cast," asserted Martyn Palmer of London's *Sunday Times,* and it was a superlative echoed by journalist David Giammarco, who enthused over Moss's portrayal of Trinity, a fierce martial–arts expert. "Not since Sigourney Weaver stomped out the vicious beasts of the *Alien* films has a female kicked such major butt on screen," the *Globe & Mail* writer declared.

Moss is Canadian by birth, and grew up in Vancouver, British Columbia. Born in 1967, she was named after a Hollies song, "Carrie Anne," that was popular at the time. She acted in children's theater, but her plans to pursue acting as an adult were sidelined by lucrative work as a model in Japan and Spain. While living in Barcelona, Moss acted in television commercials and then auditioned for a part on a CBS series that was filming in there at the time. She won the role of Tara McDonald on *Dark Justice,* and when the series returned to Los Angeles, California, for the 1992 season, Moss went there as well.

Moss took classes at Pasadena's American Academy of Dramatic Arts, but recalled her transition to Hollywood as an exceedingly difficult period in her life.

"I just didn't know anybody, not a soul," she told Palmer in the *Sunday Times.* "It was a very, very lonely time. I mean, moving to LA at just 24 and not knowing anyone, how insane is that? But I wanted to act and I just hung on in there and kept hoping." Eventually Moss landed a number of guest roles on television shows such as *L.A. Law, Silk Stalkings,* and *Baywatch,* and did some stage work as well. She even appeared in a short–lived series on the USA cable channel called *Matrix,* which had no relation to the movie that later made her famous. Her big break, ostensibly, came on a much–hyped new series for the Fox Network in 1994: *Models, Inc.* Critics savaged the show, a spin–off of the hit *Melrose Place* drama, and the *Globe & Mail*'s Giammarco described Moss's character as " an aging model embroiled in some of the most groan–inducing plot twists ever conceived outside of daytime soaps."

Moss made her big–screen debut in a little–seen mystery titled *The Soft Kill* in 1994. She also appeared a 1996 horror flick that starred a young Heather Graham, *Terrified,* and spent a season as Lucinda Scott on *F/X: The Series,* between 1996 and 1997. Other films went straight to the proverbial video bin, but Moss told Giammarco in the *Globe & Mail* interview that schlock television and B–movies served her well in her career. "I've had to deliver some of the hardest, most terrible dialogue ever written," she reflected. "When you learn how to do that, you can do anything." Reading for the role of Trinity in *The Matrix,* she said in an interview with *Palm Beach Post* writer Hap Erstein, was more or less an aberration. "I wasn't even auditioning for movies, really, because it was hard to get in the room," she recalled.

The Matrix was the brainchild of two filmmaker brothers from Chicago, Larry and Andy Wachowski. Their farfetched premise—that computers are actually running the planet, that reality as people know it was merely a "matrix," and that human behavior was programmed to maximize profit—won a surprise greenlighting by Warner Bros. studio executives. The brothers had no experience in the big–budget action–thriller genre, and were also adamant about having their actors perform all their own stunts. Moss went to seven callbacks before they cast her in the role of Trinity, and then began preparing intensely in the fall of 1997 for the film, which would not be released until some 18 months later. In order to psychologically prepare for the part, however, she revisited the Clint Eastwood *Dirty Harry* series from the 1970s and '80s. "I hadn't seen his movies since I was a kid and went with my dad and my brother," she told *Esquire*'s David Hochman. "But I remembered how still he was. Still but full of strength. I knew I needed to tap into that because I'm not a very still person."

Moss's co–stars in *The Matrix* were Laurence Fishburne (as the leader of small band of rebels who have escaped the computer–controlled Matrix and are fighting from a small place deep inside Earth) and Keanu Reeves (as the computer hacker Neo). It is Trinity's task to guide Neo into fulfill his destiny as humankind's savior, and a romance develops amidst the danger and dazzling special effects. The film was a box–office smash worldwide when it was released in the spring of 1999, with *Entertainment Weekly*'s Marc Bernardin deeming it the first successful Hollywood movie to deal credibly with the virtual–reality concept. "The genius of writer–directors Larry and Andy Wachowski's deep–thinking actioner is that they took their Big Idea and armored it in a cohesive cyberpunk/comic–book chic that had never been seen outside of Jap–animation," Bernardin asserted. The *New York Times* critic, A. O. Scott, called it a work that "succeeded by entwining traditional—and often breathtakingly innovative—action–movie motifs with the mapping of an intricate and mysterious world."

The Wachowskis had a *Matrix* sequel in the works that was eventually split into two separate films, but before reprising her Trinity role Moss appeared in a slew of films released in 2000, some of which did well with critics and audiences alike. She was a desperate, battered woman in *Memento,* which featured Guy Pearce as a short–term amnesiac named Leonard trying to find his wife's killer. Moss helped Pearce's character put together the pieces in a complex plot that unfolded in reverse in screen. "Each section of the main story begins in mid–action," noted *New Statesman* writer Jonathan Romney, "so that we do not know what is happening any more than Leonard does: it is like walking in to the middle of a film, over and over again." A sci–fi flick in which Moss starred opposite Val Kilmer, *Red Planet,* took a drubbing, however, and she also appeared in a little–seen caper–comedy with Burt Reynolds and Richard Dreyfuss, *The Crew.* But she also had a supporting role in *Chocolat,* one of the year's surprise box–office hits.

Moss began training once again for the *Matrix* sequels in the spring of 2001, learning kung–fu moves from the movie's fight choreographer, Yuen Wo Ping, of *Crouching Tiger, Hidden Dragon* fame. Often she toiled seven hours a day, but the arduous work—much of it on high wires—took its toll, and she fell and broke her leg. She was mortified that she would be re–cast, as she recalled in the *Esquire* interview. "I remember going somewhere around that time," confessed to Hochman. "I was on crutches, and a guy said, 'Hey, my girlfriend just auditioned for your part.'" He was joking, and

Moss's leg mended well enough for her to return to shooting and take on a new villain: a motorcycle. The stunt–driving school she attended failed to prepare her for the intensity of some of the scenes, especially one that required her to drive into oncoming traffic, and one chase sequence alone took eight weeks to film. "I rode a bike in the first one," she told Giammarco in the *Globe & Mail*, "but really all I had to do was pull away from a curb—and I fell off every time," she said with a laugh. "I was scared to death of them. So, of course, in this one they had me riding a motorcycle for almost two months. But it feels pretty good to have conquered my fear."

The filming of *The Matrix* sequels was stressful in other ways, Moss recalled. There were two deaths among cast members: R&B singer Aaliyah, cast as Zee, was killed in a plane crash in August of 2001, and Gloria Foster, who played the Oracle in the first *Matrix* film, died of complications from diabetes. In between those deaths, while cast and crew were far from home on location in Sydney, Australia, hijacked airliners crashed in New York, Washington, D.C., and Pennsylvania on September 11, 2001. Moss underwent a crisis of confidence, as she recalled in the interview with the *Sunday Times*. "I was a wreck," she told Palmer. "I was asking myself: 'Why am I going to work? What am I doing making a movie right now, while all this is happening?'"

The sequels, while hotly anticipated by fans of the first installment, fared less well with critics. *The Matrix Reloaded* was released in the spring of 2003, followed six months later by *The Matrix Revolutions*. The *New York Times*'s Scott called *Reloaded* "a lumpy, gaseous treatise of a movie," and *Newsweek*'s film reviewer David Ansen declared the third film not as compelling as the initial *Matrix*. "If you missed the second part, you will be hopelessly lost," Ansen wrote. "Even if you saw it, expect more confusion than your average action movie delivers." Ansen liked a fantastiscal, climactic battle scene, describing it as "a wild sequence so densely crammed with flying metal, flaming weapons, and smashed architecture it verges on abstraction." The *New York Times*'s Scott asserted, however, that the final film "feels padded. The battle for Zion goes on forever and seems designed to justify the picture's enormous military hardware budget. There is very little that is tantalizing or suspenseful. The feeling of revelation is gone, and many of the teasing implications of *Reloaded* have been abandoned."

Both *Matrix* films were enormous successes at the box office, however, and Reeve's turn as Neo was said to have revived what had been a moribund career. Moss was sometimes asked about her love scenes with the cinematic heartthrob. "I'm definitely not a big fan of that part of the work," she told Hochman in *Esquire*. "I'm such a private person, and sexuality is such a private thing. A sex scene is much harder than a fight scene. It's one thing to say, 'Kick higher,' but 'Kiss harder'—that's just crazy." The leather trench coats she and Reeves sported in the films were mentioned in a *New York Times* Style piece, and a cult–like following arose in homage to Moss's Trinity and her black latex catsuit. She was surprised to learn there was an avid Internet following for the character—who, with "Moss's endless scissor legs, angular face and thin, serious lips," noted the *Sunday Times*'s Palmer, "make her a cybergeek's S&M fantasy"—since she was vastly uninterested in computers, the Web, or any of the virtual–reality gaming elements that made *The Matrix* such a hit with a generation of filmgoers. "I'm really computer–illiterate," she admitted in the interview with Erstein for the *Palm Beach Post*. "I don't even know how to turn our computer on." Her more net–savvy mother gave her a crash course, "and I went on," Moss recalled, "and it's like, 'Oh, my God, pictures that I had never seen.' I find it a bit weird."

Moss's next film project was *Suspect Zero*, a thriller about a serial killer of other serial killers that also starred Aaron Eckhart and Ben Kingsley. Married to Steven Roy, an actor and director, Moss became a mother in 2003 as well. She was 36 years old when the final installment of *The Matrix* was released, and declared herself retired from the action–movie genre. "The first time around I didn't know what to expect," she told *Newsweek*'s Devin Gordon, "and it was really hard, but ignorance was bliss…. I'm a very strong person. But I will never do another kung fu movie again," she said with a laugh. "It's too stressful."

Sources

Books

Contemporary Theatre, Film and Television, volume 26, Gale Group, 2000.

Periodicals

Entertainment Weekly, April 9, 1999, p. 26; September 24, 1999, p. 149; June 28/July 5, 2002, p. 31.
Esquire, May 1999, p. 108; June 2003, p. 76.
Globe & Mail (Toronto, Canada), April 22, 2003.

Nation, April 26, 1999, p. 34.

New Statesman, October 23, 2000, p. 47.

Newsweek, May 5, 2003, pp. 56–58; November 10, 2003, p. 63.

New York Times, May 14, 2003; November 5, 2003.

Palm Beach Post, August 28, 2000, p. 1E.

Sunday Times (London, England), May 25, 2003, p. 12.

Time, April 5, 1999, p. 68.

—*Carol Brennan*

Takashi Murakami

Artist and designer

Born in 1962, in Tokyo, Japan. *Education:* Tokyo National University of Fine Arts and Music, B.F.A., 1986; M.F.A., 1988; Ph.D., 1993.

Addresses: *Office*—Kaikai Kiki Co. Ltd., Marunuma Geijutsuno–mori, 493 Kamiuchimagi, Asaka–shi, Saitama, Japan.

Career

Received training in the classic Japanese art form nihonga, 1980s; taught drawing, 1990s; embarked on solo career; exhibited in hundreds of galleries across the world, including the Serpentine Gallery in London, the Marianne Boesky Gallery in New York, the Boston Museum of Fine Arts, and the Tokyo Museum of Contemporary Art; worked as a guest professor in the New Genre curriculum of the UCLA art department, 1998; designed line of Louis Vuitton handbags, 2003.

Awards: Received Japan Fashion Editors Club Awards for his Louis Vuitton bag designs, 2003.

Sidelights

Japanese–born artist Takashi Murakami has become an international phenomenon by blurring the line between fine art and pop art. His edgy–yet–stunning, creepy–yet–cute cartoon–type characters appeal to a large audience and he deliberately makes his artwork accessible to all. Murakami's paintings sell in galleries for more than $250,000 and a sculpture of his fetched $1.5 million. He has also designed bags for Louis Vuitton, which sold for $4,500. Murakami's work, however, is also available on affordable coffee mugs, key chains, and stuffed animals. Because he believes artwork is more about creating goods to sell than about exhibitions, Murakami struggles to be taken seriously in some circles, although art curator Douglas Fogle called him "the most influential artist to come out of Japan in the last 15 years," according to Peter Marks of the *New York Times*.

Born in Tokyo in 1962, Murakami was raised in a family of art–lovers and artists. He has a younger brother who is also a painter. Growing up, Murakami had plenty of Western influences. His father worked at a U.S. naval base and Murakami also came of age during a time when Japanese society was filled with an ample supply of American pop culture, from rock music to films.

Inspired by a Japanese comic–book style called Manga, Murakami dreamed of becoming an animation artist but believed his drawing skills were not up to par. Hoping to improve his technique, Murakami entered the Tokyo National University of Fine Arts and Music in the 1980s. There, he studied a customary Japanese art form called nihonga. Nihonga, which dates to the late 19th century, is a style of Japanese painting that fuses both Western and Eastern art by mixing traditional Japanese subject matter with European–influenced painting techniques. Murakami earned his bachelor's degree in fine arts in 1986 and his doctorate in 1993.

In the early 1990s, Murakami taught drawing and continued painting but became disillusioned with his conventional nihonga training, believing the art form no longer appealed to the average Japanese person. Murakami wanted to make a lasting impact, so he began experimenting to find his own style. In a 2001 retrospective on his work, reprinted in *Wired*, Murakami expressed his thoughts this way: "I set out to investigate the secret of market survivability—the universality of characters such as Mickey Mouse, Sonic the Hedgehog, Doraemon, Miffy, Hello Kitty, and their knock–offs, produced in Hong Kong."

The results have been stunning. Most of Murakami's pieces contain often smirky, sometimes psychedelic, doe–eyed childlike characters rendered in dazzling, dripping Technicolor. He has a talent for creating art that is disturbing and beautiful at the same time. Though unconventional, Murakami's crazy–eyed creatures have found a place in the museum–centered art world. His signature character is a peevish Mickey Mouse lookalike called Mr. DOB, whose sculpture was sold for $1.5 million.

Not only is Murakami's style unconventional but so are his work habits. Computers play a key role in Murakami's creations, which are churned out at the Hiropon Factory, located just outside Tokyo in Saitama, Japan. A second art factory is located in New York. Murakami's art factory works like this: When Murakami has an idea, he sketches the design on paper and scans it into a computer. From there, Murakami fires up Adobe Illustrator and manipulates the piece. Murakami's artwork includes a number of recurring themes, like eyeballs, mushrooms and flowers. He keeps a digital clip–art file of these images and can simply cut and paste them into place on the computer screen. Next, he puts the colors into the file. An assistant takes over from here. The work is printed and the outlines of the images are silk–screened onto a canvas. At this point, Murakami becomes the supervisor. He watches over the piece as assistants paint on the 70 to 800 colors that make up a typical Murakami original. He may make color corrections, but seldom picks up a brush. Assistants paint on endless layers of acrylics to produce that remarkably shiny, signature sheen of a Murakami original. Some pieces take two months to produce; others take two years.

To describe his artwork, Murakami has coined the term "superflat," an acknowledgement of his style that lacks depth and perception. He believes it also reflects our technologically flat world of PDAs, flatscreen televisions, and digital billboards. The term also relates to the flattening out of boundaries in the art world.

Murakami's biggest break came when he was commissioned to create Louis Vuitton handbags. He replaced the traditional brown and gold colors with jellybean–colored logos. The bags sold for up to $4,500 apiece, though he was criticized for his commercialism.

Even though famous galleries around the world are showing his work, Murakami still battles to be taken seriously in some realms. London *Guardian* art critic Adrian Searle put it this way, according to *Newsday* writer Ariella Budick: "I recoil from its cuteness, and the sly, self–conscious and hyper–sophisticated cartoony artiness of what he does. Perhaps you need to be Japanese and addicted to Manga comics to get this stuff, or under 10 years old, or the kind of adult who likes to wear nappies, in which case this show would be an ideal environment to hang about in, sporting leaky Pampers."

Murakami, however, shrugs off such criticism. "I don't make my art intentionally childish just so I can appeal to children," he told *Newsday*. "Colorfulness, cuteness, simplicity—that's my aesthetic. I take those elements very seriously."

Demand for Murakami's work continues with respectable art houses handing him solo exhibitions, including the Serpentine Gallery in London, the Marianne Boesky Gallery in New York, the Boston Museum of Fine Arts, and the Tokyo Museum of Contemporary Art. In September of 2003, his artwork overtook New York City's Rockefeller Plaza in the form of a 30–foot–tall fiberglass sculpture of his best–known cartoonish creature, Mr. Pointy, in a show called *Reversed Double Helix*.

While some criticize Murakami for his marketing, he makes no apologies and intends to go on creating for the masses until he dies. "I am looking for the crossing point between fine art and entertainment," Murakami told Marks in the *New York Times*. "I have learned in Europe and America the way of the fine–art scene. Few people come to museums. Much bigger are movie theaters. The museum, that space is kind of old–style media, like opera. That's why I am really interested in making merchandise for ordinary people."

Selected solo exhibitions

Café Tiens!, Tokyo, Japan, 1989.

Gallery Ginza Surugadai, Tokyo, Japan, 1989.

Art Gallery at Tokyo National University of Fine Arts and Music, Tokyo, Japan, 1991.

Aoi Gallery, Osaka, Japan, 1991.

One Night Exhibition 8.23, Rontgen Kunst Institut, Tokyo, Japan, 1991.

Gallery Aires, Tokyo, Japan, 1991.

I Am Against Being For It, Gallery Hosomi Contemporary, Tokyo, Japan, 1991.

Wild, Wild, Rontgen Kunst Institut, Tokyo, Japan, 1992.

Nasubi Gallery, Tokyo, Japan, 1993.

A Very Merry Unbirthday!, Hiroshima City Museum of Contemporary Art, Hiroshima, Japan, 1993.

A Romantic Evening, Gallery Cellar, Nagoya, Japan, 1993.

Fujisan, Gallery Koto, Okayama, Japan, 1994.

Which is Tomorrow?—Fall in Love, SCAI The Bathhouse, Tokyo, Japan, 1994.

Azami, Kikyou, Ominaeshi, Aoi Gallery, Osaka, Japan, 1994.

Mr. Doomsday Balloon, Yngtingagatan 1, Stockholm, Sweden, 1995.

Crazy Z, SCAI The Bathhouse, Tokyo, Japan, 1995.

Galerie Emmanuel Perrotin, Paris, France, 1995.

NIJI, Gallery Koto, Okayama, Japan, 1995.

A Very Merry Unbirthday, To You, To Me! Ginza Komatsu, Tokyo, Japan, 1996.

727, Aoi Gallery, Osaka, Japan, 1996.

Konnichiwa, Mr. DOB, Kirin Art Plaza, Osaka, Japan, 1996.

727, Tomio Koyama Gallery, Tokyo, Japan, 1996.

Gallery Koto, Okayama, Japan, 1996.

Gavin Brown's Enterprise, New York, New York, 1996.

Feature Inc., New York, New York, 1996.

Blum & Poe, Santa Monica, California, 1997.

Gallery KOTO, Okayama, Japan, 1997.

Galerie Emmanuel Perrotin, Paris, France, 1997.

New York State University at Buffalo, New York, 1997.

Moreover, DOB Raise His Hand, Sagacho bis, Tokyo, Japan, 1998.

Back Beat: Superflat, Tomio Koyama Gallery, Tokyo, Japan, 1998.

Back Beat, Blum & Poe, Santa Monica, California, 1998.

Hiropon Project KoKo_Pity Sakurako Jet Airplane Nos. 1–6, Feature Inc., New York, New York, 1998.

The Meaning of the Nonsense of the Meaning, Center for Curatorial Studies Museum, Bard College, New York, New York, 1999.

Love & DOB, Gallery KOTO, Okayama, Japan, 1999.

Superflat, Marianne Boesky Gallery, New York, New York, 1999.

DOB's Adventures in Wonderland, Parco Department Store Gallery, Tokyo, Japan, 1999.

Second Mission Project Ko2, P.S.1 Contemporary Art Center, Long Island City, New York, 2000.

KaiKai Kiki: Superflat, ISSEY MIYAKE MEN, Tokyo, Japan, 2000.

727, Blum & Poe, Santa Monica, California, 2000.

Summon monsters? Open the Door? Heal? Or Die? Tokyo Museum of Contemporary Art, Japan, 2001.

Made in Japan, Museum of Fine Art, Boston, Massachusetts, 2001.

Wink, Grand Central Station, New York, New York, 2001.

Mushroom, Marianne Boesky Gallery, New York, New York, 2001.

KaiKai Kiki, Galerie Emmanuel Perrotin, Paris, France, 2001.

Kaikai Kiki: Takashi Murakami, Fondation Cartier pour l'art contemporain, Paris, France, 2002.

Reversed Double Helix, Rockefeller Center, New York, New York, 2003.

Superflat Monogram, Marianne Boesky Gallery, New York, New York, 2003.

Selected group exhibitions

Graduation Exhibition, Tokyo National University of Fine Arts, Tokyo, Japan, 1988.

Metropolitan Art Museum, Tokyo, Japan, 1988.

Jan Hoet in Tsurugi, Tsurugi–cho, Ishikawa, Japan, 1991.

Jan Hoet's Vision, Art Gallery Artium, Fukuoka, Japan, 1991.

Nakamura and Murakami, Metaria Square Hotel Osaka, Japan, 1992.

Artist's Shop '92, Sai Gallery, Osaka, Japan, 1992.

Mars Gallery, Tokyo, 1992.

Floating Gallery Vol. 1, Tsukishima Warehouse, Tokyo, Japan, 1993.

1st Transart Annual Painting/Crossing, Bellini Hill Gallery, Yokohama, Japan, 1993.

Nakamura and Murakami, Space Ozone, Seoul, Korea, 1993.

Nakamura and Murakami, SCAI The Bathhouse, Tokyo, Japan, 1993.

Anomaly, Rontgen Kunst Institut, Tokyo, Japan, 1993.

Tama Vivant '92, Seed Hall, Shibuya Seibu, Tokyo, Japan, 1993.

Malaria Art Show, Vol.1, February 1st Festival, Tokyo, Japan, 1993.

Artist's Shop '93, Sai Gallery, Osaka, Japan, 1993.

The Ginburart, Ginza, Tokyo, Japan, 1993.

00 Collaboration, Sagacho Exhibit Space, Tokyo, Japan, 1993.

Art Today '93, Neo–Japanology, Sezon Museum of Modern Art, Karuizawa, Nagano, Japan, 1993.

Beyond Nihonga: An Aspect of Contemporary Japanese Paintings, Tokyo Metropolitan Art Museum, Tokyo, Japan, 1993.

The Exhibition for Exhibitions, Kyoto Shijo Gallery Kyoto, Japan, 1993.

Shinjuku Syonen Art, Shinjuku Kabukicho, Tokyo, Japan, 1994.

Lest We Forget: On Nostalgia, The Gallery at Takashimaya, New York

VOCA '94, The Ueno Royal Museum, Tokyo, Japan, 1994.

The Youthful Time of Japanese Nihonga Artists from Taikan and Shunso to DOB, Koriyama City Museum of Art, Fukushima, Japan, 1994.

Open Air '94, Out of bounds, Benesse House Naoshima Contemporary Art Museum, Kagawa, Japan, 1994.

Artists in Yokohama '94, Yokohama Citizens' Gallery, Kanagawa, Japan, 1994.

Incidental Alterations: PS1 Studio Artists 1994–95, The Angel Orensanz Foundation, New York, New York, 1995.

Blind Beach, Art Space Hap, Hiroshima, Japan, 1995.

Transculture, 46th Venice Biennale, Venice, Italy, 1995.

Japan Today, Louisiana Museum of Modern Art, Humlebaek, Denmark, 1995.

Kunsternes Hus, Oslo, Norway, 1995.

Liljevalchs Konsthall, Stockholm, Sweden, 1995.

Waino Aalonoen Museum of Art, Truku, Finland, 1995.

Cutting Up, Max Protech Gallery, New York, New York, 1995.

Transculture, Benesse House, Naoshima Contemporary Art Museum, Kagawa, Japan, 1995.

Romper Room, Thread Waxing Space, New York, New York, 1996.

Tokyo Pop, The Hiratsuka Museum of Art, Kanagawa, Japan, 1996.

Ironic Fantasy, The Miyagi Museum of Art, Sedai, Japan, 1996.

The 39th Annual Yasui Prize Exhibition, Sezon Museum of Art, Tokyo, Japan, 1996.

Sharaku Interpreted by Japan's Contemporary Artists, The Japan Foundation Forum, Tokyo, Japan, 1996.

Asia–Pacific Triennial 1996, Queensland Art Gallery, Brisbane, 1996.

The 33rd 'Artists Today' Exhibition: Singularity in Plurality, Yokohama Citizens' Gallery, Kanagawa, Japan, 1997.

Japan today kunst Photograph Design, MAK—Austrian Museum of Applied Arts, Vienna, Austria, 1997.

Need for Speed, Grazer Kunstverein, Graz, Austria, 1997.

Hiropon Show '97, Shop 33, Tokyo, Japan, 1997.

The Future of Cities, Weiner Secession, Vienna, Austria, 1997.

Flying Buttress Please, Torch Gallery, Amsterdam, The Netherlands, 1997.

Super Body, Tomio Koyama Gallery, Tokyo, Japan, 1997.

Ero Pop Tokyo, George's, Los Angeles, California, 1998.

Tastes and Pursuits: Japanese Art in the 1990s, National Gallery of Modern Art, New Delhi, India, 1998.

Abstract Painting, Once Removed, Contemporary Arts Museum of Houston, Texas, 1998.

Ero Pop Christmas, NADiff, Tokyo, Japan, 1998.

50 Years of Japanese Lifestyle Postwar Fashion & Design, Ustunomiya Museum of Art, Ibaraki, Japan, 1998.

Biennale d'art Contemporain de Noumea, Noumea, New Caledonia, 1998.

The Manga Age, Museum of Contemporary Art, Tokyo, Japan, 1998.

Hiroshima City Museum of Contemporary Art, Hiroshima, Japan, 1998.

Donaiyanen! Et maintenant!: la creation contemporaine au Japon, Ecole nationale superieure des beaux–arts, Paris, France, 1998.

Art is Fun 9: Hand Craft and Time Craft, Hara Museum Arc, Gunma, Japan, 1998.

Pop Surrealism, The Aldrich Museum of Contemporary Art, Ridgefield, Connecticut, 1998.

People, Places, Things, Marianne Boesky Gallery, New York, New York, 1998.

Fluffy, Dunlop Art Gallery, Regina Canada, 1998.

Contemporarin de Bordeaux, Bordeaux, France, 1998.

PS1 Contemporary Art Center, New York, New York, 1998.

Museum of Modern Art, Humlebaek, Denmark, 1998.

Hayword Gallery, London, England, 1998.

Museum of Modern Art, Helsinki, Finland, 1998.

Lego Deluxe–Leg Exhibition, Shibuya Parco, Tokyo, Japan, 1999.

Ground Zero Japan, Contemporary Art Center, Ibaraki, Japan, 1999.

The Carnegie International 1999/2000, Carnegie Institute, Pittsburgh, Pennsylvania, 1999.

Balloon Art Festival, Shizuoko Prefectural Convention & Art Center, Shizuoka, Japan, 1999.

Pleasure Dome, Jessica Fredericks Gallery, New York, New York, 1999.

New Modernism for a New Millennium: Works by Contemporary Asian Artists from the Logan Collection, SFMOMA, San Francisco, California, 1999.

Color Me Blind! Painting in times of comics and computer games, Wüttembergischer Kunstverein, Stuttgart, Germany, 1999.

Abstract Painting Once Removed, Contemporary Arts Museum, Houston, Texas, 1999.

Painting for Joy: New Japanese Painting in the 1990s, The Japan Foundation Forum, Tokyo, Japan, 1999.

Marianne Boesky Gallery, New York, New York, 2000.

The Darker Side of Playland: Childhood Imagery from the Logan Collection, San Francisco Museum of Modern Art, California, 2000.

After Dreams, Kunsthalle Baden–Baden, Baden–Baden, Switzerland, 2000.

Yume no Ato: Was vom Traum blieb ... Zeitgenossische Kunst aus Japan, Haus am Waldsee, Berlin, Germany, 2000.

Gendai, Center for Contemporary Art, Ujazdowski Castle, Warsaw, Poland, 2000.

Twisted: Urban and Visionary Landscapes in Contemporary Painting, Van Abbe Museum, Eindhoven, The Netherlands, 2000.

Pleasure Zone, Migros Museum, Zurich, Switzerland, 2000.

00, Barbara Gladstone Gallery, New York, New York, 2000.

Urban and Visionary Landscapes in Contemporary Painting, Van Abbe Museum, Eindhoven, The Netherlands, 2000.

Balls, James Cohan Gallery, New York, 2000.

Almost Warm and Fuzzy, Des Moines Art Center, Iowa, 2000.

Superflat, Parco Gallery, Tokyo, Japan, 2000.

Let's Entertain, Walker Art Center, Minneapolis, Minnesota.

5e Biennale d'Art Contemporain de Lyon, Lyon, France, 2000.

Continental Shift, Ludwig Forum, Aachen, Germany, 2000.

One Heart, One World, United Nations, New York, New York, 2000.

Form Follows Fiction, Castello di Rivoli Museum of Contemporary Art, Italy, 2001.

Murakami/Nara, Tomio Koyama Gallery, Tokyo, Japan, 2001.

Un art populaire, Foundation Cariter pour l'art contemporain, Paris, France, 2001.

Casino 2001, 1st Quadrennial of Contemporary Art, Stedelijk Museum Voor Actuele Kunst, Ghent, Belgium, 2001.

Beau Monde: Toward A Redeemed Cosmopolitanism, Site Santa Fe Fourth International Biennial, Santa Fe, New Mexico, 2001.

Public Offerings, Museum of Contemporary Art, Los Angeles, California, 2001.

Painting at the Edge of the World, Walker Art Center, Minneapolis, Minnesota, 2001.

My Reality: The Culture of Anime, Des Moines Art Center, Iowa, 2001.

Super Flat, Los Angeles Museum of Contemporary Art, Los Angeles, California, 2001.

Almost Warm and Fuzzy: Childhood and Contemporary Art, P.S.1 Contemporary Art Center, Long Island City, New York, 2001.

Under Pressure, Swiss Institute, New York, New York, 2001.

Drawing Now: Eight Propositions, Museum of Modern Art, New York, New York, 2002.

POPJack: Warhol to Murakami, Museum of Contemporary Art, Denver, Colorado, 2002.

The Uncanny, Vancouver Art Gallery, Vancouver, British Columbia, Canada, 2002.

Reality Check: Painting in the Exploded Field, CCAC Wattis Institute for Contemporary Arts, San Francisco, California, 2002.

Chiho Aoshima, Mr. Takashi Murakami, Galerie Emmanuel Perrotin, Paris, France, 2002.

Out of the Box: 20th–Century Print Portfolios, Philadelphia Museum of Art, Philadelphia, Pennsylvania, 2002.

Selected curated exhibitions

Mr. Solo Exhibition: Frone & Perrine, Shop 33, Tokyo, Japan, 1996.

Pico 2 Show, Saga–cho bis, Tokyo, Japan, 1996.

Aya Takano Solo Exhibition: God is Coming, Shop 33, Tokyo, Japan, 1997.

Hiropon Show, Kanazawa College of Arts Manken Gallery, Ishikawa, Japan, 1997.

Hiropon Show, Iwataya Z–SIDE W&LT, Fukuoka, Tokyo, 1997.

Tokyo Sex, NAS Tokyo, Japan, 1997.

Hiropon Show, Shop 33, Tokyo, Japan, 1997.

Mr. Solo Exhibition: Oh–Edo Kunoichi Ninpocho, Shop 33, Tokyo, Japan, 1998.

Ero Pop Tokyo, George's, Los Angeles, California, 1998.

Hiropon 32.80, NADiff, Tokyo, Japan, 1999.

Hiropon Show, Parco Gallery, Nagoya, Japan, 1999.

Tokyo Girls Bravo, George's, Los Angeles, California, 1999.

Tokyo Girls Bravo, NADiff, Tokyo, Japan, 1999.

Hiropon Show, Parco Gallery, Tokyo, Japan, 1999.

Superflat, The Museum of Contemporary Art, Los Angeles, California, 2000.

Walker Art Center, Minneapolis, Minnesota, 2000.

Henry Art Gallery, Seattle, Washington, 2000.

Superflat, Parco Gallery, Tokyo, Japan, 2000.

Aya Takano Solo Exhibition: Hot Banana Fudge, NADiff, Tokyo, Japan, 2000.

Hiropon Show, Museum of Contemporary Art Tokyo, Tokyo, Japan, 2001.

Coloriage, Fondation Cartier pour l'art contemporain, Paris, France, 2002.

Sources

Periodicals

ARTnews, March 2001, pp. 134–37.

Newsday, September 22, 2003, p. B6.

New York Times, July 18, 1999; July 25, 2001, p. E1.

People, September 15, 2003, pp. 75–76.
Wired, November 2003, pp. 180–82.

Online

"Kaikai Kiki Artist Profiles: Takashi Murakami," Kaikai Kiki Co. Ltd. Online, http://www.kaikaikiki.co.jp/plofilenew/murakami/index–e.html (October 29, 2003).
"Move Over, Andy Warhol," *Time Pacific,* http://www.time.com/time/pacific/magazine/20030609/murakami.html (November 19, 2003).

"Takashi Murakami," Marianne Boesky Gallery, http://www.marianneboeskygallery.com/getpdf1505.pdf (October 29, 2003).

Transcripts

Day to Day, National Public Radio, September 15, 2003.

—*Lisa Frick*

Indra Nooyi

President and Chief Financial Officer of Pepsico

Born Indra K. Nooyi, October 28, 1955, in Madras, India; married to Raj; children: two daughters. *Education:* Madras Christian College, B.S.; Indian Institute of Management, M.B.A.; Yale University, M.S.

Addresses: *Office*—Pepsico, 700 Anderson Hill Rd., Purchase, NY 10577.

Career

Worked at British textile company Tootal in India; product manager for Johnson & Johnson in India; moved to United States to attend management school at Yale; after graduation worked at Boston Consulting Group; joined Motorola, 1986; moved to Asea Brown Boveri, 1990; joined Pepsico as strategist, 1994; became CFO of Pepsico, 2000; became president of Pepsico, 2001.

Member: Yale President's Council on International Activities; Yale School of Management Advisory Board.

Sidelights

Indra Nooyi is one of the top female executives in the United States, and the highest–ranking female executive of Indian descent. After taking a top management position at Pepsico in 1994, Nooyi oversaw major decisions that affected the direction of the food and beverage giant. She helped Pepsico spin off its fast food restaurant chains in 1997, and engineered its unloading of its bottling operations. Nooyi also handled the company's acquisition of Tropicana in 1998 and of Quaker Oats in 2001. Nooyi became Pepsico's chief financial officer in 2000, then added the title of president the next year. She is the number–two executive behind Steve Reinemund at the $20 billion company, and may be in line to run Pepsico in the future.

Nooyi was born in Madras, India, in 1955, into what she described as a conservative family. She led an unusual life for a girl of that time. She loved rock music, and played guitar in an all–girl rock band. She was also an avid cricket player. She earned an undergraduate degree at Madras Christian College, and followed this up with a master's from the Indian Institute of Management in Calcutta. This was one of only two business schools in India at that time, and it was an unusual choice for a woman, who was expected to be more interested in helping her mother around the house. Nooyi got a job with Tootal, a British textile firm, and then worked for the global consumer products company Johnson & Johnson in its Bombay office. Nooyi took on a very difficult assignment, becoming Johnson & Johnson's area product manager for its Stayfree brand sanitary pads. At that time, not only could such a product not be advertised in India, but many retailers shied away from stocking sanitary pads. Nooyi did her marketing directly, traveling to schools and colleges to educate female consumers and introduce them to the Johnson & Johnson line.

While she enjoyed her work at Johnson & Johnson, Nooyi nursed an ambition to study in the United States. She saw a magazine advertisement for Yale

University's School of Management, which was then a new program. She liked the fact that its dean was not an academic but had an industry background. Without many expectations, she applied. She was surprised to be accepted, and to get financial aid, but she was even more surprised that her parents let her go. She told Sarah Murray of the *Financial Times,* "It was unheard of for a good, conservative, south Indian Brahmin girl to do this. It would make her an absolutely unmarriageable commodity after that." Nevertheless, Nooyi went, beginning her management courses in 1978.

Despite her scholarship, Nooyi had little money and she had to work in the evenings. When she first applied for summer jobs, she had no business suit, and could not afford to buy one. So she blithely attended her interviews in a sari. Her unusual style did not seem to hold her back. Nooyi noted that by the end of her first summer job, she could afford two suits. After she graduated, Nooyi went to work for the Boston Consulting Group, and stayed with that firm for six years. In 1986 she joined the electronics firm Motorola, where she worked on strategic planning. In 1990 she took a job as a top manager at the Connecticut engineering firm Asea Brown Boveri.

In 1994, Nooyi was looking for a new job, and she landed two highly desireable offers. One was at General Electric, and the other was with Pepsico. She told Pepsico's then–CEO Wayne Calloway that she was having trouble deciding. He told her he thought General Electric was a great company, but on the other hand, he really needed her at Pepsico, and he would make it a special place for her. So Nooyi signed on, becoming Pepsico's chief strategist. She was involved in the very highest level of planning for the company's future. Pepsico had long dogged rival Coca–Cola, but had evolved into a complicated business that reached beyond its flagship Pepsi drink. Nooyi spent months reviewing the economics of different parts of the Pepsico empire. She came to a surprising decision, which was that the company should shed its restaurant division. Pepsico owned the fast food chains Pizza Hut, KFC, and Taco Bell. Pepsico's CEO wanted to hold onto the division, but Nooyi insisted that the company would be better off without it. Finally, in 1997, she got her way. She then led the company to get rid of its bottling division, fearing it was a drag on Pepsico's stock market valuation. Her next moves were the acquisition of the juice maker Tropicana and of the breakfast cereal and snack maker Quaker Oats.

The changes Nooyi made at Pepsico transformed the company. Nooyi became Pepsico's chief financial officer in 2000, and over the next year, the company's stock price rose almost 30 percent. Revenue increased about eight percent, and earnings went up by 13 percent. Pepsico now had a strong grouping of well–known snack food and drink brands, with its addition of Quaker Oats and Tropicana. "For any part of the day we will have a little snack for you," boasted Nooyi to *BusinessWeek.* The company had long done well in suburban markets. It now hoped to grow in urban areas, which required a different marketing strategy. For this, Nooyi had to work closely with chief operating officer Steve Reinemund. Reinemund became chief executive of Pepsico in 2001, and he promoted Nooyi to president. It was very important to Reinemund, a former Marine and apparently the quintessential buttoned–down businessman, to have Nooyi's more spontaneous personality and great analytical skills to balance his own insight into the future of the company. The two admittedly made an odd pair, characterized by *BusinessWeek* as "one of the most unusual management teams in Corporate America." But their opposite strengths seemed to do well for the company. Nooyi is seven years younger than Reinemund, and seems poised to become chief executive of Pepsico at some point down the road.

Sources

BusinessWeek, April 10, 2000, p. 180; January 29, 2001, p. 102.
Financial Times, January 26, 2004, p. 3.
Forbes, January 20, 2003, p. 74.
Time, December 1, 2003, p. 73.

—A. Woodward

Dean Ornish

Physician and author

Born July 16, 1953, in Dallas, TX; son of Edwin (a dentist) and Natalie (a historian) Ornish; married Shirley E. Brown (a nutritional expert and co-director of Ornish's research; divorced, 1994); married Mary Blackwell, June, 1998. *Education:* Attended Rice University; University of Texas at Austin, B.A. (summa cum laude), 1975; Baylor College of Medicine, M.D., 1980.

Addresses: *Agent*—c/o Random House, Inc., 201 E. 50th St., New York, NY 10022. *Home*—Sausalito, CA. *Office*—Preventive Medicine Research Institute, 900 Bridgeway, Ste. 2, Sausalito, CA 94965.

Career

Completed internship and residency at Massachusetts General Hospital and Harvard Medical School, early 1980s; assistant clinical professor of medicine and attending physician, University of California, San Francisco, School of Medicine, Division of General Internal Medicine, 1984—; medical staff and attending physician, Presbyterian Hospital, California Pacific Medical Center, San Francisco, 1984—; founder, president, and Bucksbaum Chair in Preventive Medicine of Preventive Medicine Research Institute, Sausalito, CA, 1984—. Named to the National Institutes of Health Planning Panel to Assess Unconventional Medical Practices, 1992.

Member: Harris County Medical Society, American Medical Students Association (founding member), American Medical Association, American College of Physicians (associate), Massachusetts Medical Society, Suffolk County Medical Society, American Association for the Advancement of Science, New York Academy of Sciences, American Heart Association, Society of Behavioral Medicine (fellow), American Heart Association, Phi Beta Kappa, Omicron Delta Kappa, Phi Kappa Phi.

Awards: Moody C. Bettis Memorial Award for Excellence in Community Medicine; Franzheim Award, The Franzheim Synergy Trust; has also won photography awards.

Sidelights

San Francisco–area physician Dean Ornish is the author of several best–selling books that tout a low–fat, high–carbohydrate diet and moderate exercise program as the best way to prevent and even reverse cardiac disease. Ornish also runs seminars and "healthy lifestyle" retreats that teach patients how to maintain both a sensible diet and positive outlook on life. Though some in the medical community were initially wary about Ornish's ideas, follow–up studies have demonstrated that his program has indeed been able to unstick some of the plaque build–up in arteries that causes a heart attack, and by 2003 several major health insurers covered the cost of enrollment. "The work has made Ornish one of the few practitioners to successfully test an Eastern style of health care," according to *Los Angeles Times* columnist Shari Roan, "which focuses on holistic healing, using traditional, Western scientific methods."

The son of a dentist, Ornish was born in Dallas, Texas, in 1953 and grew into an overachieving, academically excelling teen. An early interest in magic was supplanted by a fascination with photography, and Ornish combined the demands of school with his own business as a wedding photographer. He finished high school a National Merit scholar, and in the early 1970s, while a student at Rice University, enjoyed a budding career in rock photojournalism, with some of his images even making it into the pages of *Rolling Stone*. Yet, during his second year as a biochemistry major Ornish sank into a deep depression. "I felt I couldn't keep up," he recalled of the time in an interview with *People* writer Ron Arias. "The more I worried, the harder it was to study, and the harder it was to study, the more I worried. I couldn't sleep, and that made me crazy. Finally, I was sitting in organic chemistry and I thought, 'Of course, I'll just kill myself.'"

Fortunately, Ornish was diagnosed with mononucleosis and went back to his parents' home to recuperate before he could carry out his decision. He also began psychotherapy, but it was only when he met the man who had helped his older sister overcome her debilitating migraine headaches that his own outlook vastly improved. Under the watch of his new mentor, Swami Satchidananda, Ornish began yoga, meditation, and a vegetarian diet, and even spent time at the Swami's Virginia center. The Eastern–influenced tenets, he told Arias, hold "that peace and self–worth are there only if we can quiet the mind and body enough to experience them." With his sense of purpose now renewed, Ornish re–enrolled in college and graduated first in his class at the University of Texas at Austin in 1975.

From there, Ornish went on to medical school at Houston's Baylor College of Medicine, and began to see firsthand the long–term effects of an unhealthy Western lifestyle. As an internist in training, he recalled in a *Forbes* interview with Dyan Machan, "we'd cut people open, we'd bypass the blocked arteries. The patients would get home, eat the same foods, smoke, not manage stress, not exercise and, more often than not, the bypass would just clog up." The existing condition called was called arteriosclerosis, or hardening of the arteries, and was caused by a plaque build–up on the artery walls. The plaque was tied to the level of cholesterol in the blood, which could soar to dangerously high numbers after years of a diet high in animal fat. The coronary disease was also aggravated by smoking, stress, and a sedentary lifestyle. When Ornish was in medical school, new advances in medical technology were enabling heart surgeons to operate on these at–risk patients, who were in danger of fatal cardiac arrest. In the hours–long surgery, less damaged veins were taken from the arms and legs, and then put in place to "bypass" the damaged arteries near the heart.

Ornish began his first studies on the correlation between diet and arteriosclerosis while still in medical school at Baylor in the late 1970s. He signed up cardiac patients who were willing to try a new approach that included a strict diet and reasonable exercise program, and the results were encouraging from the start. Monitoring the plaque build–up in his subjects, he was pleased to find that it often decreased. He carried out further research while completing his internal–medicine residency at the esteemed Massachusetts General Hospital in Boston. In 1984, Ornish settled in the San Francisco Bay area, having culled $600,000 in private donations to open his Preventive Medicine Research Institute, and began to conduct further test studies.

The number of patients in Ornish's program grew, and the consistently positive results were encouraging. Those who followed the program strictly reported a lessening of angina—the chest pain associated with coronary heart disease—and Ornish found that cholesterol levels had dropped and their plaque build–up decreased by ten percent. By contrast, those in the control groups who did not follow the program showed a five–percent increase in plaque. The first mainstream media outlet to report on Ornish's findings was *Psychology Today* in 1989, and a year later the American Medical Association (AMA) also published the results of one of his studies.

Ornish decided to expand upon the suggestions in his first book, 1982's *Stress, Diet, and Your Heart*, into *Dr. Dean Ornish's Program for Reversing Heart Disease: The Only System Scientifically Proven to Reverse Heart Disease without Drugs or Surgery*. The new work was published by Random House in 1990, and sales slowly increased, partly through word–of–mouth, over the next few years. It seemed to incite a minor revolution in health–care philosophy for a generation of aging, previously skeptical Americans, with *Natural Health* writer Bill Thomson commending Ornish for delivering "a radical, promising message to doctors and patients, which was that the body, on its own, can often heal the deadliest of diseases."

Ornish's food plan countered the typical American diet, which studies show contains about 40 percent fat. Established guidelines to prevent heart disease recommend no more than a 30 percent fat–intake level. As a result, Americans are 20 times more susceptible to arteriosclerosis and other cardiac problems than in other places around the globe—such as Asia—where national diets are far leaner. Ornish counseled Americans to instead follow a diet that was low in fat, abundant in fruits, vegetables, beans, and whole grains, and absent of almost any sugar, dairy, or white–flour products. He also advised at least three hours of light to moderate exercise weekly, and one hour a day of stretching, breathing, and meditation. Ornish was also convinced that a group support system, in which participants learned better interpersonal communication skills, was crucial to reducing stress levels. "My program is not about sacrifice," he asserted to Machan in the *Forbes* article. "It's a matter of replacing something bad for you with something better."

Though the American Heart Association initially endorsed the Ornish Heart Disease Reversal Program, it cautioned that his diet was probably too strict for many to follow. Yet those who participated in the program said that it was not as difficult as it appeared, and claimed they enjoyed the marked physical improvement almost immediately. His next book, *Eat More, Weigh Less: Dr. Dean Ornish's Life Choice Program for Losing Weight Safely While Eating Abundantly*, hit bookstores in 1993 and boosted his diet–guru status immensely. He was even invited onto President Bill Clinton's staff of personal physicians; the commander–in–chief and his wife, Hillary Rodham Clinton, also asked Ornish to train the White House kitchen staff. Ornish's program moved from the Bay Area into several other American cities when forward–thinking hospitals began offering it. His research, aided by a National Institutes of Health grant, proved solid enough that several health insurers began to cover the cost of the Heart Disease Reversal Program.

Ornish's career was in high gear by 1994, but the sudden fame caused him to once again question the direction of his life, and he suffered another bout with depression after his one–year–old marriage to a fellow physician ended. In response, he cut back on his public appearances, and returned to therapy. "I've learned that when my work is ego–driven, it makes me lonely," he told *Newsweek* journalist Geoffrey Cowley for a 1998 cover story. "When I approach it in a spirit of service, I'm much happier." In the seminars he continues to run, Ornish explains why focusing on family and loved ones, and giving back to the community, helps to reduce stress levels and is even a proven life–extending strategy. He expanded on these themes in his next book, *Love and Survival: The Scientific Basis for the Healing Power of Intimacy*, which appeared in 1998. "The heart is a metaphor and symbol as well as an anatomical organ," he explained to Thomson in the *Natural Health* interview. "Interventions are most effective when they address both aspects."

Ornish's *Love and Survival* book cited a study done of one Pennsylvania community that had been founded in the 1880s by southern Italian immigrants. In Roseto, heart disease was relatively rare until the 1960s—though the diet and lifestyle of its residents were similar to patterns elsewhere where coronary–related deaths were higher. When people began moving away from Roseto, the close–knit sense of community disintegrated, and heart disease rates suddenly skyrocketed. "Love and intimacy are at the root of what makes us sick and what makes us well," Ornish told *Newsweek* in explaining what had come to be known as the Roseto effect. "I am not aware of any other factor in medicine—not diet, not smoking, not exercise—that has a greater impact." Ornish also suggested that the fact that so many more Americans live in single–person households, sometimes far away from their extended families, only adds to the problem. "There's been a radical shift in our culture in the last 50 years," he told Cathy Perlmutter in a *Prevention* interview. "We've seen a breakdown of the family. Many people don't have a job, church, synagogue, or neighborhood that they've been a part of for very long."

Ornish's findings have been published in the *American Journal of Cardiology* and Britain's *Lancet*. In 1999, his Heart Disease Reversal Program became part of a Medicare pilot project, with some 1,800 senior citizens enrolled. In 2002, he reported the results of his recent study on prostate cancer treatment in men. The disease is the number–two cause of cancer death among American men, and a program Ornish devised—a vegan diet rich in soy and tomato products, exercise, and daily meditation—showed that the blood–marker indicators decreased after three months for prostate–cancer patients. Those who were able to adhere to the diet the most closely found that their numbers dropped nearly ten percent. Some in the oncology community scoffed at Ornish's newest study, noting that in cancer, any decrease less than 50 percent is unimportant, but as Ornish told *Newsweek* writers David Noonan and Karen Springen, "You don't need it to go down," he says. "You just need it to not go up."

In his hometown of Sausalito, just across San Francisco's Golden Gate Bridge, Ornish still runs the nonprofit Preventive Medicine Research Institute. He is also a clinical professor of medicine at the University of California's San Francisco campus, and his empire has expanded to include a line of groceries called Advantage\10. His schedule remains hectic, but he still practices yoga, as he told Roan in the *Los Angeles Times* article, because it serves to remind him that "what brings me happiness is already inside me if I'd just stop disturbing it." Remarried since 1998, Ornish speaks openly about his battles with depression, and is himself awed by the trajectory of his career. In the end, he told Roan, his story "really has all the elements of a great adventure. There are life and death issues. You have your known allies and your known adversaries, and your unknown allies and unknown adversaries. It's remarkable to me to watch it unfold."

Selected writings

Stress, Diet, and Your Heart, foreword by Alexander Leaf, recipes by Martha Rose Shulman, Holt (New York City), 1982.

Dr. Dean Ornish's Program for Reversing Heart Disease: The Only System Scientifically Proven to Reverse Heart Disease without Drugs or Surgery, Random House (New York City), 1990.

Eat More, Weigh Less: Dr. Dean Ornish's Life Choice Program for Losing Weight Safely While Eating Abundantly, HarperCollins (New York City), 1993.

(With Janet Fletcher, Jean–Marc Fullsack, and Helen Roe) *Everyday Cooking with Dr. Dean Ornish: 150 Easy, Low–Fat, High–Flavor Recipes,* HarperCollins, 1996.

Love and Survival: The Scientific Basis for the Healing Power of Intimacy, HarperCollins, 1998.

Sources

Periodicals

Family Practice News, November 1, 1999, p. 1.
Forbes, May 1, 2000, p. 84.
Journal of the American Medical Association (JAMA), December 15, 1993, p. 2876.
Lancet, February 20, 1999, p. 683.
Los Angeles Times, March 10, 1996, p. 5.
Natural Health, November–December 1998, p. 112.
Newsweek, March 16, 1998, p. 50, p. 54; April 22, 2002, p. 69.
New York Times, January 13, 2003, p. C12.
People, June 5, 1995, p. 97.
Prevention, August 1998, p. 118.
Psychology Today, January–February 1989, p. 46; May 1989, p. 60.

Online

Contemporary Authors Online, The Gale Group, 2001.

—Carol Brennan

OutKast

Rap duo

Members include André 3000 (born André Benjamin, May 27, 1975, in Georgia; son of Lawrence Walker (a collections agent) and Sharon Benjamin Hodo (a real estate agent); children: Seven (son, with Erykah Badu). *Education:* Took filmmaking courses at the University of Southern California.), vocals; Big Boi (born Antwan Patton, February 1, 1975, in Savannah, GA; son of Tony Kearse (a Marine Corps officer) and Rowena Patton (a retail supervisor); children: Jordan (daughter), Bamboo (son), Cross (son)), vocals.

Addresses: *Office*—c/o Arista Records, 6 W. 57th St., New York, NY 10019.

Career

Began writing rap songs while Atlanta high–school students; released first single, "Player's Ball," on LaFace Records, 1993; released first LP, *Southernplayalisticadillacmuzik*, 1994; released *ATLiens*, 1996; released *Aquemini*, 1998; released *Stankonia*, 2000; released *Speakerboxxx/The Love Below*, 2003. Film appearances by Benjamin include: *Hollywood Homicide*, 2003; *Be Cool*, 2004.

Awards: Grammy Award for best song by a rap duo or group, National Academy of Recording Arts and Sciences, 2001, for "Ms. Jackson," and best rap album of the year, 2001, for *Stankonia*; Grammy Awards for album of the year, best rap album of the year, 2003, for *Speakerboxxx/The Love Below*, and best urban/alternative performance, 2003, for "Hey Ya!"

Sidelights

André "3000" Benjamin and Antwan "Big Boi" Patton make up OutKast, the Atlanta–bred duo whose exuberant style has reshaped the sound of contemporary rap music. Their fifth release, *Speakerboxxx/The Love Below*, was actually dual solo records from each, and became one of the best–selling records of 2003. It won not only that year's Grammy Award for Best Rap Album of the Year, it took the Album of the Year statue as well.

Propelled by the overwhelming success of André 3000's infectious dance hit, "Hey Ya!"—a third Grammy–winner that year—the CD went on to sell 3.5 million copies. Releasing a pair of solo records under their OutKast name seemed a risky move for the group, which had a loyal fan base and were one of the first successful rap acts to emerge from the Atlanta music scene, but proved once again that Benjamin and Patton had a sixth sense for turning daring musical ideas into hit records. "Every album is a risk," Benjamin told *New York Times* writer Lola Ogunnaike. "It's not like we make the easiest music to swallow."

Benjamin and Patton were both born in 1975, and would later name both a record release and their boutique label "Aquemini" after a combination of their respective astrological signs—Benjamin, born May 27, is a Gemini, while Patton's February 1 birthdate makes him an Aquarius. Benjamin was the only child of Sharon Benjamin Hodo, a real es-

tate agent, and Lawrence Walker, a collections agent. Patton's mother, Rowena, was a retail supervisor, and his father, Tony Kearse, had been a sergeant in the Marine Corps. He was the first of five children in the family, and initially dreamed of a career in pro football, or child psychology. Benjamin thought about becoming an architect before realizing that it would require him to take an abundance of math classes.

The duo met Tri–Cities High School in East Point, Georgia, a school geared toward the performing arts. It was fashion that initially brought them together: "We were preps," Patton told *People* writer Chuck Arnold. "We wore loafers, argyle socks, and V–neck sweaters with T–shirts. We were new to the school and we didn't know anybody." But it was music that cemented their friendship: both were fans of alternative hip–hop acts like De La Soul, the Brand Nubians, and A Tribe Called Quest, and also appreciated the genius of George Clinton, Bootsy Collins, and other funk greats of the 1970s.

Benjamin and Patton wrote their first rap songs in class together, and began making mix tapes in their spare time. Their first working name was "2 Shades Deep," but they learned it was taken by another act. They then dubbed themselves the Misfits, but found out that was being used as well. Taking the "misfit" idea to the dictionary, "we came across the word outcast," Benjamin recalled in an interview for *Jet* with Marti Yarbrough, "and just kept the pronunciation key spelling of it."

Around the same time that Benjamin left Tri–Cities High after the eleventh grade, he and Patton met up with an Atlanta–area production team called Organized Noize that had worked with R&B group TLC. OutKast's first single, "Player's Ball," was released by LaFace, the label of Atlanta record mogul Antonio "LA" Reid in 1993, and reached No. 1 on the Billboard rap singles chart the following year. They became the first hip–hop act ever signed to LaFace, but Benjamin and Patton were determined to chart a new course in the urban/rap/hip–hop scene. "When I look at the rap videos, it's pretty much the same video over and over," Benjamin told *Newsweek* journalist Allison Samuels. "A bunch of women in swimsuits and the guys rapping about money or jewels. Me and Big Boi wanted to change that."

Benjamin and Patton's first full LP, *Southernplayalisticadillacmuzik*, was released in 1994, and reached No. 3 on the Billboard R&B/hip–hop albums chart. It also helped to put Atlanta on the map in the urban–music scene. Before the success of OutKast and fellow Georgians the Goodie Mob, rappers from the South received short shrift in the music industry, which focused on the hard–core movers and shakers from a New York–Los Angeles axis.

OutKast hit No. 1 on the Billboard R&B/hip–hop chart two years later with their second effort, *ATLiens*. It sold 1.5 million copies, buoyed by the track "Elevators (Me and You)." Their third CD, 1998's *Aquemini* went multi–platinum, but the single "Rosa Parks" brought a lawsuit from the civil–rights heroine not long after it reached No. 19 a year later. Parks sued the duo and their label for using her name without permission, and the case would eventually go all the way to the U.S. Supreme Court. Though *Aquemini* did not produce any other hit singles, it was enthusiastically received by critics and included on several year–end polls of the best releases of 1998.

Around this same time, Benjamin dropped the "Dre" tag he had used for years in favor of the spacier "André 3000." He also became known for his flamboyant outfits, which included platinum wigs, fake–fur trousers, and an array of colorful suit–and–shirt combinations in eye–popping plaids and patterns. The outrageous wardrobe seemed an update of the funk superstar George Clinton, and Benjamin and Patton also borrowed the word "stank" from the funk heyday of the 1970s. They called their new Atlanta studio Stankonia, and dubbed their fourth release that as well.

The 17 tracks on 2000's *Stankonia* included the hits "B.O.B. (Bombs over Baghdad)" and "Ms. Jackson," and gave Benjamin and Patton two Grammy Awards, one of them for Best Rap Album of the Year. Once again, critics were ecstatic about the way in which OutKast brought together old–school with a modern twist. This release, noted *Newsweek* reviewer Lorraine Ali, "continues OutKast's journey into the weird with a sound that lies somewhere between the jamming madness of Parliament–Funkadelic, the creme de menthe vocals of Al Green, and the bumping beats of A Tribe Called Quest."

Stankonia seemed to show the two high–school pals maturing into one of rap music's more contemplative and inventive acts. The warring themes on it, one critic felt, signified the coming–of–age of the genre at a precise moment when its credibility was wavering. "With unassuming brilliance, OutKast has finessed a major rift that now runs through hip–hop," wrote *New York Times* music critic Jon Pareles. "On one side, the more commercial one, are gangsta

characters working ever more familiar variations on tales of gunplay and sex.... On the other side, in a growing backlash, are rappers who see gangsta rap reinforcing the ugliest stereotypes: no longer the defiant power fantasies of inner–city underdogs, but a demeaning show–business shtick that only pretends to be 'keeping it real.'"

Nearly three years passed before Benjamin and Patton returned with a new record—but it was a dual CD that became one of the biggest hits of the year. *Speakerboxxx/The Love Below* came out on Arista in September of 2003. *Speakerboxxx* and *The Love Below* were essentially solo CDs from Benjamin and Patton, but packaged together in a move that was initially viewed as potentially career–damaging. The two records could not have been more different in style, noted Kelefa Sanneh in a *New York Times* article. "*Speakerboxxx* is propelled by Big Boi's precise, sticky rhymes, and *The Love Below* floats along on Andre 3000's not–quite–angelic falsetto singing," Sanneh asserted, and wondered if OutKast fans would be happy with the package.

Critics loved the work, pronouncing it the duo's most daring to date, and fans voted at both cash registers and on Internet download sites. There was some cross–over between the two: Benjamin co–wrote four tracks for Patton's *Speakerboxxx*, which was the more rap–flavored half of the release. It opened with "GhettoMusick," which *Entertainment Weekly* critic Will Hermes found "a machine–gun–speed rap reclaiming '80s electrofunk from hipster ironists while targeting low–aiming rappers." Hermes found some missteps in *Speakerboxxx*, but noted its musical guest stars added to its charms. "Even the old–school tracks have a twist, whether it's Jay–Z rapping the hook of 'Flip Flop Rock,' or 'Reset,' with its dice–roll percussion and sermon by Big Boi's Georgia neighbor Cee–Lo," Hermes concluded.

Patton co–wrote the "Roses" track for Benjamin's *The Love Below*, which was a more experimental, funk– and jazz–influenced work. The project actually began as soundtrack to a film that Benjamin had co–authored. "It was an experiment, so it was fun for me and it was personal at the same time," he told *Jet*'s Yarbrough. "Originally it wasn't supposed to be catered to the OutKast fan. It wasn't supposed to be the package that I delivered because people know me for rhyming. The movie was a love story so these songs made sense." Hermes found it, from start to finish, "as strange and rich a trip as pop offers nowadays, a song cycle about love's battle against fear and (self–) deception that's frequently profound, hilarious, and very, very sexy," his *Entertainment Weekly* review asserted.

The Love Below produced the immensely successful hit single "Hey Ya!" This catchy, exuberant song became the No. 1 downloaded song on Internet music sites, and a minor pop–culture phenomenon as well, with the line "shake it like a Polaroid picture" entering the vernacular and even prompting a cautionary response from Polaroid that their instant–camera photos should actually not be shaken to speed up the drying process. In November of 2003, on a campaign stop in New England, presidential candidate General Wesley Clark even quoted the line in an attempt to show off some pop–culture credibility to younger voters.

Clark also weighed in on the topic that worried OutKast's fans: whether the two solo releases marked the end of the era for the group. But both Benjamin and Patton asserted in many interviews that their partnership was still strong, and they had no plans to part ways. "We were just showing how we'd each grown musically in our own way," Patton said of the two–disc release in the *Newsweek* interview with Samuels, and told another reporter, the *New York Times*'s Ogunnaike, that he and Benjamin were sitting on "six albums worth of material. That's plenty to work with."

By mid–February, *Speakerboxxx/The Love Below* had sold more than three million copies and spent seven weeks at No. 1 on the Billboard 200 chart. Nominated for six Grammy Awards, it won Album of the Year, Rap Album of the Year, and Best Alternative–Urban Performance for "Hey Ya!"

Patton handles the financial decisions for the business that is OutKast, which absorbs several hours weekly. This frees Benjamin to explore his creative side, such as the screenwriting project. He also started taking clarinet and saxophone lessons, and enrolled in film classes at the University of Southern California. In 2003, he appeared in a small part in the Harrison Ford movie *Hollywood Homicide,* and was later cast in *Be Cool,* the sequel to *Get Shorty.* He was also producing a Gwen Stefani solo project slated for 2004 release. Benjamin was named one of *People* magazine's "50 Most Beautiful People" in the May 10, 2004, issue.

Both Benjamin and Patton are parents. Patton, who lives in Fayetteville, Georgia, told *People*'s Arnold, "I'm a soccer dad." He has a daughter and two sons.

Benjamin has son with singer Erykah Badu, with whom he shares custody. Badu's mother was the inspiration behind OutKast's first Grammy–winning single, "Ms. Jackson." Mired in sorrow over their breakup, Benjamin wrote a song in which he promised to be a good parent despite the split. As he explained in the *People* interview, "It was about us not being together [anymore] and thinking, 'Well, what does Erykah's mom think?'" He told Arnold that he and his son's grandmother "laugh and joke about it now. Her mom will still say, 'I should be getting paid for that song.'"

Selected discography

"Player's Ball" (cassette single), LaFace Records, 1993.
Southernplayalisticadillacmuzik, LaFace Records, 1994.
ATLiens, LaFace Records, 1996.
Aquemini, LaFace Records, 1998.
Stankonia, Arista, 2000.
Speakerboxxx/The Love Below, Arista, 2003.

Sources

Periodicals

Billboard Bulletin, December 9, 2003, p. 3.
Daily Variety, May 17, 2004, p. 6.
Entertainment Weekly, September 19, 2003, p. 83; December 26, 2003, p. 78; February 6, 2004, p. 16.
Jet, February 2, 2004, p. 58.
Newsweek, October 30, 2000, p. 88; September 22, 2003, p. 86.
New York Times, October 29, 2000, p. 32; September 7, 2003, p. AR87; October 5, 2003, p. AR1.
People, February 16, 2004, p. 87; May 10, 2004.
Time, September 29, 2003, p. 71.

Online

"Clark Faces Late–Night Laugh Test," CBSNews.com, http://www.cbsnews.com/stories/2003/11/19/politics/main584458.shtml (June 18, 2004).

—*Carol Brennan*

Lindsay Owen-Jones

Chairman and Chief Executive Officer of L'Oreal S.A.

Born c. 1946 in Wallasey, England. *Education:* Oxford University, B.A., 1968; Insead, Fountainebleu, France (graduate business degree), 1969.

Addresses: *Office*—L'Oreal S.A., 41 rue Martre, 92117 Clichy, France.

Career

Began as sales representative for L'Oreal, 1969; director of Italian division, 1978–81; head of L'Oreal's U.S. subsidiary Cosmair, 1981–84; made chief executive of L'Oreal, 1984; chairman, 1988—.

Member: French Order of the Legion of Honor; Commander of the British Empire; board member, Gesparal, BNP Paribas, Sanofi–Synthelabo.

Awards: Officer, French Order of the Legion of Honor, 1998; honorary degree, Cranfield School of Management (UK), 2001; French Manager of the Year, 2002; Commander of the British Empire.

Sidelights

Lindsay Owen–Jones heads one of the largest companies in France, the cosmetics firm L'Oreal S.A. He is the first foreigner ever to reach such a rank in a major French business. Owen–Jones, an Englishman, worked his way up at L'Oreal, rising from shampoo salesman to chairman. He was only 37 when he was named chief executive officer (CEO). Owen–Jones transformed L'Oreal from a French stalwart to a powerhouse in Europe and the United States, with growing markets in Japan, China, and parts of Africa. Sales rose from $3.7 billion in his first year as CEO to more than $14 billion in 2002. L'Oreal remained consistently profitable under Owen–Jones, even as other well–known cosmetics companies floundered. Owen–Jones was responsible for some daring acquisitions, such as picking up the lackluster Maybelline brand in 1996. Maybelline quadrupled its sales over the next six years and became the number–one makeup brand in the world. Owen–Jones is esteemed for his careful long–term business planning. He has proved willing to take risks and make mistakes in the near term in order to achieve a distant goal.

Owen–Jones was born in the town of Wallasey, near Liverpool, England. His father, of Welsh descent, was an executive at a textile firm, and his mother was a teacher. He was the only son in a family that included three daughters. His parents pushed him to achieve, and always expected him to come in first in his class. When he was accepted to Oxford University amid torrid competition, his mother was not surprised, and seemingly not that anxious to congratulate him. She hoped that he would become a diplomat, and for years she was disappointed in his choice of a business career. Owen–Jones studied modern languages at Oxford, and then moved on to Insead, a prestigious business school in France. While still a graduate student, Owen–Jones met some L'Oreal employees who convinced him that the cosmetics firm did the best marketing in France. Owen–Jones told Gigi Mahon of *Barron's* that manufacturing and marketing products for women came naturally to him. "I had already discovered that I really loved women, and having been brought up with sisters I was less awe–inspired and more aware of the day–to–day. I was far less lost looking at a lipstick than most of my men friends were. So I said, hell, this sounds like more fun than selling machine tools or building nuclear plants."

Owen–Jones joined L'Oreal in 1969 as a sales representative. His job was hawking shampoo in Normandy, a rural area that did not make for the most dazzling assignment. Yet he did well, and moved on to a marketing position. Here Owen–Jones admits to making several mistakes. He tried to introduce a new hairspray, Toute Douceur, which was promoted as a "soft" spray that women applied three times a day, as opposed to a "hard" spray that went on only once. It seemed like a good way to triple hairspray sales, but Toute Douceur was evidently too soft to work well at all, and consumers rejected it. Another Owen–Jones introduction was a hair lotion packed in a pressurized glass bottle. This had to be rapidly swept off market shelves, as the product had the unfortunate tendency to explode. After several debacles, Owen–Jones was sure he was going to be fired. But instead he was promoted to head L'Oreal's Belgian division. The Belgian division had been doing badly, but Owen–Jones managed to turn it around, and it became a very profitable unit. From 1978 to 1981 he headed the Italian division, and then he moved to Cosmair, L'Oreal's United States subsidiary. Cosmair was considered L'Oreal's most important overseas division, so this was a significant promotion for Owen–Jones. Owen–Jones jumped into the competitive American market, which was dominated by Estée Lauder, Revlon, and other United States brands. Owen–Jones was able to convince major department stores to give L'Oreal's Lancôme line as much counter space as Estée Lauder. Consequently, sales for Lancôme rose by 25 percent.

Having done so well in the difficult American market, Owen–Jones was recalled to Paris in 1984 and made chief executive of L'Oreal S.A. Four years later he became chairman of the company as well. He became the only foreigner to head a major French company, and as of 2002 he was still alone in that honor. His task was to keep L'Oreal French, while at the same time making it a global player. When Owen–Jones took over L'Oreal, some 75 percent of the company's sales were in Europe, and most of that was in France. Owen–Jones made the core French brands like Lancôme, Helena Rubinstein, and L'Oreal Paris into worldwide players. At the same time, he acquired other brands which had very different images, and revved them up. Owen–Jones had L'Oreal spend $758 million in 1996 to acquire the Memphis, Tennessee–based Maybelline brand, a staple of the United States mid–price market with barely any international sales. Owen–Jones moved Maybelline headquarters out of Memphis to New York, added "New York" to the brand name, and marketed a line of hot new lipsticks and nail polishes in Japan. By 2001, Maybelline was raking in $1 billion in sales, and more than half of that came from markets in Europe and Asia. In a similar move, Owen–Jones also bought two United States hair-care companies that catered to African Americans and combined them into a new brand, Soft Sheen/Carson. L'Oreal began selling Soft Sheen/Carson in South Africa, Senegal, and other French–speaking countries, where its sales grew steadily. In another attempt to gain an international market, Owen–Jones also oversaw a marketing agreement with the Japanese cosmetics company Shu Uemura. He hoped to learn the intricacies of selling beauty products in Asia from Shu Uemura, and increase sales in Japan as well as in the burgeoning Chinese market.

Owen–Jones was scheduled to retire in 2006, when he reached the age of 60. He had done so well, it was difficult to imagine L'Oreal without him. While he had not named a successor by 2003, Owen–Jones did seem intent on sticking to the retirement schedule. He has many absorbing interests, including sailing and racing vintage cars. Owen–Jones also enjoys flying helicopters, which he describes as very difficult and dangerous. It is up to him to determine if flying and racing are more exciting than piloting a venerable beauty company from European prominence to world dominance.

Sources

Barron's, December 5, 1983, pp. 30–34.
BusinessWeek, January 13, 2003, p. 66.
Fortune, September 30, 2002, p. 141.

—A. Woodward

Chuck Palahniuk

Author

Born February 21, 1962, in Pasco, WA; son of Fred and Carol Palahniuk. *Education:* University of Oregon, journalism major, 1986.

Addresses: *Agent*—Edward Hibbert Donadio and Olson, Inc. 121 W. 27th St., Ste. 704, New York, NY 10001.

Career

Mechanic, Freightliner; published *Fight Club,* 1996; published *Survivor,* 1999; published *Invisible Monsters,* 1999; published *Choke,* 2001; published *Lullaby,* 2002; published *Diary,* 2003.

Member: The Portland Chapter of The National Cacophony Society.

Awards: PNBA Award for *Fight Club,* 1997; Bram Stoker Award for *Lullaby,* 2003.

Sidelights

The editors who read Chuck Palahniuk's unpublished manuscript, *Invisible Monsters,* were blown away by the new talent's first novel. The story was written with a provocative style and risked delving into the hidden forces that drive Americans in their daily lives. Every editor who read the book loved it, but not one of them would buy it. The tale was too twisted and no one wanted to be known for buying, much less enjoying, such a shocking story. So Palahniuk received rejection letters, praising him for his talent and wishing him luck. The young author was angry but he was not discouraged. Instead he decided to write an edgier story that would make the editors squirm even more. The result was *Fight Club,* a book about men and their primal urge to use their fists. *Fight Club,* published quickly in 1996 and adapted to screen in the cult hit of the same name, would go on to set a benchmark that many young writers aspire to today. *Booklist* wrote about the book, "Every generation frightens and unnerves its parents, and Palahniuk's first novel is Gen X's most articulate assault yet on baby–boomer sensibilities."

Palahniuk was born February 21, 1962, in Pasco, Washington. His home life was unspectacular on the surface, but underneath that façade his family held a violent and tragic secret. Palahniuk's paternal grandfather killed his wife and tried to kill Fred, Chuck's father, with a shotgun. But the boy hid under a bed as his father looked for him, the butt of the gun dragging on the floor behind him. When the disturbed man could not find his son, he shot himself. Unfortunately, this tale of violence would not be the last to touch the Palahniuk family.

Palahniuk discovered his talent with words at the University of Oregon where he studied journalism. He will not allow anyone to read his writings from that era but it is clear that his time in college was key to developing his observational skills. After graduation he went on to work at a number of odd jobs including a diesel mechanic. Palahniuk felt comfortable in more blue–collar jobs where he could be a people–watcher. He was fascinated by what drives people to behave as they do. One aspect of American life, in particular, became his obsession— the ability to recreate yourself to be what you dream you should be. "I think that the central, most American literary theme is the invention of self," he told C.P. Farley of Powells.com. "We see it in Henry James's *Bostonians*; we see it in *The Great Gatsby*; we see it in *Breakfast at Tiffany's*.... It's such an American genre, this whole idea of reinventing and creating your self based on your dream, or how you perceive yourself to be, or not to be.... So I really wanted to play with that." Perhaps an insight into why this theme appealed to him can be found in another comment he made to Farley.

"As a child my father impressed upon me that if you are going to do stupid things you are going to have to pay the price. Once he actually threatened to chop off my finger with an axe for something I'd done. And at that moment it became incredibly clear to me that I am a cause in my own life, that I had to take responsibility for myself for the rest of my life, and not blame anyone for the things that I did...." The struggle to define who he was obsessed Palahniuk and he yearned to write about it, but he did not feel he was ready to write a book.

An avid reader and lover of books, Palahniuk finally admitted to himself (with the support of some writing friends) that he wanted to write a novel of his own. Finally, in his mid–30s, he decided to commit his ideas to paper and write his first book, so he began work on *Invisible Monsters*. Palahniuk's strong need to explore the dynamics of identity in American life forced him to ask some tough questions that he had never seen addressed well in literature: How susceptible are we to the images around us? How much sway does a movie or an advertisement hold over us? Are we able to fight a force so powerful with only our own sense of identity as a defense? When he completed the book, he knew he had written a story filled with taboos but he could not have guessed at the response he was about to get.

He sent the book to a number of editors in New York City publishing houses. The feedback he got was confusing, to say the least. On one hand, everyone adored the book; on the other hand, no one wanted to touch it. It was called too risky, obscene, and unmarketable. Palahniuk was angry and disappointed by the response. So, since he loved being contrary, he decided he would write something that would disturb them even more. The result was *Fight Club*.

Written for a writers' club made up of his friends, Palahniuk crafted the tale while holding down a job as a diesel mechanic for Freightliner. *Fight Club* was the perfect book for the times. Many American men, frustrated with modern society's idea of how they should behave, were looking for a different perspective on what it means to be a man. Palahniuk tackled the issue directly and created a character who was well–behaved on the surface, but haunted by demons that made him want to fight—not for any cause in particular, just to feel the pain of it and to see if he could handle it.

Palahniuk himself had a taste for fist fights. His first big fight was in a campground when some neighboring campers were playing music too loud. Screaming became punching and Palahniuk got pounded. His cuts and bruises showed for weeks. When he went back to work he found that people could not make eye contact with him. He was mysterious to them. The bruises meant he could lose control. He was the face of chaos and he loved the feeling, so he wrote about it.

This time Palahniuk's book was published, but it only found obscurity in the marketplace, with good reviews and only passable sales. However, *Fight Club* was optioned by Hollywood and an adaptation was written by Jim Uhls. The screenplay quickly caught the eye of Brad Pitt, who identified with the listlessness of the characters and the violent reaction to life in America. *Fight Club*, the movie, was released in 1999, directed by David Fincher (also known for his films *Seven* and *Alien 3*). Though the film did not do blockbuster numbers, it was highly acclaimed and has gone on to become a huge cult hit, pulling the novel along with it. As it turned out, many men identified with the complex message of being male in a society that does not want to openly discuss the violence that exists under its civilized and mature surface. If anything, Palahniuk was trying to get a handle on what makes us consider ourselves adults, or mature. "I don't perceive that we have a lot of rituals for establishing adulthood in our society," he told Tasha Robinson of *The Onion*. "It seems for me that it's been about the impulse to rush out and buy a lot of stuff so I feel like a grownup, or commit to a relationship at age 17 so I feel like a grownup. It's about trying to, in a way, arbitrarily complete myself with a rite of passage, because there is no rite of passage that says, 'Okay, now you're an adult.'"

Palahniuk was enjoying tremendous success and found that he could write for a living, something he was skeptical would ever happen. He quickly delivered a number of books, identical in theme and similarly sharp in tone. *Survivor, Invisible Monsters* (released in a different form than when he first sent it out years before) and *Choke* all dealt with identity and how the protagonist can transform and what the consequences are of that transformation. Palahniuk had developed a reputation for making the bizarre seem realistic. His sense of violence seemed sophisticated, as if uncomfortable moments and dangerous lifestyles were just under the surface for all of us. Palahniuk is very aware of this and tries not to cross the line. To cross that line, in his opinion, is inviting failure. Violence without meaning will just lose the audience.

With great success under his belt, it appeared he was set for life. But in the midst of his success Palahniuk's family was about to be dealt another senselessly violent blow. Fred Palahniuk, Chuck's father, had started to date someone new after divorcing his wife, Carol, Chuck's mother. Fred found the woman in a newspaper ad and, to the surprise of his son, seemed to be getting along with her well. Chuck recalls his father being happier than he had ever seen him. Donna Fontaine was great match for Fred but, unfortunately, she had an abusive ex–husband, Dale Shackelford, who she put in jail for battery. After his release, Shackelford followed Donna and Fred on their way home from a date. Dale shot and killed them both. He dragged the bodies into the house and, in an attempt to make it look like an accident, set it on fire. The murderer was caught, though, and found guilty in the spring of 2001 of two counts of first–degree murder. Palahniuk attended the trial and tried to come to terms with the violence in his family, which, for him, meant working on the next book, *Lullaby.*

Lullaby was a departure from Palahniuk's theme of personal reinvention. His father's death forced him to deal with the kind of rage that made him want to kill his father's murderer. As a victim's son, it was his prerogative to ask the judge for the death sentence. Though the decision haunted him, the choice itself appealed to the writer in him. Palahniuk wanted to write a story where a character could just wish someone dead and they would die. He came up with the idea of a lulling song, or a song that can kill someone if you even hum it. *Lullaby* takes a look at what would happen if such a verse were loosed on the United States. The tale did not delve into identity as much as it did into our priorities, and our ability to act on what we decide must be done. Palahniuk did not ask for the death penalty, and, similarly, his protagonist did not use his ability to kill people he wanted to kill.

Today, Palahniuk lives on a farm in Portland, Oregon. He socializes as much as possible, opening his home to friends and family. He likes to tend to his chickens when he is not writing, which is not

very often. His novels keep him busy, taking anywhere from six weeks to four months to complete. When he is not crafting his fiction he enjoys writing articles and essays to express his strongly held and deeply considered views. He is a writer's writer and he will do it until the day he dies.

"You know, all I've ever known are really obsessive passions, so it's hard for me to imagine people who don't have some sort of obsessive passion in their life, something that they have always dreamed of doing, whether or not they're doing it," he told Powells.com's Farley. "I think that everyone's got an incredible passion, whether or not they admit it, or whether or not they're even aware of it anymore. Maybe they've just completely forgotten the fact that they wanted to do this thing when they were a child.... [M]uch of our unhappiness and destructive behavior is based on not doing what we were created to do, for whatever reason." By doing what he wants to do, Palahniuk has tackled his own rage, and given a generation of writers a unique perspective on life in America.

Selected writings

Fight Club, Henry Holt & Company, Inc. (New York City), 1999.
Invisible Monsters, W.W. Norton & Company (New York City), 1999.
Survivor, W.W. Norton & Company, 1999.
Choke, Anchor (New York City), 2002.
(Contributor) *Dog Culture: Writers on the Character of Canines,* Crown Publishing Group (New York City), 2002.
Lullaby, Anchor (New York City), 2003.
(Contributor) *Fugitives And Refugees: A Walk In Portland, Oregon,* Crown Publishing Group (New York City), 2003.
Diary, Doubleday (New York City), 2003.
Stranger Than Fiction: True Stories, Doubleday, 2004.

Sources

Periodicals

People, October 14, 2002, p. 53.
Time, September 23, 2002.

Online

"A Rhyme to Die For," *Guardian Unlimited,* http://books.guardian.co.uk/reviews/generalfiction/0,6121,799624,00.html (September 4, 2003).
"Author Interviews," Powells.com, http://www.powells.com/authors/palahniuk.html (September 4, 2003).

"Chuck Palahniuk," *Onion,* http://www.theonion avclub.com/avclub3842/avfeature_3842.html (September 4, 2003).

"Fight Club," Barnes & Noble, http://search. barnesandnoble.com/booksearch/isbninquiry. asp?isbn=0393039765 (September 4, 2003).

"Fight Club," Internet Movie Database, http:// www.imdb.com/title/tt0137523/ (September 4, 2003).

"Interview with Fight Club author Chuck Palah-niuk," DVDTalk.com, http://www.dvdtalk.com/ fightclub.html (September 4, 2003).

"Reveling in the soft white underbelly," CNN.com, http://www.cnn.com/2003/SHOWBIZ/books/ 08/27/chuck.palahniuk/index.html (September 4, 2003).

—Ben Zackheim

John Patton

Pharmaceutical researcher

Born John S. Patton, c. 1947; married; children: three. *Education:* Pennsylvania State University, B.S.; University of Rhode Island, M.S.; University of California, San Diego, Ph.D.

Addresses: *Office*—Nektar Therapeutics, 150 Industrial Rd., San Carlos, CA 94070.

Career

Did postdoctorate work in biomedicine at Harvard Medical School and University of Lund, Sweden; assistant professor in marine science and microbiology, University of Georgia, 1979–85; worked as project team leader focusing on non–invasive drug delivery, Genentech, 1985–90; founded Inhale Therapeutic Systems, 1990; changed company name to Nektar Therapeutics, 2003.

Sidelights

John Patton is a pioneer in the field of inhalable drug delivery systems. The company he founded, Nektar Therapeutics, is working on bringing to a market an inhalable form of insulin. As many as 177 million people worldwide suffer from diabetes, and many must inject themselves daily with insulin in order to survive. Patton's research may free diabetics from dealing with needles. Diabetes is the fourth–leading cause of death by disease in the United States, and its incidence is on the rise as the population ages. Patton's work may ease the lives of millions of people who need daily doses of insulin.

Patton began his career as a marine biologist. He earned a bachelor's degree in zoology and biochemistry from Pennsylvania State University, followed this up with a master's in oceanography at the University of Rhode Island, and then studied at the University of California, San Diego, Scripps Institution of Oceanography. After receiving his Ph.D. from the University of California, Patton took a postdoctorate position at Harvard Medical School, working in biomedicine. He also worked at the University of Lund, in Sweden, also in biomedicine. In 1979, Patton moved to the University of Georgia, where he was an assistant professor in the department of Marine Science and Microbiology. Patton got tenure at Georgia in 1984, but in 1985 he asked for a two–year leave of absence to take a job at the biotechnology firm Genentech, in San Francisco, California.

Genentech is considered the founder of the biotechnology industry in the United States. It started in San Francisco in 1976, where it pioneered recombinant DNA technology. Genentech offered Patton the position of Project Team Leader, working on non–invasive drug delivery systems. Patton's expertise was in the delivery of large molecules through the lungs. Patton's team at Genentech concentrated on refining the so–called pulmonary intake method of drug delivery. Chemicals inhaled deeply into the lungs go straight to the bloodstream, making this an optimal way to deliver certain pharmaceuticals. Drugs for asthma and other lung diseases are typically inhaled, and the technology for asthma inhalers had been around since the 1960s. Efforts to make an inhalable form of insulin dated back to the 1920s, but no one had been able to surmount certain physical difficulties. The advantages of this method of drug delivery were clear. Not only did the drug move quickly into the bloodstream, but pulmonary intake was painless. This made it a promising delivery method for drugs like vaccines for small children. The pain issue was also especially important in the case of insulin because of how frequently it had to be injected. Some diabetics require as many as five injections of the drug, every single day. Doctors believed some diabetics did not use all the medicine they were prescribed, because of reluctance to inject. An easier drug delivery system for diabetics would be a major breakthrough.

Patton formally resigned from his academic job in 1987, and worked at Genentech through 1990. As he got more involved in the science of inhalable drug delivery, he became convinced that an inhalable insulin was feasible. But there were still formidable obstacles. Asthma drugs could be inhaled because the precise dosage was not that important. If some hit the back of the throat instead of going down into the lungs, the user had no ill effects. Insulin could not be treated so casually. Either too much or too little insulin gave diabetics immediate effects such as dizziness or nausea, and a dose that was way off could even put the patient into shock. Also, insulin consists of large molecules. In order for the drug to reach deep into the lungs, the chemical had to be reconfigured into smaller particles. Patton was convinced these problems could be overcome. But Genentech thought devising an inhalable insulin would be too expensive. When he could not get his employer to go along with his plans, Patton decided to go into business for himself. In 1990, Patton quit his job, though he had three children nearing college age, and his wife was not employed. He sold his stock options in Genentech in order to keep going, and he and a friend, physicist Bob Platz, began making cold calls to potential investors. The pair took their business plan to countless meetings, and were turned down time and again. Patton was beginning to run out of money. Finally he met with a venture capital firm called Onset Ventures, and its team was thrilled with Patton's idea. Onset invested $650,000 in Patton's new company, which was called Inhale Therapeutic Systems. The company went public in 1994. The large New York–based pharmaceutical company Pfizer Inc. invested in Inhale, and ran its clinical trials. By the mid–1990s, Inhale was

already testing an inhalable insulin that was pumped out of a six–inch tall forced–air device. The device shot compressed air at sonic velocity, breaking the insulin into a fine powder. The patient then took a slow inhalation, dragging the insulin deep into the lungs. Inhale Therapeutics named its device Exubera.

Inhale Therapeutics Systems changed its name to Nektar Therapeutics in 2003 when it merged with Bradford Particle Design and another biotechnology company called Shearwater. Patton remained as Chief Scientific Officer of Nektar. Exubera was still in the late stages of clinical trials by 2004, awaiting approval from the Food and Drug Administration (FDA). Meanwhile, other companies were developing competing products. Questions remained about inhalable insulin, such as the long–term effects on users' lungs, and whether the higher price of the inhalable drug would keep people using the traditional injectable insulin. Patton remained firmly committed to his dream. He told Claudia Kalb and Jamie Reno of *Newsweek*, "I'm not going to quit until it's on the market and being used."

Sources

Periodicals

Newsweek, May 12, 2003, pp. E6–E11.

Online

"Breathing New Life into Medicine," *Wired,* http://www.wired.com/news/technology/0,1282,59635,00.html (April 23, 2004).

"John Patton," Onset Entrepreneurs, http://www.onset.com/entrepreneurs/john_patton.html (April 23, 2004).

"New Drugs, Devices Mount Assault on Diabetes," The Scientist, http://www.the–scientist.com/yr1997/sept/bunk_pl_970929.html (April 23, 2004).

—*A. Woodward*

Nancy Pelosi

United States House of Representatives Minority Leader

AP/Wide World Photos

Born Nancy D'Alesandro, March 26, 1940, in Baltimore, MD; daughter of Thomas Jr. (a politician) and Annunciata D'Alesandro; married Paul F. Pelosi (an investment banker), 1963; children: Nancy, Christine, Jacqueline, Paul Jr., Alexandra. *Education:* Earned degree from Trinity College, 1962.

Addresses: *Home*—San Francisco, CA, and Washington, DC. *Office*—2371 Rayburn HOB, Washington, DC 20515.

Career

Volunteer for Democratic Party in San Francisco, CA, early 1970s; managed a 1976 Maryland primary race for Democrat presidential hopeful Jerry Brown; chaired California Democratic Party, 1981–83; elected by special election to the U.S. House of Representatives from California's Eighth Congressional district, 1987, and re–elected every two years; elected minority whip by House Democrats, October, 2001, and minority leader, November, 2002.

Sidelights

Congresswoman Nancy Pelosi became the House minority leader on November 14, 2002, a momentous day in the annals of American political history. Pelosi was chosen by her Democratic Party colleagues in the U.S. House of Representatives to lead their platform for the coming Congressional term, making her the highest–ranked female elected official in American history. *New Statesman* colum-

nist Andrew Stephen described the famously liberal Californian as "a tough, experienced political operator," and even some of her Republican foes admitted that Pelosi's energetic, winning personality has earned their respect. She is known for her ability to deliver and deflect the barbed remarks common to partisan politicking with a smile. "The ability to make merry while reaching for the jugular is an essential characteristic for politicians, and friends say Ms. Pelosi learned it from one of the classic political bosses and characters of an earlier era," wrote *New York Times* journalist David Firestone.

That man was Thomas "Big Tommy" J. D'Alesandro Jr., her father. D'Alesandro represented his Baltimore, Maryland, district in the U.S. House of Representatives for years as one of President Franklin D. Roosevelt's "New Deal" Democrats. Pelosi was born in 1940 in Baltimore, the only daughter among six children. When she was seven, her father became Baltimore's new mayor, making him the first Italian American to lead the city and a hero in the strongly Italian neighborhood around Albemarle Street, where the family lived. Pelosi attended local Roman Catholic schools, and while her mother, Annunciata, hoped she might become a Roman Catholic nun, Pelosi had other plans. In an interview with *National Catholic Reporter* writer Joe Feuerherd, Pelosi said she knew from an early age that convent life was not for her. "But I thought I might want to be a priest," she told Feuerherd. "There seemed to be a little more power there, a little more discretion over what was going on in the parish."

Pelosi's father served as Baltimore mayor for 12 years, and her first experience with politics was gleaned by helping out in his campaigns. When she was 16, she attended a black–tie political event with her father, and was thrilled to find herself seated next to a young Massachusetts senator, John F. Kennedy. Otherwise Pelosi led a strict, sheltered life, and even went to a women–only Roman Catholic institution in Washington, Trinity College. She considered law school, but those plans were put aside after she married a Georgetown University graduate, Paul F. Pelosi, after she earned her degree in 1962. They settled in New York City, where her husband became an investment banker, and began a family that would quickly number five children. In 1969, they packed up and moved to the San Francisco, California, area.

Pelosi was a stay–at–home mother for years. "With five of us, she was a car–pool mom for somebody every day of the week," her son, Paul Jr., recalled in an interview with *People* magazine's J.D. Heyman. Daughter Alexandra elaborated: "We were like the kids from *The Simpsons*—she couldn't get anyone to babysit." But Pelosi found herself drawn back into politics, and began volunteering for the local Democratic Party organization in the Bay Area. She worked for a San Francisco–area Congressman, Phil Burton, and in 1976 went back to her hometown at the behest of California Democratic governor Jerry Brown, who was making a run for the White House that year. Pelosi managed Brown's Maryland campaign in the weeks leading up to the state primary, which he won.

Between 1981 and 1983, Pelosi served as chair of the California Democratic Party, and also chaired the host committee for the 1984 Democratic National Convention, held in San Francisco that July. That national nominating convention was notable for the delegates' choice of Geraldine Ferraro as presidential candidate Walter Mondale's running mate—the first time in American history that a major political party offered a female candidate on its ticket. Pelosi's own electoral victory—her first—came three years later, when she ran for Burton's former seat in the House of Representatives. Burton had died in 1983, and his wife, Sala, succeeded him to the seat in a special election that year. When Sala Burton was diagnosed with cancer, she suggested that Pelosi run for her seat in another special election planned.

Pelosi took the advice and won the seat, which represented the Eighth Congressional District of California. Her constituents included voters from the legendary Haight–Ashbury neighborhood of San Francisco, once the epicenter of the hippie counterculture in 1960s, as well as residents of Chinatown; her territory also included the city's famous Golden Gate Park and Fisherman's Wharf. She was re-elected consistently by large margins over the next 12 years, and compiled a solidly liberal voting record in Congress that scored points with her left–leaning constituents back home. Gays and lesbians are thought to comprise about 25 percent of Eighth Congressional District residents, and are ardent Democrats; in the 2000 national election, just 15 percent of voters from the district cast their ballot for Republican presidential candidate George W. Bush. Its demographics also included a large number of affluent households, and it was known as a strong donor base for the Democratic Party fund–raising efforts.

As a one of the 435 elected representatives of Congress's lower house, Pelosi consistently voted in favor of progressive social legislation, of the type often derided by conservative Republicans. She supported environmental–protection measures, increased funding for AIDS research, the legalization of same–sex unions, and the preservation of women's reproductive rights. Outspoken on human–rights matters, she once caused a stir during a 1991 visit to China when she raised a protest banner in Tiananmen Square, the site of political demonstrations two years earlier that were brutally suppressed by the Communist Chinese leadership. Labor unions also gave Pelosi high marks for her voting record on trade issues.

In the House, Pelosi served on the Appropriations Committee and later the House Intelligence committee. In October of 2001, her colleagues elected her minority whip to succeed Rep. David Bonior of Michigan, who gave up the job to make a gubernatorial run in his home state. The job of the "whip"—a term derived from the aristocratic English blood sport of fox hunting, denoting the rider whose job it was to keep the hounds on the scent of the fox—entailed making sure that House Democrats voted along party lines; the whip also sought out Republicans willing to cross party lines on certain issues. The job made her the second–ranking Democrat in House, after House minority leader Richard A. Gephardt, and the first woman ever of either party ever to hold the title. Not long after landing the post, Pelosi found herself at one of the weekly White House breakfast meetings assembled by President Bush, among top Congressional leaders of both parties. "I realized in over 200 years of our history, these meetings have taken place and a woman has never ever sat at that table," Pelosi told *WWD* writer Joanna Ramey.

Pelosi voted consistently against President Bush's policies in the first two years of the new Republican Administration. She was openly critical of his controversial tax–cut plan, and of the White House's proposed welfare and health–insurance legislation. Pelosi was also racking up points among the Democratic Party leadership as a skilled fund–raiser and tireless cross–country campaigner; in the 2002 election year, she was credited with bringing in some $8 million to Democratic Party coffers. Despite such efforts, her party lost seats in both the House and the Senate—a rarity for the Democrats in mid–term elections during a first–term Republican president, and one that had last occurred in 1902. When Gephardt announced his retirement from the post of House minority leader to devote more time to his 2004 presidential campaign, Pelosi made a bid for the job herself, and began calling on her party colleagues in the House to secure their vote.

Pelosi's rival for the job was a more centrist Democrat, Martin Frost of Texas, but Frost dropped out after Pelosi held a news conference and declared she had 105 commitments from House Democrats to confirm her as minority leader. Political analysts initially considered Pelosi a surprising choice for the post, whose task it is to unite House Democrats along a consistent party line. Her liberal voting record surprised some, but others termed it a sign that the recently trounced party was gearing up for a much more ardent, non–centrist approach to battling a Republican–controlled House, Senate, and White House. Meanwhile, Republicans were delighted with the idea that Pelosi might lead the House Democrats, citing a voting record that made for easy attack; she was even derided with the code term "San Francisco Democrat" by some of the GOP leadership.

Pelosi won the post on November 14, 2002, and was sworn in a few weeks after the 108th Congress was seated the following January. Though she and her Republican counterpart, House majority leader Tom DeLay, are often described as arch–foes, DeLay quietly showed up for her swearing–in ceremony. Despite their public images as the most ideologically opposite representatives of the mainstream American political spectrum, Pelosi and DeLay have forged a mutual respect for one another, and the Texas conservative once even accepted Pelosi's challenge to tour a San Francisco treatment center for AIDS patients in her district.

Pelosi was the first woman to hold the minority leader job in either chamber of Congress, and the rank made her, in effect, the highest-ranking politi-

cian of her gender in United States history. The *New Statesman's* Stephen cited one example of the legislative backroom dealing that is endemic to the House and Senate, terming this emblematic of "the sheer venality of American politics," but asserted that Pelosi's rise was "a chance to civilize it all." *New York Times* journalist Sheryl Gay Stolberg described Pelosi as "elegant and energetic," with "the kind of star quality that many say makes them again excited to be Democrats. Young women come to the Capitol to have their picture taken in front of her office."

In her first months on the job, Pelosi immediately went to work with her characteristic vigor, voicing party opposition to the $675–billion economic package proposed by the Bush White House, which contains such perks as an elimination of the tax on stock dividends; the Democrats, by contrast, offered an economic package that included extending unemployment–compensation benefits, tax rebates for working families, and more dollars for public transit. As House minority leader, she condemned Bush's economic record in the first half of his four–year term, asserting that the Republican–sponsored initiatives would, if implemented, bring the federal government "to a new level of recklessness and irresponsibility," the *New Statesman's* Stephen quoted her as saying.

Three months into the job, Pelosi's ability to coalesce House Democrats faced its first true challenge: the contentious issue of war with Iraq. Just after the first bombs dropped on the night of March 20, 2003, she spent hours trying to hammer out the language for a resolution that would spell out House support for the troops, while not fully endorsing the president's actions. The following September, Pelosi excoriated the President for his request to Congress to approve an $87 million aid package for military spending and reconstruction in postwar Iraq.

A grandmother of five, Pelosi and her husband divide their time between homes in the Pacific Heights neighborhood of San Francisco and a place in the Washington's Georgetown section. Belying the stereotype of cuisine–focused Italian–Americans, Pelosi stays out of the kitchen. Her daughter, Alexandra—a filmmaker whose documentary about her experiences as a reporter on the 2000 presidential campaign trail, *Journeys with George,* aired on HBO just before her mother won the House minority leader job—once told her, "'Mom, you're really a pioneer; I'm proud of you,'" Pelosi recalled in an interview with *U.S. News & World Report* writer Terence Samuel. Pelosi asked her youngest child if it was because of her status as one of the 59 elected women serving in the House, but Alexandra replied that no, she was impressed because her mother does not cook. "Well, now nobody cooks," her daughter admitted, "but you were one of the first ones to stop."

Sources

Nation, December 2, 2002, p. 11.
National Catholic Reporter, January 24, 2003, p. 3.

New Statesman, November 25, 2002, p. 35.
New York Times, November 9, 2002, p. A1, p. A16; November 10, 2002, p. 30; November 17, 2002, p. 3; April 1, 2003, p. B13; September 25, 2003.
People, December 2, 2002, pp. 217–18.
Time, May 13, 2002, p. 50.
U.S. News & World Report, June 17, 2002, p. 18.
WWD, February 5, 2002, p. 6.

—*Carol Brennan*

Stefan Persson

Executive

Born October 4, 1947, in Stockholm, Sweden; son of Erling (an entrepreneur) and Margrit Persson.

Addresses: *Office*—Hennes & Mauritz AB, Box 1421, Stockholm S–111, Sweden.

Career

Joined Hennes & Mauritz AB, Stockholm, Sweden, 1972; board chair, 1979—; served as chief executive officer, 1982–98. Also serves on the boards of the Stockholm School of Entrepreneurship, Electrolux and INGKA Holding B.V.

Awards: International Award, (U.S.) National Retail Federation, 2000.

Sidelights

Stefan Persson chairs the hugely successful clothing retailer Hennes & Mauritz AB, a company founded by his father in Sweden in 1947. Known informally as "H&M," the international chain of nearly 900 stores has mastered the art of delivering cheap but chic styles and is poised to corner this segment of the United States market. Ranked Sweden's richest private citizen, Persson is widely credited with taking the company global when he succeeded his father as chief executive officer in 1982. *BusinessWeek* writers Kerry Capell and Gerry Khermouch described H&M's successful strategy in a 2002 company profile: "Treat fashion as if it were perishable produce: Keep it fresh, and keep it mov-

ing," they wrote. "That means spotting the trends even before the trendoids do, turning the ideas into affordable clothes, and making the apparel fly off the racks."

Persson was born the same year, 1947, as H&M. His father, Erling, was the son of a butcher in Västerås, an hour or so outside of Stockholm. An entrepreneur, the senior Persson traveled to New York City just after World War II and was impressed by large department stores like Macy's and the range of women's apparel they offered. Returning to Västerås, he opened a women's clothing store, Hennes ("hers" in Swedish), which offered inexpensive but stylish apparel. It proved a hit with locals, and was soon able to open a Stockholm store, where lines around the block formed on its first day of business. "The idea of providing such garments for the average woman fitted in well with the egalitarian mood of post–war Sweden," noted *Financial Times* writer Nicholas George, who wrote that the Scandinavian country's thriving economy helped make it rise quickly to the list of the world's most affluent nations. "It is often said that if Per–Albin Hansson, the legendary Social Democratic leader, created Sweden's 'people's home' with welfare and security, Ingvar Kamprad, founder of Ikea, furnished it and Erling Persson clothed it."

The Hennes company became "H&M" in 1968 when it bought Mauritz Widforss, a Swedish hunting and gun retailer, which gave them a men's clothing line. By then, it had cautiously ventured abroad, opening stores in Norway and Denmark. Persson joined his father's company in 1972, and helped out at the launch of H&M's first London store four years later by standing outside and handing out ABBA records as a promotional stunt. He became board chair in 1979, with his father remaining chief executive officer (CEO), and began to accelerate the expansion process soon afterward. The company moved into West Germany in 1980, and by 1985 had 200 stores across the continent and in the United Kingdom. "All over northern Europe, frumpy department stores with sluggish centralised buying processes found themselves out–thought and outsold by the new arrival," noted a writer for London's *Independent* newspaper, Darius Sanai.

In 1982, Persson took the chief executive job when his father retired. H&M continued its expansion, and a period of almost exponential growth followed. Listed on the Stockholm Stock Exchange since 1974—a move made in part to avoid paying Sweden's onerous inheritance taxes—H&M shares steadily increased in value as the company posted growth rates of an astonishing 25 percent annually for a number of years. It launched children's and maternity lines in its stores, and by the late 1990s had bested competitors to become Europe's largest apparel retailer. At one point in early 2000, H&M shares were considered by some financial analysts to be the world's most highly valued stock in the retail sector. That stellar reputation plummeted a little a few months later, when Fabian Mansson, a thirty–ish former skateboard champion and chief executive officer to whom Persson had handed over his CEO title in 1998, suddenly departed. Persson, who served as board chair, and his directors then chose Rolf Eriksen, a company veteran, to replace Mansson, and returned to a more pressing concern—the launch of H&M's first United States store, "the traditional graveyard for ambitious European manufacturers and retailers," remarked Sanai in the *Independent* article.

H&M had leased a piece of prime real estate, on Fifth Avenue just across the street from Rockefeller Center, and spent heavily on a pre–launch advertising campaign geared toward an opening date of March 31, 2000. Persson was confident about entering such a tough, saturated market when he spoke to *WWD* writer Anne D'Innocenzio on the night before the flagship New York store opened to the public. "We are giving an extra edge when it comes to fashion," he told D'Innocenzio. "We are giving value for the money. Americans like to make a good deal." His instincts proved correct: When the doors opened the next day, shoppers besieged the multi-level emporium, and security personnel had to close the doors for a time because the space was above-capacity.

Part of H&M's success came from the in–house design team that Persson had established at company headquarters in Stockholm in the mid–1980s, staffed by recent design–school graduates. The company's manufacturing was then outsourced to a vast network of some 1,600 suppliers in countries like Bangladesh, China, and Turkey, where labor costs were low. Persson was also convinced that tweaking merchandise for different countries was a waste of company resources. "Everyone listens to the same type of music, watches the same films," he told D'Innocenzio in *WWD*.

Persson's father, Erling, died at age 85 in October of 2002. He and his sister, Lottie, hold some 70 percent of H&M voting shares, and 37 percent of its capital. H&M has survived economic downturns in the retail sector and has even thrived: on 2002 sales of $5.8 billion, the company turned an $833 million profit on an astonishing 550 million items sold. As H&M chair, Persson is known to run a frugal ship, albeit one staffed by 39,000 employees worldwide. Only a few executives have mobile–phone privileges, and those traveling on behalf of the company—which operates in 17 countries and began expanding into Eastern Europe in 2003—fly coach and do not submit expense–report receipts for cab rides. Persson described such budgetary concerns as "crucial," he asserted in an interview with the *Financial Times*'s George in 2001. "If we are to survive with our business idea of having the best price and value, every unnecessarily spent krona [Swedish currency] will ultimately be put on the price and threaten the whole business idea."

Sources

Periodicals

BusinessWeek, November 11, 2002, pp. 106–110.
Financial Times, May 30, 2001, p. 13; October 31, 2002, p. 27.
Independent (London, England), June 28, 2000, p. 3.
New York Times, October 2, 2002, p. C11.
WWD, March 30, 2000, p. 6.

Online

"Stefan Persson," *BusinessWeek Online*, http://www.businessweek.com/magazine/content/03_02/b3815611.htm (June 25, 2003).

—*Carol Brennan*

Mekhi Phifer

Actor

Born December 29, 1975, in New York, NY; son of Rhoda Phifer (a teacher); married Malinda Williams (divorced); children: Omi (son).

Addresses: *Office*—NBC, 30 Rockefeller Plaza, New York, NY 10112.

Career

Actor in films, including: *Clockers*, 1995; *High School High*, 1996; *Girl 6*, 1996; *Soul Food*, 1997; *Hav Plenty*, 1997; *I Still Know What You Did Last Summer*, 1998; *Hell's Kitchen*, 1998; *An Invited Guest*, 1999; *Shaft*, 2000; *Head Games*, 2001; *O*, 2001; *The Other Brother*, 2002; *8 Mile*, 2002; *Paid in Full*, 2002; *Imposter*, 2002; *Honey*, 2003. Television appearances include: *The Tuskegee Airmen* (movie), 1995; *New York Undercover*, 1996; *Homicide: Life on the Street*, 1996, 1998; *Subway Stories: Tales from the Underground* (movie), 1997; *A Lesson Before Dying* (movie), 1999; *Carmen: A Hip Hopera* (movie), 2001; *Brian's Song* (movie), 2001; *ER*, 2002—.

Awards: Rising Star Award, American Black Film Festival, 2002.

Sidelights

Prolific film and television actor Mekhi Phifer starred in more than 20 films between the year of his acting debut in Spike Lee's *Clockers* in 1995 and 2003, in which he appeared in *Honey*. In addition to his film work, he joined the regular cast of the hit NBC medical drama series *ER* in 2002 in the role of Dr. Gregory Pratt, an arrogant young M.D. whose overconfidence often lands him in hot water with his colleagues. He has also starred in numerous made–for–TV movies, and guest starred on the series *Homicide: Life on the Street*, and *New York Undercover*. In the early 2000s, he founded his own film and television production company called Ki–Kel Entertainment.

Phifer, whose first name is pronounced "Muh–KIE," explained to Amy Dawes in the *Los Angeles Daily News*, reprinted in the *Plain Dealer*, that his name "derives from the Muslim holy city of Mecca, and relates to water, and how water sustains life and is one of the strongest elements."

He grew up in New York's Harlem neighborhood. Phifer's family includes, in addition to his mother, his twin brother; they have never met their father. Phifer and his family had very little money while he was growing up, but he considered himself rich in experience and with the love of his mother. His mother taught in public schools, and after she got off work in the afternoon, she was able to spend a lot of time with her children—a factor he later said contributed to his staying out of trouble, even though many of his peers were involved in illegal activities. His home was across the street from a rough housing project, where many people he knew were involved in drug dealing and other crimes.

Phifer's mother was perhaps the strongest influence on him as he was growing up. For instance she made sure he got home at a reasonable time at night, instead of letting him stay out on the streets until late, as so many of his peers did. With his mother's help, Phifer managed to steer clear of run-ins with the law. He also worked hard at odd jobs starting at the age of 13, developing a strong work ethic. Jobs that kept him in spending money included doing building maintenance, distributing snacks at a community center, and working as a clerk at the Gap clothing chain.

Strongly interested in acting from an early age, Phifer participated in community theater productions in Harlem, and in talent contests. Before becoming a professional actor, he won a national talent contest, which resulted in his landing a record deal with Warner Bros. to cut a rap album.

Phifer got his start as a professional actor at the age of 19. He had just graduated from high school in 1994, and had been admitted to a college to study electrical engineering. He was dividing his time between working on the rap album for Warner Bros. and a construction job in New York, when he heard from a cousin who was an actor that director Spike Lee was casting his next film through an open call. Almost on a lark, he decided to accompany his cousin to the audition.

The only problem was, he did not have a set of actor's eight-by-ten-inch headshots. So, on the way to the audition, he stopped in at a Woolworth's store and had small, passport-sized pictures taken. The film for which Phifer auditioned was *Clockers,* and he was somewhat daunted at the audition to find that it was being held in a large auditorium full of professional actors, each of whom had the large, professional quality headshots that Phifer lacked; he felt less than prepared, with his, as he told the *Toronto Sun*'s Bob Thompson, "postage stamp pictures."

Even so, Phifer was noticed at the open call, and after a short interview, was told to report for a callback at a smaller audition in a week's time. At the callback, Phifer met Lee, who impressed Phifer with his style and poise. The feeling was mutual, and Lee hired Phifer to star in his film after a half dozen more callbacks. Lee later told reporters that that Phifer had a certain presence that Lee was looking for in the lead for his film. In *Clockers,* Phifer plays a young drug dealer, or "clocker," who is accused of murder. Phifer's character, called Strike, finds himself with his back to the wall, caught between the duel forces of a cop played by Harvey Keitel, and his surrogate father, who got him into drug dealing in the first place.

Following his work on *Clockers,* Phifer continued to work on his rap album. But between his acting and music careers, he lacked the time to attend college as he had originally planned. He had no regrets, however, expressing the sentiment that he had gotten an excellent education in film acting courtesy of Lee, and had gotten paid for it besides.

Phifer's first film role was by no means the last: *Clockers* launched a new career for him. Other film and television roles followed in rapid succession. His next role after *Clockers* was in the comedy *High School High,* followed by the horror film *I Still Know What You Did Last Summer.* He also appeared in 1997's *Soul Food,* in which he plays an ex-convict husband, 1998's *Hell's Kitchen, NYC,* 1999's *An Invited Guest,* and 2001's *O,* based on William Shakespeare's play *Othello,* in which he performed an update of the title character.

The "O" in *O* is an African-American basketball star at an otherwise all-white boarding school in the present day South. Phifer relished in this role the opportunity to portray a young African-American man in a positive, charismatic light—something, he told Celia McGee in the *Daily News,* that was uncommon in Hollywood. "People haven't seen a young black man in this kind of role before," he told McGee.

The film's release was delayed after the shootings at Columbine High School in Colorado. Miramax, the distributor, feared negative publicity surrounding the release of a film that featured high school violence. Finally, after two years in limbo, the film was released by Lions Gate. Phifer disagreed with the decision to delay the release of the film. His feeling was that, rather than encourage high school violence, the film would spark dialogue between parents and their children, and help to prevent violence: "Everything O does is motivated by love, not hate," he told McGee. "I hope that the R rating will bring parents and kids to the movie together and bridge some gaps. It should create mutual respect."

Phifer did not have to audition for the starring role in *O;* he landed the part after having dinner with director Tim Blake Nelson, who had become interested in Phifer after seeing him in *Soul Food.* As Nelson told Hugh Hart in the *Boston Globe,* "I liked very much Mekhi Phifer, the actor I saw in *Soul Food,* but I loved the person with whom I was sitting when we met. I knew before we parted company that day that he was going to play the role."

Other roles for Phifer at this time included 2000's *Shaft,* a remake of the 1970s detective film, and 2001's *Carmen: A Hop-Hopera,* a TV movie produced for MTV. Other television roles included parts in *The Tuskegee Airman, Subway Stories: Tales from the Underground, Brian's Song,* and *A Lesson Before Dying,* in which he starred with Don Cheadle. He also appeared in guest spots on the television series *Homicide: Life on the Street* in 1996 and 1998, and *New York Undercover,* in 1996.

Within five years of his screen debut, Phifer appeared in more than a dozen films, all the while managing to avoid the typecasting that sometimes limits African–American actors. "I never wanted to be one of these cats shuckin' and jivin'," he explained to Denene Millner in the *Daily News.* He further stated that he would never appear in a film that he could not be proud of watching, and that included films that perpetuated negative stereotypes of African Americans.

In 2002, Phifer was hired to play Dr. Gregory Pratt on the popular NBC hospital drama *ER.* Once again, Phifer welcomed the opportunity to demolish stereotypes about young African–American men, telling Eric Deggans in the *St. Petersburg Times* that it was a role he could get behind, unlike many he had turned down, including "all the stuff that perpetuates a fake stereotype." He also enjoyed the challenge of learning medical jargon and inhabiting a role that is far removed from his own personal experience.

Meanwhile, Phifer continued to appear in films, including *Imposter, Paid in Full* and *8 Mile,* all in 2002. In *8 Mile,* Phifer performed opposite rap star Eminem, who was making his acting debut. The film presents a fictionalized version of Eminem's upbringing in rough sections of Detroit. Phifer, then 27 years old, was selected as much for his street smarts as for his talents as an actor. As part of the rehearsal process, Phifer and Eminem and the rest of the cast spent a lot of time together off camera to build the spirit of camaraderie that was important to the film's performances. "We went to the malls, we went to the football games ... and spent time with each other and became friends," Phifer explained to the *Los Angeles Times.* Phifer followed up his role in *8 Mile* with a part in *Honey.* Released in 2003, the film features Phifer as the love interest of a music video choreographer.

Phifer married his costar in *An Invited Guest,* Malinda Williams, but they divorced a short time later. They had met while working together on the film *High School High* in 1996. He described himself to the *Daily News*'s McGee as "very happily divorced."

In addition to his work as an actor, Phifer also pursues careers in producing and screenwriting. He does not take his success for granted; on his shoulder is a tattoo that says "R.I.S.E.," which stands for "Robbing Is So Easy." He explained to the *Boston Globe*'s Hart that it is a reminder of his humble roots, and how easy it would be return to them.

Perhaps to hedge his bets, he has invested in the Athlete's Foot chain of shoe stores, becoming the youngest owner of the chain's shops. Phifer also founded his own film production company, called Ki–Kel Entertainment, and sells merchandise on his website, Mekhi.net. His partners in these ventures include Kelly Hilaire, whom he met on a video shoot in 1996, and the cousin who took him to the Spike Lee audition that started his acting career, Sly Phifer. In 2003, he began filming the movies *Dawn of the Dead* and *Slow Burn.*

Phifer is modest about his successes, telling the *Los Angeles Times,* "I'm not here to save the world," and that coming from "a ghetto situation," he has learned that the secret to success is to "keep it real and go with what you know."

Sources

Periodicals

Boston Globe, August 26, 2001, p. L7.
Daily News (New York), May 21, 1999, p. 60; August 23, 2001, p. 40.
Jet, July 22, 2002, pp. 59–62.
Los Angeles Times, November 7, 2002, p. E14.
Plain Dealer (Cleveland, OH), September 20, 1995, p. 6E.
St. Petersburg Times, September 26, 2002, p. 1D.
Toronto Star, November 11, 2002, p. D2.
Toronto Sun, October 3, 1995, p. 39.

Online

"Cast Biographies: Mekhi Phifer," NBC.com, http://www.nbc.com/ER/bios/Mekhi_Phifer.html (July 10, 2003).
"The Facts—Mekhi Phifer," E! Online, http://www.eonline.com/Facts/People/Bio/0,128,34922,00.html (July 10, 2003).
"Mekhi Phifer Filmography," Mekhi.net, http://www.mekhi.net (August 19, 2003).

—*Michael Belfiore*

Pink

Singer and songwriter

Born Alecia Beth Moore, September 8, 1979, in Doylestown, PA; daughter of James (an insurance salesman) and Judy (an emergency room nurse) Moore.

Addresses: *Record label*—c/o Arista Records, 888 Seventh Ave., New York, NY 10019.

Career

Began writing songs, c. 1991; made singing debut with Schools of Thought, c. 1992; stint in punk band as young teen; briefly member of Basic Instinct; signed to LaFace label as part of R&B trio Choice, 1996; became solo artist, c. 1998; released debut solo album as Pink, *Can't Take Me Home,* 2000; released *M!ssundaztood,* 2001; released *Try This,* 2003.

Awards: MTV Music Video Awards for best female video and best dance video, 2002; Grammy Award for best female rock vocal performance for "Trouble," 2004.

Sidelights

Though pop/R&B singer Pink did not always sport her signature pink hair, her reputation as a woman with edgy tendencies did not change. After a difficult early life, Pink emerged as a popular singer with a big voice and distinctive persona in the early 2000s. With three very individual albums to her credit—each of which sold into the millions world-wide—Pink was a popular black sheep. As

Lorraine Ali wrote in *Newsweek,* "A healthy dose of obstinacy and attitude—and a maybe–not–so–healthy amount of anger—have made the 23–year–old Pink (born Alecia Moore) one of the current pop scene's only credible anti–heroes."

Born in 1979, Pink was the product of the stormy marriage of James and Judy Moore. She grew up the same city she was born in, Doylestown, Pennsylvania, located outside of Philadelphia. Her parents' marital problems began when she was a toddler, but she remained especially close to and influenced by her father, a Vietnam War veteran who worked in the insurance industry. He taught her many survival skills, including how to fight, use knives and guns, and break wrists. He also played guitar and introduced her to the music of Bob Dylan and Don McLean. From an early age, Pink was seen as tough.

Before Pink was ten years old, her parents divorced. She never talked about what went wrong or consciously realized how it affected her until years later. Pink began acting out within a few years. Though she had asthma, she began smoking when she was nine years old, a habit she kept up for many years. Pink got her first tattoo when she was 12, and her tongue pierced the same year. Pink also began writing songs when she was 12. She made her singing debut with a rap group, Schools of Thought, headed by Philly club dancer/friend Skratch, when she was 13.

By the time Pink was 14, she was doing drugs and running away from home on a regular basis. She was also arrested on several occasions for rebellious misdeeds. Music remained an important part of her life. Pink explored many music scenes, from rock, punk, and rave, to hip hop, folk, R&B, and gospel. She also liked to go to clubs and hang out with skateboarders. She rode skateboards, and also participated in a number of sports including kickboxing. Pink lived with her mother after her parents' divorce, but got kicked out when she was 15 years old because of the lifestyle she was living. Pink later admitted that she was a wild and difficult teenager. After briefly living with friends and relatives, Pink moved in with her father.

By this time in her life, Pink was determined to be a musician, though she also held mundane jobs like working at McDonald's to help support herself. After stints in a punk band and as a member of Basic Instinct, a vocal group signed to MCA, she joined a woman-only R&B trio called Choice when she was 16 years old because this group seemed to have the best chance of success. In 1996, Choice was signed to the LaFace label by L.A. Reid, a successful R&B producer.

It was during her two-year stint with Choice that Pink took on her colorful nickname. There are several versions of the story of how she came to be called Pink. At the time, she had pink hair, though sources also say that she took the name because of the character Mr. Pink in *Reservoir Dogs*. Another version claimed that she was so named because she turned pink after being embarrassed in front of a boy she liked. While the name Pink stuck, she did not have as much success with Choice. The group struggled with creative conflicts, but Pink was able to rediscover her love of songwriting when one of the artists they were working with, Darryl Simmons, had her co-write a song with him, "Just To Be Loving You," for the group.

After two years, Choice could not make it work with producers. Reid believed that Pink had a chance as a solo artist and began grooming her for such a career. However, Reid and Pink each had a different vision for the direction of her solo career. It was a harsh education for Pink on how the music industry really worked. She believed that Reid wanted her to compromise who she was. Despite

their differences, Reid continued to have a hand in the way Pink's career developed even after he became president of Arista Records. Pink also joined the label.

Pink's first album, 2000's *Can't Take Me Home,* was full of slick, overproduced songs, including the first single "There You Go." Most were dance-pop-R&B numbers aimed at a teen audience. The songs did not say much and *Home* was a critical failure, but the album managed to sell two to three million records worldwide. One point of controversy among record buyers was Pink's ethnicity. She told T'cha Dunlevy of the *Gazette*, "That's part of the mystery of Pink. Nobody knows what I am. Everybody thinks I'm what they are. White people think I'm white, Spanish people think I'm Spanish. Some black people think I'm black. I don't really care. Just listen to my music."

While Pink wrote or co-wrote seven of the 13 tracks on the album, she did not like how the record sounded and wanted to take more control of her career. She did not want to be a typical created-and-controlled R&B singer, but be honest and refreshing. Despite these qualms, the success of *Can't Take Me Home* proved to Pink that she could sing and sell records.

To take charge of her career direction, Pink fired her manager and hired a new one, the successful Roger Davies. She also stood up to her record company so that she could create an album that better reflected her personality and sound. She wanted to be more rock than polished R&B/pop. Of her struggles, she told Robert Hilburn of the *Los Angeles Times*, "Everything in this business is designed to encourage you to play along. They know people are so hungry for stardom that they'll just follow the record industry game. I know because I was ready to do anything when I started out. But I found that selling records wasn't enough. I told myself after the first record that I'd rather go back home and start all over again than be trapped in a one-dimensional world any longer."

To that end, Pink chose to work with Linda Perry as a producer and co-writer of eight songs on Pink's second record, 2001's *M!ssundaztood.* Perry had been part of the rock group 4 Non Blondes which had minimal mainstream success in the early 1990s, and she had been struggling on the fringes of the music industry for a number of years. With Perry, Pink retained an R&B-dance-pop oriented sound, but she also became harder, edgier, and with a rock sound accompanying lyrics that better reflected who she was. Pink sang about herself, her rough teenage years, and her problems with her family and the music industry, often in an emotionally intense fashion.

Critics and audiences responded to the change in direction of Pink's sound. M!ssundaztood more than eight million copies worldwide, with five million copies in the United States alone. As Alexis Petridis wrote in the Guardian, "Whatever you made of the actual music on Missundaztood, it was a brave and radical career shift. Despite the mainstream, crowd–pleasing sound, there was an undeniable sense of shock about the album—it had been a long time since any pop artist had attempted to make music whose primary emotion was anger."

M!ssundaztood produced a number of hit singles for Pink. One was the first hit single "Get the Party Started," which became a club hit, then a huge pop hit. Another hit single was "Just Like a Pill," in which Pink sang about her personal insecurities. "Family Portrait," a hit worldwide, was about her parents' marital problems and its effect on her. The song was very hard for Pink to sing, but also was cathartic for her.

Following up such an intense record proved difficult for Pink. In 2003, she released Try This, an album that featured a number of musical styles recorded primarily in her own home studio. While Pink again worked with Perry on three tracks, seven songs on the record were co–written and produced by Tim Armstrong, a punk rock icon. Armstrong also played guitar and provided some vocals. The songs ranged from the punk rock–oriented "Trouble" to the R&B–type ballads "Waiting for Love" and "Love Song." "Oh My God" was recorded with rapper/performance artist Peaches, while "God is a DJ" was a pop/rock anthem.

While many critics praised Try This, others pointed out that it sounded much like Pink's second record but without the danger and the radio–friendly hooks. Still, many reviewers found much to like, including her attitude, image, and her work ethic. Joan Anderman of the Boston Globe wrote, "In a pop music landscape littered with boardroom–approved sex kittens and photo–ready rebels—yes, Pink is all that, too—the 24–year–old singer has an actual personality. She's cheeky and funny and blunt, all of which infuses her third album, Try This...." Newsweek concurred: "Thanks to boot–stomping tempos, hissing guitar and rough–and–tumble melodies, the music finally matches Pink's acerbic lyrics and overall bad attitude."

Though Pink impressed many critics, the record–buying public was less impressed. The first single, "Trouble," only reached number 16 on the Billboard Top 40 charts, and was not much of a hit on radio either. "God is a DJ" reached the top five of the charts in the United Kingdom. The slower sales of her singles did not bother Pink. She told Nekesa Mumbi Moody of the Associated Press, "I don't judge myself on how well my songs do at radio, or how much my album sells. A failure and a success is all how you look at it. I've been creative to my highest potential at this point of my life, and I'm super proud of myself for making it this far."

Pink planned on touring extensively in support of Try This and remained sure of her vision for her musical career. She told CNN.com, "I'd rather fall down for what I believe in and for what makes me tick. Is that smart? Who knows. Might not be. But there's still some fear in me—I want to be understood. I want to be heard."

Selected discography

Can't Take Me Home, Arista, 2000.
M!ssundaztood, Arista, 2001.
Try This, Arista, 2003.

Sources

Periodicals

Associated Press, November 24, 2003.
Billboard, November 15, 2003.
Boston Globe, November 11, 2003, p. F4.
Daily Telegraph (London, England), November 7, 2002, p. 25.
Gazette (Montreal, Quebec, Canada), October 17, 2000, p. 18.
Guardian, November 7, 2003, p. 17.
Independent, August 22, 2003, p. 15.
Los Angeles Times, August 23, 2003; November 9, 2003, p. E49.
Newsweek, September 1, 2003, pp. 56–57; November 10, 2003, p. 66.
People, November 10, 2003, p. 29; December 15, 2003, p. 78.
USA Today, November 23, 2001, p. 10E.

Online

"Latest News," Official Pink Website, http://www.pinkspage.com/news/index.html (February 9, 2004).

"Pink: Bio," MTV.com, http://www.mtv.com/bands/az/pink/bio.jhtml (February 9, 2004).

"Pink: Expect the unexpected," CNN.com, http://www.cnn.com/2003/SHOWBIZ/Music/11/11/music.pink.reut/index.html (February 9, 2004).

"Pink pics," AskMen.com, http://www.askmen.com/women/singer/58c_pink.html (February 9, 2004).

—A. Petruso

Lisa Marie Presley

Singer and songwriter

Born February 1, 1968, in Memphis, TN; daughter of Elvis (a rock 'n' roll star) and Priscilla (Beaulieu) Presley; married Danny Keough (a musician), 1988 (divorced, 1994); married Michael Jackson (a pop singer), May, 1994 (divorced, 1996); married Nicolas Cage (an actor), August 10, 2002 (divorced, 2002); children: Danielle, Benjamin (from first marriage). *Religion:* Scientology.

Addresses: *Agent*—William Morris Agency, One William Morris Place, Beverly Hills, CA 90212. *Office*—Elvis Presley Enterprises, Inc., P.O. Box 16508, 3734 Elvis Presley Blvd., Memphis, TN 38186–0508.

Career

Began writing songs in her 20s; signed a deal with Capitol Records, 1998; released *To Whom It May Concern,* April, 2003; also manages estate of her late father, Elvis Presley, serving as president of Elvis Presley Enterprises, Inc.

Sidelights

As the only child of Elvis Presley, the undisputed king of rock 'n' roll, Lisa Marie Presley has been in the media spotlight since the day she was born. Naturally, music has always been a theme in her life. As a youngster, Presley performed for her father, standing on a coffee table singing and imitating his moves. After his death, however, her music fell silent and she spent years toying with the idea of producing her own album, although she was nervous about the comparisons that would be made.

After a series of high–profile failed romances, including a 1994 marriage to pop singer Michael Jackson, Presley came into her own. In her mid–30s, she gathered the courage to follow in her fabled father's footsteps and released *To Whom It May Concern.* The album debuted at No. 5 on *Billboard*'s Top 200 chart in April of 2003 amid mostly positive reviews. It went on to sell more than 500,000 copies and was certified gold. The album even generated enough attention to land Presley on the cover of *Rolling Stone.*

Presley was born February 1, 1968, to Elvis and Priscilla Presley, who separated when she was four. As a child, Presley split her time between her mother's Los Angeles, California, home and her father's sprawling 14–acre Graceland estate in Memphis, Tennessee. Elvis adored and spoiled his daughter, outfitting her with jewels and pint–sized fur coats. Once, he took her aboard his private jet and flew her to Idaho so she could play in the snow. Likewise, Presley adored her father and liked to entertain him by playing songs on the piano. Other times, she grabbed a microphone and entertained herself in front of a mirror. "My dad would catch me," she told *Rolling Stone*'s Chris Heath. "I'm sure he got a kick out of it. He'd put me up on the coffee table in front of everybody and make me sing."

Life at Graceland was lax, full of freedom and luxury. Because of his tours and night concert schedule, Elvis often slept during the day, while Lisa Marie ran free. She spent a lot of time driving around the estate on a golf cart. Her father's fame afforded her a lot of fun but also a certain amount of fear. Fans and curiosity–seekers continually climbed over the front gate and rushed the estate. Frequently, Presley found strangers hiding among the trees in the woods that surrounded the home. Presley may have been scared at times, but she was also mischievous. "I was awful," she told Heath in *Rolling Stone.* "People would give me cameras to go and take pictures, and I'd take money and I'd say I was going to take a picture of my dad, and then I'd throw the camera somewhere."

Life away from Graceland was starkly different. Whereas Elvis was an easy–going parent, Priscilla, the daughter of a military officer, was strict and demanding. Lisa Marie struggled to make sense of these two worlds. One habit she developed as a child was the practice of keeping her watch perpetually set to Tennessee time, even when she was in California, where that left her two hours behind.

Presley's life changed on August 16, 1977, when Elvis Presley died of heart failure, the result of drug use. Nine–year–old Presley was at Graceland at the time of his death and has always refused to talk about that night. According to *People,* reports at the time said Lisa Marie Presley screamed, "What's wrong with my daddy?" as he lay slumped on the bathroom floor. The period following her father's death was a scary time for Presley. Thousands of fans flocked to Graceland and came through the house to catch one last glimpse of "the king" before he was buried. It was not until a few weeks later, at summer camp, that Presley finally broke down and began grieving.

After her father's death, Presley lived in California full–time, residing in Beverly Hills with her mother and her mother's new love, Marco Garibaldi. She became a brooding, lonely child. Speaking to *Newsweek* writer Lorraine Ali, Presley summed her life up this way: "I feel like I've lived four lives in one. I dealt with death early on. It wasn't just my father, it was my grandma, my grandpa, my great–grandfather, my aunts—all in a two–year period. I didn't have much of a runway into life. I was, like, a deep, dark kid who was always melancholy."

When she was young, Presley's mother joined the controversial Church of Scientology and by the time Presley was eleven, she attended the Scientology–run Apple School. By 13, Presley was using drugs and rebelled by dressing like a punk rocker. She said the albums *Dark Side of the Moon* and *The Wall* by rock group Pink Floyd became her bibles.

Presley also attended the exclusive Los Angeles–based Westlake School for Girls, although she dropped out in eleventh grade and fell deeper into drugs. At 18, however, Presley came to a crossroads one morning when she awoke to find a bunch of drugged–out people on her floor, including a cocaine dealer. "I was on a 72–hour bender," she told *Paper* magazine's Peter Davis. "Cocaine, sedatives, pot, and drinking—all at the same time." Something inside Presley snapped. She told everyone to get out, then drove to a local Church of Scientology and asked for help. As she told *Paper,* "They jumped in, not in a rehab way. It wasn't that. It was like, 'Help me … I want to stop. I want to know what I'm doing here. I want to know why I'm here. What's wrong with me? I want answers to all these questions.'" Presley credits Scientology for helping her find the answers and become a better person. Soon after her breakdown, Presley took up residence in the Scientologists' Celebrity Center on Sunset Boulevard. There, she met aspiring rocker Danny Keough. Married in 1988, the couple have two children, Danielle and Benjamin. They divorced in 1994, but remain friends, sharing custody of their children. In recent years, Presley has lived in the gated community of Hidden Hills, located near Los Angeles, and Keough has lived nearby.

For years, Presley toyed with the idea of creating an album. Though she had a recording studio in every house she lived in, she kept her singing to herself because she was scared of not being able to live up to her father's legacy. By 21, Presley began writing songs and Sony wanted to sign her to a record deal. However, she got pregnant with her second child and decided it was not the right time to go public with her songs.

Throughout her adult years, Presley continually made headlines for her disastrous marriages. In May of 1994, when she was 26, Presley married pop singer Michael Jackson in a secret ceremony in the Dominican Republic. The two had been friends for years, but critics suggested the marriage was a publicity stunt by Jackson, who at the time faced allegations of sexual misconduct with a 13–year–old boy. They divorced in 1996. Presley later called the marriage a mistake, but insisted her intentions were genuine. "I actually did fall in love with him, but I don't know what was on his menu," she told Ali in *Newsweek.* "I can't say what his intentions were with me.… My mother was like, 'Timing—hello! Wakey,

wakey!' But I rebelled against my mom, of course, and tried really hard not to think like that, not to believe that."

Her relationship troubles continued when she got involved with actor Nicolas Cage. They dated in 2001 and separated at the start of 2002. They got back together, then married on August 10, 2002. However, by November 25 of that year, Cage had filed divorce papers. Presley later called this marriage a big mistake.

While her relationships played out in public, Presley kept her songwriting and singing abilities quietly to herself. But as the 20th anniversary of her father's death approached in 1997, Presley felt pulled toward making her voice public. A memorial event was in the works and Presley wanted to do more than just walk around and shake hands. She recorded some vocals and had them mixed with her father's hit song, "Don't Cry Daddy." On the 20th anniversary of his death, about 9,000 fans heard the re–mixed soundtrack, which accompanied a video that superimposed the father–daughter duo. Afterward, producer David Foster, who put the video together, encouraged Presley to start making records.

Through Foster, Presley met producer Glen Ballard, best known for his work with Alanis Morissette. Foster signed Presley to his Java Records label at Capitol Records in 1998. The two worked together at first, but Presley eventually turned to other producers and spent several years fine–tuning the songs. "I needed to do it that way," Presley told Tamara Conniff of the *Chicago Sun–Times*. "I needed to do it under the radar. Just because I'd signed the record deal didn't mean I was anywhere near ready to put a record out. It just gave me the time to sort of find my way. I think the songs changed quite a bit. They all had face–lifts."

After nearly five years of work, Presley released the album, *To Whom It May Concern*, in April of 2003. Foster described the album this way to *People*, "Her music is a little on the dark side. She's gritty, edgy, moody." The songs resonated with audiences and received fair radio play, debuting at No. 5 on *Billboard*'s Top 200 chart. Later, the album was certified gold for selling more than 500,000 copies. Presley told the *Seattle Times* she is proud of her accomplishment: "I was this tabloid phantom prior, this sensationalistic image. And then when they hear you are going to do a record, they think, 'Oh, some celebrity kid trying to do a record.' I think they expected something far from what I delivered. They didn't have a clue to what it was about."

Listening to the songs, it becomes clear the country–rock album is largely autobiographical. In the song "So Lovely," Presley mentions her kids and in "Lights Out," she alludes to Graceland and keeping a watch two hours behind. In "Nobody Noticed It," she scolds the media for its scathing reports of her father's last days. Speaking to *Paper* magazine, Presley called making the album "enormously cathartic and therapeutic. Each song represents something. I pull from something and purge it out, and, oddly enough, it goes away when I'm done."

Despite the positive album reviews, Presley's first tour, where she opened for Chris Isaak, was less than riveting. For starters, she had never performed in front of anyone until she made the album. She did not have the luxury of most artists, who can perfect their skills over time under less scrutiny. For Presley, there were evaluations every night from reviewers looking into her dark eyes, high cheekbones, and twitchy mouth hoping to see more than a mere resemblance to the king. Also, Presley was ill with stomach problems—and the critics were waiting. "It was like a crucifixion to some degree," Presley told the *Milwaukee Journal Sentinel*'s Dave Tianen. "I was on the frying pan. Every reviewer was there every night. That's not going to happen with the normal opening act."

Besides songwriting, Presley keeps busy as president of Elvis Presley Enterprises, Inc. As the only heir to her late father's estate, her worth is estimated at more than $150 million. Once in awhile, she returns to Graceland. Presley's upstairs room—along with her father's—has not been touched and remains the same as it was when she was a child. Though public tours of Graceland are offered, the upstairs has never been open. Speaking to *Rolling Stone*, Presley said her visits bring "a beautiful sadness. It's either really painful or it's very comforting—it goes either way."

While Presley acknowledges some mistakes in her past, waiting three decades to produce an album is not one of them. This album is about her, not her birthright. It is also about finding her place in the world. "I didn't want to do anything just based on who I am," she said in a biography posted on the William Morris Agency's website. "The stuff I've been offered in my life is insane and I didn't do any of it because I didn't care. I was doing this because my heart's in this. This is what I'm good at doing. I'm good at putting myself in a song. That's it."

Selected discography

To Whom It May Concern, Capitol Records, 2003.

Sources

Periodicals

Chicago Sun–Times, September 29, 2003, p. 41.
Milwaukee Journal Sentinel (Wisconsin), September 25, 2003, p. 1E.
Newsweek, April 7, 2003, pp. 60–62.
Paper, June/July 2003, pp. 52–57.
People, May 5, 2003, pp. 81–86.

Rolling Stone, April 17, 2003, p. 52.
Seattle Times, September 19, 2003, p. H4.

Online

"Lisa Marie Presley," William Morris Agency, http://wma.com/lisa_marie_presley/Bio/LISA_MARIE_PRESLEY.pdf (February 7, 2004).

—Lisa Frick

Queer Eye for the Straight Guy cast

Television personalities

Members include Ted Allen (born in Chicago, IL); Kyan Douglas (born c. 1970, in Miami, FL); Thom Filicia (born c. 1972, in Syracuse, NY. *Education*: Syracuse University, B.A. in interior design); Carson Kressley (born 1969, in Allentown, PA. *Education*: Graduated from Gettysburg College

magna cum laude with degrees in finance and fine art); Jai Rodriguez (born David Jai Rodriguez, June 22, 1977, in Brentwood, NY).

Addresses: *Office*—Bravo c/o NBC Entertainment, 3000 W. Alameda Ave., Burbank, CA 91523.

Career

Allen began career as food critic in Chicago; worked as senior editor and restaurant critic with *Chicago* magazine; contributing editor to and co–author of column "Things a Man Should Know," *Esquire* magazine, 1997—; wrote column "In the Spirit: The Intelligent Barfly" for Women.com; also co–wrote four books. Douglas worked as a colorist at Arrojo Studio, New York City; colorist for other television shows, including *What Not To Wear* and *While You Were Out,* both on TLC; colorist for projects on *Child Magazine.* Filicia began career as designer for Parish Hadley Associates, Robert Metzger Interiors, and Bilhuber, Inc.; founded own design firm, Thom Filicia, Inc. Kressley worked as an independent stylist, then in design for men's sportswear and corporate advertising group for Polo Ralph Lauren, New York City; also worked for Neiman Marcus and Saks Fifth Avenue. Rodriguez worked as a stage actor, appearing in Toronto, Ontario, Canada, then toured Canada in *Rent,* 1998–99; also appeared in version of *Rent* on Broadway, *Zanna, Don't!,* New York City; *Spinning Into Butter,* Lincoln Center Theatre, New York City; *Sad Hotel,* White Barn Theatre; recorded first single "Love Is Good," c. 2003; appeared on soundtrack to *Zanna, Don't!.* All five cast in *Queer Eye for the Straight Guy,* 2002; first episode aired on Bravo, 2003; *Queer Eye for the Straight Guy* aired on Bravo and NBC, 2003—.

Sidelights

When the off–beat "make better" show *Queer Eye for the Straight Guy* began airing on the Bravo cable network in the summer of 2003, it was an immediate hit. *Queer Eye* features five gay men (known as the Fab 5 on the show) who are experts in certain areas that a straight man might lack knowledge: fashion, food, grooming, interior design, and culture/social skills. The five gay men who filled these roles became instant stars. They are Carson Kressley (fashion), Kyan Douglas (grooming), Thom Filicia (design), Jai Rodriguez (culture), and Ted Allen (food and wine). Each episode features the Fab 5 making over one straight man, usually for a big life event. While *Queer Eye* is a reality show (the majority of which tend to bring out the worst in people), it changes the men who participate with humor and heart. It also brings gay culture into the average American home.

When *Queer Eye* debuted in the summer of 2003, it was one of several shows that Bravo put on the air with a gay theme. It was the only really successful show, and the only one with crossover appeal. When the first hour–long episode aired on July 15, 2003, it posted Bravo's highest ratings ever with 1.6 million viewers. Viewership increased to 2.7 million viewers for the second episode, then 2.8 million for the third. These numbers prompted Bravo to increase the first season of *Queer Eye* from 13 episodes to 20 because of its popularity.

The idea for *Queer Eye* came when television/film production veteran David Collins, a gay man, overheard a conversation between a straight man and his wife. The wife pointed out to her husband that the gay men nearby were better at taking care of themselves than he was. The gay men she pointed at came over and began giving the husband advice on how to improve his life. Collins took the idea to his production company, Scout Productions, and with the help of another executive producer, David Metzler, pitched the show's concept to Bravo in early 2002.

To find the gay men to do the life makeovers, the *Queer Eye* producers put out notices everywhere in New York City, on websites, and at grooming and fashion establishments. They began with 500 potential hosts, and pared it down to 50 who auditioned for the pilot. To pick the final five, the producers looked for men who could work well together and who had chemistry. Of the men who became the final Fab 5, only Kressley and Allen appeared in the pilot, which was shot in September of 2002, and was not originally aired. The other three who worked on the pilot had chemistry issues that led to them being replaced. Despite these problems, the pilot tested well and Bravo gave the green light for the show. (The producers eventually did show the pilot, which featured commentary by Kressley, Allen, and two of the original cast, reflecting back on the episode.) To find straight men to make over, fliers were posted in New York City, where the first season was centered.

In the first two episodes that aired on Bravo, Blair Boone, an ad manager/writer for *Metrosource* magazine, served as the culture expert. He was replaced by Rodriguez (who was more enthusiastic, but not found by the producers until the first episode was already being shot). The firing of Boone shocked the other cast members, who worried about their own jobs. Boone later sought $105,000 in damages from Queer Eye LLC, which he said equals what he would have been paid for the rest of the season. "When I see the million–dollar book deal [the cast members received], I have to clench my teeth—that's what I expected to see and [to] be a part of," Boone told the *Boston Herald*.

From the beginning, Kressley emerged as the leader of the Fab 5 and was *Queer Eye*'s breakout star. Born in 1969 in Allentown, Pennsylvania, Kressley had years of experience in fashion and as a stylist. After working for years as an independent stylist, he also spent a significant amount of time working for Ralph Lauren's Polo line for men. He also was employed by Saks Fifth Avenue and Neiman Marcus in fashion jobs. Kressley had a gift for making men less afraid of fashion. Outside of work, he also was a nationally ranked, Olympic–caliber equestrian.

Each of the rest of the *Queer Eye* guys had their own niche on the show and much expertise in their selected areas. Born in Miami around 1970, Douglas grew up in Tallahassee, Florida. He received training at the Aveda Institute as a cosmetologist and colorist. He then worked as a colorist at the Arrojo Studio in New York City, among other salons. Douglas had previous television experience, working as a colorist for two shows on TLC (The Learning Channel), *What Not to Wear* and *While You Were Out*. He also worked as a colorist and did makeovers for *Child Magazine*.

Filicia has a similarly impressive background. Born around 1972 in Syracuse, New York, he is an interior designer who began his career working in high–end interior design for firms such as Robert Metzger Interiors. Filicia then founded his own design firm, Thom Filicia, Inc. His small but thriving practice designs residential and commercial interiors, and was recognized as one of the best design companies in the United States. On *Queer Eye*, Filicia does not always radically change the homes of his subjects, but makes improvements in their living spaces.

Rodriguez had a relatively high profile as an actor and singer before *Queer Eye*. Born in 1977 in Brentwood, New York, he graduated from the New York High School for the Performing Arts where he studied musical theater. Within a short time after graduation, Rodriguez was starring in the Toronto, Ontario, Canada, version of *Rent* in the role of Angel Schunard, the young drag queen who is HIV positive. Rodriguez also toured Canada in the role and appeared in the Broadway production. In addition to other roles in Broadway and Off–Broadway productions, Rodriguez is a club goer and a singer with a dance single, "Love is Good." During the filming of *Queer Eye*, he began working on his first solo album.

Like his *Queer Eye* counterparts, Allen is dedicated to making real changes in his subject's food and wine choices. Born in Chicago, Illinois, Allen has been a restaurant critic in Chicago for many years, where he worked for *Chicago* magazine as a critic and senior editor. Beginning in 1997, Allen was a contributor to the men's magazine *Esquire*. He is also the co–author of a column entitled "Things a Man Should Know," a cheeky take on food, fashion, women, and other parts of men's lives, as well as four books related to the column. Allen was nominated for two National Magazine Awards for his work in *Esquire* in 2001 and 2003. The first was for a piece on male breast cancer, and the second on a food–and–travel package.

One reason for the success of *Queer Eye* is the approach that the Fab 5 take and the men who want to be made over. The straight man usually wants to change for a reason—sometimes to impress or please a girlfriend, fiancée, or wife, other times to do well in a life situation (such as organizing an art exhibit or getting a stage musical seen by producers)—and each of the *Queer Eye* guys want to help him improve. They do not set out to change him radically, but work with much of what is already in his life and give him tools to make the changes last. Instead of calling it a makeover, the cast preferred to call it a "make better."

Unmalicious humor is a core piece of the *Queer Eye* approach. Kressley was quoted by Rob Owen of *Pittsburgh Post–Gazette* as saying, "Those things that we have some laughs with might be a little embarrassing, but in the end, the result is so great and the guys are so grateful that I think when the guys see the show they're going to want to be a part of it."

It is the Fab 5 cast which makes *Queer Eye* work on a number of levels. As Suzanne C. Ryan wrote in the *Boston Globe*, "What makes *Queer Eye* culturally significant is that its characters—a rotating cast of straight slobs and a gaggle of gay experts in food and wine, grooming, fashion, culture, and interior design—aren't actors, they're real people who are likable and appear to be good at what they do."

Each episode takes about three to four days to film, though when it airs, it seems like only 24 hours. The *Queer Eye* guys need the time to take apart who and what their subject is, how he ticks, and put his life back in order. It also takes extended amounts of time to get some of the segments together, especially those of Filicia's interior design changes.

Because of the success of *Queer Eye* on Bravo, a shorter version of each episode aired on NBC (which owned Bravo) for several weeks in July of

2003. While the 30–minute NBC version's ratings were not as great comparatively as they were on Bravo (though one episode did attract 6.7 million viewers), NBC continued to occasionally air *Queer Eye* episodes and specials.

As *Queer Eye* took off as a cultural phenomenon, the Fab 5 made over Jay Leno, the star of NBC's *The Tonight Show* in August of 2003. The cast also appeared on a number of other shows including the NBC situation comedy *Good Morning, Miami,* and *The Oprah Winfrey Show.* They also had a special on E! Entertainment Television and appeared at the Emmys.

The popularity of *Queer Eye* made it easier for the Fab 5 to obtain the products used on the show. Kressley initially had to use favors to convince designers to give him clothes for his subjects. Companies soon caught on that the products featured in the show often sold well, so they began working with the show. However, the *Queer Eye* guys only allow placement of products on the show that they like.

Success did create some problems. *Queer Eye* was quickly renewed for a second season by Bravo, but the Fab 5 wanted their contracts renegotiated. In the first season, they made only $3,000 each per episode. After some harsh words, in September of 2003 they renegotiated their contract to earn about $400,000 each for the second season of about 40 episodes. They also were paid when their shows were aired on NBC.

The stars of *Queer Eye* also used their success for their own benefit. In late 2003, they negotiated a book deal which was worth more than a million dollars. The book, called *Queer Eye for the Straight Guy: The Fab Five's Guide to Looking Better, Cooking Better, Dressing Better, Behaving Better, and Living Better,* was published on February 10, 2004. They also had potential endorsement deals in the works with companies like Almay cosmetics and Pepsi.

Individually, they also did well. Each *Queer Eye* cast member made appearances that sometimes paid $50,000 per speaking engagement. Allen had an endorsement deal with General Mills. Filicia became a spokesperson for the Pier 1 home furnishing chain, and was considering offers to start his own line of furniture. Kressley appeared in ads for Marshall Field's in Chicago, had his own book deal for his fashion wisdom, and considered offers to be a commentator on style for awards shows specials.

The draw of *Queer Eye* was proven when Super Bowl XXXVIII aired on CBS in early 2004; NBC countered with two hours of *Queer Eye.* It performed well in the ratings. Kressley was surprised by the show's success, but believed he understood why it was so popular. He told Ray Richmond of MSNBC. com, "It's happened because we have no political agenda. We're all just about having a good time and making people feel better about themselves...."

Selected writings

Queer Eye for the Straight Guy: The Fab Five's Guide to Looking Better, Cooking Better, Dressing Better, Behaving Better, and Living Better, Clarkson Potter, 2004.

Sources

Periodicals

Advertising Age, September 29, 2003, p. 3; October 20, 2003, p. 1.
Advocate, September 2, 2003, p. 40.
Adweek, November 12, 2003.
Billboard, January 24, 2004.
Boston Globe, July 24, 2003, p. D1.
BPI Entertainment News Wire, October 31, 2003.
Dayton Daily News, July 27, 2003, p. F1.
Financial Times (London, England), August 4, 2003, p. 24.
Fortune, February 9, 2004, p. 38.
Interior Design, October 2002, p. 105.
Los Angeles Times, October 15, 2003, p. E18.
Mediaweek, September 8, 2003, p. 33.
Milwaukee Journal Sentinel, September 11, 2003, p. 2A.
Newsday (New York), August 21, 2003, p. A10.
Newsweek, August 11, 2003, pp. 50–51.
New Yorker, July 28, 2003, p. 92.
New York Times, August 12, 1999, p. F1.
Ottawa Citizen, August 1, 1998, p. E1; October 4, 2003, p. J2.
People, December 1, 2003, p. 154.
Pittsburgh Post–Gazette, August 14, 2003, p. C1.
Plain Dealer (Cleveland, Ohio), January 29, 2004, p. E1.
Publishers Weekly, December 15, 2003, p. 12.
St. Louis Post–Dispatch, November 20, 2003, p. C1.
Television Week, August 11, 2003, p. 30; September 29, 2003, p. 1, p. 25.
Time, August 18, 2003, p. 20.
Variety, January 5, 1998, p. 89.

Online

"Carson enjoying 'Queer' spotlight," MSNBC.com, http://www.msnbc.com/m/pt/printthis_main. asp?storyID=960272 (September 2, 2003).

"Carson: Fashion Savant," BravoTV.com, http://www.bravotv.com/Queer_Eye_for_the_Straight_Guy/Carson_Kressley/ (February 9, 2004).

"Carson Kressley," Primetimetv.com, http://primetimetv.about.com/cs/tvstars/a/kressleycarson_p.htm (February 9, 2004).

"Jai: Culture Vulture," BravoTV.com, http://www.bravotv.com/Queer_Eye_for_the_Straight_Guy/Jai_Rodriguez/ (February 9, 2004).

"Jai Rodriguez," Primetimetv.com, http://primetimetv.about.com/cs/tvstars/a/rodriguezjai_p.htm (February 9, 2004).

"Jai Rodriguez," Tvtome.com, http://www.tvtome.com/tvtome/servlet/PersonDetail/personid-207579/ (February 9, 2004).

"Kyan Douglas," Tvtome.com, http://www.tvtome.com/tvtome/servlet/PersonDetail/personid-207576/ (February 9, 2004).

"Kyan: Grooming Guru," BravoTV.com, http://www.bravotv.com/Queer_Eye_for_the_Straight_Guy/Kyan_Douglas/ (February 9, 2004).

"NBC to air Queer Eye for the Straight Guy marathon on Superbowl Sunday," RealityTVWorld.com, http://www.realitytvworld.com/index/articles/story.php?s=2172 (February 9, 2004).

"Queer Eye's Jai Goes Pop," Rolling Stone, http://www.rollingstone.com/news/printer_friendly.asp?nid=19294 (February 9, 2004).

"Queer Eye guy to be Pier 1 spokesperson," CNN.com, http://www.cnn.com/2004/SHOWBIZ/TV/03/11/pier1.imports.ap/index.html (March 12, 2004).

"Suit vs. Queer Eye seeks $105G over culture guy's firing," Boston Herald, http://www2.bostonherald.com/inside_track/inside_track/quee09042003.htm (March 17, 2004).

"Ted Allen," Primetimetv.com, http://primetimetv.about.com/cs/tvstars/a/allented_p.htm (February 9, 2004).

"Ted: Food & Wine Connoisseur," BravoTV.com, http://www.bravotv.com/Queer_Eye_for_the_Straight_Guy/Ted_Allen/ (February 9, 2004).

"Thom: Design Doctor," BravoTV.com, http://www.bravotv.com/Queer_Eye_for_the_Straight_Guy/Thom_Felicia/ (February 9, 2004).

"Thom Filicia," PrimetimeTV.com, http://primetimetv.about.com/cs/tvstars/a/filiciathom_p.htm (February 9, 2004).

—A. Petruso

Caroline Rhea

AP/Wide World Photos

Comedian and actress

Born April 13, 1964, in Montreal, Quebec, Canada; daughter of David (an obstetrician–gynecologist) and Margery (an antiques dealer) Rhea. *Education:* Studied comedy at the New School for Social Research, New York, NY, 1989.

Addresses: *Home*—New York, NY, and Los Angeles, CA. *Office*—The Caroline Rhea Show, 30 Rockefeller Plaza, Ste. 800E, New York, NY 10112.

Career

Stand–up comedian in New York, NY, after 1988; appeared in various cable comedy showcases, including *Stand–Up Spotlight,* VH1, 1988, *Women Aloud,* Comedy Central, 1992, *Women of the Night,* HBO, 1994, and *Comic Relief VIII,* VH1, 1998. Television appearances include: *Fools for Love* (writer and host), VH1, 1993; *Pride & Joy,* NBC, 1995; *The Drew Carey Show,* ABC, 1996; *Sabrina, the Teenage Witch,* ABC and WB, 1996–2002; *Hollywood Squares,* 1998–2002; occasional substitute host of *The Rosie O'Donnell Show;* host of *The Caroline Rhea Show,* 2002—. Film appearances include: *Meatballs III,* 1987; *Man on the Moon,* 1999; *Ready to Rumble,* 2000.

Sidelights

Comedian Caroline Rhea debuted with her own talk show in the fall of 2002 after several years playing the zany Aunt Hilda on the hit television series *Sabrina, the Teenage Witch.* Prior to that, Rhea had been a veteran of the cable–comedy stand–up scene, and had won over audiences with a frank sense of humor that spared no one—including herself. She deployed that same style on the *The Caroline Rhea Show* with her guests, and sometimes even pulled pranks such as telephoning a star guest's mother. When asked by *Ladies' Home Journal* writer Marisa Sandora Carr about the tough, glutted talk–show genre, with its many notable failures, Rhea responded with the characteristic drollery that poked fun at her own family—a common theme in her jokes. "That falls into the category of things I can't control," she asserted to Carr. "My father can only knock on so many doors and tell people they have to watch his daughter's show."

Rhea (pronounced Ray) was born in 1964 and grew up in Montreal, Quebec. One of three daughters, she claims she was by no means the sole funny person in her family that sometimes even was ejected from restaurants for her physician–father's antics. "I am surprised we weren't kicked out of Canada," she once said in an interview with *Denver Post* writer Ed Will. "We are very unlike our people." After appearing in an uncredited role in *Meatballs III* Rhea moved to New York City in the late 1980s to enroll in a training program for stand–up comic aspirants at the New School for Social Research. "I always wanted to do stand–up because I thought I would be brilliantly unique," she told Will in the *Denver Post* interview. "The reality is I am just like everyone else and that is why I've had any success...."

That success came slowly, however, with more than one setback in the tough entertainment industry. Rhea began appearing at a well–known Manhattan venue, Catch a Rising Star, but waited tables and spritzed perfume at Bloomingdale's department store before her career gained momentum. By 1992 she was regularly appearing on such cable comic fare as Comedy Central's *Women Aloud,* and in 1993 served as a co–host and writer for a short–lived VH1 sketch–comedy show, *Fools for Love.* Her growing reputation as a stand–up comedian landed her two development deals for her own show, and in 1994 there was even a brief article in *Broadcasting & Cable* that Rhea was being considered as host of a talk show slated to replace Arsenio Hall.

That plan never materialized, however, but in the summer of 1995 Rhea debuted in her first steady television role, which was the result of her development deal with Disney. She played Manhattan wife and mother Carol Green in a situation comedy that aired on NBC, *Pride & Joy.* Set in a New York City apartment building, the show also starred Craig Bierko and Julie Warner as new parents; Rhea and Jeremy Piven played their quirky neighbors across the hall. The show was cancelled after a few episodes, but the following year Rhea landed the steady *Sabrina* job. Airing first on ABC and later on The WB network, the series starred Melissa Joan Hart as parentless teen witch Sabrina, who lives with her two slightly older, single, blond aunts. Sabrina learns that her entire family are spell–casters, and while training for her own "witch's license" must keep her true nature a secret from her friends and classmates. Rhea's Aunt Hilda was a bit looser than Beth Broderick's Aunt Zelda, but both proved an excellent foil for one another's comedic talents.

Rhea had a harder time appearing alongside *Sabrina, the Teenage Witch*'s talking cat, Salem. The stuffed and stiffly mobile animal often grabbed the funniest jokes in the script, and sometimes fans asked the actress if Salem was an actual cat. "I just want to look at these people," Rhea said in the interview with Will in the *Denver Post,* "and go, 'It talks. It looks like an alcoholic, arthritic rabbit wearing a hairpiece. How can you possibly think that is a real cat?' I live with two cats. That is not what they look like."

Between her *Sabrina* shooting schedule, Rhea also appeared in feature films, such as the Milos Forman 1999 biopic about the late comic Andy Kaufman,

Man on the Moon, and had a regular slot on the *Hollywood Squares* game show. For a time, her name was mentioned as a possible replacement for Kathie Lee Gifford on *Live with Regis,* but Rhea lost out to soap–opera actress Kelly Ripa. In July of 2001, however, Rosie O'Donnell's talk–show producers announced that Rhea would take over the show when O'Donnell stepped down the following year. There was a bit of confusion, as Rhea noted in an article by *Entertainment Weekly* writer Dalton Ross. "You wouldn't believe how many people ask me if the show is still gonna be called *The Rosie O'Donnell Show*," she said.

The Caroline Rhea Show debuted in September of 2002, and the comedian quickly gained positive reviews for her comic skills and forthright interview style. "At 38, the cherub–faced Rhea is funny and smart," opined *Good Housekeeping* writer Celeste Fremon, "asking as many questions as she answers, and lacing her own replies with giant servings of self–deprecating humor." Rhea often asked her guest to participate in stunts or games, and liked to bring in audience members as well. The show was taped at Rockefeller Center in New York City, and Rhea acquired an apartment in New York City to ease her commute after spending the past few years in the Los Angeles area. One of her show's running gags was her own upcoming wedding plans: Rhea had been engaged to event–planner Bob Kelty for four years, but the couple had never set a date. They quietly broke off the engagement in the spring of 2003.

Rhea crochets in her spare time and practices yoga to stay fit. She notes that moving from stand–up routines to interviewing celebrities was not much of a stretch for her. "My talk show is just like stand–up," she told *Boston Herald* Dean Johnson, "and you could not have had better training than doing stand–up comedy. With both of them, you know the basic script, and then the rest is up to you. You have to listen and respond to the people around you."

Sources

Boston Herald, September 26, 2002, p. 63.
Broadcasting & Cable, May 9, 1994, p. 10.
Denver Post, February 7, 2003.
Entertainment Weekly, September 6, 2002, p. 67.
Globe & Mail (Toronto, Canada), November 8, 1997, p. C4.
Good Housekeeping, October 2002, p. 115.
Ladies' Home Journal, September 2002, p. 62.
People, September 16, 2002, pp. 73–75; May 12, 2003, p. 181.

—*Carol Brennan*

Paola Rizzoli

Scientist

Born Paola Malanotte Rizzoli, c. 1943, in Lonigo, Vicenza, Italy. *Education:* University of Padua, Ph.D. (theoretical physics), 1968; University of California, Ph.D. (physical oceanography), 1978.

Addresses: *Office*—Massachusetts Institute of Technology, Department of Earth, Atmospheric, and Planetary Sciences, 77 Massachusetts Ave., Room 54–1416, Cambridge, MA 02139.

Career

Research scientist with the Italian National Research Council, 1969–76, and senior scientist, 1976–81; assistant professor of oceanography, Massachusetts Institute of Technology (MIT), 1981–85, associate professor, 1985–87, professor, 1990—; MIT director of the Joint Program in Oceanography and Ocean Engineering with the Woods Hole Oceanographic Institution, 1997—. Member and elected official of numerous professional and government organizations and agencies, including the American Meteorological Society and the International Association for the Physical Sciences of the Ocean.

Sidelights

Oceanographer Paola Rizzoli has led a crusade to save the beloved Italian city where she grew up, Venice, via advanced science and engineering efforts. The northern Italian port on the Adriatic Sea is actually a series of 117 islands, unwisely constructed on a 207–square–mile lagoon, and has been prone to flooding for centuries. Rizzoli specializes in ocean currents, and has contributed reams of data to support one controversial plan to keep Venice dry by the deployment of immense underwater gates.

Rizzoli has been researching Venice's problems for much of her academic career. She was born in Lonigo, a town in the province of Vicenza near Venice, and moved to the fabled city as a teenager in 1959. The area was first settled in the sixth century, and prospered immensely from its position as a trading post between East and West after the ninth century. Its riches helped build a city of stunning architectural gems during the medieval, Renaissance, and Baroque periods, which can still be viewed in the twenty–first century from the boats that serve as the city's primary method of transportation. But in modern times, Venice has been sinking precipitously due to a combination of environmental problems, both local and global. Industrialization of the Adriatic coast has contributed to the problem, as has global warming, and the city has sunk nine inches during the twentieth century; previously, it sank at the rate of one inch every 100 years. City officials regularly post warnings of *acqua alta,* or "high water," with increasing frequency, which makes Venice a dismal, soggy place to traverse.

Rizzoli earned her first degree, in physics and mathematics, in 1963 from a lyceum in Venice. She recalled one of the most notorious events in contemporary Venetian history very clearly: November 4, 1966, when an unlucky combination of storms and tides caused the waters to rise to the infamous *acqua grande* of six feet, four inches. "For three days, I was trapped in my family's apartment," she recalled in an interview with *Wired*'s Josh McHugh. "We were lucky, because it was on the third floor. The streets were full of boats." In the aftermath, countless artworks stored in museum basements were permanently ruined, while outside debris floated by and rats invaded. Only then did Venetian authorities begin seriously weighing remedies to turn back, in effect, the tide.

Rizzoli was at the forefront of the issue from the start. After graduating from the University of Padua with a Ph.D. in theoretical physics in 1968, she took a post–doctoral fellowship in Venice at the Istituto Dinamica Grandi Masse, a research institute established by the Italian government after the 1966 floods. Part of her work involved gathering data about sea tides as the chief scientist aboard research vessels that plied the Adriatic. She began constructing models of the sea to research how Adriatic tides affected the city. During the 1970s, she commuted between Venice and San Diego, where she earned another Ph.D. from the University of California's Scripps Institution of Oceanography in 1978. Her thesis topic investigated hurricanes and their oceanic counterparts, the cold/warm circular ring structures whose flows affect tides. Her work drew upon previous research done by Massachusetts Institute of Technology (MIT) scientist Edward Lorenz, and in 1981 Lorenz invited her to join the MIT faculty as an assistant professor of oceanography.

Rizzoli continued her research work on Adriatic tides in what is known as the field of oceanic hydrodynamics, while Venice officials remained deadlocked over the best solution to remedy the *acqua alta*. "No other city in the world has been studied in such detail," asserted Piero Piazzano in an article for the *UNESCO Courier*. "None has been so painstakingly dissected to determine the reasons for its rise and fall. And, it must be added, never has so much hard work produced such meager results." Sirens sound across the city on mornings when waters are expected to reach high levels, and during the 1990s this began to occur with alarming regularity. On some 60 days a year the famous piazza at St. Mark's Square is flooded, which discourages the tourism upon which the city's economy had become increasingly reliant. With all goods entering the city by boat, Venice was a famously expensive place for ordinary citizens, and many left. Its population declined from 175,000 to just 68,000 by 1998.

That same year, Rizzoli and two MIT colleagues completed an impact study that favored a proposed $5 billion engineering project to install a system of dozens of floodgates on the Adriatic seafloor. Nicknamed "MOSE," or the Modulo Sperimentale Elettromeccanico—with a nod to the biblical prophet, Moses, who parted the Red Sea—the gates would be stationed at Venice's three major inlets, the Lido, Malamocco, and Chioggia. Concrete and metal anchors weighing 300 tons each would hold down gates that were 65 feet wide; at the flick of a control–center switch, they could be filled with compressed air, which would force water to act as a barrier for threatening tides.

The start of the MOSE project was delayed for several more years due to disagreements about its potential effectiveness and possible environmental impact on the city and its canals. Scientists in the opposing camp warned that if sea levels continued to rise because of global warming, the gates might be useless in the end. Rizzoli's studies assert that at most the gates would have to be deployed a half–dozen times a year; conflicting viewpoints warn that the figure might be ten times that, which would could cause the Venetian lagoon to become stagnant. "I have become very cynical. I am afraid this project will not be completed," she told McHugh in the *Wired* article. "Not in my lifetime." Some type of system to remedy Venice's *acqua alta* was long overdue since that terrible day in 1966, she maintained. "London flooded in the 1970s, and they built the Thames River barriers five years later," she told McHugh. She noted that the early nineteenth–century English Romantic poet Lord Byron had once describe Venetians as so garrulous that they talked in their sleep. She noted that such a characteristic had hampered a practical solution to the flooding problem. "In Venice, we had our flood in 1966, and we are still talking."

Sources

Periodicals

Economist, February 8, 1992, p. 19; September 27, 2003, p. 81.
Science, March 23, 2001, p. 2315.
Time, June 2, 2003, p. 64.
UNESCO Courier, September 2000, p. 9.
Wired, August 2003, p. 128.

Online

"Paola Malanotte Rizzoli," Department of Earth, Atmospheric, and Planetary Sciences, Massachusetts Institute of Technology, http://www–paoc.mit.edu/eaps/people/person.asp?position=Faculty&who=rizzoli (February 15, 2004).
"Rizzoli, Paola M.," http://www–eaps.mit.edu/faculty/rizzoli.htm (February 15, 2004).

—*Carol Brennan*

V. Gene Robinson

Episcopal bishop

Born May 29, 1947, in Lexington, KY; son of Charles (a sharecropper) and Imogene (a sharecropper); married Isabella "Boo" Martin, 1972 (divorced, 1987); children: Ella, Jamee. *Education:* University of the South, Sewanee, B.A., 1969; General Theological Seminary, NY, M. Div., 1973. *Religion:* Episcopalian.

Addresses: *Office*—Diocesan House, 63 Green St., Concord, NH 03301.

Career

Began career as curate, Christ Church, Ridgewood, NJ, 1973; moved to New Hampshire to open girls' summer camp and horse farm, 1975; Youth Ministries Coordinator for Province I, 1978–85; coordinator of staff and ministry for the New Hampshire Episcopal Diocese bishop, 1988–2003; bishop of the New Hampshire Episcopal Diocese, 2003–.

Member: Executive secretary, Episcopal Province of New England, 1983–; Board of Trustees member, General Theological Seminary, 2001–.

Awards: The *Advocate*'s Person of the Year, 2003; National Gay and Lesbian Task Force Leadership Award, 2004.

Sidelights

V. Gene Robinson created a rift in the Anglican Communion in 2003 when he became Episcopal bishop of the New Hampshire diocese. As a gay man, his elevation to bishop represents a break from 2,000 years of Christian tradition and may force a split of the 70–million–member worldwide Anglican Communion to which it belongs. Opponents call Robinson an abomination and say he is defying the Bible's teachings by living in sin with his partner. Supporters, however, say his life's work serves as an excellent example of Christianity and they hail his elevation as a breakthrough for inclusion.

Robinson is confident the controversy will pass. "Once people see what little effect this has in their day–to–day life and in the life of their local congregation, I don't believe people will want to give up their churches just because the bishop of New Hampshire is gay," he told *Washington Times* writer Julia Duin.

From the very beginning, Robinson's life has been filled with trial and triumph. Robinson was born May 29, 1947, in Lexington, Kentucky, to tobacco sharecroppers Charles and Imogene Robinson. He was not expected to live. At ten pounds, Robinson endured a rough delivery with forceps that crushed his head and partially paralyzed his body. Believing he would die, the doctor asked Robinson's father for a name to list on the birth and death certificates. The couple thought they were having a girl and had chosen Vicki Imogene. Robinson's father figured it would not matter what the tombstone said, so he went with the chosen name, changing it to Vicky Gene. Robinson, however, struggled on. After a month in the hospital, his parents took him home, though they were told he would never walk or talk, but the paralysis eventually went away.

Growing up, Robinson attended a rural, conservative Disciples of Christ church in Nicholasville, Kentucky. By high school, he was questioning its doctrine. As Robinson told *Advocate* writer Bruce C. Steele, "I was in a fairly fundamentalist congregation, and I would ask all kinds of questions, such as 'How could a loving God send people to hell if they have never even heard of Jesus?' The response from the adults in my church was 'There are certain questions you shouldn't ask.'"

After high school, Robinson entered the University of the South, located in Sewanee, Tennessee, and became an Episcopalian. In 1969, he earned a bachelor's degree in American studies and history. That fall, he began studies at the General Theological Seminary in New York, hoping to become a minister. He also entered therapy, hoping to sort out his feelings. He wondered if he was gay. "I had been struggling with this for quite some time, and all of my significant relationships had been with men," he told the *Advocate*. "But then I got into therapy for a couple of years to cure myself. I really wanted to be married. I wanted to have children. I felt that I was in a place that I could have a mature relationship with a woman...."

Before Robinson married Isabella Martin in 1972, he warned his wife about his concerns over his sexuality, though he thought he had benefited from the counseling. In 1973, he graduated from the seminary, was ordained, and began serving at Christ Church in Ridgewood, New Jersey. In 1975, Robinson and his wife moved to New Hampshire where he began ministering to youth as co–owner and director of a girls' summer camp and horse farm. They eventually had two daughters. Over the course of the next two decades, Robinson dedicated his ministry to helping teens, AIDS patients, and congregations in conflict. He also launched "Fresh Start," a mentoring program for clergy adjusting to new positions.

By the mid–1980s, Robinson began to question his sexuality and entered counseling again. He came out to the church in 1986 after he and his wife decided to divorce. "I was increasingly feeling that I could not continue to deny who I was," Robinson told the *Advocate*. "We made a mutual decision. We felt that she deserved the opportunity to know a relationship with a heterosexual man and that I deserved the opportunity to make my life with a man."

In the late 1980s, Robinson cashed in some frequent flier miles and took a vacation to St. Croix. There, he met Mark Andrew. In time, Andrew moved to New Hampshire and the two have lived together since. They led a fairly quiet life for more than a decade until Robinson was elected bishop in June of 2003, confirmed in August, and consecrated in November of that year. Since then, other churches in the Anglican Communion have threatened to sever ties with the Episcopal Church of the United States, citing Scripture that condemns homosexuality. Church leaders from Africa to Asia have expressed anger. Peter Karanja, of the All Saints Cathedral Church in Nairobi, Kenya, summed it up this way for *Time:* "We cannot be in fellowship with them when they violate the explicit Scripture that the Anglican Church subscribes to. It's outrageous and uncalled for."

Robinson, however, believes Scripture is to be interpreted. "We take Scripture seriously, but not literally," Robinson told the *Washington Times*'s Duin, citing passages that call remarriage after divorce adultery. "We went against Scripture and 2,000 years of tradition by relaxing those rules and allowing remarriage. We used our own experience and reason to come to that conclusion." By the same measure, gay bishops should be no big deal, he believes.

No matter what happens within the Anglican Communion, Robinson plans to continue dedicating his ministry to people on the edges—not just the gay and lesbian community. His life's work has touched many people on the fringes, offering hope in the face of despair. For example, after his consecration, Robinson received a note from an 18–year–old imprisoned for killing her mother. Recalling the note to the *Advocate,* Robinson said it read, "I am neither gay nor Christian, but your election makes me think there might be a community out there who could love me despite what I've done." Robinson's election to bishop gave her hope. Robinson's supporters say this inmate is just one example of the many people touched by Robinson's ministry and that is why he was chosen to become bishop—and should remain as such.

Sources

Periodicals

Advocate, December 23, 2003, p. 34; March 30, 2004, p. 22.

New York Times, June 8, 2003, p. A1.
Time, August 18, 2003, p. 50.

Online

"Gay Canon Defends Role in Church," *Washington Times,* http://www.washingtontimes.com/functions/print.php?StoryID=20031023–114717–6294r (April 20, 2004).

"Profile: Bishop Gene Robinson," BBC News, http://news.bbc.co.uk/1/hi/world/americas/3208586.stm (April 20, 2004).

"The Rt. Rev. V. Gene Robinson," Diocese of New Hampshire, http://www.nhepiscopal.org/BishopSearch/The_Rev_Canon_V_Gene_Robinson.htm#Biography (April 20, 2004).

—Lisa Frick

Andy Roddick

AP/Wide World Photos

Professional tennis player

Born Andrew Stephen Roddick, August 30, 1982, in Omaha, NB; son of Jerry (a franchise owner) and Blanche (a teacher) Roddick.

Addresses: *Office*—Andy Roddick Foundation, 2901 Clint Moore Rd. #109, Boca Raton, FL 33496.

Career

Began playing tennis, c. 1986; played first amateur tournament, c. 1990; won Eddie Herr International, 1999; won Orange Bowl championship, 1999; ranked number–one junior player in the United States, 1999–2000; Australian Open junior men's singles winner, 2000; U.S. Open junior men's singles title, 2000; ranked number–one junior player in the world, 2000; turned professional, 2000; won first career professional men's singles title, Verizon Tennis Challenge, in Atlanta, GA, 2001; played Davis Cup tennis, 2001—; won first Grand Slam men's singles title, U.S. Open, 2003; set new world's record for fastest serve, 2004; won Queens Club, London, England, 2004.

Sidelights

Seen as one of the best young tennis players produced by the United States in the early 2000s, Andy Roddick is known for his big serve, passionate play, and fun personality. After turning professional in 2000, Roddick won a number of men's singles tournaments, though he did not win his first Grand Slam title at the U.S. Open until 2003. Roddick sometimes struggled with the demands of the

professional tour as well as his new–found fame, but after he hired Brad Gilbert as his coach in mid–2003, his game again began to improve and he set the world's record for the fastest serve in early 2004.

Born in Omaha, Nebraska, Roddick was the youngest of three sons born to Jerry and Blanche Roddick. Jerry Roddick was a private investor who owned a number of Jiffy Lube franchises, while his mother worked as a schoolteacher. Roddick lived in Nebraska until he was four years old, when the family moved to Austin, Texas. Though he left Nebraska behind, he remained a life–long, die–hard fan of the University of Nebraska's football team.

Around the time of the move to Austin, Roddick began learning to play tennis. Blanche Roddick played tennis for fun, and she encouraged each of her sons to play the sport. However, Roddick's oldest brother, Lawrence, later became a springboard diver, then worked as a chiropractor in San Antonio, Texas. His middle brother, John, played tennis at the University of Georgia, where he was a three–time All American and a highly ranked junior player. A back injury ended his career, and he later ran a tennis academy in San Antonio.

While still living in Austin, Roddick took group lessons and began competing in local amateur tournaments at the age of eight. He was very small for his age, which forced his game to emphasize the serve and using his speed to win from the baseline. Roddick was soon very interested in the sport, playing pretend games in the garage against the best players in tennis. When he was nine years old, his birthday present was a trip to watch the U.S. Open.

As a child, Roddick did not particularly stand out as a player, but he was confident of his tennis skills. In the early 1990s, he convinced Reebok to sign him for their junior program. Reebok's faith in the young player paid off. He remained signed to the company after he turned professional, through the early 2000s.

When Roddick was ten years old, he and his family moved to Boca Raton, Florida, a hot spot for tennis development. In this environment, Roddick began to develop into a solid tennis player himself. In 1997, Roddick discovered a key to his playing career. He figured out that he had a massive, hard serve when he was playing around and did not do the standard serving motion. He soon joined the junior tennis circuit, where he did very well.

While playing junior tournaments and rising in the junior ranks, Roddick continued to attend Boca Prep Academy. Coached by Tarik Benhabiles, he worked on his game every afternoon after school. However, tennis was not his only focus—he also played high school basketball. However, tennis was where he shone and the sport to which he was dedicated. By the time he was 17 years old, Roddick had a serve of 125 m.p.h. Of his young student, Benhabiles told L. Jon Wertheim of *Sports Illustrated,* "Andy's work ethic and his intensity level are tremendous for a kid his age. I tell him not to worry about the future, because if his dedication stays the same, there's no limit."

Roddick won a number of junior titles in 1999 and 2000, including the Eddie Herr International and Orange Bowl championship in 1999, and the Australian Open and U.S. Open Juniors title in 2000. He was regarded as one of the best young players in the world. At one point, Roddick was ranked number one among junior players in the world in 2000.

This success left Roddick with two choices: He could attend college as his brother, John, had and play college tennis, or turn professional. Roddick did not even consider going to college—he turned professional even before he completed high school in 2000, but only when his coach believed he was ready. One of his first tournaments he competed in as a professional was the 2000 U.S. Open, where he lost in the first round.

In 2001, Roddick began to live up to his reputation as a great young American tennis player. He beat one of the best players in the world, Pete Sampras, at a match in March of 2001. At that spring's French Open, Roddick played well. One match, against Michael Chang, gave the world a glimpse of how tough he could be. Despite suffering from debilitating cramps in the fifth set, he beat Chang. Roddick was later eliminated from the tournament.

Roddick won his first professional men's singles title in 2001, the Verizon Tennis Challenge. His victory marked the first time an American teenage player won an ATP tournament since 1992. He also won the U.S. Men's Clay Court Championships in Houston, Texas, and the Legg Mason tournament. By June of 2001, Roddick was ranked number 21 in the world, and was in the top 20 by the time of the U.S. Open. At the U.S. Open, Roddick reached the quarterfinals before losing, but was seen as a brat after yelling at the umpire and arguing a bad line call.

By the time Roddick was succeeding as a tennis player, he stood 6'2" and weighed about 180 lbs. His serve was up to 140 m.p.h. While he was no longer a small boy on the court, he also had adult concerns that reflected his outgoing personality and generous nature. In 2001, he started the Andy Roddick Foundation to help children in their educational and economic lives.

Roddick played tennis with passion and great ability to focus. A number of commentators noted how different he really was. Patrick McEnroe, his Davis Cup coach and a former professional player in his own right, told Mark Starr of *Newsweek,* "Andy plays with enthusiasm. He gets excited, he gets into it, he gets ticked off. People want to see the kind of passion he brings to the game." Sports marketing expert Dean Bonham commented to *Sports Illustrated*'s Wertheim, "He's a breath of fresh air, because there's no pretense about him. He makes no attempt to fit into a tennis-player mold."

Roddick's success and media attention hurt his game in 2002. He struggled more that year, and was unable to live up to the hype of being "the next great thing" in tennis. While he still won at least two singles titles in ATP tournaments, he was unable to break though at Grand Slam tournaments. Roddick was still able to finish in the top ten rankings for the year. The beginning of 2003 was also rough. While Roddick was able to make the semi–finals at the Australian Open, he lost in the first round of the 2003 French Open. This compelled Roddick to make a coaching change.

In June of 2003, shortly before the beginning of the Wimbledon tournament, Roddick fired Benhabiles and hired Brad Gilbert. One of the first changes that Gilbert made was adding more self–confidence to the already–competitive, speedy Roddick. Gilbert told Roddick that he had to believe he could win; he also helped Roddick work on his backhand and his play at the net, the weakest parts of his game. The short–term results were impressive. Roddick went on to win four events in the summer of 2003.

As time went on, Gilbert worked on other aspects of Roddick's game. He helped Roddick learn to adjust his game in matches and not just rely on his power to win. He also believed Roddick could improve in all areas of his game, especially his serve return and making his hard serve even harder. Roddick also began working on improving his conditioning. While Gilbert reformed Roddick's approach on the court, Roddick remained the fun–loving prankster off the court. These changes led to Roddick's biggest career victory to date.

In September of 2003, Roddick finally broke through in Grand Slam tournaments. He won his first U.S. Open, defeating Spain's Juan Carlos Ferrero in three straight sets. In addition to boosting Roddick's confidence, it also led to Roddick being ranked number two in the world. Roddick found the victory hard to believe, and went into the stands to find his coach and his parents. He told Nick Pitt of the *Australian,* "Before I won the U.S. title, there had been a lot of hype rather than substance. I got a lot of it before it was deserved, so the win was almost like validation for me, proving that maybe I was there."

Although he could have dropped out after this big win, Roddick remained committed to playing in the on–going Davis Cup tournament that pitted different countries against each other. As he had since 2001, Roddick represented the United States in the Davis Cup play. In September of 2003, Roddick lost one of his two matches against Slovakia, though his team went on to win the tournament. Roddick told Bud Collins of the *Los Angeles Times,* "Davis Cup means a lot to me. Nothing will interfere. If I feel I need rest, some time off, I'll cut down on other tournaments, but not Davis Cup."

Roddick continued to play well in late 2003 and early 2004. He won 20 straight professional matches between August and October of 2003, when he lost

in the third round of the Madrid Masters. Though injuries to his knee and hamstring forced him to pull out of several tournaments, he still played well in the ones he entered. He became the number–one ranked player in the world in November of 2003, a position he retained until February of 2004. On December 22, 2003, he was named male ITF World Champion.

Roddick lost the number–one ranking after losing at the Qatar Open in January of 2004, and losing in the quarterfinals of the Australian Open later that same month. He went into Open expecting to play well, if not win. Despite these setbacks, Roddick soon set a world's record for fastest serve. In June of 2003, he had tied the world's record of 149 m.p.h. held by Greg Rusedski. In February of 2004, Roddick broke the record in a Davis Cup match against Stefan Koubeck of Austria with a serve of 150 m.p.h.

Although he was an established tennis player with at least 12 singles titles to his name and five million dollars in winnings, Roddick continued to be a different kind of tennis player. In November of 2003, he hosted an episode of NBC's *Saturday Night Live,* a sketch comedy program. He also had a guest appearance on *Sabrina the Teenage Witch.* In 2004, Roddick was to be the subject of a reality series, *The Tour,* which followed him on the ATP tour from May to September. His then-girlfriend, pop singer Mandy Moore, declined to be featured in the television program. Roddick continued his winning ways by defeating Sebastien Grosjean at the June 13, 2004, Queens Club tournament in London, England. He went on to win a second straight RCA Championships title on July 25 of that year.

Of his life in the spotlight, Roddick told Evan Smith of *Texas Monthly,* "I can't take for granted the life that tennis has allowed me to live. Truth is, I think there are loads of kids my age who'd love to switch places with me, so I've got nothing to complain about. Of course, you always wonder what it's like to hit a home run in a playoff game or something like that, but I have no regrets." He went on to win a second straight RCA Championships title on July 25 of that year.

Sources

Periodicals

Australian, January 12, 2004, p. 20.
Los Angeles Times, September 8, 2003, p. D1; September 22, 2003, p. D13; October 17, 2003, p. D3; January 8, 2004, p. D2; January 28, 2004, p. D1.

Newsweek, August 24, 2001.

People, June 4, 2001, p. 74; December 31, 2001, p. 132; December 1, 2003, p. 105.

San Francisco Chronicle, January 18, 2004, p. B1.

Sports Illustrated, February 21, 2000, p. R6; September 15, 2003, p. 56; November 10, 2003, p. 72.

Sunday Telegraph Magazine (Sydney, Australia), January 4, 2004, p. 1.

Texas Monthly, January 2004, p. 46.

Online

"Andy Roddick sets record for fastest serve," WTNH.com, http://www.wtnh.com/global/story.asp?s=1634627&ClientType=Printable (February 9, 2004).

"Andy Roddick (USA)," ATPtennis.com, http://www.atptennis.com/en/players/playerprofiles/default2asp?playernumber=R485 (February 9, 2004).

"Andy Roddick (USA)," ATPtennis.com, http://www.atptennis.com/en/players/playerprofiles/Highlights/default2asp?playernumber=R485 (February 9, 2004).

"Andy Roddick (USA)," ATPtennis.com, http://www.atptennis.com/en/players/playerprofiles/Titles/default2asp?playernumber=R485 (February 9, 2004).

"King of Queen's," *SI.com,* http://sportsillustrated.cnn.com/2004/tennis/06/13/bc.eu.spt.ten.queens.ap (July 9, 2004).

"Roddick not alone in race for No. 1," ESPN.com, http://sports.espn.go.com/espn/print?id=1729167&type=story (February 9, 2004).

"Roddick tops Kiefer, repeats as RCA champ," *SI.com,* http://sportsillustrated.cnn.com/2004/tennis/07/25/bc.ten.indianapolis.ap/index.html (July 27, 2004).

—A. Petruso

Ilene Rosenzweig

Jeff Vespa/WireImage.com

Entrepreneur and author

Born c. 1965; daughter of Alan Rosenzweig (a legal recruiter) and Joy Zuckerman (a yoga instructor); married Rick Marin (a writer), May, 2003.

Addresses: *Home*—New York, NY, and Sag Harbor, NY. *Office*—Target Corp., 1000 Nicollet Mall, Minneapolis, MN 55403.

Career

Journalist, humorist, and lifestyle–brand co–founder. Author of the *The I Hate Madonna Handbook,* 1994; entertainment editor, *Allure* magazine, c. 1995–96; co–founded the Swellco brand with Cynthia Rowley, c. 2000; deputy editor of the *New York Times* Sunday Styles until late 2001; launched line of "Swell" products with Target stores, 2003.

Sidelights

Former fashion editor Ilene Rosenzweig created a retro–stylish, charmingly swish lifestyle brand called Swell with her clothing–designer friend Cynthia Rowley. Their "Swell" concept began its life as a book, but within a few years had morphed into a range of products for Target, the second–largest retailer in the United States. Rosenzweig and Rowley were exploring forays into other media for their tiara–topped logo, but Rosenzweig's big 2003 project was her May wedding to longtime boyfriend, journalist Rick Marin. The build–up to their nuptials coincided with Rosenzweig's PR blitz for the Target line and Marin's book tour for his newly

published *Cad: Confessions of a Toxic Bachelor.* The two traveled together on their press jaunts, and were even discussing a possible television show based on marital bliss. "With giddy savoir faire and serious business savvy," wrote *W*'s Jessica Kerwin, "Marin and Rosenzweig have turned their stylish take on modern living (indeed, their very lives) into a franchise."

Born in the mid–1960s, Rosenzweig grew up in Port Washington, New York, in a family of three children. After college, she moved to Manhattan and took a series of publishing and journalism jobs. Her first book, *The I Hate Madonna Handbook,* appeared in 1994. It was, as its title promised, a sly primer on the singer/actress's more sordid private life and career advancement through the years, and rife with inside tales of abuse. *Entertainment Weekly* writer Erica Kornberg called it a "clever, nasty, well–researched potshot" with "brilliantly vituperative chapters." By 1996, Rosenzweig was serving as *Allure* magazine's entertainment editor, but soon jumped ship to the *New York Times* to become deputy editor of its "Sunday Styles" section. She and Marin had begun dating by then, and were both at the *Times* for a period before leaving in late 2001 in a wave of resignations following executive editor Howell Raines's ascendancy.

Rosenzweig had teamed with her friend Rowley, a Chicago native whose design business began to pick up steam in the early 1990s, to create the first Swell guide in 1999. Rowley had been known to ride a motorcycle to work in New York City, but had also had a hit with her whimsical, feminine frocks. The pair merged their life and lifestyle philosophies into a tongue–in–cheek advice book, *Swell: A Girl's Guide to the Good Life.* In it, they proffered tips on entertaining, home décor, wardrobe, and a range of other topics, all with an attitude they termed "joie de vivre—only less French."

The 1999 tome sold some 120,000 copies, and launched a new phase in Rosenzweig's career. She and Rowley created the Swellco brand, and began writing an idea column for *Glamour* magazine. By mid–2002, they were hosting their own feature on the Showtime cable channel, "A Girl's Guide to Swell Movies." Their next project, *Home Swell Home: Designing Your Dream Home,* came from Rosenzweig and Rowley's "disdain for sloppy chic," noted *Record* contributor Jura Koncius or, more specifically, "all those oversize slipcovers and shapeless sofas in faded colors that started showing up in yuppie lofts and living rooms in the Nineties. The chic they espoused was sexy, not shabby."

Following the second book, Rosenzweig and Rowley launched a line of "Swell" products on the shelves of several hundred Target stores in early 2003. The whimsical housewares and clothing ranged from bathroom towels embroidered "Good," "Clean," and "Fun" to orange lycra yoga pants. The duo joined a cache of other high–profile designers creating lines for Target, including Philippe Starck, Todd Oldham, and Isaac Mizrahi. Their next venture would be *The Swell–Dressed Party,* a how–to entertaining guide. Despite what Rosenzweig and Rowley stress is their decidedly anti–Martha Stewart approach to home and hearth, Rosenzweig admits to being somewhat of a perfectionist. Hence her choice of Portofino, Italy, for her May of 2003 nuptials to Marin. "If it was in New York," Rosenzweig told *People,* "I would be stressing over cherry tomato canapés and tuna tartare. But over there it's so beautiful you don't have to worry about anything else!"

Marin detailed his first meeting with Rosenzweig in *Cad,* a brutal but comic accounting of his dating life for seven years in the 1990s. "The first time I met Ilene, she ignored me, registered such profound indifference to my presence that I backed away speechless into the party throng," Marin wrote in his book. "I'm not even sure she spoke, just threw me a nod." Rosenzweig later hired him to write a celebrity profile for *Allure,* and the two became platonic cohorts. As his book recounts, Rosenzweig failed to fall for any of his well–rehearsed dating come–ons, but the two eventually fell in love and, after dating for five years, Marin proposed to her on a beach at Shelter Island (a Long Island resort town) with a ring that had been worn by three generations of women in his family. "I do have commitment phobia," Rosenzweig recalled of the moment in an interview with *Observer* journalist Dee O'Connell, "And I was being a jerk, so I'm like, 'I'm going to wear this as a pinkie ring, this is going to be my style statement.'" After dancing on the beach and toasting their impending union with champagne, the too–big ring slipped off Rosenzweig's pinkie. They had to call in experts for help in a search that lasted 12 hours, but the ring was finally unearthed with a metal detector. "The thing that was very princely about him," she told O'Connell, "was that he didn't yell at me once."

Returning to their Flatiron district loft and summer house in Sag Harbor, Long Island, after their Italian wedding, Rosenzweig and her husband were busy at work on their next projects. Marin was working on a screenplay for *Cad,* and there was discussion of a "Swell" sitcom for a major network, and perhaps even a television show about newlywed bliss. Rosenzweig was eager to create a romantic–comedy premise that projected what she termed "a new attitude about marriage," she explained to *Los Angeles Times* writer Irene Lacher. "I think it's important to be able to show in pop culture better pictures of marriage, of commitment, that it can be fun and not dark and cynical...."

Selected writings

The I Hate Madonna Handbook, St. Martin's Press (New York City), 1994.
(With Cynthia Rowley) *Swell: A Girl's Guide to the Good Life,* Warner Books (New York City), 1999.
(With Rowley) *Home Swell Home: Designing Your Dream Home,* Atria (New York City), 2002.

Sources

DSN Retailing Today, February 24, 2003, p. 16.
Entertainment Weekly, May 13, 1994, p. 54.
HFN The Weekly Newspaper for the Home Furnishing Network, January 13, 2003, p. 4.

Los Angeles Times, October 15, 1999, p. 2; March 3, 2003, p. E1.
Newsweek, December 6, 1999, p. 77.
New York Post, August 26, 2002, p. 35.
Observer (London, England), June 8, 2003, p. 4.
People, March 24, 2003, pp. 95–96.

Record (Bergen County, NJ), October 20, 2002, p. F8.
W, February 2003, p. 110.
WWD, July 10, 2002, p. 7.

—*Carol Brennan*

Coleen Rowley

Attorney

Born Coleen Cheney, c. 1955, in Fort Belvoir, VA; daughter of Larry (a mail carrier) and Doris Cheney; married Ross Rowley, c. 1980; children: Tess, Bette, Meg, Jeb. *Education:* Wartburg College, Waverly, IA, B.A., 1977; University of Iowa Law School, J.D., 1980; completed training at the FBI Academy, 1981.

Addresses: *Office*—U.S. Federal Bureau of Investigation, Minneapolis Field Office, Ste. 1100, 111 Washington Ave. South, Minneapolis, MN 55401–2176.

Career

Began with the U.S. Federal Bureau of Investigation as an agent in Omaha, NE, 1981; also served in Jackson, MS, at the U.S. Embassy in Paris as an assistant legal attachè, and at the U.S. Consulate in Montreal; worked as a wiretap transcriber at the FBI's New York City field office after January, 1984; stationed with the Minneapolis FBI field office as a media spokesperson after 1990, and chief division counsel, 1995—.

Awards: Person of the Year, *Time* magazine, 2002.

Sidelights

Coleen Rowley, an employee of the Federal Bureau of Investigation's (FBI) Minnesota field office, unexpectedly found herself the subject of front–page headlines in the spring of 2002 when a scathing memo she wrote to her boss, FBI Director Robert S.

Mueller III, was leaked to the press. Her criticisms of the agency and its ineptitude incited a firestorm of controversy about the domestic security agency's ability to have apprised and perhaps even prevented the fateful attacks on the United States on September 11, 2001. Rowley was heralded at the end of 2002 by *Time* magazine as its "Person of the Year," along with Sherron Watkins and Cynthia Cooper, executives at Enron and WorldCom respectively, who had also come forward to criticize their organization's internal culture. Yet Rowley claimed she was anything but a hero. "I hate the term whistle–blower," she told *Time* writers Amanda Ripley and Maggie Sieger, and had said elsewhere that her outspokenness had been spurred only by guilt. "Since that fateful date of Sept. 11, 2001, I have not ceased to regret that perhaps I did not do all that I might have done," a *New York Times* report from Philip Shenon quoted her as writing.

Born in the mid–1950s on a United States military base in Virginia where her father was stationed, Rowley was the eldest of five children born to Iowans Larry and Doris Cheney. The family settled in New Hampton, a small town in north–central Iowa, where her father worked as a mail carrier. Rowley grew up in a close–knit German Lutheran family, and proved to be a strong–willed, academically gifted perfectionist from an early age. As a ten–year–old, her favorite show was *The Man from U.N. C.L.E.*, a sophisticated espionage–spoof series that ran on NBC from 1964 to 1968. Rowley actually wrote to the show and asked to join its villain–fighting, gadget–equipped team, but was told to check with the Federal Bureau of Investigation for more information about a career in spying. The FBI responded to her request with a pamphlet that clearly stated that there was no such thing as a female FBI agent. "I thought to myself, 'That's stupid,'" Rowley recalled in the *Time* interview. "I figured that would change eventually."

Rowley graduated as New Hampton Community High School's valedictorian in 1973, but was denied a Regents Scholarship to Wartburg College in Waverly, Iowa, after meeting with the committee that chose the recipients. Expected to state that she hoped to become a missionary, physician, or lawyer after she earned her degree, Rowley candidly admitted that she did not yet know what her future plans were. She enrolled in the school anyway, paying her way with the help of a state grant for those considering a career in teaching, and majored in French. None of the Regents Scholarship winners chosen over her followed through on their lofty career goals. "I tracked them," she told Ripley and Sieger in the *Time* interview. "And within a few months, not one of them was doing what they said."

Rowley, on the other hand, did enroll in law school, finishing at the University of Iowa in 1980 and marrying a fellow student, Ross Rowley, around the same time. By then the FBI was admitting female agents into its ranks, and she was accepted at its training academy in Quantico, Virginia. Her career plans were almost waylaid by an unexpected pregnancy, which happened when she stopped taking birth control pills in an effort to shave time off a two–mile run that she hoped to set a record for at the Quantico school. Rowley's husband agreed to help her with the childcare and household duties, and after she was sworn in as an FBI agent on January 19, 1981, she became the family's sole breadwinner. The pair would eventually become parents to a brood of four.

Rowley proved to be a dedicated, able FBI agent. She served in its Nebraska and Mississippi field offices, and was also posted to the U.S. Embassy in Paris as an assistant legal attachè. After a stint at the U.S. Consulate in Montreal, she was transferred to the FBI's New York City office, where she worked on the organized–crime front. To improve her fluency in Italian and Sicilian, she trained at the U.S. Department of Defense Language Institute in Monterey, California, in order to better transcribe the FBI wiretap tapes of suspected Mafia operatives. She took accused mobster Gennaro Langella on his 1984 "perp walk" before the news cameras. Transferred to the Minneapolis FBI field office in 1990, Rowley served as its media spokesperson, and after 1995 as the chief division counsel there. She fielded press inquiries regarding her colleagues' capture of longtime Symbionese Liberation Army fugitive Kathleen Soliah, and was involved in the 1997 manhunt for Andrew Cunanan, the murderer of fashion mogul Gianni Versace.

Rowley, her friends and colleagues noted, was utterly devoted to her career and to the organization. She did begin to suspect, however, that a certain bureaucratic inefficiency and poor lines of communication with FBI headquarters in Washington seemed to hamper the agents' ability to perform their jobs adequately. Those internal shortcomings were made painfully clear on September 11, 2001, when 19 men hijacked four U.S. airliners and deployed them to crash into the two World Trade Center towers in New York City and the massive Pentagon complex in Washington, D.C.; the fourth airliner was diverted to Pennsylvania and crashed into a field, killing all passengers. The attacks seemed coordinated and well–organized, and American officials claimed there had been no prior knowledge of the plan, which apparently involved a number of Middle Eastern–born men who had trained at United States flight schools.

Rowley believed otherwise. On August 13, four weeks before 9/11, officials at an Eagan, Minnesota, flight school had contacted agents at the Minneapolis FBI office, alerting them to a French–Moroccan man who had applied to the school and wanted to train on a 747 flight simulator. Her colleagues arrested the man, Zacarias Moussaoui, for overstaying his visa, and began investigating his background. They learned from French intelligence officials that Moussaoui was linked to known Islamic fundamentalist organizations overseas, and had even been placed on a watch list of suspected terrorists because of his frequent travel to and from Kuwait, Turkey, and various European countries. He was even thought to have gone to Afghanistan, which sheltered the shadowy Al Qaeda organization headed by Saudi exile Osama bin Laden, and was known to have spent time in Pakistan just before his arrival in the United States.

With Moussaoui in custody, Rowley and her colleagues attempted to get permission from FBI headquarters to search his laptop computer. Their requests for a search warrant, which could only be granted under the terms of the Foreign Intelligence Surveillance Act (FISA), were repeatedly denied; FISA rules at the time required that the FBI prove that the suspect was an agent of a terrorist group or a foreign government. Rowley and her Minnesota colleagues were adamant in their conviction that the information received from French intelligence agents met this condition, but the Washington office stonewalled in granting the request.

Three days after 9/11, Mueller, the FBI chief, asserted that his agency was surprised to learn that the hijackers had trained at United States flight schools, and that he and other officials had no inkling of this. Rowley and her fellow agents in Minneapolis were vexed. Next, a memo from an FBI agent in Phoenix, Arizona, surfaced in the media. It was dated July 5 and warned FBI headquarters about a number of Middle Eastern men who had entered the United States on student visas and were training to become pilots. Again, Mueller told the American public that there had been no warning bells sounded prior to 9/11, and because of that statement, Rowley came to believe that subordinates at headquarters had not properly briefed the FBI director. She and Minneapolis agents even tried to contact Mueller themselves, but were unable to get through. In what became a small act of rebellion, they began attaching a copy of their original August memo about Moussaoui to every single document that went to Washington.

In December of 2001, Moussaoui was charged with six counts of conspiracy for the 9/11 attacks. Mueller still claimed at the time that there was nothing the FBI could have done to prevent the tragedy, a statement that bothered Rowley. In February of 2002, the House and Senate Intelligence Committees launched a joint inquiry into why United States law–enforcement and intelligence experts had failed to detect the terrorists or their plans ahead of time. In May, Rowley was asked to come to Washington in order to meet with members of a Congressional committee behind closed doors. Wanting to present her side of the story clearly and unable to sleep because of it, she began writing down her talking points. She spent several hours drafting what would become her infamous 13–page memo. "It's at least possible we could have gotten lucky and uncovered one or two more of the terrorists in flight training prior to Sept. 11," the memo read, according to *Time,* had they been granted the search warrant to look at Moussaoui's computer. "There is at least some chance that … may have limited the Sept. 11th attacks and resulting loss of life." At her close, realizing that she might be overstepping her bounds, she tacked on a sentence requesting federal whistle–blower protection. She hand–delivered one copy to the Mueller's office, and gave two more to members of the Senate Intelligence Committee.

With a sense of relief, Rowley returned to her Minneapolis office. She learned that her memo had been leaked to the media the next day when a journalist from CNN phoned her at her desk. Stunned, she replied, "I can't help you. I don't know what you're talking about," she told *Time*'s Ripley and Sieger. Within hours, the story had hit the headlines, and

Rowley returned to Washington in early June to testify before the Senate Judiciary Committee and a battalion of news cameras. She told Congress that field–office agents like her colleagues in Minneapolis were burdened by paperwork, hampered by an ineffective computer system, and were often stymied by directives from or failed communications with the agency's D.C. headquarters.

Furthermore, Rowley described the FBI as rife with careerists, who were eager to protect their turf and unwilling to make decisions that might jeopardize their job security. "The Rowley memo casts a searing light into the depths of government ineptitude," *Time* declared. "Rowley has at least forced the FBI and the Administration to confront their failures directly and publicly, rather than sweep them under a self–stitched rug of wartime immunity." *Newsweek* writers Mark Hosenball and Michael Isikoff were equally caustic in commenting on Rowley's assessment. "Rarely has the FBI been so witheringly, and publicly, criticized by one of its own," they noted. Finally, even Mueller was forced to backtrack, telling reporters, "I cannot say for sure that there wasn't a possibility we could have come across some lead that would have led us to the hijackers," he said, according to *Time*'s Ripley and Sieger.

Rowley spurned film and book offers to tell her story, and returned to her job in Minneapolis and the arduous triathlon–training schedule that is her hobby. She remained greatly disconcerted by the controversy her memo had ignited. Some FBI agents admitted, off the record, that her criticisms were justified, but others publicly excoriated her for betraying the bureau's legendary code of loyalty and deference to superiors. "Loyalty to whoever you work for is extremely important," she conceded in the *Time* interview with Ripley and Sieger. "The only problem is, it's not *the* most important thing. And when it comes to not admitting mistakes, or covering up or not rectifying things only to save face, that's a problem."

Sources

America's Intelligence Wire, November 6, 2002.
Asia Africa Intelligence Wire, December 26, 2002.
Chicago Tribune, December 24, 2002.
Des Moines Register, February 9, 2003, p. 1.
Europe Intelligence Wire, May 15, 2003.
Maclean's, June 17, 2002, p. 13.
New American, June 17, 2002, p. 44.
New Statesman, June 10, 2002, p. 10.

Newsweek, June 3, 2002, p. 20.

New York Times, March 6, 2003, p. A1.

People, June 10, 2002, p. 73.

Star Tribune (Minneapolis, MN), March 9, 2003, p. 2B.

Strategic Finance, March 2003, p. 18.

Time, June 3, 2002, p. 24; December 30, 2002/January 6, 2003, pp. 34–42, pp. 58–60.

Time International, February 3, 2003, p. 8.

U.S. News & World Report, June 3, 2002, p. 30.

—*Carol Brennan*

Donald Rumsfeld

United States Secretary of Defense

Born Donald H. Rumsfeld, July 9, 1932, in Chicago, IL; married Joyce; children: Valerie, Marcy, Nick. *Education:* Princeton University, B.A. (politics), 1954.

Addresses: *Office*—1400 Defense Pentagon, Room 1E757, Washington, DC 20301.

Career

U.S. Navy aviator and instructor, 1954–57; administrative assistant, U.S. House of Representatives, 1957–59; investment broker, A.G. Becker & Co., 1960–62; U.S. congressman from 13th Illinois district, 1962–69; director of Office of Economic Opportunity, assistant to President Richard Nixon, 1969–70; counselor to President Nixon, director of economic stabilization program, 1971–73; U.S. ambassador to NATO, 1973–74; chief of staff for President Gerald Ford, 1974–75; Secretary of Defense, 1975–77; president, CEO, chairman of G. D. Searle & Co., 1977–85; envoy to the Middle East, 1983–84; senior advisor to the President's Panel on Strategic Systems, 1983–84; special presidential Envoy to the Middle East, 1983–84; senior adviser William Blair & Co., 1985–90; chairman and CEO of General Instrument Corporation, 1990–93; chaired U.S. Commission to Assess National Security Space Management and Organization; chairman of the board of directors of Gilead Sciences, Inc., 1997–01; Secretary of Defense, 2000—.

Member: U.S. Joint Advisory Commission on U.S./ Japan Relations, 1983–84; National Commission on Public Service, 1987–90; National Economic Commission, 1988–89; Board of Visitors of the National Defense University, 1988–92; Commission on U.S./ Japan Relations, 1989–91; U.S. Trade Deficit Review Commission, 1999–2000; Stanford board member; National Park Foundation.

Awards: Presidential Medal of Freedom, 1977; Outstanding Chief Executive Officer in the Pharmaceutical Industry, *Wall Street Transcript*, 1980; Outstanding Chief Executive Officer in the Pharmaceutical Industry, *Financial World*, 1981.

Sidelights

Donald Rumsfeld, the 21st Secretary of Defense, was sworn in on January 20, 2001. The former Navy pilot has had a lifelong commitment to public duty as the 13th Secretary of Defense under President Ford, White House Chief of Staff under President Gerald Ford, U.S. Ambassador to the North Atlantic Treaty Organization (NATO) and U.S. Congressman for Illinois. But Rumsfeld became a household name after the worst attack in history on United States soil. The terrorist attacks of September 11, 2001, were the beginning of a redefinition of national defense. Rumsfeld has been at the forefront of preparing the country for a new kind of enemy.

Born in Chicago, Illinois, to a real estate broker and homemaker, Rumsfeld's childhood was notable for an innate charisma that drew people to him. He showed an early interest in politics and the world around him when the Japanese attacked Pearl Harbor. Being a nine–year–old boy and seeing his father put aside his career to join the Navy left a deep impression on him that would shape his character and lead to a career in politics.

The young Rumsfeld was a hard worker, never happy to sit on his hands for even a moment. By the time he was a teenager he had held down 20 part–time jobs ranging from delivering newspapers to gardening. During high school he met a girl named Joyce who he would go on to marry. With high energy, focus, and excellent grades he was accepted to Princeton on academic and Naval Reserve Officer Training Corps (NROTC) scholarships.

In 1954, he started service to the U.S. Navy as a flight instructor. He ended his tenure in 1957 when he transferred to the Ready Reserve. Though he continued his Naval service in flying and administrative assignments as a reservist, he had plans for his career that would put him in a two–piece suit instead of a flight suit.

He joined the private sector for the first time as an investment banker in Chicago. Displaying his standard charm Rumsfeld quickly made friends in high places and began to hear the call of public office. At the age of 30, he ran for an Illinois seat in the U.S. House of Representatives and won. Rumsfeld arrived in Washington D.C. in 1962 and, again, found the right people to know at the right time. He joined Bob Dole, Gerald Ford, and George H.W. Bush as a young up–and–comer and the town quickly knew they had a new generation of leaders waiting in the wings. The four men became very close and those bonds, some now broken, would shape world history for decades to come.

Rumsfeld was a popular congressman and was re-elected in 1964, 1966, and 1968. But he resigned in 1969 to join President Richard Nixon's White House. His role as Director of the Office of Economic Opportunity and Assistant to the President lasted until 1970. By most accounts, Rumsfeld's performance was solid and he impressed President Nixon. In recognition of his contributions, Nixon promoted him to Counselor to the President and Director of the Economic Stabilization Program where he served until mid–1973. He got the chance to try his hand on the international scene next, by serving as the U.S. Ambassador to NATO in Brussels, Belgium, until 1974.

But in August of 1974 the White House was in chaos after the resignation of President Nixon. Rumsfeld, known for his iron–jawed leadership skills and no–nonsense style, was called back to Washington, D.C., to serve as Chairman of the transition to the Presidency of Gerald Ford. His keen sense of secrecy and politics made people uneasy. But most members of the chaotic White House knew he was doing a great job of forcing order during what some would say was a Constitutional crisis. Inevitably, with his presence making such an impact on the daily functions of the White House, Rumsfeld became Chief of Staff of the White House and a member of the President's Cabinet. Before President Ford was voted out of office Rumsfeld was appointed the 13th U.S. Secretary of Defense, the youngest in the country's history at the age of 43. He served in the position from 1975 to 1977.

Many believed Rumsfeld was positioning himself for a run for president. Indeed, most indications were that the young man was trying to pack as much experience as he could in as short a time as possible. He had already worked in very important positions on the domestic and international fronts. Even though he was young, there were very few political foes who could attack him for lack of credentials. The resignation of Nixon had left the GOP in chaos and Rumsfeld started acting like a man with a political mission. He appointed his old friend, George H.W. Bush, to head the CIA. Most insiders considered this a slap in the face for Bush since he was also positioning himself as presidential material. To most politicians, it appeared that Rumsfeld was removing his competition.

But when Ford lost to Jimmy Carter in the election of 1976, Rumsfeld decided against running for president and, in essence, disappeared from Washington. His move into the private sector was astonishing to his fellow politicians, many of whom were glad to see him go. Though he had made a deep impression on Washington, he had made his share of enemies, many in his own party who never got used to his style or his uncanny political talents. These conflicts would arise again when Rumsfeld returned to politics almost 25 years later.

Rumsfeld's sideways move into the private sector was as successful as his political career. His style of speaking has always been very direct and he dashes every point with a folksy style. That same demeanor tends to keep him at arms length from people. Many who know him acknowledge that he is, fundamentally, a mistrusting person. Still, his leadership qualities secured him positions in two *Fortune 500* companies in the years that followed his departure from the political scene.

Rumsfeld was not a power–player in Washington anymore but he kept one toe in the water at all times. He worked for the Reagan administration on a number of projects such as senior advisor to the President's Panel on Strategic Systems and special envoy to the Middle East. He also continued to be involved during President Bill Clinton's second term as a member of the U.S. Trade Deficit Review Commission and chaired the U.S. Commission to Assess National Security Space Management and Organization. These are only examples of the dozens of duties he held in the political arena which ranged from chairman of fellowships to board member of Stanford and the National Park Foundation.

But a majority of his efforts went into private industry where he became a wealthy man very quickly. Upon leaving Washington he was offered the positions of chief executive officer, president, and chairman of G.D. Searle & Company, a pharmaceutical company. Over the years, his efforts were recognized as some of the best leadership in the pharmaceutical industry by a number of business organizations. Rumsfeld moved on to serve as CEO of General Instrument Corporation from 1990 to 1993, a leader in broadband technologies. He soon joined the board of another pharmaceutical company, Gilead Sciences, Incorporated, where he focused his efforts until the call came in from Vice–President–elect Dick Cheney in 2000 to join President–elect George W. Bush's staff.

Cheney knew Rumsfeld was qualified to be Secretary of Defense. After all he had done it before as the youngest secretary in history. But Rumsfeld was 68, which meant if he were to take the job he would also become the oldest secretary in history. Cheney and Rumsfeld had stayed close and both agreed on what threats faced the world. For instance, both had lobbied President Clinton hard to consider Iraq an immediate danger to United States security. After some consideration, Rumsfeld accepted the Bush administration's offer.

Upon taking the oath of office, Rumsfeld, in his traditional fashion, announced that things were going to change. He had been a Washington insider for decades and had strong opinions about how things worked. He felt he knew what needed fixing and he set out to fix it. The only problem was that many of the enemies he had left behind when he went into the private sector were still in Washington— and they still did not like him one bit.

First, he wanted to cut defense expenditures on old weapons and move the focus to new ones that could better deal with the threats we face in the modern world. This was controversial since many in the military believed this challenged their roles as overseers. But to make matters even more tense, Rumsfeld wanted to take another look at the way the military was organized. He wanted to reshuffle United States troops in a way that could allow the country to go to war quickly, anywhere in the world. His tactics were not appreciated by people who were in a system they had lived with their entire professional careers. For any Secretary of Defense to make sweeping changes it is incumbent on them to inform congress. But many in the legislative side were complaining about being left out of the loop. Most people in Washington believed Rumsfeld was going to shoot himself in the foot with his approach to reshuffling his department and redefining its responsibilities. He had the energy to change the world but he did not necessarily have the power. Most political pros thought Rumsfeld would be out of the White House within a year.

But then disaster struck, exactly the kind of disaster for which the office of the Secretary of Defense is designed. While Rumsfeld's experience was indisputable, no one could be prepared for September 11, 2001. The morning of the attack Rumsfeld was in his office at the Pentagon. He felt the building shake and went outside to find chaos. Without knowing what had happened he helped carry some people clear of danger and was then led to the War Room where he was updated on the events of the morning. Since he is responsible for directing the defense of the United States, the world looked to him for a tactical response. When it became clear that Osama Bin Laden was behind the attacks, Afghanistan became the prime target for America's wrath. Interestingly, only hours after the 9/11 attacks, Rumsfeld was working to also put Iraq in the crosshairs. A CBS News report in September of 2002 revealed notes taken during the hours after the attacks. "Go massive," the notes read. "Sweep it all up. Things related and not.... Judge whether good enough hit S.H. (Saddam Hussein) at same time. Not only UBL (Osama Bin Laden)." Once President Bush declared the attacks as acts of war, Rumsfeld was, essentially, given the go–ahead to arrange for America's defense as he saw fit.

Being the efficient type, Rumsfeld took advantage of the times to push through the changes he had worked hard to make. The result was a new plan called the Unified Command Plan, which sought to make the rules of sizing our forces more streamlined and relevant to the threats the United States now faced. The reshuffling and top–down analysis of our military led to many more controversies, not least of which was the reinstatement of the "Star Wars" program, otherwise known as the Strategic

Defense Initiative (SDI). The program was introduced during the Reagan administration and promised to create an impenetrable shield of missile defense around the country with a series of satellites and powerful lasers that could knock down any attack from the air. SDI's confinement to the laboratory (i.e. no real world testing) was an integral part of the ABM treaty signed by the United States and the former Soviet Union. By giving SDI new life, many feared a new arms race could ignite between the two countries. Rumsfeld brushed off this kind of thinking. "No U.S. president can responsibly say that his defense policy is calculated and designed to leave the American people undefended against threats that are known to exist," Rumsfeld was reported to say in an Associated Press piece in the *New York Times*. "[Missile defense] is not so much a technical question as a matter of a president's constitutional responsibility."

Rumsfeld's power and influence in the Bush White House only increased when the war in Afghanistan ended after only a few days. With a new mandate to defend the country from weapons of mass destruction, Rumsfeld and Cheney moved to make Iraq the next target. Saddam Hussein had developed a large cache of biological weapons before the first Gulf War. Once he lost that war he was ordered by the international community to destroy all weapons of mass destruction. The United Nations was sent in to monitor their compliance. But in 1997, the inspectors were kicked out and many, Rumsfeld included, believed he was building a new arsenal. He thought if Hussein could use those weapons against the United States, he would. Which led Rumsfeld to conclude that Hussein must be removed from power. With backing from many people in the Bush administration, the path to war was laid and Rumsfeld was one of the leaders.

Once again, his gruff attitude got him in trouble. As many in the international community, including France and Germany, scoffed at the idea of preemptive war, a frustrated Rumsfeld tagged them "Old Europe." But that was the least of his problems. In his own administration he was meeting resistance with the Secretary of State, Colin Powell. Powell wanted to let the newly deployed United Nations inspectors do their work in Iraq. The media had a field day playing up the conflict and, in the end, Bush sided with Rumsfeld.

Rumsfeld did not just tell his people to get to work, he got involved. Proposal No. 177 is a series of documents that conveys, in detail, the plans of deployment and how to get what infantry where and by what date with all the weapons, people, and sup-

plies it needs. These are the kinds of documents that are usually handed off to the underlings. But Rumsfeld read every word, challenged ideas that seemed rooted in old thinking and used his authority to make the attack on Iraq a new chapter in military deployment.

When the war began on the ground on March 20, 2003, many politicians watched closely to see how Rumsfeld's influence would carry onto the battlefield. Many came out against him in the press, especially retired officers, when the advance on Baghdad slowed down. But, in the end, the Iraqi army was defeated and American troops took control of the capitol. Rumsfeld basked in the praise many gave him for the lightning–fast victory. To his supporters, the war was vindication for Rumsfeld and proved that he had been right about reorganizing the armed forces. But in the months after the defeat of the Iraqi Republican Guard, the battle became more like a guerilla war. American soldiers were asked to police the country, but various factions, both Iraqi and not, sabotaged the infrastructure and made it difficult to keep the peace. Rumsfeld's vision of armed forces that can do a little bit of everything, and do it fast and well, will go through many evaluations over the years as the United States tries to secure the peace in Iraq. However history judges him and his efforts, his name will always be tied to world history after 9/11.

To help quell the guerilla attacks, more American troops were sent to Iraq. On December 4, 2003, Rumsfeld visited Afghanistan, where he urged Afghan warlords to surrender heavy weapons, discussed plans for stopping a lingering insurgency, and pressed for economic development. The next day, he became the first senior administration official to visit the country of Georgia since a peaceful, popular revolt forced out the government of Eduard A. Shevardnadze. Rumsfeld expressed strong support for Georgia's territorial integrity in the face of rising secessionist sentiment and the presence of Russian troops on its territory. On December 13, 2004, Iraqi President Saddam Hussein was captured by American forces, who found him hiding in a hole beneath a two-room shack on a sheep farm near the Tigris River. His capture boosted United States claims that the situation in Iraq was under control.

In front of some of Europe's fiercest critics of the United States-led war in Iraq, Rumsfeld offered an impassioned defense of the conflict. He placed the blame for the war on former Iraqi President Saddam Hussein for his "deception and defiance," as well as his refusal to abandon his illegal weapons program. When it came to light that Iraqi prisoners of war had been abused by American military personnel, Rumsfeld said he would take "all measures necessary" to ensure that the abuse of detainees a Pentagon report alleged took place at a prison in Iraq "does not happen again." President Bush defended Rumsfeld against U.S. politicians and foreign leaders who demanded the secretary's resignation. On May 13, 2004, Rumsfeld visited Abu Ghraib prison in Baghdad, Iraq, the site of Iraqi-prisoner abuse. While there, he gave a rousing speech to hundreds of troops and military police, indicating that those who committed prisoner abuse would be dealt with fairly.

Sources

Periodicals

National Review, May 5, 2003.
New York Times, February 3, 2001.
Providence Journal, June 26, 2003.
Tribune, April 29, 2003.
Time, January 27, 2003, p. 22; April 14, 2003, p. 68.

Online

"Bush Administration: Donald Rumsfeld," Open secrets.org, http://www.opensecrets.org/bush/cabinet/cabinet.rumsfeld.asp (September 5, 2003).

"Bush backs Rumsfeld," CNN.com, http://www.cnn.com/2004/ALLPOLITICS/05/10/bush.pentagon/index.html (July 9, 2004).

"Donald Rumsfeld: Profile," BBC Online, http://www.bbc.co.uk/bbcfour/documentaries/profile/donald–rumsfeld.shtml (September 5, 2003).

"Donald Rumsfeld," Who2.com, http://www.who2.com/donaldrumsfeld.html (September 5, 2003).

"Experience and Drive," ABC News, http://abcnews.go.com/sections/politics/DailyNews/rumsfeld_profile.html (September 5, 2003).

"Honorable Donald Rumsfeld," Department of Defense, http://www.defenselink.mil/bios/secdef_bio.html (September 5, 2003).

"Operation Iraqi Freedom," Department of Defense's War on Terrorism, http://www.defendamerica.mil/iraq/iraqifreedom.html (September 5, 2003).

"Plans For Iraq Attack Began On 9/11," CBS News, http://www.cbsnews.com/stories/2002/09/04/september11/printable520830.shtml (September 5, 2003).

"Player Profile: Donald Rumsfeld," PBS, http://www.pbs.org/newshour/bb/middle_east/iraq/war/player5.html (September 5, 2003).

"Profile: Donald Rumsfeld," BBC Online, http://news.bbc.co.uk/1/hi/world/americas/1555349.stm (September 1, 2003).

"Rumsfeld Expresses U.S. Support for Georgia's Territorial Integrity," Embassy of the United States in Georgia, http://georgia.usembassy.gov/events/event05122003.html (July 9, 2004).

"Rumsfeld pledges detainee reforms," CNN.com, http://www.cnn.com/2004/WORLD/meast/05/04/iraq.abuse.main/index.html (July 9, 2004).

"Rumsfeld visits Iraq's Abu Ghraib prison," CNN.com, http://www.cnn.com/2004/WORLD/meast/05/13/iraq.abuse/index.html (July 9, 2004).

"Secretary of Defense: Donald Rumsfeld," University of Texas, http://www.la.utexas.edu/chenry/usme/sp2001/roles/msg00023.html (September 5, 2003).

"Speech on the 40th Munich Conference on Security Policy," Security Conference, http://www.securityconference.de/konferenzen/rede.php?menu_2004=&menu_konferenzen=&sprache=en&id=132&print=& (July 9, 2004).

Transcripts

FDCH Political Transcripts, April 17, 2003.
Fox News interview with Donald Rumsfeld, May 4, 2003.

—Ben Zackheim

Jeffrey D. Sachs

Economist

Born in 1954, in Detroit, MI; son of Theodore Sachs (an attorney); married Sonia Ehrlich, c. 1979. *Education:* Harvard College, B.A., 1976; Harvard University, M.A., 1978; Harvard University, Ph.D., 1980.

Addresses: *Office*—Earth Institute, Columbia University, 405 Low Library, MC 4335, 535 W. 116th St., New York, NY 10027.

Career

Assistant professor, Harvard University, 1980; associate professor, Harvard University, 1982; full professor, Harvard University, 1983; director of the Harvard Institute for International Development, 1995–99; director of the Center for International Development, Harvard, 1999–2002; director of Columbia University's Earth Institute as well as professor of sustainable development and of health policy and management, Columbia University, 2002—.

Member: American Academy of Arts and Sciences; Harvard Society of Fellows; Fellows of the World Econometric Society; Brookings Panel of Economists; Board of Advisors of the Chinese Economists Society; Institute of Medicine; International Financial Institutions Advisory Commission, 1999–2000; chairman of the World Health Organization's Commission on Macroeconomics and Health, 2000–01.

Awards: Honorary degrees from St. Gallen University, Switzerland, 1990, Universidad del Pacifico, Peru, 1997, Lingnan College, Hong Kong, 1998, Varna Economics University, Bulgaria, 2000, Iona College of New York, 2000; Frank E. Seidman Award in Political Economy, 1991; Commander's Cross of the Order of Merit of the Republic of Poland, 1999; Bernhard Harms Prize, Kiel, Germany, 2000.

Sidelights

Alot of people talk about how to solve the world's problems, but global economic consultant Jeffrey Sachs actually tries to do something about it. Over the past two decades, his insight and intelligence have helped many nations in their struggles for stability, leading the *New York Times Magazine* to call Sachs "probably the most important economist in the world." Sachs is regularly consulted by world leaders such as United Nations General Kofi Annan. He has also worked with Pope John Paul II and served as an economic advisor to former Russian President Boris Yeltsin. Sachs has traveled to more than 100 countries and, to keep up with the demand for his advice, does daily video conferences. In 2004, *Time* magazine named Sachs one of the 100 most influential people in the world.

Sachs was born in Detroit, Michigan, in 1954. His father, Theodore Sachs, was an attorney whose life's work centered on improving the working conditions for the labor force, such teachers, firefighters, and other public–sector workers. Sachs said his father always encouraged him to be involved in the issues of the day. Charming and popular, Sachs was Oak Park High School student council president. However, unlike most teens, he was passionate and active about politics. Sachs marched on Moratorium

Day, a day university students around the nation spent protesting the Vietnam War and calling for its end. Sachs also attended rallies that featured the legendary United Farm Worker leader Cesar Chavez.

When Sachs was a sophomore in high school, his family took a trip to Russia. There, Sachs befriended an East German student and the two became dedicated pen pals. They developed a strong connection and Sachs flew to Europe to visit his friend after he graduated from high school. During this trip, Sachs became fascinated with the concept of world economies. He began to think about how and why they were different and wondered which economic models were best.

Sachs called the visit with his pen pal a defining moment in his life. Speaking to John H. Richardson of *Esquire,* Sachs recalled the event: "He was telling me about the wonders of socialism ... and the thing I discovered was I knew nothing about these issues. I didn't know exactly what capitalism meant, what socialism meant, why we had unemployment and they didn't have unemployment. I didn't know how to answer any of that." By the time Sachs arrived at Harvard College that fall, he said his head was "swimming with this question of why different places in the world have different economic systems."

Sachs was an ambitious student. He entered Harvard in 1972. In four years, he completed his bachelor's degree and had begun his doctorate. By 1980, he was a Harvard professor, dashing off dozens of articles on economic principles—but the ideas Sachs discussed were theoretical and the problems he tackled were solved with fancy equations. In addition, Sachs tended to concentrate on the problems of the developed nations, such as finding a way to solve the 1973 United States energy crisis.

One day, however, a former student invited Sachs to attend a seminar on Bolivia aimed at discussing possible solutions to its 60,000 percent "hyperinflation." After speaking out at the seminar, Sachs was invited to go to Bolivia, forever altering the course of his life. As Sachs told *Esquire*'s Richardson, "That's what really fundamentally changed my life, my understanding of things, the day I stepped off the airplane in La Paz—July 9, 1985. And I found that the world was vastly more interesting and more complicated than my equations."

Sachs helped the government tighten its budget gap so that it would not have to print so much money to pay its debts, which in turn caused more inflation.

Sachs also begged overseas lenders to forgive a portion of Bolivia's debt. "Countries cannot be squeezed to the bone to repay debts without provoking political and social upheaval," Sachs told *Esquire*'s Richardson. He knew that the payments would plunge Bolivia back into financial collapse. Naturally, the idea did not go over well with the foreign lenders or the International Monetary Fund (IMF). Eventually, Sachs secured a debt reduction for Bolivia, which helped usher in the IMF debt–relief movement. Over the years, this program has helped countless nations.

Sachs was incredibly successful in Bolivia. His reforms drove inflation from 60,000 percent a year down to 12 percent. After this success, Poland's leaders called upon Sachs in 1989 as they worked to implement capitalism after the fall of the Berlin Wall and Communism. A few years later, Russia asked for Sachs' help, too, as have many other countries in Latin America, Eastern Europe, Asia, and Africa.

Sachs spent more than 20 years at Harvard and directed its Center for International Development. In 2002, he headed to Columbia University to run the Earth Institute, a conglomerate of 800–plus university employees in dozens of departments in the health and science fields. The Earth Institute works to help poor countries build sustainable economies, while improving human health and preserving the natural environment. "I'm focusing on a world divided between rich and poor, and a world that doesn't seem to be able to manage the natural base of our lives: air, oceans, or biodiversity," he told Alec Appelbaum of *Fast Company*.

While many economists predict gloom and doom in the fight to end poverty in developing nations, Sachs truly believes it is possible. According to Sachs, eradicating malaria, AIDS, and tuberculosis will be the key because if people are sick, they cannot work for their economies. Sachs calls these three the diseases of poverty and believes they are a cause as well as a consequence of it. Sachs believes that stopping these diseases will unleash the economic potential of some of the poorest countries. To this end, Sachs helped the United Nations start a global fund to fight AIDS, tuberculosis, and malaria. A study by Sachs and the World Health Organization concluded that if the world's richest countries raised $38 billion by 2015, they could save eight million lives per year—and expand one–third of the world's prospects for prosperity.

Sachs is irked that a lot of nations do not seem to get it. "I'm still fighting against the incredible capacity of the so–called international community to stare intense human disaster in the face and not flinch from ignoring it," he told Faith McLellan of the *Lancet*.

Despite his jet–setting, jet–lagged lifestyle, Sachs could not be happier. As he told Amy Barrett of the *New York Times Magazine:* "To have advised the pope, to be engaged with Kofi Annan—I think our world's greatest political leader—it's a joy beyond anything I could have hoped for."

Selected writings

Theoretical Issues in International Borrowing, Princeton University, 1984.

(With Michael Bruno) *Economics of Worldwide Stag-flation,* Harvard University Press, 1985.

(With Warwick McKibbin) *Global Linkages: Macroeconomic Interdependence and Cooperation in the World Economy,* The Brookings Institution, 1991.

(With Carlos Paredes) *Peru's Path to Recovery,* The Brookings Institution, 1991.

(With Felipe Larrain) *Macroeconomics in the Global Economy,* Prentice Hall, 1993.

Poland's Jump to the Market Economy, MIT Press, 1994.

(With Xiaokai Yang) *Development Economies,* Blackwell Publishers, 2003.

Sources

Periodicals

Esquire, December 2003, p. 196.
Fast Company, January 2004, p. 36.
Lancet, August 23, 2003, p. 672.
Omni, June 1991, p. 76.
New York Times Magazine, December 15, 2002, p. 45.
South China Morning Post, April 15, 2004, p. 14.

Online

"Jeffrey Sachs," Leigh Bureau, http://www.leighbureau.com/lbw/speaker_full.asp?soeajer_id=152 (May 18, 2004).

"Prof. Jeffrey D. Sachs," The Earth Institute at Columbia University, http://www.earth.columbia.edu/about/director/fullbio.html (April 20, 2004).

—Lisa Frick

Gonzalo Sanchez de Lozada

Former President of Bolivia

Born July 1, 1930, in La Paz, Bolivia; son of Enrique (a diplomat); married Ximena Iturralde Monje (a former Miss Bolivia); children: one son, one daughter. *Education:* University of Chicago, bachelor's degree, 1951. *Politics:* Nationalist Revolutionary Movement.

Addresses: *Home*—United States.

Career

Began as entrepreneur; founder and manager of Telecine Ltda., 1953–57; founder and general manager of Andean Geo–Services Ltd., 1957–62; founder and president of Compania Minera del Sur (Comsur), 1962–79; president of Comsur, 1980–82; member of parliament, 1979–80, 1982–85; senator, 1985–86; Minister for Planning and Coordination, 1986–88; party chief of the Nationalist Revolutionary Movement, 1988; President of Bolivia, 1993–97; 2002–03.

Sidelights

When Gonzalo Sanchez de Lozada became president of Bolivia in August of 2002, a social and economic crisis was brewing. With a stagnant economy, the nation of eight million had become South America's poorest country and the impoverished Indian peasants remained unconvinced that their government could help. Supporters hoped Sanchez de Lozada could work a miracle—after all, he had been president before, from 1993–97, during which time Bolivia enjoyed

moderate economic growth due to his liberal reforms. This time, however, Sanchez de Lozada's ideas were met with opposition and protestors took to the streets, demanding his resignation. The president called on his army to restore order. Bloody confrontations ensued and an estimated 70 people died. In the end, Sanchez de Lozada resigned and fled the country after only one year in office.

Gonzalo "Goni" Sanchez de Lozada was born on July 1, 1930, in La Paz, Bolivia. When he was one, his family moved to the United States when his diplomat father, Enrique, was assigned to the Bolivian embassy in Washington, D.C. Soon, the Bolivian government changed hands and the family was exiled. Enrique turned to teaching, holding positions at Harvard University and Williams College. As a result, Sanchez de Lozada spent his childhood in Washington, Boston, and Williamstown, Massachusetts. English became his first language, but his mother insisted he learn Spanish, his native tongue.

After earning a philosophy degree from the University of Chicago in 1951, Sanchez de Lozada returned to his homeland and tried several business ventures. In 1953, he founded Telecine Ltda., a documentary and commercial film production company. In 1957, he launched Andean Geo–Services Ltd., a company that took aerial photos for oil exploration companies. He found his niche in 1962 when he founded Compania Minera del Sur (Comsur), which means "Mining Company of the South." He made a fortune through Comsur, which mined zinc, tin, gold, silver, and lead. Along the way, he married a former Miss Bolivia, Ximena Iturralde Monje. They had two children.

Sanchez de Lozada's mining interests made him wealthy and influential. He turned to politics, serving in parliament from 1979–80 and 1982–85. From 1985–86, he served in the Senate and from 1986–88 was Minister for Planning and Coordination. In this capacity he gained attention for his economic reforms that halted hyperinflation.

In 1988, Sanchez de Lozada became the leader of the Nationalist Revolutionary Movement party and was elected president of Bolivia in 1993. The country was a mess. Unemployment hovered around 30 percent and 70 percent of Bolivians lived in poverty. To ease the situation, Sanchez de Lozada turned to foreign investors, hoping an influx of their money would kick–start the economy, thus creating jobs and reducing poverty.

One of his most controversial reforms involved privatizing state companies, such as YPFB, the country's gas and oil company. State companies were sold to the highest bidder, who gained management control as well as half the shares. The remaining shares were to be divided among Bolivia's adult population and held in retirement accounts. Other reforms included a new federal funding formula that sent more money to poor municipalities and Indian villages for things like schools and roads and water and electric projects. At the time, Sanchez de Lozada bragged about the reforms to *New York Times* writer Calvin Sims: "It's very exciting because we are seeing democracy working the way it should: the people are spending their money the way they want to spend it."

His term ended in 1997, but in 2002, Sanchez de Lozada became president once more. Again, the nation was in crisis, bogged by a stagnant economy. Social unrest was growing. Partway through his first year in office, Sanchez de Lozada created an uproar with his plan to let foreign investors build a $5 billion pipeline through Chile to export Bolivia's natural gas to the United States and Mexico. Some worried the plan involved corruption; others worried the revenues Bolivia was to get—estimated at $1.5 billion per year—were inadequate and that in the end, the project would benefit wealthy foreigners more than the poor peasants at home. According to the Montreal, Quebec, *Gazette*'s Larry Rohter, Bolivian Luis Alberto Javier summed up the situation this way: "We've always exported our natural resources, like silver and tin, to others, so that they get rich and we remain poor."

Bolivians also resented that Chile was involved in the proposal. The neighbors have a history of conflict, resulting from an 1879 war in which Bolivia became landlocked after losing its coastline to Chile. Sanchez de Lozada was lambasted for being too chummy with his country's long–standing rival. Bolivians were also distraught about Sanchez de Lozada's commitment to an aggressive, United States–backed coca eradication program. Coca, the raw material used for cocaine, has been a staple among Bolivia's indigenous culture for decades. It is grown legally for tea and chewing. In recent years, the eradication program had forced the closure of many coca plantations, leaving farmers even poorer.

In September of 2003, the nation's poor Indian peasants began protesting the president's policies. In time, student groups, labor unions, and opposition political parties joined the fray. Demonstrators assembled on the streets of the capital, and soldiers encircled the palace to protect the president. Soon, the demonstrations spread to other cities. Armed with dynamite, protesters blocked roads and blew up bridges, practically bringing the transportation system to a halt. In some regions, food, fuel, and hospital supplies were in short supply. Looting and fires destroyed businesses. Hoping to restore order, Sanchez de Lozada called on his army but bloody confrontations ensued and an estimated 70 people died. According to CNN, radio broadcasters took to the air, demanding the soldiers to back down. "Do not shoot," the announcers urged. "Let's stop the killing among Bolivians."

Sanchez de Lozada withdrew plans for the controversial pipeline, but it was too late. The demonstrations continued. One street protester told the *Houston Chronicle*'s John Otis that the bloodshed "was the straw that broke the camel's back. More than anything, we wanted him to leave because of the killings."

On October 17, 2003, Sanchez de Lozada stepped down from office. After his resignation, he fled to the United States. His vice president, Carlos Mesa, took over. For Sanchez de Lozada, the mess was far from over. Many Bolivians want Sanchez de Lozada brought to trial for the deaths that occurred during the uprising.

Sources

Periodicals

Economist, September 30, 1995, p. 47; October 18, 2003; January 24, 2004.

Gazette (Montreal, Quebec), August 5, 2002, p. A12; October 14, 2003, p. A18.

Houston Chronicle, October 18, 2003, p. A1.

Newsweek International, October 27, 2003, p. 37.

New York Times, March 24, 1989, p. A4; June 10, 1992, p. D16; July 16, 1995, p. 10.

Online

"Bolivian Leader Refuses to Resign," CNN.com, http://www.cnn.com/2003/WORLD/americas/10/13/bolivia.protests.ap/index.html (October 14, 2003).

—Lisa Frick

Joel Schumacher

Film director and screenwriter

Born August 29, 1939, in New York, NY; son of Francis and Marian (Kantor) Schumacher. *Education:* Attended Parsons School of Design, New York, NY; attended Fashion Institute of Technology, New York, NY.

Addresses: *Office*—Joel Schumacher Productions, 4000 Warner Blvd., Ste. 139, Rm. 26, Burbank, CA 91522.

Career

Director of films, including: *The Incredible Shrinking Woman*, 1981; *D.C. Cab*, 1983; *St. Elmo's Fire*, 1985; *The Lost Boys*, 1987; *Cousins*, 1989; *Flatliners*, 1990; *Dying Young*, 1991; *Falling Down*, 1993; *The Client*, 1994; *Batman Forever*, 1995; *A Time to Kill*, 1996; *Batman & Robin*, 1997; *8 mm*, 1999; *Flawless*, 1999; *Mauvaises Frequentations*, 1999; *Tigerland*, 2000; *Bad Company*, 2002; *Phone Booth*, 2003; *Veronica Guerin*, 2003; *Phantom of the Opera*, 2004. Director of television movies, including: *The Virginia Hill Story*, 1974; *Amateur Night at the Dixie Bar and Grill*, 1979.

Awards: National Association of Theater Owners (NATO) ShoWest Director of the Year Award, 1997; NATO ShoEast Award for Excellence in Filmmaking, 1999.

Sidelights

After more than three decades in the film industry, Joel Schumacher has earned a reputation as one of the most respected and well-liked main-stream filmmakers around. Schumacher's films are glossy; he delights moviegoers with his staggering sense of style. Movie companies love Schumacher as well because he completes his films on time and on budget. Over the years, the costume designer–turned–director has generated a long list of credits to his name, including the 1985 hit *St. Elmo's Fire*, which helped launch the careers of the "brat pack" kids, including Rob Lowe, Demi Moore, Andrew McCarthy, Judd Nelson, Ally Sheedy, and Emilio Estevez. His biggest blockbuster was 1995's *Batman Forever*, starring Val Kilmer in the feature role and Jim Carrey as his nemesis, The Riddler. That movie grossed $184 million at the box office. For Schumacher, it is a dream come true. "I'm very lucky to be here," he told Jim Schembri of the *Age*. "I have a career beyond my wildest dreams. I've wanted to make movies since I was seven. I have my health, I conquered drugs and alcohol.... I've survived an awful lot."

Schumacher was born on August 29, 1939, in New York, New York, and grew up an only child in the working–class neighborhood of Long Island City in Queens, New York. Speaking to the *New York Times*'s Bernard Weinraub, Schumacher referred to himself as an "American mongrel." Said Schumacher: "My mother was a Jew from Sweden; my father was a Baptist from Knoxville, Tennessee."

When Schumacher was four, his father died. To make ends meet, his mother went to work selling dresses. She worked six days a week and also some nights. "She was a wonderful woman, but, in a sense, I lost my mother when I lost my father," Schumacher told *Newsweek*'s Mark Miller. By the time he was eight, the unsupervised Schumacher was on the street taking care of and entertaining himself. He found comfort reading Batman comics and spent long afternoons in darkened movie theaters watching Audrey Hepburn and Cary Grant on the big screen. "Those were my two biggest obsessions before I discovered alcohol, cigarettes, and sex," Schumacher told Miller. "Then my obsessions changed a little bit. I started drinking when I was nine. I started sex when I was eleven. I started drugs in my early teens. And I left home the summer I turned 16. I went right into the beautiful-people fast lane in New York at the speed of sound. I've made every mistake in the book."

As a child, Schumacher also dabbled in entertainment. He built his own puppet theater and performed at parties. To help his mother make money, he also delivered meat for a local butcher. Walking the streets, Schumacher became interested in window displays and volunteered to dress the store windows in his neighborhood.

After he left home at 16, Schumacher lied about his age and landed a job at Macy's selling gloves in the menswear department. From there, he became a window dresser for Macy's, as well as Lord & Taylor and Saks. Later, Schumacher worked as a window dresser at Henri Bendel's and earned a scholarship to the Parsons School of Design in New York City. He also attended that city's Fashion Institute of Technology. Next, he worked as a fashion designer and helped manage a trendy boutique called Paraphernalia, long associated with Andy Warhol and Edie Sedgwick. In time, Schumacher found work with Revlon, designing packaging.

With a keen eye for style, Schumacher became a big star in the fashion world, but sunk lower into drugs. He favored speed, acid, and heroin. Schumacher refered to this period of his life—the 1960s—as his "vampire" years, according to *Newsweek*'s Miller. He stayed inside all day, covering his windows with blankets. He only went out at night. One day in 1970, something snapped, and Schumacher quit the hard-core drugs. "I guess it was the survivor in me," he told Weinraub in the *New York Times*. "I just knew I had to stop." He did, however, continue drinking, a problem that plagued him for two more decades.

In 1971, Schumacher relocated to Los Angeles, California, and got his foot in the film industry door when he landed a trial job as a costume designer

for *Play It As It Lays*, which was released in 1972. From there, he picked up jobs as a costume designer for movies like Woody Allen's *Sleeper* and *Blume in Love*, both released in 1973. Through these movies, Schumacher made contacts and landed his first directing job for the 1974 NBC–TV drama *The Virginia Hill Story*. He also began writing screenplays, including 1976's *Car Wash*, and the 1978 musical, *The Wiz*. Finally, in 1981, he got his first shot at filmmaking, directing Lily Tomlin in *The Incredible Shrinking Woman*. Reviewers frequently commented on the atypical color scheme he chose for this film.

One of Schumacher's early successes was a 1983 film about a metropolitan cab company run by a group of misfits. Called *D.C. Cab*, the film featured Mr. T. Other early hits included 1985's *St. Elmo's Fire*, and 1987's *The Lost Boys*. The latter film, a vampire flick, helped launch the careers of Corey Haim, Corey Feldman, and Kiefer Sutherland; it was a hit with the teen audience. He followed up with the 1990 thriller *Flatliners*, and the psychological drama *Falling Down*, starring Michael Douglas, in 1993.

By the early 1990s, Schumacher was coming into his own. Legendary author John Grisham asked Schumacher to adapt his best-selling legal thriller, *The Client*, for the big screen. Schumacher cast Tommy Lee Jones and Susan Sarandon in lead roles in the film that told the story of a street-savvy kid in danger because he had information about a mob killing. The movie, released in 1994, was well-received and Sarandon received an Oscar nomination for best actress.

Next, Schumacher earned directorial rights to *Batman Forever*, released in 1995. The first two installments of the series were directed by Tim Burton, but were thought to be too dark and serious. Schumacher was charged with brightening the series. Val Kilmer replaced Michael Keaton as Batman, and Jim Carrey joined the cast as The Riddler. Under Schumacher's direction, the movie became the blockbuster of the summer, raking in $184 million. *Batman & Robin* followed in 1997 but was terribly unsuccessful, putting an end to the Batman series.

Over the years, Schumacher has become known for his perceptive ability to cast unknown actors and turn them into hotshots. His films have given rise to the careers of the "brat packers," as well as Matthew McConaughey, cast in Schumacher's 1996 adaptation of another Grisham novel, *A Time to Kill*. Schumacher also "discovered" Irish actor Colin Farrell, giving him the lead in the 2000 Vietnam drama *Tigerland*, which proved to be Farrell's breakthrough performance. Schumacher later cast Farrell in his 2003 suspense thriller *Phone Booth,* which was shot in an amazing 12 days.

Another actor who gained prominence under Schumacher is comedian Chris Rock, who starred in 2002's *Bad Company.* Like many actors, Rock enjoyed working with Schumacher and was amazed by Schumacher's ability to handle the whole operation of movie–making. As Rock told *Film Journal International*'s Harry Haun: "Joel is like a general, like Patton or something. He really knows how to whip up the troops. Doing a big movie is a lot of directing. It's coordinating a whole town. It's like being a mayor, and he's totally up to the task—of being a general and making it artistic."

What makes Schumacher stand apart from other directors is his eye for style. Characters in his films appear polished and classy, yet sexy. According to Haun, a *Movieline* article by Michael Fleming once proclaimed, "Why Don't People Look in Other Movies Like They Look in Joel Schumacher Movies?" For that, Schumacher credits his childhood spent in movie theaters where he inhaled a steady diet of films with stars like Elizabeth Taylor, Paul Newman, Cary Grant, and Marilyn Monroe. As Schumacher explained to Haun, "You went to the movies and saw—Grace Kelly—these staggering images on the screen, so I think my early film influences are these archetypes—Audrey Hepburn, Gary Cooper. It's very much how I see film."

With about 20 films under his belt, Schumacher has had nearly every kind of review possible but says, for the most part, that he ignores them. Speaking with *Film Journal International*'s David Noh, Schumacher said he does not read reviews. "Woody Allen taught me a long time ago, 'Don't read them. If you believe the good, you'll believe the bad.' When they think you're a genius it's an exaggeration also, so somewhere between genius and scum is the reality of life."

After his foray into the blockbuster, high–budget world of the Batman series, Schumacher pulled back from big–name titles and returned to making grittier, chancier films. In 2003, he branched out into true crime, directing the film *Veronica Guerin,* which starred Cate Blanchett as the Irish journalist of the title. Guerin was killed by a heroin kingpin in 1996, who was angered by her investigative reporting. Schumacher made the movie in Ireland on a budget of $14 million—whereas $70 million is the average cost for a studio film. Once again, Schumacher was like a general. He kept everyone focused, shooting at 93 locations in 50 days.

The film won praise for its straightforward approach to the topic. Schumacher refused to glorify Guerin post–mortem, a trap many directors fall into. Speaking to the *Age*'s Schembri, Schumacher spoke about true stories this way: "You want to be sure that you're approaching the subject matter with integrity and not just trying to glorify the person, but trying to be honest with the facts, even if it upsets some people." Schumacher has also tried his hand at producing a musical. His film version of Andrew Lloyd Webber's musical masterpiece *The Phantom of the Opera,* was set for release in 2004.

Schumacher is also openly gay but refuses to get into discussions about how his sexuality affects him in the movie business. "It never was an issue," he told *Film Journal International*'s Noh, noting he does not believe in labels. "I think we're all villains and victims, as long as we live in a culture which keeps defining people as African–American lesbian judge, gay congressman, Jewish vice–presidential candidate, etc. You would never say that Bill Clinton was a Caucasian heterosexual WASP president, you just say he's Bill Clinton. That means the only norm is white WASP male, because everyone else must be defined. I'm totally against that."

Despite his success, Schumacher has no plans to rest on his laurels. Though he is considered a veteran filmmaker by many, Schumacher still sees himself as a student. As he told the *Guardian*'s Peter Curran: "I hope I haven't made my best one yet, I'm still trying to learn on the job. So I keep stretching and hopefully I keep making better and better films. I hope the good ones aren't behind me."

Selected screenplays

Car Wash, 1976.
Sparkle, 1976.
The Wiz, 1978.
D.C. Cab, 1983.
St. Elmo's Fire, 1985.

Sources

Periodicals

Age (Melbourne, Australia), January 16, 2004, p. 3.
Film Journal International, June 2002, p. 12; October 2003, p. 14.
New York Times, March 3, 1993, p. C13.
Newsweek, June 30, 1997, p. 76.

Online

"Cate Blanchett and Joel Schumacher," *Guardian Unlimited,* http://film.guardian.co.uk/interview/interviewpages/0,6737,998670,00.html (February 17, 2004).

"Celebs: Joel Schumacher," MSN Entertainment, http://entertainment.msn.com/celebs/celeb.aspx?c=146139&mp=f (February 23, 2004).

—*Lisa Frick*

Ryan Seacrest

Radio and television host

Born December 24, 1976, in Atlanta, GA; son of Gary (an attorney) and Connie (a homemaker) Seacrest. *Education:* Attended University of Georgia and Santa Monica College.

Addresses: *Home*—Hollywood Hills, CA. *Office*—c/o *American Idol,* P.O. Box 900, Beverly Hills, CA 90213–0900.

Career

Worked as a radio disc jockey, including: WSTR/Star 94, Atlanta, GA, c. 1992–95; KYSR–FM/Star 98.7, *Ryan Seacrest for the Ride Home,* Los Angeles, CA, 1995–2004; *Live from the Lounge,* syndicated, 2001—; KIIS–FM, Los Angeles, CA, *On–Air with Ryan Seacrest,* 2003—; *American Top 40,* syndicated, 2004—. Television appearances include: *Gladiators 2000* (host), 1994; *Extra* (part time correspondent), 1994; *Radical Outdoor Challenge* (host), ESPN, 1995; *Wild Animal Games* (host), Family Channel, 1995; *Reality Check,* 1995; *The New Edge* (host), USA and Sci–Fi, 1996; *The Click* (host), 1997; *Talk Soup* (guest host), E! Entertainment Television, 1999; *Hey Arnold!* (voice), 1999; *Melrose Place,* FOX, 1999; *Beverly Hills, 90210,* FOX, 2000; NBC Saturday Night Movie block (host), 2000; *Ultimate Revenge* (host), 2001; *American Idol* (host), FOX, 2002—; *The Tonight Show with Jay Leno* (correspondent), NBC, 2003; *American Juniors* (host), 2003; *Larry King Live* (guest host), CNN, 2003; presenter at Emmy Awards, 2003; host of New Year's Eve show, FOX, 2003; host of American Radio Music Awards, 2003; host of Radio Music Awards, 2003; *On–Air with Ryan Seacrest* (host and executive producer), syndicated, 2003-04. Also appeared in commercials for AT&T Wireless; principal, Ryan Seacrest Productions.

Sidelights

Though Ryan Seacrest came to national prominence as the host of *American Idol* in 2002, he already had established a solid reputation as a successful radio host and disk jockey (DJ) for stations in Atlanta, Georgia, and Los Angeles, California. He continued to work in both broadcasting formats for a number of years. Contradicting the common notion of a "face for radio," he was also known for his good looks and metrosexual grooming habits. The charming, easy–going Seacrest also hosted several other television shows before and after *American Idol,* including *On–Air with Ryan Seacrest,* which he also produced and owned part of.

Seacrest was born on December 24, 1976, in Atlanta, Georgia, the son of Gary and Connie Seacrest. His father worked as an attorney, while his mother was a homemaker. Seacrest and his younger sister, Meredith, were raised in the Atlanta area. From a young age, Seacrest was interested in acting and the entertainment industry. His interest was first peaked when he played King Winter in his fourth grade school musical. As a young person, Seacrest already had a goal of hosting a radio show that counted down the top records of the day.

By the time Seacrest was a student at Dunwoody High School in Atlanta, he knew he was wanted to work in radio as a disk jockey and follow in the steps of media mogul Dick Clark. At school, he read the morning announcements over the intercom and became known as "The Voice of Dunwoody High School." He also participated in many radio call–in contests. Seacrest befriended DJ Tom Sullivan and was able to move to the other side of the broadcast by working as an intern at WSTR/Star 94 while still in high school.

While he was working at WSTR, Seacrest spent a lot of time at the station and become familiar with every aspect of radio broadcasting. He made a demo tape and convinced his superiors at WSTR to hire him as a fill–in DJ for the 7 p.m. to midnight shift. Seacrest's show was soon one of the highest–rated on the station, though he was still a high school student. After graduating from Dunwoody in 1993, he continued to work for Star 94 while attending college.

Seacrest entered the University of Georgia, where he studied business. He soon added television to his resume. Though he was only a freshman in college, Seacrest was given the chance to work as a television show host. He worked on the kid–focused game show *Radical Outdoor Challenge,* which aired on EPSN in 1995. Seacrest worked on the show on weekends while attending school.

In 1995, Seacrest left both jobs and the University of Georgia behind to move to Los Angeles and try his luck in a bigger media market. He began as a part–time DJ, while continuing his business studies at Santa Monica College. Seacrest was soon hired as disc jockey as KYSR–FM/Star 98.7, and dropped out of Santa Monica College after one year. He became the afternoon drive DJ, and his show was called *Ryan Seacrest for the Ride Home.* It soon became the number–one–rated show in the market, doing the best among women aged 25–34.

While working on his successful radio show, Seacrest continued to branch out into television. In 1997, he hosted another game show for kids, *The Click,* which had an Internet theme. *The Click* was produced by Merv Griffin, who had created and produced a number of successful game shows over the years. Seacrest took advantage of the opportu-

nity to learn how television works by sitting in on production and related meetings. In 1999, Seacrest had guest appearances on a number of successful television programs, including *Talk Soup,* the E! Entertainment television show about talk shows, and the nighttime dramas *Melrose Place* and *Beverly Hills, 90210.*

Seacrest continued to have many exciting opportunities in television. He appeared on *The New Edge* on the USA network and Sci Fi, and *Wild Animal Games* on the Family Channel. He had a deal in the works for his own late–night talk show called *Seacrest @ Night,* but it was scrapped in 2000. Seacrest later admitted that a late night show would not have fit well with his talents. In 2000, he was hired as the host of a movie night block shown on NBC on Saturday nights.

While Seacrest was pursuing an ever–increasing number of opportunities in television, he continued his afternoon radio show on KYSR. In 2001, he added other hosting duties for another radio program. He was hired as the host of *Live from the Lounge,* a nationally syndicated show that appeared on Premiere Radio Networks. On the show, Seacrest interviewed celebrities.

The biggest break of Seacrest's career happened in 2002. He was hired as one of the hosts of FOX's *American Idol,* an amateur singing contest that led to a record deal for the winner. *American Idol* proved extremely popular among American television audiences, and Seacrest gained many fans, had websites dedicated to him, and enjoyed nation–wide fame. During the first season of the show, Seacrest shared hosting duties with Brian Dunkelman, a comic who was very negative; after the first season, Dunkelman was dropped and Seacrest worked subsequent seasons as the only host.

On *American Idol,* Seacrest worked with the show's judges: pop singer and choreographer Paula Abdul, musician and music producer Randy Jackson, and music producer Simon Cowell. The British Cowell was often biting in his commentary on the contestants' talents, and sometimes had conflicts with Seacrest. Despite such negativity, Seacrest emerged as a star. According to Donna Petrozzello of the *Daily News,* "The biggest winner to come out of *American Idol* isn't Kelly Clarkson. Or Ruben Studdard. Or even Clay Aiken. It's Ryan Seacrest. Since starting as host of *American Idol,* Seacrest has become an entertainment conglomerate in his own right."

While hosting *American Idol,* Seacrest brought many *American Idol*–related people to guest on his radio show. He also traveled around the United States to promote the show. A common topic of discussion about Seacrest was his appearance and the importance he placed on maintaining it. Seacrest had been a self–described "fat" kid with braces and glasses in high school, but dieted to lose weight. He admitted to enjoying clothes, shopping, eating right, and working out, and indulging in eyebrow waxes, massages, face creams, manicures, facials, and extensive hair care. In public, he made fun of himself for his sometimes–excessive grooming habits. He was named one of *People* magazine's "50 Most Beautiful People" in 2003.

More television opportunities came Seacrest's way as *American Idol* became a national phenomenon and made him a household name. In 2003, Seacrest served as host for the one–season–long *American Juniors.* This also aired on FOX and featured children competing in the same way adults did on *American Idol;* however, this program did not get the same high ratings as its predecessor and was not renewed. He was also the host of the Radio Music Awards in 2003, and was a fill–in host of *Larry King Live* on CNN that same year.

Seacrest's radio career also took off because of *American Idol.* In 2003, he was allowed to serve as the guest host of Rick Dees' top–rated, nationally syndicated morning radio show which originated in Los Angeles. Seacrest was given permission to do this despite the fact that Dees' show aired on a different station which competed with his station's morning show. By 2003, Seacrest left his afternoon radio show and Star 98.7 behind for a bigger television gig.

A long–time goal of Seacrest's was hosting his own television show, and the success of *American Idol* allowed him to do it. In 2003, with the help of FOX and his own production company—Ryan Seacrest Productions—Seacrest began hosting *On–Air with Ryan Seacrest.* This syndicated daytime talk/variety show which aired live in many markets. Seacrest had created the show and served as its executive producer.

Shot in Hollywood at a custom–built studio on the corner of Hollywood and Highland with a view of the famous Hollywood sign, *On–Air with Ryan Seacrest* was different than most daytime entertainment available. The show combined elements of other hit shows: It was seen as a modern–day *American Bandstand,* with elements of MTV's *Total Request Live,* late–night talk shows like those hosted by Craig Kilborn and Conan O'Brien, and infotainment news magazines like *Entertainment Tonight* and

Extra. The live studio audience experienced in–person interviews, performances on an outside stage, and in–house calls as well as pieces by correspondents. *On–Air with Ryan Seacrest* was supposed to air between 3 and 7 p.m. to catch a young audience that did not watch the news and had outgrown *Total Request Live.* Tag lined "We bring Hollywood to You," Seacrest's show struggled in its first year of existence. On July 27, 2004, it was announced that *On–Air with Ryan Seacrest* would end production. The show would broadcast through September 17 of that year. Seacrest also continued to host *American Idol* in its third season on FOX in 2004.

Seacrest did not neglect his radio career while working in television. Though he had left Star 98.7, in 2004 he became the host of *American Top 40,* a weekly nationally syndicated radio show which had been hosted for many years by Casey Kasem. It was one of the most popular nationally syndicated countdown shows, and Kasem had hosted it since its inception in 1970. When Seacrest took over, he changed the format to be more interactive between songs, with interviews and performances, and eliminated Kasem trademarks such as listener long–distance dedications. Seacrest recorded the program in a studio within his new television studio.

In early 2004, Seacrest added another regular job to his already busy schedule. When Dees left his morning show on KIIS–FM after many years, Seacrest was hired to replace the radio icon in the Los Angeles market. Seacrest's radio show was called *On–Air with Ryan Seacrest* like his television show, and was considered a big move up for him in radio.

Some critics believed that Seacrest was on the verge of being overexposed, if he was not already. In addition to the credits already mentioned, he appeared in commercials for AT&T Wireless, presented an award at the Emmys, and hosted both the American Radio Music Awards and the New Year's Eve show on FOX in 2003. Seacrest was even a correspondent on *The Tonight Show with Jay Leno* for one night. Seacrest dismissed such criticisms. He told Rodney Ho of the *Atlanta Journal–Constitution,* "You have to look at the broadcast world differently. In broadcast, it's conventional to be on five days a week…. I feel good about it. I'm achieving a degree of ubiquity."

Overexposure might not be a problem in his future. Seacrest's long–term goals included producing more television shows and perhaps letting someone else host them down the line. He told Hilary De Vries of the *New York Times,* "I've always had this plan of doing what Dick Clark did—producing and hosting radio and television and building a business from it." While talking to Nicholas Fonseca of *Entertainment Weekly,* Seacrest added, "I want to continue producing and conceiving and selling my own shows. I want to do this for the next 60 years."

Sources

Books

Celebrity Biographies, Baseline II, 2004.

Periodicals

Atlanta Journal–Constitution, January 12, 2004, p. 1B; March 15, 2004, p. 25.
Broadcasting & Cable, June 2, 2003, p. 21; January 5, 2004, p. 29.

Daily News (New York), January 19, 2004, p. 32.
Entertainment Weekly, January 9, 2004, pp. 46–48.
Los Angeles Times, January 19, 2004, p. E13; February 23, 2004, p. E3.
Mediaweek, November 29, 1999, p. 44; June 25, 2001, p. 27.
New York Times, January 11, 2004, sec. 2, p. 30; January 19, 2004, p. E10.
People, May 1, 2003, p. 26; May 12, 2003, p. 129; January 19, 2004, p. 69; February 16, 2004, p. 32.
Time, January 26, 2004, p. 62.
Variety, September 25, 2000, p. 48.

—*A. Petruso*

Barry Sears

Biochemist and author

Born in 1947, in Long Beach, CA; son of Dale (a floor–covering salesman) and Betty Sears; married Lynn Magnuson, 1969; children: Kristin, Kelly. *Education:* Occidental College, Los Angeles, CA, B.S.; Indiana University, Ph.D., 1969.

Addresses: *Agent*—c/o The Allen Agency, 23852 Pacific Coast Hwy., Ste. 401, Malibu, CA 90265. *Publisher*—c/o Regan Books, 10 E. 53rd St., New York, NY 10022.

Career

Did post–graduate work in biochemistry at University of Virginia; moved to Boston University School of Medicine to research structure of lipids; staff researcher at Massachusetts Institute of Technology; formed own company, Lipid Specialties, 1976; involved in various entrepreneurial ventures relating to diet and nutrition; published first book on Zone diet, 1995.

Sidelights

Dr. Barry Sears is the originator of the Zone diet, one of the most popular diets of the late 1990s and 2000s. Like another trendy diet, the Atkins plan, the Zone diet advocates that dieters restrict their intake of carbohydrates. Sears' first book on the Zone diet came out in 1995. The Zone approach was quickly championed by athletes and celebrities, and gained wide general acclaim. Sears authored nine more books in ensuing years, focusing on different aspects of the Zone diet, food science, and vitamin supplements.

Sears grew up in Long Beach, California, where he exhibited both an athletic and scientific bent. Sears's father, Dale, had been an All–American basketball player on the University of Southern California team in the 1930s, and was picked for the 1940 Olympic basketball team. Barry Sears played basketball and was an outstanding scholar as well. After graduating from Palisades High School at the age of 17, Sears went to Occidental College to major in chemistry. He played both basketball and volleyball in college, and even after he earned his Ph.D. in biochemistry from Indiana University in 1969, he continued to play volleyball at the national level. Sears's scientific work at first centered on finding the molecular structure of cholesterol and other related substances. The relationship between cholesterol and heart disease was just beginning to be understood in the early 1970s. Sears became keenly interested in understanding heart disease when his father died of a massive heart attack at the age of 53. Within several years, his father's three brothers all also died of heart attacks. This left Sears feeling that he, too, was doomed to an early death unless he could find some way to combat heart disease. Sears started working on approaches to heart disease as a researcher at Boston University's School of Medicine, and then at the Massachusetts Institute of Technology (MIT). He came upon a study published by two researchers at a San Francisco hospital that claimed that arteriosclerosis, or hardening of the arteries, had been cured in rabbits by the injection of naturally occurring fats called phospholipids. Seizing on this one study, Sears got family members to back him financially, and he started his own company in 1976, Lipid Specialties, Inc. The aim of Lipid Specialties was to come up with a phospholipid that could be created in the laboratory, and was thus patentable. A naturally occurring substance was not patentable, and so was not of interest to pharmaceutical companies. But Sears came up with several "new" phospholipids, and collaborated on animal studies of their effects with the drug manufacturer Upjohn.

In the preface to his first book, *The Zone: A Dietary Road Map,* Sears claimed that Upjohn lost interest in phospholipids because the substance would have to be injected into patients, instead of delivered in a pill. Sears had run out of his private funding, so he could not continue to study the effects of phospholipids on heart disease. He turned instead to a new venture, using phospholipid technology to deliver cancer–fighting drugs. Some drugs that were highly effective at shrinking tumors were nevertheless too toxic to help cancer patients unless they could be modified to go directly to the tumor sites. Sears' phospholipids could safely carry new cancer drugs in the bloodstream. He took out several patents for drug–delivery systems using phospholipids, and claimed in his book to hold "most of the major patents in the world for intravenous cancer–drug delivery."

But Sears' interest veered again with the awarding of the Nobel Prize for Physiology and Medicine in 1982. The prestigious award that year went to three researchers who had uncovered the functioning of a class of hormones known as eicosanoids. Eicosanoids control a variety of systems within the body, including the cardiovascular system, the immune system, and the body's system for regulating fat storage. The fatty acids Sears had been studying for years in his lipids work were also the building blocks of the eicosanoids. At this point Sears made a leap from biochemical research to nutritional science. He deduced that many diseases could be traced to an imbalance of eicosanoids. The best way to regulate eicosanoids, he theorized, was through food. In the early 1980s, Sears elaborated a theory of nutritional control of eicosanoids that evolved into the Zone diet.

The meaning of "Zone" was very broad, borrowing from several disciplines. Athletes referred to "the Zone" as a high–pitched state of physical exhilaration, when everything was going right. Sears

thought this athletic "natural high" might result from a perfect balance of eicosanoids. Getting the eicosanoids in the optimum proportions might lead to a long–term "Zone" of good health. There was also a therapeutic zone, borrowed from drug therapy. A drug might be toxic in too high a dose, yet ineffective in too low a dose. The perfect amount, falling between these quantifiable limits, was the therapeutic zone. The Zone diet was an attempt to get the body into a zone of fat–burning, artery–clearing good health by manipulating eicosanoids with food. Sears advocated thinking of food hormonally, not calorically. In other words, simply limiting calories was not enough to promote weight loss and good health. What he proposed with the Zone diet was to regulate how hormones were released in the body, specifically by limiting carbohydrates. The hormonal effect of carbohydrates, which are starchy foods like bread and pasta, is to cause the body to release insulin. Extra fat in the diet did not affect insulin, and could in fact lead to lowered cholesterol.

Sears was involved in various ventures to promote his new diet. In partnership with his brother, Doug, he began growing borage, a grain high in a particular fatty acid, in fields in Canada. He also began manufacturing nutrition bars. Meanwhile, he worked with athletes, including Stanford University's swim team, coaching them in a new way of looking at nutrition. A Zone breakfast for a competitive swimmer included lots of eggs and bacon, a small serving of fruit, and only a tiny portion of bread. Dinner might include steak, salmon, or a chicken breast, lots of vegetables, but no bread, noodles, or potatoes. Sears credited *Swimmer's World* as the first magazine to take his diet seriously. The Stanford swim team went on to win eight out of 12 national championships since aligning with Sears. The diet gained popularity in the early 1990s, spreading among athletes and becoming a trend in Hollywood.

When Sears published his first diet book (co–authored with Bill Lawren) in 1995, it was an instant best–seller. It spent 12 weeks on the *New York Times* best–seller list and went through 32 printings in its first year. It sold more than 400,000 copies in hardcover. Sears followed it up with a sequel, *Mastering the Zone*, in 1997, as well as a cookbook. When an audiotape version of *The Zone* went on sale on the cable television home–shopping network QVC, the network sold out of 15,000 copies in only 20 minutes. Celebrities who professed to follow the Zone diet included singers Madonna, Janet Jackson, and Dolly Parton, while movie star Arnold Schwarzenegger and film director Oliver Stone also became Sears acolytes. The Zone diet was both highly technical and easy to follow. Though the books gave elaborate explanations of eicosanoids and hormonal action, Sears also urged people to "eyeball" appropriate amounts of protein, estimating portion size by what would fit in the palm of their hand. The Zone mantra boiled down to 40–30–30, that is, a diet containing 40 percent carbohydrates, 30 percent fat, and 30 percent protein. This amounted to approximately twice the level of fat and protein advocated by federal dietary guidelines. And though Sears could cite few studies to back up his findings, and even his co–author disavowed much of Sears' work, it seemed to make little difference to followers of the diet. Sears was associated with various investors who made nutrition bars based on the Zone diet. These companies had substantial sales, giving some idea of the popularity of the Zone. The Balance bar, made by Bio–Foods Co., had estimated 1996 sales of $10 million. Another company making bars endorsed by Sears brought in an estimated $20 million that same year.

Sears went on to publish more books about the Zone diet, such as *Zone Food Blocks: The Quick & Easy, Mix & Match Counter for Staying in the Zone* in 1998. In 1999, he brought out *The Anti–Aging Zone*, which claimed to show readers how to use food to reverse the aging process. This was followed by *The Soy Zone, A Week in the Zone,* and *The Age–Free Zone,* all in 2000, and *The Top 100 Zone Foods: The Zone Food Science Ranking System* in 2001. In 2002 Dr. Sears published *The Omega Rx Zone: The Miracle of High–Dose Fish Oil.* This book used studies of Eskimo and Japanese diets, and concluded that certain oils found in fish could alter eicosanoid levels to decrease inflammation and increase blood flow. One caveat of this latest twist on the Zone diet was that people take supplements of pharmaceutical–grade fish oil, an expensive refined oil that was purported to be free of toxins like mercury that plague ocean fish. Phillip Whitten, who interviewed Sears about the fish oil diet for *Swim Magazine,* asked about Sears' financial ties to companies that produced pharmaceutical–grade oil. Sears admitted the connection, but seemed untroubled by it. He also seemed untroubled by the lack of research to substantiate his nutritional claims. Sears falls back on common sense as the real underpinning of his dietary system. Concluding his interview with *Swim*'s Whitten, Sears said, "The only difference between your grandmother's dietary wisdom and the Zone diet is that instead of taking cod liver oil, I recommend taking enough pharmaceutical–grade fish oil to change the balance of your eicosanoids."

Selected writings

The Zone: A Dietary Roadmap, Regan Books, 1995.
Mastering the Zone: The Next Step in Achieving Superhealth and Permanent Weight Loss, Regan Books, 1997.
Zone–Perfect Meals in Minutes, Regan Books, 1997.
Zone Food Blocks: The Quick & Easy, Mix & Match Counter for Staying in the Zone, Regan Books, 1998.
The Anti–Aging Zone, Regan Books, 1999.
A Week in the Zone, Regan Books, 2000.
The Age–Free Zone, Regan Books, 2000.
The Soy Zone, Regan Books, 2000.
The Top 100 Zone Foods: The Zone Food Science Ranking System, Regan Books, 2001.
The Omega Rx Zone: The Miracle of High–Dose Fish Oil, Regan Books, 2002.

Sources

Los Angeles, February 1997, pp. 34–37.
Men's Health, April 1996, p. 52.
Newsweek, March 6, 2000, p. 50.
People, June 17, 1996, p. 171.
Swim, May/June 1997, p. 26; July/August 2002, p. 30.

—A. Woodward

Ivan Seidenberg

Chief Executive Officer of Verizon

Born December 10, 1946, in New York, NY; married Phyllis Maisel, 1969; children: two. *Education:* City University of New York, B.A. (mathematics), 1972; Pace University, M.B.A., 1980.

Addresses: *Home*—New York, NY. *Office*—Verizon Communications, 1095 Avenue of the Americas, New York, NY 10036.

Career

Began at New York Bell as a cable splicer's helper, mid–1960s; served in the U.S. Army in Vietnam; rose through company ranks to serve as assistant vice president for marketing, 1981, vice president for federal relations, 1983, and vice president for external affairs; named president and CEO of Nynex, the successor to New York Bell, January, 1995, and chair, April, 1995; became chief executive officer of Bell Atlantic, the successor to Nynex, 1998, and co–chief executive officer of Verizon Communications, formed by the merger of Bell Atlantic with GTE Corporation, June 2000; became sole CEO, 2002.

Sidelights

Ivan Seidenberg runs Verizon Communications, the largest telephone company in the United States. Seidenberg has been with the company since its earlier incarnation as New York Bell, and rose through the ranks during a period of tremendous growth and new opportunities in the industry. He was considered instrumental in winning government regulatory approval for the series of historic

mergers that created Verizon in 2000. With some $67 billion in revenues, the publicly traded telecom giant is one of *Fortune* magazine's Top 10 companies, but has suffered along with its peers since 2001 in a flagging United States economy and moribund stock market. "The challenge facing Seidenberg," remarked *BusinessWeek*'s Steve Rosenbush, "is to survive the telecom industry's worst downturn without dismembering his creation."

Seidenberg was born in 1946 and grew up in the New York City borough of the Bronx. He began at New York Bell—which was at that time the local telephone company for New York City—in the mid–1960s as a splicer's helper, during the era when direct lines ran from customers' homes to local switching stations to main headquarters. He recalled his first day on the job as a tough one. "I didn't know anything," he told *Telephony* writer Glenn Bischoff, and just as the shift was slated to end that day, his crew was sent back out to fix a cable failure, and had to work long into the night to repair it. Despite the somewhat poor reputation New York Bell and other local phone companies had during this era, Seidenberg was impressed by the dedication of his co–workers. "It was amazing to witness the mentality of these people—and it has never changed in my 37 years with the company," he told Bischoff.

Seidenberg served two years in Vietnam before returning to New York Bell and taking college courses in the evenings. In 1972 he earned a degree in mathematics from City University of New York, and went on to earn an M.B.A. from Pace University eight years later. In all, Seidenberg spent 16 years attending college part–time, but his career at New York Bell advanced somewhat more rapidly. By 1981, he had been named assistant vice president for marketing, and two years later he was made vice president for federal relations. It was an important job at the company during a significant period: New York Bell was one of the 22 local phone companies that had been part of AT&T (American Telephone and Telegraph), the entity formed in 1875 with the invention of the telephone by Alexander Graham Bell. Known as the Bell System or "Ma Bell," it was the largest private business in the world until 1984, when a decade–long suit instigated by the U.S. Department of Justice ordered the smaller Bell companies to form seven regional holding companies, known as the "Baby Bells." New York Telephone merged with New England Telephone to become Nynex.

Seidenberg went on to serve as vice president for external affairs before being named president and CEO of Nynex in early 1995. With Nynex valued at $13.3 billion, the promotion made him head of the most successful of the Baby Bells, but after a 1996 Telecommunications Act allowed for further changes in the industry, Nynex merged the following year with Bell Atlantic, its Philadelphia–based counterpart that provided service to several mid–Atlantic states. Though the Nynex name had now given way to Bell Atlantic, Seidenberg remained chief executive officer, and continued to steer the company toward a more prosperous future. In a 1996 *Management Review* interview with Jenny C. McCune, Seidenberg hinted at the possibility of his company entering the lucrative wireless and long–distance markets—the latter dominated by names like Sprint and MCI at the time—and was an ardent supporter of less government regulation of the industry. He used an analogy with roots in another large American business sector: "Years ago, people asked, 'What happens when everybody in America has a car?' Well, April Fool," he pointed out to McCune. "Now they have two cars. In some cases, they may have three, whatever. Now we're finding people with not one, but two or three phones, fax lines. So, the intensity of changes is enormous."

Seidenberg was instrumental in another momentous telecom deal: a merger between Bell Atlantic and GTE, a leader in wireless communications and Internet networks, that was completed in 2000. The new entity was renamed Verizon Communications, and became the largest telecommunications company in the United States. *Tele.com* called Seidenberg "a chief architect in the restructuring of the telecom market" that year. Though there were some initial snags in attaining seamless service nationwide, Verizon proved an immediate success story, "the first of the old regional Bells that can legitimately claim to be a national company," noted *Fortune*'s Stephanie Mehta.

For a time, Seidenberg served as co–CEO with Charles Lee of GTE, but took over the reins completely when Lee retired in April of 2002. Seidenberg was still keenly interested in expanding into all telecommunication sectors—from local phone service and high–speed Internet access to wireless data and entertainment. Moving into new territories was almost a necessity, for traditional "landline" users were in steep decline as the twenty–first century dawned. Verizon also suffered from a general downturn in the telecommunications market in general, as the mergers of the past half–decade—combined with an overall slide in corporate stock values on Wall Street—caused debt to escalate sharply. Seidenberg's company was struggling to manage some $54 billion of its own liabilities at the close of 2002.

In early 2003, Verizon announced an ambitious plan to re–engineer its entire network, trading the old copper wire still in use for a state–of–the–art, fiber–optics network. The move would again allow Verizon to keep old customers and add a potentially large number of new ones, for the new system could deliver not just phone service but digital television, high–speed Internet access, and perhaps even affordable video calls into consumer homes. Despite the immense nature of the company, with some 236,000 employees in 14 countries, Seidenberg is known for his accessibility and polite management style. He answers staff e–mails personally, and often holds brainstorming sessions every few months with employees. Active in several charitable organizations in the New York and New Jersey area that focus on education, he lives in New York City and has two children with his wife, Phyllis. Well aware of the demands of his job, he once described his duties, according to Mehta in the *Fortune* article, as the "Chief Person in Charge of Bad News."

Sources

BusinessWeek, January 14, 2002, p. 63; October 21, 2002, p. 72; March 31, 2003, pp. 68–70.
Communications Today, September 26, 2000.

Forbes, April 16, 2001, p. 68.
Fortune, April 16, 2001, p. 162.
Independent (London, England), December 20, 2000, p. 3.
Management Review, January 1996, p. 10.

Tele.com, February 7, 2000, p. 61.
Telephony, November 18, 2002.

—*Carol Brennan*

Ron Shaich

Chief Executive Officer of Panera Bread

Born Ronald Mark Shaich, December 30, 1953, in Boston, MA; son of Joseph (a certified public accountant) and Pearl R. Shaich; married Nancy Antonacci (an education specialist), May 10, 1998; children: two. *Education:* Clark University, B.A., 1976; Harvard University, M.B.A., 1978.

Addresses: *Office*—Panera Bread Co., 6710 Clayton Rd., Richmond Heights, MO 63117.

Career

Worked as assistant to the president at Store 24 Inc., and assistant to the vice president of marketing at CVS Stores, late 1970s; served as Eastern regional manager for Original Cookie Company, Boston, MA, 1978–81; launched Cookie Jar bakery in Boston, c. 1980; Au Bon Pain Company, co–founder, 1981, co–chair until 1994, chief executive officer, 1994–99; purchased St. Louis Bread Co., 1993; renamed company Panera Bread, 1999; chair and chief executive officer, Panera Bread, 1999—.

Sidelights

Ron Shaich heads Panera Bread Company, the immensely successful chain of bakery–cafes emerging as a dominant new food purveyor on the suburban American landscape. With its artisan breads baked on site and an array of soups, salads, and sandwiches, Panera is poised to become the trend–setting leader in the growing "quick–casual" segment of the restaurant industry. "We were all eating Wonder Bread and then these artisan bread bakers came along," Shaich told *Chain Leader* journalist Margaret Littman about the success of his company. "We began to understand this drive for specialness that consumers had for specialty foodservice."

Shaich has spent much of his career in the food business. Born in December of 1953, he is the son of a certified public accountant, and earned an undergraduate degree in government and psychology from Clark University in Worcester, Massachusetts, in 1976. He began his first business on Clark's campus, running a successful convenience store for students. After earning a graduate business degree from Harvard University in 1978, he worked as an assistant to the president of Store 24, Inc. and then as an assistant to the vice president of marketing at CVS Stores.

Shaich eventually landed a job as the Eastern regional manager for the Original Cookie Company, and also opened his own Cookie Jar bakery shops in the Boston area. But as he told *Harvard Business School Bulletin* writer Susan Young about his own venture, "every morning I watched thousands of people walk by; no one bought cookies before noon. So I added fresh croissants and baguettes, two items that were not in the mainstream back then." The breads came from another Boston outfit called Au Bon Pain, a company that was started in 1976 by a French oven manufacturer whose name roughly translated as "where the good bread is." There were three Au Bon Pains in the city, but business was flagging and the investor group that owned it was ready to sell. Shaich teamed with one of the investors, a commercial real–estate veteran named Louis I. Kane, and revamped the Au Bon Pain concept, using what he learned from watching his baguette customers. "You didn't need a Harvard degree to see the opportunity," Shaich recalled in an interview with *Wall Street Journal* writer Carol Hymowitz. "Customers were coming into the store to buy a baguette and asking me to cut it from top to bottom. Then they'd take luncheon meat they'd just bought from the grocery store next door and make a sandwich."

Au Bon Pain grew quickly during the 1980s, thanks to a business plan that squeezed its outlets into busy urban locales serving the office–lunch crowd. Impressive sales–per–square–foot revenues were the result, and an initial public offering in 1991 provided an influx of cash for further expansion. By 1993, the company had grown to 250 stores, but soon began losing ground to new competitors. That same year, Shaich, who was responsible for Au Bon Pain's strategic planning and operations, made an acquisition that would herald a future direction for both himself and the food–service industry in general: Au Bon Pain bought the 19–store St. Louis Bread Company, which baked its own breads on–site and sold sandwiches made from them. Shaich told his fellow Au Bon Pain executives that they needed to unload the struggling Au Bon Pain division and concentrate on the St. Louis Bread concept, but his fellow board members balked. "I came very close to losing my job," he told Hymowitz in the *Wall Street Journal*. "The board said 'the stock is flat and maybe you are washed up.'"

In the end, Shaich convinced the others his vision had potential, and Au Bon Pain was sold to a private–equity group in 1999 for $73 million. Within weeks, St. Louis Bread—later renamed Panera Bread—was launched with several new stores that sold specialty sandwiches on an array of fresh–baked breads like ciabatta and tomato–basil. Restaurant–industry watchers and the Wall Street firms that analyze the food–service market were initially wary, believing it was merely the old Au Bon Pain with a new name. Shaich was adamant, however, that Panera's more inviting ambiance and emphasis on artisan breads like focaccia and sourdough was a new entry into the quick–casual dining sector. He also claimed he learned from his Au Bon Pain mistakes, especially the need to stay on top of food trends.

Unlike Au Bon Pain, Panera—which translates from the Spanish language as "bread basket"—settled into prime suburban locations, where business could be expected during much of the day, into the evening, and even more so on the weekends. Stores were either company–owned or franchised, and franchisees had to demonstrate a serious track record; many of those who signed on already operated successful McDonald's or Pizza Hut restaurants. The dough was delivered daily, and baked in–store. "It would be very easy to do frozen bread," Shaich told David Farkas in a *Chain Leader* article. "But we believe fresh dough is different in taste and in shelf life. As much as anything, the consumer is at the core of this decision—and they know the difference."

In its first five years in business, Shaich's Panera exceeded expectations. It posted profits of $21.7 million in 2002, and reached the $1–billion sales mark in 2003. Its stock, which was trading in 1999 for just $6 per share, was trading at $40 in early 2004. Meanwhile, the traditional fast–food chains were struggling financially. "We've been considered the poster child for the collapse of McDonald's," Shaich admitted in an interview with *St. Louis Post–Dispatch* journalist Thomas Lee. "It's so ludicrous. McDonald's problems were created 10, 15 years ago.... They focused too much on convenience and not on the food people want."

Shaich is married to Nancy Antonacci, an educational specialist, with whom he has two children. Some industry analysts wondered if Panera might stumble with the low–carbohydrate diet craze, which sent sales of breads and pastas plummeting, but the company was already planning to introduce low–carb breads and new salad choices on the menu for mid–2004. "Worried? No," Shaich told Young in the *Harvard Business School Bulletin* interview when asked about the so–called Atkins Diet revolution, which had sent bread sales plunging. "Aware of it? Yes. We have a history of being respectful of our customers' evolving preferences."

Sources

Chain Leader, May 2000, p. 103; January 2003, p. 42.
Forbes, November 13, 2000, p. 290.
Harvard Business School Bulletin, March 2004.
Inc., May 1988, p. 14; May 1990, p. 78S.
Investor's Business Daily, March 3, 2004, p. A6.
Nation's Restaurant News, July 11, 1994, p. 2; September 19, 1994, p. 172.
New York Times, May 10, 1998.
St. Louis Post–Dispatch, June 22, 2003, p. E1.
Wall Street Journal, June 10, 2003.

—Carol Brennan

Nisha Sharma

Social activist

Born c. 1982, in India; daughter of Devdutt (a factory owner) and Vidya Sharma. *Education:* Studied software engineering at a Delhi college.

Addresses: *Home*—Noida, India.

Sidelights

Nisha Sharma, a 21–year–old college student, made headlines in her native India when she called off her wedding in protest of the onerous dowry payments her future husband's family was demanding from her parents at the eleventh hour. A once prevalent custom in many cultures, the dowry—or "bride–price"—was a practice still relatively common in India, though it had been outlawed by the government in 1961. Just before her 2003 nuptials were slated to begin, an irate Sharma, dressed in her elaborate Hindu bridal costume, called the local police on her mobile phone, and her prospective groom spent what would have been his wedding night in a Delhi jail cell instead. "I never thought for a moment any of this would happen," she told *Times* of London writer Ian McKinnon a few days later. "But I don't have a moment's regret. It would have been a bad mistake."

Born in the early 1980s to Devdutt, a factory owner in the northern Indian city of Delhi, and Vidya, Sharma was a software engineering student and lived at home in Noida, a Delhi suburb. In a society where arranged marriages between families are still common among the middle class, she agreed to meet a 24–year–old computer engineer her parents had found via a newspaper ad. The couple hit it off, and marriage plans were soon underway. Munish Dalal's family initially asserted that no dowry was necessary, but it was Indian custom to give the newlyweds an array of consumer goods for their new home.

Technically, a dowry is a payment made by a bride's family to the groom, and dates back to the Anglo–Norman early medieval era in Western Europe. It came to India when the British Empire colonized this part of the Asian subcontinent, and blended with a traditional Hindu practice called the *rukhsati,* or farewell gift. After India gained independence in the post–World War II period and began a rapid modernization process, the giving of cash or goods specifically to the groom and his family was outlawed under the 1961 Dowry Prohibition Act. Despite this, the dowry remained common in the form of other types of payment to the groom and his family. The amount was linked to the bridegroom's profession (with civil servants in India commanding the highest amount) and to the thought that it was only fair to the groom's family, who had paid for his professional education and thus established him as a good income–earner for his future wife and children.

At Sharma's engagement party a week before the wedding, her family gave the Dalals a cash sum. Then, her parents agreed to buy the groom a luxury automobile, household appliances, and even a stereo, but the Dalals then allegedly requested that two of everything be given—one for Munish, and the other for his older brother. Devdutt Sharma initially agreed, as he told Lucy Ash in the *Times* of London. "I wanted Nisha to get on well with her in–laws," he admitted. "I thought it would help if they started off with the same stuff." Sharma said she knew nothing of this shopping spree at first, nor of the phone call that her future mother–in–law made to her parents the day before the planned ceremony to demand more money. Moreover, her parents then learned that Dalal was not an engineer, but rather a teacher of computer studies.

On a May day in 2003, some 2,000 guests assembled at a Delhi garden, and on the way to her wedding Sharma took a call from her brother. He told her that the Dalals had demanded a sum of $25,000, and threatened to call off the wedding if her parents did not give in. She was incensed. "I thought, 'Has he come to marry me or for the money?'" she told *People*. Behind the scenes at the wedding tent, as guests waited for the ceremony to begin, the two sides battled, and Dalal's mother and another female member of his family allegedly slapped and spit on Sharma's father. Angered, the bride called the police on her cell phone. "I've never spoken to Dad like that; why should anyone else?," she recalled of the moment in an interview with the *Times*'s Ash. "If they treated him so badly, they probably would have done the same to me, or worse."

Sharma had good reason to fear for her safety. Women's rights groups in India pegged the number of recent brides killed in just the city of Delhi alone at 150 in 2002, and 7,000 nationwide for the previous year. The deaths, often described as kitchen fires, are said to have occurred because the groom's family was unable to extort money from their in–laws after the wedding. Though the practice seems out of step with the modern era, advocates say the violence has only increased with the downturn in the global economy, which has affected India's large class of information–technology professionals. "Growing unemployment makes things worse because many young men see marriage as their main source of income and their only chance of affording all the luxury goods relentlessly advertised on Indian TV," Ash reported.

After Sharma's call to the police, Dalal was arrested later that night, and his mother and the other relative a short time later. The jilted groom now faced a maximum ten–year prison term. Meanwhile, Sharma suddenly found herself the subject of intense media interest, as well as the new standard–bearer for women's rights in modern India. Newspapers printed reports of other brides following suit and calling off their own wedding because of dowry demands, and she was inundated with film offers and even an invitation to run for political office. Sharma, however, was interested only in finishing her degree. She had also received a number of marriage proposals from young men because of the notoriety, and asserted that she would never allow herself to be the subject of dowry negotiations again—though she was not averse to another match arranged by her father. "He knows best," she told Smriti Kak, a writer for the *Tribune* of Chandigarh, India. "I will marry whoever he chooses and do what he wants me to do."

Sources

Periodicals

People, June 23, 2003, p. 65.
Times (London, England), May 16, 2003, p. 19; July 21, 2003, p. 10.

Online

"Common Girl with Uncommon Grit," Tribune Online Edition, http://www.tribuneindia.com/ 2003/20030525/herworld.htm (October 6, 2003).
"Dowry–Busting Bride Wins Star Status," CNN.com, http://www.cnn.com/2003/WORLD/asiapcf/ south/05/23/india.dowry/ (October 6, 2003).
"Dowry Demand Lands Groom in Jail," BBC.com, http://news.bbc.co.uk/1/hi/world/south_asia/ 3027683.stm (October 6, 2003).
"Nisha Sharma: 'Heroine' Seeks Oblivion," DayAfterIndia.com http://www.dayafterindia. com/june11/focus.html (October 6, 2003).

—Carol Brennan

Donald J. Sobol

Author

Born October 4, 1924, in New York, NY; son of Ira J. and Ida (Gelula) Sobol; married Rose Tiplitz (an engineer and children's author), 1955; children: Diane, Glenn, Eric, John. *Education:* Oberlin College, B.A., 1948; attended New School for Social Research, 1949–51.

Addresses: *Office*—c/o Children's Publicity, Random House, 1540 Broadway, New York, NY 10036.

Career

Author. *New York Sun,* New York City, copy boy, then reporter, 1948; *Long Island Daily News,* New York City, reporter, 1949–51; Macy's Department Store, buyer, 1953–55; freelance writer, 1955—.

Member: Authors Guild, Authors League of America.

Awards: Young Reader's Choice Award, Pacific Northwest Library Association, for *Encyclopedia Brown Keeps the Peace,* 1972; Edgar Allan Poe Award, Mystery Writers of America, for his contribution to mystery writing in the United States, 1975; Garden State Children's Book Award, for *Encyclopedia Brown Lends a Hand,* 1977; Aiken County Children's Book Award, for *Encyclopedia Brown Takes the Case,* 1977; Buckeye honor citation (grades 4–8 category), for *Encyclopedia Brown and the Case of the Midnight Visitor,* 1982.

Sidelights

Over the course of children's writer Donald J. Sobol's career, he has written a number of different kinds of books for young audiences, but he is best known for his "Encyclopedia Brown" detective series which began in 1963. Each Encyclopedia Brown book featured the brainy sleuth solving ten different short mysteries. Over the years, Brown became one of the most famous young detectives created in fiction. Brown was not Sobol's only creation. The author wrote at least 65 books on a variety of topics from history and biography to long fiction and fun facts, but many were mysteries. Other famous series of Sobol's included the "Wacky" Series, the *Encyclopedia Brown Record Books,* and the *Two–Minute Mystery* syndicated column featuring Dr. Haledijian. A very productive writer, Sobol told Adam Langer of *Book,* "I took on writing as a lifetime career on the supposition that I would write until I fell over at the typewriter."

Sobol was born on October 4, 1924, in New York City. He is the son of Ira J. Sobol, a self–made man, and his wife, Ida. Sobol and his brother and sister had a happy childhood growing up in New York City. Sobol said he was not as smart as his creation

Brown and much more interested in baseball. He attended the Ethical Culture Schools and graduated from the Fieldston School. Soon after he graduated in 1942, he joined the U.S. Army and fought in World War II. A member of the Army's Corp of Engineers, he served in the Pacific Theater and in Europe. Sobol was discharged in 1946.

After his discharge from the Army, Sobol returned to the United States and began going to college. He entered Oberlin College in Ohio. While a student at the small college, Sobol became interested in writing when he took a short story writing class taught by Professor Ralph Singleton. Singleton encouraged Sobol in his writing, though Sobol still harbored dreams of playing professional baseball. It took several years before Sobol made fiction writing the focus of his career.

Sobol earned his B.A. in 1948 from Oberlin. After graduation, he returned to New York City. Sobol's first job was at a newspaper, the *New York Sun,* as a copy boy. He was soon promoted and became a writer for the paper. In 1949, Sobol left the *Sun* and went to the *Long Island Daily News* where he also worked as a writer through 1951. In addition, Sobol wrote—sometimes under a pen name—for a number of magazines. He also continued his education at New York City's New School for Social Research from 1949 to 1951.

For his next job, Sobol moved away from journalism. He was a buyer at Macy's from 1953–55. Sobol left this job in 1955 and became a full-time writer when he married Rose Tiplitz. The couple had four children, Diane, Glenn, Eric, and John. Sobol continued to write for magazines and began working on a book.

One of the first books that Sobol published was 1957's *The Double Quest.* This was a historical children's novel set in twelfth-century England. Aimed at teenagers, the novel contained elements of the King Arthur story as well as a mystery. Another early book of Sobol's was *The Lost Dispatch: A Story of Antietam,* published in 1958. This was also a historical children's novel set at the end of the Civil War. Other books written by him were historical but not fiction, like 1959's *The First Book of Medieval Man* and 1960's *Two Flags Flying*—about the Civil War—written to help children understand these time periods.

Sobol also had a syndicated column that was published internationally between 1959 and 1968. Called *Two-Minute Mysteries,* it was Sobol's first mystery series. While the syndicated column was still being published, Sobol moved with his family to Florida in 1961. There, he continued to write many fiction and non-fiction books. In 1961, he wrote *The Wright Brothers of Kitty Hawk,* a fictional biography of the first men who flew an airplane in the United States. In 1962, he edited *The First Book of the Barbarian Invaders, A.D. 375–511.* Sometimes Sobol employed the help of his wife, Rose, who co-wrote *The First Book of Stocks and Bonds* with him. Sobol followed this with more historical facts in 1965's *Lock, Stock, and Barrel,* which contained 50 short biographical sketches of American Revolutionary War men.

In 1963, Sobol turned from these primarily non-fictional topics to mysteries. He published his first Encyclopedia Brown book that year, *Encyclopedia Brown, Boy Detective.* The book was rejected by 26 publishers before it was accepted by T. Nelson who only insisted on a few changes. *Encyclopedia Brown, Boy Detective* received praise from the first. Each of the ten stories in the book, like all those in the Encyclopedia Brown series, focused on Leroy "Encyclopedia" Brown, a ten-year-old boy who was given his nickname because of his intellectual prowess. The boy was the son of the Idaville, Florida, police chief, Chief Brown, whom he helped solve big mysteries while solving smaller ones found in every day life for local people. Brown was helped by his friend Sally Kimball, and was often at the mercy of enemy Bugs Meany.

Sobol made the Encyclopedia Brown books young-reader friendly. Many clues were given in the course of each story, and readers could find the solutions in the back of the book. The clues and mysteries were simple for those readers who were observant. Sobol also created interesting plots full of humor, puns, jokes, and details that created an atmosphere illustrating a child's life and activities. The plots were also often fast-moving and engaging. Some critics called Sobol's plots in the series formulaic, but he created Brown and his friends to be engaging for young readers, especially those who did not like reading. In a review of *Encyclopedia Brown and the Case of the Slippery Salamander,* Lauren Peterson of *Booklist* wrote, "The series' success lies in its format. Budding detectives love the excitement of trying to solve cases on their own or with a buddy.... Many youngsters also like the fact that the mysteries are only a few pages long."

Though Sobol continued to produce Encyclopedia Brown books regularly over the years, he continued to create other series as well. In 1967, he began the book series that shared the same title as his earlier syndicated column, *Two-Minute Mysteries,* featuring a character named Dr. Haledijian who solved crimes. This character was featured in several other books including 1971's *More Two–Minute Mysteries* and 1975's *Still More Two–Minute Mysteries*. Other mystery books that Sobol wrote included 1967's *Secret Agents Four,* which was a funny teenage spy fiasco book, and 1981's *Angie's First Case,* which featured a young female detective. A later mystery book for Sobol was *The Amazing Power of Asher Fine* in 1986.

Sobol also wrote other kinds of fiction and nonfiction. In 1970, he wrote *Greta the Strong,* a medieval fiction tale set in the era after King Arthur. Five years later, he published *True Sea Adventures,* 22 nonfiction stories meant to appeal to young readers. In 1979, Sobol wrote *Disasters,* about 13 disasters, ranging from the Black Death to mine cave–ins and blackouts.

Sobol later used the Encyclopedia Brown name on a number of nonfiction books featuring facts for young readers. Among the first was 1981's *Encyclopedia Brown's Second Record Book of Weird and Wonderful Facts.* In 1984, he wrote *Encyclopedia Brown's Book of Wacky Spies,* full of odd facts about spies in Germany, Great Britain, and France. *Encyclopedia Brown's Book of Wacky Cars,* published in 1987, featured true stories about cars that were weird and way out. Sobol was sometimes criticized for using the Encyclopedia Brown name to sell these books, which had next to nothing to do with the mystery series featuring that character.

Sobol's Encyclopedia Brown books were adapted for television in 1989. *Encyclopedia Brown: The Boy Detective* aired as a television movie on HBO. The series was also adapted by others for film strips and comic strips. Soon after that television movie aired, Sobol's readers caught a mistake he made in his first Encyclopedia Brown book. In 1990, first and second grade readers at a Philadelphia elementary school asked Sobol to explain how in one mystery, the villain was able to slip a boiled egg into a carton of fresh eggs that were purchased at a grocery store by the contestants of an egg–spinning contest before they were used. Sobol admitted the oversight and added a correction in subsequent editions of the book.

Sobol continued to work late in his life on the Encyclopedia Brown series and other works. He still wrote 40 hours a week while in his late 70s. He had files of clues and solutions for future mysteries yet to be written. Sobol also read a lot for himself, to find further ideas for clues. Of the aim of his books,

Sobol told a writer in *PNLA Quarterly,* as excerpted in *Children's Literature Review,* "Outwitting you, the reader, is hard, but harder still is making you laugh. I try above all else to entertain. Yes, it is nice to have a message, too. And I have one. It is that all men are brothers, and that a religion or a race cannot be blamed for the misbehavior of one of its members."

Selected writings

The Double Quest, Watts, 1957.
The Lost Dispatch: A Story of Antietam, Watts, 1958.
First Book of Medieval Man (nonfiction), Watts, 1959; revised edition published in England as *The First Book of Medieval Britain,* Mayflower, 1960.
Two Flags Flying (nonfiction), Platt, 1960.
A Civil War Sampler, Watts, 1961.
The Wright Brothers of Kitty Hawk (nonfiction), T. Nelson, 1961.
(Editor) *The First Book of the Barbarian Invaders, A.D. 375–511* (nonfiction), Watts, 1962.
(With Rose Sobol) *The First Book of Stocks and Bonds* (nonfiction), 1963.
Encyclopedia Brown, Boy Detective, T. Nelson, 1963.
(Editor) *An American Revolutionary Award Reader* (nonfiction), Watts, 1964.
Lock, Stock, and Barrel (nonfiction), Westminster, 1965.
Encyclopedia Brown And the Case of the Secret Pitch, T. Nelson, 1966.
Encyclopedia Brown Finds the Clues, T. Nelson, 1966.
Encyclopedia Brown Gets His Man, T. Nelson, 1967.
Two Minute Mysteries, Dutton, 1967.
Secret Agents Four, Four Winds Press, 1967.
(Editor) *The Strongest Man in the World,* Westminster, 1967.
Encyclopedia Brown Solves Them All, T. Nelson, 1968.
Encyclopedia Brown Keeps the Peace, T. Nelson, 1969.
Greta the Strong, Follett, 1970.
Milton, the Model A, Harvey House, 1970.
Encyclopedia Brown Saves the Day, T. Nelson, 1970.
Encyclopedia Brown Tracks Them Down, T. Nelson, 1971.
More Two–Minute Mysteries, Dutton, 1971.
Encyclopedia Brown Shows The Way, T. Nelson, 1972.
The Amazons of Greek Mythology, A.S. Barnes, 1972.
Encyclopedia Brown Takes the Case, T. Nelson, 1973.
Encyclopedia Brown Lends a Hand (aka The Case of the Exploding Plumbing), T. Nelson, 1974.
Encyclopedia Brown and the Case of the Dead Eagles, T. Nelson, 1975.
Great Sea Stories, Dutton, 1975.
Still More Two–Minute Mysteries, Dutton, 1975.
True Sea Adventures (nonfiction), T. Nelson, 1975.
Encyclopedia Brown and the Eleven: Case of the Exploding Plumbing and Other Mysteries, Dutton, 1976.

Encyclopedia Brown and the Case of the Midnight Visitor, T. Nelson, 1977.

(Editor) *The Best Animal Stories of Science Fiction and Fantasy*, Warner, 1979.

Disasters (nonfiction), Archway, 1979.

Encyclopedia Brown Carries On, Four Winds, 1980.

Angie's First Case, Four Winds, 1981.

Encyclopedia Brown Sets the Pace, Dutton, 1981.

Encyclopedia Brown's Second Record Book of Weird and Wonderful Facts (nonfiction), Random House Children's Books, 1981.

Encyclopedia Brown's Book of Wacky Crimes (nonfiction), Dutton, 1982.

Encyclopedia Brown Takes the Cake, Four Winds Press, 1983.

Encyclopedia Brown (omnibus), Angus & Robertson, 1983.

Encyclopedia Brown's Book of Wacky Spies (nonfiction), Morrow, 1984.

Encyclopedia Brown's Book of Wacky Sports (nonfiction), vol. 1, Morrow, 1984.

(With Glenn Andrews) *Encyclopedia Brown Takes the Cake!: A Cook and Case Book*, Scholastic, 1984.

Encyclopedia Brown and the Case of the Mysterious Handprints, Morrow, 1985.

Encyclopedia Brown's Third Record Book of Weird and Wonderful Facts (nonfiction), HarperCollins Juvenile Books, 1985.

Encyclopedia Brown's Book of Wacky Animals (nonfiction), Morrow, 1985.

The Amazing Power of Ashur Fine: A Fine Mystery, Macmillan, 1986.

Encyclopedia Brown's Book of Wacky Outdoors (nonfiction), Morrow, 1987.

Encyclopedia Brown's Book of Wacky Cars (nonfiction), Morrow, 1987.

Encyclopedia Brown and the Case of the Treasure Hunt, Morrow, 1988.

Encyclopedia Brown and the Case of the Disgusting Sneakers, Morrow, 1990.

Encyclopedia Brown's Book of Strange but True Crimes (nonfiction), Scholastic, 1992.

The Best of Encyclopedia Brown, Scholastic, 1993.

My Name is Amelia, Atheneum, 1994.

Encyclopedia Brown and the Case of the Two Spies, Delacorte, 1995.

Encyclopedia Brown and the Case of Pablo's Nose, Delacorte 1996.

Encyclopedia Brown and the Case of the Sleeping Dog, 1998.

Encyclopedia Brown and the Case of the Slippery Salamander, Delacorte, 1999.

Encyclopedia Brown and the Case of the Jumping Frogs, Delacorte, 2003.

Sources

Books

Children's Literature Review, vol. 4, Gale Research, 1982.

Contemporary Authors, vol. 38, Gale Research, 1993.

Fourth Book of Junior Authors & Illustrators, H.W. Wilson, 1978.

Silvey, Anita, editor, *Children's Books and Their Creators*, Houghton Mifflin, 1995.

Silvey, Anita, editor, *The Essential Guide to Children's Books and Their Creators*, Houghton Mifflin, 2002.

Something About the Author, vol. 132, Gale, 2002.

St. James Guide to Children's Writers, 5th ed., St. James Press, 1999.

Ward, Martha E. et al., *Authors of Books for Young People*, 3rd ed., Scarecrow Press, 1990.

Periodicals

Book, July–August 2003, p. 34.

Booklist, September 1, 1999, p. 134; February 1, 2004, p. 977.

Christian Science Monitor, April 6, 1984, p. B7.

Entertainment Weekly, October 24, 2003, p. 112.

Online

"Author Information," Kidsreads.com, http://www.kidsreads.com/series/series–brown–author.asp (April 7, 2004).

"Donald J. Sobol," AuthorTracke.ca, http://www.authortracker.ca/author.asp?a=authorid&b=18614 (April 7, 2004).

"Encyclopedia Brown," Thrillingdetective.com, http://www.thrillindetective.com/eyes/encyclopedia.html (April 7, 2004).

"Juvenile Books Author of the Month: Donald J. Sobol," Greenville Public Library, http://www.yourlibrary.ws/childrens_webpage/j–author102001.htm (April 7, 2004).

—A. Petruso

David Spergel

AP/Wide World Photos

Astrophysicist

Born David Nathaniel Spergel, March 25, 1961, in Rochester, NY; married Laura H. Kahn (a doctor), August 26, 1990; children: Julian, Sarah, Joshua. *Education:* Princeton University, bachelor's degree (astronomy), 1982; Harvard University, master's degree (astronomy), 1984; Harvard University, Ph.D. (astronomy), 1985; post–doctoral work, Harvard, 1986.

Addresses: *Office*—Princeton University, Department of Astrophysical Sciences, Peyton Hall—Ivy Lane, Princeton, NJ 08544–1001.

Career

Assistant professor, Princeton University, 1987–92; associate professor, Princeton University, 1992–97; visiting associate professor, University of Maryland, 1995–96; professor, Princeton University, 1997—; helped design NASA's Wilkinson Microwave Anisotropy Probe (WMAP), 1990s; began work on new NASA deep space probe, Terrestrial Planet Finder (TPF), 1999; publicly presented groundbreaking findings of WMAP, 2003.

Member: Institute for Advanced Study, 1986–88.

Awards: Alfred P. Sloan Research Fellow, 1988–92; National Science Foundation Young Investigator Award, 1988–93; Helen B. Warner Prize, 1994; Bart Bok Prize, 1994; American Astronomical Society Second Century Lecturer, 2000; John D. and Catherine T. MacArthur Foundation Fellowship, 2001.

Sidelights

Named one of the top scientists in the United States by *Time* in 2001, astrophysicist David Spergel has been at the forefront of answering fundamental questions about the origin and composition of the universe since the 1980s. A professor at Princeton University, Spergel helped to design and to examine the findings of the National Aeronautics and Space Administration's (NASA) Wilkinson Microwave Anisotropy Probe (WMAP). Launched in 2001, this robotic probe created the clearest–ever pictures of the radiation emanating from the edges of the known universe. This is the oldest radiation in the universe, and examining it in detail allowed Spergel and his team to determine, for the first time, the exact age of the universe (13.7 billion years), and the fact that the 96 percent of the universe is composed of invisible "dark matter." Spergel and his team presented their findings in February of 2003.

Spergel began his work in astrophysics as an undergraduate at Princeton University. There he developed a reputation for diving headfirst into one difficult problem after another. He has always been most comfortable when exploring the edges of what is known about the universe—and trying to push beyond them. He graduated from Princeton in 1982.

After graduating from college, Spergel headed to Harvard to continue his education in astronomy. While a Harvard student, he spent a year in England at Oxford University as a Harvard traveling scholar. He received a master's degree in astronomy in 1984. The following year he completed a Ph.D. in astronomy, also at Harvard. Upon receiving his Ph. D., Spergel spent an additional year at Harvard as a post–doctoral fellow before returning to Princeton in 1987, this time as a professor.

Spergel first made his mark while studying the structure of the Milky Way galaxy, of which the sun and 100 billion other stars is a part. Along with Leo Blitz of the University of Maryland, Spergel discovered that the Milky Way has a much more complex structure than was previously supposed. That structure includes warped edges and a band of stars around its middle section.

Next, Spergel turned his attention to the mysterious "dark matter" said to compose most of the material in the universe. It was this subject that had formed the basis of his Ph.D. thesis. He developed the idea that dark matter, theorized but never directly observed by scientists, should create a kind of cosmic wind that should blow against the Earth as it moves through space. Scientists who have continued Spergel's work on dark matter are now testing this theory.

Moving on from his investigations into dark matter, Spergel turned to the problem of why groups of galaxies form complex structures rather than spreading out evenly through the universe. The theory Spergel came up with to explain this phenomenon involved knots of warped space–time. But the theory, called "brilliant" by Time's Michael D. Lemonick was proven to be false by observational data. Spergel, true to form, instead of fighting to preserve the popularity of his theory as many scientists would do, simply moved on to the next topic.

The next topic Spergel chose moved him into an area usually reserved for engineers, not scientists. In the early 1990s, NASA brought him on the design team for the WMAP. For eight years, Spergel and his team labored to perfect the technology that would provide the best resolution of the oldest radiation in the universe.

Finally, in June of 2001, Spergel was on hand to watch a Delta rocket lift off from Cape Canaveral, Florida, carrying the fruits of many months of hard work for him and the rest of the WMAP team. The satellite, weighing 1,800 pounds, was beginning its mission to explore the extreme edge of the observable universe, a mission that would take it a million miles from home into deep space.

Also in 2001, Spergel received the coveted John D. and Catherine T. MacArthur Fellowship. Informally known as the "genius grant," the fellowship provides financial support, according to a statement issued by the MacArthur Foundation and quoted in the Daily Princetonian, to individuals who show "extraordinary originality and dedication in their creative pursuits." Spergel was one of 23 scientists, artists, scholars, and others who were awarded $500,000 each as part of the grant. The money was to be released to each recipient in installments over a period of five years, and could be used for any purpose.

Selection for the grant is through a confidential process, and requires no application. Spergel had heard rumors that he was being considered for the grant, but he did not know for sure until he received a telephone call informing him that he had won. Spergel especially appreciated the fact that the grant money came with no strings attached. He joked that he could now afford to hire someone to do his home maintenance projects instead of doing them himself. But he also said that the money would not change his life in a major way—it would just allow him more time to pursue his research.

In early 2003, Spergel and his colleagues made public their findings from their analysis of the data sent by the WMAP for the first time. The results had far–reaching implications for the field of astrophysics. Data from the probe proved, according to Spergel, that the universe did indeed start with a period of accelerated growth—a big bang, which had been theorized, but not proven. The data also allowed Spergel and his colleagues to pinpoint the age of the universe—13.7 billion years—to, as he told Tim Folger in Discover, "an accuracy of one percent. We know that ordinary matter accounts for only four percent of the mass of the universe. The rest consists of dark matter." Spergel was very excited by these results, which were beyond his wildest imaginings of what he thought would be possible to obtain when he first became an astrophysicist.

Spergel called his work on WMAP among the most satisfying experiences of his life. He also worked harder than he ever had before, rising at seven in the morning and working until two in the morning for months at a time. Many questions remained unanswered, however, including the question of what exactly is dark matter. All that was known at the time the WMAP results were made public was that dark matter seemed to be an invisible substance that, as Spergel told in *Discover*'s Folger, "seems to be driving the universe to speed up." Much remained for Spergel to investigate.

After seeing WMAP on its way, Spergel found himself addressing his next challenge. This was to work on NASA's next far–seeing robotic probe, called the Terrestrial Planet Finder (TPF). This is a probe whose mission will be to directly see, for the first time, Earth–like planets outside of the solar system. So distant and so dim are these objects, that no ordinary telescope could ever hope to see them. This is why special optics must be designed, and why only an instrument operating beyond the distorting effects of Earth's atmosphere can be used. Added to the challenge is the fact that the stars around which extrasolar planets orbit outshine the planets by millions of times, effectively drowning out the weak, reflected light from the planet.

With characteristic fervor, Spergel threw himself into this new challenge in 1999. The fact that he had never studied telescope design did not bother him. All that was required, thought Spergel, was to read up on the subject. His task was complicated by the fact that building the new space probe involved solving technical challenges that had never been faced by telescope builders before. But, Spergel told *Discover*'s Lemonick, "I had a few months with nothing special to do, so I figured it would be fun to think about something new. I took home a standard textbook, and every night after the kids went to sleep, I'd spend an hour or two reading it."

The result of Spergel's after–hours studying was the invention of a new kind of telescope that will block the light emitted by a star so that the telescope can resolve the far fainter reflected light coming from the star's orbiting planets. "This is a completely new idea," Michael Littman, an optical engineer at Princeton University told *Discover*'s Lemonick, "and once you see it, you realize how simple and elegant it is. I'm kicking myself that I didn't think of it first." Spergel, Littman, and other members of their team at Princeton unveiled a working demonstration of the revolutionary design as 2000 drew to a close,

and NASA has expressed great interest in incorporating aspects of Spergel's design into the Terrestrial Planet Finder, which it planned to launch by 2015.

One of Spergel's main objectives is to immerse himself in the study of questions whose answers will appeal to non–scientists, as well as to his colleagues. With his work on the two NASA space probes, he seemed well on his way to doing just that.

Sources

Periodicals

Daily Princetonian, October 25, 2001.
Discover, March 2002.
Time, August 20, 2001, p. 47.

Online

"America's Best: Science and Medicine: Astrophysics: David Spergel," CNN.com, http://www.cnn.com/SPECIALS/2001/americasbest/science.medicine/frameset.dspergel.exclude.html (July 10, 2003).

"Astrophysicist David Spergel Receives MacArthur Fellowship," Princeton University, http://www.princeton.edu/pr/news/01/q4/1024–spergel.htm (July 10, 2003).

"David Spergel's Home Page," Department of Astrophysical Sciences, Princeton University, http://www.astro.princeton.edu/~dns/ (August 20, 2003).

"Echo of the Big Bang," Princeton University Press, http://pup.princeton.edu/titles/7481.html (August 22, 2003).

"R&D: Discover Dialogue: David Spergel," *Discover*, http://www.discover.com/may_03/break dialogue.html (July 10, 2003).

"TPF at Princeton University," Princeton University, http://www.princeton.edu/~tpf/ (August 22, 2003).

—*Michael Belfiore*

Ed Spray

President of Scripps Networks

Born Edward A. Spray, November 28, 1941, in Seymour, IN; married Donna Cornwell, June 29, 1963; children: Brian, Catherine. *Education:* Indiana University: B.S., 1963, M.A., 1969.

Addresses: *Office*—Home and Garden Television, P.O. Box 50970, Knoxville, TN 37950.

Career

Worked as a producer and director, NBC affiliate WMAQ–TV, Chicago, IL, 1966–74; program manager, CBS affiliate WBBM–TV, Chicago, 1974–80, broadcasting director, 1980–84; programming director, CBS Television Stations, New York, NY, 1984–86; broadcasting director, KCBS–TV, Los Angeles, CA, 1986–89; vice president for program development, CBS Television Stations, Los Angeles, 1989–91; has also taught communications at Syracuse University as associate professor, 1991–94; senior vice president for programming, HGTV, Knoxville, TN, 1994–96, executive vice president, 1996–98; executive vice president for programming, Scripps Networks, 1998–2000, president, January, 2000—.

Sidelights

Television executive Ed Spray is the unsung hero behind the scenes of the cult–favorite basic–cable staple, Home and Garden Television (HGTV). Before becoming president of the Scripps Networks, owner of the home–decorating–themed channel and several others, Spray created much of HGTV's ad-

dictive in–house fare with half–hour and hour–long shows about home–buying, renovating, and a plethora of other household–related matters. HGTV, which reaches some 80 million households in the United States alone, has proved to be one of cable television's surprise hits, with ratings so impressive that its advertising revenues increased by 30 percent in 2002. Spray has been dubbed called the "the Anti–Martha"–Stewart by *Newsweek*'s Peg Tyre, and she hailed him as the creative force behind a "network that has turned remodeling into spectator sport."

Born in 1941, Spray grew up in Seymour, Indiana, and graduated from Indiana University with a degree in television production in 1963. His first job in the industry was as a television producer and director at a NBC's Chicago affiliate, WMAQ–TV, in 1966. Spray stayed there eight years, and managed to earn a master's degree from Indiana University in television journalism in 1969 as well. In 1974, he jumped ship to Chicago's CBS station, WBBM–TV, as a program manager. There, Spray was responsible for devising the hours of local, original programming that such stations were forced to rely upon on in an era when Federal Communications Commission rules prevented networks like CBS from owning and syndicating large amounts of programming. Spray's idea was to televise historical reenactments, such as the trial of Chicago White Sox star Shoeless Joe Jackson, who was accused of throwing the 1919 World Series. "It was a wonderful period," Spray told *Broadcasting & Cable* writer John M. Higgins. "This was the golden age of local programming."

Promoted to broadcasting director at WBBM in 1980, Spray spent four years on that job before heading to CBS headquarters in New York City as a programming director there. He and his wife left behind a Chicago–area house that they had bought and renovated themselves, in a years–long job that gave him firsthand knowledge that he later culled for HGTV's programming. Their house dated from 1907, and it took eight years to fully renovate. "You get started on it and never finish," he told *Broadcasting & Cable*'s Higgins. After his stint in New York, Spray was transferred to the West Coast to serve as broadcasting director at KCBS–TV in Los Angeles, California, in 1986. Three years later, he became a vice president for program development at CBS Television, which entailed buying syndicated shows for affiliate stations owned by the network, after the FCC rules had loosened. When he turned 50 years old, however, Spray lost his job in an executive re-shuffling that came in the wake of some high–stakes battles at CBS headquarters centered around controversial chief executive officer Laurence A. Tisch.

Spray jettisoned the corporate world altogether to take an associate professorship at Syracuse University in New York. He was teaching communications there when E.W. Scripps & Co., a newspaper publishing empire that dabbled in cable television, approached him to take a job as a vice president for programming at a cable channel it was creating on a shoestring budget in 1994. HGTV, as it was known, served the do–it–yourself sector of the home–renovation market, taking its cue from Public Broadcasting Corporation's popular *This Old House* and its low–key handyman star, Bob Vila. Scripps hired Spray because of his experience in creating original programming on a budget. Initially, Spray worried that executives would balk at the funds needed to devise enough appealing shows for the fledgling network, and recalled in the *Broadcasting & Cable* interview with Higgins that to him, "It was a 50–50 chance. I took it on a whim." At the time, he thought privately, that if HGTV "flops, I'll be a better teacher because I'll know more about the cable industry."

Over the next two years, Spray went to work developing a roster of accessible, compelling programs that offered friendly hosts, easy–to–understand tips, and a soothing pace that seemed to take the stress out of the task at hand. "The network's son–of–Muzak soundtrack, grinning guests, and tai chi-paced camerawork are meant to reassure viewers that a happy ending is a coat of paint away," noted Tyre in *Newsweek*. "Quick, jumpy edits are forbidden. HGTV shows college dorm rooms only after the beer signs and racy posters have been removed."

Promoted to executive vice president at HGTV in 1996, Spray was made an executive vice president for programming for all of the Scripps stations in 1998. In January of 2000 he became network president. Other channels in the line–up included the popular Food TV, the Do–It–Yourself channel, and Fine Living, a more upscale version of HGTV. The original HGTV remains one of the cable industry's most impressive success stories, with shows like "Weekend Warriors," in which a couple tackles a big project like a building a patio deck in two–day stretch, and "House Hunters," where the camera follows prospective home–buyers and their real–estate agent. In 2002, the HGTV and Food TV channels attracted some one million viewers nightly, a jump of 35 percent over the previous year. Ratings studies showed that HGTV viewers changed channels less frequently, an all–important factor in its ability to command higher advertising rates.

HGTV is even broadcast in other countries, including Latvia, and appears on the Armed Forces Network. In a paean to the pleasures of HGTV addiction, *Washington Monthly* editor Joshua Green wrote about shows like "Designing for the Sexes," a popular HGTV staple that plays off common marital squabbles, being watched by Navy personnel aboard immense warships. "The idea of rugged naval aviators, fresh from sorties over Iraq or Afghanistan, choosing to unwind before Home and Garden Television's design and decorating tips is testament to the strange power this channel holds over its viewers," Green reflected.

With 85 hours of programming to fill weekly, Spray is always on the lookout for new ideas. He has nixed some ideas for shows, including one that involved a roulette–wheel spin that decided a room's color scheme. Maintaining the appeal of his channel in a changing world remained his primary goal as network president. "Our viewers know they won't see anything anxiety–provoking or disturbing," Spray told *Newsweek*'s Tyre. "We see that when the news in the world is dark, people tune in. We're a safe haven."

Sources

Broadcasting & Cable, October 30, 2000, p. 68.
Electronic Media, January 24, 2000, p. 122.
Newsweek, November 18, 2002, pp. 64–65.
Washington Monthly, July–August 2003, p. 26.

—Carol Brennan

Philippe Starck

Designer and architect

Born January 18, 1949, in Paris, France; son of André (an airplane designer) and Jacqueline (Lanourisse) Starck; married Brigitte Laurent (died, 1992); married Nori Vaccari, April, 2000; children: Ara (first marriage), Oa (with photographer Patricia Bailer), K. (second marriage). *Education:* Studied in Ecole Nissim de Camondo in Paris, France.

Addresses: *Studio*—18/20 rue du Faubourg du Temple 75011, Paris, France.

Career

Started a company that specialized in designing inflatable furniture, 1968; design team, La Main Bleue Club, Paris, France, 1976; design team, Les Bains Douches Club, Paris, 1978; founded Starck Products, 1979; part of design team for France's president's private residence, Paris, France, 1982; founded UBIK, 1983; designer, Royalton Hotel, New York, NY, 1988; designer and architect, Paramount Hotel, New York, NY, 1990; designer and architect, Delano Hotel, Miami, FL, 1996; designer and architect, Mondrian Hotel, Los Angeles, CA, 1996; designer and architect, Hudson Hotel, CA, 2003.

Awards: Oscar du luminaire, France, 1980; three awards at Neocon, Chicago, IL, 1986; Delta de Plaia à Barcelona, Spain, 1986; Platinum Circle Award, Chicago, United States, 1987; Grand Prix National de la Création Industrielle, Paris, France, 1988; Officier des Arts et des Lettres, Paris; Design–Zentrum Nordrhein Westfalen, Germany, 1995; Primero Internacional de Diseno Barcelona, Spain, 1995; Harvard

Excellence in Design, Cambridge, MA, 1997; Commandeur dans l'Ordre des Arts et des des Lettres, Paris, 1998; Chevalier dans l'Ordre National de la Légion d'Honneur, 2000; Pratt Institute Black Alumni Award, 2001; Compasso d'Oro Italy, 2001; Red Dot Best of the Best Award, 2001; IF Design award, 2002; Observeur du design Etoile, Paris, 2002; Observeur du design Etoile, Paris, 2003.

Sidelights

If you go to Philippe Starck's online store you'll find the following product categories, all designed by Starck himself: tables, luggage, chairs, watches, books, armchairs, stationery, tableware, lamps, radios, televisions, stools, bath accessories, fine art, and even his own organic food line in packaging designed, of course, by Starck. His range of design is impressive by any standard. During Starck's 25–year career, he has applied his unique sense of design to everything from a waste management center in Paris to international hotels to paper towel dispensers. No matter what he focuses his efforts on, one gets the sense that he is playing with what is familiar to us and adding his aerodynamic, organic design to see what happens. The philosophy behind his style has always catered to the masses— good–looking but manufactured at a low cost. He has made it his life's work to change people's perception that good design is only for the wealthy or an extravagance. "When I started I was shocked that the objective of design was to create very beautiful objects to be sold to very rich people in very fancy boutiques," he told Dana Thomas of *Newsweek*. "Why couldn't these people see the vulgarity in what they were doing? I wanted to do the opposite. If I had a good idea, I wanted to give it to a million people." And he practices what he preaches. His idea of design for the masses has found life with an historic partnership with the Target superstores, placing his cutting–edge products on their shelves.

Starck is the son of an airplane designer, Andre Starck. The elder Starck's job was to think of new uses for old designs, to take fundamental designs that already existed and make them better. Perhaps this is one of the reasons his son, Philippe, is accustomed to redesigning our world. The young Starck started to show signs of an unusual eye for design from an early age. He played in his father's large workshop, which was filled with machinery, engines and spare parts that were irresistible to a curious boy. Starck's version of playtime was dismantling the machinery and putting it back together in his own way, much like his father. It was an inclination that would shape the rest of his life.

Starck, born to a well–off family that provided for him, might have shown a lot of promise at home in the workshop, but in the world around him he had a hard time fitting in. He was a recluse in school, unable to get along with his peers and, eventually, avoided going to school altogether whenever he could. "I was completely unable to adapt to society and school," he told *People*. "I spent my youth escaping."

Things did not get better for him quickly. He showed signs of depression and as he grew older he still felt like an outcast. His one escape was in his hobby. But the hobby of dismantling and remaking known objects was about to become his life's blood. His interest in working with known objects took a turn toward design when he was in his teens and he attended the prestigious school Ecole Nissim de Camondo. By the time he graduated he was considered by everyone who saw his work to be a promising new talent on the design scene. Typically for Starck, he wished to work on something cutting edge so he started a company in 1968 that specialized in designing inflatable furniture. The company did not go very far but it succeeded in getting his work out in the public eye.

Starck's eye was very natural. He liked lines in his furniture that were natural and smooth. There were other designers of the time who had a similar taste, but Starck's talent was beginning to shine and some of the big names in design were beginning to take notice. He secured an apprenticeship for Pierre Cardin in 1969, which was good for his career and also helped him put in perspective what his own tastes were. Working with Cardin's opulent—and some would say gauche—plans made Starck see what he did not want to do. Cardin's style was a turn–off for Starck and made him more determined than ever to unleash simpler lines on the world.

Even with his innate shyness Starck was beginning to blossom socially. The design world welcomed his odd mixture of personal brooding and enthusiasm for his work, traits that had made him unpopular in school. The young designer found some comfort in the aloofness of the Paris nightclub scene and, naturally, had many ideas about how the clubs themselves could improve their look. Soon, Starck found a professional niche in the Paris nightclub scene in the 1970s and gained a minor reputation with interior designs for the clubs La Main Bleue in 1976 and Les Bains Douches in 1978.

By the late 1970s Starck felt his career was not moving as fast as he wanted it to. Andy Warhol, the Manhattan–based artist, had essentially made himself a brand in the art world. Starck believed that the design industry could use a good hit of the same irony. The young designer was getting a sense of how to market himself and was slowly gaining a reputation for being a very talented (and self–serving) character in the design world. He started his own company in 1979, calling it Starck Products.

Finally, in 1982, the young designer got his big break. French president Francois Mitterrand hired him to be part of the design team on his private residence in Paris. It was a prestigious job that took his career to the next level. Not only was the president happy with the results but so was the public. With some wind at his back Starck started to secure more jobs, of note being the Café Costes restaurant which sported a spectacular staircase and Starck–designed furniture. The Costes look got the design world so excited that the Starck name began to spread and a feverish trend began in Paris. Cafes are a crucial part of life in France and competition is fierce. After Café Costes, every café in Paris had to set itself apart. Starck had started a craze and he was at the forefront of it. For the first time in his life he was able to pick the jobs that were interesting to him.

Throughout the 1980s Starck built on his reputation as the rock star of the design world. Both he and his designs were everywhere. He offered interviews to the mainstream press, which was unheard of at the time, and focused on selling himself as the "people's designer." His sense of self-marketing was refined and he was making a lot of people in his business both resentful and jealous. His success at making himself a brand confounded a community that considered itself above such nonsense. But Starck, aware of the irony of a designer being a celebrity, was out to prove something and he was not going to let the old guard slow him down.

Starck entered the next stage of his career when he partnered with American hotelier and Studio 54 co-founder Ian Schrager to design a number of hotels, including the Delano in Miami, Florida, and the Mondrian in Los Angeles, California. The projects were all huge endeavors involving hundreds of millions of dollars. They all involved creating new buildings or renovating old landmarks, both tricky and expensive endeavors. But, for the most part, his hotel work went over very well and his reputation was only furthered by his efforts. His hotels were compared to theater, with dramatic entrances and funny details that walked a fine line between tasteful and silly.

But Starck entered the big time when he broke into the western mainstream with a deal that partnered his company with the Target line of stores. Target wanted him to do a line-up of home accessories exclusively for their store. "Good design can and should be part of everyday life. I'm always looking for magic in reality," he told *People.* "For the same price, you can give a lot more love and respect and service to people." With the Target deal, Starck got to put the philosophy behind his art to the test.

Though he had been known in select circles a number of years, now he was a household name. The Starck Reality line of products included more than 50 items, such as toothbrushes and magazine racks. He told *Retail Merchandiser,* "My goal in this democratization of design is to make possible the most joyful and exciting experiences for the maximum number of people." He continued to deliver on his promise to make the Starck look accessible to everyone.

Starck's design philosophy is deeply felt and he gets very animated when he has an opportunity to talk about why he does what he does. He might seem like he is overdoing it but in interview after interview his enthusiasm for design and its effect on people shines. To Starck, the influence of design in our daily lives cannot be overestimated. He told Susannah Meadows of *Newsweek,* "A nice object will never change the life of somebody, but it helps. Everything around us has an influence on our subconscious. It will not bring back the husband, but it can send a sign of intelligence and poetry and humor."

Though he swore he would never design retail spaces he changed his tune after meeting with fashion designer Jean Paul Gaultier, who was looking for someone to craft the space of a 2,300-square-foot, first-floor brownstone on New York City's Madison Avenue. The two met a few times and Starck was impressed with how well Gaultier understood the philosophies that drive his design. "I didn't feel that fashion retail was my territory," Starck told Sheila Kim of *Interior Design,* "but Jean Paul became like a brother." The result was a partnership that created a uniquely sparse space on a city avenue that is not known for its understatement. The two men remain close friends.

Starck met his second wife, Nori Vaccari, a former New York school teacher, in 1998 at a Manhattan party. The two hit it off immediately. Starck opened up to her in a way that surprised even him. The two dated for three years before getting married in April of 2000 in Paris. They had a child, named simply K., and make their home in a loft in Paris, France. It is an ever-evolving space and Starck would have it no other way. "Things arrive, they settle, eventually they're replaced," he told *People.* "People try to finish things and don't realize that what they're finishing is their tomb. You always have to leave room for chance and necessity and relativity."

Some celebrities like to claim that success didn't change them, but Starck would probably find that boring. He wears his success in a uniquely Starck way. He makes notes on plastic paper that's made just for him. He has many homes around the world which reveal that his life is as eclectic as his designs, including a huge New York City apartment, an oyster farm in France, and a house on the Seine next to a nudist camp. He has a staff just to make sure each house has the same items as the other houses, even the same books. Perhaps the best example of how Starck handles success can be found in the fact that he refuses to do business with companies that Starck deems harmful to people. Among these blacklisted companies are ones that deal in oil, tobacco, games, and alcohol. He claims to have lost a lot of money because of his strict standards but, according to him, he does not need any more money.

In Frankfurt, Germany, in 2002, he launched his Starck 3 collection for Duravit, a collection of bath utilities and accessories. Continuing his theme of design for the people, he told a crowd of about 900 people, as quoted by Aric Chen of *Interior Design,* "It's not just about bathrooms and ceramic parts. It's a political and strategic action." His speech to launch the line of products contained an enthusiastic line that caused a bit of a stir. "I hereby declare the design war over and won. Attractive products of good quality are being made everywhere today."

But in the midst of his enthusiasm he also claims to be depressed most of the time. He still struggles with the insecurities that made him a recluse as a child. His world view is more sophisticated now but, in the end, Starck has clearly embraced nihilism. He told his Frankfurt audience, "All the things that we hold true, such as the moon, the sun, and the stars, do not exist. Nothing exists. I am afraid, like everyone else."

But, with a strong work ethic and a mission, he has found the energy to work on. The fine balance between the lightness of his work and the seriousness of his philosophy is perhaps best summed up in an answer he gave *Newsweek*'s Thomas when the journalist asked him what design he was most proud of. "The next one," Starck replied. "Because I am never, ever satisfied with what I've done."

Selected interior architecture

La Main Bleue, Paris, France, 1976.
Les Bains Douches, Paris, France, 1978.
Private residence, Elysée Palace, Paris, France, 1982.
Café Costes, Paris, France, 1982.
Manin Restaurant, Tokyo, Japan, 1986.
Café Mystique, Tokyo, Japan, 1986.
Concert Hall La Cigale, Paris, France, 1987.
Royalton Hotel, New York, NY, 1988.
Paramount Hotel, New York, NY, 1990.
Teatriz Restaurant, Madrid, Spain, 1990.
Groningen Museum, Holland, 1994.
The Peninsula Restaurant, Hong Kong, China, 1994.
Delano Hotel, Miami, FL, 1995.
Theatron Restaurant, Mexico City, Mexico, 1995.
Mondrian Hotel, Los Angeles, CA, 1996.
Asia de Cuba Restaurant, New York, NY, 1997.
Saint Martins Lane Hotel, London, England, 1999.
Mikli glasses shop, Paris, France, 1999.
Bon Restaurant, Paris, France, 2000.
Sanderson Hotel, London, England, 2000.
Hudson Hotel, New York, NY, 2000.
Clift Hotel, San Francisco, CA, 2001.
Miramar Hotel, Santa Barbara, CA, 2003.
Eurostar train, 2003.

Selected architecture

Laguiole knife factory, Paris, France, 1988.
Nani Nani building, Tokyo, Japan, 1989.
Baron Vert building, Osaka, Japan, 1992.
Asahi building, Tokyo, Japan, 1989.

Ecole Nationale des Arts Décoratifs, Paris, France, 1995.
Bordeaux Airport air traffic control tower, Bordeaux, France, 1997.
Sanderson Hotel, London, England, 2001.
Incineration plant, Paris, France, 2004.

Selected exhibitions

Georges Pompidou Museum, Paris, France.
Arts Décoratifs Museum, Paris, France.
Villa Medicis, Rome, Italy.
Museum of Munich, Germany.
Museum of Frankfurt, Germany.
Museum of Düsseldorf, Germany.
Museum of Modern Art, Kyoto, Japan.
Museum of Modern Art, New York, NY.
Design Museum, London, England.
Vitra Design Museum, Basel, Switzerland.
Vanity Case, travelling exhibition, 2002.
Georges Pompidou Museum, Paris, France, 2003.

Sources

Periodicals

Australian, March 1, 2002; March 22, 2002.
Interior Design, April 2002, p. 262; October 2002, p. 144.
Newsweek, April 1, 2002, p. 58; April 22, 2002, p. 12.
People, April 2002; November 25, 2002, p. 135.
Retailing Today, April 22, 2002, p. 4.
Retail Merchandiser, May 2002, p. 12.
Smithsonian, November 2002, p. 43.
Time, August 30, 1999.
Times, June 26, 2003.

Online

"About Philippe Starck," Cosmoworlds.com, http://www.cosmoworlds.com/philippe–starck.html (August 28, 2003).
"Biography," Philippe Starck Online, http://www.philippe–starck.com (August 28, 2003).
"Philippe Starck and design and technology," Designtechnology.org, http://www.design–technology.org/starck1.htm (August 28, 2003).
"The World is Not Enough," *New York Magazine Online*, http://www.newyorkmetro.com/nymetro/arts/columns/culturebusiness/1694/index.html (August 28, 2003).

—Ben Zackheim

Pat Summitt

AP/Wide World Photos

Head coach of the University of Tennessee at Knoxville's women's basketball team

Born Patricia Head, June 14, 1952, in Ashland City, TN; daughter of Richard and Hazel Head; married R.B. Summitt (a bank president); children: Ross Tyler. *Education:* University of Tennessee at Martin, B.S. (physical education), 1974; University of Tennessee at Knoxville, M.S. (physical education), 1975.

Addresses: *Office*—117 Stokely Athletics Center, University of Tennessee, Knoxville, TN 37996.

Career

Played basketball as a student at the University of Tennessee, 1970–74; played on silver–medal–winning U.S. World University Games team, 1973; named head coach of the University of Tennessee at Knoxville's women's basketball team, the Lady Vols, 1974; played on gold–medal–winning U.S. Pan American Games basketball team, 1975; played on silver–medal–winning U.S. women's Olympic basketball team, 1976; coached first Junior National basketball team to two gold medal wins; led U.S. national team to two gold medals and a silver medal, 1979; coached the World Championship team and helped it earn a silver medal, 1983; coached U.S. Olympic women's basketball team to first–ever gold medal, 1984; led Lady Vols to six NCAA titles, 1987, 1989, 1991, 1996, 1997, 1998; became motivational speaker for government agencies and corporations, late 1990s; commentator on the ESPN sports network, 1999; consultant to the WNBA, 2000s; became first women's basketball coach to achieve 800 career victories, 2003.

Awards: WBCA/Converse Coach of the Year, 1983, 1995; Naismith College Coach of the Year, 1987, 1989, 1994, 1998; John Bunn Award, National Basketball Hall of Fame, 1990; SEC Coach of the Year, 1993, 1995, 1998; Columbus (OH) Touchdown Club Coach of the Year, 1994, 1997, 1998; Women's Basketball Coach of the Year, Victor Awards, 1994, 1998, 2000; National Association for Sport and Physical Educator's Hall of Fame, 1996; Casey Award, Kansas City Sports Commission, 1997; Governor Ned McWherter Award of Excellence, 1997; *Sporting News* Coach of the Year, 1998; Associated Press Coach of the Year, 1998; U.S. Basketball Writers Association Coach of the Year, 1998; Wooden Award, Utah Tip–off Club, 1998; IKON/WBCA Coach of the Year, 1998; Frontier/State Farm Coach of the Year, 1998; Women's Basketball Hall of Fame, inductee, 1999; Basketball Hall of Fame, inductee, 2000; Naismith Coach of the Century, 2000.

Sidelights

Pat Summitt is the most successful coach in the history of women's basketball. From her start as coach of the University of Tennessee Lady Vols in 1974 at the age of 22, to 2003, she led her team to 800 victories, a record for a female coach. She also served as coach of the U.S women's basketball team at the 1984 Olympic games, leading it to the team's first–ever Olympic gold medal. Under her leadership, the Lady Vols have won half a dozen NCAA championships, and became the first women's basketball team to win titles three years in a row. She was inducted into the Basketball Hall of Fame in 2000.

Summitt graduated from Cheatham County High in Ashland, Tennessee, in 1970. She began her career in college sports as an undergraduate at the University of Tennessee at Martin. While a student, she played on the women's basketball team, the Lady Pacers. She graduated from college with a B.S. in physical education in 1974. During her junior year in college, in 1973, Summitt played on the silver–medal–winning U.S. World University Games basketball team in the Soviet Union. Returning from the World University Games for her senior year, Summitt began to prepare for tryouts for the 1976 U.S. Olympic team. However, a serious knee injury suffered in her fourth game of her final season as a player at Tennessee nearly shattered her plans. But the University of Tennessee provided her with the perfect place to recuperate and still stay in the game after her graduation—as head coach of the University's women's basketball team.

Summitt was just 22 years old when she named the head coach of the women's basketball program at the University of Tennessee at Knoxville. While serving as coach, she also worked toward her master's degree in physical education, taught physical education courses, and trained hard in basketball herself. By the end of the 1974–75 school year, Summitt's knee was in good enough shape for her to join the U.S. 1975 Pan American Games team. This team, with Summitt's help, won the gold medal at the games. Also in 1975, Summitt received her master's degree in physical education from the University of Tennessee. Summitt's hard work paid off when she was named to the 1976 U.S. Olympic basketball team, which won a silver medal in Montreal. Summitt also served as co–captain of the Olympic team.

The year following her Olympic win, Summitt served as the first coach of the U.S. Junior National basketball team. She led this team to two gold medal wins. Her next coaching assignment outside of Tennessee was as head of the United States national team in 1979. Playing in the William R. Jones Cup Games, the World Championships, and the Pan American Games, Summitt's team brought home two gold medals and a silver medal.

Summitt was forced to sit out the 1980 Olympics in Moscow because the United States boycotted the games in protest of the Soviet invasion of Afghani-

stan the year before. In 1983, she served as coach to the World Championship team, and helped it earn a silver medal. In 1984, Summitt returned to the Olympic Games, this time as a coach, not a player. Her team won the gold medal, marking the first–ever Olympic gold medal win for the United States women's basketball team. After clinching the gold–medal winning game, Summitt's players lifted her to their shoulders and carried her around the Los Angeles Forum, where the game was played.

Back at the University of Tennessee, Summitt coached her team to NCAA Championships in 1987 and 1989. In 1990, Summitt became the first woman to win the Basketball Hall of Fame's most highly prized award, the John Bunn Award. Summitt's team brought home no less than four NCAA titles in the 1990s—in 1991, 1996, 1997, and 1998. Under Summitt, Tennessee became the first women's basketball team to win three consecutive NCAA titles.

Over the years, Summitt proved herself again and again to be at the top of her game, and in 1997, she became the first women's college basketball coach to land on the cover of *Sports Illustrated*. Accolades piled up in the 1990s; she was three times named SEC Coach of the Year, in 1993, 1995, and 1998. Also in 1998, she was named *Sporting News* Coach of the Year and the Naismith Coach of the Year, and received numerous other honors.

Observers have attributed Summitt's unprecedented success in part to her extremely demanding coaching style. As she explained to Antonya English in the *St. Petersburg Times*, "I tell kids ... 'If you're lazy, stay as far away from me and our program as you can because you'll be miserable.' We work hard. We're not ashamed of it. We're proud of it." But Summitt has shied away from taking full credit for the successes of her team. "It bothers me," she told English, "that there has been so much focus on me.... It's about players; put the focus on the players."

In 1999, Summitt was inducted into the Women's Basketball Hall of Fame. In 2000, she was inducted into the Basketball Hall of Fame in Springfield, Massachusetts, becoming the fourth women's basketball coach in the history of the game to receive that honor. Also in 2000, Summitt was named Naismith Coach of the Century. This was also the year the Summitt celebrated her 700th victory as coach of the Lady Vols.

As the 1990s drew to a close, Summitt built a successful career as a motivational speaker. Her clients have included the Central Intelligence Agency, Federal Express, and Victoria's Secret. In the 2000s she also worked as a consultant to the WNBA, advising on player selection. In 1999, she worked as a commentator on the ESPN sports network, and in so doing, reaffirmed her commitment to coaching college basketball. "I like chemistry and the family environment," she said of college coaching to *USA Today*'s Dick Patrick, as opposed to the world of professional sports, which she found to be "cold and hard core as far as the business aspect."

Summitt passed yet another milestone in January of 2003 when she became the first women's basketball coach to pass the 800–win mark. Her record at that time stood at an astonishing 800 wins to only 161 losses in 29 seasons. By then she also had six national championships to her credit. Then 50 years old, Summitt told ecstatic fans after her 800th win that she had no plans to retire any time soon. Orange and white confetti rained down onto the court, and Summitt was presented with a cake, roses, and a ball played in the game. She later told reporters that her love of the game, and of coaching would keep her in the game indefinitely.

In addition to her coaching and speaking careers, Summitt has been active in various charitable endeavors, including the United Way, Big Brothers/ Big Sisters, the Easter Seal Society, the American Heart Association, and many other organizations. Summitt has also coauthored books, including *Reach for the Summitt,* a motivational book, and *Raise the Roof,* about the Lady Vol's 1998 season, during which the team was undefeated.

More than winning basketball games, Summitt is inspired by helping young basketball players per- form at their best. "My desire to go in and teach every day is no different right now than 10, 15, 20 years ago," she told *USA Today*'s Patrick. "I love practices. I love teaching."

Selected writings

Reach for the Summitt, Broadway Books, 1998.
Raise the Roof, Broadway Books, 1998.

Sources

Periodicals

St. Petersburg Times, March 9, 1999, p. 1C.
USA Today, December 3, 1999, p. 15C; December 20, 2002, p. 11C.

Online

"Head Coach Pat Summitt," CoachSummitt.com, http://www.coachsummitt.com (August 23, 2003).
"1980 Olympics," Fact Monster, http://www.fact monster.com/ipka/A0114780.html (October 2, 2003).
"Tennessee's Summitt is No. 1 at 800," USAToday. com, http://www.usatoday.com/sports/college/ womensbasketball/games/2003–01–14–de–paul– tennessee–summitt–800_x.htm (August 23, 2003).

—*Michael Belfiore*

Genndy Tartakovsky

Cartoon producer

Born in 1970, in Moscow, Russia; son of Boris (a dentist) and Miriam Tartakovsky; married Dawn David, 2000; children: Jacob. *Education:* Attended Columbia College, Chicago, IL; attended the California Institute of the Arts, Los Angeles, CA.

Addresses: *Office*—Cartoon Network, 1050 Techwood Dr. NW, Atlanta, GA 30318.

Career

Began animation career drawing for the *Batman* television series, c. 1991; served as creator/producer of cartoons for the cable channel Cartoon Network, including, *Dexter's Laboratory,* 1995—, *Samurai Jack,* 2001—, and *Clone Wars,* 2003—; served as supervising producer/director for the *Powerpuff Girls,* 1998—.

Sidelights

Since 1994, the Cartoon Network has remained among the top five ad–supported cable network channels. Part of that success is due to cartoon sensations like *Dexter's Laboratory* and *Samurai Jack,* both brainchilds of Russian–born animator Genndy Tartakovsky. In fact, Tartakovsky has earned such a stellar reputation in the industry that *Star Wars* creator George Lucas tapped him to create a 20–episode cartoon micro–series surrounding the legendary *Star Wars* characters. These action–packed stories ran on the Cartoon Network through the spring of 2004, while Episode III, due in 2005, was being filmed.

Tartakovsky was born in 1970, in Moscow, when Russia was still a Communist country. His father, Boris, was a dentist who took care of the Russian hockey team at a clinic where he supervised dozens of other dentists. Tartakovsky recalled that one time his father had to work on a Russian Cabinet member while soldiers stood guard outside. Because of Boris Tartakovsky's position within the government, the Tartakovsky family lived well—they had a three–bedroom apartment and ate caviar for breakfast.

Though Tartakovsky recalled his time in Russia as happy, his Jewish parents feared the family would be better off in a place not so anti–Semitic, so they moved to the United States in the mid–1970s. On the way, the family had a three–month stopover in Italy as they awaited papers. While there, Tartakovsky and his older brother, Alex, spent their days wandering through a flea market filled with other would–be immigrants selling their possessions to make money to start their new lives.

There, the Tartakovsky boys befriended an older Russian girl who spent her time sketching scenes of the crowds and peddlers. "We imitated her making sketches like you take photographs," Alex Tartakovsky told Alec Wilkinson of the *New Yorker.* "Then Genndy started drawing figures from American comic books someone was selling, and that was the main thing that became interesting to us. Just looking at the figures and then drawing pictures."

The family eventually landed in Columbus, Ohio, but Boris Tartakovsky's dental license did not transfer to the United States and he could only find work as a technician making dentures—a job that was hard to support a family of four on. Tartakovsky immersed himself in television culture and credits the tube for teaching him English. American cartoons captivated his mind and he began spending every possible moment watching them. Every morning before school and every Saturday morning Tartakovsky could be found in front of the tube.

When Tartakovsky was ten, the family moved to Chicago, Illinois, to live alongside some Russian immigrants with whom his father was acquainted. Tartakovsky, however, rebelled from his heritage and did not want to have anything to do with the other Russian kids in the neighborhood or at school. Desiring to fit into his new homeland and no longer be an outsider, Tartakovsky wanted to dress in sneakers and jeans like the American boys; he yearned to be cool. As Tartakovsky recalled to Thelma Adams of the *New York Times,* "Definitely that was a big part of my childhood: wanting to fit [in]. As an immigrant, you talk funny, you look funny, you smell funny. I wanted to do nothing but fit in and talk English and sit with everybody else."

To this end, Tartakovsky spent the better part of his youth watching television so he would have things to say to the American kids at school the next day. Often, he would check the television guide and map out his morning cartoon schedule. Even as a teen, the preoccupation continued and Tartakovsky recalled sneaking off to watch animated films like *The Jungle Book.* He recalled that he stood out in the theater because he was much older and bigger than the other moviegoers.

Growing up, Tartakovsky did more than just watch animation. He also spent a fair amount of time drawing figures from comic books. He created flip books by filling his notebooks with stick figures that dunked basketballs or ran in circles when the pages were turned quickly. Tartakovsky expressed his thoughts this way to Misha Davenport of the *Chicago Sun-Times:* "I've always tried to figure out where the idea to animate comes from. Something about watching movement you've created on screen still thrills me and there's something about telling a story through pictures that I find so appealing."

By high school, no one could deny Tartakovsky's passion for art. "Our parents noticed how much he liked to draw, so they brought him to an art teacher," Alex Tartakovsky told the *New Yorker's* Wilkinson. "After several classes they asked her opinion, and she said, 'Well, he's no Michelangelo.'"

After high school, Tartakovsky enrolled in an art–and–film school called Columbia College, located in downtown Chicago. His father had recently died of a heart attack, so Tartakovsky stayed home to live with his mother. To support himself, he began working as a theater usher and as a cook at a restaurant.

At Columbia College, Tartakovsky decided to study advertising art, figuring that would be a safe way to earn a living. Instead, he got caught up in cartooning after taking a class from Stan Hughes, an instructor who collected 16–mm classic cartoon prints. Tartakovsky would lock himself away with the cartoons, loading them onto the school's editing machines and advancing them frame–by–frame. But Tartakovsky did more than just look at the frames—he sketched each one. Through this painstaking process, Tartakovsky mastered the art of how to make a character move.

In time, Tartakovsky was accepted into the California Institute of the Arts in Los Angeles. When Tartakovsky arrived, he was blown away by the talent of the other students, most just 18 years old. He was already 20. Determined to follow his dream, Tartakovsky caught up to his peers by working twice as hard.

Tartakovsky only attended this school for two years because that was all he could afford. Next, he found work in Madrid, Spain, drawing for the *Batman* television series. It is common in the cartoon industry for some of the production work to take place overseas, where artist wages are lower. While away, Tartakovsky's mother died of cancer. His employer went bankrupt, forcing Tartakovsky to return to California. There, he landed a job at Hanna–Barbera Studios. Tartakovsky, it turns out, walked into the right place at the right time. The studio was just looking at the possibility of founding Cartoon Network.

Nearly 50 animators were invited to test out seven–minute pilots. Wondering if his work was good enough, Tartakovsky showed some of his pieces to studio executive Mike Lazzo. These pieces featured characters named Dexter and Dee Dee. Tartakovsky developed the characters as part of a CalArts assignment. He created Dee Dee first after he got an image in his head of a blond–headed, pigtailed and quite gawky ballerina dancing around. Tartakovsky gave the ballerina a nasal voice. He drew her tall, but made her short on brains. Next, Tartakovsky tried to picture her nemesis, or her opposite. He came up with Dexter, a small, thick boy genius preoccupied with science.

Tartakovsky showed Lazzo a pilot episode he had developed. In the pilot, Dexter has created a shape–shifting device in his secret lab. His sister, Dee Dee, discovers the gadget and the two wrestle for control. Each time one of them activates the device, it turns the other into a dinosaur, whale, duck or snake. In a subplot, their clueless mother wonders why the kids are not ready for school on time.

Lazzo was hooked. He told the *New Yorker* that Tartakovsky's pilot was the first fully formed cartoon to come in. "It had all the key ingredients you need a cartoon to have—it had a funny premise, it had things you could do in a cartoon and couldn't do in live action.... And, above all, it had genius timing. Genndy has a scientist's version of creativity. A cartoon can't just be a bunch of pretty pictures. In cartoons, you literally have to count frames per second to figure out when something should happen or not happen. He has a gift for that kind of delivery—it's musical. What he really has is art and science together. You never see that."

Tartakovsky has admitted that his childhood inspired the creation of Dexter and Dee Dee. Growing up, his brainy brother, now a computer engineer, always had complex toys he did not want to share. Tartakovsky says that his brother is Dexter, while he is the annoying Dee Dee.

In 1995, *Dexter's Laboratory* made its debut on the Cartoon Network and became a staple in the channel's lineup. The show ran through 2003 and earned several Emmy nominations. Tartakovsky, in fact, has been nominated for an Emmy eight times, though he has never won—and does not even mind. "I'd rather be nominated and lose than not nominated at all," he told Davenport in the *Chicago Sun–Times*. "A nomination means acceptance by your peers. I don't get caught up on whether I win or lose. Besides, I'll take good ratings over an Emmy any day."

In 2001, another Tartakovsky creation aired on the Cartoon Network. Called *Samurai Jack,* the cartoon follows a warrior, Jack, who has been banished to the future, only to find it dominated by a wicked alien force ruled by a demon named Aku. The show is populated with robots and aliens and strange creatures with magical attributes. The characters drive flying cars fortified with weapons they use in battle. The premise is that Jack is perpetually trying to find a way back home. While doing so, he is in constant battle with Aku. Unlike most cartoons, the show uses little dialogue—maybe two minutes in a

22–minute episode. The action–adventure series also proved to be an instant success. Over the years, Tartakovsky has had his hand on several other successes. He served as producer and director for the network's top–rated *Powerpuff Girls* series.

Despite his success, Tartakovsky refuses to slow down, working up to 70 hours a week because he believes in taking opportunities when they come. One opportunity of a lifetime was to produce for *Star Wars* creator George Lucas a series of animated cartoon shorts to run on the network between 2003 and 2004. The shorts, dubbed *Clone Wars,* were meant to fill in some of the storyline between *Episode II* and *Episode III* (due in 2005) of the Star Wars saga.

The task was daunting. Each episode was to run for a mere three minutes. During that time, Tartakovsky had to tell a complete story. After beginning work, Tartakovsky realized that every scene had to say something and advance the plot—there could be no scenes just for beauty's sake. Besides working with the time constraints, Tartakovsky was also faced with the challenge of creating cartoon characters that mirrored their live movie counterparts. Tartakovsky discussed the dilemmas with *Los Angeles Times* writer Charles Solomon: "We played with the style a bit to make it fit, but the biggest problem was: Do we caricature the actors or do we caricature the personalities in the movies? It became less about how does Ewan McGregor look and more about how does Obi–Wan Kenobi look as an animated character. Once we made that leap, we felt comfortable with the look." The 20 three–minute shorts debuted in November of 2003 on Cartoon Network. Lucas, too, was pleased with the results. As he told the *Los Angeles Times,* "*Clone Wars* is definitely *Star Wars,* but it clearly has Genndy's style. Visually, it's like nothing else out there."

In June of 2004, it was announced that Tartakovsky would write, produce, and direct five 12–minute animated *Clone Wars* adventures that would continue the storylines first set out in the 20–episode microseries. These installments introduced a new bad guy, General Grievous, and were scheduled to be broadcast in March of 2005. As an animator, Tartakovsky has a unique vision—and, much to the delight of his fans, that almost guarantees him a long and legendary career in the industry.

Selected animation credits

2 Stupid Dogs, art director, director, 1993.
Dexter's Laboratory, creator, executive producer, producer, director, writer, 1995.

Cow and Chicken, writer, 1997.
The Powerpuff Girls, supervising producer, story, director, 1998.
Samurai Jack, creator, executive producer, producer, writer, director, 2001.
Clone Wars, creator, 2003–04.

Sources

Periodicals

Chicago Sun–Times, November 24, 2002.
Los Angeles Times, November 7, 2003, p. E31.
New Yorker, May 27, 2002, p. 76.
New York Times, August 19, 2001, sec. 6, p. 17.
St. Louis Post–Dispatch, November 6, 2003, p. F1.

Online

"Cartoon Network," National Cable and Telecommunications Association, http://www.ncta.com/guidebook_pdfs/cartoon.pdf (May 15, 2004).
"Genndy Tartakovsky," Cartoon Network, http://www.cartoonnetwork.com/watch/studio/ap/gtartakovsky/index.html (May 15, 2004).
"Genndy Tartakovsky," TV Tome, http://www.tvtome.com/tvtome/servlet/PersonDetail/personid–18926 (May 16, 2004).
"Star Wars 'Toons Up Again," E! Online, http://www.eonline.com/News/Items/0,1,14284,00.html?eol.tkr (June 11, 2004).

—Lisa Frick

Donna Tartt

Author

Born in 1963, in Greenwood, MS; daughter of Don (a politician) and Taylor (Bousche) Tartt. *Education:* Attended University of Mississippi, c. 1981; graduated from Bennington College, 1986. *Religion:* Catholic.

Addresses: *Publisher*—Knopf Publishing, 1745 Broadway, New York, NY 10019.

Career

Began writing poetry, c. 1968; published first poem in Mississippi literary journal, c. 1976; published novels, *The Secret History,* 1992, and *The Little Friend,* 2002; other published works include short stories "A Christmas Pageant," 1993, and "A Garter Snake," 1995; and non–fiction *Sleepytown: A Southern Gothic Childhood, with Codeine,* 1992; *Basketball Season,* 1993, and *Team Spirit: Memories of Being a Freshman Cheerleader for the Basketball Team,* 1994.

Sidelights

Though author Donna Tartt only published two novels—1992's *The Secret History* and 2002's *The Little Friend*—in ten years, and a few other works in fiction and non–fiction in between, she is considered an important, influential novelist. The petite, private Tartt is a native of Mississippi, and though her first novel was set a northern college, she is considered a Southern Gothic writer. Her books also have some qualities of thrillers and suspense novels with intricate plots and interesting characters.

Tartt was born in Greenwood, Mississippi, the first of two daughters of Don Tartt, a local politician, and his wife, Taylor. When Tartt was born, she was very small in size and she was often ill throughout her childhood, suffering from such maladies as tonsillitis. Tartt was raised in Grenada, Mississippi, and spent much of her childhood with older family members, including great aunts and grandfathers. She did not have many friends her own age.

By the time she was four, Tartt began keeping a notebook, which later turned into a detailed daily journal. When she was five years old, Tartt started writing poetry. Because she was thought to be sickly, she spent many days home from school. In addition to writing, Tartt also used that time to read. She was particularly a fan of nineteenth–century British authors Charles Dickens and Thomas de Quincey. Even when she was not sick, Tartt spent much of her time reading.

At the age of 13, Tartt published her first work, a sonnet, in a Mississippi–based literary journal. While a teenager, she worked at the local library. In addition to her literary interests, Tartt was also a cheerleader for her high school basketball team when she was a freshman. In 1981, Tartt entered the University of Mississippi, where her writing talents were noticed by her professors.

One of Tartt's biggest supporters at the University of Mississippi was author Willie Morris, the school's writer–in–residence. Another professor who favored Tartt's work was Barry Hannah. Tartt sometimes took classes with graduate students and outshone them. While Tartt was emerging as a distinctive literary voice, she pleased her mother by joining a sorority.

After her first year at the University of Mississippi, Tartt transferred to a private college in Vermont, Bennington College. There, she continued to enhance her knowledge of Greek and English literature. She also became friends with at least two future important novelists, Bret Easton Ellis and Jill Eisenstadt. Ellis was already working on what would be his defining novel, *Less Than Zero*. By the end of her years at Bennington, Tartt began work on what would become her first novel, *The Secret History*.

After Tartt graduated from Bennington College in 1986, she moved to New York City, living in Greenwich Village. She also lived in Boston, Massachusetts, for a time, and went back and forth between the cities. During this period, she attended an art school in New York City for a short time, but did not have much skill as a painter and gave up this pursuit.

While living in New York City and Boston, Tartt continued to work on *The Secret History*. Ellis introduced Tartt to his literary agent, International Creative Management's Amanda Urban, who became Tartt's agent as well. When Tartt neared completion of the manuscript for *The Secret History*, Urban began a bidding war. A manuscript was circulated among those in the know, creating demand.

The Secret History was sold to the Alfred A. Knopf publishing company in 1991 for $450,000 for hardback rights. International rights were sold for $500,000, while paperback rights were sold to Ivy for $510,000. These were amazingly high numbers for a previously unpublished novelist. Tartt's novel was sold just before the American Booksellers Convention, adding to its buzz.

When *The Secret History* was published by Knopf in 1992, it had a distinctive design, including a different shape than most novels; it was proportioned so that it would stick out on a bookstore shelf. Even before it was published in September of that year, the 850–page–long novel had good word of mouth among booksellers and reviewers.

Tartt's novel was a mystery–thriller set at the fictional Hampden College, a small liberal arts college in Vermont not unlike her alma mater, Bennington College. *The Secret History*'s plot focused on a group of select college students studying with a classics scholar, Julian Morrow. The story is told from the point of view of Richard Papen, the narrator and a scholarship student from California, whom even the reader cannot trust because he wants to be accepted by the students as well as the readers.

Papen tries to befriend the already tight group of Henry, Francis, Bunny, and the twins, Camilla and Charles. Morrow had told his students about Greek bacchanals (a orgy–like celebration). Inspired by the idea of the bacchanals, the students tried to recreate such a frenzy with drugs, herbal potions, and alcohol, but a human sacrificial killing proved to be the only way they could come close to the thrilling feeling. Bunny, the only one who did not participate in the murder, is aware of what they did, and wants to tell. The four plus Papen murder Bunny, and Tartt explores the price each pays for their crimes. *The Secret History* also delves into how the campus panics after Bunny disappears and the Federal Bureau of Investigation comes on campus to investigate.

The Secret History was minimalist in the literary sense, but rich with details about colleges, romance, and Greek literature and history. Tartt's gothic thriller received mixed reviews from some critics. They believed that though she knew her material from a scholarship point of view, she lacked sufficient skill in plotting, character development, and relationships. Others believed that letting the characters remain incompletely drawn allowed readers to better identify with them.

One reviewer, Alexander Star, wrote of Tartt's novel in the *New Republic*, "Tartt records the aftereffects of unpunished crime with great skill. But her efforts to transform a chronicle of suspense into a study in sensibility are less successful.... Like her Bennington peers, Tartt offers the aroma of decadence, not its anatomy; stylish intimations of misbehavior, not visions of hell. She leaves her hero hanging out at the abyss, admiring his new sneakers."

Despite some initial critical negativity, Tartt's novel was a best seller for many months in the United States and aboard. *The Secret History* spent 13 weeks on the *New York Times* best–seller list, and three months on the *Publishers Weekly* best–seller list. The novel sold millions of copies worldwide, including more than a million in the United States (both hardcover and soft cover). Critics eventually praised it, and *The Secret History* was considered a success. The film rights were bought by Alan Pakula, but the film was not immediately made as the project passed though a number of hands in Hollywood.

After the success of *The Secret History,* Tartt stayed out of the spotlight and did not publish another novel for ten years. During that time, she lived in Manhattan, on a plantation she bought in Virginia with some of her earnings, and in France for a time. Tartt also traveled to other countries abroad. She did not completely stop writing, however; she had a few short stories published in leading magazines like the *New Yorker* and *Harper's,* and contributed poems and non–fiction works to *The Oxford Mississippian,* including a 1994 essay on cheerleading.

Many questioned how Tartt was going to follow up *The Secret History.* Though she was already working on a second novel before *The Secret History* was completed, she kept this work to herself. Tartt would not succumb to pressure to produce a novel a year. She told Charlotte Abbott of *Publishers Weekly,* "Those were not the rules I wanted to play by. I can't think of anything worse than having a big success, and then trying to rush out another big success." She was a slow writer, allowing herself to become immersed into the world of her novel over a number of years before its completion.

Tartt published her second novel, *The Little Friend,* in 2002. Tartt had built up expectations among readers and critics by taking a decade between novels. As with her first novel, she received another huge payment from her publisher, Knopf. Like *The Secret History,* the novel's story focused on intense personal relationships and murder, though this time, a child in Mississippi served as its focal point.

Set in the early 1970s, *The Little Friend* focused on the life of 12–year–old Harriet Cleve Dufresnes. Harriet lives in a small Mississippi town and becomes determined to avenge the death of her nine–year–old brother, Robin, which happened when she was an infant. Robin was found hanging in a tree in the yard of the family home. After Robin's death, Harriet's mother, Charlotte, withdrew from her family, and Harriet's father, Dix, moved away. No one was ever charged with the crime, and Harriet was raised by her three great–aunts and the family's housekeeper, Ida.

Harriet, a fan of adventure novels and Bible stories, enlists her best friend, Hely, to help her get revenge for Robin's death. Harriet decides that a former schoolmate of Robin's named Danny did the crime and decides to kill him. However, Harriet gets more than she bargained for because Danny is a drug addict (and has a brother who runs a crystal meth lab) and becomes paranoid about her following him. As a result, Harriet tries to kill him with a stolen cobra.

Tartt creates many challenges in Harriet's life. In addition to running into danger by wanting to kill Danny and deal with his drug–producing brother, her home life suffers. Ida is fired, and one of her great aunts, Libby, dies. Tartt uses these intense relationships to explore ideas about race and class in the South in this time period. She was praised for how she wrote about the South, catching its words and phrasings, and the social study aspects of it. Tartt structured it like a novel by Russian novelist Leo Tolstoy, but with a twist of the child's point of view.

Like *The Secret History, The Little Friend* generally had positive reviews. However, some critics still had problems with her plotting of the story, though others believed that the pacing reflected the setting of the novel. *The Little Friend* was seen as giving the readers more emotional currency to which they could relate. A number of reviewers compared the character of Harriet to such classic literary characters as Huck Finn and Scout La Rue. As Malcolm Jones of *Newsweek* wrote, "If *To Kill a Mockingbird* is the childhood that everyone wanted and no one really had, *The Little Friend* is childhood as it is, by turns enchanting and terrifying."

The Secret History was nominated for a number of literary prizes. They included a nomination for the Orange Fiction Prize for Property in 2003, and a place on the long list for the 2003 International Impac Dublin Literary Award. Tartt planned to follow this novel up with a novella based on the myth of Daedalus and Icarus. This was a commissioned work, done as a part of a series of books for Canongate, a Scottish publisher.

Though Tartt made her name in public as a writer, she actually spent much of her time reading, primarily books published in the nineteenth century and early twentieth century. She claimed to enjoy it more than writing in some ways, and she allowed reading to cut into her writing time. Liz Seymour of *Book* quoted Tartt's editor, Gary Fisketjon, as saying, "She's such a dedicated reader and has been reading so long it's almost in her marrow. More than even most writers, her reading informs her writing."

Selected writings

The Secret History, Knopf (New York City), 1992.
The Little Friend, Knopf (New York City), 2002.

Sources

Periodicals

Book, November–December 2002, p. 42, p. 80.
Boston Globe, November 10, 2002, p. E9.
Daily Telegraph, June 4, 2003, p. 2.
Independent (London), May 21, 2002, pp. 4–5.
Independent on Sunday (London), October 20, 2002, pp. 1–2.
New Republic, October 19, 1992, p. 47.
New Statesman, October 28, 2002, p. 48.
Newsweek, October 21, 2002, pp. 66–68.
New York Times, November 16, 1992, p. D6; October 17, 2002, p. E1; November 19, 2003, p. E2.

People, September 14, 1992, p. 28.
Publishers Weekly, September 9, 2002, p. 18.
San Francisco Chronicle, November 26, 2002, p. D1.
Sunday Star Times, November 10, 2002.
Time, August 31, 1992, p. 69; October 21, 2002, p. 74.
World Literature Today, July–September 2003, p. 100.

Online

"Donna Tartt," Mississippi Writers Page, http://www.olemiss.edu/depts/english/ms–writers/dir/tartt_donna/ (February 9, 2004).

—*A. Petruso*

Audrey Tautou

Actress

Born August 9, 1978, in Beaumont, France.

Addresses: *Agent*—c/o Claire Blondel, Artmedia 20, Avenue Rapp, 75001, Paris, France. *E–mail*—info@artmedia.fr.

Career

Actress in films, including: *Casting: Archi–dégueulasse*, 1998; *La vieille barrière*, 1998; *Vénus beauté (institut)*, 1999, aka *Venus Beauty Institute*, 2000; *Triste à mourir*, 1999; *Épouse–moi*, aka *Marry Me* 2000; *Voyous voyelles*, 2000, aka *Pretty Devils*, 2002; *Le Libertin*, aka *The Libertine*, 2000; *Le battement d'ailes du papillon*, 2000, aka *Happenstance*, 2001; *Le fabuleux destin d'Amélie Poulain*, aka *Amélie*, 2001; *Dieu est grand, je suis toute petite*, 2001, aka *God Is Great, I'm Not*, 2002; *À la folie ... pas du tout*, aka *He Loves Me ... He Loves Me Not*, 2002; *L' auberge espagnole*, 2002, aka *The Spanish Apartment*, 2003; *Dirty Pretty Things*, 2002; *Les marins perdus*, aka *Lost Seamen*, 2003; *Pas sur la bouche*, 2003; *Nowhere to Go But Up*, 2003; *Un long dimanche de fiancailles*, aka *A Very Long Engagement*, 2004. Television appearances include: *Coeur de cible* (movie), 1996; *La v´erité est un villain défaut* (movie), 1997; *Bébés boum* (movie), 1998; *Chaos technique* (movie), 1998; *Boiteux: Le baby blues* (movie), 1999.

Awards: Best Young Actress, Jeune Comedien de Cinema Festival, 1998; Cesar Award for Most Promising Actress, for *Vénus beauté (institut)*, 1999.

James Devaney/WireImage.com

Sidelights

French actress Audrey Tautou rose from being completely unknown to become a film sensation not just in her native France, but also in the United States and around the world, as a result of her work in the film *Amélie*. The film became the highest–grossing French film ever released in the United States. For her work in the film, Tautou (pronouced toe–TOO) won a Cesar Award, the French equivalent of the American Academy Award.

Born in Beaumont, France, and raised in rural Montlucon, the young Tautou was very interested in monkeys and spent her childhood dreaming of becoming a primatologist, but as she grew older, her mother told Steven Rea in the *Courier–Mail*, she was "more interested in being the monkey, rather than taking care of them." She became interested in theater and performing, acting out the lives of others.

When she was 17, Tautou took an acting course at Cours Florent in Paris. At first, she was intimidated by the city, and particularly by the huge number of other aspiring actresses, all of whom seemed to be taller and more beautiful than she was. However, a friend pointed out that this was because she was living on the same block as the Elite modeling agency. In 1998, Tautou won the Best Young Actress award in the ninth Jeune Comedien de Cinema Festival, held in Bezier, France, for her work in the film *Vieille barrière*. Director Tonie Marshall noted the award and, impressed by the young actress, gave her a role in her 1999 film *Vénus beauté (institut)*. At first, Tautou thought the director had dialed the wrong number when Marshall called the actress to offer her the role. In the film, Tautou played an impressionable hairstylist who falls in love with a much older man. She won a Cesar award for Most Promising Actress, the French equivalent of the American Academy Award, for her work in the film.

Director Jean–Pierre Jeunet was impressed by Tautou's performance in *Vénus beauté (institut)*, as well as by her fairylike appearance. Although Jeunet originally wanted English actress Emily Watson for his new film *Amélie*, Watson refused the role for unspecified reasons. Casting about for another actresss, Jeunet noticed Tautou's face on a billboard advertising *Vénus beauté (institut)*, and decided she was right for the role. He told the *Courier–Mail*'s Rea, "She was amazing during the [screen] test, exactly like she is in the film. It wasn't necessary to direct her."

In *Amélie*, Tautou played the title character, a Montmartre waitress who finds an old box of childhood treasures hidden under the floorboards of her apartment. She returns the box to its original owner and observes from a distance as his life is changed by the reunion with his beloved belongings. Struck by this transformation, Amélie comes up with more plans to change other people's lives through quirky actions and gifts, always done anonymously; most of the changes are positive, if the people deserve it, and a few are negative—also well–deserved. All is well until she meets a man, Nino, and eventually realizes she must transform her own life in the same way she has altered those of other people.

In *Movie City News*, a reporter quoted film critic Roger Ebert, who called the film "a delicious pastry of a movie, a lighthearted fantasy in which a winsome heroine overcomes a sad childhood and grows up to bring cheer to the needful and joy to herself." He described Tautou as "a fresh–faced waif who looks like she knows a secret and can't keep it." Tautou had little dialogue in the film, but this did not prevent her from being deeply expressive in the role. As Paul Fischer wrote at Dealmemo.com, "One of the many unique facets of the film is watching Tautou's visual expressiveness. With relatively minimal dialogue, the actress speaks with her face. It's an intricate, delicate performance...." Tautou explained to Fischer, "When I play a character, I try to feel the same kinds of feelings as the character, depending on her different situations. And so, those feelings come via my face." She credited the director for the film's artistry; she told Fischer, "To me, Jean–Pierre is a genius. The only thing I gave for this role was my face and voice, because his universe is so precise and so extraordinary...." She also joked to Fischer that the role was uncomplicated because she did not have much dialogue: "It was easier because I don't have to learn as many lines."

In the film, Jeunet paired Tautou with Mathieu Kassovitz as Nino. Kassovitz is a French actor who had also received a Cesar award for Most Promising Actor. Jeunet told the *Courier–Mail*'s Rea that the two actors had "beautiful chemistry" and audiences seemed to agree, packing movie houses and bringing in more than $78 million between April and December of 2001. At the Edinburgh and Toronto Film Festivals, the movie won the People's Choice Award, and was considered a potential contender for Best Foreign Film in that year's Academy Awards in the United States, although ultimately it did not win that honor. Moviegoers, however, showed their love for the film, as the real–life Montmartre cafe where Tautou's fictional character supposedly worked was mobbed by customers; so was a spice shop featured in the film. "People come into the cafe," Tautou told the *Courier–Mail*'s Rea. "They take pictures, they take pictures with the owner, some people even steal menus for souvenirs."

As a result of the film's success, Tautou found that she could no longer walk down the street without being recognized by fans. She jokingly told a *People* reporter that she realized she had made it big when she was in line at the airport: "The hostess was very nasty. When she saw me, she had this face as if she was watching the Virgin Mary." However, she told the *Courier–Mail*'s Rea that she understood why the film had made such an impact on viewers: "It's a film that makes people happy and we all need happiness in our lives, especially now." Interestingly, despite her sudden fame, Tautou has not been badgered by the press as much as she might have been in other countries. This is because French law requires that before publishing a photograph, the photographer must have the approval of its subject. Tautou told Carlo Cavagna of Aboutfilm.com, "It lets the paparazzi take the picture, but if they publish this picture, you have the choice to sue the newspaper. So me, I always sued them."

Tautou subsequently appeared in several films, including *God is Great, I'm Not, He Loves Me ... He Loves Me Not,* and *The Spanish Apartment*, as well as four others. In *Dirty Pretty Things*, directed by Stephen

Frears. Tautou played Senay, a young Turkish woman who is in England illegally, and who is struggling to make ends meet by working in a hotel. Actor Chiwetel Ejiofor played Okwe, a Nigerian illegal immigrant, who drives a cab when he is not working as an overnight clerk in the hotel. Together, they witness the criminal activity of their corrupt boss, who rents out empty hotel rooms for illegal activities; because they fear being deported, they keep quiet about this until his schemes threaten their lives.

For the role, Tautou not only had to learn to speak English, but also had to learn to speak it with a Turkish accent as well as to hide her French accent. She told the Movie City News, "It took an enormous amount of work.…. As part of my preparations, I asked to meet some Turkish women, so I could learn the rhythms of their speech." Her speech coach, Penny Dyer, taped the conversations with these women and played them over and over. After this, they went over the entire script, highlighting every vowel and consonant with different–colored markers, so that Tautou would know how to pronounce them. She noted, "The most difficult thing for me was not knowing if I was saying something right, or not, because I knew so little English to begin with." Tautou spent only three weeks preparing for the role, rehearsing each scene shortly before it was filmed. She also commented that because of her success in the role, as well as her dark hair and eyes, many observers of her work think she has a non–French ethnic origin, that she might be part–Turkish, or that she "could be from North Africa or parts of Asia, or Italy and Spain," she told Movie City News. "But, as far as I know, I'm 100–percent French."

Part of Tautou's success in the role of Senay may have come from her compassion for people like her character. She told Aboutfilm.com's Cavagna, "When you don't have any identity, any money, any passport, any work, you are nothing. There's many people who sleep on sidewalks and in their countries they were doctors, lawyers. This is very common." As an example, she cited the life of one of the cast members in the film, a woman who had been an actress in her home country and who came to London 20 years ago. Despite her acting background, she worked as a cleaning person for two decades until she got the chance to act again in *Dirty Pretty Things*.

Tautou teamed with director Jeunet again to produce *A Very Long Engagement*. The film, produced in France, included a role played by American actress Jodie Foster, who speaks French in the film. Tautou stars as Mathilde Donnay, a stubborn young woman who sets out to find out the truth about her soldier fiance, who disappeared at the end of World War I. *A Very Long Engagement* was scheduled for release in 2004.

Although Tautou did not rule out working in the United States on American films, she admitted to having turned down several offers from Hollywood. She told Aboutfilm.com's Cavagna, "When you don't speak English, you need to be brave to do a movie in English, because you think, 'Why I am going to do a movie in a foreign language? I'm going to [stink]. Where is the interest?'" In addition, according to a profile at Internet Movie Database, Tautou noted that she would be choosy about accepting such roles if she ever did take one, accepting only those that met her standards: "I certainly don't want to be in *Thingy Blah Blah 3*, if you know what I mean." She told Aboutfilm.com's Cavagna that she wasn't interested in her life as a career in the material sense, and that the American movie scene tended to overemphasize money: "You don't need to earn 20 million dollars. But, I think that if you do an American movie it's important to earn some money, but in a stupid way, to be respected." For herself, she said, "I'm interested in this work only because of the meaning I can make. After each experience, you grow up, you get enriched … and you don't know how you're going to be in six months, you don't know what you're going to want, what you're going to need."

Sources

Periodicals

Courier–Mail (Brisbane, Australia), December 1, 2001, p. M12.
People, August 25, 2003, p. 125.

Online

"An Interview with Audrey Tautou," Movie City News, http://www.moviecitynews.com/Interviews/tautou.htm (November 17, 2003).
"Audrey Tautou, Amelie Interview," Dealmemo.com, http://www.dealmemo.com/Interview/Audrey_Tautou_Amelie.htm (November 17, 2003).
"Biography for Audrey Tautou," Internet Movie Database, http://www.imdb.com/name/nm0851582/bio/ (November 17, 2003).
"Profile and Interview: Audrey Tautou," Aboutfilm.com, http://www.aboutfilm.com/features/tautou/feature.htm (November 17, 2003).

—*Kelly Winters*

Nancy Tellem

President of CBS Entertainment and CBS Productions

Born c. 1953; married to Arn Tellem (a sports agent); children: Mike, Matty (son), Eric. *Education:* Received undergraduate degree from University of California—Berkeley, and J.D. from the Hastings College of Law.

Addresses: *Office*—CBS Entertainment, 7800 Beverly Blvd., Los Angeles, CA 90036.

Career

Intern to Oakland, California, congressman Ron Dellums, in Washington, DC, 1974; worked in the legal–affairs department of Lorimar Television; served as executive vice president of business and financial affairs at Warner Bros. Television; CBS Productions President, 1997—, and president of CBS Entertainment, August, 1998—.

Sidelights

Nancy Tellem is president of CBS Entertainment, the division of the broadcast network that brings shows like *Survivor* and *Joan of Arcadia* to the airwaves. Tellem, who worked closely with former network president Les Moonves, has overseen programming for CBS's prime–time, daytime, late–night, and Saturday–morning line–up since 1998. She was named No. 3 on the Power 100 list in the 2003 Women in Entertainment issue of the *Hollywood Reporter,* which called her "a linchpin of the executive team that has orchestrated one of the great turnaround stories in network television history."

Born in the early 1950s, Tellem earned an undergraduate degree from the University of California at Berkeley, and spent one summer as a Capitol Hill intern for an Oakland, California, legislator. She went on to law school at San Francisco's Hastings College of Law, part of the University of California system, and found her niche working in the legal–affairs department of Lorimar Television, one of the most successful production companies of the 1980s. Lorimar eventually morphed into Warner Bros. Television (WBTV), and Tellem held a similar position there.

Tellem knew Moonves from her Lorimar days, and when Moonves became head of WBTV, he promoted her to executive vice president for business and financial affairs. Moonves jumped ship to CBS in 1995 to become head of its entertainment division, and two years later gave Tellem her first semi–creative post as head of CBS Productions, the unit that created original shows for the network. In early 1998 Moonves was made network president, and in August of that year named Tellem to succeed him as president of CBS Entertainment.

Tellem added the new title to concurrent duties as head of CBS Productions, which she ran with Moonves's input. Though she was now ranked as the most powerful female executive in network television, some industry insiders sniped that she was merely an aide–de–camp to Moonves. Tellem scoffed at such talk in an interview with Lawrie Mifflin of the *New York Times.* "That's a very male approach, to say 'He'll retain power,' like 'He gets all the marbles.' To me, this is a job that I do, Leslie does, and our creative team does. It's a collaborative group, and our objectives are all the same."

At the time, Tellem was only the second woman ever to hold the top entertainment post at a major broadcast network, after the notable, highly publicized failure of ABC's Jamie Tarses a few years earlier. Mifflin termed Tellem part of a new breed of television executives, "women in their forties who have climbed to executive heights without the burden of being outsiders," the New York Times journalist noted, "earning M.B.A.'s, learning the ropes on roughly equal footing with their male peers, establishing themselves as team players rather than individuals."

CBS's historic prime–time turnaround under Tellem and Moonves took time to implement. There were some early failures before Survivor, Everybody Loves Raymond, and Joan of Arcadia, and it was Tellem's job to tell the writers, actors, and technical staff that a show was going to be axed. She said in the Hollywood Reporter article that "making those calls can be incredibly difficult," but also noted the setbacks helped her help CBS find its footing eventually. "The truth of the matter is, you learn more from your failures than from your successes," she reflected.

Tellem had made CBS Productions the third–largest studio supplier in Hollywood by 2002, but she did encounter problems in her other post as entertainment president with several shows that were said to have transgressed the border between entertainment and poor taste. The first was Hitler: The Rise of Evil, which starred Robert Carlyle as Nazi German dictator Adolf Hitler. The series was based on an acclaimed book by British historian Ian Kershaw, but rabbis and other leaders in the Jewish community excoriated the network for the series, which aired during the May ratings sweeps period in 2003.

Tellem defended the miniseries, noting that it was restricted to presenting Hitler's life and career up to the onset of war in 1939. She also noted that she was the daughter of European Jews who met at medical school in Vienna, Austria, and escaped the continent when Nazi Germany began its campaign to eradicate Europe's Jewish population in the late 1930s. Many relatives on both sides of her family died in concentration camps during World War II. As she told a 2002 gathering of television critics, in her parents' home, the subject of the Holocaust was a delicate one. "The way I was brought up, even mentioning the word gave me chills," Knight Ridder/Tribune News Service writer Gail Shister quoted her as saying. "It all comes down to how it's handled. I'm a political–science buff. I'm more focused on seeing how such a figure can rise to power."

In 2003, Tellem, Moonves, and CBS also came under fire for a planned reality–TV remake of the Beverly Hillbillies, the hit 1960s sitcom about an Ozark Mountain family who become unexpected oil barons and move to the posh Los Angeles suburb. The network decided to cancel a 2004 miniseries on former President Ronald Reagan and his wife just weeks before it was set to air in February. Finally, Tellem took heat for a planned remake of the miniseries Helter Skelter, based on the bestselling book by Vincent Bugliosi about the brutal series of murders in southern California in the late 1960s by Charles Manson and his acolytes. On June 1, 2004, Tellem lost one of her associates when Moonves was named co–president and co–chief operating officer of Viacom, Inc., the parent company of CBS.

Tellem was happy that the network had some notable successes of a less controversial nature, including Joan of Arcadia, about a teenager who converses with God. She is married with three sons, and now has a counterpart at ABC, Susan Lyne, who heads entertainment programming there. Tellem's husband is high–profile sports agent Arn Tellem, who has handled endorsements and contracts for such stars as Kobe Bryant. The Tellems met when both interned in Washington during the summer of 1974, and make their family home in Pacific Palisades, California. "Nancy runs my life," her husband told Sports Illustrated writer Franz Lidz, "and I'm a source of more stress for her."

Sources

Periodicals

Broadcasting & Cable, August 24, 1998, p. 40; September 25, 2000, p. 12; January 21, 2002, p. 26.
Buffalo News, January 17, 2003, p. C7.
Daily News (Los Angeles, CA), January 20, 2004, p. U8.
Daily Variety, September 12, 2003, p. A22.
Electronic Media, October 14, 2002, p. 10.
Entertainment Weekly, April 14, 2000, p. 60.
Financial Times, January 21, 2004, p. 12.
Hollywood Reporter, December 2, 2003.
Knight–Ridder/Tribune News Service, July 15, 2002.
MediaWeek, April 12, 2004, p. 24.
New York Times, August 24, 1998.
Sports Illustrated, May 27, 2002, p. 72.

Online

"Top Entertainment Exec Shares Career Insights," Wall Street Journal, http://www.collegejournal.com/careerpaths/findcareerpath/20040331-murphy.html (April 29, 2004).

—Carol Brennan

Robert L. Tillman

President, Chief Executive Officer, and Chairman of Lowe's

B orn c. 1944. *Education:* University of North Carolina, Wilmington (UNCW), B.S.; two–year Joint Management Program of UNCW and American Management Association.

Addresses: *Office*—c/o Lowe's Companies, Inc., 1605 Curtis Bridge Rd., Wilkesboro, NC 28697.

Career

J oined Lowe's Companies as entry–level employee, 1962; worked his way up through the ranks to manager of one of the chain's most successful outlets in Wilmington, North Carolina; joined ranks of corporate management in the 1980s, serving as senior vice president of merchandising and marketing, executive vice president of merchandising, and executive vice president and chief operating officer; named to company's board of directors in 1994; became president and chief executive officer, 1996; named chairman, 1998.

Sidelights

W ith nearly 900 stores in 45 states, Lowe's Companies Inc. is the second largest home improvement chain in the United States and the country's 14th largest retailer. Largely responsible for the North Carolina–based company's phenomenal growth over the last decade has been Robert L. Tillman, president and chief executive officer of Lowe's since 1996 and its chairman since 1998. Un-

der Tillman's leadership, the Lowe's chain launched its big–store strategy, which pits it squarely against Home Depot, the industry leader. Although Home Depot is still more than twice the size of Lowe's, the smaller company has experienced extremely strong growth in recent years. In fiscal 2002, which ended January 31, 2003, Lowe's reported net income was $1.47 billion on sales of almost $26.5 billion, an increase of 43.8 percent over profit of slightly more than $1 billion a year earlier. This compared with Home Depot's fiscal 2002 net income of almost $3.7 billion on revenue of $58.2 billion, an increase of 20.4 percent over profit for fiscal 2001.

In an era when management–level personnel move from company to company at the drop of a hat, Tillman has spent his entire career with Lowe's, first joining the company as an entry–level employee in 1962. He first attracted attention from Lowe's corporate managers as the successful manager of one of the chain's outlets in Wilmington, North Carolina. Founded in 1946—more than three decades before Home Depot, which got its start in 1979—Lowe's opened its first hardware store in North Wilkesboro, North Carolina. Although it soon expanded into nearby states, for the first few decades of its existence the company focused its marketing mix on hardware, appliances, and building materials to cater to the post–war building boom. Building contractors made up the bulk of Lowe's customer base.

In 1980 Lowe's introduced its new RSVP (Retail Sales Volume and Profit) strategy, at the heart of which was a concerted effort to broaden the company's revenue base beyond building contractors to include the burgeoning do–it–yourself market. Tillman at that time was the charismatic manager of the chain's Wilmington store, one of its most successful RSVP operations. For his part, Tillman used his clout as one of the chain's star store managers to urge Lowe's management to think even bigger, building still larger stories that would offer consumers one–stop shopping for all their home improvement needs.

Later in the 1980s Tillman was plucked from the ranks of store managers and fast–tracked into corporate management, serving in a variety of marketing and merchandising positions, including senior vice president of merchandising and marketing and executive vice president of merchandising. He subsequently was named vice president and chief operating officer, in which positions he continued until 1996, when he was elected president and chief executive officer (CEO). Tillman had been tapped to join the Lowe's board of directors in 1994, and in 1998 he was given the additional responsibility of corporate chairman. After becoming CEO in the late 1990s, Tillman quickly set to work to turn his vision of a nationwide chair of super–stores into reality.

By mid–2003, Lowe's, which for decades had been seen largely as a regional hardware store operator, confined mostly to the Southeast, had spread into 45 states. Most of its growth west of the Mississippi came under Tillman's leadership, as did the company's most impressive increases in revenue and earnings. Lowe's expansion into the western United States began the year after Tillman took over as CEO when the company committed more than $1.5 billion to the creation of 100 new stores in the West. First targeted were such prime markets in Arizona, California, and Nevada as Phoenix, Tucson, Los Angeles, San Diego, and Las Vegas. Of Lowe's rationale for the westward expansion, Tillman told PR Newswire, "Heading west means introducing Lowe's to one of the home improvement industry's strongest growth regions. Moving now allows Lowe's to establish a beachhead on the West Coast, enabling our company to continue growing into new markets throughout the United States."

Lowe's move into the West was given a major boost in November of 1998 when the North Carolina–based company announced its acquisition of Eagle Hardware, a chain of 32 warehouse–scale home improvement stores confined to nine states of the western United States. In an interview with AP Online, Tillman said, "This merger allows Lowe's to accel-

erate our West Coast expansion program and gives us an immediate presence in a number of key metropolitan markets in the West." The takeover of Eagle, acquired in a $1 billion stock swap, also marked a change in strategy for Lowe's, which previously had not used acquisition to grow its network of retail outlets. Talking to Deborah Marchini of CNNfn's *Business Day,* Tillman explained that the acquisition made sense because Lowe's had no overlap with Eagle, which was based in the Pacific Northwest. "The timing was correct for Eagle and also for Lowe's to make the acquisition. It embellishes our western expansion...."

According to *BusinessWeek,* which in January of 2003 named Tillman one of corporate America's best managers, part of Lowe's recent success can be attributed to its CEO's realization that women play a key role in home improvement projects. Acting on research that showed women initiate 80 percent of home projects, Tillman moved aggressively to give Lowe's outlets greater appeal to female customers. Stores were brightened up and store offerings adjusted to include more appliances, high–end bathroom fixtures, and Laura Ashley paints.

Although Lowe's profit jumped by nearly 22 percent in the first quarter of fiscal 2003 (which ended April 30, 2003), same–store sales showed almost no increase at all, a disappointing performance attributed largely to bad weather. Total sales for the quarter were $7.2 billion, up eleven percent from the previous year, but almost all of that increase came from new stores that were not in operation a year earlier. Tillman, however, was upbeat in his assessment of the longer–term future, telling Paul Nowell of AP Online, "We remain confident that home improvement consumers will continue to invest in their homes. There are many positive signs and the housing market is strong as mortgage rates remain at 40–year lows."

On April 5, 2004, Lowe's Co. Inc. announced that Tillman would retire as chief executive officer and chairman on January 28, 2005. He was scheduled to be replaced by current Lowe's president, Robert Niblock.

Sources

Books

Complete Marquis Who's Who, Marquis Who's Who, 2003.

Periodicals

BusinessWeek, January 13, 2003, p. 63.
PR Newswire, April 21, 1998; May 30, 2003.

Online

AP Online, November 23, 1998; June 5, 2002; May 19, 2003.
Biography Resource Center Online, Gale Group, 2001.
"Improving Home Improvement," Lowe's, http://www.lowes.com/lkn?action=pg&p=About Lowes/history (July 13, 2003).

"Management Biography: Robert L. Tillman," Shareholder.com, http://www.shareholder.com/lowes/BioDetail.cfm?BioID=3791&BioType=Mgmt (July 14, 2003).

Transcripts

Business Day, CNNfn, November 25, 1998.
CNBC/Dow Jones Business Video, February 26, 2001.

—Don Amerman

Tim Tully

Neurobiologist

Born c. 1954, in Washington, IL; son of William P. and Virginia L. Tully; married Nance; children: Benjamin, Schuyler (son). *Education:* University of Illinois, B.S., 1976; University of Illinois, Ph.D., 1981.

Addresses: *Office*—Cold Spring Harbor Laboratory, One Bungtown Rd., Cold Spring Harbor, NY 11724.

Career

Completed Ph.D. at University of Illinois, 1981; postdoctoral work at Princeton, 1981–85; assistant professor at Brandeis University, 1987–91; hired at Cold Spring Harbor Laboratory, 1991; founded Helicon Therapeutics, where he serves as Chief Scientific Officer, 1997.

Member: Editorial advisory board, *Behavioral Neuroscience,* 1989–2001; editorial advisory board, *Behavior Genetics,* 1992—; editorial advisory board, *Learning & Memory,* 1995—; board of trustees, The Swartz Foundation, 1997–2000; board of directors, Helicon Therapeutics, 1997—; editorial advisory board, *Genes, Brain and Behavior,* 2001—; scientific review board, Institute for the Study of Aging, 2001—; scientific advisory board, Joekai Biotech Co., 2003—.

Awards: McKnight Scholars Award in Neuroscience, Brandeis University, 1987–90; John Merck Scholarship in the Biology of Developmental Disabilities in Children, 1990–94; Decade of the Brain Award, American Association of Neurology, 1999.

Sidelights

Tim Tully studies fruit fly memory, and hopes to gain useful insight into the workings of the human mind. He works at Cold Springs Harbor Laboratory on Long Island, New York, and also founded a private company, Helicon Therapeutics, which is developing memory enhancement drugs for human use. Tully invented a mechanized system for training fruit flies, enabling him to speed up what had been long and painstaking experiments. Tully was then able to identify a specific protein involved in making memories. Breeding flies with a specific mutation in this protein, Tully created "superflies" that learned a simple scent recognition test ten times faster than normal fruit flies. This was the world's first case of genetically enhanced memory. Tully also bred fruit flies with learning disabilities. Tully theorized that the way memory works on a molecular level is not very different from species to species. His work with fruit flies spawned research on chemicals that may help people who have memory impairment disorders such as Alzheimer's disease.

Tully grew up in Washington, Illinois, in a family of six children. Tully's close family also included 27 first cousins. Tully claimed he came to understand the basic laws of genetic inheritance from his first-hand observations of his family members. Another childhood experience that influenced his career path was an accident he suffered on Christmas Day in 1968. Tully hit his head while sledding and was knocked unconscious. When he recovered, he had a gap in his memory. He could remember everything up until December 12, but the following weeks were gone, including his memory of the presents he had opened that Christmas morning. His work as an adult combined genetics with the study of memory. Tully studied psychology and biology and the University of Illinois in Champagne–Urbana, and graduated with a double degree. He stayed at the University of Illinois for his graduate work, and earned his Ph.D. in genetics in 1981. Tully then moved to the East Coast, first to postdoctoral study at Princeton, and then in 1987 taking an assistant professorship at Brandeis University, in Waltham, Massachusetts, near Boston.

Looking only at his discoveries, Tully's work seems exciting, but the day–to–day labor of working with fruit flies was tedious and slow. Geneticists had been studying learning in fruit flies since the 1970s, when a biologist at the California Institute of Technology discovered that their behavior could be trained. The basis for fruit fly training went even further back, to the early 20th century Russian scientist Petrovich Pavlov. In Pavlov's famous experiment, he fed hungry dogs after ringing a bell. He found that the dogs learned to associate the sound of the bell with food, and they would salivate whenever they heard the ring. Similarly, the California biologist found that fruit flies could be taught to associate odors with an electric stimulus. Researchers exposed the flies to an odor, and then administered an electric shock. The flies learned to associate the odor with the shock, and demonstrated their learning by flying away from the odor. Researchers were able to breed several strains of fruit fly that had trouble learning. But it was not entirely clear whether these deficient flies had difficulties with memory, or whether they had some other problem. By the late 1980s, some scientists were skeptical that fruit fly experiments would ever be precise enough to yield interesting results. Tully was able to take a big step forward by first mechanizing the fruit fly training process. This did two things: It standardized the training, so the experiments were more reliable, and it freed Tully from the exacting work of dealing with the flies hour after hour. With his computerized system, a machine stimulated the flies at preprogrammed intervals, allowing much bigger scale, more complex experiments than had been attempted before.

In 1991, Tully took a position at Cold Spring Harbor Laboratories, a leading neuroscience research institute. In his new large and well–funded lab, Tully and his colleagues began to focus on specific genes related to memory in fruit flies. Tully and Jerry Yin eventually identified a gene that encoded a protein known as CREB. CREB seemed to be cru-cial to the formation of different types of memory, from short term to long term. With careful breeding, Tully and Yin produced flies that had distinct mutations in the gene that controlled CREB. In flies where the CREB protein was essentially turned off, the creatures showed seriously impaired memory formation. In 1994 Tully published his research on fruit flies which had the CREB protein permanently switched on, as it were. These flies seemed to exhibit photographic memory. Whereas normal fruit flies had to be exposed to an odor and accompanying electric shock ten times in order to learn to avoid the odor, Tully's "superflies" learned after only one session. Other scientists confirmed the importance of CREB by performing similar studies on sea slugs and mice.

Tully's superfly research hinted that specific chemicals could be used to enhance memory. This was exceedingly important for the millions of people afflicted with Alzheimer's disease and other memory–impairment syndromes. While continuing to work at Cold Spring Harbor, Tully formed a private pharmaceutical research company, Helicon Therapeutics, in 1997. The potential market for memory–enhancing drugs was enormous, and Helicon quickly raised more than $20 million in private stock placements. The company screened some 200,000 compounds, looking for chemicals that might safely boost CREB and so enhance memory in humans. By 2004 the company had one potential drug in preclinical trials, meaning it was possibly only a few years away from releasing an important new pharmaceutical.

Tully's work held out hope for people with many types of brain disorders, from strokes to autism to head injury, and for people concerned with the common mild memory impairment that comes with age. Researchers also speculated that someday, even people with normal memory might be able to take a pill to make them be able to learn better. In the meantime, Tully maintained a down–to–earth attitude about what people should do to preserve their memories. He advised respondents to a science hotline question–and–answer session to get plenty of physical exercise as the best way to preserve brain function into old age. He also suggested that keeping mentally active might help preserve short–term memory function.

Tully was also keenly aware that genetic work on brain function had its detractors. As a student at the University of Illinois, he had taken part in a study of scientific racism, and he was well aware of the animosity between people who believed genes controlled intelligence and the other camp, which held that environment was the prime influence on how smart individuals became. Tully believed that genetic and environmental interactions were extremely complex. Just because memory and thus learning had a genetic element did not at all imply that intelligence was out of our individual control. His scientific work led him to advocate an educational system that put a premium on individual liberty. "The same educational method will not work the same for you and me," he told the *Christian Science Monitor*. "And if it doesn't work for me, it's not necessarily because I'm stupid. It's because there's a different system that will work better for me." His research opened up new vistas in the control of brain disorders, and also led to some moral thickets. If normal people could enhance their learning power with a pill, would that be cheating? Who would control access to such pills? These questions were broader than what one scientist alone could answer. Although Tully had kept his head down for years, focusing on flies in test tubes, he was well aware of the larger issues of his research.

Sources

Periodicals

Christian Science Monitor, August 27, 1998, p. B3.
Science, September 27, 1991, pp. 1486–87.
Sciences, May/June 1996, pp. 37–42.
Scientific American, September 2003, pp. 54–65.

Online

"A Gene You Won't Forget," Public Broadcasting System, http://www.pbs.org/saf/1202/hotline/hotline.htm (February 17, 2004).
"Tim Tully, Ph.D.," Cold Spring Harbor Laboratory, http://www.cshl.org/gradschool/tully_.html (February 17, 2004).
"Viagra for the Brain," *Forbes.com,* http://www.forbes.com/global/2002/0204/060_print.html (February 17, 2004).

—A. Woodward

Gabrielle Union

Actress

Born Gabrielle Monique Union, October 29, 1972, in Omaha, NB; daughter of Sylvester E. (a military sergeant and business executive) and Teresa (a phone company manager) Union; married Chris Howard (a sports therapist), May 5, 2001. *Education:* Attended the University of Nebraska–Lincoln; University of California at Los Angeles, B.S. (sociology), c. 1995; attended Cuesta College, San Luis Obispo, CA.

Addresses: *Fan mail*—4570 Van Nuys Blvd., Ste. 171, Sherman Oaks, CA 91403.

Career

Actress in films, including: *She's All That*, 1999; *10 Things I Hate About You*, 1999; *Love & Basketball*, 2000; *Bring It On*, 2000; *The Brothers*, 2001; *Two Can Play That Game*, 2001; *Deliver Us from Eva*, 2002; *Abandon*, 2002; *Welcome to Collinwood*, 2002; *Cradle 2 the Grave*, 2003; *Bad Boys II*, 2003. Television appearances include: *7th Heaven*, 1996–99; *H–E Double Hockey Sticks* (movie), 1999; *City of Angels*, 2000. Television guest appearances include: *Saved by the Bell: The New Class*, 1995; *Moesha*, 1996; *Malibu Shores*, 1996; *Star Trek: Deep Space Nine*, 1997; *ER*, 2000; *Friends*, 2001; *Sister, Sister*; *Clueless*; *Good Behavior*; *Dave's World*; *Hitz*.

Awards: AOL Time Warner Rising Star Award, American Black Film Festival's Film Life Movie Awards, 2003.

Steve Granitz/WireImage.com

Sidelights

Although actress Gabrielle Union did not intend to have a career in acting, an internship at a modeling agency in Los Angeles, California, led to a guest role on the television series *Saved by the Bell: The New Class* in 1995, a number of other television roles, and a promising film career. After appearing in a number of roles in teen movies such as 1999's *She's All That* and 2000's *Bring It On*, Union had roles in successful ensemble works, including 2001's *Two Can Play That Game* and 2002's *Deliver Us from Eva*. She co–starred in her first blockbuster film *Bad Boys II* in 2003. Union also had the distinction of being the first African–American actor or actress to appear on NBC's hit situation comedy *Friends* in 2001, as a woman who dated two of the male characters on the show.

Union is the middle of three daughters of Sylvester E. Union, and his wife, Teresa; she was born in 1972. Union's father served in the military to the rank of sergeant, and later worked as a manager at Western Union and AT&T. Union's mother also worked as a manager at the phone company. Union was born into one of the most famous black families in Omaha, Nebraska, a descendant of Emma Early Bryant–Fisher.

In 1981, Union's father was transferred to an office in Pleasanton, California, where she spent the rest of her childhood. Though she grew up in California, she spent her summers in Nebraska. Her heartland roots remained important to her. Union told Tony Moton of the *Omaha World Herald,* "From the time we left, it was important to my parents I stay familiar with my family. Basically, I didn't want to lose my Midwestern values. Home is where the heart is, and we are very much Nebraskans, rather than Californians."

In both Nebraska and California, sports were an important part of Union's childhood. She played basketball, softball, and soccer, among other sports. By the time she was in high school, she focused on soccer, basketball, and track. Union's father especially encouraged her in her pursuit of athletics, but taught her a lesson that helped her when she began acting in Hollywood. Union told Clarissa Cruz in *Entertainment Weekly,* "[My father] said, 'You are the only black person in the whole class. You're gonna have to prove to them every day that you're just as smart, if not smarter. Just as good, if not better. Just as fast, if not faster.' So not only am I trying to beat all my classmates, I'm trying to prove to my dad that I'm living up to his expectations."

After graduating from high school in Pleasanton, Union went back to Nebraska for college. She spent a semester at the University of Nebraska–Lincoln, where she played soccer. She then returned to California, where she transferred to the University of California at Los Angeles (UCLA). Union also attended Cuesta College in San Luis Obispo, California.

While a young college student, Union was the victim of a horrific crime. In 1992, when she was 19 years old, Union had a summer job at a Payless shoe store. As she was closing the store one night, a man with a gun came in, robbed the store, and sexually assaulted her. The rapist was an employee of another Payless store and had also raped another female Payless employee. He later turned himself in, and was convicted of the crime. Because Payless had not told its employees of the potential problem, Union was able to win a lawsuit against the company for gross negligence. Union was able to overcome the emotional trauma of the assault with the help of a college rape survivor group, and she later spoke out in support of rape victims after she began her acting career.

Union studied sociology at UCLA, and intended to go to law school after completing her degree. During her senior year, she had an internship at a mod-

eling agency, where she was often mistaken for a model. After Union earned her bachelor's degree, her former employer asked her if she wanted to try modeling. Facing the burden of student loans and still hoping to go do law school, she agreed. This led to an acting career. Though she had no training in drama, Union soon had an agent and was auditioning for acting roles.

On Union's first audition, she impressed the casting agent and landed her first television role: a guest spot on the syndicated show *Saved by the Bell: The New Class.* Union continued to work in television in the late 1990s, primarily in guest–starring roles on programs such as *Sister, Sister* and *Moesha.* In 1996, Union had her first recurring role on television, playing Keesha Hamilton, the eldest daughter of the Reverend Hamilton, an African Methodist Episcopal minister, on the family oriented drama *7th Heaven.* She credited her success in acting in part to her photographic memory as well as her outgoing personality.

In 1999, Union landed her first film role in the teen comedy *She's All That,* as Katie, the mean friend of the lead played by Freddie Prinze, Jr. Many of Union's early film roles were as teenagers, though by this time Union was in her mid–twenties. Despite her age, she was believable in these parts because of her youthful appearance. Other roles Union played in the teen genre included Chastity in 1999's *10 Things I Hate About You* and a groupie after Omar Epps' character Q in 2000's *Love & Basketball.*

Many of Union's teen roles were as mean–spirited girls. In *10 Things I Hate About You*—a modern teen version of William Shakespeare's play *The Taming of the Shrew*—Union's Chastity betrays her best friend Bianca (played by Larisa Oleynik) by stealing her boyfriend. Of her roles as the bad girl in teen movies, Union told the *Omaha World–Herald*'s Moton, "I would rather play a snobby black girl going to school and being [cruel] rather than being a drug dealer's pregnant girlfriend. I don't want to be involved in anything that perpetuates stereotypes of minorities."

In 2000, Union appeared in her breakthrough film, *Bring It On.* While this was again a teen flick, it was also athletic, focusing on cheerleading, and Union had a leading role. She played Isis, the head of an inner–city cheerleading squad, the Comets. She and her team aspire to make the national competition with their flashy moves despite the lack of funds to get there. Even though Union had been athletic for much of her life, she found that training for the role was demanding. Her hard work paid off when her performance was praised in the press, and *Bring It On* did well at the box office.

After this teen film role, Union briefly returned to television for her first lead in a television series. She played Dr. Courtney Ellis on the short–lived medical drama series *City of Angels* on CBS in 2000. Though the show was cancelled after a half season, Union was the primary female and it was her first real adult role. The following year, she had a breakthrough role as the first black character in her guest–starring role on the long–running NBC hit situation comedy *Friends*. Her character dated two of the male leads, Joey and Ross, on the show.

When Union returned to film in 2001, she appeared in adult roles in several ensemble films featuring primarily African–American casts. In 2001's *The Brothers,* a film about four men and their relationships with women, Union played freelance photographer Denise Johnson, an independent and self–sufficient woman. Union's Johnson is attempting to convince her boyfriend, a pediatrician named Jackson (played by Morris Chestnut) to commit to a relationship, though this was something he has desperately shied away from as he preferred to play the field. Later that year, Union appeared in the ensemble comedy *Two Can Play That Game* as Conny, a woman attempting to steal Keith, the boyfriend of the main character and narrator, Shante Smith (played by Vivica A. Fox). Smith declares war to win back her man from Conny, her professional nemesis.

As Union's professional life continued to soar, her personal life was also blossoming. On May 5, 2001, she married Chris Howard, a former professional football player who had played for the Jacksonville Jaguars. The running back became a sport therapist and worked for Fox Sports after his athletic career ended. The pair had met at a party in Jacksonville in 1999.

In 2002, Union had the leading role in another black ensemble comedy, *Deliver Us from Eva.* As the title character, Eva Dandridge, she played the oldest of four sisters who gave up her life to raise them after the death of their parents in a car accident. When the movie begins, the women are adults, but Union's Eva still rules their lives. The younger sisters' boyfriends and husbands conspire to get rid of Eva by paying Ray (played by rapper/actor LL Cool J) to romance her and get her out of town. They eventually fall in love with each other in this loose take on Shakespeare's *Taming of the Shrew.*

Union's next film roles were smaller, but more challenging and diverse. In 2002, she played the best friend of the lead character played by Katie Holmes in *Abandon,* a psychological thriller set at a college. Union was similarly challenged in that year's *Welcome to Collinwood,* playing a teenaged blind girl named Michelle. The film starred William H. Macy, and her character was the younger sister of a character played by Isaiah Washington. Union researched the role by spending time with a young, blind, African–American girl at the Braille Institute. Union went to the opposite end of the movie spectrum in 2003, when she co–starred in the action film *Cradle 2 the Grave,* which also featured Chinese martial arts star Jet Li and rapper/actor DMX. This film, which opened at number one at the box office, focused on a jewel theft.

While many of Union's films to this point in her career had been small to medium Hollywood pictures, in 2003, she co–starred in her first Hollywood blockbuster. She had the high–profile role of Sydney Burnett in *Bad Boys II,* the sequel to the 1995 box office smash, *Bad Boys.* Her character was the younger half–sister of Marcus Burnett (played by comedian/actor Martin Lawrence) and the love interest of his Miami Police Department partner, Mike Lowrey (played by actor/rapper Will Smith). Union's character is an undercover federal agent on assignment to bust a drug dealer in Miami, whose life and career are put in jeopardy. Union's success in this film was seen as paving the way to bigger projects in the future.

Though a rising starlet in Hollywood, Union remains down to earth, enjoying shopping at Target and sipping Capri Sun juice drink. She insists on living very practically, and remains levelheaded about money. Though her future in acting looks bright, she has plans if her career ever ends, including perhaps getting a master's degree. Of her prospects in show business, Mark Brown, the director of *Two Can Play That Game,* told Kelly Carter of *USA Today,* "She just came on the scene and exploded. I think she has a very promising future, certainly as a leading lady. She has star appeal."

Sources

Books

Celebrity Biographies, Baseline II, 2003.

Periodicals

Chicago Sun–Times, March 23, 2001, p. 31; September 7, 2001, p. 33; January 29, 2003, p. 39; February 7, 2003, p. 30.
Daily News (New York), February 7, 2003, p. 60.

Entertainment Weekly, April 25, 2003, pp. 71–72.
Hollywood Reporter, July 18, 2002.
Jet, February 17, 2003, p. 58; August 4, 2003, p. 34.
Newsday (New York), July 18, 2003, p. B3.
Omaha World Herald (Nebraska), July 11, 1999, p. 1e.
People, March 10, 2003, p. 37; August 11, 2003, pp. 75–76.
USA Today, September 7, 2001, p. 2E; July 18, 2003, p. 4E.

Online

"Sizzlin' Sixteen 2002," E! Online, http://www.eonline.com/Features/Features/Sizzlin2002/Girls/union.html (December 18, 2003).

—*A. Petruso*

Jay Walker

Chairman of Walker Digital Corporation

Born Jay S. Walker, November 5, 1955, in Yonkers, NY; married Eileen; children: two. *Education:* Cornell University, B.S., 1977.

Addresses: *Office*—Walker Digital LLC, 1177 High Ridge Rd., Ste. 128, Stamford, CT 06905.

Career

Started own newspaper while still in college; developed marketing for publishing industry journal *Folio*; founded Visual Technologies Corporation, 1981; founded Catalog Media Corporation, 1986; co–founded NewSub Services (later Synapse Group), 1991; founded Walker Digital, a business–model think tank, 1995; founded Priceline.com, 1998; left Priceline, 2001.

Awards: Named Entrepreneur of the Year by Ernst & Young, 1998; Direct Marketer of the Year, 1999; Yonkers Legend Award, 2002.

Sidelights

Jay Walker was one of the leading lights of the dot–com boom, founding what was one of the highest–flying Internet companies of the late 1990s, Priceline.com. The website debuted a unique marketing technique known as buyer–driven commerce, where consumers use the Internet to name the price they are willing to pay on given items, and their offers are either accepted or rejected. Priceline.com began by selling airline tickets. This provided a use-

ful way for airlines to fill seats that would otherwise go empty and consumers had a convenient way to buy discounted tickets. Priceline.com in turn spawned Priceline WebHouse Club Inc., which extended the buyer–driven model to gasoline and grocery sales.

Walker became an instant billionaire when Priceline went public in 1999, and at one time his net worth was estimated at more than $10 billion. However, the good times were short–lived. Walker was forced to close Priceline WebHouse in October of 2000 after it lost millions of dollars, and a few months later Walker stepped down from his chairmanship of Priceline. Priceline's stock price tumbled from a one–time high of $162 to below $3, and Walker sold his stake in the company to investors in Hong Kong. After being hailed as a genius, Walker found himself "the poster boy for the dot–com train wreck," in the words of Steven Levy, writing for *Newsweek*. Walker returned to running Walker Digital Corporation, a private research firm he started in 1995. Walker Digital specializes in developing patentable business models. Walker holds 200 patents in a variety of fields, one of few living inventors in the world with such a record. In 2003, he found himself in the headlines again as he boosted a plan to provide security to vulnerable sites such as power plants with an Internet–based surveillance system called US HomeGuard.

Walker grew up in Yonkers, New York, and showed his entrepreneurial spirit even as a young boy. Walker's mother's family had fled from Germany just before World War II, and his maternal grandfather had started a new life in New York as a Realtor. On the other side of the family, his paternal grandmother was one of the original investors in RCA. RCA was the seminal radio and television corporation that rode the crest of the Roaring Twenties stock boom much as Walker's Priceline was the toast of the Internet technology boom some 70 years later. Walker began honing his salesmanship while still an adolescent, going door–to–door hawking candles, seeds, and jelly. Later he delivered newspapers, covering a four–mile route by bike in all kinds of weather, 365 days a year. In high school, Walker was active in student government. He took on an unusual role as the student representative to contentious talks between the teacher's union and the city of Yonkers, as the municipal government tried to sort out a crisis in school funding.

Walker graduated from high school in 1973 and moved on to Cornell University, in Ithaca, New York. Though he graduated with a degree in industrial relations, Walker had a very unusual course of study. His career goal, he told Bob Chuvala of the *Westchester County Business Journal,* had been to become the administrative assistant for a wealthy person. "I decided I needed to learn a set of skills that would make me very attractive," he told Chuvala, "[to] somebody who was highly accomplished." Consequently, he learned how to take dictation, how to program a computer, the rudiments of contract and commercial law, and how to fly a single engine plane. Walker put all that aside briefly, dropping out of Cornell in order to launch a free weekly paper in Ithaca. Walker claimed to have overseen a paid staff of 175 and reached a circulation of 25,000 with his *Midweek Observer* before the local daily paper, run by the Gannett Corporation, decided to bring out its own weekly and so put Walker out of business. Walker returned to college courses and graduated in 1977, in debt to the tune of $150,000 for his failed media venture.

After graduation Walker moved to New York City and worked on the marketing staff of a magazine called *Folio,* a trade journal catering to periodical publishers. After four years at *Folio,* Walker went into business for himself again, starting a company he called Visual Technologies Corporation. Visual

Technologies sold interactive glass sculptures. The round objects responded to human touch by emitting flashes of electromagnetic light. They were sold through the Sharper Image catalogue, a vendor of high–end technological toys and gadgets. But by 1986 Visual Technologies filed for bankruptcy. The sculptures had proven too expensive to manufacture, and Visual Technologies went under, $5.3 million in the red. For the next two years, Walker ran another company, Catalog Media Corporation. His idea was to expand the marketing reach of catalogs, number one by selling ad space in them, just as in magazines, and number two, to sell catalogs in bookstores. Neither of these ideas seemed to catch fire. Catalog Media teamed up with Trans World Airlines (TWA) to offer discounted airfare coupons to consumers who purchased a set amount of goods from particular catalogs. TWA brought suit against Catalog Media, however, claiming that the company had violated the contract and was instead selling the discounted coupons in bulk to travel agents. The case was settled out of court, and Catalog Media disbanded in 1988.

Beginning in 1991, Walker formed a business partnership with Michael Loeb, who remained a staunch backer for years. Loeb was the son of *Fortune* magazine editor Marshall Loeb, who was also a significant investor in more than one Walker company. Walker and Michael Loeb went into business together with a company called NewSub Services (later Synapse Group), which marketed magazine subscriptions through credit card companies. This venture seemed to go well, but Walker was not content to stop there. In 1995 he founded yet another company, Walker Digital. He modeled this firm after Thomas Edison's laboratory in Menlo Park. The inventor was a hero to Walker, and he wanted his new company to be fertile ground for all kinds of inventions relating to new technologies and new ways of doing business. Not *what* was sold but *how* things were sold was the key element. One early Walker Digital business scheme was a way of increasing sales at fast–food outlets with software that could add incremental prices for side–dishes and extras. However, buyer–driven pricing was the real revolution to come out of Walker Digital.

Buyer–driven pricing as a modern sales technique evidently did not originate with Walker, but with Bill Perell, who founded the company Marketel in San Francisco in 1991. Marketel took bids over phone and fax for airline tickets, letting consumers offer what they were willing to pay, and matching the bids up with potential empty seats. But Marketel only lasted seven months before it went out of business. Walker revamped the idea for the Internet, and his company spent some $2.5 million developing a patent for the buyer–driven business model. Walker Digital received its patent in 1998, marking the first time the U.S. Patent Office had ever granted a patent for a business method. Walker had been talking up his idea to airlines while the patent was being considered, and by April of 1998 Priceline.com was ready for business. Airlines had thousands of empty seats every day, some on flights at odd times, some to unpopular destinations. Priceline.com allowed consumers to offer their own price for a ticket, though they had to accept whatever the airline gave them. This meant that flyers could get cheap tickets as long as they were willing to let the airline decide when they took off, and how many stops they made on the way. Walker dubbed the system "consumer freight," according to *Fortune*'s Peter Elkind.

In its first year, Priceline was only able to satisfy seven percent of its bidders, meaning only one in 14 people who tried Priceline got a seat. And Priceline was subsidizing the price of the tickets, losing roughly $30 on each ticket sold. But nothing could deter Jay Walker. He hired actor William Shatner, who had played Captain Kirk on the original *Star Trek* television show, to pitch Priceline. The actor was reluctant to talk to Walker, so Walker paid him to meet him for a drink in a Manhattan bar. Shatner was so impressed by Walker's vision that he signed on to do the ads, taking his $500,000 fee in stock. Walker also hired some veteran financiers to run the company. He hired Richard Braddock, former president of Citicorp, as chairman and chief executive, and Walker himself stepped back to an advisory role as vice chairman.

The fledgling company was losing money rapidly, but it seemed to have a stellar future. It attracted private capital, and in 1999 it went public. Priceline's share price started the day at $16 and went up and up. Two days later, Walker's share in the firm was valued at $5.2 billion, and Priceline itself was valued at $11.8 billion. Walker bought a third Mercedes–Benz and began building a baronial mansion. He was featured on magazine covers as the new guru of the Internet, and Priceline's stock continued to rise. Next Walker started a new company in late 1999, Priceline WebHouse, which extended the name–your–price model to sales of groceries and gasoline. WebHouse was plagued with technological problems and was unable to cope with the surge of enthusiastic users. It also subsidized the products it sold, losing about a million dollars every week. Walker sold his own Priceline stock to raise money for WebHouse, putting about $125 million in the ailing firm, while other private investors added some $30 million. Priceline's share price be-

gan to sink in late 2000 as investor enthusiasm for technology stocks waned. Shortly after moving WebHouse's staff into luxurious new headquarters, Walker announced that he was closing the company while he still had cash left to pay its vendors. On December 31, 2001, Walker announced that he was resigning from his vice chairman position at Priceline. Its share price had dived to only a couple of dollars, and Walker's own fortune shot from the billions to just the millions.

After selling his stake in Priceline to investors from Hong Kong, Walker returned to the company he founded in 1995, Walker Digital. Walker Digital continued to apply for patents for business models, as it worked with customers in the grocery, retail, restaurant, financial services, and gaming industries. Walker was apparently undaunted by his spectacular rise and fall. In 2003 he began hawking an Internet–based surveillance system to the United States government's Department of Homeland Security. His plan, called US HomeGuard, proposed putting cameras at some 47,000 sensitive points, including around water reservoirs, nuclear power plants, and airports. People would be paid to watch images from the camera at home, using an Internet hookup, and report any suspicious activity. Walker proposed that the government pay his company $40 million to set up a test network. *Wired* magazine's Jessie Scanlon called the idea "intriguing," and it was just the sort of unexpected thing Walker might be expected to spearhead.

Sources

Periodicals

Fortune, September 6, 1999, pp. 193–202; November 13, 2000, pp. 127–38.
Inc., November 1, 1998.
Newsweek, October 30, 2000, p. 78.
Travel Weekly, January 4, 2001, p. 22.
Wall Street Journal, April 1, 1999, p. B4; October 16, 2000, p. A1, p. A8; February 23, 2001, p. A1, p. A8.
Westchester County Business Journal, April 8, 2002, p. 26.
Wired, June 2003, p. 56.

Online

"About Jay Walker," WalkerDigital.com, http://www.walkerdigital.com/our–company–jay.asp (October 2, 2003).

—A. Woodward

Ben Wallace

Professional basketball player

Born September 10, 1974, in White Hall, AL; son of Sadie Wallace; married Chanda, 2001. *Education:* Attended Cuyahoga Community College; attended Virginia Union University. *Religion:* Baptist.

Addresses: *Office*—c/o Detroit Pistons, Palace of Auburn Hills, 2 Championship Dr., Auburn Hills, MI 48326.

Career

Signed as a free agent with Washington Bullets (later renamed Wizards), 1996; played for Orlando Magic, 1999–2000; played for Detroit Pistons, 2000—.

Awards: Division II All–American first–team honors; Defensive Player of the year, *Basketball Digest,* 2001–02; Defensive Player of the year, 2002–03; NBA All–Star team, 2003.

Sidelights

An undersized basketball center listed at six feet, nine inches tall, Ben Wallace has become a National Basketball Association (NBA) star the hard way—he earned it. Wallace signed as a free agent out of college with the Washington Wizards and has also played for the Orlando Magic and Detroit Pistons. Relying on hustle and a tough work ethic, Wallace has become a defensive standout in the league. *Sports Illustrated*'s L. Jon Wertheim called Wallace a "sequoia who plays both ends of the floor with inelegance and Rasputin persistence." Wallace earned Defensive Player of the Year honors for the 2001–02 and 2002–03 NBA seasons and was named to the league's All–Star team for the first time in 2003.

Wallace was born in the small town of White Hall, Alabama, the youngest of eight brothers and the tenth of eleven children. Wallace's penchant for playing hard and going after all loose balls on the basketball court started when he played pick–up games with his brothers. "As the little brother, I knew they weren't going to pass to me," Wallace told Wertheim in *Sports Illustrated.* "If I wanted to see the ball, I'd have to get a steal, a rebound, or save the ball from going out of bounds."

Wallace and his brothers worked on local farms to earn money. In the summer before his junior year in high school, Wallace wanted to attend a basketball camp held by Charles Oakley. So, to make the $50 fee for the camp, Wallace cut peoples' hair for $3 each.

After high school, Wallace entered Cuyahoga Community College in Ohio where he was a two–year starter. In the junior–college venue, Wallace quickly proved himself to be a man among boys, averaging 24 points per game (ppg), 17 rebounds per game (rpg), and seven block shots per game (bpg) in his second year. Wallace then went on to Virginia Union University, where he earned Division II All–American first–team honors as he led the team to the Final Four championship games in Division II college basketball.

Not a prolific scorer and suspected of being shorter than his listed height, Wallace was not drafted out of college by the NBA. The Washington Wizards, however, signed him as a free agent. Although he was nearly cut in training camp, Wallace made the team as a reserve forward, playing in only 34 games his first year. By the next year, however, Wallace began to assert himself and gained more playing time. He also became a fan favorite known especially for his defensive hustle in rebounding and blocking shots. During his three seasons at Washington, Wallace averaged 3.5 ppg, 5.2 rpg, and 1.2 bpg.

Despite his hustle and growing maturation as an NBA player, he was traded by Washington to the Orlando Magic in August of 1999. He played in 81 games for the Magic in the 1999–2000 season and averaged 8.2 rpg, which was twentieth in the league that year. The next year, however, Wallace was traded along with Chucky Atkins to the Detroit Pistons in exchange for their star player Grant Hill. During his first season with the Pistons, Wallace led the NBA with 13.2 rebounds a game and as the end of the 2002–2003 season approached, Wallace's name was being mentioned for the league's Most Valuable Player award. He became the first Piston player in franchise history to lead the club in rebounds, steals, and blocks.

Wallace's breakout year, however, came in the 2001–2002 season with the Detroit Pistons when *Basketball Digest* named him the NBA's Defensive Player of the Year. Playing as an undersize center, Wallace not only led the league in rebounding with an average of 13 per game, but also in blocked shots with 2.33 per game. As pointed out by Brett Ballantini in *Basketball Digest*, "seven–footers have owned" the shot blocking statistic since it was first recorded in 1973–74. Ballantini went on to note that Wallace "has broken that mold and shattered the notion of what a power forward (in center's clothing) can accomplish on the defensive end."

Rick Carlisle, former Pistons head coach, told Ballantini, "For a guy his size, the number of blocked shots he gets is phenomenal. Pound for pound, he's the best defensive player I've ever seen in my life."

That season, Wallace helped the Pistons to their first Central Division title since 1989–90. According to USA Basketball, the Pistons improved from a 32–win season in 2000–01 to a 50–win season, the first 50–plus–win season for the team since 1996–97.

Wallace is also only the fourth player in NBA basketball who won both the rebounding and block shot titles the same year, putting him in the company of NBA greats Kareem Abdul–Jabbar, Bill Walton, and Hakeem Olajuwon.

For a big man who plays ferocious defense, Wallace is a quiet and modest individual who devoutly practices his Baptist faith. Married and a father, Wallace also has maintained his childlike love of cartoons and remote–control cars. But, it is hard work that has made him a success on the court. "In the NBA, 75 percent of the players don't want to work," Charles Oakley told Wertheim in *Sports Illustrated*. "When you get a guy like Ben who goes overtime, he's going to stand out."

Wallace has become immensely popular among basketball fans, who immediately recognize his trademark flowing Afro haircut. In the NBA store in New York City, Wallace's jersey is in the top 20 in sales. He has done advertisements for American Express, Sega, and others.

Wallace led the league in rebounding for most of the 2003 season and hovered at third in blocked shots. On April 23, 2003, Wallace was named the 2002–03 Defensive Player of the Year, an honor that marked the second consecutive season he earned the award. He is only the sixth player in NBA history to win the award in back–to–back seasons; he recorded a league–leading 15.4 rebounds, the highest regular season average since Dennis Rodman's 16.1 rpg in 1996–97, 3.15 blocks (second in the NBA), and 1.42 steals per game. When he was named a member of the 2003 All–Star Game, he became the first undrafted player in NBA history to be voted a starter in the event. For the 2003–04 season, Wallace ranked number one in offensive rebounds, and number two in defensive rebounds, total rebounds, blocks, rebounds per game, and blocks per game. Wallace has one goal in mind: "[I'm] just staying aggressive, playing basketball with lots of energy and having fun working the game, without getting too caught up in this or that, Xs and Os," Wallace told Joanne C. Gerstner in the *Detroit News*. "I'm just at a point in time where I am not worrying about making mistakes." Wallace's hard work paid off: the Detroit Pistons defeated the Los Angeles Lakers in the NBA Finals in 2004. The Pistons won in five games, clinching the victory on June 15, 2004, with a 100-87 win. It was the team's first title in 14 years and Coach Larry Brown's first title ever.

Sources

Periodicals

Basketball Digest, Summer 2002.
Cincinnati Post, June 16, 2004, p. B1.
New York Post, June 16, 2004, p. 128.
Sports Illustrated, March 9, 1998; February 10, 2003, pp. 42–44.

Online

"Ben Wallace," NBA.com, http://www.nba.com/ playerfile/ben_wallace/index.html?nav=page (February 20, 2004).

"Ben Wallace," USA Basketball, http://www. usabasketball.com/biosmen/ben_wallace_bio. html (February 20, 2004).

"Wallace Does Much More than Just Take Up Space," *Philadelphia Daily News,* http://www. philly.com/mld/dailynews/sports/5179757.htm (February 20, 2004).

"Wallace Has Developed into Marketing Magnet," *Detroit News,* http://www.detnews.com/2003/ pistons/0302/21/h04–91177.htm (February 20, 2004).

"Wallace Keeps Getting Stronger," *Detroit News,* http://www.detnews.com/2003/pistons/0303/ 26/c06–119749.htm (February 20, 2004).

"Wallace Named Defensive Player of the Year," NBA.com, http://www.nba.com/news/wallace_ 030423.html (February 20, 2004).

—*Marie L. Thompson*

Mike Weir

Professional golfer

Born Michael Richard Weir, May 12, 1970, in Sarnia, Ontario, Canada; son of Richard and Rowie Weir; married Bricia; children: Elle Marisa, Lily. *Education:* Brigham Young University, Provo, Utah, B.S. (recreation management), 1993.

Addresses: *Home*—Draper, Utah. *Office*—c/o Professional Golfers' Association of America, 100 Avenue of the Champions, Palm Beach Gardens, FL 33418. *Website*—http://www.mikeweir.com/.

Career

Turned professional, 1992; joined the Canadian Tour, 1993; joined PGA's U.S. Tour, earning close to $220,000 his rookie season, 1998; won first PGA Tour title at Air Canada Championship, 1999; became first Canadian to play in the Presidents Cup team competition, 2000; won second victory on PGA Tour at WGC–American Express Championship, 2000; became first Canadian golfer to be rated among the world's top 10 after ending season with a win at the Tour Championship, 2001; dropped to 42nd in world rankings after lackluster play, 2002; vaulted to top ranks of world golfers with wins at Bob Hope Chrysler Classic, Nissan Open, and the Masters, 2003.

Awards: Canadian Juvenile Champion, 1986; Ontario Junior Champion, 1988; Ontario Amateur Champion, 1990, 1992; Western Athletic Conference Player of the Year, 1992; Infinity Players Championship winner, 1993; Canadian Tour Rookie of the Year, 1993; BC Tel Pacific Open winner, 1997; Canadian Masters winner, 1997; Air Canada Championship, 1999; World Golf Championship, 2000; Canadian Press Male Athlete of the Year, 2000, 2001; PGA Tour Championship, 2001; Canadian Press Male Athlete of the Year, 2001; Bob Hope Chrysler Classic winner, 2003; Nissan Open winner, 2003; Masters Tournament winner, 2003.

Sidelights

In just over a decade, Mike Weir has managed to become one of the greatest professional golfers ever to come out of Canada. The crowning glory of his pro golfing career thus far came in April of 2003 when he won the prestigious Masters Tournament in Augusta, Georgia, a feat no golfer from Canada had ever accomplished. But that was just the high point for Weir in 2003, who got his winning season off to an early start with victories at the Bob Hope Chrysler Classic and Nissan Open for prize monies of just over $1.6 million for those two tournaments alone. In fact, by the end of June, Weir's winnings on the 2003 PGA tour had topped $4 million, making him the number–one golfer on the tour in terms of earnings. Not too shabby for a golfer who in the mid–1990s was fighting tooth and nail just to stay in the pro game, struggling so hard that at times he was forced to call upon his wife to caddy for him.

Only minutes after his win at Augusta, Weir received a congratulatory phone call from an ecstatic Canadian Prime Minister Jean Chretien. According to the *Toronto Star,* Weir then told reporters, "It's such a thrill, something I've dreamed of since I was a little kid. This win is a win for me and my family, but it is a big win for Canada and Canadian golf and the fans that have been very supportive of me."

Weir's winning ways in 2003 make it somewhat hard to believe that the five–foot, nine–inch golfer struggled for years just to qualify for the PGA's U.S. Tour. "It took me five years going to [PGA] qualifying school to get out here," the golfer told Pierre LeBrun of the *Canadian Press,* as posted online at Slam! Sports. "And I can remember many times that I was missing cut after cut on the Australian Tour and I was by myself and didn't have any money. You're out on the range by yourself practicing until you can't see a shot five feet in front of you." Weir's persistence paid off, and in 1998 he made his debut on the PGA Tour. It was hardly the most auspicious beginning. He made only 13 of 27 cuts and wound up 131st on the tour's money list for 1998.

He was born Michael Richard Weir on May 12, 1970, in Sarnia in the southern part of the Canadian province of Ontario. His father, Richard, worked for a local chemical company, while his mother, Rowie, stayed at home to look after Mike and his two older brothers, Jim and Craig. Enthusiastic about sports as a boy, Weir's first great love was hockey. According to his father, Weir was also a fine baseball player. He was first introduced to the game of golf at the age of eight when his father took him to a par–three course not far from the family's home in Sarnia. Recognizing Mike's budding interest in—and natural aptitude for—golf, his father bought his youngest son a secondhand set of left–handed clubs. When the family moved a few years later to nearby Bright's Grove, Richard signed up for a family membership at the local Huron Oaks Golf Club so his three sons could have access to all the recreational facilities—an exercise center, swimming pool, and golf course—available there.

Mike was soon spending all his spare time at Huron Oaks. As the club's pro, Steve Bennett, recalled for Bob Verdi of *Golf Digest,* "He was there a lot, hitting balls, chipping, putting. Not many kids his age would spend hours practicing. Mike did." Since Weir showed up at the golf course almost every day, Bennett hired the boy to do odd jobs around the club. When Weir balked at picking up range balls in the rain, Bennett suspended him from his job for a week. "Mike never had to be talked to about responsibility after that," Bennett told Verdi.

Before long, Weir had set his sights on a career as a professional golfer. He was so serious about perfecting his game that at age 13 he wrote a letter to Jack Nicklaus to ask whether he should continue playing left–handed or make an effort to switch to his right; Nicklaus advised Weir to stick with his natural swing. Three years later, when he was 16, Weir won the 1986 Canadian juvenile championship. In 1988 he captured the Ontario junior championship and won the province's amateur championship two years after that. When it came time to pick a college, Weir decided to enroll at Brigham Young University (BYU) on a golf scholarship. The Mormon–supported school in Provo, Utah, had already helped to groom other Canadian golfers, including Brent Franklin, Jim Nelford, Richard Zokol, and Rick Gibson.

As a sophomore at BYU, Weir met his future wife, Bricia, a native of Mexico who grew up mostly in Los Angeles, California, and is herself an accomplished athlete, having played on the amateur tennis circuit before she was married. Her background in sports helps her to understand her husband's obsession with golf and his quest to perfect his game. As she told Michael Clarkson of the *Toronto Star,* "Sports is an obsession. Athletes tend to be obsessive, to try to get better and better." The Weirs, who decided to make their home in Utah after finishing college, live in Draper. They have two daughters, Elle Marisa and Lily.

During his collegiate golfing career, Weir won three events and finished among the top ten a total of 19 times. Even before graduating, the young golfer in 1992 announced his decision to turn professional. After receiving his bachelor's degree in recreation management in 1993, he pooled some of his own money with $10,000 from a sponsor in London, Ontario, and a car lent to him by a dealer in Timmins to join the Canadian Tour. The investment proved to be a wise one: Weir capped off his debut season on the tour with a one–stroke win at the Infinity Players Championship and was named Rookie of the Year. But Weir longed to join the PGA's U.S. Tour, and so at the end of the Canadian Tour in 1993, he headed off to the PGA Tour qualifying school in Palm Springs, California. It turned out to be a crushing disappointment. Weir's father, Richard, recounted to *London Free Press* reporter John Herbert this low point in his son's career: "He was first alternate at the final stage and didn't get to play. One hundred and ninety–seven players and nobody drops out. They kept telling him somebody would drop out; it always happens. But it didn't."

Although Weir continued to play on the Canadian Tour and elsewhere around the world, the going was particularly rough for him and his wife during the mid–1990s as he struggled to take his game to the next level. In his interview with LeBrun in *Canadian Press,* Weir recalled those dark years. "I can remember clearly one moment that seemed to crystallize things for me. It was on the practice range at the 1994 Canadian Open and I was hitting balls next to Nick Price. I was watching how the ball just exploded off his clubface, and it occurred to me that there was no way I could ever think of beating this guy if I didn't change some things. So I did."

Determined to improve his swing, Weir was persuaded by a mutual friend to pay a visit in early 1996 to golf coach Mike Wilson, who was then an instructor at the David Leadbetter Golf Academy in Palm Desert, California. Together, Weir and Wilson, with input from sports psychologist Rich Gordin, mapped out a plan to help the Canadian golfer improve all aspects of his game. Wilson and Gordin both remain key members of "Team Weir" today. Wilson, a native of Albuquerque, New Mexico, now teaches golf under his own name in Palm Desert and is the personal coach not only for Weir but for other pro golfers, including J.P. Hayes and Paul Stankowski.

The master plan to improve Weir's game began to pay off in 1997. That year, the golfer won the Order of Merit on the Canadian Tour. However, it was not until 1998 that he finally managed to break into the PGA's U.S. Tour. That breakthrough, Weir told the *London Free Press,* as quoted online at Slam! Sports, was his most memorable moment in golf until winning the Masters in 2003. It was his sixth attempt at qualifying and making it onto the tour was more memorable for him than any of the tournaments he had previously won. "It had been a childhood dream for so long, and I have worked so hard at getting there. To play the way I did under the extreme pressure of Q–school [qualifying school] is something I'm very proud of. I was right on the bubble in the final round, close to the cut line, so it was the most pressure–packed round I have ever played. I hit some unbelievable shots that day."

In 1999, his second year on the PGA Tour, Weir posted his first win, a two–stroke victory at the Air Canada Championship. It was the first win by a Canadian on the PGA Tour since 1992 and helped push Weir's earnings for the year to just under $1.5 million. For the 1999 tour as a whole, he finished in the top ten seven times. Things only got better in 2000 when Weir racked up earnings of more than $2.5 million and ended up 21st in the world golf rankings. Making 2000 particularly sweet for Weir was his victory at the final event of the 2000 PGA Tour—the World Golf Championship in Spain, an event at which he bested such world–class golfers as Tiger Woods, Vijay Singh, and Lee Westwood.

Weir's earnings on the PGA Tour in 2001 edged up to almost $2.8 million, but more significantly he broke into the ranks of the world's top ten golfers for the first time, largely on the strength of his win at the PGA Tour Championship. Weir's win came in a four–way playoff against Ernie Els, Sergio Garcia, and David Toms. It was also his first PGA Tour win on American soil. In recognition of his play for the year, Weir won the 2001 Canadian Press Male Athlete of the Year Award. After three successive years of consistently improving performance, 2002 was something of a come–down for Weir, who slipped from the ranks of the world's top ten pro golfers to 42nd place. His earnings on the tour dropped below $1 million, totaling only $844,000, and putting him in 78th place on the PGA money list.

However, Weir's lackluster performance in 2002 made his burst of brilliance in 2003 seem all the more impressive. He recorded his first win of the 2003 season at the Bob Hope Chrysler Classic in late January–early February, picking up $810,000 for his victory. Just three weeks later, he earned another $810,000 paycheck for winning the Nissan Open. The high point of Weir's 2003 season came with his surprising win at the Masters in Augusta. In winning the famed green jacket reserved for Masters winners, Weir accomplished what no Canadian had ever done. To get the job done at Augusta, Weir had to best Len Mattiace in a high–pressure play–off round at the end of the tournament. Shortly after he'd won the day, Weir told S.L. Price of *Sports Illustrated,* "It was just a gut–wrenching day, [with] a lot of comeback putts that I needed to make and was able to make. To do that coming down the stretch, knowing what a great score Len's had today, that's what I'm really proud of." On February 22, 2004, Weir won the Nissan Open by one shot. The victory made him the first repeat winner in nine years.

Sources

Periodicals

Atlanta Journal and Constitution, April 14, 2003, p. D1.
Golf Digest, July 2001.
London Free Press (Ontario, Canada), June 7, 2003.
Press (Canterbury, New Zealand), April 15, 2003, p. 8.
PR Newswire, April 28, 2003.
Sports Illustrated, April 21, 2003, p. 36.
Tampa Tribune, April 14, 2003.
Toronto Star, April 1, 2000; April 14, 2003; May 9, 2003.

Online

Biography Resource Center Online, Gale Group, 2003.

"Career Highlights," MikeWeir.com, http://www.mikeweir.com/aboutme/bio.sps?section=aboutme&sid=450&lid=1&aid=0 (July 1, 2003).

"Mike Weir," ESPN.com, http://sports.espn.go.com/golf/players/profile?playerId=453 (July 1, 2003).

"Mike Weir has come a long way since having his wife caddy for him," Slam! Sports, http://slam.canoe.ca/Slam030413/glf_weir–cp.html (July 2, 2003).

"Mike Weir's Golf Swing Highlights," Beau Productions, http://beauproductions.com/golfswingsws/mikeweir/videos/weir.wmv (July 1, 2003).

"Mike Weir," *SI.com,* http://sportsillustrated.cnn.com/golf/pga/bios/2003/bio1209.html (July 2, 2003).

"Oh Canada!" *SI.com,* http://sportsillustrated.cnn.com/augusta/news/2003/04/13/masters_sunday_ap/ (July 14, 2003).

"Special things for Mike Weir," Slam! Sports, http://cnews.canoe.ca/Slam030607/glf_weir4–sun.html (July 2, 2003).

"Weir holds off late charge to win Nissan Open," *SI.com,* http://sportsillustrated.cnn.com/2004/golf/02/22/nissan.sunday.ap/index.html (July 9, 2004).

"Welcome to Team Weir" MikeWeir.com, http://www.mikeweir.com/static/default.sps?section=teamweir&sid=450&lid=1&page=teamweir (July 3, 2003).

—Don Amerman

Treat Williams

Actor and director

Born Robert Treat Williams, December 1, 1951, in Rowayton, CT; married Pamela Van Sant; children: Gill, Eleanor Claire. *Education:* Attended Franklin and Marshall College.

Addresses: *Agent*—United Talent Agency, 9560 Wilshire Blvd., 5th Floor, Beverly Hills, CA 90212. *Home*—Park City, Utah.

Career

Actor on stage, including: *Grease,* 1973; *Over Here; The Pirates of Penzance; Oleanna; Captains Courageous,* 1999; *Stephen Sondheim's Follies,* 2001; *War Letters,* 2002.

Film appearances include: *The Eagle Has Landed,* 1976; *The Ritz,* 1976; *Deadly Hero,* 1976; *1941,* 1979; *The Empire Strikes Back* (uncredited), 1980; *Why Would I Lie?,* 1980; *The Pursuit of D.B. Cooper,* 1981; *Prince of the City,* 1981; *Faerie Tale Theatre,* 1982; *Once Upon a Time in America,* 1984; *Flashpoint,* 1984; *Smooth Talk,* 1985; *The Men's Club,* 1986; *Bermuda: Cave of the Sharks,* 1987; *Dead Heat,* 1988; *Sweet Lies,* 1988; *Heart of Dixie,* 1989; *The Third Solution,* 1989; *Beyond the Ocean,* 1990; *Where the Rivers Flow North,* 1993; *Hand Gun,* 1994; *Things to Do in Denver When You're Dead,* 1995; *The Taming Power of the Small,* 1995; *Mister Dog,* 1995; *Mulholland Falls,* 1996; *The Phantom,* 1996; *Cannes Man,* 1996; *The Devil's Own,* 1997; *Deep Rising,* 1998; *Deep End of the Ocean,* 1999; *Skeletons in the Closet,* 2000; *Critical Mass,* 2000; *Crash Point Zero,* 2000; *The Substitute: Failure Is Not An Option* (straight–to–video), 2001; *Venomous,* 2001; *The Circle,* 2001; *Gale Force* (straight–to–video), 2002; *Hollywood Ending,* 2002.

Television appearances include: *Hair* (movie), 1979; *Dempsey* (movie), 1983; *A Streetcar Named Desire* (movie), 1984; *Some Men Need Help* (movie), 1985; *J. Edgar Hoover* (movie), 1987; *Echoes in the Darkness* (movie), 1987; *Third Degree Burn* (movie), 1989; *Drug Wars: The Camarena Story* (miniseries), 1990; *Max and Helen* (movie), 1990; *Eddie Dodd,* 1991; *Final Verdict* (movie), 1991; *Tales from the Crypt,* 1992; *Till Death Do Us Part,* 1992; *The Water Engine,* 1992; *Batman: The Animated Series* (voice), 1992; *Deadly Matrimony* (movie), 1992; *Bonds of Love* (movie), 1993; *Road to Avonlea,* 1993; *Good Advice,* 1993; *Parallel Lives* (movie), 1994; *Texan* (movie), 1994; *Vault of Horror I* (movie), 1994; *In the Shadow of Evil* (movie), 1995; *Johnny's Girl* (movie), 1995; *The Late Shift* (movie), 1996; *Escape: Human Cargo* (movie), 1998; *The Substitute 2: School's Out* (movie), 1998; *36 Hours to Die* (movie), 1999; *The Substitute 3: Winner Takes All* (movie), 1999; *Journey to the Center of the Earth* (movie), 1999; *UC: Undercover,* 2002; *Going to California,* 2002; *Guilty Hearts* (miniseries), 2002; *Everwood,* 2002—. Producer of television programs, including: *Bonds of Love,* 1993. Director of television films, including: *Texan,* 1994.

Awards: Best new director, Aspen Short Film Festival, for *Texan,* 1994; best short film, Fort Lauderdale Film Festival, for *Texan,* 1994; best performer in a Broadway production, Drama League Awards, for

Captains Courageous, 1998; best performer in a Broadway production, Drama League Awards, for *Stephen Sondheim's Follies,* 2001; best actor in a TV show, Family Television Awards, for *Everwood,* 2003.

Sidelights

Treat Williams has been a renowned actor on Broadway, in films, and on television for more than 30 years. Along the way he has been seen in such greats as the television version of *Hair, A Streetcar Named Desire, Mulholland Falls, Deep End of the Ocean,* and Woody Allen's *Hollywood Ending.* It was the WB television series *Everwood,* however, that brought him to the attention of audiences everywhere. He has received much critical acclaim and several award nominations for his portrayal of the endearing Dr. Andy Brown, a surgeon who moved his family from New York City to a small town in Colorado after his wife died.

Williams was named after his ancestor Robert Treat Payne (1731–1814), one of the men who signed the Declaration of Independence. Williams was born on December 1, 1951, in Rowayton, Connecticut. He grew up there attending prep–school before he went on to Franklin and Marshall College in Pennsylvania. While there he joined the Fulton Repertory Theatre Troupe in Lancaster. He thoroughly explored his love of acting while part of the Troupe and so after graduation he moved to New York City to try acting as a full–time career. Soon after his move, in 1973, he made his Broadway debut in the musical *Grease.* He started out as an understudy to John Travolta but later ended up taking over the role of Danny Zuko himself. His plan to enter the New York acting scene began with great success. He was later seen in productions of *Over Here,* a play that featured the Andrews Sisters, *The Pirates of Penzance,* and *Oleanna.*

Williams decided to try his hand at film acting and soon after made his film debut in the farcical movie *The Ritz* in 1976. He played a private detective who was tracking a mobster through ridiculous situations. It was in 1979's television version of *Hair,* however, that Williams caught the public's eye. He was nominated for a Golden Globe award for New Star of the Year for his portrayal of the character Berger, the leader of a group of hippies. Around the same time, Williams, who has always been interested in singing as well as acting, formed a rock band with Kevin Kline, Rex Smith, Peter Riegert, and Mary Elizabeth Mastrantonio called Crime & Punishment.

Williams had early success in his chosen profession, but he was said to have really come into his own when he played Detective Daniel Ciello in the Sid-

ney Lumet film, *Prince of the City,* in 1981. At the time he gained much critical acclaim and "was pegged as the next Pacino," according to *Entertainment Weekly.* He was nominated for his second Golden Globe award for Best Actor in a Leading Role for his portrayal of Det. Ciello. It seemed like stardom was just around the corner for Williams. Unfortunately he went through a period where he told *Entertainment Weekly* that he was interested in little more than "chasing the ongoing party," along with all the drugs that partying provides, and it was a little while before he cleaned himself up and really pursued his acting whole–heartedly again.

Williams was involved in a string of movies that did not receive much praise. But he was given his next big break when he played Stanley Kowalski in the television version of *A Streetcar Named Desire* in 1984. He was nominated for his third Golden Globe for Best Actor in a Leading Role in a Mini–Series or Television Movie for his portrayal of the aggressive Kowalski. Also in the 1980s Williams was much–admired for his lead in the television movie *J. Edgar Hoover.*

In 1994 Williams expanded his area of expertise by trying his hand at directing—he directed Showtime's *Texan* for the Chanticleer Series. The film is about a retired pilot who discovers that his wife has been lying to him. He won two awards for the film: Best New Director at the Aspen Short Film Festival and Best Short Film at the Fort Lauderdale Film Festival.

Williams returned to acting with the black comedy *Things to Do in Denver When You're Dead.* In the movie Williams played a rather psychotic character named Critical Bill who uses corpses as punching bags. He was next seen in the controversial movie *Mulholland Falls,* a murder mystery set in Los Angeles, California, in which Williams played a wicked army colonel. Then in 1996 Williams played the villain Xander Drax in the movie *The Phantom,* based on the comic strip, alongside Billy Zane, Kristy Swanson, and Catherine Zeta–Jones. Although none of these films received the applause of critics, they have all become cult favorites in their genres.

The next movie for which Williams received critical acclaim was 1996's television movie *The Late Shift,* a movie that dramatized the fight between men who wanted to take over *The Tonight Show* after Johnny Carson left it. Williams played agent Michael Ovitz, a role in which Dick Cavett in the *New York Times* said Williams was "smart and smooth." Williams was nominated for an Emmy award for his portrayal of the legendary agent. He was also nominated for a Golden Satellite Award for Best Performance by an Actor in a Supporting Role in a Series, Mini–Series, or Motion Picture Made for Television.

As the 1990s came to a close Williams was also seen in the 1998 underwater action flick *Deep Rising,* and he made a cameo appearance in the Festival film *Cannes Man,* alongside such actors as Johnny Depp and Dennis Hopper. Williams received good reviews for the 1999 film, *The Deep End of the Ocean,* alongside Michelle Pfeiffer. The movie was based on the book by Jacquelyn Mitchard. Mitchard's book was the first selection for talk show host Oprah Winfrey's book club because it was considered something that would have mass appeal. The story is about a family that is thrown into turmoil when the wife, played by Pfeiffer, loses her three–year–old son when she takes her eyes off him for a minute at her high school reunion. Williams plays the husband. *New York Times'* Janet Maslin said the film was paced "so simply and determinedly that its early scenes are like a string of picture postcards, each one depicting a new phase of the family's ordeal."

Also in 1999, Williams played Theodore Lytton in the television miniseries *Journey to the Center of the Earth.* The movie was based on the novel by Jules Verne in which explorers travel to the center of the planet to discover an ancient civilization. After a few more movies that did not quite receive rave reviews, Williams took part in the 2002 television miniseries *Guilty Hearts* with Marcia Gay Harden and Olympia Dukakis. Based on a true story, Williams played a doctor who meets an unhappily married woman at church with whom he starts an affair. After the doctor's wife finds out about the affair, she is mysteriously murdered.

Williams returned to the theater in the musical *Captains Courageous,* which opened at the Manhattan Theatre Club in New York City in 1999. It was a musical based on the novel by Rudyard Kipling about a rich, obnoxious boy who falls off a ship and meets up with a Portuguese seaman and his mates on a New England fishing boat. Williams played the part of the Portuguese fisherman. Peter Marks wrote in the *New York Times* that Williams gave "a pleasingly uncomplicated performance." The music was well received, and Williams was said to be "always appealing ... possessed of a pleasant, delicate singing voice." Marks continued, "Mr. Williams proves a warmly embraceable father figure, soft and masculine, too." Williams received a Drama League Award for the part.

The next musical Williams was seen in was 2001's *Stephen Sondheim's Follies,* a play about two couples who go to a showgirl reunion where they are forced to face the truth about their unhappy marriages. According to Rex Reed of the *New York Observer* "Mr. Williams, as the neglected husband guilty of extramarital affairs for the warmth and affection he never got at home, has a masculine vulnerability that is gruff, charming and tender, often at the same time, and his show–stopping baggy–pants number 'The God–Why–Don't–You–Love–Me Blues,' is the kind of stuff that made Bert Lahr famous." He received a Drama League Award for his performance.

In 2002 Woody Allen offered Williams a part in his film, *Hollywood Ending.* The movie is about a director whose career has taken a turn for the worst. His ex–wife tries to get him a job with her new studio chief fiancée, played by Williams. Elvis Mitchell wrote in the *New York Times* that "Mr. Williams [takes] the conniving unflappability of his performance in *The Late Shift* to a frightening and impressive level."

Also in 2002 Williams received another big break for his career: he was offered the part of Dr. Andrew Brown on the WB series, *Everwood.* When Williams first read the script he was taken by it immediately and he was chosen for the role almost as quickly. The *New York Times'* Neil Genzlinger wrote that the actor "has rarely looked as comfortable as he does in *Everwood,* a promising new drama full of wry touches." *Entertainment Weekly* affirmed that "Treat Williams is soaring again.... His performance in *Everwood* is ... confident yet casual, thoughtful and generous."

Everwood is filmed in Utah, and when the show was signed on for a second season Williams moved his family from New York City to the Salt Lake City area (mirroring the show's premise) so that he could be near his family and filming at the same time. The show became an immediate hit. When asked about why the show has been so successful, Williams told *Entertainment Weekly,* "I think there's a yearning for places that are clean, pure, innocent. I know I feel that. And I think that's what people see in *Everwood.*" CNN.com said of his performance, "Williams is likable even when his character isn't rational." Williams was nominated for a SAG Award for Outstanding Performance by a Male Actor in a Drama Series in both 2003 and 2004. He was also honored at the Family Television Awards for his portrayal of Dr. Brown. According to Ken Tucker in *Entertainment Weekly,* "Really, if you're not watching *Everwood,* you're not missing a guilty pleasure: You're missing pure pleasure."

When he is not busy acting on stage, on television, and in film, Williams loves to fly. He is a certified commercial pilot, helicopter pilot, and a flight instructor. He has a 39 Texan T–6 World War II–era plane and a twin–engine Seneca. He is married to Pamela Van Sant with whom he has two children: a son, Gill, and a daughter, Eleanor Claire.

Sources

Periodicals

Entertainment Weekly, June 27/July 4, 2003, p. 70.
Guardian (London, England), May 16, 2002.
New York Observer, April 23, 2001.
New York Times, February 24, 1996; June 7, 1996; February 10, 1997; January 2, 1998; February 17, 1999; February 28, 1999; March 12, 1999; September 13, 1999; April 6, 2001; May 1, 2002; September 16, 2002.
PR Newswire, December 17, 2001; January 6, 2003; March 31, 2003; August 18, 2003.

Online

"Careerists on Broadway: Love's labors," CNN.com, http://www.cnn.com/2001/CAREER/trends/04/12/broadway/index.html (February 23, 2004).

"Cast bio: Treat Williams," TheWB.com, http://www.thewb.com/Faces/CastBio/0,7930,63675,00.html (February 25, 2004).

"Everwood," *Entertainment Weekly,* http://www.ew.com/ew/article/review/tv/0,6115,350657_3│6379││0_0_,00.html (February 26, 2004).

"Everwood," *Entertainment Weekly,* http://www.ew.com/ew/article/review/tv/0,6115,535757_3│6379││0_0_,00.html (February 26, 2004).

"List of SAG Award nominations," CNN.com, http://www.cnn.com/2003/SHOWBIZ/Movies/01/28/list.sag.nominations/index.html (January 28, 2003) (February 23, 2004).

"Quirky mobsters punch up *Things to do in Denver,*" CNN.com, http://www.cnn.com/SHOWBIZ/Movies/9512/denver/index.html (February 23, 2004).

"The Tricks Are On Treat," *Entertainment Weekly,* http://www.ew.com/ew/report/0,6115,293216_1│6379││0_0_,00.html (February 26, 2004).

"This week's reviews: 'Quitting,' 'Hairspray' songs, more," CNN.com, http://www.cnn.com/2002/SHOWBIZ/News/09/18/people.review.pp/index.html (February 23, 2004).

"Treat Williams," Hollywood.com, http://www.hollywood.com/celebs/bio/celeb/1676284 (February 26, 2004).

"Treat Williams," IMDB.com, http://www.imdb.com/name/nm0001852/ (February 25, 2004).

"Treat Williams," MSN.com, http://entertainment.msn.com/celebs/celeb.aspx?c=235053 (February 25, 2004).

"Treat Williams," Telusplanet.net, http://www.telusplanet.net/public/albear1/TREATWILLIAMS.html (March 5, 2004).

—*Catherine V. Donaldson*

Yao Ming

Professional basketball player

Born September 12, 1980, in China; son of Yao Zhi Yuan (father, a former basketball player, an engineer) and Fang Feng Di (mother, a former basketball player, a Chinese sports research institute official).

Addresses: *Office*—Houston Rockets, 2 Greenway Plaza, Ste. 400, Houston, TX 77046.

Career

Trained as a basketball player in Chinese state athletic schools, 1990s; became a player for the China Basketball Association team the Shanghai Sharks; named league's Most Valuable Player twice, 1990s; played on the Chinese national team in the Olympics, 2000; joined the Houston Rockets, a National Basketball Association (NBA) team, 2002; named to the NBA All–Star team, 2003.

Awards: Western Conference Rookie of the Month, December, 2002, February, 2003; NBA All–Rookie First Team, 2003; NBA All–Star team, 2003.

Sidelights

Chinese basketball player Yao Ming became the first foreigner to be the number–one draft pick of the National Basketball Association (NBA) in June of 2002. He was picked by the Houston Rockets, and in his first season became one of the NBA's top players. Already a star in his homeland, 22–year–old Yao received international attention for his

prowess on American basketball courts. His talents include an agility unusual for a player of his great stature (seven feet, five inches). In his first season with the Rockets, Yao received numerous honors, including Western Conference Rookie of the month twice, and spots on the NBA All–Rookie First Team and the NBA All–Star team. In addition to playing with the Rockets, Yao continued to play internationally for the Chinese national basketball team, and became a sought–after endorser of products ranging from credit cards to computers.

Yao comes from a family of basketball players; both of his parents played for the Chinese national team. His mother, herself six feet two inches (some sources say six feet three inches), was captain of the Chinese national women's basketball team. Yao's father is six feet ten inches (some sources say six feet seven inches), and found work as an engineer after retiring from basketball. Yao, his parents' only child, grew up in Shanghai, China. His family was of limited means while Yao was growing up. Their home was a small apartment whose doorways were not tall enough to accommodate its inhabitants unless they stooped. The government food ration coupons the family had to live on were not enough to feed the Yaos' growing boy, and so Yao's mother had to depend on handouts from food stalls that were about to throw out food at the end of each day. Yao was exceptionally tall from an early age—passing the five–foot–five mark by the time he was nine years old. He was even born tall—nearly two feet long. He reached the seven foot mark by the time he was 17 years old.

Although basketball might have seemed a natural career for a boy who was unusually tall, and whose parents had both been players, Yao was slow to approach the game. He was shy and unaggressive as a boy, and was often tormented by his classmates. His early interests were not athletic. Instead he immersed himself in military history books. But when Yao was nine years old, he was scouted by Chinese sports officials, who declared that Yao was to play basketball. Sent to one of the thousands of state–run sports schools in China, Yao was made to learn the game of basketball, and pushed through endless drills. The courts he played in were unheated, and frequently got so cold that the balls Yao played with could no longer bounce.

In his teens, when Yao's training was deemed complete, he was sent to play for the Shanghai Sharks. This was the China Basketball Association (CBA) team based in Yao's hometown. By the time Yao was 21 years old, he had been named Most Valuable Player (MVP) in the CBA twice. In 2000, Yao played for China in the Summer Olympics in Australia.

In his final year with the Sharks, Yao stunned fans by scoring every shot he took—all 21 one of them. No one could remember when anyone had ever accomplished such a feat. Yao played a total of 122 games with the CBA, averaging 23.4 points and 15.4 rebounds per game. His record in the 2000–01 season was 4.8 blocked shots per game, more than any other player in the league. He held the number–two position in scoring, with 32.4 points per game, and in rebounds, with 19.0 per game. *Time International*'s Hannah Beech went as far as to call him "China's Incredible Hulk of the hardcourt."

Yao was the number–one draft pick when he joined the NBA in June of 2002, and the Houston Rockets won the lottery to pick him. He was the first player from a foreign league ever to be an NBA number–one draft pick. Yao is the third Chinese player to join the NBA. Two other Chinese basketball players proceeded him by a few months into the NBA. These were Wang Zhizhi, who joined the Dallas Mavericks, and Mengke Bateer, who went to play for the Denver Nuggets.

When Yao was drafted by the Rockets, there was some uncertainty about whether the team could jump through the bureaucratic hoops required by the Chinese government to get him to the United States, or whether the Chinese government would allow him to stay once he was there. But Yao was worth fighting for; he had proven himself to be a top–notch player who, as Carroll Dawson, the general manager of the Rockets, told Brent Zwerneman in the *San Antonio Express–News,* had "quickness, size and agility." His agility and speed were especially impressive considering his large size. Yao also had the advantage of being an excellent entrée for the NBA into China's market of more than a billion citizens. With Yao on the Rockets, the team's owners saw an opportunity to open the world's biggest market to Yao–themed basketball merchandise, and to greatly expand the number of viewers for NBA advertisers. "It's the largest population base in the world by a fair amount," Russ Granik, the NBA deputy commissioner, told Jere Longman in the *New York Times.* "On top of that, we know there are a lot of basketball fans there." These factors provided the incentive for the Rockets to work hard to get Yao.

Before releasing their star player, Chinese officials wanted to be sure that Yao would receive the attention they thought he deserved. They also wanted him to play in a city that had a large Asian population. After an extended period of negotiations, during which Chinese officials determined that Yao would be the NBA's number–one draft pick, the officials at last consented to let their star basketball player go. In June of 2002, Yao signed a four–year, $15.6 million contract (some sources say $17.8 million) with the Houston Rockets. The deal included a $350,000 transfer fee the NBA had to pay Yao's old team in China, and it also called for Yao to turn over at least half of his earnings to Chinese government sports authorities. He would also continue to play occasionally on the Chinese national team in international competitions.

Because his commitments with the Shanghai Sharks kept him in China until just nine days before the opening of the NBA's 2002–03 season in October of 2002, Yao did not have a chance to practice with his American teammates much before being thrown into his first NBA games. Consequently, his first six games were less than spectacular: his per–game point average was less than four. But in a November game against the Los Angeles Lakers, Yao finally hit his stride, scoring in all nine of his attempted shots, for a total of 20 points and six rebounds.

The Rockets' hopes for Yao as a major draw among Chinese fans were realized when ratings for NBA games shown on Chinese television hit an all–time high during his first season with the Rockets. This demonstrated beyond a doubt that the NBA, whose ratings were sagging at home, had tapped into a vast new potential market. The Rockets played to that market by hiring Mandarin Chinese–speaking executives, posting billboards in Chinese, and setting in motion a weekly interview series in which Yao would answer questions in Mandarin. In addition, the team began to print ticket information and statistics in Mandarin. Les Alexander, the owner of the Rockets, went as far as to say to Longman in the *New York Times* that Yao had presented the Rockets with "the best co–branding opportunity in the world."

Yao's success in the United States has provided opportunities for businesses based in China as well. For instance, the Rockets signed an exclusive deal with the Chinese beer maker Yanjing to be the exclusive supplier of imported beer served at Rockets games. American importers of the beer were ecstatic when, propelled by Yao's popularity, the beer became a hot–selling item in all of its normal outlets as well as at the Rockets games.

But Yao's success was by no means limited to his ability to make money for his handlers. In a single season with the Rockets, Yao forced opposing team members to devise new strategies to counter his unusual combination of reach and speed. In his first year as a Rocket, Yao was named to the All–Star team in the position of starting center, and was twice named Rookie of the Month. He ended his first season with an average of 13.5 points per game and 8.2 rebounds. Also during his first season, he scored the highest field goal percentage in six consecutive games in the history of the NBA when he made 31 of 35 attempts—an accuracy of 88.6 percent.

Along with his new status as an international basketball star, Yao has had to adjust to life in the United States. Back in China, he lived his entire life either with his parents, or in the dormitories of the state schools. But although he has said that he is appalled by the traffic jams on the Houston highways, he has adapted to life in Texas quite well, downing the massive steaks for which the state is famous, and enjoying the range of shopping opportunities unavailable to him until arriving in his adopted country. Although he still lived with his parents during his first season with the NBA, home now consisted of a large house in an exclusive

Houston housing development—a far cry from the cramped apartment he grew up in. He enjoyed newfound wealth and independence, even though under the deal he made with Chinese officials he has had to send a large part of his income from both his salary as a player and from his product endorsements back home.

Yao has proved just as popular among American sports fans as he has among fans in China. American basketball fans have found in him a refreshing change to the boisterous grandstanding of many American players. American corporations, too, have found in him a wholesome endorser of their products, and he has lent his image to advertisements for everything from Visa credit cards to Apple computers. On October 23, 2003, the shoe company Reebok announced it had signed a multi–year endorsement contract with Yao. Other immigrants from China have expressed the hope that Yao's popularity will help him be a kind of cultural ambassador to the United States, presenting a positive image of Chinese people. As Chinese–American politician Gordon Quan told Longman in the *New York Times*, "I think people like Yao can build a bridge of better understanding. He will represent what China is to a lot of people—big, powerful, smart, talented." But more important to Yao than endorsement deals or his status as a representative of Chinese culture in the United States is the game of basketball. As he told Josh Tyrangiel in *Time*, "I think it's all pretty boring. I'd much rather be playing basketball."

Sources

Periodicals

New York Times, December 15, 2002; February 26, 2003.
People, December 16, 2002, p. 84.
San Antonio Express–News, June 25, 2002, p. 1C.
Seattle Times, November 29, 2002, p. E1.
Time, February 10, 2003, pp. 68–71.
Time International, April 28, 2003, p. 34.

Online

"Reebok signs Yao Ming," CNNMoney.com, http://money.cnn.com/2003/10/23/news/companies/yao_reebok.reut/index.html (October 23, 2003).

—*Michael Belfiore*

Tim and Nina Zagat

Restaurant critics

Born Eugene H. Zagat Jr., c. 1940, in New York; son of Eugene Zagat, Sr.; married Nina Safronoff (an attorney), 1965; children: Ted, John. *Education:* Yale University Law School, J.D., 1966. Born Nina Safronoff, c. 1942, in New York; married Tim Zagat (an attorney), 1965; children: Ted, John. *Education:* Yale University Law School, J.D., 1966.

Addresses: *Office*—Zagat Survey, L.L.C., 4 Columbus Circle, New York, NY 10019.

Career

Tim Zagat worked as a corporate attorney in Paris, France, c. 1966–70, and in New York City until 1987; Nina Zagat was an attorney specializing in estate law in Paris, c. 1966–70, and in New York City until 1990; began eponymous New York City restaurant guide, 1979; established as Zagat Survey L.L.C., 1982; Tim Zagat served as chair of New York City's visitor's bureau in the late 1990s.

Sidelights

Husband–and–wife attorneys Tim and Nina Zagat created the influential restaurant guides that bear their name, and which inspire both fear and loathing among restaurateurs. The 25th edition of the *Zagat New York City Restaurant Survey* was published in 2004, and marked their company's growth from a two–page list of Manhattan eateries given away free to friends into an expansive travel– and–leisure empire that rates restaurants and hotels in numerous cities around the world. "The rever-

berations of the Zagat enterprise are felt in every quarter of the restaurant world," wrote Steven A. Shaw in *Commentary*. "Even at the most elite levels, owners and chefs know that Zagat rankings are more important to success, not to say survival, than the reviews of all the city's newspapers combined."

Both Zagats (pronounced zuh–GAT) are New York–area natives. Tim, a corporate lawyer, grew up in the city, while estate–specialist Nina, née Safronoff, was a product of Long Island. They began dating during their first year at Yale University's School of Law in the early 1960s, and were married in 1965. Both landed jobs at the Paris offices of their respective law firms after graduating in 1966, and the budding gourmands eagerly delved into that city's fabled cuisine. "We thought we were going to be there for only six months, so we grabbed every opportunity to try different restaurants," Nina told *FSB* writer Carlye Adler. "We kept a list as a hobby during the two years we wound up living there."

Back in New York by the early 1970s, the Zagats organized monthly dinners for friends and colleagues who were fellow food–lovers. They called their group the Downtown Wine Tasting Association, and it grew in size over the decade. One evening in the late 1970s, "somebody with the benefit of his tenth glass of wine started criticizing the food critic of *The New York Times*," Tim recalled in an interview with *Newsweek International*'s Vibhuti Patel. "So I, also on my tenth glass of wine, said, hey, why not do a survey by our friends, who all eat out and travel extensively. Hundreds of real people sharing their experiences seemed a better way to rate a restaurant than one 'critic.'"

In some accounts of that apocryphal night, the fellow tablemate was Ivan Karp, the influential art dealer, but the end–product was the same: the Zagats came up with a survey questionnaire, and passed it around to a hundred friends and colleagues. They invited them to rate New York City's restaurants, from the inexpensive to the extravagant, and then tabulated the results. Each establishment was ranked on a numerical scale that rated its food, decor, service, and cost factor. Also included were brief blurbs from survey participants on various aspects of the restaurant, strung together in terse but informative prose. Two stalwarts of the era, a steakhouse called Luchow's and a candlelit tourist landmark called Sign of the Dove, both earned abysmal ratings. "Those restaurants were awful," agreed *Fortune* writer Mark Gimein in a 2004 profile of the Zagat empire. "How awful? In 1973 a New York businessman chose to be arrested rather than pay for the charred and 'pea–sized' Chateaubriand he was served at Sign of the Dove. The charges were dismissed when nobody from the restaurant showed up to defend the food. Zagat's is part of the reason that few places that bad are still in business."

The Zagats gave the first three editions of their guides away for free to their friends and colleagues, but word–of–mouth caused demand for copies of the rankings and survey forms to grow exponentially. "When Citibank called, my first thought was, am I over the limit?" Tim recalled in an interview with *Restaurants & Institutions* writer Laura Yee. "But what they wanted was 10,000 copies." By 1982, some 600 amateur restaurant critics were reviewing New York dining spots for them, and the Zagats were so inundated with data that they had to outsource the tabulation work. At that point, Nina—"the practical visionary," as her husband described her to Yee—decided that they might be able to sell a bound edition to at least recoup their expenses.

The two attorneys went to work on finding a publisher for their idea, but their proposal was met with rejection. "And we had very good contacts," Tim told *FSB*'s Adler. "Our respective law firms had publishing houses that we were close to. But most national publishers don't like local books, and the track record of publishing restaurant guides up to that time had not been very good." Even a family member in the book business turned them down, and so they decided to print and sell it themselves. In their Toyota Corolla station wagon, they took boxes of the first official *Zagat New York City Restaurant Survey*, with its distinctive burgundy cover, to the small bookstores that once dominated Madison and Lexington avenues. They sold 7,500 copies the first year, and 18,000 the second.

A turning point came in 1985, when the *Zagat Guide* outsold the *New York Times* restaurant guide and was featured in a *New York* magazine cover story. From there, sales jumped from 40,000 annually to 75,000 a month, and Nina decided that expanding into other cities would alleviate the tax they would have to pay on their new business's healthy profit. They found contacts in Chicago, San Francisco, and Los Angeles to review eating establishments there, and those editions proved equally successful. Tim quit his law firm in 1987 to manage the Zagat empire full–time, with Nina following three years later.

In the early 1990s, the Zagats were intrigued by the new possibilities of online information sources, and signed content–licensing deals with America Online, Prodigy, and other service providers, before eventually establishing their own fee–based website. They ventured into global territory as well, and were publishing information on restaurants and hotels for some 45 cities around the world by 2000. At that point, intrigued by possibilities of wireless technology, they invited in investors—among them prestigious venture–capital firms—and began raising capital for a well–executed expansion. They even hired a marketing person whose resume included executive stints at Verizon and American Express to serve as the company's first–ever chief executive officer.

Some 200,000 people submit recommendations to Zagat Survey, L.L.C., a number that reached such epic proportions with the introduction of online submission forms. But the Zagats also work hard at balancing those numbers by surveying the data with the help of an advisory staff that includes members of food and wine clubs and corporate executives who dine out frequently at some of the best restaurants on the planet. The *Zagat Guide* does have its share of critics in the highly competitive restaurant world of New York City. "Zagateers," as the survey respondents are known, are not required to document whether or not they have actually dined at the restaurant in question. Detractors claim that its data–gathering process is flawed, and that the highest ratings are heavily skewed to those places tourists seem to prefer, such as Union Square Café, which has stellar cuisine but also rather atypically unpretentious service for a pricey Manhattan eatery. "Nor is there anything," noted Shaw in the *Commentary* article, "to prevent determined people from voting multiple times for their friends' restaurants, evaluating restaurants visited long ago or ranked according to the opinions of others, or engaging in conduct calculated to teach a restaurant a lesson—or make it number one."

The *Zagat New York City Restaurant Survey* is usually dismissed by establishment food critics in the highly competitive restaurant scene in that city, but diners there swear allegiance to it, and it sells some 650,000 copies annually. The 2004 *Survey*, celebrating its 25th year, caused somewhat of an uproar when its rankings became public in late 2003: a small bistro in Brooklyn wound up ranking as high as Le Bernardin, Daniel, and Jean Georges, three of the city's internationally renowned restaurants. The newest *Zagat* gave Grocery, a small 30–seat eatery in the Carroll Gardens section of the borough, a 28 out of a possible score of 30. That result even made the front page of the *New York Times,* whose food critic William Grimes went back for a visit and adjusted his previous opinion, granting that there had been marked improvement since his first visit three years before. But as Grimes concluded that ranking Grocery on par with a place with that offers one of North America's most sumptuous dining experiences was not assessing the situation fairly. "For what it is, the Grocery is about as good as it can be," Grimes wrote. "So in one sense, the Zagat voters are correct. The Grocery deserves a nearly perfect score. But perfection at one culinary level does not compare with perfection at a higher level.... [T]he perfect three–minute pop song cannot grip the imagination and hold it the way a three–minute polonaise by Chopin can."

The Zagats assert that the eponymous guides are for the paying customer, not the food–world insider. Their system, Tim asserted in an interview with *Restaurants & Institutions* writer Nancy Ross Ryan, "is inherently more accurate than any critic. A critic can only have a limited number of experiences in a limited number of restaurants during certain times of the year." He also noted that New York's top restaurant critics are not exactly members of a secret cabal. "It's a joke to say that the major critics are anonymous," Tim told Ryan. "They're not. They get the best seat and the best service. The critics will retort that the chef can't learn to cook just for them. True. But imagine the guy from Dubuque sitting next to a major New York critic.... One is going to get yesterday's salmon and the other is going to be offered the specially prepared, just–in fresh sea trout."

Such egalitarian, honest opinions give their rankings a far truer character, the Zagats claim, and Shaw, writing in *Commentary,* declared that such was the conundrum presented by the success of the *Zagat* guide. "It is the vision of great chefs that ultimately creates educated consumers and hence the demand for better and better cuisine," Shaw declared. "Under the sway of a Zagat–style survey, however, a restaurant that wants to survive and flourish will find itself pandering to average tastes...."

The Zagats live on Central Park West and dine out often, but still do not participate in their restaurant surveys. Though company revenues are unknown, they are estimated to hover around $20 million annually. They publish *Zagat Guides* for some 70 cities around the world, with sister publications rating hotels, spas, airlines, and rental–car companies. In 2003, they launched a survey of movies, music, and theater. One of their two sons, Ted, also works for the company and published the first *Zagat Guide* to New York City nightclubs and bars. As Yee noted in her *Restaurants & Institutions* article, the Zagats' vision found a perfect audience in the 1990s. "Since the guide debuted," she noted, "dining out, a $360 billion industry, has become a national pastime, a form of entertainment. American food has grown up, garnered respect, and spawned a generation of celebrity chefs."

Tim Zagat dismissed the idea that their empire was anything but preconceived. "I wouldn't say we were smart," he told Yee in *Restaurants & Institutions.* "I would say we worked hard." What began as a hobby remains one for him and his wife, he told a journalist for *Entrepreneur,* Bob Weinstein. While he agreed that the right product and a sound business sense were vital to the success of any enterprise, what was "more important is doing something you love. That's the only thing that kept us going. That's why we worked so hard at improving the books. When you're not quite sure where it will all wind up, what keeps you going is the pleasure of doing something you enjoy. And the real kicker is when you turn profitable and look at the bottom line, and it's all yours."

Sources

BusinessWeek, November 20, 2000, p. 146; December 9, 2002, p. 44.
Commentary, November 2000, p. 47.

Entrepreneur, August 1996, p. 120.
Fortune, January 12, 2004, p. 46.
FSB, December 1, 1999, p. 56.
Newsweek International, June 4, 2001, p. 64.
New York Times, November 11, 1998; October 20, 2003, p. A1, p. B9.

People, September 6, 1999, p. 117.
Restaurants & Institutions, September 1, 1993, p. 22; May 1, 2000, p. 29.

—*Carol Brennan*

Elias A. Zerhouni

United States government official

Born Elias Adam Zerhouni, April 12, 1951, in Nedroma, Algeria; married to Nadia Azza (a pediatrician); children: three. *Education:* University of Algiers, M.D., 1975.

Addresses: *Office*—Office of the Director, National Institutes of Health, 9000 Rockville Pike, Bethesda, MD 20892.

Career

Instructor in radiology, Johns Hopkins University School of Medicine, 1978–79, assistant professor of radiology, 1979–81, associate professor, 1985–92, professor, 1992–2002; also served as vice dean for clinical affairs, 1996–99, chair of radiology department, 1996–2002, vice dean for research, 1999–2000, and executive vice dean, 2000–2002; appointed director of the National Institutes of Health by United States President George W. Bush, 2002.

Sidelights

An unexpected presidential appointment gave Maryland radiologist and researcher Elias A. Zerhouni the directorship of the National Institutes of Health (NIH) in 2002. As head of the immense governmental agency, which conducts and funds research in medicine and the life sciences, the Algerian–born physician was one of a handful of Muslim Arab–Americans in the administration of President George W. Bush. "There is a clear belief in the Koran that through knowledge you can improve not just medicine, but the lot of man," Zerhouni re-

flected in a statement that appeared on a website devoted to Muslims in America. "My work in medicine and at NIH is profoundly connected to my belief in Islam."

Born in 1951, Zerhouni is a native of the Algerian city of Nedroma, and was a competitive swimmer during his teens. In addition to Arabic, he also speaks French fluently—a legacy of the North African land's colonial history—and learned English as well. When he completed his medical studies at the University of Algiers, he applied for and won residency at Johns Hopkins University, considered one of the leading medical and teaching facilities in the United States.

Zerhouni arrived in the United States in 1975, bringing his wife, Nadia, and just $300 with him. Three years later, he finished his residency in diagnostic radiology and began teaching at the university as well. He was at the forefront of important new advances in diagnostic radiology, gaining expertise in CAT scans (computer axial tomography) and magnetic resonance imaging (MRI), each of which speeded the diagnostic process immensely without the need for exploratory surgery. In addition to teaching, Zerhouni also conducted his own research, developing techniques and devices that helped radiologists more accurately assess pulmonary tumors and heart functions.

In 1992, Zerhouni was made a full professor at Johns Hopkins, and eventually became a vice dean and chair of its radiology department. Over the next decade, he emerged as a respected administrator at the school of medicine, creating a strategic plan for research and winning funds for new and advanced facilities. His efforts attracted the attention of the White House, which nominated him to become the new director of the National Institutes of Health (NIH) in March of 2002. He was approved by Senate vote on May 2, 2002, and sworn in 18 days later.

The NIH director's office had been vacant for two years. Some Washington political observers believed that the Bush Administration's delay in filling the post was linked to finding a suitable candidate who shared the White House line on embryonic stem–cell research. Scientists were eager to explore the possibilities that such cells, which come from human embryos that went unused in in–vitro fertilization (IVF) techniques, might yield. These are cells that develop in embryos within the first two weeks of the life stage, and they provide the building blocks for some of the 200 other cells in the human body. Stem–cell therapies, it is believed, might bring important advances in the treatment of spinal–cord injuries, some forms of blindness, diabetes, and Alzheimer's and Parkinson's diseases.

Many religious groups, from American conservative Christians to the seat of the Roman Catholic church at the Vatican, oppose certain aspects of embryonic stem–cell research. Linking it to human cloning, they object on the grounds that scientists are attempting to tamper with the sanctity of human life. Some also believe that unregulated research might inspire women to undergo IVF procedures, and then sell the results. In August of 2001, President Bush signed an order that served as a compromise, in effect, but one that pleased neither side: federal funding on any future stem–cell research would be limited to projects that used the 78 existing colonies of stem cells.

The president's appointment of Zerhouni to the NIH post several months later was also viewed as a compromise. "Dr. Zerhouni shares my view that human life is precious and should not be exploited or destroyed for the benefits of others," Bush said, according to an article by *Virginian Pilot* journalist Liz Szabo. Zerhouni has consistently defended White House policy on the matter, and noted that confining federally funded research to the existing lines was adequate for the time being. If scientific progress was slowed by lack of laboratory resources, he said in late 2003, "I'll be the first to go the president and say we have reached a point where we need a debate here," the *New York Times* quoted him as saying. Such assertions prompted some to term the doctor an ideal person for the politically sensitive NIH post. Writing in the *San Francisco Chronicle*, Keay Davidson noted that Zerhouni "has demonstrated a mastery of Washingtonspeak—the ability to discuss controversial topics without alienating anyone."

Zerhouni supervises an agency with 27 separate institutes and centers, such as the National Institute on Aging and the National Cancer Institute, and which funds more than 2,000 biomedical projects around the world. It employs 18,000 people and has a Congressionally mandated budget of $27 billion. In September of 2003, Zerhouni introduced a "roadmap" for future medical research, a plan designed to bring together scientists working in molecular biology and clinical medicine. In an interview with the *New York Times'* Denise Grady two months earlier, Zerhouni had termed "life sciences … the core challenge of the 21st century. For thousands of years medicine has relied on what? On the fact that you have a core of people to whom you come when a disease has declared itself." In the future, he asserted—thanks to advances in molecular biology— "we're going to have to understand what I call the subclinical phase of diseases, where the disease is evolving in you but you feel nothing."

Zerhouni's wife is also a doctor and they are the parents of three children. He became a naturalized United States citizen in the early 1980s. In the *New York Times* interview with Grady, he reflected back on his career path that led him to the prestigious NIH post. "I think America treated me well, and I think you have to be grateful and have a sense of duty…. Some people ask me, 'What did you think about this? You're an immigrant, you're not born here, you've come through the ranks at Hopkins and then you're picked at N.I.H.' I say, 'Look, it says more about America than it says about me.'"

Sources

Periodicals

Lancet, August 2, 2003, p. 381; October 25, 2003, p. 1382.
New York Times, July 15, 2003; November 28, 2003, p. A35.
San Francisco Chronicle, November 11, 2002, p. A3.
Science, May 10, 2002, p. 997; September 27, 2002, p. 2197.

Science & Government Report, January 15, 2003.
Virginian Pilot, March 27, 2002, p. A3.

Online

"About the NIH Director," National Institutes of Health, http://copr.nih.gov/message_from_director.shtm (March 24, 2004).

"Director's Page," National Institutes of Health, http://www.nih.gov/about/director/ (March 22, 2004).

"Dr. Elias Zerhouni," Muslims in America, http://www.opendialogue.com/english/zerhouni.html (March 22, 2004).

—Carol Brennan

Obituaries

Ivan Allen Jr.

Born Ivan Earnest Allen Jr., March 15, 1911, in Atlanta, GA; died July 2, 2003, in Atlanta, GA. Mayor and business owner. As mayor of Atlanta, Georgia, from 1962 to 1970, Ivan Allen Jr. presided over that city's peaceful desegregation. He ended segregation at City Hall, testified before Congress in favor of civil rights laws, and forged friendships with Martin Luther King, Jr. and other black leaders. His leadership also encouraged economic development in the city and attracted major–league sports teams, helping to make Atlanta the progressive, dynamic city it is today.

"Over the turbulent waters of the 1960s, Ivan Allen was the human bridge from the old South to the new in Atlanta," author Gary M. Pomerantz, who wrote a book about the Allen family, told Douglas Martin in the *New York Times*. "Literally on his back, he carried the city's white establishment to a more enlightened day." Sam A. Williams, president of the Metro Atlanta Chamber of Commerce, told the *Atlanta Journal–Constitution*, "He really built this city. He was what made us different from Birmingham and the rest of the South. He put us on the map of the world." Born in Atlanta in 1911, Allen was the only child of Ivan Sr. and Irene Beaumont Allen. His father was a state senator and owner of a major local office supply company. Allen graduated from the Georgia Institute of Technology and joined his father's company in 1933. He married Louise Richardson in 1936, the same year he became treasurer of the Georgia State Hospital Authority and worked for Georgia's governor, Eugene Talmadge. During World War II, he served as a quartermaster in Atlanta and as a division director in the Selective Service System. From 1945 to 1946, he worked as an aide to another governor, Ellis Arnall.

Allen became president of the family company, Ivan Allen Co., in 1946, and its sales more than quadrupled in five years. He briefly ran for governor in the 1950s as a segregationist, but he did not get much support. His political philosophy later changed. He was elected president of Atlanta's Chamber of Commerce in 1960, and pushed for new expressways, rapid transit, a stadium, and a plan for school integration. In March of 1961, he negotiated an agreement to desegregate Atlanta's lunch counters.

He ran for mayor that year against segregationist Lester Maddox. Maddox got the most support from white Atlanta residents, but the black community, which made up 40 percent of the city, carried Allen to victory. On January 2, 1962, Allen took office and immediately ordered the "white" and "colored" signs at Atlanta's city hall be taken down, integrated the city hall cafeteria, and allowed the city's black police officers to arrest whites for the first time. While mayor, he also hired Atlanta's first black firefighters.

There was one blemish on his racial policies: late in 1962 he erected a fence to separate a black neighborhood from a white neighborhood, but he took it down in the face of legal challenges a few months later. The same year, he took on a solemn responsibility: when more than 100 Atlanta leaders on an art appreciation tour died in a plane crash near Paris, France, Allen went to France to help identify the bodies and bring them home.

Allen heeded President John F. Kennedy's call and testified before Congress in favor of the bill that would become the 1964 Civil Rights Act. He was the only prominent Southern politician to do so, and his testimony was not welcomed by many whites in Atlanta. "When President Kennedy wrote

Profiles in Courage, he was writing about men like you," Senator John Pastore of Rhode Island told Allen at the time, according to the *Atlanta Journal–Constitution.* When Martin Luther King, Jr. won the Nobel Peace Prize in 1964, Allen helped organize a 1,500–person dinner to honor him. Though other white leaders in the city had been hesitant to embrace King, many attended the dinner, making it a turning point in Atlanta's race relations. During a 1966 riot in Summerhill, a black neighborhood in the city, Allen walked the streets, refusing to wear a riot helmet as the police did, and was thrown from a car while trying to pacify a crowd.

Allen helped bring major–league baseball, football, and basketball to Atlanta, attracting the Braves from Milwaukee in 1965, the Falcons football team in 1966, and basketball's Hawks in 1968. The city's population grew more than 30 percent while he was mayor, and more than 50 new buildings appeared downtown. New freeways were built and the airport was expanded.

After two terms, Allen decided not to run for re–election, and he left office in 1970 and returned to his office–supply business. King's widow, Coretta Scott King, honored him with the Martin Luther King Jr. Nonviolent Peace Prize in 1981. Allen's company was bought by the office–supply giant Staples Inc. in 1998. The Atlanta City Council debated renaming a downtown street Ivan Allen Jr. Boulevard in 2000, but Allen declined.

After lapsing into a coma, Allen died on July 2, 2003, at the age of 92 in a retirement home in Atlanta, Georgia, one week after his old opponent, Maddox, and Atlanta's first black mayor, Maynard Jackson, also died. He is survived by his wife, sons Hugh and Beaumont, seven grandchildren, and four great–grandchildren. Another son, Ivan III, died in 1992. **Sources:** *Atlanta Journal-Constitution,* July 3, 2003, p. A1; CNN.com, http://www.cnn.com/2003/ALLPOLITICS/07/02/allen.obit.ap/index.html (July 7, 2003); *Los Angeles Times,* July 3, 2003, p. B14; *New York Times,* July 3, 2003, p. A21.

—*Erick Trickey*

Manuel Alvarez Bravo

Born February 4, 1902, in Mexico City, Mexico; died of natural causes, October 19, 2002, in Mexico City, Mexico. Photographer. Manuel Alvarez Bravo's photographs represented the height of Mexican photography during the 1930s and '40s. One of the leading surrealist artists on the North American continent, his work was also praised for its realism because of its intense focus on the everyday lives of Mexico's diverse population.

The son of a high school teacher, Alvarez Bravo left school by the age of 13 and began work in a government office. For a short time, he studied music and painting at the National Academy of Fine Arts. Working as a clerk to support himself, Alvarez Bravo continued to show an interest in art. He learned basic photography from a family friend who had given him a camera. Eventually he bought his own camera and was lucky enough to receive training from some of Europe's finest photographers.

Alvarez Bravo learned European photographic techniques from Hugo Brehme, whom Alvarez Bravo met when he was 21. Brehme also introduced Alvarez Bravo to Wilhelm Kahlo, who, like Brehme, was another German–born photographer making his home in Mexico. Kahlo was the father of the famous painter Frida Kahlo who—along with muralist Diego Rivera—strongly influenced Mexican art during the early post–Revolutionary years.

Alvarez Bravo continued to meet other photographers who had a great influence on him. In particular, the Italian photographer Tina Modotti bolstered Alvarez Bravo's career. As principal photographer for *Mexican Folkways,* she helped get his work published in the magazine. *Mexican Folkways* focused on Mexican popular art and customs as well as showcasing the muralists of the time. When Modotti was deported from Mexico in 1930 for her political beliefs, Alvarez Bravo took over her duties.

Alvarez Bravo began exhibiting his works in the mid–1920s. In 1926, he won an award for regional photography at an exhibition. An introduction to American photographer Edward Weston (who was Modotti's beau at the time), led to an exhibit at the Berkeley Art Museum with Weston, along with Imogen Cunningham and Dorothea Lange. His first one–man exhibition came in 1932 in Mexico City. Soon afterward he met the American photographer Paul Strand and French portraitist Henri Cartier–Bresson. Alvarez Bravo exhibited with Cartier–Bresson in 1934 at the Palace of Fine Arts in Mexico City. In 1935, the two exhibited again, along with Walker Evans, in New York.

In the 1930s, Alvarez Bravo began a teaching career that lasted for more than 30 years. He taught at various schools including the San Carlos Academy, the Center of Cinematographic Studies of the National Autonomous University of Mexico, and the Central School of Art. His unusual teaching style combined with his anonymity caused many students to eschew his classes. When most students were wanting to study filmmaking, Alvarez Bravo was taking them out to the countryside, having them set up cameras, and then waiting for something to happen.

Alvarez Bravo's work grew from many influences. As a child growing up during the Mexican revolution, he encountered death almost daily. Mexico had lost more than a million people in the conflict, and many bodies lay decomposing in the countryside where he played. The influence of his international contemporaries led to the creation of photographs that were filled with symbolism. His work was also guided by his association with Mexico's left–wing intellectual and political community.

Early in his career Alvarez Bravo sought out the intimate details of daily life in Mexico City. Photographs like *The Crouched Ones*, which shows workers sitting at a counter with their backs to the camera, is extraordinary because the lighting and composition make them appear decapitated as well as chained to their chairs.

As he matured, Alvarez Bravo became interested in creating meaning, however ambivalent, and began setting up scenes to be photographed. One of his most famous photographs made in this fashion is *The Good Reputation Sleeping*. The photograph was commissioned by French surrealist André Breton for the cover of his catalogue of the surrealist exhibition in Mexico City. In the photograph, a woman lies nude on a sidewalk, bandages are wrapped about her, and cacti are placed around her body.

In the 1940s, Alvarez Bravo began to focus on the Mexican landscape using wide–angle cameras. Praised from the beginning for his ability to link the past and the present in his work, these later photographs exemplified this strength in his work. His 1957 print *Kiln Two* shows two brick–making ovens with smoke pouring out their pointed tops. The photo harks back to Mexico's ancient history by referencing Mayan temples while also representing the effect of industrialization on the country.

Late in his life Alvarez Bravo found it hard to travel. He continued to photograph, but he worked primarily in his studio or his backyard photographing nudes as well as objects that were sent to him from colleagues, friends, and admirers. Although Alvarez Bravo enjoyed his work and did not complain,

Jonathan Kandell of the *New York Times* reported that Alvarez Bravo said, "But the countryside, the daily life of the street is so much richer than ... doing nudes."

Despite having exhibited in the United States with some of its top photographers during the '20s and '30s, Alvarez Bravo eventually became unknown to many. In 1971, he was reintroduced to the United States and a wider audience when the Norton Simon Museum (at that time called the Pasadena Art Museum) launched a retrospective. The retrospective eventually traveled to the Museum of Modern Art in New York. Alvarez Bravo was honored again more than 30 years later on his 100th birthday with exhibitions at the J. Paul Getty Museum as well as other American museums

Alvarez Bravo married Lola Martinez de Anda in 1925, and divorced her in 1934. He then married and later divorced Doris Heyden. His widow is Colette Urbajtel whom he married in 1962. Alvarez Bravo died on October 19, 2002, at the age of 100. He is survived by his wife and five children. Alvarez Bravo was a leader in Mexico's artistic renaissance; his work focused on specifically Mexican subjects. Weston Naef, a curator for the J. Paul Getty Museum told the *New York Times*, "For Alvarez Bravo almost all of his greatest pictures were made within 100 miles of his home.... [He was] completely committed to a body of work that had its grounding in the soil from which he came." **Sources:** *Los Angeles Times*, October 21, 2002, p. B9; *New York Times*, October 21, 2002, p. A20; *Times* (London), http://www.timesonline.co.uk (October 25, 2002); *Washington Post*, October 22, 2002, p. B6.

—*Eve M. B. Hermann*

Idi Amin

Born c. 1925, in Koboko, Uganda; died from multiple organ failure, August 16, 2003, in Jidda, Saudi Arabia. Dictator. Idi Amin ruled Uganda for eight years through terror and mayhem. He drove the once–prosperous nation over the brink of financial ruin and initiated a level of chaos from which Uganda has struggled to escape. A global pariah, Amin was sanctioned by countless nations and condemned by human rights organizations. His place in history was guaranteed by a combination of unfortunate timing and charismatic bullying.

Born Idi Amin Dada in northern Uganda, near Sudan and Congo, his father was a member of the Kakwa tribe while his mother came from the Lugbara tribe. Amin lived with his mother after his parents separated. She is said to have worked as a cane cutter and lived with several different military men. In the cities in which they lived, they stayed within the Nubian settlements—tribes with which he eventually became closely linked during his rule.

Amin had very little formal education; reports vary on the actual grade level that he reached. In his early 20s, between 1944 and 1946, he joined the King's African Rifles, the British colonial regiment of East Africa. One report states that he joined as a cook, another that he was a private. Because he had not been well educated, Amin found it difficult to advance within the ranks. This obstacle was eventually overcome and he was made corporal in 1949.

In the 1950s he reportedly fought against the Mau Mau guerrillas in Kenya. By the end of the 1960s, as Uganda was facing the end of British colonial rule, Amin was promoted several more times. In 1957 or 1959 he was promoted to sergeant major. The British military considered Amin a possible candidate for a leadership role and gave him the rank of "effendi"—reserved exclusively for noncommissioned officers native to Uganda. From 1951 to 1960, Amin used his 6' 4" frame to hold the title of Ugandan heavyweight boxing champion, a title that earned him some amount of fame and respect in his country.

In 1963, Uganda gained independence from Britain and its first prime minister took control of the country. With Prime Minister Milton Obote's approval, Amin was promoted to major and sent to both Britain and Israel for further training. During this time he earned his paratrooper wings. Obote found a helpful ally in Amin and in 1964 promoted him to colonel. Amin was also given command over the army and air force.

In February of 1966, members of Parliament brought charges of misappropriation of funds against Amin. He was accused of stealing hundreds of thousands of dollars worth of gold and ivory from guerrillas in the Congo whom he was supposed to be arming. In reaction to the charges, Prime Minister Obote suspended the Constitution and Amin arrested the ministers who had originally brought the charges. Amin was now in complete control of the military and the police. By April of that year, Amin and Obote had forced the King of Baganda, with whom the prime minister had a power–sharing agreement, into exile and consolidated power under Obote. Obote promoted Amin to brigadier general and then major general.

Amin and Obote worked closely together for several years but eventually Obote began to harbor suspicions regarding Amin's intentions. The prime minister initiated an inquiry into the whereabouts of millions of dollars missing from the military budget. In January of 1971, while Obote was away at a conference in Singapore, Amin took control of Uganda. The power grab was initially looked upon favorably by other African nations as well as some in Britain and Israel who had lucrative business contracts with Uganda. Eventually this pleasure would turn to horror as Amin's death squads took their toll on the country's population and his bizarre public behavior dissolved international opinion, leading some to call him a buffoon, sociopath, and murderer.

In 1972, only a year after taking power, he began to exhibit the behavior that eventually earned him scorn and condemnation. He asked Israel for monetary and military aid. When they refused he expelled as many as 500 Israelis from Uganda, launching invectives against Zionism and the Jewish people. That same year he deported more than 40,000 Ugandan born Indians and Pakistanis. Since they comprised the majority of the business and merchant class in Uganda, the economy was severely disabled.

As his rule continued, his behavior became more erratic and bizarre. He presented himself with so many awards and medals that at times his uniform ripped from the weight. He publicly humiliated a group of British businessmen by forcing them to carry him on a throne. Others he forced to bow before him and swear allegiance. He offered to become king of Scotland. All the while he also hurled insults at world leaders.

Beneath the show of buffoonery Amin showed himself to be a calculating and frightening dictator. Those who opposed him or were from rival tribes were often the focus of death squads. Hundreds of thousands of people were murdered, executed, or disappeared during his rule. He campaigned against the Anglican Church, arresting and murdering its leaders and deporting many of the clergy. The number of Ugandans killed during his tenure is estimated to range anywhere from 100,000 to 500,000.

His confidence was severely shaken in 1976 when Israeli commandoes successfully rescued 102 hostages from a hijacked plane that had landed in Uganda. The commandoes had subverted Ugandan forces and destroyed war planes owned by the

Ugandan Air Force. In retaliation he killed a 73–year–old woman who had been a hostage and was recovering in a Ugandan hospital.

As his tenure continued he faced mounting internal pressure. Several unsuccessful takeovers were put down. His army had become restless and ready for rebellion. In 1978 he decided to invade Tanzania, to keep his army occupied and focused. Tanzanian troops, along with the help of Ugandan exiles, were able to stop the invasion and mounted a counter–invasion that led to the takeover of the Ugandan city of Kampala on April 12, 1979. Amin was forced to flee. In exile, Amin was granted asylum in Saudi Arabia under the condition that he refrain from politics.

Amin remained in Saudi Arabia until his death, living in the city of Riyadh. He spent his exile reading from the Koran, watching television, and playing the accordion. Amin is reported to have had at least four wives and more than 30 children. David Lamb of the *Los Angeles Times* described Amin as follows, "More a tribal chief than a president, he was a master showman who loved center stage and knew how to use the international media." He died on August 16, 2003, without ever facing charges for the crimes he committed in Uganda. **Sources:** *Chicago Tribune,* August 17, 2003, sec. 1, p. 3; *Los Angeles Times,* August 16, 2003, p. A1, p. A5; *New York Times,* August 17, 2003, p. A22; *Times* (London), August 18, 2003, p. 25; *Washington Post,* August 17, 2003, p. C11.

—*Eve M. B. Hermann*

Robert C. Atkins

Born Robert Coleman Atkins, October 17, 1930, in Columbus, OH; died after suffering a severe head injury, April 17, 2003, in New York, NY. Doctor and author. Dr. Robert C. Atkins was the author of one of the most influential weight–loss programs of the twentieth century. The Atkins diet claimed that people would shed pounds by exercising and cutting out starches in favor of eating more protein, even if the meals were laced with higher amounts of fat and cholesterol. On his plan, meat, eggs and cheese are encouraged, while bread, potatoes, pasta and fruit are generally off–limits.

This low–carbohydrate diet was unconventional and ran counter to most of the tenets of Western mainstream medicine. The medical community berated the Atkins diet for years as dangerous, but research from a few small studies released in February of 2003 found that cardiovascular risk factors decreased and cholesterol profiles actually improved.

Though Atkins' first book, *Dr. Atkins' Diet Revolution: The High Calorie Way to Stay Thin Forever* was published in 1972, "low–carb" didn't become a buzzword until the late 1990s and early 2000s, after publication of *Dr. Atkins' New Diet Revolution* in 1999. Various editions of the book sold more than 15 million copies, making it one of the top 50 titles ever published. It spent five years on the *New York Times*'s best–seller list.

Atkins was born in Columbus, Ohio, and moved to Dayton, Ohio, in the seventh grade. His father was a restaurant owner. As a teen, Atkins considered becoming a comedian and even performed one summer at resorts in the Adirondacks after graduating from college. He received a pre–medical bachelor's degree from the University of Michigan in 1951. He went on to specialize in cardiology at Cornell University Medical School, earning his medical degree in 1955 after training at Rochester and Columbia University Hospitals and St. Luke's Hospital in New York.

In 1959, Atkins opened his own practice on the Upper East Side of Manhattan in New York City. He told an interviewer once that he began a low–carbohydrate diet in 1963 to counter obesity and depression. The program he followed was initiated by Dr. Alfred W. Pennington, who found that 20 test subjects lost an average of 22 pounds in 100 days by eliminating sugar and starch. A version of the diet was published in the *Journal of the American Medical Association.*

After six weeks on the plan, Atkins said, he lost 27 pounds and turned his practice into an obesity clinic. He appeared on the *Tonight* show and in several magazines, including *Vogue* in 1970. This led to one million requests for copies of his diet plan. The thrust of the diet is that people may eat as much as two–thirds of their calories from fat, but very few carbohydrates—which is more than double the usual recommendation. Atkins claimed that without carbohydrates, the body would burn its own fat. Meanwhile, in 1973, the American Medical Association labeled the diet "potentially dangerous." Other critics over the years included the American Dietetic Association and the American Heart Association. These groups and others claimed that the Atkins plan wouldn't work over the long term and that it could cause health problems ranging from bad breath and constipation to osteoporosis and heart problems.

Between the late 1970s and the 1990s, Atkins opened an alternative healing clinic and fell out of the public eye, although he did continue to publish books. During this time, he was sued several times by unhappy clients, and temporarily lost his medical license in 1993 after another doctor filed a complaint. The doctor treated the patient for an air bubble that had blocked a vessel in her brain after she received ozone treatment from Atkins, who said it would kill cancer cells. A judge reinstated the license.

When Atkins released his 1999 book, adherents included celebrities like Jennifer Aniston and Brad Pitt. Restaurant–goers followed, brushing away the breadbasket in favor of steaks, bunless hamburgers, cheese, and eggs. The diet hit at a time when more Americans were overweight than ever before: The *Journal of the American Medical Association* reported in 2002 that 64.5 percent of Americans were overweight, compared with 55.9 percent in 1994.

However, health concerns resurfaced among medical professionals. The American Heart Association in 2001 issued a strong recommendation against following high–protein diets such as Atkins' and others, including the Zone, Protein Power, and Sugar Busters. Atkins' final book, *Atkins for Life,* published posthumously, addressed the controversy by advocating a diet with more lean meats and nutrient–rich vegetables. He also advocated taking 20 nutritional supplements a day, and he himself took 60 daily.

No long–term studies on the Atkins diet had been completed by the time of the author's death, so it was still unknown whether people could maintain the weight loss over time and not suffer negative health effects. Six smaller studies, including one conducted at Duke University, showed that subjects on the Atkins diet lost weight and lowered their cholesterol without harming their health.

The National Institutes of Health in 2003 began a large study, but that same year, the *Journal of the American Medical Association* published a report by a team of doctors from Yale and Stanford universities suggesting that Atkins dieters lost weight because they ate fewer calories overall, not because they consumed fewer carbohydrates. The study did not espouse or condemn the Atkins plan.

One year before his death, Atkins suffered a cardiac arrest and had to be revived. In an official statement, he attributed it to cardiomyopathy, a heart condition caused by an infection rather than clogged arteries. At age 72, Atkins died on April 17, 2003, in New York, New York, after slipping on pavement and suffering severe head injuries. Subsequently, he underwent surgery to remove a blood clot from his brain, but never regained consciousness. He is survived by his wife, Veronica, and his mother, Norma. **Sources:** *Chicago Tribune,* April 18, 2003, sec. 1, p. 6; CNN.com, http://www.cnn.com/2003/HEALTH/04/10/atkins.hospital.reut/index.html (April 10, 2003); *Independent,* April 19, 2003, p. 22; *Los Angeles Times,* April 18, 2003, p. B11; *New York Times,* April 18, 2003, p. D9; *Washington Post,* April 18, 2003, p. B7.

—*Geri Koeppel*

Luciano Berio

Born October 24, 1925, in Oneglia, Italy; died May 27, 2003, in Rome, Italy. Composer. For some five decades before his death, Luciano Berio was one of the twentieth century's most prolific composers, and considered Italy's leading musical pioneer of his era. Writing in a primarily modernist style, Berio produced large–scale orchestral works, operas, and chamber music, but it was his solo voice compositions for which he became particularly renowned. Berio's works "combined innovative imagination and analytical depth with a richly sensuous feeling for sound and form," declared Paul Griffiths in the *New York Times.*

Berio was born in 1925 in Oneglia, a town on Italy's northwest Ligurian coast. Both his father and grandfather were accomplished musicians, and Berio was initially trained by the latter as a youngster. He planned to become a pianist, but injured his hand while serving in the Italian Army during the final days of World War II. After the war's end, he studied composition at the Milan Conservatory, where he met his first wife, the American singer Cathy Berberian. After their 1950 marriage, they began traveling to New York City often, and there Berio came to know the Italian composer Luigi Dallapiccola, and was influenced by Dallapiccola's atonal style. One of Berio's first works was 1953's *Chamber Music,* a vocal piece with clarinet, cello, and harp based on the writings of Irish author James Joyce, which he wrote for Berberian to perform. Berio and Berberian later welcomed the birth of their daughter.

During the 1950s, Berio became deeply involved in European avant–garde music. After 1955, he ran a Milan studio for electronic music with Italian composer Bruno Maderna, whom he knew through summers spent at an academy for modernist composers and musicians in Darmstadt, West Germany. Some of Berio's most complex works came out of this era, including *Tempi Concertati* (1958–59) for flute, violin, two pianos and four instrumental groups. At Darmstadt he also came to know Pierre Boulez, Karlheinz Stockhausen, and other leading names in European music, and Stockhausen's daring electronica compositions were particularly influential on the direction of Berio's work. In 1958 he debuted what became "one of the early classics of tape music," according to Griffiths, *Thema (Omaggio a Joyce),* another work drawn from the Irish writer's free–form prose. That year, the first in Berio's important "Sequenza" series was introduced as well, which were complex works for one instrument that showcased the history, style, and mood of each, beginning with the flute.

Berio spent a much of the 1960s living and working in the United States. He taught at Mills College in California in the early 1960s, where his students included future composer Steve Reich and Grateful Dead bassist Phil Lesh. After 1964 and the end of his first marriage, Berio lived in New York City with his second wife, Susan Oyama, a union that produced a son and daughter. For a number of years he was a professor of composition at the esteemed Juilliard School, and founded its Juilliard Ensemble, which performed many of his works under his baton. Over the years he increasingly drew from the pantheon of musical forms of the past, including Giuseppe Verdi's operas, the early modernist works from Igor Stravinsky, and even Gustav Mahler's romantic symphonies. He continued to find inspiration in literary works as well, and his *Sinfonia* for orchestra and vocal octet (1968–9) incorporated Mahler's "'Resurrection" Symphony as well as the words of dramatist Samuel Beckett. "The result was Mahler transformed," Mark Swed noted in the *Los Angeles Times,* "and a work that was credited with kicking off the contemporary genres of post–Modernism and New Romanticism."

Berio's first full–scale opera, simply titled *Opera,* debuted with the Santa Fe Opera in 1970. In 1971, he and Oyama divorced. After 1972, he lived and worked primarily in Italy, settling in a town near Siena called Radicondoli. He married Talia Pecker in the mid–1970s; they had two sons. His sole excursion was a few years in the 1970s spent running Boulez's computer–music institute in Paris, France, but in 1980 Berio established his own electronic studio in Florence, which he named Tempo Reale. His

most important works of the decade are considered *Una vera storia* ("A True Story"), which had its premiere in Florence in 1982, and *Un re in Ascolto* ("A King Listens"), which debuted at the prestigious Salzburg Festival in Austria in 1984. Both operas were collaborations between Berio and Italy's foremost living writer of the time, Italo Calvino.

After 2000 Berio served as president of the National Academy of St. Cecilia, a venerable Roman institution that includes an orchestra, library, school, and array of other musical organizations. He was also a frequent guest conductor with the Los Angeles Philharmonic for a number of years, and was working on an orchestration for a Monteverdi opera commissioned by the Los Angeles Opera artistic director Placido Domingo just before his death in 2003. The famed tenor sometimes teased the avant–gardist about his style. "'Luciano,'" Domingo recalled in the *Los Angeles Times* article, "'write for me some melodic music that I can sing,' I would say to him. And he would reply, 'Placido, everything I write sounds melodic to me.'"

Berio died on May 27, 2003; he was 77. He is survived by his third wife, Talia Pecker Berio; daughters Cristina and Marina; sons Stefano, Dani, and Yoni; four grandchildren, and one great–grandchild. **Sources:** *Chicago Tribune,* May 30, 2003, section 1, p. 11; *Guardian* (London, England), May 29, 2003, p. 27; *Los Angeles Times,* May 28, 2003, p. B10; *New York Times,* May 28, 2003, p. A21; May 30, 2003, p. A2, June 5, 2003, p. A2.

—*Carol Brennan*

David Brinkley

Born David McClure Brinkley, July 10, 1920, in Wilmington, NC; died after complications from a fall, June 11, 2003, in Houston, TX. Broadcast journalist. Veteran American newscaster David Brinkley helped define an entire era of television news reporting. His long stint as co–anchor of NBC's nightly *Huntley–Brinkley Report* between 1956 and 1970 set the standard for an entire generation of on–air journalists. Brinkley, noted *Washington Post* writer Bart Barnes, "was known for a wry sense of humor, pithy observations and a low–key, matter-of–fact style of reporting and commentary that lacked pretense and pomposity. He was supremely self–confident, not easily impressed, and he came across as less enamored of himself than many of his colleagues."

Born in 1920, Brinkley was a native of Wilmington, North Carolina, and the last of seven children in his family. His father, scion of an old Southern fortune, died when Brinkley was eight, and the household was left penniless when it turned out that the elder Brinkley had made many unsecured loans to friends. Brinkley's mother was an austere, religious woman who disapproved of her bookworm son's reading habits on the grounds that using electric light bulbs at night attracted mosquitoes, and he was at times forced to go outside and read under the light of the street lamp. He began writing for the local newspaper while still in high school, and after graduation spent a year at the University of North Carolina and then the North Carolina National Guard, from which he was discharged when misdiagnosed with a kidney ailment.

In 1942, Brinkley went to work for the United Press wire service in Atlanta, Georgia, and moved on to its bureaus in Charlotte, North Carolina, and Nashville, Tennessee. In 1943, he traveled to Washington, D.C., to interview for a job with CBS Radio; when CBS turned him down he went to NBC to ask for an interview, and was hired immediately. A quick study, Brinkley was soon given the White House beat, and after World War II became one of the few radio reporters to move successfully into the new medium of television. The cameras, lights, and teleprompters confounded some of his former colleagues, but Brinkley confessed later that he made his first mistakes on shows like *America United* in the late 1940s, which was broadcast locally in the District of Columbia area when, he claimed, there were but a few hundred households with television sets.

Brinkley was anchoring NBC's 15–minute nightly news broadcast by the early 1950s, and covering major news stories on assignment. In 1956, he was paired with NBC's Los Angeles–area newscaster, Chet Huntley, at the Democratic National Convention. Their on–air repartee struck a chord with viewers, and the network received an unprecedented amount of mail commending their coverage; even the *New York Times* pegged Brinkley as a rising star. Thus in October of that year, Brinkley and Huntley debuted on *The Huntley–Brinkley Report,* which would become the leading news program in American living rooms nightly for more than a decade.

Brinkley and Huntley's half–hour broadcast of the day's news—twice as long as most at the time—featured Brinkley's liberal, often irreverent commentary that served to take television journalism out of the era of news "readers" who simply recited copy and into the modern era of intelligent, measured critical analysis. Brinkley wrote all of his own copy, often underlining certain words for emphasis, which gave him a distinctive style. "With his unconventional cadence and dry, reedy tone, Brinkley broke with the mellifluous tradition of earlier broadcasting and spawned generations of imitators," declared Richard T. Cooper in the *Los Angeles Times.* His delivery was even mimicked by comedians, and both he and Huntley enjoyed immense celebrity during the 1960s. Brinkley reported from Washington, and Huntley from New York, and their trademark sign–off—"Good night, Chet," followed by "Good night, David"—became a national catchphrase. Brinkley later admitted both he and Huntley loathed it as a bit of forced froth.

The Huntley–Brinkley Report ended when Huntley retired in 1970. Brinkley floundered at NBC for the next decade, since news executives were busy grooming a new generation of broadcast journalists, but ABC was eager to hire him in 1981 when he was finally released from his contract. He was given his own show, *This Week with David Brinkley,* which once more set a new standard for its genre. The Sunday–morning chatfest topped the ratings as Brinkley moderated a panel comprised of well–known journalists in a discussion of the week's top story. He retired from the network in 1997, ending his run as the longest–serving anchor or host of a daily or weekly national television program in American broadcast history.

Brinkley wrote with characteristic frankness about his career in journalism in a 1995 autobiography. He had only one notable gaffe in his 40–plus–year career: late on ABC's election–night coverage in 1996, he fumed over a re–elected Bill Clinton's lengthy speech, terming the President "a bore," not realizing that his microphone was on. He later apologized for the remark, but ran afoul of his former colleagues a year later when he appeared in a series of feel–good ads for agribusiness giant Archer Daniels Midland Company. He wrote three books, including a 1988 bestseller, *Washington Goes to War,* about the transformation of the United States capital during World War II from a slow–moving Southern burg to the epicenter of global power. Throughout his career, Brinkley won ten Emmy awards, three George Peabody awards, and, in 1992, the Presidential Medal of Freedom.

At his Wyoming home in January of 2003, a wheelchair–bound Brinkley was rescued from a fire by a sheriff's deputy, who broke a window to take him to safety. He died on June 11, 2003, in Houston, Texas, at age 82 after complications suffered in a fall. He is survived by his second wife, Susan Benfer Brinkley, three sons from his first marriage, and a stepdaughter he adopted. His assessment of the dominant news source of his generation is often quoted by detractors of television journalism. "The one function that TV news performs very well," Brinkley once said, according to Barnes in the *Washington Post,* "is that when there is no news, we give it to you with the same emphasis as if there were." **Sources:** CNN.com, http://www.cnn.com/2003/SHOWBIZ/TV/06/12/obit.brinkley/index.html (June 12, 2003); *Entertainment Weekly,* June 27/July 4, 2003, p. 16; E! Online, http://www.eonline.com/News/Items/0,1,11965,00.html?tnews (June 12, 2003); *Independent* (London, England), June 14, 2003, p. 17; *Los Angeles Times,* June 13, 2003, p. A1; *New York Times,* June 13, 2003, p. A30; *Washington Post,* June 13, 2003, p. A1, p. A11.

—*Carol Brennan*

Charles Bronson

Born Charles Buchinsky, November 3, 1921, in Ehrenfeld, PA; died from pneumonia, August 30, 2003, in Los Angeles, CA. Actor. Charles Bronson gained superstar status in the United States in 1974 with the release of the film *Death Wish.* His role as the liberal–minded architect who becomes a vigilante was reprised in four sequels and brought him stardom but also criticism for the violence portrayed in the films. His was a career spent playing rough and tough gunslingers and outlaws while his private life was spent raising children and painting. He never quite broke out of the tough–guy mold although he was often praised in roles that showed more depth and subtlety.

Bronson grew up in the coal–mining town of Ehrenfeld, Pennsylvania, in the poorer part of the area called Scooptown. One of 15 children, he grew up in harsh conditions and experienced extreme poverty. His parents had immigrated to the United States from Lithuania to work in the mines. Bronson, whose given name was Buchinsky, lost his father when he was ten years old. When he was 16, he joined his older brothers working in the coal mines.

In 1943, Bronson was drafted into the Army. First stationed in Kingman, Arizona, Bronson soon found himself part of the 760th Flexible Gunnery Training Squadron. He was stationed in Guam, and took part

in regular bombing raids on Japanese territories. When he returned home he floated from job to job, from bricklayer to cook to onion picker. A chance meeting with some actors from Philadelphia gave him his introduction to theater and acting.

Spurred on by hopes of earning the high salary paid to film actors, Bronson moved to California and joined the Pasadena Playhouse. He took acting lessons and acted in several plays. In 1951, he earned a small role in the film *You're in the Navy Now* starring Gary Cooper. In that film he was billed as Charles Buchinski. By 1954, he had officially changed his name to Bronson. The impetus for his name change was a fear that his Slavic–sounding name would bring him unwarranted attention from the House Un–American Activities Committee, which was busily blacklisting members of the Communist Party in Hollywood circles at the time.

Throughout the 1950s Bronson appeared in numerous guest roles on television including TV Westerns like *Bonanza, Big Valley, Gunsmoke,* and *Rawhide.* He also took on small roles in films including one as the laboratory assistant to Vincent Price in the horror movie *The House of Wax.* His role in the 1958 film *Machine Gun Kelly* brought him some recognition, but it was not until the 1960s that Bronson began appearing in more substantial roles. Unfortunately, with co–stars like Steve McQueen, Richard Burton, and Yul Brynner, Bronson found it difficult to move into the limelight despite turning in credible performances.

In 1960, Bronson starred as one of seven mercenaries hired to protect a Mexican village from bandits. *The Magnificent Seven,* a remake of Japanese director Akira Kirosawa's *Seven Samurai,* was an incredible success but Bronson was overshadowed by his co–stars. His roles in later films like *The Great Escape, The Sandpiper, Battle of the Bulge,* and *The Dirty Dozen* also earned critical acclaim but starring roles seemed to elude him.

In 1968, Bronson went to France at the request of French actor Alain Delon who had seen Bronson in *Machine Gun Kelly* and wanted to make a film with him. It was a bold step that ended up paying off for Bronson. He and Delon starred in the film *Adieu l'ami,* which became a hit in Europe. Bronson starred in several other films made in France, Italy, and Spain, including the Spaghetti western *Once Upon a Time in the West.* His European films made him an unlikely sex symbol with nicknames that translated as "The Brute" and "Sacred Monster." In 1972, he was named by the Hollywood Foreign Press Association as the number–one box office attraction in the world outside of Hollywood. The previous year he had received a Golden Globe award for most popular actor in the world.

Well into his 50s and a European icon, Bronson returned to the United States in the mid–1970s to become a major Hollywood film star. In 1974 he starred in *Mr. Majestyk* as a farmer fighting against the thuggish practices of men who want to run him off his property. Playing a good man who is pushed too far and fights back violently was a theme continued in his other film of 1974—*Death Wish.* Seeming to hit the tenor of the time, his character was widely cheered by crowds who lived vicariously through him. Muggers, thieves, and a wide range of other criminals faced death at the hands of Bronson's Paul Kersey. When critics roundly criticized the violence, Bronson remained unfazed.

Bronson's film career continued into the 1980s, but his popularity waned and actors such as Arnold Schwarzenegger and Sylvester Stallone replaced him as leading action heroes. In the 1990s most of his roles were in television with the exception of *Death Wish V,* which was released in 1994, and a small but touching performance in *The Indian Runner,* directed by actor/director Sean Penn. His final performance came in 1999, in the television drama *Family of Cops III,* the third installment of a trilogy of television movies made starring Bronson as the patriarch of a family of police officers.

Bronson divorced his first wife, actress Harriet Tendler, in 1968 and married actress Jill Ireland. Bronson and Ireland were married until 1990 when she died of cancer. In 1998, he married Kim Weeks, who survives him along with his four children, two step-sons, and two grandchildren. Bronson may be remembered most for his violent action films like the *Death Wish* series, but he was also part of some of Hollywood's classic Western and military films of the '60s. An unlikely sex symbol, Bronson's popularity spanned decades and continents. He died on August 30, 2003, in Los Angeles, California, at the age of 81. **Sources:** *Chicago Tribune,* September 1, 2003, sec. 4, p. 9; E! Online, http://www.eonline.com/News/Items/0,1,12416,00.html?tnews (September 2, 2003); *Los Angeles Times,* September 1, 2003, p. B13; *New York Times,* September 2, 2003, p. C10; *People,* September 15, 2003, pp. 69-70; *Times* (London), September 2, 2003, p. 27.

—*Eve M. B. Hermann*

Dee Brown

Born February 28, 1908, in Alberta, LA; died of congenital heart failure, December 12, 2002, Little Rock, AR. Author. Dee Brown's 1970 book *Bury My Heart at Wounded Knee* created a new outlook on the history of the American West. By focusing on the history of the United States from the perspective of Native Americans, Brown's book brought to light stories of racism, displacement, and abuse that had been ignored. In his lifetime, Brown wrote 29 books. In his nonfiction he often took a point of view that challenged conventional ideas on the topic, whether it be the national railroad or women on the frontier. His many fiction books were often based on historical fact.

When Brown was five years old, his father died, forcing his mother to move to Ouachita County, Arkansas, where her family lived. While his mother worked days at a local store, Brown's grandmother took care of him. Her father had known the legendary frontiersman and politician Davy Crocket, and she told the stories she knew about him as well as ones from the Civil War.

Like many children of his generation, Brown spent a lot of time at the movies, enjoying films that portrayed cowboys as heroes of the West, conquering the savage Indians. Brown had friends who were Native American and they explained to him that the Indians on the big screen did not represent real Indians. His social consciousness raised, Brown went on to found his own tabloid at the age of 15. He and his cousin bought a hand press with which they published editorials attacking local entities like the oil companies for environmental degradation.

After high school, Brown worked as a reporter and printer for the newspaper in Harrison, Arkansas. From there he went on to Arkansas State Teachers College, where he studied history and worked in the library. After graduation he was faced with the Depression and floated from job to job, eventually ending up in Washington, D.C. He worked at the U.S. Department of Agriculture's library until he was drafted by the Army. During the Depression, Brown married Sara Baird Stroud; they had two children.

Brown would work at the library, and after his children went to bed, he would write. He placed third in a short story contest and attracted the attention of literary agents. He was commissioned to write a satirical book about bureaucracy in the federal government. By the time Brown finished the book, public sentiment about the government had changed due to the war in Europe. A satire would not be so easily accepted in those patriotic times. The book was cancelled. Instead, Brown published a novel he wrote in two months called *Wave the Banner High,* about Davy Crockett.

In 1942, Brown was drafted into the Army. For most of World War II, he worked as a librarian at the Aberdeen Proving Ground. After the war was over, Brown collaborated with Martin F. Schmitt on three books. From 1948 to 1955, they published *Fighting Indians of the West, Trail–Driving Days,* and *The Settlers' West.* The book were created using photographs from the National Archives compiled by Schmitt and commentary provided by Brown.

Throughout the '50s and '60s, Brown continued to write while working as a librarian at the agriculture library for the University of Illinois at Champaign–Urbana. During that time he earned his master's degree in library science. His focus was almost exclusively on the history of the West, but he always approached the topic from a perspective that was different from what was traditionally taught or portrayed. This approach was not always welcomed. Further research was blocked by the railroad companies once they learned that Brown's book, *Hear That Lonesome Whistle Blow,* was highly critical of the exploitive practices of the railroad companies. Other nonfiction books written in this vein were *Gentle Tamers: Women of the Old Wild West* and *Grierson's Raid: A Cavalry Adventure of the Civil War.*

In 1970, Brown's most influential book was published. Years of research, compiling speeches and documentation plus two years of writing, produced the almost 500–page chronicle of Native American reaction to the settlement of whites into their territories. *Bury My Heart at Wounded Knee: An Indian History of the American West* was a best–seller. Since its publication it has sold more than five million copies and been translated into 15 languages.

Bury My Heart at Wounded Knee focused on the mistreatment that Native Americans suffered between 1860 and 1890. Racist practices, lies, deception, and carelessness were highlighted. The book added another dimension to the historical perception of the American frontier. It changed scholarly attitudes toward the West. Finally, it engaged a generation of Native Americans. University of Arkansas at Little Rock professor C. Fred Williams told Elaine Woo of the *Los Angeles Times,* "The effect of *Bury My Heart* was essentially to give voice to the American Indians. They were always an important part of the American West, usually as the indirect object. Dee Brown [made] them the direct object."

Brown retired from his position as librarian and professor at University of Illinois in 1972 and returned to Arkansas. He continued writing, publishing his last book, *The Way to a Bright Star,* in 1998. He contributed to many anthologies and collections, including *Growing Up Western, Dee Brown's Civil War Anthology,* and *Dee Brown's Folktales of the Native Americans, Retold For Our Times.*

Brown's wife died in 2001. He died on December 12, 2002, at the age of 94 from congenital heart failure. He is survived by his son, daughter, sister, and a grandson. Brown wrote many historically valuable books, but *Bury My Heart at Wounded Knee* had an invaluable and extensive impact on how Native American history is viewed. **Sources:** *Chicago Tribune,* December 14, 2002, p. 11; *Los Angeles Times,* December 14, 2002, p. B20; *New York Times,* December 14, 2002, p. A27; *Times* (London), December 17, 2002, p. 28; *Washington Post,* December 14, 2002, p. B6.

—*Eve M. B. Hermann*

Benny Carter

Born Bennett Lester Carter, August 8, 1907, in New York, NY; died of bronchitis and other ailments, July 12, 2003, in Los Angeles, CA. Musician and arranger. Award–winning jazz musician and arranger Benny Carter had a distinctive sound that was showcased most famously in his 1937 song "Honeysuckle Rose." His 1961 album, *Further Definitions,* which critics consider a masterpiece, remains one of jazz's most influential recordings.

Carter was the only son and the youngest of three children in his family. He grew up in one of the roughest Manhattan neighborhoods at that time, San Juan Hill, near what is now Lincoln Center. His formal education ceased after the eighth grade. His mother taught him piano and, through his cousin, Theodore (Cuban) Bennett, and Bubber Miley, a neighbor who played with Duke Ellington, Carter developed an interest in the trumpet. He saved for months and bought a trumpet at a pawn shop when he was 13, but, when he failed to master it after a weekend's effort, he traded it for a C–melody saxophone (having been told, erroneously, that that instrument was easier to learn). Carter, who was for the most part self–taught, counted Frankie Trumbauer as an early inspiration. By the age of 15 he was sitting in at night spots around Harlem.

In 1925, Carter married his first wife, who died of pneumonia three years later. He briefly attended Wilberforce College in Ohio, where he played with the Wilberforce Collegians, then toured with Horace Henderson. After brief stints with James P. Johnson, Earl Hines, and Ellington, he worked for more than a year with the Charlie Johnson Orchestra, his first full–time job. Carter formed his own group for New York's Arcadia ballroom in 1928 and somehow managed to teach himself to arrange music. That same year he recorded his first records, with the Charlie Johnson group, including two of his own arrangements. Later that year, he began working in a band led by pioneering big band arranger Fletcher Henderson, Horace Henderson's brother. The band was revitalized by Carter's innovative writing, especially his scores for the saxophone section, and he became an influential arranger who also wrote for Ellington and Benny Goodman. Shortly after joining the band, the 21–year–old Carter was chosen by its members to replace the leader, who had walked out during a tour.

In 1931, Carter became the musical director for the Detroit–based McKinney's Cotton Pickers. Having mastered the alto sax, he now took up the trumpet, and within a couple of years was recording trumpet parts that rivaled his alto work. On both instruments, he became known for envisioning a solo as a whole while still retaining spontaneity. The next year he returned to New York and began assembling his own orchestra, which eventually included swing stars such as Teddy Wilson, Dicky Wells, Chu Berry, and Sid Catlett. As was true of all the bands Carter led, the group, with its high musical standards, became known as a "musicians' band." He was helping to codify what would become the style and essence of swing music, stripping away the elaborate embellishment of dance bands, streamlining rhythm, and making improvisation and composition equal. Unfortunately, the band struggled for commercial success, especially during the Depression, and Carter was compelled to disband it.

At this time, an opportune invitation sent Carter to Paris, France, to play with the Willie Lewis Orchestra at a club called Chez Florence. After nine months, at the instigation of music critic Leonard Feather, he moved to England to work as an arranger for the BBC dance orchestra, writing a prodigious three to six arrangements weekly for a period of ten months. As he spent the next three years traveling throughout Europe, Carter became pivotal in spreading jazz abroad and changing its face permanently. He visited with American musicians such as his friend Coleman Hawkins and played and recorded with leading French, British, and Scandinavian jazz musicians. He also led the first international interracial group in Holland. Carter credited Doc Cheatham, with whom he played during this period, as his greatest influence on trumpet. He did not own a trumpet at the time, so Carter would use Cheatham's.

In 1938 Carter returned to New York to find the big band sound that he had helped to craft sweeping the nation. He recorded with Lionel Hampton and formed another orchestra, which played the Savoy Ballroom in Harlem for two years. His arrangements were much in demand, and appeared on recordings by Ellington, Goodman, Count Basie, Glenn Miller, Tommy Dorsey, and Gene Krupa. Though he only had one major hit in the big–band era (a novelty song called "Cow–Cow Boogie," sung by Ella Mae Morse), during the 1930s Carter composed and/or arranged many of the pieces that became Swing Era classics, such as "When Lights Are Low," "Blues in My Heart," and "Lonesome Nights."

In 1941, Carter stripped down to a sextet that included bebop groundbreakers Kenny Clarke and Dizzy Gillespie. He also wrote arrangements for a radio show, *Your Hit Parade*. In 1942 he reorganized his band and moved to California, settling in Hollywood, where he would live for the rest of his life. In the mid–1940s, Carter's band included such leading modernists as Miles Davis, Art Pepper, Max Roach, and J.J. Johnson, all of whom have expressed a debt to Carter as an important mentor.

In Hollywood, Carter moved steadily into studio work. He was among the first African–American arrangers for films and in the 1950s led the integration of white and black musicians unions. In 1943 he wrote arrangements for and played on the soundtrack of the film *Stormy Weather*, although he did not receive a screen credit. From 1946, when he surrendered full–time work as leader of a big band, until 1970, he was virtually out of the public eye. He arranged scores for dozens of movies and, beginning in 1959, television programs. Among his film credits are *The Snows of Kilamanjaro*, *The Flower Drum Song*, and Martin Scorsese's *Too Late Blues*. Among his television credits are *M Squad*, the Alfred Hitchcock series, *Banyon*, *Ironside*, and *The Chrysler Theater*. He also toured occasionally as a soloist and with the Jazz at the Philharmonic ensemble. Carter's arrangements were used by almost every significant popular jazz and blues singer of the era, including Billie Holiday, Ray Charles, Peggy Lee, Sarah Vaughan, Billy Eckstine, and Mel Tormé.

In 1969, Carter was persuaded by Morroe Berger, a sociology professor at Princeton University who had done his master's thesis on jazz, to spend a weekend at the college as part of some classes, seminars, and a concert. This led to a new outlet for Carter's talent: teaching. For the next nine years he visited Princeton five times, most of them brief stays except for one in 1973 when he spent a semester there as a visiting professor. In 1974 Princeton awarded him an honorary master of humanities degree. He conducted workshops and seminars at several other universities and was a visiting lecturer at Harvard for a week in 1987.

Carter's touring career was revitalized by his academic work. The U.S. State Department sponsored his tour of the Middle East in 1975, and the following year he played in a nightclub in New York City for the first time in more than three decades. Over the next 20 years Carter made dozens of new records, and much of his early work was reissued. He continued touring worldwide.

Carter received numerous accolades. In 1978, Carter was invited to the White House to lead a band as part of President Jimmy Carter's commemoration of the Newport Jazz Festival's 25th anniversary. In 1982, when Carter turned 75, New York's WKCR radio station commemorated his birthday by playing his music constantly for 177 hours. Carter received a Grammy Lifetime Achievement Award in 1987 from the National Academy of Recording Arts and Sciences. In 1994, he won a Grammy for "Elegy in Blue." In 1996, Carter was among five recipients of the Kennedy Center Honors in Washington, D.C. That same year, the lauded documentary on Carter, *Symphony in Riffs,* was released on home video. In 2000 he was presented with the National Medal of Arts by President Bill Clinton.

Carter was married five times, with three of the marriages ending in divorce. In 1979, he married his fifth wife, Hilma Ollila Arons, whom he met in 1940 when she went to the Savoy Ballroom to hear his band. Carter died at a Los Angeles hospital on July 12, 2003, just a month shy of his 96th birthday. He is survived by his wife, a daughter, a granddaughter, and a grandson. Nicknamed The King by fellow musicians early in his career, Carter was beloved not only for his musical genius, but also for his reserved, dignified, and modest personality.

Sources: ASCAP, http://ascap.com (January 5, 2004); Benny Carter, http://bennycarter.com (January 5, 2004); *Los Angeles Times,* July 14, 2003, p. B9; *New York Times,* July 14, 2003, p. A19; Riverwalk: Live from the Landing, http://riverwalk.org (January 5, 2004); *Salon.com,* http://salon.com (January 5, 2004); Rutgers University at Newark, http://newarkwww.rutgers.edu (January 5, 2004); *Village Voice,* http://villagevoice.com (January 5, 2004); *Washington Post,* July 15, 2003, p. B7.

—*Amanda de la Garza*

Nell Carter

Born Nell Ruth Hardy, September 13, 1948, in Birmingham, AL; died of natural causes likely caused by heart disease and complications from diabetes, January 23, 2003, in Beverly Hills, CA. Actress and singer. Broadway and television performer Nell Carter was best known for her role as a sassy housekeeper on the television sitcom *Gimme a Break,* which ran on NBC from 1981 to 1987. Carter also won a Tony award in 1978 for her stage performance in the Fats Waller musical review, *Ain't Misbehavin'.* The rotund, four–foot, eleven–inch actress had a powerful, sultry singing voice and a strong stage presence; she deftly handled roles in drama, comedy, and musicals with equal capability.

Carter, the fifth of nine children, grew up in Birmingham, Alabama. When she was a toddler, her father died of electrocution after stepping on a live power line in a field next to their home. She was raped at gunpoint at age 15, and that same year, four of her friends died when a bomb planted by segregationists exploded in a church. Later, Carter would say she found solace in listening to music, having a fondness for her mother's Dinah Washington and B.B. King tunes as well as her brother's Elvis Presley records.

From a young age, Carter sang in church groups, on the gospel circuit and on a weekly radio program, *The Y Teens.* Later, she performed in coffeehouses. At age 19, she moved to New York City to study acting at Bill Russell's School of Drama. There, she began to appear at nightclubs like Reno Sweeney, the Village Gate, Dangerfield's, the Apartment, and the Rainbow Room.

Carter's Broadway debut came in the short–lived 1971 musical *Soon,* which counted then–unknowns Richard Gere and Peter Allen in the cast. Carter also had bit parts in the films *Jesus Christ Superstar* in 1973 and *Hair* in 1979. She studied drama in London before being cast in *Ain't Misbehavin'*, a compilation of songs by, and associated with, jazz star Fats Waller. It opened in February of 1978 at the Manhattan Theater Club and moved to the Longacre Theater on Broadway three months later, where it ran four years.

In 1978, Carter won a Tony Award for best featured actress for her performance in *Ain't Misbehavin'* and won an Emmy Award in 1982 for the television version of the show. Her rendition of the quietly soulful "Mean to Me" was considered one of the musical's highlights. Her other theater credits included *Hello Dolly!, Don't Bother Me, I Can't Cope,* and *Bubbling Brown Sugar.*

In addition to her stage roles, Carter appeared in a handful of television shows in the late 1970s and early 1980s, including the soap opera *Ryan's Hope* in 1978 and 1979 and in the television series *The Misadventures of Sheriff Lobo* in 1980. She played the role of Nell Harper on *Gimme a Break* from 1981 to 1987, portraying an African–American woman caring for the three daughters of a white widower, who was also the town's police chief. For this, she garnered Emmy nominations in 1982 and 1983. One episode, in 1985, was broadcast live—the first for a situation comedy in almost 30 years.

After *Gimme a Break* went off the air in 1987, Carter took various parts in films, on television shows, and on stage. She did a voice–over for the 1992 animated movie *Bebe's Kids,* had film roles in 1995's *The Grass Harp* and 1996's *The Proprietor,* and appeared in episodes of the television shows *Hanging with Mr. Cooper, Ally McBeal,* and *Reba.* In 1997 she played villainous orphanage manager Miss Hannigan in the revival of the play *Annie.*

Even later in her career, Carter kept active with cabaret performances and concerts. Before her death, she was in rehearsals at a theater in Long Beach, California, to play Mama in *Raisin,* a 1973 musical version of the play, *A Raisin in the Sun.* In an obituary in the *Los Angeles Times,* her manager stated she had lost 170 pounds over the previous year and was eager to express her dramatic range in the production.

Eating disorders, alcohol and drug addiction, and other health concerns plagued Carter for years. In a 1994 interview, she admitted that she first tried cocaine the night she won her Tony Award. She fi-

nally managed to get clean with help from a 12–step program. In 1992, Carter had two brain surgeries to fix an aneurysm, and that same year, her grandmother died after suffering from Alzheimer's disease. In 1997, Carter learned she had diabetes.

Carter was married in 1982 and divorced in 1992, then married again that same year. She was divorced again in 1993. In 1989 and 1990, she adopted two sons, Joshua and Daniel. Carter died on January 23, 2003, at the age of 54; a coroner's report later ruled her death was due to natural causes likely caused by heart disease and complications from diabetes. She is survived by an adult daughter, Tracy, and her two sons. **Sources:** *Chicago Tribune,* January 24, 2003, sec. 1, p. 11; CNN.com, http://www.cnn.com/2003/SHOWBIZ/TV/05/06/nell.carter.ap/index.html (May 6, 2003); E! Online, www.eonline.com/News/Items/0,1,11735,00.html?tnews (May 7, 2003); *Independent,* February 7, 2003, p. 18; *Los Angeles Times,* January 24, 2003, p. B14; *New York Times,* January 24, 2003, p. C19; *Washington Post,* January 24, 2003, p. B8.

—*Geri Koeppel*

June Carter Cash

Born Valerie June Carter, June 23, 1929, in Maces Springs, VA; died of complications following open–heart surgery, May 15, 2003, in Nashville, TN. Singer and songwriter. June Carter Cash, perhaps best known as the wife of country–music legend Johnny Cash, was an accomplished performer in her own right in the years before her marriage. Venerated by nearly every country–music star who emerged out of the Nashville scene since the mid–twentieth century, Cash was deemed "a link from the bedrock of the genre's history to its most respected modern practitioners" by *Entertainment Weekly* after her death.

Cash was born in 1929 in Maces Spring, Virginia, where her father Ezra farmed, but her mother, aunt and uncle had already formed a music group by then called the Carter Family that enjoyed some regional fame. The group's growing success led the family to relocate to Texas when Cash was ten years old, in order to be nearer to a powerful radio station in Del Rio, XERA, whose country–music programming could be heard as far north as Saskatchewan, Canada. Cash's group, led by her famous parent, "Mother" Maybelle Carter, were a string–based ensemble and had their own show on XERA for a number of years, and Cash sang her own numbers and played the autoharp. The group broke up in 1943, but Cash and her sisters continued to perform with Maybelle, and made frequent appearances on the stage of Nashville's legendary Grand Ole Opry.

Cash sometimes joked that her voice was the weakest of the bunch, and so she honed her comic talents to compensate. Her performing style caught on, and she had her first solo hit in 1949, "Baby It's Cold Outside," which was a duet with an act called Homer and Jethro. She wed singer Carl Smith, with whom she had a daughter, Carlene, but the couple were divorced by 1957 and Cash then wed her second husband, Rip Nix, a Nashville police officer; they had a daughter named Rozanna. Her stage presence attracted the attention of leading theater and film director Elia Kazan, who suggested she pursue a performing career outside of the music business. Cash studied under Lee Strasberg, head of the famed Actors' Studio in New York, and also at the Neighborhood Playhouse in that city. In 1961, she was offered a slot on a planned television variety show for which an unknown Woody Allen was part of the comic–writing team, but Cash declined it in order to take a job touring with country–music star Johnny Cash.

Cash had met her future husband backstage at the Grand Ole Opry in 1956; by the early 1960s Johnny had enjoyed tremendous success but was plagued by addictions to prescription drugs and alcohol. On tour, June would hide his pills and even flush them down the toilet. She co–wrote his 1963 hit "Ring of Fire" with Merle Kilgore and the song became indelibly associated with his career. "Instead of the usual seraphic love language of teen–angels," noted her New York Times obituary by Ben Ratliff, "it used images of suffering and hellfire and is probably the most complicated popular love song in country music."

Both Cash's marriage to Nix and Johnny Cash's ended, and he proposed to her on stage one night in London, Ontario. They were wed in 1968, not long after their duet "Jackson," from the 1967 LP Carryin' On, won a Grammy. The duo won their second Grammy for the 1970 hit "If I Were a Carpenter," and though Cash performed frequently with her husband onstage for much of the following decade, she stopped making solo records almost entirely. She continued to take the occasional film

and television role after the birth of their son, John Carter Cash, in 1970, and appeared in a small but compelling part as the deeply religious mother of Robert Duvall's minister character in the 1997 film The Apostle.

In a 1996 gig with her husband at the House of Blues in Hollywood, Cash sang a new song she had written about the vagaries of fame, "I Used to Be Somebody," which led to a new record deal. Her 1999 release Press On, won the Grammy in the folk–music category. "I've been really happy just traveling with John and being Mrs. Johnny Cash all these years," Los Angeles Times writer Geoff Boucher quoted her as saying. "But I'm also really happy and surprised that someone wanted me to make another album, and I'm real proud of what I've done."

Cash and her husband had homes in Nashville, in the Clinch Mountain area of Virginia, and in Jamaica. In 2003, she underwent surgery to replace a heart valve, and never recovered; she passed away at the age of 73. Cash is survived by her two daughters, a son, four stepdaughters, and several grandchildren. Her death was mourned as the passing of one of country's most beloved performers, and her husband died just four months later. Those close to the family claim he never recovered from her death. As he wrote in his autobiography, according to the Los Angeles Times's Boucher, "What June did for me was post signs along the way, lift me when I was weak, encourage me when I was discouraged, and love me when I was alone and felt unlovable." **Sources:** CNN.com, http://www.cnn.com/2003/SHOWBIZ/Music/05/15/june.carter.cash.obit.ap/index.html (May 16, 2003); Entertainment Weekly, May 30, 2003; Los Angeles Times, May 16, 2003, p. B13; New York Times, May 16, 2003, p. A23; People, June 2, 2003, p. 89; September 29, 2003, p. 78; Times (London), http://www.timesonline.co.uk (May 18, 2003); Washington Post, May 16, 2003, p. B6.

—Carol Brennan

James Coburn

Born August 31, 1928, in Laurel, NE; died from a heart attack, November 18, 2002, in Beverly Hills, CA. Actor. James Coburn appeared in more than 80 films throughout his career. He was most often recognized for his gritty, masculine roles in films like The Magnificent Seven, The Great Escape, and Major

Dundee. His popularity waned in the 1970s, and in the 1980s he was sidelined by rheumatoid arthritis. Overcoming the crippling effects of arthritis, Coburn made a comeback in the 1990s, eventually earning an Academy Award for his performance in *Affliction.*

Coburn grew up in Compton, California, where his family had moved after leaving Laurel, Nebraska. His first acting role came early, when he was four years old, playing Herod in a school play. In his teens, he worked in a movie theater performing various roles from janitor to ticket taker. From those inauspicious beginnings, he went on to study acting at Los Angeles City College and the University of Southern California. In the early 1950s, Coburn served in the military. Stationed in Texas, he worked as a public information officer.

In 1955, Coburn finished his military duty and promptly moved to New York where he studied acting with master teacher Stella Adler. His experience there included stage plays and appearances in episodes of the dramatic television series *Studio One* and *General Electric Theatre.* After a few years in New York, Coburn returned to Los Angeles where he continued to work in television. He had roles on *Wagon Train, The Rifleman,* and *Alfred Hitchcock Presents.*

In 1959, Coburn made his film debut in *Ride Lonesome.* This taut, well–written, B–Western has earned a reputation as one of the best examples of the genre. Coburn turned in a memorable performance as Whit, a dim–witted outlaw seeking a pardon by helping to turn in a fugitive. That same year he had another supporting role in the minor Western *Face of a Fugitive.*

In 1960, Coburn became a star with his role in the classic Western directed by John Sturges, *The Magnificent Seven.* Appearing onscreen with superstars Yul Brenner and Steve McQueen, Coburn held his own as Britt, a knife–wielding mercenary. Even though he had only a few lines, Coburn exuded a cool menace as one of the seven men hired to protect a village from outlaws. Coburn went on to play roles in several other films directed by Sturges, including the World War II epic *The Great Escape.*

In 1966, Coburn starred in *Our Man Flint,* a satirical spoof of James Bond films. As the epitome of the suave super agent, Coburn used his lanky good looks, toothy grin, and baritone voice to play the ultra–cool Derek Flint. The film was wildly successful and was followed by a less successful sequel, *In Like Flint.* E! Online wrote of the film, "It was Coburn's greatest hit, made him a full–blown pop–culture icon and proved that he could do funny as well as menace."

Coburn's career began to wane during the 1970s, although he continued to appear in films throughout the decade. In 1971, he played explosives expert Sean Mallory in Sergio Leone's action film set in Mexico, *A Fistful of Dynamite.* In 1973, he portrayed the outlaw–turned–sheriff Pat Garrett in Sam Peckinpah's *Pat Garrett and Billy the Kid.* As the decade progressed, Coburn was appearing in smaller roles in less important films so he tried his hand at directing and writing. In 1974, he directed episodes of *The Rockford Files,* the popular crime drama starring James Garner. He co–wrote the story for *Circle of Iron* with his friend, martial–arts expert Bruce Lee.

The onset of rheumatoid arthritis in the early 1980s almost sidelined Coburn. He continued to appear in movies and on television, but the crippling effects of the arthritis limited his roles to those in which he moved very little. He supplemented his income with voice work and appearances in commercials. Coburn, who had indulged a lifelong interest in eastern religions, yoga, and meditation, turned to alternative therapies to relieve his arthritis. Although his right hand was crippled, Coburn eventually conquered his arthritis through a combination of sulphur pills, diet, and exercise.

With his arthritis under control, Coburn made his comeback in the 1990s as a character actor. He appeared in *Young Guns II, Hudson Hawk, Sister Act 2,* and *Maverick.* He also made appearances on television. Even though he was working regularly, many of the roles were small and did not use Coburn to his fullest potential. The film *Affliction,* in which Coburn had a supporting role as Nick Nolte's alcoholic father, gave Coburn a chance to shine. He earned an Academy Award for Best Supporting Actor in 1998 for his portrayal of Glen Whitehouse, a verbally and physically abusive man.

In the 2000s, Coburn continued to work hard. He made notable appearances on television and in film. He appeared in dramas such as *Proximity, The Man from Elysian Fields,* and his final film, released after his death, *The American Gun.* He was the voice of Henry J. Waternoose, III, in the successful computer–animated film *Monsters, Inc.* Continuing to show his less serious side, he also appeared in the 2002 comedy *Snow Dogs.*

Coburn married Beverly Kelly in 1959; they divorced in 1979. He married Paula Murad in 1993. Coburn died on November 18, 2002, of a heart attack while listening to music at home; he was 74. He is survived by his wife; his son, James; stepdaughter, Lisa; and two grandchildren. His long career in acting took him from dramatic Westerns to comedic spoofs, and throughout it all he made it look easy. His manager Hillard Elkins told CNN.com, "He was a guy who looked like he was casual, but he studied and he worked and he understood character." **Sources:** CNN.com, http://www.cnn.com/2002/SHOWBIZ/Movies/11/18/obit.coburn.ap/index.html (November 19, 2002); E! Online, http://www.eonline.com/News/Items/0,1,10862,00.html?eol.tkr (November 20, 2002); *New York Times*, November 20, 2002, p. A21; *People*, December 12, 2002, p. 70; *Times* (London), http://www.timesonline.co.uk (November 20, 2002).

—Eve M. B. Hermann

Richard Crenna

Born November 30, 1926, in Los Angeles, CA; died of heart failure, January 17, 2003, in Los Angeles, CA. Actor. Richard Crenna's career spanned more than 60 years from the heyday of radio to the rise of television. He was an actor, a director, a producer, and an active member of the Screen Actors Guild. His varied career included television situation comedies and dramas as well as made–for–TV movies. He acted in films and may be most remembered for his role as Colonel Trautman in Sylvester Stallone's Rambo series.

Crenna grew up in Los Angeles, where his mother managed a small chain of family owned hotels. His father was a pharmacist. While in junior high Crenna signed up for drama classes, because he thought he could goof off while hanging out with the prettiest girls. He became a child radio actor when he was recruited with a number of classmates to play a part on the *Boy Scout Jamboree*. Crenna was a member of the show's Beaver Patrol for the next eleven years.

Crenna finished high school and studied English at the University of Southern California. During this time he continued to work in radio productions. He had roles in shows like *Gunsmoke, Red Ryder, One Man's Family,* and *I Love A Mystery*. He sometimes worked in as many as eight shows a week.

In 1948, Crenna began playing the role that would define him for the next four years. As Walter Den-

ton in the situation comedy *Our Miss Brooks* starring Eve Arden, Crenna played the epitome of the geeky, socially awkward teenage boy. When the show was transferred to television in 1952, Arden insisted that Crenna come along despite being well into his 20s. He left the successful series in 1956 at nearly 30 years of age.

In 1957, Crenna starred in the popular comedy series, *The Real McCoys*. As Luke, the grandson of a Virginia farmer who transplants the family to California, Crenna was finally able to portray an adult. The show lasted six seasons, ending in 1963. To combat boredom, Crenna took up directing, trying his hand at several episodes of the series. He continued to direct throughout his career, including episodes of *Wendy and Me, No Time for Sergeants,* and *The Andy Griffith Show*.

Crenna's first dramatic role came in the short–lived series *Slattery's People*. Unfortunately, the show lasted less than two seasons. Throughout the '60s Crenna appeared in several films, returning to television in made–for–TV movies and short series over the next 20 years. He made attempts to return to situation comedy in the '70s, '80s, and '90s, but none of the shows were successful. In 1985, he earned an Emmy for Outstanding Actor in a Limited Series or Special for his portrayal of a cop who is sexually assaulted in *The Rape of Richard Beck*. In 2000, he began making appearances on the CBS drama *Judging Amy* as Jared Duff, the love interest of Tyne Daly's character.

Crenna had made his big–screen debut in 1950 playing a bit part in the Fred Astaire film *Let's Dance*. He appeared in several other films in supporting roles throughout the '50s. He played baseball star "Dizzy" Dean's brother in *The Pride of St. Louis*. His roles in the films *It Grows on Trees* and *Over–Exposed* were well received. In 1956, he played Walter Denton for the last time in the movie version of *Our Miss Brooks*.

Being part of the successful television series *The Real McCoys* left Crenna little time to make films. After the series ended and *Slattery's People* was cancelled, Crenna portrayed the grouchy yet brave Captain Collins in the 1966 Steve McQueen film *The Sand Pebbles*. He followed up with a performance opposite Audrey Hepburn in the suspense/thriller *Wait Until Dark*.

In the 1980s, Crenna's supporting roles in films received the most critical acclaim. In 1981, he played the despicable and doomed husband of Matty

Walker (Kathleen Turner's screen debut) in the steamy film noir *Body Heat*. In 1984, he appeared with Matt Dillon in *The Flamingo Kid*. For his role as a cardsharp who leads Dillon astray, Crenna earned a Golden Globe nomination.

In 1982, Crenna appeared in the film *First Blood*. The film starred Sylvester Stallone as Rambo, a Vietnam veteran who takes revenge on the police department of a small town. The film was wildly successful and followed by two sequels. Crenna appeared in all three films as Colonel Samuel Trautman, the only person for whom Rambo has any loyalty. Dennis McLellan of the *Los Angeles Times* reported that Crenna said of the movie's success, "This film series has given me the kind of recognition I've never before had as an actor. I feel like I'm part of a cult happening. It's like being a part of the Woodstock of the '80s on the big screen." In 1993, Crenna even parodied the roll in the film *Hot Shots! Part Deux*.

Crenna died on January 17, 2003, from heart failure while hospitalized with pancreatic cancer; he was 75. He is survived by his wife of more than 40 years, Penni; his son, Richard; daughters Sean and Maria; and three granddaughters. His daughter summarized the breadth of Crenna's career to Corey Kilgannon of the *New York Times*, "He had such a full career because he lived for his work. If you never saw him on the screen as an actor, you surely heard him through radio roles and voiceovers." **Sources:** *Los Angeles Times,* January 19, 2003, p. B16; *New York Times,* January 20, 2003, p. A21; *Times* (London), http://www. timesonline.co.uk (January 28, 2003); *Washington Post,* January 17, 2002, p. C9.

—*Eve M. B. Hermann*

Hume Cronyn

Born July 18, 1911, in London, Ontario, Canada; died of prostate cancer, Fairfield, CT, on June 15, 2003. Actor, writer, and director. Hume Cronyn's long and varied career spanned seven decades and encompassed roles in theater, film, and television. In addition to acting, Cronyn was a talented director and writer. His marriage to Jessica Tandy lasted for 52 years and the two actors created many memorable roles starring opposite each other.

Cronyn came from a privileged Canadian family; his mother was a member of the Labatt's brewery family and his father, also named Hume, was a prominent Canadian banker as well as a politician. Cronyn's interest in theater was encouraged while he was growing up. His parents took him to London, England, to see performances when he was 15 years old. Despite his love of theater, Cronyn followed his father's wishes by studying law at McGill University in Montreal, Canada.

Short and compact, Cronyn was a talented athlete and a star on the McGill University boxing team. He was even nominated for a spot on the 1932 Canadian Olympic boxing team. By 1932, though, Cronyn—who had been spending summers in the United States studying acting—had made a decision about his future. He chose to quit college, move to New York City, and take a chance on being an actor.

Cronyn had made his theater debut in 1931 in the play *Up Pops the Devil,* playing a paperboy. From 1932 to 1934, he studied at the American Academy of Dramatic Arts as well as under the Austrian drama coach Max Reinhardt. He appeared in as many plays as possible where he could find work and made his Broadway debut in 1934 in *Hippers' Holiday,* playing a janitor. In 1939, he made a critically acclaimed appearance in Anton Chekov's *Three Sisters* as the brother, Andrea Prozoroff.

In 1940, Cronyn met the British actress Jessica Tandy and sparked a relationship that would last more than 50 years. Together Tandy and Cronyn established a reputation for performing the classics as well as a successful run of more experimental stage works. In 1946, Cronyn directed Tandy in a Los Angeles, California, production of Tennessee Williams' *Portrait of a Madonna.* The role earned her critical acclaim and helped further her Broadway career. They starred in their first Broadway production together in 1951 in the comedy *The Fourposter.* For their performances in *The Gin Game* they were both nominated for Tony Awards.

The couple went on to co-star in film and television as well. In 1954 they appeared in *The Marriage,* a short-lived NBC series—the first ever to be telecast in color. In the 1980s they appeared in several films including *The World According to Garp, Batteries Not Included, Cocoon,* and *Cocoon: The Return.* In 1991, they made the CBS movie *To Dance With the White Dog* and were both nominated for Emmy Awards. Tandy died three years later, in 1994, from cancer. The two actors earned membership in the Theater Hall of Fame as well as lifetime achievement awards from the Kennedy Center and the Tony Awards.

In 1943, Cronyn made his film debut in Alfred Hitchcock's *Shadow of a Doubt*. The next year he appeared in another Hitchcock film called *Lifeboat* and was also nominated for a best supporting actor Academy Award for his role in *The Seventh Cross*. Other notable films that Cronyn appeared in include 1943's *Phantom of the Opera*, 1946's *The Postman Always Rings Twice*, and 1963's *Cleopatra*. Cronyn's television appearances in the 1950s included starring in two episodes of the *Alfred Hitchcock Presents* series. He also appeared in several dramas including *The Bridge of San Luis Rey, The Moon and Sixpence*, and *Juno and the Paycock*.

By the 1960s, Cronyn was beginning to earn awards for his work in theater. In 1961, he was awarded the Barter Theater Award for outstanding contribution to the theater. He also won the New York Drama League Medal for his role in *Big Fish, Little Fish* playing a homosexual art instructor. In 1964, Cronyn won a Tony Award playing Polonious in Shakespeare's *Hamlet*.

Cronyn was a tireless worker and was not slowed when in 1969 his left eye had to be removed due to cancer. He meticulously prepared for each of his roles, trying to pin down the smallest nuances of his characters. In between acting jobs he kept himself busy writing or directing. CNN.com reported that he said, "I fill my life with a lot of 'busyness' in between jobs. Then I work very hard. Some of it is quite unhealthy. It's compulsive.... I'm a little old to change."

Cronyn was also an experienced writer and worked with Hitchcock on the scripts for two of his films, *Rope* and *Under Capricorn*. He also wrote the play *Foxfire* in which he and Tandy starred on stage and in a television adaptation. He also co-wrote *The Dollmaker*, a television movie starring Jane Fonda. In 1991, he published his memoir, *A Terrible Liar*.

Cronyn died on June 15, 2003, of prostate cancer. He was 91 years old. Cronyn's first marriage, to Emily Woodruff in 1935, ended in divorce. Cronyn is survived by his third wife, author Susan Cooper (whom he married in 1996), three children, two stepchildren, eight grandchildren, and five great-grandchildren. His attention to detail and his energetic dedication to all aspects of performance earned him a permanent and acclaimed spot in entertainment history. **Sources:** CNN.com, http://www.cnn.com/2003/SHOWBIZ/Movies/06/16/obit.cronyn.ap/index.html (March 12, 2004); E! Online, http://www.eonline.com/News/Items/0,1,11992,00.

html?eol.tkr (March 12, 2004); *Independent* (London, England), June 18, 2003, p. 16; *Los Angeles Times,* June 17, 2003, p. B12; *New York Times,* June 17, 2003, p. A1; *Washington Post,* June 17, 2003, p. B7.

—*Eve M. B. Hermann*

Celia Cruz

Born October 21, 1925, in Havana, Cuba; died of brain cancer, July 16, 2003, in Fort Lee, NJ. Singer. Cuban–born singing star Celia Cruz has been hailed as the queen of salsa, rumba, and Latin music, and an inadvertent symbol of the Cuban–American community's exile spirit. Cruz, who fled the Caribbean island nation in 1960, became a world–famous singer with an energetic, flamboyant stage presence that brought audiences to their feet. "Cruz is undisputedly the best–known and most influential female figure in the history of Afro–Cuban music," declared *Billboard*'s Leila Cobo.

Though sometimes evasive about her age, news sources reported that Cruz was 77 when she died in 2003, which placed her birth date at October 21, 1925. A native of Havana, Cuba, she grew up in a household headed by her father, a railroad stoker. The family was of Afro–Cuban heritage, descendants of the Africans who were forcibly brought to the island nation to work in its vast sugar fields in centuries past, and eventually grew to include 14 children, some of them Cruz's cousins. As the second eldest child, she would often have to put the younger ones to bed, and would sing them to sleep.

In her teens, Cruz entered and won first prize in a radio contest, "La hora del té," by singing a tango song. She began entering other amateur contests, and though her mother was encouraging, her father strongly disapproved of her ambitions to become a singer in Cuba's strong salsa scene. This musical style merged elements from traditional Spanish music with the African rhythms that came from the island's former slave population, and exemplified national character traits of both exuberance and a penchant for romantic melancholy. Cruz's father hoped instead that she would become a teacher, and so to placate him Cruz entered the local teachers' college for a time, but quit when her singing career began to take off in earnest. From 1947 to 1950 she studied music theory, voice and piano at the National Conservatory of Music in Havana.

Cruz's break came when La Sonora Matancera, a popular Cuban band, hired her as their lead vocalist in 1950. She had a tough time at first, because female singers were a relative rarity in Cuban music and she replaced a singer with a popular following. Irate fans even wrote to the radio station that broadcast La Sonora Matancera performances, but as Cruz told Cobo in *Billboard,* she was unfazed. "I could [not] care less. This was my job—the job of my dreams and the job that fed me." Even an American record company executive that signed the band was uneasy with the proposition of a rumba track with a female singer, so the band's leader, Rogelio Martínez, promised to pay Cruz out of his own pocket for the session if the record failed to catch on, but the song was a hit.

Both La Sonora Matancera and Cruz became stars in Cuba. Throughout the 1950s, they played regularly at Havana's famed Tropicana nightclub, appeared in films, and toured extensively throughout Latin America. These heady years ended in 1959 when Communist leader Fidel Castro seized power and Cuba became a socialist state. A year and a half later, Cruz was with La Sonora Matancera on a Mexican tour when they defected en masse on July 15, 1960. The band settled in the United States, and Cruz soon became a naturalized citizen. Castro was irate that one of his country's most popular musical acts had made such a public statement against his regime, and vowed that none would ever be granted entry back into Cuba again. Cruz tried to return when her mother died in 1962, but was unable to secure government permission. That same year, she wed Pedro Knight, La Sonora Matancera's trumpet player, who would eventually become her manager and musical director for much of her career.

At first, Cruz remained relatively unknown in the United States outside of the Cuban exile community, but that changed when she joined the Tito Puente Orchestra in the mid–1960s. The popular percussionist and bandleader from Puerto Rico had a large following across Latin America, and as the frontperson, Cruz again became a dynamic focus for the act.

Cruz recorded several albums with Puente, including *Cuba Y Puerto Rico Son* in 1966. But it was her stage presence that made her such a compelling figure in Latin music. She had a strong, husky voice that could hold its own against a hard–working rhythm section, and was a tireless dancer, storyteller, and audience–rouser. Fans adored her glitzy stage outfits, often sewn from yards of fabric and embellished with sequins, feathers, or lace. Reportedly she never wore the same one twice. High heels and towering wigs only added to the diminutive singer's allure. Her signature shout, "Azucar!"

(Sugar!), came from a dining experience at a Miami restaurant, when her Cuban waiter asked if she took sugar in her coffee. As she recalled in the *Billboard* interview with Cobo, "I said, 'Chico, you're Cuban. How can you even ask that? With sugar!' And that evening during my show—I always talk during the show so the horn players can rest their mouths—I told the audience the story and they laughed. And one day, instead of telling the story, I simply walked down the stairs and shouted 'Azucar!'"

By the 1970s, the salsa sound had caught on with a new generation of Latin Americans, riding a resurgence of ethnic pride and interest in the music of their parents' era. Cruz even appeared at Carnegie Hall for a 1973 staging of *Hommy—A Latin Opera,* the Spanish–language adaptation of the hit rock opera from the Who, *Tommy.* For a number of years, she was signed to the Fania label, a salsa–source powerhouse co–owned by trombonist Willie Colón, with whom she recorded an acclaimed 1974 work, *Celia and Willie.* She performed regularly with the Fania All–Stars, including a 1976 concert at Yankee Stadium in the Bronx that was recorded and released as a double album. The singer also appeared annually at a New York City salsa–fest held at Madison Square Garden.

Cruz lived in the New York City area, but was also a star in Miami and performed there often. For Cuban–Americans, she seemed to symbolize the trajectory of its large exile community centered in southern Florida—many of whom, like her, had fled the Castro regime and then achieved personal and professional success in their adopted homeland. Most were avowed foes of Castro and asserted, as Cruz had also done, that they would never to return to Cuba unless it became a democracy.

Over the years, Cruz worked with a roster of performers that proved her crossover appeal, though she never sang in anything but her native Spanish language. She recorded or collaborated with Brazilian star Caetano Veloso, R&B singer Patti LaBelle, Wyclef Jean of the Fugees, producer Emilio Estefan, the tenor Luciano Pavarotti, and even former Talking Heads singer David Byrne. In the 1992 film *The Mambo Kings,* she was cast as a nightclub owner, and she also appeared in 1995's *The Perez Family.* Her awards included a Grammy for best tropical Latin album of 1989 for *Ritmo en el corazón,* a collaboration with conga player Ray Barretto, and she took three consecutive Latin Grammy awards when the honors were established in 2000, including best salsa album of 2002 for *La Negra Tiene Tumbao,* which spawned a hit single of the same name.

Cruz was not slowed by age, and still toured heavily and recorded well into her seventies. "My life is singing," she told Knight–Ridder/Tribune News Service reporter Mario Tarradell in 2002. "I don't plan on retiring. I plan to die on a stage. I can have a headache. But when it's time to sing and I step on that stage, there's no more headache. As long as I'm doing what I want to do, I feel good." Her final album was *Regalo de Alma* ("Gift from the Soul"), recorded in early 2003 when she was already suffering from cancer. She died on July 16, 2003, at her home in Fort Lee, New Jersey. She had requested that her funeral include two public viewings—one in New York City, and a second in Miami; thousands turned out for each.

"For the almost two million Cubans who live outside the island," noted Ojito in the *New York Times,* "Cruz was an icon.... She embodied what Cubans view as some of their best qualities: strong family ties, an impeccable work ethic and a joy in living, even in the face of calamity." **Sources:** *Billboard,* July 26, 2003; *Contemporary Hispanic Biography,* vol. 1, Gale, 2002; *Economist,* July 26, 2003; *Entertainment Weekly,* August 1, 2003; Knight-Ridder/Tribune News Service, July 16, 2003; July 19, 2003; July 22, 2003; *New York Times,* July 17, 2003, p. C13; *People,* August 4, 2003, pp. 69-70; *Time,* July 11, 1998.

—Carol Brennan

Buddy Ebsen

Born Christian Rudolph Ebsen, April 2, 1908, in Belleville, IL; died of pneumonia, July 6, 2003, in Torrance, CA. Actor and dancer. Buddy Ebsen's career spanned more than 60 years, encompassing the latter days of vaudeville, Broadway success, and a brief foray into film. He is most popularly remembered for his television role as hillbilly–turned–millionaire Jed Clampett of the long–running situation comedy *The Beverly Hillbillies. People* reported that Ebsen, referring to the common refrain uttered by Clampett, once said, "I can walk on any stage in the English–speaking world and say, 'Well, doggies!' and I'm home free."

Nicknamed "Buddy" early on by an aunt, Ebsen didn't intend to make a career out of performing. Early on he had decided to become a doctor despite the fact that his father operated a dance school where he took ballet lessons as a young child. When

he was ten years old the family moved to Orlando, Florida, where his father opened another dance school. After graduating from high school, Ebsen went on to attend the University of Florida as well as Rollins College. He was taking pre–medical courses, inspired by a childhood illness suffered by his sister, when he was forced to withdraw because of the Depression.

Ebsen decided to take up dancing and try his luck in New York. His early training in his father's school served him well and in 1928 he had his first role in New York in the chorus of a show called *Whoopee.* Inspired by his success, Ebsen invited his sister, Vilma, to join him and together they created a winning dance routine. They toured the vaudeville circuit and played at supper clubs as well as performing in the legendary variety production called the Ziegfeld Follies. Eventually the two were invited to Hollywood where they appeared in the MGM film *Flying Colors.* Their act was one of the standout features of the film. They also earned rave reviews for their appearance in the film *Broadway Melody of 1936.*

Unfortunately, the contract they signed with MGM stated that one of them could be terminated at any time. Vilma was sent packing back to New York where she retired from performing and married. Ebsen stayed in Hollywood. In 1936, he married Ruth Cambridge and had two daughters with her. After that marriage ended in divorce, Ebsen married Nancy Wolcott in 1945. Wolcott and Ebsen had four daughters and one son and were divorced in 1985. Ebsen later married Dorothy Knott, to whom he remained married until his death.

Ebsen's biggest role may have been the one he lost. He was originally cast as the Scarecrow in *The Wizard of Oz.* Ray Bolger, who was playing the Tin Man, pleaded with him to exchange roles until Ebsen finally agreed. Unfortunately for Ebsen, the makeup that made him silver was made from aluminum and after a couple weeks of filming, his lungs became lined with the metallic dust. He found it nearly impossible to breathe and was soon hospitalized. He spent two weeks in the hospital in an oxygen tent and then several more weeks recovering. By the time he was well, Jack Haley had been cast as the Tin Man. However, Ebsen was still in the film in a way; since he had pre–recorded the songs, it is his voice that is featured on the soundtrack, not Haley's. Plus, as Ebsen later told the *Los Angeles Times,* "I suspect I'm still in a couple of the long shots because you couldn't tell who was in there and it cost a lot of money to reshoot."

After losing his place in one of film history's most enduring films, Ebsen ended up losing again. In 1938, Louis B. Mayer told Ebsen that MGM needed to own him. It meant signing an exclusive contract that would prevent Ebsen from working for any other studio. Ebsen declined by saying, as reported in the *Washington Post,* "I'll tell you what kind of a fool I am, Mr. Mayer, I can't be owned." With those words, Ebsen took leave of Hollywood, where Mayer succeeded in blackballing him from film roles at any studio.

During the 1940s, Ebsen toured again as a dancer and performed in shows throughout the country. The *New York Times* reported Ebsen's recollection of that time, "I probably enjoyed show business the most when I was doing plays like *The Male Animal* and *Good Night, Ladies,* when people would lay down their money and laugh and you'd see them walk out happy." Ebsen served a three-year tour of duty with the Coast Guard on the U.S.S. Pocatello in the North Pacific. In his down time while at sea, he wrote sketches for variety shows and musicals that he helped stage.

In the mid-'50s, Ebsen returned to Hollywood. A director recommended to Walt Disney that Ebsen play Davy Crockett in Disney's weekly special *Davy Crockett.* When Fess Parker was chosen instead, Ebsen was given the role of Crockett's friend, George Russel. Nearly forgotten for more than 20 years, Ebsen became a hero to children throughout the United States. Children everywhere played at being Crockett and Russel, wearing coonskin hats and singing the show's theme song.

Ebsen found other roles in Hollywood, including a small but poignant role in *Breakfast at Tiffany's.* In that film he played the husband of Audrey Hepburn's Holly Golightly. For the most part though, film was beginning its decline and television was becoming more popular. In 1962, Ebsen would step into his career-defining role as Jed Clampett, the wise and jovial head of the family in the hit television series *The Beverly Hillbillies.* Despised by the critics and advertisers, but loved by audiences, *Beverly Hillbillies* ran for nine seasons, ending in 1971. In 1973, Ebsen took on another role in a successful television series. He played the ex-private investigator pulled from retirement by the disappearance of his son in the show *Barnaby Jones.* The show aired for seven years, until 1980. He later appeared regularly on another detective series, *Matt Houston.*

Never one to sit still, Ebsen occupied himself in his later years with writing, painting, and running his business that manufactured ocean-going catamarans. He authored a popular novel in 2001 called *Kelly's Quest* as well as his biography, *The Other Side of Oz.* Ebsen died on July 6, 2003, from pneumonia; he was 95. He is survived by his seven children and third wife, Dorothy. **Sources:** *Independent* (London, England), July 8, 2003, p. 16; *Los Angeles Times,* July 8, 2003, p. B12; *New York Times,* July 8, 2003, p. B8; *People,* July 21, 2003, p. 82; *Washington Post,* July 8, 2003, p. B7.

—*Eve M. B. Hermann*

Howard Fast

Born Howard Melvin Fast, November 11, 1914, in New York, NY; died of natural causes, March 12, 2003, in Old Greenwich, CT. Author. Prolific author Howard Fast wrote more than 80 books, many of them best-sellers, over the course of a career that spanned nearly 70 years. Through many of his works ran a strong liberal streak, the legacy of Fast's left-leaning political convictions that landed him in trouble with the Federal Bureau of Investigation (FBI) in the 1940s. In his 1990 memoir, *Being Red,* he chronicled his experiences as a member of the American Communist Party, an association he formally relinquished in 1956. "In the party I found ambition, narrowness, and hatred," he wrote, according to the *Independent.* "I also found love and dedication and high courage and integrity—and some of the noblest human beings I have ever known."

Born in 1914, Fast was one of four children of a laborer father and an English-born mother. The family was poor, a condition that grew bleaker after his mother died when he was 12. As a teen during the Great Depression, Fast left New York and traveled cross-country by riding railroad cars with other freight hobos. He returned to the area and found success when his first novel, *Two Villages,* was accepted for publication by Dial Press in 1933, the year he turned 18. His first commercial success, however, came in 1939 with *Conceived in Liberty,* a historical novel that fictionalized the American Revolutionary Army's experience at Valley Forge, Pennsylvania.

Other works from early in Fast's career also delved into Revolutionary War times and were a success with both the reading public and the critical establishment, such as the 1942 bestseller about Army general and future United States president George Washington, *The Unvanquished. Citizen Tom Paine,* which appeared the following year, was an even greater career triumph, and was said to have helped restore this Revolutionary War pamphleteer's reputation. Moving on to the post–Civil War Reconstruction era, Fast's 1944 best–seller, *Freedom Road,* chronicled the life of a former slave who becomes a United States Senator and target of 1870s Ku Klux Klan riders. It was later made into a 1979 television mini–series that starred Muhammad Ali.

During World War II, Fast worked in the Office of War Information as a scriptwriter for Voice of America radio broadcasts, but ran afoul of the government when he joined the American Communist Party. He was investigated by a Congressional committee that was rooting out alleged subversives in 1945, and refused to cooperate with its demand to turn over records of the Joint Anti–Fascist Refugee Committee, which had collected funds for victims of the Spanish Civil War in the 1930s. A series of court challenges followed, and the FBI compiled a 1,000–plus–page dossier on Fast and pressured his New York publishers to shun him. He was even jailed for three months in 1950 on a contempt of Congress charge. A hero to many of the left for his defiance, Fast was awarded the Stalin International Peace Prize in 1953, making him the sole American to earn it after actor–singer Paul Robeson.

Fast's career was revived that same year with the publication of his novel *Spartacus,* about a slave who leads a revolt the against powerful Roman Empire in late antiquity. It was later made into a successful 1960 movie of the same name that starred Kirk Douglas and was director Stanley Kubrick's first major blockbuster film. By then Fast had left the Communist Party, disillusioned after revelations that came out of the Soviet Union about the millions who had been persecuted under Soviet leader Josef Stalin. "I was part of a generation that believed in socialism and finally found that belief corroded and destroyed," a *New York Times* obituary by Mervyn Rothstein quoted him as saying in a 1981 interview. "That is not renouncing Communism or socialism. It's reaching a certain degree of enlightenment about what the Soviet Union practices."

After 1957, Fast lived in California, where he enjoyed success as a screenwriter for such films as 1968's *Penelope,* which starred Natalie Wood. He also wrote news articles, children's stories, poetry, and a successful fictional family saga beginning in 1977 with *The Immigrants.* He also was the author of detective novels under the pseudonym E. V. Cun-

ningham that featured Masao Masuto, a Zen Buddhist police detective in Beverly Hills. In all, Fast sold more than 80 million books around the globe, a figure that included sales of his final work, *Greenwich,* in 2000. Its story centered around a dinner party in the posh Connecticut enclave of the same name, where Fast and his wife, Bette, had lived since 1980. Widowed in 1994, he wed Mercedes O'Connor in 1999.

Fast died on March 12, 2003; he was 88. He is survived by his second wife, his daughter, Rachel; his son, Jonathan; three stepsons, and three grandchildren. The inexhaustible author claimed never to have been plagued by writer's block. "The only thing that infuriates me," his *New York Times* obituary quoted him as saying "is that I have more unwritten stories in me than I can conceivably write in a lifetime." **Sources:** *Independent* (London, England), March 14, 2003, p. 18; *Los Angeles Times,* March 14, 2003, p. B13; *New York Times,* March 13, 2003, p. C12; *Washington Post,* March 14, 2003, p. B7.

—Carol Brennan

Althea Gibson

Born August 25, 1927, in Silver, SC; died of respiratory failure, September 28, 2003, in East Orange, NJ. Professional tennis player. Althea Gibson broke the color barrier in the world of tennis in the 1950s. She was the first black athlete ever to compete in a United States national championship match, and went on to win both the U.S. women's title and two Wimbledon Cups. An entire generation passed before another African American woman attained such ranks in the sport.

Gibson's path to fame was a remarkable one. Born to South Carolina sharecropper parents in 1927, she grew up in Harlem, the largely African–American section of New York City, where her father found work as a garage attendant. In a stroke of luck, the street on which their tenement apartment building sat on West 143rd Street had been closed off as a designated play area, and volunteers from the Police Athletic League (PAL) set up a paddle tennis court right in front of the building's stoop. Gibson took up the game at the age of nine, and three years later won the city paddle tennis title. Impressed by her natural athleticism, a PAL volunteer brought her to the Cosmopolitan Tennis Club in 1941, which was a local tennis facility open to both blacks and whites.

Gibson improved quickly under her coach at the Cosmopolitan, but was rebellious at home. She often defied her parents by skipping school and even staying out all night, and finally ran away from home. After a stint in a Roman Catholic shelter for teenaged girls, she became a ward of the city and was given a small rent stipend to live on her own. She was forced to take menial jobs to make ends meet but continued with her athletic training, and in 1942 won the first tennis tournament she ever entered. That title, the New York junior women's, was granted by the American Tennis Association (ATA), an organization for black players. At the time, the United States Lawn Tennis Association (USTA) had no minority members.

In 1946, at the age of 19, Gibson was put in contact with two affluent black physicians, who sponsored both her and another promising young tennis player named Arthur Ashe. Gibson moved in with one of the families in North Carolina in order to finish high school, and went on to Florida A&M College. She continued to compete in ATA events, winning ten national championship titles in a row, and her prowess earned her a measure of media attention. There were calls for her to be allowed to enter the USTA's National Grass Court Championships at Forest Hills, New York, which was the precursor to the United States Open. But USTA officials declared that first Gibson must compete in a preliminary event—the catch being that organizers of such an event would have to extend an invitation. When none came, several USTA players rallied to the cause, led by Alice Marble, a former Wimbledon and U.S. Nationals titleholder. Gibson made her debut on the courts of Forest Hills on August 28, 1950. She did well, very nearly unseating the current Wimbledon champion at the time, Louise Brough. The next year Gibson advanced all the way to Wimbledon, the legendary English event, but lost in the quarterfinals. After finishing her Florida A&M degree in 1953, she was able to devote more time to her game, and emerged as a fearsome opponent over the next few years. "The lean and muscular young woman had a dominating serve," noted *New York Times* writer Robert Mcg. Thomas Jr., "and her long, graceful reach often stunned opponents."

In 1956, Gibson won her first French championship, and the following year won both the singles and doubles titles at Wimbledon. She was feted with a ticker–tape parade in New York City when she returned, and went on to win the U.S. Open that summer as well. Hailed in the press as a pioneering black athlete and inspiration to the civil–rights movement, Gibson was nevertheless wary of being linked to any cause. She won Wimbledon again in 1958 as well as the U.S. singles title, but there was no prize money in the sport at the time. She turned pro soon afterward, playing exhibition matches at the halftime shows of Harlem Globetrotters games.

Gibson served as New Jersey state athletic commissioner until 1992, and recreation director for her town of East Orange. Twice married, she had no children, and suffered a series of financial setbacks in her later years, but supporters rallied to help her once again when her plight became public knowledge. Remarkably, her feat at Wimbledon was not repeated until 1990, when Zina Garrison became the second black woman in history to make it the finals there. Nine years later, American tennis prodigy Serena Williams repeated Gibson's achievement and became the first black woman to win a U.S. Open title in 41 years; in 2000, Serena's sister, Venus, won Wimbledon.

Gibson suffered strokes in her later years and was rarely seen in public after 1990. She died on September 28, 2003, at the age of 76 in an East Orange hospital following treatment for an infection and a respiratory ailment. She is survived by a brother and a sister, as well as by the Foundation bearing her name that she helped establish that provides athletic and educational opportunities to urban youth. Following the news of Gibson's death, Venus Williams released a statement to the media. "I am honored to have followed in such great footsteps," Williams declared, according to *Los Angeles Times* writer Diane Pucin. "Her accomplishments set the stage for my success, and through players like myself and Serena and many others to come, her legacy will live on." **Sources:** *Chicago Tribune*, September 29, 2003, sec. 1, p. 1, p. 7; *Los Angeles Times*, September 29, 2003, p. A1, p. A21; *New York Times*, September 29, 2003, p. A21, October 2, 2003, p. A2; *People*, October 13, 2003, p. 94; *Washington Post*, September 29, 2003, p. A1, p. A6.

—Carol Brennan

Martha Griffiths

Born Martha Wright, January 29, 1912, in Pierce City, MO; died April 22, 2003, in Armada, MI. United States Representative. Martha Griffiths entered Congress in 1955, was re–elected nine times, and served through 1974. A feisty, piercingly intelligent thinker and speaker, Griffiths was a long–time fighter for women's rights, and successfully worked to bring women under the protection of the 1964 Civil Rights Act. She also backed the Equal Rights Amendment, and was involved in pushing it through Congress after almost 50 years of controversy. Griffiths was the daughter of a letter carrier in Pierce City, Missouri, and while still in high school, became noted for her debating ability. In college at the University of Missouri at Columbia, she excelled in political science. After graduating, she married her college sweetheart, Hicks G. Griffiths, in 1934. Both studied law at the University of Michigan; they were the first married couple to graduate from that university's law school. Griffiths was admitted to the Michigan bar in 1941, and subsequently worked in Detroit, Michigan, as a contract negotiator for army ordnance during World War II. She and her husband went into private practice together after the war, and in 1948 joined a friend, G. Mennen Williams, to run his successful campaign for the Michigan governor's seat.

In 1946, Griffiths made her own foray into Democratic politics, running for a seat in the Michigan legislature. She lost, but was not discouraged. On her second bid for office, she won. In 1952, her re-election campaign attracted national interest, as she traveled across her district in a house trailer, serving refreshments to prospective voters. Although she lost this campaign, she used the trailer tactic successfully in 1954 when she ran for Congress, winning the Detroit seat. In Congress, she became most interested in issues that affected women, and made it her goal to change laws that were unfair to them. For example, she was outraged to discover that when a man who was covered by Social Security died, his dependent children received benefits—but when a woman who was covered by the program died, her children received nothing. If a man died, his widow had to pay taxes on any money he left her, but if a woman died, her husband paid nothing. If a man divorced his wife after decades of marriage, she did not receive any of his Social Security payments. Griffiths worked to eliminate these disparities, and succeeded.

In 1964, Griffiths began working to add a ban on sex discrimination to the Civil Rights Act. Another member of Congress, Howard W. Smith from Virginia, opposed this amendment but told Griffiths he would work with her to convince Southern congress members to support it. Behind the scenes, however, his apparent agreement with Griffiths was part of a plan to defeat the amendment by making it look foolish. In February of 1954, he made light of women's issues on the House floor, joking that he would introduce a bill that would increase the supply of men in the country so that the 2.6 million unmarried women in the United States would be able to find husbands. Another member of Congress re-

marked that after being married for 49 years, he always had the last two words in any discussion, and those words were "Yes, dear."

In response, Griffiths noted that these comments about the amendment only made it more obvious that women were treated as second–class citizens, and commented that without the amendment, the Civil Rights Act would protect African–American women, but not white women, from discrimination. According to Elaine Woo in the Los Angeles Times, Griffiths said, "A vote against this amendment today by a white man is a vote against his wife or his widow or his daughter or his sister." As a result, the amendment passed by a vote of 168 to 133.

In 1970, Griffiths began working on behalf of the beleaguered Equal Rights Amendment, which had been under debate since 1923, when women were allowed to vote for the first time. The amendment had cleared the Senate twice, but had never made it to a vote in Congress. Invoking a rarely used tactic, Griffiths gathered enough signatures to ensure that the amendment would receive one hour of debate on the House floor. On August 10, 1974, the amendment was approved in Congress by a vote of 346 to 15; the Senate approved it two years later. However, in 2003, it had still been ratified by only 35 states, three fewer than the number required to add it to the U.S. constitution.

In 1974, Griffiths retired from Congress to serve on various corporate boards. She returned to politics in 1982, when Michigan gubernatorial candidate James Blanchard asked her to be his running mate. Griffiths was so popular among her constituents that some observers said Blanchard would not have won without her on the ticket. The two teamed up again for a successful second term, but in a third bid for office, Blanchard didn't invite Griffiths to join him. Then 78, she had begun suffering from poor health and had endured a series of strokes. According to the Los Angeles Times's Woo, Griffiths was angered by Blanchard's rejection, and commented, "The biggest problem in politics is that you help some s.o.b. get what he wants, and then he throws you off the train." Later, she noted, "He has a right to do what he wants to do. And after the election, we'll see what he should have done." Blanchard lost that election. According to the Los Angeles Times's Woo, Griffiths was a woman who broke many barriers. She was the first woman appointed to the Detroit Recorder's Court, the first woman sent to Congress from her district, the first woman seated on the House Ways and Means Committee, and the first woman chosen to serve as Michigan's lieutenant governor. Griffiths died on April 22, 2003, at her home in Armada, Michigan, at the age of 91, after several years of failing health; her husband passed away in 1996. **Sources:** *Chicago Tribune*, April 24, 2003; *Los Angeles Times*, April 25, 2003, p. B13; *New York Times*, April 25, 2003, p. B11; *Washington Post*, April 25, 2003, p. B9. —*Kelly Winters*

Buddy Hackett

Born Leonard Hacker on August 31, 1924, in Brooklyn, NY; died June 30, 2003, in Malibu, CA. Comedian. For more than 50 years Buddy Hackett kept audiences roaring with laughter. He worked his way up from a joke–telling waiter in the Catskills of New York to a headliner on the stages of Las Vegas, Nevada. He was a veteran of early television and even had his own show for a while. Like other excellent comedians, Hackett could turn in a formidable dramatic performance and did so in the film *God's Little Acre.* As his act matured, so did the language and he became one of the first popular comedians to perform R–rated routines.

Born and raised in Brooklyn, Hackett was the son of an upholsterer. Growing up he used humor to defend himself against kids who teased him about his height and weight. In high school, he played on the football team. During the summers he would work at vacation resorts in the Catskill Mountains in northern New York. As a waiter he learned how to keep people laughing. Eventually he was good enough that he was hired on as a "tummler." In the role of tummler he was responsible for keeping the guests—even the most jaded patrons—laughing at all times.

Hackett apprenticed in his father's upholstery business for a while and then went to serve in the military in World War II. After three years of service, he returned home where he saw the original Broadway production of the musical *Oklahoma!.* Inspired by the musical to make show business his life, he changed his name from Leonard Hacker to Buddy Hackett and found an agent.

Hackett made his comedy debut at a club called the Pink Elephant in Brooklyn. Insecure about his own material, Hackett first started performing with routines that were written for him. He could never make the material work and was consistently playing to unsatisfied houses. Realizing that he needed to develop his own material, Hackett ended up writing routines for himself that were much more successful. With his agent's help, he started getting gigs at prominent East Coast clubs like the Riviera, where he was a hit.

Sensing that there were too many stand–up acts on the East Coast, Hackett headed to California. With fewer competitors and some experience under his belt, Hackett became a favorite at the Billy Gray Band Box, an important club in Los Angeles. His success there led to an offer in 1946 to become one of the comedic trio the Three Stooges after one of its members had suffered a stroke. Hackett turned the offer down and focused on developing his own style.

By the 1950s, Hackett was performing regularly in Las Vegas as well as headlining at clubs across the country. Despite a full touring schedule, he found time to appear in movies throughout the '50s and '60s. He made his film debut in 1953 in *Walking My Baby Back Home.* Some of his other films included *All Hands on Deck, Muscle Beach Party,* and *The Love Bug.* For the most part, his roles in films were comedic. However, he surprised audiences and critics alike with his performance as the poor farmer Pluto Swint in the dramatic film *God's Little Acre,* as well as the character Marcellus Washburn in *The Music Man.* In later years he appeared in the Bill Murray film *Scrooged* and contributed his voice to the animated film *The Little Mermaid* as Scuttle the seagull; he also appeared in 1998's *Paulie,* a film about a talking parrot.

Hackett appeared regularly on television. He made frequent appearances on CBS's *Jackie Gleason Show* when he replaced Art Carney as Gleason's partner. He was also a regular guest on *The Tonight Show* when it was hosted by Jack Paar and later when Johnny Carson was the host. In 1956, NBC premiered a situation comedy starring Hackett called *Stanley.* The show only lasted for a season but it launched a long–lasting career for comedienne Carol Burnett, who played Hackett's girlfriend. He continued to make guest appearances on television into the 1990s and 2000s. He appeared in episodes of *Just Shoot Me, Sabrina the Teenage Witch,* and *The Late Late Show with Craig Kilborn.* In 1999, he appeared in the satirical television show *Action,* which was a hit with critics but did not last. His last television appearance was on the 2003 reality television show *Last Comic Standing,* where he scouted for comedic talent.

Hackett first appeared on Broadway in 1954 in the play *Lunatics and Lovers.* His role in that play about the New York underground lasted 336 performances. In 1960, he appeared in *Viva Madison Avenue.* His 1964 role in *I Had a Ball* as a fortune–teller was often credited as being the only reason that the roundly panned play lasted for six months.

Hackett started spicing up his act with crass language and riffing on more mature themes as a way of protecting his material. He was well known for his ability to improvise, and often went onstage with only a vague idea of what his act was going to be for the evening. Fellow Las Vegas veteran Steve Lawrence explained to Tom Vallance of the *Independent*, "Buddy was in innovator. In his time, he was the most creative comic that I've ever seen. He was also a groundbreaker with a lot of taboos we grew up with. But he always did it in a way that was hysterical."

Hackett died on June 30, 2003, at his home in Malibu, California; he was 78. He is survived by his wife of 48 years, Sherry Cohen; three children, and two grandchildren. He innovated the use of off–color language and topics in comedy routines while also proving that he was a skilled actor. He told Vallance of the *Independent*, "I found out that if you made people laugh, they like you. Most people got to like me because I made them laugh. When they didn't, I hit them." **Sources:** CNN.com, http://www.cnn.com/2003/SHOWBIZ/TV/07/01/obit.hackett.ap/index.html (July 1, 2003); E! Online, http://www.eonline.com/News/Items/0,1,12079,00.html?eol.tkr, (July 2, 2003); *Independent* (London, England), July 2, 2003, p. 14; *Washington Post,* July 2, 2003, p. B7.

—*Eve M. B. Hermann*

Richard Harris

Born Richard St. John Harris, October 1, 1930, in Limerick, Ireland; died of Hodgkin's disease, October 25, 2002, in London, England. Actor. To a generation of filmgoers, Anglo–Irish star Richard Harris was the leading man of his generation: vigorous, eloquent, and fiercely independent. To their grandchildren, however, he personified the kindly Albus Dumbledore, headmaster of the Hogwarts School in the first two *Harry Potter* movies. Harris had an erratic career, with several stage successes but some notable screen flops, and enjoyed a degree of infamy for his hard–living ways and witty, barb–laden television talk–show appearances. "Although the critics generally had high praise for his acting," declared his *New York Times* obituary writer Richard Severo, "some seemed to suggest that Richard Harris the man—noted for his interest in pub crawling, strong spirits, and strong, spirited women—was far more intriguing than most of the scripts he got."

Born in the city of Limerick as one of eight children in his family, Harris was the son of a local flour–mill owner whose business later fell on hard times.

In his youth, he was a talented rugby player, but at age 22 was struck down by tuberculosis. He read voraciously during his convalescence, and decided that he would like to become a theater director. Unable to find a course in the field, he studied acting at the London Academy of Music and Dramatic Art instead, and struggled to survive there financially. For a time, he even slept in a coal cellar, the room where coal delivery trucks once dumped fuel briquettes for residential heating. His first successes came on the London stage in the late 1950s, and he soon came to be considered one of Britain's new "Angry Young Men," along with Albert Finney, Peter O'Toole, and other rising young actors making a name for themselves in gritty, realist stage and film dramas.

In the early 1960s, Harris won parts in Hollywood films such as *The Guns of Navarone* and *Mutiny on the Bounty,* which gave him a chance to work—and trade taunts—with his longtime idol, Marlon Brando. In 1963, he was nominated for an Academy Award for his lead role in *This Sporting Life,* about a loutish rugby player, but within a few years would become indelibly associated with *Camelot,* the hit stage musical. He reprised his role as the mythical King Arthur in the film version, though the finished product was generally deemed a travesty by most critics. In a savvy move, however, Harris acquired the performance rights to it, which allowed him to live off royalty income for many years.

Fans of Harris consider his role as an English toff seized by the Sioux in the 1970 film *A Man Called Horse* as one of his best, and his career nadir to be *Orca, Killer Whale,* a 1977 ocean thriller that cast him alongside Charlotte Rampling and a poorly disguised animatronic cetacean. As the decade progressed, Harris earned a reputation as a heavy drinker, and it was said that shooting schedules for his films usually had to be extended by at least a week to account for the days Harris would be unable to work. He later admitted to cocaine abuse as well, and claimed to have once tossed thousands of dollars' worth of it down the toilet in an attempt to break the habit. Twice he had almost died and been given last rites, the Roman Catholic sacrament for those near death, but he eventually curbed his substance–abuse habits to an occasional pint of Guinness.

Television interviews with Harris usually contained a colorful story or two, and he was frank about his disdain for acting as a profession. "If anyone ever asks my advice, I tell them, 'Don't take yourself too seriously,'" the *New York Times*'s Severo quoted him as saying in an interview that appeared in London's

Mirror newspaper a few months before his death. Harris also enjoyed a riposte–laden, years–long war of words with actor Michael Caine. "He makes films you wouldn't rent on video," Harris once said of the *Blame It On Rio* star, according to Severo, while Caine liked to assert that Harris and Richard Burton had squandered their own thespian talents in the bottle.

Later in his career Harris enjoyed a bit of a revival, taking parts that cast him in the wise, elder–statesman role. He appeared in Ridley Scott's *Gladiator* as Marcus Aurelius, and played the benevolent headmaster in *Harry Potter and the Sorcerer's Stone* in 2001 and *Harry Potter and the Chamber of Secrets* in 2002. A few months prior to the sequel's release, Harris was diagnosed with lymphatic cancer, and was under treatment in London for it. He lived in the city—at a Savoy Hotel suite for many years that he liked to reach by freight elevator—as well as in the Bahamas. In 1957 he wed Elizabeth Rees–Williams, the daughter of a lord, with whom he had three sons, and there was also a seven–year marriage to actress Ann Turkel in the 1970s. "I have made 72 movies in my life," CNN.com quoted him as saying, "and been miscast twice—as a husband." Harris died on October 25, 2002, in London, England, of Hodgkin's disease; he was 72. He is survived by his sons from his first marriage: Damien, Jared, and Jamie. **Sources:** *Chicago Tribune,* October 27, 2002, sec. 4, p. 9; CNN.com, http://www.cnn.com/2002/SHOWBIZ/Movies/10/25/harris.obit/index.html (October 28, 2002); *Independent* (London, England), October 28, 2002, p. 14; *Los Angeles Times,* October 26, 2002, p. B20; *New York Times,* October 26, 2002, p. B8; *People,* November 11, 2002, pp. 77-78; *Washington Post,* October 26, 2002, p. B7.

—*Carol Brennan*

George Roy Hill

Born December 20, 1921, in Minneapolis, MN; died December 27, 2002, in New York, NY. Film director. George Roy Hill won the best director Oscar for 1973's *The Sting,* which reunited the stellar acting team of Paul Newman and Robert Redford, who first came together in Hill's *Butch Cassidy and the Sundance Kid,* a hit film released in 1969. Both films landed on the list of top ten grossing films of all time, making Hill the first director to have two films on the list.

Hill grew up in Minneapolis, the son of George R. and Helen Frances Owens Hill. He loved adventure at an early age, and was especially drawn to

aviation. He spent much of his free time at the small airport outside of Minneapolis getting to know aviators and airplanes. He became a pilot himself at the age of 16. He also loved classical music, and he studied music while a student at Yale University and sang in the school's glee club. Also at Yale, he led a drama club. He graduated from college in 1943 with a bachelor of arts degree, and immediately joined the Marine Corps, where he served in the South Pacific during World War II as a pilot, transporting supplies and troops.

Returning from the war, Hill moved to Texas, where he worked for a time as a newspaper reporter. Not long after moving to Texas, however, he again relocated, this time to Dublin, Ireland, where he continued his study of music, adding literature to the mix at Trinity College. He returned to the United States in 1949 after completing a bachelor's degree in literature, and went to work as an actor. He received good reviews in an Off–Broadway play by Strindberg called *The Creditors,* and went on tour with a reparatory company specializing in Shakespeare. It was while working with the Shakespeare company that Hill met his future wife, Louisa Horton. They married on April 7, 1951, and subsequently divorced in 1978.

Following his theater work, Hill moved on to radio, where he became a regular on a soap opera. But the outbreak of the Korean War interrupted Hill's career in radio; the Marines recalled him to active duty, where he served a year and a half at a flight training facility in North Carolina. Returning to civilian life as a major, Hill found work in the burgeoning television industry, where he worked as a writer and director. One of his early efforts was a drama called *My Brother's Keeper,* which was based on his experiences in the military, and in which he also acted. The show was aired on the Kraft Television Theater.

Eventually becoming a prominent television writer and director, Hill earned Emmy awards for writing and directing *A Night to Remember,* a drama about the sinking of the *Titanic.* Hill returned to theater in 1957, directing *Look Homeward, Angel* on Broadway. This play, written by Ketti Frings, and based on a novel by Thomas Wolfe, won a Pulitzer Prize. Other Broadway directing gigs followed, including *A Period of Adjustment* by Tennessee Williams. That play brought Hill to Hollywood in 1962 when he was called upon to direct the film version. The film featured Jane Fonda in her first major film role. Hill remained primarily a film director for the rest of his career as a director. His credits in the 1960s included *Toys in the Attic,* released in 1963, and 1966's *Hawaii.*

Hill finished the 1960s with the resoundingly successful *Butch Cassidy and the Sundance Kid*. That film represented a milestone not just in Hill's career as a director, but also for the genre of the Western film. Instead portraying its main characters as stereotypical Western outlaws, it presented Newman and Redford as free spirits for whom robbing banks was fun. The film, a tremendous box office success, was credited with reviving what was then perceived as the dying art of the Western film. It won four Academy awards, including one for best song for "Raindrops Keep Falling on My Head," written by Burt Bacharach and Hal David. The film also received nominations for best picture and best director.

Hill next put Newman and Redford together in *The Sting*, which featured the duo as conmen involved in the con of their lives to escape from a murderous gangster. This film was credited with bringing back to popularity the music of ragtime composer Scott Joplin. It received no less than ten Academy nominations, winning a total of seven, including those for best picture, best director, original screenplay, and best musical score.

Although the Newman/Redford films were very successful at the box office and earned numerous Academy awards, they were not liked by every critic, including longtime *New Yorker* writer Pauline Kael, who criticized both films for focusing on the relationship between the Newman and Redford characters at the expense of female characters. Hill responded by expressing exasperation at the idea that he should stop the action in the films just to introduce female characters who did not advance the plot.

Other films directed by Hill included *The World According to Garp*, released in 1982, and *Slap Shot*, released in 1977. The latter film, which was about hockey players, and starred Newman, was initially not well received, but it gained popularity in the years following its release. The last film Hill directed was *Funny Farm* which was released in 1988, starring Chevy Chase. After completing this film, Hill retired from filmmaking to teach at Yale.

Hill died on December 27, 2002, in New York City of complications related to Parkinson's disease at the age of 81. He is survived by his sons, George Roy III and John Andrew Steele; his daughters, Frances and Owens; and 12 grandchildren. **Sources:** *Chicago Tribune*, December 28, 2002, sec. 2, p. 11; *New York Times*, December 28, 2002, p. A20; *Washington Post*, December 28, 2002, p. B7.

—*Michael Belfiore*

Bob Hope

Born Leslie Townes Hope, May 29, 1903, in Eltham, England; died from complications due to pneumonia, July 27, 2003, in Toluca Lake, CA. Comedian and actor. Known as "Mr. Entertainment," "The King of Comedy," or "ol' ski nose," Bob Hope entertained the world for more than 70 years. He earned his stripes as a young vaudevillian comedian, did a turn on Broadway, made it to Hollywood, then onto radio and eventually television. Always busy, always touring, Hope logged more than a million miles of travel visiting American troops wherever they were stationed across the globe. Jack Kroll of *Newsweek* said of Hope, "His greatness was in his rapid–fire delivery, his rhythm, his fervent enjoyment of himself."

Born Leslie Townes Hope, he moved to Cleveland, Ohio, with his family when he was four years old. His father, William Henry Hope, was a stonemason who moved to the United States with hopes of finding employment. Hope's mother, Avis Townes Hope, had been a concert singer. She taught Hope to sing and dance when he was young and often had him perform for visitors.

Hope held several jobs as a teenager including selling newspapers and shoes. He also worked at a meat market, a drugstore, and as a golf caddy. Eventually he was drawn to entertainment, spurred on by an award he won imitating silent screen star Charlie Chaplin. His first shot at stardom came as part of a duo who performed the opening act for entertainer Fatty Arbuckle's traveling show. Afterward his duo joined the vaudeville circuit. It did not take Hope long to decide to try a solo act and he spent some lean times in Chicago, Illinois, perfecting his routine.

Hope eventually changed his name from Leslie to Bob. He wrote about his reasons for changing the name in *The Bob Book*, excerpted by *E! Online*: "I thought, 'Hey, Leslie's a girl's name! I think what I'll do is change it to Bob. It's more chummy' … Leslie had a little question mark behind it, you know?" Hope said the name change made all the difference in his career. He claims his earnings for each show increased and that he was booked more often.

By 1932 Hope was playing parts on Broadway in shows like *Ballyhoo*, *Roberta*, and *Say When*. In 1936 he and comedienne Fanny Brice shared billing in the *Ziegfeld Follies*. That same year he turned in a memorable performance in *Red, Hot, and Blue* opposite comedian Jimmy Durante and singer/performer

Ethel Merman. His use of the ad–libbed one–liner infuriated Merman but pleased audiences. That role earned him a ticket to Hollywood.

In Hollywood, Hope had a role in the film *The Big Broadcast of 1938*. It wasn't his greatest film but his theme song, "Thanks for the Memory," was first sung in that film. In addition to film roles, including the highly successful horror comedy *The Cat and the Canary*, Hope was spending some time in front of the mike for NBC. He was so popular on radio that in 1938 NBC gave him his own radio show. His show soon became the number–one radio show in America. In 1952, Hope signed a two million dollar contract with NBC Radio—the largest ever for a radio star. Hope broadcast regularly until 1956.

Hope's film career took off in 1940 with the release of *The Road to Singapore*, a musical comedy pairing Hope with singer/actor Bing Crosby. Crosby and Hope, along with actress Dorothy Lamour, made a total of seven "Road" movies. Incredibly popular, these movies propelled Hope to the top of Hollywood's list of moneymakers. One of his most popular films made without Crosby was the 1948 movie *Paleface*. Hope's character in this film was cast in the same mold as that of his "Road" movies in which he had played a coward who made the best of his situation by joking and smirking while always trying to get the girl. *Paleface* was followed by the less successful *Son of Paleface*.

Success in radio and film did not lead to complacency for Hope. Instead he seemed to work even harder. In 1941 he made his first foray into entertaining U.S. servicemen. Until the mid–1990s, Hope traveled the world to deliver his one–liners to military personnel eager for distraction in the midst of wars and military actions, as well as during peacetime. From 1948 to 1972, he hosted annual Christmas shows at military bases overseas. The last of Hope's Christmas shows for the military was held in 1983.

Although Hope never won an Academy Award for any of his roles in more than 50 films, he was an integral part of their ceremonies from 1940 to 1978. He was the emcee and co–host of 20 Academy of Motion Picture Arts and Sciences awards ceremonies. For his contributions on screen and off, the Academy awarded Hope with five special honors. In addition to two honorary Oscars and two special awards throughout his career, Hope was also given the Jean Hersholt Humanitarian Award in 1959.

For the majority of his career, Hope kept his politics private. For all of his career he enjoyed the friendship of presidents from Eisenhower to Clinton. In the 1970s he was a frequent golf partner of Richard Nixon and Gerald Ford. Hope had publicly supported Nixon's policy in Vietnam and organized a pro–Vietnam rally in Washington in 1970 called "Honor America Day." In 1971, he offered $10 million to North Vietnam for the release of prisoners of war. In 1972, he was a major fund–raiser for Nixon's presidential re–election.

Politics aside, Hope was one of the most honored entertainers in history, a fact that is recognized by the *Guinness Book of World Records*. Throughout his career Hope received more than 2,000 awards and honors. Some of his honors include the Congressional Medal of Honor, Knighthood, and being named an honorary veteran as well as part of American folklore. The Navy christened a ship and the Air Force a plane in his name in 1997. The United Service Organization's building in Washington D.C., is also named in his honor.

Hope is survived by his wife of 70 years, Dolores Reade, as well as his four children and four grandchildren. Hope made a significant and positive impact on generations of fans. He died on July 27, 2003, at the age of 100. Kroll wrote of Hope, "It sometimes seemed as if he'd ambled through the entire 20th century with a golf club in his hand, a sheaf of written–to–order wisecracks in his pocket and that so–false–it–was–true grin on his face." **Sources:** E! Online, http://www.eonline.com/Features/Specials/Hope/Why/index.html (July 28, 2003); E! Online, http://www.eonline.com/News/Items/0,1,12223,00.html (July 28, 2003); *Los Angeles Times*, July 29, 2003, p. A1, p. A20; *Newsweek*, August 11, 2003, pp. 62-63; *New York Times*, July 29, 2003, p. A1, p. A22; *Washington Post*, July 29, 2003, p. A1, p. A7.

—*Eve M. B. Hermann*

Roy Harris Jenkins

Born November 11, 1920, in Abersychan, Monmouthshire, Wales; died of a suspected heart attack, January 5, 2003, in East Hendred, Oxfordshire, England. Politician and author. Roy Harris Jenkins, also known as Lord Jenkins of Hillhead, was a figure of tremendous influence in British politics in the post–World War II era. As a leading Labour Party name, Jenkins tried unsuccessfully to unite his ardently leftist party toward a more reasonable center. In Britain he is sometimes referred to as "the best prime minister we never had," according to his *New York Times* obituary by Paul Lewis.

Jenkins came from South Wales, where his coal–miner father rose to a position of prominence in the national miners' union and even served in Parliament. He fulfilled his parents' expectations of a stellar career himself after earning a degree from Oxford's Balliol College in 1941 and serving on the famous codebreaking team at Bletchley Manor during World War II. Joining the British Labour Party, Jenkins lost his first bid for a seat in Parliament in 1945, but was elected three years later from a district in South London. Between 1950 and 1976 he represented voters of Stetchford constituency in the city of Birmingham as a Member of Parliament (MP). During his first decade in the House of Commons, Jenkins worked to modernize British censorship laws that dated back to the Victorian era.

Jenkins was politically allied with Labour leader Hugh Gaitskell, a centrist like himself, but enjoyed a less cordial relationship with Gaitskell's successor after 1963, Harold Wilson. Both men were at odds politically—Jenkins, for example, supported Britain's entry into the European Economic Community (EEC), the forerunner of the European Union—and Wilson was said to have been wary that Jenkins might try to usurp his party leadership. When Wilson and Labour won the 1964 elections, he appointed Jenkins to serve as Britain's aviation minister. As such, Jenkins convinced a reluctant Wilson government that it was indeed bound to honor the terms of a contract to build an expensive new supersonic airplane with French aerospace interests, later christened the Concorde.

Jenkins was made Home Secretary in 1965, and worked to liberalize archaic British laws in the midst of a dramatically changing society. His office made strides in legalizing women's reproductive rights, easing divorce restrictions, and decriminalizing homosexuality. His era as Home Secretary was later derided by Labour's foes, the Conservative (Tory) Party, as the start of what it considered Britain's far too permissive era. But other issues derailed the Wilson government: in 1967, an economic crisis loomed when the pound sterling was devalued, and Jenkins and the Chancellor of the Exchequer, James Callaghan, traded jobs with one another. Jenkins worked to deliver a balanced budget, but the austerity measures came too slowly to improve matters with the British public, and Labour lost the 1970 national elections.

Still serving as a Birmingham MP, Jenkins turned to championing England's formal entry into the EEC. Many in his party were opposed to the prospect of a federated Europe, and Jenkins sided with Tory MPs in a historic Commons vote on the matter in October of 1971. For it, he "was elevated in the media into a politician of principle," noted Dennis Kavanagh in London's *Independent* newspaper. Wilson and the Labour Party returned to power in 1974, and Jenkins again served as the cabinet's Home Secretary. After a street in Birmingham was rocked by a Irish Republican Army bomb attack, he introduced the harsh Prevention of Terrorism Act to combat the internal threat.

Yet the Labour Party was bitterly divided at the time over many issues, of both the pragmatic economic kind and thornier ideological ones. Wilson resigned in early 1976, and Jenkins stood for election to succeed him, but came in third. That same year, however, he was appointed President of the European Commission, the first British politician to hold the Brussels job. Always a visionary, he made a 1977 speech arguing for monetary union across Europe, which began finally in 1998 with the introduction of a common currency, the Euro.

Jenkins returned in 1981 to a Britain sharply divided after the rise of arch–conservative Tory leader Margaret Thatcher in 1979. The Labour Party had drifted far to the left, and had lost a record number of Parliament seats. To remedy this, Jenkins co–founded a splinter party, the Social Democrats, with a more centrist political stance, but it sputtered out after a few years.

Jenkins had also enjoyed a long second career as an astute biographer of past prime ministers, from William Gladstone to Winston Churchill. In 1987 he was made chancellor of Oxford University, and created a life peer that same year, which gave him a seat in the House of Lords. His own memoirs, the aptly titled *A Life at the Centre,* appeared in 1991. In it, he wrote of his years–long attempt to rid the Labour platform of some of its more entrenched socialist ideals, the same ones that made middle–class voters wary. It was a strategy later successfully adopted by a younger Labour politician, Tony Blair, whom Jenkins had befriended in the late 1970s.

Jenkins and other Labour politicians were sometimes derided for enjoying a posh life on weekends while championing the common laborer in Parliament, but in turn he criticized colleagues who adopted working–class accents to appeal to voters. A competitive tennis player, he owned an estate in

Oxfordshire that boasted a croquet lawn, and was a dedicated gastronome. Since 1945 he was the spouse of Jennifer Morris, whom he had met at Balliol, and they had two sons and a daughter. His death on January 5, 2003, at the age of 82 prompted Blair to term him, according to the Richard Pearson of the *Washington Post*, "one of the most remarkable people ever to grace British politics." **Sources:** *Chicago Tribune*, January 6, 2003, sec. 1, p. 10; *Independent* (London, England), January 6, 2003, p. 14; *Los Angeles Times*, January 6, 2003, p. B9; *New York Times*, January 6, 2003, p. A19; *Washington Post*, January 6, 2003, p. B5.

—Carol Brennan

Elia Kazan

Born Elia Kazanjoglous, September 7, 1909, in Constantinople, Turkey; died of natural causes, September 28, 2003, in Manhattan, NY. Director and author. Director of stage and screen, Elia (pronounced EE–lee–yah) Kazan played an important role in bringing to life some of America's most treasured plays and movies. His intimate work with playwrights such as Arthur Miller and Tennessee Williams transformed Broadway. Kazan was also known for his skill in dealing with actors and helped bring up some of the cinema's enduring stars, including Marlon Brando and Warren Beatty. Controversy followed Kazan for decades after his decision in the 1950s to testify before the House Un–American Activities Committee (HUAC), but his career never suffered.

When Kazan was four years old his father, a rug merchant, moved to New York from Constantinople, Turkey, and shortened the family name from Kazanjoglous to Kazan. The family lived in the Greek section of Harlem for a short time before moving to the suburb of New Rochelle. Despite the shortened name and growing up in the suburbs of New York, Kazan always considered himself an outsider. Expected to become a rug merchant like his father, Kazan decided to take a different route.

Kazan had an interest in film and literature and after high school he entered Williams College. At college, Kazan's sense of isolation and separateness was further enhanced. He was not invited to join a fraternity and instead worked as a bartender and waiter at their social gatherings. Kazan attributed some of his desire to succeed to the revenge fantasies he harbored during his days in college. He de-

cided to study performing arts after seeing the influential film *Battleship Potemkin*. He graduated with honors in 1930 and attended Yale University Drama School for two years before heading to New York.

In New York, Kazan joined the Group Theatre. He studied as an actor with them and also worked as part of the stage crew. It was with the Group Theatre, which included famed actor and teacher Lee Strasberg and writer Clifford Odets, that Kazan became devoted to the "Method" form of acting—one which asked the actor to find a matching internal emotional truth to mimic the emotion exhibited by the character. Kazan eventually became disillusioned with the Group Theatre, particularly with the influence that the Communist Party held over the group.

Kazan began directing plays in 1935. During that time he was also acting in plays, including several written by Group Theatre member Odets such as *Paradise Lost*, *Golden Boy*, and *Night Music*. In 1940 he had his first film role, playing a gangster in *City for Conquest*. Despite offers to remain in Hollywood and continue acting, Kazan passed up a long–term contract with Warner Brothers and chose to concentrate on directing. He returned to New York. His first critical success came in 1942 with the comedy *Cafe Crown*. That same year his direction of *Skin of Our Teeth* won the New York Drama Critics Award.

It was not long before Kazan was noticed by Hollywood again—this time for his direction. In 1945 he made his directing debut with *A Tree Grows in Brooklyn*, in which he used actual locations in the city for some of the film's scenes instead of sets. The lead actors of the film won Academy Awards for their performances and Kazan went on to direct several other critically acclaimed as well as popularly successful films in the 1940s. Kazan continued to pioneer on–location filming with *Boomerang!*, which was shot in Connecticut. In 1947, Kazan won an Academy Award for Best Director for *Gentleman's Agreement*, which starred film icon Gregory Peck. The film addressed the issue of anti–Semitism and also won Best Picture. In 1949, Kazan directed *Pinky*, which successfully tackled issues of racism.

While his film career was gaining steam, Kazan continued directing award–winning Broadway plays. In 1947, he won a Tony award for his direction of Arthur Miller's *All My Sons*. His long collaboration with playwright Tennessee Williams began around this time, including his direction of *A Streetcar Named Desire*, *Camino Real*, *Cat on a Hot Tin Roof*, and *Sweet Bird of Youth*. Kazan also directed the highly successful production of Miller's *Death of a Salesman*. In 1948, Kazan, along with Lee Strasberg and others, formed the Actors Studio, which produced such stars as Al Pacino and Robert De Niro.

On April 10, 1952, Kazan made the most controversial decision of his life. On that day he appeared before HUAC and listed the names of eight former associates of his, calling them Communists. His personal relationships suffered the most. The testimony led to a long-standing rift between him and Miller. On the other hand, Kazan's directing career suffered little. He went on to direct such films as *On the Waterfront*, which won eight Oscars. In 1956, his film *East of Eden* introduced the young James Dean to filmgoing audiences.

Despite continuing success on Broadway—he won the New York Drama Critics award for *Sweet Bird of Youth* in 1959—Kazan became frustrated with the financial burdens and restrictions becoming prevalent in Broadway productions. He abandoned Broadway and began focusing on writing novels and screenplays. He also left the Actors Studio to co-direct the Lincoln Center Repertory Company. After two disastrous years with the Lincoln Center's first acting company, Kazan resigned.

Through the 1960s and 1970s, Kazan focused even more on writing. As a writer, Kazan wrote six novels and an autobiography. His novels *America, America* and *The Arrangement* were turned into films, which he also directed. One of the last films he directed was *The Last Tycoon*, made in 1976, starring De Niro. In his 1988 autobiography, Kazan said he turned to writing because he was tired of interpreting the work of others.

In 1999, Kazan faced controversy again when he was given a special award by the Motion Picture Academy. Even after 40 years, Kazan was still seen by some as a traitor and his award was protested. Others, including director Martin Scorcese and De Niro, supported the award and Kazan. During the award presentation many audience members withheld applause in protest, while others gave him a standing ovation.

Kazan was married three times. His first wife, playwright Molly Day Thacher, died in 1963 after a 31-year marriage. His second wife, actress Barbara Loden, died after 13 years of marriage. He is survived by his third wife, Frances Rudge, four children, three step-children, six grandchildren, and two great-grandchildren. Kazan died on September 28, 2003, of natural causes; he was 94. Bart Barnes

of the *Washington Post* wrote, "[Kazan was] widely acclaimed as one of the 20th century's most innovative and influential American artists." His direction bolstered the work of American playwrights, introduced some of stage and screen's most influential actors, and created a kind of filmmaking that has influenced generations of movie makers. **Sources:** E! Online, http://www.eonline.com/News/Items/0,1,12590,00.html?eol.tkr (September 9, 2003); *New York Times*, September 29, 2003, p. A1, p. A20; *Washington Post*, September 29, 2003, p. A1, p. A9.

—*Eve M. B. Hermann*

Jean Kerr

Born Bridget Jean Collins, July 10, 1922, in Scranton, PA; died of pneumonia, January 5, 2003, in White Plains, NY. Author and playwright. Jean Kerr mined the absurdities of suburban life for comic effect in her 1957 best-seller, *Please Don't Eat the Daisies*. It went on to incarnations as a feature film and even a television series, and remained Kerr's best legacy as a writer whose "bright one-liners and playful romantic comedies have appealed to readers and theatergoers for decades," noted her *Washington Post* obituary. The mother of six was modest about her success, saying once of her career, "It's pretty good for a girl who tried writing to justify not doing the dishes," according to *Los Angeles Times* journalist Myrna Oliver.

Kerr grew up in Scranton, Pennsylvania, the daughter of Irish immigrants, and studied at Marywood College there. She met her future husband, a playwright and professor of drama at Catholic University in Washington, D.C., when she enrolled in its master's program in the early 1940s. She and Walter Kerr wed, and moved to the New York City area after she earned her graduate degree in 1945. They collaborated on a 1946 play, *Song of Bernadette*, based on the true story of a teenager who saw an apparition of the Virgin Mary at a grotto in Lourdes, France. Adapted from a book of the same name that had already been made into a popular 1943 film, their play was panned by critics and closed after just three nights.

Kerr and her husband had better luck with a 1949 musical comedy revue *Touch and Go*, but she was soon sidetracked by a growing family that would eventually number five boys and a daughter, including a set of twins. In Larchmont, New York—one of the towns in posh Westchester County that serve as Manhattan's suburban respite—they bought a quirky, elaborate manse built by an inventor that featured turrets, a warren of rooms, two–story fireplace, and even a carillon. Life there, with the children and their pets and her husband's thriving career as a Broadway playwright and director, became the basis for Kerr's amusing articles for a women's magazine, which in turn became her 1957 book, *Please Don't Eat the Daisies*. It featured what a writer for London's *Independent* newspaper, Tom Vallance, termed her "hilariously droll essays," perhaps best exemplified by something she once told an interviewer about becoming a mother: "The thing about having a baby," Vallance quoted her as saying, "is that, thereafter, you have it." Kerr's book was turned into a 1960 movie starring Doris Day and David Niven, and later a television series that ran on NBC from 1965 to 1967.

Kerr, pleased to earn enough income to afford child–care help, often parked her Chevrolet a few blocks away from her home for peace and quiet, and wrote there in longhand. "There is nothing to do but write, after I get the glove compartment tidied up," *New York Times* writer Robert Berkvist quoted her as once saying. She borrowed the title for her second collection of essays, 1960's *The Snake Has All the Lines*, from an exchange with her young son, who came home from school one day and announced he had won the part of Adam, the biblical first man, in a school play. She congratulated him for landing the plum role, but he groused, "the snake has all the lines," according to Oliver's *Los Angeles Times* obituary. This and Kerr's subsequent works remained popular with readers, in part because she possessed "an unquestioned gift," asserted Berkvist in his *New York Times* tribute, "for finding the comic in the commonplace anxieties of suburbia and married life."

Other works written from Kerr's Chevrolet office included *Penny Candy* and *How I Got to Be Perfect*, published in 1978, and she still wrote for the stage as well. *Mary, Mary,* a smash Broadway play about a divorced couple who realize they are still enamored of one another, ran for four years in the early 1960s and was one of the longest–running shows on Broadway of the decade; it, too, became a Hollywood film with Debbie Reynolds as the lead. Her last produced play, 1980's *Lunch Hour,* was a romantic comedy set in the Hamptons that starred Sam Waterston and Gilda Radner.

Kerr's husband eventually became a Pulitzer Prize–winning theater critic for the *New York Times.* On the subject of taking her husband's suggestions about her plays in progress, she once told an inter-

viewer that he "can't save me from failure, but he can save me from disgrace," according to the *Los Angeles Times*'s Oliver. Widowed in 1996, Kerr faced a far tougher critic in one of her sons, Christopher, who once wrote a book report on *Please Don't Eat the Daisies* for school. "This is about a woman who lives in Larchmont with four wonderful children," he asserted, according to Vallance's *Independent* obituary. "While it is funny, it is exaggerated to the point of being flat lies." Kerr died on January 5, 2003, of pneumonia; she was 80. She is survived by five sons, a daughter, two brothers, and eleven grandchildren. **Sources:** *Chicago Tribune,* January 7, 2003, sec. 2, p. 9; *Independent* (London, England), January 10, 2003, p. 18; *Los Angeles Times,* January 8, 2003, p. B10; *New York Times,* January 7, 2003, p. C14; *Washington Post,* January 8, 2003, p. B6.

—*Carol Brennan*

Bill Mauldin

Born William Henry Mauldin, October 29, 1921, in Mountain Park, NM; died of pneumonia, January 22, 2003, in Newport Beach, CA. Cartoonist. Pulitzer Prize–winning editorial cartoonist Bill Mauldin received thousands of letters from fellow World War II veterans in the months before his 2003 death expressing enduring gratitude for his morale–boosting cartoons that ran in the Army newspaper. Mauldin's "Willie" and "Joe" were a pair of disheveled, long–suffering American soldiers with a wicked insubordinate streak, much like their creator. "Mauldin's characters offered a counterpoint to the clean–cut, gung–ho fighting man put forth by the Army publicity machine," declared *Los Angeles Times* writer Mike Anton.

Mauldin hailed from Mountain Park, New Mexico, where he was born in 1921. His handyman father drank, and his parents' marriage was a tempestuous one. Afflicted with rickets as a child, Mauldin was a gaunt, weak child and once overheard his father's friend say of him, "If that was my son, I would drown him," a *Times* of London article reported. He never forgot the sting of the remark, and later credited it with instilling in him a determination to make something of himself. By his teen years, when the family was living in Phoenix, Arizona, Mauldin was taking a correspondence course in drawing, and after being ejected from his high school for a prank involving a lit cigarette and a biology–classroom skeleton, Mauldin headed to the Chicago Academy of Fine Arts with a loan from his grandmother.

Mauldin began earning a modest income from magazine–illustration work, and considered himself ineligible for military service—because of his sickly childhood—once World War II began in 1941. He became a member of the Arizona Guard, which required no physical exam, but when it was federalized, he found himself a member of the Oklahoma–based 45th Division of the U.S. Army. Sent overseas in 1943, he participated in the invasion of Italy, was wounded at Salerno and earned a Purple Heart, and attained the rank of sergeant. He also served on the staff of *Stars and Stripes,* the Army newspaper, and his comical cartoons about the daily grind of Army life in Europe soon attracted a cult following. His soldiers, Willie and Joe, were ordinary infantrymen fighting the Nazi German menace, and when not dodging enemy fire were plagued by the soldiers' everyday miseries: bad food, rain, and the officious inanities of their superior officers. "During the war, he excoriated self–important generals ..., glamour–dripping Air Force pilots in leather jackets, and cafe owners in liberated countries who rewarded the thirsty G.I.'s who had freed them by charging them double for brandy," noted Richard Severo in the *New York Times.* "He was nothing short of beloved by his fellow enlisted men." Even the Allied commander in Europe, General Dwight D. Eisenhower, was a fan of the strip, and shielded Mauldin when the cartoons came under fire from General George S. Patton, who thought the duo served to depict the rank and file of the United States military in a unflattering light.

Mauldin's work also ran Stateside in several daily newspapers, and he earned his first Pulitzer Prize in 1945 for what *Washington Post* staff writer Claudia Levy called "a typical Mauldin effort showing dispirited infantrymen slogging through a downpour and was captioned, 'Fresh American troops, flushed with victory.'" He had actually planned to have Willie and Joe become casualties in the final days of the war, but his editors talked him out of that idea. The series made his name, but Mauldin later said he was uneasy with the fame that it brought. "I never quite could shake off the guilt feeling that I had made something good out of the war," the *New York Times* quoted him as saying.

After the end of the war, Mauldin found work as a syndicated newspaper cartoonist and revived Willie and Joe during the 1950–53 Korean War. He appeared in a few films, including *The Red Badge of Courage,* and worked for the *St. Louis Post–Dispatch* as its editorial cartoonist after 1958. He won his second Pulitzer Prize the following year for a cartoon sympathetic to the plight of harassed Soviet writer Boris Pasternak, author of the Nobel prize–winning *Doctor Zhivago.* In 1962, Mauldin joined the *Chicago Sun–Times,* and his cartoons remained faithfully subversive over the next quarter–century: he poked fun at segregationists in the American South during the civil rights era, the politicians involved in the 1974 Watergate scandal, and even the staunchly conservative bent of some United States veterans' organizations. Perhaps the most famous image of Mauldin's career appeared just after the assassination of President John F. Kennedy in 1963, a captionless illustration showing the subject of Washington, D.C's stately Lincoln Memorial collapsed in grief.

Mauldin made a tour of Vietnam in 1965 when his son was serving in the military, and visited American troops stationed in Saudi Arabia during the 1991 Persian Gulf War. His pen satirized the United States' involvement in the first conflict with Iraq, and sometimes mocked the American president at the time, George H. W. Bush. Hampered by a hand injury, he retired from the *Sun–Times* in 1991. He was diagnosed with Alzheimer's disease and living in a nursing home in Orange County, California, in 2002 when a campaign was launched by a longtime fan of Wiille and Joe; veterans' organizations publicized his plight, and he received thousands of letters from former soldiers and fans of his World War II work.

Mauldin was married three times (and divorced twice): a brief union during World War II, a second one to Natalie Evans in 1947, who died in an automobile accident, and to Christine Lund after 1972. Mauldin died on January 22, 2003, of complications from Alzheimer's disease, pneumonia, and other ailments; he was 81. He is survived by seven sons; his daughter died in 2001. One of his sons told Anton in the *Los Angeles Times,* that his father's "philosophy in his work was always, 'If it's big, hit it.' He grew up a little guy. He understood the little guy." **Sources:** CNN.com, http://www.cnn.com/2003/US/West/01/22/mauldin.obit.ap/index.html (January 23, 2003); *Los Angeles Times,* January 23, 2003, p. A1, p. A8; *New York Times,* January 23, 2003, p. B7; *Times* (London), http://www.timesonline.co.uk (January 24, 2003); *Washington Post,* January 23, 2003, p. B6.

—*Carol Brennan*

Daniel Patrick Moynihan

Born March 16, 1927, in Tulsa, OK; died of a ruptured appendix, March 26, 2003, in Washington, DC.

Professor and United States Senator. During his more than 40 years in government and teaching, Daniel Patrick Moynihan was known for his erudite, opinionated, and entertaining speaking style, as well as for his willingness to criticize presidential administrations of both parties, and his often controversial views on race relations. Although he was not known as an original researcher, the 18 books he wrote or edited sparked intense debate and further research and action on the part of those who read them. His campaign to turn Washington D.C.'s Pennsylvania Avenue into a lasting monument renewed the city and remains today as a legacy to his interest in architecture. Moynihan was born in Tulsa, Oklahoma, in 1927, the son of a newspaperman. Later in that year, his father moved the family to New York City, where he worked writing advertising copy. In 1937, when Moynihan was ten, his father abandoned the family, leaving them in poverty. They moved into a series of Manhattan apartments, and Moynihan helped to support the family by shining shoes in Times Square. Moynihan graduated from high school with honors in 1943, and then worked as a stevedore at Piers 48 and 49 in Manhattan.

After attending City College in Manhattan for a year, Moynihan enlisted in the Navy and received officer training at Middlebury College and at Tufts University. The following year, with the end of World War II, he was discharged, worked at a bar his mother had bought, and then earned his B.A. at Tufts in 1948. In 1949, he earned an M.A. at the Fletcher School of Law and Diplomacy at Tufts. In 1950, he received a Fulbright Scholarship to attend the London School of Economics. Upon returning to the United States in 1953, he worked on Robert F. Wagner's mayoral campaign and then wrote speeches for W. Averell Harriman's successful gubernatorial campaign in 1954, later becoming Harriman's chief aide. While working there, he met Elizabeth Brennan, and they married in May of 1955. In 1961, after completing his Ph.D. in international relations at Syracuse University, he began working in the Labor Department in Washington, D.C., eventually becoming the department's assistant secretary. While there, he became interested in the architecture of office spaces, and then in the architecture of public buildings and public spaces. This interest would endure for the rest of his life, and would give rise to one of his most enduring projects: transforming Washington's dingy Pennsylvania Avenue into a grand boulevard that connected the U.S. Capitol and the White House.

Moynihan was also interested in immigration and ethnic diversity, and became controversial for his views on the problems facing African–American families. Noting the high levels of unemployment, welfare, and unmarried mothers among African Americans, he wrote that America had destroyed these families through the historical legacy of slavery, and that it was the responsibility of the government to adopt policies to enhance the stability and resources of these families. His views were roundly criticized by liberal observers, and in 1965 he left the administration. In 1966, he moved to Harvard University, where he served as director of the Joint Center for Urban Studies and became a tenured professor in the Graduate School of Education. He continued to spar with liberals on his views regarding African–American issues.

When Republican Richard M. Nixon was elected president, Moynihan, who viewed himself as a liberal Democrat, joined the White House staff as assistant to the president for urban affairs. His friends and his wife were startled by his alliance with Nixon, and his wife refused to move to Washington. While working with Nixon, Moynihan pushed for a Family Assistance Plan for poor families; the program went nowhere. So did Moynihan's suggestion that the United States end the war in Vietnam.

In 1970 he went back to Harvard, where he shifted his interests to foreign affairs; he was instrumental in negotiating an end to India's huge food aid debt to the United States. In 1975 he became the United States' ambassador to the United Nations. As ambassador, he became famous for his blunt replies to criticism of the United States by other countries. United States Secretary of State Henry Kissinger disliked Moynihan's confrontational tactics, and Moynihan retired in February of 1976. He then ran for the Democratic nomination for the Senate, won easily, and won again three more times. As a senator, he worked to rectify a shortfall of Federal money to New York. He was also noted for his criticism of all four presidents under whom he served.

In 1977, Moynihan decided that President Jimmy Carter did not realize how evil the Soviet Union was, and over the ensuing years, he noted that the Soviet Union's empire seemed to be crumbling from the inside. As a result, he believed that vast military spending to protect the United States against the Soviets was no longer necessary, and he was sharply critical of President Ronald Reagan's emphasis on military spending at the expense of domestic spending. In 1990, he was similarly critical of President George H.W. Bush's decision to invade Iraq. When President Bill Clinton sought to establish a national health insurance program, Moynihan was against the program, commenting that the administration should first reform welfare. Despite this criticism, in 2000, President Clinton awarded Moynihan the Medal of Freedom, the United States' highest civilian honor.

Moynihan died on March 26, 2003, as a result of complications arising from a ruptured appendix; he was 76. He is survived by his wife, Elizabeth; their children, Timothy, Maura, and John; and two grandchildren. He was buried at Arlington National Cemetery with full military honors, including a 21–gun salute and a musical tribute by the Navy Band. **Sources:** *Independent* (London, England), March 28, 2003, p. 20; *Los Angeles Times*, March 27, 2003, p. B16; *New York Times*, March 27, 2003, p. A1; April 1, 2003, p. D9; *Washington Post*, April 27, 2003, p. A1, p. A6.

—*Kelly Winters*

Donald O'Connor

Born Donald David Dixon Ronald O'Connor, August 28, 1925, in Chicago, IL; died of heart failure, September 27, 2003, in Woodland Hills, CA. Singer, dancer, and actor. Donald O'Connor was a singer, dancer, and actor best known for his jaunty, spirited solo in the film *Singin' in the Rain*. He also starred in several of the well–loved *Francis the Talking Mule* movies. In all, he made more than 70 motion pictures and won the Emmy, Peabody, Golden Globe, and Sylvania awards. O'Connor was honored with two stars on the Hollywood Walk of Fame. Born in Chicago, Illinois, O'Connor was the youngest of seven children born to John Edward O'Connor, a circus strongman, dancer, and comedian, and Effie Irene Crane O'Connor, a circus acrobat, tightrope walker, bareback rider, and dancer, and was carried onstage for applause when he was three days old. When he was six months old, his father suffered a heart attack and died in the middle of a performance. His mother continued to act, and eventually involved O'Connor in her act when he was about one year old. The two traveled throughout the United States to perform on the vaudeville circuit, and O'Connor was performing as a singer and dancer by the age of three. Although his mother passed on some rudimentary education to him, he spent most of his time learning the tricks of the show–business trade: tap–dancing, soft–shoe, and handstands. As a result, he could not relate to ordinary children, who attended school, did not work, and did not know how to dance. One tragic event, other than the death of his father, marred his childhood: his sister was hit by a car and killed.

By the time he was 12, O'Connor had a song–and–dance act with his brothers, Billy and Jack, and the three boys made a short film in 1937. In 1938, after a Hollywood talent scout saw him perform at the Biltmore Hotel in Los Angeles, O'Connor appeared in his first big film, *Sing You Sinners,* playing Bing Crosby's younger brother. In the following year, he appeared in the Gary Cooper film, *Beau Geste.* That same year, his brother, Billy, died from scarlet fever, and the family act broke up in 1940. O'Connor, now on his own, got a contract with Universal for $200 a week, and gradually earned more noteworthy roles.

On February 7, 1944, O'Connor married Gwendolyn Carter; they had a daughter, Donna, and divorced ten years later. In the 1940s, according to Richard Severo in the *New York Times,* the *New York World–Telegram* called him "the funniest man around right now" and he received favorable reviews in *Variety.* O'Connor was drafted near the end of World War II, and spent his time in the service entertaining combat troops. While he was in the service, Universal continued to pay him his salary of $50 a day.

After the war O'Connor returned to films, and usually received favorable reviews even when the movies he appeared in bombed. Some of the motion pictures he appeared in were 1947's *Something in the Wind,* starring Deanna Durbin; 1948's *Feudin', Fussin' and A'Fightin',* and 1949's *Yes Sir, That's My Baby. I Love Melvin,* released in 1953, was panned by both critics and audiences, but both loved the roller–skating tap dance he performed in it. In 1954, O'Connor was so well–known and well–liked that he was asked to be master of ceremonies at that year's Academy Awards.

In 1950, O'Connor began starring in a long series of films co–starring a talking mule. The first, *Francis,* was followed by five sequels; for a sixth installment, O'Connor decided not to participate, and his role as the film's human lead was taken by Mickey Rooney. In the 1950s, O'Connor also began appearing in television roles. According to the *New York Times'* Severo, *New York Herald Tribune* television critic John Crosby called O'Connor "one of the greatest all–around talents in show business."

O'Connor made his immortal scene in *Singin' in the Rain* in 1952. Starring with Gene Kelly and Debbie Reynolds, O'Connor danced across the screen in the "Make 'Em Laugh" number. In 2002, according to Robert W. Welkos in the *Los Angeles Times,* O'Connor said, "No one ever thought [the film] would be this big or make this kind of splash." O'Connor choreographed the routine, which included dancing up walls and doing backflips.

In 1956, O'Connor married again, this time to Gloria Noble; this marriage would last for the rest of his life. They would eventually have three children, Alicia, Donald Frederick, and Kevin. O'Connor's career sagged in the late 1950s when Hollywood musicals went out of style, although he did appear in the title role of *The Buster Keaton Story* in 1957. He remained out of the public eye for some time after this film, although in 1981, he reappeared briefly in *Ragtime,* and in 1983, he appeared on Broadway in a revival of *Show Boat.*

O'Connor, who had started drinking during his stint in the armed forces, eventually became an alcoholic. When he recognized this, in 1979, he stopped drinking, but as a result of the drinking and his poor eating habits, he had developed heart disease. In 1990, he had successful quadruple–bypass surgery, began exercising, changed his diet, and continued to maintain sobriety. In 1997, O'Connor appeared in the comedy *Out to Sea,* which starred Walter Matthau and Jack Lemmon.

In 1992, according to the *New York Times'* Severo, O'Connor said that as he got older his views of what a good part was had changed. "Now I'm looking for the parts where I die and they talk about me for the rest of the movie," he joked. At the age of 78, O'Connor died of heart failure on September 27, 2003, at the Motion Picture Country Home and Hospital in Woodland Hills, CA. He is survived by his wife, Gloria; four children, his niece, Patty O'Connor Norton; and four grandchildren. **Sources:** *Los Angeles Times,* September 28, 2003, p. B22; *New York Times,* September 29, 2003, p. A19; *Times* (London), September 29, 2003, p. 26; *Washington Post,* September 28, 2003, p. C11.

—*Kelly Winters*

Robert Palmer

Born Robert Allen Palmer, January 19, 1949, in Batley, Yorkshire, England; died after a heart attack, September 26, 2003, in Paris, France. Singer. British rocker Robert Palmer was firmly entrenched in the vintage American soul style early in his career. He later enjoyed a streak of 1980s hits that owed much of their appeal to the stylized MTV videos that ac-

companied them. "With his suavely grainy voice and songs like 'Addicted to Love,' 'Bad Case of Loving You' and 'Simply Irresistible,' Mr. Palmer presented himself as a pop Romeo," noted *New York Times* writer Jon Pareles. "The 1986 video clip for 'Addicted to Love,' which showed Mr. Palmer backed by a band of deadpan models in little black dresses, cemented his image."

Palmer was born in England in 1949 but spent much of his childhood living on the Mediterranean island of Malta, where his father served as an intelligence operative attached to the British Navy. His interest in music was spurred in part by American Forces Network broadcasts, an English–language radio service for United States troops stationed in Europe which featured an intoxicating mix of American soul, R&B, and jazz.

After the family returned to England when Palmer was 12, he began taking guitar lessons and joined his first band, the Mandrakes, three years later. In 1968, he became the singer for the Alan Bown Set, and a year later joined a jazz–rock group called Dada. That band morphed into the unfortunately named Vinegar Joe, which nevertheless enjoyed some minor success as a compelling live act, thanks to Palmer. Yet the singer eschewed the rock lifestyle that brought many of his peers down in the early 1970s. "I loved the music, but the excesses of rock 'n' roll never really appealed to me at all," *Los Angeles Times* writer Dennis McLellan quoted him as saying. "I couldn't see the point of getting up in front of a lot of people when you weren't in control of your wits."

In 1974, Palmer released his first solo record, *Sneakin' Sally Through the Alley,* whose Helmut Newton-esque cover photograph of the singer and an attractive female emerging from a tunnel near Heathrow Airport established his image as the alluring, elegantly dressed gentleman rock star. The work was recorded in New Orleans with top musicians, but failed to score any major hits. He did nominally better with his next release, *Pressure Drop,* a 1976 collection of tracks with distinct reggae overtones. By then Palmer, his wife, and children were living in New York City, but decamped to the Bahamas in 1978. His next effort of that year, *Double Fun,* yielded his first Top 20 hit in United States with "Every Kinda People," a Caribbean–influenced track that became a staple of easy–listening radio for years.

Palmer returned to the grittier side of rock with 1979's *Secrets,* and he had another hit with "Bad Case of Lovin' You (Doctor Doctor)," a cover of a

Moon Martin song. In the early 1980s, he teamed with Gary Numan to write some songs, but Palmer's records during this era were critical and commercial flops. It was only when he joined the supergroup Power Station in late 1984, whose line–up included John Taylor and Andy Taylor from Duran Duran, that Palmer began to gain transatlantic fame. The group's releases, "Some Like It Hot" and the T. Rex cover "Bang a Gong (Get It On)," were massive hits in 1985, but Palmer had assumed the project was just a lark and was uninterested in touring to capitalize on the unexpected chart success. Instead he went to work on another solo LP titled *Riptide,* also released in 1985, which gave him a No. 1 hit with "Addicted to Love" and a Grammy Award for best male rock vocal performance.

The video for "Addicted to Love" caused a stir when it first aired on MTV, and remained on the music channel's heavy–rotation list for months. It featured a slickly suited Palmer in front of a passel of nearly identical models, each of whom wore tight black dresses and sported blood–red lipstick. Palmer's "band" nominally played instruments or otherwise detachedly gyrated to the music, and feminists criticized the video as blatantly sexist. It had been shot by a highly regarded fashion photographer, Terence Donovan, who reprised the look in two other videos for Palmer, "I Didn't Mean to Turn You On" and "Simply Irresistible." The latter song earned him his second Grammy Award in 1988.

Palmer went on to release a slew of other solo LPs, but none attained the chart success of *Riptide* or its successor, *Heavy Nova.* His last record was the blues–tinged *Drive* in 2003. By then Palmer, divorced for a number of years, was living in Switzerland with his longtime girlfriend, Mary Ambrose, who was featured on the cover of his 1994 album, *Honey.* In September of that year, he traveled to England to film a television documentary about his musical career called *My Kinda People,* and was staying at a Paris hotel with Ambrose when he died of a heart attack on September 26, 2003. Just two weeks earlier, Palmer had undergone a medical checkup and was pronounced in good health. He is survived by Ambrose, his parents, and a son and daughter. Tributes from the many musicians who knew and respected him poured in when news of his death emerged. "He was a fabulous singer," longtime friend Sting told *People.* "A gentleman. And underrated." **Sources:** *Chicago Tribune,* September 27, 2003, sec. 2, p. 10; E! Online, http://www.eonline.com/News/Items/0,1,12576,00.html?tnews (September 29, 2003); *Los Angeles Times,* September 27, 2003, p. B20; *New York Times,* September 27, 2003, p. A25; *People,* October 13, 2003, p. 94; *Times* (London), http://www.timesonline.co.uk (September ber 26, 2003); *Washington Post,* September 27, 2003, p. B7.

—Carol Brennan

Suzy Parker

Born Cecilia Ann Renee Parker, October 28, 1932, in Long Island City, NY; died May 3, 2003, in Montecito, CA. Fashion model. Suzy Parker, an American fashion model of the 1950s, became one of the first superstars of her profession. The flame–haired beauty, known for her outspoken pronouncements on the vagaries of her industry, went on to a career in film and television before settling in the Santa Barbara, California, area to become a wife and mother. Parker, noted the *Washington Post*'s Richard Pearson, "refused to take her profession entirely seriously, maintaining that she was no more than 'an animated clothes hanger.'"

Parker was born in 1932, but later shaved a year off of her age, causing many of the death notices to give her age as 69 when she died in 2003. Her stepdaughter, Pamela Dillman Harman, also explained that Parker was a native of Long Island City, not San Antonio, Texas, as she had often claimed. Harman told Dennis McLellan in the *Los Angeles Times,* "She liked to cast a mystery over her background." Parker spent her high–school years in Jacksonville, Florida, and it was her older sister, Dorian Leigh, who first broke into the modeling field in the 1940s. Leigh was responsible for introducing her then–15–year–old younger sibling to Eileen Ford, head of a well–known Manhattan modeling agency, and Parker began modeling during her summer vacations in New York.

Parker's career took off after legendary *Harper's Bazaar* editor Diana Vreeland put her on the cover. She was photographed for that magazine and for *Vogue* in their typically lavish editorial spreads, and traveled frequently to Paris, France, to work with designers Christian Dior and Coco Chanel. Parker's high cheekbones, green eyes, and auburn hair gazed out coolly from magazine covers, Revlon ads, and a host of other sources, often photographed by the best fashion photographers of the day, including Horst P. Horst and Richard Avedon. She quickly became the standard–bearer for a new postwar American style, succeeding in an age "in which elegance and exclusivity were being pushed aside by sexiness and availability, and she could do both looks equally convincingly," noted the *Times* of London, which also called her "the epitome of the new American woman: healthy, assured, and in charge of her life."

Parker was said to be the first model ever to earn $200 an hour, and reportedly took home the then–astronomical figure of $100,000 during her top years. For a model, Parker achieved a level of international celebrity that had solely been the provenance of film and stage stars before her; she was one of the first fashion muses to attain household–name status. Yet she was also forthright about her profession and a host of other topics. She once told a reporter that she believed the institution of marriage destroys love, but then press reports surfaced that she was actually secretly wed at the time to French writer Pierre de la Salle; further evidence emerged that she had also been married briefly at 17 to her high–school boyfriend, Charles Staton. Mlle. Chanel was godmother to Parker's daughter with de la Salle, Georgia.

Eager to move beyond the confines of the fashion world, Parker tried her hand behind the camera lens for a time, apprenticing at the Paris studio of famed art photographer Henri Cartier–Bresson, and then working as an editor at French *Vogue*. She made her first film appearance in the Audrey Hepburn–Fred Astaire classic *Funny Face,* about a beatnik turned fashion model. Parker's personality was said to have been the basis for the character, with Astaire playing the Avedon–type role. She went on to star in 1957's *Kiss Them for Me* alongside Cary Grant, which was panned by critics, and in *Ten North Frederick* with Gary Cooper. "Parker's trademark in photographs and later on the movie screen was icy sophistication, often likened to that of Grace Kelly," noted *New York Times* writer Douglas Martin, "but in person she exuded a girl–next–door prettiness and a sort of wacky loquaciousness."

Parker also appeared in a 1963 episode of the *Twilight Zone,* but was married that year to actor Bradford Dillman (whom she met when they both appeared in the film, *A Circle of Deception*), and cut back on her work considerably after the wedding. They had three children together, and the household included her daughter Georgia as well as Dillman's son and daughter from a previous marriage. The family moved out of the Hollywood area and north to Montecito in 1968, where she spent the remainder of her life. "She was a fabulous model and did enjoy that work because she was so good at it," Harman told the *Los Angeles Times'* McLellan. After the stab at acting, as Harman noted, her stepmother "decided 'OK, I'm going to give up on this and devote my talents to being the best wife and mother,' and she really was that."

Parker died on May 3, 2003; she was 70. She is survived by her husband, daughter Georgia from a previous marriage, daughter Dinah and sons Charles and Christopher (with Dillman), stepchildren Jeffrey and Pamela, and four grandchildren. Ill for a number of years before her death, Parker was eulogized as the first "supermodel," the term later coined in the 1980s to describe highly paid fashion divas like Linda Evangelista and Christy Turlington. Yet Avedon, who had photographed them all, asserted that Parker "gave emotion and reality to the history of fashion photography," the *Los Angeles Times'* McLellan quoted him as saying. "She invented the form, and no one has surpassed her."
Sources: *Chicago Tribune,* May 7, 2003; CNN.com, http://www.cnn.com/2003/SHOWBIZ/Movies/05/05/obit.parker.ap/index.html (May 7, 2003); *Los Angeles Times,* May 6, 2003, p. B13, May 7, 2003; *New York Times,* May 6, 2003, p. C17; *Times* (London, England), http://www.timesonline.co.uk (May 9, 2003); *Washington Post,* May 9, 2003, p. B8.

—*Carol Brennan*

Gregory Peck

Born Eldred Gregory Peck on April 5, 1916, in La Jolla, CA; died June 12, 2003, in Los Angeles, CA. Actor. Gregory Peck seemed to embody the soul of the principled, upright, all–American man in some of his most notable roles. He was an imposing figure with a smooth, deep voice—a perfect match for the silver screen. His skill and presence were rewarded early with several Academy Award nominations, but it was not until he played the role for which he is most remembered that he won the coveted award.

As Atticus Finch, the Southern lawyer defending the innocence of a wrongly accused man in *To Kill a Mockingbird,* actor and character seemed inseparable. For Peck it was a career defining role. Not only did his character stand up against the entrenched racism of his small town, he was also charged with raising a child on his own. The tenderness and the empathy he showed as Finch earned him the Best Actor Academy Award in 1962. CNN.com reported that Peck said of the role, "I put everything I had into it ... everything I'd learned in 46 years of living, about family life and fathers and children. And my feelings about racial justice and inequality and opportunity."

Peck grew up in a broken home. His parents separated when he was three years old and later divorced. During his early childhood he split his time between his mother, his father, and his maternal grandmother. At the age of ten, he was sent to

St. John's Military Academy in Los Angeles, California. From there he went on to attend the University of California at Berkeley where he studied English. Theater was never an interest of his until a director asked him to take a part in an adaptation of *Moby Dick*. CNN.com reported Peck said of the experience, "I don't know why I said yes. I guess I was fearless, and it seemed like it might be fun. I wasn't any good, but I ended up doing five plays my last year in college."

That brief experience with theater hooked Peck and after graduating from college he headed to New York to become an actor. He worked several odd jobs to support himself, including ushering at Radio City Music Hall, guiding tours at the NBC studios, and as a model. He was awarded a scholarship at the Neighborhood Playhouse and studied there for two years. His movement instructor was the innovative choreographer Martha Graham. During one of his classes with her she pushed on his back during a stretching exercise and caused an injury that eventually exempted Peck from military service. With some of Hollywood's most prestigious leading men serving in the war, Peck ably stepped into the role of leading man.

His star rose quickly. A year after leaving California he received the best actor award from the Barter Theater in Abingdon, Virginia. Two years later, in 1942, he debuted on Broadway in *Morning Star*. Soon afterward he was invited to Hollywood and made his film debut in 1944 in *Days of Glory*, playing a Russian fighting the Nazis. That same year, at age 28, he was nominated for an Academy Award for his role as a young priest in *Keys of the Kingdom*. By the end of the 1940s, he would collect nominations for three more films: *The Yearling, Gentleman's Agreement*, and *Twelve O'Clock High*.

Peck became one of the first stars to defy the studio system by refusing to sign with any single studio. He was also extremely careful in choosing his roles, trying to avoid typecasting himself. By the time he won his Oscar in 1962 he became one of the few actors with the power to command a million–dollar salary.

A committed activist, Peck dedicated himself to political causes throughout his career—supporting Democratic candidates, as well as social justice issues. At one point he was even being asked to run for office, but declined. President Lyndon Johnson named Peck to the National Council of the Arts and awarded him the Medal of Freedom, the United States' highest civilian honor. While he was a favorite of Johnson's, Peck earned a place on President Richard Nixon's infamous "enemies list" for his activities.

While the late 1960s were lean times for Peck's film career, he was incredibly involved behind the scenes by his membership in several entertainment industry associations. From 1967 to 1969 he served on the board of the American Film Institute, of which he was also a founding chairman. He was also president of the Motion Picture Academy of Arts and Sciences from 1967 to 1970. In 1968, the Motion Picture Academy awarded him the Jean Hersholt Humanitarian Award for his contribution to causes such as civil rights.

The 1970s produced only one real hit for Peck. In 1976, he played the father in the horror film *The Omen* in which his son is the reincarnation of Satan. The film was one of the most popular movies of the decade. He continued to accept roles here and there into the 1980s and 1990s. In 1983, he played President Abraham Lincoln in a television miniseries about the civil war called *The Blue and The Gray*. In 1987, he played a president again in *Amazing Grace and Chuck*. In 1989 he appeared as writer Ambrose Bierce in the film *Old Gringo*. His last role in a television version of *Moby Dick*, for which he won critical raves. It was ironic that he performed in this adaptation, since his first acting role had been in a play based on the same novel.

Peck married for the first time in 1942. That marriage lasted 13 years and produced three sons. After his divorce, he married the French journalist Veronique Passani in 1955. His marriage to Passani lasted until his death and resulted in two children, a son and a daughter. In 1975, Peck's oldest son from his first marriage committed suicide.

Peck received numerous lifetime achievement awards including ones from the Screen Actors Guild, the American Film Institute, and the Kennedy Center. In 2003, just weeks before his death, Peck's character, Atticus Finch, was named the number–one film hero by the American Film Institute. Peck died on June 12, 2003, in his sleep at his home in Los Angeles, California; he was 87. He is survived by his wife, three sons, and a daughter. **Sources:** CNN.com, http://www.cnn.com/2003/SHOWBIZ/Movies/06/12/obit.peck/index.html (June 13, 2003); E! Online, http://www.eonline.com/News/Items/0,1,11969,00.html?tnews (June 13, 2003); *Entertainment Weekly*, June 27/July 4, 2003, pp. 10-11;

Los Angeles Times, June 13, 2003, p. A1, p. A2, p. A27; *New York Times,* June 13, 2003, p. A1, p. A27; *People,* June 30, 2003, pp. 46-49; *Washington Post,* June 13, 2003, p. A1, p. A10.

—*Eve M. B. Hermann*

Sam Phillips

Born Samuel Cornelius Phillips, January 5, 1923, in Florence, AL; died of respiratory failure, July 30, 2003, in Memphis, TN. Record label executive. Recording studio owner Sam Phillips founded Sun Records in 1952 and is credited with discovering Elvis Presley and with being an instrumental part of the launch of the rock 'n' roll genre. He brought wide attention to the then–neglected rhythm and blues and African–American country music, helping to bring these musical styles and traditions to white Americans. He helped launch the careers of Jerry Lee Lewis, Carl Perkins, Johnny Cash, Roy Orbison, and Charlie Rich, among many others.

Phillips grew up in Florence, Alabama, where he was the youngest of eight children; his parents were poor tenant farmers. According to Claudia Luther in the *Los Angeles Times,* Phillips said that he felt "an awakening of my spirit" when he heard the singing of African Americans who worked alongside him and his parents, picking cotton in the fields. He wondered what it would have been like for him if he had been born African American, and experienced the same hardships. As he grew older, he decided that the music of poor people—both black and white—"was absolutely the greatest thing we had in the South," according to Luther. However, at the time, this music was not recorded, and few people considered it valuable or interesting.

Phillips originally hoped to become a criminal defense lawyer, but poverty and his father's death prevented him from pursuing the education needed for such a career. He got a job at a radio station in Muscle Shoals, Alabama, and in 1945 moved to station WREC in Memphis, Tennessee. Witnessing that city's vibrant musical scene, he became determined to have this music get national—and eventually international—recognition. In 1949 he started a business, Memphis Recording Service, working there at night after his shift at the radio station. He recorded anything he could make a little money from, mostly weddings and $2–a–side personal recordings; he also recorded political speeches, and once he even

recorded a car muffler and testified in court about its loudness in decibels. His motto was "We Record Anything, Anywhere, Anytime." However, he also began recording local musicians performing black gospel, white gospel, blues, and what was known at the time as "hillbilly music." These artists included B.B. King, Roscoe Gordon, Howlin' Wolf, and Ike Turner's band. According to Douglas Martin in the *New York Times,* his ambition was to record "the real gutbucket stuff that other labels weren't putting out." Phillips renamed his company Sun Records in 1952.

However, Phillips soon found that the potential of his recordings of "race" music—blues and R&B—were limited because of the prevalent racism of the time. Although many white fans liked the music, they were reluctant to buy it because it was performed by African Americans. Phillips decided that if he could find white artists who could perform the music, he could break down this barrier. When Elvis Presley, then a shy 18–year–old who wanted to make a record for his mother's birthday, showed up in 1953, Phillips did not think he would be the one to do it, despite the fact that he had a very unusual voice. Presley worked with Phillips during the next year without much success, until he recorded "That's All Right" in July of 1954. Phillips took the record to radio station WHBQ, where it received such enthusiastic calls from listeners that the DJ ended up playing it many times in a row. In 1956, because of mounting debts, Phillips sold Presley's contract to RCA Records for $35,000, a tiny fraction of what it would eventually be worth.

After recording Presley, Phillips recorded Carl Perkins, Johnny Cash, Roy Orbison, Jerry Lee Lewis, and Charlie Rich. He also recorded rockabilly artists Billy Lee Riley and Sonny Burgess. Because of his work with these artists, Phillips was in the first group of ten people to be inducted into the Rock 'n' Roll Hall of Fame in 1986, and was the only person also to be a member of the country, blues, and rockabilly Halls of Fame.

Phillips was forced to close his studio after bigger labels began siphoning off his performers by offering them much bigger contracts than he could afford; he sold it to producer Shelby Singleton of Nashville in 1969. Today, the studio is a tourist site for those interested in the history of rock 'n' roll. Phillips went on to other business ventures, and spent many of his later years operating a radio station in Memphis. He lived quietly, although he occasionally appeared at events honoring Presley after Presley's death in 1977.

According to the *Los Angeles Times'* Luther, Phillips did not purposely set out to create a new kind of music. "I think I was conscious of letting out the insides, emotional insides, of people, and that was a challenge to a great extent. Oh, man, I loved the music. I loved it. I dearly loved it. So this was a beautiful experience. It still is, to see the influence it's had around the world." On July 30, 2003, at the age of 80, Phillips died of respiratory failure in Memphis, Tennessee. He is survived by his wife, Rebecca; sons Knox and Jerry, two granddaughters, and a great–grandson. **Sources:** *Los Angeles Times,* July 31, 2003, p. A1, p. A20; *New York Times,* August 1, 2003, p. A19; *Times* (London), August 1, 2003, p. 35; *Washington Post,* August 1, 2003, p. B4.

—*Kelly Winters*

George Plimpton

Born George Ames Plimpton, March 18, 1927, in New York, NY; died September 26, 2003, in New York, NY. Author, editor, and actor. American writer and editor George Plimpton was best known by the American public for his non–fiction books and articles that were the result of what he termed "participatory journalism." He took part as an amateur in professional sporting and entertainment events and wrote about his experiences for the general public. Plimpton was also the founding editor of the *Paris Review,* an influential literary journal, which he oversaw until his death.

Plimpton was born in New York City, the son of Francis T.P. Plimpton and his wife, Pauline Ames. The family was socially prominent. Plimpton's father worked as both a corporate lawyer and, during the 1960s, as a deputy U.S. representative to the United Nations. Plimpton attended a high–profile prep school, Phillips Exeter Academy, but was expelled. He later entered Harvard University where he remained until he left to serve in World War II.

Between 1945 and 1948, Plimpton was a soldier in the United States Army. He was stationed primarily in Italy, where he worked as a tank driver. After his discharge, Plimpton returned to Harvard and finished his undergraduate education. He also served as editor of the *Harvard Lampoon.* When Plimpton graduated in 1950, he then entered Cambridge University in England where he earned another bachelor's degree and a master's degree from King's College.

While on a break from Cambridge in 1953, Plimpton was hired as the first editor of the *Paris Review* after it was founded by Peter Matthiessen and Harold L. Humes. The quarterly publication never had a large circulation but soon became influential in literary circles. In addition to publishing authors when they were up and coming, including Jack Kerouac, Jay McInerney, and Philip Roth, Plimpton also put in print lengthy interviews with established literary figures such as Ernest Hemingway in which they talked about their craft. Plimpton's association with the *Paris Review* led to friendships with many famous writers, though the periodical was also a financial drain on those involved because it was never profitable and involved much creative fundraising by Plimpton and others.

The *Paris Review's* headquarters moved from Paris, where it had its first offices, to wherever Plimpton was based. When he returned to the United States in the late 1950s, the magazine soon followed. Plimpton did not just work on the *Paris Review,* but also worked in other writing–related positions. From 1956–58, he taught at Barnard College at Columbia University. He was an associate of *Horizon* magazine from 1959–61. He was later an editor and writer of *Harper's* magazine from 1972–81.

Plimpton also had his own writing career. In 1955, he published a children's book, *The Rabbit's Umbrella.* Fiction, however, was not to be his main focus. Beginning in the late 1950s, Plimpton began doing participatory journalism pieces, first for magazines like *Sports Illustrated* and later in his own books. One of his first experiences was boxing with light heavyweight champion Archie Moore in 1959, the same year he pitched to all–star players at Major League Baseball's All–Star Game and to leading players of the day like Willie Mays.

Plimpton's first participatory book was 1961's *Out of My League,* which chronicled his experiences in baseball. Such books helped establish Plimpton as a writer with the American public, doing what they could only imagine and describing his experiences for their pleasure. Plimpton went on to play goalie for two professional hockey teams, the Boston Bruins and the Edmonton Oilers, basketball with the Boston Celtics, tennis against a professional, and in pro–am golf tournaments.

One of Plimpton's best–known books was 1963's *Paper Lion.* In this tome, he chronicled his experiences trying out for and playing third string quarterback for the Detroit Lions, a professional football team. He tried to keep his season–long experience under wraps, but was found out. Nonetheless, the book was popular enough to be made into a film in 1968.

Plimpton did not only participate in sports. He also tried his hand at taming a lion, being a clown, and using a trapeze for a circus. He also played orchestral instruments with the New York Philharmonic for a tour, which was then directed by perfectionist Leonard Bernstein. He was once kicked out for missing his cue, but talked his way back in to performing.

Plimpton also played a role in more serious news events. A life–long friend of Robert F. Kennedy, he was present when Kennedy, then a Democratic presidential candidate in 1968, was assassinated by Sirhan Sirhan. Plimpton was one of two men who grabbed the assassin, held him down, and took the gun from his hand.

In the 1960s, Plimpton also began another career, as an actor. His first role was as an extra in *Lawrence of Arabia,* and he went on to appear in a number of small roles in films including a gunman in 1970's *Rio Lobo* and a psychiatrist in 1997's *Good Will Hunting.* By the 1990s, Plimpton had a recurring role on the hit NBC television series *ER.*

Another writing incident that brought Plimpton prominence occurred in 1985, the result of a April Fool's joke. He made up a pitcher who was also Tibetan Monk who could throw a baseball harder than anyone else, 168 mph, and published his work in *Sports Illustrated.* Some fell for his creation, and the whole experience inspired him to write a novel, 1987's *The Curious Case of Sidd Finch*

Plimpton continued to do participatory journalism, run the *Paris Review,* and work on other literary–related projects until his death. He died on September 26, 2003, in his sleep at his apartment in Manhattan after suffering from heart problems; he was 76. Upon Plimpton's death, his friend Norman Mailer told Mary Rourke and Claudia Luther of the *Los Angeles Times,* "George had a rare gift. He was so open to life and all of its new and unexpected situations." Plimpton's 20–year marriage to Freddy Medora Espy ended in divorce in 1988. He is survived by his second wife, Sara Whitehead Dudley, two children from his first marriage, Medora Ames and Taylor Ames, and two from his second marriage, twins Olivia Hartley and Laura Dudley.

Sources: *Chicago Tribune,* September 27, 2003, sec. 1, pp. 1-2; *Independent* (London), October 1, 2003, p. 20; *Los Angeles Times,* September 27, 2003, p. A1, p. A16; *New York Times,* September 27, 2003, p. A13; *People,* October 13, 2003, p. 93; *Washington Post,* September 27, 2003, p. B7.

—*A. Petruso*

Karel Reisz

Born in 1926, in Ostrava, Czechoslovakia; died of a blood disorder, November 25, 2002, in London, England. Film director. Karel Reisz was a Czech émigré–auteur who made several notable films in British New Wave cinema of the early 1960s. Later in his career he made a few Hollywood works that were hailed by critics, such as 1981's *The French Lieutenant's Woman.* Though the director made "only eleven features in his four–decade career," noted *New York Times* journalist Rick Lyman about Reisz, "they were noted for their polish, ambition, and psychological acuity."

Reisz's surname is pronounced "rice," revealing his German–Jewish roots in the city of Ostrava, a mining and industrial city in what was then the Moravian part of Czechoslovakia. His father was a lawyer there, and both parents, suspecting an imminent invasion of Czechoslovakia by neighboring Nazi Germany in 1938, sent the 12–year–old Reisz and his brother to England as part of the "Kindertransport" program. Reisz's trip was sponsored by a Quaker school in London, where he quickly learned English. After the war's end, the boys learned that both parents had died at Auschwitz, the German–run concentration camp in Poland.

At his London school Reisz first began making 16–millimeter films, and belonged to the Oxford Film Society during his time at the renowned university. There, with future directors Tony Richardson and Lindsay Anderson, he founded *Sequence,* the film society's magazine. After earning a chemistry degree from Oxford's Emmanuel College, Reisz became a schoolteacher in London, but wrote film reviews on the side. He left the teaching profession in the early 1950s to take a job as the program director of England's National Film Theater. He also became a highly regarded film–editing professional, and even authored a seminal textbook on it.

At the National Film Theater, Reisz teamed with Anderson and Richardson again to launch its "Free Cinema" film series, which promoted the work of young auteurs, including themselves. The Free Cinema term soon came to be used to define a new style of British filmmaking, characterized by daring works that tackled gritty, working–class themes. Reisz's own first film was a 1958 documentary, *We Are the Lambeth Boys,* about a youth club in London. Two years later he earned critical acclaim for *Saturday Night and Sunday Morning,* which was actor Albert Finney's first starring role as a loutish, put–upon factory worker. Lyman, writing in the *New York Times,* termed it "one of the seminal works of the British New Wave." Reisz's bleak, honest portrayal of life in an industrial city—based on Alan Sillitoe's novel—popularized the memorable line, "Don't let the bastards grind you down."

Reisz worked again with Finney four years later in 1964's murder–thriller, *Night Must Fall.* His next work starred a young Vanessa Redgrave as the socialite wife of an unstable artist in 1967's *Morgan: A Suitable Case for Treatment!* Redgrave also worked with Reisz on an ill–fated biopic about the modern dancer Isadora Duncan, who died in 1927 when her long scarf became entangled in the spokes of her car's wheel. The finished version of *Isadora* clocked in at three hours at its 1968 debut, and earned terrible reviews. Reisz cut nearly an hour from it and re–released it under the title *The Loves of Isadora,* but this version also failed at the box office. The expensive debacle seemed to mark the end of one period of Reisz's career. As film critic Richard Schickel told the *Los Angeles Times* writer Dennis McLellan, Reisz did not produce enough "hits" later in his career to become a household name, but during the 1960s, "the spirit of the time matched his sensibility: a director trying to make movies that didn't fit the conventional mold," Schickel asserted. "But it was a relatively brief moment where people took him with great seriousness."

Reisz even retreated from filmmaking altogether for a time, but returned in 1974 with *The Gambler,* the first of his works made in the United States. A critical favorite, it starred James Caan as professor with a gambling addiction. *Who'll Stop the Rain,* a 1978 drama that featured Nick Nolte as a Vietnam veteran turned drug smuggler, also earned Reisz praise. Perhaps his best–known work was *The French Lieutenant's Woman,* released in 1981 to enthusiastic critical acclaim. An adaptation of a novel from John Fowles, with a screenplay written by playwright Harold Pinter, this story of repressed desires was set in nineteenth–century England and the modern era and featured a young Meryl Streep and a relative unknown, Jeremy Irons, in dual roles.

Reisz also made *Sweet Dreams,* the 1985 biopic about late country–and–western star Patsy Cline, and cast Nolte in another film, 1990's *Everybody Wins,* from a script by playwright Arthur Miller. Over the next decade, Reisz directed works for the stage by Pinter and Miller.

Reisz's marriage to Julia Coppard ended in divorce; he married actress Betsy Blair in 1963. Reisz died on November 25, 2002, of a blood disorder; he was 76. He is survived by his wife; sons from his first marriage, Matthew, Toby, and Barney; a stepdaughter, Kerry; and seven grandchildren. **Sources:** *Chicago Tribune,* November 28, 2002, sec. 1, p. 13; *Los Angeles Times,* November 28, 2002, p. B13; *New York Times,* November 28, 2002, p. C11; *Washington Post,* November 29, 2002, p. B7.

—*Carol Brennan*

John Schlesinger

Born John Richard Schlesinger, February 16, 1926, in London, England; died of complications from a stroke, July 25, 2003, in Palm Springs, CA. Director and actor. Known for such films as *Midnight Cowboy, Sunday, Bloody Sunday,* and *Darling,* John Schlesinger was a brave, honest, and sometimes controversial director who won an Oscar for *Midnight Cowboy* and was nominated for several other awards throughout his career. He started out as an actor, before he found his place in the world of directing where "his stylish, groundbreaking films will be remembered for their riveting displays of all–too–human emotions," David Ansen wrote in *Newsweek.*

Schlesinger was born in London to a father who was a pediatrician and an amateur musician and a mother who was also a musician. His father played the cello and his mother played the violin; they both encouraged his interest in the arts. Schlesinger himself played the piano, but he originally wanted to be an architect, although that plan went by the wayside when he was given a camera at the age of ten. He served with the Royal Engineers during World War II where he made an amateur film, *Horrors.* After he left the military he attended Balliol College at Oxford University where he studied English Literature. There he made experimental films, many of which he won awards for, and was even elected president of the university's drama society, with whom he toured America. After graduation he started his career as a British stage and film actor before he was hired by the BBC as a freelance documentarian.

A Kind of Loving was the film that established Schlesinger as a mainstream movie director. The movie, starring Alan Bates, is about a man who realizes how unprepared he is for children when he marries his girlfriend because she gets pregnant. *A Kind of Loving* won the Berlin Film Festival's Golden Bear Award in 1962. He next made 1963's *Billy Liar,* a film about a man who avoids responsibility by daydreaming. His next film, *Darling,* helped actress Julie Christie rise to stardom in 1965 when she won an Oscar for her performance as a model who becomes disillusioned with her life.

In 1969 Schlesinger won an Oscar for Best Director for what was probably his best–known work, *Midnight Cowboy.* The film starred Jon Voight as Joe Buck (a role that is said to have made Voigt's career) and Dustin Hoffman as Ratso Rizzo. The movie, about a man from Texas becoming a prostitute in order to survive in New York, was rated X for its adult themes and content, but it won the Oscar for Best Picture, and was nominated for six others. It also won an Oscar for Best Adapted Screenplay. It is the only X–rated film to receive the best picture award. "The film's homosexual theme was regarded as scandalous, but the tale ... was embraced by critics and Hollywood despite its shocking sequences," wrote CNN.com. The film was later re–rated to R, without cuts, because audiences had become more accepting of such issues in movies.

He went on to direct such films as 1967's *Far From the Madding Crowd,* based on the Thomas Hardy novel, and 1985's *The Falcon and the Snowman,* which was based on the true story of a CIA employee and his drug dealer friend who become spies for the Soviet Union. In 1971, his film *Sunday, Bloody Sunday,* for which he received an Oscar nomination for best director, was released. It was a groundbreaking movie about a man, played by Murray Head, who is in love with both an older woman (Glenda Jackson) and a young male doctor (Peter Finch). According to the *Times* of London, "A passionate kiss between Finch and Murray Head signaled one of the cinema's first mature treatments of homosexuality and enabled Schlesinger, himself gay, 'to express myself publicly.'" It was the first movie to deal with homosexuality as normal, rather than horrible or funny.

Schlesinger also directed such greats as 1975's *The Day of the Locust,* based on Nathanael West's account of young actors trying to make it in Hollywood, 1976's *Marathon Man,* a thriller starring Laurence Olivier as a Nazi war criminal and Dustin Hoffman as the innocent man Olivier tortures for information, and 1979's *Yanks,* about American soldiers stationed in Britain during World War II. Another memorable film by Schlesinger was 1995's *Cold Comfort Farm,* done for BBC Films. The movie is about a young orphan who moves in with an odd country family and then proceeds to clean up all their problems. *Daily Variety* called the film a "small–scale triumph." In 2000 he completed the last film he would direct, *The Next Best Thing,* a movie about a straight woman who decides to have a child with her gay friend, which starred Madonna and Rupert Everett.

When he was not making films, Schlesinger also directed theater, opera, and British television productions, as well as a Paul McCartney music video. He was also one of the eight directors who made the 1972 Munich Olympic film *Visions of Eight.* When asked what he wanted in his life, CNN.com wrote that Schlesinger said in 1970, "I'm only interested in one thing—that is tolerance.... It's important to get people to care a little for someone else. That's why I'm more interested in the failures of this world than the successes." He spent his career fighting those limitations and stretching the minds of audiences around the world. While he did it he led actors that were unknown into the spotlight. Schlesinger's films "were beacons for actors, who gave some of their finest performances in his work," wrote Mel Gussow in the *New York Times.*

Schlesinger suffered a stroke in December of 2000 and his health never fully returned. He was so ill in 2002 that he was unable to attend the British Academy of Film and Television Arts awards ceremony even though he was being given a lifetime achievement award. Schlesinger was in and out of the Desert Regional Medical Center in Palm Springs for 90 days before he died of complications from a stroke on July 25, 2003; he was 77. Schlesinger is survived by his brother, Roger; his sister, Hilary; and his life partner of 35 years, Michael Childers. It is generally agreed that Schlesinger made a great contribution to world cinema, and as Hoffman was quoted as saying in United Press International, "Shakespeare said it best in Hamlet, 'We will never see the likes of him again.'" **Sources:** CNN.com, http://www.cnn.com/2003/SHOWBIZ/Movies/07/25/obit.schlesinger.ap/index.html (July 25,

2003); *Daily Variety,* July 28, 2003, p. 6; *Entertainment Weekly,* August 8, 2003, p. 19; Knight Ridder/Tribune News Service, July 25, 2003; *Los Angeles Times,* July 26, 2003, p. B22; *Newsweek,* August 4, 2003, p. 12; *New York Times,* July 26, 2003, p. A15; *Times* (London), http://www.timesonline.co.uk (July 26, 2003); United Press International, July 28, 2003; *Washington Post,* July 26, 2003, p. B7.

—*Catherine V. Donaldson*

Carol Shields

Born Carol Ann Warner, June 2, 1935, in Oak Park, IL; died of breast cancer, July 16, 2003, in Victoria, BC, Canada. Author. Canadian–American novelist Carol Shields wrote several acclaimed works over the course of a career that cancer prematurely ended in 2003. As a writer, she eschewed literary fireworks and narrative dazzle for stories instead about women who struggled to make sense of their place in the world. One of those, *The Stone Diaries,* won the 1995 Pulitzer Prize for literature. "In her hands the commonplace turned into extraordinary," *New York Times* writer Christopher Lehmann–Haupt asserted.

Shields lived a life not unlike many of her heroines during her first four decades: she was born into a comfortable middle–class household in Oak Park, a suburb of Chicago, in 1935. Her father managed a candy factory, and her mother taught school. A talented writer during her teens, she went to Hanover College in Indiana, but during a semester abroad at England's Exeter University she met a Canadian student, Don Shields, whom she married in 1957. The pair settled in Ottawa, Ontario, Canada, and began a family.

Shields became the mother of five children, but began yearning for a life outside the home after she read Betty Friedan's groundbreaking 1963 feminist tract, *The Feminine Mystique.* In 1968, at the age of 33, Shields decided to return to school for her master's degree. She also began writing poetry and short stories. One of her first jobs was editing a small literary journal from her home. "It was a jobette, really," the *Scotsman's* David Robinson quoted her as saying. "I worked in a spare room upstairs. I became the Mother Who Typed."

After earning her master's degree from the University of Ottawa in 1975, Shields turned some of her unused thesis material about Canadian poet Susanna Moodie into the plotline of her first novel, *Small Ceremonies,* which was published in Canada in 1976. It was followed by *The Box Garden* and *Happenstance,* each of which also failed to earn more than a passing mention by the literary establishment. "There were reviews that called them 'domestic' novels and 'women's' novels," the *Scotsman's* Robinson quoted Shields as saying, "and spoke of them quite lightly.... I love domesticity. I love the idea of home, and I think that is, in the end, what serious novels are about: the search for home."

Shields' novels gained a following in Canada, then the United States, particularly with a 1987 novel, *Mary Swann,* about a murdered poetess. An esteemed British publisher discovered her work and began issuing her back list, and as a result, Shields' novels caught on with United Kingdom readers as well. Her 1994 novel, *The Stone Diaries,* cemented her reputation, taking awards on both sides of the Atlantic. Its plot followed one woman's eight–decade–long story of a life largely unfulfilled. Daisy Goodwill Flett's recollections of moving from daughter to wife to mother struck a chord with readers, and the work became a bestseller. It was shortlisted for the Man Booker Prize, one of Britain's top literary honors, and won the National Book Critics Circle Award in the United States and Canada's Governor General Literary Award. Shields's dual citizenship also made her eligible for Pulitzer, which she won in 1995 for *The Stone Diaries.* The financial windfall from the book's success bought Shields a vacation home in France, which she dubbed "Chateau Pulitzer."

Not long after her 1997 novel, *Larry's Party*—her first to center on a male protagonist—won Britain's prestigious Orange Prize for the best book by a woman writer in the English language of the past year, Shields was diagnosed with breast cancer. Two years later, in 2000, she retired from the University of Manitoba, where she had taught for the past 20 years, and settled in picturesque British Columbia with her husband, who had also retired as an engineering professor. She continued to work, despite undergoing surgery, radiation treatment, and chemotherapy, completing another acclaimed novel, *Unless.* Published in 2002, it detailed the difficulties of a woman whose daughter has dropped out of college to live as a homeless person. She stands on a Toronto street corner, a silent beggar, wearing a sign that proclaims "Goodness." The work was shortlisted for both the Orange and Booker prizes. Shields claimed her illness had halted her schedule, at least temporarily. "I've stopped writing several times, through some of the worst phases," *Los Angeles Times* journalist Dennis McLellan quoted her as saying. "But I always start again. It's a kind of consolation. And there's something about wanting to go home to write that final book."

Shields was 68 when she died at her home in Victoria, British Columbia. She is survived by her husband, one son, four daughters, and eleven grandchildren, and left a novel in progress about an elderly writer in Chicago. Unlike the heroine of *The Stone Diaries*, Shields did not feel she led an unfulfilled life. "I don't feel I've missed out at all," her *Independent* obituary by Clare Colvin quoted her as saying. "I've got my friends, my family, my writing…. I think I've done pretty well." **Sources:** *Chicago Tribune*, July 18, 2003, sec. 3, p. 12; CNN. com, http://www.cnn.com/2003/SHOWBIZ/books/07/17/arts.canada.shields.reut/index.html (July 17, 2003); *Independent* (London, England), July 18, 2003, p. 17; *Los Angeles Times*, July 18, 2003, p. B12; *New York Times*, July 18, 2003, p. C11; *Scotsman* (Edinburgh, Scotland), July 18, 2003, p. 18; *Time*, May 27, 2002, p. 61; *Washington Post*, July 18, 2003, p. B7.

—*Carol Brennan*

Bill Shoemaker

Born William Lee Shoemaker, August 19, 1931, in Fabens, TX; died of natural causes, October 12, 2003, in San Marino, CA. Professional jockey. Hall of Fame jockey Bill Shoemaker, known as "The Shoe," rode 8,833 winning horses and won the Kentucky Derby four times. He also won two Preakness Stakes, five Belmont Stakes, and the Breeders' Cup Classic. Shoemaker was noted for his grace, his rapport with horses, and his seemingly effortless riding style.

Born in an adobe shack in Fabens, Texas, in 1931, Shoemaker weighed one pound, 13 ounces at birth; the doctor who attended his birth said he would not survive. His grandmother, in defiance of the doctor's decree, created a makeshift incubator for him when she wrapped him in a blanket and placed him on a pillow near the lid of a warm oven.

Shoemaker lived with various relatives while his father looked for work during the Depression; he learned to ride at his grandfather's ranch, where he was sent out on a horse to pick up the mail. After his parents divorced, he lived with his father in El Monte, California. Although he remained small

throughout his life—topping out at 4'11" and wearing a size 2 1/2 shoe—he was strong, and became a member of his high school boxing and wrestling teams, never losing a match. When he was 14, a classmate suggested that he had the perfect build to be a jockey, and Shoemaker began working at the Suzy Q Ranch in La Puente, California. He found that he loved the thoroughbred horses there, and without telling his father, quit school for a job at the ranch that paid $75 a month.

Two years later, he got a job as an exercise rider at the Bay Meadows track in San Mateo, California, working with trainer Hurst Philpot and future Hall of Fame jockey Johnny Adams. He loved the job, and knew he wanted to ride for the rest of his life. He began riding at Golden Gate Fields, where he won his first race. His first win only netted him $120, but by the end of his career, he had made more than $123 million. One secret of his success was that he continued to learn and improve with every season. He also possessed a notably even temper and calm disposition, an asset during stressful races.

Another asset was his understanding of horses. According to Bill Christine in the *Los Angeles Times*, horse breeder Rex Ellsworth said that Shoemaker "knew when a horse was doing his best or loafing. When a horse was doing his best, Shoe left him alone. When a horse loafed, Shoe would get after him. I never worried when Shoe rode one of my horses, because I knew he'd do a perfect job." Adam Bernstein, writing in the *Washington Post*, quoted sportswriter Jim Murray, who said, "No one ever rode a running horse the way Willie Lee Shoemaker does. Not Geronimo, the James brothers, the Pony Expressers, the Buffalo hunters, the Lone Ranger, Paul Revere, or the Headless Horseman of Sleepy Hollow. He is history's all-time cavalryman."

Shoemaker's stellar career was interrupted several times by injuries. In 1968, he broke a thigh bone when his mount fell on him. His doctor used a child-sized metal pin to repair the injury, and Shoemaker went through physical rehabilitation for the next 13 months. He returned to racing and won his first two races, but in April of 1969 he was thrown from his horse and suffered a broken pelvis, a ruptured bladder, and temporary paralysis in his left leg. After this injury, he came back to racing and rode winning races for the next 20 years.

In 1986, when many thought the 54-year-old Shoemaker's career was on the decline, he rode a horse named Ferdinand in the Kentucky Derby. Ferdinand was a long shot, with a 17-to-1 chance of winning. Shoemaker rode him so effectively that Ferdinand won by more than two lengths. Shoemaker thus became the oldest jockey ever to win the Derby. Because of the length of his career, he was also one of the youngest jockeys to win the Derby.

In 1990, Shoemaker considered retiring from riding and becoming a trainer. He made a farewell tour of racetracks all over the United States, ending with a final race at his home track in Santa Anita, California, where he finished fourth; it was the last of a record–setting 40,350 races. After his last ride, he began training horses, and had his first winner in June of 1990 at Hollywood Park. However, in April of 1991, after a round of golf, he left the course to meet friends for dinner, and while driving, crashed and rolled his Ford Bronco. At the time, his blood alcohol level was twice the legal limit. He suffered multiple injuries, including a broken neck, and was paralyzed from the neck down.

Later that year, seated in a wheelchair, which he operated by turning his head and breathing into a tube, Shoemaker resumed training, but was limited by the fact that he couldn't ride the horses himself in order to assess their ability. In 1997, realizing that the physical rigors of training were too much for him, he retired.

On October 12, 2003, at age 72, Shoemaker died in his sleep at his home in San Marino, California, near the Santa Anita racetrack. Shoemaker was married and divorced three times. He is survived by his only child, Amanda, from his third marriage, and his brother, Lonnie. **Sources:** *Independent* (London), October 14, 2003, p. 18; *Los Angeles Times,* October 13, 2003, p. A1, p. A10; *New York Times,* October 13, 2003, p. B8; *San Francisco Chronicle,* October 13, 2003, p. C1; *SI.com,* http://www.sportsillustrated.com/2003/more/10/12/obit_shoemaker.ap/index.html (October 13, 2003); *Washington Post,* October 13, 2003, p. B4.

—*Kelly Winters*

Nina Simone

Born Eunice Kathleen Waymon, February 21, 1933, in Tryon, NC; died in her sleep of natural causes, April 21, 2003, in Carry–le–Rouet, France. Singer and pianist. Soulful singer Nina Simone had one top–20 hit during her lifetime—a 1959 version of George Gershwin's "I Loves You, Porgy," but her powerful voice and commanding presence has continued to influence other musicians to this day. She blended jazz, blues, gospel, and European art songs with emotional honesty, and in the 1960s, was known for incorporating civil rights protests into her songs.

Simone was the sixth of seven children born to John Divine Waymon, a barber and dry cleaner, and Mary Kate Waymon, a Methodist minister. In her autobiography, *You Put a Spell on Me,* she wrote, "Everything that happened to me as a child involved music. Everybody played music. There was never any formal training; we learned to play the same way we learned to walk, it was that natural." When she was six years old, Simone became the pianist for her church, but it was apparent that even among her musically talented family, she had a greater gift. Recognizing that Simone would benefit from formal training with a piano teacher, but also realizing that the family could not afford the lessons, Simone's mother arranged to clean the home of a British piano teacher in exchange for lessons for her daughter.

Inspired by the lessons, the talented Simone hoped to be the first African–American concert pianist. She earned a one–year scholarship at the Juilliard School of Music in New York City, but ran out of money and could not continue studying there. She was not accepted into her dream school, the prestigious Curtis Institute of Music in Philadelphia; for the rest of her life, she believed racism was the reason for her rejection. She dropped her plans for a classical piano career and began singing in clubs. In 1954, she began playing and singing at the Midtown, an Irish pub in Atlantic City, New Jersey. She took the stage name Simone partly in honor of her favorite actress, Simone Signoret, and partly to hide her nightclub singing from her mother, whose religious sensibilities forbade it.

When she started at the club, she assumed she had been hired simply to play the piano, but the manager explained to her that she had to sing as well as play. She began singing, at first in the style of Billie Holiday and other artists she admired. Although the patrons of the club were often indifferent to her music, she sang what she wanted to hear, often playing in a strictly classical style to accompany her folk, gospel, or jazz–inspired singing. This unique mixture of musical styles became her signature.

Simone's Midtown performances quickly brought her to the attention of jazz fans and record executives; she began singing in Philadelphia, then in Greenwich Village in New York City. In 1958, she was offered her first recording contract, with Bethlehem Records. In 1959, she recorded her most famous song, a rendition of George Gershwin's "I Loves You, Porgy." Other hits included "I Put a Spell on You," "My Baby Just Cares for Me," "Gin House Blues," "Forbidden Fruit," and "Please Don't Let Me Be Misunderstood." After leaving Bethlehem Records, she recorded for the Colpix, Philips, and RCA labels and began a thriving concert career.

In the 1960s, as the civil rights movement unfolded, Simone became politically active, and began singing about social issues. When civil rights leader Medgar Evers was assassinated, she wrote "Mississippi Goddam" in protest; she later wrote "Sunday in Savannah" and sang Langston Hughes' "Backlash Blues" in response to continuing racism in American society.

Simone had been married to her manager, Andy Stroud, for a decade by 1970, but the marriage ended in divorce; because of her singing career, she had missed much of her daughter's childhood. In addition, the civil rights movement had lost some of the fire it had held in the 1960s, as many of its heroes died or did not speak out as loudly. Discouraged by this lack of momentum, Simone left the United States, beginning a 15-year period of life as an expatriate in various countries, including Barbados, Liberia, Egypt, Turkey, the Netherlands, and Switzerland; ultimately, in 1994, she settled in the south of France.

In 2000, Simone returned to the United States for a rare appearance at the Wiltern Theatre. Her daughter, Lisa, who uses the single stage name Simone, joined her for several songs. Jazz critic Don Heckman wrote, according to Geoff Boucher in the *Los Angeles Times,* that the concert was "an experience that has as much to do with a soul-stirring, spirit-raising, shamanistic ritual as it does with a mere program of music.... But she could have come on to a stage with nothing more than her piano and a companion and the crowd would have been just as pleased, the music no less assertive and challenging."

Simone died in her sleep of natural causes on April 21, 2003, at her home in southern France; she was 70. She is survived by three brothers, a sister, and her daughter. **Sources:** *Entertainment Weekly,* May 2, 2003; *Los Angeles Times,* April 22, 2003, p. B11; *New York Times,* April 22, 2003, p. A27; Ninasimone.com, http://www.ninasimone.com/rca.html (December 30, 2003); *Times* (London, England), http://www.timesonline.co.uk (April 22, 2003); *Washington Post,* April 22, 2003, p. B6. —*Kelly Winters*

Walter Sisulu

Born Walter Max Ulyate Sisulu, May 18, 1912, in Transkei, South Africa; died May 6, 2003, in Soweto, South Africa. Activist. Walter Sisulu was a South African political leader who, as a result of his activism, spent more than 25 years in prison. With Nelson Mandela, he helped guide the African National Congress's campaign against apartheid, but he was less well-known than Mandela, perhaps because he preferred to work behind the scenes. Together, they transformed the African National Congress (ANC) from a banned liberation movement into the ruling party of South Africa. Sisulu was born in the Transkei in South Africa, a former British protectorate, now known as the Eastern Cape, the son of a white construction worker and an African maid. Shortly after Sisulu's birth, his father left his mother. Under the racist designations then used in South Africa, Sisulu's mixed heritage made him a "Coloured," thus setting him apart from his all-black peers. He was angry at his father for abandoning the family, and also at the rest of his family for appeasing whites. These factors fueled his youthful desire to become an activist and work for social change in South Africa.

Sisulu identified with his African heritage as a member of the Xhosa people. He was initiated into the Xhosa under the tutelage of his uncle, who was a village leader. After a brief education at an Anglican mission school, he left at the age of 15 to find work to support his family. He took whatever work he could find, laboring as a paint mixer, delivery person, gold miner, and baker. While working, he continued his studies through correspondence courses. During his time as a baker, he tried to organize the workers into a union, and as a result, was fired. In 1940, he started his own real-estate business in Johannesburg, selling land to black Africans before the apartheid system (which enforced strict racial segregation) took away their rights of ownership. During this time, he also became involved in the ANC, an activist organization that aimed to improve the rights and lives of black South Africans. As a member of the ANC, in 1941 he helped recruit activist Nelson Mandela to the cause, acting as a mentor to the younger man, paying his school tuition, introducing him to his first wife (a cousin of Sisulu's) and even arranging for Mandela to find lodgings in his mother's home. Together, they founded the ANC Youth League, which espoused a rather militant approach to the ANC's campaign against the oppressive South African government. According to Bill Keller in the *New York Times*, Sisulu later said of Mandela, "I had no hesitation, the moment I met him, that this is the man I need … for leading the African people."

In 1944, Sisulu married his wife, Albertina; Mandela, who later became president of South Africa, was his best man. As Sisulu became more involved in political causes, Albertina took over the jobs of supporting their family and raising their children. From 1949 to 1954, Sisulu served as secretary general of the ANC. In addition, Sisulu was a founder of the ANC's armed wing, Umkhunto we Sizwe. As a result of his activities, Sisulu, along with Mandela, was a defendant in South Africa's Treason Trial, a four-year trial in which 156 people were charged with high treason against the government. Although all the defendants were acquitted in 1961, Sisulu was often placed under house arrest in the ensuing years. In 1963, he went underground, hiding from the government. Later that year, he, Mandela, and other anti-apartheid activists were arrested, and convicted of treason. The government demanded that they be sentenced to death, but instead, they were sentenced to life in prison. During his long prison term, Sisulu's wife and children were subjected to arrests, banning orders, and government harassment. Sisulu was released from Pullsmoor Prison on October 15, 1989. Mandela was released four months later, and apartheid began to crumble.

When Mandela was elected president of South Africa in 1994, he made Sisulu one of his closest advisors, although Sisulu's age and poor health prevented him from taking an official position in the new government. Behind the scenes, Sisulu emphasized moderation and reconciliation in the years after apartheid was over. According to the *New York Times*'s Keller, he said, "Bitterness does not do your cause any good. That doesn't mean you don't get angry. But you don't let it get in the way of your policy."

Sisulu died on May 5, 2003, at his home in Soweto, near Johannesburg, at the age of 90; he had suffered from a long illness. According to Nita Lelyveld of the *Los Angeles Times*, Mandela said, "His absence has created a void. A part of me is gone." Sisulu is survived by his wife, Albertina; a daughter, Lindiwe; four sons, Zwelakhe, Max, Mlungisi, and Nonku-

luleko; and three adopted children. **Sources:** *Chicago Tribune,* May 6, 2003, sec. 1, p. 11; *Los Angeles Times,* May 6, 2003, p. B12; *New York Times,* May 6, 2003, p. C17; *Times* (London, England), http://www.timesonline.co.uk (May 7, 2003).

—Kelly Winters

Robert Stack

Born January 13, 1919, in Los Angeles, CA; died of heart failure, May 14, 2003, in Bel Air, CA. Actor. Actor Robert Stack was known for his portrayal of determined, crime fighter Eliot Ness in the 1960s television series *The Untouchables,* as well as for his role as host of another series, *Unsolved Mysteries.* His work on *The Untouchables* won him an Emmy award in 1960.

Stack was born in Los Angeles, California, in 1919, a fifth-generation Californian. His great-grandfather founded one of the city's first opera houses, and his grandmother was a noted opera singer. His father, James, was an advertising executive, but Stack's parents divorced when he was only a year old. When he was three, he moved with his mother to Paris, France, where she studied singing. Stack's older brother, James, stayed in the United States with their father. When Stack was six, he and his mother returned to the United States; he had learned to speak fluent French while in Paris, but now had to learn English. His parents remarried, but his father died when Stack was ten. His mother, believing that Stack needed to have male role models in his life, encouraged him to become involved in sports.

Among these mentors and role models were actor Spencer Tracy, producers Darryl Zanuck and Walter Wagner (with whom he played polo) and actors Gary Cooper, Fred MacMurray, and Clark Gable (who shot skeet with him). Stack attended the University of Southern California for a year, then joined a theater group in Hollywood and studied singing. His teacher told him that if he wanted to hear truly talented singers, he should go to Universal Studios. At the time, the studio was looking for a man who could play a prince, and when producer Joe Pasternak saw Stack standing around the set, he asked Stack to audition. He won the lead, acting opposite Deanna Durbin in *First Love* and giving the teenaged actress her first on-screen kiss, an event that generated national attention. He followed this with a string of movies, including *The Mortal Storm,* a drama that depicted the evils of the German Nazi dictatorship. As a result, according to a *Times* reporter, Stack once said, "I found out I was on Hitler's hitlist."

Stack served as a gunnery officer in the Navy during World War II and then returned to films, playing the lead in *The Bullfighter and the Lady* in 1951 as well as in the first commercial 3–D movie *Bwana Devil* in 1952, and appearing in a supporting role in *The High and the Mighty,* which starred John Wayne, in 1953. In 1956 he appeared in *Written on the Wind,* a melodrama starring Lauren Bacall and Rock Hudson, and received a Best Supporting Actor Oscar nomination for his work in that film. In that same year, he married his wife, Rosemarie. In later years, they would be well known in Hollywood for their long and happy marriage.

From 1959 to 1963, Stack starred as steely–eyed, determined Eliot Ness on the television series *The Untouchables,* which was based on the real–life investigator, set in Prohibition–era Chicago, and which featured Ness fighting bootleggers and mobsters. Initially, Stack didn't want the part; at the time, television was a relatively new medium, and television actors did not receive the respect accorded to film actors. Stack's agent insisted, however, and he took the part. John Milius, a longtime friend of Stack's, told *Los Angeles Times* writer Dennis McLellan that as an actor, Stack had "unshakable dignity. At the same time, there was something dangerous about [him]. You can call it whatever you want—macho or whatever it is—but Bob had prowess; he had an authority in what he did. I don't know whether it came from a certain moral center or what." However, Milius also noted that Stack had an excellent sense of humor to balance this stoic dignity. Stack became so renowned for his role as Ness, and so identified with the part, that he found it hard to find other work after the series ended. Stack later starred in three other television series, *The Name of the Game* from 1968 to 1971, *Most Wanted* from 1976 to 1977, and *Strike Force* from 1981 to 1982, as well as hosting *Unsolved Mysteries* from 1987 to 2002. He also appeared in the 1980 comedy film *Airplane,* a satire of the 1970s genre of "disaster movies," and in the 1988 comedy *Caddyshack II.* In both these films, he mocked his earlier screen image as Ness.

In his later years, Stack suffered from ill health. He underwent radiation treatment for prostate cancer, and when he suffered two blocked arteries, his doctor said that heart surgery would be too risky because of the after–effects of the radiation. He died of heart failure at his home in Bel Air, California, on May 14, 2003; he was 84. He is survived by his wife, children Elizabeth and Charles, and his brother, James. **Sources:** *Los Angeles Times,* May 16, 2003, p. B12; *New York Times,* May 16, 2003, p. A23; *Times* (London, England), May 19, 2003, http://www.timesonline.co.uk (May 19, 2003); *Washington Post,* May 16, 2003, p. B6;

—Kelly Winters

William Steig

Born November 14, 1907, in Brooklyn, NY; died of natural causes, October 3, 2003, in Boston, MA. Author and illustrator. As one of the most admired cartoonists of all time, Steig spent seven decades drawing for the *New Yorker* magazine. He touched generations of readers with his tongue–in–cheek pen–and–ink drawings, which often expressed states of mind like shame, embarrassment or anger. Later in life, Steig turned to children's books, working as both a writer and illustrator. His 1990 book *Shrek!* was adapted for the big screen and won a 2001 Academy Award for best animated feature film.

Born in Brooklyn, New York, Steig was the son of Polish–Jewish immigrants Joseph and Laura Ebel Steig. The future illustrator first took up drawing as a teenager, working as a cartoonist for his high school newspaper. Steig's parents were laborers—his father painted houses and his mother worked as a seamstress. As such, they did not want Steig or his three brothers to become laborers for fear they would be exploited by businessmen. They were not to become businessmen, either, for fear they would exploit laborers. Instead, the brothers were encouraged to become artists. For two years, Steig attended the City College of New York, where he earned All–American honors in water polo. From there, he attended the National Academy of Design in New York for three years and spent a week at the Yale School of Fine Arts.

Steig turned to drawing after the Depression set in around 1929 and the family needed money. He had intended to go to sea and become a beachcomber, but he felt a duty to take care of his parents and younger brother. In 1930, he sold his first cartoon to the *New Yorker* for $40 and was subsequently hired as a staff cartoonist. That first cartoon depicted one prison inmate lamenting to another, "My son's incorrigible, I can't do a thing with him." Over the next 70 years, Steig produced 1,600 drawings and 117 covers for the magazine. He first gained notoriety for his series of "Small Fry" cartoons that depicted hard–nosed brats. They arrived in 1931 and stayed for 30 years, appearing both inside and on the cover.

In his 60s, Steig began writing children's books and published more than 25. His first book used letters to stand for words. Published in 1968, it was titled "CDB!" which meant "See the bee." Most often, however, his books featured animal heroes like brave pigs, dogs, donkeys or other strange creatures. Steig focused on animal characters because he felt it gave him more freedom to do wackier things. He also thought children were amused by watching animals behave like the humans they knew.

His third book, 1969's *Sylvester and the Magic Pebble,* won the Caldecott Medal in 1970, the highest honor a children's picture book can capture. It tells the story of a donkey who turns into a stone. Another favorite was *The Amazing Bone,* published in 1976, which is about a day–dreaming pig on the way home from school. Another beloved book was 1982's *Doctor De Soto,* which featured the dilemmas of a mouse dentist treating a hungry fox. Deemed semi–autobiographical, Steig's last book, *When Everybody Wore a Hat,* came out a few months before his death.

For Steig, writing children's books was "as easy as pie," he once told the *Boston Globe.* "A small book, if you're functioning well, you can write pretty quickly, a few days or a few weeks. The illustrating is more time–consuming: I hate to illustrate my books, because I find it hard to repeat scenes and characters. It looks bad to me."

Steig's children's books were also wildly popular because of the crazy, complicated language he used—words like lunatic, palsied, sequestration, and cleave. Kids love the sound of those words even if they do not quite understand the meaning. Steig's descriptions were also clever. He once described a beached whale as "breaded with sand."

Throughout the course of his career, Steig compiled his cartoons and drawings into books. Some of them were published first in the *New Yorker.* Others were deemed too dark to be printed there. Most of these collections centered on the cold, dark psychoanalytical truth about relationships. They featured husbands and wives fighting and parents snapping at their kids. His first adult book, *Man About Town,* was published in 1932, followed by *About People,*

published in 1939, which focused on social outsiders. *Sick of Each Other,* published in 2000, included a drawing depicting a wife holding her husband at gunpoint, saying, "Say you adore me."

According to the *Los Angeles Times,* fellow *New Yorker* artist Edward Sorel once wrote a review of Steig in which he said: "If we consider his entire oeuvre: his prolific output; the inventiveness of his stories, so often involving transformation; his precise and demanding language; and the sheer beauty of his pictures, then his legacy can only be described as unprecedented."

Steig also liked to take credit for changing the focus of the contemporary greeting card industry. According to the *Washington Post,* Steig said, "Greeting cards used to be all sweetness and love. I started doing the complete reverse—almost a hate card—and it caught on."

Over the course of his life, Steig married four times. His first wife was Elizabeth Mead, sister of anthropologist Margaret Mead. They married in 1936, had a son and a daughter, and divorced. In 1950, he married Kari Homestead and they had one daughter before their 1963 divorce. In 1964, he married Stephanie Healey and they divorced in 1966. His fourth wife was Jeanne Doron, whom he married in 1969. They had one son and two daughters and remained together until his death.

Steig continued to work well into his last year. At age 95, he died on October 3, 2003, at his home in Boston, Massachusetts. He is survived by his wife, Jeanne; two children from his first marriage, Lucy and Jeremy; a daughter from his second marriage, Maggie; and two grandchildren. **Sources:** *Boston Globe,* October 5, 2003, p. D18; *Independent* (London, England), October 7, 2003, p. 16; *Los Angeles Times,* October 5, 2003, p. B16; *New York Times,* October 5, 2003, p. A39; *Washington Post,* October 6, 2003, p. B5.

—*Lisa Frick*

Joe Strummer

Born John Graham Mellor, August 21, 1952, in Ankara, Turkey; died of a heart attack, December 22, 2002, in Broomfield, Somerset, England. Musician, actor, and activist. As the guitarist, lead singer, and a songwriter for the British punk band the Clash, Joe Strummer brought unique political sensibilities to raucous punk music, as well as diverse musical influences from reggae to rockabilly. Although Clash songs such as "Rock the Casbah" and "Train in Vain," gained the group widespread fame in the United States, the group's most avid following was in Great Britain, where they had 16 Top 40 hits. Upon hearing of Strummer's death, British singer Billy Bragg was quoted in *Daily Variety* as saying: "Without Joe there's no political Clash, and without the Clash the whole political edge of punk would have been severely dulled."

The son of a British diplomat, Strummer was born John Graham Mellor in Ankara, Turkey, and attended several London boarding schools. In the early 1970s, he began performing on London street corners and subway stations and formed the rock band 101ers, which became a popular band in the pubs of England. By then, he had assumed his new name of Joe Strummer, reportedly to reflect his guitar playing. In 1976, he helped form the Clash after seeing the British punk band the Sex Pistols. The band quickly became popular and opened for the Sex Pistols during their infamous "Anarchy tour" in the summer of 1976. But, unlike many punk bands with questionable musical ability, the Clash, thanks to the song writing of Strummer and Clash co-founder Mick Jones, evolved from writing three-chord punk anthems to songs influenced by reggae, blues, and rap.

The band signed with CBS Records and quickly recorded their debut album, *The Clash*, which *Rolling Stone* magazine called the "definitive punk album" in 1977. However, CBS Record's parent company in the United States, Columbia Records, refused to release the album in America, partly due to the band's lyrics and its outlaw persona. For example, the British hit, "White Riot," included such lyrics as "all the power's in the hands of people rich enough to buy it."

Despite this setback, the album became a best-selling import in America. A BBC biography of the Clash noted that critics "recognized that they had brilliantly distilled the anger, depression and energy of mid-'70s England" and "had infused the messages and sloganeering with strong tunes and pop hooks."

The band's breakthrough in the United States came in 1979 with their album *London Calling*, which included their first American hit single, "Train in Vain." The band followed with the albums *Sandinista!*, which included the title song about Nicara-

guan Sandinistas fighting the American–backed enemy, and *Combat Rock*, which included the hits "Rock the Casbah" and "Should I Stay or Should I Go."

Strummer and Jones worked both as a team and individually in writing the group's songs, delivering messages of social consciousness and anti–racism. A BBC News article summed up the Clash and Strummer's songs saying that "the message was brutally honest ... and for those who did not buy into it, there was always the damn good rock music."

Although successful and firm fixtures on the music scene, the band began to undergo internal division until Jones left the band in 1983. The band called it quits three years later in 1986. Strummer continued writing music and performing, including forming the short–lived band Latino Rockabilly War, performing with the Pogues, and releasing a solo album titled *Earthquake Weather*.

Strummer was introduced to the film world when he wrote two songs for the movie *Sid & Nancy*, a film about the tragic end of the former Sex Pistols' bass player and his girlfriend. Strummer continued to compose for films and then began acting, appearing in the movies *Candy Mountain, Walker, Straight to Hell*, and *Mystery Train*. Strummer reappeared on the music scene in 1999 with a new band, the Mescaleros, and the album *Rock Art and the X–Ray Style*. They later released *Global a Go–Go*.

Throughout his career, Strummer never lost his edge in terms of his combative personality and the hard–hitting social commentary in his lyrics. Phil Gallo and Debra Johnson reported in *Daily Variety* that during a performance in the fall of 2002 at the Troubador, "Strummer proved his punk attitude has never deflated, pulling an abusive patron onstage and challenging him to a fist fight."

Singer Bragg also noted in London's *Guardian Unlimited*, "I have a great admiration for the man. His most recent records are as political and edgy as anything he did with the Clash. His take on multicultural Britain in the 21st century is far ahead of anybody else."

Throughout his life, Strummer remained active in social causes and outspoken against racism. At the time of his death, he was scheduled to collaborate with Bono from the band U2 on a Nelson Mandela tribute song for an AIDS fund–raiser in South

Africa. He was also interested in environmental issues. Future Forests, which Strummer helped found, announced plans to plant trees and name a forest after him, creating a "living memorial on the Isle of Skye in Scotland."

The Clash had often received lucrative offers to re-unite, but never did. However, the band was going to perform together again for their induction into the Rock and Roll Hall of Fame on March 10, 2003. An article on CNN.com quoted Bono telling the British Press Association, "The Clash was the greatest rock band. They wrote the rule book for U2."

Strummer died on December 22, 2002, in England, of a heart attack; he was 50. He is survived by his wife, Lucinda, and three children. Although Strummer never again reached the fame or audiences that he did with the Clash, his legacy in rock music is unquestionable. Tom Sinclair, writing in *Entertainment Weekly,* noted that Strummer's musical efforts post–Clash "felt anticlimactic almost by definition. He had embodied rock commitment so completely that no second act seemed possible." **Sources:** BBC News, http://news.bbc.co.uk/2/hi/entertainment/2600955.stm (February 4, 2003); BBC News, http://news.bbc.co.uk/2/hi/entertainment/2601287.stm (February 4, 2003); *Cincinnati Post,* January 21, 2003; CNN.com, http://www.cnn.com/2002/SHOWBIZ/Music/12/23/obit.strummer (February 4, 2003); *Daily Variety,* December 24, 2002; *Entertainment Weekly,* January 10, 2003; *Guardian Unlimited,* http://www.guardian.co.uk/arts/news/story/0,117117,864833,00.html (February 4, 2003).

—*David A. Petechuk*

Rene Thom

Born Rene Frederic Thom, September 2, 1923, in Montbeliard, France; died of vascular disease, October 25, 2002, in Bures–sur–Yvette, France. Mathematician. Considered one of the leading thinkers in the field of topology, a branch of mathematics, Thom became best known for applying geometric principals to the most vexing problems of society and in nature. Perhaps his best–known theory was one he called catastrophe theory, which was an attempt to describe mathematically how epidemics, earthquakes, revolutions, and other violent events can arise out of seemingly peaceful circumstances. If it were possible to explain such events mathematically, Thom reasoned, it might also become possible to predict and even prevent these events. Thom won the highest prize in mathematics, the Fields Medal, in 1958.

Thom was born in a small town in France near Switzerland's border. His parents were shopkeepers. He took to mathematics at an early age, by some accounts learning to visualize shapes in four–dimensional space by the age of ten. His mathematical talents won him a scholarship. He received a university degree in mathematics in 1940, shortly before Hitler invaded France. He went on to earn a degree in philosophy in 1941. He continued his studies at the Ecole Normale Superieure in Paris, where he was a student from 1943 to 1946. Also during this time, he married and started a family. He finally completed his studies in 1951, when he received a Ph.D. Soon afterward, he traveled to the United States for a year of post–doctoral work at Princeton University, where he met Albert Einstein. Returning to France, Thom became a professor and continued his research.

In the 1950s, Thom, working with Hassler Whitney, created two new branches of mathematics called differential topology and singularity theory. These theories allow researchers to mathematically manipulate spheres in higher dimensions of space beyond the three that we live in. Higher dimensional spheres are called manifolds, and Thom created a way to examine the intersections of manifolds that have been mapped onto one another. The points where the manifolds intersect are called singularities, and, along with manifolds, are considered essential to a deep understanding of geometry. This work led to Thom's being awarded the Fields Medal in 1958. This is the highest honor that can be awarded to mathematicians, equivalent to the Nobel Prize.

In 1964, Thom joined the faculty of the Institut des Hautes Etudes Scientifique (Institute of Advanced Scientific Studies), which is one of the most renowned scientific institutions in France. Thom remained at this institution, based in Bures–sur–Yvette, outside of Paris, for the remainder of his career. It was here that Thom began work on what was to become one of his best–known theories: catastrophe theory. This theory, which applied the principals of manifolds and singularities to the problem of predicting catastrophic events, was codified in a book called *Structural Stability and Morphogenesis,* which was published in 1972. The work eventually sold well enough to qualify it as a best–seller.

Although the book did well, the theory it described did not live up to the hopes many had for it. Not only did it not adequately describe chaotic events, but, according to many critics, it also depended too much on gut feeling and not enough on rigorous mathematics. Thom himself provided ammunition to this criticism by declaring, according to Martin Weil in the *Washington Post,* "If one must choose between rigor and meaning, I shall unhesitatingly choose the latter."

Although Thom's catastrophe theory failed to illuminate the causes of events its proponents hoped to better understand, including prison riots, hurricanes, and stock market crashes, it did focus attention on the analysis of how small events in large systems, such as weather patterns and social movements, can have large repercussions for the system as a whole. Many have credited Thom with planting the seeds of a theory that has proven much more successful than his in describing such events: chaos theory.

Perhaps one of Thom's greatest achievements was to fire the imaginations of others, including the painter Salvador Dali, who, in 1983, honored Thom in a painting called "Topological Abduction of Europe: Homage to Rene Thom." The work depicted one of Thom's equations superimposed on a chaotic landscape.

Thom made no secret of the fact that he was often more attracted to the deeper philosophical meaning behind mathematics than in the strict, rigorous mathematics practiced by his colleagues. To inspire was his aim. This was perhaps best summed up in the final sentence of his book, which was quoted in the *Times* after his death: "At a time when so many scholars in the world are calculating, is it not desirable that some, who can, dream?"

In his writings, he described one of the factors that led to his delving more deeply into the philosophical underpinnings of mathematics than into the rigors of its execution. This was the realization that one of his colleagues so dazzled students with his supreme command of the technicalities of mathematics, that Thom felt he could never hope to compete. Instead, Thom decided, he would "tackle more general notions," according to the *Washington Post*'s Weil.

In the final years of his active life, Thom focused almost exclusively on philosophy and linguistics. Circulatory problems at the end of his life led to the amputation of one foot, and caused him lose much of his memory. In addition to the Fields Medal, he won the Grand Prix Scientifique de la Ville de Paris in 1974, and was named an honorary member of the London Mathematical Society in 1990.

Thom died on October 25, 2002, in Bures–sur–Yvette, France, of vascular disease at the age of 79. He is survived by his wife, Suzanne; his daughters, Francoise and Elizabeth; and his son, Christian. **Sources:** *Guardian* (London), November 14, 2002, p. 28; *New York Times,* November 10, 2002, p. 46; *Times* (London), November 15, 2002, p. 41; *Washington Post,* November 17, 2002, p. C10.

—*Michael Belfiore*

Strom Thurmond

Born James Strom Thurmond, December 5, 1902, in Edgefield, SC; died of natural causes, June 26, 2003, in Edgefield, SC. Politician. Former U.S. Senator Strom Thurmond died in June of 2003, just months after his historic record as a 47–year member of Congress ended with his retirement. The South Carolina Republican was once a staunch segregationist, but modified his views as civil–rights legislation went into effect across the land in the 1960s. "Times change and people change, and people who can't change don't stay in office long," *Washington Post* obituary writer J. Y. Smith quoted him as saying.

Born in Edgefield, South Carolina, in 1902, Thurmond was the son of a judge and grew up in a town that produced many of the state's governors. He earned a horticulture degree from the forerunner of Clemson University in 1923, and began his career as a teacher and coach before winning his first political race as superintendent of Edgefield county schools in 1928. After studying on his own to pass the state bar exam, he served as county attorney for Edgefield from 1930 to 1938. He also spent part of the decade in the state house and as an appellate judge.

After returning from World War II a decorated veteran who took part in the D–Day invasion of France, Thurmond immediately re–entered politics in his home state. He was a Democrat during this first half of his long political career. In the years after the American Civil War, the party was firmly associated with white Southern political power, and Thurmond courted votes by taking up the issue of segregation of the races, but once in office often acted more progressively. Elected South Carolina governor in 1946, he put one of the toughest prosecutors in the state on a 1947 lynching case involving 28 whites who had killed a black man.

Perhaps the most infamous period in Thurmond's political career came during the 1948 presidential race. Incumbent Democrat Harry S Truman had recently enacted civil–rights reforms, including a historic desegregation of the armed forces, that were vehemently opposed by many white Southerners. At that year's Democratic National Convention, many Southern delegates walked out when calls were made to adopt civil–rights reform as a plank in the party's platform. Thurmond joined the breakaway group, called the States' Rights Democratic Party, and was nominated as its candidate for the White House. The "Dixiecrat" party, as it was called, staunchly opposed desegregation efforts and federal measures that would force all states to comply. Speaking on behalf of Southerners, Thurmond asserted that "all the laws of Washington and all the bayonets of the Army cannot force the Negro into our homes, into our schools, our churches, and our places of recreation and amusement," the *New York Times* writer Adam Clymer quoted him as saying.

Thurmond and the Dixiecrats won a million popular votes, 39 electoral ones, and placed third in the race, but it did not fail to return Truman to the White House. Over the next decade, Thurmond remained a strong opponent of court rulings and federal laws that attempted to desegregate the South. His stance, he asserted, was not based on any personal racial bias, but rather against federal involvement in state matters. With his gubernatorial term set to expire in 1951, Thurmond entered South Carolina's 1950 Senate race, but lost. He won a seat four years later as write–in candidate, making him the first and only U.S. Senator to enter the chamber as a write–in candidate. As the civil–rights struggle gained momentum, Thurmond responded with vigor, once speaking on the Senate floor for more than 24 hours straight in a filibuster to delay voting, but the first federal civil rights bill since 1875 passed anyway.

Thurmond decamped to the Republican Party in 1964, when President Lyndon B. Johnson signed the historic Civil Rights Act into law that year. "The party of our fathers is dead," the *New York Times* obituary by Clymer quoted Thurmond as saying. Within a few years, however, Thurmond was also courting minority voters himself. Recognizing that the 1965 Voting Rights Act gave new political power to blacks in the South and that the white hold on political power in the South was eroding, he became one of the first Southern senators to hire an African American on his staff in 1971. Thurmond was elected to the Senate seven more times after his 1954 write–in bid, usually by strong margins. He began his last six–year term in early 1997, returning to his seat as chair of the Senate Armed Services. Previously, he had chaired the Senate Judiciary Committee and served as president pro tempore of the Senate. He sponsored few important bills during his career, but was known as a champion "pork–barrel" politician, able to secure federal funds for his home state. The final day of his career in Congress arrived on November 19, 2002 and, in honor of his service, Thurmond was given the gavel and allowed to preside over the Senate that day, though his party did not have the majority at the time. He closed the year's session with the words, "That's all," according to Clymer in the *New York Times.*

Thurmond died at age 100 on June 26, 2003, of natural causes in his hometown of Edgefield. Among many of the other records he held, one ended that day: Thurmond was the last living American politician elected by veterans of U.S. Civil War, which came during his 1928 run for Edgefield County school superintendent. He was widowed in 1960 when his spouse of 20–some years, Jean Crouch, in died of cancer. Eight years later Thurmond wed former Miss South Carolina Nancy Moore, with whom he had four children. Three survived him, and six months after Thurmond's death a 78–year–old California woman stepped forward to admit that she was Thurmond's daughter as well. The incident was a final coda on one of America's most revered and once–jeered politicians, for Essie Mae Washington–Williams was the product of a liaison between a 22–year–old Thurmond and the African–American maid in his parents' home. **Sources:** *Chicago Tribune,* June 26, 2003, sec. 1, p. 1; CNN.com, http://www.cnn.com/2003/ALLPOLITICS//06/26/thurmond.obit/index.html (June 27, 2003); http://www.cnn.com/SPECIALS/2003/special.strom.thurmond/stories/bio/index.html (June 27, 2003); *Independent* (London, England), June 28, 2003, p. 20; *Los Angeles Times,* June 27, 2003, p. A1; July 1, 2003, p. A2; *New York Times,* June 28, 2003, p. A13; July 1, 2003, p. A2; December 20, 2003, p. A1; *People,* July 14, 2003, p. 123; *Washington Post,* June 27, 2003, p. A1.

—*Carol Brennan*

Paul Wellstone

Born Paul David Wellstone, July 21, 1944, in Washington, DC; died in a plane crash, October 25, 2002, in Eveleth, MN. United States Senator. Paul Wellstone, a Democratic senator from Minnesota, was known for his strongly liberal positions and beliefs. During his eleven years in the Senate, he championed human rights as a foreign policy issue, supported abortion rights and gun control, and opposed both the Persian Gulf War in 1991 and the war on Iraq in 2002.

Wellstone was born in Washington, D.C., and grew up in the capitol's suburbs, in Arlington, Virginia. After finishing high school in his hometown, he went on to earn a bachelor's degree from the University of North Carolina in 1965. He continued his studies at North Carolina, completing a Ph.D. in political science in 1969. Along the way, he became a champion collegiate wrestler, and married Sheila Ison. Wellstone's politics were also shaped during this time by the civil rights and anti–Vietnam War movements of the 1960s. This was reflected in the topic of his dissertation, which was called *Black Militants in the Ghetto: Why They Believe in Violence.*

Wellstone's first career was as a college professor. After earning his doctorate, he joined the faculty of Carlton College in Northfield, Minnesota, not far from the Twin Cities of Minneapolis and St. Paul. He taught there for a total of 21 years—up until the time he was elected to the U.S. Senate. At Carlton, he became known for his political activism, joining protests against the Vietnam war and against other United States military actions, including the bombing of Cambodia. In the service of this last cause, he was arrested for civil disobedience.

It was during his time at Carlton that Wellstone developed the oratorical style for which he became known as a senator—asking questions, engaging his listeners, and challenging them to get involved in the issues he discussed. As a precursor to his political career, Wellstone co–chaired Jesse Jackson's 1988 presidential campaign in Minnesota, switching his efforts to helping the campaign of Michael Dukakis after he, not Jackson, received the Democratic nomination. Two years after that presidential campaign, Wellston ran his own campaign for Senate, unseating the incumbent, republican Rudy Boschwitz.

Wellstone was elected to his first term in the Senate with an unorthodox, populist campaign that upset a much–better–funded Republican incumbent. Wellstone won that first campaign with 50 percent of the vote to Boschwitz's 48 percent. Among his campaign promises were statements that he would create controversy, fight for liberal causes, and serve in the Senate for only two terms. He ran again in 1996 after his first term was up, again beating Boschwitz with 50 percent of the vote, this time to Boschwitz's 41 percent. At the time of his death, Wellstone was on his way toward breaking one of his campaign promises by running for a third term.

Most observers agreed that Wellstone, who began his first term in office in 1991, made good on his promise to fight for the causes he believed in, even when he appeared to have little chance of winning.

For instance, he was one of the few in Congress to vote in October of 2002 against authorizing President George W. Bush to invade Iraq. He also strongly opposed the first President Bush on the first Persian Gulf War in 1991. He opposed the North American Free Trade Agreement (NAFTA) in 1993, and was an advocate for gun control laws and a proponent of abortion rights.

Between the two wars in the Persian Gulf, Wellstone became known as a fierce advocate for advancing human rights as a foreign policy issue, for seeking to increase government funding for health care, welfare, and education. Not one for compromise, Wellstone often gave impassioned speeches advancing his views on the Senate floor, even in cases where it was clear that his cause would not win. "He was always the last guy standing with the last amendment," Senator Byron L. Dorgan, a democrat from North Dakota, told Nick Anderson in the *Los Angeles Times.* "It was always about children, or the poor."

Wellstone considered the idea of running for president in 2000, but decided against it after doctors advised him that the ruptured disk in his back for which he was being treated would not stand up to the rigors of campaign travel. Wellstone published a memoir in 2001 called *The Conscience of a Liberal.*

Wellstone died in a plane crash in a rural area of Minnesota on October 25, 2002, while on his way to a funeral for the father of a state legislator. Also killed in the crash were Wellstone's wife, Sheila, their daughter, Marcia, as well five other people on board the plane. The twin–engine, propeller plane went down without warning in a freezing drizzle in Minnesota's North Woods. The plane had been attempting to land in Eveleth, Minnesota, and it came down about two miles short of the runway.

At the time of his death, Wellstone was heavily campaigning for his third term as a U.S. Senator, even though, as he had publicly revealed, he suffered from a mild form of multiple sclerosis. Both President Bush and his Republican party invested heavily in trying to defeat him. According to polls, he had a good chance of defeating his challenger, Republican Norm Coleman. The race would have been a close one, and on it depended the fate of the Democrats' control of the Senate; a win by Wellstone would have preserved the Democrats' single–seat Senate lead, while a loss would allow the Republicans to take control. After Wellstone's death, Coleman was elected to fill Wellstone's vacant Senate seat.

Wellstone died at the age of 58. He is survived by two sons, David and Mark, and six grandchildren. **Sources:** *Chicago Tribune,* October 26, 2002, p. 1, p. 12; *Los Angeles Times,* October 26, 2002, p. A16; *New York Times,* October 26, 2002, p. A19; *Washington Post,* October 26, 2002, p. A1, p. A6.

—*Michael Belfiore*

Barry White

Born Barry Eugene Carter, September 12, 1944, in Galveston, TX; died of kidney failure, July 4, 2003, in Los Angeles, CA. Singer. Soul seducer Barry White put out a string of hits during the disco heyday of the 1970s that redefined the term "romantic" music. With his deep bass voice and come–hither croons, White was not the pioneer of "the erotically charged love song," noted *Entertainment Weekly* writer Tom Sinclair, but his hits "simultaneously raised the bar for all subsequent bedroom ballads and changed the rules of the game for the R&B love men who sang them."

Though White was born in Galveston, Texas, in 1944, he and his younger brother, Darryl, grew up in a single–parent household in the rough South–Central neighborhood of Los Angeles, California. He was a talented musician from an early age, playing piano on a hit record called "Goodnight My Love" from Jesse Belvin when he was just eleven, and directing the choir at his Baptist church in his teens. Lured by street life, he spent seven months in a juvenile–detention lock–up at age 16 for stealing tires. One day while there, however, he heard the Elvis Presley song, "It's Now or Never," and felt as if the song was a message urging him to turn his life around, which he did from that day forward. His brother never managed to extricate himself, and died years later in a senseless shooting in the same Los Angeles neighborhood. Reflecting back on his own good fortune, White liked to say that he had been "born under a sign named blessed," according to *People.*

As a young man, White sang in a soul outfit called the Upfronts, and served as songwriter, arranger, and producer for a number of other minor bands of the era. Two 1965 solo tracks released under the name Barry Lee failed to catch on, and thereafter White concentrated on his career as a talent scout for the Mustang and Bronco record labels. He helped launch a female R&B group called Love Unlimited in the early 1970s, producing their 1972 hit "Walkin' in the Rain With the One I Love;" one of

the women, Glodean James, eventually became his second wife. Offered a solo deal, White was initially wary about performing again, but headed back into the studio anyway. The result was 1973's *I've Got So Much to Give* and its hit single, "I'm Gonna Love You Just a Little More, Baby." He also formed a side project called the Love Unlimited Orchestra, whose 1973 instrumental, "Love's Theme" went to No. 1 and was said to have ushered in the disco era.

A string of hit LPs and singles followed White's debut LP over the next few years, including "Can't Get Enough of Your Love, Babe," "You're My First, My Last, My Everything," and "It's Ecstasy When You Lay Down Next to Me." They were lushly orchestrated R&B ballads in which "White created a fantasy world of opulence and desire," the *New York Times'* Jon Pareles noted. "As strings played hovering chords, guitars echoed off into the distance, and drums provided a muffled heartbeat, Mr. White spoke in his bottomless bass and crooned the reassuring sentiments" of his love songs. And though White's "canyon–deep, butter–smooth vocals emphasized his songs' sexually charged verbal foreplay," noted a CNN.com writer, White always asserted that they were merely paeans to his wife, Glodean.

During the course of his long career in the music business, White earned an astounding 106 gold albums, 41 of which also attained platinum status. After disco died out, his fame did for a time as well, but he was a respected figure nonetheless who was tapped to produce Marvin Gaye's next album just days before the former Motown star was slain in 1984. White's own comeback began in 1993 with an appearance on the animated series *The Simpsons,* and his 1994 LP, *The Icon Is Love,* sold two million copies. Its single, "Practice What You Preach," reached No. 1. His past hits were mined for the popular *Ally McBeal* television series, and he even appeared as himself on an episode of the show. A 1999 record, *Staying Power,* earned him two long–awaited Grammy awards.

An immense man, White suffered from high blood pressure, and his health declined. In 2002, he was forced to drop out of a planned concert tour, and was hospitalized in September of that year. He died at age 58 of kidney failure the following July at Cedars–Sinai Medical Center in Los Angeles. Divorced from his second wife, he was father to six children from those two unions and step–father to one child; his ninth child, a daughter, was born just weeks before his death to his companion, Catherine Denton. Long heralded as the king of the "make–out" song, White claimed he was anything but a Romeo himself and preferred the quiet life. In his spare time, *Chicago Tribune* obituary writer Richard Cromelin quoted him as saying, he liked to "play video games. I love my fish. I deal with my dogs. I stay home. I spend time with my children. I'm not a party animal." **Sources:** *Billboard Bulletin,* July 7, 2003, p. 1; *Chicago Tribune,* July 5, 2003, sec. 1, p. 4; CNN.com, http://www.cnn.com/2003/SHOWBIZ/Music/07/04/obit.barry.white.ap/index.html (July 7, 2003); *Daily Variety,* July 7, 2003, p. 4; *Entertainment Weekly,* July 18, 2003, p. 17; E! Online, http://www.eonline.com/News/Items/0,1,12100,00.html (July 7, 2003); *Los Angeles Times,* July 5, 2003, p. B21; *New York Times,* July 5, 2003, p. A13; *People,* July 21, 2003, p. 71; *Times* (London, England) http://www.thetimesonline.co.uk (July 7, 2003); *Washington Post,* July 5, 2003, p. B7.

—Carol Brennan

Warren Zevon

Born Warren William Zevon, January 24, 1947, in Chicago, IL; died of lung cancer, September 7, 2003, in Los Angeles, CA. Singer and songwriter. Acclaimed musician Warren Zevon was best known for his 1978 hit "Werewolves of London," but the wry humor and tumbling piano riffs in it were hallmarks of many of his other songs, which went largely unappreciated over the course of his long career.

Zevon's roots were in Chicago, where he was born in 1947 to a mother who belonged to the Mormon church but had married a boxer of Russian–Jewish heritage. Zevon's father earned a living as a gambler, and his son later claimed he had links to organized crime as well. The family eventually resettled in Los Angeles, California, where the musically gifted young Zevon earned poor grades at Fairfax High School. After he quit school during his junior year, his father presented him with a sports car he had won in a card game. Zevon drove the Corvette cross–country to New York City to become part of the burgeoning folk–music scene there. He eventually wound up back in southern California in the late 1960s, where he formed a duo called Lyme and Cybelle. It had little success, but Zevon's songwriting talents were noticed by others, and one of his works was recorded by the Turtles and became the B–side to their hit "Happy Together." The royalties from "Like the Seasons" provided a lucrative source of income for him for years.

Zevon released his first LP, *Wanted Dead or Alive,* in 1969. The record was produced by the legendary Kim Fowley, but was a commercial flop. Zevon turned to writing commercial jingles for clients that included the winemaker Gallo, and in the early 1970s took a job as music director and keyboard player for the Everly Brothers. At the time, the two brothers were still touring steadily but not speaking to one another. Zevon's own personal life was disintegrating as well, and his penchant for vodka became debilitating. At one point, tired of the Los Angeles scene, he and his wife fled to Spain, where he played in bars there. He was convinced to come back to record another album by his friend, the singer and songwriter Jackson Browne, who had urged a budding record label mogul named David Geffen to sign Zevon to his Asylum Records label.

The resulting LP, *Warren Zevon,* was produced by Browne and released in 1976. It featured a roster of well–known musical guests who knew and respected Zevon from his previous work as a songwriter and session musician, including the Eagles' Glenn Frey, Stevie Nicks and Lindsey Buckingham of Fleetwood Mac, Beach Boy Carl Wilson, and Bonnie Raitt. The record failed to make a dent on the charts, but four of its tracks were recorded by Linda Ronstadt, including "Poor, Poor Pitiful Me." Zevon's next work, *Excitable Boy,* was the biggest commercial success of his career. It included the 1978 hit "Werewolves of London" as well as "Roland the Headless Thompson Gunner" and "Lawyers, Guns and Money." These and the majority of Zevon's oeuvre, noted *New York Times* writer Jon Pareles, "were terse, action–packed, gallows–humored tales that could sketch an entire screenplay in four minutes and often had death as a punch line." Such songs, asserted Greg Kot in the *Chicago Tribune,* "had a profound effect on the singer–songwriter pop of the '70s. In an ocean of male sensitivity, as defined by Jackson Browne, James Taylor, and other gentle crooners, Zevon brought a room–wrecking sense of abandon, dissolution, and desperation to his songs..."

That desperation was still spilling over into his personal life, and twice Zevon entered substance–abuse rehabilitation programs. His marriage ended, and this bleak period of his life found expression in his LP 1980 release, *Bad Luck Streak in Dancing School.* He eventually remarried—to an actress from the hit television series *Knot's Landing* named Kim Lankford—and after a five–year period of inactivity since his 1982 release, *The Envoy,* released *Sentimental Hygiene* in 1987. Some members of R.E.M., still in the relatively unknown alternative–rock era of their career, played on it, and they also worked with Zevon on another project whose songs were released as the self–titled *Hindu Love Gods* in 1990.

Zevon spent the rest of the 1990s releasing albums of his songs that barely cracked the Billboard Top 200, but were favorites with critics, musicians, and longtime fans of his work. Cigarettes were the one habit he had failed to kick, and in August of 2002 he was diagnosed with lung cancer. Doctors told him that it was in advanced stages and inoperable, but Zevon went ahead with plans to record his thirteenth studio record. Appearing on it were a pantheon of music legends, including Browne, Bruce Springsteen, Don Henley, Ry Cooder, Dwight Yoakam, Emmylou Harris, and Tom Petty.

Over the course of his career, Zevon's songs had been known for their morbid humor, including "I'll Sleep When I'm Dead" and "Life'll Kill Ya," but he avoided dwelling on his fate when he wrote and recorded *The Wind.* "I feel the opposite of regret," he told the *Los Angeles Times* not long after the diagnosis of his fatal illness, according to his obituary by Geoff Boucher. "I was the hardest–living rocker on my block for a while.... Then for 18 years I was a sober dad of some amazing kids. Hey, I feel like I've lived a couple of lives."

Released in late August of 2003, *The Wind* debuted in the *Billboard* Top 20, but the 56–year–old Zevon died days later at his home in Los Angeles on September 7, 2003. Posthumously, Zevon won Grammy Awards for Best Contemporary Folk Album for *The Wind* and Best Rock Performance by a Duo or Group with Vocal for the track "Disorder in the House," which he sang with Springsteen. He is survived by his two former wives, two children, and two grandchildren. **Sources:** *Chicago Tribune,* September 9, 2003, sec. 1, p. 5; CNN.com, http://www.cnn.com/2003/SHOWBIZ/Music/09/08/obit.zevon.ap/index.html (September 8, 2003); E! Online, http://www.eonline.com/News/Items/0,1,12457,00.html?eol.tkr (September 9, 2003); *Los Angeles Times,* September 8, 2003, p. B9; *New York Times,* September 9, 2003, p. A29; *Times* (London), September 9, 2003, p. 31; *Washington Post,* September 9, 2003, p. B6.

—*Carol Brennan*

Cumulative Nationality Index

This index lists all newsmakers alphabetically under their respective nationalities. Indexes in softbound issues allow access to the current year's entries; indexes in annual hardbound volumes are cumulative, covering the entire *Newsmakers* series.

Listee names are followed by a year and issue number; thus **1996**:3 indicates that an entry on that individual appears in both 1996, Issue 3, and the 1996 cumulation. For access to newsmakers appearing earlier than the current softbound issue, see the previous year's cumulation.

AFGHAN
Karzai, Hamid **2002**:3

ALGERIAN
Zeroual, Liamine **1996**:2

AMERICAN
Aaliyah **2001**:3
Abbey, Edward
  Obituary **1989**:3
Abbott, George
  Obituary **1995**:3
Abbott, Jim **1988**:3
Abdul, Paula **1990**:3
Abercrombie, Josephine **1987**:2
Abernathy, Ralph
  Obituary **1990**:3
Abraham, S. Daniel **2003**:3
Abraham, Spencer **1991**:4
Abrams, Elliott **1987**:1
Abramson, Lyn **1986**:3
Abzug, Bella **1998**:2
Achtenberg, Roberta **1993**:4
Ackerman, Will **1987**:4
Acuff, Roy
  Obituary **1993**:2
Adair, Red **1987**:3
Adams, Patch **1999**:2
Adams, Scott **1996**:4
Addams, Charles
  Obituary **1989**:1
Affleck, Ben **1999**:1
Agassi, Andre **1990**:2
Agee, Tommie
  Obituary **2001**:4
Agnew, Spiro Theodore
  Obituary **1997**:1
Aguilera, Christina **2000**:4
Aiello, Danny **1990**:4
Aikman, Troy **1994**:2
Ailes, Roger **1989**:3
Ailey, Alvin **1989**:2
  Obituary **1990**:2
Ainge, Danny **1987**:1
Akers, John F. **1988**:3
Akers, Michelle **1996**:1

Akin, Phil
  Brief Entry **1987**:3
Alba, Jessica **2001**:2
Albee, Edward **1997**:1
Albert, Marv **1994**:3
Albert, Stephen **1986**:1
Albom, Mitch **1999**:3
Albright, Madeleine **1994**:3
Alda, Robert
  Obituary **1986**:3
Alexander, Jane **1994**:2
Alexander, Jason **1993**:3
Alexander, Lamar **1991**:2
Alexie, Sherman **1998**:4
Ali, Laila **2001**:2
Ali, Muhammad **1997**:2
Alioto, Joseph L.
  Obituary **1998**:3
Allaire, Paul **1995**:1
Allard, Linda **2003**:2
Allen, Bob **1992**:4
Allen, Debbie **1986**:2
Allen, Joan **1998**:1
Allen, John **1992**:1
Allen, Mel
  Obituary **1996**:4
Allen, Ray **2002**:1
Allen, Steve
  Obituary **2001**:2
Allen, Tim **1993**:1
Allen, Woody **1994**:1
Allen Jr., Ivan
  Obituary **2004**:3
Alley, Kirstie **1990**:3
Allred, Gloria **1985**:2
Alter, Hobie
  Brief Entry **1985**:1
Altman, Robert **1993**:2
Altman, Sidney **1997**:2
Alvarez, Aida **1999**:2
Ambrose, Stephen **2002**:3
Ameche, Don
  Obituary **1994**:2
Amory, Cleveland
  Obituary **1999**:2
Amos, Tori **1995**:1
Amos, Wally **2000**:1

Amsterdam, Morey
  Obituary **1997**:1
Anastas, Robert
  Brief Entry **1985**:2
Ancier, Garth **1989**:1
Anderson, Gillian **1997**:1
Anderson, Harry **1988**:2
Anderson, Laurie **2000**:2
Anderson, Marion
  Obituary **1993**:4
Anderson, Poul
  Obituary **2002**:3
Andreessen, Marc **1996**:2
Andrews, Maxene
  Obituary **1996**:2
Angelos, Peter **1995**:4
Angelou, Maya **1993**:4
Angier, Natalie **2000**:3
Aniston, Jennifer **2000**:3
Annenberg, Walter **1992**:3
Anthony, Earl
  Obituary **2002**:3
Anthony, Marc **2000**:3
Antonini, Joseph **1991**:2
Applegate, Christina **2000**:4
Applewhite, Marshall Herff
  Obituary **1997**:3
Arad, Avi **2003**:2
Archer, Dennis **1994**:4
Arden, Eve
  Obituary **1991**:2
Aretsky, Ken **1988**:1
Arison, Ted **1990**:3
Arkoff, Samuel Z.
  Obituary **2002**:4
Arledge, Roone **1992**:2
Arlen, Harold
  Obituary **1986**:3
Arman **1993**:1
Armstrong, C. Michael **2002**:1
Armstrong, Henry
  Obituary **1989**:1
Armstrong, Lance **2000**:1
Arnaz, Desi
  Obituary **1987**:1
Arnold, Tom **1993**:2
Arquette, Patricia **2001**:3

Boies, David **2002**:1
Boitano, Brian **1988**:3
Bolger, Ray
  Obituary **1987**:2
Bollinger, Lee C. **2003**:2
Bolton, Michael **1993**:2
Bombeck, Erma
  Obituary **1996**:4
Bonds, Barry **1993**:3
Bonet, Lisa **1989**:2
Bonilla, Bobby **1992**:2
Bon Jovi, Jon **1987**:4
Bonner, Robert **2003**:4
Bono, Sonny **1992**:2
  Obituary **1998**:2
Bontecou, Lee **2004**:4
Boone, Mary **1985**:1
Booth, Shirley
  Obituary **1993**:2
Bopp, Thomas **1997**:3
Bose, Amar
  Brief Entry **1986**:4
Bosworth, Brian **1989**:1
Botstein, Leon **1985**:3
Boudreau, Louis
  Obituary **2002**:3
Bowe, Riddick **1993**:2
Bowles, Paul
  Obituary **2000**:3
Bowman, Scotty **1998**:4
Boxcar Willie
  Obituary **1999**:4
Boxer, Barbara **1995**:1
Boyer, Herbert Wayne **1985**:1
Boyington, Gregory Pappy
  Obituary **1988**:2
Boyle, Gertrude **1995**:3
Boyle, Lara Flynn **2003**:4
Boyle, Peter **2002**:3
Boynton, Sandra **2004**:1
Bradford, Barbara Taylor **2002**:4
Bradley, Bill **2000**:2
Bradley, Todd **2003**:3
Bradley, Tom
  Obituary **1999**:1
Bradshaw, John **1992**:1
Brady, Sarah and James S. **1991**:4
Brady, Tom **2002**:4
Brandy **1996**:4
Braun, Carol Moseley **1993**:1
Bravo, Ellen **1998**:2
Braxton, Toni **1994**:3
Brazile, Donna **2001**:1
Bremen, Barry **1987**:3
Bremer, L. Paul **2004**:2
Brennan, Edward A. **1989**:1
Brennan, Robert E. **1988**:1
Brennan, William
  Obituary **1997**:4
Brenneman, Amy **2002**:1
Breyer, Stephen
  Gerald **1994**:4 **1997**:2
Bridges, Lloyd
  Obituary **1998**:3
Brinkley, David
  Obituary **2004**:3
Bristow, Lonnie **1996**:1
Brokaw, Tom **2000**:3
Bronfman, Edgar, Jr. **1994**:4
Bronson, Charles
  Obituary **2004**:4
Brooks, Albert **1991**:4

Brooks, Diana D. **1990**:1
Brooks, Garth **1992**:1
Brooks, Gwendolyn **1998**:1
  Obituary **2001**:2
Brooks, Mel **2003**:1
Brower, David **1990**:4
Brown, Bobbi **2001**:4
Brown, Dan **2004**:4
Brown, Dee
  Obituary **2004**:1
Brown, Edmund G., Sr.
  Obituary **1996**:3
Brown, J. Carter
  Obituary **2003**:3
Brown, James **1991**:4
Brown, Jerry **1992**:4
Brown, Jim **1993**:2
Brown, John Seely **2004**:1
Brown, Judie **1986**:2
Brown, Les **1994**:3
Brown, Les
  Obituary **2001**:3
Brown, Paul
  Obituary **1992**:1
Brown, Ron
  Obituary **1996**:4
Brown, Ron **1990**:3
Brown, Willie **1996**:4
Brown, Willie L. **1985**:2
Browner, Carol M. **1994**:1
Browning, Edmond
  Brief Entry **1986**:2
Bryant, Kobe **1998**:3
Brynner, Yul
  Obituary **1985**:4
Buchanan, Pat **1996**:3
Buck, Linda **2004**:2
Buckley, Betty **1996**:2
Buckley, Jeff
  Obituary **1997**:4
Buffett, Jimmy **1999**:3
Buffett, Warren **1995**:2
Bullock, Sandra **1995**:4
Bundy, McGeorge
  Obituary **1997**:1
Bundy, William P.
  Obituary **2001**:2
Bunshaft, Gordon **1989**:3
  Obituary **1991**:1
Burck, Wade
  Brief Entry **1986**:1
Burger, Warren E.
  Obituary **1995**:4
Burk, Martha **2004**:1
Burnett, Carol **2000**:3
Burnison, Chantal Simone **1988**:3
Burns, Charles R.
  Brief Entry **1988**:1
Burns, Edward **1997**:1
Burns, George
  Obituary **1996**:3
Burns, Ken **1995**:2
Burns, Robin **1991**:2
Burr, Donald Calvin **1985**:3
Burroughs, William S.
  Obituary **1997**:4
Burroughs, William S. **1994**:2
Burstyn, Ellen **2001**:4
Burton, Tim **1993**:1
Burum, Stephen H.
  Brief Entry **1987**:2

Buscaglia, Leo
  Obituary **1998**:4
Buscemi, Steve **1997**:4
Busch, August A. III **1988**:2
Busch, August Anheuser, Jr.
  Obituary **1990**:2
Busch, Charles **1998**:3
Bush, Barbara **1989**:3
Bush, George W., Jr. **1996**:4
Bush, Jeb **2003**:1
Bush, Millie **1992**:1
Bushnell, Candace **2004**:2
Bushnell, Nolan **1985**:1
Buss, Jerry **1989**:3
Butcher, Susan **1991**:1
Butler, Brett **1995**:1
Butler, Octavia E. **1999**:3
Butterfield, Paul
  Obituary **1987**:3
Caan, James **2004**:4
Caen, Herb
  Obituary **1997**:4
Caesar, Adolph
  Obituary **1986**:3
Cage, John
  Obituary **1993**:1
Cage, Nicolas **1991**:1
Cagney, James
  Obituary **1986**:2
Cain, Herman **1998**:3
Calhoun, Rory
  Obituary **1999**:4
Caliguiri, Richard S.
  Obituary **1988**:3
Callaway, Ely
  Obituary **2002**:3
Calloway, Cab
  Obituary **1995**:2
Calloway, D. Wayne **1987**:3
Cameron, David
  Brief Entry **1988**:1
Cammermeyer, Margarethe **1995**:2
Campanella, Roy
  Obituary **1994**:1
Campbell, Bebe Moore **1996**:2
Campbell, Ben Nighthorse **1998**:1
Campbell, Bill **1997**:1
Canfield, Alan B.
  Brief Entry **1986**:3
Cantrell, Ed
  Brief Entry **1985**:3
Caplan, Arthur L. **2000**:2
Capriati, Jennifer **1991**:1
Caras, Roger
  Obituary **2002**:1
Caray, Harry **1988**:3
  Obituary **1998**:3
Carcaterra, Lorenzo **1996**:1
Card, Andrew H., Jr. **2003**:2
Carey, Drew **1997**:4
Carey, Mariah **1991**:3
Carey, Ron **1993**:3
Carlin, George **1996**:3
Carlisle, Belinda **1989**:3
Carlson, Richard **2002**:1
Carmona, Richard **2003**:2
Carnahan, Jean **2001**:2
Carnahan, Mel
  Obituary **2001**:2
Carpenter, Mary-Chapin **1994**:1
Carradine, John
  Obituary **1989**:2

Cruise, Tom **1985**:4
Crumb, R. **1995**:4
Cruz, Nilo **2004**:4
Cruzan, Nancy
  Obituary **1991**:3
Crystal, Billy **1985**:3
Cugat, Xavier
  Obituary **1991**:2
Culkin, Macaulay **1991**:3
Cunningham, Merce **1998**:1
Cunningham, Michael **2003**:4
Cunningham, Randall **1990**:1
Cunningham, Reverend William
  Obituary **1997**:4
Cuomo, Mario **1992**:2
Curran, Charles E. **1989**:2
Curren, Tommy
  Brief Entry **1987**:4
Curry, Ann **2001**:1
Curtis, Ben **2004**:2
Curtis, Jamie Lee **1995**:1
Cusack, John **1999**:3
Cyrus, Billy Ray **1993**:1
Dafoe, Willem **1988**:1
Dahmer, Jeffrey
  Obituary **1995**:2
Daily, Bishop Thomas V. **1990**:4
D'Alessio, Kitty
  Brief Entry **1987**:3
Daly, Carson **2002**:4
D'Amato, Al **1996**:1
Damon, Matt **1999**:1
Danes, Claire **1999**:4
Daniels, Faith **1993**:3
Daniels, Jeff **1989**:4
Danza, Tony **1989**:1
D'Arby, Terence Trent **1988**:4
Darden, Christopher **1996**:4
Daschle, Tom **2002**:3
Davenport, Lindsay **1999**:2
David, Larry **2003**:4
Davis, Angela **1998**:3
Davis, Bette
  Obituary **1990**:1
Davis, Eric **1987**:4
Davis, Geena **1992**:1
Davis, Miles
  Obituary **1992**:2
Davis, Noel **1990**:3
Davis, Paige **2004**:2
Davis, Patti **1995**:1
Davis, Sammy, Jr.
  Obituary **1990**:4
Davis, Terrell **1998**:2
Day, Dennis
  Obituary **1988**:4
Day, Pat **1995**:2
Dean, Laura **1989**:4
Dearden, John Cardinal
  Obituary **1988**:4
DeBartolo, Edward J., Jr. **1989**:3
DeCarava, Roy **1996**:3
De Cordova, Frederick **1985**:2
Dees, Morris **1992**:1
DeGeneres, Ellen **1995**:3
de Kooning, Willem **1994**:4
  Obituary **1997**:3
De La Hoya, Oscar **1998**:2
Delany, Sarah
  Obituary **1999**:3
DeLay, Tom **2000**:1
Dell, Michael **1996**:2

DeLuca, Fred **2003**:3
de Mille, Agnes
  Obituary **1994**:2
Deming, W. Edwards **1992**:2
  Obituary **1994**:2
Demme, Jonathan **1992**:4
De Niro, Robert **1999**:1
Dennehy, Brian **2002**:1
Dennis, Sandy
  Obituary **1992**:4
Denver, John
  Obituary **1998**:1
de Passe, Suzanne **1990**:4
Depp, Johnny **1991**:3
Dern, Laura **1992**:3
Dershowitz, Alan **1992**:1
Desormeaux, Kent **1990**:2
Destiny's Child **2001**:3
Deutch, John **1996**:4
Devine, John M. **2003**:2
DeVita, Vincent T., Jr. **1987**:3
De Vito, Danny **1987**:1
Diamond, I.A.L.
  Obituary **1988**:3
Diamond, Selma
  Obituary **1985**:2
Diaz, Cameron **1999**:1
DiBello, Paul
  Brief Entry **1986**:4
DiCaprio, Leonardo Wilhelm **1997**:2
Dickerson, Nancy H.
  Obituary **1998**:2
Dickey, James
  Obituary **1998**:2
Dickinson, Brian **1998**:2
Diebenkorn, Richard
  Obituary **1993**:4
Diemer, Walter E.
  Obituary **1998**:2
Diesel, Vin **2004**:1
DiFranco, Ani **1997**:1
Diggs, Taye **2000**:1
Diller, Barry **1991**:1
Diller, Elizabeth and Ricardo
  Scofidio **2004**:3
Dillon, Matt **1992**:2
DiMaggio, Joe
  Obituary **1999**:3
Di Meola, Al **1986**:4
Dinkins, David N. **1990**:2
Disney, Lillian
  Obituary **1998**:3
Disney, Roy E. **1986**:3
Divine
  Obituary **1988**:3
Dixie Chicks **2001**:2
Dr. Demento **1986**:1
Dr. Dre **1994**:3
Doherty, Shannen **1994**:2
Dolan, Terry **1985**:2
Dolan, Tom **2001**:2
Dolby, Ray Milton
  Brief Entry **1986**:1
Dole, Bob **1994**:2
Dole, Elizabeth Hanford **1990**:1
Dolenz, Micky **1986**:4
Donahue, Tim **2004**:3
Donahue, Troy
  Obituary **2002**:4
Donghia, Angelo R.
  Obituary **1985**:2
Donnellan, Nanci **1995**:2

Dorati, Antal
  Obituary **1989**:2
Dorris, Michael
  Obituary **1997**:3
Dorsey, Thomas A.
  Obituary **1993**:3
Doubleday, Nelson, Jr. **1987**:1
Douglas, Buster **1990**:4
Douglas, Marjory Stoneman **1993**:1
  Obituary **1998**:4
Douglas, Michael **1986**:2
Dove, Rita **1994**:3
Dowd, Maureen Brigid **1997**:1
Downey, Bruce **2003**:1
Downey, Morton, Jr. **1988**:4
Dravecky, Dave **1992**:1
Drescher, Fran **1995**:3
Drexler, Clyde **1992**:4
Drexler, Millard S. **1990**:3
Dreyfuss, Richard **1996**:3
Drysdale, Don
  Obituary **1994**:1
Duarte, Henry **2003**:3
Dubrof, Jessica
  Obituary **1996**:4
Duchovny, David **1998**:3
Dudley, Jane
  Obituary **2002**:4
Duff, Hilary **2004**:4
Duffy, Karen **1998**:1
Dukakis, Michael **1988**:3
Dukakis, Olympia **1996**:4
Duke, David **1990**:2
Duke, Doris
  Obituary **1994**:2
Duke, Red
  Brief Entry **1987**:1
Duncan, Tim **2000**:1
Duncan, Todd
  Obituary **1998**:3
Dunham, Carroll **2003**:4
Dunlap, Albert J. **1997**:2
Dunne, Dominick **1997**:1
Dunst, Kirsten **2001**:4
Dupri, Jermaine **1999**:1
Durocher, Leo
  Obituary **1992**:2
Durrell, Gerald
  Obituary **1995**:3
Duval, David **2000**:3
Duvall, Camille
  Brief Entry **1988**:1
Duvall, Robert **1999**:3
Dykstra, Lenny **1993**:4
Dylan, Bob **1998**:1
Earle, Sylvia **2001**:1
Earnhardt, Dale
  Obituary **2001**:4
Earnhardt, Dale, Jr. **2004**:4
Eastwood, Clint **1993**:3
Eaton, Robert J. **1994**:2
Eazy-E
  Obituary **1995**:3
Ebert, Roger **1998**:3
Ebsen, Buddy
  Obituary **2004**:3
Eckert, Robert A. **2002**:3
Eckstine, Billy
  Obituary **1993**:4
Edelman, Marian Wright **1990**:4
Edmonds, Kenneth Babyface **1995**:3
Edwards, Bob **1993**:2

Furman, Rosemary
Brief Entry **1986**:4
Furyk, Jim **2004**:2
Futrell, Mary Hatwood **1986**:1
Futter, Ellen V. **1995**:1
Gabor, Eva
Obituary **1996**:1
Gacy, John Wayne
Obituary **1994**:4
Gaines, William M.
Obituary **1993**:1
Gale, Robert Peter **1986**:4
Galindo, Rudy **2001**:2
Gallagher, Peter **2004**:3
Gallo, Robert **1991**:1
Galvin, John R. **1990**:1
Galvin, Martin
Brief Entry **1985**:3
Gandolfini, James **2001**:3
Gandy, Kim **2002**:2
Ganzi, Victor **2003**:3
Garbo, Greta
Obituary **1990**:3
Garcia, Andy **1999**:3
Garcia, Cristina **1997**:4
Garcia, Jerry **1988**:3
Obituary **1996**:1
Garcia, Joe
Brief Entry **1986**:4
Gardner, Ava Lavinia
Obituary **1990**:2
Gardner, David and Tom **2001**:4
Gardner, Randy **1997**:2
Garner, Jennifer **2003**:1
Garnett, Kevin **2000**:3
Garofalo, Janeane **1996**:4
Garr, Teri **1988**:4
Garrison, Jim
Obituary **1993**:2
Garson, Greer
Obituary **1996**:4
Garzarelli, Elaine M. **1992**:3
Gates, Bill **1993**:3 **1987**:4
Gates, Robert M. **1992**:2
Gathers, Hank
Obituary **1990**:3
Gault, Willie **1991**:2
Gebbie, Kristine **1994**:2
Geffen, David **1985**:3 **1997**:3
Gehry, Frank O. **1987**:1
Geisel, Theodor
Obituary **1992**:2
Gellar, Sarah Michelle **1999**:3
Geller, Margaret Joan **1998**:2
George, Elizabeth **2003**:3
Gephardt, Richard **1987**:3
Gerba, Charles **1999**:4
Gerberding, Julie **2004**:1
Gere, Richard **1994**:3
Gergen, David **1994**:1
Gerstner, Lou **1993**:4
Gertz, Alison
Obituary **1993**:2
Gerulaitis, Vitas
Obituary **1995**:1
Getz, Stan
Obituary **1991**:4
Giamatti, A. Bartlett **1988**:4
Obituary **1990**:1
Giannulli, Mossimo **2002**:3
Gibson, Althea
Obituary **2004**:4

Gibson, Kirk **1985**:2
Gibson, William Ford, III **1997**:2
Gifford, Kathie Lee **1992**:2
Gilbert, Walter **1988**:3
Gilford, Jack
Obituary **1990**:4
Gill, Vince **1995**:2
Gillespie, Dizzy
Obituary **1993**:2
Gillespie, Marcia **1999**:4
Gillett, George **1988**:1
Gilruth, Robert
Obituary **2001**:1
Gingrich, Newt **1991**:1 **1997**:3
Ginsberg, Allen
Obituary **1997**:3
Ginsburg, Ruth Bader **1993**:4
Gish, Lillian
Obituary **1993**:4
Giuliani, Rudolph **1994**:2
Glaser, Elizabeth
Obituary **1995**:2
Glass, David **1996**:1
Glass, Philip **1991**:4
Glasser, Ira **1989**:1
Glaus, Troy **2003**:3
Gleason, Jackie
Obituary **1987**:4
Glenn, John **1998**:3
Gless, Sharon **1989**:3
Glover, Danny **1998**:4
Glover, Savion **1997**:1
Gobel, George
Obituary **1991**:4
Gober, Robert **1996**:3
Goetz, Bernhard Hugo **1985**:3
Goizueta, Roberto **1996**:1
Obituary **1998**:1
Goldberg, Gary David **1989**:4
Goldberg, Leonard **1988**:4
Goldberg, Whoopi **1993**:3
Goldblum, Jeff **1988**:1 **1997**:3
Golden, Thelma **2003**:3
Goldhaber, Fred
Brief Entry **1986**:3
Goldman, William **2001**:1
Goldman-Rakic, Patricia **2002**:4
Goldwater, Barry
Obituary **1998**:4
Gomez, Lefty
Obituary **1989**:3
Gooden, Dwight **1985**:2
Gooding, Cuba, Jr. **1997**:3
Goodman, Benny
Obituary **1986**:3
Goodman, John **1990**:3
Goody, Joan **1990**:2
Goody, Sam
Obituary **1992**:1
Gordon, Dexter **1987**:1 **1990**:4
Gordon, Gale
Obituary **1996**:1
Gordon, Jeff **1996**:1
Gore, Albert, Jr. **1993**:2
Gore, Albert, Sr.
Obituary **1999**:2
Gore, Tipper **1985**:4
Goren, Charles H.
Obituary **1991**:4
Gorman, Leon
Brief Entry **1987**:1
Gossett, Louis, Jr. **1989**:3

Gould, Chester
Obituary **1985**:2
Gould, Gordon **1987**:1
Gould, Stephen Jay
Obituary **2003**:3
Grace, J. Peter **1990**:2
Graden, Brian **2004**:2
Grafton, Sue **2000**:2
Graham, Bill **1986**:4
Obituary **1992**:2
Graham, Billy **1992**:1
Graham, Donald **1985**:4
Graham, Heather **2000**:1
Graham, Katharine Meyer **1997**:3
Obituary **2002**:3
Graham, Lauren **2003**:4
Graham, Martha
Obituary **1991**:4
Gramm, Phil **1995**:2
Grammer, Kelsey **1995**:1
Granato, Cammi **1999**:3
Grange, Red
Obituary **1991**:3
Grant, Amy **1985**:4
Grant, Cary
Obituary **1987**:1
Grant, Charity
Brief Entry **1985**:2
Grant, Rodney A. **1992**:1
Graves, Michael **2000**:1
Graves, Nancy **1989**:3
Gray, Hanna **1992**:4
Gray, John **1995**:3
Gray, Macy **2002**:1
Graziano, Rocky
Obituary **1990**:4
Green, Richard R. **1988**:3
Greenberg, Hank
Obituary **1986**:4
Greenberg, Robert **2003**:2
Green Day **1995**:4
Greene, Brian **2003**:4
Greenspan, Alan **1992**:2
Gregorian, Vartan **1990**:3
Gregory, Cynthia **1990**:2
Gregory, Dick **1990**:3
Grier, Pam **1998**:3
Griffey, Ken Jr. **1994**:1
Griffith, Melanie **1989**:2
Griffiths, Martha
Obituary **2004**:2
Grisham, John **1994**:4
Grodin, Charles **1997**:3
Groening, Matt **1990**:4
Gross, Terry **1998**:3
Grove, Andrew S. **1995**:3
Grucci, Felix **1987**:1
Gruden, Jon **2003**:4
Grusin, Dave
Brief Entry **1987**:2
Guccione, Bob **1986**:1
Guccione, Bob, Jr. **1991**:4
Guest, Christopher **2004**:2
Guggenheim, Charles
Obituary **2003**:4
Gumbel, Bryant **1990**:2
Gumbel, Greg **1996**:4
Gund, Agnes **1993**:2
Gunn, Hartford N., Jr.
Obituary **1986**:2
Guyer, David
Brief Entry **1988**:1

Gwynn, Tony **1995**:1
Haas, Robert D. **1986**:4
Hackett, Buddy
  Obituary **2004**:3
Hackman, Gene **1989**:3
Hackney, Sheldon **1995**:1
Hagelstein, Peter
  Brief Entry **1986**:3
Hagler, Marvelous Marvin **1985**:2
Hahn, Jessica **1989**:4
Hair, Jay D. **1994**:3
Ha Jin **2000**:3
Hakuta, Ken
  Brief Entry **1986**:1
Haldeman, H. R.
  Obituary **1994**:2
Hale, Alan **1997**:3
Hale, Clara
  Obituary **1993**:3
Haley, Alex
  Obituary **1992**:3
Hall, Anthony Michael **1986**:3
Hall, Arsenio **1990**:2
Hall, Gus
  Obituary **2001**:2
Halston
  Obituary **1990**:3
Hamilton, Margaret
  Obituary **1985**:3
Hamilton, Scott **1998**:2
Hamm, Mia **2000**:1
Hammer, Armand
  Obituary **1991**:3
Hammer, Jan **1987**:3
Hammer, M. C. **1991**:2
Hammond, E. Cuyler
  Obituary **1987**:1
Hammond, John
  Obituary **1988**:2
Hampton, Lionel
  Obituary **2003**:4
Hanauer, Chip **1986**:2
Hancock, Herbie **1985**:1
Handler, Daniel **2003**:3
Handler, Ruth
  Obituary **2003**:3
Hanks, Tom **1989**:2 **2000**:2
Hanna, William
  Obituary **2002**:1
Hannah, Daryl **1987**:4
Hardaway, Anfernee **1996**:2
Harden, Marcia Gay **2002**:4
Haring, Keith
  Obituary **1990**:3
Harker, Patrick T. **2001**:2
Harkes, John **1996**:4
Harmon, Mark **1987**:1
Harmon, Tom
  Obituary **1990**:3
Harriman, Pamela **1994**:4
Harriman, W. Averell
  Obituary **1986**:4
Harris, Barbara **1996**:3
Harris, Barbara **1989**:3
Harris, E. Lynn **2004**:2
Harris, Ed **2002**:2
Harris, Emmylou **1991**:3
Harris, Katherine **2001**:3
Harris, Patricia Roberts
  Obituary **1985**:2
Harris, Thomas **2001**:1
Harry, Deborah **1990**:1

Hart, Mary
  Brief Entry **1988**:1
Hart, Melissa Joan **2002**:1
Hart, Mickey **1991**:2
Hartman, Phil **1996**:2
  Obituary **1998**:4
Harvard, Beverly **1995**:2
Harvey, Paul **1995**:3
Harwell, Ernie **1997**:3
Haseltine, William A. **1999**:2
Hassenfeld, Stephen **1987**:4
Hastert, Dennis **1999**:3
Hatch, Orin G. **2000**:2
Hatch, Richard **2001**:1
Hatem, George
  Obituary **1989**:1
Hawk, Tony **2001**:4
Hawke, Ethan **1995**:4
Hawkins, Jeff and
  Donna Dubinsky **2000**:2
Hawkins, Screamin' Jay
  Obituary **2000**:3
Hawn, Goldie Jeanne **1997**:2
Hayes, Helen
  Obituary **1993**:4
Hayes, Isaac **1998**:4
Hayes, Robert M. **1986**:3
Hayes, Woody
  Obituary **1987**:2
Hayse, Bruce **2004**:3
Hayworth, Rita
  Obituary **1987**:3
Headroom, Max **1986**:4
Healey, Jack **1990**:1
Healy, Bernadine **1993**:1
Healy, Timothy S. **1990**:2
Heard, J.C.
  Obituary **1989**:1
Hearst, Randolph A.
  Obituary **2001**:3
Heat-Moon, William Least **2000**:2
Heche, Anne **1999**:1
Heckerling, Amy **1987**:2
Heckert, Richard E.
  Brief Entry **1987**:3
Hefner, Christie **1985**:1
Heid, Bill
  Brief Entry **1987**:2
Heifetz, Jascha
  Obituary **1988**:2
Heinz, H J.
  Obituary **1987**:2
Heinz, John
  Obituary **1991**:4
Helgenberger, Marg **2002**:2
Heller, Joseph
  Obituary **2000**:2
Heller, Walter
  Obituary **1987**:4
Helms, Bobby
  Obituary **1997**:4
Helms, Jesse **1998**:1
Helmsley, Leona **1988**:1
Heloise **2001**:4
Helton, Todd **2001**:1
Hemingway, Margaux
  Obituary **1997**:1
Henderson, Rickey **2002**:3
Hennessy, John L. **2002**:2
Henning, Doug
  Obituary **2000**:3
Hensel Twins **1996**:4

Henson, Brian **1992**:1
Henson, Jim **1989**:1
  Obituary **1990**:4
Hepburn, Katharine **1991**:2
Hernandez, Willie **1985**:1
Hero, Peter **2001**:2
Hershey, Barbara **1989**:1
Hershiser, Orel **1989**:2
Herzog, Doug **2002**:4
Heston, Charlton **1999**:4
Hewitt, Jennifer Love **1999**:2
Hewlett, William
  Obituary **2001**:4
Highsmith, Patricia
  Obituary **1995**:3
Hilbert, Stephen C. **1997**:4
Hilfiger, Tommy **1993**:3
Hill, Anita **1994**:1
Hill, Faith **2000**:1
Hill, George Roy
  Obituary **2004**:1
Hill, Grant **1995**:3
Hill, Lauryn **1999**:3
Hill, Lynn **1991**:2
Hillegass, Clifton Keith **1989**:4
Hills, Carla **1990**:3
Hines, Gregory **1992**:4
Hinton, Milt
  Obituary **2001**:3
Hirschhorn, Joel
  Brief Entry **1986**:1
Hirt, Al
  Obituary **1999**:4
Hiss, Alger
  Obituary **1997**:2
Hoffa, Jim, Jr. **1999**:2
Hoffman, Abbie
  Obituary **1989**:3
Hoffs, Susanna **1988**:2
Hogan, Ben
  Obituary **1997**:4
Hogan, Hulk **1987**:3
Holbrooke, Richard **1996**:2
Holden, Betsy **2003**:2
Holl, Steven **2003**:1
Holmes, John C.
  Obituary **1988**:3
Holtz, Lou **1986**:4
Holyfield, Evander **1991**:3
Hooker, John Lee **1998**:1
  Obituary **2002**:3
hooks, bell **2000**:2
Hootie and the Blowfish **1995**:4
Hope, Bob
  Obituary **2004**:4
Horne, Lena **1998**:4
Horner, Jack **1985**:2
Hornsby, Bruce **1989**:3
Horovitz, Adam **1988**:3
Horowitz, Paul **1988**:2
Horowitz, Vladimir
  Obituary **1990**:1
Horrigan, Edward, Jr. **1989**:1
Horwich, Frances
  Obituary **2002**:3
Houseman, John
  Obituary **1989**:1
Houston, Cissy **1999**:3
Houston, Whitney **1986**:3
Howard, Desmond Kevin **1997**:2
Howard, Ron **1997**:2

Kerr, Jean
  Obituary **2004**:1
Kerr, Walter
  Obituary **1997**:1
Kerrey, Bob **1986**:1 **1991**:3
Kerrigan, Nancy **1994**:3
Kesey, Ken
  Obituary **2003**:1
Kessler, David **1992**:1
Ketcham, Hank
  Obituary **2002**:2
Kevorkian, Jack **1991**:3
Keyes, Alan **1996**:2
Kidd, Jason **2003**:2
Kid Rock **2001**:1
Kilborn, Craig **2003**:2
Kilby, Jack **2002**:2
Kilmer, Val **1991**:4
Kilts, James M. **2001**:3
Kimsey, James V. **2001**:1
King, Bernice **2000**:2
King, Coretta Scott **1999**:3
King, Don **1989**:1
King, Larry **1993**:1
King, Mary-Claire **1998**:3
King, Stephen **1998**:1
Kingsborough, Donald
  Brief Entry **1986**:2
Kingsley, Patricia **1990**:2
Kinison, Sam
  Obituary **1993**:1
Kiraly, Karch
  Brief Entry **1987**:1
Kirk, David **2004**:1
Kissinger, Henry **1999**:4
Kissling, Frances **1989**:2
Kistler, Darci **1993**:1
Kite, Tom **1990**:3
Klass, Perri **1993**:2
Klein, Calvin **1996**:2
Kline, Kevin **2000**:1
Kloss, Henry E.
  Brief Entry **1985**:2
Kluge, John **1991**:1
Knievel, Robbie **1990**:1
Knight, Bobby **1985**:3
Knight, Philip H. **1994**:1
Knight, Ted
  Obituary **1986**:4
Knight, Wayne **1997**:1
Knowles, John
  Obituary **2003**:1
Koch, Bill **1992**:3
Koch, Jim **2004**:3
Kohnstamm, Abby **2001**:1
Koogle, Tim **2000**:4
Koons, Jeff **1991**:4
Koontz, Dean **1999**:3
Koop, C. Everett **1989**:3
Kopits, Steven E.
  Brief Entry **1987**:1
Koplovitz, Kay **1986**:3
Kopp, Wendy **1993**:3
Koppel, Ted **1989**:1
Kordich, Jay **1993**:2
Koresh, David
  Obituary **1993**:4
Kornberg, Arthur **1992**:1
Kors, Michael **2000**:4
Kostabi, Mark **1989**:4
Kovacevich, Dick **2004**:3
Kozinski, Alex **2002**:2

Kozol, Jonathan **1992**:1
Kramer, Larry **1991**:2
Kramer, Stanley
  Obituary **2002**:1
Krantz, Judith **2003**:1
Kravitz, Lenny **1991**:1
Krim, Mathilde **1989**:2
Kroc, Ray
  Obituary **1985**:1
Krol, John
  Obituary **1996**:3
Kroll, Alexander S. **1989**:3
Krone, Julie **1989**:2
Kruk, John **1994**:4
Krzyzewski, Mike **1993**:2
Kubrick, Stanley
  Obituary **1999**:3
Kudrow, Lisa **1996**:1
Kulp, Nancy
  Obituary **1991**:3
Kunitz, Stanley J. **2001**:2
Kunstler, William **1992**:3
Kunstler, William
  Obituary **1996**:1
Kuralt, Charles
  Obituary **1998**:3
Kurzban, Ira **1987**:2
Kurzweil, Raymond **1986**:3
Kushner, Tony **1995**:2
Kutcher, Ashton **2003**:4
Kwoh, Yik San **1988**:2
Kyser, Kay
  Obituary **1985**:3
Lachey, Nick and
  Jessica Simpson **2004**:4
LaDuke, Winona **1995**:2
Laettner, Christian **1993**:1
Lafley, A. G. **2003**:4
LaFontaine, Pat **1985**:1
Lagasse, Emeril **1998**:3
Lahiri, Jhumpa **2001**:3
Lahti, Christine **1988**:2
Laimbeer, Bill **2004**:3
Lake, Ricki **1994**:4
Lalas, Alexi **1995**:1
Lamb, Wally **1999**:1
Lamour, Dorothy
  Obituary **1997**:1
L'Amour, Louis
  Obituary **1988**:4
Lancaster, Burt
  Obituary **1995**:1
Land, Edwin H.
  Obituary **1991**:3
Lander, Toni
  Obituary **1985**:4
Landers, Ann
  Obituary **2003**:3
Landon, Alf
  Obituary **1988**:1
Landon, Michael
  Obituary **1992**:1
Landrieu, Mary L. **2002**:2
Landry, Tom
  Obituary **2000**:3
Lane, Burton
  Obituary **1997**:2
Lane, Nathan **1996**:4
Lang, Eugene M. **1990**:3
Lange, Jessica **1995**:4
Lange, Liz **2003**:4
Langer, Robert **2003**:4

Langevin, James R. **2001**:2
Langston, J. William
  Brief Entry **1986**:2
Lanier, Jaron **1993**:4
Lansbury, Angela **1993**:1
Lansdale, Edward G.
  Obituary **1987**:2
Lansing, Sherry **1995**:4
Lanza, Robert **2004**:3
LaPaglia, Anthony **2004**:4
Lardner Jr., Ring
  Obituary **2001**:2
Larroquette, John **1986**:2
Larson, Jonathan
  Obituary **1997**:2
LaSalle, Eriq **1996**:4
Lauder, Estee **1992**:2
Lauper, Cyndi **1985**:1
Lauren, Ralph **1990**:1
Lawless, Lucy **1997**:4
Lawrence, Martin **1993**:4
Laybourne, Geraldine **1997**:1
Lazarus, Charles **1992**:4
Lazarus, Shelly **1998**:3
Lear, Frances **1988**:3
Leary, Denis **1993**:3
Leary, Timothy
  Obituary **1996**:4
Lederman, Leon Max **1989**:4
Lee, Brandon
  Obituary **1993**:4
Lee, Henry C. **1997**:1
Lee, Pamela **1996**:4
Lee, Peggy
  Obituary **2003**:1
Lee, Spike **1988**:4
Leguizamo, John **1999**:1
Lehane, Dennis **2001**:4
Leibovitz, Annie **1988**:4
Leigh, Jennifer Jason **1995**:2
Lelyveld, Joseph S. **1994**:4
Lemmon, Jack **1998**:4
  Obituary **2002**:3
Lemon, Ted
  Brief Entry **1986**:4
LeMond, Greg **1986**:4
Leno, Jay **1987**:1
Leonard, Elmore **1998**:4
Leonard, Sugar Ray **1989**:4
Lerner, Michael **1994**:2
Leslie, Lisa **1997**:4
Letterman, David **1989**:3
Levin, Gerald **1995**:2
Levine, Arnold **2002**:3
Levine, James **1992**:3
Levinson, Barry **1989**:3
Levitt, Arthur **2004**:2
Lewis, Edward T. **1999**:4
Lewis, Henry
  Obituary **1996**:3
Lewis, Huey **1987**:3
Lewis, John
  Obituary **2002**:1
Lewis, Juliette **1999**:3
Lewis, Loida Nicolas **1998**:3
Lewis, Ray **2001**:3
Lewis, Reggie
  Obituary **1994**:1
Lewis, Reginald F. **1988**:4
  Obituary **1993**:3
Lewis, Richard **1992**:1

Lewis, Shari **1993**:1
  Obituary **1999**:1
LeWitt, Sol **2001**:2
Leyland, Jim **1998**:2
Liberace
  Obituary **1987**:2
Libeskind, Daniel **2004**:1
Lichtenstein, Roy **1994**:1
  Obituary **1998**:1
Lieberman, Joseph **2001**:1
Lightner, Candy **1985**:1
Lilly, John C.
  Obituary **2002**:4
Liman, Arthur **1989**:4
Limbaugh, Rush **1991**:3
Lin, Maya **1990**:3
Lincoln, Blanche **2003**:1
Lindbergh, Anne Morrow
  Obituary **2001**:4
Lindros, Eric **1992**:1
Lindsay, John V.
  Obituary **2001**:3
Lines, Ray **2004**:1
Ling, Bai **2000**:3
Ling, Lisa **2004**:2
Lipinski, Tara **1998**:3
Lipkis, Andy
  Brief Entry **1985**:3
Lipsig, Harry H. **1985**:1
Lipton, Martin **1987**:3
Lithgow, John **1985**:2
Little, Cleavon
  Obituary **1993**:2
Liu, Lucy **2000**:4
LL Cool J **1998**:2
Lobell, Jeanine **2002**:3
Locklear, Heather **1994**:3
Lodge, Henry Cabot
  Obituary **1985**:1
Loewe, Frederick
  Obituary **1988**:2
Lofton, Kenny **1998**:1
Logan, Joshua
  Obituary **1988**:4
Long, Nia **2001**:3
Long, Shelley **1985**:1
Longo, Robert **1990**:4
Lopes, Lisa
  Obituary **2003**:3
Lopez, George **2003**:4
Lopez, Jennifer **1998**:4
Lopez, Nancy **1989**:3
Lord, Bette Bao **1994**:1
Lord, Jack
  Obituary **1998**:2
Lord, Winston
  Brief Entry **1987**:4
Lords, Traci **1995**:4
Lott, Trent **1998**:1
Louganis, Greg **1995**:3
Louis-Dreyfus, Julia **1994**:1
Love, Courtney **1995**:1
Love, Susan **1995**:2
Loveless, Patty **1998**:2
Lovett, Lyle **1994**:1
Lowe, Edward **1990**:2
Lowe, Rob **1990**:4
Lowell, Mike **2003**:2
Loy, Myrna
  Obituary **1994**:2
Lucas, George **1999**:4
Lucci, Susan **1999**:4

Luce, Clare Boothe
  Obituary **1988**:1
Lucid, Shannon **1997**:1
Lucke, Lewis **2004**:4
Ludlum, Robert
  Obituary **2002**:1
Lukas, D. Wayne **1986**:2
Lupino, Ida
  Obituary **1996**:1
Lutz, Robert A. **1990**:1
Lynch, David **1990**:4
Lynn, Loretta **2001**:1
Mac, Bernie **2003**:1
MacCready, Paul **1986**:4
MacDonald, Laurie and Walter
  Parkes **2004**:1
MacDowell, Andie **1993**:4
MacKinnon, Catharine **1993**:2
MacMurray, Fred
  Obituary **1992**:2
MacNelly, Jeff
  Obituary **2000**:4
MacRae, Gordon
  Obituary **1986**:2
Macy, William H. **1999**:3
Madden, John **1995**:1
Maddux, Greg **1996**:2
Madonna **1985**:2
Maglich, Bogdan C. **1990**:1
Magliozzi, Tom and Ray **1991**:4
Maguire, Tobey **2002**:2
Maher, Bill **1996**:2
Mahony, Roger M. **1988**:2
Maida, Adam Cardinal **1998**:2
Mailer, Norman **1998**:1
Majerle, Dan **1993**:4
Malkovich, John **1988**:2
Malloy, Edward Monk **1989**:4
Malone, John C. **1988**:3 **1996**:3
Malone, Karl **1990**:1 **1997**:3
Maltby, Richard, Jr. **1996**:3
Mamet, David **1998**:4
Mancini, Henry
  Obituary **1994**:4
Mankiller, Wilma P.
  Brief Entry **1986**:2
Mann, Sally **2001**:2
Mansfield, Mike
  Obituary **2002**:4
Mansion, Gracie
  Brief Entry **1986**:3
Manson, Marilyn **1999**:4
Mantegna, Joe **1992**:1
Mantle, Mickey
  Obituary **1996**:1
Mapplethorpe, Robert
  Obituary **1989**:3
Maraldo, Pamela J. **1993**:4
Maravich, Pete
  Obituary **1988**:2
Marchand, Nancy
  Obituary **2001**:1
Marcus, Stanley
  Obituary **2003**:1
Marier, Rebecca **1995**:4
Marin, Cheech **2000**:1
Marineau, Philip **2002**:4
Maris, Roger
  Obituary **1986**:1
Marky Mark **1993**:3
Marriott, J. Willard
  Obituary **1985**:4

Marriott, J. Willard, Jr. **1985**:4
Marsalis, Branford **1988**:3
Marsalis, Wynton **1997**:4
Marshall, Penny **1991**:3
Marshall, Susan **2000**:4
Marshall, Thurgood
  Obituary **1993**:3
Martin, Billy **1988**:4
  Obituary **1990**:2
Martin, Casey **2002**:1
Martin, Dean
  Obituary **1996**:2
Martin, Dean Paul
  Obituary **1987**:3
Martin, Judith **2000**:3
Martin, Lynn **1991**:4
Martin, Mary
  Obituary **1991**:2
Martin, Steve **1992**:2
Martinez, Bob **1992**:1
Marvin, Lee
  Obituary **1988**:1
Mas Canosa, Jorge
  Obituary **1998**:2
Master P **1999**:4
Masters, William H.
  Obituary **2001**:4
Matalin, Mary **1995**:2
Mathews, Dan **1998**:3
Mathis, Clint **2003**:1
Matlin, Marlee **1992**:2
Matlovich, Leonard P.
  Obituary **1988**:4
Matthau, Walter **2000**:3
Matthews, Dave **1999**:3
Mattingly, Don **1986**:2
Matuszak, John
  Obituary **1989**:4
Mauldin, Bill
  Obituary **2004**:2
Maxwell, Hamish **1989**:4
Mayes, Frances **2004**:3
Maynard, Joyce **1999**:4
McAuliffe, Christa
  Obituary **1985**:4
McCain, John S. **1998**:4
McCall, Nathan **1994**:4
McCarron, Chris **1995**:4
McCarthy, Carolyn **1998**:4
McCarthy, Jenny **1997**:4
McCartney, Bill **1995**:3
McCartney, Linda
  Obituary **1998**:4
McCloskey, J. Michael **1988**:2
McCloskey, James **1993**:1
McCloy, John J.
  Obituary **1989**:3
McColough, C. Peter **1990**:2
McConaughey, Matthew
  David **1997**:1
McCourt, Frank **1997**:4
McCrea, Joel
  Obituary **1991**:1
McDermott, Alice **1999**:2
McDonald, Camille **2004**:1
McDonnell, Sanford N. **1988**:4
McDonough, William **2003**:1
McDormand, Frances **1997**:3
McDougall, Ron **2001**:4
McDuffie, Robert **1990**:2
McElligott, Thomas J. **1987**:4
McEntire, Reba **1987**:3 **1994**:2

McFarlane, Todd **1999**:1
McFerrin, Bobby **1989**:1
McGillis, Kelly **1989**:3
McGinley, Ted **2004**:4
McGowan, William **1985**:2
McGowan, William G.
  Obituary **1993**:1
McGraw, Tim **2000**:3
McGuire, Dorothy
  Obituary **2002**:4
McGwire, Mark **1999**:1
McIntyre, Richard
  Brief Entry **1986**:2
McKee, Lonette **1996**:1
McKenna, Terence **1993**:3
McKinney, Cynthia A. **1997**:1
McKinney, Stewart B.
  Obituary **1987**:4
McLaughlin, Betsy **2004**:3
McMahon, Jim **1985**:4
McMahon, Vince, Jr. **1985**:4
McMillan, Terry **1993**:2
McMillen, Tom **1988**:4
McMurtry, James **1990**:2
McNamara, Robert S. **1995**:4
McNealy, Scott **1999**:4
McRae, Carmen
  Obituary **1995**:2
McSally, Martha **2002**:4
McVeigh, Timothy
  Obituary **2002**:2
Meadows, Audrey
  Obituary **1996**:3
Meier, Richard **2001**:4
Meisel, Steven **2002**:4
Mellinger, Frederick
  Obituary **1990**:4
Mello, Dawn **1992**:2
Mellon, Paul
  Obituary **1999**:3
Melman, Richard
  Brief Entry **1986**:1
Mengers, Sue **1985**:3
Menninger, Karl
  Obituary **1991**:1
Menuhin, Yehudi
  Obituary **1999**:3
Merchant, Natalie **1996**:3
Meredith, Burgess
  Obituary **1998**:1
Merrick, David
  Obituary **2000**:4
Merrill, James
  Obituary **1995**:3
Merritt, Justine
  Brief Entry **1985**:3
Messing, Debra **2004**:4
Metallica **2004**:2
Mfume, Kweisi **1996**:3
Michelman, Kate **1998**:4
Michener, James A.
  Obituary **1998**:1
Mickelson, Phil **2004**:4
Midler, Bette **1989**:4
Mikulski, Barbara **1992**:4
Milano, Alyssa **2002**:3
Milbrett, Tiffeny **2001**:1
Milburn, Rodney Jr.
  Obituary **1998**:2
Milland, Ray
  Obituary **1986**:2

Millard, Barbara J.
  Brief Entry **1985**:3
Miller, Andre **2003**:3
Miller, Arthur **1999**:4
Miller, Bebe **2000**:2
Miller, Bode **2002**:4
Miller, Dennis **1992**:4
Miller, Merton H.
  Obituary **2001**:1
Miller, Nicole **1995**:4
Miller, Rand **1995**:4
Miller, Reggie **1994**:4
Miller, Roger
  Obituary **1993**:2
Miller, Sue **1999**:3
Mills, Malia **2003**:1
Mills, Wilbur
  Obituary **1992**:4
Minner, Ruth Ann **2002**:2
Minnesota Fats
  Obituary **1996**:3
Minsky, Marvin **1994**:3
Misrach, Richard **1991**:2
Mitchell, Arthur **1995**:1
Mitchell, George J. **1989**:3
Mitchell, John
  Obituary **1989**:2
Mitchell, Joni **1991**:4
Mitchelson, Marvin **1989**:2
Mitchum, Robert
  Obituary **1997**:4
Mizrahi, Isaac **1991**:1
Moakley, Joseph
  Obituary **2002**:2
Moby **2000**:1
Mohajer, Dineh **1997**:3
Molinari, Susan **1996**:4
Monaghan, Tom **1985**:1
Mondavi, Robert **1989**:2
Monica **2004**:2
Monk, Art **1993**:2
Monroe, Bill
  Obituary **1997**:1
Monroe, Rose Will
  Obituary **1997**:4
Montana, Joe **1989**:2
Montgomery, Elizabeth
  Obituary **1995**:4
Moody, John **1985**:3
Moody, Rick **2002**:2
Moon, Warren **1991**:3
Moonves, Les **2004**:2
Moore, Archie
  Obituary **1999**:2
Moore, Clayton
  Obituary **2000**:3
Moore, Demi **1991**:4
Moore, Julianne **1998**:1
Moore, Mandy **2004**:2
Moore, Mary Tyler **1996**:2
Moore, Michael **1990**:3
Moose, Charles **2003**:4
Morgan, Dodge **1987**:1
Morgan, Robin **1991**:1
Morita, Noriyuki Pat **1987**:3
Moritz, Charles **1989**:3
Morris, Dick **1997**:3
Morris, Mark **1991**:1
Morrison, Sterling
  Obituary **1996**:1
Morrison, Toni **1998**:1

Morrison, Trudi
  Brief Entry **1986**:2
Mortensen, Viggo **2003**:3
Mosbacher, Georgette **1994**:2
Mosley, Walter **2003**:4
Moss, Cynthia **1995**:2
Moss, Randy **1999**:3
Motherwell, Robert
  Obituary **1992**:1
Mott, William Penn, Jr. **1986**:1
Mottola, Tommy **2002**:1
Mourning, Alonzo **1994**:2
Moyers, Bill **1991**:4
Moynihan, Daniel Patrick
  Obituary **2004**:2
Mulcahy, Anne M. **2003**:2
Muldowney, Shirley **1986**:1
Mullis, Kary **1995**:3
Mumford, Lewis
  Obituary **1990**:2
Muniz, Frankie **2001**:4
Murdoch, Rupert **1988**:4
Murphy, Eddie **1989**:2
Murray, Arthur
  Obituary **1991**:3
Murray, Bill **2002**:4
Musburger, Brent **1985**:1
Muskie, Edmund S.
  Obituary **1996**:3
Nader, Ralph **1989**:4
Nance, Jack
  Obituary **1997**:3
Napolitano, Janet **1997**:1
Nauman, Bruce **1995**:4
Navratilova, Martina **1989**:1
Neal, James Foster **1986**:2
Nechita, Alexandra **1996**:4
Neeleman, David **2003**:3
Neiman, LeRoy **1993**:3
Nelson, Harriet
  Obituary **1995**:1
Nelson, Rick
  Obituary **1986**:1
Nelson, Willie **1993**:4
Nemerov, Howard
  Obituary **1992**:1
Neuharth, Allen H. **1986**:1
Nevelson, Louise
  Obituary **1988**:3
Newhouse, Samuel I., Jr. **1997**:1
New Kids on the Block **1991**:2
Newman, Arnold **1993**:1
Newman, Joseph **1987**:1
Newman, Paul **1995**:3
Newton, Huey
  Obituary **1990**:1
Nichols, Mike **1994**:4
Nicholson, Jack **1989**:2
Nielsen, Jerri **2001**:3
Nipon, Albert
  Brief Entry **1986**:4
Nirvana **1992**:4
Nixon, Pat
  Obituary **1994**:1
Nixon, Richard
  Obituary **1994**:4
Nolan, Lloyd
  Obituary **1985**:4
Nolte, Nick **1992**:4
Noonan, Peggy **1990**:3
North, Alex **1986**:3
North, Oliver **1987**:4

Wasserstein, Wendy **1991**:3
Waterman, Cathy **2002**:2
Waters, John **1988**:3
Waters, Maxine **1998**:4
Watkins, Sherron **2003**:1
Watson, Elizabeth **1991**:2
Watterson, Bill **1990**:3
Wattleton, Faye **1989**:1
Watts, J.C. **1999**:2
Wayans, Damon **1998**:4
Wayans, Keenen Ivory **1991**:1
Wayne, David
  Obituary **1995**:3
Weaver, Sigourney **1988**:3
Webb, Wellington E. **2000**:3
Webber, Chris **1994**:1
Weber, Pete **1986**:3
Wegman, William **1991**:1
Weicker, Lowell P., Jr. **1993**:1
Weil, Andrew **1997**:4
Weill, Sandy **1990**:4
Weinstein, Bob and Harvey **2000**:4
Weintraub, Jerry **1986**:1
Weitz, Bruce **1985**:4
Welch, Bob **1991**:3
Welch, Jack **1993**:3
Wells, David **1999**:3
Wells, Linda **2002**:3
Wells, Mary
  Obituary **1993**:1
Wells, Sharlene
  Brief Entry **1985**:1
Wellstone, Paul
  Obituary **2004**:1
Welty, Eudora
  Obituary **2002**:3
Wenner, Jann **1993**:1
West, Cornel **1994**:2
West, Dorothy **1996**:1
West, Dottie
  Obituary **1992**:2
Wexler, Nancy S. **1992**:3
Whaley, Suzy **2003**:4
Whelan, Wendy **1999**:3
Whitaker, Forest **1996**:2
White, Barry
  Obituary **2004**:3
White, Bill **1989**:3
White, Byron
  Obituary **2003**:3
White, Jaleel **1992**:3
White, Reggie **1993**:4
White, Ryan
  Obituary **1990**:3
Whitestone, Heather **1995**:1
Whitman, Christine Todd **1994**:3
Whitman, Meg **2000**:3
Whitmire, Kathy **1988**:2
Whitson, Peggy **2003**:3
Whittle, Christopher **1989**:3
Wiesel, Elie **1998**:1
Wiest, Dianne **1995**:2
Wigand, Jeffrey **2000**:4
Wigler, Michael
  Brief Entry **1985**:1
Wilder, Billy
  Obituary **2003**:2
Wilder, L. Douglas **1990**:3
Wildmon, Donald **1988**:4
Wilkens, Lenny **1995**:2

Williams, Anthony **2000**:4
Williams, Doug **1988**:2
Williams, Edward Bennett
  Obituary **1988**:4
Williams, G. Mennen
  Obituary **1988**:2
Williams, Hosea
  Obituary **2001**:2
Williams, Joe
  Obituary **1999**:4
Williams, Ricky **2000**:2
Williams, Robin **1988**:4
Williams, Serena **1999**:4
Williams, Ted
  Obituary **2003**:4
Williams, Treat **2004**:3
Williams, Vanessa L. **1999**:2
Williams, Venus **1999**:2
Williams, Willie L. **1993**:1
Williamson, Marianne **1991**:4
Willis, Bruce **1986**:4
Willson, S. Brian **1989**:3
Wilson, August **2002**:2
Wilson, Brian **1996**:1
Wilson, Carl
  Obituary **1998**:2
Wilson, Cassandra **1996**:3
Wilson, Edward O. **1994**:4
Wilson, Flip
  Obituary **1999**:2
Wilson, Jerry
  Brief Entry **1986**:2
Wilson, Owen **2002**:3
Wilson, Pete **1992**:3
Wilson, William Julius **1997**:1
Winans, CeCe **2000**:1
Winfrey, Oprah **1986**:4 **1997**:3
Winger, Debra **1994**:3
Winston, George **1987**:1
Winter, Paul **1990**:2
Witherspoon, Reese **2002**:1
Witkin, Joel-Peter **1996**:1
Wolf, Naomi **1994**:3
Wolf, Stephen M. **1989**:3
Wolfe, Tom **1999**:2
Wolfman Jack
  Obituary **1996**:1
Womack, Lee Ann **2002**:1
Wong, B.D. **1998**:1
Wood, Elijah **2002**:4
Woodard, Lynette **1986**:2
Woodcock, Leonard
  Obituary **2001**:4
Woodruff, Robert Winship
  Obituary **1985**:1
Woods, James **1988**:3
Woods, Tiger **1995**:4
Woodson, Ron **1996**:4
Woodwell, George S. **1987**:2
Worth, Irene
  Obituary **2003**:2
Worthy, James **1991**:2
Wright, Steven **1986**:3
Wright, Will **2003**:4
Wrigley, William, Jr. **2002**:2
Wu, Harry **1996**:1
Wyle, Noah **1997**:3
Wynette, Tammy
  Obituary **1998**:3

Wynn, Keenan
  Obituary **1987**:1
Wynn, Stephen A. **1994**:3
Wynonna **1993**:3
Yamaguchi, Kristi **1992**:3
Yamasaki, Minoru
  Obituary **1986**:2
Yankovic, Weird Al **1985**:4
Yankovic, Frank
  Obituary **1999**:2
Yard, Molly **1991**:4
Yeager, Chuck **1998**:1
Yearwood, Trisha **1999**:1
Yetnikoff, Walter **1988**:1
Yoakam, Dwight **1992**:4
Yokich, Stephen P. **1995**:4
York, Dick
  Obituary **1992**:4
Young, Coleman A.
  Obituary **1998**:1
Young, Loretta
  Obituary **2001**:1
Young, Robert
  Obituary **1999**:1
Young, Steve **1995**:2
Youngblood, Johnny Ray **1994**:1
Youngman, Henny
  Obituary **1998**:3
Zagat, Tim and Nina **2004**:3
Zahn, Paula **1992**:3
Zamboni, Frank J.
  Brief Entry **1986**:4
Zamora, Pedro
  Obituary **1995**:2
Zanker, Bill
  Brief Entry **1987**:3
Zanuck, Lili Fini **1994**:2
Zappa, Frank
  Obituary **1994**:2
Zech, Lando W.
  Brief Entry **1987**:4
Zellweger, Renee **2001**:1
Zemeckis, Robert **2002**:1
Zerhouni, Elias A. **2004**:3
Zetcher, Arnold B. **2002**:1
Zevon, Warren
  Obituary **2004**:4
Ziff, William B., Jr. **1986**:4
Zigler, Edward **1994**:1
Zinnemann, Fred
  Obituary **1997**:3
Zinni, Anthony **2003**:1
Zito, Barry **2003**:3
Zucker, Jeff **1993**:3
Zucker, Jerry **2002**:2
Zuckerman, Mortimer **1986**:3
Zwilich, Ellen **1990**:1

ANGOLAN
Savimbi, Jonas **1986**:2 **1994**:2

ARGENTINIAN
Barenboim, Daniel **2001**:1
Bocca, Julio **1995**:3
Duhalde, Eduardo **2003**:3
Herrera, Paloma **1996**:2
Maradona, Diego **1991**:3
Pelli, Cesar **1991**:4

Carrey, Jim **1995**:1
Cavanagh, Tom **2003**:1
Cerovsek, Corey
  Brief Entry **1987**:4
Cherry, Don **1993**:4
Chretien, Jean **1990**:4 **1997**:2
Christensen, Hayden **2003**:3
Coffey, Paul **1985**:4
Copps, Sheila **1986**:4
Cronenberg, David **1992**:3
Cronyn, Hume
  Obituary **2004**:3
Dewhurst, Colleen
  Obituary **1992**:2
Dion, Celine **1995**:3
Eagleson, Alan **1987**:4
Ebbers, Bernie **1998**:1
Egoyan, Atom **2000**:2
Erickson, Arthur **1989**:3
Fonyo, Steve
  Brief Entry **1985**:4
Foster, David **1988**:2
Fox, Michael J. **1986**:1 **2001**:3
Frank, Robert **1995**:2
Frye, Northrop
  Obituary **1991**:3
Fuhr, Grant **1997**:3
Garneau, Marc **1985**:1
Gatien, Peter
  Brief Entry **1986**:1
Giguere, Jean-Sebastien **2004**:2
Gilmour, Doug **1994**:3
Graham, Nicholas **1991**:4
Granholm, Jennifer **2003**:3
Green, Tom **1999**:4
Greene, Graham **1997**:2
Greene, Lorne
  Obituary **1988**:1
Gretzky, Wayne **1989**:2
Haney, Chris
  Brief Entry **1985**:1
Harris, Michael Deane **1997**:2
Hayakawa, Samuel Ichiye
  Obituary **1992**:3
Hennessy, Jill **2003**:2
Hextall, Ron **1988**:2
Hull, Brett **1991**:4
Jennings, Peter Charles **1997**:2
Johnson, Pierre Marc **1985**:4
Jones, Jenny **1998**:2
Juneau, Pierre **1988**:3
Jung, Andrea **2000**:2
Karsh, Yousuf
  Obituary **2003**:4
Keeler, Ruby
  Obituary **1993**:4
Kent, Arthur **1991**:4 **1997**:2
Kielburger, Craig **1998**:1
Korchinsky, Mike **2004**:2
Lalonde, Marc **1985**:1
Lang, K.D. **1988**:4
Lanois, Daniel **1991**:1
Lemieux, Claude **1996**:1
Lemieux, Mario **1986**:4
Levesque, Rene
  Obituary **1988**:1
Levy, Eugene **2004**:3
Lewis, Stephen **1987**:2
Mandel, Howie **1989**:1
Markle, C. Wilson **1988**:1
Martin, Paul **2004**:4
McKinnell, Henry **2002**:3

McLachlan, Sarah **1998**:4
McLaren, Norman
  Obituary **1987**:2
McLaughlin, Audrey **1990**:3
McTaggart, David **1989**:4
Messier, Mark **1993**:1
Morgentaler, Henry **1986**:3
Morissette, Alanis **1996**:2
Moss, Carrie-Anne **2004**:3
Mulroney, Brian **1989**:2
Munro, Alice **1997**:1
Myers, Mike **1992**:3 **1997**:4
O'Donnell, Bill
  Brief Entry **1987**:4
Ondaatje, Philip Michael **1997**:3
Parizeau, Jacques **1995**:1
Peckford, Brian **1989**:1
Peterson, David **1987**:1
Pocklington, Peter H. **1985**:2
Pratt, Christopher **1985**:3
Raffi **1988**:1
Randi, James **1990**:2
Reisman, Simon **1987**:4
Reitman, Ivan **1986**:3
Reuben, Gloria **1999**:4
Rhea, Caroline **2004**:1
Richard, Maurice
  Obituary **2000**:4
Roy, Patrick **1994**:2
Rypien, Mark **1992**:3
Sainte-Marie, Buffy **2000**:1
Sakic, Joe **2002**:1
Shaffer, Paul **1987**:1
Shields, Carol
  Obituary **2004**:3
Short, Martin **1986**:1
Strong, Maurice **1993**:1
Sutherland, Kiefer **2002**:4
Tilghman, Shirley M. **2002**:1
Trudeau, Pierre
  Obituary **2001**:1
Twain, Shania **1996**:3
Vander Zalm, William **1987**:3
Vardalos, Nia **2003**:4
Vickrey, William S.
  Obituary **1997**:2
Villeneuve, Jacques **1997**:1
Weir, Mike **2004**:1
Whitehead, Robert
  Obituary **2003**:3
Williams, Lynn **1986**:4
Wilson, Bertha
  Brief Entry **1986**:1
Wood, Sharon
  Brief Entry **1988**:1
Young, Neil **1991**:2
Yzerman, Steve **1991**:2

CHADIAN
  Deby, Idriss **2002**:2

CHILEAN
  Arrau, Claudio
    Obituary **1992**:1
  Pinochet, Augusto **1999**:2

CHINESE
  Chan, Jackie **1996**:1
  Chen, Joan **2000**:2
  Chen, T.C.
    Brief Entry **1987**:3

Deng Xiaoping **1995**:1
  Obituary **1997**:3
Fang Lizhi **1988**:1
Gao Xingjian **2001**:2
Gong Li **1998**:4
Hatem, George
  Obituary **1989**:1
Hou Hsiao-hsien **2000**:2
Hu Jintao **2004**:1
Hu Yaobang
  Obituary **1989**:4
Hwang, David Henry **1999**:1
Jiang Quing
  Obituary **1992**:1
Jiang Zemin **1996**:1
Lee, Ang **1996**:3
Lee, Henry C. **1997**:1
Lord, Bette Bao **1994**:1
Lucid, Shannon **1997**:1
Tan Dun **2002**:1
Weihui, Zhou **2001**:1
Wei Jingsheng **1998**:2
Woo, John **1994**:2
Wu, Harry **1996**:1
Yao Ming **2004**:1
Ye Jianying
  Obituary **1987**:1
Yen, Samuel **1996**:4
Zhao Ziyang **1989**:1

COLOMBIAN
  Botero, Fernando **1994**:3
  Juanes **2004**:4
  Leguizamo, John **1999**:1
  Pastrana, Andres **2002**:1
  Schroeder, Barbet **1996**:1
  Shakira **2002**:3
  Uribe, Alvaro **2003**:3

CONGOLESE
  Kabila, Joseph **2003**:2
  Kabila, Laurent **1998**:1
    Obituary **2001**:3
  Mobutu Sese Seko
    Obituary **1998**:4

COSTA RICAN
  Arias Sanchez, Oscar **1989**:3

COTE D'IVOIRIAN
  Gbagbo, Laurent **2003**:2

CROATIAN
  Ivanisevic, Goran **2002**:1
  Tudjman, Franjo
    Obituary **2000**:2
  Tudjman, Franjo **1996**:2

CUBAN
  Acosta, Carlos **1997**:4
  Canseco, Jose **1990**:2
  Castro, Fidel **1991**:4
  Cruz, Celia
    Obituary **2004**:3
  Cugat, Xavier
    Obituary **1991**:2
  Estefan, Gloria **1991**:4
  Garcia, Andy **1999**:3
  Garcia, Cristina **1997**:4

Goizueta, Roberto **1996**:1
Obituary **1998**:1
Gutierrez, Carlos M. **2001**:4
Saralegui, Cristina **1999**:2
Zamora, Pedro
Obituary **1995**:2

CYPRIAN
Chalayan, Hussein **2003**:2
Kyprianou, Spyros
Obituary **2003**:2

CZECH
Albright, Madeleine **1994**:3
Hammer, Jan **1987**:3
Hasek, Dominik **1998**:3
Havel, Vaclav **1990**:3
Hingis, Martina **1999**:1
Hrabal, Bohumil
Obituary **1997**:3
Jagr, Jaromir **1995**:4
Klima, Petr **1987**:1
Kukoc, Toni **1995**:4
Maxwell, Robert
Obituary **1992**:2
Porizkova, Paulina
Brief Entry **1986**:4
Reisz, Karel
Obituary **2004**:1
Serkin, Rudolf
Obituary **1992**:1
Stoppard, Tom **1995**:4
Trump, Ivana **1995**:2
Zatopek, Emil
Obituary **2001**:3

DANISH
Borge, Victor
Obituary **2001**:3
Kristiansen, Kjeld Kirk **1988**:3
Lander, Toni
Obituary **1985**:4

DOMINICAN
Sosa, Sammy **1999**:1

DOMINICAN REPUBLICAN
Balaguer, Joaquin
Obituary **2003**:4

DUTCH
de Kooning, Willem **1994**:4
Obituary **1997**:3
Heineken, Alfred
Obituary **2003**:1
Koolhaas, Rem **2001**:1
Parker, Colonel Tom
Obituary **1997**:2

EGYPTIAN
Ghali, Boutros Boutros **1992**:3
Mubarak, Hosni **1991**:4
Rahman, Sheik Omar Abdel- **1993**:3

ENGLISH
Adams, Douglas
Obituary **2002**:2
Altea, Rosemary **1996**:3
Amanpour, Christiane **1997**:2

Ambler, Eric
Obituary **1999**:2
Amis, Kingsley
Obituary **1996**:2
Andrews, Julie **1996**:1
Ashcroft, Peggy
Obituary **1992**:1
Ashwell, Rachel **2004**:2
Atkinson, Rowan **2004**:3
Barker, Clive **2003**:3
Beckham, David **2003**:1
Bee Gees, The **1997**:4
Berners-Lee, Tim **1997**:4
Blair, Tony **1996**:3 **1997**:4
Bloom, Orlando **2004**:2
Bonham Carter, Helena **1998**:4
Bowie, David **1998**:2
Brown, Tina **1992**:1
Burgess, Anthony
Obituary **1994**:2
Burnett, Mark **2003**:1
Bush, Kate **1994**:3
Caine, Michael **2000**:4
Campbell, Naomi **2000**:2
Carey, George **1992**:3
Charles, Prince of Wales **1995**:3
Clapton, Eric **1993**:3
Coldplay **2004**:4
Collins, Jackie **2004**:4
Comfort, Alex
Obituary **2000**:4
Cook, Peter
Obituary **1995**:2
Costello, Elvis **1994**:4
Cowell, Simon **2003**:4
Crawford, Michael **1994**:2
Crisp, Quentin
Obituary **2000**:3
Cushing, Peter
Obituary **1995**:1
Davis, Crispin **2004**:1
Dee, Janie **2001**:4
Diana, Princess of Wales **1993**:1
Obituary **1997**:4
Dido **2004**:4
Driver, Minnie **2000**:1
Elliott, Denholm
Obituary **1993**:2
Entwistle, John
Obituary **2003**:3
Everett, Rupert **2003**:1
Everything But The Girl **1996**:4
Faldo, Nick **1993**:3
Fielding, Helen **2000**:4
Fiennes, Ralph **1996**:2
Finney, Albert **2003**:3
Fonteyn, Margot
Obituary **1991**:3
Freud, Lucian **2000**:4
Frieda, John **2004**:1
Gielgud, John
Obituary **2000**:4
Grant, Hugh **1995**:3
Gray, David **2001**:4
Greene, Graham
Obituary **1991**:4
Guinness, Alec
Obituary **2001**:1
Harris, Richard
Obituary **2004**:1
Harrison, George
Obituary **2003**:1

Harvey, Polly Jean **1995**:4
Headroom, Max **1986**:4
Hebard, Caroline **1998**:2
Hempleman-Adams, David **2004**:3
Hill, Benny
Obituary **1992**:3
Hornby, Nick **2002**:2
Houser, Sam **2004**:4
Hoyle, Sir Fred
Obituary **2002**:4
Hughes, Ted
Obituary **1999**:2
Hume, Basil Cardinal
Obituary **2000**:1
Humphry, Derek **1992**:2
Hurley, Elizabeth **1999**:2
Irons, Jeremy **1991**:4
Jacques, Brian **2002**:2
John, Elton **1995**:4
Lane, Ronnie
Obituary **1997**:4
Lasdun, Denys
Obituary **2001**:4
Law, Jude **2000**:3
Lawson, Nigella **2003**:2
Leach, Penelope **1992**:4
Leakey, Mary Douglas
Obituary **1997**:2
le Carre, John **2000**:1
LeVay, Simon **1992**:2
Lewis, Lennox **2000**:2
Lupino, Ida
Obituary **1996**:1
Lyne, Adrian **1997**:2
Major, John **1991**:2
Malone, Jo **2004**:3
Marsden, Brian **2004**:4
McCartney, Paul **2002**:4
McCartney, Stella **2001**:3
McDowall, Roddy
Obituary **1999**:1
McEwan, Ian **2004**:2
McKellen, Ian **1994**:1
Mercury, Freddie
Obituary **1992**:2
Milligan, Spike
Obituary **2003**:2
Minghella, Anthony **2004**:3
Montagu, Ashley
Obituary **2000**:2
Moore, Dudley
Obituary **2003**:2
Moss, Kate **1995**:3
Newkirk, Ingrid **1992**:3
Newton-John, Olivia **1998**:4
Northam, Jeremy **2003**:2
Nunn, Trevor **2000**:2
Oasis **1996**:3
Ogilvy, David
Obituary **2000**:1
Oliver, Jamie **2002**:3
Osborne, John
Obituary **1995**:2
Osbournes, The **2003**:4
Owen-Jones, Lindsay **2004**:2
Palmer, Robert
Obituary **2004**:4
Park, Nick **1997**:3
Patten, Christopher **1993**:3
Penrose, Roger **1991**:4
Pleasence, Donald
Obituary **1995**:3

Porter, George
  Obituary **2003**:4
Princess Margaret, Countess of
  Snowdon
  Obituary **2003**:2
Pullman, Philip **2003**:2
Queen Elizabeth the Queen Mother
  Obituary **2003**:2
Redgrave, Lynn **1999**:3
Reisz, Karel
  Obituary **2004**:1
Richards, Keith **1993**:3
Ritchie, Guy **2001**:3
Roth, Tim **1998**:2
Saatchi, Maurice **1995**:4
Sacks, Oliver **1995**:4
Schlesinger, John
  Obituary **2004**:3
Scott, Ridley **2001**:1
Seal **1994**:4
Seymour, Jane **1994**:4
Smith, Paul **2002**:4
Smith, Zadie **2003**:4
Springer, Jerry **1998**:4
Springfield, Dusty
  Obituary **1999**:3
Stewart, Patrick **1996**:1
Sting **1991**:4
Stoppard, Tom **1995**:4
Strummer, Joe
  Obituary **2004**:1
Sullivan, Andrew **1996**:1
Taylor, Elizabeth **1993**:3
Thompson, Emma **1993**:2
Tilberis, Elizabeth **1994**:3
Trotman, Alex **1995**:4
Uchida, Mitsuko **1989**:3
Ware, Lancelot
  Obituary **2001**:1
Watson, Emily **2001**:1
Westwood, Vivienne **1998**:3
Wiles, Andrew **1994**:1
Wilkinson, Tom **2003**:2
Wilmut, Ian **1997**:3
Winslet, Kate **2002**:4

FIJI ISLANDER
Singh, Vijay **2000**:4

FILIPINO
Aquino, Corazon **1986**:2
Lewis, Loida Nicolas **1998**:3
Macapagal-Arroyo, Gloria **2001**:4
Marcos, Ferdinand
  Obituary **1990**:1
Natori, Josie **1994**:3
Ramos, Fidel **1995**:2
Salonga, Lea **2003**:3

FINNISH
Kekkonen, Urho
  Obituary **1986**:4
Ollila, Jorma **2003**:4
Torvalds, Linus **1999**:3

FRENCH
Adjani, Isabelle **1991**:1
Agnes B **2002**:3
Arnault, Bernard **2000**:4
Baulieu, Etienne-Emile **1990**:1

Becaud, Gilbert
  Obituary **2003**:1
Besse, Georges
  Obituary **1987**:1
Binoche, Juliette **2001**:3
Bourgeois, Louise **1994**:1
Brando, Cheyenne
  Obituary **1995**:4
Calment, Jeanne
  Obituary **1997**:4
Cardin, Pierre **2003**:3
Chagall, Marc
  Obituary **1985**:2
Chirac, Jacques **1995**:4
Colbert, Claudette
  Obituary **1997**:1
Cousteau, Jacques-Yves
  Obituary **1998**:2
Cousteau, Jean-Michel **1988**:2
Cresson, Edith **1992**:1
Delors, Jacques **1990**:2
Deneuve, Catherine **2003**:2
Depardieu, Gerard **1991**:2
Dubuffet, Jean
  Obituary **1985**:4
Duras, Marguerite
  Obituary **1996**:3
Fekkai, Frederic **2003**:2
Gaultier, Jean-Paul **1998**:1
Godard, Jean-Luc **1998**:1
Grappelli, Stephane
  Obituary **1998**:1
Guillem, Sylvie **1988**:2
Indurain, Miguel **1994**:1
Klarsfeld, Beate **1989**:1
Lefebvre, Marcel **1988**:4
Malle, Louis
  Obituary **1996**:2
Mercier, Laura **2002**:2
Mitterrand, Francois
  Obituary **1996**:2
Nars, Francois **2003**:1
Petrossian, Christian
  Brief Entry **1985**:3
Picasso, Paloma **1991**:1
Ponty, Jean-Luc **1985**:4
Prost, Alain **1988**:1
Rampal, Jean-Pierre **1989**:2
Reza, Yasmina **1999**:2
Rothschild, Philippe de
  Obituary **1988**:2
Rykiel, Sonia **2000**:3
Simone, Nina
  Obituary **2004**:2
Starck, Philippe **2004**:1
Tautou, Audrey **2004**:2
Thom, Rene
  Obituary **2004**:1
Thomas, Michel **1987**:4
Ungaro, Emanuel **2001**:3
Villechaize, Herve
  Obituary **1994**:1
Xenakis, Iannis
  Obituary **2001**:4

GERMAN
Barbie, Klaus
  Obituary **1992**:2
Becker, Boris
  Brief Entry **1985**:3
Beuys, Joseph
  Obituary **1986**:3

Blobel, Gunter **2000**:4
Boyle, Gertrude **1995**:3
Brandt, Willy
  Obituary **1993**:2
Breitschwerdt, Werner **1988**:4
Casper, Gerhard **1993**:1
Dietrich, Marlene
  Obituary **1992**:4
Etzioni, Amitai **1994**:3
Frank, Anthony M. **1992**:1
Graf, Steffi **1987**:4
Grass, Gunter **2000**:2
Gursky, Andreas **2002**:2
Hahn, Carl H. **1986**:4
Hess, Rudolph
  Obituary **1988**:1
Honecker, Erich
  Obituary **1994**:4
Kiefer, Anselm **1990**:2
Kinski, Klaus **1987**:2
  Obituary **1992**:2
Klarsfeld, Beate **1989**:1
Klemperer, Werner
  Obituary **2001**:3
Kohl, Helmut **1994**:1
Krogner, Heinz **2004**:2
Lagerfeld, Karl **1999**:4
Max, Peter **1993**:2
Mengele, Josef
  Obituary **1985**:2
Mutter, Anne-Sophie **1990**:3
Newton, Helmut **2002**:1
Nuesslein-Volhard, Christiane **1998**:1
Pfeiffer, Eckhard **1998**:4
Pilatus, Robert
  Obituary **1998**:3
Polke, Sigmar **1999**:4
Rey, Margret E.
  Obituary **1997**:2
Richter, Gerhard **1997**:2
Sander, Jil **1995**:2
Schily, Otto
  Brief Entry **1987**:4
Schrempp, Juergen **2000**:2
Schroder, Gerhard **1999**:1
Tillmans, Wolfgang **2001**:4
Werner, Ruth
  Obituary **2001**:1
Witt, Katarina **1991**:3
Zetsche, Dieter **2002**:3

GHANIAN
Annan, Kofi **1999**:1
Chambas, Mohammed ibn **2003**:3

GREEK
Huffington, Arianna **1996**:2
Papandreou, Andrea
  Obituary **1997**:1

GUATEMALAN
Berger, Oscar **2004**:4
Menchu, Rigoberta **1993**:2

GUINEA-BISSAUNI
Makeba, Miriam **1989**:2
Ture, Kwame
  Obituary **1999**:2

HAITIAN
Aristide, Jean-Bertrand **1991**:3
Cedras, Raoul **1994**:4
Preval, Rene **1997**:2

HONG KONGER
Chow Yun-fat **1999**:4
Lee, Martin **1998**:2

HUNGARIAN
Dorati, Antal
Obituary **1989**:2
Fodor, Eugene
Obituary **1991**:3
Gabor, Eva
Obituary **1996**:1
Grove, Andrew S. **1995**:3
Polgar, Judit **1993**:3
Solti, Georg
Obituary **1998**:1

ICELANDIC
Bjork **1996**:1
Finnbogadottir, Vigdis
Brief Entry **1986**:2

INDIAN
Chopra, Deepak **1996**:3
Devi, Phoolan **1986**:1
Obituary **2002**:3
Durrell, Gerald
Obituary **1995**:3
Gandhi, Indira
Obituary **1985**:1
Gandhi, Rajiv
Obituary **1991**:4
Gandhi, Sonia **2000**:2
Gowda, H. D. Deve **1997**:1
Mahesh Yogi, Maharishi **1991**:3
Mehta, Zubin **1994**:3
Mother Teresa **1993**:1
Obituary **1998**:1
Musharraf, Pervez **2000**:2
Narayan, R.K.
Obituary **2002**:2
Nooyi, Indra **2004**:3
Prowse, Juliet
Obituary **1997**:1
Rajneesh, Bhagwan Shree
Obituary **1990**:2
Ram, Jagjivan
Obituary **1986**:4
Rao, P. V. Narasimha **1993**:2
Rushdie, Salman **1994**:1
Sharma, Nisha **2004**:2
Vajpayee, Atal Behari **1998**:4
Wahid, Abdurrahman **2000**:3

INDONESIAN
Habibie, Bacharuddin Jusuf **1999**:3
Megawati Sukarnoputri **2002**:2
Megawati Sukarnoputri **2000**:1

IRANIAN
Ebadi, Shirin **2004**:3
Khatami, Mohammed **1997**:4
Khomeini, Ayatollah Ruhollah
Obituary **1989**:4
McCourt, Frank **1997**:4

Rafsanjani, Ali Akbar
Hashemi **1987**:3
Schroeder, Barbet **1996**:1

IRAQI
Hussein, Saddam **1991**:1
Kamel, Hussein **1996**:1
Saatchi, Maurice **1995**:4

IRISH
Adams, Gerald **1994**:1
Ahern, Bertie **1999**:3
Beckett, Samuel Barclay
Obituary **1990**:2
Bono **1988**:4
Branagh, Kenneth **1992**:2
Brosnan, Pierce **2000**:3
Byrne, Gabriel **1997**:4
de Valois, Dame Ninette
Obituary **2002**:1
Enya **1992**:3
Farrell, Colin **2004**:1
Geldof, Bob **1985**:3
Heaney, Seamus **1996**:2
Herzog, Chaim
Obituary **1997**:3
Hume, John **1987**:1
Huston, John
Obituary **1988**:1
Jordan, Neil **1993**:3
McGuinness, Martin **1985**:4
Neeson, Liam **1993**:4
O'Connor, Sinead **1990**:4
O'Sullivan, Maureen
Obituary **1998**:4
Robinson, Mary **1993**:1
Trimble, David **1999**:1
U **2002**:4

ISRAELI
Arens, Moshe **1985**:1
Arison, Ted **1990**:3
Barak, Ehud **1999**:4
Begin, Menachem
Obituary **1992**:3
Herzog, Chaim
Obituary **1997**:3
Levinger, Moshe **1992**:1
Levy, David **1987**:2
Mintz, Shlomo **1986**:2
Netanyahu, Benjamin **1996**:4
Peres, Shimon **1996**:3
Rabin, Leah
Obituary **2001**:2
Rabin, Yitzhak **1993**:1
Obituary **1996**:2
Shcharansky, Anatoly **1986**:2

ITALIAN
Agnelli, Giovanni **1989**:4
Armani, Giorgio **1991**:2
Bartoli, Cecilia **1994**:1
Benetton, Luciano **1988**:1
Benigni, Roberto **1999**:2
Berio, Luciano
Obituary **2004**:2
Berlusconi, Silvio **1994**:4
Capra, Frank
Obituary **1992**:2
Cavalli, Roberto **2004**:4
Ciampi, Carlo Azeglio **2004**:3

Clemente, Francesco **1992**:2
Coppola, Carmine
Obituary **1991**:4
Fabio **1993**:4
Fano, Ugo
Obituary **2001**:4
Fellini, Federico
Obituary **1994**:2
Ferrari, Enzo **1988**:4
Ferretti, Alberta **2004**:1
Ferri, Alessandra **1987**:2
Fo, Dario **1998**:1
Gardenia, Vincent
Obituary **1993**:2
Gassman, Vittorio
Obituary **2001**:1
Gucci, Maurizio
Brief Entry **1985**:4
Lamborghini, Ferrucio
Obituary **1993**:3
Leone, Sergio
Obituary **1989**:4
Masina, Giulietta
Obituary **1994**:3
Mastroianni, Marcello
Obituary **1997**:2
Michelangeli, Arturo
Benedetti **1988**:2
Montand, Yves
Obituary **1992**:2
Pavarotti, Luciano **1997**:4
Pozzi, Lucio **1990**:2
Prada, Miuccia **1996**:1
Rizzoli, Paola **2004**:3
Sinopoli, Giuseppe **1988**:1
Staller, Ilona **1988**:3
Tomba, Alberto **1992**:3
Versace, Donatella **1999**:1
Versace, Gianni
Brief Entry **1988**:1
Obituary **1998**:2
Zanardi, Alex **1998**:2
Zeffirelli, Franco **1991**:3

JAMAICAN
Marley, Ziggy **1990**:4
Tosh, Peter
Obituary **1988**:2

JAPANESE
Akihito, Emperor of Japan **1990**:1
Aoki, Rocky **1990**:2
Doi, Takako
Brief Entry **1987**:4
Hirohito, Emperor of Japan
Obituary **1989**:2
Honda, Soichiro
Obituary **1986**:1
Hosokawa, Morihiro **1994**:1
Isozaki, Arata **1990**:2
Itami, Juzo
Obituary **1998**:2
Katayama, Yutaka **1987**:1
Koizumi, Junichiro **2002**:1
Kurosawa, Akira **1991**:1
Obituary **1999**:1
Masako, Crown Princess **1993**:4
Matsuhisa, Nobuyuki **2002**:3
Mitarai, Fujio **2002**:4
Miyake, Issey **1985**:2
Miyazawa, Kiichi **1992**:2
Mori, Yoshiro **2000**:4

Morita, Akio
Obituary **2000**:2
Morita, Akio **1989**:4
Murakami, Takashi **2004**:2
Nagako, Empress Dowager
Obituary **2001**:1
Nomo, Hideo **1996**:2
Obuchi, Keizo
Obituary **2000**:4
Obuchi, Keizo **1999**:2
Oe, Kenzaburo **1997**:1
Sasakawa, Ryoichi
Brief Entry **1988**:1
Shimomura, Tsutomu **1996**:1
Suzuki, Ichiro **2002**:2
Suzuki, Sin'ichi
Obituary **1998**:3
Takada, Kenzo **2003**:2
Takei, Kei **1990**:2
Takeshita, Noburu
Obituary **2001**:1
Tanaka, Tomoyuki
Obituary **1997**:3
Toyoda, Eiji **1985**:2
Uchida, Mitsuko **1989**:3
Yamamoto, Kenichi **1989**:1

JORDANIAN
Abdullah II, King **2002**:4
al-Abdullah, Rania **2001**:1
Hussein I, King **1997**:3
Obituary **1999**:3

KENYAN
Kibaki, Mwai **2003**:4
Moi, Daniel arap **1993**:2

KOREAN
Chung Ju Yung
Obituary **2002**:1
Kim Dae Jung **1998**:3
Kim Il Sung
Obituary **1994**:4
Kim Jong Il **1995**:2
Pak, Se Ri **1999**:4

LATVIAN
Baryshnikov, Mikhail Nikolaevich
1997:3

LEBANESE
Berri, Nabih **1985**:2
Jumblatt, Walid **1987**:4
Sarkis, Elias
Obituary **1985**:3

LIBERIAN
Doe, Samuel
Obituary **1991**:1

LIBYAN
Qaddhafi, Muammar **1998**:3

LITHUANIAN
Landsbergis, Vytautas **1991**:3

MADAGASCAN
Ravalomanana, Marc **2003**:1

MALAWI
Banda, Hastings **1994**:3

MALAYSIAN
Ngau, Harrison **1991**:3
Yeoh, Michelle **2003**:2

MEXICAN
Alvarez Bravo, Manuel
Obituary **2004**:1
Catlett, Elizabeth **1999**:3
Colosio, Luis Donaldo **1994**:3
Esquivel, Juan **1996**:2
Felix, Maria
Obituary **2003**:2
Fox, Vicente **2001**:1
Graham, Robert **1993**:4
Hayek, Salma **1999**:1
Kahlo, Frida **1991**:3
Paz, Octavio **1991**:2
Salinas, Carlos **1992**:1
Santana, Carlos **2000**:2
Tamayo, Rufino
Obituary **1992**:1
Zedillo, Ernesto **1995**:1

MOROCCAN
King Hassan II
Obituary **2000**:1

MOZAMBICAN
Chissano, Joaquim **1987**:4
Dhlakama, Afonso **1993**:3
Machel, Samora
Obituary **1987**:1

NAMIBIAN
Nujoma, Sam **1990**:4

NEW ZEALANDER
Campion, Jane **1991**:4
Castle-Hughes, Keisha **2004**:4
Crowe, Russell **2000**:4
Jackson, Peter **2004**:4
Shipley, Jenny **1998**:3

NICARAGUAN
Astorga, Nora **1988**:2
Cruz, Arturo **1985**:1
Obando, Miguel **1986**:4
Robelo, Alfonso **1988**:1

NIGERAN
Abacha, Sani **1996**:3
Babangida, Ibrahim
Badamosi **1992**:4
Obasanjo, Olusegun **2000**:2
Okoye, Christian **1990**:2
Olajuwon, Akeem **1985**:1
Sade **1993**:2
Saro-Wiwa, Ken
Obituary **1996**:2

NORWEGIAN
Brundtland, Gro Harlem **2000**:1
Cammermeyer, Margarethe **1995**:2
Olav, King of Norway
Obituary **1991**:3

PAKISTANI
Bhutto, Benazir **1989**:4
Zia ul-Haq, Mohammad
Obituary **1988**:4

PALESTINIAN
Arafat, Yasser **1989**:3 **1997**:3
Freij, Elias **1986**:4
Habash, George **1986**:1
Husseini, Faisal **1998**:4
Nidal, Abu **1987**:1
Sharon, Ariel **2001**:4
Terzi, Zehdi Labib **1985**:3

PANAMANIAN
Blades, Ruben **1998**:2

PERUVIAN
Fujimori, Alberto **1992**:4
Perez de Cuellar, Javier **1991**:3
Testino, Mario **2002**:1

POLISH
Begin, Menachem
Obituary **1992**:3
Eisenstaedt, Alfred
Obituary **1996**:1
John Paul II, Pope **1995**:3
Kieslowski, Krzysztof
Obituary **1996**:3
Kosinski, Jerzy
Obituary **1991**:4
Masur, Kurt **1993**:4
Niezabitowska, Malgorzata **1991**:3
Rosten, Leo
Obituary **1997**:3
Sabin, Albert
Obituary **1993**:4
Singer, Isaac Bashevis
Obituary **1992**:1
Walesa, Lech **1991**:2

PORTUGUESE
Saramago, Jose **1999**:1

PUERTO RICAN
Alvarez, Aida **1999**:2
Del Toro, Benicio **2001**:4
Ferrer, Jose
Obituary **1992**:3
Julia, Raul
Obituary **1995**:1
Martin, Ricky **1999**:4
Novello, Antonia **1991**:2
Trinidad, Felix **2000**:4

ROMANIAN
Ceausescu, Nicolae
Obituary **1990**:2
Codrescu, Andre **1997**:3

RUSSIAN
Brodsky, Joseph
Obituary **1996**:3
Gorbachev, Raisa
Obituary **2000**:2
Gordeeva, Ekaterina **1996**:4
Grinkov, Sergei
Obituary **1996**:2
Kasparov, Garry **1997**:4

Kasyanov, Mikhail **2001**:1
Konstantinov, Vladimir **1997**:4
Kournikova, Anna **2000**:3
Lapidus, Morris
    Obituary **2001**:4
Lebed, Alexander **1997**:1
Primakov, Yevgeny **1999**:3
Putin, Vladimir **2000**:3
Safin, Marat **2001**:3
Sarraute, Nathalie
    Obituary **2000**:2
Schneerson, Menachem Mendel
    1992:4
    Obituary **1994**:4
Titov, Gherman
    Obituary **2001**:3

RWANDAN
    Kagame, Paul **2001**:4

SALVADORAN
    Duarte, Jose Napoleon
        Obituary **1990**:3

SCOTTISH
    Coldplay **2004**:4
    Connery, Sean **1990**:4
    McGregor, Ewan **1998**:2
    Ramsay, Mike **2002**:1
    Rowling, J.K. **2000**:1

SENEGALESE
    Senghor, Leopold
        Obituary **2003**:1

SOMALIAN
    Iman **2001**:3

SOUTH AFRICAN
    Barnard, Christiaan
        Obituary **2002**:4
    Blackburn, Molly
        Obituary **1985**:4
    Buthelezi, Mangosuthu
        Gatsha **1989**:3
    Coetzee, J. M. **2004**:4
    de Klerk, F.W. **1990**:1
    Duncan, Sheena
        Brief Entry **1987**:1
    Fugard, Athol **1992**:3
    Hani, Chris
        Obituary **1993**:4
    Makeba, Miriam **1989**:2
    Mandela, Nelson **1990**:3
    Mandela, Winnie **1989**:3
    Matthews, Dave **1999**:3
    Mbeki, Thabo **1999**:4
    Oppenheimer, Harry
        Obituary **2001**:3
    Paton, Alan
        Obituary **1988**:3
    Ramaphosa, Cyril **1988**:2
    Sisulu, Walter
        Obituary **2004**:2
    Slovo, Joe **1989**:2
    Suzman, Helen **1989**:3
    Tambo, Oliver **1991**:3
    Theron, Charlize **2001**:4

Treurnicht, Andries **1992**:2
Woods, Donald
    Obituary **2002**:3

SOVIET
    Asimov, Isaac
        Obituary **1992**:3
    Chernenko, Konstantin
        Obituary **1985**:1
    Dalai Lama **1989**:1
    Dubinin, Yuri **1987**:4
    Dzhanibekov, Vladimir **1988**:1
    Erte
        Obituary **1990**:4
    Federov, Sergei **1995**:1
    Godunov, Alexander
        Obituary **1995**:4
    Gorbachev, Mikhail **1985**:2
    Grebenshikov, Boris **1990**:1
    Gromyko, Andrei
        Obituary **1990**:2
    Karadzic, Radovan **1995**:3
    Milosevic, Slobodan **1993**:2
    Molotov, Vyacheslav Mikhailovich
        Obituary **1987**:1
    Nureyev, Rudolf
        Obituary **1993**:2
    Sakharov, Andrei Dmitrievich
        Obituary **1990**:2
    Smirnoff, Yakov **1987**:2
    Vidov, Oleg **1987**:4
    Yeltsin, Boris **1991**:1
    Zhirinovsky, Vladimir **1994**:2

SPANISH
    Almodovar, Pedro **2000**:3
    Banderas, Antonio **1996**:2
    Blahnik, Manolo **2000**:2
    Carreras, Jose **1995**:2
    Cela, Camilo Jose
        Obituary **2003**:1
    Chillida, Eduardo
        Obituary **2003**:4
    Cruz, Penelope **2001**:4
    Dali, Salvador
        Obituary **1989**:2
    de Pinies, Jamie
        Brief Entry **1986**:3
    Domingo, Placido **1993**:2
    Juan Carlos I **1993**:1
    Lopez de Arriortua, Jose Ignacio
        1993:4
    Miro, Joan
        Obituary **1985**:1
    Moneo, Jose Rafael **1996**:4
    Montoya, Carlos
        Obituary **1993**:4
    Samaranch, Juan Antonio **1986**:2
    Segovia, Andres
        Obituary **1987**:3
    Wences, Senor
        Obituary **1999**:4

SRI LANKAN
    Bandaranaike, Sirimavo
        Obituary **2001**:2
    Ondaatje, Philip Michael **1997**:3
    Wickramasinghe, Ranil **2003**:2

SUDANESE
    Turabi, Hassan **1995**:4

SWEDISH
    Bergman, Ingmar **1999**:4
    Cardigans, The **1997**:4
    Carlsson, Arvid **2001**:2
    Garbo, Greta
        Obituary **1990**:3
    Hallstrom, Lasse **2002**:3
    Lindbergh, Pelle
        Obituary **1985**:4
    Lindgren, Astrid
        Obituary **2003**:1
    Olin, Lena **1991**:2
    Palme, Olof
        Obituary **1986**:2
    Persson, Stefan **2004**:1
    Renvall, Johan
        Brief Entry **1987**:4
    Sorenstam, Annika **2001**:1

SWISS
    del Ponte, Carla **2001**:1
    Federer, Roger **2004**:2
    Frank, Robert **1995**:2
    Vollenweider, Andreas **1985**:2

SYRIAN
    al-Assad, Bashar **2004**:2
    Assad, Hafez
        Obituary **2000**:4
    Assad, Hafez al- **1992**:1
    Assad, Rifaat **1986**:3

TAHITIAN
    Brando, Cheyenne
        Obituary **1995**:4

TAIWANESE
    Chen Shui-bian **2001**:2
    Ho, David **1997**:2
    Lee Teng-hui **2000**:1

TANZANIAN
    Nyerere, Julius
        Obituary **2000**:2

TRINIDADIAN
    Ture, Kwame
        Obituary **1999**:2

TUNISIAN
    Azria, Max **2001**:4

TURKISH
    Ocalan, Abdullah **1999**:4

UGANDAN
    Amin, Idi
        Obituary **2004**:4
    Museveni, Yoweri **2002**:1

UKRAINIAN
    Baiul, Oksana **1995**:3

VENEZUELAN
    Herrera, Carolina **1997**:1
    Perez, Carlos Andre **1990**:2

Cumulative Occupation Index

This index lists all newsmakers alphabetically by their occupations or fields of primary activity. Indexes in softbound issues allow access to the current year's entries; indexes in annual hardbound volumes are cumulative, covering the entire *Newsmakers* series.

Listee names are followed by a year and issue number; thus **1996**:3 indicates that an entry on that individual appears in both 1996, Issue 3, and the 1996 cumulation. For access to newsmakers appearing earlier than the current softbound issue, see the previous year's cumulation.

ART AND DESIGN

Adams, Scott **1996**:4
Addams, Charles
　Obituary **1989**:1
Agnes B **2002**:3
Allard, Linda **2003**:2
Alvarez Bravo, Manuel
　Obituary **2004**:1
Anderson, Laurie **2000**:2
Arman **1993**:1
Armani, Giorgio **1991**:2
Ashwell, Rachel **2004**:2
Aucoin, Kevyn **2001**:3
Avedon, Richard **1993**:4
Azria, Max **2001**:4
Badgley, Mark and
　James Mischka **2004**:3
Baldessari, John **1991**:4
Banks, Jeffrey **1998**:2
Barbera, Joseph **1988**:2
Barks, Carl
　Obituary **2001**:2
Barnes, Ernie **1997**:4
Barry, Lynda **1992**:1
Bean, Alan L. **1986**:2
Beuys, Joseph
　Obituary **1986**:3
Blahnik, Manolo **2000**:2
Blass, Bill
　Obituary **2003**:3
Bohbot, Michele **2004**:2
Bontecou, Lee **2004**:4
Boone, Mary **1985**:1
Botero, Fernando **1994**:3
Bourgeois, Louise **1994**:1
Bowie, David **1998**:2
Boynton, Sandra **2004**:1
Brown, Bobbi **2001**:4
Brown, J. Carter
　Obituary **2003**:3
Bunshaft, Gordon **1989**:3
　Obituary **1991**:1
Cameron, David
　Brief Entry **1988**:1
Campbell, Ben Nighthorse **1998**:1
Campbell, Naomi **2000**:2
Cardin, Pierre **2003**:3

Castelli, Leo
　Obituary **2000**:1
Catlett, Elizabeth **1999**:3
Cavalli, Roberto **2004**:4
Chagall, Marc
　Obituary **1985**:2
Chalayan, Hussein **2003**:2
Chast, Roz **1992**:4
Chatham, Russell **1990**:1
Chia, Sandro **1987**:2
Chihuly, Dale **1995**:2
Chillida, Eduardo
　Obituary **2003**:4
Christo **1992**:3
Claiborne, Liz **1986**:3
Clemente, Francesco **1992**:2
Cole, Kenneth **2003**:1
Cooper, Alexander **1988**:4
Crumb, R. **1995**:4
Dali, Salvador
　Obituary **1989**:2
Davis, Paige **2004**:2
DeCarava, Roy **1996**:3
de Kooning, Willem **1994**:4
　Obituary **1997**:3
Diebenkorn, Richard
　Obituary **1993**:4
Diller, Elizabeth and Ricardo
　Scofidio **2004**:3
Donghia, Angelo R.
　Obituary **1985**:2
Duarte, Henry **2003**:3
Dubuffet, Jean
　Obituary **1985**:4
Dunham, Carroll **2003**:4
Eisenman, Peter **1992**:4
Eisenstaedt, Alfred
　Obituary **1996**:1
Ellis, Perry
　Obituary **1986**:3
Engelbreit, Mary **1994**:3
Erickson, Arthur **1989**:3
Erte
　Obituary **1990**:4
Eve **2004**:3
Fekkai, Frederic **2003**:2
Ferretti, Alberta **2004**:1

Field, Patricia **2002**:2
Finley, Karen **1992**:4
Fisher, Mary **1994**:3
Ford, Tom **1999**:3
Foster, Norman **1999**:4
Frank, Robert **1995**:2
Frankenthaler, Helen **1990**:1
Freud, Lucian **2000**:4
Frieda, John **2004**:1
Gaines, William M.
　Obituary **1993**:1
Gaultier, Jean-Paul **1998**:1
Gehry, Frank O. **1987**:1
Giannulli, Mossimo **2002**:3
Gober, Robert **1996**:3
Golden, Thelma **2003**:3
Goody, Joan **1990**:2
Gould, Chester
　Obituary **1985**:2
Graham, Nicholas **1991**:4
Graham, Robert **1993**:4
Graves, Michael **2000**:1
Graves, Nancy **1989**:3
Greenberg, Robert **2003**:2
Groening, Matt **1990**:4
Guccione, Bob **1986**:1
Gund, Agnes **1993**:2
Gursky, Andreas **2002**:2
Halston
　Obituary **1990**:3
Handford, Martin **1991**:3
Haring, Keith
　Obituary **1990**:3
Hilfiger, Tommy **1993**:3
Hockney, David **1988**:3
Holl, Steven **2003**:1
Hughes, Robert **1996**:4
Isozaki, Arata **1990**:2
Jacobs, Marc **2002**:3
Jahn, Helmut **1987**:3
Johnson, Betsey **1996**:2
Johnson, Philip **1989**:2
Jordan, Charles M. **1989**:4
Judge, Mike **1994**:2
Kahlo, Frida **1991**:3
Kamali, Norma **1989**:1
Karan, Donna **1988**:1

Karsh, Yousuf
  Obituary 2003:4
Kashuk, Sonia 2002:4
Kaskey, Ray
  Brief Entry 1987:2
Katz, Alex 1990:3
Kelly, Ellsworth 1992:1
Kelly, Patrick
  Obituary 1990:2
Kent, Corita
  Obituary 1987:1
Keplinger, Dan 2001:1
Ketcham, Hank
  Obituary 2002:2
Kiefer, Anselm 1990:2
Klein, Calvin 1996:2
Koolhaas, Rem 2001:1
Koons, Jeff 1991:4
Kors, Michael 2000:4
Kostabi, Mark 1989:4
Lagerfeld, Karl 1999:4
Lang, Helmut 1999:2
Lange, Liz 2003:4
Lapidus, Morris
  Obituary 2001:4
Lasdun, Denys
  Obituary 2001:4
Lauren, Ralph 1990:1
Leibovitz, Annie 1988:4
LeWitt, Sol 2001:2
Libeskind, Daniel 2004:1
Lichtenstein, Roy 1994:1
  Obituary 1998:1
Lin, Maya 1990:3
Lobell, Jeanine 2002:3
Longo, Robert 1990:4
MacNelly, Jeff
  Obituary 2000:4
Mann, Sally 2001:2
Mansion, Gracie
  Brief Entry 1986:3
Mapplethorpe, Robert
  Obituary 1989:3
Mauldin, Bill
  Obituary 2004:2
Max, Peter 1993:2
McCartney, Linda
  Obituary 1998:4
McCartney, Stella 2001:3
McDonough, William 2003:1
McFarlane, Todd 1999:1
Meier, Richard 2001:4
Meisel, Steven 2002:4
Mellinger, Frederick
  Obituary 1990:4
Mercier, Laura 2002:2
Miller, Nicole 1995:4
Mills, Malia 2003:1
Miro, Joan
  Obituary 1985:1
Misrach, Richard 1991:2
Miyake, Issey 1985:2
Mizrahi, Isaac 1991:1
Moneo, Jose Rafael 1996:4
Moore, Henry
  Obituary 1986:4
Motherwell, Robert
  Obituary 1992:1
Mumford, Lewis
  Obituary 1990:2
Murakami, Takashi 2004:2
Nars, Francois 2003:1

Natori, Josie 1994:3
Nauman, Bruce 1995:4
Nechita, Alexandra 1996:4
Neiman, LeRoy 1993:3
Nevelson, Louise
  Obituary 1988:3
Newman, Arnold 1993:1
Newton, Helmut 2002:1
Nipon, Albert
  Brief Entry 1986:4
Ogilvy, David
  Obituary 2000:1
Oldham, Todd 1995:4
Ono, Yoko 1989:2
Parker, Suzy
  Obituary 2004:2
Pedersen, William 1989:4
Pei, I.M. 1990:4
Pelli, Cesar 1991:4
Penn & Teller 1992:1
Picasso, Paloma 1991:1
Polke, Sigmar 1999:4
Portman, John 1988:2
Potok, Anna Maximilian
  Brief Entry 1985:2
Pozzi, Lucio 1990:2
Prada, Miuccia 1996:1
Pratt, Christopher 1985:3
Predock, Antoine 1993:2
Puryear, Martin 2002:4
Queer Eye for the
  Straight Guy cast 2004:3
Radocy, Robert
  Brief Entry 1986:3
Raimondi, John
  Brief Entry 1987:4
Raskin, Jef 1997:4
Rauschenberg, Robert 1991:2
Rhodes, Zandra 1986:2
Richter, Gerhard 1997:2
Ringgold, Faith 2000:3
Ritts, Herb 1992:3
Roberts, Xavier 1985:3
Roche, Kevin 1985:1
Rockwell, David 2003:3
Rosenberg, Evelyn 1988:2
Rosenzweig, Ilene 2004:1
Rothenberg, Susan 1995:3
Rouse, James
  Obituary 1996:4
Rowley, Cynthia 2002:1
Rykiel, Sonia 2000:3
Saatchi, Charles 1987:3
Salgado, Sebastiao 1994:2
Schnabel, Julian 1997:1
Schulz, Charles
  Obituary 2000:3
Schulz, Charles M. 1998:1
Serrano, Andres 2000:4
Shaw, Carol 2002:1
Sherman, Cindy 1992:3
Slick, Grace 2001:2
Smith, Paul 2002:4
Smith, Willi
  Obituary 1987:3
Spade, Kate 2003:1
Spiegelman, Art 1998:3
Starck, Philippe 2004:1
Stella, Frank 1996:2
Sui, Anna 1995:1
Takada, Kenzo 2003:2

Tamayo, Rufino
  Obituary 1992:1
Testino, Mario 2002:1
Thiebaud, Wayne 1991:1
Tillmans, Wolfgang 2001:4
Tompkins, Susie
  Brief Entry 1987:2
Trudeau, Garry 1991:2
Truitt, Anne 1993:1
Twombley, Cy 1995:1
Tyler, Richard 1995:3
Ungaro, Emanuel 2001:3
Valvo, Carmen Marc 2003:4
Venturi, Robert 1994:4
Versace, Donatella 1999:1
Versace, Gianni
  Brief Entry 1988:1
  Obituary 1998:2
von Furstenberg, Diane 1994:2
Vreeland, Diana
  Obituary 1990:1
Wagner, Catherine F. 2002:3
Walker, Kara 1999:2
Wang, Vera 1998:4
Warhol, Andy
  Obituary 1987:2
Washington, Alonzo 2000:1
Waterman, Cathy 2002:2
Watterson, Bill 1990:3
Wegman, William 1991:1
Westwood, Vivienne 1998:3
Wilson, Peter C.
  Obituary 1985:2
Wintour, Anna 1990:4
Witkin, Joel-Peter 1996:1
Yamasaki, Minoru
  Obituary 1986:2

BUSINESS

Abraham, S. Daniel 2003:3
Ackerman, Will 1987:4
Agnelli, Giovanni 1989:4
Ailes, Roger 1989:3
Akers, John F. 1988:3
Akin, Phil
  Brief Entry 1987:3
Allaire, Paul 1995:1
Allard, Linda 2003:2
Allen, Bob 1992:4
Allen, John 1992:1
Alter, Hobie
  Brief Entry 1985:1
Alvarez, Aida 1999:2
Amos, Wally 2000:1
Ancier, Garth 1989:1
Andreessen, Marc 1996:2
Annenberg, Walter 1992:3
Antonini, Joseph 1991:2
Aoki, Rocky 1990:2
Arad, Avi 2003:2
Aretsky, Ken 1988:1
Arison, Ted 1990:3
Arledge, Roone 1992:2
Armstrong, C. Michael 2002:1
Arnault, Bernard 2000:4
Ash, Mary Kay 1996:1
Ashwell, Rachel 2004:2
Aurre, Laura
  Brief Entry 1986:3
Ballmer, Steven 1997:2
Banks, Jeffrey 1998:2
Barad, Jill 1994:2

Pfeiffer, Eckhard 1998:4
Phelan, John Joseph, Jr. 1985:4
Phillips, Sam
  Obituary 2004:4
Pierce, Frederick S. 1985:3
Pittman, Robert W. 1985:1
Pocklington, Peter H. 1985:2
Popcorn, Faith
  Brief Entry 1988:1
Pope, Generoso 1988:4
Porizkova, Paulina
  Brief Entry 1986:4
Porsche, Ferdinand
  Obituary 1998:4
Porter, Sylvia
  Obituary 1991:4
Portman, John 1988:2
Potter, Michael 2003:3
Prada, Miuccia 1996:1
Pratt, Jane 1999:1
Presser, Jackie
  Obituary 1988:4
Pressler, Paul 2003:4
Pritzker, A.N.
  Obituary 1986:2
Proctor, Barbara Gardner 1985:3
Puck, Wolfgang 1990:1
Questrom, Allen 2001:4
Quinn, Jane Bryant 1993:4
Radocy, Robert
  Brief Entry 1986:3
Rand, A. Barry 2000:3
Rapp, C.J.
  Brief Entry 1987:3
Rawlings, Mike 2003:1
Raymond, Lee R. 2000:3
Redenbacher, Orville
  Obituary 1996:1
Redstone, Sumner 1994:1
Regan, Judith 2003:1
Rhodes, Zandra 1986:2
Riggio, Leonard S. 1999:4
Riney, Hal 1989:1
Riordan, Richard 1993:4
Roberts, Xavier 1985:3
Roddick, Anita 1989:4
Roedy, Bill 2003:2
Rooney, Art
  Obituary 1989:1
Roosevelt, Franklin D., Jr.
  Obituary 1989:1
Ross, Percy
  Brief Entry 1986:2
Ross, Steven J.
  Obituary 1993:3
Rossellini, Isabella 2001:4
Rothschild, Philippe de
  Obituary 1988:2
Rothstein, Ruth 1988:2
Rowland, Pleasant 1992:3
Rowley, Coleen 2004:2
Saatchi, Maurice 1995:4
Sachs, Jeffrey D. 2004:4
Sagansky, Jeff 1993:2
Sander, Jil 1995:2
Sanger, Steve 2002:3
Sasakawa, Ryoichi
  Brief Entry 1988:1
Scardino, Marjorie 2002:1
Schlessinger, David
  Brief Entry 1985:1
Schoenfeld, Gerald 1986:2

Schott, Marge 1985:4
Schrempp, Juergen 2000:2
Schultz, Howard 1995:3
Schwab, Charles 1989:3
Schwinn, Edward R., Jr.
  Brief Entry 1985:4
Sculley, John 1989:4
Sedelmaier, Joe 1985:3
Seidenberg, Ivan 2004:1
Shaich, Ron 2004:4
Siebert, Muriel 1987:2
Simmons, Russell and
  Kimora Lee 2003:2
Smale, John G. 1987:3
Smith, Frederick W. 1985:4
Smith, Jack 1994:3
Smith, Roger 1990:3
Snider, Stacey 2002:4
Spade, Kate 2003:1
Spector, Phil 1989:1
Spray, Ed 2004:1
Starck, Philippe 2004:1
Steel, Dawn 1990:1
  Obituary 1998:2
Steinberg, Leigh 1987:3
Steinbrenner, George 1991:1
Stempel, Robert 1991:3
Stern, David 1991:4
Stewart, Martha 1992:1
Stonesifer, Patty 1997:1
Stroh, Peter W. 1985:2
Strong, Maurice 1993:1
Sullivan, Andrew 1996:1
Summers, Anne 1990:2
Tagliabue, Paul 1990:2
Takada, Kenzo 2003:2
Tanny, Vic
  Obituary 1985:3
Tartikoff, Brandon 1985:2
  Obituary 1998:1
Tellem, Nancy 2004:4
Thalheimer, Richard
  Brief Entry 1988:3
Thomas, Dave 1986:2 1993:2
  Obituary 2003:1
Thomas, Michel 1987:4
Tilberis, Elizabeth 1994:3
Tillman, Robert L. 2004:1
Tisch, Laurence A. 1988:2
Tompkins, Susie
  Brief Entry 1987:2
Toyoda, Eiji 1985:2
Trask, Amy 2003:3
Traub, Marvin
  Brief Entry 1987:3
Treybig, James G. 1988:3
Trotman, Alex 1995:4
Trotter, Charlie 2000:4
Troutt, Kenny A. 1998:1
Trump, Donald 1989:2
Trump, Ivana 1995:2
Turlington, Christy 2001:4
Turner, Ted 1989:1
Tyler, Richard 1995:3
Tyson, Don 1995:3
Unz, Ron 1999:1
Upshaw, Gene 1988:1
Vagelos, P. Roy 1989:4
Veeck, Bill
  Obituary 1986:1
Versace, Donatella 1999:1

Versace, Gianni
  Brief Entry 1988:1
  Obituary 1998:2
Vinton, Will
  Brief Entry 1988:1
Vischer, Phil 2002:2
von Furstenberg, Diane 1994:2
Wachner, Linda 1988:3 1997:2
Waitt, Ted 1997:4
Waldron, Hicks B. 1987:3
Walgreen, Charles III
  Brief Entry 1987:4
Walker, Jay 2004:2
Walton, Sam 1986:2
  Obituary 1993:1
Wang, An 1986:1
  Obituary 1990:3
Ware, Lancelot
  Obituary 2001:1
Watkins, Sherron 2003:1
Weill, Sandy 1990:4
Weinstein, Bob and Harvey 2000:4
Weintraub, Jerry 1986:1
Welch, Jack 1993:3
Westwood, Vivienne 1998:3
Whitman, Meg 2000:3
Whittle, Christopher 1989:3
Williams, Edward Bennett
  Obituary 1988:4
Williams, Lynn 1986:4
Wilson, Jerry
  Brief Entry 1986:2
Wilson, Peter C.
  Obituary 1985:2
Wintour, Anna 1990:4
Wolf, Stephen M. 1989:3
Woodcock, Leonard
  Obituary 2001:4
Woodruff, Robert Winship
  Obituary 1985:1
Wrigley, William, Jr. 2002:2
Wynn, Stephen A. 1994:3
Yamamoto, Kenichi 1989:1
Yetnikoff, Walter 1988:1
Zagat, Tim and Nina 2004:3
Zamboni, Frank J.
  Brief Entry 1986:4
Zanker, Bill
  Brief Entry 1987:3
Zetcher, Arnold B. 2002:1
Zetsche, Dieter 2002:3
Ziff, William B., Jr. 1986:4
Zuckerman, Mortimer 1986:3

DANCE
Abdul, Paula 1990:3
Acosta, Carlos 1997:4
Ailey, Alvin 1989:2
  Obituary 1990:2
Allen, Debbie 1998:2
Astaire, Fred
  Obituary 1987:4
Baryshnikov, Mikhail
  Nikolaevich 1997:3
Bennett, Michael
  Obituary 1988:1
Bissell, Patrick
  Obituary 1988:2
Bocca, Julio 1995:3
Campbell, Neve 1998:2
Cunningham, Merce 1998:1

Davis, Sammy, Jr.
  Obituary **1990**:4
Dean, Laura **1989**:4
de Mille, Agnes
  Obituary **1994**:2
de Valois, Dame Ninette
  Obituary **2002**:1
Dudley, Jane
  Obituary **2002**:4
Englund, Richard
  Obituary **1991**:3
Fagan, Garth **2000**:1
Farrell, Suzanne **1996**:3
Feld, Eliot **1996**:1
Fenley, Molissa **1988**:3
Ferri, Alessandra **1987**:2
Flatley, Michael **1997**:3
Fonteyn, Margot
  Obituary **1991**:3
Forsythe, William **1993**:2
Fosse, Bob
  Obituary **1988**:1
Garr, Teri **1988**:4
Glover, Savion **1997**:1
Godunov, Alexander
  Obituary **1995**:4
Graham, Martha
  Obituary **1991**:4
Gregory, Cynthia **1990**:2
Guillem, Sylvie **1988**:2
Herrera, Paloma **1996**:2
Hewitt, Jennifer Love **1999**:2
Hines, Gregory **1992**:4
Jackson, Janet **1990**:4
Jamison, Judith **1990**:3
Joffrey, Robert
  Obituary **1988**:3
Jones, Bill T. **1991**:4
Kaye, Nora
  Obituary **1987**:4
Keeler, Ruby
  Obituary **1993**:4
Kelly, Gene
  Obituary **1996**:3
Kistler, Darci **1993**:1
Lander, Toni
  Obituary **1985**:4
MacMillan, Kenneth
  Obituary **1993**:2
Madonna **1985**:2
Marshall, Susan **2000**:4
Miller, Bebe **2000**:2
Mitchell, Arthur **1995**:1
Morris, Mark **1991**:1
Murray, Arthur
  Obituary **1991**:3
North, Alex **1986**:3
Nureyev, Rudolf
  Obituary **1993**:2
Parker, Sarah Jessica **1999**:2
Parsons, David **1993**:4
Perez, Rosie **1994**:2
Prowse, Juliet
  Obituary **1997**:1
Rauschenberg, Robert **1991**:2
Renvall, Johan
  Brief Entry **1987**:4
Robbins, Jerome
  Obituary **1999**:1
Rogers, Ginger
  Obituary **1995**:4
Stroman, Susan **2000**:4

Takei, Kei **1990**:2
Taylor, Paul **1992**:3
Tharp, Twyla **1992**:4
Tudor, Antony
  Obituary **1987**:4
Tune, Tommy **1994**:2
Varone, Doug **2001**:2
Verdi-Fletcher, Mary **1998**:2
Verdon, Gwen
  Obituary **2001**:2
Whelan, Wendy **1999**:3

EDUCATION

Abramson, Lyn **1986**:3
Alexander, Lamar **1991**:2
Bakker, Robert T. **1991**:3
Bayley, Corrine
  Brief Entry **1986**:4
Billington, James **1990**:3
Bollinger, Lee C. **2003**:2
Botstein, Leon **1985**:3
Bush, Millie **1992**:1
Campbell, Bebe Moore **1996**:2
Casper, Gerhard **1993**:1
Cavazos, Lauro F. **1989**:2
Cheek, James Edward
  Brief Entry **1987**:1
Cheney, Lynne V. **1990**:4
Clements, George **1985**:1
Cole, Johnetta B. **1994**:3
Coles, Robert **1995**:1
Commager, Henry Steele
  Obituary **1998**:3
Curran, Charles E. **1989**:2
Davis, Angela **1998**:3
Delany, Sarah
  Obituary **1999**:3
Deming, W. Edwards **1992**:2
  Obituary **1994**:2
Dershowitz, Alan **1992**:1
Dove, Rita **1994**:3
Drucker, Peter F. **1992**:3
Edelman, Marian Wright **1990**:4
Edwards, Harry **1989**:4
Etzioni, Amitai **1994**:3
Feldman, Sandra **1987**:3
Fernandez, Joseph **1991**:3
Folkman, Judah **1999**:1
Fox, Matthew **1992**:2
Fulbright, J. William
  Obituary **1995**:3
Futrell, Mary Hatwood **1986**:1
Futter, Ellen V. **1995**:1
Ghali, Boutros Boutros **1992**:3
Giamatti, A. Bartlett **1988**:4
  Obituary **1990**:1
Goldhaber, Fred
  Brief Entry **1986**:3
Gray, Hanna **1992**:4
Green, Richard R. **1988**:3
Gregorian, Vartan **1990**:3
Gund, Agnes **1993**:2
Hackney, Sheldon **1995**:1
Hair, Jay D. **1994**:3
Harker, Patrick T. **2001**:2
Hayakawa, Samuel Ichiye
  Obituary **1992**:3
Healy, Bernadine **1993**:1
Healy, Timothy S. **1990**:2
Heaney, Seamus **1996**:2
Heller, Walter
  Obituary **1987**:4

Hennessy, John L. **2002**:2
Hill, Anita **1994**:1
Hillegass, Clifton Keith **1989**:4
Horwich, Frances
  Obituary **2002**:3
Hunter, Madeline **1991**:2
Janzen, Daniel H. **1988**:4
Jordan, King **1990**:1
Justiz, Manuel J. **1986**:4
Kemp, Jan **1987**:2
King, Mary-Claire **1998**:3
Kopp, Wendy **1993**:3
Kozol, Jonathan **1992**:1
Lagasse, Emeril **1998**:3
Lamb, Wally **1999**:1
Lang, Eugene M. **1990**:3
Langston, J. William
  Brief Entry **1986**:2
Lawrence, Ruth
  Brief Entry **1986**:3
Laybourne, Geraldine **1997**:1
Leach, Penelope **1992**:4
Lerner, Michael **1994**:2
Levine, Arnold **2002**:3
MacKinnon, Catharine **1993**:2
Malloy, Edward Monk **1989**:4
Marier, Rebecca **1995**:4
McAuliffe, Christa
  Obituary **1985**:4
McMillan, Terry **1993**:2
Morrison, Toni **1998**:1
Mumford, Lewis
  Obituary **1990**:2
Nemerov, Howard
  Obituary **1992**:1
Nye, Bill **1997**:2
Owens, Delia and Mark **1993**:3
Pagels, Elaine **1997**:1
Paglia, Camille **1992**:3
Paige, Rod **2003**:2
Parizeau, Jacques **1995**:1
Peter, Valentine J. **1988**:2
Riley, Richard W. **1996**:3
Rodin, Judith **1994**:4
Rosendahl, Bruce R.
  Brief Entry **1986**:4
Rowland, Pleasant **1992**:3
Scheck, Barry **2000**:4
Schuman, Patricia Glass **1993**:2
Shalala, Donna **1992**:3
Sherman, Russell **1987**:4
Silber, John **1990**:1
Simmons, Adele Smith **1988**:4
Simmons, Ruth **1995**:2
Smoot, George F. **1993**:3
Sowell, Thomas **1998**:3
Spock, Benjamin **1995**:2
  Obituary **1998**:3
Steele, Shelby **1991**:2
Swanson, Mary Catherine **2002**:2
Tannen, Deborah **1995**:1
Thiebaud, Wayne **1991**:1
Thomas, Michel **1987**:4
Tilghman, Shirley M. **2002**:1
Tribe, Laurence H. **1988**:1
Tyson, Laura D'Andrea **1994**:1
Unz, Ron **1999**:1
Van Duyn, Mona **1993**:2
Vickrey, William S.
  Obituary **1997**:2
Warren, Robert Penn
  Obituary **1990**:1

West, Cornel **1994**:2
Wexler, Nancy S. **1992**:3
Wiesel, Elie **1998**:1
Wigand, Jeffrey **2000**:4
Wiles, Andrew **1994**:1
Wilson, Edward O. **1994**:4
Wilson, William Julius **1997**:1
Wu, Harry **1996**:1
Zanker, Bill
  Brief Entry **1987**:3
Zigler, Edward **1994**:1

FILM
Abbott, George
  Obituary **1995**:3
Adjani, Isabelle **1991**:1
Affleck, Ben **1999**:1
Aiello, Danny **1990**:4
Alda, Robert
  Obituary **1986**:3
Alexander, Jane **1994**:2
Alexander, Jason **1993**:3
Allen, Debbie **1998**:2
Allen, Joan **1998**:1
Allen, Woody **1994**:1
Alley, Kirstie **1990**:3
Almodovar, Pedro **2000**:3
Altman, Robert **1993**:2
Ameche, Don
  Obituary **1994**:2
Anderson, Judith
  Obituary **1992**:3
Andrews, Julie **1996**:1
Aniston, Jennifer **2000**:3
Applegate, Christina **2000**:4
Arad, Avi **2003**:2
Arden, Eve
  Obituary **1991**:2
Arkoff, Samuel Z.
  Obituary **2002**:4
Arlen, Harold
  Obituary **1986**:3
Arnaz, Desi
  Obituary **1987**:1
Arnold, Tom **1993**:2
Arquette, Patricia **2001**:3
Arquette, Rosanna **1985**:2
Arthur, Jean
  Obituary **1992**:1
Ashcroft, Peggy
  Obituary **1992**:1
Astaire, Fred
  Obituary **1987**:4
Astor, Mary
  Obituary **1988**:1
Atkinson, Rowan **2004**:3
Autry, Gene
  Obituary **1999**:1
Aykroyd, Dan **1989**:3 **1997**:3
Bacall, Lauren **1997**:3
Backus, Jim
  Obituary **1990**:1
Bacon, Kevin **1995**:3
Baddeley, Hermione
  Obituary **1986**:4
Bailey, Pearl
  Obituary **1991**:1
Bakula, Scott **2003**:1
Baldwin, Alec **2002**:2
Bale, Christian **2001**:3
Ball, Lucille
  Obituary **1989**:3

Banderas, Antonio **1996**:2
Banks, Tyra **1996**:3
Barker, Clive **2003**:3
Barkin, Ellen **1987**:3
Barr, Roseanne **1989**:1
Barrymore, Drew **1995**:3
Baryshnikov, Mikhail
  Nikolaevich **1997**:3
Basinger, Kim **1987**:2
Bassett, Angela **1994**:4
Bateman, Justine **1988**:4
Bates, Kathy **1991**:4
Baxter, Anne
  Obituary **1986**:1
Beatty, Warren **2000**:1
Belushi, Jim **1986**:2
Benigni, Roberto **1999**:2
Bening, Annette **1992**:1
Bennett, Joan
  Obituary **1991**:2
Bergen, Candice **1990**:1
Bergman, Ingmar **1999**:4
Bernardi, Herschel
  Obituary **1986**:4
Bernhard, Sandra **1989**:4
Bernsen, Corbin **1990**:2
Berry, Halle **1996**:2
Bialik, Mayim **1993**:3
Bigelow, Kathryn **1990**:4
Binoche, Juliette **2001**:3
Birch, Thora **2002**:4
Black, Jack **2002**:3
Blades, Ruben **1998**:2
Blanc, Mel
  Obituary **1989**:4
Blanchett, Cate **1999**:3
Bloom, Orlando **2004**:2
Bogosian, Eric **1990**:4
Bolger, Ray
  Obituary **1987**:2
Bonet, Lisa **1989**:2
Bonham Carter, Helena **1998**:4
Booth, Shirley
  Obituary **1993**:2
Bowie, David **1998**:2
Boyle, Lara Flynn **2003**:4
Boyle, Peter **2002**:3
Branagh, Kenneth **1992**:2
Brandauer, Klaus Maria **1987**:3
Bridges, Lloyd
  Obituary **1998**:3
Bronson, Charles
  Obituary **2004**:4
Brooks, Albert **1991**:4
Brooks, Mel **2003**:1
Brosnan, Pierce **2000**:3
Brown, James **1991**:4
Brown, Jim **1993**:2
Brynner, Yul
  Obituary **1985**:4
Buckley, Betty **1996**:2
Bullock, Sandra **1995**:4
Burnett, Carol **2000**:3
Burns, Edward **1997**:1
Burns, George
  Obituary **1996**:3
Burns, Ken **1995**:2
Burr, Raymond
  Obituary **1994**:1
Burstyn, Ellen **2001**:4
Burton, Tim **1993**:1

Burum, Stephen H.
  Brief Entry **1987**:2
Buscemi, Steve **1997**:4
Byrne, Gabriel **1997**:4
Caan, James **2004**:4
Caesar, Adolph
  Obituary **1986**:3
Cage, Nicolas **1991**:1
Cagney, James
  Obituary **1986**:2
Caine, Michael **2000**:4
Calhoun, Rory
  Obituary **1999**:4
Campbell, Naomi **2000**:2
Campbell, Neve **1998**:2
Campion, Jane **1991**:4
Candy, John **1988**:2
  Obituary **1994**:3
Capra, Frank
  Obituary **1992**:2
Carey, Drew **1997**:4
Carlin, George **1996**:3
Carradine, John
  Obituary **1989**:2
Carrey, Jim **1995**:1
Carson, Lisa Nicole **1999**:3
Caruso, David **1994**:3
Carvey, Dana **1994**:1
Cassavetes, John
  Obituary **1989**:2
Castle-Hughes, Keisha **2004**:4
Cattrall, Kim **2003**:3
Caulfield, Joan
  Obituary **1992**:1
Cavanagh, Tom **2003**:1
Chan, Jackie **1996**:1
Channing, Stockard **1991**:3
Chase, Chevy **1990**:1
Cheadle, Don **2002**:1
Chen, Joan **2000**:2
Cher **1993**:1
Chiklis, Michael **2003**:3
Chow Yun-fat **1999**:4
Christensen, Hayden **2003**:3
Clay, Andrew Dice **1991**:1
Cleese, John **1989**:2
Close, Glenn **1988**:3
Coburn, James
  Obituary **2004**:1
Coco, James
  Obituary **1987**:2
Coen, Joel and Ethan **1992**:1
Colbert, Claudette
  Obituary **1997**:1
Coleman, Dabney **1988**:3
Connelly, Jennifer **2002**:4
Connery, Sean **1990**:4
Connick, Harry, Jr. **1991**:1
Cooper, Chris **2004**:1
Coppola, Carmine
  Obituary **1991**:4
Coppola, Francis Ford **1989**:4
Coppola, Sofia **2004**:3
Corbett, John **2004**:1
Cosby, Bill **1999**:2
Costner, Kevin **1989**:4
Cox, Courteney **1996**:2
Craven, Wes **1997**:3
Crawford, Broderick
  Obituary **1986**:3
Crenna, Richard
  Obituary **2004**:1

Ryan, Meg **1994**:1
Ryder, Winona **1991**:2
Salonga, Lea **2003**:3
Sandler, Adam **1999**:2
Sarandon, Susan **1995**:3
Savage, Fred **1990**:1
Savalas, Telly
Obituary **1994**:3
Schlesinger, John
Obituary **2004**:3
Schneider, Rob **1997**:4
Schroeder, Barbet **1996**:1
Schumacher, Joel **2004**:3
Schwarzenegger, Arnold **1991**:1
Schwimmer, David **1996**:2
Scorsese, Martin **1989**:1
Scott, George C.
Obituary **2000**:2
Scott, Randolph
Obituary **1987**:2
Scott, Ridley **2001**:1
Seidelman, Susan **1985**:4
Sevigny, Chloe **2001**:4
Seymour, Jane **1994**:4
Shaffer, Paul **1987**:1
Sharkey, Ray
Obituary **1994**:1
Shawn, Dick
Obituary **1987**:3
Sheedy, Ally **1989**:1
Sheen, Martin **2002**:1
Shepard, Sam **1996**:4
Shields, Brooke **1996**:3
Shore, Dinah
Obituary **1994**:3
Short, Martin **1986**:1
Shue, Andrew **1994**:4
Shyamalan, M. Night **2003**:2
Silverman, Jonathan **1997**:2
Silvers, Phil
Obituary **1985**:4
Silverstone, Alicia **1997**:4
Sinatra, Frank
Obituary **1998**:4
Singleton, John **1994**:3
Sinise, Gary **1996**:1
Siskel, Gene
Obituary **1999**:3
Slater, Christian **1994**:1
Smirnoff, Yakov **1987**:2
Smith, Kevin **2000**:4
Smith, Will **1997**:2
Smits, Jimmy **1990**:1
Snipes, Wesley **1993**:1
Sobieski, Leelee **2002**:3
Soderbergh, Steven **2001**:4
Sondheim, Stephen **1994**:4
Sorkin, Aaron **2003**:2
Sorvino, Mira **1996**:3
Sothern, Ann
Obituary **2002**:1
Southern, Terry
Obituary **1996**:2
Spacek, Sissy **2003**:1
Spacey, Kevin **1996**:4
Spade, David **1999**:2
Spader, James **1991**:2
Spheeris, Penelope **1989**:2
Spielberg, Steven **1993**:4 **1997**:4
Stack, Robert
Obituary **2004**:2
Staller, Ilona **1988**:3

Stallone, Sylvester **1994**:2
Steel, Dawn **1990**:1
Obituary **1998**:2
Steiger, Rod
Obituary **2003**:4
Stevenson, McLean
Obituary **1996**:3
Stewart, Jimmy
Obituary **1997**:4
Stewart, Patrick **1996**:1
Stiles, Julia **2002**:3
Stiller, Ben **1999**:1
Sting **1991**:4
Stone, Oliver **1990**:4
Stone, Sharon **1993**:4
Stoppard, Tom **1995**:4
Streep, Meryl **1990**:2
Streisand, Barbra **1992**:2
Strummer, Joe
Obituary **2004**:1
Studi, Wes **1994**:3
Styne, Jule
Obituary **1995**:1
Susskind, David
Obituary **1987**:2
Sutherland, Kiefer **2002**:4
Swank, Hilary **2000**:3
Tanaka, Tomoyuki
Obituary **1997**:3
Tandy, Jessica **1990**:4
Obituary **1995**:1
Tarantino, Quentin **1995**:1
Tautou, Audrey **2004**:2
Taylor, Elizabeth **1993**:3
Taylor, Lili **2000**:2
Theron, Charlize **2001**:4
Thiebaud, Wayne **1991**:1
Thompson, Emma **1993**:2
Thompson, Fred **1998**:2
Thornton, Billy Bob **1997**:4
Thurman, Uma **1994**:2
Tilly, Jennifer **1997**:2
Tomei, Marisa **1995**:2
Travolta, John **1995**:2
Tucci, Stanley **2003**:2
Tucker, Chris **1999**:1
Tucker, Forrest
Obituary **1987**:1
Turner, Janine **1993**:2
Turner, Kathleen **1985**:3
Turner, Lana
Obituary **1996**:1
Turturro, John **2002**:2
Tyler, Liv **1997**:2
Ullman, Tracey **1988**:3
Union, Gabrielle **2004**:2
Urich, Robert **1988**:1
Obituary **2003**:3
Vanilla Ice **1991**:3
Van Sant, Gus **1992**:2
Vardalos, Nia **2003**:4
Varney, Jim
Brief Entry **1985**:4
Obituary **2000**:3
Vaughn, Vince **1999**:2
Ventura, Jesse **1999**:2
Vidal, Gore **1996**:2
Vidov, Oleg **1987**:4
Villechaize, Herve
Obituary **1994**:1
Vincent, Fay **1990**:2
Voight, Jon **2002**:3

Walker, Nancy
Obituary **1992**:3
Wallis, Hal
Obituary **1987**:1
Warhol, Andy
Obituary **1987**:2
Washington, Denzel **1993**:2
Wasserman, Lew
Obituary **2003**:3
Waters, John **1988**:3
Watson, Emily **2001**:1
Wayans, Damon **1998**:4
Wayans, Keenen Ivory **1991**:1
Wayne, David
Obituary **1995**:3
Weaver, Sigourney **1988**:3
Wegman, William **1991**:1
Weinstein, Bob and Harvey **2000**:4
Weintraub, Jerry **1986**:1
Whitaker, Forest **1996**:2
Wiest, Dianne **1995**:2
Wilder, Billy
Obituary **2003**:2
Wilkinson, Tom **2003**:2
Williams, Robin **1988**:4
Williams, Treat **2004**:3
Williams, Vanessa L. **1999**:2
Willis, Bruce **1986**:4
Wilson, Owen **2002**:3
Winfrey, Oprah **1986**:4 **1997**:3
Winger, Debra **1994**:3
Winslet, Kate **2002**:4
Witherspoon, Reese **2002**:1
Wolfman Jack
Obituary **1996**:1
Wong, B.D. **1998**:1
Woo, John **1994**:2
Wood, Elijah **2002**:4
Woods, James **1988**:3
Wyle, Noah **1997**:3
Wynn, Keenan
Obituary **1987**:1
Yeoh, Michelle **2003**:2
Young, Loretta
Obituary **2001**:1
Young, Robert
Obituary **1999**:1
Zanuck, Lili Fini **1994**:2
Zeffirelli, Franco **1991**:3
Zellweger, Renee **2001**:1
Zemeckis, Robert **2002**:1
Zeta-Jones, Catherine **1999**:4
Zucker, Jerry **2002**:2

LAW
Abzug, Bella **1998**:2
Achtenberg, Roberta **1993**:4
Allred, Gloria **1985**:2
Angelos, Peter **1995**:4
Archer, Dennis **1994**:4
Astorga, Nora **1988**:2
Babbitt, Bruce **1994**:1
Bailey, F. Lee **1995**:4
Baker, James A. III **1991**:2
Bikoff, James L.
Brief Entry **1986**:2
Blackmun, Harry A.
Obituary **1999**:3
Boies, David **2002**:1
Bradley, Tom
Obituary **1999**:1

Brennan, William
Obituary **1997**:4
Breyer, Stephen
Gerald **1994**:4 **1997**:2
Brown, Willie **1996**:4
Brown, Willie L. **1985**:2
Burger, Warren E.
Obituary **1995**:4
Burnison, Chantal Simone **1988**:3
Campbell, Kim **1993**:4
Cantrell, Ed
Brief Entry **1985**:3
Casey, William
Obituary **1987**:3
Casper, Gerhard **1993**:1
Clark, Marcia **1995**:1
Clinton, Bill **1992**:1
Clinton, Hillary Rodham **1993**:2
Cochran, Johnnie **1996**:1
Colby, William E.
Obituary **1996**:4
Cuomo, Mario **1992**:2
Darden, Christopher **1996**:4
Dees, Morris **1992**:1
del Ponte, Carla **2001**:1
Dershowitz, Alan **1992**:1
Deutch, John **1996**:4
Dole, Elizabeth Hanford **1990**:1
Dukakis, Michael **1988**:3
Eagleson, Alan **1987**:4
Ehrlichman, John
Obituary **1999**:3
Ervin, Sam
Obituary **1985**:2
Estrich, Susan **1989**:1
Fairstein, Linda **1991**:1
Fehr, Donald **1987**:2
Fieger, Geoffrey **2001**:3
Florio, James J. **1991**:2
Foster, Vincent
Obituary **1994**:1
France, Johnny
Brief Entry **1987**:1
Freeh, Louis J. **1994**:2
Fulbright, J. William
Obituary **1995**:3
Furman, Rosemary
Brief Entry **1986**:4
Garrison, Jim
Obituary **1993**:2
Ginsburg, Ruth Bader **1993**:4
Giuliani, Rudolph **1994**:2
Glasser, Ira **1989**:1
Gore, Albert, Sr.
Obituary **1999**:2
Grisham, John **1994**:4
Harvard, Beverly **1995**:2
Hayes, Robert M. **1986**:3
Hill, Anita **1994**:1
Hills, Carla **1990**:3
Hirschhorn, Joel
Brief Entry **1986**:1
Hoffa, Jim, Jr. **1999**:2
Hyatt, Joel **1985**:3
Ireland, Patricia **1992**:2
Ito, Lance **1995**:3
Janklow, Morton **1989**:3
Kennedy, John F., Jr. **1990**:1
Obituary **1999**:4
Kennedy, Weldon **1997**:3
Kunstler, William **1992**:3

Kunstler, William
Obituary **1996**:1
Kurzban, Ira **1987**:2
Lee, Henry C. **1997**:1
Lee, Martin **1998**:2
Lewis, Loida Nicolas **1998**:3
Lewis, Reginald F. **1988**:4
Obituary **1993**:3
Lightner, Candy **1985**:1
Liman, Arthur **1989**:4
Lipsig, Harry H. **1985**:1
Lipton, Martin **1987**:3
MacKinnon, Catharine **1993**:2
Marshall, Thurgood
Obituary **1993**:3
McCloskey, James **1993**:1
Mitchell, George J. **1989**:3
Mitchell, John
Obituary **1989**:2
Mitchelson, Marvin **1989**:2
Morrison, Trudi
Brief Entry **1986**:2
Nader, Ralph **1989**:4
Napolitano, Janet **1997**:1
Neal, James Foster **1986**:2
O'Connor, Sandra Day **1991**:1
O'Leary, Hazel **1993**:4
O'Steen, Van
Brief Entry **1986**:3
Panetta, Leon **1995**:1
Pirro, Jeanine **1998**:2
Powell, Lewis F.
Obituary **1999**:1
Puccio, Thomas P. **1986**:4
Quayle, Dan **1989**:2
Raines, Franklin **1997**:4
Ramaphosa, Cyril **1988**:2
Ramo, Roberta Cooper **1996**:1
Rehnquist, William H. **2001**:2
Reno, Janet **1993**:3
Rothwax, Harold **1996**:3
Scalia, Antonin **1988**:2
Scheck, Barry **2000**:4
Schily, Otto
Brief Entry **1987**:4
Sheehan, Daniel P. **1989**:1
Sheindlin, Judith **1999**:1
Sirica, John
Obituary **1993**:2
Skinner, Sam **1992**:3
Slater, Rodney E. **1997**:4
Slotnick, Barry
Brief Entry **1987**:4
Souter, David **1991**:3
Starr, Kenneth **1998**:3
Steinberg, Leigh **1987**:3
Stern, David **1991**:4
Stewart, Potter
Obituary **1986**:1
Strauss, Robert **1991**:4
Tagliabue, Paul **1990**:2
Thomas, Clarence **1992**:2
Thompson, Fred **1998**:2
Tribe, Laurence H. **1988**:1
Vincent, Fay **1990**:2
Violet, Arlene **1985**:3
Wapner, Joseph A. **1987**:1
Watson, Elizabeth **1991**:2
White, Byron
Obituary **2003**:3
Williams, Edward Bennett
Obituary **1988**:4

Williams, Willie L. **1993**:1
Wilson, Bertha
Brief Entry **1986**:1

MUSIC

Aaliyah **2001**:3
Abdul, Paula **1990**:3
Ackerman, Will **1987**:4
Acuff, Roy
Obituary **1993**:2
Aguilera, Christina **2000**:4
Albert, Stephen **1986**:1
Allen, Peter
Obituary **1993**:1
Amos, Tori **1995**:1
Anderson, Marion
Obituary **1993**:4
Andrews, Julie **1996**:1
Andrews, Maxene
Obituary **1996**:2
Anthony, Marc **2000**:3
Arlen, Harold
Obituary **1986**:3
Arnaz, Desi
Obituary **1987**:1
Arrau, Claudio
Obituary **1992**:1
Arrested Development **1994**:2
Ashanti **2004**:1
Astaire, Fred
Obituary **1987**:4
Autry, Gene
Obituary **1999**:1
Backstreet Boys **2001**:3
Badu, Erykah **2000**:4
Baez, Joan **1998**:3
Bailey, Pearl
Obituary **1991**:1
Baker, Anita **1987**:4
Barenboim, Daniel **2001**:1
Bartoli, Cecilia **1994**:1
Basie, Count
Obituary **1985**:1
Battle, Kathleen **1998**:1
Beastie Boys, The **1999**:1
Becaud, Gilbert
Obituary **2003**:1
Beck **2000**:2
Bee Gees, The **1997**:4
Benatar, Pat **1986**:1
Bennett, Tony **1994**:4
Berio, Luciano
Obituary **2004**:2
Berlin, Irving
Obituary **1990**:1
Bernhard, Sandra **1989**:4
Bernstein, Leonard
Obituary **1991**:1
Berry, Chuck **2001**:2
Bjork **1996**:1
Blades, Ruben **1998**:2
Blakey, Art
Obituary **1991**:1
Blige, Mary J. **1995**:3
Bolton, Michael **1993**:2
Bon Jovi, Jon **1987**:4
Bono **1988**:4
Bono, Sonny **1992**:2
Obituary **1998**:2
Borge, Victor
Obituary **2001**:3
Botstein, Leon **1985**:3

Bowie, David **1998**:2
Bowles, Paul
  Obituary **2000**:3
Boxcar Willie
  Obituary **1999**:4
Boyz II Men **1995**:1
Brandy **1996**:4
Branson, Richard **1987**:1
Braxton, Toni **1994**:3
Brooks, Garth **1992**:1
Brown, James **1991**:4
Brown, Les
  Obituary **2001**:3
Buckley, Jeff
  Obituary **1997**:4
Buffett, Jimmy **1999**:3
Bush, Kate **1994**:3
Butterfield, Paul
  Obituary **1987**:3
Cage, John
  Obituary **1993**:1
Calloway, Cab
  Obituary **1995**:2
Cardigans, The **1997**:4
Carey, Mariah **1991**:3
Carlisle, Belinda **1989**:3
Carpenter, Mary-Chapin **1994**:1
Carreras, Jose **1995**:2
Carter, Benny
  Obituary **2004**:3
Carter, Nell
  Obituary **2004**:2
Carter, Ron **1987**:3
Cash, Johnny **1995**:3
Cash, June Carter
  Obituary **2004**:2
Cerovsek, Corey
  Brief Entry **1987**:4
Chapman, Tracy **1989**:2
Cheatham, Adolphus Doc
  Obituary **1997**:4
Cher **1993**:1
Clapton, Eric **1993**:3
Clarke, Stanley **1985**:4
Clarkson, Kelly **2003**:3
Cleveland, James
  Obituary **1991**:3
Cliburn, Van **1995**:1
Clooney, Rosemary
  Obituary **2003**:4
Cobain, Kurt
  Obituary **1994**:3
Coldplay **2004**:4
Cole, Natalie **1992**:4
Collins, Albert
  Obituary **1994**:2
Combs, Sean Puffy **1998**:4
Como, Perry
  Obituary **2002**:2
Connick, Harry, Jr. **1991**:1
Coolio **1996**:4
Copland, Aaron
  Obituary **1991**:2
Coppola, Carmine
  Obituary **1991**:4
Corea, Chick **1986**:3
Costello, Elvis **1994**:4
Cowell, Simon **2003**:4
Crawford, Michael **1994**:2
Cray, Robert **1988**:2
Crosby, David **2000**:4

Crothers, Scatman
  Obituary **1987**:1
Crow, Sheryl **1995**:2
Crowe, Russell **2000**:4
Cruz, Celia
  Obituary **2004**:3
Cugat, Xavier
  Obituary **1991**:2
Cyrus, Billy Ray **1993**:1
D'Arby, Terence Trent **1988**:4
Davis, Miles
  Obituary **1992**:2
Davis, Sammy, Jr.
  Obituary **1990**:4
Day, Dennis
  Obituary **1988**:4
Dean, Laura **1989**:4
Denver, John
  Obituary **1998**:1
de Passe, Suzanne **1990**:4
Destiny's Child **2001**:3
Dido **2004**:4
DiFranco, Ani **1997**:1
Di Meola, Al **1986**:4
Dimitrova, Ghena **1987**:1
Dion, Celine **1995**:3
Dixie Chicks **2001**:2
Dr. Demento **1986**:1
Dr. Dre **1994**:3
Dolenz, Micky **1986**:4
Domingo, Placido **1993**:2
Dorati, Antal
  Obituary **1989**:2
Dorsey, Thomas A.
  Obituary **1993**:3
Duff, Hilary **2004**:4
Duncan, Todd
  Obituary **1998**:3
Dupri, Jermaine **1999**:1
Dylan, Bob **1998**:1
Eazy-E
  Obituary **1995**:3
Eckstine, Billy
  Obituary **1993**:4
Edmonds, Kenneth Babyface **1995**:3
Eldridge, Roy
  Obituary **1989**:3
Elliott, Missy **2003**:4
Eminem **2001**:2
Eno, Brian **1986**:2
Entwistle, John
  Obituary **2003**:3
En Vogue **1994**:1
Enya **1992**:3
Ertegun, Ahmet **1986**:3
Esquivel, Juan **1996**:2
Estefan, Gloria **1991**:4
Etheridge, Melissa **1995**:4
Eve **2004**:3
Everything But The Girl **1996**:4
Falco
  Brief Entry **1987**:2
Farrell, Perry **1992**:2
Fender, Leo
  Obituary **1992**:1
Fitzgerald, Ella
  Obituary **1996**:4
Fleming, Renee **2001**:4
Ford, Tennessee Ernie
  Obituary **1992**:2
Foster, David **1988**:2
Franklin, Aretha **1998**:3

Franklin, Melvin
  Obituary **1995**:3
Garbage **2002**:3
Garcia, Jerry **1988**:3
  Obituary **1996**:1
Geffen, David **1985**:3 **1997**:3
Geldof, Bob **1985**:3
Getz, Stan
  Obituary **1991**:4
Gibb, Andy
  Obituary **1988**:3
Gifford, Kathie Lee **1992**:2
Gift, Roland **1990**:2
Gill, Vince **1995**:2
Gillespie, Dizzy
  Obituary **1993**:2
Glass, Philip **1991**:4
Goodman, Benny
  Obituary **1986**:3
Goody, Sam
  Obituary **1992**:1
Gordon, Dexter **1987**:1 **1990**:4
Gore, Tipper **1985**:4
Graham, Bill **1986**:4
  Obituary **1992**:2
Grant, Amy **1985**:4
Grappelli, Stephane
  Obituary **1998**:1
Gray, David **2001**:4
Gray, Macy **2002**:1
Grebenshikov, Boris **1990**:1
Green Day **1995**:4
Grusin, Dave
  Brief Entry **1987**:2
Guccione, Bob, Jr. **1991**:4
Guest, Christopher **2004**:2
Hammer, Jan **1987**:3
Hammer, M. C. **1991**:2
Hammond, John
  Obituary **1988**:2
Hampton, Lionel
  Obituary **2003**:4
Hancock, Herbie **1985**:1
Harris, Emmylou **1991**:3
Harrison, George
  Obituary **2003**:1
Harry, Deborah **1990**:1
Hart, Mary
  Brief Entry **1988**:1
Hart, Mickey **1991**:2
Harvey, Polly Jean **1995**:4
Hawkins, Screamin' Jay
  Obituary **2000**:3
Hayes, Isaac **1998**:4
Heard, J.C.
  Obituary **1989**:1
Heid, Bill
  Brief Entry **1987**:2
Heifetz, Jascha
  Obituary **1988**:2
Helfgott, David **1997**:2
Helms, Bobby
  Obituary **1997**:4
Hewitt, Jennifer Love **1999**:2
Hill, Faith **2000**:1
Hill, Lauryn **1999**:3
Hinton, Milt
  Obituary **2001**:3
Hirt, Al
  Obituary **1999**:4
Hoffs, Susanna **1988**:2

Raffi **1988**:1
Raitt, Bonnie **1990**:2
Ramone, Joey
  Obituary **2002**:2
Rampal, Jean-Pierre **1989**:2
Rashad, Phylicia **1987**:3
Raskin, Jef **1997**:4
Rattle, Simon **1989**:4
Red Hot Chili Peppers **1993**:1
Redman, Joshua **1999**:2
Reed, Dean
  Obituary **1986**:3
Reese, Della **1999**:2
Reznor, Trent **2000**:2
Rich, Buddy
  Obituary **1987**:3
Rich, Charlie
  Obituary **1996**:1
Richards, Keith **1993**:3
Riddle, Nelson
  Obituary **1985**:4
Rimes, LeeAnn **1997**:4
Robbins, Jerome
  Obituary **1999**:1
Robinson, Earl
  Obituary **1992**:1
Roedy, Bill **2003**:2
Rogers, Roy
  Obituary **1998**:4
Rose, Axl **1992**:1
Ruffin, David
  Obituary **1991**:4
RuPaul **1996**:1
Sade **1993**:2
Sainte-Marie, Buffy **2000**:1
Salerno-Sonnenberg, Nadja **1988**:4
Salonga, Lea **2003**:3
Santana, Carlos **2000**:2
Satriani, Joe **1989**:3
Scholz, Tom **1987**:2
Seal **1994**:4
Seger, Bob **1987**:1
Segovia, Andres
  Obituary **1987**:3
Selena
  Obituary **1995**:4
Serkin, Rudolf
  Obituary **1992**:1
Shaffer, Paul **1987**:1
Shakira **2002**:3
Shakur, Tupac
  Obituary **1997**:1
Sherman, Russell **1987**:4
Shocked, Michelle **1989**:4
Shore, Dinah
  Obituary **1994**:3
Simmons, Russell and Kimora Lee
  2003:2
Simon, Paul **1992**:2
Simone, Nina
  Obituary **2004**:2
Sinatra, Frank
  Obituary **1998**:4
Sinopoli, Giuseppe **1988**:1
Smith, Kate
  Obituary **1986**:3
Smith, Will **1997**:2
Snider, Dee **1986**:1
Snoop Doggy Dogg **1995**:2
Snow, Hank
  Obituary **2000**:3

Solti, Georg
  Obituary **1998**:1
Sondheim, Stephen **1994**:4
Spears, Britney **2000**:3
Spector, Phil **1989**:1
Springfield, Dusty
  Obituary **1999**:3
Staples, Roebuck Pops
  Obituary **2001**:3
Stern, Isaac
  Obituary **2002**:4
Sting **1991**:4
Strait, George **1998**:3
Streisand, Barbra **1992**:2
Strummer, Joe
  Obituary **2004**:1
Styne, Jule
  Obituary **1995**:1
Sun Ra
  Obituary **1994**:1
Suzuki, Sin'ichi
  Obituary **1998**:3
Tan Dun **2002**:1
Tesh, John **1996**:3
Thomas, Michael Tilson **1990**:3
Tiffany **1989**:1
TLC **1996**:1
Tone-Loc **1990**:3
Torme, Mel
  Obituary **1999**:4
Tosh, Peter
  Obituary **1988**:2
Travis, Randy **1988**:4
Tritt, Travis **1995**:1
Tune, Tommy **1994**:2
Turner, Tina **2000**:3
Twain, Shania **1996**:3
Twitty, Conway
  Obituary **1994**:1
Tyner, Rob
  Obituary **1992**:2
U **2002**:4
Uchida, Mitsuko **1989**:3
Ullman, Tracey **1988**:3
Upshaw, Dawn **1991**:2
Valente, Benita **1985**:3
Van Halen, Edward **1985**:2
Vanilla Ice **1991**:3
Vaughan, Sarah
  Obituary **1990**:3
Vaughan, Stevie Ray
  Obituary **1991**:1
Vega, Suzanne **1988**:1
Vollenweider, Andreas **1985**:2
von Karajan, Herbert
  Obituary **1989**:4
von Trapp, Maria
  Obituary **1987**:3
Walker, Junior
  Obituary **1996**:2
Washington, Grover, Jr. **1989**:1
Wasserman, Lew
  Obituary **2003**:3
Weintraub, Jerry **1986**:1
Wells, Mary
  Obituary **1993**:1
West, Dottie
  Obituary **1992**:2
White, Barry
  Obituary **2004**:3
Williams, Joe
  Obituary **1999**:4

Williams, Vanessa L. **1999**:2
Willis, Bruce **1986**:4
Wilson, Brian **1996**:1
Wilson, Carl
  Obituary **1998**:2
Wilson, Cassandra **1996**:3
Winans, CeCe **2000**:1
Winston, George **1987**:1
Winter, Paul **1990**:2
Womack, Lee Ann **2002**:1
Wynette, Tammy
  Obituary **1998**:3
Wynonna **1993**:3
Xenakis, Iannis
  Obituary **2001**:4
Yankovic, Weird Al **1985**:4
Yankovic, Frank
  Obituary **1999**:2
Yearwood, Trisha **1999**:1
Yoakam, Dwight **1992**:4
Young, Neil **1991**:2
Zappa, Frank
  Obituary **1994**:2
Zevon, Warren
  Obituary **2004**:4
Zinnemann, Fred
  Obituary **1997**:3
Zwilich, Ellen **1990**:1

**POLITICS AND
GOVERNMENT--FOREIGN**
Abacha, Sani **1996**:3
Abdullah II, King **2002**:4
Adams, Gerald **1994**:1
Ahern, Bertie **1999**:3
Akihito, Emperor of Japan **1990**:1
al-Abdullah, Rania **2001**:1
al-Assad, Bashar **2004**:2
Albright, Madeleine **1994**:3
Amin, Idi
  Obituary **2004**:4
Annan, Kofi **1999**:1
Aquino, Corazon **1986**:2
Arafat, Yasser **1989**:3 **1997**:3
Arens, Moshe **1985**:1
Arias Sanchez, Oscar **1989**:3
Aristide, Jean-Bertrand **1991**:3
Assad, Hafez
  Obituary **2000**:4
Assad, Hafez al- **1992**:1
Assad, Rifaat **1986**:3
Astorga, Nora **1988**:2
Babangida, Ibrahim
  Badamosi **1992**:4
Balaguer, Joaquin
  Obituary **2003**:4
Banda, Hastings **1994**:3
Bandaranaike, Sirimavo
  Obituary **2001**:2
Barak, Ehud **1999**:4
Barbie, Klaus
  Obituary **1992**:2
Begin, Menachem
  Obituary **1992**:3
Berger, Oscar **2004**:4
Berlusconi, Silvio **1994**:4
Berri, Nabih **1985**:2
Bhutto, Benazir **1989**:4
Blair, Tony **1996**:3 **1997**:4
Bolkiah, Sultan Muda
  Hassanal **1985**:4
Bouchard, Lucien **1999**:2

Pol Pot
  Obituary **1998**:4
Preval, Rene **1997**:2
Primakov, Yevgeny **1999**:3
Princess Margaret, Countess of
  Snowdon
  Obituary **2003**:2
Putin, Vladimir **2000**:3
Qaddhafi, Muammar **1998**:3
Queen Elizabeth the Queen Mother
  Obituary **2003**:2
Rabin, Leah
  Obituary **2001**:2
Rabin, Yitzhak **1993**:1
  Obituary **1996**:2
Rafsanjani, Ali Akbar
  Hashemi **1987**:3
Rahman, Sheik Omar Abdel- **1993**:3
Ram, Jagjivan
  Obituary **1986**:4
Ramos, Fidel **1995**:2
Rao, P. V. Narasimha **1993**:2
Ravalomanana, Marc **2003**:1
Reisman, Simon **1987**:4
Robelo, Alfonso **1988**:1
Robinson, Mary **1993**:1
Saleh, Ali Abdullah **2001**:3
Salinas, Carlos **1992**:1
Sanchez de Lozada, Gonzalo **2004**:3
Sarkis, Elias
  Obituary **1985**:3
Saro-Wiwa, Ken
  Obituary **1996**:2
Savimbi, Jonas **1986**:2 **1994**:2
Schily, Otto
  Brief Entry **1987**:4
Schroder, Gerhard **1999**:1
Sharon, Ariel **2001**:4
Shipley, Jenny **1998**:3
Silva, Luiz Inacio Lula da **2003**:4
Simpson, Wallis
  Obituary **1986**:3
Sisulu, Walter
  Obituary **2004**:2
Slovo, Joe **1989**:2
Staller, Ilona **1988**:3
Strauss, Robert **1991**:4
Suu Kyi, Aung San **1996**:2
Suzman, Helen **1989**:3
Takeshita, Noburu
  Obituary **2001**:1
Tambo, Oliver **1991**:3
Terzi, Zehdi Labib **1985**:3
Thatcher, Margaret **1989**:2
Treurnicht, Andries **1992**:2
Trimble, David **1999**:1
Trudeau, Pierre
  Obituary **2001**:1
Tudjman, Franjo
  Obituary **2000**:2
Tudjman, Franjo **1996**:2
Turabi, Hassan **1995**:4
Uribe, Alvaro **2003**:3
Vajpayee, Atal Behari **1998**:4
Vander Zalm, William **1987**:3
Wahid, Abdurrahman **2000**:3
Walesa, Lech **1991**:2
Wei Jingsheng **1998**:2
Werner, Ruth
  Obituary **2001**:1
Wickramasinghe, Ranil **2003**:2
William, Prince of Wales **2001**:3

Wilson, Bertha
  Brief Entry **1986**:1
Ye Jianying
  Obituary **1987**:1
Yeltsin, Boris **1991**:1
Zedillo, Ernesto **1995**:1
Zeroual, Liamine **1996**:2
Zhao Ziyang **1989**:1
Zhirinovsky, Vladimir **1994**:2
Zia ul-Haq, Mohammad
  Obituary **1988**:4
Chirac, Jacques **1995**:4

POLITICS AND GOVERNMENT--U.S.
Abraham, Spencer **1991**:4
Abrams, Elliott **1987**:1
Abzug, Bella **1998**:2
Achtenberg, Roberta **1993**:4
Agnew, Spiro Theodore
  Obituary **1997**:1
Ailes, Roger **1989**:3
Albright, Madeleine **1994**:3
Alexander, Lamar **1991**:2
Alioto, Joseph L.
  Obituary **1998**:3
Allen Jr., Ivan
  Obituary **2004**:3
Alvarez, Aida **1999**:2
Archer, Dennis **1994**:4
Ashcroft, John **2002**:4
Aspin, Les
  Obituary **1996**:1
Atwater, Lee **1989**:4
  Obituary **1991**:4
Babbitt, Bruce **1994**:1
Baker, James A. III **1991**:2
Baldrige, Malcolm
  Obituary **1988**:1
Banks, Dennis J. **1986**:4
Barry, Marion **1991**:1
Barshefsky, Charlene **2000**:4
Beame, Abraham
  Obituary **2001**:4
Begaye, Kelsey **1999**:3
Bennett, William **1990**:1
Benson, Ezra Taft
  Obituary **1994**:4
Bentsen, Lloyd **1993**:3
Berger, Sandy **2000**:1
Berle, Peter A.A.
  Brief Entry **1987**:3
Biden, Joe **1986**:3
Bonner, Robert **2003**:4
Bono, Sonny **1992**:2
  Obituary **1998**:2
Boxer, Barbara **1995**:1
Boyington, Gregory Pappy
  Obituary **1988**:2
Bradley, Bill **2000**:2
Bradley, Tom
  Obituary **1999**:1
Brady, Sarah and James S. **1991**:4
Braun, Carol Moseley **1993**:1
Brazile, Donna **2001**:1
Bremer, L. Paul **2004**:2
Brennan, William
  Obituary **1997**:4
Brown, Edmund G., Sr.
  Obituary **1996**:3
Brown, Jerry **1992**:4
Brown, Ron
  Obituary **1996**:4

Brown, Ron **1990**:3
Brown, Willie **1996**:4
Brown, Willie L. **1985**:2
Browner, Carol M. **1994**:1
Buchanan, Pat **1996**:3
Bundy, McGeorge
  Obituary **1997**:1
Bundy, William P.
  Obituary **2001**:2
Bush, Barbara **1989**:3
Bush, George W., Jr. **1996**:4
Bush, Jeb **2003**:1
Caliguiri, Richard S.
  Obituary **1988**:3
Campbell, Ben Nighthorse **1998**:1
Campbell, Bill **1997**:1
Card, Andrew H., Jr. **2003**:2
Carey, Ron **1993**:3
Carmona, Richard **2003**:2
Carnahan, Jean **2001**:2
Carnahan, Mel
  Obituary **2001**:2
Carter, Billy
  Obituary **1989**:1
Carter, Jimmy **1995**:1
Casey, William
  Obituary **1987**:3
Cavazos, Lauro F. **1989**:2
Chamberlin, Wendy **2002**:4
Chavez, Linda **1999**:3
Chavez-Thompson, Linda **1999**:1
Cheney, Dick **1991**:3
Cheney, Lynne V. **1990**:4
Christopher, Warren **1996**:3
Cisneros, Henry **1987**:2
Clark, J. E.
  Brief Entry **1986**:1
Clinton, Bill **1992**:1
Clinton, Hillary Rodham **1993**:2
Clyburn, James **1999**:4
Cohen, William S. **1998**:1
Collins, Cardiss **1995**:3
Connally, John
  Obituary **1994**:1
Conyers, John, Jr. **1999**:1
Cuomo, Mario **1992**:2
D'Amato, Al **1996**:1
Daschle, Tom **2002**:3
DeLay, Tom **2000**:1
Dinkins, David N. **1990**:2
Dolan, Terry **1985**:2
Dole, Bob **1994**:2
Dole, Elizabeth Hanford **1990**:1
Dukakis, Michael **1988**:3
Duke, David **1990**:2
Ehrlichman, John
  Obituary **1999**:3
Elders, Joycelyn **1994**:1
Engler, John **1996**:3
Ervin, Sam
  Obituary **1985**:2
Estrich, Susan **1989**:1
Falkenberg, Nanette **1985**:2
Farmer, James
  Obituary **2000**:1
Farrakhan, Louis **1990**:4
Faubus, Orval
  Obituary **1995**:2
Feinstein, Dianne **1993**:3
Fenwick, Millicent H.
  Obituary **1993**:2
Ferraro, Geraldine **1998**:3

Starr, Kenneth **1998**:3
Stephanopoulos, George **1994**:3
Stewart, Potter
  Obituary **1986**:1
Stokes, Carl
  Obituary **1996**:4
Strauss, Robert **1991**:4
Suarez, Xavier
  Brief Entry **1986**:2
Sullivan, Louis **1990**:4
Sununu, John **1989**:2
Swift, Jane **2002**:1
Taylor, Maxwell
  Obituary **1987**:3
Tenet, George **2000**:3
Thomas, Clarence **1992**:2
Thomas, Helen **1988**:4
Thompson, Fred **1998**:2
Thurmond, Strom
  Obituary **2004**:3
Tower, John
  Obituary **1991**:4
Townsend, Kathleen
  Kennedy **2001**:3
Tsongas, Paul Efthemios
  Obituary **1997**:2
Tutwiler, Margaret **1992**:4
Tyson, Laura D'Andrea **1994**:1
Udall, Mo
  Obituary **1999**:2
Ventura, Jesse **1999**:2
Violet, Arlene **1985**:3
Wallace, George
  Obituary **1999**:1
Washington, Harold
  Obituary **1988**:1
Waters, Maxine **1998**:4
Watts, J.C. **1999**:2
Webb, Wellington E. **2000**:3
Weicker, Lowell P., Jr. **1993**:1
Wellstone, Paul
  Obituary **2004**:1
Whitman, Christine Todd **1994**:3
Whitmire, Kathy **1988**:2
Wilder, L. Douglas **1990**:3
Williams, Anthony **2000**:4
Williams, G. Mennen
  Obituary **1988**:2
Wilson, Pete **1992**:3
Yard, Molly **1991**:4
Young, Coleman A.
  Obituary **1998**:1
Zech, Lando W.
  Brief Entry **1987**:4
Zerhouni, Elias A. **2004**:3
Zinni, Anthony **2003**:1

RADIO
Albert, Marv **1994**:3
Albom, Mitch **1999**:3
Ameche, Don
  Obituary **1994**:2
Autry, Gene
  Obituary **1999**:1
Backus, Jim
  Obituary **1990**:1
Barber, Red
  Obituary **1993**:2
Becker, Brian **2004**:4
Bell, Art **2000**:1
Blanc, Mel
  Obituary **1989**:4

Campbell, Bebe Moore **1996**:2
Caray, Harry **1988**:3
  Obituary **1998**:3
Cherry, Don **1993**:4
Codrescu, Andre **1997**:3
Cosell, Howard
  Obituary **1995**:4
Costas, Bob **1986**:4
Crenna, Richard
  Obituary **2004**:1
Day, Dennis
  Obituary **1988**:4
Dr. Demento **1986**:1
Donnellan, Nanci **1995**:2
Durrell, Gerald
  Obituary **1995**:3
Edwards, Bob **1993**:2
Fleming, Art
  Obituary **1995**:4
Ford, Tennessee Ernie
  Obituary **1992**:2
Gobel, George
  Obituary **1991**:4
Goodman, Benny
  Obituary **1986**:3
Gordon, Gale
  Obituary **1996**:1
Graham, Billy **1992**:1
Granato, Cammi **1999**:3
Grange, Red
  Obituary **1991**:3
Greene, Lorne
  Obituary **1988**:1
Gross, Terry **1998**:3
Harmon, Tom
  Obituary **1990**:3
Harvey, Paul **1995**:3
Harwell, Ernie **1997**:3
Hill, George Roy
  Obituary **2004**:1
Hope, Bob
  Obituary **2004**:4
Houseman, John
  Obituary **1989**:1
Hughes, Cathy **1999**:1
Imus, Don **1997**:1
Ives, Burl
  Obituary **1995**:4
Kasem, Casey **1987**:1
Keyes, Alan **1996**:2
King, Larry **1993**:1
Kyser, Kay
  Obituary **1985**:3
Levesque, Rene
  Obituary **1988**:1
Limbaugh, Rush **1991**:3
Magliozzi, Tom and Ray **1991**:4
Milligan, Spike
  Obituary **2003**:2
Nelson, Harriet
  Obituary **1995**:1
Olson, Johnny
  Obituary **1985**:4
Osgood, Charles **1996**:2
Paley, William S.
  Obituary **1991**:2
Parks, Bert
  Obituary **1992**:3
Porter, Sylvia
  Obituary **1991**:4
Quivers, Robin **1995**:4
Raphael, Sally Jessy **1992**:4

Raye, Martha
  Obituary **1995**:1
Riddle, Nelson
  Obituary **1985**:4
Roberts, Cokie **1993**:4
Saralegui, Cristina **1999**:2
Schlessinger, Laura **1996**:3
Seacrest, Ryan **2004**:4
Sevareid, Eric
  Obituary **1993**:1
Shore, Dinah
  Obituary **1994**:3
Smith, Buffalo Bob
  Obituary **1999**:1
Smith, Kate
  Obituary **1986**:3
Stern, Howard **1988**:2 **1993**:3
Swayze, John Cameron
  Obituary **1996**:1
Tom and Ray Magliozzi **1991**:4
Totenberg, Nina **1992**:2
Wolfman Jack
  Obituary **1996**:1
Young, Robert
  Obituary **1999**:1

RELIGION
Abernathy, Ralph
  Obituary **1990**:3
Altea, Rosemary **1996**:3
Applewhite, Marshall Herff
  Obituary **1997**:3
Aristide, Jean-Bertrand **1991**:3
Beckett, Wendy (Sister) **1998**:3
Benson, Ezra Taft
  Obituary **1994**:4
Bernardin, Cardinal Joseph **1997**:2
Berri, Nabih **1985**:2
Browning, Edmond
  Brief Entry **1986**:2
Burns, Charles R.
  Brief Entry **1988**:1
Carey, George **1992**:3
Chavis, Benjamin **1993**:4
Chittister, Joan D. **2002**:2
Chopra, Deepak **1996**:3
Clements, George **1985**:1
Cleveland, James
  Obituary **1991**:3
Coffin, William Sloane, Jr. **1990**:3
Cunningham, Reverend William
  Obituary **1997**:4
Curran, Charles E. **1989**:2
Daily, Bishop Thomas V. **1990**:4
Dalai Lama **1989**:1
Dearden, John Cardinal
  Obituary **1988**:4
Dorsey, Thomas A.
  Obituary **1993**:3
Eilberg, Amy
  Brief Entry **1985**:3
Farrakhan, Louis **1990**:4
Fox, Matthew **1992**:2
Fulghum, Robert **1996**:1
Graham, Billy **1992**:1
Grant, Amy **1985**:4
Hahn, Jessica **1989**:4
Harris, Barbara **1996**:3
Harris, Barbara **1989**:3
Healy, Timothy S. **1990**:2
Huffington, Arianna **1996**:2

Hume, Basil Cardinal
    Obituary **2000**:1
Hunter, Howard **1994**:4
Irwin, James
    Obituary **1992**:1
Jackson, Jesse **1996**:1
John Paul II, Pope **1995**:3
Jumblatt, Walid **1987**:4
Kahane, Meir
    Obituary **1991**:2
Khomeini, Ayatollah Ruhollah
    Obituary **1989**:4
Kissling, Frances **1989**:2
Koresh, David
    Obituary **1993**:4
Krol, John
    Obituary **1996**:3
Lefebvre, Marcel **1988**:4
Levinger, Moshe **1992**:1
Mahesh Yogi, Maharishi **1991**:3
Mahony, Roger M. **1988**:2
Maida, Adam Cardinal **1998**:2
Malloy, Edward Monk **1989**:4
McCloskey, James **1993**:1
Mother Teresa **1993**:1
    Obituary **1998**:1
Obando, Miguel **1986**:4
O'Connor, Cardinal John **1990**:3
O'Connor, John
    Obituary **2000**:4
Perry, Harold A.
    Obituary **1992**:1
Peter, Valentine J. **1988**:2
Rafsanjani, Ali Akbar
    Hashemi **1987**:3
Rahman, Sheik Omar Abdel- **1993**:3
Rajneesh, Bhagwan Shree
    Obituary **1990**:2
Reed, Ralph **1995**:1
Reese, Della **1999**:2
Robertson, Pat **1988**:2
Robinson, V. Gene **2004**:4
Rogers, Adrian **1987**:4
Runcie, Robert **1989**:4
    Obituary **2001**:1
Schneerson, Menachem
    Mendel **1992**:4
    Obituary **1994**:4
Scott, Gene
    Brief Entry **1986**:1
Sharpton, Al **1991**:2
Shaw, William **2000**:3
Smith, Jeff **1991**:4
Spong, John **1991**:3 **2001**:1
Stallings, George A., Jr. **1990**:1
Swaggart, Jimmy **1987**:3
Turabi, Hassan **1995**:4
Violet, Arlene **1985**:3
Wildmon, Donald **1988**:4
Williamson, Marianne **1991**:4
Youngblood, Johnny Ray **1994**:1

SCIENCE
Abramson, Lyn **1986**:3
Adams, Patch **1999**:2
Adamson, George
    Obituary **1990**:2
Allen, John **1992**:1
Altman, Sidney **1997**:2
Atkins, Robert C.
    Obituary **2004**:2
Bakker, Robert T. **1991**:3

Ballard, Robert D. **1998**:4
Barnard, Christiaan
    Obituary **2002**:4
Baulieu, Etienne-Emile **1990**:1
Bayley, Corrine
    Brief Entry **1986**:4
Bean, Alan L. **1986**:2
Beattie, Owen
    Brief Entry **1985**:2
Berkley, Seth **2002**:3
Berle, Peter A.A.
    Brief Entry **1987**:3
Berman, Jennifer and Laura **2003**:2
Bettelheim, Bruno
    Obituary **1990**:3
Blobel, Gunter **2000**:4
Bloch, Erich **1987**:4
Boyer, Herbert Wayne **1985**:1
Bristow, Lonnie **1996**:1
Brown, John Seely **2004**:1
Buck, Linda **2004**:2
Burnison, Chantal Simone **1988**:3
Carlsson, Arvid **2001**:2
Carson, Ben **1998**:2
Cerf, Vinton G. **1999**:2
Chaudhari, Praveen **1989**:4
Chu, Paul C.W. **1988**:2
Coles, Robert **1995**:1
Collins, Eileen **1995**:3
Colwell, Rita Rossi **1999**:3
Comfort, Alex
    Obituary **2000**:4
Conrad, Pete
    Obituary **2000**:1
Cousteau, Jacques-Yves
    Obituary **1998**:2
Cousteau, Jean-Michel **1988**:2
Cram, Donald J.
    Obituary **2002**:2
Cray, Seymour R.
    Brief Entry **1986**:3
    Obituary **1997**:2
Davis, Noel **1990**:3
DeVita, Vincent T., Jr. **1987**:3
Diemer, Walter E.
    Obituary **1998**:2
Djerassi, Carl **2000**:4
Douglas, Marjory Stoneman **1993**:1
    Obituary **1998**:4
Downey, Bruce **2003**:1
Duke, Red
    Brief Entry **1987**:1
Durrell, Gerald
    Obituary **1995**:3
Earle, Sylvia **2001**:1
Fang Lizhi **1988**:1
Fano, Ugo
    Obituary **2001**:4
Fauci, Anthony S. **2004**:1
Fields, Evelyn J. **2001**:3
Fiennes, Ranulph **1990**:3
Fisher, Mel **1985**:4
Folkman, Judah **1999**:1
Fossey, Dian
    Obituary **1986**:1
Foster, Tabatha
    Obituary **1988**:3
Futter, Ellen V. **1995**:1
Gale, Robert Peter **1986**:4
Gallo, Robert **1991**:1
Garneau, Marc **1985**:1
Geller, Margaret Joan **1998**:2

Gerba, Charles **1999**:4
Gerberding, Julie **2004**:1
Gilbert, Walter **1988**:3
Gilruth, Robert
    Obituary **2001**:1
Glenn, John **1998**:3
Goldman-Rakic, Patricia **2002**:4
Goodall, Jane **1991**:1
Gould, Gordon **1987**:1
Gould, Stephen Jay
    Obituary **2003**:3
Greene, Brian **2003**:4
Hagelstein, Peter
    Brief Entry **1986**:3
Hair, Jay D. **1994**:3
Hale, Alan **1997**:3
Hammond, E. Cuyler
    Obituary **1987**:1
Haseltine, William A. **1999**:2
Hatem, George
    Obituary **1989**:1
Hawking, Stephen W. **1990**:1
Healy, Bernadine **1993**:1
Ho, David **1997**:2
Horner, Jack **1985**:2
Horowitz, Paul **1988**:2
Hounsfield, Godfrey **1989**:2
Hoyle, Sir Fred
    Obituary **2002**:4
Irwin, James
    Obituary **1992**:1
Jacobs, Joe **1994**:1
Janzen, Daniel H. **1988**:4
Jarvik, Robert K. **1985**:1
Jemison, Mae C. **1993**:1
Jorgensen, Christine
    Obituary **1989**:4
Keith, Louis **1988**:2
Kessler, David **1992**:1
Kevorkian, Jack **1991**:3
King, Mary-Claire **1998**:3
Klass, Perri **1993**:2
Koop, C. Everett **1989**:3
Kopits, Steven E.
    Brief Entry **1987**:1
Kornberg, Arthur **1992**:1
Krim, Mathilde **1989**:2
Kwoh, Yik San **1988**:2
Laing, R.D.
    Obituary **1990**:1
Langer, Robert **2003**:4
Langston, J. William
    Brief Entry **1986**:2
Lanza, Robert **2004**:3
Leakey, Mary Douglas
    Obituary **1997**:2
Leakey, Richard **1994**:2
Lederman, Leon Max **1989**:4
LeVay, Simon **1992**:2
Levine, Arnold **2002**:3
Lilly, John C.
    Obituary **2002**:4
Lorenz, Konrad
    Obituary **1989**:3
Love, Susan **1995**:2
Lucid, Shannon **1997**:1
Maglich, Bogdan C. **1990**:1
Marsden, Brian **2004**:4
Masters, William H.
    Obituary **2001**:4
McIntyre, Richard
    Brief Entry **1986**:2

Menninger, Karl
  Obituary **1991**:1
Minsky, Marvin **1994**:3
Montagu, Ashley
  Obituary **2000**:2
Morgentaler, Henry **1986**:3
Moss, Cynthia **1995**:2
Mullis, Kary **1995**:3
Ngau, Harrison **1991**:3
Nielsen, Jerri **2001**:3
Novello, Antonia **1991**:2
Nuesslein-Volhard, Christiane **1998**:1
Nye, Bill **1997**:2
Ornish, Dean **2004**:2
Owens, Delia and Mark **1993**:3
Patton, John **2004**:4
Pauling, Linus
  Obituary **1995**:1
Penrose, Roger **1991**:4
Perutz, Max
  Obituary **2003**:2
Peterson, Roger Tory
  Obituary **1997**:1
Pinker, Steven A. **2000**:1
Plotkin, Mark **1994**:3
Porter, George
  Obituary **2003**:4
Pough, Richard Hooper **1989**:1
Profet, Margie **1994**:4
Prusiner, Stanley **1998**:2
Quill, Timothy E. **1997**:3
Radecki, Thomas
  Brief Entry **1986**:2
Redenbacher, Orville
  Obituary **1996**:1
Redig, Patrick **1985**:3
Richter, Charles Francis
  Obituary **1985**:4
Rifkin, Jeremy **1990**:3
Rizzoli, Paola **2004**:3
Rock, John
  Obituary **1985**:1
Rosenberg, Steven **1989**:1
Rosendahl, Bruce R.
  Brief Entry **1986**:4
Sabin, Albert
  Obituary **1993**:4
Sacks, Oliver **1995**:4
Sagan, Carl
  Obituary **1997**:2
Sakharov, Andrei Dmitrievich
  Obituary **1990**:2
Salk, Jonas **1994**:4
  Obituary **1995**:4
Schank, Roger **1989**:2
Schenk, Dale **2002**:2
Schroeder, William J.
  Obituary **1986**:4
Schultes, Richard Evans
  Obituary **2002**:1
Sears, Barry **2004**:2
Shepard, Alan
  Obituary **1999**:1
Shimomura, Tsutomu **1996**:1
Shirley, Donna **1999**:1
Sidransky, David **2002**:4
Skinner, B.F.
  Obituary **1991**:1
Smoot, George F. **1993**:3
Soren, David
  Brief Entry **1986**:3
Spelke, Elizabeth **2003**:1

Spergel, David **2004**:1
Spock, Benjamin **1995**:2
  Obituary **1998**:3
Steger, Will **1990**:4
Steptoe, Patrick
  Obituary **1988**:3
Sullivan, Louis **1990**:4
Szent-Gyoergyi, Albert
  Obituary **1987**:2
Thom, Rene
  Obituary **2004**:1
Thompson, Lonnie **2003**:3
Thompson, Starley
  Brief Entry **1987**:3
Thomson, James **2002**:3
Toone, Bill
  Brief Entry **1987**:2
Tully, Tim **2004**:3
Vagelos, P. Roy **1989**:4
Venter, J. Craig **2001**:1
Vickrey, William S.
  Obituary **1997**:2
Waddell, Thomas F.
  Obituary **1988**:2
Weil, Andrew **1997**:4
Wexler, Nancy S. **1992**:3
Whitson, Peggy **2003**:3
Wigand, Jeffrey **2000**:4
Wigler, Michael
  Brief Entry **1985**:1
Wiles, Andrew **1994**:1
Wilmut, Ian **1997**:3
Wilson, Edward O. **1994**:4
Woodwell, George S. **1987**:2
Yeager, Chuck **1998**:1
Yen, Samuel **1996**:4
Zech, Lando W.
  Brief Entry **1987**:4

SOCIAL ISSUES
Abbey, Edward
  Obituary **1989**:3
Abernathy, Ralph
  Obituary **1990**:3
Ali, Muhammad **1997**:2
Allred, Gloria **1985**:2
Amory, Cleveland
  Obituary **1999**:2
Anastas, Robert
  Brief Entry **1985**:2
Aristide, Jean-Bertrand **1991**:3
Baez, Joan **1998**:3
Baird, Bill
  Brief Entry **1987**:2
Baldwin, James
  Obituary **1988**:2
Ball, Edward **1999**:2
Banks, Dennis J. **1986**:4
Bayley, Corrine
  Brief Entry **1986**:4
Bellamy, Carol **2001**:2
Ben & Jerry **1991**:3
Bergalis, Kimberly
  Obituary **1992**:3
Berresford, Susan V. **1998**:4
Biehl, Amy
  Obituary **1994**:1
Blackburn, Molly
  Obituary **1985**:4
Block, Herbert
  Obituary **2002**:4
Bly, Robert **1992**:4

Bradshaw, John **1992**:1
Brady, Sarah and James S. **1991**:4
Bravo, Ellen **1998**:2
Bristow, Lonnie **1996**:1
Brooks, Gwendolyn **1998**:1
  Obituary **2001**:2
Brower, David **1990**:4
Brown, Jim **1993**:2
Brown, Judie **1986**:2
Burk, Martha **2004**:1
Bush, Barbara **1989**:3
Cammermeyer, Margarethe **1995**:2
Caplan, Arthur L. **2000**:2
Caras, Roger
  Obituary **2002**:1
Carter, Amy **1987**:4
Carter, Rubin **2000**:3
Chavez, Cesar
  Obituary **1993**:4
Chavez-Thompson, Linda **1999**:1
Chavis, Benjamin **1993**:4
Cleaver, Eldridge
  Obituary **1998**:4
Clements, George **1985**:1
Clinton, Hillary Rodham **1993**:2
Coffin, William Sloane, Jr. **1990**:3
Cole, Johnetta B. **1994**:3
Coles, Robert **1995**:1
Connerly, Ward **2000**:2
Coors, William K.
  Brief Entry **1985**:1
Cozza, Stephen **2001**:1
Crisp, Quentin
  Obituary **2000**:3
Cruzan, Nancy
  Obituary **1991**:3
Davis, Angela **1998**:3
Dees, Morris **1992**:1
Devi, Phoolan **1986**:1
  Obituary **2002**:3
Dickinson, Brian **1998**:2
Dorris, Michael
  Obituary **1997**:3
Douglas, Marjory Stoneman **1993**:1
  Obituary **1998**:4
Downey, Morton, Jr. **1988**:4
Duncan, Sheena
  Brief Entry **1987**:1
Ebadi, Shirin **2004**:3
Edelman, Marian Wright **1990**:4
Edwards, Harry **1989**:4
Elders, Joycelyn **1994**:1
Ellison, Ralph
  Obituary **1994**:4
Ensler, Eve **2002**:4
Erin Brockovich-Ellis **2003**:3
Etzioni, Amitai **1994**:3
Evers-Williams, Myrlie **1995**:4
Falkenberg, Nanette **1985**:2
Faludi, Susan **1992**:4
Farrakhan, Louis **1990**:4
Faubus, Orval
  Obituary **1995**:2
Faulkner, Shannon **1994**:4
Ferrell, Trevor
  Brief Entry **1985**:2
Filipovic, Zlata **1994**:4
Finley, Karen **1992**:4
Fisher, Mary **1994**:3
Fonyo, Steve
  Brief Entry **1985**:4
Foreman, Dave **1990**:3

Gordeeva, Ekaterina **1996**:4
Gordon, Jeff **1996**:1
Graf, Steffi **1987**:4
Granato, Cammi **1999**:3
Grange, Red
   Obituary **1991**:3
Graziano, Rocky
   Obituary **1990**:4
Greenberg, Hank
   Obituary **1986**:4
Gretzky, Wayne **1989**:2
Griffey, Ken Jr. **1994**:1
Grinkov, Sergei
   Obituary **1996**:2
Gruden, Jon **2003**:4
Gumbel, Greg **1996**:4
Gwynn, Tony **1995**:1
Hagler, Marvelous Marvin **1985**:2
Hamilton, Scott **1998**:2
Hamm, Mia **2000**:1
Hanauer, Chip **1986**:2
Hardaway, Anfernee **1996**:2
Harkes, John **1996**:4
Harmon, Tom
   Obituary **1990**:3
Harwell, Ernie **1997**:3
Hasek, Dominik **1998**:3
Hawk, Tony **2001**:4
Hayes, Woody
   Obituary **1987**:2
Helton, Todd **2001**:1
Hempleman-Adams, David **2004**:3
Henderson, Rickey **2002**:3
Henin-Hardenne, Justine **2004**:4
Hernandez, Willie **1985**:1
Hershiser, Orel **1989**:2
Hewitt, Lleyton **2002**:2
Hextall, Ron **1988**:2
Hill, Grant **1995**:3
Hill, Lynn **1991**:2
Hingis, Martina **1999**:1
Hogan, Ben
   Obituary **1997**:4
Hogan, Hulk **1987**:3
Holtz, Lou **1986**:4
Holyfield, Evander **1991**:3
Howard, Desmond Kevin **1997**:2
Howser, Dick
   Obituary **1987**:4
Hughes, Sarah **2002**:4
Hull, Brett **1991**:4
Hunter, Catfish
   Obituary **2000**:1
Indurain, Miguel **1994**:1
Inkster, Juli **2000**:2
Irvin, Michael **1996**:3
Ivanisevic, Goran **2002**:1
Iverson, Allen **2001**:4
Jackson, Bo **1986**:3
Jackson, Phil **1996**:3
Jagr, Jaromir **1995**:4
Jenkins, Sally **1997**:2
Jeter, Derek **1999**:4
Johnson, Earvin Magic **1988**:4
Johnson, Jimmy **1993**:3
Johnson, Kevin **1991**:1
Johnson, Keyshawn **2000**:4
Johnson, Larry **1993**:3
Johnson, Michael **2000**:1
Johnson, Randy **1996**:2
Jones, Jerry **1994**:4
Jones, Marion **1998**:4

Jordan, Michael **1987**:2
Joyner, Florence Griffith **1989**:2
   Obituary **1999**:1
Joyner-Kersee, Jackie **1993**:1
Kallen, Jackie **1994**:1
Kanokogi, Rusty
   Brief Entry **1987**:1
Kasparov, Garry **1997**:4
Kelly, Jim **1991**:4
Kemp, Jack **1990**:4
Kemp, Jan **1987**:2
Kemp, Shawn **1995**:1
Kerrigan, Nancy **1994**:3
Kidd, Jason **2003**:2
King, Don **1989**:1
Kiraly, Karch
   Brief Entry **1987**:1
Kite, Tom **1990**:3
Klima, Petr **1987**:1
Knievel, Robbie **1990**:1
Knight, Bobby **1985**:3
Koch, Bill **1992**:3
Konstantinov, Vladimir **1997**:4
Kournikova, Anna **2000**:3
Kroc, Ray
   Obituary **1985**:1
Krone, Julie **1989**:2
Kruk, John **1994**:4
Krzyzewski, Mike **1993**:2
Kukoc, Toni **1995**:4
Laettner, Christian **1993**:1
LaFontaine, Pat **1985**:1
Laimbeer, Bill **2004**:3
Lalas, Alexi **1995**:1
Landry, Tom
   Obituary **2000**:3
Lemieux, Claude **1996**:1
Lemieux, Mario **1986**:4
LeMond, Greg **1986**:4
Leonard, Sugar Ray **1989**:4
Leslie, Lisa **1997**:4
Lewis, Lennox **2000**:2
Lewis, Ray **2001**:3
Lewis, Reggie
   Obituary **1994**:1
Leyland, Jim **1998**:2
Lindbergh, Pelle
   Obituary **1985**:4
Lindros, Eric **1992**:1
Lipinski, Tara **1998**:3
Lofton, Kenny **1998**:1
Lopez, Nancy **1989**:3
Louganis, Greg **1995**:3
Lowell, Mike **2003**:2
Lukas, D. Wayne **1986**:2
Madden, John **1995**:1
Maddux, Greg **1996**:2
Majerle, Dan **1993**:4
Malone, Karl **1990**:1 **1997**:3
Mantle, Mickey
   Obituary **1996**:1
Maradona, Diego **1991**:3
Maravich, Pete
   Obituary **1988**:2
Maris, Roger
   Obituary **1986**:1
Martin, Billy **1988**:4
   Obituary **1990**:2
Martin, Casey **2002**:1
Mathis, Clint **2003**:1
Mattingly, Don **1986**:2

Matuszak, John
   Obituary **1989**:4
McCarron, Chris **1995**:4
McCartney, Bill **1995**:3
McGwire, Mark **1999**:1
McMahon, Jim **1985**:4
McMahon, Vince, Jr. **1985**:4
Messier, Mark **1993**:1
Mickelson, Phil **2004**:4
Milbrett, Tiffeny **2001**:1
Milburn, Rodney Jr.
   Obituary **1998**:2
Miller, Andre **2003**:3
Miller, Bode **2002**:4
Miller, Reggie **1994**:4
Minnesota Fats
   Obituary **1996**:3
Monaghan, Tom **1985**:1
Monk, Art **1993**:2
Montana, Joe **1989**:2
Moon, Warren **1991**:3
Moore, Archie
   Obituary **1999**:2
Morgan, Dodge **1987**:1
Moss, Randy **1999**:3
Mourning, Alonzo **1994**:2
Muldowney, Shirley **1986**:1
Musburger, Brent **1985**:1
Navratilova, Martina **1989**:1
Newman, Paul **1995**:3
Nomo, Hideo **1996**:2
Norman, Greg **1988**:3
O'Donnell, Bill
   Brief Entry **1987**:4
Okoye, Christian **1990**:2
Olajuwon, Akeem **1985**:1
Olson, Billy **1986**:3
O'Malley, Susan **1995**:2
O'Neal, Shaquille **1992**:1
Pak, Se Ri **1999**:4
Palmer, Jim **1991**:2
Paterno, Joe **1995**:4
Patrick, Danica **2003**:3
Pavin, Corey **1996**:4
Payton, Walter
   Obituary **2000**:2
Peete, Calvin **1985**:4
Penske, Roger **1988**:3
Piazza, Mike **1998**:4
Pierce, Mary **1994**:4
Pincay, Laffit, Jr. **1986**:3
Pippen, Scottie **1992**:2
Pocklington, Peter H. **1985**:2
Polgar, Judit **1993**:3
Prost, Alain **1988**:1
Rafter, Patrick **2001**:1
Retton, Mary Lou **1985**:2
Rice, Jerry **1990**:4
Richard, Maurice
   Obituary **2000**:4
Riggs, Bobby
   Obituary **1996**:2
Riley, Pat **1994**:3
Ripken, Cal, Jr. **1986**:2
Ripken, Cal, Sr.
   Obituary **1999**:4
Roberts, Steven K. **1992**:1
Robinson, David **1990**:4
Robinson, Frank **1990**:2
Robinson, Sugar Ray
   Obituary **1989**:3
Roddick, Andy **2004**:3

Langer, Robert **2003**:4
Lanier, Jaron **1993**:4
MacCready, Paul **1986**:4
McGowan, William **1985**:2
McLaren, Norman
   Obituary **1987**:2
Minsky, Marvin **1994**:3
Moody, John **1985**:3
Morita, Akio
   Obituary **2000**:2
Morita, Akio **1989**:4
Newman, Joseph **1987**:1
Noyce, Robert N. **1985**:4
Ollila, Jorma **2003**:4
Pack, Ellen **2001**:2
Palmisano, Samuel J. **2003**:1
Parsons, Richard **2002**:4
Perlman, Steve **1998**:2
Perry, William **1994**:4
Pfeiffer, Eckhard **1998**:4
Ramsay, Mike **2002**:1
Raskin, Jef **1997**:4
Rifkin, Jeremy **1990**:3
Ritchie, Dennis and Kenneth
   Thompson **2000**:1
Roberts, Brian L. **2002**:4
Roberts, Steven K. **1992**:1
Rutan, Burt **1987**:2
Schank, Roger **1989**:2
Schmidt, Eric **2002**:4
Scholz, Tom **1987**:2
Schroeder, William J.
   Obituary **1986**:4
Sculley, John **1989**:4
Seidenberg, Ivan **2004**:1
Semel, Terry **2002**:2
Shirley, Donna **1999**:1
Sinclair, Mary **1985**:2
Taylor, Jeff **2001**:3
Tito, Dennis **2002**:1
Titov, Gherman
   Obituary **2001**:3
Tom and Ray Magliozzi **1991**:4
Toomer, Ron **1990**:1
Torvalds, Linus **1999**:3
Treybig, James G. **1988**:3
Walker, Jay **2004**:2
Wang, An **1986**:1
   Obituary **1990**:3
Wright, Will **2003**:4
Yamamoto, Kenichi **1989**:1

TELEVISION

Affleck, Ben **1999**:1
Alba, Jessica **2001**:2
Albert, Marv **1994**:3
Albom, Mitch **1999**:3
Alda, Robert
   Obituary **1986**:3
Alexander, Jane **1994**:2
Alexander, Jason **1993**:3
Allen, Debbie **1998**:2
Allen, Steve
   Obituary **2001**:2
Allen, Tim **1993**:1
Alley, Kirstie **1990**:3
Altman, Robert **1993**:2
Amanpour, Christiane **1997**:2
Ameche, Don
   Obituary **1994**:2
Amsterdam, Morey
   Obituary **1997**:1

Ancier, Garth **1989**:1
Anderson, Gillian **1997**:1
Anderson, Harry **1988**:2
Anderson, Judith
   Obituary **1992**:3
Andrews, Julie **1996**:1
Angelou, Maya **1993**:4
Aniston, Jennifer **2000**:3
Applegate, Christina **2000**:4
Arden, Eve
   Obituary **1991**:2
Arledge, Roone **1992**:2
Arlen, Harold
   Obituary **1986**:3
Arnaz, Desi
   Obituary **1987**:1
Arnold, Tom **1993**:2
Arquette, Rosanna **1985**:2
Atkinson, Rowan **2004**:3
Autry, Gene
   Obituary **1999**:1
Axthelm, Pete
   Obituary **1991**:3
Aykroyd, Dan **1989**:3 **1997**:3
Azaria, Hank **2001**:3
Bacall, Lauren **1997**:3
Backus, Jim
   Obituary **1990**:1
Bacon, Kevin **1995**:3
Baddeley, Hermione
   Obituary **1986**:4
Bailey, Pearl
   Obituary **1991**:1
Bakula, Scott **2003**:1
Ball, Lucille
   Obituary **1989**:3
Baranski, Christine **2001**:2
Barbera, Joseph **1988**:2
Barkin, Ellen **1987**:3
Barney **1993**:4
Barr, Roseanne **1989**:1
Barrymore, Drew **1995**:3
Basinger, Kim **1987**:2
Bassett, Angela **1994**:4
Bateman, Justine **1988**:4
Baxter, Anne
   Obituary **1986**:1
Beatty, Warren **2000**:1
Belushi, Jim **1986**:2
Belzer, Richard **1985**:3
Bergen, Candice **1990**:1
Berle, Milton
   Obituary **2003**:2
Bernardi, Herschel
   Obituary **1986**:4
Bernsen, Corbin **1990**:2
Bernstein, Leonard
   Obituary **1991**:1
Berry, Halle **1996**:2
Bialik, Mayim **1993**:3
Bixby, Bill
   Obituary **1994**:2
Black, Carole **2003**:1
Blades, Ruben **1998**:2
Blaine, David **2003**:3
Blanc, Mel
   Obituary **1989**:4
Blanchett, Cate **1999**:3
Bloodworth-Thomason,
   Linda **1994**:1
Bloom, Orlando **2004**:2
Bochco, Steven **1989**:1

Bolger, Ray
   Obituary **1987**:2
Bonet, Lisa **1989**:2
Bono, Sonny **1992**:2
   Obituary **1998**:2
Booth, Shirley
   Obituary **1993**:2
Boyle, Lara Flynn **2003**:4
Boyle, Peter **2002**:3
Bradshaw, John **1992**:1
Brandy **1996**:4
Brenneman, Amy **2002**:1
Bridges, Lloyd
   Obituary **1998**:3
Brinkley, David
   Obituary **2004**:3
Brokaw, Tom **2000**:3
Bronson, Charles
   Obituary **2004**:4
Brooks, Mel **2003**:1
Brosnan, Pierce **2000**:3
Brown, Les **1994**:3
Buckley, Betty **1996**:2
Bullock, Sandra **1995**:4
Burnett, Carol **2000**:3
Burnett, Mark **2003**:1
Burns, George
   Obituary **1996**:3
Burns, Ken **1995**:2
Burr, Raymond
   Obituary **1994**:1
Butler, Brett **1995**:1
Caan, James **2004**:4
Caine, Michael **2000**:4
Calhoun, Rory
   Obituary **1999**:4
Campbell, Neve **1998**:2
Campion, Jane **1991**:4
Candy, John **1988**:2
   Obituary **1994**:3
Carey, Drew **1997**:4
Carlin, George **1996**:3
Carrey, Jim **1995**:1
Carson, Lisa Nicole **1999**:3
Carter, Chris **2000**:1
Carter, Nell
   Obituary **2004**:2
Caruso, David **1994**:3
Carvey, Dana **1994**:1
Cassavetes, John
   Obituary **1989**:2
Cattrall, Kim **2003**:3
Caulfield, Joan
   Obituary **1992**:1
Cavanagh, Tom **2003**:1
Chancellor, John
   Obituary **1997**:1
Channing, Stockard **1991**:3
Chase, Chevy **1990**:1
Chavez, Linda **1999**:3
Cher **1993**:1
Cherry, Don **1993**:4
Chiklis, Michael **2003**:3
Child, Julia **1999**:4
Cho, Margaret **1995**:2
Chow Yun-fat **1999**:4
Christensen, Hayden **2003**:3
Chung, Connie **1988**:4
Clarkson, Kelly **2003**:3
Clay, Andrew Dice **1991**:1
Cleese, John **1989**:2
Clooney, George **1996**:4

Close, Glenn **1988**:3
Coca, Imogene
 Obituary **2002**:2
Coco, James
 Obituary **1987**:2
Colasanto, Nicholas
 Obituary **1985**:2
Coleman, Dabney **1988**:3
Connery, Sean **1990**:4
Convy, Bert
 Obituary **1992**:1
Cook, Peter
 Obituary **1995**:2
Cooper, Chris **2004**:1
Copperfield, David **1986**:3
Coppola, Francis Ford **1989**:4
Corbett, John **2004**:1
Cosby, Bill **1999**:2
Cosell, Howard
 Obituary **1995**:4
Costas, Bob **1986**:4
Couric, Katherine **1991**:4
Cousteau, Jacques-Yves
 Obituary **1998**:2
Cowell, Simon **2003**:4
Cox, Courteney **1996**:2
Cox, Richard Joseph
 Brief Entry **1985**:1
Crawford, Broderick
 Obituary **1986**:3
Crawford, Cindy **1993**:3
Crawford, Michael **1994**:2
Crenna, Richard
 Obituary **2004**:1
Crichton, Michael **1995**:3
Cronkite, Walter Leland **1997**:3
Crothers, Scatman
 Obituary **1987**:1
Crystal, Billy **1985**:3
Curry, Ann **2001**:1
Curtis, Jamie Lee **1995**:1
Cushing, Peter
 Obituary **1995**:1
Dalton, Timothy **1988**:4
Daly, Carson **2002**:4
Damon, Matt **1999**:1
Danes, Claire **1999**:4
Daniels, Faith **1993**:3
Daniels, Jeff **1989**:4
Danza, Tony **1989**:1
David, Larry **2003**:4
Davis, Bette
 Obituary **1990**:1
Davis, Geena **1992**:1
Davis, Paige **2004**:2
Davis, Sammy, Jr.
 Obituary **1990**:4
Day, Dennis
 Obituary **1988**:4
De Cordova, Frederick **1985**:2
DeGeneres, Ellen **1995**:3
Depardieu, Gerard **1991**:2
Depp, Johnny **1991**:3
De Vito, Danny **1987**:1
Dewhurst, Colleen
 Obituary **1992**:2
Diamond, Selma
 Obituary **1985**:2
DiCaprio, Leonardo Wilhelm **1997**:2
Dickerson, Nancy H.
 Obituary **1998**:2
Diller, Barry **1991**:1

Disney, Roy E. **1986**:3
Doherty, Shannen **1994**:2
Dolenz, Micky **1986**:4
Douglas, Michael **1986**:2
Downey, Morton, Jr. **1988**:4
Drescher, Fran **1995**:3
Duchovny, David **1998**:3
Duff, Hilary **2004**:4
Duffy, Karen **1998**:1
Dukakis, Olympia **1996**:4
Duke, Red
 Brief Entry **1987**:1
Durrell, Gerald
 Obituary **1995**:3
Duvall, Robert **1999**:3
Eastwood, Clint **1993**:3
Ebert, Roger **1998**:3
Ebsen, Buddy
 Obituary **2004**:3
Eisner, Michael **1989**:2
Elfman, Jenna **1999**:4
Ellerbee, Linda **1993**:3
Elliott, Denholm
 Obituary **1993**:2
Engstrom, Elmer W.
 Obituary **1985**:2
Evans, Dale
 Obituary **2001**:3
Eve **2004**:3
Fallon, Jimmy **2003**:1
Farley, Chris
 Obituary **1998**:2
Fawcett, Farrah **1998**:4
Fell, Norman
 Obituary **1999**:2
Ferrell, Will **2004**:4
Ferrer, Jose
 Obituary **1992**:3
Field, Sally **1995**:3
Finney, Albert **2003**:3
Firestone, Roy **1988**:2
Fishburne, Laurence **1995**:3
Fisher, Carrie **1991**:1
Flanders, Ed
 Obituary **1995**:3
Fleiss, Mike **2003**:4
Fleming, Art
 Obituary **1995**:4
Flockhart, Calista **1998**:4
Fonda, Bridget **1995**:1
Ford, Tennessee Ernie
 Obituary **1992**:2
Fosse, Bob
 Obituary **1988**:1
Foster, Jodie **1989**:2
Foster, Phil
 Obituary **1985**:3
Fox, Michael J. **1986**:1 **2001**:3
Fox, Vivica **1999**:1
Foxworthy, Jeff **1996**:1
Foxx, Jamie **2001**:1
Foxx, Redd
 Obituary **1992**:2
Franciscus, James
 Obituary **1992**:1
Frankenheimer, John
 Obituary **2003**:4
Franz, Dennis **1995**:2
Freeman, Morgan **1990**:4
Freleng, Friz
 Obituary **1995**:4

Funt, Allen
 Obituary **2000**:1
Gabor, Eva
 Obituary **1996**:1
Gallagher, Peter **2004**:3
Gandolfini, James **2001**:3
Garcia, Andy **1999**:3
Gardenia, Vincent
 Obituary **1993**:2
Garner, Jennifer **2003**:1
Garofalo, Janeane **1996**:4
Gellar, Sarah Michelle **1999**:3
Gere, Richard **1994**:3
Gifford, Kathie Lee **1992**:2
Gilford, Jack
 Obituary **1990**:4
Gillett, George **1988**:1
Gish, Lillian
 Obituary **1993**:4
Gleason, Jackie
 Obituary **1987**:4
Gless, Sharon **1989**:3
Glover, Danny **1998**:4
Gobel, George
 Obituary **1991**:4
Goldberg, Gary David **1989**:4
Goldberg, Leonard **1988**:4
Goldberg, Whoopi **1993**:3
Goldblum, Jeff **1988**:1 **1997**:3
Goodman, John **1990**:3
Gordon, Gale
 Obituary **1996**:1
Goren, Charles H.
 Obituary **1991**:4
Gossett, Louis, Jr. **1989**:3
Graden, Brian **2004**:2
Graham, Billy **1992**:1
Graham, Lauren **2003**:4
Grammer, Kelsey **1995**:1
Grange, Red
 Obituary **1991**:3
Grant, Rodney A. **1992**:1
Graziano, Rocky
 Obituary **1990**:4
Green, Tom **1999**:4
Greene, Graham **1997**:2
Greene, Lorne
 Obituary **1988**:1
Griffith, Melanie **1989**:2
Grodin, Charles **1997**:3
Groening, Matt **1990**:4
Guest, Christopher **2004**:2
Gumbel, Bryant **1990**:2
Gumbel, Greg **1996**:4
Gunn, Hartford N., Jr.
 Obituary **1986**:2
Hackett, Buddy
 Obituary **2004**:3
Hackman, Gene **1989**:3
Haley, Alex
 Obituary **1992**:3
Hall, Anthony Michael **1986**:3
Hall, Arsenio **1990**:2
Hamilton, Margaret
 Obituary **1985**:3
Hamilton, Scott **1998**:2
Hammer, Jan **1987**:3
Hanks, Tom **1989**:2 **2000**:2
Hanna, William
 Obituary **2002**:1
Harmon, Mark **1987**:1

Hart, Mary
  Brief Entry **1988**:1
Hart, Melissa Joan **2002**:1
Hartman, Phil **1996**:2
  Obituary **1998**:4
Hatch, Richard **2001**:1
Hawn, Goldie Jeanne **1997**:2
Hayek, Salma **1999**:1
Hayes, Helen
  Obituary **1993**:4
Hayes, Isaac **1998**:4
Headroom, Max **1986**:4
Heche, Anne **1999**:1
Hefner, Christie **1985**:1
Helgenberger, Marg **2002**:2
Hennessy, Jill **2003**:2
Henning, Doug
  Obituary **2000**:3
Henson, Brian **1992**:1
Henson, Jim **1989**:1
  Obituary **1990**:4
Hepburn, Katharine **1991**:2
Hershey, Barbara **1989**:1
Heston, Charlton **1999**:4
Hewitt, Jennifer Love **1999**:2
Hill, Benny
  Obituary **1992**:3
Hill, George Roy
  Obituary **2004**:1
Hill, Lauryn **1999**:3
Hope, Bob
  Obituary **2004**:4
Horwich, Frances
  Obituary **2002**:3
Hoskins, Bob **1989**:1
Houseman, John
  Obituary **1989**:1
Houston, Cissy **1999**:3
Howard, Ron **1997**:2
Howard, Trevor
  Obituary **1988**:2
Hudson, Rock
  Obituary **1985**:4
Huffington, Arianna **1996**:2
Hughley, D.L. **2001**:1
Humphries, Barry **1993**:1
Hunt, Helen **1994**:4
Hunter, Holly **1989**:4
Hurley, Elizabeth **1999**:2
Hurt, William **1986**:1
Huston, Anjelica **1989**:3
Hutton, Timothy **1986**:3
Ifill, Gwen **2002**:4
Ireland, Jill
  Obituary **1990**:4
Irons, Jeremy **1991**:4
Irwin, Steve **2001**:2
Isaacson, Walter **2003**:2
Itami, Juzo
  Obituary **1998**:2
Jackson, Janet **1990**:4
Jackson, Samuel L. **1995**:4
James, Jesse **2004**:4
Janney, Allison **2003**:3
Jennings, Peter Charles **1997**:2
Jillian, Ann **1986**:4
Johnson, Don **1986**:1
Jones, Cherry **1999**:3
Jones, Chuck **2001**:2
Jones, Jenny **1998**:2
Jones, Tom **1993**:4
Jones, Tommy Lee **1994**:2

Judd, Ashley **1998**:1
Judge, Mike **1994**:2
Julia, Raul
  Obituary **1995**:1
Juneau, Pierre **1988**:3
Kahn, Madeline
  Obituary **2000**:2
Kasem, Casey **1987**:1
Katzenberg, Jeffrey **1995**:3
Kavner, Julie **1992**:3
Kaye, Danny
  Obituary **1987**:2
Kaye, Sammy
  Obituary **1987**:4
Keaton, Michael **1989**:4
Keitel, Harvey **1994**:3
Keith, Brian
  Obituary **1997**:4
Kelley, DeForest
  Obituary **2000**:1
Keno, Leigh and Leslie **2001**:2
Kent, Arthur **1991**:4 **1997**:2
Kidman, Nicole **1992**:4
Kilborn, Craig **2003**:2
King, Larry **1993**:1
King, Stephen **1998**:1
Kinison, Sam
  Obituary **1993**:1
Klemperer, Werner
  Obituary **2001**:3
Klensch, Elsa **2001**:4
Kloss, Henry E.
  Brief Entry **1985**:2
Knight, Ted
  Obituary **1986**:4
Knight, Wayne **1997**:1
Koplovitz, Kay **1986**:3
Koppel, Ted **1989**:1
Kordich, Jay **1993**:2
Kudrow, Lisa **1996**:1
Kulp, Nancy
  Obituary **1991**:3
Kuralt, Charles
  Obituary **1998**:3
Kutcher, Ashton **2003**:4
Lachey, Nick and
  Jessica Simpson **2004**:4
Lagasse, Emeril **1998**:3
Lahti, Christine **1988**:2
Lake, Ricki **1994**:4
Landon, Michael
  Obituary **1992**:1
Lange, Jessica **1995**:4
Lansbury, Angela **1993**:1
LaPaglia, Anthony **2004**:4
Larroquette, John **1986**:2
LaSalle, Eriq **1996**:4
Lawless, Lucy **1997**:4
Lawrence, Martin **1993**:4
Lawson, Nigella **2003**:2
Laybourne, Geraldine **1997**:1
Leach, Penelope **1992**:4
Leach, Robin
  Brief Entry **1985**:4
Leary, Denis **1993**:3
Lee, Pamela **1996**:4
Leguizamo, John **1999**:1
Leigh, Jennifer Jason **1995**:2
Lemmon, Jack **1998**:4
  Obituary **2002**:3
Leno, Jay **1987**:1
Letterman, David **1989**:3

Levinson, Barry **1989**:3
Levy, Eugene **2004**:3
Lewis, Juliette **1999**:3
Lewis, Richard **1992**:1
Lewis, Shari **1993**:1
  Obituary **1999**:1
Liberace
  Obituary **1987**:2
Ling, Lisa **2004**:2
Little, Cleavon
  Obituary **1993**:2
Liu, Lucy **2000**:4
LL Cool J **1998**:2
Locklear, Heather **1994**:3
Long, Shelley **1985**:1
Lopez, George **2003**:4
Lopez, Jennifer **1998**:4
Lord, Jack
  Obituary **1998**:2
Lords, Traci **1995**:4
Louis-Dreyfus, Julia **1994**:1
Loy, Myrna
  Obituary **1994**:2
Lucci, Susan **1999**:4
Lupino, Ida
  Obituary **1996**:1
Lynch, David **1990**:4
Mac, Bernie **2003**:1
MacMurray, Fred
  Obituary **1992**:2
MacRae, Gordon
  Obituary **1986**:2
Macy, William H. **1999**:3
Madden, John **1995**:1
Maher, Bill **1996**:2
Malkovich, John **1988**:2
Malone, John C. **1988**:3 **1996**:3
Mandel, Howie **1989**:1
Mantegna, Joe **1992**:1
Marchand, Nancy
  Obituary **2001**:1
Martin, Dean
  Obituary **1996**:2
Martin, Mary
  Obituary **1991**:2
Martin, Steve **1992**:2
Matlin, Marlee **1992**:2
Matthau, Walter **2000**:3
McCarthy, Jenny **1997**:4
McDormand, Frances **1997**:3
McDowall, Roddy
  Obituary **1999**:1
McGillis, Kelly **1989**:3
McGinley, Ted **2004**:4
McGregor, Ewan **1998**:2
McKee, Lonette **1996**:1
McKellen, Ian **1994**:1
Meadows, Audrey
  Obituary **1996**:3
Meredith, Burgess
  Obituary **1998**:1
Messing, Debra **2004**:4
Midler, Bette **1989**:4
Milano, Alyssa **2002**:3
Milland, Ray
  Obituary **1986**:2
Miller, Dennis **1992**:4
Milligan, Spike
  Obituary **2003**:2
Minogue, Kylie **2003**:4
Mitchum, Robert
  Obituary **1997**:4

Montgomery, Elizabeth
Obituary **1995**:4
Moonves, Les **2004**:2
Moore, Clayton
Obituary **2000**:3
Moore, Demi **1991**:4
Moore, Dudley
Obituary **2003**:2
Moore, Julianne **1998**:1
Moore, Mary Tyler **1996**:2
Morita, Noriyuki Pat **1987**:3
Mortensen, Viggo **2003**:3
Moss, Carrie-Anne **2004**:3
Moyers, Bill **1991**:4
Muniz, Frankie **2001**:4
Murdoch, Rupert **1988**:4
Murphy, Eddie **1989**:2
Musburger, Brent **1985**:1
Myers, Mike **1992**:3 **1997**:4
Nance, Jack
Obituary **1997**:3
Neeson, Liam **1993**:4
Nelson, Harriet
Obituary **1995**:1
Nelson, Rick
Obituary **1986**:1
Nelson, Willie **1993**:4
Newton-John, Olivia **1998**:4
Nichols, Mike **1994**:4
Nolan, Lloyd
Obituary **1985**:4
Nolte, Nick **1992**:4
Northam, Jeremy **2003**:2
Norville, Deborah **1990**:3
Nye, Bill **1997**:2
O'Brien, Conan **1994**:1
O'Connor, Carroll
Obituary **2002**:3
O'Donnell, Rosie **1994**:3
Oldman, Gary **1998**:1
Olin, Ken **1992**:3
Oliver, Jamie **2002**:3
Olivier, Laurence
Obituary **1989**:4
Olmos, Edward James **1990**:1
Olsen, Mary-Kate and Ashley **2002**:1
Olson, Johnny
Obituary **1985**:4
O'Reilly, Bill **2001**:2
Osbournes, The **2003**:4
Osgood, Charles **1996**:2
O'Sullivan, Maureen
Obituary **1998**:4
Otte, Ruth **1992**:4
Ovitz, Michael **1990**:1
Paley, William S.
Obituary **1991**:2
Palmer, Jim **1991**:2
Pantoliano, Joe **2002**:3
Park, Nick **1997**:3
Parker, Sarah Jessica **1999**:2
Parker, Trey and Matt Stone **1998**:2
Parks, Bert
Obituary **1992**:3
Pauley, Jane **1999**:1
Paulsen, Pat
Obituary **1997**:4
Paxton, Bill **1999**:3
Peller, Clara
Obituary **1988**:1
Penn, Sean **1987**:2
Perez, Rosie **1994**:2

Perry, Luke **1992**:3
Perry, Matthew **1997**:2
Peterson, Cassandra **1988**:1
Pfeiffer, Michelle **1990**:2
Phifer, Mekhi **2004**:1
Philbin, Regis **2000**:2
Phoenix, River **1990**:2
Obituary **1994**:2
Pierce, David Hyde **1996**:3
Pierce, Frederick S. **1985**:3
Pinchot, Bronson **1987**:4
Pinkett Smith, Jada **1998**:3
Pitt, Brad **1995**:2
Pittman, Robert W. **1985**:1
Plato, Dana
Obituary **1999**:4
Pleasence, Donald
Obituary **1995**:3
Plimpton, George
Obituary **2004**:4
Poitier, Sidney **1990**:3
Potts, Annie **1994**:1
Povich, Maury **1994**:3
Powter, Susan **1994**:3
Price, Vincent
Obituary **1994**:2
Priestly, Jason **1993**:2
Prince, Faith **1993**:2
Prinze, Freddie, Jr. **1999**:3
Pryor, Richard **1999**:3
Quaid, Dennis **1989**:4
Queen Latifah **1992**:2
Queer Eye for the
Straight Guy cast **2004**:3
Quinn, Martha **1986**:4
Quivers, Robin **1995**:4
Radecki, Thomas
Brief Entry **1986**:2
Radner, Gilda
Obituary **1989**:4
Raimi, Sam **1999**:2
Randi, James **1990**:2
Raphael, Sally Jessy **1992**:4
Rashad, Phylicia **1987**:3
Raye, Martha
Obituary **1995**:1
Reasoner, Harry
Obituary **1992**:1
Redgrave, Lynn **1999**:3
Redgrave, Vanessa **1989**:2
Reed, Donna
Obituary **1986**:1
Reed, Robert
Obituary **1992**:4
Reese, Della **1999**:2
Reeve, Christopher **1997**:2
Reiner, Rob **1991**:2
Reiser, Paul **1995**:2
Remick, Lee
Obituary **1992**:1
Reuben, Gloria **1999**:4
Reubens, Paul **1987**:2
Rhea, Caroline **2004**:1
Ricci, Christina **1999**:1
Richards, Michael **1993**:4
Riddle, Nelson
Obituary **1985**:4
Ripa, Kelly **2002**:2
Ritter, John **2003**:4
Rivera, Geraldo **1989**:1
Robbins, Tim **1993**:1
Roberts, Cokie **1993**:4

Roberts, Doris **2003**:4
Roberts, Julia **1991**:3
Robertson, Pat **1988**:2
Robinson, Max
Obituary **1989**:2
Rock, Chris **1998**:1
Rock, The **2001**:2
Roddenberry, Gene
Obituary **1992**:2
Rogers, Fred **2000**:4
Rogers, Roy
Obituary **1998**:4
Roker, Al **2003**:1
Roker, Roxie
Obituary **1996**:2
Rolle, Esther
Obituary **1999**:2
Rollins, Howard E., Jr. **1986**:1
Romano, Ray **2001**:4
Rose, Charlie **1994**:2
Rourke, Mickey **1988**:4
Rowan, Dan
Obituary **1988**:1
Rudner, Rita **1993**:2
Russell, Keri **2000**:1
Ryan, Meg **1994**:1
Sagansky, Jeff **1993**:2
Sajak, Pat
Brief Entry **1985**:4
Sandler, Adam **1999**:2
Saralegui, Cristina **1999**:2
Sarandon, Susan **1995**:3
Savage, Fred **1990**:1
Savalas, Telly
Obituary **1994**:3
Sawyer, Diane **1994**:4
Schaap, Dick
Obituary **2003**:1
Schneider, Rob **1997**:4
Schwimmer, David **1996**:2
Scott, Gene
Brief Entry **1986**:1
Seacrest, Ryan **2004**:4
Sedelmaier, Joe **1985**:3
Seinfeld, Jerry **1992**:4
Sevareid, Eric
Obituary **1993**:1
Seymour, Jane **1994**:4
Shaffer, Paul **1987**:1
Shandling, Garry **1995**:1
Sharkey, Ray
Obituary **1994**:1
Shawn, Dick
Obituary **1987**:3
Sheedy, Ally **1989**:1
Sheen, Charlie **2001**:2
Sheindlin, Judith **1999**:1
Shepherd, Cybill **1996**:3
Shields, Brooke **1996**:3
Shore, Dinah
Obituary **1994**:3
Short, Martin **1986**:1
Shriver, Maria
Brief Entry **1986**:2
Shue, Andrew **1994**:4
Silverman, Jonathan **1997**:2
Silvers, Phil
Obituary **1985**:4
Silverstone, Alicia **1997**:4
Sinise, Gary **1996**:1
Siskel, Gene
Obituary **1999**:3

Candy, John **1988**:2
  Obituary **1994**:3
Carrey, Jim **1995**:1
Carson, Lisa Nicole **1999**:3
Carter, Nell
  Obituary **2004**:2
Cassavetes, John
  Obituary **1989**:2
Caulfield, Joan
  Obituary **1992**:1
Cavanagh, Tom **2003**:1
Channing, Stockard **1991**:3
Close, Glenn **1988**:3
Coco, James
  Obituary **1987**:2
Connery, Sean **1990**:4
Convy, Bert
  Obituary **1992**:1
Cook, Peter
  Obituary **1995**:2
Cooper, Chris **2004**:1
Coppola, Carmine
  Obituary **1991**:4
Costner, Kevin **1989**:4
Crawford, Broderick
  Obituary **1986**:3
Crawford, Cheryl
  Obituary **1987**:1
Crawford, Michael **1994**:2
Crisp, Quentin
  Obituary **2000**:3
Cronyn, Hume
  Obituary **2004**:3
Cruz, Nilo **2004**:4
Culkin, Macaulay **1991**:3
Cusack, John **1999**:3
Cushing, Peter
  Obituary **1995**:1
Dafoe, Willem **1988**:1
Dalton, Timothy **1988**:4
Daniels, Jeff **1989**:4
Davis, Paige **2004**:2
Day-Lewis, Daniel **1989**:4 **1994**:4
Dee, Janie **2001**:4
Dench, Judi **1999**:4
De Niro, Robert **1999**:1
Dennis, Sandy
  Obituary **1992**:4
Depardieu, Gerard **1991**:2
Dern, Laura **1992**:3
De Vito, Danny **1987**:1
Dewhurst, Colleen
  Obituary **1992**:2
Diggs, Taye **2000**:1
Douglas, Michael **1986**:2
Dukakis, Olympia **1996**:4
Duncan, Todd
  Obituary **1998**:3
Duvall, Robert **1999**:3
Ebsen, Buddy
  Obituary **2004**:3
Elliott, Denholm
  Obituary **1993**:2
Ephron, Henry
  Obituary **1993**:2
Fawcett, Farrah **1998**:4
Feld, Kenneth **1988**:2
Ferrer, Jose
  Obituary **1992**:3
Fiennes, Ralph **1996**:2
Fierstein, Harvey **2004**:2
Finney, Albert **2003**:3

Fishburne, Laurence **1995**:3
Fisher, Carrie **1991**:1
Flanders, Ed
  Obituary **1995**:3
Flockhart, Calista **1998**:4
Fo, Dario **1998**:1
Fosse, Bob
  Obituary **1988**:1
Foster, Sutton **2003**:2
Freeman, Morgan **1990**:4
Fugard, Athol **1992**:3
Gabor, Eva
  Obituary **1996**:1
Gallagher, Peter **2004**:3
Gardenia, Vincent
  Obituary **1993**:2
Garr, Teri **1988**:4
Geffen, David **1985**:3 **1997**:3
Gere, Richard **1994**:3
Gielgud, John
  Obituary **2000**:4
Gilford, Jack
  Obituary **1990**:4
Gleason, Jackie
  Obituary **1987**:4
Glover, Danny **1998**:4
Glover, Savion **1997**:1
Gobel, George
  Obituary **1991**:4
Goldberg, Whoopi **1993**:3
Goldblum, Jeff **1988**:1 **1997**:3
Gossett, Louis, Jr. **1989**:3
Grammer, Kelsey **1995**:1
Grant, Cary
  Obituary **1987**:1
Grant, Hugh **1995**:3
Greene, Graham **1997**:2
Gregory, Dick **1990**:3
Hall, Anthony Michael **1986**:3
Hamilton, Margaret
  Obituary **1985**:3
Harris, Richard
  Obituary **2004**:1
Harrison, Rex
  Obituary **1990**:4
Havel, Vaclav **1990**:3
Hawke, Ethan **1995**:4
Hayes, Helen
  Obituary **1993**:4
Hennessy, Jill **2003**:2
Henning, Doug
  Obituary **2000**:3
Hepburn, Katharine **1991**:2
Hill, George Roy
  Obituary **2004**:1
Hines, Gregory **1992**:4
Hopkins, Anthony **1992**:4
Horne, Lena **1998**:4
Hoskins, Bob **1989**:1
Houseman, John
  Obituary **1989**:1
Houston, Cissy **1999**:3
Humphries, Barry **1993**:1
Hunt, Helen **1994**:4
Hunter, Holly **1989**:4
Hurt, William **1986**:1
Hwang, David Henry **1999**:1
Irons, Jeremy **1991**:4
Irwin, Bill **1988**:3
Itami, Juzo
  Obituary **1998**:2

Ives, Burl
  Obituary **1995**:4
Jackman, Hugh **2004**:4
Jackson, Samuel L. **1995**:4
Janney, Allison **2003**:3
Jay, Ricky **1995**:1
Jillian, Ann **1986**:4
Jones, Cherry **1999**:3
Jones, Tommy Lee **1994**:2
Julia, Raul
  Obituary **1995**:1
Kahn, Madeline
  Obituary **2000**:2
Kavner, Julie **1992**:3
Kaye, Danny
  Obituary **1987**:2
Kaye, Nora
  Obituary **1987**:4
Kazan, Elia
  Obituary **2004**:4
Keeler, Ruby
  Obituary **1993**:4
Keitel, Harvey **1994**:3
Kerr, Jean
  Obituary **2004**:1
Kilmer, Val **1991**:4
Kinski, Klaus **1987**:2
  Obituary **1992**:2
Kline, Kevin **2000**:1
Kramer, Larry **1991**:2
Kushner, Tony **1995**:2
Lahti, Christine **1988**:2
Lane, Burton
  Obituary **1997**:2
Lane, Nathan **1996**:4
Lange, Jessica **1995**:4
Lansbury, Angela **1993**:1
Larson, Jonathan
  Obituary **1997**:2
Lawless, Lucy **1997**:4
Leary, Denis **1993**:3
Leigh, Jennifer Jason **1995**:2
Lithgow, John **1985**:2
Little, Cleavon
  Obituary **1993**:2
Lloyd Webber, Andrew **1989**:1
Loewe, Frederick
  Obituary **1988**:2
Logan, Joshua
  Obituary **1988**:4
Lord, Jack
  Obituary **1998**:2
MacRae, Gordon
  Obituary **1986**:2
Macy, William H. **1999**:3
Maher, Bill **1996**:2
Malkovich, John **1988**:2
Maltby, Richard, Jr. **1996**:3
Mamet, David **1998**:4
Mantegna, Joe **1992**:1
Marshall, Penny **1991**:3
Martin, Mary
  Obituary **1991**:2
McDormand, Frances **1997**:3
McDowall, Roddy
  Obituary **1999**:1
McGillis, Kelly **1989**:3
McGregor, Ewan **1998**:2
McKee, Lonette **1996**:1
McKellen, Ian **1994**:1
Merrick, David
  Obituary **2000**:4

Messing, Debra **2004**:4
Midler, Bette **1989**:4
Minghella, Anthony **2004**:3
Montand, Yves
   Obituary **1992**:2
Montgomery, Elizabeth
   Obituary **1995**:4
Moore, Dudley
   Obituary **2003**:2
Moore, Mary Tyler **1996**:2
Moss, Carrie-Anne **2004**:3
Neeson, Liam **1993**:4
Newman, Paul **1995**:3
Nichols, Mike **1994**:4
Nolan, Lloyd
   Obituary **1985**:4
Nolte, Nick **1992**:4
North, Alex **1986**:3
Northam, Jeremy **2003**:2
Nunn, Trevor **2000**:2
O'Donnell, Rosie **1994**:3
Oldman, Gary **1998**:1
Olin, Ken **1992**:3
Olin, Lena **1991**:2
Olivier, Laurence
   Obituary **1989**:4
Osborne, John
   Obituary **1995**:2
O'Sullivan, Maureen
   Obituary **1998**:4
Pacino, Al **1993**:4
Page, Geraldine
   Obituary **1987**:4
Papp, Joseph
   Obituary **1992**:2
Parks, Suzan-Lori **2003**:2
Paulsen, Pat
   Obituary **1997**:4
Peck, Gregory
   Obituary **2004**:3
Penn, Sean **1987**:2
Penn & Teller **1992**:1
Perkins, Anthony
   Obituary **1993**:2
Peters, Bernadette **2000**:1
Pfeiffer, Michelle **1990**:2
Picasso, Paloma **1991**:1
Pinchot, Bronson **1987**:4
Pleasence, Donald
   Obituary **1995**:3
Poitier, Sidney **1990**:3
Preminger, Otto
   Obituary **1986**:3
Preston, Robert
   Obituary **1987**:3
Price, Vincent
   Obituary **1994**:2
Prince, Faith **1993**:2
Quaid, Dennis **1989**:4
Radner, Gilda
   Obituary **1989**:4
Rashad, Phylicia **1987**:3
Raye, Martha
   Obituary **1995**:1
Redford, Robert **1993**:2
Redgrave, Lynn **1999**:3
Redgrave, Vanessa **1989**:2
Reeves, Keanu **1992**:1
Reilly, John C. **2003**:4
Reitman, Ivan **1986**:3
Reza, Yasmina **1999**:2
Richards, Michael **1993**:4

Ritter, John **2003**:4
Robbins, Jerome
   Obituary **1999**:1
Roberts, Doris **2003**:4
Roker, Roxie
   Obituary **1996**:2
Rolle, Esther
   Obituary **1999**:2
Rudner, Rita **1993**:2
Rudnick, Paul **1994**:3
Ruehl, Mercedes **1992**:4
Salonga, Lea **2003**:3
Sarandon, Susan **1995**:3
Schoenfeld, Gerald **1986**:2
Schwimmer, David **1996**:2
Scott, George C.
   Obituary **2000**:2
Seymour, Jane **1994**:4
Shaffer, Paul **1987**:1
Shawn, Dick
   Obituary **1987**:3
Shepard, Sam **1996**:4
Short, Martin **1986**:1
Silvers, Phil
   Obituary **1985**:4
Sinise, Gary **1996**:1
Slater, Christian **1994**:1
Smith, Anna Deavere **2002**:2
Snipes, Wesley **1993**:1
Sondheim, Stephen **1994**:4
Spacey, Kevin **1996**:4
Steiger, Rod
   Obituary **2003**:4
Stewart, Jimmy
   Obituary **1997**:4
Stewart, Patrick **1996**:1
Stiller, Ben **1999**:1
Sting **1991**:4
Stoppard, Tom **1995**:4
Streep, Meryl **1990**:2
Streisand, Barbra **1992**:2
Stritch, Elaine **2002**:4
Styne, Jule
   Obituary **1995**:1
Susskind, David
   Obituary **1987**:2
Tandy, Jessica **1990**:4
   Obituary **1995**:1
Taylor, Elizabeth **1993**:3
Taylor, Lili **2000**:2
Thompson, Emma **1993**:2
Tomei, Marisa **1995**:2
Tucci, Stanley **2003**:2
Tune, Tommy **1994**:2
Ullman, Tracey **1988**:3
Urich, Robert **1988**:1
   Obituary **2003**:3
Vardalos, Nia **2003**:4
Vogel, Paula **1999**:2
Walker, Nancy
   Obituary **1992**:3
Washington, Denzel **1993**:2
Wasserstein, Wendy **1991**:3
Wayne, David
   Obituary **1995**:3
Weaver, Sigourney **1988**:3
Weitz, Bruce **1985**:4
Wences, Senor
   Obituary **1999**:4
Whitaker, Forest **1996**:2
Whitehead, Robert
   Obituary **2003**:3

Wiest, Dianne **1995**:2
Wilkinson, Tom **2003**:2
Williams, Treat **2004**:3
Willis, Bruce **1986**:4
Wong, B.D. **1998**:1
Woods, James **1988**:3
Worth, Irene
   Obituary **2003**:2
Wyle, Noah **1997**:3
Youngman, Henny
   Obituary **1998**:3
Zeffirelli, Franco **1991**:3

WRITING

Adams, Douglas
   Obituary **2002**:2
Adams, Scott **1996**:4
Albom, Mitch **1999**:3
Alexie, Sherman **1998**:4
Amanpour, Christiane **1997**:2
Ambler, Eric
   Obituary **1999**:2
Ambrose, Stephen **2002**:3
Amis, Kingsley
   Obituary **1996**:2
Amory, Cleveland
   Obituary **1999**:2
Anderson, Poul
   Obituary **2002**:3
Angelou, Maya **1993**:4
Angier, Natalie **2000**:3
Asimov, Isaac
   Obituary **1992**:3
Atkins, Robert C.
   Obituary **2004**:2
Atwood, Margaret **2001**:2
Axthelm, Pete
   Obituary **1991**:3
Bacall, Lauren **1997**:3
Bakker, Robert T. **1991**:3
Baldwin, James
   Obituary **1988**:2
Ball, Edward **1999**:2
Baraka, Amiri **2000**:3
Barber, Red
   Obituary **1993**:2
Barker, Clive **2003**:3
Barry, Dave **1991**:2
Barry, Lynda **1992**:1
Beckett, Samuel Barclay
   Obituary **1990**:2
Bloodworth-Thomason,
   Linda **1994**:1
Blume, Judy **1998**:4
Bly, Robert **1992**:4
Blyth, Myrna **2002**:4
Bombeck, Erma
   Obituary **1996**:4
Bowles, Paul
   Obituary **2000**:3
Boynton, Sandra **2004**:1
Bradford, Barbara Taylor **2002**:4
Bradshaw, John **1992**:1
Branagh, Kenneth **1992**:2
Brodsky, Joseph
   Obituary **1996**:3
Brokaw, Tom **2000**:3
Brooks, Gwendolyn **1998**:1
   Obituary **2001**:2
Brown, Dan **2004**:4
Brown, Dee
   Obituary **2004**:1

Brown, Tina **1992**:1
Buffett, Jimmy **1999**:3
Burgess, Anthony
  Obituary **1994**:2
Burroughs, William S.
  Obituary **1997**:4
Burroughs, William S. **1994**:2
Buscaglia, Leo
  Obituary **1998**:4
Busch, Charles **1998**:3
Bush, Millie **1992**:1
Bushnell, Candace **2004**:2
Butler, Octavia E. **1999**:3
Byrne, Gabriel **1997**:4
Caen, Herb
  Obituary **1997**:4
Campbell, Bebe Moore **1996**:2
Caplan, Arthur L. **2000**:2
Carcaterra, Lorenzo **1996**:1
Carey, George **1992**:3
Carlson, Richard **2002**:1
Carver, Raymond
  Obituary **1989**:1
Castaneda, Carlos
  Obituary **1998**:4
Castillo, Ana **2000**:4
Cela, Camilo Jose
  Obituary **2003**:1
Chabon, Michael **2002**:1
Chatwin, Bruce
  Obituary **1989**:2
Chavez, Linda **1999**:3
Cheney, Lynne V. **1990**:4
Child, Julia **1999**:4
Chopra, Deepak **1996**:3
Clancy, Tom **1998**:4
Clark, Mary Higgins **2000**:4
Clavell, James
  Obituary **1995**:1
Cleaver, Eldridge
  Obituary **1998**:4
Codrescu, Andre **1997**:3
Coetzee, J. M. **2004**:4
Cole, Johnetta B. **1994**:3
Coles, Robert **1995**:1
Collins, Billy **2002**:2
Collins, Jackie **2004**:4
Comfort, Alex
  Obituary **2000**:4
Condon, Richard
  Obituary **1996**:4
Cook, Robin **1996**:3
Cornwell, Patricia **2003**:1
Cosby, Bill **1999**:2
Covey, Stephen R. **1994**:4
Cowley, Malcolm
  Obituary **1989**:3
Crichton, Michael **1995**:3
Cronenberg, David **1992**:3
Cruz, Nilo **2004**:4
Cunningham, Michael **2003**:4
Dahl, Roald
  Obituary **1991**:2
Darden, Christopher **1996**:4
David, Larry **2003**:4
Davis, Patti **1995**:1
Delany, Sarah
  Obituary **1999**:3
Dershowitz, Alan **1992**:1
Diamond, I.A.L.
  Obituary **1988**:3

Diamond, Selma
  Obituary **1985**:2
Dickey, James
  Obituary **1998**:2
Dickinson, Brian **1998**:2
Djerassi, Carl **2000**:4
Dorris, Michael
  Obituary **1997**:3
Douglas, Marjory Stoneman **1993**:1
  Obituary **1998**:4
Dove, Rita **1994**:3
Dowd, Maureen Brigid **1997**:1
Drucker, Peter F. **1992**:3
Dunne, Dominick **1997**:1
Duras, Marguerite
  Obituary **1996**:3
Durrell, Gerald
  Obituary **1995**:3
Ebert, Roger **1998**:3
Edwards, Bob **1993**:2
Eggers, Dave **2001**:3
Elliott, Missy **2003**:4
Ellison, Ralph
  Obituary **1994**:4
Ellroy, James **2003**:4
Ephron, Nora **1992**:3
Epstein, Jason **1991**:1
Etzioni, Amitai **1994**:3
Evans, Joni **1991**:4
Evans, Robert **2004**:1
Fabio **1993**:4
Falconer, Ian **2003**:1
Faludi, Susan **1992**:4
Fast, Howard
  Obituary **2004**:2
Fielding, Helen **2000**:4
Filipovic, Zlata **1994**:4
Fish, Hamilton
  Obituary **1991**:3
Fisher, Carrie **1991**:1
Flynt, Larry **1997**:3
Fo, Dario **1998**:1
Fodor, Eugene
  Obituary **1991**:3
Foote, Shelby **1991**:2
Forbes, Steve **1996**:2
Foxworthy, Jeff **1996**:1
Franken, Al **1996**:3
Frankl, Viktor E.
  Obituary **1998**:1
Franzen, Jonathan **2002**:3
Frazier, Charles **2003**:2
Friedan, Betty **1994**:2
Frye, Northrop
  Obituary **1991**:3
Fugard, Athol **1992**:3
Fulbright, J. William
  Obituary **1995**:3
Fulghum, Robert **1996**:1
Gaines, William M.
  Obituary **1993**:1
Gao Xingjian **2001**:2
Garcia, Cristina **1997**:4
Geisel, Theodor
  Obituary **1992**:2
George, Elizabeth **2003**:3
Gibson, William Ford, III **1997**:2
Gillespie, Marcia **1999**:4
Ginsberg, Allen
  Obituary **1997**:3
Goldman, William **2001**:1
Gore, Albert, Jr. **1993**:2

Goren, Charles H.
  Obituary **1991**:4
Grafton, Sue **2000**:2
Graham, Billy **1992**:1
Graham, Katharine Meyer **1997**:3
  Obituary **2002**:3
Grass, Gunter **2000**:2
Gray, John **1995**:3
Greene, Graham
  Obituary **1991**:4
Grisham, John **1994**:4
Grodin, Charles **1997**:3
Guccione, Bob, Jr. **1991**:4
Ha Jin **2000**:3
Haley, Alex
  Obituary **1992**:3
Handford, Martin **1991**:3
Handler, Daniel **2003**:3
Harris, E. Lynn **2004**:2
Harris, Thomas **2001**:1
Hart, Mickey **1991**:2
Havel, Vaclav **1990**:3
Hayakawa, Samuel Ichiye
  Obituary **1992**:3
Heaney, Seamus **1996**:2
Heat-Moon, William Least **2000**:2
Heller, Joseph
  Obituary **2000**:2
Heloise **2001**:4
Herzog, Chaim
  Obituary **1997**:3
Highsmith, Patricia
  Obituary **1995**:3
hooks, bell **2000**:2
Hornby, Nick **2002**:2
Hrabal, Bohumil
  Obituary **1997**:3
Hughes, Robert **1996**:4
Hughes, Ted
  Obituary **1999**:2
Humphries, Barry **1993**:1
Humphry, Derek **1992**:2
Hwang, David Henry **1999**:1
Ice-T **1992**:3
Ivins, Molly **1993**:4
Jacques, Brian **2002**:2
Jay, Ricky **1995**:1
Jen, Gish **2000**:1
Jenkins, Sally **1997**:2
Jennings, Peter Charles **1997**:2
Jewel **1999**:2
Johnson, Diane **2004**:3
Jones, Gayl **1999**:4
Jones, Jenny **1998**:2
Jong, Erica **1998**:3
Jordan, Neil **1993**:3
Jurgensen, Karen **2004**:3
Kael, Pauline **2000**:4
  Obituary **2002**:4
Kahane, Meir
  Obituary **1991**:2
Kasparov, Garry **1997**:4
Kazan, Elia
  Obituary **2004**:4
Kennedy, John F., Jr. **1990**:1
  Obituary **1999**:4
Kent, Arthur **1991**:4 **1997**:2
Kerr, Jean
  Obituary **2004**:1
Kerr, Walter
  Obituary **1997**:1

Cumulative Subject Index

This index lists all newsmakers by subjects, company names, products, organizations, issues, awards, and professional specialties. Indexes in softbound issues allow access to the current year's entries; indexes in annual hardbound volumes are cumulative, covering the entire *Newsmakers* series.

Listee names are followed by a year and issue number; thus **1996**:3 indicates that an entry on that individual appears in both 1996, Issue 3, and the 1996 cumulation. For access to newsmakers appearing earlier than the current softbound issue, see the previous year's cumulation.

ABC Television
Arledge, Roone **1992**:2
Diller, Barry **1991**:1
Funt, Allen
Obituary **2000**:1
Philbin, Regis **2000**:2
Pierce, Frederick S. **1985**:3

ABT
See: American Ballet Theatre

Abortion
Allred, Gloria **1985**:2
Baird, Bill
Brief Entry **1987**:2
Baulieu, Etienne-Emile **1990**:1
Brown, Judie **1986**:2
Falkenberg, Nanette **1985**:2
Kissling, Frances **1989**:2
Morgentaler, Henry **1986**:3
Terry, Randall **1991**:4
Wattleton, Faye **1989**:1
Yard, Molly **1991**:4

Abscam
Neal, James Foster **1986**:2
Puccio, Thomas P. **1986**:4

Academy Awards
Affleck, Ben **1999**:1
Allen, Woody **1994**:1
Almodovar, Pedro **2000**:3
Ameche, Don
Obituary **1994**:2
Andrews, Julie **1996**:1
Arlen, Harold
Obituary **1986**:3
Arthur, Jean
Obituary **1992**:1
Ashcroft, Peggy
Obituary **1992**:1
Astor, Mary
Obituary **1988**:1
Barbera, Joseph **1988**:2
Baryshnikov, Mikhail
Nikolaevich **1997**:3

Bates, Kathy **1991**:4
Baxter, Anne
Obituary **1986**:1
Beatty, Warren **2000**:1
Benigni, Roberto **1999**:2
Bergman, Ingmar **1999**:4
Berlin, Irving
Obituary **1990**:1
Binoche, Juliette **2001**:3
Booth, Shirley
Obituary **1993**:2
Brooks, Mel **2003**:1
Brynner, Yul
Obituary **1985**:4
Burstyn, Ellen **2001**:4
Cagney, James
Obituary **1986**:2
Caine, Michael **2000**:4
Capra, Frank
Obituary **1992**:2
Cassavetes, John
Obituary **1989**:2
Cher **1993**:1
Coburn, James
Obituary **2004**:1
Connelly, Jennifer **2002**:4
Connery, Sean **1990**:4
Cooper, Chris **2004**:1
Copland, Aaron
Obituary **1991**:2
Coppola, Carmine
Obituary **1991**:4
Coppola, Francis Ford **1989**:4
Coppola, Sofia **2004**:3
Crawford, Broderick
Obituary **1986**:3
Damon, Matt **1999**:1
Davis, Bette
Obituary **1990**:1
Davis, Geena **1992**:1
Del Toro, Benicio **2001**:4
Demme, Jonathan **1992**:4
Dench, Judi **1999**:4
De Niro, Robert **1999**:1
Dennis, Sandy
Obituary **1992**:4

Diamond, I.A.L.
Obituary **1988**:3
Douglas, Michael **1986**:2
Duvall, Robert **1999**:3
Eastwood, Clint **1993**:3
Elliott, Denholm
Obituary **1993**:2
Fellini, Federico
Obituary **1994**:2
Ferrer, Jose
Obituary **1992**:3
Field, Sally **1995**:3
Fosse, Bob
Obituary **1988**:1
Gielgud, John
Obituary **2000**:4
Gish, Lillian
Obituary **1993**:4
Goldberg, Whoopi **1993**:3
Goldman, William **2001**:1
Gooding, Cuba, Jr. **1997**:3
Gossett, Louis, Jr. **1989**:3
Grant, Cary
Obituary **1987**:1
Guggenheim, Charles
Obituary **2003**:4
Hackman, Gene **1989**:3
Hanks, Tom **1989**:2 **2000**:2
Harden, Marcia Gay **2002**:4
Hawn, Goldie Jeanne **1997**:2
Hayes, Helen
Obituary **1993**:4
Hayes, Isaac **1998**:4
Hepburn, Audrey
Obituary **1993**:2
Hepburn, Katharine **1991**:2
Heston, Charlton **1999**:4
Hill, George Roy
Obituary **2004**:1
Hope, Bob
Obituary **2004**:4
Hopkins, Anthony **1992**:4
Houseman, John
Obituary **1989**:1
Hurt, William **1986**:1
Huston, Anjelica **1989**:3

Vinton, Will
  Brief Entry **1988**:1
Whittle, Christopher **1989**:3

AFL-CIO
  See: American Federation of Labor
  and Congress of Industrial
  Organizations

African National Congress
  Buthelezi, Mangosuthu
    Gatsha **1989**:3
  Hani, Chris
    Obituary **1993**:4
  Mandela, Nelson **1990**:3
  Mbeki, Thabo **1999**:4
  Sisulu, Walter
    Obituary **2004**:2
  Slovo, Joe **1989**:2
  Tambo, Oliver **1991**:3

Agriculture
  Davis, Noel **1990**:3

AIDS
  See: Acquired Immune Deficiency
  Syndrome

AIDS Coalition to Unleash Power
  Kramer, Larry **1991**:2

AIM
  See: American Indian Movement
  Peltier, Leonard **1995**:1

A.J. Canfield Co.
  Canfield, Alan B.
    Brief Entry **1986**:3

ALA
  See: American Library Association

Albert Nipon, Inc.
  Nipon, Albert
    Brief Entry **1986**:4

Alcohol abuse
  Anastas, Robert
    Brief Entry **1985**:2
  Bradshaw, John **1992**:1
  Lightner, Candy **1985**:1
  MacRae, Gordon
    Obituary **1986**:2
  Mantle, Mickey
    Obituary **1996**:1
  Welch, Bob **1991**:3

ALL
  See: American Life League

Alternative medicine
  Jacobs, Joe **1994**:1
  Weil, Andrew **1997**:4

Alvin Ailey Dance Theatre
  Jamison, Judith **1990**:3

AMA
  See: American Medical Association

Amazon.com, Inc.
  Bezos, Jeff **1998**:4

**American Academy and Institute of
Arts and Letters**
  Brooks, Gwendolyn **1998**:1
    Obituary **2001**:2
  Cunningham, Merce **1998**:1
  Dickey, James
    Obituary **1998**:2
  Foster, Norman **1999**:4
  Graves, Michael **2000**:1
  Mamet, David **1998**:4
  Roth, Philip **1999**:1
  Vonnegut, Kurt **1998**:4
  Walker, Alice **1999**:1
  Wolfe, Tom **1999**:2

American Airlines
  Crandall, Robert L. **1992**:1

American Ballet Theatre
  Bissell, Patrick
    Obituary **1988**:2
  Bocca, Julio **1995**:3
  Englund, Richard
    Obituary **1991**:3
  Feld, Eliot **1996**:1
  Ferri, Alessandra **1987**:2
  Godunov, Alexander
    Obituary **1995**:4
  Gregory, Cynthia **1990**:2
  Herrera, Paloma **1996**:2
  Kaye, Nora
    Obituary **1987**:4
  Lander, Toni
    Obituary **1985**:4
  Parker, Sarah Jessica **1999**:2
  Renvall, Johan
    Brief Entry **1987**:4
  Robbins, Jerome
    Obituary **1999**:1
  Tudor, Antony
    Obituary **1987**:4

American Book Awards
  Alexie, Sherman **1998**:4
  Baraka, Amiri **2000**:3
  Child, Julia **1999**:4
  Kissinger, Henry **1999**:4
  Walker, Alice **1999**:1
  Wolfe, Tom **1999**:2

American Civil Liberties Union
  Abzug, Bella **1998**:2
  Glasser, Ira **1989**:1

American Express
  Chenault, Kenneth I. **1999**:3
  Weill, Sandy **1990**:4

**American Federation of Labor and
Congress of Industrial Organizations**
  Chavez-Thompson, Linda **1999**:1
  Sweeney, John J. **2000**:3

American Indian Movement
  Banks, Dennis J. **1986**:4

American Library Association
  Blume, Judy **1998**:4
  Heat-Moon, William Least **2000**:2
  Schuman, Patricia Glass **1993**:2
  Steel, Danielle **1999**:2

American Life League
  Brown, Judie **1986**:2

American Medical Association
  Bristow, Lonnie **1996**:1

**Amer-I-can minority empowerment
program**
  Brown, Jim **1993**:2

American Museum of Natural History
  Futter, Ellen V. **1995**:1

American Music Awards
  Ashanti **2004**:1
  Badu, Erykah **2000**:4
  Boyz II Men **1995**:1
  Brooks, Garth **1992**:1
  Cole, Natalie **1992**:4
  Franklin, Aretha **1998**:3
  Jackson, Alan **2003**:1
  Jackson, Michael **1996**:2
  Jewel **1999**:2
  Loveless, Patty **1998**:2
  McEntire, Reba **1987**:3 **1994**:2
  Newton-John, Olivia **1998**:4
  Parton, Dolly **1999**:4
  Spears, Britney **2000**:3
  Strait, George **1998**:3
  Turner, Tina **2000**:3
  Yoakam, Dwight **1992**:4

American Power Boat Association
  Copeland, Al **1988**:3
  Hanauer, Chip **1986**:2

America Online
  Case, Steve **1995**:4 **1996**:4
  Kimsey, James V. **2001**:1

America's Cup
  Bond, Alan **1989**:2
  Conner, Dennis **1987**:2
  Turner, Ted **1989**:1

Amnesty International
  Healey, Jack **1990**:1
  Wiesel, Elie **1998**:1

Anaheim Angels baseball team
Glaus, Troy **2003**:3
Vaughn, Mo **1999**:2

ANC
See: African National Congress

Anheuser-Busch, Inc.
Busch, August A. III **1988**:2
Busch, August Anheuser, Jr.
Obituary **1990**:2

Animal rights
Amory, Cleveland
Obituary **1999**:2
Caras, Roger
Obituary **2002**:1
Hurley, Elizabeth **1999**:2
Newkirk, Ingrid **1992**:3
Steel, Danielle **1999**:2

Animal training
Burck, Wade
Brief Entry **1986**:1
Butcher, Susan **1991**:1

Anthropology
Beattie, Owen
Brief Entry **1985**:2
Castaneda, Carlos
Obituary **1998**:4
Cole, Johnetta B. **1994**:3
Leakey, Richard **1994**:2
Montagu, Ashley
Obituary **2000**:2

AOL
See: America Online

Apartheid
Biehl, Amy
Obituary **1994**:1
Blackburn, Molly
Obituary **1985**:4
Buthelezi, Mangosuthu
Gatsha **1989**:3
Carter, Amy **1987**:4
de Klerk, F.W. **1990**:1
Duncan, Sheena
Brief Entry **1987**:1
Fugard, Athol **1992**:3
Hoffman, Abbie
Obituary **1989**:3
Makeba, Miriam **1989**:2
Mandela, Winnie **1989**:3
Paton, Alan
Obituary **1988**:3
Ramaphosa, Cyril **1988**:2
Suzman, Helen **1989**:3
Tambo, Oliver **1991**:3
Treurnicht, Andries **1992**:2
Woods, Donald
Obituary **2002**:3

APBA
See: American Power Boat
Association

Apple Computer, Inc.
Jobs, Steve **2000**:1
Perlman, Steve **1998**:2
Raskin, Jef **1997**:4
Sculley, John **1989**:4

Archaeology
Soren, David
Brief Entry **1986**:3

Architecture
Bunshaft, Gordon **1989**:3
Obituary **1991**:1
Cooper, Alexander **1988**:4
Diller, Elizabeth and Ricardo
Scofidio **2004**:3
Eisenman, Peter **1992**:4
Erickson, Arthur **1989**:3
Foster, Norman **1999**:4
Gehry, Frank O. **1987**:1
Goody, Joan **1990**:2
Graves, Michael **2000**:1
Holl, Steven **2003**:1
Isozaki, Arata **1990**:2
Jahn, Helmut **1987**:3
Johnson, Philip **1989**:2
Kiefer, Anselm **1990**:2
Lapidus, Morris
Obituary **2001**:4
Lasdun, Denys
Obituary **2001**:4
Libeskind, Daniel **2004**:1
Lin, Maya **1990**:3
McDonough, William **2003**:1
Meier, Richard **2001**:4
Moneo, Jose Rafael **1996**:4
Mumford, Lewis
Obituary **1990**:2
Pedersen, William **1989**:4
Pei, I.M. **1990**:4
Pelli, Cesar **1991**:4
Portman, John **1988**:2
Predock, Antoine **1993**:2
Roche, Kevin **1985**:1
Rockwell, David **2003**:3
Rouse, James
Obituary **1996**:4
Venturi, Robert **1994**:4
Yamasaki, Minoru
Obituary **1986**:2

Argus Corp. Ltd.
Black, Conrad **1986**:2

Arizona state government
Hull, Jane Dee **1999**:2

Arkansas state government
Clinton, Bill **1992**:1

Artificial heart
Jarvik, Robert K. **1985**:1
Schroeder, William J.
Obituary **1986**:4

Artificial intelligence
Minsky, Marvin **1994**:3

Association of Southeast Asian Nations
Bolkiah, Sultan Muda
Hassanal **1985**:4

Astronautics
Bean, Alan L. **1986**:2
Collins, Eileen **1995**:3
Conrad, Pete
Obituary **2000**:1
Dzhanibekov, Vladimir **1988**:1
Garneau, Marc **1985**:1
Glenn, John **1998**:3
Lucid, Shannon **1997**:1
McAuliffe, Christa
Obituary **1985**:4
Whitson, Peggy **2003**:3

Astronomy
Bopp, Thomas **1997**:3
Geller, Margaret Joan **1998**:2
Hale, Alan **1997**:3
Hawking, Stephen W. **1990**:1
Hoyle, Sir Fred
Obituary **2002**:4
Marsden, Brian **2004**:4
Smoot, George F. **1993**:3

AT&T
Allen, Bob **1992**:4
Armstrong, C. Michael **2002**:1

Atari
Bushnell, Nolan **1985**:1
Kingsborough, Donald
Brief Entry **1986**:2
Perlman, Steve **1998**:2

Atlanta Braves baseball team
Lofton, Kenny **1998**:1
Maddux, Greg **1996**:2
Sanders, Deion **1992**:4
Turner, Ted **1989**:1

Atlanta Falcons football team
Sanders, Deion **1992**:4

Atlanta Hawks basketball team
Maravich, Pete
Obituary **1988**:2
McMillen, Tom **1988**:4
Turner, Ted **1989**:1
Wilkens, Lenny **1995**:2

Atlantic Records
Ertegun, Ahmet **1986**:3

Automobile racing
Earnhardt, Dale, Jr. **2004**:4
Ferrari, Enzo **1988**:4
Fittipaldi, Emerson **1994**:2
Gordon, Jeff **1996**:1
Muldowney, Shirley **1986**:1
Newman, Paul **1995**:3
Penske, Roger **1988**:3
Porsche, Ferdinand
Obituary **1998**:4
Prost, Alain **1988**:1
St. James, Lyn **1993**:2

Carnival Cruise Lines
Arison, Ted **1990**:3

Car repair
Magliozzi, Tom and Ray **1991**:4

Cartoons
Addams, Charles
Obituary **1989**:1
Barbera, Joseph **1988**:2
Barry, Lynda **1992**:1
Blanc, Mel
Obituary **1989**:4
Chast, Roz **1992**:4
Disney, Roy E. **1986**:3
Freleng, Friz
Obituary **1995**:4
Gaines, William M.
Obituary **1993**:1
Gould, Chester
Obituary **1985**:2
Groening, Matt **1990**:4
Judge, Mike **1994**:2
MacNelly, Jeff
Obituary **2000**:4
Mauldin, Bill
Obituary **2004**:2
Parker, Trey and Matt Stone **1998**:2
Schulz, Charles
Obituary **2000**:3
Schulz, Charles M. **1998**:1
Spiegelman, Art **1998**:3
Tartakovsky, Genndy **2004**:4
Trudeau, Garry **1991**:2
Watterson, Bill **1990**:3

Catholic Church
Beckett, Wendy (Sister) **1998**:3
Bernardin, Cardinal Joseph **1997**:2
Burns, Charles R.
Brief Entry **1988**:1
Clements, George **1985**:1
Cunningham, Reverend William
Obituary **1997**:4
Curran, Charles E. **1989**:2
Daily, Bishop Thomas V. **1990**:4
Dearden, John Cardinal
Obituary **1988**:4
Fox, Matthew **1992**:2
Healy, Timothy S. **1990**:2
Hume, Basil Cardinal
Obituary **2000**:1
John Paul II, Pope **1995**:3
Kissling, Frances **1989**:2
Krol, John
Obituary **1996**:3
Lefebvre, Marcel **1988**:4
Mahony, Roger M. **1988**:2
Maida, Adam Cardinal **1998**:2
Obando, Miguel **1986**:4
O'Connor, Cardinal John **1990**:3
O'Connor, John
Obituary **2000**:4
Peter, Valentine J. **1988**:2
Rock, John
Obituary **1985**:1
Stallings, George A., Jr. **1990**:1

CAT Scanner
Hounsfield, Godfrey **1989**:2

Cattle rustling
Cantrell, Ed
Brief Entry **1985**:3

Caviar
Petrossian, Christian
Brief Entry **1985**:3

CBC
See: Canadian Broadcasting Corp.

CBS, Inc.
Cox, Richard Joseph
Brief Entry **1985**:1
Cronkite, Walter Leland **1997**:3
Moonves, Les **2004**:2
Paley, William S.
Obituary **1991**:2
Reasoner, Harry
Obituary **1992**:1
Sagansky, Jeff **1993**:2
Tellem, Nancy **2004**:4
Tisch, Laurence A. **1988**:2
Yetnikoff, Walter **1988**:1

CDF
See: Children's Defense Fund

Center for Equal Opportunity
Chavez, Linda **1999**:3

Centers for Living
Williamson, Marianne **1991**:4

Central America
Astorga, Nora **1988**:2
Cruz, Arturo **1985**:1
Obando, Miguel **1986**:4
Robelo, Alfonso **1988**:1

Central Intelligence Agency
Carter, Amy **1987**:4
Casey, William
Obituary **1987**:3
Colby, William E.
Obituary **1996**:4
Deutch, John **1996**:4
Gates, Robert M. **1992**:2
Inman, Bobby Ray **1985**:1
Tenet, George **2000**:3

Centurion Ministries
McCloskey, James **1993**:1

Cesar Awards
Adjani, Isabelle **1991**:1
Deneuve, Catherine **2003**:2
Depardieu, Gerard **1991**:2
Tautou, Audrey **2004**:2

Chanel, Inc.
D'Alessio, Kitty
Brief Entry **1987**:3
Lagerfeld, Karl **1999**:4

Chantal Pharmacentical Corp.
Burnison, Chantal Simone **1988**:3

Charlotte Hornets basketball team
Bryant, Kobe **1998**:3
Johnson, Larry **1993**:3
Mourning, Alonzo **1994**:2

Chef Boy-ar-dee
Boiardi, Hector
Obituary **1985**:3

Chess
Kasparov, Garry **1997**:4
Polgar, Judit **1993**:3

Chicago Bears football team
McMahon, Jim **1985**:4
Payton, Walter
Obituary **2000**:2

Chicago Bulls basketball team
Jackson, Phil **1996**:3
Jordan, Michael **1987**:2
Kukoc, Toni **1995**:4
Pippen, Scottie **1992**:2

Chicago Blackhawks
Hasek, Dominik **1998**:3

Chicago Cubs baseball team
Caray, Harry **1988**:3
Obituary **1998**:3
Sosa, Sammy **1999**:1

Chicago, Ill., city government
Washington, Harold
Obituary **1988**:1

Chicago White Sox baseball team
Caray, Harry **1988**:3
Obituary **1998**:3
Leyland, Jim **1998**:2
Thomas, Frank **1994**:3
Veeck, Bill
Obituary **1986**:1

Child care
Hale, Clara
Obituary **1993**:3
Leach, Penelope **1992**:4
Spock, Benjamin **1995**:2
Obituary **1998**:3

Children's Defense Fund
Clinton, Hillary Rodham **1993**:2
Edelman, Marian Wright **1990**:4

Chimpanzees
Goodall, Jane **1991**:1

Choreography
Abdul, Paula **1990**:3
Ailey, Alvin **1989**:2
Obituary **1990**:2
Astaire, Fred
Obituary **1987**:4
Bennett, Michael
Obituary **1988**:1
Cunningham, Merce **1998**:1
Dean, Laura **1989**:4

de Mille, Agnes
Obituary **1994**:2
Feld, Eliot **1996**:1
Fenley, Molissa **1988**:3
Forsythe, William **1993**:2
Fosse, Bob
Obituary **1988**:1
Glover, Savion **1997**:1
Graham, Martha
Obituary **1991**:4
Jamison, Judith **1990**:3
Joffrey, Robert
Obituary **1988**:3
Jones, Bill T. **1991**:4
MacMillan, Kenneth
Obituary **1993**:2
Mitchell, Arthur **1995**:1
Morris, Mark **1991**:1
Nureyev, Rudolf
Obituary **1993**:2
Parsons, David **1993**:4
Ross, Herbert
Obituary **2002**:4
Takei, Kei **1990**:2
Taylor, Paul **1992**:3
Tharp, Twyla **1992**:4
Tudor, Antony
Obituary **1987**:4
Tune, Tommy **1994**:2
Varone, Doug **2001**:2

Christian Coalition
Reed, Ralph **1995**:1

Christic Institute
Sheehan, Daniel P. **1989**:1

Chrysler Motor Corp.
Eaton, Robert J. **1994**:2
Iacocca, Lee **1993**:1
Lutz, Robert A. **1990**:1

CHUCK
See: Committee to Halt Useless
College Killings

Church of England
Carey, George **1992**:3
Runcie, Robert **1989**:4
Obituary **2001**:1

**Church of Jesus Christ of Latter-Day
Saints**
See: Mormon Church

CIA
See: Central Intelligence Agency

Cincinatti Bengals football team
Esiason, Boomer **1991**:1

Cincinnati Reds baseball team
Davis, Eric **1987**:4
Rose, Pete **1991**:1
Schott, Marge **1985**:4

Cinematography
Burum, Stephen H.
Brief Entry **1987**:2
Markle, C. Wilson **1988**:1
McLaren, Norman
Obituary **1987**:2

Civil rights
Abernathy, Ralph
Obituary **1990**:3
Abzug, Bella **1998**:2
Allen Jr., Ivan
Obituary **2004**:3
Allred, Gloria **1985**:2
Aquino, Corazon **1986**:2
Baldwin, James
Obituary **1988**:2
Banks, Dennis J. **1986**:4
Blackburn, Molly
Obituary **1985**:4
Buthelezi, Mangosuthu
Gatsha **1989**:3
Chavez, Linda **1999**:3
Chavis, Benjamin **1993**:4
Clements, George **1985**:1
Connerly, Ward **2000**:2
Davis, Angela **1998**:3
Dees, Morris **1992**:1
Delany, Sarah
Obituary **1999**:3
Duncan, Sheena
Brief Entry **1987**:1
Farmer, James
Obituary **2000**:1
Faubus, Orval
Obituary **1995**:2
Glasser, Ira **1989**:1
Griffiths, Martha
Obituary **2004**:2
Harris, Barbara **1989**:3
Healey, Jack **1990**:1
Hoffman, Abbie
Obituary **1989**:3
Hume, John **1987**:1
Jordan, Vernon, Jr. **2002**:3
King, Bernice **2000**:2
King, Coretta Scott **1999**:3
Kunstler, William **1992**:3
Makeba, Miriam **1989**:2
Mandela, Winnie **1989**:3
Marshall, Thurgood
Obituary **1993**:3
McGuinness, Martin **1985**:4
Pendleton, Clarence M.
Obituary **1988**:4
Ram, Jagjivan
Obituary **1986**:4
Shabazz, Betty
Obituary **1997**:4
Sharpton, Al **1991**:2
Shcharansky, Anatoly **1986**:2
Simone, Nina
Obituary **2004**:2
Slovo, Joe **1989**:2
Stallings, George A., Jr. **1990**:1
Steele, Shelby **1991**:2
Sullivan, Leon
Obituary **2002**:2
Suzman, Helen **1989**:3

Ture, Kwame
Obituary **1999**:2
Washington, Harold
Obituary **1988**:1
West, Cornel **1994**:2
Williams, G. Mennen
Obituary **1988**:2
Williams, Hosea
Obituary **2001**:2
Wu, Harry **1996**:1

Civil War
Foote, Shelby **1991**:2

Claymation
Park, Nick **1997**:3
Vinton, Will
Brief Entry **1988**:1

Cleveland Ballet Dancing Wheels
Verdi-Fletcher, Mary **1998**:2

Cleveland Browns football team
Brown, Jim **1993**:2

Cleveland Cavaliers basketball team
Wilkens, Lenny **1995**:2

Cleveland city government
Stokes, Carl
Obituary **1996**:4

Cleveland Indians baseball team
Belle, Albert **1996**:4
Boudreau, Louis
Obituary **2002**:3
Greenberg, Hank
Obituary **1986**:4
Lofton, Kenny **1998**:1
Veeck, Bill
Obituary **1986**:1

Cliff's Notes
Hillegass, Clifton Keith **1989**:4

Climatology
Thompson, Starley
Brief Entry **1987**:3

Clio Awards
Proctor, Barbara Gardner **1985**:3
Riney, Hal **1989**:1
Sedelmaier, Joe **1985**:3

Cloning
Lanza, Robert **2004**:3
Wilmut, Ian **1997**:3

Coaching
Bowman, Scotty **1998**:4
Brown, Paul
Obituary **1992**:1
Chaney, John **1989**:1

Hayes, Woody
    Obituary **1987**:2
Holtz, Lou **1986**:4
Howser, Dick
    Obituary **1987**:4
Jackson, Phil **1996**:3
Johnson, Jimmy **1993**:3
Knight, Bobby **1985**:3
Leyland, Jim **1998**:2
Lukas, D. Wayne **1986**:2
Martin, Billy **1988**:4
    Obituary **1990**:2
McCartney, Bill **1995**:3
Paterno, Joe **1995**:4
Schembechler, Bo **1990**:3
Shula, Don **1992**:2
Tarkenian, Jerry **1990**:4
Walsh, Bill **1987**:4

Coca-Cola Co.
Goizueta, Roberto **1996**:1
    Obituary **1998**:1
Keough, Donald Raymond **1986**:1
Woodruff, Robert Winship
    Obituary **1985**:1

Coleman Co.
Coleman, Sheldon, Jr. **1990**:2

Colorado Avalanche hockey team
Lemieux, Claude **1996**:1

Colorization
Markle, C. Wilson **1988**:1

Columbia Pictures
Pascal, Amy **2003**:3
Steel, Dawn **1990**:1
    Obituary **1998**:2
Vincent, Fay **1990**:2

Columbia Sportswear
Boyle, Gertrude **1995**:3

Comedy
Alexander, Jason **1993**:3
Allen, Steve
    Obituary **2001**:2
Allen, Tim **1993**:1
Allen, Woody **1994**:1
Anderson, Harry **1988**:2
Arnold, Tom **1993**:2
Atkinson, Rowan **2004**:3
Barr, Roseanne **1989**:1
Belushi, Jim **1986**:2
Belzer, Richard **1985**:3
Benigni, Roberto **1999**:2
Berle, Milton
    Obituary **2003**:2
Bernhard, Sandra **1989**:4
Black, Jack **2002**:3
Bogosian, Eric **1990**:4
Borge, Victor
    Obituary **2001**:3
Brooks, Albert **1991**:4
Brooks, Mel **2003**:1
Burns, George
    Obituary **1996**:3
Busch, Charles **1998**:3
Butler, Brett **1995**:1

Candy, John **1988**:2
    Obituary **1994**:3
Carey, Drew **1997**:4
Carrey, Jim **1995**:1
Carvey, Dana **1994**:1
Chase, Chevy **1990**:1
Cho, Margaret **1995**:2
Clay, Andrew Dice **1991**:1
Cleese, John **1989**:2
Cook, Peter
    Obituary **1995**:2
Cosby, Bill **1999**:2
Crystal, Billy **1985**:3
DeGeneres, Ellen **1995**:3
Diamond, Selma
    Obituary **1985**:2
Dr. Demento **1986**:1
Fallon, Jimmy **2003**:1
Farley, Chris
    Obituary **1998**:2
Foster, Phil
    Obituary **1985**:3
Foxworthy, Jeff **1996**:1
Foxx, Jamie **2001**:1
Foxx, Redd
    Obituary **1992**:2
Franken, Al **1996**:3
Gleason, Jackie
    Obituary **1987**:4
Gobel, George
    Obituary **1991**:4
Goldberg, Whoopi **1993**:3
Gordon, Gale
    Obituary **1996**:1
Gregory, Dick **1990**:3
Hackett, Buddy
    Obituary **2004**:3
Hall, Arsenio **1990**:2
Hill, Benny
    Obituary **1992**:3
Hope, Bob
    Obituary **2004**:4
Hughley, D.L. **2001**:1
Humphries, Barry **1993**:1
Irwin, Bill **1988**:3
Jones, Jenny **1998**:2
Kinison, Sam
    Obituary **1993**:1
Lawrence, Martin **1993**:4
Leary, Denis **1993**:3
Leguizamo, John **1999**:1
Leno, Jay **1987**:1
Letterman, David **1989**:3
Lewis, Richard **1992**:1
Lopez, George **2003**:4
Mac, Bernie **2003**:1
Mandel, Howie **1989**:1
Martin, Steve **1992**:2
McCarthy, Jenny **1997**:4
Miller, Dennis **1992**:4
Milligan, Spike
    Obituary **2003**:2
Morita, Noriyuki Pat **1987**:3
Murphy, Eddie **1989**:2
Murray, Bill **2002**:4
Myers, Mike **1992**:3 **1997**:4
O'Brien, Conan **1994**:1
O'Donnell, Rosie **1994**:3
Parker, Trey and Matt Stone **1998**:2
Paulsen, Pat
    Obituary **1997**:4
Penn & Teller **1992**:1

Peterson, Cassandra **1988**:1
Pryor, Richard **1999**:3
Reiser, Paul **1995**:2
Reubens, Paul **1987**:2
Rhea, Caroline **2004**:1
Richards, Michael **1993**:4
Rock, Chris **1998**:1
Rogers, Ginger
    Obituary **1995**:4
Rowan, Dan
    Obituary **1988**:1
Rudner, Rita **1993**:2
Sandler, Adam **1999**:2
Schneider, Rob **1997**:4
Seinfeld, Jerry **1992**:4
Shandling, Garry **1995**:1
Shawn, Dick
    Obituary **1987**:3
Short, Martin **1986**:1
Silvers, Phil
    Obituary **1985**:4
Skelton, Red
    Obituary **1998**:1
Smigel, Robert **2001**:3
Smirnoff, Yakov **1987**:2
Spade, David **1999**:2
Tucker, Chris **1999**:1
Wayans, Keenen Ivory **1991**:1
Williams, Robin **1988**:4
Wilson, Flip
    Obituary **1999**:2
Wright, Steven **1986**:3
Yankovic, Weird Al **1985**:4
Youngman, Henny
    Obituary **1998**:3

Comic Books
Arad, Avi **2003**:2
Barks, Carl
    Obituary **2001**:2
Smith, Kevin **2000**:4
Washington, Alonzo **2000**:1

Committee for the Scientific Investigation of Claims of the Paranormal
Randi, James **1990**:2

Committee to Halt Useless College Killings
Stevens, Eileen **1987**:3

Communitarianism
Etzioni, Amitai **1994**:3

Compaq Computer Corp.
Pfeiffer, Eckhard **1998**:4

CompuServe Inc.
Bloch, Henry **1988**:4
Ebbers, Bernie **1998**:1

ComputerLand Corp.
Millard, Barbara J.
    Brief Entry **1985**:3

Computers
Akers, John F. **1988**:3
Andreessen, Marc **1996**:2
Barrett, Craig R. **1999**:4

Landry, Tom
Obituary **2000**:3
Smith, Emmitt **1994**:1

Doubleday Mystery Guild
Grafton, Sue **2000**:2

Dance Theatre of Harlem
Fagan, Garth **2000**:1
Mitchell, Arthur **1995**:1

Datsun automobiles
See: Nissan Motor Co.

Dell Computer Corp.
Dell, Michael **1996**:2

DEC
See: Digital Equipment Corp.

Democratic National Committee
Brown, Ron
Obituary **1996**:4
Brown, Ron **1990**:3
Waters, Maxine **1998**:4

Denver Broncos football team
Barnes, Ernie **1997**:4
Davis, Terrell **1998**:2
Elway, John **1990**:3

Department of Commerce
Baldrige, Malcolm
Obituary **1988**:1
Brown, Ron
Obituary **1996**:4

Department of Education
Cavazos, Lauro F. **1989**:2
Riley, Richard W. **1996**:3

Department of Defense
Cohen, William S. **1998**:1
Perry, William **1994**:4

Department of Energy
O'Leary, Hazel **1993**:4

Department of Health, Education, and Welfare
Harris, Patricia Roberts
Obituary **1985**:2
Ribicoff, Abraham
Obituary **1998**:3

Department of Health and Human Services
Kessler, David **1992**:1
Sullivan, Louis **1990**:4

Department of Housing and Urban Development
Achtenberg, Roberta **1993**:4
Harris, Patricia Roberts
Obituary **1985**:2
Kemp, Jack **1990**:4
Morrison, Trudi
Brief Entry **1986**:2

Department of the Interior
Babbitt, Bruce **1994**:1

Department of Labor
Dole, Elizabeth Hanford **1990**:1
Martin, Lynn **1991**:4

Department of State
Christopher, Warren **1996**:3
Muskie, Edmund S.
Obituary **1996**:3

Department of Transportation
Dole, Elizabeth Hanford **1990**:1
Schiavo, Mary **1998**:2

Depression
Abramson, Lyn **1986**:3

Desilu Productions
Arnaz, Desi
Obituary **1987**:1
Ball, Lucille
Obituary **1989**:3

Detroit city government
Archer, Dennis **1994**:4
Maida, Adam Cardinal **1998**:2
Young, Coleman A.
Obituary **1998**:1

Detroit Lions football team
Ford, William Clay, Jr. **1999**:1
Sanders, Barry **1992**:1
White, Byron
Obituary **2003**:3

Detroit Pistons basketball team
Hill, Grant **1995**:3
Laimbeer, Bill **2004**:3
Rodman, Dennis **1991**:3 **1996**:4
Thomas, Isiah **1989**:2
Vitale, Dick **1988**:4 **1994**:4
Wallace, Ben **2004**:3

Detroit Red Wings hockey team
Bowman, Scotty **1998**:4
Federov, Sergei **1995**:1
Ilitch, Mike **1993**:4
Klima, Petr **1987**:1
Konstantinov, Vladimir **1997**:4
Yzerman, Steve **1991**:2

Detroit Tigers baseball team
Fielder, Cecil **1993**:2
Gibson, Kirk **1985**:2
Greenberg, Hank
Obituary **1986**:4
Harwell, Ernie **1997**:3
Hernandez, Willie **1985**:1
Ilitch, Mike **1993**:4
Monaghan, Tom **1985**:1
Schembechler, Bo **1990**:3

Digital Equipment Corp.
Olsen, Kenneth H. **1986**:4

Diets
Atkins, Robert C.
Obituary **2004**:2
Gregory, Dick **1990**:3
Ornish, Dean **2004**:2
Powter, Susan **1994**:3
Sears, Barry **2004**:2

Dilbert cartoon
Adams, Scott **1996**:4

Dinosaurs
Bakker, Robert T. **1991**:3
Barney **1993**:4
Crichton, Michael **1995**:3
Henson, Brian **1992**:1

Diplomacy
Abrams, Elliott **1987**:1
Albright, Madeleine **1994**:3
Astorga, Nora **1988**:2
Baker, James A. III **1991**:2
Begin, Menachem
Obituary **1992**:3
Berri, Nabih **1985**:2
Carter, Jimmy **1995**:1
de Pinies, Jamie
Brief Entry **1986**:3
Dubinin, Yuri **1987**:4
Ghali, Boutros Boutros **1992**:3
Gromyko, Andrei
Obituary **1990**:2
Harriman, Pamela **1994**:4
Harriman, W. Averell
Obituary **1986**:4
Harris, Patricia Roberts
Obituary **1985**:2
Holbrooke, Richard **1996**:2
Jumblatt, Walid **1987**:4
Kekkonen, Urho
Obituary **1986**:4
Keyes, Alan **1996**:2
Kim Dae Jung **1998**:3
Lansdale, Edward G.
Obituary **1987**:2
Le Duc Tho
Obituary **1991**:1
Lewis, Stephen **1987**:2
Lodge, Henry Cabot
Obituary **1985**:1
Lord, Winston
Brief Entry **1987**:4
Luce, Clare Boothe
Obituary **1988**:1
Masako, Crown Princess **1993**:4
McCloy, John J.
Obituary **1989**:3
Molotov, Vyacheslav Mikhailovich
Obituary **1987**:1
Palme, Olof
Obituary **1986**:2
Paz, Octavio **1991**:2
Perez de Cuellar, Javier **1991**:3
Strauss, Robert **1991**:4
Taylor, Maxwell
Obituary **1987**:3
Terzi, Zehdi Labib **1985**:3
Williams, G. Mennen
Obituary **1988**:2
Zeroual, Liamine **1996**:2
Zhao Ziyang **1989**:1

Discovery Channel
Otte, Ruth **1992**:4

Disney/ABC Cable Networks
Laybourne, Geraldine **1997**:1

DNA Testing
Scheck, Barry **2000**:4

DNC
See: Democratic National
Committee

Documentaries
Burns, Ken **1995**:2
Moore, Michael **1990**:3

Dolby Laboratories, Inc.
Dolby, Ray Milton
Brief Entry **1986**:1

Domino's Pizza
Monaghan, Tom **1985**:1

Donghia Companies
Donghia, Angelo R.
Obituary **1985**:2

Drama Desk Awards
Allen, Debbie **1998**:2
Allen, Joan **1998**:1
Bishop, Andre **2000**:1
Brooks, Mel **2003**:1
Crisp, Quentin
Obituary **2000**:3
Fagan, Garth **2000**:1
Fierstein, Harvey **2004**:2
Foster, Sutton **2003**:2
Janney, Allison **2003**:3
Kline, Kevin **2000**:1
Lane, Nathan **1996**:4
LaPaglia, Anthony **2004**:4
Nunn, Trevor **2000**:2
Peters, Bernadette **2000**:1
Salonga, Lea **2003**:3
Smith, Anna Deavere **2002**:2
Spacey, Kevin **1996**:4
Wong, B.D. **1998**:1

DreamWorks SKG
Katzenberg, Jeffrey **1995**:3
Ostin, Mo **1996**:2
Spielberg, Steven **1993**:4 **1997**:4

Drug abuse
Barrymore, Drew **1995**:3
Bennett, William **1990**:1
Bradshaw, John **1992**:1
Burroughs, William S.
Obituary **1997**:4
Hirschhorn, Joel
Brief Entry **1986**:1
Phoenix, River **1990**:2
Obituary **1994**:2

Drunk driving
Anastas, Robert
Brief Entry **1985**:2
Lightner, Candy **1985**:1

Druze
Jumblatt, Walid **1987**:4

Duds n' Suds
Akin, Phil
Brief Entry **1987**:3

Duke University basketball team
Krzyzewski, Mike **1993**:2

Dun & Bradstreet
Moritz, Charles **1989**:3

DuPont
See: E.I. DuPont de Nemours & Co.

Dwarfism
Kopits, Steven E.
Brief Entry **1987**:1

Earth First!
Foreman, Dave **1990**:3
Hayse, Bruce **2004**:3

eBay
Whitman, Meg **2000**:3

Ecology
Abbey, Edward
Obituary **1989**:3
Allen, John **1992**:1
Brower, David **1990**:4
Foreman, Dave **1990**:3
Janzen, Daniel H. **1988**:4
Lipkis, Andy
Brief Entry **1985**:3
McCloskey, J. Michael **1988**:2
McIntyre, Richard
Brief Entry **1986**:2
McTaggart, David **1989**:4
Mott, William Penn, Jr. **1986**:1
Nader, Ralph **1989**:4
Plotkin, Mark **1994**:3
Wilson, Edward O. **1994**:4
Woodwell, George S. **1987**:2

Economics
Delors, Jacques **1990**:2
Garzarelli, Elaine M. **1992**:3
Greenspan, Alan **1992**:2
Heller, Walter
Obituary **1987**:4
Kim Dae Jung **1998**:3
Lalonde, Marc **1985**:1
Parizeau, Jacques **1995**:1
Porter, Sylvia
Obituary **1991**:4
Reisman, Simon **1987**:4
Sachs, Jeffrey D. **2004**:4
Sowell, Thomas **1998**:3
Tyson, Laura D'Andrea **1994**:1

Edmonton Oilers hockey team
Coffey, Paul **1985**:4
Gretzky, Wayne **1989**:2
Pocklington, Peter H. **1985**:2

E. F. Hutton Group, Inc.
Fomon, Robert M. **1985**:3

E.I. DuPont de Nemours & Co.
Heckert, Richard E.
Brief Entry **1987**:3

Emmy Awards
Albert, Marv **1994**:3
Alexander, Jane **1994**:2
Alexander, Jason **1993**:3
Allen, Debbie **1998**:2
Anderson, Judith
Obituary **1992**:3
Arledge, Roone **1992**:2
Aykroyd, Dan **1989**:3 **1997**:3
Azaria, Hank **2001**:3
Ball, Lucille
Obituary **1989**:3
Baranski, Christine **2001**:2
Barbera, Joseph **1988**:2
Berle, Milton
Obituary **2003**:2
Bochco, Steven **1989**:1
Boyle, Peter **2002**:3
Brooks, Mel **2003**:1
Burnett, Carol **2000**:3
Burnett, Mark **2003**:1
Carter, Chris **2000**:1
Carter, Nell
Obituary **2004**:2
Chase, Chevy **1990**:1
Chiklis, Michael **2003**:3
Child, Julia **1999**:4
Coca, Imogene
Obituary **2002**:2
Coco, James
Obituary **1987**:2
Copperfield, David **1986**:3
Cosby, Bill **1999**:2
Cronkite, Walter Leland **1997**:3
Davis, Bette
Obituary **1990**:1
De Cordova, Frederick **1985**:2
De Vito, Danny **1987**:1
Dewhurst, Colleen
Obituary **1992**:2
Field, Patricia **2002**:2
Field, Sally **1995**:3
Finney, Albert **2003**:3
Flanders, Ed
Obituary **1995**:3
Fosse, Bob
Obituary **1988**:1
Foster, Jodie **1989**:2
Frankenheimer, John
Obituary **2003**:4
Franz, Dennis **1995**:2
Freleng, Friz
Obituary **1995**:4
Gandolfini, James **2001**:3
Gellar, Sarah Michelle **1999**:3
Gless, Sharon **1989**:3
Gobel, George
Obituary **1991**:4
Goldberg, Gary David **1989**:4
Goldberg, Leonard **1988**:4
Gossett, Louis, Jr. **1989**:3
Grammer, Kelsey **1995**:1
Grodin, Charles **1997**:3
Guest, Christopher **2004**:2
Hanks, Tom **1989**:2 **2000**:2
Hartman, Phil **1996**:2
Obituary **1998**:4
Heche, Anne **1999**:1

Helgenberger, Marg **2002**:2
Henning, Doug
  Obituary **2000**:3
Hopkins, Anthony **1992**:4
Howard, Trevor
  Obituary **1988**:2
Janney, Allison **2003**:3
Jennings, Peter Charles **1997**:2
Johnson, Don **1986**:1
Jones, Tommy Lee **1994**:2
Kavner, Julie **1992**:3
Kaye, Danny
  Obituary **1987**:2
Knight, Ted
  Obituary **1986**:4
Koppel, Ted **1989**:1
Kuralt, Charles
  Obituary **1998**:3
LaPaglia, Anthony **2004**:4
Larroquette, John **1986**:2
Lemmon, Jack **1998**:4
  Obituary **2002**:3
Letterman, David **1989**:3
Levinson, Barry **1989**:3
Levy, Eugene **2004**:3
Lewis, Shari **1993**:1
  Obituary **1999**:1
Liberace
  Obituary **1987**:2
Lucci, Susan **1999**:4
Malkovich, John **1988**:2
Mantegna, Joe **1992**:1
McFarlane, Todd **1999**:1
Meredith, Burgess
  Obituary **1998**:1
Messing, Debra **2004**:4
Midler, Bette **1989**:4
Miller, Arthur **1999**:4
Moore, Julianne **1998**:1
Moore, Mary Tyler **1996**:2
Murray, Bill **2002**:4
Myers, Mike **1992**:3 **1997**:4
North, Alex **1986**:3
O'Brien, Conan **1994**:1
O'Connor, Carroll
  Obituary **2002**:3
O'Connor, Donald
  Obituary **2004**:4
Olmos, Edward James **1990**:1
Olson, Johnny
  Obituary **1985**:4
Page, Geraldine
  Obituary **1987**:4
Paulsen, Pat
  Obituary **1997**:4
Pryor, Richard **1999**:3
Redgrave, Vanessa **1989**:2
Ritter, John **2003**:4
Rivera, Geraldo **1989**:1
Roberts, Doris **2003**:4
Rock, Chris **1998**:1
Rolle, Esther
  Obituary **1999**:2
Rollins, Howard E., Jr. **1986**:1
Romano, Ray **2001**:4
Rose, Charlie **1994**:2
Saralegui, Cristina **1999**:2
Schulz, Charles M. **1998**:1
Scott, George C.
  Obituary **2000**:2
Seymour, Jane **1994**:4

Silvers, Phil
  Obituary **1985**:4
Sinatra, Frank
  Obituary **1998**:4
Sorkin, Aaron **2003**:2
Springer, Jerry **1998**:4
Stack, Robert
  Obituary **2004**:2
Stein, Ben **2001**:1
Stiller, Ben **1999**:1
Streep, Meryl **1990**:2
Susskind, David
  Obituary **1987**:2
Tharp, Twyla **1992**:4
Tillstrom, Burr
  Obituary **1986**:1
Vieira, Meredith **2001**:3
Vonnegut, Kurt **1998**:4
Walker, Nancy
  Obituary **1992**:3
Walters, Barbara **1998**:3
Ward, Sela **2001**:3
Weitz, Bruce **1985**:4
Wilson, Flip
  Obituary **1999**:2
Witt, Katarina **1991**:3
Woods, James **1988**:3
Young, Robert
  Obituary **1999**:1

Encore Books
  Schlessinger, David
    Brief Entry **1985**:1

Energy Machine
  Newman, Joseph **1987**:1

Entrepreneurs
  Akin, Phil
    Brief Entry **1987**:3
  Allen, John **1992**:1
  Alter, Hobie
    Brief Entry **1985**:1
  Aoki, Rocky **1990**:2
  Arison, Ted **1990**:3
  Aurre, Laura
    Brief Entry **1986**:3
  Bauer, Eddie
    Obituary **1986**:3
  Ben & Jerry **1991**:3
  Berlusconi, Silvio **1994**:4
  Black, Conrad **1986**:2
  Bloomberg, Michael **1997**:1
  Boiardi, Hector
    Obituary **1985**:3
  Bose, Amar
    Brief Entry **1986**:4
  Branson, Richard **1987**:1
  Buffett, Warren **1995**:2
  Burr, Donald Calvin **1985**:3
  Bushnell, Nolan **1985**:1
  Campeau, Robert **1990**:1
  Clark, Jim **1997**:1
  Covey, Stephen R. **1994**:4
  Craig, Sid and Jenny **1993**:4
  Cray, Seymour R.
    Brief Entry **1986**:3
    Obituary **1997**:2
  Cummings, Sam **1986**:3
  Dell, Michael **1996**:2
  DiFranco, Ani **1997**:1

Ertegun, Ahmet **1986**:3
Garcia, Joe
  Brief Entry **1986**:4
Gates, Bill **1993**:3 **1987**:4
Gatien, Peter
  Brief Entry **1986**:1
Gillett, George **1988**:1
Graham, Bill **1986**:4
  Obituary **1992**:2
Guccione, Bob **1986**:1
Haney, Chris
  Brief Entry **1985**:1
Herrera, Carolina **1997**:1
Hilbert, Stephen C. **1997**:4
Honda, Soichiro
  Obituary **1986**:1
Hughes, Mark **1985**:3
Hyatt, Joel **1985**:3
Ilitch, Mike **1993**:4
Inatome, Rick **1985**:4
Isaacson, Portia
  Brief Entry **1986**:1
Jacuzzi, Candido
  Obituary **1987**:1
Jones, Arthur A. **1985**:3
Katz, Lillian **1987**:4
Kerkorian, Kirk **1996**:2
Kingsborough, Donald
  Brief Entry **1986**:2
Knight, Philip H. **1994**:1
Koplovitz, Kay **1986**:3
Kurzweil, Raymond **1986**:3
Mahesh Yogi, Maharishi **1991**:3
Markle, C. Wilson **1988**:1
Marriott, J. Willard
  Obituary **1985**:4
McGowan, William **1985**:2
McIntyre, Richard
  Brief Entry **1986**:2
Melman, Richard
  Brief Entry **1986**:1
Monaghan, Tom **1985**:1
Moody, John **1985**:3
Morgan, Dodge **1987**:1
Murdoch, Rupert **1988**:4
Murray, Arthur
  Obituary **1991**:3
Olsen, Kenneth H. **1986**:4
Paulucci, Jeno
  Brief Entry **1986**:3
Penske, Roger **1988**:3
Pocklington, Peter H. **1985**:2
Radocy, Robert
  Brief Entry **1986**:3
Roberts, Xavier **1985**:3
Roddick, Anita **1989**:4
Sasakawa, Ryoichi
  Brief Entry **1988**:1
Schlessinger, David
  Brief Entry **1985**:1
Smith, Frederick W. **1985**:4
Tanny, Vic
  Obituary **1985**:3
Thalheimer, Richard
  Brief Entry **1988**:3
Thomas, Michel **1987**:4
Tompkins, Susie
  Brief Entry **1987**:2
Trump, Donald **1989**:2
Trump, Ivana **1995**:2
Turner, Ted **1989**:1
Waitt, Ted **1997**:4

Wilson, Jerry
  Brief Entry **1986**:2
Wilson, Peter C.
  Obituary **1985**:2
Wynn, Stephen A. **1994**:3
Zanker, Bill
  Brief Entry **1987**:3

Environmentalism
  Ben & Jerry **1991**:3
  Brower, David **1990**:4
  Denver, John
    Obituary **1998**:1
  Douglas, Marjory Stoneman **1993**:1
    Obituary **1998**:4
  Erin Brockovich-Ellis **2003**:3
  Foreman, Dave **1990**:3
  Gore, Albert, Jr. **1993**:2
  Hair, Jay D. **1994**:3
  Hayse, Bruce **2004**:3
  Korchinsky, Mike **2004**:2
  McDonough, William **2003**:1
  Ngau, Harrison **1991**:3
  Plotkin, Mark **1994**:3
  Puleston, Dennis
    Obituary **2002**:2
  Strong, Maurice **1993**:1
  Strummer, Joe
    Obituary **2004**:1
  Vitousek, Peter **2003**:1

Environmental Protection Agency
  Browner, Carol M. **1994**:1

EPA
  See: Environmental Protection
  Agency

Episcopal Church
  Browning, Edmond
    Brief Entry **1986**:2
  Harris, Barbara **1996**:3
  Harris, Barbara **1989**:3
  Spong, John **1991**:3 **2001**:1

Espionage
  Philby, Kim
    Obituary **1988**:3

Esprit clothing
  Krogner, Heinz **2004**:2
  Tompkins, Susie
    Brief Entry **1987**:2

Essence magazine
  Gillespie, Marcia **1999**:4
  Lewis, Edward T. **1999**:4
  Taylor, Susan L. **1998**:2

Estee Lauder
  Burns, Robin **1991**:2
  Lauder, Estee **1992**:2

Ethnobotany
  Plotkin, Mark **1994**:3

European Commission
  Delors, Jacques **1990**:2

Euthanasia
  Cruzan, Nancy
    Obituary **1991**:3
  Humphry, Derek **1992**:2
  Kevorkian, Jack **1991**:3

Excel Communications
  Troutt, Kenny A. **1998**:1

Exploration
  Ballard, Robert D. **1998**:4
  Fiennes, Ranulph **1990**:3
  Hempleman-Adams, David **2004**:3
  Steger, Will **1990**:4

ExxonMobil Oil
  Raymond, Lee R. **2000**:3

Fabbrica Italiana Automobili Torino SpA
  Agnelli, Giovanni **1989**:4

Faith Center Church
  Scott, Gene
    Brief Entry **1986**:1

Fallon McElligott
  McElligott, Thomas J. **1987**:4

Famous Amos Chocolate Chip Cookies
  Amos, Wally **2000**:1

Fashion
  Agnes B **2002**:3
  Allard, Linda **2003**:2
  Armani, Giorgio **1991**:2
  Avedon, Richard **1993**:4
  Bacall, Lauren **1997**:3
  Badgley, Mark and James Mischka **2004**:3
  Banks, Jeffrey **1998**:2
  Benetton, Luciano **1988**:1
  Blahnik, Manolo **2000**:2
  Blass, Bill
    Obituary **2003**:3
  Bohbot, Michele **2004**:2
  Cameron, David
    Brief Entry **1988**:1
  Cardin, Pierre **2003**:3
  Cavalli, Roberto **2004**:4
  Chalayan, Hussein **2003**:2
  Charron, Paul **2004**:1
  Claiborne, Liz **1986**:3
  Cole, Kenneth **2003**:1
  Crawford, Cindy **1993**:3
  D'Alessio, Kitty
    Brief Entry **1987**:3
  Duarte, Henry **2003**:3
  Ellis, Perry
    Obituary **1986**:3
  Erte
    Obituary **1990**:4
  Eve **2004**:3
  Ferretti, Alberta **2004**:1
  Ford, Tom **1999**:3
  Gaultier, Jean-Paul **1998**:1
  Giannulli, Mossimo **2002**:3
  Gucci, Maurizio
    Brief Entry **1985**:4
  Haas, Robert D. **1986**:4

Halston
  Obituary **1990**:3
Herrera, Carolina **1997**:1
Hilfiger, Tommy **1993**:3
Jacobs, Marc **2002**:3
Johnson, Betsey **1996**:2
Kamali, Norma **1989**:1
Karan, Donna **1988**:1
Kelly, Patrick
  Obituary **1990**:2
Klein, Calvin **1996**:2
Klensch, Elsa **2001**:4
Korchinsky, Mike **2004**:2
Kors, Michael **2000**:4
Krogner, Heinz **2004**:2
Lagerfeld, Karl **1999**:4
Lang, Helmut **1999**:2
Lange, Liz **2003**:4
Lauren, Ralph **1990**:1
McLaughlin, Betsy **2004**:3
Mellinger, Frederick
  Obituary **1990**:4
Mello, Dawn **1992**:2
Miller, Nicole **1995**:4
Mills, Malia **2003**:1
Miyake, Issey **1985**:2
Mizrahi, Isaac **1991**:1
Murakami, Takashi **2004**:2
Natori, Josie **1994**:3
Nipon, Albert
  Brief Entry **1986**:4
Oldham, Todd **1995**:4
Parker, Suzy
  Obituary **2004**:2
Persson, Stefan **2004**:1
Picasso, Paloma **1991**:1
Porizkova, Paulina
  Brief Entry **1986**:4
Potok, Anna Maximilian
  Brief Entry **1985**:2
Prada, Miuccia **1996**:1
Pressler, Paul **2003**:4
Queer Eye for the
  Straight Guy cast **2004**:3
Rhodes, Zandra **1986**:2
Rykiel, Sonia **2000**:3
Sander, Jil **1995**:2
Smith, Paul **2002**:4
Smith, Willi
  Obituary **1987**:3
Spade, Kate **2003**:1
Sui, Anna **1995**:1
Takada, Kenzo **2003**:2
Tilberis, Elizabeth **1994**:3
Tompkins, Susie
  Brief Entry **1987**:2
Trump, Ivana **1995**:2
Tyler, Richard **1995**:3
Valvo, Carmen Marc **2003**:4
Versace, Donatella **1999**:1
Versace, Gianni
  Brief Entry **1988**:1
  Obituary **1998**:2
von Furstenberg, Diane **1994**:2
Wachner, Linda **1988**:3 **1997**:2
Wang, Vera **1998**:4
Westwood, Vivienne **1998**:3

FBI
  See: Federal Bureau of Investigation

Genentech, Inc.
Boyer, Herbert Wayne **1985**:1

General Electric Co.
Fudge, Ann **2000**:3
Immelt, Jeffrey R. **2001**:2
Welch, Jack **1993**:3

General Motors Corp.
Devine, John M. **2003**:2
Estes, Pete
Obituary **1988**:3
Jordan, Charles M. **1989**:4
Lutz, Robert A. **1990**:1
Moore, Michael **1990**:3
Smith, Jack **1994**:3
Smith, Roger **1990**:3
Stempel, Robert **1991**:3

Genetics
Boyer, Herbert Wayne **1985**:1
Gilbert, Walter **1988**:3
Haseltine, William A. **1999**:2
King, Mary-Claire **1998**:3
Kornberg, Arthur **1992**:1
Krim, Mathilde **1989**:2
Nuesslein-Volhard, Christiane **1998**:1
Rifkin, Jeremy **1990**:3
Rosenberg, Steven **1989**:1
Wigler, Michael
Brief Entry **1985**:1

Genome Corp.
Gilbert, Walter **1988**:3

Geology
Rosendahl, Bruce R.
Brief Entry **1986**:4

Georgetown University
Healy, Timothy S. **1990**:2

Georgetown University basketball team
Thompson, John **1988**:3

Gesundheit! Institute
Adams, Patch **1999**:2

Gianni Versace Group
Versace, Donatella **1999**:1
Versace, Gianni
Brief Entry **1988**:1
Obituary **1998**:2

Gillett Group
Gillett, George **1988**:1

GM
See: General Motors Corp.

Golden Globe Awards
Affleck, Ben **1999**:1
Bacall, Lauren **1997**:3
Bakula, Scott **2003**:1
Beatty, Warren **2000**:1
Blanchett, Cate **1999**:3
Bronson, Charles
Obituary **2004**:4

Burnett, Carol **2000**:3
Caine, Michael **2000**:4
Carter, Chris **2000**:1
Cattrall, Kim **2003**:3
Cheadle, Don **2002**:1
Cher **1993**:1
Chiklis, Michael **2003**:3
Connelly, Jennifer **2002**:4
Cooper, Chris **2004**:1
Coppola, Sofia **2004**:3
Cosby, Bill **1999**:2
Curtis, Jamie Lee **1995**:1
Damon, Matt **1999**:1
Danes, Claire **1999**:4
Dench, Judi **1999**:4
De Niro, Robert **1999**:1
Dennehy, Brian **2002**:1
Depardieu, Gerard **1991**:2
Duvall, Robert **1999**:3
Elfman, Jenna **1999**:4
Farrow, Mia **1998**:3
Fell, Norman
Obituary **1999**:2
Fiennes, Ralph **1996**:2
Finney, Albert **2003**:3
Flockhart, Calista **1998**:4
Garner, Jennifer **2003**:1
Goldberg, Whoopi **1993**:3
Hallstrom, Lasse **2002**:3
Hanks, Tom **1989**:2 **2000**:2
Harris, Ed **2002**:2
Heston, Charlton **1999**:4
Irons, Jeremy **1991**:4
Jackson, Peter **2004**:4
Johnson, Don **1986**:1
Jolie, Angelina **2000**:2
Keaton, Diane **1997**:1
Lansbury, Angela **1993**:1
Lemmon, Jack **1998**:4
Obituary **2002**:3
Lucas, George **1999**:4
Luhrmann, Baz **2002**:3
Matlin, Marlee **1992**:2
Matthau, Walter **2000**:3
Minghella, Anthony **2004**:3
Moore, Dudley
Obituary **2003**:2
Moore, Mary Tyler **1996**:2
Norton, Edward **2000**:2
O'Connor, Donald
Obituary **2004**:4
Pakula, Alan
Obituary **1999**:2
Peters, Bernadette **2000**:1
Redgrave, Lynn **1999**:3
Ritter, John **2003**:4
Roberts, Julia **1991**:3
Russell, Keri **2000**:1
Sheen, Martin **2002**:1
Spacek, Sissy **2003**:1
Streisand, Barbra **1992**:2
Sutherland, Kiefer **2002**:4
Swank, Hilary **2000**:3
Taylor, Lili **2000**:2
Thompson, Emma **1993**:2
Ullman, Tracey **1988**:3
Washington, Denzel **1993**:2

Golden State Warriors basketball team
Sprewell, Latrell **1999**:4
Webber, Chris **1994**:1

Golf
Azinger, Paul **1995**:2
Baker, Kathy
Brief Entry **1986**:1
Callaway, Ely
Obituary **2002**:3
Chen, T.C.
Brief Entry **1987**:3
Couples, Fred **1994**:4
Curtis, Ben **2004**:2
Duval, David **2000**:3
Faldo, Nick **1993**:3
Furyk, Jim **2004**:2
Hogan, Ben
Obituary **1997**:4
Kite, Tom **1990**:3
Lopez, Nancy **1989**:3
Martin, Casey **2002**:1
Mickelson, Phil **2004**:4
Norman, Greg **1988**:3
Pak, Se Ri **1999**:4
Pavin, Corey **1996**:4
Peete, Calvin **1985**:4
Sarazen, Gene
Obituary **1999**:4
Singh, Vijay **2000**:4
Snead, Sam
Obituary **2003**:3
Strange, Curtis **1988**:4
Webb, Karrie **2000**:4
Weir, Mike **2004**:1
Whaley, Suzy **2003**:4
Woods, Tiger **1995**:4

Gorillas
Fossey, Dian
Obituary **1986**:1

Gospel music
Dorsey, Thomas A.
Obituary **1993**:3
Franklin, Aretha **1998**:3
Houston, Cissy **1999**:3
Reese, Della **1999**:2
Staples, Roebuck Pops
Obituary **2001**:3

W.R. Grace & Co.
Grace, J. Peter **1990**:2

Grammy Awards
Aguilera, Christina **2000**:4
Anderson, Marion
Obituary **1993**:4
Anthony, Marc **2000**:3
Arrested Development **1994**:2
Ashanti **2004**:1
Badu, Erykah **2000**:4
Baker, Anita **1987**:4
Battle, Kathleen **1998**:1
Beck **2000**:2
Bee Gees, The **1997**:4
Benatar, Pat **1986**:1
Bennett, Tony **1994**:4
Berry, Chuck **2001**:2
Blades, Ruben **1998**:2
Bolton, Michael **1993**:2
Bono **1988**:4
Boyz II Men **1995**:1
Brandy **1996**:4
Braxton, Toni **1994**:3

Labor
Bieber, Owen **1986**:1
Carey, Ron **1993**:3
Eagleson, Alan **1987**:4
Fehr, Donald **1987**:2
Feldman, Sandra **1987**:3
Hoffa, Jim, Jr. **1999**:2
Huerta, Dolores **1998**:1
Kielburger, Craig **1998**:1
Martin, Lynn **1991**:4
Nussbaum, Karen **1988**:3
Presser, Jackie
Obituary **1988**:4
Ramaphosa, Cyril **1988**:2
Rothstein, Ruth **1988**:2
Saporta, Vicki
Brief Entry **1987**:3
Steinberg, Leigh **1987**:3
Upshaw, Gene **1988**:1
Williams, Lynn **1986**:4

Labour Party (Great Britain)
Blair, Tony **1996**:3 **1997**:4
Jenkins, Roy Harris
Obituary **2004**:1
Livingstone, Ken **1988**:3
Maxwell, Robert **1990**:1

Ladies Professional Golf Association
Baker, Kathy
Brief Entry **1986**:1
Inkster, Juli **2000**:2
Lopez, Nancy **1989**:3
Pak, Se Ri **1999**:4
Sorenstam, Annika **2001**:1
Webb, Karrie **2000**:4
Whaley, Suzy **2003**:4

Language instruction
Thomas, Michel **1987**:4

Lasers
Gould, Gordon **1987**:1
Hagelstein, Peter
Brief Entry **1986**:3

Law enforcement
Cantrell, Ed
Brief Entry **1985**:3
France, Johnny
Brief Entry **1987**:1
Harvard, Beverly **1995**:2
Rizzo, Frank
Obituary **1992**:1
Watson, Elizabeth **1991**:2
Williams, Willie L. **1993**:1

Learning Annex
Zanker, Bill
Brief Entry **1987**:3

Lear's magazine
Lear, Frances **1988**:3

Lego toy system
Kristiansen, Kjeld Kirk **1988**:3

Lenin Peace Prize
Kekkonen, Urho
Obituary **1986**:4

Lettuce Entertain You Enterprises, Inc.
Melman, Richard
Brief Entry **1986**:1

Leukemia research
Gale, Robert Peter **1986**:4

Levi Strauss & Co.
Haas, Robert D. **1986**:4
Marineau, Philip **2002**:4

Liberal Democratic Party (Japan)
Miyazawa, Kiichi **1992**:2

Liberal Party (Canada)
Chretien, Jean **1990**:4 **1997**:2
Peterson, David **1987**:1

Liberal Party (South Africa)
Paton, Alan
Obituary **1988**:3

Library of Congress
Billington, James **1990**:3
Dickey, James
Obituary **1998**:2
Van Duyn, Mona **1993**:2

Likud Party (Israel)
Netanyahu, Benjamin **1996**:4

Lillian Vernon Corp.
Katz, Lillian **1987**:4

Limelight clubs
Gatien, Peter
Brief Entry **1986**:1

Lincoln Savings and Loan
Keating, Charles H., Jr. **1990**:4

Linguistics
Tannen, Deborah **1995**:1

Literacy
Bush, Millie **1992**:1
Kozol, Jonathan **1992**:1

Little People's Research Fund
Kopits, Steven E.
Brief Entry **1987**:1

Little Caesars pizza restaurants
Ilitch, Mike **1993**:4

Live Aid
Bono **1988**:4
Dylan, Bob **1998**:1
Geldof, Bob **1985**:3
Graham, Bill **1986**:4
Obituary **1992**:2

L.L. Bean Co.
Gorman, Leon
Brief Entry **1987**:1

Lloyd's of London
Davison, Ian Hay **1986**:1

Loews Corp.
Tisch, Laurence A. **1988**:2

Log Cabin Republicans
Tafel, Richard **2000**:4

Lone Ranger
Moore, Clayton
Obituary **2000**:3

Los Angeles city government
Bradley, Tom
Obituary **1999**:1
Riordan, Richard **1993**:4

Los Angeles Dodgers baseball team
Hershiser, Orel **1989**:2
Nomo, Hideo **1996**:2
Welch, Bob **1991**:3

Los Angeles Express football team
Young, Steve **1995**:2

Los Angeles Kings hockey team
Gretzky, Wayne **1989**:2

Los Angeles Lakers basketball team
Bryant, Kobe **1998**:3
Buss, Jerry **1989**:3
Chamberlain, Wilt
Obituary **2000**:2
Johnson, Earvin Magic **1988**:4
Riley, Pat **1994**:3
Worthy, James **1991**:2

Los Angeles Museum of Contemporary Art
Isozaki, Arata **1990**:2

Los Angeles Raiders football team
Gault, Willie **1991**:2
Upshaw, Gene **1988**:1

Los Angeles Sparks basketball team
Leslie, Lisa **1997**:4

Louisiana Legislature
Duke, David **1990**:2

Louisiana state government
Roemer, Buddy **1991**:4

Luis Vuitton
Arnault, Bernard **2000**:4

LPGA
See: Ladies Professional Golf Association

National Union for the Total
Independence of Angola
    Savimbi, Jonas **1986**:2 **1994**:2

National Union of Mineworkers
    Ramaphosa, Cyril **1988**:2

National Wildlife Federation
    Hair, Jay D. **1994**:3

Native American issues
    Banks, Dennis J. **1986**:4
    Begaye, Kelsey **1999**:3
    Brown, Dee
      Obituary **2004**:1
    Campbell, Ben Nighthorse **1998**:1
    Castaneda, Carlos
      Obituary **1998**:4
    Grant, Rodney A. **1992**:1
    Greene, Graham **1997**:2
    LaDuke, Winona **1995**:2
    Mankiller, Wilma P.
      Brief Entry **1986**:2
    Peltier, Leonard **1995**:1
    Sidney, Ivan
      Brief Entry **1987**:2
    Studi, Wes **1994**:3

NATO
    See: North Atlantic Treaty
    Organization

Nautilus Sports/Medical Industries
    Jones, Arthur A. **1985**:3

Navajo Nation
    Begaye, Kelsey **1999**:3

Nazi Party
    Hess, Rudolph
      Obituary **1988**:1
    Klarsfeld, Beate **1989**:1
    Mengele, Josef
      Obituary **1985**:2

NBC Television Network
    Brokaw, Tom **2000**:3
    Curry, Ann **2001**:1
    Gumbel, Greg **1996**:4
    Tartikoff, Brandon **1985**:2
      Obituary **1998**:1

NCPAC
    See: National Conservative Political
    Action Committee

NCTV
    See: National Coalition on
    Television Violence

NDP
    See: New Democratic Party
    (Canada)

NEA
    See: National Education Association

Nebraska state government
    Kerrey, Bob **1986**:1 **1991**:3
    Orr, Kay **1987**:4

Nebula Awards
    Asimov, Isaac
      Obituary **1992**:3
    Brooks, Mel **2003**:1

Negro American League
    Pride, Charley **1998**:1

NEH
    See: National Endowment for the
    Humanities

Netscape Communications Corp.
    Andreessen, Marc **1996**:2
    Barksdale, James L. **1998**:2
    Clark, Jim **1997**:1

Neurobiology
    Goldman-Rakic, Patricia **2002**:4
    LeVay, Simon **1992**:2
    Tully, Tim **2004**:3

New Democratic Party (Canada)
    Lewis, Stephen **1987**:2
    McLaughlin, Audrey **1990**:3

New England Patriots football team
    Bledsoe, Drew **1995**:1
    Brady, Tom **2002**:4

Newfoundland provincial government
    Peckford, Brian **1989**:1

New Hampshire state government
    Sununu, John **1989**:2

New Jersey Devils hockey team
    Lemieux, Claude **1996**:1

New Orleans Saints football team
    Williams, Ricky **2000**:2

New York City Ballet
    Kistler, Darci **1993**:1
    Whelan, Wendy **1999**:3

New York City Board of Education
    Green, Richard R. **1988**:3

New York City government
    Dinkins, David N. **1990**:2
    Fairstein, Linda **1991**:1
    Giuliani, Rudolph **1994**:2
    Kennedy, John F., Jr. **1990**:1
      Obituary **1999**:4

New Yorker magazine
    Brown, Tina **1992**:1
    Chast, Roz **1992**:4
    Shawn, William
      Obituary **1993**:3
    Steig, William
      Obituary **2004**:4

New York Giants football team
    Collins, Kerry **2002**:3
    Taylor, Lawrence **1987**:3

New York Islanders hockey team
    LaFontaine, Pat **1985**:1

New York Knicks basketball team
    Bradley, Bill **2000**:2
    Ewing, Patrick **1985**:3
    McMillen, Tom **1988**:4
    Riley, Pat **1994**:3
    Sprewell, Latrell **1999**:4

New York Mets baseball team
    Agee, Tommie
      Obituary **2001**:4
    Bonilla, Bobby **1992**:2
    Carter, Gary **1987**:1
    Doubleday, Nelson, Jr. **1987**:1
    Gooden, Dwight **1985**:2
    Piazza, Mike **1998**:4
    Ryan, Nolan **1989**:4

New York Philharmonic Orchestra
    Masur, Kurt **1993**:4

New York Public Library
    Gregorian, Vartan **1990**:3
    Healy, Timothy S. **1990**:2

New York Rangers hockey team
    Messier, Mark **1993**:1

New York City public schools
    Fernandez, Joseph **1991**:3

New York State Government
    Cuomo, Mario **1992**:2
    Florio, James J. **1991**:2
    Pataki, George **1995**:2
    Rothwax, Harold **1996**:3

New York Stock Exchange
    Fomon, Robert M. **1985**:3
    Phelan, John Joseph, Jr. **1985**:4
    Siebert, Muriel **1987**:2

New York Times
    Dowd, Maureen Brigid **1997**:1
    Lelyveld, Joseph S. **1994**:4
    Sulzberger, Arthur O., Jr. **1998**:3

New York Titans football team
    Barnes, Ernie **1997**:4

New York Yankees baseball team
    DiMaggio, Joe
      Obituary **1999**:3
    Gomez, Lefty
      Obituary **1989**:3
    Howser, Dick
      Obituary **1987**:4
    Jeter, Derek **1999**:4
    Mantle, Mickey
      Obituary **1996**:1
    Maris, Roger
      Obituary **1986**:1

Martin, Billy **1988**:4
Obituary **1990**:2
Mattingly, Don **1986**:2
Steinbrenner, George **1991**:1
Torre, Joseph Paul **1997**:1
Wells, David **1999**:3

NFL
See: National Football League

NHLPA
See: National Hockey League
Players Association

NHRA
See: National Hot Rod Association

NIH
See: National Institutes of Health

Nike, Inc.
Hamm, Mia **2000**:1
Knight, Philip H. **1994**:1 9 to 5
Bravo, Ellen **1998**:2
Nussbaum, Karen **1988**:3

Nissan Motor Co.
Katayama, Yutaka **1987**:1

No Limit (record label)
Master P **1999**:4

Nobel Prize
Altman, Sidney **1997**:2
Arias Sanchez, Oscar **1989**:3
Beckett, Samuel Barclay
Obituary **1990**:2
Begin, Menachem
Obituary **1992**:3
Blobel, Gunter **2000**:4
Carlsson, Arvid **2001**:2
Cela, Camilo Jose
Obituary **2003**:1
Coetzee, J. M. **2004**:4
Cram, Donald J.
Obituary **2002**:2
Ebadi, Shirin **2004**:3
Fo, Dario **1998**:1
Gao Xingjian **2001**:2
Grass, Gunter **2000**:2
Heaney, Seamus **1996**:2
Hounsfield, Godfrey **1989**:2
Kilby, Jack **2002**:2
Kissinger, Henry **1999**:4
Kornberg, Arthur **1992**:1
Lederman, Leon Max **1989**:4
Lorenz, Konrad
Obituary **1989**:3
Menchu, Rigoberta **1993**:2
Morrison, Toni **1998**:1
Mother Teresa **1993**:1
Obituary **1998**:1
Mullis, Kary **1995**:3
Nuesslein-Volhard, Christiane **1998**:1
Oe, Kenzaburo **1997**:1
Pauling, Linus
Obituary **1995**:1
Paz, Octavio **1991**:2
Perutz, Max
Obituary **2003**:2

Porter, George
Obituary **2003**:4
Prusiner, Stanley **1998**:2
Sakharov, Andrei Dmitrievich
Obituary **1990**:2
Saramago, Jose **1999**:1
Singer, Isaac Bashevis
Obituary **1992**:1
Suu Kyi, Aung San **1996**:2
Szent-Gyoergyi, Albert
Obituary **1987**:2
Trimble, David **1999**:1
Walesa, Lech **1991**:2
Wiesel, Elie **1998**:1

NORAID
See: Irish Northern Aid Committee

North Atlantic Treaty Organization
Galvin, John R. **1990**:1

NOW
See: National Organization for
Women

NRA
See: National Rifle Association

NRC
See: Nuclear Regulatory
Commission

NPR
See: National Public Radio
Tom and Ray Magliozzi **1991**:4

NSF
See: National Science Foundation

Nuclear energy
Gale, Robert Peter **1986**:4
Hagelstein, Peter
Brief Entry **1986**:3
Lederman, Leon Max **1989**:4
Maglich, Bogdan C. **1990**:1
Merritt, Justine
Brief Entry **1985**:3
Nader, Ralph **1989**:4
Palme, Olof
Obituary **1986**:2
Rickover, Hyman
Obituary **1986**:4
Sinclair, Mary **1985**:2
Smith, Samantha
Obituary **1985**:3
Zech, Lando W.
Brief Entry **1987**:4

Nuclear Regulatory Commission
Zech, Lando W.
Brief Entry **1987**:4

NUM
See: National Union of
Mineworkers

NWF
See: National Wildlife Federation

Oakland A's baseball team
Canseco, Jose **1990**:2
Caray, Harry **1988**:3
Obituary **1998**:3
Stewart, Dave **1991**:1
Welch, Bob **1991**:3
Zito, Barry **2003**:3

Oakland Raiders football team
Matuszak, John
Obituary **1989**:4
Trask, Amy **2003**:3
Upshaw, Gene **1988**:1

Obie Awards
Albee, Edward **1997**:1
Baldwin, Alec **2002**:2
Bergman, Ingmar **1999**:4
Close, Glenn **1988**:3
Coco, James
Obituary **1987**:2
Daniels, Jeff **1989**:4
Dewhurst, Colleen
Obituary **1992**:2
Diller, Elizabeth and Ricardo
Scofidio **2004**:3
Dukakis, Olympia **1996**:4
Duvall, Robert **1999**:3
Ensler, Eve **2002**:4
Fierstein, Harvey **2004**:2
Fo, Dario **1998**:1
Fugard, Athol **1992**:3
Hurt, William **1986**:1
Hwang, David Henry **1999**:1
Irwin, Bill **1988**:3
Kline, Kevin **2000**:1
Leguizamo, John **1999**:1
Miller, Arthur **1999**:4
Pacino, Al **1993**:4
Parks, Suzan-Lori **2003**:2
Shepard, Sam **1996**:4
Streep, Meryl **1990**:2
Tune, Tommy **1994**:2
Turturro, John **2002**:2
Vogel, Paula **1999**:2
Washington, Denzel **1993**:2
Woods, James **1988**:3

Occidental Petroleum Corp.
Hammer, Armand
Obituary **1991**:3

Oceanography
Cousteau, Jacques-Yves
Obituary **1998**:2
Cousteau, Jean-Michel **1988**:2
Fisher, Mel **1985**:4

Office of National Drug Control Policy
Bennett, William **1990**:1
Martinez, Bob **1992**:1

Ogilvy & Mather Advertising
Lazarus, Shelly **1998**:3

Ohio State University football team
Hayes, Woody
Obituary **1987**:2

Oil
Adair, Red **1987**:3
Aurre, Laura
Brief Entry **1986**:3
Hammer, Armand
Obituary **1991**:3
Jones, Jerry **1994**:4

Olympic games
Abbott, Jim **1988**:3
Ali, Muhammad **1997**:2
Armstrong, Lance **2000**:1
Baiul, Oksana **1995**:3
Baumgartner, Bruce
Brief Entry **1987**:3
Benoit, Joan **1986**:3
Blair, Bonnie **1992**:3
Boitano, Brian **1988**:3
Bradley, Bill **2000**:2
Conner, Dennis **1987**:2
Davenport, Lindsay **1999**:2
De La Hoya, Oscar **1998**:2
DiBello, Paul
Brief Entry **1986**:4
Dolan, Tom **2001**:2
Drexler, Clyde **1992**:4
Eagleson, Alan **1987**:4
Edwards, Harry **1989**:4
Evans, Janet **1989**:1
Ewing, Patrick **1985**:3
Freeman, Cathy **2001**:3
Gault, Willie **1991**:2
Graf, Steffi **1987**:4
Granato, Cammi **1999**:3
Grinkov, Sergei
Obituary **1996**:2
Hamilton, Scott **1998**:2
Hamm, Mia **2000**:1
Holyfield, Evander **1991**:3
Hughes, Sarah **2002**:4
Johnson, Michael **2000**:1
Jordan, Michael **1987**:2
Joyner, Florence Griffith **1989**:2
Obituary **1999**:1
Joyner-Kersee, Jackie **1993**:1
Kerrigan, Nancy **1994**:3
Kiraly, Karch
Brief Entry **1987**:1
Knight, Bobby **1985**:3
Laettner, Christian **1993**:1
LaFontaine, Pat **1985**:1
Lalas, Alexi **1995**:1
Leonard, Sugar Ray **1989**:4
Leslie, Lisa **1997**:4
Lewis, Lennox **2000**:2
Lindbergh, Pelle
Obituary **1985**:4
Lipinski, Tara **1998**:3
Louganis, Greg **1995**:3
Milbrett, Tiffeny **2001**:1
Milburn, Rodney Jr.
Obituary **1998**:2
Miller, Bode **2002**:4
Retton, Mary Lou **1985**:2
Rudolph, Wilma
Obituary **1995**:2
Runyan, Marla **2001**:1
Samaranch, Juan Antonio **1986**:2
Shea, Jim, Jr. **2002**:4
Street, Picabo **1999**:3
Strobl, Fritz **2003**:3
Strug, Kerri **1997**:3

Summitt, Pat **2004**:1
Swoopes, Sheryl **1998**:2
Thomas, Debi **1987**:2
Thompson, John **1988**:3
Tomba, Alberto **1992**:3
Van Dyken, Amy **1997**:1
Waddell, Thomas F.
Obituary **1988**:2
Witt, Katarina **1991**:3
Woodard, Lynette **1986**:2
Yamaguchi, Kristi **1992**:3

ON Technology
Kapor, Mitch **1990**:3

Ontario provincial government
Eagleson, Alan **1987**:4
Peterson, David **1987**:1

Opera
Anderson, Marion
Obituary **1993**:4
Bartoli, Cecilia **1994**:1
Battle, Kathleen **1998**:1
Berio, Luciano
Obituary **2004**:2
Carreras, Jose **1995**:2
Domingo, Placido **1993**:2
Fleming, Renee **2001**:4
Pavarotti, Luciano **1997**:4
Upshaw, Dawn **1991**:2
Zeffirelli, Franco **1991**:3

Operation Rescue
Terry, Randall **1991**:4

Orlando Magic basketball team
Hardaway, Anfernee **1996**:2

Painting
Bean, Alan L. **1986**:2
Botero, Fernando **1994**:3
Chagall, Marc
Obituary **1985**:2
Chatham, Russell **1990**:1
Chia, Sandro **1987**:2
Dali, Salvador
Obituary **1989**:2
de Kooning, Willem **1994**:4
Obituary **1997**:3
Diebenkorn, Richard
Obituary **1993**:4
Dubuffet, Jean
Obituary **1985**:4
Frankenthaler, Helen **1990**:1
Freud, Lucian **2000**:4
Graves, Nancy **1989**:3
Haring, Keith
Obituary **1990**:3
Hockney, David **1988**:3
Kahlo, Frida **1991**:3
Katz, Alex **1990**:3
Kelly, Ellsworth **1992**:1
Kiefer, Anselm **1990**:2
Kostabi, Mark **1989**:4
Lichtenstein, Roy **1994**:1
Obituary **1998**:1
Longo, Robert **1990**:4
Miro, Joan
Obituary **1985**:1

Motherwell, Robert
Obituary **1992**:1
Murakami, Takashi **2004**:2
Nechita, Alexandra **1996**:4
Neiman, LeRoy **1993**:3
Ono, Yoko **1989**:2
Polke, Sigmar **1999**:4
Pozzi, Lucio **1990**:2
Pratt, Christopher **1985**:3
Rauschenberg, Robert **1991**:2
Rothenberg, Susan **1995**:3
Schnabel, Julian **1997**:1
Stella, Frank **1996**:2
Tamayo, Rufino
Obituary **1992**:1
Thiebaud, Wayne **1991**:1
Twombley, Cy **1995**:1
Warhol, Andy
Obituary **1987**:2
Wegman, William **1991**:1

Pakistan People's Party
Bhutto, Benazir **1989**:4

Paleontology
Bakker, Robert T. **1991**:3
Gould, Stephen Jay
Obituary **2003**:3
Horner, Jack **1985**:2

Palestine Liberation Organization
Arafat, Yasser **1989**:3 **1997**:3
Habash, George **1986**:1
Husseini, Faisal **1998**:4
Hussein I, King **1997**:3
Obituary **1999**:3
Redgrave, Vanessa **1989**:2
Terzi, Zehdi Labib **1985**:3

Palimony
Marvin, Lee
Obituary **1988**:1
Mitchelson, Marvin **1989**:2

Palm Computing
Hawkins, Jeff and Donna Dubinsky **2000**:2

Paralegals
Furman, Rosemary
Brief Entry **1986**:4

Paramount Pictures
Diller, Barry **1991**:1
Lansing, Sherry **1995**:4
Steel, Dawn **1990**:1
Obituary **1998**:2

Parents' Music Resource Center
Gore, Tipper **1985**:4
Snider, Dee **1986**:1

Parents of Murdered Children
Hullinger, Charlotte
Brief Entry **1985**:1

Paris Opera Ballet Company
Guillem, Sylvie **1988**:2

Tanny, Vic
Obituary **1985**:3
Wilson, Jerry
Brief Entry **1986**:2

Physics
Chaudhari, Praveen **1989**:4
Chu, Paul C.W. **1988**:2
Fang Lizhi **1988**:1
Fano, Ugo
Obituary **2001**:4
Hawking, Stephen W. **1990**:1
Horowitz, Paul **1988**:2
Lederman, Leon Max **1989**:4
Maglich, Bogdan C. **1990**:1
Penrose, Roger **1991**:4
Sakharov, Andrei Dmitrievich
Obituary **1990**:2

PhytoFarms
Davis, Noel **1990**:3

Pittsburgh, Pa., city government
Caliguiri, Richard S.
Obituary **1988**:3

Pittsburgh Penguins hockey team
Jagr, Jaromir **1995**:4
Lemieux, Mario **1986**:4

Pittsburgh Pirates baseball team
Leyland, Jim **1998**:2
Stargell, Willie
Obituary **2002**:1

Pittsburgh Steelers football team
Rooney, Art
Obituary **1989**:1
White, Byron
Obituary **2003**:3
Woodson, Ron **1996**:4

Pixillation
McLaren, Norman
Obituary **1987**:2

Pixar Animation Studios
Jobs, Steve **2000**:1
Varney, Jim
Brief Entry **1985**:4
Obituary **2000**:3

Pizza Kwik, Ltd.
Paulucci, Jeno
Brief Entry **1986**:3

Pizza Time Theatres, Inc.
Bushnell, Nolan **1985**:1

Planned Parenthood Federation of America
Maraldo, Pamela J. **1993**:4
Wattleton, Faye **1989**:1

Playboy Enterprises
Hefner, Christie **1985**:1
Ingersoll, Ralph II **1988**:2
Melman, Richard
Brief Entry **1986**:1

Pleasant Company
Rowland, Pleasant **1992**:3

PLO
See: Palestine Liberation
Organization

PMRC
See: Parents' Music Resource Center

Poetry
Angelou, Maya **1993**:4
Bly, Robert **1992**:4
Brooks, Gwendolyn **1998**:1
Obituary **2001**:2
Burroughs, William S.
Obituary **1997**:4
Codrescu, Andre **1997**:3
Collins, Billy **2002**:2
Dickey, James
Obituary **1998**:2
Dove, Rita **1994**:3
Dylan, Bob **1998**:1
Ginsberg, Allen
Obituary **1997**:3
Heaney, Seamus **1996**:2
Hughes, Ted
Obituary **1999**:2
Jewel **1999**:2
Kunitz, Stanley J. **2001**:2
Milligan, Spike
Obituary **2003**:2
Mortensen, Viggo **2003**:3
Nemerov, Howard
Obituary **1992**:1
Paz, Octavio **1991**:2
Sapphire **1996**:4
Senghor, Leopold
Obituary **2003**:1
Van Duyn, Mona **1993**:2
Walker, Alice **1999**:1

Polaroid Corp.
Land, Edwin H.
Obituary **1991**:3

Pole vaulting
Olson, Billy **1986**:3

Pop art
Castelli, Leo
Obituary **2000**:1
Lichtenstein, Roy **1994**:1
Obituary **1998**:1
Richter, Gerhard **1997**:2
Warhol, Andy
Obituary **1987**:2

Popular Front for the Liberation of Palestine
Habash, George **1986**:1

Pornography
Flynt, Larry **1997**:3

Portland, Ore., city government
Clark, J. E.
Brief Entry **1986**:1

Portland Trail Blazers basketball team
Drexler, Clyde **1992**:4
Wilkens, Lenny **1995**:2

POWER
See: People Organized and Working
for Economic Rebirth

President's Council for Physical Fitness
Schwarzenegger, Arnold **1991**:1

Presidential Medal of Freedom
Annenberg, Walter **1992**:3
Cagney, James
Obituary **1986**:2
Cheek, James Edward
Brief Entry **1987**:1
Copland, Aaron
Obituary **1991**:2
Cronkite, Walter Leland **1997**:3
Ellison, Ralph
Obituary **1994**:4
Fulbright, J. William
Obituary **1995**:3
Kissinger, Henry **1999**:4
Luce, Clare Boothe
Obituary **1988**:1
Ormandy, Eugene
Obituary **1985**:2
Rickover, Hyman
Obituary **1986**:4
Rumsfeld, Donald **2004**:1
Salk, Jonas **1994**:4
Obituary **1995**:4
Sinatra, Frank
Obituary **1998**:4
Smith, Kate
Obituary **1986**:3
Strauss, Robert **1991**:4
Wasserman, Lew
Obituary **2003**:3

Primerica
Weill, Sandy **1990**:4

Princeton, N.J., city government
Sigmund, Barbara Boggs
Obituary **1991**:1

Pritzker Prize
Bunshaft, Gordon **1989**:3
Obituary **1991**:1
Foster, Norman **1999**:4
Johnson, Philip **1989**:2
Koolhaas, Rem **2001**:1
Pritzker, A.N.
Obituary **1986**:2
Roche, Kevin **1985**:1
Venturi, Robert **1994**:4

Procter & Gamble Co.
Lafley, A. G. **2003**:4
Smale, John G. **1987**:3

Proctor & Gardner Advertising, Inc.
Proctor, Barbara Gardner **1985**:3

Professional Bowlers Association
Weber, Pete **1986**:3

Professional Golfers Association
Azinger, Paul **1995**:2
Chen, T.C.
  Brief Entry **1987**:3
Couples, Fred **1994**:4
Curtis, Ben **2004**:2
Furyk, Jim **2004**:2
Norman, Greg **1988**:3
Peete, Calvin **1985**:4
Sarazen, Gene
  Obituary **1999**:4
Singh, Vijay **2000**:4
Stewart, Payne
  Obituary **2000**:2
Strange, Curtis **1988**:4
Weir, Mike **2004**:1

Professional Flair
Verdi-Fletcher, Mary **1998**:2

Progress and Freedom Foundation
Huffington, Arianna **1996**:2

Project Head Start
Zigler, Edward **1994**:1

Promise Keepers
McCartney, Bill **1995**:3

Psychedelic drugs
Castaneda, Carlos
  Obituary **1998**:4
Leary, Timothy
  Obituary **1996**:4
McKenna, Terence **1993**:3

Psychiatry
Bettelheim, Bruno
  Obituary **1990**:3
Coles, Robert **1995**:1
Frankl, Viktor E.
  Obituary **1998**:1
Laing, R.D.
  Obituary **1990**:1
Menninger, Karl
  Obituary **1991**:1

Psychology
Pinker, Steven A. **2000**:1

Public Broadcasting Service
Barney **1993**:4
Gunn, Hartford N., Jr.
  Obituary **1986**:2
Lewis, Shari **1993**:1
  Obituary **1999**:1
Rogers, Fred **2000**:4
Rose, Charlie **1994**:2
Trotter, Charlie **2000**:4

Public relations
Kingsley, Patricia **1990**:2

Publishing
Annenberg, Walter **1992**:3
Black, Conrad **1986**:2
Brown, Tina **1992**:1
Davis, Crispin **2004**:1
Doubleday, Nelson, Jr. **1987**:1
Epstein, Jason **1991**:1
Evans, Joni **1991**:4
Forbes, Malcolm S.
  Obituary **1990**:3
Forbes, Steve **1996**:2
Gaines, William M.
  Obituary **1993**:1
Graham, Donald **1985**:4
Guccione, Bob **1986**:1
Guccione, Bob, Jr. **1991**:4
Hamilton, Hamish
  Obituary **1988**:4
Hefner, Christie **1985**:1
Hillegass, Clifton Keith **1989**:4
Ingersoll, Ralph II **1988**:2
Kennedy, John F., Jr. **1990**:1
  Obituary **1999**:4
Lear, Frances **1988**:3
Levin, Gerald **1995**:2
Lewis, Edward T. **1999**:4
Macmillan, Harold
  Obituary **1987**:2
Maxwell, Robert
  Obituary **1992**:2
Maxwell, Robert **1990**:1
Morgan, Dodge **1987**:1
Morgan, Robin **1991**:1
Murdoch, Rupert **1988**:4
Neuharth, Allen H. **1986**:1
Newhouse, Samuel I., Jr. **1997**:1
Onassis, Jacqueline Kennedy
  Obituary **1994**:4
Pope, Generoso **1988**:4
Pratt, Jane **1999**:1
Regan, Judith **2003**:1
Rowland, Pleasant **1992**:3
Steinem, Gloria **1996**:2
Sullivan, Andrew **1996**:1
Summers, Anne **1990**:2
Tilberis, Elizabeth **1994**:3
Wenner, Jann **1993**:1
Whittle, Christopher **1989**:3
Wintour, Anna **1990**:4
Ziff, William B., Jr. **1986**:4
Zuckerman, Mortimer **1986**:3
Zwilich, Ellen **1990**:1

Pulitzer Prize
Abbott, George
  Obituary **1995**:3
Albee, Edward **1997**:1
Albert, Stephen **1986**:1
Angier, Natalie **2000**:3
Barry, Dave **1991**:2
Bennett, Michael
  Obituary **1988**:1
Block, Herbert
  Obituary **2002**:4
Brooks, Gwendolyn **1998**:1
  Obituary **2001**:2
Caen, Herb
  Obituary **1997**:4
Chabon, Michael **2002**:1

Coles, Robert **1995**:1
Copland, Aaron
  Obituary **1991**:2
Cruz, Nilo **2004**:4
Cunningham, Michael **2003**:4
Dove, Rita **1994**:3
Ebert, Roger **1998**:3
Faludi, Susan **1992**:4
Geisel, Theodor
  Obituary **1992**:2
Haley, Alex
  Obituary **1992**:3
Kushner, Tony **1995**:2
Lahiri, Jhumpa **2001**:3
Lelyveld, Joseph S. **1994**:4
Logan, Joshua
  Obituary **1988**:4
Mailer, Norman **1998**:1
Mamet, David **1998**:4
Marsalis, Wynton **1997**:4
Mauldin, Bill
  Obituary **2004**:2
McCourt, Frank **1997**:4
Merrill, James
  Obituary **1995**:3
Michener, James A.
  Obituary **1998**:1
Miller, Arthur **1999**:4
Morrison, Toni **1998**:1
Papp, Joseph
  Obituary **1992**:2
Parks, Suzan-Lori **2003**:2
Proulx, E. Annie **1996**:1
Quindlen, Anna **1993**:1
Roth, Philip **1999**:1
Royko, Mike
  Obituary **1997**:4
Safire, William **2000**:3
Shepard, Sam **1996**:4
Shields, Carol
  Obituary **2004**:3
Smiley, Jane **1995**:4
Sondheim, Stephen **1994**:4
Trudeau, Garry **1991**:2
Tyler, Anne **1995**:4
Updike, John **2001**:2
Van Duyn, Mona **1993**:2
Vogel, Paula **1999**:2
Walker, Alice **1999**:1
Wasserstein, Wendy **1991**:3
Welty, Eudora
  Obituary **2002**:3
Wilson, August **2002**:2
Wilson, Edward O. **1994**:4

Quebec provincial government
Bouchard, Lucien **1999**:2
Johnson, Pierre Marc **1985**:4
Levesque, Rene
  Obituary **1988**:1

Radical Party (Italy)
Staller, Ilona **1988**:3

Radio One, Inc.
Hughes, Cathy **1999**:1

Random House publishers
Evans, Joni **1991**:4

RCA Corp.
Engstrom, Elmer W.
Obituary **1985**:2

Real estate
Bloch, Ivan **1986**:3
Buss, Jerry **1989**:3
Campeau, Robert **1990**:1
Portman, John **1988**:2
Trump, Donald **1989**:2

Reebok U.S.A. Ltd., Inc.
Fireman, Paul
Brief Entry **1987**:2

Renaissance Motion Pictures
Raimi, Sam **1999**:2

RENAMO
Dhlakama, Afonso **1993**:3

Renault, Inc.
Besse, Georges
Obituary **1987**:1

Republican National Committee
Abraham, Spencer **1991**:4
Atwater, Lee **1989**:4
Obituary **1991**:4
Molinari, Susan **1996**:4

Resistancia Nacional Mocambican
See: RENAMO

Restaurants
Aoki, Rocky **1990**:2
Aretsky, Ken **1988**:1
Bushnell, Nolan **1985**:1
Copeland, Al **1988**:3
Fertel, Ruth **2000**:2
Kaufman, Elaine **1989**:4
Kerrey, Bob **1986**:1 **1991**:3
Kroc, Ray
Obituary **1985**:1
Lagasse, Emeril **1998**:3
Melman, Richard
Brief Entry **1986**:1
Petrossian, Christian
Brief Entry **1985**:3
Puck, Wolfgang **1990**:1
Shaich, Ron **2004**:4
Thomas, Dave **1986**:2 **1993**:2
Obituary **2003**:1
Zagat, Tim and Nina **2004**:3

Retailing
Charron, Paul **2004**:1
Drexler, Millard S. **1990**:3
Marcus, Stanley
Obituary **2003**:1
Persson, Stefan **2004**:1

Reuben Awards
Gould, Chester
Obituary **1985**:2
Schulz, Charles
Obituary **2000**:3

Revlon, Inc.
Duffy, Karen **1998**:1
Perelman, Ronald **1989**:2

Rhode Island state government
Violet, Arlene **1985**:3

Richter Scale
Richter, Charles Francis
Obituary **1985**:4

Ringling Brothers and Barnum & Bailey Circus
Burck, Wade
Brief Entry **1986**:1
Feld, Kenneth **1988**:2

RJR Nabisco, Inc.
Horrigan, Edward, Jr. **1989**:1

Robotics
Kwoh, Yik San **1988**:2

Rock Climbing
Hill, Lynn **1991**:2

Rockman
Scholz, Tom **1987**:2

Roller Coasters
Toomer, Ron **1990**:1

Rolling Stone magazine
Wenner, Jann **1993**:1

Rotary engine
Yamamoto, Kenichi **1989**:1

Running
Benoit, Joan **1986**:3
Joyner, Florence Griffith **1989**:2
Obituary **1999**:1
Knight, Philip H. **1994**:1
Zatopek, Emil
Obituary **2001**:3

Russian Federation
Putin, Vladimir **2000**:3
Yeltsin, Boris **1991**:1

SADD
See: Students Against Drunken Driving

Sailing
Alter, Hobie
Brief Entry **1985**:1
Conner, Dennis **1987**:2
Koch, Bill **1992**:3
Morgan, Dodge **1987**:1
Turner, Ted **1989**:1

St. Louis Blues hockey team
Fuhr, Grant **1997**:3
Hull, Brett **1991**:4

St. Louis Browns baseball team
Veeck, Bill
Obituary **1986**:1

St. Louis Cardinals baseball team
Busch, August A. III **1988**:2
Busch, August Anheuser, Jr.
Obituary **1990**:2
Caray, Harry **1988**:3
Obituary **1998**:3
McGwire, Mark **1999**:1

St. Louis Rams football team
Warner, Kurt **2000**:3

San Antonio Spurs basketball team
Duncan, Tim **2000**:1
Robinson, David **1990**:4

San Antonio, Tex., city government
Cisneros, Henry **1987**:2

San Diego Chargers football team
Barnes, Ernie **1997**:4
Bell, Ricky
Obituary **1985**:1
Unitas, Johnny
Obituary **2003**:4

San Diego Padres baseball team
Dravecky, Dave **1992**:1
Gwynn, Tony **1995**:1
Kroc, Ray
Obituary **1985**:1
Sheffield, Gary **1998**:1

San Francisco city government
Alioto, Joseph L.
Obituary **1998**:3
Brown, Willie **1996**:4

San Francisco 49ers football team
DeBartolo, Edward J., Jr. **1989**:3
Montana, Joe **1989**:2
Rice, Jerry **1990**:4
Walsh, Bill **1987**:4
Young, Steve **1995**:2

San Francisco Giants baseball team
Bonds, Barry **1993**:3
Dravecky, Dave **1992**:1

SANE/FREEZE
Coffin, William Sloane, Jr. **1990**:3

Save the Children Federation
Guyer, David
Brief Entry **1988**:1

SBA
See: Small Business Administration

Schottco Corp.
Schott, Marge **1985**:4

Schwinn Bicycle Co.
Schwinn, Edward R., Jr.
Brief Entry **1985**:4

Harriman, W. Averell
  Obituary **1986**:4
Putin, Vladimir **2000**:3
Sakharov, Andrei Dmitrievich
  Obituary **1990**:2
Smith, Samantha
  Obituary **1985**:3
Vidov, Oleg **1987**:4

Speed skating
Blair, Bonnie **1992**:3

Spin magazine
Guccione, Bob, Jr. **1991**:4

Spinal-cord injuries
Reeve, Christopher **1997**:2

Starbucks Coffee Co.
Schultz, Howard **1995**:3

Strategic Defense Initiative
Hagelstein, Peter
  Brief Entry **1986**:3

Stroh Brewery Co.
Stroh, Peter W. **1985**:2

Students Against Drunken Driving
Anastas, Robert
  Brief Entry **1985**:2
Lightner, Candy **1985**:1

Submarines
Rickover, Hyman
  Obituary **1986**:4
Zech, Lando W.
  Brief Entry **1987**:4

Sun Microsystems, Inc.
McNealy, Scott **1999**:4

Sunbeam Corp.
Dunlap, Albert J. **1997**:2

Suicide
Applewhite, Marshall Herff
  Obituary **1997**:3
Dorris, Michael
  Obituary **1997**:3
Hutchence, Michael
  Obituary **1998**:1
Quill, Timothy E. **1997**:3

Sundance Institute
Redford, Robert **1993**:2

Sunshine Foundation
Sample, Bill
  Brief Entry **1986**:2

Superconductors
Chaudhari, Praveen **1989**:4
Chu, Paul C.W. **1988**:2

Supreme Court of Canada
Wilson, Bertha
  Brief Entry **1986**:1

Surfing
Curren, Tommy
  Brief Entry **1987**:4

SWAPO
See: South West African People's
  Organization

Swimming
Evans, Janet **1989**:1
Van Dyken, Amy **1997**:1

Tampa Bay Buccaneers football team
Bell, Ricky
  Obituary **1985**:1
Gruden, Jon **2003**:4
Johnson, Keyshawn **2000**:4
Testaverde, Vinny **1987**:2
Williams, Doug **1988**:2
Young, Steve **1995**:2

Tandem Computers, Inc.
Treybig, James G. **1988**:3

Teach for America
Kopp, Wendy **1993**:3

Tectonics
Rosendahl, Bruce R.
  Brief Entry **1986**:4

Teddy Ruxpin
Kingsborough, Donald
  Brief Entry **1986**:2

Tele-Communications, Inc.
Malone, John C. **1988**:3 **1996**:3

Televangelism
Graham, Billy **1992**:1
Hahn, Jessica **1989**:4
Robertson, Pat **1988**:2
Rogers, Adrian **1987**:4
Swaggart, Jimmy **1987**:3

Temple University basketball team
Chaney, John **1989**:1

Tennis
Agassi, Andre **1990**:2
Ashe, Arthur
  Obituary **1993**:3
Becker, Boris
  Brief Entry **1985**:3
Capriati, Jennifer **1991**:1
Courier, Jim **1993**:2
Davenport, Lindsay **1999**:2
Federer, Roger **2004**:2
Gerulaitis, Vitas
  Obituary **1995**:1

Gibson, Althea
  Obituary **2004**:4
Graf, Steffi **1987**:4
Henin-Hardenne, Justine **2004**:4
Hewitt, Lleyton **2002**:2
Hingis, Martina **1999**:1
Ivanisevic, Goran **2002**:1
Kournikova, Anna **2000**:3
Navratilova, Martina **1989**:1
Pierce, Mary **1994**:4
Riggs, Bobby
  Obituary **1996**:2
Roddick, Andy **2004**:3
Sabatini, Gabriela
  Brief Entry **1985**:4
Safin, Marat **2001**:3
Sampras, Pete **1994**:1
Seles, Monica **1991**:3
Williams, Serena **1999**:4
Williams, Venus **1998**:2

Test tube babies
Steptoe, Patrick
  Obituary **1988**:3

Texas Rangers baseball team
Rodriguez, Alex **2001**:2
Ryan, Nolan **1989**:4

Texas State Government
Bush, George W., Jr. **1996**:4
Richards, Ann **1991**:2

Therapeutic Recreation Systems
Radocy, Robert
  Brief Entry **1986**:3

Timberline Reclamations
McIntyre, Richard
  Brief Entry **1986**:2

Time Warner Inc.
Ho, David **1997**:2
Levin, Gerald **1995**:2
Ross, Steven J.
  Obituary **1993**:3

TLC Beatrice International
Lewis, Loida Nicolas **1998**:3

TLC Group L.P.
Lewis, Reginald F. **1988**:4
  Obituary **1993**:3

Today Show
Couric, Katherine **1991**:4
Gumbel, Bryant **1990**:2
Norville, Deborah **1990**:3

Tony Awards
Abbott, George
  Obituary **1995**:3
Alda, Robert
  Obituary **1986**:3
Alexander, Jane **1994**:2
Alexander, Jason **1993**:3

Allen, Debbie **1998**:2
Allen, Joan **1998**:1
Bacall, Lauren **1997**:3
Bailey, Pearl
   Obituary **1991**:1
Bennett, Michael
   Obituary **1988**:1
Bloch, Ivan **1986**:3
Booth, Shirley
   Obituary **1993**:2
Brooks, Mel **2003**:1
Brynner, Yul
   Obituary **1985**:4
Buckley, Betty **1996**:2
Burnett, Carol **2000**:3
Carter, Nell
   Obituary **2004**:2
Channing, Stockard **1991**:3
Close, Glenn **1988**:3
Crawford, Cheryl
   Obituary **1987**:1
Crawford, Michael **1994**:2
Cronyn, Hume
   Obituary **2004**:3
Dench, Judi **1999**:4
Dennis, Sandy
   Obituary **1992**:4
Dewhurst, Colleen
   Obituary **1992**:2
Fagan, Garth **2000**:1
Ferrer, Jose
   Obituary **1992**:3
Fiennes, Ralph **1996**:2
Fierstein, Harvey **2004**:2
Fishburne, Laurence **1995**:3
Flanders, Ed
   Obituary **1995**:3
Fosse, Bob
   Obituary **1988**:1
Foster, Sutton **2003**:2
Gleason, Jackie
   Obituary **1987**:4
Glover, Savion **1997**:1
Harrison, Rex
   Obituary **1990**:4
Hepburn, Katharine **1991**:2
Hines, Gregory **1992**:4
Hwang, David Henry **1999**:1
Irons, Jeremy **1991**:4
Jackman, Hugh **2004**:4
Kahn, Madeline
   Obituary **2000**:2
Keaton, Diane **1997**:1
Kline, Kevin **2000**:1
Kushner, Tony **1995**:2
Lane, Nathan **1996**:4
Lansbury, Angela **1993**:1
LaPaglia, Anthony **2004**:4
Lithgow, John **1985**:2
Mantegna, Joe **1992**:1
Matthau, Walter **2000**:3
McKellen, Ian **1994**:1
Merrick, David
   Obituary **2000**:4
Midler, Bette **1989**:4
Miller, Arthur **1999**:4
Moore, Dudley
   Obituary **2003**:2
Nichols, Mike **1994**:4

Nunn, Trevor **2000**:2
Pacino, Al **1993**:4
Papp, Joseph
   Obituary **1992**:2
Parker, Mary-Louise **2002**:2
Peters, Bernadette **2000**:1
Preston, Robert
   Obituary **1987**:3
Prince, Faith **1993**:2
Reza, Yasmina **1999**:2
Robbins, Jerome
   Obituary **1999**:1
Ruehl, Mercedes **1992**:4
Salonga, Lea **2003**:3
Sondheim, Stephen **1994**:4
Spacey, Kevin **1996**:4
Stoppard, Tom **1995**:4
Stritch, Elaine **2002**:4
Stroman, Susan **2000**:4
Styne, Jule
   Obituary **1995**:1
Tune, Tommy **1994**:2
Verdon, Gwen
   Obituary **2001**:2
Wasserstein, Wendy **1991**:3
Wayne, David
   Obituary **1995**:3
Whitehead, Robert
   Obituary **2003**:3
Wong, B.D. **1998**:1
Worth, Irene
   Obituary **2003**:2

Toronto Blue Jays baseball team
Ainge, Danny **1987**:1
Carter, Joe **1994**:2
Wells, David **1999**:3

Toronto Maple Leafs hockey team
Gilmour, Doug **1994**:3

Tour de France
Armstrong, Lance **2000**:1
Indurain, Miguel **1994**:1
LeMond, Greg **1986**:4

Toyota Motor Corp.
Toyoda, Eiji **1985**:2

Toys and games
Barad, Jill **1994**:2
Bushnell, Nolan **1985**:1
Hakuta, Ken
   Brief Entry **1986**:1
Haney, Chris
   Brief Entry **1985**:1
Hassenfeld, Stephen **1987**:4
Kingsborough, Donald
   Brief Entry **1986**:2
Kristiansen, Kjeld Kirk **1988**:3
Lazarus, Charles **1992**:4
Roberts, Xavier **1985**:3
Rowland, Pleasant **1992**:3

Toys R Us
Eyler, John. H., Jr. **2001**:3
Lazarus, Charles **1992**:4

Track and field
Johnson, Michael **2000**:1
Jones, Marion **1998**:4
Joyner, Florence Griffith **1989**:2
   Obituary **1999**:1

Trade negotiation
Hills, Carla **1990**:3
Reisman, Simon **1987**:4

Tradex
Hakuta, Ken
   Brief Entry **1986**:1

Travel
Arison, Ted **1990**:3
Fodor, Eugene
   Obituary **1991**:3
Steger, Will **1990**:4

Treasure Salvors, Inc.
Fisher, Mel **1985**:4

TreePeople
Lipkis, Andy
   Brief Entry **1985**:3

Trevor's Campaign
Ferrell, Trevor
   Brief Entry **1985**:2

Trivial Pursuit
Haney, Chris
   Brief Entry **1985**:1

Twentieth Century-Fox Film Corp.
Diller, Barry **1991**:1
Goldberg, Leonard **1988**:4

UAW
   See: United Auto Workers

UFW
   See: United Farm Workers
Chavez, Cesar
   Obituary **1993**:4

Ultralight aircraft
MacCready, Paul **1986**:4
Moody, John **1985**:3

UN
   See: United Nations

Uncle Noname (cookie company)
Amos, Wally **2000**:1

UNICEF
Bellamy, Carol **2001**:2
Hepburn, Audrey
   Obituary **1993**:2

Union Pacific Railroad
Harriman, W. Averell
Obituary **1986**:4

UNITA
See: National Union for the Total
Independence of Angola

United Airlines
Friend, Patricia A. **2003**:3
Wolf, Stephen M. **1989**:3

United Auto Workers
Bieber, Owen **1986**:1
Woodcock, Leonard
Obituary **2001**:4
Yokich, Stephen P. **1995**:4

United Farm Workers
Chavez, Cesar
Obituary **1993**:4
Huerta, Dolores **1998**:1

United Federation of Teachers
Feldman, Sandra **1987**:3

United Nations
Albright, Madeleine **1994**:3
Annan, Kofi **1999**:1
Astorga, Nora **1988**:2
Bailey, Pearl
Obituary **1991**:1
de Pinies, Jamie
Brief Entry **1986**:3
Fulbright, J. William
Obituary **1995**:3
Ghali, Boutros Boutros **1992**:3
Gromyko, Andrei
Obituary **1990**:2
Lewis, Stephen **1987**:2
Lodge, Henry Cabot
Obituary **1985**:1
Perez de Cuellar, Javier **1991**:3
Terzi, Zehdi Labib **1985**:3

United Petroleum Corp.
Aurre, Laura
Brief Entry **1986**:3

United Press International
Thomas, Helen **1988**:4

United Steelworkers of America
Williams, Lynn **1986**:4

University Network
Scott, Gene
Brief Entry **1986**:1

University of Chicago
Gray, Hanna **1992**:4

University of Colorado football team
McCartney, Bill **1995**:3

University of Las Vegas at Nevada basketball team
Tarkenian, Jerry **1990**:4

University of Michigan football team
Harmon, Tom
Obituary **1990**:3
McCartney, Bill **1995**:3
Schembechler, Bo **1990**:3

University of Notre Dame
Holtz, Lou **1986**:4
Malloy, Edward Monk **1989**:4

University of Pennsylvania
Rodin, Judith **1994**:4

University of Tennessee
Alexander, Lamar **1991**:2

University of Wisconsin
Shalala, Donna **1992**:3

UNIX
Ritchie, Dennis and Kenneth
Thompson **2000**:1

Untouchables
Ram, Jagjivan
Obituary **1986**:4

UPI
See: United Press International

Urban design
Cooper, Alexander **1988**:4

USA Network
Herzog, Doug **2002**:4
Koplovitz, Kay **1986**:3

U.S. Civil Rights Commission
Pendleton, Clarence M.
Obituary **1988**:4

U.S. Department of Transportation
Slater, Rodney E. **1997**:4

U.S. House of Representatives
Abzug, Bella **1998**:2
Aspin, Les
Obituary **1996**:1
Bono, Sonny **1992**:2
Obituary **1998**:2
Clyburn, James **1999**:4
Collins, Cardiss **1995**:3
Conyers, John, Jr. **1999**:1
DeLay, Tom **2000**:1
Fenwick, Millicent H.
Obituary **1993**:2
Ferraro, Geraldine **1998**:3
Foley, Thomas S. **1990**:1
Frank, Barney **1989**:2
Fulbright, J. William
Obituary **1995**:3
Gephardt, Richard **1987**:3
Gingrich, Newt **1991**:1 **1997**:3
Gore, Albert, Sr.
Obituary **1999**:2
Hastert, Dennis **1999**:3
Hyde, Henry **1999**:1
Jackson, Jesse, Jr. **1998**:3

Jordan, Barbara
Obituary **1996**:3
Langevin, James R. **2001**:2
McCarthy, Carolyn **1998**:4
McKinney, Cynthia A. **1997**:1
McKinney, Stewart B.
Obituary **1987**:4
McMillen, Tom **1988**:4
Mfume, Kweisi **1996**:3
Mills, Wilbur
Obituary **1992**:4
O'Neill, Tip
Obituary **1994**:3
Pelosi, Nancy **2004**:2
Pepper, Claude
Obituary **1989**:4
Quayle, Dan **1989**:2
Ros-Lehtinen, Ileana **2000**:2
Roybal-Allard, Lucille **1999**:4
Sanchez, Loretta **2000**:3
Sanders, Bernie **1991**:4
Udall, Mo
Obituary **1999**:2
Waters, Maxine **1998**:4
Watts, J.C. **1999**:2

U.S. National Security Adviser
Berger, Sandy **2000**:1

U.S. Office of Management and Budget
Raines, Franklin **1997**:4

U.S. Postal Service
Frank, Anthony M. **1992**:1

U.S. Public Health Service
Koop, C. Everett **1989**:3
Novello, Antonia **1991**:2
Sullivan, Louis **1990**:4

U.S. Senate
Abrams, Elliott **1987**:1
Biden, Joe **1986**:3
Boxer, Barbara **1995**:1
Bradley, Bill **2000**:2
Braun, Carol Moseley **1993**:1
Campbell, Ben Nighthorse **1998**:1
Cohen, William S. **1998**:1
D'Amato, Al **1996**:1
Dole, Bob **1994**:2
Ervin, Sam
Obituary **1985**:2
Feinstein, Dianne **1993**:3
Fulbright, J. William
Obituary **1995**:3
Glenn, John **1998**:3
Goldwater, Barry
Obituary **1998**:4
Hatch, Orin G. **2000**:2
Heinz, John
Obituary **1991**:4
Helms, Jesse **1998**:1
Jackson, Jesse **1996**:1
Kassebaum, Nancy **1991**:1
Kemp, Jack **1990**:4
Lott, Trent **1998**:1
McCain, John S. **1998**:4
Mikulski, Barbara **1992**:4
Mitchell, George J. **1989**:3
Morrison, Trudi
Brief Entry **1986**:2

Muskie, Edmund S.
Obituary **1996**:3
Nunn, Sam **1990**:2
Pepper, Claude
Obituary **1989**:4
Quayle, Dan **1989**:2
Ribicoff, Abraham
Obituary **1998**:3
Snowe, Olympia **1995**:3
Thompson, Fred **1998**:2
Tower, John
Obituary **1991**:4

U.S. Supreme Court
Blackmun, Harry A.
Obituary **1999**:3
Brennan, William
Obituary **1997**:4
Breyer, Stephen
Gerald **1994**:4 **1997**:2
Burger, Warren E.
Obituary **1995**:4
Flynt, Larry **1997**:3
Ginsburg, Ruth Bader **1993**:4
Marshall, Thurgood
Obituary **1993**:3
O'Connor, Sandra Day **1991**:1
Powell, Lewis F.
Obituary **1999**:1
Rehnquist, William H. **2001**:2
Scalia, Antonin **1988**:2
Souter, David **1991**:3
Stewart, Potter
Obituary **1986**:1
Thomas, Clarence **1992**:2

U.S. Trade Representative
Barshefsky, Charlene **2000**:4

U.S. Treasury
Bentsen, Lloyd **1993**:3

USW
See: United Steelworkers of America

Utah Jazz basketball team
Malone, Karl **1990**:1 **1997**:3
Maravich, Pete
Obituary **1988**:2
Stockton, John Houston **1997**:3

U2
Bono **1988**:4
U **2002**:4

Vampires
Rice, Anne **1995**:1

Venezuela
Perez, Carlos Andre **1990**:2

Veterinary medicine
Redig, Patrick **1985**:3

Viacom, Inc.
Redstone, Sumner **1994**:1

Vietnam War
Dong, Pham Van
Obituary **2000**:4

Vigilantism
Goetz, Bernhard Hugo **1985**:3
Slotnick, Barry
Brief Entry **1987**:4

Virgin Holdings Group Ltd.
Branson, Richard **1987**:1

Virginia state government
Robb, Charles S. **1987**:2
Wilder, L. Douglas **1990**:3

Vogue magazine
Wintour, Anna **1990**:4

Volkswagenwerk AG
Hahn, Carl H. **1986**:4
Lopez de Arriortua, Jose Ignacio
1993:4

Volleyball
Kiraly, Karch
Brief Entry **1987**:1

Voyager aircraft
Rutan, Burt **1987**:2

Vanity Fair magazine
Brown, Tina **1992**:1

Virtual reality
Lanier, Jaron **1993**:4

Wacky WallWalker
Hakuta, Ken
Brief Entry **1986**:1

Wall Street Analytics, Inc.
Unz, Ron **1999**:1

Wallyball
Garcia, Joe
Brief Entry **1986**:4

Wal-Mart Stores, Inc.
Glass, David **1996**:1
Walton, Sam **1986**:2
Obituary **1993**:1

Walt Disney Productions
Disney, Roy E. **1986**:3
Eisner, Michael **1989**:2
Katzenberg, Jeffrey **1995**:3

Wang Laboratories, Inc.
Wang, An **1986**:1
Obituary **1990**:3

War crimes
Barbie, Klaus
Obituary **1992**:2
Hess, Rudolph
Obituary **1988**:1
Karadzic, Radovan **1995**:3

Klarsfeld, Beate **1989**:1
Mengele, Josef
Obituary **1985**:2
Milosevic, Slobodan **1993**:2

Warnaco
Wachner, Linda **1988**:3 **1997**:2

Washington Bullets basketball team
McMillen, Tom **1988**:4
O'Malley, Susan **1995**:2

Washington, D.C., city government
Barry, Marion **1991**:1
Williams, Anthony **2000**:4

Washington Post
Graham, Donald **1985**:4
Graham, Katharine Meyer **1997**:3
Obituary **2002**:3

Washington Redskins football team
Monk, Art **1993**:2
Rypien, Mark **1992**:3
Smith, Jerry
Obituary **1987**:1
Williams, Doug **1988**:2
Williams, Edward Bennett
Obituary **1988**:4

Watergate
Dickerson, Nancy H.
Obituary **1998**:2
Ehrlichman, John
Obituary **1999**:3
Ervin, Sam
Obituary **1985**:2
Graham, Katharine Meyer **1997**:3
Obituary **2002**:3
Haldeman, H. R.
Obituary **1994**:2
Mitchell, John
Obituary **1989**:2
Neal, James Foster **1986**:2
Nixon, Richard
Obituary **1994**:4
Thompson, Fred **1998**:2

Water skiing
Duvall, Camille
Brief Entry **1988**:1

Wayne's World
Myers, Mike **1992**:3 **1997**:4

WebTV Networks Inc.
Perlman, Steve **1998**:2

Wendy's International
Thomas, Dave **1986**:2 **1993**:2
Obituary **2003**:1

Who Wants to be a Millionaire
Philbin, Regis **2000**:2

Windham Hill Records
Ackerman, Will **1987**:4

Wine making
    Lemon, Ted
      Brief Entry **1986**:4
    Mondavi, Robert **1989**:2
    Rothschild, Philippe de
      Obituary **1988**:2

WNBA
    See: Women's National Basketball
    Association

**Women's National Basketball
Association**
    Cooper, Cynthia **1999**:1
    Laimbeer, Bill **2004**:3
    Swoopes, Sheryl **1998**:2

Women's issues
    Allred, Gloria **1985**:2
    Baez, Joan **1998**:3
    Boxer, Barbara **1995**:1
    Braun, Carol Moseley **1993**:1
    Burk, Martha **2004**:1
    Butler, Brett **1995**:1
    Cresson, Edith **1992**:1
    Davis, Angela **1998**:3
    Doi, Takako
      Brief Entry **1987**:4
    Faludi, Susan **1992**:4
    Faulkner, Shannon **1994**:4
    Ferraro, Geraldine **1998**:3
    Finley, Karen **1992**:4
    Finnbogadottir, Vigdis
      Brief Entry **1986**:2
    Flynt, Larry **1997**:3
    Friedan, Betty **1994**:2
    Furman, Rosemary
      Brief Entry **1986**:4
    Grant, Charity
      Brief Entry **1985**:2
    Griffiths, Martha
      Obituary **2004**:2
    Harris, Barbara **1989**:3
    Hill, Anita **1994**:1
    Ireland, Jill
      Obituary **1990**:4

Jong, Erica **1998**:3
Kanokogi, Rusty
    Brief Entry **1987**:1
Love, Susan **1995**:2
MacKinnon, Catharine **1993**:2
Marier, Rebecca **1995**:4
Mikulski, Barbara **1992**:4
Monroe, Rose Will
    Obituary **1997**:4
Morgan, Robin **1991**:1
Nasrin, Taslima **1995**:1
Nussbaum, Karen **1988**:3
Paglia, Camille **1992**:3
Profet, Margie **1994**:4
Steinem, Gloria **1996**:2
Summers, Anne **1990**:2
Wattleton, Faye **1989**:1
Wolf, Naomi **1994**:3
Yard, Molly **1991**:4

Woods Hole Research Center
    Woodwell, George S. **1987**:2

World Bank
    McCloy, John J.
      Obituary **1989**:3
    McNamara, Robert S. **1995**:4

World Cup
    Hamm, Mia **2000**:1

World Health Organization
    Brundtland, Gro Harlem **2000**:1

World of Wonder, Inc.
    Kingsborough, Donald
      Brief Entry **1986**:2

World Wrestling Federation
    Austin, Stone Cold Steve **2001**:3
    Chyna **2001**:4
    Hogan, Hulk **1987**:3
    McMahon, Vince, Jr. **1985**:4
    Ventura, Jesse **1999**:2

Wrestling
    Austin, Stone Cold Steve **2001**:3
    Baumgartner, Bruce
      Brief Entry **1987**:3
    Chyna **2001**:4
    Hogan, Hulk **1987**:3
    McMahon, Vince, Jr. **1985**:4
    Rock, The **2001**:2
    Ventura, Jesse **1999**:2

WWF
    See: World Wrestling Federation

Xerox
    Allaire, Paul **1995**:1
    Brown, John Seely **2004**:1
    McColough, C. Peter **1990**:2
    Mulcahy, Anne M. **2003**:2
    Rand, A. Barry **2000**:3

Yahoo!
    Filo, David and Jerry Yang **1998**:3
    Koogle, Tim **2000**:4
    Semel, Terry **2002**:2

Young & Rubicam, Inc.
    Kroll, Alexander S. **1989**:3

Zamboni ice machine
    Zamboni, Frank J.
      Brief Entry **1986**:4

ZANU
    See: Zimbabwe African National
    Union

Ziff Corp
    Ziff, William B., Jr. **1986**:4

Zimbabwe African National Union
    Mugabe, Robert **1988**:4

Cumulative Newsmakers Index

This index lists all newsmakers included in the entire *Newsmakers* series.

Listee names are followed by a year and issue number; thus **1996**:3 indicates that an entry on that individual appears in both 1996, Issue 3, and the 1996 cumulation.

Lindgren, Astrid 1907-2002
  Obituary **2003**:1
Lindros, Eric 1973- **1992**:1
Lindsay, John V. 1921-2000
  Obituary **2001**:3
Lines, Ray 1960(?)- **2004**:1
Ling, Bai 1970- **2000**:3
Ling, Lisa 1973- **2004**:2
Lipinski, Tara 1982- **1998**:3
Lipkis, Andy
  Brief Entry **1985**:3
Lipsig, Harry H. 1901- **1985**:1
Lipton, Martin 1931- **1987**:3
Lithgow, John 1945- **1985**:2
Little, Cleavon 1939-1992
  Obituary **1993**:2
Liu, Lucy 1968- **2000**:4
Livi, Yvo
  See Montand, Yves
Living Colour **1993**:3
Livingstone, Ken 1945- **1988**:3
Lizhi, Fang
  See Fang Lizhi
LL Cool J 1968- **1998**:2
Lloyd Webber, Andrew 1948- **1989**:1
Lobell, Jeanine 1964(?)- **2002**:3
Locklear, Heather 1961- **1994**:3
Lodge, Henry Cabot 1902-1985
  Obituary **1985**:1
Loewe, Frederick 1901-1988
  Obituary **1988**:2
Lofton, Kenny 1967- **1998**:1
Lofton, Ramona
  See Sapphire
Logan, Joshua 1908-1988
  Obituary **1988**:4
Long, Nia 1970- **2001**:3
Long, Shelley 1950(?)- **1985**:1
Longo, Robert 1953(?)- **1990**:4
Lon Nol
  Obituary **1986**:1
Lopes, Lisa 1971-2002
  Obituary **2003**:3
Lopes, Lisa Left Eye
  See TLC
Lopez, George 1963- **2003**:4
Lopez, Ignacio
  See Lopez de Arriortua, Jose Ignacio
Lopez, Inaki
  See Lopez de Arriortua, Jose Ignacio
Lopez, Jennifer 1970- **1998**:4
Lopez, Nancy 1957- **1989**:3
Lopez de Arriortua, Jose
  Ignacio 1941- **1993**:4
Lord, Bette Bao 1938- **1994**:1
Lord, Jack 1920-1998
  Obituary **1998**:2
Lord, Winston
  Brief Entry **1987**:4
Lords, Traci 1968- **1995**:4
Lorenz, Konrad 1903-1989
  Obituary **1989**:3
Lott, Trent 1941- **1998**:1
Louganis, Greg 1960- **1995**:3
Louis-Dreyfus, Julia 1961(?)- **1994**:1
Love, Courtney 1964(?)- **1995**:1
Love, Susan 1948- **1995**:2
Loveless, Patty 1957- **1998**:2
Lovett, Lyle 1958(?)- **1994**:1
Lowe, Edward 1921- **1990**:2
Lowe, Rob 1964(?)- **1990**:4
Lowell, Mike 1974- **2003**:2

Loy, Myrna 1905-1993
  Obituary **1994**:2
Lucas, George 1944- **1999**:4
Lucci, Susan 1946(?)- **1999**:4
Luce, Clare Boothe 1903-1987
  Obituary **1988**:1
Lucid, Shannon 1943- **1997**:1
Lucke, Lewis 1951(?)- **2004**:4
Ludlum, Robert 1927-2001
  Obituary **2002**:1
Luhrmann, Baz 1962- **2002**:3
Lukas, D. Wayne 1936(?)- **1986**:2
Lukas, Darrell Wayne
  See Lukas, D. Wayne
Lupino, Ida 1918(?)-1995
  Obituary **1996**:1
Lutz, Robert A. 1932- **1990**:1
Lynch, David 1946- **1990**:4
Lyne, Adrian 1941- **1997**:2
Lynn, Loretta 1935(?)- **2001**:1
Mac, Bernie 1957- **2003**:1
Macapagal-Arroyo, Gloria 1947- ... **2001**:4
MacCready, Paul 1925- **1986**:4
MacDonald, Laurie and
  Walter Parkes **2004**:1
MacDowell, Andie 1958(?)- **1993**:4
MacDowell, Rosalie Anderson
  See MacDowell, Andie
Machel, Samora 1933-1986
  Obituary **1987**:1
MacKinnon, Catharine 1946- ... **1993**:2
Macmillan, Harold 1894-1986
  Obituary **1987**:2
MacMillan, Kenneth 1929-1992
  Obituary **1993**:2
Macmillan, Maurice Harold
  See Macmillan, Harold
MacMurray, Fred 1908-1991
  Obituary **1992**:2
MacNelly, Jeff 1947-2000
  Obituary **2000**:4
MacRae, Gordon 1921-1986
  Obituary **1986**:2
Macy, William H. **1999**:3
Madden, John 1936- **1995**:1
Maddux, Greg 1966- **1996**:2
Madonna 1958- **1985**:2
Maglich, Bogdan C. 1928- **1990**:1
Magliozzi, Ray
  See Magliozzi, Tom and Ray
Magliozzi, Tom
  See Magliozzi, Tom and Ray
Magliozzi, Tom and Ray **1991**:4
Maguire, Tobey 1975- **2002**:2
Maher, Bill 1956- **1996**:2
Mahesh Yogi, Maharishi 1911(?)- ... **1991**:3
Mahony, Roger M. 1936- **1988**:2
Maida, Adam Cardinal 1930- ... **1998**:2
Mailer, Norman 1923- **1998**:1
Majerle, Dan 1965- **1993**:4
Majid, Hussein Kamel
  See Kamel, Hussein
Major, John 1943- **1991**:2
Makeba, Miriam 1934- **1989**:2
Malkovich, John 1953- **1988**:2
Malle, Louis 1932-1995
  Obituary **1996**:2
Malloy, Edward Monk 1941- **1989**:4
Malone, Jo 1964(?)- **2004**:3
Malone, John C. 1941- **1988**:3 **1996**:3
Malone, Karl 1963- **1990**:1 **1997**:3
Maltby, Richard, Jr. 1937- **1996**:3

Mamet, David 1947- **1998**:4
Mancini, Henry 1924-1994
  Obituary **1994**:4
Mandel, Howie 1955- **1989**:1
Mandela, Nelson 1918- **1990**:3
Mandela, Winnie 1934- **1989**:3
Mankiller, Wilma P.
  Brief Entry **1986**:2
Mann, Sally 1951- **2001**:2
Mansfield, Mike 1903-2001
  Obituary **2002**:4
Mansion, Gracie
  Brief Entry **1986**:3
Manson, Marilyn 1969- **1999**:4
Mantegna, Joe 1947- **1992**:1
Mantle, Mickey 1931-1995
  Obituary **1996**:1
Mapplethorpe, Robert 1946-1989
  Obituary **1989**:3
Maradona, Diego 1961(?)- **1991**:3
Maraldo, Pamela J. 1948(?)- ... **1993**:4
Maravich, Pete 1948-1988
  Obituary **1988**:2
Marchand, Nancy 1928-2000
  Obituary **2001**:1
Marcos, Ferdinand 1917-1989
  Obituary **1990**:1
Marcus, Stanley 1905-2002
  Obituary **2003**:1
Marier, Rebecca 1974- **1995**:4
Marin, Cheech 1946- **2000**:1
Marineau, Philip 1946- **2002**:4
Maris, Roger 1934-1985
  Obituary **1986**:1
Mark, Marky
  See Marky Mark
Markle, C. Wilson 1938- **1988**:1
Markle, Clarke Wilson
  See Markle, C. Wilson
Marky Mark 1971- **1993**:3
Marley, Ziggy 1968- **1990**:4
Marriott, J. Willard 1900-1985
  Obituary **1985**:4
Marriott, J. Willard, Jr. 1932- ... **1985**:4
Marriott, John Willard
  See Marriott, J. Willard
Marriott, John Willard, Jr.
  See Marriott, J. Willard, Jr.
Marrow, Tracey
  See Ice-T
Marsalis, Branford 1960- **1988**:3
Marsalis, Wynton 1961- **1997**:4
Marsden, Brian 1937- **2004**:4
Marsh, Dorothy Marie
  See West, Dottie
Marshall, Penny 1942- **1991**:3
Marshall, Susan 1958- **2000**:4
Marshall, Thurgood 1908-1993
  Obituary **1993**:3
Martin, Alfred Manuel
  See Martin, Billy
Martin, Billy 1928-1989 .... **1988**:4
  Obituary **1990**:2
Martin, Casey 1972- **2002**:1
Martin, Dean 1917-1995
  Obituary **1996**:2
Martin, Dean Paul 1952(?)-1987
  Obituary **1987**:3
Martin, Judith 1938- **2000**:3
Martin, Lynn 1939- **1991**:4
Martin, Mary 1913-1990
  Obituary **1991**:2

Puente, Tito 1923-2000
  Obituary **2000**:4
Puleston, Dennis 1905-2001
  Obituary **2002**:2
Pullman, Philip 1946- **2003**:2
Puryear, Martin 1941- **2002**:4
Putin, Vladimir 1952- **2000**:3
Puzo, Mario 1920-1999
  Obituary **2000**:1
Pynchon, Thomas 1937- **1997**:4
Qaddhafi, Muammar 1942- **1998**:3
Quaid, Dennis 1954- **1989**:4
Quayle, Dan 1947- **1989**:2
Quayle, James Danforth
  See Quayle, Dan
Queen Elizabeth the Queen Mother
  1900-2002
  Obituary **2003**:2
Queen Latifah 1970(?)- **1992**:2
Queer Eye for the
  Straight Guy cast **2004**:3
Questrom, Allen 1940- **2001**:4
Quill, Timothy E. 1949- **1997**:3
Quindlen, Anna 1952- **1993**:1
Quing, Jiang
  See Jiang Quing
Quinlan, Karen Ann 1954-1985
  Obituary **1985**:2
Quinn, Anthony 1915-2001
  Obituary **2002**:2
Quinn, Jane Bryant 1939(?)- **1993**:4
Quinn, Martha 1959- **1986**:4
Quivers, Robin 1953(?)- **1995**:4
Ra, Sun
  See Sun Ra
Rabbitt, Eddie 1941-1998
  Obituary **1998**:4
Rabin, Leah 1928-2000
  Obituary **2001**:2
Rabin, Yitzhak 1922-1995 .... **1993**:1
  Obituary **1996**:2
Radecki, Thomas
  Brief Entry **1986**:2
Radner, Gilda 1946-1989
  Obituary **1989**:4
Radocy, Robert
  Brief Entry **1986**:3
Raffi 1948- **1988**:1
Rafsanjani, Ali Akbar Hashemi
  1934(?)- **1987**:3
Rafter, Patrick 1972- **2001**:1
Rahman, Sheik Omar Abdel-
  1938- **1993**:3
Raimi, Sam 1959- **1999**:2
Raimondi, John
  Brief Entry **1987**:4
Raines, Franklin 1949- **1997**:4
Raitt, Bonnie 1949- **1990**:2
Rajneesh, Bhagwan Shree 1931-1990
  Obituary **1990**:2
Ram, Jagjivan 1908-1986
  Obituary **1986**:4
Ramaphosa, Cyril 1953- **1988**:2
Ramaphosa, Matamela Cyril
  See Ramaphosa, Cyril
Ramo, Roberta Cooper 1942- **1996**:1
Ramone, Joey 1951-2001
  Obituary **2002**:2
Ramos, Fidel 1928- **1995**:2
Rampal, Jean-Pierre 1922- **1989**:2
Ramsay, Mike 1950(?)- **2002**:1
Rand, A. Barry 1944- **2000**:3

Randi, James 1928- **1990**:2
Rao, P. V. Narasimha 1921- **1993**:2
Raphael, Sally Jessy 1943- **1992**:4
Rapp, C.J.
  Brief Entry **1987**:3
Rapp, Carl Joseph
  See Rapp, C.J.
Rasa Don
  See Arrested Development
Rashad, Phylicia 1948- **1987**:3
Raskin, Jef 1943(?)- **1997**:4
Rattle, Simon 1955- **1989**:4
Rauschenberg, Robert 1925- **1991**:2
Ravalomanana, Marc 1950(?)- **2003**:1
Rawlings, Mike 1954- **2003**:1
Ray, Amy
  See Indigo Girls
Ray, James Earl 1928-1998
  Obituary **1998**:4
Raye, Martha 1916-1994
  Obituary **1995**:1
Raymond, Lee R. 1930- **2000**:3
Reasoner, Harry 1923-1991
  Obituary **1992**:1
Redenbacher, Orville 1907-1995
  Obituary **1996**:1
Redfield, James 1952- **1995**:2
Redford, Robert 1937- **1993**:2
Redgrave, Lynn 1943- **1999**:3
Redgrave, Vanessa 1937- **1989**:2
Red Hot Chili Peppers **1993**:1
Redig, Patrick 1948- **1985**:3
Redman, Joshua 1969- **1999**:2
Redstone, Sumner 1923- **1994**:1
Reed, Dean 1939(?)-1986
  Obituary **1986**:3
Reed, Donna 1921-1986
  Obituary **1986**:1
Reed, Ralph 1961(?)- **1995**:1
Reed, Robert 1933(?)-1992
  Obituary **1992**:4
Reese, Della 1931- **1999**:2
Reeve, Christopher 1952- **1997**:2
Reeves, Keanu 1964- **1992**:1
Reeves, Steve 1926-2000
  Obituary **2000**:4
Regan, Judith 1953- **2003**:1
Rehnquist, William H. 1924- **2001**:2
Reich, Robert 1946- **1995**:4
Reid, Vernon
  See Living Colour
Reilly, John C. 1965- **2003**:4
Reiner, Rob 1947- **1991**:2
Reiser, Paul 1957- **1995**:2
Reisman, Simon 1919- **1987**:4
Reisman, Sol Simon
  See Reisman, Simon
Reisz, Karel 1926-2002
  Obituary **2004**:1
Reitman, Ivan 1946- **1986**:3
Remick, Lee 1936(?)-1991
  Obituary **1992**:1
Reno, Janet 1938- **1993**:3
Renvall, Johan
  Brief Entry **1987**:4
Retton, Mary Lou 1968- **1985**:2
Reuben, Gloria 1964- **1999**:4
Reubens, Paul 1952- **1987**:2
Rey, Margret E. 1906-1996
  Obituary **1997**:2
Reza, Yasmina 1959(?)- **1999**:2
Reznor, Trent 1965- **2000**:2

Rhea, Caroline 1964- **2004**:1
Rhodes, Zandra 1940- **1986**:2
Ribicoff, Abraham 1910-1998
  Obituary **1998**:3
Ricci, Christina 1980- **1999**:1
Rice, Anne 1941- **1995**:1
Rice, Condoleezza 1954- **2002**:1
Rice, Jerry 1962- **1990**:4
Rich, Bernard
  See Rich, Buddy
Rich, Buddy 1917-1987
  Obituary **1987**:3
Rich, Charlie 1932-1995
  Obituary **1996**:1
Richard, Maurice 1921-2000
  Obituary **2000**:4
Richards, Ann 1933- **1991**:2
Richards, Keith 1943- **1993**:3
Richards, Michael 1949(?)- **1993**:4
Richter, Charles Francis 1900-1985
  Obituary **1985**:4
Richter, Gerhard 1932- **1997**:2
Rickover, Hyman 1900-1986
  Obituary **1986**:4
Riddle, Nelson 1921-1985
  Obituary **1985**:4
Ridenhour, Carlton
  See Public Enemy
Ridge, Tom 1945- **2002**:2
Rifkin, Jeremy 1945- **1990**:3
Riggio, Leonard S. 1941- **1999**:4
Riggs, Bobby 1918-1995
  Obituary **1996**:2
Riley, Pat 1945- **1994**:3
Riley, Richard W. 1933- **1996**:3
Rimes, LeeAnn 1982- **1997**:4
Riney, Hal 1932- **1989**:1
Ringgold, Faith 1930- **2000**:3
Ringwald, Molly 1968- **1985**:4
Riordan, Richard 1930- **1993**:4
Ripa, Kelly 1970- **2002**:2
Ripken, Cal, Jr. 1960- **1986**:2
Ripken, Cal, Sr. 1936(?)-1999
  Obituary **1999**:4
Ripken, Calvin Edwin, Jr.
  See Ripken, Cal, Jr.
Ritchie, Dennis
  See Ritchie, Dennis and
  Kenneth Thompson
Ritchie, Dennis and
  Kenneth Thompson **2000**:1
Ritchie, Guy 1968- **2001**:3
Ritter, John 1948- **2003**:4
Ritts, Herb 1954(?)- **1992**:4
Rivera, Geraldo 1943- **1989**:1
Rizzo, Frank 1920-1991
  Obituary **1992**:1
Rizzoli, Paola 1943(?)- **2004**:3
Robards, Jason 1922-2000
  Obituary **2001**:3
Robb, Charles S. 1939- **1987**:2
Robbins, Harold 1916-1997
  Obituary **1998**:1
Robbins, Jerome 1918-1998
  Obituary **1999**:1
Robbins, Tim 1959- **1993**:1
Robelo, Alfonso 1940(?)- **1988**:1
Roberts, Brian L. 1959- **2002**:4
Roberts, Cokie 1943- **1993**:4
Roberts, Corinne Boggs
  See Roberts, Cokie
Roberts, Doris 1930- **2003**:4

Sullivan, Leon 1922-2001
   Obituary **2002**:2
Sullivan, Louis 1933- **1990**:4
Sulzberger, Arthur O., Jr. 1951- **1998**:3
Summers, Anne 1945- **1990**:2
Summitt, Pat 1952- **2004**:1
Sumner, Gordon Matthew
   See Sting
Sun Ra 1914(?)-1993
   Obituary **1994**:1
Sununu, John 1939- **1989**:2
Susskind, David 1920-1987
   Obituary **1987**:2
Sutherland, Kiefer 1966- **2002**:4
Suu Kyi, Aung San 1945(?)- **1996**:2
Suzman, Helen 1917- **1989**:3
Suzuki, Ichiro 1973- **2002**:2
Suzuki, Sin'ichi 1898-1998
   Obituary **1998**:3
Svenigsson, Magnus
   See Cardigans, The
Svensson, Peter
   See Cardigans, The
Swaggart, Jimmy 1935- **1987**:3
Swank, Hilary 1974- **2000**:3
Swanson, Mary Catherine 1944- ... **2002**:2
Swayze, John Cameron 1906-1995
   Obituary **1996**:1
Sweeney, John J. 1934- **2000**:3
Swift, Jane 1965(?)- **2002**:1
Swoopes, Sheryl 1971- **1998**:2
Synodinos, Emitrios George
   See Snyder, Jimmy
Szent-Gyoergyi, Albert 1893-1986
   Obituary **1987**:2
Tafel, Richard 1962- **2000**:4
Tagliabue, Paul 1940- **1990**:2
Takada, Kenzo 1938- **2003**:2
Takei, Kei 1946- **1990**:2
Takeshita, Noburu 1924-2000
   Obituary **2001**:1
Tamayo, Rufino 1899-1991
   Obituary **1992**:1
Tambo, Oliver 1917- **1991**:3
Tan, Amy 1952- **1998**:3
Tanaka, Tomoyuki 1910-1997
   Obituary **1997**:3
Tan Dun 1957- **2002**:1
Tandy, Jessica 1901-1994 .... **1990**:4
   Obituary **1995**:1
Tannen, Deborah 1945- **1995**:1
Tanny, Vic 1912(?)-1985
   Obituary **1985**:3
Tarantino, Quentin 1963(?)- **1995**:1
Taree, Aerle
   See Arrested Development
Tarkenian, Jerry 1930- **1990**:4
Tartakovsky, Genndy 1970- **2004**:4
Tartikoff, Brandon 1949-1997 .... **1985**:2
   Obituary **1998**:1
Tartt, Donna 1963- **2004**:3
Tautou, Audrey 1978- **2004**:2
Taylor, Elizabeth 1932- **1993**:3
Taylor, Jeff 1960- **2001**:3
Taylor, Lawrence 1959- **1987**:3
Taylor, Lili 1967- **2000**:2
Taylor, Maxwell 1901-1987
   Obituary **1987**:3
Taylor, Paul 1930- **1992**:3
Taylor, Susan L. 1946- **1998**:2
Tellem, Nancy 1953(?)- **2004**:4

Teller
   See Penn & Teller
Tenet, George 1953- **2000**:3
Teresa, Mother
   See Mother Teresa
Terry, Randall **1991**:4
Terzi, Zehdi Labib 1924- **1985**:3
Tesh, John 1952- **1996**:3
Testaverde, Vinny 1962- **1987**:2
Testino, Mario 1954- **2002**:1
Thalheimer, Richard 1948-
   Brief Entry **1988**:3
Tharp, Twyla 1942- **1992**:4
Thatcher, Margaret 1925- **1989**:2
Theron, Charlize 1975- **2001**:4
Thiebaud, Wayne 1920- **1991**:1
Tho, Le Duc
   See Le Duc Tho
Thom, Rene 1923-2002
   Obituary **2004**:1
Thomas, Clarence 1948- **1992**:2
Thomas, Danny 1914-1991
   Obituary **1991**:3
Thomas, Dave **1986**:2 **1993**:2
   Obituary **2003**:1
Thomas, Debi 1967- **1987**:2
Thomas, Derrick 1967-2000
   Obituary **2000**:3
Thomas, Frank 1968- **1994**:3
Thomas, Helen 1920- **1988**:4
Thomas, Isiah 1961- **1989**:2
Thomas, Michael Tilson 1944- **1990**:3
Thomas, Michel 1911(?)- **1987**:4
Thomas, R. David
   See Thomas, Dave
Thomas, Rozonda Chilli
   See TLC
Thomas, Thurman 1966- **1993**:1
Thomas, Todd (Speech)
   See Arrested Development
Thomason, Linda Bloodworth
   See Bloodworth-Thomason, Linda
Thompson, Emma 1959- **1993**:2
Thompson, Fred 1942- **1998**:2
Thompson, Hunter S. 1939- **1992**:1
Thompson, John 1941- **1988**:3
Thompson, Kenneth
   See Ritchie, Dennis and Kenneth
   Thompson
Thompson, Lonnie 1948- **2003**:3
Thompson, Starley
   Brief Entry **1987**:3
Thomson, James 1958- **2002**:3
Thorn, Tracey 1962-
   See Everything But The Girl
Thornton, Billy Bob 1956(?)- **1997**:4
Thurman, Uma 1970- **1994**:2
Thurmond, Strom 1902-2003
   Obituary **2004**:3
Tiffany 1972- **1989**:1
Tilberis, Elizabeth 1947(?)- **1994**:3
Tilghman, Shirley M. 1946- **2002**:1
Tillman, Robert L. 1944(?)- **2004**:1
Tillmans, Wolfgang 1968- **2001**:4
Tillstrom, Burr 1917-1985
   Obituary **1986**:1
Tilly, Jennifer 1958(?)- **1997**:2
Timmerman, Jacobo 1923-1999
   Obituary **2000**:3
Tisch, Laurence A. 1923- **1988**:2
Tito, Dennis 1940(?)- **2002**:1

Titov, Gherman 1935-2000
   Obituary **2001**:3
TLC **1996**:1
Tom and Ray Magliozzi **1991**:4
Tomba, Alberto 1966- **1992**:3
Tomei, Marisa 1964- **1995**:2
Tompkins, Susie
   Brief Entry **1987**:2
Tone-Loc 1966- **1990**:3
Toomer, Ron 1930- **1990**:1
Toone, Bill
   Brief Entry **1987**:2
Torello, Juan Antonio Samaranch
   See Samaranch, Juan Antonio
Torme, Mel 1925-1999
   Obituary **1999**:4
Torre, Joseph Paul 1940- **1997**:1
Torvalds, Linus 1970(?)- **1999**:3
Tosh, Peter 1944-1987
   Obituary **1988**:2
Totenberg, Nina 1944- **1992**:2
Tower, John 1926-1991
   Obituary **1991**:4
Townsend, Kathleen Kennedy
   1951- **2001**:3
Toyoda, Eiji 1913- **1985**:2
Trask, Amy 1961- **2003**:3
Traub, Marvin
   Brief Entry **1987**:3
Travers, P.L. 1899(?)-1996
   Obituary **1996**:4
Travers, Pamela Lyndon
   See Travers, P.L.
Travis, Randy 1959- **1988**:4
Travolta, John 1954- **1995**:2
Treurnicht, Andries 1921- **1992**:2
Treybig, James G. 1940- **1988**:3
Tribe, Laurence H. 1941- **1988**:1
Trimble, David 1944- **1999**:1
Trinidad, Felix 1973- **2000**:4
Tritt, Travis 1964(?)- **1995**:1
Trotman, Alex 1933- **1995**:4
Trotter, Charlie 1960- **2000**:4
Troutt, Kenny A. 1948- **1998**:1
Trudeau, Garry 1948- **1991**:2
Trudeau, Pierre 1919-2000
   Obituary **2001**:1
Truitt, Anne 1921- **1993**:1
Trump, Donald 1946- **1989**:2
Trump, Ivana 1949- **1995**:2
Truscott-Jones, Reginald Alfred John
   See Milland, Ray
Tsongas, Paul Efthemios 1941-1997
   Obituary **1997**:2
Tucci, Stanley 1960- **2003**:2
Tucker, Chris 1973(?)- **1999**:1
Tucker, Forrest 1919-1986
   Obituary **1987**:1
Tudjman, Franjo 1922-1999
   Obituary **2000**:2
Tudjman, Franjo 1922- **1996**:2
Tudor, Antony 1908(?)-1987
   Obituary **1987**:4
Tully, Tim 1954(?)- **2004**:3
Tune, Tommy 1939- **1994**:2
Turabi, Hassan 1932(?)- **1995**:4
Ture, Kwame 1941-1998
   Obituary **1999**:2
Turlington, Christy 1969(?)- **2001**:4
Turner, Janine 1962- **1993**:2
Turner, Kathleen 1954(?)- **1985**:3

Webber, Andrew Lloyd
  See Lloyd Webber, Andrew
Webber, Chris 1973- **1994**:1
Webber, Mayce Edward Christopher
  See Webber, Chris
Weber, Pete 1962- **1986**:3
Wegman, William 1942(?)- **1991**:1
Weicker, Lowell P., Jr. 1931- **1993**:1
Weihui, Zhou 1973- **2001**:1
Wei Jingsheng 1950- **1998**:2
Weil, Andrew 1942- **1997**:4
Weill, Sandy 1933- **1990**:4
Weill, Sanford
  See Weill, Sandy
Weinstein, Bob
  See Weinstein, Bob and Harvey
Weinstein, Bob and Harvey **2000**:4
Weinstein, Harvey
  See Weinstein, Bob and Harvey
Weintraub, Jerry 1937- **1986**:1
Weir, Mike 1970- **2004**:1
Weitz, Bruce 1943- **1985**:4
Welch, Bob 1956- **1991**:3
Welch, Jack 1935- **1993**:3
Wells, David 1963- **1999**:3
Wells, Linda 1958- **2002**:3
Wells, Mary 1943-1992
  Obituary **1993**:1
Wells, Sharlene
  Brief Entry **1985**:1
Wellstone, Paul 1944-2002
  Obituary **2004**:1
Welty, Eudora 1909-2001
  Obituary **2002**:3
Wences, Senor 1896-1999
  Obituary **1999**:4
Wenner, Jann 1946- **1993**:1
Werner, Ruth 1907-2000
  Obituary **2001**:1
West, Cornel 1953- **1994**:2
West, Dorothy 1907- **1996**:1
West, Dottie 1932-1991
  Obituary **1992**:2
Westwood, Vivienne 1941- **1998**:3
Wexler, Nancy S. 1945- **1992**:3
Whaley, Suzy 1966- **2003**:4
Whelan, Wendy 1967(?)- **1999**:3
Whitaker, Forest 1961- **1996**:2
White, Alan
  See Oasis
White, Barry 1944-2003
  Obituary **2004**:3
White, Bill 1934- **1989**:3
White, Byron 1917-2002
  Obituary **2003**:3
White, Jaleel 1976- **1992**:3
White, Reggie 1961- **1993**:4
White, Ryan 1972(?)-1990
  Obituary **1990**:3
Whitehead, Robert 1916-2002
  Obituary **2003**:3
Whitestone, Heather 1973(?)- **1995**:1
Whitman, Christine Todd
  1947(?)- **1994**:3
Whitman, Meg 1957- **2000**:3
Whitmire, Kathryn Jean
  See Whitmire, Kathy
Whitmire, Kathy 1946- **1988**:2
Whitson, Peggy 1960- **2003**:3
Whittle, Christopher 1947- **1989**:3
Wickramasinghe, Ranil 1949- **2003**:2
Wiesel, Elie 1928- **1998**:1

Wiest, Dianne 1948- **1995**:2
Wigand, Jeffrey 1943(?)- **2000**:4
Wigler, Michael
  Brief Entry **1985**:1
Wilder, Billy 1906-2002
  Obituary **2003**:2
Wilder, L. Douglas 1931- **1990**:3
Wilder, Lawrence Douglas
  See Wilder, L. Douglas
Wildmon, Donald 1938- **1988**:4
Wiles, Andrew 1953(?)- **1994**:1
Wilkens, Lenny 1937- **1995**:2
Wilkinson, Tom 1948- **2003**:2
William, Prince of Wales 1982- **2001**:3
Williams, Anthony 1952- **2000**:4
Williams, Doug 1955- **1988**:2
Williams, Douglas Lee
  See Williams, Doug
Williams, Edward Bennett 1920-1988
  Obituary **1988**:4
Williams, G. Mennen 1911-1988
  Obituary **1988**:2
Williams, Gerhard Mennen
  See Williams, G. Mennen
Williams, Hosea 1926-2000
  Obituary **2001**:2
Williams, Joe 1918-1999
  Obituary **1999**:4
Williams, Lynn 1924- **1986**:4
Williams, Ricky 1977- **2000**:2
Williams, Robin 1952- **1988**:4
Williams, Serena 1981- **1999**:4
Williams, Ted 1918-2002
  Obituary **2003**:4
Williams, Treat 1951- **2004**:3
Williams, Vanessa L. 1963- **1999**:2
Williams, Venus 1980- **1998**:2
Williams, Willie L. 1944(?)- **1993**:1
Williamson, Marianne 1953(?)- **1991**:4
Willis, Bruce 1955- **1986**:4
Willson, S. Brian 1942(?)- **1989**:3
Wilmut, Ian 1944- **1997**:3
Wilson, August 1945- **2002**:2
Wilson, Bertha
  Brief Entry **1986**:1
Wilson, Brian 1942- **1996**:1
Wilson, Carl 1946-1998
  Obituary **1998**:2
Wilson, Cassandra 1955- **1996**:3
Wilson, Edward O. 1929- **1994**:4
Wilson, Flip 1933-1998
  Obituary **1999**:2
Wilson, Jerry
  Brief Entry **1986**:2
Wilson, Owen 1968- **2002**:3
Wilson, Pete 1933- **1992**:3
Wilson, Peter C. 1913-1984
  Obituary **1985**:2
Wilson, William Julius 1935- **1997**:1
Wimbish, Doug
  See Living Colour
Winans, CeCe 1964- **2000**:1
Winfrey, Oprah 1954- **1986**:4 **1997**:3
Winger, Debra 1955- **1994**:3
Winslet, Kate 1975- **2002**:4
Winston, George 1949(?)- **1987**:1
Winter, Paul 1939- **1990**:2
Wintour, Anna 1949- **1990**:4
Witherspoon, Reese 1976- **2002**:1
Witkin, Joel-Peter 1939- **1996**:1
Witt, Katarina 1966(?)- **1991**:3
Wolf, Naomi 1963(?)- **1994**:3

Wolf, Stephen M. 1941- **1989**:3
Wolfe, Tom 1930- **1999**:2
Wolfman Jack 1938-1995
  Obituary **1996**:1
Womack, Lee Ann 1966- **2002**:1
Wong, B.D. 1962- **1998**:1
Woo, John 1945(?)- **1994**:2
Wood, Daniel
  See New Kids on the Block
Wood, Elijah 1981- **2002**:4
Wood, Sharon
  Brief Entry **1988**:1
Woodard, Lynette 1959(?)- **1986**:2
Woodcock, Leonard 1911-2001
  Obituary **2001**:4
Woodruff, Robert Winship 1889-1985
  Obituary **1985**:1
Woods, Donald 1933-2001
  Obituary **2002**:3
Woods, James 1947- **1988**:3
Woods, Tiger 1975- **1995**:4
Woodson, Ron 1965- **1996**:4
Woodward, Thomas Jones
  See Jones, Tom
Woodwell, George S. 1928- **1987**:2
Worrell, Ernest P.
  See Varney, Jim
Worth, Irene 1916-2002
  Obituary **2003**:2
Worthy, James 1961- **1991**:2
Wright, Eric
  See Eazy-E
Wright, Steven 1955- **1986**:3
Wright, Will 1960- **2003**:4
Wrigley, William, Jr. 1964(?)- **2002**:2
Wu, Harry 1937- **1996**:1
Wyle, Noah 1971- **1997**:3
Wynette, Tammy 1942-1998
  Obituary **1998**:3
Wynn, Francis Xavier Aloysius James
  Jeremiah Keenan
  See Wynn, Keenan
Wynn, Keenan 1916-1986
  Obituary **1987**:1
Wynn, Stephen A. 1942- **1994**:3
Wynonna 1964- **1993**:3
Xenakis, Iannis 1922-2001
  Obituary **2001**:4
Xuxa 1963(?)- **1994**:2
Yamaguchi, Kristi 1971- **1992**:3
Yamamoto, Kenichi 1922- **1989**:1
Yamasaki, Minoru 1912-1986
  Obituary **1986**:2
Yang, Jerry
  See Filo, David and Jerry Yang
Yankovic, Weird Al 1959- **1985**:4
Yankovic, Frank 1915-1998
  Obituary **1999**:2
Yao Ming 1980- **2004**:1
Yard, Molly **1991**:4
Yauch, Adam
  See Beastie Boys, The
Yeager, Chuck 1923- **1998**:1
Yearwood, Trisha 1964- **1999**:1
Ye Jianying 1897-1986
  Obituary **1987**:1
Yeltsin, Boris 1931- **1991**:1
Yen, Samuel 1927- **1996**:4
Yeoh, Michelle 1962- **2003**:2
Yetnikoff, Walter 1933- **1988**:1
Yoakam, Dwight 1956- **1992**:4

Yogi, Maharishi Mahesh
  See Mahesh Yogi, Maharishi
Yokich, Stephen P. 1935- **1995**:4
York, Dick 1923-1992
  Obituary **1992**:4
Young, Adrian 1969-
  See No Doubt
Young, Andre
  See Dr. Dre
Young, Coleman A. 1918-1997
  Obituary **1998**:1
Young, Loretta 1913-2000
  Obituary **2001**:1
Young, Neil 1945- **1991**:2
Young, Robert 1907-1998
  Obituary **1999**:1
Young, Steve 1961- **1995**:2
Youngblood, Johnny Ray 1948- **1994**:1
Youngman, Henny 1906(?)-1998
  Obituary **1998**:3
Yzerman, Steve 1965- **1991**:2
Zagat, Tim and Nina **2004**:3
Zahn, Paula 1956(?)- **1992**:3

Zamboni, Frank J.
  Brief Entry **1986**:4
Zamora, Pedro 1972-1994
  Obituary **1995**:2
Zanardi, Alex 1966- **1998**:2
Zanker, Bill
  Brief Entry **1987**:3
Zanker, William I.
  See Zanker, Bill
Zanuck, Lili Fini 1954- **1994**:2
Zappa, Frank 1940-1993
  Obituary **1994**:2
Zarnocay, Samuel
  See Kaye, Sammy
Zatopek, Emil 1922-2000
  Obituary **2001**:3
Zech, Lando W.
  Brief Entry **1987**:4
Zedillo, Ernesto 1951- **1995**:1
Zeffirelli, Franco 1923- **1991**:3
Zellweger, Renee 1969- **2001**:1
Zemeckis, Robert 1952- **2002**:1
Zerhouni, Elias A. 1951- **2004**:3

Zeroual, Liamine 1951- **1996**:2
Zeta-Jones, Catherine 1969- **1999**:4
Zetcher, Arnold B. 1940- **2002**:1
Zetsche, Dieter 1953- **2002**:3
Zevon, Warren 1947-2003
  Obituary **2004**:4
Zhao Ziyang 1919- **1989**:1
Zhirinovsky, Vladimir 1946- **1994**:2
Zia ul-Haq, Mohammad 1924-1988
  Obituary **1988**:4
Ziff, William B., Jr. 1930- **1986**:4
Zigler, Edward 1930- **1994**:1
Zinnemann, Fred 1907-1997
  Obituary **1997**:3
Zinni, Anthony 1943- **2003**:1
Zito, Barry 1978- **2003**:3
Zucker, Jeff 1965(?)- **1993**:3
Zucker, Jerry 1950- **2002**:2
Zuckerman, Mortimer 1937- **1986**:3
Zwilich, Ellen 1939- **1990**:1
Zylberberg, Joel
  See Hyatt, Joel